Waste Regulation Law

Butterworths Environmental Law Series

Waste Regulation Law

Duncan Laurence
BSc, MSc, PhD, MInstWM

Environmental Protection Agency
Republic of Ireland

Consultant Editor
Prof Robert G Lee LLB

Cardiff Law School
Consultant: Hammond Suddards

Butterworths
London, Dublin, Edinburgh
1999

United Kingdom	Butterworths, a Division of Reed Elsevier (UK) Ltd, Halsbury House, 35 Chancery Lane, LONDON WC2A 1EL and 4 Hill Street, EDINBURGH EH2 3JZ
Australia	Butterworths, a Division of Reed International Books Australia Pty Ltd, CHATSWOOD, New South Wales
Canada	Butterworths Canada Ltd, MARKHAM, Ontario
Hong Kong	Butterworths Asia (Hong Kong), HONG KONG
India	Butterworths India, NEW DELHI
Ireland	Butterworth (Ireland) Ltd, DUBLIN
Malaysia	Malayan Law Journal Sdn Bhd, KUALA LUMPUR
New Zealand	Butterworths of New Zealand Ltd, WELLINGTON
Singapore	Butterworths Asia, SINGAPORE
South Africa	Butterworths Publishers (Pty) Ltd, DURBAN
USA	Lexis Law Publishing, CHARLOTTESVILLE, Virginia

A CIP Catalogue record for this book is available from the British Library.

ISBN 0 406 02457 X

Typeset by Phoenix Photosetting, Chatham, Kent
Printed and bound in Great Britain by Redwood Books, Trowbridge, Wiltshire

Visit us at our website: http://www.butterworths.co.uk

I would like to dedicate this book to my wife Clare, for her patience, her support and for never once questioning (at least out loud) the value of this enterprise.

PREFACE

This book has been written over a period when British waste management law has been subject to massive change. The main provisions contained in Part II of the Environmental Protection Act 1990 (hereinafter the 'EPA 1990') were enacted in 1994, with additional requirements on scrapyards entering into force in 1995. The entire country's regulatory infrastructure has undergone a structural hiatus with the implementation of the Environment Act 1995 and the formation of the Environment Agency and Scottish Environment Protection Agency in 1996. An entirely new system for regulating special waste also commenced in that year. Since then, minor changes to the legislation have been made regularly each year and now the relevant secondary legislation extends to at least 24 statutory instruments. Given this context, a national understanding of the relevant provisions is still developing and only recently have judgments on these provisions become a regular feature of the law reports.

This book was written, first and foremost, to provide a guide through the complexities of British waste management law. Although a very detailed coverage of the legislation is undertaken in individual chapters, Chapter 1 and the introductions to the subsequent chapters are designed to provide a suitable lead in for those encountering the provisions for the first time.

The volume was written with three audiences in mind: lawyers, the regulatory community and industry. For lawyers, this book offers in-depth evaluation of the legislation and also of the relevant case law. But it hopes also to broaden the lawyer's understanding of the context within which the law operates by relating the legislation to the manner by which waste regulation is conducted in Britain.

The second audience for which the book was written is the regulatory community. Given its complexity, many regulators require a detailed guide to the law, particularly a quick and easy access to key legal points, coupled with cross-referencing to appropriate cases. This need appears all the more crucial given the sprawling nature of the statutory provisions and the copious amendments made to the legislation. The book also concentrates on particular points where problems have arisen in the past and suggests possible solutions to these issues.

The third audience is the 'regulated', in other words the waste management industry and those numerous industrial activities which themselves generate waste. Operators of waste management facilities work within one of the most tightly regulated sectors. Virtually no other activity would receive a twice weekly inspection from a policing authority as is the case with a major co-disposal landfill. Any manager of a waste management facility now requires a detailed knowledge of the relevant legislation and of the wording of the licence or registration under which the facility is operated. The nature of the legislation may mean that legal restraints affect the business on a daily basis. This high profile interface means that, like regulatory officials, each manager has to develop expertise in this area. Exclusive reliance on the legal profession is expensive and generally results in a reactive approach to dealing with problems. It is more efficient to develop an understanding of the legal framework of environmental controls on business so that expensive court outings are avoided.

The provisions in s 34 of the EPA 1990 on the duty of care (see Chapter 3) affect wastes generated by all industrial or commercial premises. For this reason, any person in industry or commerce responsible for the disposal or recovery of wastes will need to be conversant with the legislation and the relevant Code of Practice. This function will also include the checking of the credentials of the intended recipients of waste and deciding whether the proposed destination is legitimate. Such a task requires a considerable understanding of the nature of waste management licensing and the statutory system of exemptions and exclusions from the licensing provisions. In addition, virtually every company produces scrap metal from time to time. This material is usually controlled waste (see Chapter 2); hence the duty of care applies, controlled waste carriers must be used and the intended destination for this material must either possess a waste management licence or an appropriate exemption. The facets of the legislation just described are the subject of half of this volume.

The 'regulated' audience for this book includes the construction and scrap metal industries. Although neither industry has in the past often considered itself akin to commercial waste management companies, the legislation has significant effects on the manner in which both construction and metal reclamation companies operate. This book recognises the significant impact of the waste management legislation on both of these industrial sectors. For the construction industry, particular problem areas are highlighted and given special attention throughout the text. A similar approach is made in respect of the scrap metal industry, with an entire chapter being devoted to a discussion of statutory exemptions from waste management licences for metal recycling facilities.

This book sets out the British legislation as it stands on 31 August 1999. When I was originally approached by Butterworths in the autumn of 1992 to write a waste law book, a slimmer volume was envisaged. It is telling of the manner by which British waste legislation has developed that this account is at least double the length originally planned. The level of embellishment which has occurred since the enactment of the Waste Management Licensing Regulations in 1994 was not apparent at the contract stage. For example, the earlier Collection and Disposal of Waste Regulations 1988 set down 23 simply worded paragraphs of exemptions from waste disposal licences on a three page Schedule. By contrast the Waste Management Licensing Regulations 1994 set out 45 paragraphs of exemptions over twelve pages and these have been subject to amendments in the last five years on no less than eleven occasions. Increased complexity is also exemplified in the Special Waste Regulations 1996, which are in parts nearly incomprehensible to a person attempting to read them for the first time. Since 1994, no less than seven Circulars have been published to provide explanatory material on the provisions which make up British waste management law. One Circular is 199 pages in length. Indeed, if I had realised at the time Butterworths commissioned this book what was intended by the Department of the Environment, I might have readily passed the task of completing this volume onto some other unfortunate.

It now seems that most of the major changes in the British waste regulatory system have now been made. Indeed, the then Conservative Government had gone on record to indicate that it was its intention that the regulations should be given time to bed down and consolidate. How likely this will be, only time will tell. But in the short term it seems distinctly possible that the only changes will be in four areas.

The first major forthcoming change to British waste law will involve the entry into force of the Pollution Prevention and Control Act 1999. While the Act itself received

Royal Assent a few weeks before this book went to press, the extensive regulations setting out implementation had not been finalised. In respect of the currency of this book, it needs to be appreciated that only a small number of new waste management facilities will be subject to the Pollution Prevention and Control Act 1999 from October 1999. The long lead-in time for existing facilities – which might extend up to 2007 unless 'substantial change' at particular facilities are envisaged – will mean that most waste management facilities currently subject to Part II of the EPA 1990 will continue to be regulated by the provisions described in the forthcoming chapters for at least a couple of years. Indeed, it seems likely that the majority of existing landfills will not transfer into the new regime at all, but will instead be embraced by the Landfill Directive when its transposition commences in 2001.

The second area of statutory change is contaminated land, with the implementation of Part IIA of the EPA 1990 at the end of 1999. Contaminated land regulation and control – while an important new area of environmental law – is a subject in itself and hence has been deliberately omitted from the account below.

The third area of regulatory uncertainty concerns the UK's transposition of the Landfill Directive. Although adopted in April 1999, transposition is not until July 2001 and hence the necessary changes to the British legislation will not be available until much nearer that date.

Finally, further minor legislative changes are expected on waste definitions, special waste and exemptions from waste management licences. In respect of the definition of waste, these changes are covered in Chapter 2. The other changes – where they have been announced – receive mention in the footnotes to other chapters. When these amendments are to be made remains uncertain, and the establishment of the Welsh Assembly and the Scottish Parliament inevitably means that further minor legislative changes will be delayed until towards the end of 1999.

These factors make the publication of this book not only timely, but ensure that its contents will comprehensively describe the bulk of the national waste management provisions for the next few years without becoming dated.

There is an observable trend, as evidenced by the formation of the Agencies in both Scotland and England and Wales, to approach environmental regulation in a comprehensive and holistic manner. However, and perhaps ironically, the scope of environmental law books is tending to be in the other direction. As Andrew Bryce noted in his review of Mumma A (1995) *Environmental Law: Meeting UK and EC Requirements* (JEL (1996) Vol 8 No 1 p 201), it may be that the days of a single volume, comprehensive account of environmental law are diminishing. Instead, specialist books are appearing on particular topics. This is not, of course, a criticism of the authors of the more generalised texts. More, it is a reflection of the increasing depth and complexity of environmental law in particular areas, where the level of detail necessary to get to grips with the provisions cannot be accommodated in a single volume and where writing such a tome presents an inordinate challenge to the author. For these reasons, this book deals with British waste legislation on its own and unashamedly does not attempt to reflect on the Environment Agency's wider enforcement powers. Nor does it consider the regulatory powers of bodies other than the Agency, such as local authorities. Instead, this book attempts to replace any deficiency in breadth of coverage by way of an emphasis on depth. This book therefore attempts to dissect and analyse both the primary and secondary legislation in some considerable detail. Hence a number of chapters are based solely on a discussion of single sections of the EPA 1990: s 33 in the case of the Agency's enforcement powers at licensed and unlicensed waste management facilities (see Chapter 7), s 34 in relation to the duty of care (see Chapter 3) and s 75 in respect of waste definitions (see Chapter 2). Indeed the coverage of just these three sections of the EPA 1990 occupies about one third of this book.

But to an author, the increased emphasis on the depth of coverage greatly increases the risk of misinterpretation. A facet of much of the EPA 1990 and the subsidiary regulations is that many of the provisions have yet to be subject to detailed analysis in court. The majority of cases do not get beyond the magistrates' or crown courts and few are subject to detailed consideration at the level of the Divisional Court and above. As will be shown, not all of the provisions of legislation are readily understandable and certain of them are not substantiated by way of explanatory circular. Inevitably, some of the provisions can be read in more than one way. Although a range of people have helped in various ways with the manuscript, it should be emphasised that what is being presented here is the author's interpretation. No doubt a different view may well be possible and that a definitive interpretation will only emerge judicially with time.

Like many books on environmental law, it has proved a difficult task to decide which areas of the law should be included and which excluded. Areas of overlap are considerable, not only in respect of allied areas such as land use planning and development control or the transport of hazardous goods, but also in relation to criminal law and evidence. Furthermore, overlaps exist with civil law and such matters as judicial review, civil liability and so on. Given the artificiality of the boundaries between air, water and land pollution, it is easy to stray into the legislation on Integrated Pollution Control and Part I of the EPA 1990 or that concerning the protection of surface waters. Although all the above have considerable relevance to the law affecting waste management, they have to be either limited or excluded for space reasons. Fortunately, many of these matters are amply covered by other texts.

I would like to acknowledge a whole range of people who have helped with this book. A number of my ex-colleagues at what was then Lancashire County Council Waste Regulation Authority viewed some of the early draft chapters and, since then, some have been kind enough to furnish me with further comments. Others working in consultancies and waste management companies have also provided assistance. Hence I would particularly like to mention Keith Ashcroft, Sheila Bethwaite, Steve Burns, Sarah Dewar, Dr Sarah Drewry, Gill Edwards, Sue Hindle, James Hunt, Graham Piggin, Andy Stokes and Jeremy Walker. Thanks should also go to a number of environmental lawyers who have been kind enough to forward me transcripts of relevant judgments. I would like to acknowledge the assistance of my colleague at the Environmental Protection Agency, Dr Matt Crowe. Mention should also be made of Lancashire County Council for allowing me to work part-time for 18 months whilst producing the preliminary draft of this book. It is my hope that similarly enlightened opportunities are available to staff of the Environment Agency.

A particularly large thanks should, of course, go to my consultant editor – Professor Bob Lee of the Cardiff Law School – whose patience, comments and encouragement have exceeded many times over any material reward he is likely to receive from the publishers.

I would also like to mention the assistance and encouragement of the publishers, Butterworths.

In the end, although many people provided valuable assistance and comments, the responsibility for the final text rests solely with the writer. Whilst every endeavour has been made to make the forthcoming account accurate and readable, comments and suggestions for improvements in the text would be very much welcomed. Butterworths permitting, the next edition will hopefully iron out those parts of the book where the legislation warrants a more extensive or clearer analysis. It is my hope that readers who wish to contribute to this process will either contact me directly or through the publishers.

Finally, a word of explanation seems appropriate as to how someone who resides in the Republic of Ireland has come to write a book on British waste regulation law. The answer stems from the nature of my professional life since I graduated from the University of East Anglia's School of Environmental Sciences in 1981. Between that time and 1985, I undertook a MSc thesis and – subsequently – a PhD on industrial waste management. The latter involved me being attached to one of the larger waste regulation authorities, the then West Midlands County Council. I then moved on to the University of Lancaster, spending five years looking at national and European Community waste regulation policy issues from a more academic standpoint. In 1990 I joined Lancashire County Council's waste regulation staff, initially as a Licensing Officer and later as the section's Research and Planning Officer. I left Britain for Ireland at a time when Ireland's Waste Management Act 1996 was due to enter the statute book. Since then I have been involved with the Environmental Protection Agency in the establishment of an entirely new system of waste licensing in Ireland (see Laurence D (1999) 'Implementing Community Law: Waste Regulation in Ireland and Britain', in *World Wide Wastes – Proceedings of the Institute of Wastes Management 101st Annual Conference and Exhibition*, Torbay, 8–11 June 1999). Although the legislative framework is different in places, it shares a commonality of origin in the transposition of European Community environmental law. Furthermore, the common international theme of the effective regulation of the waste management industry has allowed me to make the following detailed commentary on the more recent developments in the British legislation.

Duncan Laurence
Wexford
31 August 1999

Contents

Contents

Table of statutes

Table of statutory instruments

Table of European Communities and other legislation

Other Legislation

Table of cases

M

Decisions of the European Court of Justice are listed below numerically. These decisions are also included in the preceding alphabetical list

Chronological List of Statutory Instruments

1971
Indictment Rules 1971, SI 1971/1253

1973
Diseases of Animals (Waste Food) Order 1973, SI 1973/1936

1976
Control of Pollution Act 1974 (Commencement No 5) Order 1976, SI 1976/731
Control of Pollution (Licensing of Waste Disposal) Regulations 1976, SI 1976/732

1977
Control of Pollution (Licensing of Waste Disposal) (Scotland) Regulations 1977, SI 1977/2006

1978
Pollution Control and Local Government (Northern Ireland) Order 1978, SI 1978/1049

1980
Animal Products and Poultry Products Order 1980, SI 1980/14
Control of Pollution (Special Waste) Regulations 1980, SI 1980/1709
Town and Country Planning (Prescription of County Matters) Regulations 1980, SI 1980/2010

1982
Importation of Animal Products and Poultry Products (Amendment) Order 1982, SI 1982/948

1984
Prevention of Pollution (Reception Facilities) Order 1984, SI 1984/862

1985
Deposits in the Sea (Exemptions) Order 1985, SI 1985/1699
Waste Regulation and Disposal (Authorities) Order 1985, SI 1985/1884

1987
Dangerous Substances in Harbour Areas Regulations 1987, SI 1987/37
Diseases of Animals (Waste Food) (Amendment) Order 1987, SI 1987/232
Control of Pollution (Landed Ships' Waste) Regulations 1987, SI 1987/402

1988
Collection and Disposal of Waste Regulations 1988, SI 1988/819
Transfrontier Shipment of Hazardous Waste Regulations 1988, SI 1988/1562
Town and Country Planning General Development Order 1988, SI 1988/1813
Merchant Shipping (Prevention of Pollution by Garbage) Regulations 1988, SI 1988/2292
Merchant Shipping (Reception Facilities for Garbage) Regulations 1988, SI 1988/2293

1989
Control of Pollution (Landed Ships' Waste) (Amendment) Regulations 1989, SI 1989/65
Road Traffic (Carriage of Explosives) Regulations 1989, SI 1989/615
Sludge (Use in Agriculture) Regulations 1989, SI 1989/1263

1990
Sludge (Use in Agriculture) (Amendment) Regulations 1990, SI 1990/880

1991
Environmental Protection (Prescribed Process and Substances) Regulations 1991, SI 1991/472
Environmental Protection (Applications, Appeals and Registers) Regulations 1991, SI 1991/507
Environmental Protection (Amendment of Regulations) Regulations 1991, SI 1991/836
Litter (Animal Droppings) Order 1991, SI 1991/961

Environmental Protection Act 1990 (Commencement No 8) Order 1991, SI 1991/1319
Control of Explosives Regulations 1991, SI 1991/1531
Control of Pollution (Amendment) Act 1989 (Commencement) Order 1991, SI 1991/1618
Controlled Waste (Registration of Carriers and Seizure of Vehicles) Regulations 1991, SI 1991/1624
Environmental Protection Act 1990 (Commencement No 10) Order 1991, SI 1991/2829
Environmental Protection (Duty of Care) Regulations 1991, SI 1991/2839

1992

Controlled Waste Regulations 1992, SI 1992/588
Environmental Protection (Prescribed Processes and Substances) (Amendment) Regulations 1992, SI 1992/614
Control of Pollution (Licensing of Waste Disposal) (Scotland) Amendment Regulations 1992, SI 1992/1368
Asbestos (Prohibitions) Regulations 1992, SI 1992/3067
Environmental Information Regulations 1992, SI 1992/3240
Animal By-Products Order 1992, SI 1992/3303

1993

Environmental Protection Act 1990 (Commencement No 13) Order 1993, SI 1993/274
Controlled Waste (Amendment) Regulations 1993, SI 1993/566
Environmental Protection (Prescribed Processes and Substances) (Amendment) Regulations 1993, SI 1993/1749
Environmental Protection (Prescribed Processes and Substances) (Amendment) (No 2) Regulations 1993, SI 1993/2405

1994

Waste Management Licensing Regulations 1994, SI 1994/1056
Environmental Protection Act 1990 (Commencement No 15) Order 1994, SI 1994/1096
Transfrontier Shipment of Waste Regulations 1994, SI 1994/1137
Environmental Protection (Prescribed Processes and Substances Etc) (Amendment) Regulations 1994, SI 1994/1271
Environmental Protection (Prescribed Processes and Substances Etc) (Amendment) (No 2) Regulations 1994, SI 1994/1329
Environmental Protection Act 1990 (Commencement No 15) (Amendment) Order 1994, SI 1994/2487
Importation of Animal Products and Poultry Products (Amendment) Order 1994, SI 1994/2920
Environmental Protection Act 1990 (Commencement No 15) (Amendment No 2) Order 1994, SI 1994/3234
Chemicals (Hazard Information and Packaging for Supply) Regulations 1994, SI 1994/3247

1995

Waste Management Licensing (Amendment etc) Regulations 1995, SI 1995/288
Waste Management Licensing (Amendment No 2) Regulations 1995, SI 1995/1950
Environment Act 1995 (Commencement No 1) Order 1995, SI 1995/1983
Environmental Protection Act 1990 (Commencement No 17) Order 1995, SI 1995/2152
Environment Act 1995 (Commencement No 2) Order 1995, SI 1995/2649
Environmental Protection (Prescribed Processes and Substances) (Amendment) Regulations 1995, SI 1995/3247

1996

Environment Act 1995 (Commencement No 5) Order 1996, SI 1996/186
Environmental Agency (Transfer Date) Order 1996, SI 1996/234
Environment Licences (Suspension and Revocation) Regulations 1996, SI 1996/508
Environment Act 1995 (Consequential Amendments) Regulations 1996, SI 1996/593
Waste Management Regulations 1996, SI 1996/634
Environmental Protection (Applications, Appeals and Registers) (Amendment) Regulations 1996, SI 1996/667
Animal By-Products (Amendment) Order 1996, SI 1996/827
Waste Management Licensing (Scotland) Regulations 1996, SI 1996/916
Special Waste Regulations 1996, SI 1996/972
Environment Act 1995 (Consequential and Transitional Provisions) (Scotland) Regulations 1996, SI 1996/973
Environmental Protection (Applications, Appeals and Registers) (Amendment No 2) Regulations 1996, SI 1996/979
Chemicals (Hazardous Information and Packaging for Supply) (Amendment) Regulations 1996, SI 1996/1092
Waste Management Licensing (Amendment) Regulations 1996, SI 1996/1279

Landfill Tax Regulations 1996, SI 1996/1527
Landfill Tax (Qualifying Material) Order 1996, SI 1996/1528
Landfill Tax (Contaminated Land) Order 1996, SI 1996/1529
Special Waste (Amendment) Regulations 1996, SI 1996/2019
Environmental Protection (Prescribed Processes and Substances Etc) (Amendment) (Petrol Vapour Recovery) Regulations 1996, SI 1996/2678

1997
Special Waste (Amendment) Regulations 1997, SI 1997/251
Special Waste (Scotland) Regulations 1997, SI 1997/257
Waste Management (Miscellaneous Provisions) Regulations 1997, SI 1997/351
Producer Responsibility Obligations (Packaging Waste) Regulations 1997, SI 1997/648
Chemicals (Hazardous Information and Packaging for Supply) (Amendment) Regulations 1997, SI 1997/1460
Waste Management Licensing (Amendment) Regulations 1997, SI 1997/2203
Waste and Contaminated Land (Northern Ireland) Order 1997, SI 1997/2778
Animal By-Products (Amendment) Order 1997, SI 1997/2894
Merchant Shipping (Port Waste Reception Facilities) Regulations 1997, SI 1997/3018

1998
Landfill Tax (Amendment) Regulations 1998, SI 1998/61
Environment Act 1995 (Commencement No 11) Order 1995, SI 1998/604
Controlled Waste (Registration of Carriers and Seizure of Vehicles) (Amendment) Regulations 1998, SI 1998/605
Waste Management Licensing (Amendment) Regulations 1998, SI 1998/606
Environmental Protection (Prescribed Processes and Substances) (Amendment) (Hazardous Waste Incineration) Regulations 1998, SI 1998/767
Merchant Shipping (Prevention of Pollution by Garbage) Regulations 1998, SI 1998/1377
Environmental Information (Amendment) Regulations 1998, SI 1998/1447
Groundwater Regulations 1998, SI 1998/2746
Chemicals (Hazard Information and Packaging for Supply) (Amendment) Regulations 1998, SI 1998/3106

1999
Environmental Assessment (Scotland) Regulations 1999, SSI 1999/1
Chemicals (Hazard Information and Packaging for Supply) (Amendment) Regulations 1999, SI 1999/197
Town and Country Planning (Environmental Impact Assessment) (England and Wales) Regulations 1999, SI 1999/293
Waste Management Licences (Consultation and Compensation) Regulations 1999, SI 1999/481
Animal By-Products Order 1999, SI 1999/646
Environment Act 1995 (Commencement No 14) Order 1999, SI 1999/803
Environment Act 1995 (Consequential Amendment) Regulations 1999, SI 1999/1108
Producer Responsibility Obligations (Packaging Waste) (Amendment) Regulations 1999, SI 1999/1361
Landfill Tax (Site Restoration and Quarries) Order 1999, SI 1999/2075

Chapter 1

Introduction

INTRODUCTION

1.01 All human activities produce waste. Some wastes may be environmentally hazardous in themselves. Others may present significant hazards only if deposited together in large quantities. Inappropriately landfilled household waste, for example, may present a significant threat to water supplies and a gas hazard to neighbouring properties. Conversely, large amounts of other wastes are biologically and environmentally inert. A particular feature of the environmental control of wastes is that, unlike other air or water pollutants, they are infinitely transportable and may even be traded as commodities. The result is that they may pose a threat to the environment far away from their source. They need to be disposed of or recycled somewhere and often at significant cost. And in spite of the fact that wastes are universal, no one wants to live near a waste management facility of any kind.

1.02 Given this context, the transport and disposal of wastes must be subject to legal controls. As wastes are universal, this legislation impinges upon every commercial and industrial organisation in Britain. It may affect a small builder or a large construction company, an owner-driver of a skip vehicle or a stock-market quoted waste disposal company, the local corner shop or the largest manufacturing plant in the country. For example, the Department of the Environment has estimated[1] that between 1 and 1.5 million businesses in Britain are affected by the provisions in the Environmental Protection Act 1990 on the duty of care[2].

1 Department of the Environment (1991) *The Duty of Care: A Draft Circular, A Consultation Paper and Draft Regulations under s 34(5)* (22 July 1991), Annex B, Compliance Cost Assessment, para A10.
2 EPA 1990, s 34: see Chapter 3.

1.03 The fact that wastes are universal means that waste law is complex and is getting more so. This complexity must match up to a waste disposal and reclamation system whose subtleties and interactions are often little appreciated by those less familiar with the waste management industry. This is especially true now that legislative intervention is rightly being extended from a focus solely on waste disposal facilities towards processes involving waste minimisation, recycling and reclamation. Given the increased emphasis by national policy makers on recycling and recovery[1], this trend will continue. Alongside waste to energy facilities, other recovery operations are by no means environmentally benign activities and therefore often warrant significant statutory control.

1 See for example Department of the Environment (1995) *Making Waste Work: A strategy for Sustainable Waste Management in England and Wales*, Cm 3040, HMSO, London.

1.04 The purpose of this chapter is to orient the reader prior to the more detailed discussion of the legislation which follows in later chapters. The chapter sets out not only to summarise the statutory provisions and to describe the regulatory bodies responsible for them, it also attempts to introduce the system of British waste management in order to provide an understanding of the context within which the waste management legislation operates. It will demonstrate the fact that waste regulation law affects all industrial sectors and therefore requires compliance by a very large number of different bodies and individuals. It also provides a perspective on the size and significance of the regulatory task facing the Environment Agency and the Scottish Environment Protection Agency in the forthcoming years.

LEGISLATIVE TRADITIONS

The development of British waste regulation law

1.05 The statutory controls contained in Part II of the Environmental Protection Act 1990 (hereinafter 'the EPA 1990') represent the third version of the British regulatory system which specifically focused on waste management. Prior to 1972, waste regulation was put into effect only by general legislation, such as that emanating from the land use planning process and by way of the Public Health Act 1936[1]. That neither of these proved particularly effective is illustrated by the case of the Malkins Bank site in Cheshire. This site had been receiving an uncontrolled variety of toxic wastes since 1932, with the result that half of the site was covered to a depth of 15 metres with various chemicals. By 1970, the smell of 'rotten eggs and tomcats'[2] could be detected several miles away, with periodic minor explosions from deposited drums. A useful snapshot of typical industrial waste disposal practices up to the mid 1970s is contained in the Department of the Environment's publication *Co-operative Programme of Research on the Behaviour of Hazardous Wastes in Landfill Sites*[3]. It would appear that Malkins Bank was by no means untypical of industrial waste landfills at that time.

1 See Technical Committee on the Disposal of Solid Toxic Wastes (1970) *Disposal of Solid Toxic Wastes*, the Ministry of Housing and Local Government and the Scottish Development Department, London, HMSO (generally known as the 'Key Report').
2 See Wilson D C, Smith E T and Pearce K W (1981) 'Uncontrolled Hazardous Waste Sites: A perspective of the Problem in the UK' *Chemistry and Industry*, No 1, Jan 1981, pp 18–23.
3 Department of the Environment (1978) *Co-operative Programme of Research on the Behaviour of Hazardous Wastes in Landfill Sites*, HMSO, London.

1.06 The first statute specifically aimed at controlling waste management practices was the Deposit of Poisonous Waste Act 1972. This Act was essentially a stop-gap measure, being rushed through Parliament in a record 11 days in the face of widespread public concern about the fly-tipping of hazardous waste[1]. The Act for the first time provided for a notification procedure to track and control toxic waste movements, and also made it an offence to deposit poisonous, noxious or polluting wastes in a manner which gave rise to an environmental hazard[2]. The Act empowered local authorities to act as the enforcing agency.

1 For an interesting account of the campaign for controls see Open University (1978) *Environmental Control and Public Health Course Unit 10 Toxic Wastes*, Appendix 1, Oxford University Press.
2 See Department of the Environment (1972) *Deposit of Poisonous Waste Act 1972*, Circular 70/72, HMSO, London.

1.07 More comprehensive legislation followed the Deposit of Poisonous Waste Act 1972 in the form of the Control of Pollution Act 1974. Part I of the 1974 Act introduced a system of waste disposal licences for waste management facilities[1] and provided the backbone of waste regulatory controls until 1994. The toxic waste notification system under the Deposit of Poisonous Waste Act 1972 continued until 1981, when it was replaced by the Control of Pollution (Special Waste) Regulations 1980[2].

1 Waste disposal licensing was enacted in 1976: Control of Pollution Act 1974 (Commencement No 5) Order 1976 (SI 1976/731).
2 SI 1980/1709: subsequently repealed by SI 1996/972.

1.08 Although the Control of Pollution Act 1974 provided an invaluable start to the formalisation and control of waste management activities, by the 1980s it was apparent that waste regulation was in the doldrums. A series of highly critical reports from a variety of Select Committees[1], along with the Royal Commission on Environmental Pollution[2] and the Hazardous Waste Inspectorate[3], were a feature of the environmental history of that decade. A reasonable summary of the problems is apparent from the first paragraph of one of the Environment Committee's reports[4]:

'Never, in any of our enquiries into environmental problems, have we experienced such consistent and universal criticism of existing legislation and of central and local government as we have during the course of this inquiry.'[5]

Eventually in 1994 – and it took a long time – the Control of Pollution Act 1974 was replaced by Part II of the EPA 1990 and the associated regulations which are the subject of this volume. Waste regulation was subsequently moved from local government to the Environment Agency and the Scottish Environment Protection Agency in 1996.

1 See House of Lords Select Committee on Science and Technology (1981) *Hazardous Waste Disposal*, Vols I–III, HMSO, London; House of Commons Environment Committee (1989) *Toxic Waste* Vols I–III, HMSO, London; House of Commons Welsh Affairs Committee (1990) *Toxic Waste Disposal in Wales*, HMSO, London.
2 Royal Commission on Environmental Pollution (1985) *Managing Waste: The Duty of Care*, HMSO, London.
3 Hazardous Waste Inspectorate (1985) *First Report Hazardous Waste Management – An Overview*, Department of the Environment, London; Hazardous Waste Inspectorate (1986) *Second Report, Hazardous Waste Management '. . . Ramshackle & Antediluvian'?*, Department of the Environment, London; Department of the Environment (1988) *The Hazardous Waste Inspectorate Third Report*, HMSO, London.
4 House of Commons Environment Committee (1989) *Toxic Waste* Vol I, HMSO, London, page xi, para 1.
5 See also Laurence D S (1987) 'The Department of the Environment: Ramshackle or Antediluvian?' *Wastes Management*, January 1987, pp 28–35.

1.09 For many years, a formal national waste policy for Britain was notable by its absence. However, in December 1995, a White Paper, *Making Waste Work: A Strategy of Sustainable Waste Management in England and Wales*[1], was published. *Making Waste Work* set out to provide a framework in which the statutory controls mesh with the waste planning roles of the Agency and local authorities and also with the landfill tax[2]. The Strategy, amongst other things, contains a series of targets for waste management up to the year 2005. Two primary targets are singled out; a 'landfill diversion target' and a waste recovery target[3]. These require that the amount of controlled waste passing to landfill be reduced from 70% to 60% and that 40% of household waste be recovered, both by 2005. It was expected that the primary engine for the delivery of these goals was to be the landfill tax. A further target was to be set in 1998, which was for the overall reduction of controlled waste, but this was postponed[4].

1 Department of the Environment (1995), Cm 3040, HMSO, London.
2 The landfill tax is discussed at para 1.100 below.
3 Department of the Environment (1995), para 1.38ff.
4 'Waste Targets in doubt as Waste Strategy put back to 1999' *Ends Report* 276, Jan 1998, p 32.

1.10 In June 1998, a further consultation paper was published – *Less Waste, More Value*[1]. Separate strategies are proposed for Scotland, Wales and Northern Ireland. The lack of progress in these matters since *Making Waste Work* was starkly highlighted in June 1998 by the House of Commons Select Committee on the Environment[2]. In a report which in tone seems to parallel the critical Reports of Select Committees in the late 1980s, the Committee expressed the view that[3]:

'. . . waste management in this country is still characterised by inertia, careless administration and ad-hoc, rather than science-based, decisions. Lip service alone, in far too many instances, has been paid to the principles of reducing waste and diverting it from disposal. Central government has lacked the commitment, and local government the resources, to put a sustainable waste management strategy into practice.'

In July 1999, *A Way with Waste – A Draft Waste Strategy for England and Wales* was finally published[4]. It is to be finalised in 2000.

1   Department of the Environment, Transport and the Regions (1998) *Less Waste, More Value*, DETR Sales, London.
2   House of Commons Environment, Transport and Regional Affairs Committee (1998) *Sustainable Waste Management* 6th Report, Vols I–III, Stationery Office, London. See also Department of the Environment, Transport and the Regions (1998) *Sustainable Waste Management, The Government's Response*, Cm 4058, Stationery Office, London.
3   House of Commons Environment, Transport and Regional Affairs Committee (1998) *Sustainable Waste Management* 6th Report, Stationery Office, London, Vol 1, para 17.
4   Department of the Environment, Transport and the Regions, London.

1.11   Finally, mention should be made of the new system for the regulation of contaminated land[1]. Provisions to effect a modern control regime on the identification and clean-up of contaminated land have been awaited for most of the 1990s, being much delayed due to their commercial implications. However, it now appears that they will enter into force in December 1999[2]. These provisions will operate in parallel to the waste management licensing system under Part II of the EPA 1990, with boundaries being set to prevent overlap[3]. For the reasons discussed in the preface, a detailed discussion of these matters is beyond the scope of this book.

1   EPA 1990, s 78A, as amended by the Environment Act 1995, s 57.
2   *Hansard* 27 April 1999 col 91.
3   EPA 1990, s 78YB, as amended by the Environment Act 1995, s 57.

European Community influences

The Community policy context

1.12   In parallel to the British developments, the 1970s saw the start of, and the 1980s the maturation of, the European Community's environmental policy. The first European Environment Programme was started in July 1973[1], being justified on several different grounds. Firstly, as a parallel to the Treaty of the European Community's emphasis on economic expansion, there was a need to effect an improvement in the quality of life of Community citizens as well as their standards of living. The second reason concerned the possibility that member states with high environmental standards might find themselves at a competitive disadvantage to countries with laxer standards. Conversely, there was also a need to safeguard against a member state obstructing free trade by using its environmental legislation as a market barrier[2].

1   Although until the Single European Act came into force in 1987, there was no mention of a Community environment policy within the EC Treaty.
2   That this is a genuine concern is apparent from the cases on waste definitions: see Chapter 2.

1.13   The international aspects of global environmental policy-making were also being increasingly recognised at this time. Discharges to major European rivers – such as the Rhine – and the whole issue of acid rain provided a context to the need for an environment component in Community policy making. The vast volume of residuals generated by member states made Community waste management practices one of a number of obvious candidates for initiatives. It has been estimated that 1.2 billion tonnes of non-agricultural waste is generated annually in the Community[1], of which 22 million tonnes is hazardous[2].

1 See OECD (1997) *OECD Environmental Data Compendium 1997* OECD, Paris, figure extracted for 15 EC member states from data contained in Table 7.1A.
2 See OECD (1997) *OECD Environmental Data Compendium 1997* OECD, Paris, figure extracted for 14 EC member states (no data provided for France) from data contained in Table 7.3.

1.14 The extensive internal waste trade between member states particularly called for Community-wide action in this area. From a UK perspective, the issue of cross-border waste movements is much less significant than elsewhere in Europe. The total amount of waste entering the UK is relatively small. However, within the European Community as a whole, the total number of cross-border waste movements of *hazardous waste* (*not* all wastes) has been estimated as being about 100,000 annually, or approximately one movement every five minutes. A number of industrial conurbations are close to member states' borders. And certain countries in the Community – or close to it – are significantly deficient in their waste management infrastructure. Accordingly, they may attract wastes from more 'developed' member states, where environmental controls are more sophisticated and where 'Not in My Backyard' (NIMBY) pressures from concerned citizens are perhaps most acute.

1.15 The need for international controls on cross-border waste movements was well exemplified by an incident in 1983 involving the temporary loss of 41 barrels of dioxin contaminated waste from a major industrial accident at Seveso in Italy[1].

1 Anon (1986) 'Carrier's Wife Paid to Reveal Seveso Dioxin in Plan Brokered by German Interior Minister', *International Environment Reporter* 9 (1) p 8.

1.16 Since the Single European Act came into force in 1987, Community waste management policy has been effectively a subset of the obligations on environmental protection provided for in the amended Treaty[1]. An overall indication of the direction of Community waste management policy is supplied by the five successive Environmental Action Programmes[2] and by the 1989 Community Strategy on Waste Management[3]. The latter was reviewed in 1996[4], being the subject of a Council resolution in 1997[5] which covers a further five-year period.

1 Contained in Title XIX of the EC Treaty, particularly in Article 174 (previously Title XVI and Article 130(r)).
2 *Programme of Action of the European Communities on the Environment* (OJ C112/1 20.12.73); *European Community Action Programme on the Environment (1977–1981)* (OJ C139/3 13.6.77); *EEC Third Environmental Action Programme (1983–1987)* (OJ C46 17.2.83); *EEC Fourth Environmental Action Programme (1987–1992)* (OJ C328/1 7.12.87); *Towards Sustainability – A European Community Programme of Policy and Action in relation to the Environment and Sustainable Development* (OJ C138/5 17.5.93). The latter runs until the year 2000.
3 Commission of the European Communities (1989) *A Community Strategy for Waste Management*, SEC(89) 934 Final, 18 September 1989; Council Resolution of 7 May 1990 on Waste Policy (90C 122/02) (OJ C122/2 18.5.90).
4 *Communication from the Commission on the Review of the Community Strategy for Waste Management* draft Council Resolution on Waste Policy, Brussels 30.07.96, COM(96) 399 Final.
5 *Council Resolution of 24 February 1997 on a Community Strategy for Waste Management* (OJ C76 11 March 1997), p 1.

1.17 Community waste management policy at the outset had a dual objective: a resource conservation strategy and a disposal policy. This was explicitly reinforced by the Fifth Action Programme. Consequently, the Community Strategy on Waste Management[1] suggests a series of Strategic Guidelines:

(1) *Waste Prevention* by the use of 'clean' technologies and by waste minimisation;
(2) *Recycling and Re-use* by the effective re-utilisation of waste after it arises;
(3) *Optimisation of Final Disposal Methods and Technologies* by the expansion of physical, chemical and biological waste pre-treatment. Landfill should be a last resort;
(4) *Effective Regulation of Waste Transportation*;
(5) *Remedial Action on Contaminated Dump Sites*.

Typically, the above guidelines are condensed into the form of a simple, three level hierarchy. This is composed – in order of priority – of waste prevention, recycling and final disposal. The centrality of the hierarchy in policy-making was re-confirmed in 1996 by the Communication from the Commission which reviewed the Waste Strategy[2]. However, like many individual countries, until recently the emphasis of Community waste management policy has been placed on attaining an effective regulatory framework aimed particularly at controlling waste *disposal* activities and waste movements. Indeed, the Communication from the Commission was itself critical of the slowness of progress in respect of the upper elements of the hierarchy[3], noting in particular that waste generation rates across the Community are still increasing.

1   Commission of the European Communities (1989) *A Community Strategy for Waste Management*, SEC(89) 934 Final, 18 September 1989, sections IV to VIII.
2   *Communication from the Commission on the Review of the Community Strategy for Waste Management* draft Council Resolution on Waste Policy, Brussels 30.07.96, COM(96) 399 Final, para 20.
3   *Communication from the Commission on the Review of the Community Strategy for Waste Management* draft Council Resolution on Waste Policy, Brussels 30.07.96, COM(96) 399 Final, para 33.

EC policy implementation

1.18   The implementation of Community waste management initiatives started in the mid 1970s by way of a series of Directives which primarily required the establishment of structures and responsibilities by member states. The most significant of these initiatives is the Directive on Waste[1], which is sometimes referred to as the 'Waste Framework Directive'[2]. This was followed by Directives on Toxic and Dangerous Waste[3], PCBs[4] and waste oils[5].

1   Council Directive of 15 July 1975 on Waste (75/442/EEC) (OJ L194/39 25.7.75) (as amended by Council Directive of 18 March 1991 amending Directive 75/442/EEC on Waste (91/156/EEC) (OJ L78/32 26.3.91)) and by Commission Decision of 24 May 1996 adapting Annexes IIA and IIB to Council Directive 75/442/EEC on Waste (96/350/EEC) (OJ L135/32 6.6.96).
2   Note that, despite the Directive on Waste being substantially amended by Directive 91/156, it retains its original number (75/442/EEC): see, for example, the title of the subsequent decision to establish a Waste Catalogue: 'Commission Decision of 20 December 1993 establishing a list of waste pursuant to Article 1(a) of Council Directive *75/442/EC on waste*'.
3   Council Directive of 20 March 1978 on Toxic and Dangerous Waste, (OJ L84/43 31.3.78) (repealed by Council Directive of 12 December 1991 on Hazardous Waste (91/689/EEC) (OJ L377/20 31.12.91).
4   Council Directive of 6 April 1976 on the disposal of polychlorinated biphenyls and polychlorinated terphenyls (76/403/EEC) (OJ L108 26.4.76) (repealed by Council Directive of 16 September 1996 on the disposal of polychlorinated biphenyls and polychlorinated terphenyls (PCB/PCT) (96/59/EC) (OJ L243 p 31).
5   Council Directive of 16 June 1975 on the disposal of waste oils (75/439/EEC) (OJ L194/23 25.7.85) (subsequently amended by Council Directive of 22 December 1986 amending Directive 75/439/EEC on the disposal of waste oils (87/101/EEC) (OJ L42/43 12.2.87).

1.19   Initially, the Directive on Waste had little influence on British practices as, ironically from a 1990s perspective, the control system in place in Britain was ahead of many member states and the Directive on Waste was partly based on British practice[1]. Indeed, the first time a Directive changed UK waste regulation practices was in 1981 when the Directive on Toxic and Dangerous Waste[2] caused the repeal of the Deposit of Poisonous Waste Act 1972 and its replacement by the Control of Pollution (Special Waste) Regulations 1980[3].

1   See Haigh N (1998) *Manual of European Environmental Policy: The EC and Britain* Cartermill Publishing, London, paras 5.3-4 and 5.3-6.
2   Council Directive on Toxic and Dangerous Waste (78/319) (OJ L84/43 31.3.78).
3   SI 1980/1709.

1.20   Since then, Community instigated environmental law has attained a fundamental and wide-ranging influence over the UK's system of environmental controls. Britain's early lead in these matters dropped rapidly in the 1980s. Indeed, the integration of many Community environmental provisions has been problematic ever since, despite virtually all of them being subject to the UK's earlier prior agreement at the Council of Ministers. For example, the implementation of the waste management licensing system under the EPA 1990 was delayed for a year due to technical problems involved with the matching of that Act to the provisions of the Directive on Waste.

1.21   In hindsight, many of the original waste management directives could be readily criticised for their vagueness. Key problems centred upon a lack of clear definitions of 'waste', 'toxic waste' and of the nature of acceptable disposal. Even after the wording of the Directive on Waste was tightened in 1991[1], the overall environmental objective for member states' waste management controls, namely disposal or recovery '... without endangering human health and without using processes or methods which could harm the environment ...'[2] is clearly very open ended and hence likely to be subject to varied interpretation between countries.

1   By way of Council Directive of 18 March 1991 amending Directive 75/442/EEC on Waste (91/156/EEC) (OJ L78/32 26.3.91).
2   Council Directive of 15 July 1975 on Waste (75/442/EEC), (OJ L194/39 25.7.75) (as amended by Council Directive of 18 March 1991 amending Directive 75/442/EEC on Waste (91/156/EEC) (OJ L78/32 26.3.91)) and by Commission Decision of 24 May 1996 adapting Annexes IIA and IIB to Council Directive 75/442/EEC on Waste (96/350/EEC) (OJ L135/32 6.6.96), Article 4.

1.22   There is therefore an observable trend for the embellishment of the Community provisions, due to the need to respond to the lack of uniform transposition of Directives into national law by member states. Generally, the later Community initiatives are characterised by their greater precision and leave member states with proportionately less discretion. For example, since the late 1980s, a series of Directives emerged which have been specifically aimed at defining acceptable practices at particular types of waste management facility. There are now two Directives on municipal waste incineration[1], and a Directive on hazardous waste incineration[2]. There was also a succession of proposals for a Directive on landfill[3]. However, by the Autumn of 1996, the draft Landfill Directive had become so weakened and internally confused that it was not surprising that the European Parliament vetoed it by a majority of 445 votes to 18[4].

1   Council Directive of June 1989 on the Prevention of Air Pollution from New Municipal Waste Incineration Plants (89/369/EEC); Council Directive of 21 June 1989 on the Reduction of Air Pollution from Existing Municipal Incineration Plans, (89/429/EEC) (OJ L203/50).
2   Council Directive 94/67/EC of 16 December 1994 on the Incineration of Hazardous Waste (OJ L365/34 31.12.94). It is proposed to replace this Directive – along with the two on municipal waste incincerators: see Proposal for a Council Directive on the Incineration of Waste (OJ C372/11 2.12.98) and Proposal for a Council Directive amending Directive 94/67/EC on the Incineration of Hazardous Waste (OJ C13/6 17.1.98). Since these were published, a more recent proposal is to merge these draft Directives. There is also a proposed Council Directive on Port Reception Facilities for Ship-Generated Waste and Cargo Residues (OJ C271/79 31.8.98).

3   Proposal for a Council Directive on the Landfill of Waste, COM(91)102 (OJ C190/1 22.7.91).
    A number of other drafts were also circulated.
4   *ENDS Report* 256 May 1996, p 38.

1.23   A significantly different proposal for a Landfill Directive swiftly emerged in the
winter of 1996, being formally published in 1997[1]. Ironically, given certain member
states' opposition to the earlier proposal, the new proposal is more stringent and wider
ranging in its potential effect. For example, while the earlier version was controversial
for the reason that it wished to restrict co-disposal[2] practices at landfills, the revised
version will extensively reduce the intake of biodegradable wastes at most landfills
(see Table 1.0)[3]. Adopted in 1999, the Directive will need to be transposed into
national law by 16 July 2001[4].

1   Proposal for the Council Directive on the Landfill of Waste (OJ C156/10 24.5.97).
2   The mixing of particular types of hazardous waste with household and other similar wastes.
3   The Directive was considered by the House of Lords Select Committee on the European
    Communities (1998) *Sustainable Landfill* 17th Report 97–98, Stationery Office, London.
4   Council Directive 1999/31/EC on the Landfill of Waste (OJ L182/1 16.7.99) Article 18.

Table 1.0

Landfill Directive Biodegradable Waste Reduction Targets[1]		
Target	To be Achieved by	Derogation for UK[2]
75%	2006	2010
50%	2009	2013
35%	2016	2020

1   Council Directive 99/31/EC on the Landfill of Waste (OJ L182/1 16.7.99), Article 5.2.
2   Article 5.2 of the Landfill Directive would indicate that the UK – and some other member states –
    due to a high reliance on landfill (see para 1.44 below) would obtain a derogation on the targets in
    accordance to the dates set out in the Table.

1.24   There have also been attempts to tighten up on the subject of regulation, namely
by way of defining 'waste' and 'hazardous waste' in much greater detail than hitherto.
A new definition of waste was promulgated in the 1991 amendments to the Directive
on Waste[1], albeit that it still does not fully standardise waste definitions between
member states. The latter criticism is itself raised by the 1996 Communication on the
Waste Strategy[2]. A redefinition of hazardous waste occurred in 1995 when the earlier
Toxic and Dangerous Waste Directive[3] was repealed and replaced by a Directive on
Hazardous Waste[4].

1   Council Directive of 18 March 1991 amending Directive 75/442/EEC on Waste (91/156/EEC)
    (OJ L78/32 26.3.91).
2   Communication from the Commission on the review of the Community Strategy for Waste
    Management. Draft Council Resolution on Waste Policy 30.7.1996, Com(96) 399 Final, para 13.
3   Council Directive of 20 March 1978 on Toxic and Dangerous Waste, (OJ L84/43 31.3.78).
4   Council Directive of 12 December 1991 on Hazardous Waste (91/689/EEC) (OJ L377/20 31.12.91);
    Council Directive 94/31/EC of 27 June 1994 amending Directive 91/689/EEC on Hazardous Waste
    (OJ L168/28 2.7.94).

1.25   A final initiative of relevance is a Directive on Integrated Pollution Prevention
and Control (IPPC)[1]. Unlike the other Directives already referred to, this is more
general in its environmental protection requirements, perhaps reflecting the reality that
member states were not likely to agree a more stringent version. The IPPC Directive
will require the implementation of an integrated pollution control regime on a range of
waste management facilities. These include:

- all hazardous waste disposal facilities in excess of 10 tonnes per day capacity[2];
- hazardous waste recovery facilities in excess of 10 tonnes per day capacity which involve the processing of waste solvents, acids and bases, 'components used for pollution abatement' and waste oil, along with processes which use waste to generate energy[3];
- non-hazardous waste landfills, other than those which accept only inert wastes, of an input rate in excess of 10 tonnes per day or 25,000 tonnes total capacity[4];
- municipal waste incinerators of a capacity of over 3 tonnes per hour[5];
- disposal processes involving biological and physico-chemical waste treatment[6].

Member states are required to transpose the Directive on 30 October 1999[7]. New facilities proposed after that date, along with existing plant where 'substantial changes' are envisaged, will need to comply fully prior to operation[8]. Existing plants have eight years from date of transposition in which to comply[9]. As the IPPC Directive and the proposed Landfill Directive have the potential to overlap, the latter contains a provision[10] to the effect that the requirements of the IPPC Directive are met when there is compliance with the Landfill Directive[11].

1 Council Directive 96/61/EC of 24 September 1996 concerning Integrated Pollution Prevention and Control (OJ L257/26 10.10.96).
2 Directive 96/61, Annex 1, para 5.1.
3 Directive 96/61, Annex 1, para 5.1 as cross-referred to operations R1, R5, R6, R8 and R9 in Annex IIB of Directive 75/442.
4 Directive 96/61, Annex 1, para 5.4.
5 Directive 96/61, Annex 1, para 5.2.
6 Directive 96/61, Annex 1, para 5.3 as cross-referred to operations D8 and D9 in Annex IIA of Directive 75/442.
7 Directive 96/61, Article 21.
8 Directive 96/61, Article 20.
9 Directive 96/61, Articles 5 and 12(2).
10 Council Directive 99/31/EC on the Landfill of Waste (OJ L182/1 16.7.99), Article 1(2).
11 The implementation in Britain of the elements of the IPPC Directive which effect waste management facilities is considered further at para 1.93ff.

Reducing Community waste generation

1.26 As already noted, most of the Community initiatives have focused upon definitions and upon the control of particular waste management processes. Many such initiatives address waste management options which are low down in the waste management hierarchy proposed in the Community Waste Strategy. Initiatives aimed at progressing activities towards the upper echelons of the waste hierarchy – like waste minimisation and recycling – have been somewhat longer in their gestation. However, it seems likely that Community-lead activity will increase in respect of this matter in the next decade. A start was made in 1994, by way of a Directive[1] which attempted to instigate more widespread recycling of the 25 million tonnes of packaging waste produced each year by member states[2].

1 The European Parliament and Council Directive 94/62 of 20 December 1994 on Packaging and Packaging Waste (OJ L365/10 31.12.94).
2 Figure extrapolated from Table 7.1B of OECD (1997) *OECD Environmental Data Compendium 1997*, OECD, Paris.

1.27 In the 1980s, a number of member states commenced the independent drafting of legislation to restrict the production of waste packaging and to encourage its re-use and recycling. Such initiatives were aided by a judgment of the European Court which permitted Denmark unilaterally to ban metal drink cans and to require that all drinks containers be refillable[1]. Rather than allow such unilateral actions by individual member states and the trade barriers that are often an inevitable consequence, as well as to attempt to create and maintain stable European-wide markets for recycled materials, the Commission attempted to regain some of the initiative by way of its own proposal for a Packaging Directive[2]. In 1996 the Directive replaced an earlier, and rather anodyne, beverage containers Directive[3].

1 *Commission EC v Denmark*: 302/86 [1988] ECR 4607, [1990] 2 JEL No 1 p 89.
2 The European Parliament and Council Directive 94/62 of 20 December 1994 on Packaging and Packaging Waste (OJ L365/10 31.12.94).
3 Council Directive of 27 June 1985 on Containers of Liquids for Human Consumption (85/339) (OJ L176/18 6.7.85), which was repealed by Article 23 of Directive 94/62.

1.28 The Packaging Directive contains ambitious recycling targets, requiring that between 50% and 65% of packaging waste be removed from the waste stream for recovery within five years of June 1996[1]. In addition, between 25% and 45% of such waste has to be recycled[2]. The distinction between 'recovery' and 'recycling' is principally that the former includes incineration with energy generation[3]. A more ambitious longer term target for the next five years is to be determined in the year 2000[4]. It would appear that this Directive is very much seen as the first in a series, which will set targets for the reduction and recovery of different waste types[5].

1 Directive 94/62, Article 6(1)(a).
2 Directive 94/62, Article 6(1)(b).
3 Directive 94/62, Article 3(6), 3(7) and 3(8).
4 Directive 94/62, Article 6(3).
5 Communication from the Commission on the review of the Community Strategy for Waste Management. Draft Council Resolution on Waste Policy 30.7.1996, Com(96) 399 Final, para 70.

1.29 Mention should also be made to proposed Directives on end of life vehicles[1] and electronic waste[2]. While these proposals are likely to be subject to change in order to attain the agreement of member states, these provisions illustrate the process of interweaving of the Directive on Waste's regulatory structures (eg objectives of preventing 'environmental pollution', permits, definition of waste) with a resources policy component aimed at stimulating enhanced reclamation and/or waste reduction. Both proposed Directives are founded on the definition of waste in the Directive on Waste[3], and require that end of life vehicles and electronic wastes always pass to an authorised facility for collection or dismantling. The latter is required to be operated in a manner which will neither cause pollution nor otherwise contravene the Directive on Waste[4]. Hence technical requirements for such facilities – for example impermeable surfacing or degassing of chlorinated fluorocarbons – are set out. The draft vehicles Directive requires that 're-use and recovery'[5] is to account for 85% by weight of a vehicle by 2005 and 95% by 2015. Targets are also proposed in the draft Directive for the re-use and recycling of electronic wastes. If nothing else, the existence of these proposals clearly illustrates the fact that the definition of 'waste' in the Directive on Waste extends to materials of economic value which pass to recycling facilities[6].

1 Proposal for a Council Directive on end of life vehicles (97/C 337/02) OJ C337/3 7.11.97: see Pocklington D 'An Assessment of the Proposed European Legislation on End-of-Life Vehicles' EELR May 1998 p 138.
2 Proposal for a Directive on Waste from Electrical and Electronic Equipment. It is understood that this proposal has yet to be published in the Official Journal of the European Communities.
3 It is notable that this is less explicit in the proposed Directive on electronic waste. However, it is implicit due to the use of cross-references to the requirements of the Directive on Waste in respect of collection facilities not causing environmental pollution and being subject to the Directive's system of permits.
4 Council Directive of 15 July 1975 on Waste (75/442/EEC) (OJ L194/39 25.7.75), as amended by Council Directive of 18 March 1991 amending Directive 75/442/EEC on Waste (91/156/EEC) (OJ L78/32 26.3.91), Article 4.

5   Ie including combustion for the purposes of energy recovery.
6   A point developed extensively in Chapter 2.

1.30   An essential prerequisite to any system which attempts to establish national waste recovery targets is a common statistical base which is readily comparable between countries. While there remains no common and unified definition of waste across all member states[1], a European Waste Catalogue was finalised[2] in 1994 with the objective of setting down the foundations of Community-wide waste management statistics[3]. In 1999, a formalised methodology for the compilation of waste statistics was proposed as a draft council Regulation[4].

1   Chapter 2 shows this deficit is unlikely to be rectified in the short term, if at all.
2   Commission Decision of 20 December 1993 establishing a list of wastes pursuant to Article 1(a) of Council Directive 75/442/EEC on Waste (Decision 94/3) (OJ L5/15 7.1.94).
3   Communication from the Commission on the review of the Community Strategy for Waste Management. Draft Council Resolution on Waste Policy 30.7.1996, Com(96) 399 Final, para 83.
4   Proposal for a Council Regulation (EC) on Waste Management Statistics (OJ C87/22 29.3.99).

Transfrontier waste controls

1.31   Finally, reference should be made to the Community's control system on international waste movements. A major policy problem for certain member states was the need to adequately regulate cross-border movements of waste. In 1984, the extensive international waste trade became the specific subject of a Directive[1], which was a response to the considerable volume of waste moved internally within the Community and a reaction to the 41 wandering Seveso drums[2]. When the Toxic and Dangerous Waste Directive was being drafted, it was felt that existing legislation and a number of ad-hoc conventions between member states presented a sufficient level of control[3]. The Seveso drum incident therefore called into question the efficacy of member states' and the Community's existing regulatory framework.

1   Council Directive of 6 December 1984 on the Supervision and Control within the European Community of the Transfrontier Shipment of Hazardous Waste (OJ L326/31 13.12.84), as amended by the Council Directive of 22 July 1985 adapting to technical progress Council Directive 84/631/EEC on the supervision and control within the European Community of the transfrontier shipment of hazardous waste (85/469/EEC) (OJ L272/1 12.10.85); Council Directive of 12 June 1986 amending Directive 84/631/EEC on the supervision and control within the European Community of the transfrontier shipment of hazardous waste (86/279/EEC) (OJ L181/13 4.7.86); Council Directive of 23 December 1986 adapting to technical progress for the second time Council Directive 84/631/EEC on the supervision and control within the European Community of the transfrontier shipment of hazardous waste, (87/112/EEC) (OJ L48/31 17.2.87).
2   See para 1.15.
3   Haigh N (1987) *EEC Environmental Policy and Britain* 2nd edn, Longman, p 147.

1.32   However, the policy approach at Community level towards transfrontier waste movements was markedly different in the 1980s to that observed in the 1990s. Until roughly late 1989, it was proposed that the free trade provisions concomitant with the creation of the Single Market should apply to international shipments of wastes as well as goods. This meant the creation of a type of 'Euro-Waste Free Market', a concept of highly dubious practical and political validity[1]. Eventually, practical realities prevailed. The 1989 Waste Strategy proposed[2] what has become known as the 'proximity principle': that wastes should be disposed of[3] as close to their origin as is possible.

1   The proposal failed to take into account that such measures, which effectively legitimate the trade, would also stimulate movements to member states whose infrastructure and regulatory controls are at best rudimentary.
2   Commission of the European Communities (1989) *A Community Strategy for Waste Management*, SEC(89) 934 Final, 18 September 1989, p 23.

3 Typically, the proximity principle does not apply to waste movements destined for recycling: Article 5 of the Directive on Waste (as amended) refers only to 'disposal' activities, not recovery facilities. Similarly Article 4 of Council Regulation 259/93 allows member states to prevent cross-border waste movements only in respect of disposal sites.

1.33 Although the proximity principle was enshrined in the Directive on Waste when it was amended in 1991[1], the enactment of the principle in respect of cross-border waste movements was mainly driven by extra-Community institutions in the form of the United Nations Environment Programme and the OECD[2]. Indeed, the Transfrontier Directive[3] had to be scrapped entirely with the ratification by the Community of the Basel Convention[4]. All member states are parties to the Basel Convention, which is aimed at protecting less developed countries from the indiscriminate dumping of 'developed' countries' waste. As explained in Chapter 5, the Basel Convention requires that European countries should be looking inwardly to provide the infrastructure to dispose of Europe's residuals. To accord with the Convention, and the subsequent OECD Decision on wastes passing to recovery[5], the Community's cross border control system had to be expanded to address all transfrontier waste movements, not only those involving hazardous wastes. In addition, a significant change was made to the tradition by which Community provisions were transposed. A Regulation, rather than a Directive, was selected as a vehicle by which to enact this policy[6]. The Council Regulation on Transfrontier Waste Shipments (Regulation 259/93)[7] is perhaps the most complex of all the provisions of the Community on environmental protection. It is discussed in detail in Chapter 5.

1 Council Directive of 15 July 1975 on Waste (75/442/EEC) (OJ L194/39 25.7.75) as amended by Council Directive of 18 March 1991 amending Directive 75/442/EEC on Waste (91/156/EEC) (OJ L78/32 26.3.91), Article 5.
2 Organisation for Economic Co-operation and Development.
3 Council Directive of 6 December 1984 on the Supervision and Control within the European Community of the Transfrontier Shipment of Hazardous Waste (OJ L326/31 13.12.84).
4 1989 Convention on the Control of Transboundary Movements of Hazardous Wastes and their Disposal (1 JEL No 2 (1989), pp 255–277).
5 OECD Decision on the Control of Transfrontier Movements of Waste Destined for Recovery Operations (OECD C(92)39/Final as amended by Decision C(93)74/Final 23.7.93, Decision C(94) 153 28.7.94 and Decision C(96)231 10.12.96: see para 5.21ff).
6 Directives require transposition by a member state's own legislation, Regulations are directly applicable in all member states and do not require transposition: see EC Treaty Article 249 (formerly Article 189).
7 Council Regulation (EEC) No 259/93 of 1 February 1993 on the supervision and control of shipments of waste within, into and out of the European Community (OJ L30/1 6.2.93).

THE WASTE MANAGEMENT INDUSTRY IN BRITAIN[1]

1.34 In parallel to the development of both domestic and Community legislation, the British waste industry has become increasingly sophisticated over the last three decades. Until the implementation of the EPA 1990, there were, in effect, three quite distinct and separate branches of the waste management industry. The first consisted of the private sector waste disposal companies, which ranged from owner-driver skip operators to major public limited companies. These dealt extensively in the carriage and disposal of commercial and industrial waste, also providing a limited household waste disposal infrastructure. The second sector of the waste industry centred upon the local authorities, which collected virtually all household waste and whose household waste disposal sites also provided a significant outlet for commercial and industrial wastes gathered by the private sector. The final component was the recycling industry which covered the reclamation of scrap metal, vehicle dismantling, waste paper processing, plastics recovery and other similar activities.

1   This section provides a variety of statistics on the waste industry which have been compiled from a range of sources. As there appears little consensus as to the exact breadth of the industry – for example whether the scrap metal industry is included and also the contribution resultant from construction activities – inevitable discrepancies between figures arise. No attempt has been made below to reconcile such problems. The information is presented solely to illustrate the magnitude and variety of the 'waste industry' (however defined).

1.35   By the 1990s the distinction between the public and private sector operators has become much less sharp, particularly in England and Wales. This decade also saw the start of the integration of some of the recycling industry within certain waste disposal companies.

1.36   The duality involving the private and public sectors was significantly affected by two related government policy initiatives. Firstly, the compulsory competitive tendering system established in the 1980s for local authority refuse collection introduced much more private sector involvement[1]. Secondly, under s 32 of the EPA 1990, local authorities in England and Wales were required to divest themselves of their waste disposal infrastructure, including landfills, household waste incinerators, transfer stations and civic amenity sites[2]. The legislation left the local authorities with what were essentially two options. The first was to form a Local Authority Waste Disposal Company (LAWDC) which, whilst wholly controlled by the local authority, was operated at 'arms length' to it, by way of an independent board of directors[3]. The alternative solution was to sell off the waste management assets to the private sector. Both of the options have been extensively utilised, and most LAWDCs have been subsequently sold by their local authority masters.

1   By way of the provisions contained in the Local Government Act 1988.
2   Transfer stations are facilities whereby waste is deposited by collection vehicles, being bulked up for long-distance transport into larger capacity vehicles. Civic amenity sites are facilities where the public can dispose of those wastes which are not gathered by the normal household waste collection rounds.
3   See Department of the Environment (1991) *Competition for Local Authority Waste Disposal Contracts and New Arrangements for Disposal Operations* Circular 8/91, HMSO, London.

1.37   Besides the traditional differentiation between the public and private sector waste industry, activities involving recycling and reclamation did not, in the past, consider themselves to be part of the national waste management industry. The perception was that this sector dealt with 'secondary raw materials', not wastes[1]. Historic roots and ownership were often quite distinct and, until the late 1980s, much of the recycling industry was subject to considerably less formal regulation.

1   This distinction was perhaps the cause of the case of *R v Rotherham Metropolitan Borough Council, ex p Rankin* [1990] 1 PLR 93 where the planning permission of a solvent recovery facility was the subject of a judicial review due to a failure to advertise the application as 'bad neighbour' development under the Town and Country Planning Act 1971.

1.38   However, this distinction has also been subject to change, albeit that actual industrial restructuring appears by no means over. Structural change is likely to be encouraged by the recognition of the contribution of the recycling industry towards the delivery of the national waste strategy and to the Landfill Directive's biodegradable waste diversion targets. Given the increased emphasis on recycling and reclamation at the expense of the option of final disposal, particularly disposal by way of landfill[1], commercial providers of waste management capacity are increasingly looking at the provision of integrated reclamation and disposal systems. Hence the traditional structural boundaries between the waste management and the recycling industry are breaking down. For example, in the 1990s a number of waste paper merchants were purchased by certain companies which had been hitherto focused upon landfill site management. Further integration would seem inevitable in the next decade. Finally, the waste regulatory provisions of the EPA 1990 acknowledge that many recycling activities involve materials falling within the statutory meaning of controlled wastes. Many of these activities are also sources of pollution, particularly land contamination, and hence statutory controls are applicable to them.

1   See para 1.09.

1.39   The structure of the waste industry remains interesting. Firstly, a very large number of organisations are involved in different facets of the industry. The extent and texture of the private sector involvement is shown in Table 1.1. Secondly, while a small number of large public limited companies appear to dominate the market, this tends to disguise the major presence of smaller operators. Indeed, market research has described the waste management sector as 'highly fragmented' in respect of other UK industries and the waste industry overseas[1]. A report published in 1997 indicated that no single company had a national market share in excess of 6% and that, while the then ten major companies exhibited a 43% market share, the remainder of the sector was characterised by a myriad of smaller concerns[2], many of which operated only a local presence. Indeed, dominance of small companies is particularly evident in the case of motor vehicle dismantling and in skip hire. Overall, it is estimated that about 77,000 people are employed in the waste industry[3].

1   Department of Trade and Industry (1997) *The Competitiveness of the UK Waste Management Industry*, DTI, London, p 50.
2   Department of Trade and Industry (1997) *The Competitiveness of the UK Waste Management Industry*, DTI, London, p 50.
3   Department of Trade and Industry (1997) *The Competitiveness of the UK Waste Management Industry*, DTI, London, para 2.5.

Table 1.1

Estimated Numbers of Organisations involved in Waste Management[1]	
Waste Disposal Services	1838
Waste Paper Merchants	315
Waste Product Reclaimers	86
Waste Food Processors	24
Waste Materials Merchants	42
Waste Oil and Solvent Services	88
Scrap and General Merchants	2035
Tank Cleaning and Servicing	93
Asbestos Removal and Disposal	159
Commercial Cleaning and Maintenance	2738
Demolition Services	652
Total	8070

1   From Holmes J (1995) *The UK Waste Management Industry*, Institute of Wastes Management, Northampton, Table 21, as compiled from information supplied by British Telecom. Excludes general road haulage companies. Some double counting has been caused by multiple entries in Telecom's database. By contrast, the DTI estimate that there are about 3500 firms who make up the core of the British waste management industry (see Department of Trade and Industry (1997) *The Competitiveness of the UK Waste Management Industry*, DTI, London, p 45). However, it is evident that the DTI are using a narrower definition of 'the waste industry' and it seems that scrap metal and waste paper processors are, for example, excluded.

1.40   Mergers have been an extensive feature of this industrial sector since the late 1970s[1] and it seems inevitable that restructuring will continue. Water privatisation in the 1980s caused providers of water services to diversify. Increasing inward invest-ment by French and US firms has also been a feature[2].

1 Department of Trade and Industry (1997) *The Competitiveness of the UK Waste Management Industry*, DTI, London, p 43.
2 Department of Trade and Industry (1997) *The Competitiveness of the UK Waste Management Industry*, DTI, London, para 2.5. See also, for example, Miller-Bakewell M (1997) 'French take the lead' *The Waste Manager*, March 1997, pp 10–11; Owen D (1997) 'The French are coming' *The Waste Manager*, September 1997, pp 12–13.

1.41 The removal and subsequent management of controlled wastes in the UK is estimated to cost about £3.5 billion annually[1], accounting for an estimated 0.5% of GDP[2]. These very significant figures stem from the universal nature of wastes in an industrial society, and the vast volume generated annually. It is estimated that approxi-mately 423 million tonnes of waste are produced annually in the UK[3], of which 245 million tonnes have been claimed by the Department of the Environment to fall within the definition of 'controlled waste'[4]. Only controlled waste is subject to Part II of the EPA 1990[5] and to the waste regulatory system which will be fully described in later chapters.

1 Department of Trade and Industry (1997) *The Competitiveness of the UK Waste Management Industry*, DTI, London, para 1.2; see also Department of the Environment (1992) *Waste Management Paper No 1 – A Review of Options*, 2nd edn, HMSO, London, para 2.44.
2 Department of Trade and Industry (1997) *The Competitiveness of the UK Waste Management Industry*, DTI, London, para 1.2 and Annex B.
3 Department of the Environment, Transport and the Regions (1998) *Digest of Environmental Statistics No 20*, Stationery Office, London, Table 7.1.
4 Department of the Environment (1995) *Making Waste Work: A Strategy for Sustainable Waste Management in England and Wales*, Cm 3040, HMSO, London, para 1.16.
5 See Chapter 2.

1.42 A breakdown of the UK's major waste arisings is contained in Table 1.2. It can be seen that the two largest types of waste arising are agricultural wastes and wastes from mines and quarries. Neither of these are subject to the EPA 1990, for the reason that they are not defined as 'controlled wastes'[1]. Of the controlled wastes shown in Table 1.2, wastes from construction and demolition activities, as well as wastes from other industrial sources, are the most significant. Indeed, these quantities dwarf the 29 million tonnes of household waste which arises annually from UK domestic properties.

1 EPA 1990, s 75(7): this position is expected to change, see para 2.29ff.

1.43 It is easy to underestimate the contribution of the construction and demolition industry in UK waste management, despite the fact that this sector produces as much controlled waste as all of the remainder of the country's industrial activities. The EPA 1990 places significant constraints on the manner by which construction and demoli-tion companies are able to deal with the wastes they generate. It is for this reason that a number of sections of the forthcoming chapters focus on the implications for this industrial sector of particular elements of the EPA 1990 and subsidiary regulations.

1.44 Landfill is by far the dominant disposal route for all controlled waste produced in the UK[1] and, according to the Department of the Environment, landfill accounts for the disposal of 120 million tonnes of waste per year[2]. It has been estimated that the national landfill market is worth £700 million annually[3].

1 Department of the Environment (1995) *Making Waste Work: A Strategy for Sustainable Waste Management in England and Wales*, Cm 3040, HMSO, London, para 1.17.

2 Department of the Environment (1995) *Making Waste Work: A Strategy for Sustainable Waste Management in England and Wales*, Cm 3040, HMSO, London, para 2.189.
3 Department of Trade and Industry (1997) *The Competitiveness of the UK Waste Management Industry*, DTI, London, para 1.2.

Table 1.2

Estimated Waste Arisings in the UK[1]

Waste Type	Quantity (mt: million tonnes)	Percentage of Total	Controlled Waste
Agricultural Waste	80 mt	19%	No
Construction and Mining and Quarrying Waste	74 mt	17%	No
Demolition Waste	70 mt	17%	Yes
Dredged Spoils	51 mt	12%	Yes
Industrial Waste	50 mt	12%	Yes
Sewage Sludge	35 mt	8%	some[2]
Household Waste	26 mt	6%	Yes
Commercial Waste	15 mt	4%	Yes
Power Station Ash	13 mt	3%	Yes
Blast Furnace Ash and Slag	6 mt	1%	Yes
Other Municipal Waste	2 mt	>1%	Yes
Total	423 mt[3]		

1 Department of the Environment, Transport and the Regions (1998) *Digest of Environmental Statistics* No 20, Stationery Office, London, Table 7.1.
2 Although the Department of the Environment's White Paper *Making Waste Work* suggests that all sewage sludge is a controlled waste (see Department of the Environment (1995) *Making Waste Work: A Strategy for Sustainable Waste Management in England and Wales*; Cm 3040, HMSO, London, Figure 1.1 and paras 1.1.5, 1.16), this is not strictly correct. As is discussed in Chapter 2, sewage sludge spread on farmland under the Sludge (Use in Agriculture) Regulations 1989 (SI 1989/1263) is not a controlled waste when managed in accordance with the Regulations (see the Controlled Waste Regulations, SI 1992/588, reg 7(1)(b) and see para 2.223ff).
3 It would appear that rounding in the figures as originally published causes them not to fully add-up.

1.45   The significance of the landfill disposal route and the other waste management options is shown in Table 1.3. Besides the domination by landfill as the management option for all of the major categories of controlled waste, another feature of note from the Table is the very small quantity of waste currently subject to incineration. Furthermore, despite the increasing prevalence of infrastructure such as bottle and waste paper banks throughout British towns, the amount of household waste recycled still remains a stubbornly small proportion of the total[1].

1 A more recent survey suggests that 6.5% of the 29 million tonnes of household waste is recycled: Department of the Environment, Transport and the Regions (1998) *Municipal Waste Management 1997/98*, DETR publications sales, London.

1.46   Finally, brief mention should be made of waste management prices. As noted earlier, waste management in the UK costs about £3.5 billion each year. Table 1.4 presents example prices for some common types of wastes. However, there will be considerable variations in prices nationally due to geographical differences and the level of competition between operators[1]. Since the implementation of the landfill tax,

Table 1.3

Major Waste Management Options for Controlled Wastes[1]

Type of waste	Landfill	Incineration	Recycle/ Re-use	Other
Household	90%	5%	5%	–
Commercial	85%	7.5%	7.5%	–
Construction and Demolition	63%	–	30%	7%
Industrial	73%	1%	18%	6%
All Controlled Wastes	70%	2%	21%	7%

1   Department of the Environment (1995) *Making Waste Work: A Strategy for Sustainable Waste Management in England and Wales*, Cm 3040, HMSO, London, Figure 1.2. The figures in the Table exclude sewage sludge and dredgings.

virtually no mixed skip waste – for example unsorted industrial waste such as packaging or builder's waste from a house renovation – passes directly to landfill. The cost of such an activity, which would be well in excess of £100 per load, is too great. Instead as much material as possible is subject to pre-sorting at waste transfer stations. This is in order to prevent the entire contents being subject to the £10[1] per tonne landfill tax, as would have been the case if delivered directly to landfill. Hence, the inert materials are recovered or pass to landfill at the lower tax rate of £2 per tonne. Recyclable materials are abstracted and as little as possible sent to landfill at the highest rate of the landfill tax. While the landfill tax has caused a major structural shift in the national arrangements for the management of non-hazardous biodegradable wastes, the disposal of many hazardous wastes is an even more costly exercise. These matters illustrate the financial incentive for unauthorised dumping and hence the key role the law plays in making this as unattractive an option as possible[2].

1   1999 figure: this is to rise annually by £1 per tonne up to 2004.
2   Prices involving biodegradable waste disposal to landfill will rise further with the implementation of the Landfill Directive.

Table 1.4

Common Waste Management Prices

Example	Total[1] (£)
30m³ container of non-special industrial waste	£200[2]
8m³ builders' skip	£85[3]
Mini-skip	£45[4]

1   Prices expressed per load, including landfill tax.
2   Assumes waste is not compacted and payload is 4–5 tonnes only.
3   Assumes significant non-inert waste content and payload of 1–2 tonnes.
4   Assumes significant non-inert waste content and payload of 0.5 tonnes.

1.47   While not part of the bone-fide waste management infrastructure, a small industry has grown up which attempts to exploit the financial benefits of unauthorised disposal activities. Although there does not appear to be a significant involvement in organised crime in British waste management outside certain major cities, a minority of small-scale operators are extensively involved in fly-tipping. Others are involved in illicit sorting and bulking-up activities as a way of avoiding spiralling landfill charges. Fortunately, the materials involved are often construction, demolition and less environmentally significant industrial wastes. However, this activity is not only a considerable nuisance to the public and landowners. The policing of unauthorised waste management activities occupies a critical amount of the Environment Agency's waste regulation staff time, and remediation is also a significant public expense. For example, the clearance of fly-tipped wastes in Britain in 1991 was estimated to cost local authorities and landowners at least £20m per year[1]. Chapters 7 and 12 discuss the legal provisions by which the Environment Agency is able to respond to this issue.

1   Department of the Environment (1991) *The Duty of Care: A Draft Circular, A Consultation Paper and Draft Regulations under s 34(5)* (22 July 1991) Annex B, Compliance Cost Assessment, para A2.

THE STATUTORY ROLES

1.48   Although the main focus of the control system contained in the EPA 1990 is the Environment Agency, it will be seen that, in practice, the system is far more intricate. For the system to work effectively, a partnership needs to exist between the various statutory bodies. The roles do, to a certain extent, overlap and boundaries are not always clearly delineated in the relevant legislation.

The Environment Agency

1.49   On 1 April 1996, with the commencement of the relevant sections of the Environment Act 1995, the Environment Agency in England and Wales[1] was created, along with the Scottish Environment Protection Agency[2]. These two Agencies were formed out of a number of the earlier pollution control bodies whose powers, property and staff transferred over. In England, the single largest body to transfer was the National Rivers Authority[3]. The functions of this body transferred wholesale and these included[4] the policing of water quality by way of the Water Resources Act 1991, along with significant other powers in respect of flood defence[5].

1   By way of SI 1995/1983 and SI 1996/186.
2   By SI 1995/2649 and SI 1996/186.
3   In Scotland, the equivalent bodies were the River Purification Authorities: however flood defence functions were not transferred.
4   The following more significant NRA functions transferred (Environment Act 1995, s 2(1)(a)): Pts II (water resources management), III (pollution control) and IV (flood defence) of the Water Resources Act 1991; the functions under the Land Drainage Act 1991 (including functions under s 138(8) of the Water Act 1989); and functions under the Diseases of Fish Act 1937, the Sea Fisheries Regulation Act 1966 and the Salmon and Freshwater Fisheries Act 1975; functions as navigation authority, harbour authority or conservancy authority passed to the NRA by way of Pt III of the Water Act 1989.
5   Transferred by the Environment Act 1995, ss 2 and 3 and by SI 1996/234.

1.50   Also transferred were the functions under Part I of the EPA 1990 of Her Majesty's Inspectorate of Pollution[1], along with those of the Inspectorate's duties under the Radioactive Substances Act 1993[2]. Part I of the EPA 1990 established a system of Integration Pollution Control (IPC) authorisations for major items of industrial plant. IPC authorisations cover much of the more significant controlled waste combustion and hazardous waste recovery infrastructure, involving hazardous waste incinerators, other incinerators of over one tonne per hour capacity[3], cement kilns, solvent recovery facilities and plants manufacturing fuel from waste[4].

1   Environment Act 1995, s 2(1)(d), (f) and (g).
2   Environment Act 1995, s (1)(e).
3   Including all of the national household waste incinerator infrastructure and similar clinical waste
     disposal facilities.
4   See SI 1991/972, Sch 1 as amended by SIs 1991/836, 1992/614, 1993/1749, 1993/2405, 1994/1271,
     1994/1329, 1995/3247, 1996/2678 and 1998/767.

1.51   The functions of 'waste regulation authorities' were also transferred[1]. Prior to
the formation of the two Agencies, there were 80[2] separate waste regulation authorities
(WRAs)[3]. Their functions were contained in the Control of Pollution (Amendment)
Act 1989, Part II of the EPA 1990 and in other regulations[4]. These enactments were the
main waste regulatory powers, covering waste management licensing, controlled
waste carrier and broker registration, powers in respect of unauthorised disposal activities and so on. In England, the functions transferred mainly from the County Councils[5] and from the district councils in Wales[6].

1   Environment Act 1995, s 2(1)(b).
2   Department of the Environment (1995) *Making Waste Work: A Strategy for Sustainable Waste*
     Management in England and Wales, Cm 3040, HMSO, London, para 4.28.
3   The English shire counties, the Welsh and Scottish district councils, varying arrangements in the
     metropolitan areas.
4   Principally SIs 1989/1263, 1990/880, 1991/1624, 1991/2839, 1992/588, 1994/1056, 1994/1137,
     1995/288, 1995/1950 and 1996/634.
5   As constituted by the EPA 1990, s 30(1)(a).
6   EPA 1990, s 30(1)(f). Different arrangements existed in the metropolitan areas (EPA 1990,
     s 30(1)(c),(d) and (e)) and in London (EPA 1990, s 30(1)(b)).

1.52   Although all of these functions transferred, the use of the term 'waste regulation authority' is retained in the EPA 1990. However, the EPA 1990 was amended so
that there are now only two such authorities: the Environment Agency in England and
Wales[1] and the Scottish Environment Protection Agency[2]. Both Agencies are allowed
to make charges to recover their costs in enacting specified functions and there are
slight differences in the rates apportioned[3].

1   EPA 1990, s 30(1)(a) as amended by the Environment Act 1995, s 120(1) and Sch 22, para 62(2).
2   EPA 1990, s 30(1)(b) as amended by the Environment Act 1995, s 120(1) and Sch 22, para 62(2).
3   See Environment Agency (1999) *Waste Management Licensing (Charges) Scheme 1999–2000*,
     Environment Agency, Bristol and Scottish Environment Protection Agency (1999) *Waste Management*
     Charging (Scotland) Scheme 1999, SEPA, Stirling and see para 9.142ff.

1.53   The Environment Agency also gained certain new functions in respect of waste
management. Section 92 of the Environment Act 1995 introduced a provision[1] which
requires the Agency to provide advice to the Secretary of State on the production of a
national waste strategy for England and Wales[2]. This function superseded the waste
management planning provisions contained in s 50 of the EPA 1990, which the Environment Act 1995 repealed[3]. The Agency also became responsible for the oversight of
the 'producer responsibility scheme' contained in s 93 of the Environment Act 1995.
The scheme is enacted by way of secondary legislation[4] and, at the time of writing, is
mainly concerned with the implementation of the Packaging Directive[5]. The Agency
will also have significant functions in respect of the Pollution Prevention and Control
Act 1999[6], as well as the new contaminated land regime[7] when it is implemented.

1   EPA 1990, s 44A.
2   EPA 1990, s 44A(6). By contrast SEPA itself produces the strategy for Scotland (EPA 1990, s 44B).
3   Environment Act 1995, s 120(1), Sch 22, para 78.
4   The Producer Responsibility Obligations (Packaging Waste) Regulations 1997 (SI 1997/648), as
     amended by the Producer Responsibility Obligations (Packaging Waste) (Amendment) Regulations
     1999 (SI 1999/1361).

5 The European Parliament and Council Directive 94/62 of 29 December 1994 on Packaging and Packaging Waste, (OJ L365/10 31.12.94).
6 See para 1.93ff.
7 EPA 1990, Part IIA as amended by the Environment Act 1995, s 57.

1.54 Finally, certain functions which were hitherto the domain of central government also became the Environment Agency's responsibility[1]. For waste management, one of the most significant was the responsibility for the monitoring of the spreading of sewage sludge[2]. In addition, the Agency is now responsible for the production of technical guidance in the form of Waste Management Papers[3]. Prior to April 1996, these documents were drafted by the Department of the Environment.

1 Environment Act 1995, s 2(1)(h).
2 Environment Act 1995, s 3(2)(b): sewage sludge spreading is controlled under the Sludge (Use in Agriculture) Regulations 1989 (as amended by SI 1990/880 and, particularly, SI 1995/593, reg 5), being previously under the domain of the Ministry of Agriculture, Fisheries and Food.
3 Department of the Environment (1995) *Making Waste Work: A Strategy for Sustainable Waste Management in England and Wales*, Cm 3040, HMSO, London, para 4.31. A full listing of the Waste Management Papers is contained in Appendix I.

The Secretary of State

1.55 Besides general policy-making and the drafting of legislation, the Secretary of State[1] has one principal function in relation to the regulation of waste management activities. The Secretary of State deals with appeals by persons aggrieved in respect of the Environment Agency's determination of waste management licences[2] and controlled waste carrier[3] and broker registrations[4]. These appeals have been delegated to the Planning Inspectorate in Bristol[5]. Usually, the Inspectorate will consider the evidence and determine the appeal on behalf of the Secretary of State. However, as is the case with planning appeals, the Secretary of State can 'recover' the appeal and determine it in-house. Instances where this might occur[6] include cases of national importance or significant local controversy, cases subject to 'significant legal difficulties', or where policy precedents may be involved.

1 In England, the Secretary of State for the Environment, Transport and the Regions. Different arrangements will apply – post devolution – in Wales.
2 EPA 1990, s 43 as amended by Environment Act 1995, s 120(1), Sch 22, para 77. See para 9.126ff.
3 Control of Pollution (Amendment) Act 1989.
4 SI 1994/1056, reg 20.
5 Environment Act 1995, s 114: see also Department of the Environment (1996) *Waste Management Licences: The Appeals Procedure Guidance.*
6 Department of the Environment (1996) *Waste Management Licences: The Appeals Procedure Guidance*, Appendix 4, para 4.2. Examples given include appeals concerning financial provision elements of waste management licences (financial provision is discussed at para 8.177ff), questions involving assessment of the technical competence of a licensee (see para 8.130ff), the use of new disposal techniques and licence surrender (see para 9.93ff).

1.56 In addition to the appellate function, the EPA 1990 contained significant default powers to ensure that specified actions were undertaken by the local authority-based waste regulation authorities[1]. These powers were never used and were repealed by the Environment Act 1995[2]. However, powers which permit the Secretary of State to give the Agency directions as to the content of waste management licences[3] and whether a licence should be suspended or revoked[4] are retained in the EPA 1990.

1 EPA 1990, s 72.
2 Environment Act 1995, s 120(1), Sch 22, para 87.
3 EPA 1990, s 35(7) and (8).
4 EPA 1990, s 38(7) and 42(8).

1.57   The Secretary of State also has the inevitable policy-making role, which is enacted by way of legislation and published guidance. The draft National Waste Strategy has already been mentioned[1]. The Environment Agency is required to undertake national waste arisings surveys in order to generate greater confidence in the statistical basis of the figures which will form the foundation of the finalised Strategy[2]. Once on a statutory footing, the Strategy will satisfy the requirement of s 44A of the EPA 1990[3], that the Secretary of State produce a strategy 'as soon as possible'[4]. It seems unlikely that this will occur before mid 2000 at the earliest.

1   Department of the Environment (1995) *Making Waste Work: A Strategy for Sustainable Waste Management in England and Wales*, Cm 3040, HMSO, London.
2   EPA 1990, s 44A(6).
3   As amended by the Environment Act 1995, s 92.
4   EPA 1990, s 44A(1). See House of Commons Environment, Transport and the Regions Committee (1998) *Sustainable Waste Management* 6th Report, Vols I–III, Stationery Office, London.

The local authorities

1.58   Despite losing their waste regulatory functions in 1996, local authorities continue to play a significant role in waste management. In particular, the British legislation closely interweaves the development control and waste management licensing provisions. It will prove vitally important that the Environment Agency and local authorities are able to work in partnership and in the manner intended by the legislation.

The planning authority

1.59   In England, waste management is a county matter for the purposes of the Town and Country Planning Act 1990[1]. Being so defined, the development control aspects of such facilities are the responsibility of the county council, rather than the district councils which deal with most other planning issues. The only exceptions are where a particular development is located in a London metropolitan district or where a unitary planning authority, or a national park authority has been created. In these instances, these bodies will have responsibility for the development control aspects of waste management facilities in parallel to their other planning functions. In Wales it is done by the 22 unitary authorities, which are either county or county borough councils; and in Scotland planning is undertaken by the 32 unitary authorities.

1   See Town and Country (Prescription of County Matters) Regulations 1980, SI 1980/2010.

1.60   Planning Policy Guidance Note 23 lists the activities which in 'the Department's view'[1] are county matters when involving the deposit or processing of waste[2]:

–   scrap yards;
–   clinical and other types of waste incinerator;
–   landfill and land raising sites;
–   waste storage facilities;
–   sewage treatment plants;
–   dredging tips;
–   recycling and waste reception centres; and
–   concrete crushing and blacktop processing centres.

However, in practice, certain English local authorities still maintain that some of the activities listed are not in fact 'county matters'. For example, it is not uncommon to encounter the assertion that responsibility for the enforcement of planning permissions at scrapyards remains with the district council[3].

1 Ie the Department of the Environment.
2 Department of the Environment *Planning Policy Guidance: Planning and Pollution Control* (PPG 23), HMSO, London, Annex 7, para 7. This is due to be superseded: see Department of the Environment, Transport and the Regions (1998) *Planning Policy Guidance: Planning and Waste Management* (PPG 10), Consultation Paper, DETR, London.
3 See also *R v Berkshire County Council, ex p Wokingham District Council* [1997] Env LR 545.

1.61 As part of the planning authorities' assessment of planning applications, regard must be had to the contents and policies of the National Waste Strategy[1]. The Strategy is a material consideration in such deliberations.

1 Department of the Environment (1995) *Making Waste Work: A Strategy for Sustainable Waste Management in England and Wales*, Cm 3040, HMSO, London, para 1.113ff.

The Waste Collection Authority

1.62 In England, the collection authority is usually the district council[1] or, where created, the unitary authority. However, in London the principal collection authorities are the London Boroughs. In Wales[2] and Scotland[3], it is the unitary authority.

1 EPA 1990, s 30(3)(a).
2 EPA 1990, s 30(3)(bb), as amended by the Local Government (Wales) Act 1994, s 22(3) and s 68(8), Sch 9, para 17(3).
3 EPA 1990, s 30(3)(c), as amended by the Local Government etc (Scotland) Act 1994, s 180(1), Sch 13, para 167(3).

1.63 As their name suggests, these bodies have the duty to arrange for the collection of household waste[1] and discretionary powers in respect of commercial[2] and industrial waste collection[3]. They also have duties in respect of the emptying of septic tanks and privies[4]. The collection authority is required to deliver waste to disposal facilities in the manner determined by the waste disposal authority[5]. The only exception is where the collection authority has made its own arrangements for the waste's recycling[6]. Each collection authority is also required to produce a recycling plan for its area[7].

1 EPA 1990, s 45(1)(a).
2 EPA 1990, s 45(1)(b).
3 EPA 1990, s 45(2).
4 EPA 1990, s 45(6).
5 EPA 1990, s 48(1).
6 EPA 1990, s 48(2).
7 EPA 1990, s 49.

The Waste Disposal Authority

1.64 The waste disposal authority (WDA) is usually the County Council in England[1]. The exception is the metropolitan areas. The arrangements for London are set out in the Waste Regulation and Disposal (Authorities) Order 1985[2], with different arrangements applying to the City of London and London boroughs outside the Order[3]. For Merseyside and Manchester, the WDA is the joint board set up between the districts[4]. In the other metropolitan areas, the WDA is the district council[5]. The county or county borough council is the waste disposal authority in Wales[6], and a unitary council in Scotland has similar responsibilities[7].

1 EPA 1990, s 30(2).
2 EPA 1990, ss 30(2)(b)(i) and 30(4), and SI 1985/1884.
3 EPA 1990, s 30(2)(b).
4 EPA 1990, s 30(2)(c) and (d): the exception is the metropolitan borough of Wigan, where that council is the WDA.
5 EPA 1990, s 30(2)(e).

6   EPA 1990, s 30(2)(f), as amended by the Local Government (Wales) Act 1994, s 22(3), Sch 9,
    para 17(2).
7   EPA 1990, s 30(2)(g), as amended by the Local Government etc (Scotland) Act 1994, s 180(1), Sch 3,
    para 167(3).

1.65   In England and Wales, the function of the waste disposal authority is the management of contracts for the disposal of waste collected by the waste collection authorities[1]. This is done by way of a tendering process for one or more fixed-term disposal contracts to which there must be free competition. Once the contract is awarded, the disposal authority is required to monitor the performance of the appointed contractor and, near to the expiry date of the contract, undertake the re-tendering process.

1   See the EPA 1990, Sch 2, Pt II, and see Department of the Environment (1991) *Competition for Local
    Authority Waste Disposal Contracts and New Arrangements for Disposal Operations* Circular 8/91,
    HMSO, London.

1.66   The system in Scotland is somewhat different, in that the WDA can operate its own waste disposal infrastructure[1]. According to Circular 11/94[2], the continuation of the system whereby WDAs are allowed to operate their own facilities was widely supported by respondents to the earlier consultation exercises. In addition, it was also claimed that this arrangement took into account the small and dispersed population in Scotland and that it was not possible to set up market competition similar to that introduced in England and Wales.

1   In England and Wales, the EPA 1990 requires that this function is done by local authority waste
    disposal companies (LAWDCs) or by the private sector.
2   Annex 4, para 4.20.

1.67   Where the Scottish WDA operates a waste management facility, the site was – up to 1996 – controlled by a 'resolution' issued under s 54 of the EPA 1990 rather than by a waste management licence[1]. This provision was subsequently superseded and all such facilities now need to possess licences[2], even though a backlog of unprocessed applications remained throughout 1998[3].

1   Interestingly, Circular 11/94 indicates that the system of exemptions from waste management licences
    does not apply to facilities owned or operated by the Scottish WDAs (see Circular 11/94, Annex 4,
    para 4.81). Presumably this assertion stemmed from the wording of s 54(2) of the EPA 1990, which
    required that 'any' land under the control of the WDA on which waste is deposited, treated, kept or
    disposed of should have been subject to a resolution.
2   EPA 1990, s 54, as amended by Environment Act 1995, Sch 23, para 18 (commenced by
    SI 1996/186).
3   See SEPA (1998) *Corporate Plan 1998/99* SEPA, Stirling, p 21.

Local air pollution control

1.68   In England and Wales, a limited number of waste management facilities will be jointly regulated by the Agency and the local authority. These are industrial plants which are too small to fall within the Agency's system of integrated pollution control authorisations[1]. These processes are subject to an authorisation by the local authority in respect only of their air pollution aspects[2] under a system termed Local Authority Air Pollution Control (LAAPC)[3]. The responsibility for authorisation then lies with the London Boroughs, the district councils or unitary authorities in England and Wales[4]. The other environmental aspects of the operation of such waste management facilities are regulated by the Agency through the powers set out in Part II of the EPA 1990.

1   EPA 1990, Pt I.
2   EPA 1990, s 4(11).

3   EPA 1990, s 4(3).
4   However, in Scotland, the system is different, as SEPA absorbed both the IPC processes and those
    lesser processes subject to LAAPC: see the Environment Act 1995, s 21(1)(h).

1.69   The nature of these activities is set out in the Environmental Protection (Prescribed Processes and Substances) Regulations 1991[1]. The processes, in England and Wales, subject to controls by way of the local authorities are on the Part B list and hence are often referred to as 'Part B Processes'. Examples of waste management facilities which are subject to joint local authority/Agency regulation include[2]:

–   any waste oil burner of less than 3 megawatts;
–   burning of non-hazardous waste as fuel in a facility of between 0.4 and 3
     megawatts
–   certain specified non-hazardous waste incinerators of between 50kgs per hour and
     1 tonne per hour capacity;
–   small iron and steel furnaces, including foundries; and
–   small non-ferrous metal furnaces.

In the case of those activities which involve waste recovery, the preliminary storage elements are often subject to the system of statutory exemptions from the need for the site to possess a waste management licence[3].

1   SI 1991/472, as amended by SIs 1991/836, 1992/614, 1993/1749, 1993/2405, 1994/1271, 1994/1329,
    1994/3247, 1996/2678 and 1998/767.
2   SI 1991/472 (as amended), Sch 1.
3   SI 1994/1056, reg 17: see Chapter 10.

The Ministry of Agriculture, Fisheries and Food

1.70   In England, the Ministry of Agriculture, Fisheries and Food[1] has certain key responsibilities in waste management, particularly in respect of by-products or secondary raw materials which do not fall within the definition of controlled waste.

1   In Wales, the Welsh National Assembly, and in Scotland, the Scottish Executive.

1.71   Firstly, the Ministry is responsible for the correct management of all[1] agricultural wastes which, by way of s 75 of the EPA 1990, fall outside the Agency's statutory remit. While the Agency has primary responsibility for the management of 'controlled wastes', any waste from a premises covered by the Agriculture Act 1947 is excluded from this definition[2].

1   This is due for amendment in order to ensure that 'non-natural' substances used in farming are
    controlled wastes: see para 2.60ff.
2   EPA 1990, s 75(7).

1.72   Secondly, a significant reclamation industry where the control over the transport of wastes is left in the hands of the Ministry is that which deals with animal by-products, such as rendering. Usually, this sector is not involved in the processing of controlled wastes, for the reason that such by-products are raw materials for other commercial uses[1]. In England, the regulation of this industry is undertaken by the Ministry, in conjunction with local authorities, primarily by way of the Animal By-Products Order 1999[2]. The environmental impact of the actual animal waste plants themselves is controlled under Part I of the EPA 1990[3], where the air pollution impacts are dealt with by the local authorities under Part B authorisations[3].

1   See Circular 11/94, Annex 4, para 4.91: waste definitions are discussed in Chapter 2.
2   SI 1999/646.
3   And by SI 1991/472, Sch 1, Section 6.9. In Scotland, this is the responsibility of SEPA.

1.73   However, in a certain number of limited instances, animal by-products may fall within the definition of controlled waste, particularly when they are to be disposed of or subject to activities such as land-spreading. Again, the carriage of these materials is generally[1] covered by the Animal By-Products Order 1999[2] and hence is subject to the Ministry's control. However, the regulation of the final destination of these materials, such as incineration or land-spreading, is mainly overseen by the Agency[3].

1   See SI 1994/1056, regs 21 and 22 and para 6.14ff.
2   SI 1999/646.
3   See Chapter 10.

1.74   The third waste regulatory function of the Ministry is the policing of the dumping of waste at sea under the Food and Environment Protection Act 1985. This Act carried out the UK's obligations under what were the London Convention on the Prevention of Marine Pollution by Dumping of Waste and Other Matter 1972 and the Oslo Convention for the Prevention of Marine Pollution by Dumping from Ships and Aircraft 1972. Both Conventions were superseded in March 1998 by the Convention for the Protection of the Marine Environment of the North East Atlantic ('Ospar Convention'). Signed in Paris in 1992, the Ospar Convention required the cessation of the disposal of sewage sludge to sea by December 1998[1]. Industrial waste dumping at sea by the UK ceased in 1992. However, the responsibility for the policing of these provisions remains with the Ministry as does the function of the control of the offshore disposal of materials such as dredgings.

1   Ospar Convention, Annex II, Article 3(2)(c).

1.75   Other than actual disposal of waste at sea, the Ministry of Agriculture, Fisheries and Food also regulates waste disposal activities where wastes are deposited on the coastline. The boundary of jurisdiction between the Agency and the Ministry is set down by the statutory definitions of 'sea' and 'land' in the Food and Environment Protection Act 1985[1] and in the EPA 1990[2] respectively. Oddly, the definitions overlap so that the area between the low and high spring tides – the foreshore – is under joint control[3].

1   Food and Environment Protection Act 1985, s 24.
2   EPA 1990, s 29(8).
3   See Circular 11/94 Annex 3, para 3.3: see para 7.45ff.

AN OVERVIEW OF BRITISH WASTE REGULATION LAW

1.76   Waste management is one of the most highly regulated of all industrial activities. Embellishment of the legislation has been the norm rather than the exception throughout the 1990s, despite a government whose overall philosophy was claimed to be deregulatory. The following is intended to be a summary of the main provisions of the EPA 1990 and subsidiary regulations, with the precise detail of the relevant enactments being picked up later in subsequent chapters. For clarity, a simple waste production-carriage-disposal/recovery model will be used to structure the summary. It should be emphasised that the section below is very much an overview of the principal provisions and their effects. The picture is, in fact, significantly more complex, and reference should be made to the relevant chapters for the full account. Also presented within this discussion are certain key statistics which illustrate the context within which the legislation operates.

Waste production

1.77 To be subject to the statutory controls contained in Part II of the EPA 1990, a substance must fall within the definition of 'controlled waste'[1]. Controlled waste is legally defined as material that has been discarded by the holder. It includes wastes passing to recovery facilities, with any discarded material remaining defined as waste regardless of whether a recipient has a use for it. Only after the application of the actual recovery process does the reclaimed material re-enter the commercial cycle.

1 EPA 1990, s 75: see Chapter 2.

1.78 A proportion of controlled waste falls within the definition of 'special waste' contained in the Special Waste Regulations 1996[1]. This material is so defined for the reason that it may present immediate hazards to human health and to the environment. Much of this waste emanates from industrial processes. The inherent hazards of special waste mean that the material must be subject to careful handling throughout the waste's lifecycle. Given the hazardous nature of the material, there are often major costs involved in the management of this type of waste. The total quantity of special waste arising in England and Wales in 1997/98 was 5.6 million tonnes[2]. Under the earlier definition which was superseded by the 1996 Regulations, it was estimated that approximately 100,000 British firms annually produce special waste[3]. This is expected now to be a considerable under-estimate[4].

1 SI 1996/972 as amended by SI 1996/2019: see Chapter 4.
2 Personal communication to author from Environment Agency.
3 Department of the Environment (1985) *A Report of the Review of the Control of Pollution (Special Waste) Regulations 1980*, Department of the Environment, London, para 35.
4 Under the earlier definition contained in the Control of Pollution (Special Waste) Regulations 1980 (SI 1980/1709), about 2 million tonnes of special waste was produced each year (see Department of the Environment, Transport and the Regions (1998) *Digest of Environmental Statistics*, No 20, Stationery Office, London, Table 7.6).

Waste carriage

1.79 When controlled waste is to be moved, the person undertaking the transportation normally has to be registered with the Agency as a controlled waste carrier[1]. The registration can be cancelled by the Agency if the carrier has been involved in significant unauthorised waste management activities. A provision of similar effect applies to persons involved in the brokerage of waste movements[2]. About 79,000 waste carriers and nearly 2,000 brokers are registered with the Environment Agency[3].

1 Control of Pollution (Amendment) Act 1989: see Chapter 6.
2 SI 1994/1056, reg 20: see Chapter 6.
3 Environment Agency (1998) *1997–98 Annual Report and Accounts*, Environment Agency, Bristol, Appendix V. About 6,000 carriers and brokers are registered with SEPA: SEPA (1999) *Corporate Plan 1999–2000*, SEPA, Stirling, Figure 11.

1.80 When controlled waste is transferred, the EPA 1990 imposes a 'duty of care' on each of the parties in the transaction[1]. The duty requires that each holder should take reasonable steps to ensure that the waste is correctly managed. A failure to exercise the duty is an offence under s 34 of the EPA 1990. When waste is transferred, it should usually be consigned only to a registered waste carrier or to a disposal or recovery facility subject to the requisite licence or registration.

1 EPA 1990, s 34: see Chapter 3.

1.81 As part of the duty of care, any transfer of waste between parties should be subject to written documentation in the form of a transfer note[1]. Where special wastes are transferred, the transfer note is replaced by a consignment note, which is used to ensure that the movement of the material is tracked by the Agency from 'cradle to grave'[2].

1 Environmental Protection (Duty of Care) Regulations 1991 (SI 1991/2839): see para 3.118.
2 SI 1996/972 as amended by SI 1996/2019: see para 4.62.

1.82 As mentioned briefly earlier in this chapter, some controlled waste is traded internationally. Like special waste, the majority of these movements are subject to a tracking documentation procedure[1]. Other than a variety of environmentally innocuous wastes – such as wastepaper – which pass to recovery, both the importing and exporting countries are able to approve in advance any transfrontier waste shipment. This prevents waste being abandoned in a particular state by unscrupulous operators. While no waste is exported from the UK for disposal, waste can be exported for the purposes of recovery and reclamation[2]. The UK also accepts waste from a number of other countries for recovery or final disposal. However, it is government policy that no imported wastes pass direct to landfill[3]. In 1996, approximately 76,000 tonnes of hazardous waste was imported[4], mainly for high temperature incineration or chemical treatment and recovery.

1 By way of Council Regulation (EEC) No 259/93 of 1 February 1993 on the Supervision and Control of Shipments of Waste within, into and out of the European Community (OJ L30/1 6.2.93) and the Transfrontier Shipment of Waste Regulations 1994 (SI 1994/1137): see Chapter 5.
2 Department of the Environment (1996) *United Kingdom Management Plan for Exports and Imports of Waste*, HMSO, London, Chapters 3 and 4.
3 Department of the Environment (1996) *United Kingdom Management Plan for Exports and Imports of Waste*, HMSO, London, para 5.31.
4 Department of the Environment, Transport and the Regions (1998) *Digest of Environmental Statistics*, No 20, Stationery Office, London, Table 7.9: however, no figures appear to be published on imports of non-hazardous wastes.

Waste disposal/recovery

1.83 All waste management facilities must have an appropriate licence or registration, which is normally issued by the Agency. Sites without the benefit of such authorisations can be subject to enforcement proceedings by the Agency, principally by way of s 33 of the EPA 1990[1].

1 See Chapter 7.

1.84 The majority of the larger controlled waste disposal and recovery facilities are required under the EPA 1990 to possess waste management licences[1]. This includes landfills, treatment plants and transfer stations, as well as the more significant scrapyards and motor vehicle dismantlers. These licences are only granted when the site has a valid planning status and when the Agency is satisfied that pollution of the environment or harm to human health will not result from the activity subject to the licence application[2]. In addition, the operator has to be a 'fit and proper' person to hold and retain the waste management licence[3].

1 EPA 1990, s 33.
2 EPA 1990, s 36: see Chapter 8.
3 EPA 1990, s 36 and s 74.

1.85 A waste management licence is subject to a range of conditions which ensure that the site is operated in a manner which prevents environmental pollution and harm to human health. The Agency regularly visits these facilities in order to verify compliance[1]. Legal action can be instituted in respect of non-compliance with licence conditions[2]. Alternatively, the licence can be modified, suspended or revoked by the Agency[3]. Charges are payable to the Agency for licence applications[4] and to cover the costs of its inspection function[5]. Table 1.5 shows estimates of the types and numbers of licensed waste management facilities in existence[6].

1   See para 12.27: 140,000 inspection visits were undertaken in England and Wales by the Environment Agency in 1997/98 (see Environment Agency (1998) *1997–98 Annual Report and Accounts* Environment Agency, Bristol, Appendix V). The equivalent figure for Scotland is 12,500 (see SEPA (1999) *Corporate Plan 1999/2000*, SEPA, Stirling, Figure 11).
2   EPA 1990, s 33 and see Chapter 7.
3   See Chapter 9.
4   Including applications for licence modification.
5   Environment Act 1995, s 41: see para 9.142ff.
6   While no breakdown is given, the Environment Agency had 7,353 licences in force in the financial year 1997/98 (see Environment Agency (1998) *1997–98 Annual Report and Accounts*, Environment Agency, Bristol, Appendix V.

Table 1.5

Licensed Waste Management Facilities in England and Wales (1998/99)[1]

Type of Waste Management Facility	Number of Licensed Waste Management Activities
Landfill	2868
Transfer Station (including Civic Amenity)	3646
Treatment facilities	754
Incineration	93
Scrapyard/Vehicle Dismantler	1941
Total	9302

1   The information in this Table has been provided from the Site File Database and is reproduced courtesy of Landmark Information Group Ltd. There is likely to be some discrepancy with the information presented from Environment Agency sources elsewhere in this chapter due to the survey methodology used. However, while national statistics were collated up to 1994 – see Department of the Environment (1994) *Digest of Environmental Protection and Water Statistics*, HMSO, London, Table 7.3 – it would appear that these are the only available statistics. From correspondence with the Environment Agency, it seems that this information is no longer centrally collected. The data presented in the Table relate to 8584 waste management licences – some of these will cover more than one of the activities referred to in the Table.

1.86 The conditions of a waste management licence apply throughout the life of a facility and into its post-closure period. They will continue indefinitely until the licensee has successfully applied to the Agency for the surrender of the licence[1]. The licence only becomes of no effect when a 'certificate of completion' has been issued by the Agency. For landfills accepting biodegradable waste, it is unlikely that certificates of completion will be issued for many years, for the reason that biodegradation operates slowly over the decades after filling has ceased.

1   EPA 1990, s 39: see para 9.93ff.

1.87 The content of waste management licences is mainly left to the Agency's discretion. In exercising its discretion, the Agency must have regard to guidance issued by the Department of the Environment[1] in the form of Waste Management Papers[2]. These documents set down the basic principles which determine the content of a waste management licence[3].

1   EPA 1990, ss 35(8) and 74(5): see para 8.225.
2   Since the Agency was established in 1996, the production of Waste Management Papers is now an Agency function.
3   In respect of the drafting of licences, the most significant Waste Management Papers are Department of the Environment (1994) *Licensing of Waste Management Facilities* Waste Management Paper No 4, 3rd edn, HMSO, London; Department of the Environment (1995) *Licensing of Metal Recycling Sites* Waste Management Paper No 4A, HMSO, London; Department of the Environment (1993) *Landfill Completion* Waste Management Paper No 26A, HMSO, London; and Department of the Environment (1995) *Landfill Design, Construction and Operational Practices* Waste Management Paper No 26B, HMSO, London. At the time of writing (Summer 1999), two further Waste Management Papers – *Landfill Monitoring* and *Landfill Restoration and Post-Closure Management* – are in preparation. In addition, a draft Paper on landfill co-disposal is in existence, but it appears that this will not be proceeded with, due to the imminent implementation of the Landfill Directive (see 'Written Evidence by the Environment Agency' in House of Lords Select Committee on the European Communities (1998) *Sustainable Landfill* 17th Report, Stationery Office, London, para 3.14).

1.88   A number of waste management facilities, such as large incinerators, solvent recovery plants and cement kilns, are not subject to the provisions on waste management licensing. Instead, they are presently[1] controlled by the Agency through Integrated Pollution Control (IPC) authorisations. These are issued under Part I of the EPA 1990. To avoid a duplication of controls, the legislation excludes these activities from Part II of the EPA 1990 with respect to waste management licences[2].

1   Such facilities will become permitted under the Pollution Prevention and Control Act 1999 over the period to 2007 (see para 1.93).
2   By way of the EPA 1990, s 33(3) and SI 1994/1056, reg 16: see para 10.14ff.

1.89   A number of other, smaller facilities involving the combustion of controlled wastes are under joint Agency and local authority control[1]. These are facilities such as pet crematoria and other small incinerators, where an authorisation under Part I of the EPA 1990 is issued by the local authority in respect of atmospheric emissions. The remainder of the operation of the plant, such as waste storage and intermediate processing, is subject to a waste management licence[2].

1   This does not apply in Scotland, where SEPA controls the entire activity.
2   See para 10.17.

1.90   The relevant legislation classes those processes which are subject to Part I of the EPA 1990 as being *excluded* from waste management licensing[1]. Along with exclusions, there are a series of activities which are subject to *exemptions* from the need to possess a waste management licence[2]. The latter are all relatively small operations, mainly involved in controlled waste recovery and associated storage. They are defined in a long and intricate list contained in the Waste Management Licensing Regulations 1994[3]. Examples include household waste recycling infrastructure such as bottle banks and the land-spreading of specified industrial wastes[4]. Should an activity be operated in a manner which breaches the requirements for exemption, a waste management licence is required[5]. The absence of such a licence in these circumstances can lead to possible prosecution by the Agency[6]. About 28,500 exempt facilities were in existence in England and Wales at the end of the financial year 1997/98[7].

1   EPA 1990, s 33(3) and SI 1994/1056, reg 16.
2   EPA 1990, s 33(3) and SI 1994/1056, reg 17: see Chapters 10 and 11.
3   SI 1994/1056, reg 17 and Sch 3, as amended.
4   See Chapter 10.
5   SI 1994/1056, reg 17: see para 10.32.
6   By way of the EPA 1990, s 33: see Chapter 7.
7   Environment Agency (1998) *1997–98 Annual Report and Accounts*, Environment Agency, Bristol, Appendix V.

1.91 Although a number of the smaller scrapyards and motor vehicle dismantlers are able to benefit from the system of exemptions from licensing, the control system over these activities is somewhat more onerous than is the case for the other exempt operations[1]. The relevant legislation sets down in some detail the technical requirements which must be complied with for the exemption to hold. Record-keeping requirements are also prescribed. In addition, the Agency must receive an annual fee to cover the cost of inspecting the facility to ensure the continuation of the conditions of exemption. About 1,400 metal recycling sites benefit from this provision in England and Wales[2].

1 SI 1994/1056, regs 17 and 18, Sch 3, as amended by SIs 1995/288, 1996/972 and 1998/606: see Chapter 11.
2 Environment Agency (1998) *1997–98 Annual Report and Accounts* Environment Agency, Bristol, Appendix V.

1.92 All exempt activities need to be subject to registration[1]. Usually, registration will be with the Agency itself. However, a small number of exempt activities have a deemed registration with the local authority.

1 SI 1994/1056, reg 18: see paras 10.24ff and 11.88ff.

The Pollution Prevention and Control Act 1999

1.93 The Pollution Prevention Control Act 1999 gained Royal Assent just at the time this book was going to press. The result was that the drafts of the extensive subsidiary regulations to implement this new pollution control regime were yet to be published and that the form by which these new provisions would be interleaved with the EPA 1990 was not clear. Such factors cause only a limited description of these changes to be set out below.

1.94 The Pollution Prevention and Control Act 1999 transposes Council Directive 96/61[1] on integrated pollution prevention and control (the 'IPPC Directive') into national law. The date of transposition is set by the Directive at 30 October 1999[2]. Perhaps reflecting the realities of the shift of power from national government to the European Community, the Pollution Prevention and Control Act 1999 extensively relies on the making of secondary legislation to ensure the full enactment of the new pollution control regime. The result is that the text of the Act is relatively short, being mainly concerned with enabling powers which allow the Secretary of State to make regulations. This facet proved to be constitutionally controversial, causing delays in the Parliamentary process, with the Act obtaining Royal Assent just before the Summer Parliamentary recess. An allied effect of the style of drafting means that, in the absence of the secondary legislation, it is not possible to make a detailed account of how the new system is to work in practice. Devolution in Wales and Scotland will also mean that there may be differences in the format of the regulations as compared to those made for England.

1 Council Directive 96/61/EC of 24 September 1996 concerning integrated pollution prevention and control, OJ L257/26 10.10.96.
2 Council Directive 96/61, Article 21(1) and 22.

1.95 Ultimately, the Pollution Prevention and Control Act 1999 will cause the repeal of Part I of the EPA 1990. The system of Integrated Pollution Control (IPC) authorisations will transfer into the new regime in accordance with the requirements of the IPPC Directive. The latter requires all affected facilities to fully comply with its regime from between October 1999 to October 2007. From the end of October 1999 any new facility must obtain a permit under the Pollution Prevention and Control Act 1999 which reflects the requirements of the Directive[1]. Existing facilities are to be brought under the IPPC umbrella between 1999 and 2007, with the Directive leaving the exact dates within this timeframe to member states[2]. However, existing installations where 'substantial change' is proposed should have the requirements of the Directive reflected in any permit issued[3]. Member states are left with discretion as to how the concept of 'substantial change' is to be defined, subject to the proviso in the Directive that it is a change of sufficient magnitude to have '... significant negative effects on human beings and the environment'[4].

1   Directive 96/61/EC, Article 4.
2   Directive 96/61/EC, Article 5.
3   Directive 96/61/EC, Article 12.
4   Directive 96/61/EC, Article 2(10)(b).

1.96   The long lead-in time for existing facilities in the IPPC Directive will mean that the regulations stemming from the Pollution Prevention and Control Act 1999 will cause the progressive phase-in of the new regime for existing facilities over the period to 2007. Conversely new facilities – as well as existing facilities subject to a 'substantial change' – will need to make applications for permits under the new regime. Accordingly, the regimes contained in Part I of the EPA 1990 and the Pollution Prevention and Control Act 1999 will operate in parallel for some time, until the latter causes the repeal of the former[1].

1   Pollution Prevention and Control Act 1999, s 6(2).

1.97   Like Part I of the EPA 1990[1], the Pollution Prevention Control Act 1999 embraces a wide variety of major industrial processes, along with the more significant waste management activities. It has been estimated that the IPPC Directive would ultimately affect the following existing British waste management activities: 600 disposal or recovery facilities of capacities in excess of ten tonnes per day; eight municipal waste incinerators and 130 waste treatment plants[2]. About 1000 landfills[3] are also covered by the Directive. However, the Landfill Directive[4] causes its requirements to override those of the IPPC Directive[5]. This factor suggests that the current system of landfill licensing under the EPA 1990 will probably continue unchanged until at least 2002, when transposition of the Landfill Directive is to be commenced. As noted, the two exceptions to this general rule will be new landfills constructed after October 1999 and existing facilities where they are to be subject to 'substantial change'.

1   See paras 1.50, 10.14ff.
2   See Department of the Environment, Transport and the Regions *UK Implementation of Directive 96/61 on IPPC: Consultation Paper* July 1997, DETR, Annex A.
3   Originally it was thought that the figure was 3000 – see *UK Implementation of Directive 96/61 on IPPC: Consultation Paper*, Annex A – but this seems to have been an over-estimate.
4   Council Directive 1999/31/EC of 26 April 1999 on the Landfill of Waste, OJ L182/1 16.7.99.
5   See Landfill Directive 1999/31/EC, Article 1.2 and para 1.25.

1.98   In practice, the gradual implementation of the Pollution Prevention Control Act 1999 over the waste sector means that the waste management licensing system set out in this book will continue to apply for some time[1]. Only a small number of proposed waste facilities which are currently in the pipeline or are to be subject to 'substantial change' fall within the new regime in the short term[2]. Besides setting out appropriate mechanisms whereby the new permitting system will operate, the subsidiary regulations will need to make amendments to Part II of the EPA 1990 and associated secondary legislation. This is to ensure – in a manner similar to that already in existence with respect to waste management facilities under Part I of the EPA 1990[3] – that there are clear administrative boundaries between the two regimes.

1   In a manner similar to that applying to facilities subject to Part I of the EPA 1990, many of the non-licensing requirements of Part II of the EPA 1990 continue to apply to waste movements to facilities subject to permits under the Pollution Prevention and Control Act 1999 (definition of waste, duty of care, special waste, provisions on transfrontier waste shipment, broker and carrier registration: see Chapters 2–6). Furthermore, the concept of 'fit and proper person' (see para 8.112ff) applies to waste management facilities permitted under the Pollution Prevention and Control Act 1999.
2   For example, SEPA estimates that only two permits in total under the Pollution Prevention and Control Act 1999 will be in force in the financial year 2000/01, with this figure increasing to 27 the year after (see SEPA (1999) *Corporate Plan 1999–2000*, SEPA, Stirling, figure 20).
3   See SI 1994/1056, reg 16 and see para 10.14ff.

1.99   The Pollution Prevention and Control Act 1999 also contains provisions affect-ing time-limited waste management licences[1]. It is understood that the Environment Agency discovered it had about 200 licences which contain time limitations[2], but where waste management activities were still occurring. These licences are those which were originally waste disposal licences under the Control of Pollution Act 1974 and became – or should have become[3] – waste management licences under the EPA 1990 by way of the latter's transitional provisions[4]. The continued existence of time limitations on these licences would be against the general scheme of the EPA 1990 which required a licence to continue in existence until its surrender was formally accepted by the Agency[5], thereby ensuring that the environmental protection measures of the licence remain in place until any pollution liability ceased. Hence the Pollution Prevention and Control Act 1999 contains provisions which override any expiry date of an affected licence[6]. The Agency is required to formally notify all affected licensees[7].

1   Pollution Prevention and Control Act 1999, s 4: the provisions only relate to licences in England and Wales (Pollution Prevention and Control Act 1999, s 4(1)(c), (2)(b)).
2   For example, a condition may require that the licence expires when the planning permission runs out. The facility may still need environmental monitoring and the maintenance of environmental control measures – such as gas or leachate management – to continue.
3   These provisions effect a licence originally granted under the Control of Pollution Act 1974 which either: (a) became a waste management licence with expiry occurring after that date or (b) should have become a waste management licence but was in fact precluded from doing so due to the expiry date being set at before the enactment of waste management licensing under the EPA 1990. Although seemingly not apparent to either the licensee or the Agency, waste management activities at these facilities continued into 1998/99. In some cases, the existence of the expiry date was found to have precluded certain licences from transferring to waste management licences in 1994. Provision is contained in the Pollution Prevention and Control Act 1999 (s 4(6)(a) and (e) and (7)) to protect an operator from enforcement action caused by a licence's earlier expiry in these circumstances.
4   EPA 1990, s 77: see para 9.82.
5   See paras 1.86 and 9.93ff.
6   Pollution Prevention and Control Act 1999, s 4(1), (3) and (4).
7   Pollution Prevention and Control Act 1999, s 4(9).

The landfill tax

1.100   As was explained in the Preface, the purpose of this book is to consider in detail the regulatory system by which wastes in Britain are controlled. The focus there-fore is upon the powers and duties of the Environment Agency and the Scottish Envi-ronment Protection Agency. The landfill tax, being a fiscal measure, does not itself regulate the operation of landfills nor achieve the imposition of environmentally acceptable conditions on them. It acts as an economic incentive which is intended to divert wastes to other, more financially attractive, waste management solutions. However, given the magnitude of the tax and its topicality, it is perhaps appropriate to include a brief account of the provisions. But this can be no more than a summary. The precise details can be found in the primary and secondary legislation itself, while two useful guides to the provisions have been written by HM Customs and Excise[1].

1 HM Customs and Excise, *A General Guide to the Landfill Tax* Notice LFT1, Customs & Excise, Newcastle; HM Customs and Excise, *Reclamation of Contaminated Land* Information Note 1/97 (the notes published prior to the commencement of tax have all been superseded: see Notice LFT1, page 1): see also HM Customs and Excise, *Review of the Landfill Tax: Report*, March 1998, HM Customs and Excise, Newcastle and the House of Commons Environment, Transport and Regional Affairs Committee Report (1999) *The Operation of the Landfill Tax*, 13th Report, Stationery Office, London.

1.101   The tax is administered by HM Customs and Excise[1], not by the Environment Agency. It is claimed that the tax stems from government policy that industrial activities should follow the principle of 'sustainable development'[2]. The concept of the landfilling of biodegradable wastes is one of the more obvious industrial practices which contravenes this principle. Biodegradation of wastes in landfills may take a number of generations to achieve. The result is that future generations may have to undertake long-term monitoring of old landfills, along with any remedial work required.

1 Finance Act 1996, s 39(2).
2 See Department of the Environment (1995) *Making Waste Work. A Strategy for Sustainable Waste Management in England and Wales*, Cm 3040, HMSO, London. Sustainable development has been defined (see, for example, *Making Waste Work*, para 1.5) as 'development that meets the needs of the present without compromising the ability of future generations to meet their own needs'.

1.102   Given the predominance of landfill as the most significant UK disposal practice[1], it is not possible readily to substitute alternative solutions immediately and with wide effect[2]. However, as noted at para 1.09, the government White Paper *Making Waste Work* has set a target for the reduction of the use of landfill as a disposal option for controlled wastes from 70% to 60%, with the landfill tax being the key policy instrument to effect this change[3].

1 See para 1.44 above.
2 And even if this were possible, landfill would be still required to deal with any residues. For example, between 20% and 30% by weight of the input to a municipal waste incineration plant ends up as post-combustion ash. Recycling facilities and composting plants will also produce a significant unusable percentage of waste.
3 Department of the Environment (1995) *Making Waste Work. A Strategy for Sustainable Waste Management in England and Wales*, Cm 3040, HMSO, London, para 1.40.

1.103   The provisions on the landfill tax came into force in October 1996[1]. Their statutory basis is primarily the Finance Act 1996[2], being supported by a succession of statutory instruments[3]. The tax was intended to affect about 100 million tonnes of controlled waste[4] and raised £426m in the year 1997/98[5].

1 Finance Act 1996, s 40(1)(d), as amended by SI 1996/1529, Finance Act 1997, Sch 5, SI 1996/2100, SI 1998/61 and SI 1999/2075.
2 Part III and Sch 5.
3 Landfill Tax Regulations 1996 (SI 1996/1527); Landfill Tax (Qualifying Material) Order 1996 (SI 1996/1528); Landfill Tax (Contaminated Land) Order 1996 (SI 1996/1529); Landfill Tax (Amendment) Regulations 1998 (SI 1998/61); and Landfill Tax (Site Restoration and Quarries Order) 1999 (SI 1999/2075).
4 HM Customs and Excise (1995) *Landfill Tax: A Consultation Paper*, published HM Customs and Excise, 21 March 1995, para 1.7.
5 See *ENDS Report* 289, Feb 1999, pp 17–20.

1.104   All persons who are liable for the tax were required to register with Customs and Excise[1] by 1 August 1996[2], with the Finance Act 1996 containing penalties in respect of failure to register[3]. There are two bands of the tax[4]. From April 1999, the general tax rate was £10 per tonne of waste deposited at landfills, with a further annual increase of £1 per tonne for each year until 2004. However, the tax rate is reduced to £2 per tonne for waste which falls within the definition of 'qualifying material'[5]. 'Qualifying material' is composed of waste which is commonly regarded as 'inactive or inert'[6], being defined in the Landfill Tax (Qualifying Material) Order 1996[7]. While the full list is shown in Table 3.1 of Chapter 3, examples of qualifying material are wastes composed of uncontaminated rock, soils, concrete etc. These materials are most typical of wastes from demolition or construction industry activities[8].

1   Finance Act 1996, s 47(3): the requirements of registration are set down in SI 1996/1527, Pt II.
2   SI 1996/1527, reg 4(4).
3   Finance Act 1996, Sch 5 para 21.
4   Finance Act 1996, s 42(1).
5   Finance Act 1996, s 42(2).
6   Finance Act 1996, s 42(4).
7   SI 1996/1528 (see also Finance Act 1996, s 63).
8   However, certain types of construction and demolition industry wastes are by no means inactive or inert. While the presence of items such as small pieces of wood, soil mixed with small quantities of grass, plaster attached to bricks etc, allow the whole load to be subject to the lower rate of £2 per tonne, generally the full £10 per tonne tax is to be levied where non-inert materials are present (see HM Customs and Excise (1997) *A General Guide to the Landfill Tax*, Notice LFT1, para 2.3).

1.105   Certain controlled wastes deposited at sites which fall within the definition of landfills[1] are exempt from the tax. These wastes include material removed by way of dredging activities[2] and waste from commercial mining or quarrying operations[3]. Pet cemeteries are also exempted[4]. In defined circumstances[5], waste from contaminated land reclamation may also fall within an exemption, as does inert wastes used to restore landfill sites and old quarries[6].

1   Defined in the Finance Act 1996, s 65.
2   Finance Act 1996, s 43.
3   Finance Act 1996, s 44.
4   Finance Act 1996, s 45.
5   Finance Act 1996, ss 43A and 43B, as amended by SI 1996/1529: see also HM Customs and Excise, *Reclamation of Contaminated Land* Information Note 1/97, Customs and Excise, Newcastle.
6   See SI 1999/2075.

1.106   The most imaginative aspect of the tax involves the right of taxpayers to accrue tax credits by way of making contributions to 'environmental bodies'[1]. A taxpayer is entitled to a 90% tax credit[2], up to a ceiling of 20% of the total contributions in a 12-month period[3]. The nature of 'environmental bodies' is set down in the Landfill Tax Regulations 1996[4]. They must be non-profit making and controlled neither by the contributor nor by a local authority. Briefly, to qualify as such a body, its objectives must involve land reclamation; research and development; education or dissemination of information on sustainable waste management practices; and the provision of, or improvement of, public amenity areas or buildings of historic interest in the vicinity of existing landfills. However, these works must be entirely separate from either activities which landfill taxpayers are otherwise required to undertake by way of waste management licences or the clean-up of pollution for which the taxpayers themselves were responsible for. In all cases, any organisation intending to operate as an environmental body must receive the prior blessing of the regulatory body ENTRUST, as must the projects themselves[5].

1   Finance Act 1996, s 53; SI 1996/1527, Pt VII: see HM Customs and Excise (1997) *A General Guide to the Landfill Tax* Notice LFT1, para 2.3, para 10.1ff.
2   SI 1996/1527, reg 31(2).
3   SI 1996/1527, reg 31(3).

4   SI 1996/1527, reg 33.
5   ENTRUST publish a useful guide to the environmental body scheme: *Interpretations and Precedents to the Landfill Tax Regulations.*

1.107   Finally, there are stiff penalties for avoidance of the tax[1], being backed by Customs and Excise's substantial statutory investigative powers. Penalties involve both criminal and civil sanctions. Taxpayers involved in fraudulent tax evasion – and those who assist such persons – are liable to fines and/or imprisonment. On summary conviction, the maximum fine of the statutory maximum[2] or three times the unpaid tax (whichever is greater) can be imposed, and/or imprisonment of a period up to six months[3]. On conviction on indictment, a penalty of 'any amount' can be imposed and/or a custodial sentence of up to seven years[4]. There are similar offences in respect of the making of false statements and entering into contracts which involve landfills where it is known that tax evasion will occur. In parallel to these criminal sanctions, the Finance Act 1996 allows for a range of additional civil penalties in respect of tax evasion[5]. Convictions under these provisions can also affect a licensee's status as being a 'fit and proper person' to hold a waste management licence[6].

1   Finance Act 1996, Sch 5, Pt IV.
2   Currently £5,000.
3   Finance Act 1996, Sch 5, para 16(1)(a).
4   Finance Act 1996, Sch 5, para 16(1)(b).
5   Finance Act 1996, Sch 5, para 18.
6   SI 1997/351, reg 2 and see para 8.117ff.

WASTE MANAGEMENT IN NORTHERN IRELAND

1.108   At the time of writing (Summer 1999), the arrangements for the control of waste management in Northern Ireland still remain at a point of transition, with implementation being retarded this time by the lack of progress on the formation of the Northern Ireland Assembly. Wholly new legislation, in the form of the Waste and Contaminated Land (Northern Ireland) Order 1997[1], awaits full commencement[2]. Although the Order's provisions closely follow the substance of the EPA 1990 and subsidiary provisions, the lack of commencement means that a detailed description of the provisions is excluded from this volume. The Pollution Control and Local Government (Northern Ireland) Order 1978[3] remains mainly in force. These provisions have an essential similarity to the much discredited Control of Pollution Act 1974's powers. This problem exemplifies the trend for the province to significantly lag behind the rest of the UK in both the enactment of modern legislation and the comprehensive transposition of European Community obligations[4].

1   SI 1997/2778 (NI 19).
2   See SR 1998/288, Art 2; SR 1998/390, Art 2.
3   SI 1978/1049 (NI 19) as amended by SI 1985/1208 (NI 15), Sch 3 para 17 and SI 1997/2778, Sch 6.
4   See Morrow K and Turner S 'The more things change, the more they stay the same? Environmental Law, Policy and Funding in Northern Ireland' (1998) 10 JEL 1, 41–59, and see also House of Commons Environment Committee, *Environmental Issues in Northern Ireland* Session 1990–91, HMSO, London.

1.109   With a small number of exceptions, Northern Ireland's provisions are entirely separate from those effecting England and Wales or Scotland. Hence the powers contained in Part II of the EPA 1990, which set down the system of waste management licensing, are excluded from applying to the province[1]. Until September 1998, the control of special wastes was undertaken by the Pollution Control (Special Waste) (Northern Ireland) Regulations 1981[2], which were broadly similar to the earlier British Special Waste Regulations 1980[3]. These have been replaced by the Special Waste

(Northern Ireland) Regulations 1998[4]. Other provisions – such as controlled waste carrier and broker registration – are not yet in force[5].

1 EPA 1990, s 164(4): the only exception is the powers in the EPA 1990 for the Secretary of State to make regulations covering the record-keeping of imports involving special waste: EPA 1990, s 62(2)(e). Similarly, the Control of Pollution (Amendment) Act 1989 (s 11(4)), the Waste Management Licensing Regulations 1994 (SI 1994/1056, reg 1(6)) and the Special Waste Regulations 1996 (SI 1996/972, reg 1(2)) do not apply.
2 SR 1992/254.
3 SI 1980/1709.
4 SR 1998/289.
5 In Winter 1998, a consultation paper on the Controlled Waste (Registration of Carriers and Seizure of Vehicles) Regulations was issued by the Northern Ireland Office.

1.110 There are two exceptions to the general rule that Northern Ireland has its own waste management legislation. The first involves the Transfrontier Shipment of Waste Regulations 1994[1], which fully apply to the province as well as to Britain[2]. Secondly, the landfill tax was enacted in Northern Ireland in 1996, at the same time as it applied to Britain.

1 SI 1994/1137.
2 These provisions are discussed in Chapter 5.

1.111 It is proposed that the administration of the waste regulation function will be extensively reorganised in the near future. In addition to the reforms contained in the Waste and Contaminated Land Order 1997, it is proposed that the administration of waste regulation is to be centralised. Hence the district councils will lose their regulatory functions, with waste regulation being subsumed into a centralised agency, the Department of the Environment and Heritage Service. At the time of writing (Summer 1999), the Department is responsible for special waste controls[1]. The remaining waste regulatory functions have yet to transfer, including the local authorities' responsibilities for transfrontier waste shipments.

1 SR 1998/289; the Department is also responsible for drafting the waste strategy (see SR 1998/390).

A POSTSCRIPT

1.112 While it has proved relatively straightforward to summarise the relevant statutory provisions at para 1.76ff above, in reality British waste management law has, in the period from 1991, developed into a highly convoluted and complex system. Indeed, complexity is now such that persons less than familiar with the statutory provisions are confronted with significant difficulties. An obvious question to ask is why has this particular industrial sector been subject to such complicated regulations? This question becomes particularly pertinent as much of it occurred under a Conservative government with an explicit deregulatory policy agenda. Although it may be superficially attractive to blame the European Community's environmental directives as the source of the labyrinth, this is not strictly correct. While the Community has had a significant influence on the shape of the legislation, it has had only a partial role in creating complexity in the British statutory provisions.

1.113 The principal driving force towards complication would appear to be the law-making style of the government at that time. From the nature of the regulatory provisions, and also from the 199-page Circular which accompanies the Waste Management Licensing Regulations 1994[1], it would appear that government policy was to codify and formalise what was hitherto left to the regulators' discretion. The legislation is increasingly attempting to identify and embrace each and every possible permutation and combination of waste transaction and to produce regulatory procedures which embrace them.

1   Department of the Environment (1994) *Environmental Protection Act 1990: Part II Waste Management Licensing The Framework Directive on Waste* Circular 11/94, HMSO, London.

1.114   Regulatory complexity is particularly obvious in respect of the system of registered exemptions from waste management licences[1] and in the Special Waste Regulations 1996[2]. In respect of the exemptions, it is a consequence primarily of the requirements of the EPA 1990 in respect of the duty of care[3]. The duty of care requires, *inter alia*, that virtually every transfer of waste beyond the curtilage of any premises should involve only 'authorised persons'. Having established this requirement, the nature of all 'authorised persons' has then to be defined in detail. This has resulted in the requirement that every site, large or small, environmentally trivial or otherwise, must be classified within the legislation. This applies as much to a bottle bank as to a major landfill involved in the deposit of hazardous waste. As noted, many of the more environmentally innocuous activities do not require licensing, being instead registered with the Agency[4].

1   SI 1994/1056, reg 17 and Sch 3.
2   SI 1996/972 as amended by SI 1996/2019
3   EPA 1990, s 34.
4   See para 1.89.

1.115   To some extent, the elaboration caused by the duty of care has been supplemented by the European provisions. As is discussed in Chapter 12, the Directive on Waste[1] requires that every waste recovery and disposal operation must be subject to either a permit or registration with the competent authority. The fact that this requirement applies to all activities – no matter if they are one-off isolated events – has been confirmed by the European Court[2].

1   Council Directive of 15 July 1975 on Waste (75/442/EEC) (OJ L194/39 25.7.75) as amended by Council Directive of 18 March 1991 amending Directive 75/442/EEC on Waste (91/156/EEC) (OJ L78/32 26.3.91), Articles 9, 10 and 11.
2   *Ministère Public v Oscar Traen* [1988] 3 CMLR 511: discussed at para 12.05.

1.116   Up to the period when the EPA 1990 was brought into force, the actions of most regulatory authorities were informed by way of a purposive interpretation of the statutory remit. Even within the current British legislation, there is no explicit statutory duty on the Environment Agency to search out every possible potentially licensable waste management activity[1]. Certainly, under the earlier Control of Pollution Act 1974, action could be taken if damage to the environment was implicated or if what was going on was a bona fide commercial scale waste management operation. If it was not, then it could be ignored. This was particularly the case with waste recovery activities of low potential environmental significance[2].

1   See para 12.09.
2   However, having removed much of the regulators' discretion on these matters, the guidance issued with the Waste Management Licensing Regulations 1994 and the Environment Act 1995 also appears to suggest that the Agency should utilise its discretion even more widely: for example, in Circular 11/94 regulators are cautioned about pursuing what are 'technical' offences, where the environment has not been affected (see Circular 11/94, para 17 and para 12.34ff).

1.117   The tendency throughout the early 1990s for the codification of all conceivable permutations of waste transaction has resulted in statutory provisions of some considerable length and complexity. Examples include provisions which exclude from the requirement to hold a waste management licence the discharge of sewage from railway carriages[1] and the burial of a dead domestic cat in a private garden[2]. Whether it is strictly necessary to go this far is a moot point. It seems doubtful that litigation on this matter would be likely or well-received in a court of law. It also does seem rather unlikely that a successful complaint for an infraction of the Directive on Waste would be upheld by the European Court of Justice on such a trivial matter.

1   SI 1994/1056, Sch 3, para 31: see para 10.250.
2   SI 1994/1056, Sch 3, para 37: see para 10.232.

1.118   While the embellishment of the legislation is an observable trend, so is increasing complexity. Although a certain amount of complexity is an inevitable facet of the regulation of a £3.5 billion industry, complexity is also a direct result of the manner by which the Community provisions are integrated with the EPA 1990 in the relevant legislation, principally the Waste Management Licensing Regulations 1994[1]. Despite the fact that the Bill which resulted in the EPA 1990 and the amendments to the Directive on Waste[2] were being drafted concurrently, this is not at all apparent from the wording of the EPA 1990. Indeed, it would appear that the EPA 1990 was drafted in isolation of what was being developed in the European dimension. Certainly, the British and European legislation do not sit particularly comfortably together, with the Directive being exclusively transposed in the form of 'bolt on' provisions contained mainly in the Schedules to the Waste Management Licensing Regulations 1994.

1   SI 1994/1056 as amended by SIs 1994/1137, 1995/288, 1995/1950, 1996/593, 1996/634, 1996/972, 1996/1279, 1997/251, 1997/351, 1997/2203, 1998/606 and 1998/2746.
2   By way of Directive 91/156.

1.119   The result is that it is very difficult to grasp quickly the principles of the regulatory system, as it is not immediately apparent where the key parts of the legislation are to be located. For example, while the main powers to grant waste management licences are contained in s 35 and s 36 of the EPA 1990[1], further highly significant provisions are contained in the Waste Management Licensing Regulations 1994, particularly reg 15 in respect of groundwater protection[2] and reg 19 – in conjunction with Schedule 4 – in relation to the implementation of the 'relevant objectives' of the Directive on Waste[3].

1   See para 8.29ff.
2   See para 8.70ff.
3   See para 8.50ff.

1.120   An additional problem is the confusing terminology scattered around the EPA 1990 and Waste Management Licensing Regulations 1994. Again, this is a function of the less than satisfactory reconciliation of the EPA 1990 and the Directive on Waste. Certainly, there has been no attempt to rationalise terminology to a common base. For example, some sections refer to 'recycling', others to 'recovery'. The Waste Management Licensing Regulations 1994 set out to describe waste 'disposal' operations and include waste treatment under this heading[1]. But s 29(6) of the EPA 1990, which provides a list of key definitions in the primary legislation, makes a distinction between 'disposal' and 'treatment' operations. In addition, 'recycling and re-use' is viewed as a subset of 'treatment' in that section. By contrast, the Waste Management Licensing Regulations 1994 indicate that recovery and disposal operations are subject to quite distinct definitional approaches.

1   SI 1994/1056, Sch 4, Parts III and IV; see Tables 2.5 and 2.6 in Chapter 2.

1.121 It should also be observed that, in certain instances, the transposition of the Community provisions could be described as somewhat half-hearted. The manner by which the requirements for registration of exempted activities is drafted, involving a maximum penalty of a £10 fine[1], is somewhat mocking of the requirements of the provisions on registration contained in the Directive on Waste. As is shown in Chapter 2, the revised definition of waste – particularly that involving 'Directive waste'[2] – is subject to an unclear and highly ambiguous definition. However, it follows the wording of the Directive exactly and hence results in transposition of EC law in its 'pure' form. That this change undermined a bundle of case law – much of which ironically already followed the tenet of the Directive – was obviously viewed as of much lesser significance by those responsible for the drafting of the legislation. Although Circular 11/94 sets out to clarify matters, this guidance is sometimes heavily qualified – and in places contradictory – as to be less than satisfactory[3]. Furthermore, the guidance is of little application where it is most needed, in a court of law.

1   Besides this low level of fine, the provisions are drafted in a manner which makes them unlikely to be subject to proceedings: see para 10.24.
2   SI 1994/1056, reg 1(3): see para 2.35.
3   See para 2.103ff.

1.122 Overall, the more one reads the EPA 1990, the Waste Management Licensing Regulations 1994 and Circular 11/94, the more one comes to the conclusion that, in general, they do not sit happily with the requirements of the Directive on Waste. What can be seen is that, in the drafting of the legislation, there appears to be a fundamental lack of confidence on behalf of the legislators in how the transposition of Community law should have been handled. Rather than undertake a careful analysis of the provisions of the EPA 1990 Act in the light of the Directive on Waste and then plug any identifiable gaps by way of secondary legislation to ensure compliance with the Community provisions, a 'belt and braces' approach has been favoured. This involved adding virtually all of the significant elements of the Directive as an additional layer of secondary legislation. This duality of approach can then act as some form of insurance against infraction proceedings at the European Court of Justice. Although it may prove politically valuable to keep the UK out of the Court, whether the legislation constitutes good law-making is doubtful, mainly because key elements of the provisions of British waste management law have ended up scattered amongst obscure paragraphs contained in the schedules of secondary legislation. Overall, the lack of a coherent approach seems likely to cause difficulties to all parties. It has also significantly contributed to the length of the account of the provisions which follow in subsequent chapters.

1.123 Finally, it also will be apparent from the forthcoming chapters that, although waste management is highly regulated, certain elements of the legislation have been subject to deliberate dilution, with the result that their application fails to serve fully the provisions' purpose or intent. Indeed, in the case of the duty of care there is a feeling that the dilution process has gone too far, particularly in respect, for example, of the transfer note system. Although it is not absolutely clear of their effects, the amendments made to s 34 of the EPA 1990 by the Deregulation and Contracting Out Act 1994 appear[1] to undermine the fundamental purpose of the transfer note system, namely the comprehensive, written and traceable documentation of waste movements between parties. Similarly, when the Code of Practice on the duty of care was revised in 1996, the re-drafted version actually sets out to highlight the weaknesses in the legislation, in order to be somehow deregulatory.

1   See para 3.157ff.

1.124   A potential outcome of the difficulties outlined above is that a duality of compliance may emerge. Certain companies may wish to follow the spirit of the legislation and not sail close to the edges of grey areas. This need becomes particularly apparent with companies which are wishing to attain quality management standards and accredited environmental management systems such as contained in ISO 14001[1] or EMAS[2]. However, companies with other objectives seem able to exploit those grey areas to their commercial advantage. Although this is an inevitable facet of any regulatory system, the rather half-hearted manner by which certain statutory provisions are cast appears to encourage this dichotomy. One effect is that companies wishing to ensure total compliance do so at some internal cost to themselves[3]. The result is a playing field of waste management law which is by no means level and whose gradient has been cast by legislators as deliberately uncertain. Whether this arrangement will ensure a societal net benefit in commercial or environmental terms remains to be seen.

1   International Standard Organisation *Environmental Management Systems – Specification with Guidance for Use* ISO 14001, International Standards Organisation, Switzerland.
2   Council Regulation (EEC) No 1836/93 of 29 June 1993 allowing voluntary participation by companies in the industrial sector in a Community eco-management and audit scheme (OJ L168/1 10.7.93).
3   And still bear the risk of inadvertently contravening one of the more obscure requirements of the relevant legislation.

Chapter 2

The definition of waste and controlled waste

INTRODUCTION

2.01 The foundation of UK waste management law is the definition of waste. The fact that a substance falls within this definition is fundamental to whether it is subject to Part II of the EPA 1990. The definition of waste therefore determines such matters as whether a particular industrial operation is to be subject to a waste management licence[1], if the duty of care[2] is to apply to a transaction involving specified materials and is also one of the criteria in deciding whether their transportation is to be by way of a registered waste carrier[3].

1 See Chapter 8.
2 EPA 1990, s 34: see Chapter 3.
3 Control of Pollution (Amendment) Act 1989: see Chapter 6. Oddly, the landfill tax contains its own separate definition of waste, which is somewhat different from that contained in the EPA 1990 and Waste Management Licensing Regulations 1994: see Finance Act 1996, s 64, HM Customs and Excise (1997) *A General Guide to the Landfill Tax* Notice LFT1, para 1.3, and para 2.168.

2.02 The definition of waste was one of the few sections of the Control of Pollution Act 1974[1] whose wording was incorporated verbatim into the EPA 1990[2]. However, when Part II of the EPA 1990 was enacted in 1994, this definition was circumscribed by the Waste Management Licensing Regulations 1994[3]. The Department of the Environment's stated purpose of the additional provisions[4] was to fully embrace the definition contained in the Directive on Waste[5]. However, it is claimed that the relevant provisions constitute a temporary solution[6], which is fortunate given the tortuous nature of the chosen statutory mechanism[7]. A more permanent solution is contained in the Environment Act 1995[8]. When the relevant provisions are commenced, the latter Act would result in s 75 of the EPA 1990 being subject to significant amendment.

1 Control of Pollution Act 1974, s 30.
2 Control of Pollution Act 1974, s 75.
3 SI 1994/1056, regs 1(3) and 24(8).
4 Circular 11/94, Annex 2, para 2.4.
5 Article 1(a) of Council Directive of 15 July 1975 on Waste (75/442/EEC) (OJ L194/39 25.7.95) as amended by Directive 91/156 (OJ L78/32 26.3.91).
6 See Circular 11/94, Annex 2, para 2.4.
7 See para 2.31 below.
8 Environment Act 1995, Sch 22, para 88: see para 2.43 below.

2.03 Although the amendments made by the Environment Act 1995 will considerably straighten the route by which waste is statutorily defined, the question of waste definitions remains one of the most complex and difficult components of the regulatory regime. However, it is important not to over-state the problem, nor to lose focus of the fact that difficulties arise principally in respect of substances passing to recovery. The debate arises from both national and Community legislation centring the definition of waste on substances which are held to be 'discarded'. As will be shown, precedent indicates that this term has a special meaning different from common usage. For materials consigned to disposal facilities, the fact that – being 'discarded' – they are defined as wastes will often be obvious and hence the relevant legislation leaves little scope for argument. Indeed, in the case of many substances passing to recovery, this also holds true. Therefore while the detailed treatment in this chapter expresses the nature of the current controversy over waste definitions, this debate has relevance mainly to the waste recovery sector, being focused on those materials which are close to the borderline between 'wastes' and 'economic goods'. Within this context, it does, of course, have particular relevance to the increasing trend towards the diversion of wastes from disposal to recovery facilities[1].

1 See paras 1.26ff and 1.38.

2.04 The difficulties relating to the definition of waste in the context of waste recovery do not necessarily derive from an inadequate legal definition in national or Community legislation. The problem stems from the realities of waste management, particularly the variety and complexity of commercial transactions involving substances which may or may not be defined as 'wastes'. This highly variable texture provides significant challenges to a legislator attempting to devise a workable but comprehensive waste definition, and facing the challenge of balancing two conflicting requirements. On the one hand, it is important to derive a definition which comprehensively covers those substances which need to be the subject of environmental controls; but on the other hand, it is all too easy to produce a legal definition which inappropriately restricts the legitimate trade in economic goods through normal commercial transactions.

2.05 Virtually every country has struggled with the drafting of a comprehensive legal definition of waste and it is perhaps correct to say that none have produced a wording which is entirely satisfactory. This was acknowledged in 1996 at EC level by the Commission's draft Resolution on Waste Policy[1]:

'The discussion on the distinction between waste and goods has been going on for almost twenty years now. No satisfactory definition has yet to be found to determine when a material becomes waste and when waste becomes a good again . . . Notwithstanding the inherent difficulty of this question, practical implications necessitate further efforts involving all parties concerned, including international organisations, towards finding such a definition.'

1 *Communication from the Commission on the Review of the Community Strategy for Waste Management. Draft Council Resolution on Waste Policy* (1996) COM(96) 399 Final. 30.07.96, para 13.

2.06 The principal difficulty is that the dividing line between what are often termed 'goods' and 'wastes' is never clear-cut and may even overlap. In the absence of legislative intervention, economic circumstances would often dictate where that line is, but these circumstances – and hence the dividing line itself – will vary considerably in time and space. An example concerns waste paper, a commodity whose price is unstable and highly cyclical. High prices may be paid by secondary users of waste paper at certain times. But at other times holders of waste paper may end up paying a third party to take the material away. A second example is bonemeal, a by-product of the rendering of animal carcasses. Until the BSE crisis, this material was sold extensively as an animal feed supplement. Since concerns were raised that bonemeal may harbour the agent responsible for BSE, by the winter of 1998 340,000 tonnes of bonemeal were in storage awaiting disposal in Britain[1]. Bonemeal became regarded as a waste in the middle of 1996 for the reason that the material became surplus, due to the collapse of its market[2].

1   'First Big Contract to Dispose of Waste from the BSE Cull' *ENDS Report* 285, October 1998, p 15;
    see also 'The Environmental Impact of the BSE Crisis' *ENDS Report* 268, May 1997, p 21.
2   Since May 1996, the location of the storage of bonemeal is, for example, exempted from the need to
    be subject to a waste management licence: SI 1994/1056, Sch 3, para 17 as amended by
    SI 1996/1279, reg 2: see para 10.92ff.

2.07   The value of wastes or raw materials is also not just a function of gate prices.
There are other determining factors including transport costs, the quantities of the
material involved, technological innovation and the availability of appropriate waste
management infrastructure. All these aspects have a fundamental influence on whether
substances are to be seen as wastes or goods.

2.08   In the past, there has been a tendency to view wastes as being defined as valueless articles. Although a lack of value may be a useful indicator that something is
waste, focusing solely on value has become increasingly inappropriate for a number of
reasons. Firstly, if wastes are to be defined as valueless, the unstable value of some
substances may cause them to switch in or out of regulatory controls. Clearly, it is
untenable to construct a workable statutory definition – or indeed to centre a waste
control system – on this basis.

2.09   Secondly, there is an observable trend of competition between the recycling and
disposal infrastructure for the business of waste holders. Since the implementation of
statutory controls in the 1970s, waste disposal prices have increased considerably.
This trend will continue with further advances in the sophistication of the national
waste management infrastructure, along with public opposition factors which restrict
the supply of new disposal sites, legal restrictions such as the Landfill Directive and
economic mechanisms such as the landfill tax. The result has been a stimulated interest
in the possibility of reprocessing what were hitherto economically marginal
substances. Examples include energy recovery from paint wastes as secondary fuel in
cement manufacture, the chemical recovery of zinc-based wastes from galvanising
and the composting of household waste.

2.10   Often materials such as these have a negative value when sent for reprocessing: the holder still has to pay to have the materials taken away. In cases where
a holder must pay for certain wastes to pass to recycling or recovery, it seems unarguable that such materials should be subject to statutory control. Paying to take these
wastes away will always create an incentive on the holder to get rid of the material for
free. And a potentially attractive way of undertaking this would be indiscriminate
unauthorised disposal. In addition, even if the holder receives some payment for the
wastes, the financial incentive for uncontrolled dumping may still exist. Although the
materials have a value, the value may be small. The value may also be totally dependent on the existence of the outlet which is prepared to pay for the materials. Should
that outlet close (or should the supply of wastes exceed the outlet's requirements), the
waste materials will regain their negative value. The incentive for inappropriate
disposal therefore continues.

2.11   Furthermore, while many countries acknowledge the desirability of the use of
the recycling route at the expense of disposal[1], recycling and other recovery processes
are by no means environmentally benign. These operations can be highly polluting,
whilst the residues resulting from the processes require careful handling and disposal.
Clear evidence of this could be found at many UK car dismantlers and scrap yards,

where the indiscriminate discharge of materials such as oil has made such sites one of the major sources of contaminated land in the country.

1   See Department of the Environment (1995) *Making Waste Work A Strategy for Sustainable Waste Management in England and Wales*, Cm 3040, HMSO, London and see para 1.09.

2.12   'Sham recycling' is also not unknown, particularly in countries which focus their controls solely on waste disposal installations. Materials are accepted at such plants, ostensibly for recovery, but where the amount of waste being recovered – if any – is very small. The residues are then disposed of in a way which avoids statutory control. The export of wastes from one country to another for sham recycling is a global problem. Hence EC controls on transfrontier waste movements[1] allow an intended recipient country to formally object to such shipments on the grounds that the proportion of waste being recovered is very small, that the value of the recovered materials is low or that there is a disproportionate cost involved in the disposal of the non-recoverable residues[2].

1   See Chapter 5.
2   Council Regulation 259/93, Article 7(4)(a): see para 5.154.

2.13   All the above factors lead to the conclusion that the activities of the waste re-cycling industry requires statutory control. Equally, it should be clear that wastes with a positive value must be addressed by waste management law.

2.14   However, there becomes a point where the value of the waste material is so significant that there is no financial incentive for the holder to consider unauthorised disposal. Many industries are based on the processing of intermediate products from other processes. The chemical industry in particular relies on the use of by-products – or more rightly 'co-products' – in a significant variety of ways. There are hundreds of possible examples, including alkali production. Caustic soda production by way of the electrolytic decomposition of salt solutions produces copious quantities of chlorine as a co-product. As both materials are produced together, an excessive demand for chlorine, particularly for PVC production, will mean that unwanted caustic soda will need to be stored[1]. The converse also applies, whereby an excessive demand for caustic soda may cause stocks of chlorine to build up. When the economics of the storage of the surplus materials become unfavourable, the production processes them-selves may be curtailed, causing prices to increase. What is notable in this example is that the market provides controls. Regulatory intervention of an environmental nature has only a very indirect role (if at all) in this instance, relating primarily to general process emissions.

1   See Heaton C R (1986) *The Chemical Industry*, Blackie, London, p 132.

2.15   Moreover, innovation will always attempt to find uses for particular sub-stances. The market may itself provide significant incentives for such innovation, but regulation also has a role in this process. Finding new uses for by-products has been the basis of the chemical industry since its inception. Two examples of early chemical industry activities illustrates this point. In the 19th century, the Leblanc process was used to manufacture soda, an essential industrial feedstock. The process resulted in the production of vast quantities of hydrochloric acid, as a by-product of the action of sulphuric acid on sodium chloride. Originally, these acid gases were vented to the atmosphere causing significant environmental destruction to vegetation in proximity to any alkali works. Eventually, these releases were subject to control under the Alkali Works Act 1863. The development of water-based scrubbing systems to achieve the Alkali Works Act 1863's 95% acid removal target resulted in the production of a by-product hydrochloric acid, for which end uses quickly developed. Likewise, the early production of town gas resulted in an obnoxious waste in the form of coal tar. Eventually, innovation resulted in the re-use of significant quantities; as one commentator enthused: '. . . black and apparently useless coal-tar was to prove to the organic chemist an almost unbelievably rich treasure house'[1]. Processed coal tar formed the basis for consumables as diverse as shampoos, disinfectants and creosote.

1   Williams T I (1952) *The Chemical Industry: Past and Present*, republished by E P Publishing in 1972, Wakefield, p 63.

2.16   Industrial innovations such as these cause hitherto residual materials to become commodities of sufficient value as to make regulatory control no longer appropriate. Hence substances generated in these circumstances should not be caught within the ambit of waste management legislation. Conversely, 95% of all wastes will never attain the status of a valuable commodity until processed and hence their status under the control regime will be pretty obvious. This will be the case even with extensive recycling[1]. However, whilst it may be self-evident when waste management controls should or should not apply in many cases, the dividing line between goods and wastes is virtually impossible to determine on a practical basis. Even if it was possible, economic circumstances and industrial innovation will dictate that prices will fluctuate and cause the boundary to shift.

1   The implementation of German packaging waste recovery legislation ordinance in the late 1980s caused segregated packaging waste to pass to France, the UK and other locations due to a lack of recovery infrastructure in Germany itself to cope with the additional volumes generated.

2.17   As will be seen, both Community and British law attempts to address these realities. From EC case law, it is clear[1] that wastes of economic value which pass to recovery may fall within the regulatory controls which emanate from the Directive on Waste[2]. British case law in respect of the EPA 1990 and the earlier Control of Pollution Act 1974[3] has come to a similar conclusion. However, there is a reluctance to set down hard and fast rules. Indeed, it may be that the economic factors detailed above will cause any legal case to turn on its own facts. Restraint by the judiciary in setting down wide rules may be appropriate for these reasons. As will be discussed below, the Department of the Environment has made a valiant attempt to provide guidance by way of Annex 2 of Circular 11/94[4]. But like most country's waste definitions, this guidance does not – and the realities of waste management ensures that it cannot – provide a definitive view of when a substance is a waste or a potentially re-usable product.

1   See para 2.78ff below.
2   Council Directive of 15 July 1975 on Waste, 75/442/EEC (OJ L194/39 25.7.75) as amended by Council Directive of 18 March 1991 amending Directive 75/442/EEC on Waste, (91/156/EEC) (OJ L78/32 26.3.91) and by Commission Decision of 24 May 1996 adapting Annexes IIA and IIB of Council Directive 75/442/EEC on Waste (OJ L135/32 6.6.96).
3   See para 2.168.
4   Department of the Environment (1994) *Environmental Protection Act 1990 Waste Management Licensing The Framework Directive on Waste*, Circular 11/94, HMSO, London.

2.18   The last word on the subject of the interface between 'wastes' and 'goods' should be left to Schiemann J[1]. In a judicial review involving the validity of a solvent recovery plant's planning permission, the meaning of 'trade waste' was considered. For the appellants, it was argued that the solvents were trade waste as they were useless due to the impurities gained from the prior use of the material in other industrial contexts. For the recovery plant operator as defendant, the solvents were viewed as raw materials, as they constituted the chemical feedstocks on which the solvent recovery company was dependent for its existence[2]. Faced with this conflict, Schiemann J noted[3]:

> 'The argument at times reminded me of those black and white lithographs by Escher which depict fishes or swallows depending on whether one is concentrating on the black or the white. Some would say the picture was of fishes; others would say it was of swallows. The right answer is that it is both fishes and swallows. Similarly here the solvents are perhaps rightly regarded as being both trade waste and raw materials.'

1   *R v Rotherham Metropolitan Borough Council, ex p Rankin* [1990] 1 PLR 93.
2   *R v Rotherham Metropolitan Borough Council, ex p Rankin* [1990] 1 PLR 93 at 95F/G.
3   *R v Rotherham Metropolitan Borough Council, ex p Rankin* [1990] 1 PLR 93 at 99C/D.

THE DEFINITION OF WASTE UNDER THE DIRECTIVE ON WASTE

2.19   Waste was first defined in EC law in 1975 in the Directive on Waste[1]. However, the definition in Article 1 was originally cast only in very general terms and resulted in each member state defining waste differently. There were also significantly different approaches on how far individual member states' definitions encompassed 'wastes' passing to recovery and re-use. The contrasts created particular difficulties for the control of movements of waste between member states[2]. The result of this was that the Directive on Waste was extensively modified in April 1993[3]. The modifications covered virtually the whole Directive, including the definition of waste.

1   Council Directive of 15 July 1975 on Waste (75/442/EEC), (OJ L194/39 25.7.75).
2   Now controlled by EC Regulation 259/93: see Chapter 5. The earlier legislation – principally Council Directive of 6 December 1984 on the Supervision and Control within the European Community of the Transfrontier Shipment of Hazardous Waste (OJ L326/31 13.12.84) – was dependent upon member states' individual definitions of waste.
3   See Council Directive of 18 March 1991 amending Directive 75/442/EEC on Waste (91/156/EEC) (OJ L78/32 26.3.91), Article 2(1).

Article 1 of the Directive

2.20   Article 1 of the Directive on Waste[1] provides the key definition. As will be seen, the wording of this Article is now enshrined into British law[2]. Article 1(a) states that:

> 'Waste shall mean any substance or object in the categories set out in Annex I which the holder discards or intends or is required to discard.'

It is of note that this contains two requirements, both of which must be satisfied for a substance to be a waste. Firstly, the substance must fall within one of the categories of the Annex I (see Table 2.1). Secondly, it must be discarded in the manner set down.

1   Council Directive of 15 July 1975 on Waste (75/442/EEC), (OJ L194/39 25.7.75); as amended by Council Directive of 18 March 1991 amending Directive 75/442/EEC on Waste (91/156/EEC) (OJ L78/32 26.3.91).
2   See para 2.29ff below.

Table 2.1

Directive 75/442 on Waste
Annex I Categories of Waste

Q1   Production or consumption residues not otherwise specified below
Q2   Off-specification products
Q3   Products whose date for appropriate use has expired
Q4   Materials spilled, lost or having undergone other mishap, including materials, equipment, etc contaminated as a result of mishap
Q5   Materials contaminated or soiled as a result of planned actions (eg residues from cleaning operations, packing materials, containers, etc)
Q6   Unusable parts (eg reject batteries, exhausted catalysts, etc)
Q7   Substances which no longer perform satisfactorily (eg contaminated acids, contaminated solvents, exhausted tempering salts, etc)
Q8   Residues of industrial processes (eg slags, still bottoms etc)
Q9   Residues from pollutant abatement processes (eg scrubber sludges, baghouse dusts, spent filters, etc)
Q10 Machining/finishing residues (eg lathe turnings, mill scales, etc)
Q11 Residues from raw materials extraction and processing (eg mining residues, oil field slops, etc)
Q12 Adulterated materials (eg oils contaminated with PCBs, etc)
Q13 Any materials, substances or products whose use has been banned by law
Q14 Products for which the holder has no further use (eg agricultural, household, office, commercial and shop discards, etc)
Q15 Contaminated materials, substances or products resulting from remedial action with respect to land
Q16 Any materials, substances or products which are not contained in the above categories

2.21   From even a cursory glance at the Annex I list[1], it will be apparent the list of substances therein is all-embracing. Items Q1 and Q16 make this clear. Hence the question of the definition of waste in reality turns on whether the holder is somehow discarding the material. The Directive leaves the term 'discarding' to have its ordinary meaning. However, the concept of waste as a whole under the Directive has been subject to a series of European Court judgments[2]. While these will be discussed later[3], it should be noted at this stage that Article 1(a) states that whether a substance is a waste is a decision made by the 'holder' of the waste. It is argued below that this is not a decision to be taken by the recipient of a waste transaction, unless that person can fall within the somewhat restricted category of 'holder'. The identity of the 'holder' is considered further at para 2.156 below.

1   See Table 2.1.
2   *Vessoso and Zanetti* Cases C-206/88 and C-207/88 ([1990] ECR I-1461) and see also Case C-359/88 (ECR 1990 I-1509); *EC v Germany* [1995] ECR 1-1097; *EC v Belgium* [1993] 5 JEL 133-148; *Criminal Proceedings Against Tombesi* [1998] Env LR 59; *Inter-Environnement Wallonie ASBL v Region Wallone* [1998] Env LR 623.
3   See para 2.156.

2.22   Article 1(a) of the Directive on Waste also requires the European Commission to draw up a list of wastes 'belonging to the categories listed in Annex I'. This list was published in December 1993 as the European Waste Catalogue (EWC)[1]. The EWC is reproduced in full in Appendix II. It has no legal status with respect to deciding when a substance may be a waste[2]. Its use is more to categorise wastes by their nature and source. Hence the Directive on Hazardous Wastes[3] sets out that certain of these wastes should be considered to be hazardous wastes. It will also have potential future use in the provision of EC-wide statistical data on waste arisings and movements[4].

1   Commission Decision of 20 December 1993 establishing a List of Waste pursuant to Article 1(a) of Council Directive 75/442/EEC on Waste (94/3/EC), (OJ L5/15).
2   Introductory Note 3 to the Annex to Commission Decision 94/3 states '... the inclusion of a material in the EWC does not mean that the material is a waste in all circumstances. The entry is only relevant when the definition of waste has been satisfied'.
3   Council Directive of 12 December 1991 on Hazardous Waste (Directive 91/689/EEC), (OJ L377/20 31.12.91) and see, in particular, Council Decision of 22 December 1994 establishing a list of Hazardous Waste pursuant to Article 1(4) of Council Directive 91/689/EEC (94/904/EC), (OJ L356/14 31.12.94).
4   It is expected that it will be published in a revised form in 2000, being combined with the Hazardous Waste List (EC Decision 94/904: see para 4.16). In addition, a separate Council Regulation (OJ C87/22 29.3.99) has been proposed in order to attain EC-wide uniformity in the collation of waste statistics.

Exclusions

2.23   Not all substances fall within the definition of waste contained in the Directive on Waste. Exclusions are set out in Article 2(1):

'(a)   gaseous effluents emitted into the atmosphere;
(b)   where they are already covered by other legislation:
    (i)   radioactive waste;
    (ii)   waste resulting from prospecting, extraction, treatment and storage of mineral resources and the working of quarries;
    (iii)   animal carcasses and the following agricultural waste: faecal matter and other natural, non-dangerous substances used in farming;
    (iv)   waste waters, with the exception of waste in liquid form;
    (v)   decommissioned explosives.'

Like the primary definition of waste in Article 1, these exclusions have a significance in British law. They are therefore returned to later at para 2.48, but, at this juncture, the somewhat inconsistent drafting of Article 2 and the Annex I list should be noted. Despite Article 2 excluding most mining and agricultural waste from the Directive, items Q11 and Q14 in Annex I of the Directive[1] include mining residues and agricultural discards as categories of waste.

1   See Table 2.1.

Disposal and recovery facilities

2.24   In its amended form, the Directive on Waste also became much more explicit to the effect that, as well as having application to disposal facilities, it also applied to waste management by recovery and reclamation. Disposal and recovery operations were distinguished by way of individual definitional lists contained in the Directive's Annexes IIA and IIB (see Tables 2.2 and 2.3). The Directive also made clear that both types of activity require a permit, but that member states can establish a separate system for the registration of certain types of recovery activity[1]. While there is no direct connection between the definition of waste in Article 1 of the Directive and these Annexes, their presence on the legislation indicates that wastes can be 'discarded' not only to disposal facilities but also to recovery activities. This important point is returned to later[2].

1   Council Directive of 15 July 1975 on Waste (75/442/EEC), (OJ L194/39 25.7.75) (as amended by Council Directive of 18 March 1991 amending Directive 75/442/EEC on Waste (91/156/EEC), (OJ L78/32 26.3.91) Article 11: this matter is discussed at para 10.07ff.
2   See para 2.91.

Table 2.2[1]

Directive 75/442 on Waste
Annex IIA – Disposal Operations

D1 Deposit into or onto land (eg landfill, etc)
D2 Land treatment (eg biodegradation of liquid or sludgy discards in soils, etc)
D3 Deep injection (eg injection of pumpable discards into wells, salt domes, or naturally occurring repositories, etc)
D4 Surface impoundment (eg placement of liquid or sludgy discards into pits, ponds or lagoons etc)
D5 Specially engineered landfill (eg placement into lined discrete cells which are capped and isolated from one another and the environment, etc)
D6 Release into a water body except seas/oceans
D7 Release into seas/oceans including sea bed insertion
D8 Biological treatment not specified elsewhere in this Annex which results in final compounds or mixtures which are discarded by means of any of the operations numbered D1 to D12
D9 Physico-chemical treatment not specified elsewhere in this Annex which results in final compounds or mixtures which are discarded by means of any of the operations numbered D1 to D12 (eg evaporation, drying, calcination, etc)
D10 Incineration on land
D11 Incineration at sea
D12 Permanent storage (eg emplacement of containers in a mine, etc)
D13 Blending or mixture prior to submission to any of the operations numbered D1 to D13
D14 Repackaging prior to submission to any of the operations numbered D1 to D13
D15 Storage pending any of the operations numbered D1 to D14 (excluding temporary storage, pending collection, on the site where it is produced)

1 As amended by Commission Decision of 24 May 1996 adapting Annexes IIA and IIB of Council Directive 75/442/EEC on Waste (OJ L135/32 6.6.96), Article 1.

Table 2.3[1]

Directive 75/442 on Waste
Annex IIB Operations Which May Lead to Recovery

R1 Use principally as a fuel or other means to generate energy
R2 Solvent reclamation/regeneration
R3 Recycling/reclamation of organic substances which are not used as solvents (including composting and other biological transformation processes)
R4 Recycling/reclamation of metals and metal compounds
R5 Recycling/reclamation of other inorganic materials
R6 Regeneration of acids or bases
R7 Recovery of components used for pollution abatement
R8 Recovery of components from catalysts
R9 Oil refining or other reuses of oil
R10 Land treatment resulting in the benefit to agriculture or ecological improvement
R11 Use of wastes obtained from any of the operations numbered R1 to R10
R12 Exchange of wastes for submission to any of the operations numbered R1 to R11
R13 Storage of wastes pending any of the operations numbered R1 to R12 (excluding temporary storage, pending collection, on the site where it is produced)

1 As amended by Commission Decision of 24 May 1996 adapting Annexes IIA and IIB of Council Directive 75/442/EEC on Waste (OJ L135/32 6.6.96), Article 1.

Transfrontier waste shipments

2.25 In respect of international waste shipments, it should be noted that a slightly different definition of waste appears to apply to wastes moved across frontiers under Council Regulation 259/93[1]. This is discussed at para 5.41ff.

1 Council Regulation (EEC) No 259/93 of 1 February 1993 on the supervision and control of shipments of waste within, into and out of the European Community (OJ L30/1 6.2.93).

EC law and waste definitions

2.26 Because the definition of waste in Community law is contained in a Directive, the definition will normally require to be transposed into the law of each of the Community's member states. Indeed, most member states' national law acknowledges this principle and transposes the definition accordingly.

2.27 However, the European Court in *Tombesi*[1] appears to call this principle into question[2]. This is because of the explicit cross reference to Article 1 of the Directive on Waste by Council Regulation 259/93 on transfrontier waste shipments[3]. The Regulation indicates that, for its purposes, waste is to be defined by way of the Directive on Waste. Whilst Regulation 259/93 pertains to the control of international waste movements[4], the European Court has acknowledged that certain of its provisions also apply to movements within member states. While specified Titles of the Regulation are excluded from having application within a member state, the court has held that Title I – which contains the reference to the definition of waste in the Directive on Waste – is not referred to in these exclusions[5]. Hence the court found[6]:

'Accordingly, it must be concluded that, in order to ensure that the national systems for supervision and control of shipments of waste conform with minimum criteria, Article 2(a) in Title I of Regulation No 259/93, referring to Article 1(a) of Directive 75/442, as amended, laid down a common definition of the concept of waste which is of direct application, *even to shipments within any member state.*'[7]

1 *Criminal Proceedings against Tombesi and others* [1998] Env LR 59 at 87, paras 47 and 48: discussed at para 2.84.
2 See also *Beside BV and I M Besselsen v Minister of Volkshuisvesting* [1999] Env LR 328 at 352, para 27: see para 5.53ff.
3 Council Regulation (EEC) No 259/93 of 1 February 1993 on the supervision and control of shipments of waste within, into and out of the European Community (OJ L30/1 6.2.93), Article 2(a).
4 See Chapter 5.
5 See *Tombesi* [1998] Env LR 59 at 87, paras 44 to 46 and see Regulation 259/93's Title III and Article 13.
6 *Tombesi* [1998] Env LR 59 at 87, para 46.
7 Author's emphasis. See also *Mayer Parry Recycling Ltd v Environment Agency* [1999] Env LR 489 at 492, para 5.

2.28 The precise ramifications of this matter in respect of Britain would seem to invite analysis. Although they are limited in practice due to the British and European provisions having a practically identical basis[1], there may be potential for conflict in the following instance. As is discussed later[2], the national definition of waste is narrower than that set down in the Directive on Waste in respect of certain agricultural wastes, along with wastes from mining and quarrying. These are explicitly excluded from the EPA 1990's definition of 'controlled waste'[3]. What is not clear is whether these exclusions are simply over-ridden by the finding of *Tombesi* that the definition of waste in the Directive on Waste has direct application. If this is correct, then it may be that the exclusions in the EPA 1990 have fallen into some sort of legal limbo.

However, this interpretation – if right – certainly has not received acknowledgement from either the Department of the Environment or the Agency.

1 See *Mayer Parry Recycling Ltd v Environment Agency* [1999] Env LR 489 at 494, para 12.
2 See paras 2.57, 2.61 and 2.73.
3 EPA 1990, s 75.

THE DEFINITION OF WASTE UNDER THE EPA 1990

2.29   Section 75 of the EPA 1990 sets out the definition for two important concepts: 'waste' and 'controlled waste'. The following sections will consider the meaning of the term 'waste': 'controlled waste' will be dealt with later at para 2.190. Although 'waste' has been defined in environmental law since the Control of Pollution Act 1974 entered into force, the definition of waste was significantly changed by the Waste Management Licensing Regulations 1994[1]. As noted earlier, the wording of the definition is to be further amended by the Environment Act 1995[2]. In anticipation that this change will be implemented in the near future, the following sections set out the existing system of waste definitions and then proceed to consider the outcome of the expected modifications.

1 SI 1994/1056, reg 1(3).
2 Environment Act 1995, Sch 22, para 88.

2.30   The changes made in 1994 to the statutory definition of waste cast doubt on whether earlier British case law on waste definitions can be extensively relied upon. This affects a very significant body of precedents on British waste regulation law[1].

1 *Long v Brooke* [1980] Crim LR 109; *Ashcroft v Michael McErlain* (1985), unreported; *Berridge Incinerators v Nottinghamshire County Council* (1987), unreported; *Kent County Council v Queenborough Rolling Mill Co Ltd* (1990) 89 LGR 306; *Ashcroft v Michael McErlain* (1985), unreported; *Thanet District Council v Kent County Council* [1993] Env LR 391; *Cheshire County Council v Armstrong's Transport (Wigan) Ltd* [1995] Env LR 62; *Meston Technical Services v Warwickshire County Council* (10 March 1995, unreported), QBD.

Definition 1: s 75 of the EPA 1990 and the Waste Management Licensing Regulations 1994

2.31   Waste is currently defined by way of a combination of s 75 of the EPA 1990, the Waste Management Licensing Regulations 1994[1] and the Directive on Waste itself. Although the primary legislation lays down the principal definition, this is greatly circumscribed by the Regulations.

1 SI 1994/1056.

2.32   It has already been noted that the definition of waste in s 75 of the EPA 1990 is a verbatim copy of that contained in the Control of Pollution Act 1974[1]. It would seem that the latter definition was itself derived from the Radioactive Substances Act 1960[2]. Section 75(2) of the EPA 1990 states that waste:

'. . . includes –

    (a)   any substance which constitutes a scrap material or an effluent or other unwanted surplus substance arising from the application of any process; and

    (b)   any substance or article which requires to be disposed of as being broken, worn out, contaminated or otherwise spoiled;

but does not include a substance or article which is an explosive within the meaning of the Explosives Act 1875.'

1   Control of Pollution Act 1974, s 31.
2   Now replaced by the Radioactive Substances Act 1993 – radioactive waste is defined in s 47(1).

2.33   It should be noted that the definition of waste starts with the words 'waste includes. . .'. Therefore it can embrace other materials besides those listed in sub-sections (a) and (b) of s 75(2)[1]. At present, the burden of proof is upon the defence when disputes arise about waste definitions[2]:

> 'Any thing which is discarded or otherwise dealt with as if it were waste shall be presumed to be waste unless the contrary is proved.'

1   Confirmed in *Ashcroft v Michael McErlain Ltd* (30 January 1985, unreported), QBD: although a case involving the definition of waste under the Control of Pollution Act 1974, the definition in s 30(1) of that Act is identical to that in s 75(2) of the EPA 1990. May LJ held that the term 'waste' is to be construed primarily in respect of its ordinary everyday meaning, but this meaning is, when necessary, extended to include the substances and articles referred to in the definition itself (ie in s 30(a) and (b) of the Control of Pollution Act 1974 and, by analogy, s 75(2)(a) and (b) of the EPA 1990). Accordingly, May LJ considered for meaning of the word 'waste' in the light of the definition contained in the *Shorter Oxford Dictionary*.
2   EPA 1990, s 75(3).

2.34   Having set down the definition of waste, the EPA 1990 introduces and defines the term 'controlled waste'[1]. Controlled waste is held to mean 'household, industrial and commercial waste or any such waste'. Household, industrial and commercial wastes are then subject to individual definitions[2]. Section 75(8) allows the Secretary of State to make regulations which allocate substances to the different categories of controlled waste. This provision resulted in the Controlled Waste Regulations 1992[3]. The definitions used in s 75 of the EPA 1990 and in the Controlled Waste Regulations 1992 make it clear that controlled waste[4] is a sub-set of the category of waste. Hence certain substances may be 'wastes', but not 'controlled wastes'. Agricultural and mining wastes are examples[5]. At this juncture it is sufficient to appreciate that the EPA 1990 only deals with controlled waste and that this category is divided into three types: household, commercial and industrial waste. While these categories are subject to detailed interpretation in the Controlled Waste Regulations 1992, the definitions contained therein do not affect the meaning of the word 'waste' in the EPA 1990. Hence the three types of controlled waste are discussed, alongside the Controlled Waste Regulations 1992, at para 2.190 below.

1   EPA 1990, s 75(4).
2   EPA 1990, s 75(5), (6) and (7).
3   SI 1992/588.
4   See para 2.190 below.
5   Although s 63(2) of the EPA 1990 sets down offences in respect of the inappropriate management of waste which does not fall within the definition of controlled waste, this sub-section has yet to be commenced.

2.35   Although the provisions of s 75 of the EPA 1990 were enacted in May 1991[1], the breadth of the meaning of 'waste' and 'controlled waste' in s 75 was significantly changed by the Waste Management Licensing Regulations 1994[2]. A purpose of the 1994 Regulations was to transpose the Directive on Waste into British law more clearly[3]. The Waste Management Licensing Regulations 1994 changed the scope of the controlled waste definition, by way of the introduction of the term 'Directive waste'. While the definition of waste in s 75(2) of the EPA 1990 remains, it is effectively over-ridden by the meaning of Directive waste. Hence, as one commentator put it[4], the definition contained in s 75(2) is 'in a kind of legal limbo or condemned cell awaiting its final demise'.

1   Environmental Protection Act (Commencement No 8) Order, SI 1991/1319.
2   SI 1994/1056, reg 1(3).
3   The importance of the implementation of the Directive is made clear by the title of the associated Circular 11/94: *Environmental Protection Act 1990: Part II Waste Management Licensing. The Framework Directive on Waste.*
4   Cheyne I and Purdue M (1995) 'Fitting Definition to Purpose: the Search for a Satisfactory Definition of Waste', *JEL*, Vol 7, No 2, p 154.

2.36   The notion of 'Directive waste' was wholly new, with Regulation 1(3) of the Waste Management Licensing Regulations 1994 requiring that Directive waste:

'. . . means any substance or object in the categories set out in Part II of Schedule 4[1] which the producer or the person in possession of it discards or intends or is required to discard but with the exception of anything excluded from the scope of the Directive by Article 2 of the Directive[2], and "discard" has the same meaning as in the Directive, and "producer" means anyone whose activities produce Directive waste or who carries out preprocessing, mixing or other operations resulting in a change in its nature or composition[3].'

1   See Table 2.4: it should be noted that there are minor differences between the list of wastes in Annex 1 of the Directive, Sch 4, Pt II of the Waste Management Licensing Regulations 1994 and, when para 95 of Sch 22 of the Environment Act 1995 is enacted, Sch 2B of the EPA 1990.
2   Ie the Directive on Waste: SI 1994/1056, reg 1(3).
3   The Waste Management Licensing Regulations 1994 also define 'waste' as meaning Directive waste when the term is used within those regulations: SI 1994/1056, reg 1(3).

Table 2.4

Waste Management Licensing Regulations 1994, Schedule 4, Part II
Substances or Objects which are Waste when Discarded etc

1.	Production or consumption residues not otherwise specified in this Part of this Schedule (Q1).
2.	Off-specification products (Q2).
3.	Products whose date for appropriate use has expired (Q3).
4.	Materials spilled, lost or having undergone other mishap, including any materials, equipment, etc, contaminated as a result of the mishap (Q4).
5.	Materials contaminated or soiled as a result of planned actions (eg residues from cleaning operations, packing materials, containers, etc) (Q5).
6.	Unusable parts (eg reject batteries, exhausted catalysts, etc) (Q6).
7.	Substances which no longer perform satisfactorily (eg contaminated acids, contaminated solvents, exhausted tempering salts, etc) (Q7).
8.	Residues of industrial processes (eg slags, still bottoms etc) (Q8).
9.	Residues from pollution abatement processes (eg scrubber sludges, baghouse dusts, spent filters, etc) (Q9).
10.	Machining or finishing residues (eg lathe turnings, mill scales, etc) (Q10).
11.	Residues from raw materials extraction and processing (eg mining residues, oil field slops, etc) (Q11).
12.	Adulterated materials (eg oils contaminated with PCBs, etc) (Q12).
13.	Any materials, substances or products whose use has been banned by law (Q13).
14.	Products for which the holder has no further use (eg agricultural, household, office, commercial and shop discards, etc) (Q14).
15.	Contaminated materials, substances or products resulting from remedial action with respect to land (Q15).
16.	Any materials, substances or products which are not contained in the above categories (Q16).

(Note: the reference in brackets at the end of each paragraph of this Part of this Schedule is the number of the corresponding paragraph in Annex 1 of the Directive.)

2.37 As will be discussed at para 2.75 below, this whole definition pivots on an interpretation of the word 'discard'. The Waste Management Licensing Regulations 1994[1] integrate into the Directive waste definition the requirement that '... "discard" has the same meaning as in the Directive ...'. However, it should be appreciated that the term is not defined in the Directive. Accordingly, this phrase requires that an interpretation of the term is made in accordance with the purpose and intent of the Directive[2]. This rather complex matter is discussed at para 2.106 below.

1 SI 1994/1056, reg 1(3).
2 See Circular 11/94, Annex II, paras 2.11 and 2.17.

2.38 As noted, the Directive waste concept is used to modify the definition of 'controlled waste'[1]. This is achieved by way of an amendment to Controlled Waste Regulations 1992[2]:

'For the purposes of Part II of the Act, waste which is not Directive waste shall not be treated as household waste, industrial waste or commercial waste.'

Accordingly, waste other than Directive waste cannot be a controlled waste.

1 SI 1994/1056, reg 24.
2 SI 1992/588, reg 7A as amended by SI 1994/1056, reg 24(8).

2.39 It will be immediately apparent that the definition of Directive waste[1] is close to that contained in Article 1 of the Directive on Waste[2]. Not surprisingly therefore, whether a substance falls within the category of Directive waste in British law turns on whether:

1   it is somehow discarded[3];
2   it falls within Part II of Schedule 4 (see Table 2.4); and
3   it is not excluded by virtue of Article 2 of the Directive on Waste.

While the kernel of the Directive's Article 1 is reiterated in the Directive waste definition, the text of exclusions contained in Article 2 is not repeated in the Waste Management Licensing Regulations 1994, requiring that the Directive must itself be consulted. Accordingly, the detailed provisions of no less than four legislative items have to be considered in any legal proceedings which turn on questions of waste definitions: the EPA 1990, the Waste Management Licensing Regulations 1994, the Directive on Waste and the Controlled Waste Regulations 1992[4].

1 SI 1994/1056, reg 1(3).
2 See para 2.20 above.
3 An interpretation of 'discarding' is to be found at para 2.75 below.
4 SI 1992/588.

2.40 While the exclusions from the Directive on Waste in Article 2 have already been described briefly at para 2.23 above, Circular 11/94[1] sets down additional guidance on how that Article is to be interpreted. This has important ramifications, particularly given the key role of the definition of waste in setting down boundaries to the application of the statutory controls contained in Part II of the EPA 1990. Given the significance of the exclusions and the controversy one of these has generated in respect of emissions of effluent treatment plants, these exclusions are considered at para 2.48 below.

1 *Environmental Protection Act 1990: Part II Waste Management Licensing The Framework Directive on Waste*, Circular 11/94, HMSO, London, para 1.12.

2.41 The Waste Management Licensing Regulations 1994 also make one further modification to ensure that Directive waste is embedded throughout Part II of the EPA 1990. Regulation 19 and Schedule 4 to the Regulations modifies the meaning of the term 'waste' when it is used in Part II of the EPA 1990[1]. It ensures that any references to 'waste'[2] in Part II are interpreted so as to 'include' a reference to Directive waste[3]. The purpose of this would appear to be to extend the definition of Directive waste to apply whenever the EPA 1990 makes use of the term 'waste'[4]. However, this additional modification would appear to be superfluous. As noted earlier, the amended Controlled Waste Regulations 1992 make clear that controlled waste must always constitute Directive waste[5].

1   SI 1994/1056, Sch 4, para 9(2).
2   Note that the term 'waste' is used, not 'controlled waste'.
3   SI 1994/1056, Sch 4, para 9(2).
4   Circular 11/94 does not provide its own explanation.
5   SI 1992/588, reg 7A, as amended by SI 1994/1056, reg 24(8).

2.42 Finally, the Waste Management Licensing Regulations 1994 contain similar lists of waste disposal and recovery activities as those contained in Annexes IIA and IIB of the Directive on Waste. Like the Directive on Waste, the wording of the definition of wastes in the Waste Management Licensing Regulations 1994 does not make a direct connection with these lists. However, the lists serve the vital purpose in demonstrating that the legislation envisages that wastes can be discarded when they are passed to recovery facilities. The lists contained in the Schedules of the 1994 Regulations are shown in Tables 2.5 and 2.6. It will be apparent that the wording is slightly different to that set out in the Directive on Waste. While this was the case when the Waste Management Licensing Regulations 1994 came into force (see Tables 2.5 and 2.6), more significant disparities are apparent since the Annexes to the Directive on Waste were updated in 1996[1].

1   By Commission Decision of 24 May 1996 adapting Annexes IIA and IIB of Council Directive 75/442/EEC on Waste (OJ L135/32 6.6.96), Article 1. Compare Tables 2.5 and 2.6 with Tables 2.2 and 2.3.

Definition 2: s 75 of the EPA 1990 as amended by the Environment Act 1995

2.43 The definition of 'waste' in s 75 of the EPA 1990 is to be subject to amendment by the Environment Act 1995[1]. This amendment would appear to make the concept of 'Directive waste' no longer necessary and obviates the convoluted manner by which the Waste Management Licensing Regulations 1994 were used for this purpose. At the time of writing (Summer 1999), these provisions have not been subject to commencement. However, for completeness the proposals are discussed below.

1   Environment Act 1995, Sch 22, para 88.

2.44 The amended s 75(2) of the EPA 1990[1] requires waste to be defined in the following manner:

' "Waste" means any substance or object in the categories set out in Schedule 2B to this Act which the holder discards or intends or is required to discard; and for the purposes of this definition –

"holder" means the producer of the waste or the person who is in possession of it; and "producer" means any person whose activities produce waste or any person who carries out pre-processing, mixing or other operations resulting in a change in the nature or composition of this waste.'

The lists of categories of waste contained in Schedule 2B of the amended EPA 1990 is reproduced in Table 2.7. The list is taken directly from Annex I of the Directive on Waste. Although broadly similar to both the Annex and to the list contained in the Waste Management Licensing Regulations 1994[2], certain minor differences between the lists of waste should be noted. But in any case, as para 2.21 has made clear, virtually any material will fit within this classification, particularly given the wording of Categories 1 and 16.

1   As amended by the Environment Act 1995, Sch 22 and para 88(2).
2   SI 1994/1056, Sch 4, Pt II: see Table 2.4.

Table 2.5

Waste Management Licensing Regulations 1994, Schedule 4, Part III: Waste Disposal Operations

1   Tipping of waste above or underground (eg landfill, etc) (D1)
2   Land treatment of waste (eg biodegradation of liquid or sludge discards in soils, etc) (D2)
3   Deep injection *of waste*[1] (eg injection of pumpable discards into wells, salt domes, or naturally occurring repositories, etc) (D3)
4   Surface impoundment of *waste* (eg placement of liquid or sludge discards into pits, ponds or lagoons etc) (D4)
5   Specially engineered landfill of *waste* (eg placement into lined discrete cells which are capped and isolated from one another and the environment, etc) (D5)
6   Release of solid *waste* into a water body except seas or oceans (D6)
7   Release of waste into seas or oceans including sea bed insertion (D7)
8   Biological treatment not listed elsewhere in this *Part of this Schedule* which results in final compounds or mixtures which are disposed of by means of the operations listed in this *Part of this Schedule* (D8)
9   Physico-chemical treatment not listed elsewhere in this *Part of this Schedule* which results in final compounds or mixtures which are disposed of by means of any of the operations listed in this *Part of this Schedule* (eg evaporation, drying, calcination, etc) (D9)
10 Incineration of *waste* on land (D10)
11 Incineration of *waste* at sea (D11)
12 Permanent storage of *waste* (eg emplacement of containers in a mine, etc) (D12)
13 Blending or mixture of waste prior to the waste being submitted to any of the operations listed in this *Part of this Schedule* (D13)
14 Repackaging of *waste* prior to the waste being submitted to any of the operations listed in this *Part of this Schedule* (D13)
15 Storage of waste pending any of the operations *listed* in this *Part of this Schedule*, but excluding temporary storage, pending collection, on the site where it is produced (D14).

1   The italicised words show the differences between the wording of the Directive on Waste, Annex IIA in its original form and Part III of Sch 4 of the Waste Management Licensing Regulations 1994. Additional disparities now exist since the Directive was amended in 1996.

2.45   In comparison to the unamended version of s 75(2) of the EPA 1990, which held that the definition of waste 'includes' certain substances, it will be noted that the amendment states that waste 'means' those substances which are discarded. Hence whilst a dictionary definition of waste was appropriate under the earlier definition[1], this approach is no longer applicable.

1   See *Ashcroft v McErlain* (30 January 1985, unreported), QBD and para 2.178.

Table 2.6

Waste Management Licensing Regulations 1994, Schedule 4, Part IV: Waste Recovery
Operations

1 Reclamation or regeneration of solvents (R1)
2 Recycling or reclamation of organic substances which are not used as solvents (R2)
3 Recycling or reclamation of metals and metal compounds (R3)
4 Recycling or reclamation of other inorganic materials (R4)
5 Regeneration of acids or bases (R5)
6 Recovery of components used for pollution abatement (R6)
7 Recovery of components from catalysts (R7)
8 *Re-refining, or other re-uses, of oil which is waste*[1] (R8)
9 Use of waste principally as a fuel or for other means of generating energy (R9)
10 Spreading of *waste* on land resulting in benefit to agriculture or ecological improvement,
   including composting and other biological transformation processes, except in the case
   of waste excluded under Article 2(1)(b)(iii)[2] *of the Directive* (R10)
11 Use of wastes obtained from any of the operations listed in paragraphs 1 to 10 of this
   Part of this Schedule (R10)
12 Exchange of wastes for submission to any of the operations listed in Paragraphs 1 to 11
   of this Part of this Schedule (R11)
13 Storage of materials intended for submission to any operation listed *in this Part of this
   Schedule,* but excluding temporary storage, pending collection, on the site where it is
   produced (R13)

1 The italicised words show the differences between the wording of the Directive on Waste, Annex IIA
   in its original form and Part III of Sch 4 of the Waste Management Licensing Regulations 1994.
   Additional disparities now exist since the Directive was amended in 1996.
2 Article 2(1)(b)(iii) excludes animal carcasses, faecal matter and other natural, non-dangerous
   substances used in farming from the provisions of the Directive on Waste: see paras 2.23 and 2.48.

2.46   A second effect of the amendments to be made to s 75 of the EPA 1990 is that
the burden of proof in establishing whether a material is or is not a waste is altered. In
the unamended s 75(3) of the EPA 1990[1] the burden of proof was on the defendant.
This being so, the burden could be discharged in court on the basis of the criteria of the
balance of probabilities[2]. However, the Environment Act 1995 will repeal s 75(3)[3].
This change places the duty upon the prosecution to prove that a material is a waste.
The criteria in this instance will be more stringent: whether a substance is a waste must
be proved 'beyond reasonable doubt'.

1 And also in the Control of Pollution Act 1974, s 30.
2 See *R v Carr-Briant* [1943] 2 All ER 156; *R v Dunbar* [1957] 2 All ER 737; *R v Hudson* [1965] 1 All
   ER 721.
3 Environment Act 1995, Sch 22, para 88(3).

2.47   Finally, a rather odd provision is to be added to the end of s 75 of the EPA 1990.
The Environment Act 1995 proposes a new s 75(11), which requires:

'Subsection (2)[1] above is substituted, and Schedule 2B[2] to this Act is inserted, for
the purpose of assigning to "waste" in this Part the meaning which it has in the
Directive on Waste by virtue of paragraphs (a) to (c) of Article 1[3], and Annex I[4] to,
that Directive, and those provisions shall be construed accordingly.'

The purpose of this sub-section is not entirely evident and it would appear that it is not
essential to the operation of the remainder of the amended s 75. However, it may just

provide a further pointer that the British definition of waste must be construed by way of the Directive[5].

1 EPA 1990, s 75(2)
2 See Table 2.6.
3 As discussed at para 2.20ff, para (a) requires that waste is defined as a material which the holder discards, paras (b) and (c) respectively define the term 'producer' and 'holder'.
4 See Table 2.1.
5 It should also be noted that, unlike the definition of Directive waste in the Waste Management Licensing Regulations 1994 (SI 1994/1056, reg 1(3)), the Environment Act 1995 does not set out any explicit reference to the exclusions contained in Article 2 of the Directive on Waste (see para 2.23). Whether s 75(11) is intended to do this is not clear. However, it may be that, when the amendment to s 75 of the EPA 1990 is enacted, a reference to Article 2 could be contained in any new regulations, using the general power in the European Communities Act 1972 to modify primary legislation to transpose EC law.

Table 2.7

Environmental Protection Act 1990
Schedule 2B[1]

Categories of Waste
1 Production or consumption residues not otherwise specified below
2 Off-specification products
3 Products whose date for appropriate use has expired
4 Materials spilled, lost or having undergone other mishap, including any materials, equipment, etc, contaminated as a result of the mishap
5 Materials contaminated or soiled as a result of planned actions (eg residues from cleaning operations, packing materials, containers, etc)
6 Unusable parts (eg reject batteries, exhausted catalysts, etc)
7 Substances which no longer perform satisfactorily (eg contaminated acids, contaminated solvents, exhausted tempering salts, etc)
8 Residues of industrial processes (eg slags, still bottoms etc)
9 Residues from pollution abatement processes (eg scrubber sludges, baghouse dusts, spent filters, etc)
10 Machining/finishing residues (eg lathe turnings, mill scales, etc)
11 Residues from raw materials extraction and processing (eg mining residues, oil field slops, etc)
12 Adulterated materials (eg oils contaminated with PCBs, etc)
13 Any materials, substances or products whose use has been banned by law
14 Products for which the holder has no further use (eg agricultural, household, office, commercial and shop discards, etc)
15 Contaminated materials, substances or products resulting from remedial action with respect to land
16 Any materials, substances or products which are not contained in the above categories

1 As amended by the Environment Act 1995, Sch 22, para 95 (not commenced).

Exclusions from the definition of waste

2.48 At para 2.23, it was noted that Article 2 of the Directive on Waste excludes certain materials from the definition of waste. In the Waste Management Licensing Regulations 1994[1] there is also explicit cross reference to those exclusions contained in the definition of Directive waste. This makes it essential that Article 2 of the Directive on Waste must be considered for details of the stipulated statutory exclusions. Unfortunately Article 2 is not a model of clear drafting and Circular 11/94[2] provides 2,000 words of non-statutory interpretation. In certain instances the basis of this interpretation would not seem to be firmly founded on the actual wording of the provisions.

1   SI 1994/1056, reg 1(3).
2   *Environmental Protection Act 1990: Part II Waste Management Licensing The Framework Directive on Waste*, Circular 11/94, HMSO, London, para 1.12.

2.49   In addition, it has been noted that the proposed amendment to the definition of waste contained in the Environment Act 1995 does not contain an explicit cross reference to Article 2 of the Directive[1]. Accordingly, it is not clear at present as to how the exclusions contained in Article 2 are to be handled when s 75 of the EPA 1990 is amended by the Environment Act 1995.

1   Environment Act 1995, Sch 22, para 88.

2.50   The full wording of Article 2 of the Directive on Waste is to be found at para 2.23 above. In summary, Article 2 excludes:

(a)   gaseous effluents emitted to the atmosphere;
(b)   radioactive waste;
(c)   waste from prospecting, extraction, etc of mineral resources and from quarries;
(d)   animal carcasses, agricultural waste, faecal matter and other natural, non-hazardous substances used in farming;
(e)   waste waters, but not liquid waste;
(f)   decommissioned explosives.

However, with the exception only of gaseous effluents, the other five types of waste are only to be excluded by the Directive when they are 'already covered by other legislation'[1]. Circular 11/94 provides a detailed interpretation of this phrase[2]. It notes that, to satisfy the criteria of being already covered by relevant legislation, that legislation must pre-date the date on which the Directive on Waste's amendments were adopted: 18 March 1991[3]. The Circular also views the reference to 'other legislation' as embracing both national and Community provisions[4]. Finally, to be 'covered' the Circular requires that the legislation must provide a level of control at least equivalent to the requirements of the Directive on Waste[5].

1   Council Directive of 15 July 1975 on Waste (75/442/EEC), (OJ L194/39 25.7.75) (subsequently amended by Council Directive of 18 March 1991 amending Directive 75/442/EEC on Waste (91/156/EEC), (OJ L78/32 26.3.91), Article 2(1).
2   Circular 11/94, Annex I, para 1.15ff.
3   Circular 11/94 (Annex 1, para 1.15) allows for subsequently published consolidating legislation to fall within this rule, provided that the earlier provisions were enacted prior to March 1991. The Water Resources Act 1991 is an example: although coming into force in December 1991, its provisions on trade effluent consents are derived from the Water Act 1989.
4   Circular 11/94, Annex 1, para 1.15: whether this is strictly correct seems doubtful. The definition of waste is central to the control of transfrontier waste movement under Regulation 259/93 (see Chapter 5). In this context the 'other legislation' being referred to must be Community legislation. If it were national legislation, a major purpose of Regulation 259/93 – namely the implementation of an even system of Community-wide controls on transfrontier waste movements – would be defeated.
5   Circular 11/94, Annex 1, para 1.16.

Gaseous emissions

2.51   These are entirely excluded from the ambit of the Directive on Waste[1]. Circular 11/94 however notes[2] that this does not preclude emissions from waste management facilities from being under statutory control. More, the purpose of the exclusion in the

Directive is intended to ensure that the Directive does not address atmospheric emissions in general. Emissions from waste management facilities, whilst not themselves falling within the definition of waste, can of course be addressed by waste management licence conditions. As is discussed in Chapter 8, these conditions may be necessary to ensure that pollution of the environment and harm to human health do not result from the activity[3].

1   Council Directive of 15 July 1975 on Waste (75/442/EEC), (OJ L194/39 25.7.75) (subsequently amended by Council Directive of 18 March 1991 amending Directive 75/442/EEC on Waste (91/156/EEC), (OJ L78/32 26.3.91), Article 2(1)(a).
2   Circular 11/94, Annex 1, para 1.13.
3   They are also required by the Directive on Waste: see Article 4 and see Circular 11/94, Annex 1, para 1.13.

2.52   Despite the blanket exclusion contained in Article 2, the Circular considers that the definition of waste may embrace the emission of ozone depleting substances in certain instances[1]. Chlorofluorocarbons (CFCs) emitted from refrigerators during dismantling or maintenance are given as an example[2]. However, the Circular considers that the legislation is somewhat restrictive in its application and does not apply to incidental releases of CFC from plant under normal usage. These emissions are considered not to fall within the definition of waste[3]. But CFCs emitted due to maintenance or from end of life equipment are considered by Circular 11/94 to be within the national definition of waste. Accordingly, it asserted that the EPA 1990's control mechanisms such as the duty of care[4] apply in these instances. The precise basis of this assertion is not made absolutely clear, but it may stem from the fact that CFCs are liquid within the confines of a refrigeration unit. They become gaseous only under room temperature and pressure.

1   Circular 11/94, Annex 4, para 4.95ff.
2   A second example in the Circular is waste solvents: however, the Circular is much less specific in this instance (see Circular 11/94, Annex 4, para 4.95ff).
3   Circular 11/95, Annex 4, para 4.103.
4   EPA 1990, s 34: see Chapter 3.

Radioactive waste

2.53   Radioactive waste is excluded from Article 2 of the Directive and hence from the definition of Directive waste[1]. However, this exclusion is subject to the proviso in the Directive that such waste is covered by 'other legislation'. Circular 11/94 considers that this is satisfied by the existence of the current statutory provisions on health and safety and also by the Radioactive Substances Act 1993[2].

1   SI 1994/1056, reg 1(3). See also para 4.53.
2   Circular 11/94, Annex 1, para 1.17(a). The Circular refers to the Radioactive Substances Act 1960, which was superseded in August 1993 by the Radioactive Substances Act 1993: see the Radioactive Substances Act 1993, s 49(1) and Sch 4.

2.54   In addition to the exclusion contained in the Directive, s 78 of the EPA 1990 provides a further, parallel, exclusion for radioactive waste. Section 78 requires that Part II of the EPA 1990 does not apply to radioactive waste within the meaning of the Radioactive Substances Act 1993[1]. However, the Minister is given powers to modify this provision by way of regulations[2]. At the time of writing, no such regulations have been made.

1   EPA 1990, s 78 as amended by the Radioactive Substances Act 1993, s 49(1) and Sch 4.
2   EPA 1990, s 78.

Mineral working and quarrying waste

2.55 Like radioactive waste, 'waste resulting from prospecting, extraction, treatment and storage of mineral resources and the working of quarries' is excluded from the definition of Directive waste where it has been addressed by other legislation. Circular 11/94 points to the Town and Country Planning Acts and to the Mines and Quarries (Tips) Act 1969 as providing the principal regulatory framework[1].

1 Circular 11/94, Annex 1, para 1.17(b).

2.56 It is acknowledged in the Circular that the Directive on Waste only provides for the exclusion of wastes in respect of quarrying and, more importantly, mineral waste[1]. The specific reference to 'mineral resources' is held to mean that non-mineral wastes from mines and quarries are not subject to the exclusion contained in the Directive. The Circular provides canteen and office wastes, used tyres, machinery and waste oils as examples of these wastes. Such materials from these sources are therefore subject to the Directive on Waste.

1 Circular 11/94, Annex 1, para 1.17(b).

2.57 However, the wording of the EPA 1990 itself precludes these wastes falling within the concepts of controlled waste or Directive waste. Section 75(7) states that wastes from any mine or quarry cannot be controlled waste. As Part II only applies to substances which are both Directive waste and controlled waste[1], wastes from these sources are not covered by national law[2].

1 See SI 1992/588, reg 7A as amended by SI 1994/1056, reg 24(8) and see para 2.190ff.
2 See also Environment Agency *Special Wastes: A technical guidance note on their definition and classification* (1999) Environment Agency, Bristol, para 3.3.5.

2.58 Circular 11/94 discusses this matter[1], stating that the Department of the Environment is to issue a consultation paper to ensure that the British legislation precisely follows the Directive's requirements. The Circular states that regulations would be made to address this shortfall later in 1994. At the time of writing (Summer 1999), the regulations are still awaited.

1 Circular 11/94, paras 25–28, Annex 1, para 1.17(b).

2.59 Finally, it would appear that the Circular's views of the exclusion from the Directive in respect of mining and quarrying wastes is open to potential question. As noted, the Circular views the exclusion as applying only to 'mineral wastes' and for this reason, waste from mineral workings which is composed of materials such as oils, tyres, etc are claimed to be wastes which are subject to the Directive[1]. However, it would appear that the phrase in Article 2 of the Directive in respect of these exclusions – '... waste resulting from prospecting, extraction, treatment and storage of mineral resources and the working of quarries' – can be read differently[2]. In contrast to what is stated in the Circular, this phrase may mean that any waste from prospecting, extraction, (etc) of mineral resources is to be totally excluded from the Directive. Similarly, it may also indicate that any waste from quarrying is excluded. This would include tyres, oils, machinery etc from these sources.

1 See in particular Circular 11/94, Annex 1, para 1.17(b).
2 Directive on Waste, Article 2(1)(b)(ii).

Agricultural waste

2.60 The Directive on Waste requires that 'animal carcasses and the following agricultural waste: faecal matter and other natural, non-dangerous substances used in farming' are excluded from the scope of the Directive when they are covered by 'other legislation'[1]. Circular 11/94 states that animal carcasses are covered both by the Animal Waste Directive (90/667/EEC) and the Animal By-Products Order 1992[2]. Hence it is asserted that such wastes are excluded from the definition of Directive waste, 'whether or not the waste is from agricultural premises'[3]. However, the wording of the relevant exclusion indicates that, excepting animal carcasses, other animal wastes can be Directive waste when they stem from non-agricultural sources[4]. An example might be bonemeal or tallow, both of which are, since the BSE crises, unwanted by-products from the rendering industry[5].

1   Council Directive of 15 July 1975 on Waste (75/442/EEC), (OJ L194/39 25.7.75) (as amended by Council Directive of 18 March 1991 amending Directive 75/442/EEC on Waste (91/156/EEC), (OJ L78/32 26.3.91), Article 2(1)(b)(iii).
2   SI 1992/3303: the Animal By-Products Order 1992 has been replaced by the Animal By-Products Order 1999 (SI 1999/646). It is discussed in general terms at para 6.18.
3   Circular 11/94, Annex 1, para 1.1.7(c). Animal carcasses stemming from premises used in agriculture, along with other wastes emanating from these sources also cannot be controlled waste under the EPA 1990: see EPA 1990, s 75(7)(c).
4   Wastes from agricultural premises cannot be controlled waste under s 75(7) of the EPA 1990.
5   The temporary storage of these materials is exempt from waste management licensing: see SI 1994/1056, Sch 3, para 17 as amended by SI 1996/1279, reg 2 and see para 10.92ff.

2.61   A second result of the wording of Article 2 of the Directive is that 'non-natural' wastes and 'dangerous' wastes used in farming are not excluded from the ambit of the Directive[1]. Examples of the former wastes might be oil, tyres, scrap machinery, while 'dangerous' wastes would cover pesticides, herbicides, veterinary products and asbestos roofing materials[2]. However, s 75 of the EPA 1990[3] explicitly precludes any agricultural waste being held to constitute a controlled waste[4]. Like mining and quarrying wastes, Circular 11/94 indicates that proposals to ensure compliance with the Directive were to be issued in 1994. But nothing has so far emerged, despite a more recent statement[5] that reiterates the intention to extend the definition in respect of agricultural wastes.

1   See Council Directive of 15 July 1975 on Waste (75/442/EEC), (OJ L194/39 25.7.75) (subsequently amended by Council Directive of 18 March 1991 amending Directive 75/442/EEC on Waste (91/156/EEC), (OJ L78/32 26.3.91), Article 2(1)(b)(iii) and see Circular 11/94, Annex 1, para 1.17(c).
2   If these materials constituted controlled wastes any 'dangerous' waste would be likely to be a special waste: see Chapter 4.
3   EPA 1990, ss 75(7)(c) and 75(8).
4   See also Circular 11/94 para 28, Annex 1, para 1.17(c). The Environment Agency has stated that 'all' agricultural waste is excluded from the definition of special wastes: see Environment Agency, *Special Wastes: A technical guidance note on their definition and classification*, Environment Agency (1999), Bristol, para 3.3.5.
5   See Department of the Environment (1997) *The Sustainable Use of Soil, The Government's Response to the 19th Report of the Royal Commission on Environmental Pollution* Stationery Office, London, para 31.

Waste waters and liquid waste

2.62   The exclusion in the Directive for 'waste waters, with the exception of waste in liquid form' from the EPA 1990's definition of waste has by far generated the most comment since the Directive waste concept was introduced in 1994. This particular exclusion – described by one commentator as 'singularly obscure'[1] – is an obvious attempt to set the boundary between the control system of the Directive on Waste and that enacted by other Directives concerned with general discharges to the aquatic environment. However, as will be shown below, the boundary can be at best described as vague.

1   Burnett-Hall R (1995) *Environmental Law*, Sweet & Maxwell, London, para 11–106.

2.63 The starting point is to note that 'waste waters' are only excluded by Article 2 of the Directive when they are 'already covered by other legislation'[1]. In respect of the Community law, Circular 11/94 stresses that the main item of legislation addressing the disposal of waste waters[2] is the Dangerous Substances Directive[3], which addresses discharges to water bodies. A second is the Directive on Urban Waste Water Treatment[4].

1   Council Directive of 15 July 1975 on Waste (75/442/EEC), (OJ L194/39 25.7.75) (as amended by
    Council Directive of 18 March 1991 amending Directive 75/442/EEC on Waste (91/156/EEC),
    (OJ L78/32 26, 29.3.91), Article 2(1)(b).
2   Circular 11/94, Annex I, para 1.17(d).
3   Council Directive of 4 May 1976 on Pollution caused by the Discharge of Certain Dangerous
    Substances into the Aquatic Environment (Directive 76/464/EEC), (OJ L129/12 18.5.76).
4   Council Directive of 21 May 1991 concerning Urban Waste Water Treatment (91/271/EEC),
    (OJ L135/40 30.5.91).

2.64 In respect of national legislation, Circular 11/94[1] concludes that the Water Resources Act 1991 is sufficient to ensure that all 'waste waters' discharged to controlled waters[2] or to the sea are outside the scope of the definition of Directive waste[3].

1   Circular 11/94, Annex 1, para 1.17(d).
2   Defined in s 104(1) of the Water Resources Act 1991: controlled waters include groundwater.
3   Circular 11/94, Annex 1, para 1.17(d).

2.65 The position in respect of discharges of waste waters or liquid wastes to sewers is, however, considerably less clear. Circular 11/94 states that discharges of waste waters to sewers where eventual treatment is subject to the Urban Waste Water Treatment Directive are covered by 'other legislation'. Hence they are excluded from the definition of Directive waste[1].

1   Circular 11/94, Annex 1, para 1.17(d).

2.66 However, problems arise in respect of Article 2 of the Directive on Waste's reference to 'liquid waste'. While 'waste waters' are beyond that Directive, 'liquid waste' is not. The lack of any precise boundary between these terms is the source of some difficulty. Certainly, 'liquid waste' – using the terminology of the Directive – can fall within the concept of 'Directive waste'[1].

1   For example SI 1994/1056, reg 16(1)(c) absolves disposal activities involving liquid waste from the
    need to possess a waste management licence when they are subject to a consent under the Water
    Resources Act 1991: see para 10.18.

2.67 A potential problem arises in respect of inputs to effluent treatment plants at industrial premises. This equipment is essential to many industrial activities. Effluent treatment is undertaken to ensure that the resultant discharge is suitable for conveyance by the sewerage network and environmentally acceptable at the final destination, the sewage treatment plant. It seems clear from the British legislation that the outflowing material from an effluent treatment plant is either not Directive waste – due to the discharge being covered by a trade effluent consent – or is Directive waste but the discharge is exempted from a waste management licence by the Waste Management Licensing Regulations 1994[1]. However, by definition, the treatment plant itself is changing the chemical or physical composition of the inflowing waters, thereby converting the intake into 'waste waters'. Hence this treatment process can be potentially identified as falling within one or more of the disposal activities listed in Annex IIA of the Directive[2]. Accordingly, it seems possible that the material entering the plants – which may not be 'waste water' at that stage – may be identifiable as Directive waste.

1   SI 1994/1056, reg 16(1)(c).
2   See Table 2.5.

2.68   This matter was drawn to the attention of regulatory bodies by the Department of the Environment in a letter dated 26 May 1995. The letter suggested that a trade effluent consent was not sufficient to exempt the incoming liquor entering a trade effluent plant from the provisions of the EPA 1990 on waste management licensing. The consent only pertained to waste water discharges from the plant, not what is passing to it. Accordingly, the letter indicated that certain plants may need waste management licences.

2.69   The contents of the Department of the Environment's letter was by no means inconsequential. A vast number of industrial premises possess such plants which, if the letter was correct, would need waste management licences[1]. In addition, they cannot be subject to the EPA 1990's lesser registration system[2] for the reason that the Waste Management Licensing Regulations 1994 do not contain a suitable provision[3]. Along with the huge workload for both regulatory bodies and the regulated in making and processing licence applications, a further difficulty was that the legislation contained transitional provisions in respect of certificates of technical competence. To benefit from these provisions, all operators needed to identify themselves by specified dates[4]. If the deadline was missed, a treatment plant operator would face considerable difficulties as a full certificate to technical competence would be necessary in order for the plant to legally continue in operation.

1   An exception is trade effluent plants subject to authorisations under Pt I of the EPA 1990. All processes subject to such authorisations are excluded from needing waste management licences by SI 1994/1056, reg 16(1)(a): see para 10.14ff.
2   See Chapter 10.
3   See Department of the Environment letter of the 26 May 1995, para 8. In addition, the Directive on Waste only countenances the registration of disposal and recovery facilities at the place of production (Article 11). Waste water treatment plants are more obviously classifiable as disposal operations, not recovery facilities. In addition, for wastes subject to the Directive on Hazardous Waste, disposal at the place of production is not allowed under registration – permits are always needed (see Directive 91/689 Article 3(1)). The latter restriction is taken up in British law by SI 1994/1056, reg 17(3A), as amended by SI 1996/972, Sch 3.
4   See para 8.144ff.

2.70   However, in 1996 the Department of the Environment appeared to retract this interpretation of the legislation, holding that the possession of the discharge consent under the Water Resources Act 1991[1] or a sewer discharge consent issued under Part IV of the Water Industry Act 1991 were, in fact, sufficient to ensure that the waste water is covered by 'other legislation'. Hence as 'waste waters' are excluded from the Directive waste definition, no waste management licence was required[2].

1   Control of Pollution Act 1974, Pt II in Scotland .
2   The Department of the Environment's press release is reproduced in the *Wastes Manager*, August 1996, p 7; see also *ENDS Report* 258, July 1996, pp 27–28, 'DOE goes full circle on licensing of effluent treatment plants'.

2.71   Not surprisingly however, this matter has not been definitively resolved. For example, it has been rightly pointed out that, whilst 'waste waters' can be exempted from the Directive waste definition, 'waste in liquid form' cannot be[1]. For example, it is suggested that electroplating or steel pickling liquors are 'waste in liquid form' even when passed to an effluent plant for treatment and sewer discharge[2]. Secondly, it has been noted that the Directive's provisions which result in the exclusion of activities covered by 'other legislation' is acceptable only where the coverage is sufficient to fulfil the objectives of the Directive on Waste[3]. This seems not to be possible under the wording of the Water Resources Act 1991. For example, the Directive requires that nuisances and odours from waste management activities are controlled[4]. However, these matters are not addressed by the Water Resources Act 1991's discharge consent system[5].

1 See *ENDS Report* 258, July 1996, pp 27–28, 'DOE goes full circle on licensing of effluent treatment plants'.
2 These materials would be special wastes. Article 3(1) of the Hazardous Waste Directive (91/689) requires the disposal of such materials at the site of production to be subject to a permit which satisfies Article 9 of the Directive on Waste – not a registration. Hence it seems doubtful that a discharge consent would satisfy the requirements of the Directive in respect of such permits. Separately Burnett-Hall has argued that non-aqueous organic solvent wastes cannot be 'waste waters', due to the absence of significant water content. Hence he asserts that the purpose of the phrase 'waste in liquid form' is to describe non-aqueous effluents: see Burnett-Hall R (1995) *Environmental Law*, Sweet & Maxwell, London, para 11–106.
3 Indeed Circular 11/94 (Annex 1, para 1.15) itself acknowledges that, to be adequately 'covered' by other legislation, that legislation must provide 'an effective means of pursuing the aims of the [Waste] Directive'.
4 Council Directive of 15 July 1975 on Waste (75/442/EEC), (OJ L194/39 25.7.75) (as amended by Council Directive of 18 March 1991 amending Directive 75/442/EEC on Waste (91/156/EEC), (OJ L78/32 26.3.91), Article 4.
5 See Water Resources Act 1991, s 88 and Sch 10, para 2(5).

2.72 How this matter is to be resolved is not immediately apparent. Primarily it stems from the root of many of the interpretative difficulties presented by the Waste Management Licensing Regulations 1994. As Chapter 1 has argued[1], the use of verbatim references from the Directive on Waste is not helpful when the Article subject to the reference is not itself clear.

1 See para 1.21.

Decommissioned explosives

2.73 Decommissioned explosives are excluded from the Directive on Waste when they are 'already covered by other legislation'[1]. Circular 11/94 indicates[2] that decommissioned explosives are subject to 'other legislation' in the form of the Explosives Act 1875 itself, along with the Control of Explosives Regulations 1991 (SI 1991/1531) and the Road Traffic (Carriage of Explosives) Regulations 1989 (SI 1989/615). The provisions of the Health and Safety at Work Act etc 1974 are also viewed as having application.

1 Council Directive of 15 July 1975 on Waste (75/442/EEC), (OJ L194/39 25.7.75) (as amended by Council Directive of 18 March 1991 amending Directive 75/442/EEC on Waste (91/156/EEC), (OJ L78/32 26.3.91), Article 2(b)(v).
2 Circular 11/94, Annex 1, para 1.17(e).

2.74 In addition to the Circular's guidance, s 75(2)(b) of the EPA 1990 holds that all explosives within the meaning of Explosives Act 1875 are excluded from the national definition of waste[1]. The Explosives Act 1875 embraces the following substances[2]:

'(1) Gunpowder, nitro-glycerine, dynamite, gun-cotton, blasting powders, fulminate of mercury or other metals, coloured fires, and every other substance, whether similar to the above mentioned or not, used or manufactured with a view to produce a practical effect by explosion or a pyrotechnic effect; and

(2) includes fog-signals, fireworks, fuses, rockets, percussion caps, detonators, cartridges, ammunition of all descriptions, and every adaptation or preparation of any explosive as above defined.'

As noted at para 2.43, s 75(2) is due for replacement by an amendment contained in the Environment Act 1995[3]. The intended replacement to s 75(2) does not contain a reference to the exclusion in respect of the Explosives Act 1875. It is therefore not clear from the Environment Act 1995 as to how this exclusion will be continued when s 75 is amended.

1   See para 2.32ff above.
2   Explosives Act 1875, s 3.
3   Environment Act 1995, Sch 22, para 88(2).

WHEN IS WASTE 'DISCARDED'?

2.75   The kernel to the understanding of both the current definition of Directive waste and the proposed amendment to s 75 of the EPA 1990 is the fact that, in order for a substance to be a waste[1], it must be discarded. Alternatively, the definition of waste requires that it must be intended to be discarded or required to be discarded[2].

1   Controlled waste is always Directive waste: SI 1992/588, reg 7A as amended by SI 1994/1056, reg 24(8).
2   While the definition of waste in respect of the landfill tax (see Finance Act 1996, s 64) is different to that contained in s 75 of the EPA 1990, the definition pivots on whether a waste holder has 'the intention of discarding the material' (Finance Act 1996, s 64(1)).

2.76   The question of 'discarding' can sometimes be complex and difficult in respect of substances passing to recovery facilities. Firstly, the concept of discarding is itself less than clear in its scope and application. Secondly, the legislation does not make immediately clear the identity of the person taking the decision to discard. However, it seems vital to the wording of the definition of waste that such a person is correctly identified. The following sections will attempt to analyse these two, highly significant, issues. What should become apparent is that the term 'discarding' must have a special meaning in the context of the legislation, which is different from its common language usage. Furthermore, the definition of waste is closely linked to the actions of the person who generates the waste at first instance. Of lesser significance will be the actions of other individuals who receive waste from the original generator.

2.77   Although the matters to be considered below are somewhat involved, the point made early on in this chapter is worth reiterating. It is often unnecessary to undertake a detailed consideration of the legal principles behind the legislation. Often whether or not waste is discarded will be self-evident. This will particularly be the case when waste is passed to disposal facilities or is fly-tipped. Therefore only in the more involved cases – particularly those in respect of substances passing to recovery or re-use – will recourse be needed to the detailed interpretation set out below.

'Discarding' and waste recovery

2.78   Prior to the extensive amendment of the Directive on Waste by Directive 91/156[1], the original definition of waste contained in Article 1 was considered by the European Court of Justice in *Vessoso and Zanetti*[2]. As will be shown, this case applies equally to the definition in its amended form.

1   Council Directive of 18 March 1991 amending Directive 75/442/EEC on Waste (91/156/EEC), (OJ L78/32 26.3.91).

2	*Criminal Proceedings against G Vessoso and G Zanetti* Cases C-206/88 and C-207/88, [1990] ECR
	I-1461; see also *Criminal Proceedings against E Zanetti* Case 359/88 [1990] ECR I-1509: as the
	cases were similar, the Advocate General issued a single opinion (see [1990] ECR I-1461 at 1466).

2.79	*Vessoso and Zanetti* concerned a referral to the European Court of cases
concerning waste carriers who were involved in the salvage of materials and the
recovery of wastes. Cases 206/88 and 207/88[1] involved the collection and storage of
general salvaged materials. In case 359/88[2], the materials in question were spent
hydrochloric acids from galvanising[3], which were to be re-used in ferric chloride
manufacture. The recovery plant did not have the benefit of an appropriate authorisation. In all the cases, the defendants claimed that a permit was not needed for the
recovery operation as the materials being delivered did not constitute waste.

1	*Criminal Proceedings against G Vessoso and G Zanetti* [1990] ECR I-1461.
2	*Criminal Proceedings against E Zanetti and ors* [1990] ECR I-1509.
3	Galvanising is a surface coating process involving the application of zinc onto a metal substrate. It
	results in a zinc/hydrochloric acid waste stream of some significant toxicity. Usually these wastes are
	special wastes: special waste is discussed in Chapter 4.

2.80	In the lower court it was argued that the relevant Italian decree should be inter-
preted in the light of the requirements of the Directive on Waste[1] and the Directive on
Toxic and Dangerous Waste[2], particularly as the Decree transposed the Directives'
requirements into Italian law. Reviewing the text of both Directives, the European
Court confirmed their application to materials which have a positive value and which
pass to recycling or recovery. The court held that the aim of both Directives, as set out
in their recitals[3], was:

'... namely the protection of human health and the safeguarding of the environment, would be jeopardized if the application of those directives were dependent on
whether or not the holder[4] intended to exclude all economic re-utilisation by others
of the substances or objects of which he disposes.'

Accordingly, the concept of waste under the two Directives[5]:

'... does not presume that the holder disposing of a substance or an object intended
to exclude all economic re-utilisation of the substance or object by others.'

1	Directive 75/442 prior to amendment by Council Directive of 18 March 1991 amending Directive
	75/442/EEC on Waste (91/156/EEC) (OJ L78/32 26.3.91).
2	Directive 78/319 now repealed by Directive 91/689: see para 4.03.
3	See *Vessoso and Zanetti* [1990] ECR I-1461 at 1478, para 12.
4	It is very important to realise that the word 'holder' had only a general meaning in the Directive on
	Waste in its unamended form. The use of the term in the *Zanetti* decision – and the context of that use
	– is not the same as is applicable under the subsequent amendments made to the Directive on Waste
	by Directive 91/156. In the Directive as amended, 'holder' is tightly defined: this important point is
	discussed at para 2.156ff below.
5	See *Vessoso and Zanetti* [1990] ECR I-1461 at 1478, para 13.

2.81	Although the definition of waste considered in *Vessoso and Zanetti* has been
considerably changed by the amendments instigated by Directive 91/156, the European Court of Justice's decision still holds. This is explicitly made clear in *EC
Commission v Germany*[1] and later in *Tombesi*[2] and in *Inter-Environnement Wallonie*[3].

1	[1995] ECR I-1097, para 23.
2	*Criminal Proceedings against Tombesi* [1998] Env LR 59 at 87, para 47.
3	*Inter-Environnement Wallonie ASBL v Region Wallone* [1998] Env LR 623 at 650, para 31.

2.82	*EC Commission v Germany*[1] involved an action by the Commission in respect
of non-compliance with the now-repealed Transfrontier Directive[2] and the Directive

on Toxic and Dangerous Wastes[3], along with incorrect transposition of the Directive on Waste. The latter was caused by German national law excluding certain waste substances from the ambit when they were to be subject to reclamation.

1   [1995] ECR I-1097.
2   Council Directive of 6 December 1994 on the Supervision and Control within the European Community of the Transfrontier Shipment of Hazardous Waste (84/631/EEC), (OJ L326/41 13.12.84).
3   Council Directive on Toxic and Dangerous Waste (78/319/EEC), (OJ L84/43 31.3.78).

2.83   The European Court found against Germany in respect of the alleged inadequacies relating to the transposition of the definition of waste into national law. It reaffirmed the fact that national legislation which excludes objects capable of economic reutilisation is not compatible with the Directive on Waste[1]. It also stated that these principles – as laid down in *Vessoso and Zanetti* – still have application, despite the changes made to the Directive on Waste by Directive 91/156[2].

1   *EC Commission v Germany* [1995] ECR I-1097 at 1132, para 22.
2   *EC Commission v Germany* [1995] ECR I-1097 at 1132, para 23.

2.84   The judgment of *Criminal Proceedings against Tombesi*[1] closely follows the earlier findings of the European Court described above. Hence it confirms that materials which pass to recovery processes can fall within the definition of waste in Article 1 of the Directive on Waste[2]. *Tombesi* relates to a succession of cases concerning quite disparate circumstances, all of which involved Italian nationals. For example, Case C-304/94 pertained to the unauthorised disposal of waste from marble working, which appears to have been dumped or used for the construction of embankments; Case 330/94 involved the handling of toxic wastes arising from the operation of electrostatic precipitators; Case C-342/94 addressed the unlicensed reprocessing by grinding of olive oil residues; and Case C-224/95 related to the unauthorised transportation of copper cable and other metal scrap. All the cases were referred to the European Court due to the Italian Court wishing to seek guidance, under Article 177[3] of the Treaty establishing the European Community, on whether the relevant national legislation was compatible with the Directive on Waste.

1   [1998] Env LR 59 at 87, para 47.
2   Council Directive of 15 July 1975 on Waste (75/442/EEC), (OJ L194/39 25.7.75) (as amended by Council Directive of 18 March 1991 amending Directive 75/442/EEC on Waste (91/156/EEC), (OJ L78/32 26.3.91).
3   Now Article 234 since the Treaty of Amsterdam came into effect.

2.85   The European Court held that all recovery and disposal activities require permits under the Directive on Waste where the materials involved have been discarded[1]:

'... the system of supervision and control established by Directive 75/442, as amended, is intended to cover all objects and substances discarded by their owners, even if they have a commercial value and are collected on a commercial basis for recycling, reclamation or re-use.'

Hence land reclamation[2] and embankment construction fall within the Directive's concepts of waste disposal or recovery operations when they involve substances which have been discarded[3].

1   *Tombesi* [1998] Env LR 59 at 88, para 52.
2   Termed in the judgment 'landfill tipping in hollows in the ground'.
3   The court did not however rule on the nature of the word 'discard': see para 2.132 below.

2.86 Moreover, it was held that a claim by the current holder that the materials might have some use does not preclude the materials continuing to remain within the definition of waste. This was particularly the case where a holder did not actually have a particular destination in mind. The court also felt that this interpretation extended to residues which had been subject to simple processing operations. One of the cases considered by the court involved waste being subject to a grinding process, with the resultant residue being held to remain defined as waste. Again, this finding was particularly pertinent in instances when the end use for the residues appears undefined[1]. While the court's findings in this respect offer little explanation, what appears to be addressed here are circumstances familiar to many Environment Agency officers at transfer stations. Often operators claim that stored materials such as bricks, wood etc are not wastes as they are to pass to unspecified re-use. In parallel to the claim that the materials are not to be viewed as waste is the implication that the provisions of the EPA 1990 do not apply.

1   See the final two lines of para 52 of the court's judgment. These are more readily understood if considered in the light of Italian lower court's questions 5 and 6 contained in para 30 of the ECJ's judgment. The latter questions are themselves subject to some useful explanation by the Advocate General in para 61 of his Opinion.

2.87 The *Vessoso, Tombesi* and *EC Commission v Germany* cases found support in the subsequent European Court judgment of *Inter-Environnement Wallonie ASBL v Region Wallone*[1]. The latter centred upon a complaint to the national court by an environment group that one of the Belgian regional authorities had incorrectly transposed the Directive on Waste into national law. The case was referred to the European Court for determination. The relevant national law required that authorisations for waste management facilities were restricted to off-site disposal and recovery activities, explicitly excluding all disposal and recovery processes which were an integral part of an industrial production process.

1   *Inter-Environnement Wallonie ASBL v Region Wallone* [1998] Env LR 623.

2.88 Not surprisingly given the content of Article 11 of the Directive on Waste and Article 3 of the Hazardous Waste Directive[1], the European Court found the regional authority to have incorrectly transposed Community law. However, the Court's decision – as well as the opinion of the Advocate General[2] – assists in the understanding of how the definition of waste is to be approached.

1   Council Directive of 12 December 1991 on Hazardous Waste (91/689/EEC), (OJ L377/20 31.12.91).
2   See para 2.132ff.

2.89 The court held that the definition of waste in the Directive on Waste 'turns on the meaning of the word "discard" '[1] and that 'discard' covers both wastes passing to disposal and to recovery[2]. It was also held that the Directive on Waste applies to all disposal and recovery activities at the place of production in the circumstances specified by its articles and regardless of whether they had a potential for environmental damage[3]. The approach of *Vessoso, Tombesi* and *EC Commission v Germany* was followed, to the effect that the definition of waste in the Directive 'is not to be understood as excluding substances and objects which were capable of economic reutilisation'[4]. To this finding was added the following: '[t]hat conclusion does not undermine the distinction which must be drawn . . . between waste recovery within the meaning of Directive 75/442, as amended, and normal industrial treatment of products which are not waste, no matter how difficult that distinction may be'[5]. While the Advocate General pressed the court to actually set out some guidelines[6], little further assistance to this effect was given in the court's own judgment.

1   *Inter-Environnement Wallonie ASBL v Region Wallone* [1998] Env LR 623 at 649, para 26.
2   *Inter-Environnement Wallonie ASBL v Region Wallone* [1998] Env LR 623 at 649, para 27.
3   *Inter-Environnement Wallonie ASBL v Region Wallone* [1998] Env LR 623 at 650, para 30.
4   *Inter-Environnement Wallonie ASBL v Region Wallone* [1998] Env LR 623 at 650, para 31.
5   *Inter-Environnement Wallonie ASBL v Region Wallone* [1998] Env LR 623 at 650, para 33.
6   *Inter-Environnement Wallonie ASBL v Region Wallone* [1998] Env LR 623 at 641, para 69.

2.90   The question of division between waste and goods was also considered by the European Court in *EC Commission v Belgium*[1]. The facts of the case and the focus of the judgment are somewhat different to the *Vessoso and Zanetti, Tombesi* and *Inter-Environnement Wallonie* judgments. *Kingdom of Belgium* confirms that, under the EC Treaty, there is no distinction between 'goods' and 'wastes': recyclable materials fall as much under the provisions pertaining to the free movement of 'goods' as do wastes, even those of a negative value. The court considered a ban on the cross-border traffic of certain wastes and the claim by the Belgian authorities that such a ban on imported 'wastes' passing to final disposal did not contravene the EC Treaty's provisions on the free movement of goods. It was argued that 'goods' and 'wastes' were quite different entities. The court held that it is impossible to view 'goods' as somehow distinguishable from 'wastes', even where wastes of a negative value are to pass to disposal[2]:

> 'It is important to consider ... that the distinction between recyclable and non-recyclable wastes raises, from a practical point of view, a serious difficulty in application, particularly in its application to controls at the frontier. In effect, such a distinction is founded on uncertain elements, changeable over the course of time, as a result of technical progress. Moreover, the recyclable character or otherwise of a waste depends equally on the cost entailed in the recycling, which arises from the profitability of the envisaged re-utilisation, so much so that its estimation is necessarily subjective and dependent on unstable factors.
> It should be concluded in consequence that wastes, recyclable or not, must be considered as products the movement of which, in conformance with Article 30 of the Treaty, cannot in principle be prevented.'

In essence, the court has confirmed the entirely separate finding, alluded to at para 2.18, of Schiemann J in *R v Rotherham Metropolitan Borough Council, ex p Rankin*[3]. What is a waste to one person may be an economic good to another. However, for the purposes of the legal definition, the fact that the Directive on Waste defines waste primarily from the point of view of the original producer[4] means that, once so defined, a material stays waste until it has been recovered.

1   Case 2/90 [1993] 5 JEL 133-148.
2   *EC Commission v Belgium*, paras 27 and 28.
3   [1990] 1 PLR 93. See also Marina Wheeler's analysis of the *Belgium* judgment in (1993) JEL 5, particularly at p 143.
4   See para 2.156 below.

A special meaning for 'discarding'

2.91   It will be evident by now that the term 'discard' is central to Article 1 of the Directive on Waste, as well as to the definitions in British law of Directive waste and the proposed amendment to s 75 of the EPA 1990[1]. The phrase is used in the British provisions primarily because it is the term adopted by the Directive on Waste[2]. As noted, it is essential to understand that the term embraces wastes passing to either disposal or recovery. For those disposal operations listed in the Directive's Annex IIA[3], the notion of 'discarding' is a reasonably obvious concept. However, in respect of the waste recovery activities set down in Annex IIB[4], the term needs to be approached carefully. If 'discarding' is given its ordinary, everyday meaning of 'throwing away something'[5], the term sits somewhat incongruously with the lengthy list of recovery operations set down in the Directive's Annex IIB. It is also a little anomalous in the context of the Directive's Article 11, which envisages that as well as disposing of it, someone can discard waste and pass it to a recovery process on that person's own premises[6]. Finally, an overtly narrow definition of the term does not satisfactorily accord with the European Court's consistent finding[7] that the concept of waste can involve substances of positive financial value passing to recovery processes.

1   It is also central to the definition of waste for the landfill tax: see the Finance Act 1996, s 64(1).
2   Circular 11/94, Annex 1, para 1.4.
3   Which is reproduced in the Waste Management Licensing Regulations 1994 (SI 1994/1056) as Sch 4, Pt III: see Table 2.5.
4   SI 1994/1056, Sch 4, Pt IV and Table 2.6.
5   For example, two different dictionaries have the verb 'to discard' as meaning:
      'reject or get rid of as unwanted or superfluous' (*Concise Oxford Dictionary*, 1995 edition)
      'to get rid of as useless or undesirable' (*Collins Concise Dictionary*, 1997 edition).
6   This might include burning it as a fuel: see item R9 in Table 2.6.
7   *Vessoso and Zanetti* [1990] ECR 1-1461 and [1990] ECR 1-1509; *Criminal Proceedings against Tombesi and others* [1998] Env LR 59; *Inter-Environnement Wallonie ASBL v Region Wallone* [1998] Env LR 623.

2.92   Therefore, while the concept of discarding applies reasonably well to the notion of disposal activities, these factors suggest that an extended definition of 'discarding' must be considered and applied in respect of waste recovery. In other words, discarding must have a special meaning in the context of the legislation. That it is now necessary to consider this meaning in detail is primarily caused by the drafting of the Directive on Waste (and consequently British national law) which make only an implicit – but not explicit – connection between the definition of waste and the fact that the definition must be considered in the context of waste recovery processes.

2.93   Where problems arise in the interpretation of Community legislation, it is appropriate to consider texts drafted in the languages of other member states[1]. Circular 11/94 points to this, highlighting inconsistencies between the English and French versions of the Directive.

1   See *Bestruur der Sociale Verzeringsbank v J H van der Vecht* [1967] ECR 345 at 354; *Stauder v City of Ulm* [1969] ECR 419 at 424; *R v Bouchereau* [1977] ECR 1999 at 2010 para 14; *Wörsdorfer v Raad van Arbeid* [1979] ECR 2717 at 2724, para 6; *CILFIT srl v Ministry of Health* [1982] ECR 3415 at 3430, para 18ff; *Rockfon A/S v Specialarbejderbundet i Danmark* [1995] ECR I-4291 at I-4317, para 28; *R v Customs and Excise Comrs, ex p EMU Tabac* [1998] QB 791 at 814H/815A, para 36. See also *North Kerry Milk Products v Minister of Agriculture and Fisheries* [1977] ECR 425 at 435, para 11 and *Mayer Parry Recycling Ltd v Environment Agency* [1999] Env LR 489 at 497, para 22.

2.94   An exact synonym to the English term 'discard' does not figure in the French version of Article 1(a) of the Directive. As Circular 11/94 notes[1], the term used in the French version is *se défaire*. This means 'to get rid of' and could be used in the context of advertising an item for sale in a local paper as much as sending waste to a specialist disposal contractor. A term of equivalent meaning to the French is also used in the German version of Article 1(a): *entledigen*.

1   Circular 11/94, Annex 2, para 2.17; as Carnwath J notes in *Mayer Parry Recycling Ltd v the Environment Agency* [1999] Env LR 489 at 498, para 26, the Italian version translates in a similar manner to the French.

2.95   It is therefore apparent that discarding must have an extended meaning. Indeed, Circular 11/94 considers that[1]:

'. . . the concept of discarding should be interpreted as meaning also "disposing of" or "getting rid of".'

While neither of these concepts are contained in the relevant legislation, the notion of a holder 'disposing of' waste seems to be applicable in respect of waste recovery and hence for those operations set out in the Directive's Annex IIB. Indeed, the term 'dispose of' was used in the original Directive prior to its amendment to cover not only operations such as waste storage and 'tipping', but also 'transformation operations necessary for . . . [waste's] re-use, recovery and recycling'[2].

1   Circular 11/94, Annex 2, para 2.17.
2   Directive on Waste, Article 1(b) (prior to amendment by Council Directive of 18 March 1991 amending Directive 75/442/EEC on Waste (91/156/EEC), (OJ L78/32 26.3.91).

2.96   The Circular's views on this matter seem consistent with the *Tombesi*, *Wallonie* and *Mayer Parry Recycling Ltd v Environment Agency*[1] decisions. Similarly Fluck sees discarding in the following terms[2]:

'Discarding . . . does not mean "getting rid of an object" . . . but . . . "releasing an object from its original intended purpose in order to recover or dispose or it" or "re-dedicating an object for recovery or disposal".'

However, the context would indicate that it also embraces the 'getting rid of' element, but that this should be regarded a sub-set of the wider options set out by Fluck above.

1   [1999] Env LR 489 at 505, para 46, discussed at para 2.136 below.
2   Fluck J (1994) 'The Term "Waste" in EC Law', *European Environmental Review*, March 1994, pp 79–84 at 82, col 1.

2.97   It seems likely that the term 'discard' was chosen for the English version of the Directive as a 'best fit' solution to a linguistic conundrum[1]. As mentioned earlier, a more appropriate phrase might be 'dispose of'[2]. But this may have been rejected by those drafting the amendments to the Directive on Waste as confusing in the context of other amendments proposed to be made to the text. For example, 'Disposal Operations' were to be listed in Annex IIA and are distinct from 'Operations which lead to Recovery' in Annex IIB. According to Fluck[3], although 'disposal' could legitimately encompass recovery activities in English, to translate the term directly into French and German would not be linguistically appropriate. The direct translation of 'disposal' could not be used to subsume waste recovery in those languages.

1   A point acknowledged by Carnwath J in *Mayer Parry Recycling Ltd v Environment Agency* [1999] Env LR 489 at 498, para 30.
2   Used in Article 1(a) of the Directive on Waste in its unamended form, applying both to disposal and recovery: see Article 1(b).
3   Fluck J (1994) 'The Term "Waste" in EC Law', *European Environmental Law Review* March 1994, pp 79–84 at 80, col 1.

2.98   As the term 'disposal' was already allocated elsewhere in the Directive, coupled with the fact that 'disposal' would not happily translate from English whilst retaining the required nuances, a compromise synonym was used. But as is a feature of all compromises, the result is never perfect.

2.99   In any case, because the legislation was in the form of a Directive, rather than a regulation, it might be thought that there was less need to ensure that a comprehensive single term is available in all languages. Being a Directive, the expectation would be that member states would provide their own subsidiary legislation and hence could iron out any linguistic difficulties or ambiguities at the transposition stage[1]. Hence the suggestion in Circular 11/94[2] that the concept of discarding encompasses the terms of 'disposing of' or 'getting rid of'. However, in the end, the Department of the Environment chose instead to transpose the Directive's literal translation verbatim and leave these other meanings to be addressed by non-statutory guidance.

1 In *Tombesi* [1998] Env LR 56 at 76, para 56 Jacobs A-G reflects that imprecision in the definition of 'recovery' could be addressed by member states – rather than at EC level – as part of the concept of subsidiarity (see also *Wallonie* [1998] Env LR 623 at 641, paras 69 and 70, at 644, para 82).
2 Circular 11/94, Annex 2, para 2.17.

2.100 The differences in the drafting of the Directive in different languages do little to attain the goal of a unified European-wide waste definition. Equally, it has already been noted that the English translation of the Directive contains ambiguity in a key article and that the Department of the Environment itself recognised this matter prior to the finalisation of the Waste Management Licensing Regulations 1994[1]. However, in the light of prior knowledge that there was likely to be difficulties, it is somewhat astonishing that a decision was taken to leave the matter to non-statutory guidance and by the problematic consideration of the intent of the Directive. Indeed, by raising the issue of the lack of symmetry between this key term in different member states' languages[2], the Circular could be taken to imply that in order to understand the definition of waste in the Directive, translations from other member state's languages need to be considered. This seems a rather tall order for the lower British courts. It is also one which is inappropriately demanding given the centrality of waste definitions to the British waste controls system.

1 See Circular 11/94, Annex 2, para 2.17.
2 See Circular 11/94, Annex 2, para 2.17.

2.101 Finally, Circular 11/94 proposes that, as well as the 'disposal' and the 'getting rid of' elements, the term should be interpreted by way of an assessment of the fundamental purpose of the Directive[1]. This matter is discussed later at para 2.106ff below.

1 Circular 11/94, Annex 2, paras 2.11 and 2.17.

2.102 In conclusion, what will be apparent is the vagueness of this key element of the Directive on Waste. A consequence of this looseness is the notion of a unified European waste definition is still some way off, despite the stated objective of the amendments made to the Directive on Waste in 1991 being that[1]:

'. . . common terminology and a definition of waste are needed in order to improve the efficiency of waste management in the Community.'

1 See Council Directive of 18 March 1991 amending Directive 75/442/EEC on Waste (91/156/EEC) (OJ L78/32 26.3.91), citation seven.

Annex 2 to Circular 11/94

2.103 Given that the term 'discard' is problematical in its interpretation, Annex 2 to Circular 11/94 attempts, at some length and complexity, to set down guidelines. It also tries to portray the important dividing line between instances when substances are waste and when they are secondary raw materials. The Annex remains an important source of guidance[1], despite being published prior to the *Tombesi* and *Wallonie* decisions[2]. The following discussion is written in order to set out the Circular's stance on the definition of waste and for this reason it is not combined into an evaluation of the implications of the later judgments. However, the latter are returned to[3], when the important matter of materials passing to direct re-use is considered.

1   Carnwath J early on in *Mayer Parry Recycling Ltd v Environment Agency* [1999] Env LR 489 at 497,
    para 23, dismisses Annex 2 of the Circular in the light of the *Tombesi* and *Inter-Environnement
    Wallonie* decisions as '. . . largely overtaken by two recent decisions of the European Court . . .'.
    However – and rather oddly in the light of this assertion – he later quotes approving a number of
    paragraphs of the Annex (Annex 2, paras 2.31, 2.47, 2.15), which he describes as '[t]his guidance
    seems to me in line with the approach of the European Court' (at para 50 of *Mayer Parry*).
2   However, it embraces the foundation of this burgeoning area of Community law by way of its
    discussion of the *Vessoso and Zanetti* judgment.
3   See para 2.131.

2.104   While Circular 11/94 remains an important contribution to the waste definition debate, operational experience with its Annex 2 since 1994 would suggest that
it invites both unwarranted selective quotation and highly detailed – and perhaps inappropriate – legalistic interpretations of its advice. Although referring to a Department
of the Environment Circular on gypsy encampments, the following observation by
McCullough J is apt in this context also[1]:

'These circulars were intended to provide . . . general guidance. Their paragraphs
are to be read with common sense. Words are to be given their ordinary meaning and
the sense and purpose of a paragraph as a whole, and indeed of a circular as a whole,
is of greater importance than any individual phrase, or sentence contained in it.'

Indeed, the need to consider Circular 11/94's guidance as a whole is itself acknowledged in the Annex 2 of that document[2].

1   *Mid-Bedfordshire District Council v Secretary of State for the Environment* (unreported): quotation
    from Nott S M & Morgan P H (1984) '*The Significance of Department of the Environment Circulars
    in the Planning Process*', JPL 1984, pp 622–632.
2   Circular 11/94, Annex 2, paras 2.10 and 2.53.

2.105   Annex 2 is quite different from the other Annexes of the Circular for the
reason that it extensively sets out to interpret one word in the statute: 'discard'.
Indeed, Annex 2 spends nearly 7,000 words undertaking such a task. Given the vari-
abilities in waste/goods lifecycles, it sets itself an ambitious task. Essentially, it is
trying to set out a series of decision rules which have application to any waste transaction. For example, the Annex attempts to explain why there is no transaction of
'waste' when returnable bottles are taken back to the corner shop or when clothes
pass to charity shops; the nature of the difference between selling an old car to a
garage for repair or selling it to a vehicle dismantler; why 13 million tonnes of fuel
ash from power stations[1] is to be viewed as waste when passing to landfill but not
when destined for building block manufacture and so on. If for no other reason, the
complexity and texture of waste transactions mean that the guidance is not likely to
be definitive. And it seems fair to say that inconsistencies set in towards the final
half of Annex 2.

1   Government Statistical Service (1998) *Digest of Environmental Statistics*, No 20, Stationery Office,
    London, Table 7.1.

2.106   It has been noted earlier that both the definition of Directive waste[1] and the
proposed amendment to s 75 of the EPA 1990[2] state that the term 'waste' has the
meaning in the Directive, but that the Directive does not contain any explicit definition. Instead, the reference to the Directive in the British definition of waste has the
purpose of prompting the courts to consider an interpretation which is closest to the
Directive's objectives and purpose[3]. Circular 11/94 makes reference in this respect to
how the European Court would approach the question of whether or not a substance or
article was 'discarded'[4], but the sentiment is also apt for the national courts:

'. . . in reaching a judgment on the meaning of 'discard' the determinant consideration would be an interpretation which in the opinion of the European Court of
Justice best furthered the purpose of the Directive. . .'.

1   SI 1994/1056, reg 1(3).
2   EPA 1990, s 75(11) as to be inserted by the Environment Act 1995, Sch 22, para 88.
3   See Circular 11/94, Annex 2, paras 2.11, 2.14, 2.31 and 2.39.
4   Circular 11/94, Annex 2, para 2.17.

2.107   Early on in Annex 2, the Circular sets down its own purposive interpretation
of the Directive on Waste. According to the Circular, the Directive is intended to
address and control those wastes which pose[1]:

'. . . a threat to human health or the environment which is different from the threat
posed by substances or objects which are not waste. This threat arises from the
particular propensity of waste to be disposed of or recovered in ways which are
potentially harmful to human health or the environment *and from the fact that the
producers of the substances or objects concerned will normally no longer have the
self interest necessary to ensure the provision of appropriate safeguards*' [emphasis
in original].

1   Circular 11/94, Annex 2, para 2.14.

2.108   In other words, the Circular is saying that wastes are those substances which
the holder may no longer have a self interest in disposing of or recovering properly.
This important facet is perhaps the major determinant to the whole waste-goods
delineation. On the one hand, a scrap transformer containing PCBs would present a
significant disposal cost to the holder. Being subject to such a cost, and being
unwanted, the producer will not have the self interest to take care of it[1]. Conversely,
one tonne of titanium scrap may be of such value that any regulations aimed at
ensuring its appropriate storage and recovery would be superfluous. Between these
two poles, a dividing line is located. As already alluded to at para 2.06 above, the location of that dividing line is uncertain, but clearly from cases such as *Vessoso and
Zanetti*[2] it does not mean that wastes are restricted to substances which have a negative
value. The dividing line will be where economic self interest sets in to exclude the
possibility that the holder 'loses' the material. Exactly where this line is located is not
settled by the Circular. As noted at the beginning of this chapter, it will be inherently
variable and an inevitable consequence may be that it may need to be approached on a
case-by-case basis.

1   It would seem that the 'self-interest' being referred to in the quotation from the Circular is economic
    self-interest. Self-interest created by other means such as by way of fear of prosecution would
    produce a circular argument of somewhat ludicrous outcome. A holder would be allowed to determine
    that a substance should not be waste due to the holder's fear of prosecution under the EPA 1990.
    However once the material was so classified, prosecution would no longer be possible
2   See para 2.87ff and Circular 11/94, Annex 2, paras 2.43–2.45.

2.109   Having set out the purpose of the Directive, the Circular then considers the
circumstances when it will be appropriate to hold that a person 'discards or intends or
is required to discard' substances which constitute waste.

2.110   In the context of disposal operations, the question of discarding appears relatively easy to assess. As Circular 11/94 states[1], if any substance falling within the
Directive's Annex I list[2] passes to one of the disposal operations listed in Annex IIA of
the Directive[3] it is being discarded as waste[4]. Similarly, if the waste is abandoned or
flytipped, it can be assumed that it has been discarded[5].

1   Circular 11/94, Annex 2, para 2.23.
2   See Table 2.1: reproduced in SI 1994/1056 as Sch 4, Pt II.
3   See Table 2.2; reproduced in British law by SI 1994/1056, Sch 4, Pt III.
4   Obviously common sense has to be applied. While item Q16 in Table 2.1 implies that any
     conceivable substance or object could fall in that list, it is not implying that construction materials
     used to build or maintain disposal facilities will be waste.
5   Circular 11/94, Annex 2, para 2.24.

2.111   The approach taken for waste recovery is, not surprisingly, less straightforward. As noted above, the dividing line between waste and goods clearly exists but has an uncertain location on the positive side of £0.00. What is also clear is that there may be circumstances when materials passing to those recovery activities listed in Table 2.3 may not necessarily be wastes[1]. Examples given in the Circular include 'Use principally as a fuel ...' and 'Spreading on land resulting in benefit to agriculture ...'[2].

1   Circular 11/94, Annex 2, para 2.27.
2   Circular 11/94, Annex 2, para 2.25: although it quotes the phrases as set out in the original version of
     Annex IIB of the Directive (see Table 2.3), the Circular has mistakenly omitted to recognise the fact
     that these terms have been qualified by the words 'of waste' when that Annex was reproduced in the
     Waste Management Licensing Regulations 1994 (see Table 2.6).

2.112   In order to differentiate between products and wastes passing to recycling or disposal, the Circular introduces the concept of a 'substance which falls out of the commercial cycle or out of the chain of utility' as a way of describing wastes[1]. These substances should be seen as quite distinct from other materials that exist within the Circular's term of 'normal commercial cycle', which describes transactions involving goods[2]. Such a distinction is necessary for the reason alluded to above: that some of the waste recovery operations listed in the Directive[3] include 'normal commercial cycle' users which involve the processing of economic goods. The recovery of components from catalysts might be an example[4].

1   Circular 11/94, Annex 2, para 2.14.
2   See Circular 11/94, Annex 2, para 2.15: described in *Mayer Parry Recycling Ltd v Environment
     Agency* [1999] Env LR 489 at 506, para 50 as in line with the *Tombesi* and *Inter-Environnement
     Wallonie* decisions.
3   See SI 1994/1056, Sch 4, Pt IV: see also Table 2.6.
4   Item R7 in Table 2.6.

2.113   Single trip and returnable bottles are used in the Circular[1] as a way of illustrating the effect of the notion that wastes can be identified as substances which have fallen out of the normal commercial cycle. Returnable bottles are not discarded when they are returned to a retailer. Nor do they fall out of a normal commercial cycle of drink production, consumption, bottle re-use and refilling[2]. By contrast, if single trip bottles are taken to a bottle bank, then they should be viewed as being taken out of the normal commercial cycle. Therefore, bottles deposited in these circumstances will be defined as waste.

1   Circular 11/94, Annex 2, para 2.21.
2   Naturally, they will eventually become waste at the end of their useful life.

2.114   At first glance this example might be viewed as making unnecessarily fine distinctions. A very extensive network of bottle banks exist, many of which serve transfer stations, which then pass bottles back to purpose-built glass recovery plants. Clearly, with the national recycling target for the year 2000 supposedly set at a level of 25% of all recyclable domestic refuse[1], bottle banks may in the future be viewed as integral to the 'normal commercial cycle' of glass bottle making and drinks production/consumption.

1   Department of the Environment (1990) *This Common Inheritance*, 1990 White Paper on the
    Environment, HMSO, London.

2.115   A second concept is put forward in the Circular, which helps to clarify the
difficulty outlined in the previous paragraph. The concept of a 'specialised recovery
operation' is introduced[1]. This term could be criticised as somewhat unfortunate as it
includes all types of recovery operations, be they solvent distillation units or 'low
tech' operations involving bottle banks or land spreading. But the Circular's purpose
of using this term is to describe those recovery facilities or operations which 'wholly
or partly derive their justification from the recovery of waste'[2].

1   See Circular 11/94, Annex 2, paras 2.28 and 2.30.
2   See Circular 11/94, Annex 2, para 2.30: the following paragraph (2.31) which develops on this matter
    is described in *Mayer Parry Recycling Ltd v Environment Agency* [1999] Env LR 489 at 505, para 49
    and 506, para 50 as in line with the *Tombesi* and *Inter-Environnement Wallonie* decisions.

2.116   The utility of the distinction involving specialised recovery is perhaps best
illustrated by the bottles example. In the case of returnable bottles which are collected
by commercial outlets and sent back to the manufacturer, there is no obvious
'specialised recovery operation' going on. There is no plant identifiable in the lifecycle
of the bottles which wholly or partly derives its justification from waste recovery. The
bottle cleaning and re-filling plant is an adjunct to drinks production. In addition, this
operation is part of the 'normal commercial cycle' of drinks manufacture.

2.117   By contrast, a bottle bank and other associated recycling infrastructure is to be
viewed as a 'specialised recovery operation'. It wholly derives its justification from
waste recovery. It also deals exclusively with materials that have fallen out of the
normal commercial cycle and which have been discarded by the holder.

2.118   The Circular's concepts of 'specialised recovery operation' and 'normal
commercial cycle' are useful in the resolution of many of the more complex cases
involving substances which are closer to 'by-products' and than 'true' waste. A simple
example might be a sawmill, which produces metal scrap from surplus or worn out
machinery and also large quantities of sawdust. The scrap is sent to a scrap metal
dealer. Clearly, it is being both discarded and is passing to a specialised recovery operation[1]. The sawdust passes regularly to pet shops in local towns. Although it might be
argued that this material is discarded, an application of the concepts proposed by the
Circular would indicate that this end use is part of the 'normal commercial cycle'.
Certainly, the sawdust appears not to be being sent to a 'specialised recovery operation'. When these factors are coupled to Circular 11/94's analysis of the nature of
waste, it would appear that the particular circumstances of sawdust re-use does not
involve the re-use of 'waste' within the meaning set down in the EPA 1990 and associated regulations.

1   Item 3 'Recycling or reclamation of metals and metal compounds (R3)' on Sch 4, Pt IV of the Waste
    Management Licensing Regulations 1994 (see Table 2.6).

2.119   Accordingly, five fundamental concepts can be elucidated from Circular
11/94:

(1)   wastes are substances or objects which the producer no longer has the economic
      self-interest to safeguard;
(2)   substances which fall out of the normal commercial cycle or chain of utility are to
      be viewed as discarded and thus 'waste';

(3) any discarded substance passing to a waste disposal operation – as distinct from a recovery operation – is a waste;

(4) any discarded substance sent to a facility which involves a specialised recovery operation is a waste;

(5) substances which pass to other forms of re-use which are not based on a specialised recovery operation may or may not be waste.

The first four items described above have obvious utility, being conceptually simple and widely applicable. The idea of specialised recovery operation is a particularly attractive way of setting boundaries between normal commercial cycle activities and a waste management operation. For example, a frequent complaint from many motor vehicle dismantlers concerns the justification for their premises being held to be dealing with controlled waste, but that a garage repairing vehicles is not. Certain garages may accept or purchase accident damaged vehicles in the same manner as vehicle dismantlers. Parts of the vehicles are used to repair others. But, unlike the garage, the dismantler is clearly identifiable as a specialised recovery operation. By contrast, the garage's purchase of the occasional insurance write-off for parts recovery is incidental to the premises' principal function[1].

1   However, this type of delineation is a matter of degree. The question of boundaries to separate specialised recovery operations from economic re-use is returned to below.

2.120   However, although these four concepts are relatively straightforward, the most difficult area is the fifth and final item: whether substances passing to end users other than specialised recovery involve the acceptance of waste. Unfortunately, it is this area which is subject to a less than satisfactory treatment in the Circular.

2.121   The difficulty can be illustrated by comparing two essentially similar cases. Returning to the sawmill example referred to earlier, it will be apparent that the sawdust destined for pet shops is not subject to a specialised recovery operation. To the producer, the material is of a low value, which may be either positive or negative, being dependent upon other factors such as quantity, transportation, market demand etc, but generally the actual value is less than significant. Although the Circular does not use this example, it would seem correct to state that the arguments raised by its Annex 2 point to the conclusion that sawdust is not a waste when arising in these circumstances.

2.122   The second example involves the use of spent solvents as boiler fuel supplements. For the purposes of this illustration, there is no form of pre-processing and neither is there any significant adaptation of existing boilers[1]. It might be concluded that, like the sawdust example, this operation is within the normal commercial cycle, particularly as there is no identifiable specialised recovery operation. Therefore, on these grounds it might be argued that the solvents are not waste.

1   On-site or off-site re-use would fall into this example. Article 11 of the Directive on Waste allows for the recovery of waste on the producer's premises: see Circular 11/94, Annex 2, para 2.39ff.

2.123   However, although the circumstances of these materials' re-use are similar, it seems unarguable that the solvents should be considered to be waste. If they fell within the definition of waste, they would be special wastes due to factors such as toxicity[1]. Of importance to the determination of this question would be whether persons are paid to take these materials away. Alternatively, they might be purchased by a third party only for a small sum. All these factors would suggest that they fall within the purpose and the controls of the Directive on Waste. The grounds are those set down early in

Annex 2 of the Circular[2], that the holder has little or no self interest to ensure that the materials are safeguarded and that the materials present a potential environmental hazard.

1   The nature of special wastes is discussed in Chapter 4.
2   See Circular 11/94, Annex 2, para 2.14.

2.124   What would also appear from these examples is that the concepts of normal commercial cycle and specialised recovery operation do not connect particularly well to the Circular's assessment of the purposes of the Directive. Indeed, the issue about the status of wastes and by-products significantly tests both the logic and internal consistency of the Circular. The key part of Annex 2 in these respects is the sub-section entitled 'Products and By-Products'[1].

1   Circular 11/94, Annex 2, para 2.32ff.

2.125   In that sub-section it is noted that, despite the fact that a holder may have no use for a substance or object and wishes to pass it to another user, the material may not be waste as it might not actually be discarded[1]. Such materials remain in the normal commercial cycle. The Circular then sets out four categories to which these more borderline materials can be assigned. The categories are[2]:

(a)   *Worn but functioning substances or objects which are still useable – 'albeit after repair' – for the purpose for which they were made.* This category encompasses substances or objects sold by the holder. An example in the Circular is an old car which is sold on for repair. The Circular asserts that this category can cover products which are given away. The transfer of clothes to a charity would fall within this heading[3]. However, this classification excludes cases where the holder has to pay for the material to be removed[4].

(b)   *Substances or objects which can be put to use without resorting to a specialised recovery operation.* Substances or objects in this category are not to be considered as discarded, being either sold or given away. However, it would appear that materials for which the recipient receives payment are excluded[5]. In any case, this category excludes[6] operations which are aimed principally at relieving the holder from the burden of otherwise disposing of it. Of particular significance to such a question is whether, if the source of the material was cut-off, an alternative product would be used instead. If no alternative was substituted, it would seem that the original material was a waste[7]. Examples in the Circular of transactions which fall outside the definition of waste include by-products from food and drink processing passed to animal feed, animal by-products used by the rendering industry and fuel ash from power stations which passes to breeze block manufacture.

(c)   *Substances or objects which are incapable for further use unless subject to a specialised recovery operation.* Substances within this category can either have a positive or negative value. They are out of the commercial cycle and are discarded by the holder. Hence they are defined as waste and remain waste until recovered.

(d)   *Substances or objects which the holder does not want AND[8] for which payment has to be made for their removal.* In these circumstances, the Circular views these materials as waste on the grounds that such materials have been passed to the commercial waste management infrastructure.

1   Circular 11/94, Annex 2, para 2.33.
2   Circular 11/94, Annex 2, para 2.33.
3   See Circular 11/94, Annex 2, para 2.36: but this assertion appeared somewhat at variance to the exemption in the Waste Management Licensing Regulations 1994 (SI 1994/1056), Sch 3, para 28 for the 'storage of returned goods' (see in particular Circular 11/94's discussion at Annex 5, para 5.184).

As originally worded, this provision embraced storage prior to 're-use or submission to a recovery operation'. In 1996, this was changed (by SI 1996/972, Sch 3) to 'recovery or disposal', with the term 're-use' being dropped.

4 This is covered by category (d).
5 Circular 11/94, Annex 2, para 2.33(b)(ii).
6 Circular 11/94, Annex 2, para 2.37.
7 An example might be materials transferred for use as a fuel. Would additional primary fuel be needed if the transfer ceased? Similarly, if the transaction of materials land spreading ceased, would alternative land conditioners be sought? See Circular 11/94, Annex 2, paras 2.37 and 2.38.
8 The emphasis is present in the Circular. However, the second element of the relevant sub-paragraph states (Circular 11/94, Annex 2, para 2.33(d)(ii)) '... the fact that a payment is made by the product may be evidential in relation to intent *but it is not necessarily crucial*' [author's emphasis]. This appears to be a rather unsatisfactory contradiction to the emphasis on the word 'and' contained in the title to this category in the Circular.

2.126 From the above, it can be seen that wastes will be principally found only in categories (c) and (d) above. However, this form of categorisation is not entirely satisfactory[1]. Categories (a) to (d) are not mutually exclusive. Furthermore, the presence in the Circular of extensive caveats in the explanatory text contradict and weaken the decision rules. Finally, the system of exemptions in the Waste Management Licensing Regulations 1994 for facilities which do not need waste management licences[2] allow for the exemption of the 'beneficial use of waste' if it can be 'put to that use without further treatment'[3]. The fact that this exemption exists at all appears to call into question the Circular's analysis of whether direct re-use involved substances classified as wastes. After all, the Waste Management Licensing Regulations 1994 and the Circular are contemporaneous[4].

1 See Cheyne I and Purdue M (1995) 'Fitting Definition to Purpose: The Search for a Satisfactory Definition of Waste' JEL, Vol 7, No 2, pp 145–168, at 163–164.
2 See Chapter 10.
3 SI 1994/1056, Sch 3, para 15(1): see para 10.189.
4 This exemption is explained in Circular 11/94, Annex 5, para 5.121ff.

2.127 The problems caused by these contradictions can be illustrated by the sawdust example used above. Once removed from the holder, the sawdust certainly might be able to be put to use immediately. This type of transaction may well be covered by category (b). However, it is equally conceivable that the sawmill does not want the material and is happy to pay a small amount for its removal. In this case, category (d) appears to have application. Again, this difficulty leads to the question of the value of the material. Should the above categories be taken literally, if the sawdust is removed at a cost of 1p per tonne, then it falls into category (d). If it is given away for nothing, it is allocated to category (b). This is a less than satisfactory basis for a statutory definition of anything. These types of problem[1] have tended to cause a general disillusionment with Annex 2 of the Circular as a whole. This is a pity, as a significant amount of its advice has considerable power and utility.

1 Likewise, para 2.46 of Annex 2 of the Circular unequivocally states that, once a substance becomes defined as a waste, it remains so defined until it is somehow recovered or treated. However, this is directly contradicted by para 2.50 which notes that, in certain instances, a change of intention by a subsequent holder of the waste – without any associated change made to the waste's nature and composition – is enough to affect whether it should continue to be defined as waste.

2.128 It also seems that, while Circular 11/94's concepts such as specialised recovery operation narrow down the breadth of the waste/goods boundary, they also throw up other areas requiring delineation. For example, an increasingly unclear area is where the concept of 'specialised recovery operation' ends and where re-use without specialised recovery commences. This is not helped by Annex 2's definition of specialised recovery[1] as constituting an operation which wholly or *partly* derives its justification from the recovery of waste [author's emphasis].

1 Circular 11/94, Annex 2, para 2.30.

2.129 These difficulties can be illustrated by the case of the solvent wastes referred to earlier. It was noted that no modification of the boilers was undertaken to allow these materials to be burnt. It would seem that, if the burners of a boiler were adapted specifically to accept solvents as well as primary fuel, the adaptation would involve a 'specialised recovery operation'. But if this assertion is correct, it seems valid to apply the same principles to the sawdust from the sawmill. If a person supplying pet shops bags this material up for retail sale, surely this is also a specialised recovery operation?

2.130 But the factor of most fundamental importance has been omitted from the above discussion. And this perhaps exemplifies the danger of taking various paragraphs of Annex 2 on their own and subjecting them to individualised detailed analysis. The primary issue concerns the objectives of the Directive and their fulfilment. The Circular's view of these objectives has already been quoted and indicates that the Directive relates to substances or objects which a holder no longer has a reason to safeguard by way of economic self-interest. A second objective is to ensure that public health and the environment are subject to protection from materials generated in those circumstances. These factors perhaps can be used to distinguish between the circumstances of the sawdust and the solvents. The sawdust transaction does not need controlling for the reason that human health and the environment are unlikely to be affected by it. Conversely, the chemical nature of the solvents, coupled with their low economic value, would indicate that these materials should be subject to the Directive and hence a member state's statutory controls. This factor is regardless of whether there is any identifiable specialised recovery operation involved as an adjunct to the combustion process. The question of specialised recovery is essentially irrelevant to this latter debate. As McCullough J has noted[1], Department of the Environment Circulars need to be read with common sense.

1 *Mid-Bedfordshire District Council v Secretary of State for the Environment*: see para 2.104 above.

Wastes and by-products passing to recovery and direct re-use

2.131 The matter of waste definitions becomes acutely difficult in respect of materials which can be put to direct re-use without any form of intermediate recovery process to make them suitable. This difficulty has already been alluded to in the discussion of Annex II of Circular 11/94. It is a particular problem for the materials reclamation industry, effecting – for example – the very extensive re-use of scrap for ferrous and non-ferrous metal production. It is argued on behalf of the industry that the incoming materials should never be regarded as waste, particularly as these are often of value and are traded like other commodities. The industry also asserts that waste management controls have applied 'by stealth', in the sense that the definition of waste was drafted inadvertently too widely and catches an industrial sector where additional regulatory control is environmentally unjustified. Whilst it has already been discussed that the activities of the reclamation industry may not be environmentally benign, what does seem clear is that the industry should at least know where it stands. In this respect, the vagueness of the definition of waste in the Directive on Waste in respect of substances passing to recovery or to direct re-use has caused a developing problem of countries unilaterally adopting different rules[1], thereby creating possible barriers to the very extensive global trade in reclaimable materials[2]. While Circular 11/94 attempted to address, by way of non-statutory guidance, the matter of direct re-use through the concepts of 'normal commercial cycle' and 'specialised recovery operation', it will be apparent that the argument presented in its Annex 2 becomes flawed and self-contradictory. Since the Circular was published in 1994, a somewhat different approach has evolved via the European Court of Justice.

1 See OECD (1998) *Final Guidance Document for Distinguishing Waste from Non-Waste* Env/EPOC/WMP(98)1/Rev1, OECD, Paris and see also Bontoux Land Leone F (1997) *The Legal Definition of Waste and its Impact on Waste Management in Europe*, Office of the Official Journal of the European Communities, Luxembourg, EUR 17716 EN.
2 See, for example, *R v Environment Agency, ex p Dockgrange Ltd, Mayer Parry Ltd and the Robinson Group Ltd*, [1998] 10 JEL 1 146, discussed at para 5.51ff.

2.132 This approach has been promulgated in Advocate General Jacobs's successive opinions in *Tombesi*[1] and *Inter-Environnement Wallonie*[2]. It significantly down-plays the need to obtain a definitive understanding of the word 'discard' in the statutory definition of waste. In its stead is the identification of a link between the definition of waste and the disposal and recovery processes listed in Annexes IIA and IIB of the Directive on Waste (see Tables 2.2 and 2.3). It has already been noted that neither the wording of the Directive nor the British legislation makes this direct connection[3]. Furthermore this is simply an opinion of the Advocate General and not a decision of the European Court as a whole. However, the concept has been given application in British law by Carnwath J's judgment of *Mayer Parry Recycling Ltd v Environment Agency*[4].

1 [1998] Env LR 59.
2 [1998] Env LR 623. It also raises a rather fundamental issue concerning the role of the European Court of Justice in a process which appears near to one of altering the scope of existing legislation in what might be viewed as furthering policy goals. Given the consensus – as identified in *Tombesi* and *Wallonie* – in member states' views on the need for some form of exclusion for by-products used directly in other industrial processes, it could be argued that it is up to those member states to amend the relevant legislation. This seems to be particularly pertinent in this instance where it seems that the drafting inadvertently over-stepped the intended boundary between wastes and goods. It is at least arguable that the placing of restrictions on that boundary for practical – and often deregulatory – reasons is a policy matter, not a matter of law for the European Court of Justice.
3 See OECD (1998) *Final guidance Document for Distinguishing Waste from non-Waste*, Waste Management Policy Group, OECD, Paris and Cheyne I and Purdue M (1995) *Fitting Definition to Purpose: The Search for a Satisfactory Definition of Waste* 7 JEL 149-168 at 157-159; see also Waite A (1994) 'Crucial Need to Understand the meaning of "Waste"' *Law and the Waste Industry* IWM/UKELA Supplement, Institute of Wastes Management, Northampton.
4 [1999] Env LR 489.

2.133 The approach of linking the definition of wastes to operations covered by Annex IIA and Annex IIB of the Directive, whilst down-playing the significance of the term 'discard', has been christened the '*Euro Tombesi* bypass'[1]. It seems to have been a consequence of submissions made to the European Court by member states in *Inter-Environnement Wallonie*, which appeared to Advocate General Jacobs to exhibit a consensus – at least in their basis[2]. A similar basis of consensus of OECD states as set out in a 1996 draft of a report of the OECD Waste Management Policy Group[3] was also acknowledged[4]. The *Euro Tombesi* bypass develops from non-controversial conclusion that the term 'discard' has a special meaning within the confines of the legislation, embracing waste passing to both disposal and recovery operations[5]. The 'bypass' element is then introduced, being well-expressed by the Advocate General in *Tombesi*[6] '[t]he scope of the term "waste" therefore, depends on what is meant by "disposal operation" and "recovery operation"'.

1   See Van Calster G 'The *Euro Tombesi* Bypass and the Basel Relief Routes' *European Business Law Review* 1997, pp 137–143.
2   *Wallonie* [1998] Env LR 623 at 641, para 71.
3   Published in 1998 as *Final Guidance Document for Distinguishing Waste from Non-Waste* Env/EPOC/WMP(98)1/Rev1, OECD, Paris.
4   *Wallonie* [1998] Env LR 623 at 641, para 71ff.
5   *Tombesi* [1998] Env LR 59 at 74, para 50; *Wallonie* [1998] Env LR 623 at 639, para 60.
6   *Tombesi* [1998] Env LR 59 at 74, para 50.

2.134   The *Euro Tombesi* bypass holds that, by definition, a material consigned to a disposal process in Annex IIA of the Directive is obviously a waste[1]. Similarly any material sent to a recovery process is a waste if the recovery process features on Annex IIB. The latter is particularly important for the reason that – so the argument goes – should a material not be consigned to a process which is identifiable in Annex IIB, that material is not a waste[2]. Hence the Advocate General found that materials which can be transferred to another person and used in their present state – in other words without any form of processing to make them suitable – are not 'recovered'. The Advocate General uses the example of a motor car sold to another person[3].

1   Other than those materials which are used to construct the process – quarry stone for landfill roads is an example. This also illustrates the need to at least consider 'discarding' within this approach.
2   '... *the sole question* [author's emphasis] is whether the substance at issue is subject to a disposal or recovery operation within the meaning of Annex IIA or B' *Tombesi* [1998] Env LR 59, per Advocate General Jacobs at 77, para 57.
3   *Tombesi* [1998] Env LR 59 at 74, para 52.

2.135   This approach would ensure that many substances which are used directly in industrial processes do not fall within the definition of waste. Examples might be scrap metal used as a furnace feed in a foundry or chemical by-products used in chemical manufacture. It is argued that neither appears readily classifiable in Annex IIB. To follow Circular 11/94's parlance, these transactions are within the 'normal commercial cycle' and do not involve specialised recovery operations. Defining materials arising in these circumstances as not being wastes is conceptually useful for the obvious reason that waste management controls would not apply.

2.136   The Advocate General's position was subject to extensive consideration and approval in *Mayer Parry Recycling Ltd v Environment Agency*[1] by Carnwath J. This case involved a large recycling company which undertook diverse scrap processing operations including sorting, cutting, crushing, separation and baling. The matter before the court was whether four broad types of scrap metal accepted by the recycling company fell within the definition of waste under Community and national law. The four types were[2]:

(a)   scrap metal which required no additional processing which was suitable for direct use as a feedstock to iron and steel manufacture and 'not subject to any further recovery operation within the meaning of Annex IIB';
(b)   scrap metal destined for further treatment by processes such as sorting, crushing, fragmentisation or baling, with a view to being later used in iron and steel manufacture;
(c)   scrap metal contaminated with oils and cutting fluids which requires specialist processing (eg oil removal) prior to smelting or which is subject to other special measures in order to protect human health and the environment
(d)   scrap contaminated with small quantities of other foreign matter such as plastic, wood, concrete, soil etc.

1   [1999] Env LR 489.
2   *Mayer Parry Recycling Ltd v Environment Agency* [1999] Env LR 489 at 506, para 52.

2.137   The Environment Agency did not dispute that it considered scrap metal type (a) above not to be waste[1]. In argument, it followed the Advocate General's opinion in the *Tombesi* and *Wallonie* cases '. . . in putting the emphasis not on the term 'discard', but on the description in Annex IIB of recovery operations'[2]. Hence as Mayer Parry Recycling Ltd's operations readily classified under the heading of Annex IIB 're-cycling/reclamation of metals and metal compounds', the company was dealing in waste. But where the scrap metal can be used in a furnace without further processing, the Agency was stated as accepting that it '. . . is a raw material which is not destined for a recovery operation . . .'[3].

1   *Mayer Parry Recycling Ltd v Environment Agency* [1999] Env LR 489 at 507, para 53.
2   *Mayer Parry Recycling Ltd v Environment Agency* [1999] Env LR 489 at 504, para 42.
3   *Mayer Parry Recycling Ltd v Environment Agency* [1999] Env LR 489 at 504, para 43.

2.138   By contrast, it was argued on behalf of Mayer Parry Recycling Ltd that the key to the issue was the need to pin-down the concept in the definition of waste of 'discarding'. It was claimed that discarding involved a person getting rid of something as unwanted or not needed and that this was an incorrect description of how scrap metal is considered when consigned to a reprocessor. Therefore, while something could be sold and remain defined as waste, the sale of the metal scrap is an inherent part of 'the mainstream of the commercial recycling industry'[1] and not part of the national waste management system.

1   *Mayer Parry Recycling Ltd v Environment Agency* [1999] Env LR 489 at 504, at para 44: in other words – to use Circular 11/94's parlance – that it is within the 'normal commercial cycle'.

2.139   Being bound by the earlier decisions of the European Court[1], Carnwath J sided with the Environment Agency. Given that the Agency did not argue the point, the court found that scrap metal type (a)[2] was not waste[3]. The three other types of scrap were considered to fall within the definition of waste under Community and national law. The court held that[4]:

> 'The general concept is now reasonably clear. The term "discard" is used in a broad sense equivalent to "get rid of", but it is coloured by the examples of waste given in Annex I[5] and the Waste Catalogue, which indicate that it is concerned generally with materials which have ceased to be required for their original purpose, normally because they are unsuitable, unwanted or surplus to requirements. That broad category is however limited by the context, which shows that the purpose is to control disposal and recovery of such materials. Accordingly, materials which are to be re-used (rather than finally disposed of), but which do not require any recovery operation before being put to their new use, are not treated as waste[6]. Similarly, materials which are made ready for re-use by a recovery operation, cease to be waste when the recovery operation is complete[7].'

1   *Mayer Parry Recycling Ltd v Environment Agency* [1999] Env LR 489 at 505, para 45.
2   See para 2.136.
3   *Mayer Parry Recycling Ltd v Environment Agency* [1999] Env LR 489 at 509, para 61.
4   *Mayer Parry Recycling Ltd v Environment Agency* [1999] Env LR 489 at 505, para 46.
5   See Table 2.1.
6   An argument also made by Fluck J (1994) 'The Term "Waste" in EC Law' *European Environmental Law Review* 79 at 82, col 1.
7   If not complete, the material would of course remain waste. Precisely how recovery is to be viewed as 'complete' is a problematic area: see para 2.145.

2.140   Given the analysis made earlier in this chapter, the general outcome of the *Mayer Parry* litigation is not particularly surprising. However, what is significant is that, while Carnwath J considered alternative language meanings of the word 'discard', much less significance is made of both the importance of the word[1] and also the matter of waste definitions being subjective and being viewed through the actions or the intentions of the holder of the waste[2]. In *Mayer Parry*, it is confirmed that the term has a special meaning different from the ordinary English use, which requires '. . . regard [to be taken] to the background and other language versions'[3]. The *Tombesi* and *Wallonie* decisions were subject to detailed analysis, with an emphasis being placed on Advocate General Jacobs' two opinions[4]. What is particularly interesting are the following paragraphs of Carnwath J's judgment and the adoption of the *Euro Tombesi* bypass. In considering the four types of material listed above, he states[5]:

> 'Turning to the facts of the case, *all*[6] the materials referred to . . . are potentially within the definition of waste, in the sense that they are "got rid of" by their original users, *because they are not wanted or needed for their original purpose*[7]. Thus, manufacturers get rid of surplus material, such as borings and offcuts, because they are not needed for their primary product; materials in a building about to be demolished are no longer needed by the original owner, and the vehicle dismantler handles cars which have reached the end of their useful life for their original purpose. Accordingly, the issue in this case turns on the scope of the term "recovery". In so far as the discarded materials do not require any recovery operation, as the Agency concedes, they are not treated as waste at all. Insofar as they do require recovery operations, they remain waste until those recovery operations are complete.'

This finding raises some quite fundamental matters. Indeed, it might suggest that, in the absence of the judicial cross-connection between the wording of the definition of waste in the Directive and the Annex IIB recovery operations, all the materials listed in (a) to (d) above – including scrap metal delivered directly from a large manufacturing business to iron and steel production – would be waste. Carnwath J clearly indicates that he viewed them as all being discarded. Hence whether this finding is upheld in the long term may well be dependent on whether the European Court does or does not adopt the *Euro Tombesi* bypass in any future case.

1   In *Mayer Parry Recycling Ltd v Environment Agency* [1999] Env LR 489 at 497, para 23 Carnwath J notes that '[t]he definition of "waste" . . ., and in particular the meaning (if any) [author's emphasis] to be given to the word "discard", has given rise to much controversy and academic debate'.
2   See comment by Purdue M in the commentary to *Tombesi* in [1998] 10 JEL 140.
3   *Mayer Parry Recycling Ltd v Environment Agency* [1999] Env LR 489 at 498, para 30; see also 503, para 41.
4   *Mayer Parry Recycling Ltd v Environment Agency* [1999] Env LR 489 at 499, para 32; 503, para 40.
5   *Mayer Parry Recycling Ltd v Environment Agency* [1999] Env LR 489 at 505, paras 47 and 48.
6   Author's emphasis.
7   Author's emphasis.

2.141   There are also major other practical difficulties with this approach. While van Calster[1], van Rossem[2] and, subsequently, Carnwath J[3] assert that the European Court in *Wallonie* adopted the *Euro Tombesi* bypass, all the court in the *Wallonie* case appears to do is to hold that:

(a)   '. . . the scope of the term "waste" turns on the meaning of the term "discard" '[4];
(b)   'the term "discard" covers both disposal and recovery of a substance or object'[5];
(c)   the list of categories of waste in Annex I[6] of the Directive and the disposal and recovery operations in Annexes IIA and IIB '. . .does not in principle exclude any kind of residue, industrial by-product or other substance arising from production processes'[7];
(d)   the Directive applies not only to disposal or recovery of waste by 'specialist undertakings' but also at the place of production[8];

(e) there is nothing in the Directive to indicate that it does not apply to production processes involving disposal or recovery operations which do not have the potential for environmental harm[9];

(f) from precedent, the definition of waste in the Directive is not to be understood as excluding materials capable of economic reutilisation[10];

(g) it is concluded that substances forming part of industrial processes may be waste under the Directive[11];

(h) this conclusion does not undermine the necessary distinction between waste recovery under the Directive and 'normal industrial treatment of products'[12];

(i) the court considers that a substance is not excluded from the definition of waste under the Directive 'by the mere fact' that it forms an integral part of an industrial production process[13].

What is notable here is the court's omission from both its discussion and its conclusions of any reference to the restriction that wastes are substances which pass solely to disposal and recovery processes, as defined in the Directive's Annexes IIA and IIB.

1 Van Calster G (1997) 'The EC Definition of Waste: the Euro Tombesi By-Pass and the Basel Relief Routes' *European Business Law Review* 137–143 at 139.
2 See van Rossem's commentary on the *Tombesi* case at (1998) JEL 10 141–145 at 143.
3 *Mayer Parry Recycling Ltd v Environment Agency* [1999] Env LR 489 at 503, para 40, where Carnwath J considered that the *Wallonie* judgment '... moves much closer than the *Tombesi* judgment to express adoption of the Advocate General's approach'.
4 *Wallonie* [1998] Env LR 623 at 641, para 26.
5 *Wallonie* [1998] Env LR 623 at 641, para 27: van Rossem quotes this and the previous paragraph as evidence of the Euro Tombesi bypass (see at 1998 JEL 10 at 143).
6 See Table 2.1.
7 *Wallonie* [1998] Env LR 623 at 641, para 28.
8 *Wallonie* [1998] Env LR 623 at 641, para 29.
9 *Wallonie* [1998] Env LR 623 at 641, para 30.
10 *Wallonie* [1998] Env LR 623 at 641, para 31.
11 *Wallonie* [1998] Env LR 623 at 641, para 32.
12 *Wallonie* [1998] Env LR 623 at 641, para 33.
13 *Wallonie* [1998] Env LR 623 at 641, para 34.

2.142   Secondly, as van Rossem points out[1] it is not possible to ignore the notion of discarding completely. To do so would mean that anything passing to disposal or recovery, including chemicals, fuel oil or any other raw material used in the process would be waste.

1 Van Rossem R's commentary on the *Tombesi* case at (1998) JEL 10 141–145 at 143.

2.143   Perhaps more fundamentally, the adoption of the *Euro Tombesi* bypass has the danger that it has simply moved the focus of the problem away from the word 'discard' and onto the definition of the nature of an Annex IIB recovery operation[1]. In this respect a difficulty is created by Annex IIB being cast in non-exhaustive terms[2]: a point acknowledged by the Advocate General in *Tombesi*[3]. That Annex IIB incompletely covers all types of waste recovery is alluded to, for example, by the Department of the Environment, who has noted that the blending of wastes is a process which is excluded from the list of recovery operations[4].

1 See van Rossem's comment on the *Tombesi* case at (1998) JEL 10 141–145 at 142.
2 The header to Annex IIB states 'This Annex is intended to list recovery operations as they are carried out in practice'.
3 *Tombesi* [1998] Env LR 59 at 74, para 51 and 75, para 55. But note that this is not the case with the British legislation due to SI 1994/1056, Sch 4, para 9: see para 2.41.
4 Department of the Environment (1996) *United Kingdom Management Plan for the Exports and Imports of Waste*, HMSO, London, para 6.34.

2.144   There are also major difficulties in defining 'recovery'. Firstly, it has been noted that Carnwath J found that wastes are involved when they are consigned to an Annex IIB recovery process. If it is accepted that 'recovery' means a process as defined by Annex IIB and that 'Recycling/Reclamation of metals and metal compounds' is found in Category R4 of that Annex[1], how should an electric arc furnace be viewed? Such a furnace takes a charge of up to 100% scrap iron – there is no primary iron ore added. Surely this furnace is making the scrap useable as steel once again? Indeed, it seems to serve no other purpose[2].

1   Council Directive of 15 July 1975 on Waste (75/442/EEC) (OJ L194/39 25.7.75), as amended by Council Directive of 18 March 1991 amending Directive 75/442/EEC on Waste (91/156/EEC) (OJ L78/32 26.3.91) and by Commission Decision of 26 May 1996 adapting Annexes IIA and IIB to Council Directive 75/442/EEC on Waste (96/350/EEC) (OJ L135/32 6.6.96).
2   Even if the furnace accepted scrap metal which had been completely recovered by the likes of Mayer Parry Recycling Ltd, if it took other scrap metal direct from a factory or materials which had not been 'completely' recovered, it would be licensable on the basis of the logic used by Carnwath J to hold that Mayer Parry Recycling Ltd was licensable: it takes waste. In any event, such an undertaking would seem also to fall within the definition of a 'specialised recovery operation' in Circular 11/94: operations which '... wholly or partly derive their justification from the recovery of waste' (Circular 11/94, Annex 2, para 2.30).

2.145   A second difficulty is in determining the nature of recovery. As Carnwath J acknowledges[1] '... materials which are made ready for re-use by a recovery operation, cease to be waste when the recovery operation is complete'. The question arises as to what is meant by 'complete'. If not 'complete', the material will remain a waste. That recovery may be partial is well recognised in the legislation. Perhaps the best example is in respect of transfrontier waste shipments and Regulation 259/93[2]. The Regulation specifies the grounds available to a country to raise a formal objection to a proposed international waste shipment, which includes that[3]:

> '... the ratio of the recoverable and non-recoverable waste, the estimated value of the materials to be finally recovered or the cost of the recovery and the cost of the disposal of the non-recoverable fractions do not justify the recovery under economic and environmental considerations.'

As guidance to the Agency when making decisions in the context of Regulation 259/93, the relevant statutory document[4] contains a section entitled 'Genuine Recovery Operations'. This sets out a number of criteria by which the Agency is to judge whether a proposed recovery operation is legitimate. Clearly, the existence of this section shows that recovery – despite being classifiable in Annex IIB of the Directive on Waste – may not always be genuine[5].

1   *Mayer Parry Recycling Ltd v Environment Agency* [1999] Env LR 489 at 505, para 46.
2   Council Regulation (EEC) No 259/93 of 1 February 1993 on the supervision and control of shipments of waste within, into and out of the European Community (OJ L30/1 6.2.93); see Chapter 5.
3   Council Regulation (EEC) No 259/93 of 1 February 1993 on the supervision and control of shipments of waste within, into and out of the European Community (OJ L30/1 6.2.93), Article 7(4)(a): see para 5.154.
4   Department of the Environment (1996) *United Kingdom Management Plan for the Exports and Imports of Waste*, HMSO, London, para 6.4ff; see para 5.37ff.
5   See also para 6.20ff – entitled 'Sham Recovery' – of Department of the Environment (1996) *United Kingdom Management Plan for the Exports and Imports of Waste*, HMSO, London.

2.146   These factors mean that there has to be found a dividing line between 'complete' recovery – where the outflowing materials are not wastes – and other types of more partial recovery where the materials arising from the process remain waste. As Carnwath J notes in *Mayer Parry*, once the recycling company had '... restored the material to a form which is suitable for sale as raw material to steelworks or other manufacturers, the presumption is that the task of recovery is complete and the material ceases to be waste[1]. But it seems clear that this will not always be the case. For example, it has already been noted that in 1996 the Department of the Environment[2] took the view that a waste blending process to form 'secondary liquid fuel' (SLF) prior to consignment to combustion in cement manufacture was insufficient to take SLF outside the national definition of waste[3]. Likewise, the European Court in *Tombesi* did not consider that a grinding process applied to specified wastes was sufficient to cause the end product to be excluded from the definition of waste under the Directive on Waste[4].

1   *Mayer Parry Recycling Ltd v The Environment Agency* [1999] Env LR 489 at 506, para 51; see also para 54. Likewise in *Durham County Council v Thomas Swann & Co Ltd* [1995] Env LR 72 at 76, 'properly cleaned' reclaimed chemical drums were found to be no longer waste.
2   Department of the Environment (1996) *United Kingdom Management Plan for the Exports and Imports of Waste*, HMSO, London.
3   See *Kent County Council v Queenborough Rolling Mill Co Ltd* [1990] LGR 306: discussed at para 2.173.
4   [1998] Env LR 59 at 88, para 54.

2.147   The establishment of the boundary between direct re-use in a process and recovery as set out in Annex IIB is also problematic. The Advocate General acknowledges[1] that the distinction between these concepts is 'somewhat artificial', describing the difference as 'somewhat fragile'[2]. This factor is also acknowledged by Carnwath J[3]: 'The difficulty at this point is in drawing a clear line between the recovery operations, and industrial operations for which recycled scrap is used as a raw material'. Hence he falls back onto Circular 11/94's concepts of 'specialised recovery operation' and 'normal commercial cycle' to provide assistance.

1   See *Tombesi* [1998] Env LR 59 at 75, para 54.
2   See also *Wallonie* [1998] Env LR 623 at 650, para 33 and the Advocate General in *EC Commission v Germany* [1995] ECR I-1097 at 1109, para 34.
3   See *Mayer Parry Recycling Ltd v Environment Agency* [1999] Env LR 489 at 505, para 49: later in the judgment Carnwath J describes recovery and 'normal industrial treatment' as having a 'difficult distinction' (para 56) in the context of further processing by a scrap end-user. He comments 'I do not think there can be a wholly logical resolution to these issues' (para 57).

2.148   A further difficulty, well illustrated by van Rossem[1], is that certain Annex IIB operations themselves involve direct use of materials in their existing form: examples include the reuse of oil (R9), use principally as a fuel (R1) and the spreading of waste on land (R10)[2]. None of these appear to involve recovery prior to direct use[3]. However, in *Tombesi*, the Advocate General clearly considered that the notion of recovery was different to re-use and that, to be embraced by the former term, some form of positive processing must be involved[4]: '... what is entailed by "recovery" is a process by which goods are restored to their previous state or transformed into a usable state or by which certain usable components are extracted or produced. It follows that ... goods which are transferred to another person and put to continued use in their existing form are not "recovered" ...'. If this approach is to be followed strictly, the already environmentally problematic area of the landspreading of wastes[5] might fall out of statutory control entirely.

1   (1998) 10 JEL at 142.
2   Council Directive of 15 July 1975 on Waste (75/442/EEC) (OJ L194/39 25.7.75), Annex IIB, as amended by Council Directive of 18 March 1991 amending Directive 75/442/EEC on Waste (91/156/EEC) (OJ L78/32 26.3.91) and by Commission Decision of 26 May 1996 adapting Annexes IIA and IIB to Council Directive 75/442/EEC on Waste (96/350/EEC) (OJ L135/32 6.6.96): see Table 2.3.

3 Note the difference in construction of these categories to the others: the latter are prefixed by the verbs 'recycling', 'reclamation', 'regeneration' and 'recovery'.
4 See *Criminal Proceedings against Tombesi* [1998] Env LR 59 at 74, para 52.
5 See para 10.138ff.

2.149 If the view is taken that wastes are restricted to those substances passing to the disposal and recovery operations listed in Annex IIA and IIB of the Directive on Waste, a very significant question arises as to the status of activities which are not described by these Annexes. Should this restrictive approach be followed, then by definition materials passing to operations outside Annexes IIA and IIB are not waste. Inevitably, this means that such activities do not fall within the requirements of the Directive on Waste for permits or registrations. As mentioned, the blending of waste would be excluded[1]. But it seems obvious that this restrictive approach defeats the purpose of the Directive, namely to comprehensively control all types of waste management activity. It also causes questions to be raised as to how some of the British waste management provisions are to be construed. On the one hand, it might be argued that activities outside Annexes IIA and IIB are not licensable. For example, Burnett-Hall[2] has asserted that – despite acknowledging that there are provisions in the legislation which indicate to the contrary[3] – no waste management licence is ever needed for the storage of waste at the site of production, pending its removal. As is evident from Tables 2.2 and 2.3, these activities are excluded from Annexes IIA and IIB of the Directive. The only alternative explanation as to why certain waste management activities which involve non-Annex IIB operations[4] are included in the British provisions might revolve around the assertion that they have legitimately gone further than strictly required by the Directive. In both *Tombesi*[5] and *Wallonie*[6], the Advocate General indicates the legitimacy of such an action as part of the concept of subsidiarity: '[a]s the Directive stands at present, I think it must to some extent be left to member states to develop more detailed criteria to apply the term "recovery operation" to the various situations which may occur in practice'[7].

1 Department of the Environment (1996) *United Kingdom Management Plan for the Exports and Imports of Waste*, HMSO, London, para 6.34.
2 Burnett-Hall R (1997) 'Waste Controls and Development Projects' *IWM/UKELA Proceedings*, Institute of Wastes Management, Northampton pp 13–14.
3 SI 1994/1056, Sch 3, para 41 allows a general exemption from licensing for waste stored on the premises of production, except where quantities of special waste exceed defined limits (see para 10.55ff). Should such limits be exceeded, the implication certainly is that a waste management licence is needed.
4 Examples include the exemption from licensing in respect of '... the beneficial use of waste if ...it is to be put to that use without further treatment ...' (SI 1994/1056, Sch 3, para 15: see para 10.189).
5 [1998] Env LR 59 at 76, para 56.
6 [1998] Env LR 623 at 641, para 69.
7 [1998] Env LR 623 at 641, para 69.

2.150 Finally, by focusing the definition of waste towards the disposal or recovery process at the end of a waste life-cycle, problems may arise in determining the status of consignments intercepted prior to their arrival at their destination[1]. A number of chapters of this book concern themselves with controls on wastes prior disposal or recovery. It seems difficult to base the statutory definition of waste on the intended end-use of a substance, particularly when there may be no evidence as to what that end-use is to be. For example, how can one know that wastes are involved in the case of a haulier stopped in transit to determine whether that person should possess a registration under the Control of Pollution (Amendment) Act 1989[2]?

1   See Purdue M (1998) JEL 158: '. . . the question of what constitutes waste should apparently be
    determined *before* the disposal operation takes place'; see also Waite A (1994) 'Crucial need to
    Understand the Meaning of "Waste"' *IWM UKELA Annual Supplement* October 1994, pp 4–5. This
    matter is also alluded to by the Advocate General in *Tombesi* [1998] Env LR 59 at 75/76, para 55.
2   See para 6.53 and Figure 6.1. In *Environment Agency v Short* [1999] Env LR 300 it was
    unsuccessfully argued that timber from demolition work which was claimed to be destined for use in
    domestic fires was not controlled waste. However, there was no elaborate rehearsal of any of the
    above argument in this judgment.

2.151   The conceptual difficulty just described is likely to be most acutely felt in
respect of statutory control over transfrontier waste movements. As is explained in
Chapter 5, wastes passing internationally to recovery may be subject to three different
control procedures and even may be banned entirely by non-EC countries. The focus
of these procedures is as much on the control of waste prior to shipment and in transit
as it is to its arrival. A consideration of the status of scrap metal in the context of transfrontier waste controls well illustrates the difficulty. International movements of all
waste into and out of the Community are subject to Regulation 259/93[1]. The least
onerous control procedures apply to those substances on the 'Green List' of the Regulation[2]. Besides electing to unilaterally ban such wastes from entering their sover-
eignty, non-OECD countries may alternatively require that they are dealt with under
the more stringent system of 'Amber List' or 'Red List' controls[3]. The Green List is
reproduced in Appendix III, Table 1. What is clear is that virtually every type of metal
scrap features on it, including high value precious metals such as gold, silver and platinum, as well as scrap iron, steel, copper, aluminium and so on. Electronic scrap,
textiles, rubber and waste paper also feature.

1   Council Regulation (EEC) No 259/93 of 1 February 1993 on the supervision and control of shipments
    of waste within, into and out of the European Community (OJ L30/1 6.2.93) see Chapter 5.
2   Council Regulation (EEC) No 259/93 of 1 February 1993 on the supervision and control of shipments
    of waste within, into and out of the European Community (OJ L30/1 6.2.93), Article 16 (as amended
    by Council Regulation (EC) No 120/97 of 20 January 1997 amending Regulation (EC) No 259/93 on
    the supervision and control of shipments of waste, within, into and out of the European Community
    (OJ L22/14 24.1.97) and Commission Regulation (EC) No 2408/98 of 6 November 1998 amending
    Annex V to Council Regulation (EEC) 259/93 on the supervision and control of shipments of waste
    within, into and out of the European Community (OJ L298/19 7.11.98)); see para 5.136ff.
3   See para 5.137ff.

2.152   Like virtually all other elements of national and international waste management legislation, the application of Regulation 259/93 is dependent on whether wastes
are involved. Should a country wish to exercise its right to ban some or all of these
wastes from crossing their border[1], it would seem highly anomalous that they can only
exercise such a right in respect of, for example, a consignment of scrap iron passing to
an Annex IIB recovery process, but not when an identical material is to pass to direct
re-use[2]. Furthermore, should such a shipment get intercepted in transit, the *Euro
Tombesi* bypass would imply that the shipper is subject to criminal penalties only if it
could be proved – somehow – that the material is going to pass to an identifiable
Annex IIB recovery process. This seems to be a very shaky foundation for such an
important concept as the transfrontier waste shipment controls.

1   As they are allowed to under Regulation 259/93, Art 17: see para 5.137ff and see also Council
    Regulation 1420/99 of 29 April 1999 establishing common rules and procedures to apply to certain
    non-OECD waste, OJ L166/6 1.7.1999 and Commission Regulation (EC) No 1547/99 of 12 July
    1999 determining the control procedures under Council Regulation (EC) No 259/93 to apply to
    shipments of certain types of waste to certain countries to which OECD Decision C(92)39Final does
    not apply (OJ L185/1 17.7.1999).
2   Should such an approach be adopted, examples of undesirable transactions which might legitimately
    occur include asbestos roofing sheets being consigned for re-use in buildings, sulphuric acid 'wastes'

to be used for low grade steel cleaning purposes, 'spent' cyanides to be used for poor quality steel hardening and so on. Many wastes contain active ingredients. But often – as in the case of the steel cleaning and hardening example – they are depleted such that they operate too slowly to be of use in a Western commercial context.

2.153 Overall, it may be that the exclusion of the direct re-use of by-products from waste management controls is conceptually useful due to the loose definition of waste in Community law and in a climate of deregulation and concerns about burdens on business. But, as will be apparent, the focus away from the term 'discarding' onto the term 'recovery' opens up its own difficulties. In respect of this dilemma, the whole issue of waste management controls and the reclamation industry needs to be kept in perspective. As is made clear in Chapter 1, the scrap industry is already part of the 'waste industry' (however defined)[1]. These sectors will move closer and become more integrated with the increased emphasis by policy makers on recycling and by rising waste disposal prices caused by such mechanisms as the landfill tax[2] and the Landfill Directive[3]. It is also increasingly clear that policy-makers are becoming less willing to consider this industry as a special case: the British exemption and licensing system of metal recycling facilities[4], as well as the proposed Directives on End of Life Vehicles and Electronic Wastes[5], exemplify this trend. Many scrap processing plants are highly polluting if inadequately controlled[6] – those that are not can be subject to the system of registration set out by the Directive on Waste[7]. Virtually all large carriers of scrap metal have already obtained registration under the Control of Pollution (Amendment) Act 1989 on the grounds that sometimes they will carry scrap which is controlled waste[8]. Finally, scrap metal furnaces do not need waste management licences anyway. Instead they have always required authorisation under Pt I of the EPA 1990[9].

1 See para 1.37ff. Interestingly a 1997 Resolution of the European Steel and Coal Consulative Committee on the classification of scrap (OJ C356/8 22.11.97) clearly regards *all* EC scrap as currently falling within the Community definition of waste.
2 See para 1.100ff.
3 See para 1.23ff.
4 See Chapter 11.
5 See para 1.29.
6 Besides land contamination, a developing problem, although outside the remit of the EPA 1990 (see para 2.53), is radioactive contamination due to improper dismantling of scrap containing radioactive sources from, for example, medical equipment.
7 See Chapter 11.
8 See Chapter 6, also para 3.148ff and see *Mayer Parry Recycling Ltd v Environment Agency* [1999] Env LR 489 at 576, para 28 to Appendix 1.
9 But, if it is accepted that a scrap furnace is embraced by the Directive on Waste, the 'relevant objectives' of the Directive will need to be followed in any authorisation: see para 12.22.

2.154 In addition, the nature of the correct issue at stake here needs careful analysis. There seems little dispute that, in respect of the reclamation industry, the legislation as it is currently drafted has the potential to cause uncertainty. But Purdue and Cheyne[1] make a very valid and widely applicable point in their analysis of Annex 2 of Circular 11/94:

'The Circular suggests as an example the transfer of used clothes for charitable purposes, and argues that it would be "artificial and unnecessary" to regulate such transfers. This is certainly true, but it does not necessarily mean that such transfers should be excluded from the general definition of waste. The issue is only whether such transfers should be subject to regulation.'

Hence it seems valid to argue that legislators should address particular problem areas[2] and that the courts should not supersede this role. For example, one of the main objections by the metal recycling industry against being subject to waste management controls does not seem to be whether the actual facilities should be licensed[2]. More it is over such matters as controlled waste transfer notes or special waste controls. If it really does cost £8,400 per facility to operate the duty of care transfer note system[3] and that there is no environmental benefit from this system, then surely this can be addressed by way of minor changes to national law?

1   Purdue M and Cheyne I 'Fitting Definition to Purpose: The Search for a Satisfactory Definition of Waste' (1995) JEL 149 at 167.
2   It may be that the latter argument was unsuccessfully fought when scrapyards become licensable and a 'last stand' has been made in the form of *Mayer Parry Recycling Ltd v Environmental Agency* [1999] Env LR 489.
3   See 'Barriers to Sustainable Waste Management: A Plea for Recycling', Memorandum by the British Secondary Metals Association, in House of Commons Environment, Transport and Regional Affairs Committee Session 1997–98, Sixth Report *Sustainable Waste Management*, Volume III, p 309. Transfer notes are discussed at para 3.118.

2.155   Given the centrality of waste definitions to the entire waste control system, it does seem particularly undesirable to tinker with that foundation on the ad hoc, case-by-case basis which is the inevitable product of litigation. As the above discussion has hopefully shown, national and international waste management law has subtle cross-connections which may not always be apparent – or relevant – to either party in any particular proceedings. The resultant judgment – especially at the level of the lower courts – may inadvertently conflict with national obligations under particular treaties. Whilst the most obvious example of the latter is Community law, other provisions such as the Basel Convention[1] or decisions of the OECD[2] may come into play, particularly where recoverable materials are concerned. A court may not be made aware of the whole picture and hence be unable to act accordingly. The most desirable approach may well be to assess whether there is a genuine need to alter existing laws in the name of 'over-regulation' and to fine-tune national or international law accordingly.

1   The Basel Convention on the Control of Transboundary Movements of Hazardous Wastes and their Disposal: see para 5.12ff.
2   OECD Decision on the Control of Transfrontier Movements of Waste Destined for Recovery Operations: see para 5.21ff.

The role of the waste producer in the discarding of waste

2.156   An important matter which does not seem to have received adequate attention in the *Tombesi*, *Wallonie* and *Mayer Parry* decisions is that the definition of waste in the Directive on Waste is constructed in a manner which is subjective. Instead, the European Court has attempted to look for objective rules. But the wording clearly shows that the focus of the definition is upon the waste 'holder' and that waste is involved when that person discards, intends to discard or is required to discard a particular substance.

2.157   The matter of how the concept of the 'holder' operates in the wording of the definition of waste needs to be approached carefully. The term 'holder' is defined in the Directive on Waste[1] as meaning:

'. . . the producer of the waste or the natural or legal person who is in possession of it.'

Likewise, the term 'producer' in this context is also defined[2] as meaning:

'. . . anyone whose activities produce waste ("original producer") and/or anyone who carries out pre-processing, mixing or other operations resulting in a change in the nature or composition of this waste.'

1   Council Directive of 15 July 1975 on Waste (75/442/EEC), (OJ L194/39 25.7.75) (as amended by
    Council Directive of 18 March 1991 amending Directive 75/442/EEC on Waste (91/156/EEC),
    (OJ L78/32 26.3.91), Article 1(b)).
2   Council Directive of 15 July 1975 on Waste (75/442/EEC), (OJ L194/39 25.7.75) (as amended by
    Council Directive of 18 March 1991 amending Directive 75/442/EEC on Waste (91/156/EEC),
    (OJ L78/32 26.3.91), Article 1(c)).

2.158   Like the Directive, both the current definition of waste in the Waste Management Licensing Regulations 1994 and the amendment proposed in the Environment
Act 1995 approach the identity of the person undertaking the discarding process in this
fashion. The Waste Management Licensing Regulations 1994 require that the
discarding process is enacted by 'the producer or person in possession' of the waste.
The proposed amendment to s 75(2) of the EPA 1990 is similar, but introduces the
Directive's term 'holder' to encompass both the producer and any other person in
possession of the waste. Both the current and proposed definitions of waste also
contain the Directive's definition of waste 'producer'. In the Waste Management
Licensing Regulations 1994[1] this individual constitutes 'anyone whose activities
produce Directive waste or who carries out preprocessing, mixing or other operations
resulting in a change in its nature or composition'[2].

1   SI 1994/1056, reg 1(3).
2   The Environment Act 1995 contains a slightly different wording which is closer to the Directive: 'any
    person whose activities produce waste or any person who carries out preprocessing, mixing or other
    operations resulting in a change in the nature or composition of this waste' (Environment Act 1995,
    Sch 22, para 88(2), which will replace s 75(2) of the EPA 1990).

2.159   It should therefore be evident that there is an array of what appear to be overlapping terms contained in the legislation. The term 'producer' can have two identities.
In addition, there are also persons defined as acting as 'holders' and also being in
possession of waste. Although the correct identity of the person who makes the decision to discard waste is a fundamental concept in waste definitions[1], it is unfortunate
that this person is not always readily identifiable from the face the legislation. The
result is that confusion is an easy outcome.

1   The term also has significance in relation to other enactments which make up British waste regulation
    law, including the Controlled Waste (Registration of Carriers and Seizure of Vehicles) Regulations
    1991 (waste 'producers' are exempt from carrier registration unless they are to transport building and
    demolition waste: SI 1991/1624, reg 2(1)(b): see para 6.10ff) and the Duty of Care (EPA 1990, s 34:
    see para 3.79ff). Difficulties may occur in deciding the primary responsibilities for the transfer note
    system under the duty of care) and in the identification of persons acting as waste brokers
    (SI 1994/1056, Sch 5: see para 3.101ff). The Special Waste Regulations 1996 (SI 1996/972), however,
    instead use the term 'consignor': see para 4.73.

2.160   However, there would appear to be a consistency of emphasis in the texts of
repealed, current and proposed definitions of waste to the effect that waste should be
primarily defined in terms of the producer's point of view[1]. Whilst at first sight this
may not be immediately apparent from *Vessoso and Zanetti*[2], a full consideration of
the context of the judgment of the European Court would also point to this conclusion. Although this matter has yet to be subject to detailed judicial interpretation, it is
difficult to envisage a workable definition of waste stemming from an alternative
approach.

1   Although the landfill tax relates to a different wording for the definition of waste (see the Finance Act
    1996, s 64 and see HM Customs and Excise (1997) *A General Guide to the Landfill Tax*, Notice
    LFT1, para 1.3) follows the approach that waste is to be defined from the producer's point of view.
2   Discussed at para 2.78 above.

2.161 From para 2.78 above, it will be recalled that the *Vessoso* judgment related to the definition of waste contained in the Directive on Waste[1] in its unamended form. While the judgment addressed the question of whether recyclable materials of value could be wastes, it did not directly investigate the identity of the person in a waste transaction who takes the decision that a substance should be a waste. In the unamended Directive, the definition of waste was cast loosely and, for this reason, the wording was subject to significant tightening by Directive 91/156 in 1993. However, it is important to appreciate that it was the original definition of waste which was considered by the European Court in *Vessoso*. This definition held that[2]:

'. . . "waste" means any substance or object which the holder disposes of or is required to dispose of pursuant to the provisions of national law in force.'

What is important to note is that the term 'holder', unlike the case of the amended definition, was not defined, being left to have its ordinary meaning. Accordingly, in *Vessoso* it was held that[3]:

'. . . the protection of human health and the safeguarding of the environment, would be jeopardized if the application of those directives were dependent on whether or not the holder intended to exclude all economic re-utilisation by others of the substances or objects of which he disposes.'

This essentially means that the purpose of the Directive on Waste would be thwarted if the Directive is not to apply in instances where a holder wishes to consign waste to recovery. In essence, an identical substance cannot be defined as a waste when it passes to disposal but not when it is sent for recovery. This is perhaps the fundamental point of *Vessoso and Zanetti*.

1   Council Directive of 15 July 1975 on Waste (75/442/EEC), (OJ L194/39 25.7.75).
2   Council Directive of 15 July 1975 on Waste (75/442/EEC), (OJ L194/39 25.7.75) as amended by Council Directive of 15 July 1975 on Waste (75/442/EEC), (OJ L194/39 25.7.75) as amended by Council Directive of 18 March 1991 amending Directive 75/442/EEC on Waste (91/156/EEC), (OJ L78/32 26.3.91), Article 1(a).
3   *Criminal Proceedings against G Vessoso and G Zanetti* [1990] ECR I-1461 at 1478, para 12.

2.162 By analogy, therefore, it would similarly defeat the purpose of the Directive if it were possible for persons to receive a waste – in their capacity as the subsequent holders in a waste transaction – and be able to subjectively reconfigure the legal status of a waste to a raw material without actually changing its nature. If this was permissible, the subsequent holder would be in a position to unilaterally determine whether or not the material in question should be subject to legislative control. That this is inappropriate was also a conclusion of the European Court in *Tombesi*[1]. An inapplicably wide utilisation of this principle would cause most, if not all, waste recycling facilities to fall outside statutory controls when they were recovering 'wastes' of a positive value. For obvious reasons, this is a highly undesirable scenario and one which the Court in *Vessoso and Zanetti* clearly found against[2]. Accordingly, this analysis would suggest that, once the original producer determined that a substance is a waste, it remains so defined until it is subject to some form of processing which significantly changes its nature or composition. Any other interpretation of the legislation would appear to invite the possibility of substances switching in or out of statutory controls. Other individuals can only take the decision to discard a material in exceptional circumstances. This argument appears to become more attractive when the permissible roles under the legislation of subsequent waste holders are analysed.

1 *Criminal Proceedings against Tombesi* [1998] Env LR 59 at 88 para 54: see also *Environment Agency v Short* [1999] Env LR 300 which involved an unsuccessful argument that timber apparently destined for domestic fires was not waste.
2 The argument that a material remains defined as waste until processed also finds support in Circular 11/94 (see Annex 2, para 2.46).

The role of other waste holders in 'discarding'

2.163 If the definition of waste solely revolved around the intent of the original producer, there would be no need to consider the influence of the actions of other parties in waste transactions, particularly how they relate to, and affect, the manner by which waste is defined. However, the legislation permits other individuals to take decisions which may determine whether a substance is or is not to be considered as waste. As suggested above, the opportunities available to re-define a particular material from being a waste to constituting products or goods should be viewed as highly restricted in practice and must be subject to a careful analysis. Both the provisions of the Directive on Waste and British law have potential to cause confusion in these respects. As noted, the problem stems from the manner in which the Directive introduces the array of persons who can ostensibly determine whether a substance is or is not discarded. Persons who appear to be allowed to make such a decision are:

(a) the waste producer, who can either be:

   (i) a person whose activities produce waste[1]; or

   (ii) anyone who carries out pre-processing, mixing or other operations resulting in a change in the nature or composition of the waste; or

(b) a person who is in possession of the waste.

But these – particularly item (b) – need to be read in the light of the above argument, which has suggested that once a material has been discarded by the producer it is waste. It remains waste when in the hands of the carrier, even if the carrier has a use for it. It stays as waste when it is delivered to a disposal or recovery facility. Being waste when it arrives, the recipient site will need to satisfy the requirements on permits or registrations as required by Articles 9, 10 and 11 of the Directive on Waste. The fact that a recipient of the waste has a use for the incoming material does not mean that it is no longer waste. The material stays waste until processed.

1 Referred to in Article 1(b) of the Directive as the 'original producer'.

2.164 The arrangement just described appears to be envisaged by the dual meaning allocated by the legislation to the term 'waste producer'. The 'waste producer' is held in the Directive on Waste to be either the original producer '... and/or anyone who carries out pre-processing, mixing or other operations resulting in a change in the nature or composition of this waste'[1]. The purpose of the latter phrase is in respect of any site where waste is not subject to final disposal, but where it is to be subject to some form of intermediate processing or recovery. For example, it has particular application at waste transfer stations, sites where the 'mixing' of waste takes place[2]. It also applies to recovery and treatment plants where wastes may be not only subject to 'mixing', but where 'pre-processing' and 'other operations resulting in a change in the nature or composition' of the waste occur. Accordingly, the legislation is allowing for the fact that, when waste is processed, the identity of the producer moves on from the original producer to the operator of the waste management facility which caused the nature of the waste to be transformed. As the identity of the producer has changed, the status of the material as a waste is reassessed in the light of the circumstances of the 'new' producer. Whether a substance is waste depends on whether the 'new' producer discards, intends or is required to discard it.

1 There are some minor, but not significant, differences in the precise wording in the equivalent phrase in the Waste Management Licensing Regulations 1994 and in the amendment to the EPA 1990 found in the Environment Act 1995.
2 Transfer stations can be either disposal or recovery facilities under the Directive on Waste, see Annexes IIA and IIB, Items D15 and R13 (Tables 2.2 and 2.3 above).

2.165 But it seems essential that, when the identity of the producer is to change and when materials which were hitherto wastes are to be reclassified as goods, the operations undertaken on the material have satisfied the test of causing a significant change in the 'nature or composition' of the waste. If no such change has occurred, the material stays waste as defined by the original producer[1]. To use Carnwath J's term in *Mayer Parry Recycling Ltd v Environment Agency*[2]: the recovery process must be 'complete'. Therefore, for example, the Waste Management Licensing Regulations 1994 contain an exemption from waste management licensing in respect of shredding, chipping etc of waste plant matter, including wood and bark[3]. The exemption also extends to the storage of the resultant materials, which has a notable contrast to many other exemptions which solely exempt storage prior to processing[4]. The existence of the post-processing storage element in the exemption for plant matter clearly indicates that the legislation views such materials as remaining as defined as waste when produced in these circumstances[5].

1 This argument finds support in *Tombesi* (see para 2.84ff above), where the application of a simple grinding process was not considered sufficient to cause a substance to fall out of the definition of waste. It is also given credence in respect of the landfill tax: see HM Customs and Excise (1997) *A General Guide to the Landfill Tax*, Notice LFT1, para 1.3.
2 [1999] Env LR 489 at 505, para 46: see para 2.136.
3 SI 1994/1056, Sch 3, para 21(1): see para 10.203ff.
4 For example, contrast the wording of SI 1994/1056, Sch 3, paras 21(2)–22(2) on silver recovery (see para 10.197).
5 See Circular 11/94, Annex 5, para 5.164.

2.166 Finally, there is the question of the purpose of the provisions of the legislation which appear to allow that the discarding decision to be open to not only the producer of the waste but also a person who is in possession of it[1]. It would seem that the objective here is to address other occasions when a person may be in possession of waste, but not have produced it in the sense of either causing its production by an industrial process or by way of consumption activities. An example of such an instance might be a person who purchased an industrial unit containing waste or where someone wishes to remove waste which was flytipped on their land[2].

1 Directive on Waste, Article 1(c) (as amended by Directive 91/156, Article 1); SI 1994/1056, reg 1(3); Environment Act 1995, Sch 22, para 88(2).
2 Any more extensive interpretation of the role of the 'person in possession of the waste' would lead to the following difficulty. It has already been noted that, in Article 1(b) of the Directive (and in the British legislation), the producer is defined as the original producer '... and/or anyone who carries out pre-processing, mixing or other operations resulting in a change in the nature or composition of this waste'. If the term 'person in possession of the waste' was to have an inordinately wide meaning, the final portion of the Directive's definition of waste producer would serve no purpose.

2.167 This analysis would therefore suggest that the legislation is in fact envisaging a hierarchical list of waste producers. At first instance, the discarding decision is always to be undertaken by the original producer. Only in exceptional circumstances will other persons be in a position to make such a determination. These circumstances will usually be when the composition of the waste has been changed by specified processing at a waste management facility – where these activities satisfy the criteria of the legislation concerning pre-processing, mixing or other operations which alter the nature of the waste. In this case, the material may no longer be considered to be waste due to the success of the recovery process. Alternatively, it will remain as waste as the operator of the facility – as the new producer – discards it. The hierarchical approach would indicate that, only when it is not possible to categorise a person in these terms, does it become the person who is in possession of the waste who is able to make the discarding decision. This will be probably only where there is no producer identifiable within the other categories just described[1].

1 It should be noted that the idea of a hierarchical approach to responsibilities for waste features in other EC waste management law. The Council Regulation on Transfrontier Waste Shipments (Regulation 259/93: see para 5.79) identifies notifiers – persons responsible for the correct completion of the required pre-notification and waste tracking document – in this fashion (Regulation 259/93, Article 2(g)).

Defining waste: some British case law

2.168 Unfortunately, other than the *Mayer Parry* judgment[1], there have been few cases turning on the question of the national definition of waste since the EPA 1990 was enacted[2]. However, despite the exact wording being changed since the concept of Directive waste was promulgated in British law, the approach that waste is defined mainly from the point of view of the original holder has conceptual similarity to that contained in the Control of Pollution Act 1974[3]. Therefore, case law derived from that definition can be used to illustrate this general approach. The key issue is whether the producer has somehow 'discarded' the material in the first instance. This can be either a conscious decision or can be implied from the producer's actions.

1 *Mayer Parry Recycling Ltd v Environment Agency* [1999] Env LR 489: see para 2.136.
2 There have been a number of decisions on waste definitions under the Landfill Tax by the VAT and Duties Tribunal: *Taylor Woodrow Construction Northern Ltd v Customs and Excise Comrs* (12 November 1998, Manchester Tribunal Centre); *ICI Chemicals and Polymers Ltd v Customs and Excise Comrs* ([1998] V & DR 310, Manchester Tribunal Centre; *FI Gamble and Sons Ltd v Customs and Excise Comrs* ([1998] V & DR 481, London Tribunal Centre), *Darfish Ltd v Customs and Excise Comrs* (Manchester Tribunal Centre, 26 March 1999: under appeal to the High Court). However, the definition of waste is different in the Finance Act 1996 and hence these are not discussed in detail below.
3 Control of Pollution Act 1974, s 30(1).

2.169 Given that the earlier precedents stemming from the Control of Pollution Act 1974 will have less relevance due to changes resultant from the introduction of the concept of 'Directive waste' by the Waste Management Licensing Regulations 1994, they have not been integrated into the earlier discussion. Instead they are summarised below in general terms to show the approach taken by the Courts in the past. However, the similarities in the objectives of the Control of Pollution Act 1974 and the EPA 1990 allow analogies to be drawn between the earlier case law and the EPA 1990's provisions.

2.170 In *Long v Brooke*[1], Chapman J in Bradford Crown Court found that waste should be defined under the Control of Pollution Act 1974 from the point of view of the producer. *Long v Brooke* involved the deposition of soil and sub-soil as part of the restoration of an old quarry. The defendant, who owned the quarry, was approached by a developer who wished to dispose of a large quantity of these materials. The defendant was paid for the deposition in the quarry, but it was claimed that such a payment was off-set by the cost of hiring plant to undertake the restoration activities.

1   [1980] Crim LR 109. Affirmed in the Scottish case of *H.L. Friel & Son v Inverclyde District Council* [1994] SCLR 561 at 564E.

2.171   At the Crown Court, it was argued that, from the point of view of the recipient of the soil, its deposition in the quarry would restore the quarry. Hence the soil was of value to the recipient. However, Chapman J found that the definition of waste in the Control of Pollution Act 1974 viewed waste from the point of view of the person discarding the material. Hence if the soil was surplus to the developer, it should be seen as a waste. This is regardless of whether the recipient actually wanted the material. Accordingly, the quarry owner was convicted of contravening the Control of Pollution Act 1974.

2.172   In *Berridge Incinerators*[1], the approach of *Long v Brooke* was affirmed by Crawford J in the Divisional Court. The *Berridge* case involved a complex dispute over whether Berridge Incinerators Ltd had valid planning permission – and hence whether the incineration facility could actually be issued a waste disposal licence under the Control of Pollution Act 1974 – for its continued activities. As part of the judgment, Crawford J considered the definition of waste under the Control of Pollution Act 1974 and noted:

> 'It is, of course, a truism that one man's waste is another man's raw material. The fact that a price is paid by the collector of material to its originator is, no doubt, relevant; but I do not regard it as crucial. If I have an old fireplace to dispose of to a passing rag and bone man, its character as a waste is not affected by whether or not I can persuade the latter to pay me 50 pence for it. In my judgement, the correct approach is to regard the material from the point of view of the person who produces it. Is it something which is produced as a product, or even as a by-product of his business, or is it something to be disposed of as useless? I notice that this was the approach adopted by His Honour Judge Chapman QC in the Crown Court (*Long v Brook . . .*) and I respectfully agree with it.'

Besides the affirmation of the Crown Court's decision in *Long v Brooke*, the *Berridge* judgment clearly confirms that wastes are not to be seen as restricted to substances which possess a negative value. If a person is receiving a discarded material for payment, that material may be a waste. This reasoning seems also very much in line with *Vessoso and Zanetti*[2].

1   *Berridge Incinerators Ltd v Nottinghamshire County Council*, 14 April 1987, unreported, QBD.
2   See para 2.78 above.

2.173   The case of *Kent County Council v Queenborough Rolling Mill*[1] took an essentially similar approach to the *Berridge Incinerators* judgment. The rolling mill company wished to increase the height of some of its land by importing materials from a construction site. The construction site was located on an old pottery, and contained extensive deposits of waste china clay, broken china, concrete and general rubbish. These materials were sorted by a contractor and only substances such as china clay, pottery, concrete and ballast were sent to the Queenborough Site. The site did not have the benefit of a waste disposal licence under the Control of Pollution Act 1974[2]. No payment was made by the Company to the contractor for the material.

1   *Kent County Council v Queenborough Rolling Mill Company Ltd* (1990) 89 LGR 306. Affirmed in the Scottish case of *H.L. Friel & Son Ltd v Inverclyde District Council* 1994 SCLR 561 at 564E.
2   Under the EPA 1990 it would probably be exempt from the need to possess a waste management licence: see SI 1994/1056, Sch 3 (para 10.112).

2.174 On conviction at the lower court, the Company appealed. The grounds were that the excavated materials from the old pottery were not controlled wastes, mainly for the reason that they were put to a useful purpose and that they had been pre-sorted.

2.175 The Divisional Court found that the use to which the materials were put was 'irrelevant in this situation'[1]. The material had been originally discarded by the pottery and lain there for many years. The nature of the material had to be considered when it was removed from the construction site. It was decided that, at the time of its excavation, the material was waste within the meaning of s 30 of the Control of Pollution Act 1974: 'The usefulness . . . of the deposit as fill on the receiving site did not change the character of the material.'[2] Hence once the deposited material was defined as waste, it remains so defined. While the sorting process of the wastes resulted in one stream of the sorted material being consigned for land reclamation, it was held that the sorted material still should be viewed as 'controlled waste'. The judgment makes clear that the separation of materials into different factions after excavation did not cause its nature as waste to be changed[3].

1 *Kent County Council v Queenborough Rolling Mill Company Ltd* (1990) 89 LGR 306 at 315.
2 *Kent County Council v Queenborough Rolling Mill Company Ltd* (1990) 89 LGR 306 at 315.
3 *Kent County Council v Queenborough Rolling Mill Company Ltd* (1990) 89 LGR 306 at 315:
however, and rather confusingly, Pill J then adds 'Different considerations might apply if material is recycled or reconstituted before the deposit complained of'.

2.176 It will be apparent that this judgment seems consistent with the later decision of *Tombesi* that an intermediate process involving grinding was not sufficient to take a material out of the definition of waste. In addition, the facts of *Queenborough Rolling Mill* also can be used to provide a demonstration of the manner in which the definition of waste under the EPA 1990 causes the identity of the waste producer to transfer when 'pre-processing, mixing and other operations' have been completed on the waste[1]. It would seem correct to assert that the contractors supplying the waste to the rolling mill company would become the 'producer' of this waste once the waste passed through their sorting process[2].

1 See also *HL Friel v Inverclyde District Council* 1994 SCLR 561 at 564C/D.
2 The contractors are clearly persons who received the waste produced originally by the pottery and who undertook activities which constitute '. . .pre-processing, mixing or other operations resulting in a change in the nature or composition of . . . waste'.

2.177 Whether the material passed to the rolling mill company remains defined as waste under the amended definition in the EPA 1990 turns on whether the contractors, as waste producer, can be viewed as 'discarding' the material. In this example the waste was given away. This might be used to suggest that the sorted materials were being discarded[1].

1 This assertion may receive support from the extensive list of activities which are exempt from the requirement of the EPA 1990 to possess a waste management licence (EPA 1990, s 33(3) and SI 1994/1056, reg 17 and Sch 3: see Chapter 10). Of particular significance are those activities involving the re-use of wastes from the construction industry (para 10.110ff discusses these activities).

2.178 If nothing else, the judgment in *Ashcroft v Michael McErlain Ltd*[1] showed that excavation materials from construction sites were not – under the Control of Pollution Act 1974 – always to be viewed as waste. Michael McErlain Ltd had been contracted to excavate a field to allow a link road to be constructed from the highway to a site of a proposed factory. The excavation material was immediately transported from the site by the company. It was deposited at a riding school in order to raise the level of a paddock and to improve drainage.

1   *Ashcroft v Michael McErlain Ltd* (30 January 1985, unreported), QBD.

2.179   May LJ held that, while excavated soils could constitute waste, on the facts of this particular case the soil removed was not so defined. He used a dictionary to provide guidance on the nature of 'waste' and asked the question whether the excavated material was matter which had been eliminated or thrown aside[1]. In the instant case, he held that the material was not waste, mainly for the fact that someone had an immediate use for it. If the soil had been stockpiled and someone had come along later and asked for it, May LJ felt that it may well have been waste: but this was not the issue here.

1   A reason for this was that the definition of waste in the Control of Pollution Act 1974 states that waste 'includes' certain listed items. Hence other items not listed could also fall within the definition. Accordingly, May LJ placed primary emphasis on the ordinary meaning of the term 'waste'. This approach may no longer appropriate in the context of either Directive waste or the proposed amendment to s 75(2) of the EPA 1990. Both these make clear that the term waste 'means' the various items listed. Accordingly, items outside that list cannot be waste.

2.180   May LJ appears to be saying that the soil only becomes waste after it has had some physical operation done to it. And in this respect he appears to rely more on the dictionary definition of waste than the definition contained in s 30 of the Control of Pollution Act 1974[1]. By relying on the dictionary definition, he makes extensive use of the word 'discarded' and sees this in the context of piling the soil up at the roadside or placing it in skips. However, this might be criticised as a rather narrow view. Firstly, although clearly not 'discarded' at the point prior to excavation, the soil was *unwanted* when it was in situ and before it has been disturbed, primarily because it was in the way of a proposed access road to a factory. It is usual practice in the construction industry, mainly for the reason to avoid the double-handling of the excavated material, that an outlet for excavation material is found prior to the excavation starting.

1   Indeed May LJ's extensive use of the Dictionary definition appears to be almost at the expense of the definition contained in the statute itself.

2.181   While this decision appears open to criticism in respect of the statutory provisions extant at that time, it is useful to consider the effect of either the Directive waste concept or the proposed amendment to s 75 of the EPA 1990 on this circumstances of this decision. As noted, May LJ appeared to consider that a substance became waste only after a physical act of discarding. In the light of the changes made to the definition of waste in 1994, this may no longer be the case. Both the new and proposed definitions state that waste is a substance which the holder 'discards or intends or is required to discard'. It may well be possible to argue that the material in *McErlain* was *intended to be* discarded. This intention perhaps is sufficient to make it waste as soon as excavation works commenced.

2.182   Although the case of *Cheshire County Council v Armstrong's Transport (Wigan) Ltd*[1] was also made under the Control of Pollution Act 1974, this case may have considerable relevance to an appreciation of the word 'discard' in the amended statutory definition of waste. This is a consequence of the manner by which Butler-Sloss LJ sets out her decision, with the *ratio decidendi* appearing to be readily applicable as much to the Directive waste concept and the proposed amendment to s 75(2) of the EPA 1990 as it did to the Control of Pollution Act 1974. In this respect, this judgment could be viewed as somewhat distinct from those others summarised in this section.

1   [1995] Env LR 62.

2.183   In *Cheshire County Council*, the defendant company were subcontracted to undertake two activities at a site were existing flats were to be demolished and replaced by new housing association accommodation. The first activity was to remove all the miscellaneous demolition waste for licensed disposal. There was no suggestion that this was not done correctly. Secondly, the company was contracted to crush all the concrete resultant from the demolition of the flats. Once crushed, the concrete was to be re-utilised at the site to provide the footings for the new buildings.

2.184   It was originally envisaged that the concrete was to be crushed on site. But the company was advised by the local borough council of the nuisance this operation would cause to residents. Accordingly, the crushing machinery was relocated. These activities duly proceeded at a separate site, with a temporary crushing plant being installed. Broken concrete and crushed material was stored on the site, with the latter being returned to the original site of demolition to provide the foundations.

2.185   Summonses were issued by the County Council against Armstrong Transport, with the principal allegation being the company's failure to obtain a waste disposal licence for the crushing facility[1]. At both the Magistrates' Court and the Divisional Court, the case turned on whether 'waste' was being dealt with.

1   This type of activity would now usually be exempt under the Waste Management Licensing Regulations 1994: see para 10.117ff.

2.186   Butler-Sloss LJ held that a number of factors must be satisfied for a material to fall within the definition of 'waste'[1]:

'It has to be that which is disposed of, discarded, got rid of, not needed any more, by the person who is in the process of discarding it or disposing of it. It has to be of no further use to that person who has possibly produced and is certainly discarding the material. In my judgement, both the *Kent County Council* case and *Long v Brooke* are to be distinguished from the present facts. The one contract which this respondent engaged in was a contract to remove waste and dispose of it in such a way as the respondent chose, and also to remove concrete blocks, crush them and return them to the site. As the magistrates said in their opinion, the concrete throughout the whole process remained the property of the housing association or the demolition contractor. The respondent never regarded the concrete as waste to be disposed of; they could not have sold it; they could not have disposed of it in any way they chose and they were under the obligation of the contract to return it to the original site from where it had been removed. That, in my judgment, is far removed from the interpretation of "waste" in section 30 of the Control of Pollution Act, which requires that the substances should be unwanted, to be disposed of, or to be discarded. In this particular case, quite simply, it was to be taken away, processed, and returned.'

This finding appears to have been subsequently affirmed by *Meston Technical Services Ltd v Warwickshire County Council*[2], where the Divisional Court held:

'Reading the judgment [ie *Cheshire County Council*] as a whole, what the learned Lord Justice [ie Butler-Sloss LJ] had in mind in my view was the approach to the material by the owners of it. Their state of mind, as summarised in the [*Cheshire CC*] judgment, was such that the material did not constitute waste.'

1   *Cheshire County Council v Armstrong's Transport (Wigan) Ltd* [1995] Env LR 62, at 65.
2   (10 March 1995, unreported), QBD: discussed below.

2.187   Finally, *Meston Technical Services Ltd v Warwickshire County Council*[1] involved a solvent recovery facility which was subject to a waste disposal licence under the Control of Pollution Act 1974. Waste was deposited in drums outside the area of the premises which was subject to the licence and also in breach of conditions of the site's licence. These actions contravened s 3 of the Control of Pollution Act 1974. The case turned on whether the materials deposited were 'waste' under the Control of Pollution Act 1974. For the defendants it was claimed that the deposited solvents were in fact 'materials to be sold on' for other purposes, rather than wastes.

1   *Meston Technical Services Ltd v Warwickshire County Council* (10 March 1995, unreported), QBD.

2.188   Two points were put before the Divisional Court. However due to the replacement of the Control of Pollution Act 1974 by the EPA 1990, only one remains relevant. It was claimed on behalf of the solvent recovery company that a material constituted waste only where there was an intention by the person in possession the material to dispose of it or abandon it. If the material was valuable to the solvent recovery company, it was not waste and hence it was argued that *Meston* should be viewed as analogous to *Cheshire County Council v Armstrong's Transport (Wigan) Ltd*[1].

1   See para 2.182 above .

2.189   However, the Divisional Court considered that the facts of *Meston* were quite different from *Cheshire County Council*:

'I do not regard the *Cheshire County Council* case as authority for the proposition that, provided the depositor (the defendant) does not regard the material as waste and he proposes to make use of it by sale or in some other way, the material is taken out of the category of waste. That appears to me to be contrary to the reasoning both in the *Kent County Council*[1] decision and the *Cheshire County Council decision*.'[2]

Accordingly the appellants were convicted. Although the court does not appear to have been referred to *Vessoso and Zanetti*[3], in the light of that judgment it would seem to have been difficult to decide *Meston* in any other manner.

1   *Kent County Council v Queenborough Rolling Mills*: see para 2.173.
2   See also *HL Friel & Son Ltd v Inverclyde District Council* 1994 SCLR 561 at 564C/F.
3   [1990] ECR I-1461.

CONTROLLED WASTE

Controlled waste and the Controlled Waste Regulations 1992

2.190   While considerable significance must be placed on the understanding of the definition of waste, the term 'controlled waste' also needs to be approached carefully. This is because the sole focus of the EPA 1990's waste management control system is upon controlled wastes. Items such as waste management licences, the duty of care, and carrier registration do not pertain to substances which are not embraced by this highly important term.

2.191 'Controlled waste' is defined in s 75 of the EPA 1990[1]:

' "Controlled waste" means household, industrial and commercial waste or any such waste.'

The Waste Management Licensing Regulations 1994 cause wastes which are not 'Directive waste'[2] not to be household, industrial or commercial wastes[3].

1 EPA 1990, s 75(4).
2 See para 2.35.
3 SI 1992/588, reg 7A, as amended by SI 1994/1056, reg 24(8).

2.192 The terms 'household, industrial and commercial waste' are subject to their own individual definitions in the EPA 1990[1]. These primarily relate to the types of premises from which waste is produced and will be individually covered later in this section. Besides these definitions, s 75(8) of the EPA 1990 allows the Secretary of State to make regulations which assign particular classes of waste to any of these three categories. The current provisions are the Controlled Waste Regulations 1992[2]. The Regulations both extend the breadth of the categories of household, industrial and commercial wastes and also provide demarcation as to which category a particular type of waste belongs. The Regulations are accompanied by their own Circular: Circular 14/92[3].

1 EPA 1990, s 75(5), (6) and (7).
2 SI 1992/588: the predecessor regulations were the Collection and Disposal of Waste Regulations 1988 (SI 1988/819), which themselves superseded the Control of Pollution (Licensing of Waste Disposal) Regulations 1976 (SI 1976/732).
3 *The Environmental Protection Act 1990 – Parts II and IV The Controlled Waste Regulations*, HMSO, London.

2.193 Subject to a small number of specific exceptions, the penal requirements of Pt II of the EPA 1990 do not differentiate between the three types of controlled waste. However, on some occasions care must be taken to ensure the waste in question fits into one of the three categories. Otherwise the EPA 1990 will not apply.

2.194 The manner in which the statutory definition of 'controlled waste' is to be approached was considered in *Thanet District Council v Kent County Council*[1]. Although *Thanet District Council* concerned the Control of Pollution Act 1974 and the Collection and Disposal of Waste Regulations 1988[2], the case is of relevance to the EPA 1990 and the Controlled Waste Regulations 1992. The wording of the relevant sub-sections of the two Acts[3] are virtually identical and the Controlled Waste Regulations 1992 serve the same purpose as the earlier Collection and Disposal of Waste Regulations 1988.

1 *Thanet District Council v Kent County Council* [1993] Env LR 391.
2 SI 1988/819.
3 Control of Pollution Act 1974, s 30(1) and the EPA 1990, s 75(4).

2.195 *Thanet District Council* concerned a composting plant and transfer station operated by the local authority. Along with litter, the District Council collected large quantities of seaweed from local beaches and mixed the material with straw for the purposes of producing a compost. The premises did not have the benefit of a waste disposal licence under the Control of Pollution Act 1974.

2.196 The case turned on the question of whether seaweed fell within the definition of controlled waste under s 30(1) of the Control of Pollution Act 1974. Of key significance was the phrase in s 30(1) that ' "Controlled waste" means household, industrial and commercial waste or any such waste'. Wright J held[1]:

'In my judgement, the expression "any such waste", in the context of section 30(1) of the 1974 Act, means that "controlled waste" is to be defined as household, industrial and commercial waste or any combination or permutation of these three classes of waste.'

Accordingly, for a material to fall within the categories of controlled waste, it must appear either in the definitions of household, industrial or commercial wastes in the primary legislation or in the regulations which set out the nature of these wastes in more detail. Wright J considered the purpose of the power in the Control of Pollution Act 1974 to make regulations which serve to assign wastes to one of the three controlled waste categories[2]. He concluded that this is[3]:

'. . . to make it clear that various materials and substances, which would not ordinarily be thought of as amounting to household, industrial and commercial waste at all, are nevertheless to be treated as though they were.'

Hence it was found that, seaweed, a substance which neither fitted into any categories of waste in the Control of Pollution Act 1974 nor those contained in the relevant regulations, could not be a controlled waste[4].

1   *Thanet District Council v Kent County Council* [1993] Env LR 391, at 394.
2   In the case of the Control of Pollution Act 1974, s 30(4), which is equivalent to the EPA 1990, s 75(8).
3   *Thanet District Council v Kent County Council* [1993] Env LR 391, at 395.
4   The seaweed composting process therefore did not require a waste disposal licence under the Control of Pollution Act 1974.

2.197   In addition to the fact that wastes which are neither encompassed by the definitions given in the EPA 1990 nor described in the Controlled Waste Regulations 1992 cannot be controlled wastes, the EPA 1990 explicitly requires that certain other wastes cannot be controlled wastes: wastes from mines and quarries or from agricultural premises are examples[1]. Likewise, the Controlled Waste Regulations 1992 also contain their own exclusions[2]. For example, they generally exclude sewage from being a controlled waste[3] unless the Controlled Waste Regulations 1992 explicitly state to the contrary[4]. The latter exclusion has some quite significant impacts on the manner by which waste management licences impinge upon the water industry. It is discussed separately at para 2.223 below for this reason.

1   The EPA 1990 precludes any regulations made under s 75 from encompassing wastes from these sources (EPA 1990, s 75(8)): however, there may be at least some doubt as to whether these exclusions still hold in the face of Community law: see para 2.26.
2   Oddly, the Controlled Waste Regulations 1992 themselves reiterate the exclusion already contained in s 75 of the EPA 1990 in respect of wastes from mines and quarries and agricultural wastes (SI 1992/588, reg 1(4)(a)).
3   And to a lesser extent sewage sludge and septic tank wastes: see para 2.223ff.
4   SI 1992/588, reg 1(4)(b).

2.198   Although the main function of the Controlled Waste Regulations 1992 is to delineate the breadth of the categories of household, commercial and industrial wastes, the Regulations also perform other tasks. Of significance are the subtle changes made by the Controlled Waste Regulations 1992 to the household, industrial and commercial waste classification in respect of specified sections of the EPA 1990. These primarily affect wastes arising at domestic properties[1], sewage and other similar materials[2] and also animal by-products[3]. These are discussed separately at para 2.218ff below.

1   SI 1992/588, regs 2(2) and 3(3).
2   SI 1992/588, regs 1(4) and 7(1).
3   SI 1992/588, reg 7(3).

2.199   A final function of the Controlled Waste Regulations 1992 is to set up decision criteria for instances when commercial charges can be made by waste collection authorities[1] for the removal of different types of waste. While the removal of household waste from domestic properties is generally free[2], collection costs can be recouped in respect of other materials such as garden waste, large objects etc[3]. These provisions are not discussed further here as they are outside the general theme of this book[4].

1   The functions of collection authorities are described at para 1.62ff.
2   EPA 1990, s 45(3).
3   The circumstances when this applies are set down in SI 1992/588, reg 4 and Sch 2.
4   However, Sch 2 to the Controlled Waste Regulations 1992, which sets down the type of household waste for which charges can be made, could be used to provide clarification when ambiguities arise in respect of how household waste is to be categorised.

Household waste

2.200   Subject to any additional meanings given to the term 'household waste' by way of subsidiary regulations[1], the term is defined in the EPA 1990 as meaning[2] waste from domestic properties[3], caravans[4], residential or nursing homes, educational establishments and hospitals.

1   EPA 1990, s 75(8).
2   EPA 1990, s 75(5).
3   'That is to say, a building or self-contained part of a building which is used wholly for the purposes of living accommodation'.
4   As defined in s 29(1) of the Caravan Sites and Control of Development Act 1960.

2.201   These sources are substantiated and/or clarified by way of reg 2 and Schedule 1 to the Controlled Waste Regulations 1992. Schedule 1 is reproduced here in Table 2.8, alongside the other types of household waste as contained in the EPA 1990 itself. It can be seen that, while the most important source of household waste is domestic properties, such waste is also generated by premises including places of religious worship, small private garages, houseboats and camp sites.

2.202   It is important to appreciate that not all substances stemming from the activities shown in Table 2.8 are household wastes in all circumstances. Some of the headings used in the Table are very general and simply describe any waste type which is not specified elsewhere in the Regulations as industrial or commercial waste. This is made clear by the construction of the Controlled Waste Regulations 1992 and was confirmed by Wright J in *Thanet District Council*[1]. For example reg 5 stipulates that, with a minor exception for waste produced by householders themselves in respect only of the duty of care[2], all construction and demolition wastes are industrial wastes, even when generated from works carried out at domestic properties[3]. Septic tank sludge is similarly restricted to be household waste only in respect of the duty of care.

1   *Thanet District Council v Kent County Council* [1993] Env LR 391, at 395: see para 2.194 above.
2   EPA 1990, s 34: see para 3.23ff.
3   SI 1992/588, reg 5(2)(a): confirmed by Circular 14/92, Annex 1, para 1.19 and Annex 2, para 2.28.

2.203   Although neither the EPA 1990 nor the Controlled Waste Regulations 1992 are as explicit as is the case for construction and demolition wastes, certain other wastes cannot be regarded as household wastes. For example, while s 75(2)(c) of the EPA 1990 indicates that waste from a hospital is generally household waste, the Controlled Waste Regulations 1992 require that waste from a hospital laboratory is always industrial waste[1]. Similarly clinical waste from hospitals is always industrial waste[2].

1   SI 1992/588, reg 5(1) and Sch 3, para 2.
2   SI 1992/588, reg 5(1); see Circular 14/92, Annex 1, para 1.4; Annex 2, para 2.11.

Table 2.8

Household Waste

(A) *Wastes Listed in the EPA 1990*[1]
– waste from a domestic property[2];
– a caravan[3] which is 'usually and for the time being' situated on a caravan site;
– a residential home;
– premises forming part of[4] a university, school or other educational establishment;
– premises forming part of a hospital[5] or nursing home.

(B) *Wastes Listed in the Schedule 1 to the Controlled Waste Regulations 1992*
1. Waste from a hereditament or premises exempted from local non-domestic rating by virtue of –

(a) in England and Wales, paragraph 11 of Schedule 5 of the Local Government Finance Act 1988 (places of religious worship etc);
(b) in Scotland, section 22 of the Valuation and Rating (Scotland) Act 1956 (churches etc).

2. Waste from premises occupied by a charity[6] and wholly or mainly used for charitable purposes.
3. Waste from any land belonging to or used in connection with domestic property[7], a caravan[8] or a residential home.
4. Waste from a private garage which either has a floor area of 25 square metres or less or is used wholly or mainly for the accommodation of a private motor vehicle.
5. Waste from a private storage premises used wholly or mainly for the storage of articles of domestic use.
6. Waste from a moored vessel used wholly for the purposes of living accommodation.
7. Waste from a camp site[9].
8. Waste from a prison or other penal institution.
9. Waste from a hall or other premises used wholly or mainly for public meetings.
10. Waste from a royal palace.
11. Waste arising from the discharge by a local authority of its duty under section 89(2) of the EPA 1990[10].

1 EPA 1990, s 75(5).
2 'That is to say, a building or self-contained part of a building which is used wholly for the purposes of living accommodation': EPA 1990, s 75(5)(a).
3 As defined in s 29(1) of the Caravan Sites and Control of Development Act 1960: EPA1990, s 75(5)(b).
4 See Circular 14/92, Annex 1, para 1.4.
5 But excluding clinical waste: SI 1992/588, reg 5(1) and Sch 3, para 8.
6 Defined in SI 1992/588, reg 1(2) as any body of persons or trust established for charitable purposes only.
7 For definition see the EPA 1990, s 75(5)(a), Interpretation Act 1978, s 11 and Circular 14/92, Annex 1, para 1.6.
8 For definition see the EPA 1990, s 75(5)(b), Interpretation Act 1978, s 11 and Circular 14/92, Annex 1, para 1.6.
9 Defined in SI 1992/588, reg 1(2) as land on which tents are pitched for human habitation and land incidental to this use.
10 Circular 14/92, Annex 1, para 1.17 states that this includes collected dog faeces.

2.204 There is some uncertainty as to whether waste from residential dwellings on farms is always household waste. While a farmhouse might fall within the definition of 'domestic property' under s 75(5)(a), 75(7) and (8) of the EPA 1990 explicitly prevent the term 'controlled waste' encompassing wastes emanating from premises subject to the Agriculture Act 1947[1]. It may be that this exclusion extends to wastes arising from the residential aspects of the farm as a whole[2].

1 In Scotland, the Agriculture (Scotland) Act 1948.
2 As noted at para 2.43 above, this matter is expected to be addressed by way of amendments to the EPA 1990 in order to fully enact the Directive on Waste.

Industrial waste

2.205 Industrial waste is also defined in s 75 of the EPA 1990[1]. The most important category of industrial waste is that which arises from any 'factory'[2]. The EPA 1990 requires that the term 'factory' is to be interpreted in accordance with the Factories Act 1961. Section 175 of the Factories Act 1961[3] covers both the factory premises and the area within the premises' curtilage. In the Factories Act 1961, factories are held to be places where persons are employed in 'manual labour[4] in any process for or incidental to' various listed industrial activities. The definition extends to premises located in the open air[5]. The work carried on must be by way of a trade or for the purposes of gain[6] and to which an employer has a right of access and control[7]. A list is provided in the Factories Act 1961 of factory-type activities, which includes:

(a) the making of any article or of part of an article;
(b) the 'altering, repairing, ornamenting, finishing, cleaning or washing or the breaking up or demolition of any article';
(c) adapting articles for sale; and
(d) slaughtering and places where animals are confined which are neither agricultural premises[8] nor markets.

Having covered the broad classes of factory, the Factories Act 1961 also lists a range of other industrial activities which are to be treated as falling within the definition of a factory[9].

1 EPA 1990, s 75(6)(a).
2 EPA 1990, s 75(6)(a).
3 The term's crucial importance to health and safety legislation means that there is considerable case law on s 175 of the Factories Act 1961. For reasons of brevity, this material is not explored extensively below.
4 While 'manual labour' involves work with the hands, it describes both skilled and unskilled work: *J and F Stone Lighting and Radio v Haygarth* [1966] 3 All ER 539.
5 Factories Act 1961, s 175(7).
6 See for example *Hendon Corpn v Stranger* [1948] 1 All ER 377, CA: a research establishment is to be regarded as a factory.
7 Factories Act 1961, s 175(1).
8 Defined by the Agriculture Act 1947 (Agriculture (Scotland) Act 1948).
9 Factories Act 1961, s 175(2).

2.206 Of particular significance to the manner by which industrial waste is defined is the fact that the definition of a factory in the Factories Act 1961 is much broader than just manufacturing. It should be noted that the Factories Act 1961 encompasses activities involving altering, repair, washing, breaking up, demolition, etc. Hence building sites, vehicle garages, drum washing facilities, car dismantlers, demolition sites are all sources of industrial wastes under s 75(6) of the EPA 1990.

2.207 However, it should be appreciated that the definition of factory under the Factories Act 1961 does not extend to farms[1]. In addition to this exclusion, it has already been noted that s 75(7) of the EPA 1990 requires that wastes from agricultural premises cannot be controlled waste. The EPA 1990 thus contains what appears to be a duplicate exclusion. Similarly, the EPA 1990 prevents any waste from a mine or quarry being a controlled waste[2].

1 See the Factories Act 1961, s 175(1) and (2), and see for example *Kerr v Mitchell* [1959] NI 21, CA.
2 EPA 1990, s 75(7).

2.208 Besides requiring that wastes from factories subject to the Factories Act 1961 are industrial wastes[1], the EPA 1990 indicates that a range of other types of industrial activity are sources of industrial waste. These are any premises which are used for the purposes or used in connection with the following activities:

(a) public transport[2];
(b) the supply of electricity, gas, water, or the provision of sewerage services[3];
(c) postal or telecommunications services provided to the public[4].

It would appear that these are included in s 75 for the reason that not all of the activities may be covered by the definition of a factory under the Factories Act 1961.

1 EPA 1990, s 75(6)(a).
2 EPA 1990, s 75(6)(b).
3 EPA 1990, s 75(6)(c).
4 EPA 1990, s 75(6)(d).

2.209 The Controlled Waste Regulations 1992 also add breadth to the definition of industrial waste contained in the primary legislation[1], as well as assigning certain wastes to the industrial waste category[2]. Virtually all these wastes are listed[3] in Schedule 3. Outside of Schedule 3, construction and demolition wastes also fall[4] within the definition of industrial waste[5]. All these types of industrial waste are listed in Table 2.9.

1 See for example SI 1992/588, Sch 3, para 3(1): 'Waste from a workshop ... not being a factory within the meaning of section 175 of the Factories Act 1961 because the people working there are not employees ...'.
2 SI 1992/588, reg 5.
3 The exception is construction and demolition waste which is made an industrial waste by way of SI 1992/588, reg 5(2)(a).
4 SI 1992/588, reg 5(2): construction and demolition wastes are household waste when produced by householders for the purposes only of the duty of care; see SI 1992/588, reg 2 and para 3.25ff.
5 See also *Environment Agency v Short* [1999] Env LR 300.

Table 2.9

Industrial Waste

(A) *Wastes Listed in s 75(6) of the EPA 1990*
– waste from any factory[1],
– waste from any premises used for the purposes of or used in connection with:
   (a) public transport[2];
   (b) the supply of electricity, gas, water, or the provision of sewerage services[3];
   (c) postal or telecommunications services provided to the public[4].

(B) *Waste Listed in the Controlled Waste Regulations 1992*
(i) Regulation 5(2):
   – Waste arising from works of construction[5] or demolition, including waste arising from work preparatory thereto[6,7];
   – septic tank sludge[8].

Table 2.9 – *contd*

Industrial Waste

(ii) Schedule 3[9]:
   1. Waste from premises used for maintaining vehicles, vessels or aircraft, not being waste from a private garage to which paragraph 4 of Schedule 1 applies[10].
   2. Waste from a laboratory.
   3. (1) Waste from a workshop or similar premises not being a factory within the meaning of section 175 of the Factories Act 1961 because the people working there are not employees or because the work there is not carried on by way of trade or for purposes of gain.
      (2) In this paragraph, 'workshop' does not include premises at which the principal activities are computer operations or the copying of documents by photographic or lithographic means.
   4. Waste from premises occupied by a scientific research association approved by the Secretary of State under section 508 of the Income and Corporation Taxes Act 1988.
   5. Waste from dredging operations.
   6. Waste arising from tunnelling or from any other excavation.
   7. Sewage not falling within a description in regulation 7[11] which:
      (a) is treated, kept or disposed of in or on land, other than by means of a privy, cesspool or septic tank;
      (b) is treated, kept or disposed of by means of mobile plant; or
      (c) has been removed from a privy or cesspool.
   8. Clinical waste other than:
      (a) clinical waste from a domestic property, caravan, residential home or from a moored vessel used wholly for the purposes of living accommodation;
      (b) waste[12] collected under section 22(3) of the Control of Pollution Act 1974 or section 25(2) of the Local Government and Planning (Scotland) Act 1982[13]; or
      (c) waste[12] collected under sections 89, 92(9) or 93.
   9. Waste arising from any aircraft, vehicle or vessel[14] which is not occupied for domestic purposes.
   10. Waste which has previously formed part of any aircraft, vehicle or vessel[14] and which is not household waste.
   11. Waste removed from land on which it has previously been deposited and any soil with which such waste has been in contact, other than:
      (a) waste[15] collected under section 22(3) of the Control of Pollution Act 1974; or section 25(2) of the Local Government and Planning (Scotland) Act 1982[13]; or
      (b) waste collected under sections 89, 92(9) or 93[16].
   12. Leachate from a deposit of waste.
   13. Poisonous or noxious waste arising from any of the following processes undertaken on premises used for the purposes of a trade or business:
      (a) mixing or selling paints;
      (b) sign writing;
      (c) laundering or dry cleaning;
      (d) developing photographic film or making photographic prints;
      (e) selling petrol, diesel fuel, paraffin, kerosene, heating oil or similar substances; or
      (f) selling pesticides, herbicides or fungicides.
   14. Waste from premises used for the purposes of breeding, boarding, stabling or exhibiting animals.
   15. (1) Waste oil, waste solvent or scrap metal[17] other than:
      (a) waste from a domestic property, caravan or residential home;
      (b) waste falling within paragraphs 3 to 6 of Schedule 1[18].
      (2) In this paragraph–
      'waste oil' means mineral or synthetic oil which is contaminated, spoiled or otherwise unfit for its original purpose; and 'waste solvent' means solvent which is contaminated, spoiled or otherwise unfit for its original purpose.

Table 2.9 – *contd*

Industrial Waste

16. Waste arising from the discharge by the Secretary of State of his duty under section 89(2)[19].
17. Waste imported into Great Britain.
18. (1) Tank washings or garbage landed in Great Britain[20].

(2) In this paragraph–

'tank washings' has the same meaning as in paragraph 36 to Schedule 3 to the Waste Management Licensing Regulations 1994[21]; 'garbage' has the same meaning as in regulation 1(2) of the Merchant Shipping (Reception Facilities for Garbage) Regulations 1988[22].

1 Within the meaning of the Factories Act 1961: EPA 1990, s 75(6)(a).
2 EPA 1990, s 75(6)(b).
3 EPA 1990, s 75(6)(c).
4 EPA 1990, s 75(6)(d).
5 'Construction' is defined as including improvement, repair or alternation: SI 1992/588, reg 1(2).
6 SI 1992/588, reg 5(2)(a).
7 For the purposes of the duty of care (EPA 1990, s 34(2)), such waste is household waste, but only when it is produced by the householder on the premises (see paras 2.220 and 3.25). However, in any other case, construction and demolition waste is industrial waste.
8 But for exclusions see para 2.223.
9 SI 1992/588, Sch 3.
10 Ie wastes described as household waste: see Table 2.8 above.
11 Ie SI 1992/588, reg 7: discussed at para 2.227 below.
12 Ie clinical waste collected as litter – see para 2.230 below.
13 As amended by SI 1994/1056, reg 24(9).
14 'Vessel' includes a hovercraft (SI 1992/588, reg 1(2)).
15 Ie litter.
16 EPA 1990, ss 89, 92(9) or 93: these section relate to litter: see para 2.230 below.
17 The Controlled Waste Regulations 1992 include a reference to reg 7(2). This is now superfluous as this refers to the deadline when scrap metal became a controlled waste – October 1995 – which has long passed. Scrap metal has the same meaning as in s 9(2) of the Scrap Metal Dealers Act 1964 (SI 1992/588, reg 1(2)): this is discussed at para 11.30.
18 Paras 3–6 of Table 2.8.
19 EPA 1990, s 89(2) refers to litter abatement.
20 See para 10.105ff.
21 As amended by SI 1996/972, reg 24.
22 Note that the Merchant Shipping (Reception Facilities for Garbage) Regulations 1988 have been revoked and replaced by the Merchant Shipping (Port Waste Reception Facilities) Regulations 1997 (SI 1997/3018); see reg 16.

2.210 From Table 2.9, it will be seen that certain important waste streams are assigned to be industrial wastes. Examples include most clinical wastes[1], excavation wastes, wastes removed from places where it had already been deposited, leachate and waste imported into Britain.

1 Defined as meaning (SI 1992/588, reg 1(2)):
'(a) any waste which consists wholly or partly of human or animal tissue, blood swabs or dressings, or syringes, needles or other sharp instruments, being waste which unless rendered safe may prove hazardous to any person coming into contact with it; and
(b) any other waste arising from medical, nursing, dental, veterinary, pharmaceutical or similar practice, investigation, treatment, care, teaching or research, or the collection of blood for transfusion, being waste which may cause infection to any person coming into contact with it'.

2.211 A minority of the categories which are set down in the Schedule as industrial wastes are a little odd. For example, paragraph 13[1] contains the term 'poisonous or noxious wastes'. The use of the phrase is rather anomalous[2] as it is not subject to any definition. It is also hard to understand why the term 'special wastes' was not used.

1   See Table 2.9, para 13.
2   Possibly this is an anachronism stemming from the Control of Pollution Act, whereby s 3(3) set out more stringent penalties in respect of persons who deposited waste of a 'poisonous, noxious or polluting' nature in a manner which presented an environmental hazard.

2.212   Similarly, the terms 'waste oil' and 'waste solvent' are defined in a manner which departs from the general approach taken in the EPA 1990 and in the Controlled Waste Regulations 1992 in respect of other wastes. The Schedule to the Regulations explicitly states that solvents and oils are only industrial wastes when they are discarded[1] and when they are 'contaminated, spoiled or otherwise unfit for ... [the] original purpose'[2].

1   This seems rather tautological as, if they were not discarded, they would not be waste under the EPA 1990 anyway.
2   SI 1992/588, Sch 3, para 15(2).

2.213   Finally, it should be noted that certain wastes from domestic properties fall within the industrial wastes classification. The most obvious example is construction industry wastes[1]. These waste types are discussed further at para 2.202.

1   SI 1992/588, reg 5(2)(a): an exception is the duty of care – see reg 2(2)(a).

Commercial waste

2.214   Section 75(7) of the EPA 1990 defines commercial waste, but allows regulations to be made which enlarge the scope of the definition[1]. In the EPA 1990, the term 'commercial waste' is held to mean:

'... waste from premises used wholly or mainly for the purposes of a trade or business or the purposes of sport, recreation or entertainment.'

There is an obvious contrast in the drafting between the definition of commercial waste and the meanings given to household and industrial waste. The definitions of household and industrial waste in s 75 of the EPA 1990 are composed of inclusive lists[2]. By contrast, the term commercial waste is approached in the EPA 1990 in a way which makes it a residual category for those substances which are not household or industrial wastes. Hence s 75(7) of the EPA 1990 requires that any waste which is a household or industrial waste cannot be a commercial waste[3]. Secondly, waste from any mine or quarry and waste from premises used for agriculture[4] cannot be a commercial waste[5].

1   EPA 1990, s 75(8).
2   Which are then subject to supplementation by the Controlled Waste Regulations 1992.
3   EPA 1990, s 75(7)(a) and (b).
4   Within the meaning of the Agriculture Act 1947 or, in Scotland, the Agriculture (Scotland) Act 1948.
5   EPA 1990, s 75(7)(c).

2.215   Although there are contrasts between the way the EPA 1990 itself approaches the definition of commercial waste, the Controlled Waste Regulations 1992 set down the usual list of wastes which fall within the commercial waste category[1]. This is contained in Schedule 4, which is reproduced here as Table 2.10.

1   SI 1992/588, reg 6 and Sch 4.

Table 2.10

Commercial Waste

(A) *Section 75(7) of the EPA 1990*
Waste which is not household waste or industrial waste[1], but which stems from premises used wholly or mainly for the purposes of:
− a trade or business;
− sport, recreation or entertainment.

(B) *Controlled Waste Regulations 1992, Schedule 4*
1. Waste from an office or showroom.
2. Waste from a hotel within the meaning of–
   (a) in England and Wales, section 1(3) of the Hotel Proprietors Act 1956; and
   (b) in Scotland, section 139(1) of the Licensing (Scotland) Act 1976.
3. Waste from any part of a composite hereditament[2], or, in Scotland, of part residential subjects[3], which is used for the purposes of a trade or business.
4. Waste from a private garage which either has a floor area exceeding 25 square metres or is not used wholly or mainly for the accommodation of a private motor vehicle.
5. Waste from premises occupied by a club, society or any association of persons (whether incorporated or not) in which activities are conducted for the benefit or its members.
6. Waste from premises (not being premises from which waste is by virtue of the Act or any other provision of these Regulations to be treated as household or industrial waste) occupied by –
   (a) a court;
   (b) a government department;
   (c) a local authority;
   (d) a body corporate or an individual appointed by or under any enactment to discharge any public functions; or
   (e) a body incorporated by a Royal Charter.
7. Waste from a tent pitched on land other than a camp site[4].
8. Waste from a market or fair.
9. Waste[5] collected under s 22(3) of the Control of Pollution Act 1974 or s 25(2) of the Local Government and Planning (Scotland) Act 1982[6].

1   Nor agricultural waste or waste from mining and quarrying.
2   Composite hereditament is defined in SI 1992/588, reg 1(2) as having the same meaning as in s 64(9) of the Local Government Finance Act 1988.
3   Part residential subjects are defined in SI 1992/588, reg 1(2) as the same as that contained in s 99(1) of the Local Government Finance Act 1992.
4   Camp site is defined in SI 1992/588, reg 1(2) as land on which tents are pitched for human habitation and land incidental to this use.
5   Ie litter: see para 2.230 below.
6   As amended by SI 1994/1056, reg 24(9).

Re-defining particular types of controlled waste

2.216   It has already been noted at para 2.156ff above that, once a material is defined as waste, it remains so defined until it is subject to a processing operation which effects its chemical or physical properties. Even after processing it may still be a waste. An example would be waste arising from domestic properties, received at a transfer station or civic amenity site[1] and then subsequently passed on for landfill. However this type of operation may affect which of the categories of household, commercial or industrial waste a substance is assigned to. Both s 75 of the EPA 1990 and the Controlled Waste Regulations 1992 cause certain controlled wastes to become re-categorised after intermediate processing. Hence waste collected from a domestic property is normally household waste. Once it has been processed at a transfer station or civic amenity site and consigned for disposal, it will remain defined as waste. However, as explained at para 2.164, the operator of the transfer station or civic amenity site will become the waste producer[2]. Accordingly, when the waste is removed from such a facility, the material will be an industrial waste. This is because the EPA 1990[3] requires that wastes stemming from the premises covered by the Factories Act 1961 are all industrial wastes[4].

1 The primary purpose of civic amenity site is as a disposal facilities open for use by the public for the deposition of their household wastes.
2 As currently required by reg 1(3) of the Waste Management Licensing Regulations 1994 (SI 1994/1056: see para 2.31ff) and, when enacted, by the amended s 75(2) of the EPA 1990 (to be amended by Sch 22, para 88(1) of the Environment Act 1995: see para 2.43ff above).
3 EPA 1990, s 75(6)(a).
4 As noted at para 2.164 above, the operator of the facility will now become the waste producer, for the reason that the transfer operations involve mixing etc.

2.217 There are also other examples of cases where the type of controlled waste switches identity. Any waste excavated from a landfill will always be an industrial waste[1], even when it was household waste when originally deposited.

1 SI 1992/588, reg 5(1) and Sch 3, para 11.

MISCELLANEOUS PROVISIONS FOR PARTICULAR TYPES OF WASTE

2.218 As already discussed earlier in this chapter, there are exclusions for certain wastes from the controlled waste definition by way of the reference to the Directive on Waste[1] and as contained in the primary legislation[2]. These are supplemented by a range of additional exclusions contained in the Controlled Waste Regulations 1992 themselves.

1 See para 2.48ff.
2 EPA 1990, s 75(7).

2.219 These exclusions also go hand in hand with the series of exemptions from the need for recipient sites to possess waste management licences. The result is that some wastes are not controlled waste in stipulated circumstances, thereby disapplying the provisions of the EPA 1990 entirely. In other instances, the material may fall within the controlled waste definition, but the requirements of the Act are lifted in respect of the need for the intended destination to possess a waste management licence. In the latter case, the duty of care[1] and the requirements of carrier registration[2] still apply when the waste is in transit. Whilst exemptions from licensing are discussed in Chapters 10 and 11, the following sections will discuss the exclusions contained in the Controlled Waste Regulations 1992 which pertain to particular waste types.

1 EPA 1990, s 34: see Chapter 3.
2 See Chapter 5.

The disposal of household waste by the householder at a domestic premises

2.220 The EPA 1990 contains a general provision which permits householders to dispose of household wastes on their own properties without needing a waste management licence[1]. As is explained in Chapter 7, s 33 sets down the EPA 1990's primary offence in respect of the unauthorised use of land for waste disposal purposes. Within s 33, householders are permitted to undertake minor disposal operations on their properties, provided that certain requirements are satisfied[2]. The most important is that the waste emanates from the dwelling and that the disposal operation is done by the occupier or with that person's permission. This would allow for bonfires and the use of compost heaps for example. However, in all cases, the exclusion in s 33 applies only to 'household waste', not to other controlled wastes such as industrial waste. Given that the disposal of certain hazardous wastes at domestic properties is highly undesirable, the Controlled Waste Regulations 1992 cause the reclassification of these wastes from being household waste into the category of industrial wastes[3]. Being industrial wastes, they fall outside the exemption contained in s 33 of the EPA 1990, thereby making the disposal by householders of these wastes on their properties an offence under s 33(1). The particular wastes which are subject to this re-classification are[4]: any mineral or synthetic oil or grease; asbestos; and clinical waste[5]. Being industrial wastes, the exemption under s 33(2) no longer applies[6].

1 EPA 1990, s 33(2).
2 EPA 1990, s 33(2): see para 7.04.
3 SI 1992/588, reg 3(1): see Circular 14/92, Annex 1, para 1.21.
4 SI 1992/588, reg 3(1).
5 Defined as meaning (SI 1992/588, reg 1(2)):
    '(a) any waste which consists wholly or partly of human or animal tissue, blood swabs or dressings, or syringes, needles or other sharp instruments, being waste which unless rendered safe may prove hazardous to any person coming into contact with it; and
    (b) any other waste arising from medical, nursing, dental, veterinary, pharmaceutical or similar practice, investigation, treatment, care, teaching or research, or the collection of blood for transfusion, being waste which may cause infection to any person coming into contact with it'.
6 EPA 1990, s 33(2) is considered further at para 7.04.

2.221 In the case of construction[1] and demolition waste, the Controlled Waste Regulations 1992 hold that these materials are industrial waste[2]. This means that householders cannot benefit from the exception from waste management licensing contained in s 33(2) of the EPA 1990. Accordingly, rubble disposal by householders on their premises is not allowed. However, the rubble must, for obvious reasons, fall within the definition of waste for the EPA 1990 to apply[3].

1 Defined in SI 1992/588, reg 1(1) as including wastes arising from improvement, repair or alteration.
2 SI 1992/588, reg 5: see Circular 14/92, Annex 1, para 1.19. The only exception is in respect of the duty of care: see SI 1992/588, reg 2(2) and see para 2.227 below.
3 As *Cheshire County Council v Armstrong Transport (Wigan) Ltd* [1995] Env LR 62 has shown – see para 2.182 above – rubble is not always classed as waste under the EPA 1990.

Household waste and the duty of care

2.222 The Controlled Waste Regulations 1992 exempt construction and demolition waste and septic tank sludge from the duty of care[1] when these materials are produced by householders. This is done by classifying wastes generated in these circumstances as household waste, taking advantage of the exclusion of the duty of care granted under s 34(2) of the EPA 1990 for household wastes of that nature[2]. The wording only lifts the duty of care's requirements in respect of an 'occupier of domestic property', not third parties involved in the removal of the material[3]. In instances other than when the duty of care applies, these materials are normally[4] industrial wastes[5].

1 EPA 1990, s 34.
2 EPA 1990, s 34(2) is considered further at para 3.23.
3 See EPA 1990, s 34(2) and SI 1992/588, reg 2(2).
4 Septic tank sludge may not constitute an industrial waste when disposed of at a sewage treatment works or when landspread on farmland (see para 2.228).
5 SI 1992/588, reg 5(2)(a).

Sewage sludge, sewage and septic tank sludge

2.223 The Controlled Waste Regulations 1992 have important ramifications on the manner by which sewage and sewage-related wastes are subject to the EPA 1990. They contain provisions which exempt those substances from the definition of controlled waste, with the result that the provisions of the EPA 1990 do not apply. However, this exemption is done selectively and with varying effect.

Sewage treatment

2.224 The most important exclusion from the definition of controlled waste relates to sewage, sludge and septic tank sludge[1] which is treated, kept or disposed of within the curtilage of a sewage works[2]. Being outside the controlled waste definition, the storage and disposal infrastructure of a sewage treatment works does not require a waste management licence for the receipt of these materials[3]. However, in order for the incoming wastes to remain beyond the definition of controlled waste, the exclusion requires that the treating, keeping and disposal operations must be 'an integral part of the operation of . . . [the] works' and must not be undertaken by mobile plant. Provided these requirements are followed, these wastes are neither industrial nor commercial wastes.

1 The Controlled Waste Regulations 1992 (SI 1992/588, reg 1(2)) require that 'sludge' and 'septic tank sludge' has the same meaning as in the Sludge (Use in Agriculture) Regulations 1989 (SI 1989/1263).
2 SI 1992/588, reg 7(1)(a).
3 However, if the works accepted other substances which fell within the controlled waste definition, a licence or exemption from licensing would be needed under s 33 of the EPA 1990: see Chapters 7 and 8.

2.225 In a small number of circumstances, sewage itself[1] may be a controlled waste. The instances when it should be so defined are when it is specifically referred to in the Controlled Waste Regulations 1992. Otherwise, sewage is not so defined[2]. As noted, the Controlled Waste Regulations 1992 state that sewage is not a controlled waste when it is treated, kept or disposed of integrally within a sewage works[3]. However, sewage sludge becomes an industrial waste where it is treated, kept or disposed of on land other than a sewage works where the land in question is not a privy, cesspool or septic tank[4]. Similarly, sewage is to be regarded as an industrial waste when it is treated, kept or disposed of by mobile plant[5]. Finally, sewage is an industrial waste when it has been removed from a privy or cesspool[6]. This would mean that the duty of care applies, that appropriately registered waste carriers are to be used and that the destination of the waste is subject either to a waste management licence or a registration as an exempt facility[7].

1 Including matter in or from privies: SI 1992/588, reg 1(4)(b).
2 EPA 1990, s 75(8).
3 SI 1992/588, reg 5(1) and Sch 3, para 7.
4 SI 1992/588, Sch 3, para 7(a).
5 SI 1992/588, Sch 3, para 7(b).
6 SI 1992/588, Sch 3, para 7(c).
7 The disposal of this material in these circumstances cannot be 'integral' to the operation of a sewage treatment works: see SI 1992/588, reg 7(1)(a).

Sewage sludge spreading

2.226 The Controlled Waste Regulations 1992 also affect the final disposal of sewage sludge. Sewage sludge is the residual matter resultant from the biological treatment of sewage[1]. An estimated 35 million tonnes[2] of this sludge arise in the United Kingdom each year[3], significantly more than the quantity of household waste generated nationally. In 1996, nearly 50% of the United Kingdom's sludge passed to farmland for crop nutrient purposes[4].

1 In the Controlled Waste Regulations 1992 it is termed as 'sludge' (SI 1992/588, reg 1(2)), being given the meaning contained in the Sludge (Use in Agriculture) Regulations 1989: 'residual sludge from sewage plants treating domestic or urban waste waters and other sewage plants treating waste waters of a composition similar to domestic and urban waste waters': SI 1989/1263, reg 2(1).
2 Wet weight.
3 Government Statistical Service (1998) *Digest of Environmental Protection Statistics*, No 20, Stationery Office, Table 7.1.
4 The other disposal options were landfill (9%), sea disposal (24%), incineration (8%) and other uses such as land reclamation, forestry, compost products (9%): see Government Statistical Service (1998) *Digest of Environmental Statistics*, No 20, Stationery Office, Table 7.8. Note that since 31 December 1998 the sea disposal of sewage sludge by Britain has ceased.

2.227 Sewage sludge disposal to farmland is mainly subject to control by way of the Sludge (Use in Agriculture) Regulations 1989[1]. On the formation of the Agency in 1996, the responsibility for the enforcement of these Regulations was transferred from the Ministry of Agriculture, Fisheries and Food[2]. To avoid duplication between the EPA 1990 and the Sludge (Use in Agriculture) Regulations 1989, the Controlled Waste Regulations 1992 require that any sewage sludge subject to the Sludge (Use in Agriculture) Regulations 1989 is neither a commercial or industrial waste[3]. However, the prerequisite of this exclusion is that the sludge is 'supplied or used' in accordance with the Sludge (Use in Agriculture) Regulations 1989. Hence if the sludge is not dealt with in the manner set out in the Sludge (Use in Agriculture) Regulations 1989, it becomes an industrial waste[4], causing the EPA 1990's regulatory provisions to apply. It also seems that if sewage sludge is stored at an intermediate location, it falls into the category of industrial waste. It is not being 'supplied or used' in these circumstances. As is described at para 10.166, an exemption from the need to possess a waste management licence specifically addresses storage of sewage sludge in these circumstances[5]. A second effect of the Controlled Waste Regulations 1992's provisions is that sewage sludge becomes an industrial waste when spreading is to occur on land which is not subject to the Sludge (Use in Agriculture) Regulations 1989. An example would be when the spreading occurred on land other than land used for agriculture. The term 'agriculture' in the Sludge (Use in Agriculture) Regulations 1989 applies only to the growing of all types of commercial food crops, including crops for stock rearing purposes[6]. Hence the spreading of sludge on other types of farmland or on other land[7] would involve the deposition of controlled wastes. The EPA 1990 would apply in these circumstances[8].

1 SI 1989/1263 as amended by SI 1990/880, SI 1996/593 and SI 1996/973.
2 Environment Act 1995, s 2(2)(e).
3 SI 1992/588, reg 7(1)(b).
4 For the reason that the sewage treatment works is subject to s 75(6)(c) of the EPA 1990, which states that premises involved in sewerage services are sources of industrial wastes: see also Circular 14/92, Annex 2, para 2.30.
5 SI 1994/1056, Sch 3, para 8(1).
6 SI 1989/1263, reg 2(1).
7 Eg for land reclamation purposes.
8 Often such spreading activities are exempt from waste management licences under Sch 3 of SI 1994/1056: see para 10.138ff.

Septic tank sludge spreading

2.228 The approach taken by the Controlled Waste Regulations 1992 in respect of septic tank sludge is somewhat narrower[1]. The Controlled Waste Regulations 1992 require that septic tank sludge is neither a commercial or industrial waste[2] when it is 'used' on agricultural land within the meaning of the Sludge (Use In Agriculture) Regulations 1989[3]. It should be noted that the term utilised by the Controlled Waste Regulations 1992 is 'used', rather than 'supplied or used' as was the case of sewage sludge (see above). Accordingly, septic tank sludge remains an industrial waste up to the point it is used[4]. This is confirmed by Circular 14/94[5] and also by the fact that the place of storage of the sludge prior to use is specifically exempted by the Waste Management Licensing Regulations 1994 from the need to possess a waste management licence[6]. Accordingly, the control system contained in the EPA 1990 applies, including the duty of care and, where appropriate, carrier registration.

1   'Septic tank sludge' has the same meaning (SI 1992/588, reg 1(2)) as in the Sludge (Use in Agriculture Regulations 1989 (SI 1989/1263, as amended by SI 1990/880): 'residual sludge from septic tanks and other similar installations of the treatment of sewage'.
2   It is not a houschold waste for any purpose other than the duty of care: SI 1991/588, reg 2(2).
3   SI 1992/588, reg 7(1)(c) as amended by SI 1995/288, reg 2(2).
4   SI 1992/588, reg 5(2).
5   Annex 2, para 2.28.
6   SI 1994/1056, Sch 3, para 7(7): this exemption is discussed at para 10.148.

Animal by-products

2.229   Many animal by-products will not normally fall within the definition of waste[1]. In addition, items such as hides or meat for pet food are in the normal commercial cycle and hence are not discarded. But in certain limited circumstances, it is conceivable that they would do so[2]. The Controlled Waste Regulations 1992 state[3] that animal by-products[4] are not commercial or industrial wastes with respect only to the duty of care[5]. However, to be excluded from the duty of care, the wastes must be collected and transported in accordance with the Animal By-Products Order 1992. Collection and transportation in a manner which is not in accordance with the Order causes the penal provisions of both the Order itself and also the EPA 1990 to apply. This matter is discussed further at para 3.27ff.

1   See para 2.60 above.
2   See Circular 11/94, Annex 4, paras 4.91–4.94.
3   SI 1992/588, reg 7(3).
4   As defined in Article 3(1) of the Animal By-Products Order 1992 (SI 1992/3303). Note that while the reference to the Animal By-Products Order 1992 remains in the legislation, that Order has been replaced by the Animal By-Products Order 1999 (SI 1999/646).
5   EPA 1990, s 34.

Street cleansing wastes

2.230   The Controlled Waste Regulations 1992 make clear that litter and other cleansing wastes are controlled waste[1]. This is to ensure that waste management licences, the duty of care and carrier registration apply to the material when collected[2]. Street cleansing is undertaken primarily by way of powers contained in Part IV of the EPA 1990. Section 89 of the EPA 1990 requires local authorities, the Highways Agency, designated statutory undertakers and occupiers of premises located in litter control areas to keep the highway and other land free of litter and debris. There is also a duty on the local authority and Highways Agency to maintain the cleanliness of the highway. The nature of litter control areas are set down in s 90 of the EPA 1990 and these may be designated by the relevant local authority. Under s 92 of the EPA 1990 litter authorities can serve abatement notices on occupiers of land to have the litter removed. Similarly, litter control notices can be served under s 93 of the EPA 1990 on sources of litter such as fast food outlets. A number of the provisions in Part IV encompass dog faeces[3], by way of the Litter (Animal Droppings) Order 1991[4].

1   See SI 1992/588, reg 6, Sch 4, para 9; reg 8.
2   See Circular 14/92, Annex 4, para 4.3.
3   See Circular 14/92, Annex 4, para 4.2.
4   SI 1991/961.

2.231   Regulation 8 of the Controlled Waste Regulations 1992 sets out a somewhat complicated decision methodology in respect of waste collected under these powers. Depending upon the particular section in Part IV of the EPA 1990 under which the street cleansing wastes were collected, litter falls into one of the three categories of household, commercial or industrial waste. The purpose of this delineation is to decide whether the waste collection authority can make a charge for the removal of the materials[1].

1   See SI 1992/588, reg 8(d), EPA 1990, s 45 and Circular 14/92, Annex 4, para 4.6ff. As this aspect is outside the theme of this book, it is not considered further.

2.232   However, what is important to note is that the Controlled Waste Regulations 1992 make clear that street cleansing wastes fall within one of the categories of controlled waste. Waste arising by way of the duty in s 89(2) of the EPA 1990 for local authorities and the Highways Agency to ensure that streets and roads are kept clean are household wastes[1]. In this respect, the Controlled Waste Regulations 1992 plugged a significant loophole in the earlier Collection and Disposal of Waste Regulations 1988[2].

1   SI 1992/588, Sch 1, para 11.
2   SI 1988/819: see the unreported Crown Court case of *David Thomas Watkins v Taff Ely Borough Council* (1991).

Chapter 3

The duty of care

INTRODUCTION

3.01 Experience of the Control of Pollution Act 1974 in the 1980s indicated a huge disparity in the quality of waste management across the country[1]. A common view of waste transactions was succinctly summarised by the Third Report of the Hazardous Waste Inspectorate[2]:

'Too many producers' principal concern about waste is to get it off the premises, at the cheapest possible price, and then forget about it.'

There was often a perception that it was not the waste producer's problem if the material was subsequently incorrectly disposed of or even fly-tipped. Certain companies appeared to consider that virtually any waste materials could be placed together in collection containers, tending to neglect the correct labelling of the contents. Such activities could result in a waste carrier delivering unsuitable wastes to a disposal site or cause worse outcomes. All these issues came to be addressed by what is known as the 'duty of care'.

1   See House of Lords Select Committee on Science and Technology (1981) *Hazardous Waste Disposal*, Vols I–III, HMSO, London; The Hazardous Waste Inspectorate (1985) *First Report Hazardous Waste Management – An Overview*, Department of the Environment, London; Royal Commission on Environmental Pollution (1985) *Managing Waste: The Duty of Care*, HMSO, London; House of Commons Environment Committee (1989) *Toxic Waste* Vols I–III, HMSO, London; House of Commons Welsh Affairs Committee (1990) *Toxic Waste Disposal in Wales*, HMSO, London.
2   Department of the Environment (1988) *The Hazardous Waste Inspectorate Third Report*. HMSO, London, p 15.

3.02 Credit for the parentage of the duty of care should go primarily to the Royal Commission on Environmental Pollution. In its 11th Report[1] the Commission considered approvingly the duty of care placed upon employers by the Health and Safety at Work etc Act 1974[2]. It proposed that an analogous general duty should be applicable on the producers of waste to ensure the occurrence of correct disposal. The Commission envisaged that this responsibility would require the producer to take all reasonable steps to ensure that its waste was subsequently managed and disposed of without harm to the environment[3]. In many ways this was a reflection of the failure of the Control of Pollution Act 1974 to correctly apportion the blame for many incidents: on those responsible for the production of the waste.

1   Royal Commission on Environmental Pollution (1985) *Managing Waste: The Duty of Care* 11th Report Cmnd 9675, HMSO, London, pp 38, 106–107.
2   Health and Safety at Work etc Act 1974, s 2.
3   Royal Commission on Environmental Pollution (1985) *Managing Waste: The Duty of Care* 11th Report Cmnd 9675, HMSO, London p 109.

3.03 The Royal Commission's recommendations were eventually enshrined in legislation by way of s 34 of the EPA 1990, which was fully enacted by April 1992[1]. Within s 34, the Commission's proposals were extended to make the duty applicable to all parties in waste management, not just the waste producer.

1   Environmental Protection Act 1990 (Commencement No 10) Order 1991, SI 1991/2829.

3.04   It is interesting to note that the duty of care is perhaps one of the few areas of UK waste control which significantly depart from, and builds on, the baseline of statutory requirements set by EC law[1]. The duty emanates solely from the EPA 1990, not from any EC environmental provision.

1   Mainly the Directive on Waste 75/442 as amended by Directive 91/156.

3.05   In summary, s 34 of the EPA 1990 requires all parties in waste management to take measures applicable to them which are 'reasonable in the circumstances'[1]. These measures are directed to four objectives:

–   to prevent other persons contravening s 33 of the EPA 1990;
–   to prevent the 'escape' of waste from the holder's control;
–   to transfer waste only to correctly authorised persons such as waste management licence holders or registered waste carriers; and
–   at the time of the transfer, to pass over an adequate written description of the waste which will prevent others contravening s 33 and will prevent the waste 'escaping'.

1   EPA 1990, s 34(1).

3.06   The provisions of s 34 of the EPA 1990[1] are substantiated by the Environmental Protection (Duty of Care) Regulations 1991[2], which are accompanied by their own Circular[3] and also by a statutory Code of Practice. The latter is now in its second edition, with the first edition being superseded in March 1996[4]. Although published nearly two years after the 1994 enactment of the new waste management licensing system, the revised Code of Practice finally took on board the changes associated with the implementation of Part II of the EPA 1990.

1   Section 34 of the EPA 1990 has been subject to minor amendment by s 33 of the Deregulation and Contracting Out Act 1994 and also s 120 and para 65 of Sch 22 of the Environment Act 1995.
2   SI 1991/2839.
3   Circular 19/91 *Environmental Protection Act 1990 Section 34 The Duty of Care* HMSO, London.
4   Department of the Environment (1996) *Waste Management The Duty of Care A Code of Practice*, 2nd edn, HMSO, London. Hereinafter the Code is referred to as the 'Code of Practice' in the footnotes to this chapter.

3.07   The Code of Practice provides essential advice on how the elements of the duty of care should be addressed by parties to waste transactions. It attempts to embrace the diversity of waste transactions and also the wide variety of circumstances in which waste arises, by setting out guidelines on the nature of measures which may be applicable to each party and which may be reasonable.

3.08   An important element of the duty is a system which attempts to provide formal written documentation of waste movements. This builds upon the requirement in s 34(1) of the EPA 1990 that written descriptions are handed over when wastes are transferred between parties. The nature of this written description usually makes up part of a document known as a 'transfer note'. The information to be contained on such a note is prescribed by the Environmental Protection (Duty of Care) Regulations 1991.

3.09   The purpose of transfer notes is to set out an 'audit trail' which aids the Agency in the detection of offences. For example, when inappropriate waste is deposited at a disposal site, the notes can be used to identify the carrier and, if need be, trace the producer. However, an amendment made to s 34 of the EPA 1990 by the Deregulation and Contracting Out Act 1994 has meant that such an exercise is not always possible[1].

1   This is discussed fully at para 3.157ff.

3.10 Transactions involving special waste[1] do not need to be documented by transfer notes[2]. Special waste consignment notes suffice. However, the remainder of the duty of care applies. Hence the Code of Practice not only supplies valuable advice on how parties should check up on each other when special waste is to be moved, it also sets down guidelines which may be applicable to the description of wastes contained in special waste consignment notes. In addition, previous holders of special waste are allowed – by way of the Waste Management Licensing Regulations 1994[3] – access to the records of disposal or recovery facilities in respect of their waste.

1 See Chapter 4.
2 SI 1991/2839, reg 2(3) as amended by SI 1996/972, reg 23: this includes waste which falls within the definition of special waste but which is transported internationally under the notification document set down by EC Regulation 259/93: see para 3.159 below. The movement of special waste without a consignment note – or with a defectively completed note – contravenes both the duty of care and the Special Waste Regulations: see SI 1996/972, reg 18 and para 4.183.
3 SI 1994/1056, Sch 4, para 14(1)(b), as amended by SI 1996/972, reg 25 and Sch 3: see para 4.172ff.

3.11 In all of these respects, it is important to note that the duty of care relates mainly to times when wastes are transferred between different parties. Its requirements will principally bite when a producer, carrier and disposal site are not the same individuals. If the producer arranges waste to be moved to a merchant disposal site using the producer's own transport, then the waste is only transferred when it has been passed over to the site. If the producer uses its own transport to take the waste to its own disposal site, then no transfer of waste has occurred. When no transfer of waste occurs, the only time the duty pertains is if waste 'escapes'[1].

1 EPA 1990, s 34(1)(b): see para 3.45 below.

3.12 Interesting questions arise as to the status of the Code of Practice in relation to its use in court[1]. While s 34(10) of the EPA 1990 allows the Code to be admissible in evidence, it is not clear whether its use is restricted to proceedings under s 34 only or extends to any litigation under Part II of the EPA 1990[2]. Certainly, the wording of s 34(10) places no restrictions on its use. Hence it may well be that the Code can be used in respect of proceedings under s 33, the principal enforcement provision in the EPA 1990 for waste management sites[3]. For example, the Code could be used to cast useful light on whether defendants can rely on the statutory defences contained in s 33(7) of the EPA 1990. Of particular significance would be Code's influence on assertions by defendants that they 'took all reasonable precautions and exercised all due diligence to avoid the commission of the offence'[4].

1 See also Baldwin R and Houghton J 'Circular Arguments: the Status and Legitimacy of Administrative Rules' (1986) *Public Law* 239.
2 Or for transfrontier shipments under Regulation 259/93: see Chapter 5.
3 See Chapter 7.
4 EPA 1990, s 33(7)(a); other examples of possible uses of the Code include the determination of the adequacy of waste descriptions on special waste consignment notes or on transfrontier notification documents.

3.13 Secondly, there is also a question of whether the Code can not only be used in respect of offences under s 34 of the EPA 1990, but can also be utilised to cast light on some of the terms used in Part II of the EPA 1990[1]. At a number of places, the Code provides additional clarification of the legislation. It sets down meanings for certain terms which are undefined either in s 34 itself or elsewhere in the EPA 1990 and associated regulations. For example, while the term 'waste producer' is not defined in respect of s 34, the Code indicates that it should be viewed as having the same meaning[2] as the definition contained in reg 1(3) of the Waste Management Licensing Regulations 1994[3]. The

Code also sets out an explanation of s 34 itself in Annex A. How much reliance the prosecution or defence can place on these clarifications is not clear.

1 Only the Introduction and the Appendix are not to be regarded as part of the Code of Practice: see Code of Practice page 3, para i and the first paragraph of page 64. The Appendix should be noted also as distinct from the Code's Annex A to E.
2 Code of Practice, para B.2 and also see the Code's glossary of terms on page 62.
3 SI 1994/1056: see para 3.79 below.

3.14 While the Code adds considerably to the information that can presented in court proceedings, it is not the only source of guidance. As will be seen below, Circular 19/91 provides significant clarification on certain aspects of the duty of care. Indeed, in places it goes further than the Code of Practice itself[1]. However, it should be appreciated that the advice of the Circular is of considerably lower standing than that contained in the Code. As noted, only the Code is explicitly required by s 34(10) of the EPA 1990 to be considered in court proceedings.

1 See, for example, para 3.111 below on construction and demolition activities.

3.15 Finally, it should be noted that both the Duty of Care Circular and the Code of Practice play down the role of regulatory bodies in enforcing the duty[1]. This is because the duty is specifically designed to be self-policing. Circular 19/91 notes[2]:

'All waste holders will wish to protect themselves against the consequences of misbehaviour by another party in the waste chain, and will have every incentive to check on others and on the waste itself and to document the steps they have taken against the possibility of a criminal inquiry.'

Accordingly, the Circular's policy appears to be one of allowing the duty to police itself and for the enforcing authorities to use s 34 of the EPA 1990 mainly in the context of offences involving beaches of s 33 of that Act[3]. Whether the envisaged self-regulation is being achieved is very much an open question. Surveys taken since 1993 consistently illustrate widespread ignorance of the requirements of the duty of care by industry in general[4].

1 See Circular 19/91, para 33 and Code of Practice, para 5.11.
2 Circular 19/91, para 33.
3 See Circular 19/91, para 34 and see Code of Practice, para 5.11.
4 See, for example, Leach B and Edwards P 'A Duty to Hear' (1993) *Surveyor* 29 July 1993, pp 10–12; Bland M 'A Duty, but who Cares?' (1995) *Wastes Management* November 1995, pp 37–38; ' "Duty of Care" Rules on Transfer Notes Flouted' *Ends Report* 251 December 1995, pp 13–14; Lowe S 'Small Change' (1997) *The Waste Manager* December 97/January 1998 Issue, pp 18–20.

THE PRINCIPAL OFFENCE

3.16 The offence of contravening the duty of care is set down in s 34(1) of the EPA 1990:

'. . . it shall be the duty of any person[1] who imports, produces, carries, keeps, treats, or disposes of controlled waste or, as a broker, has control of such waste, to take all such measures applicable to him in that capacity as are reasonable in the circumstances –

(a) to prevent any contravention by any other person of section 33 above[2];
(b) to prevent the escape of the waste from his control or that of any other person; and
(c) on the transfer of waste, to secure –

(i) that the transfer is only to an authorised person or to a person for authorised transport purposes; and

(ii) that there is transferred such a written description of the waste as will enable other persons to avoid a contravention of that section and to comply with the duty as respects the escape of waste.'

1 'Person' includes bodies corporate or unincorporate: Interpretation Act 1978, Sch 1.
2 EPA 1990, s 33; see Chapter 7.

3.17 The caveats of applicability and reasonableness in s 34(1) of the EPA 1990 preclude the need for s 34 to have separate sub-sections setting down statutory defences. Instead, the Secretary of State is permitted to issue the Code of Practice 'for the purpose of providing to persons practical guidance on how to discharge the duty imposed on them . . .'[1]. As noted earlier, the Code of Practice is admissible in court, and '. . . if any provision of such a code appears to the court to be relevant to any question arising in the proceedings it shall be taken into account in determining that question'[2]. This does not mean that the provisions of the Code should be slavishly followed. More it means that the Code gives an indication of a level and standard of behaviour which can be classed as acceptable waste management in the late 1990s[3]. Indeed, as the Code of Practice itself notes[4]: 'The legal obligation is to comply with the duty of care itself rather than with the code.'

1 EPA 1990, s 34(7).
2 EPA 1990, s 34(10).
3 See Circular 19/91, para 15. The Highway Code has a similar function under road traffic law.
4 Code of Practice, 2nd edn, page 3, para iv.

3.18 It should be noted that s 34(6) of the EPA 1990 creates two offences: (a) an offence of failing to comply with s 34(1)[1]; and (b) a separate offence of non-compliance with any regulations made by the Secretary of State under powers contained in s 34(5). Section 34(5) allows the Secretary of State to prescribe the information to be contained in transfer notes. The sub-section also allows time periods to be set down for the keeping of such documents and for the furnishing of them to the Agency on request. These requirements are all fulfilled by the Environmental Protection (Duty of Care) Regulations 1991[2].

1 Ie the duty of care itself.
2 SI 1991/2839.

3.19 The two offences contained in s 34 of the EPA 1990 have certain contrasts. In particular, it should be appreciated that an offence under s 34(1) only occurs if persons fail to take steps which are (a) applicable to them, and (b) which are reasonable in the circumstances. These provisions are discussed further below. What should be noted at this juncture is that there are no similar prerequisites in respect of the non-compliance with any regulations made under s 34(5). *Any* breach of the Environmental Protection (Duty of Care) Regulations 1991[1] is an offence. In addition, there are no statutory defences in respect of non-compliance with the Duty of Care Regulations.

1 SI 1991/2839.

3.20 A person who fails to comply either with the Duty itself, or with any regulations made under powers contained in s 34(5) of the EPA 1990 is liable[1] on summary conviction to a fine not exceeding the statutory maximum[2] and on conviction on indictment to an unlimited fine. Unlike the main provisions contained in s 33 of the EPA 1990, s 34 does not allow the courts to impose custodial sentences.

1   EPA 1990, s 34(6).
2   Currently £5,000.

Directors' (etc) liability and offences caused by the default of others

3.21   The provisions of ss 157 and 158 of the EPA 1990 apply to the duty of care. Hence directors, managers, secretaries etc can be held personally liable where an offence has been caused by their consent, neglect or connivance[1]. As the Code of Practice notes, 'employers are responsible for the acts and omissions of their employees. They therefore should provide adequate equipment, training and supervision to ensure that their employees observe the duty of care'[2].

1   EPA 1990, s 157: see para 7.156ff.
2   Code of Practice, para A.8.

3.22   Section 158 of the EPA 1990, states that, where a person commits an offence due to the act or default of another, the second person can be found guilty of the offence. This is regardless of whether the first person was charged[1].

1   EPA 1990, s 158: see para 7.173ff.

EXCLUSIONS FROM THE DUTY

Occupiers of domestic properties

3.23   The duty of care applies to virtually all commercial parties in a waste life cycle. However, a significant exclusion relates to 'an occupier of a domestic property as respects the household waste produced on the property'[1].

1   EPA 1990, s 34(2).

3.24   It is particularly important to recognise the boundaries created by that phrase. Firstly, the exclusion applies only to 'domestic properties' and their 'occupiers'[1]. Secondly, the material must be 'household waste' produced on the property. The nature of 'household waste' is defined in s 75(8) of the EPA 1990 and further prescribed by the Controlled Waste Regulations 1992[2]. Under s 75(8) of the EPA 1990, there are five sources of household waste. These are waste from a domestic property, from a caravan, from a residential home, from an educational establishment and from a hospital or nursing home. But as the exclusion in s 34(2) solely addresses household wastes from 'domestic properties'[3], only this category of waste is outside the duty of care. Hence the duty applies to household waste emanating from caravans, residential homes, educational establishments, hospitals and nursing homes[4]. It would seem entirely right that the duty of care should therefore apply in these instances. To do otherwise would exempt from the duty significant types of waste which require proper controls, such as clinical waste from residential homes.

1   The word 'occupier' is discussed at para 12.108.
2   SI 1992/588, reg 2(1) and Sch 1: see Chapter 2.
3   A 'domestic property' is defined in s 75(5)(a) of the EPA 1990 as meaning '... a building or self-contained part of a building which is used wholly for the purposes of living accommodation ...'.
4   It should be also be noted that the Controlled Waste Regulations 1992 (SI 1992/588), Sch 1, para 3 refer to caravans and residential homes as separate entities from domestic properties.

Construction waste, demolition waste and septic tank sludge from domestic properties

3.25 Subject to one exception, the EPA 1990 views these waste types as 'industrial wastes', even if they arise from domestic properties[1]. The exclusion for householders as occupiers of domestic properties from the duty of care only applies to 'household waste'[2]. It does not apply to 'industrial wastes'. The objective of totally excluding a householder from the duty of care in respect of construction, demolition and septic tank wastes is undertaken by way of Regulation 2(2) of the Controlled Waste Regulations 1992[3]. Regulation 2(2) prescribes that construction[4] and demolition waste, along with septic tank sludge, are to be treated as household waste '. . . for the purposes only of s 34(2) . . .'[5]. Being household wastes in these circumstances, they are thus outside the scope of the duty[6].

1 SI 1992/588, reg 5(2): see Circular 14/92 *The Environmental Protection Act 1990 Parts II and IV. The Controlled Waste Regulations 1992*, HMSO, London, Annex 1, para 1.19 and see paras 2.202, 2.209.
2 EPA 1990, s 34(2).
3 SI 1992/588.
4 Defined as including 'improvement, repair or alteration': SI 1992/588, reg 1(2).
5 SI 1992/588, reg 2(2).
6 By way of the general exclusion for household waste contained in s 34(2).

3.26 However, it is important that the extent of this provision is not interpreted too widely. What the provision achieves is to absolve the householder[1] from the duty of care in respect of these, and other, wastes produced on that person's property. As the Code of Practice makes clear, this provision does not exempt[2]:

'(a) a householder disposing of waste that is not from his property (for example, waste from his workplace; or waste from a neighbour's property); or

(b) someone who is not the occupier of the property (for example, a builder carrying out works to a house he does not occupy . . .).'

In the case of the latter, the builder is the producer of the waste. As such persons are not normally the occupier[3] of the premises in which they are working, the waste arising from the construction or demolition works falls within the definition in the Controlled Waste Regulations 1992 of industrial waste[4]. Hence the duty of care applies.

1 When falling within the circumstances described at para 3.23 above.
2 Code of Practice, para A.9 and see also Circular 19/91, para 10.
3 The nature of occupiers is discussed at para 12.108.
4 SI 1992/588, reg 5(2)(a).

Animal by-products

3.27 The second type of waste to be excluded from the duty of care are wastes which are composed of animal by-products[1]. These are excluded by way of an amendment made to the Controlled Waste Regulations 1992[2] by the Waste Management Licensing Regulations 1994[3]. As has been discussed in Chapter 2[4], the principal purpose of the 1992 Regulations was to allocate certain wastes to the categories set down in s 75 of the EPA 1990: household waste, commercial waste and industrial waste[4].

1 Note that Circular 11/94, Annex 4, para 4.91 suggests that many animal by-products will not be wastes on the grounds that they are not discarded: see also Chapter 2.
2 SI 1992/588, reg 7(3).
3 SI 1994/1056, reg 24(7).
4 See para 2.190ff.

3.28   The effect of the amendment to the Controlled Waste Regulations 1992 is to require that animal by-products are not be treated as industrial or commercial wastes for the purposes of s 34 of the EPA 1990[1]. However, this is not a blanket exclusion and the duty can apply to animal by-products only in certain limited instances. The 1992 Regulations[2] state that the duty does not apply to animal by-products when 'collected and transported in accordance with Schedule 2 of the Animal By-Products Order 1992'[3]. Accordingly, if transportation is in manner which is outside the requirements of the Order, the duty of care applies.

1   SI 1992/588, reg 7(3) as amended by SI 1994/1056, reg 24(7).
2   SI 1992/588, reg 7(3).
3   While the reference to the 1992 Order (SI 1992/3303, as amended by SI 1996/827 and SI 1997/2894) remains in SI 1992/588, the Order has been consolidated by SI 1999/646 as the Animal By-Products Order 1999, with the 1992 Order being revoked (see SI 1999/646, art 35 and Sch 6, Pt I).

3.29   While the Animal By-Products Order 1992 is discussed further at para 6.14ff. in relation to the registration of waste carriers, it should be noted that, *inter alia*, it contains a number of requirements on waste transporters which would potentially overlap with the duty of care[1]. For example, the Order requires that containers transporting animal by-products should not leak. Accordingly, it would seem that, if wastes which were animal by-products were being transported in leaking containers, both the Order and the duty of care's requirements on the escape on waste[2] would apply. Hence an offence would be committed under both sets of legislation. There are also other overlaps, including the requirement of the Order that transactions of animal by-products are formally documented.

1   Circular 11/94, Annex 4, para 4.92; Code of Practice, para A.10.
2   EPA 1990, s 34(1)(b).

Scrap metal

3.30   Up to the end of September 1995, the duty of care did not apply to 'scrap metal'[1]. This was again by way of the Controlled Waste Regulations 1992 which exempted scrap metal from being a household, commercial or industrial waste[2].

1   As defined by the Scrap Metal Dealers Act 1964: see para 11.31.
2   SI 1992/588, regs 3(2) and 7(2), as amended by SI 1995/288, reg 2(1).

3.31   Although the deadline has now passed, it should be noted that the Code of Practice singles out scrap metal for additional guidance[1]. Much of this additional guidance pertains only to the documentation of scrap metal transactions, and hence it is discussed elsewhere at para 3.148 below.

1   Code of Practice, Section 7.

ELEMENTS OF THE DUTY OF CARE

3.32   It has already been noted that there are a number of items that are required to be fulfilled in order to comply with s 34(1) of the EPA 1990. These requirements, whose stringency of compliance varies, depend on the type of person and the role of the person in a waste transaction. The Code of Practice provides advice in respect of these matters. How that advice relates to the elements of the duty and impinges upon its parties is expanded upon further below.

'Reasonable in the circumstances': the Code of Practice

3.33 One of the difficulties in fulfilling the Royal Commission's proposal for a duty of care was that the wording of the duty should have a variable level of applicable stringency. This is necessary mainly for reasons of natural justice and for the duty to fulfil its objectives. Not all parties in waste management will be as knowledgeable about the waste they produce and how it should be managed. One person industrial organisations cannot be expected to understand as much about the legal and environmental implications of waste management as might a major chemical company or waste disposal contractor. For example, tracking a waste carrier's vehicle to a disposal site, the evaluation of the conditions of the site's licence and the interpretation of a full chemical analysis would not necessarily be reasonable actions for a self-employed individual. However, a company producing large amounts of hazardous waste might consider such actions as routine.

3.34 The EPA 1990 takes on board these realities by requiring a party to the duty '. . . to take all such measures applicable to him in that capacity as are reasonable in the circumstances . . .'[1]. This term applies to the four requirements of the duty as described earlier[2]: preventing others contravening s 33 of the EPA 1990; preventing the escape of waste; transferring waste only to duly authorised individuals; and, at the same time, transferring written descriptions of the waste between parties. However, it does not apply to compliance with the Environmental Protection (Duty of Care) Regulations 1991[3].

1 EPA 1990, s 34(1).
2 EPA 1990, s 34(1).
3 See para 3.19.

3.35 Therefore it can be seen that, in respect of s 34(1) itself, a party to the duty is required to take measures which are 'applicable to him in that capacity'. The measures which are applicable will vary with the party's relationship to the waste. They will depend upon whether the person is a producer, carrier, disposer and so on[1]. The capacity of the holder of the waste is a function of who the holder is, the degree of control which that person can exercise over what happens to the waste and the nature of that individual's involvement with the waste[2].

1 See Circular 19/91, para 9.
2 Code of Practice, para A.13: see also the discussion of 'reasonable precautions' in the context of s 33 of the EPA 1990 at para 7.145ff.

3.36 Besides measures applicable to a holder of waste, the second requirement of s 34(1) of the EPA 1990 involves the need for a party to the duty to take actions which are 'reasonable in the circumstances'. There are normally four circumstances which affect what actions are to be seen as reasonable. They are[1]:

(a) the nature of the waste;
(b) the dangers it presents in handling and treatment;
(c) how it is dealt with; and
(d) what the holder might reasonably be expected to know or foresee.

The Code of Practice concentrates particularly on the last item listed, extensively addressing questions of knowledge and foresight.

1 Code of Practice, para A.12.

3.37 Although the duty of care varies in the stringency of its application and is dependent on the identity of the parties to it, certain minimum standards can be identified from the Code of Practice itself. They are therefore applicable to all individuals affected by the duty. The Code of Practice suggests a number of ways by which a person can obtain help in order to ensure compliance with the duty. However, the Code emphasises that the responsibility for compliance with the duty rests with the person holding the waste. It cannot be passed on to others, such as consultants or laboratories, whose function should be viewed as advisory[1]. This would seem to hold even if a person was relying upon a waste broker to deal with a waste transaction.

1   See Code of Practice, paras 6.1 and 6.2.

3.38   A summary of the basic questions every waste holder should ask is contained early on in the Code of Practice[1]:

– Does the waste need a special container to prevent its escape or to protect it from the elements?
– What type of container would suit the waste?
– Can the waste be safely mixed with other wastes or should it be segregated?
– Can the waste be safely crushed?
– Can the waste be safely incinerated or are there special requirements for its incineration, such as minimum temperatures and combustion time?
– Can the waste be disposed of safely to landfill with other waste? and
– Is the waste's physical state likely to change in storage?

1   Code of Practice, para 1.4.

Preventing a contravention of s 33 of the EPA 1990

3.39   It has already been noted that the duty of care has a succession of requirements. The first of these is to ensure that persons take steps which are applicable to them and reasonable in the circumstances to prevent a contravention 'by any other person' of s 33 of the EPA 1990[1].

1   EPA 1990, s 34(1)(a).

3.40   A detailed discussion of s 33 of the EPA 1990 is to be found in Chapter 7. In summary, s 33(1) forbids persons from depositing, keeping, treating or disposing of waste other than at premises subject to waste management licences or which are exempt from the need to possess such licences[1]. A breach of s 33(1) can also occur if the deposit, treatment, keeping or disposal of the waste is not in accordance with a waste management licence. Contravention of s 33(1) can also happen where waste is treated, kept or disposed of in a manner which causes pollution of the environment or harm to human health[2]. Finally, s 33(6) is contravened when a licence condition is breached.

1   EPA 1990, s 33(1) and SI 1994/1056, regs 16 and 17.
2   EPA 1990, s 33(1)(c).

3.41   From *Shanks & McEwan (Southern Waste Services) Ltd v Environment Agency*[1], it is clear that it is not necessary for a successful prosecution under s 34 of the EPA 1990 that someone actually commits an offence under s 33 as well. Inappropriate waste being intercepted immediately prior to deposit at a facility does not absolve the carrier or the producer from potential liability. However, a breach of s 33 of the EPA 1990 only triggers an offence in respect of the duty of care in certain, quite specific, circumstances[2]. These circumstances involve two fundamental requirements. For a prosecution to succeed, it must be shown, firstly, that applicable and reasonable steps have not been taken *and*, secondly, that this omission has caused 'any other person' to contravene s 33. In the absence of these two elements, there is no offence under s 34(1)(a)[3]. A key concept to the understanding of this part of s 34 is the requirement that one person's act must always cause 'another person' to contravene s 33 of the EPA 1990. This principle is perhaps best illustrated by example. If a waste producer hides some inappropriate waste amongst other materials which are removed and later deposited at a landfill by a waste carrier, this action will violate the requirement of s 34(1) directly. The producer's actions caused the other person – the carrier in this example – to contravene s 33. Hence the producer has contravened s 34(1)(a) of the duty. By contrast, s 34(1)(a) will not be breached if a producer takes away waste and fly-tips it. The producer will not be affected by s 34(1)(a) – as no 'other person'[4] has contravened s 33(1)[5]. Finally, a disposal facility who allows a carrier to deposit waste in contravention of the facility's waste management licence would appear to be embraced by s 34. The disposal facility has caused another person – namely the carrier – to deposit waste in contravention to s 33 of the EPA 1990. These examples also illustrate the fact that – unlike in s 34(1)(c)[6] – the offence in s 34(1)(a) places responsibilities throughout the chain of waste managers. Hence 'any other person' in that sub-section can refer to anyone 'upstream' or 'downstream' in a waste lifecycle[7].

1   *Shanks & McEwan (Southern Waste Services) Ltd v Environment Agency* [1999] Env LR 138 at 144.
2   EPA 1990, s 34(1)(a).
3   But there may be offences under s 34(1)(b) or (c): see below.
4   Ie a person other than the producer.
5   But the producer may instead be liable in these circumstances under s 34(1)(b): see para 3.45. Furthermore, an offence under s 34(1)(a) will be committed where a landowner 'knowingly permitted' the producer to make the deposit (see Chapter 7). In this case, the land owner is breaching s 33 of the EPA 1990, with the producer being open to proceedings for non-compliance with s 34(1)(a)
6   See para 3.61.
7   See *Shanks & McEwan (Southern Waste Services) Ltd v Environment Agency* [1999] Env LR 138 at 144.

3.42 It will also be apparent that the reference in s 34(1)(a) of the EPA 1990 to s 33 causes some overlap in possible offences. For example, if a carrier deposits waste at a licensed facility in contravention of a licence condition, that person will have caused an offence against s 33. An offence will also occur against s 34.

3.43 However, there are also obvious limitations as to how far breaches of a condition of a waste management licence will also be breaches of the duty of care. These boundaries arise due to the obvious practical limitations on what might be seen as steps which are 'applicable' or 'reasonable' in s 34(1) of the EPA 1990. These limitations are essentially one of fact, being judged by the criteria set down in s 34(1) and by way of the Code of Practice. Clearly, a carrier deliberately depositing the wrong sort of waste at a site run by a third party is an obvious example of a breach of the duty. Conversely, it would not be likely that, for example, an offence would be created under s 34 by a person delivering waste to a site where the licence holder was not complying with licence conditions in respect of landfill gas monitoring. In the latter example, it is difficult to conceive that any steps taken by the carrier would fall foul of s 34's criteria of being 'applicable to him in that capacity as are reasonable in circumstances'[1].

1   EPA 1990, s 34(1).

3.44 Finally, it needs to be appreciated that s 34(1)(a) is written in a manner which excludes certain waste management facilities from its ambit. As noted, s 34(1)(a) cross-refers to s 33 of the EPA 1990 and hence covers the delivery of waste to facilities

subject to waste management licences or appropriate exemptions, along with unauthorised disposal. However, the taking of wastes to sites which possess other types of
permits, particularly facilities subject to Integrated Pollution Control (IPC) authorisations under the Part I of the EPA 1990, is not an offence under s 34(1)(a). These facilities, which include hazardous waste incinerators and cement kilns, are entirely
excluded from s 33[1]. Hence, if inappropriate waste is delivered to such a facility, there
is no contravention of s 34(1)(a)[2].

1   SI 1994/1056, reg 16 as amended by SI 1995/288, reg 3(4).
2   Section 34(1)(a) of the EPA 1990 only refers to a contravention of s 33 of the Act. IPC facilities are
     excluded from s 33 by s 33(3) and SI 1994/1056, reg 16: see para 10.14ff.

Preventing the escape of waste[1]

3.45   The second element of EPA 1990, s 34 is the requirement that a party to the duty
prevents the 'escape' of waste 'from his control and that of any other person'[2]. Again,
this component is subject to the requirement on the party to take measures which are
applicable in that capacity and which are reasonable in the circumstances.

1   See Laurence D 'Waste and Strays' (1993) *Surveyor*, 1 April 1993, p 11.
2   EPA 1990, s 34(1)(b).

3.46   The provision on waste escaping is the only part of s 34 which addresses waste
when it is held by only one party. It is independent of any notion of waste being transferred. Essentially the requirement pertaining to the 'escape' of waste is aimed at the
circumstances where waste may be blown off a moving lorry, or from poor storage at
the producer's premises. Alternatively, it would address circumstances where waste
has leaked from storage tanks or drums or has been subject to a deliberate release[1].
Whether an uncontrolled outbreak of leachate from a landfill[2] could be seen as falling
under the duty has not been tested in the courts[3].

1   An example might be a release of CFCs from the processing of scrap refrigerators: see Circular
     11/94, Annex 1, para 1.13 and Annex 4, para 4.95ff.
2   A controlled waste under reg 5 and Sch 3 of SI 1992/588.
3   EPA 1990, s 33(1)(c) might be used to address such an issue more forcefully in terms of sentencing
     (see para 7.11). However, it should be noted that an action under s 34(1)(b) would not require the
     prosecution to show evidence of harm to human health or pollution of the environment. All that s 34
     requires is evidence that waste has escaped and hence this type of prosecution may have lower
     evidential requirements in some circumstances.

3.47   In order to ensure that waste should not escape, the Code of Practice requires[1]
that protection measures should be taken against:

−   the waste's container wearing or corroding;
−   accidental spills or leaks or the leaching of unprotected waste by rainfall;
−   accident or weather breaking open the container and allowing waste to escape;
−   the waste blowing away or falling while stored or transported; and
−   the scavenging of waste by vandals, thieves, children, trespassers or animals.

The requirements of the Code of Practice with respect of waste left outside the
premises and awaiting collection are quite clear. Materials stored in these circumstances[2]:

> '. . . should be in containers that are strong and secure enough to resist not only wind
> and rain but also animal disturbance, especially for food waste. All containers left
> outside for collection will therefore need to be secured or sealed. For example
> drums with lids, bags tied up, skips covered.'

Furthermore[3]:

'... holders should take particular care to secure waste material attractive to scavengers, for example building or demolition materials and scrap metal.'

1   Code of Practice, para 2.1.
2   Code of Practice, para 2.7.
3   Code of Practice, para 2.3.

Securing compliance with the duty when waste is transferred

3.48   This part of the duty and, in particular, the Code of Practice breaks down into two basic elements. The first involves the actions required to be taken prior to the use of a carrier or waste management site for the first time. The second element concerns the checks needed to ensure that the first and subsequent loads of waste dispatched end up where they should do. As will be seen, a greater emphasis is placed in the Code on the selection process for a legitimate carrier or waste management facility. Once such a person is selected, checking up on the continued integrity of the waste transaction is only to be undertaken occasionally, unless the holder of the waste has knowledge or suspicion that all may not be well. The following two sections describe these elements.

Establishing a transfer to authorised persons or for authorised transportation purposes

3.49   Section 34(1)(c) of the EPA 1990 requires that waste only passes to an authorised person or to a person for authorised transportation purposes[1]. Again, the prerequisite is for the holder of the waste to take steps which are applicable and which are reasonable in the circumstances to ensure that only the envisaged types of transfer occur.

1   The notion that the duty of care only applies to persons who are lawfully acting as transferor or transferee has been described as 'totally misconceived': see *R v Hertfordshire County Council, ex p Green Environmental Industries* [1998] 2 Env LR 153 at 165.

3.50   Generally, transfers of wastes to 'authorised persons' will be to registered waste carriers or to holders of waste management licences[1]. However, the waste collection authority[2], persons who have been exempted or excluded from the requirement to hold either a waste management licence[3] or from carrier registration[4] and a waste disposal authority in Scotland[5] are all authorised persons. Besides these categories, the Secretary of State is empowered to prescribe other classes of individuals as authorised persons[6]. No such persons have as yet been prescribed.

1   EPA 1990, s 34(3)(b), (d).
2   EPA 1990, s 34(3)(a).
3   EPA 1990, s 34(3)(c): such persons are exempt or excluded under s 33(3) of the EPA 1990 and regs 16 and 17 of SI 1994/1056 (see para 10.04).
4   EPA 1990, s 34(3)(e): see para 6.08ff.
5   EPA 1990, s 34(3)(f).
6   EPA 1990, s 34(3A): as amended by the Environment Act 1995, s 120 and Sch 22, para 65.

3.51   As well as transfers to an authorised person, wastes can be passed to someone 'for authorised transportation purposes'. This provision covers the small number of cases where a transfer between parties does not need to involve a registered waste carrier[1]. 'Authorised transportation purposes' are therefore defined in s 34 of the EPA 1990 as meaning instances where waste is moved to a different place within the same premises, between the point of disembarkation to where the waste has landed in Britain and the transport by air or sea from Britain to elsewhere[2].

1   As registered under the Control of Pollution (Amendment) Act 1989: see Chapter 6 and para 6.22.
2   EPA 1990, s 33(4): the wording is similar to s 2 of the Control of Pollution (Amendment) Act 1989.

3.52   The question of 'authorised transportation purposes' involving the movement of waste within the same premises[1] has been noted as being potentially problematic[2]. Often a collection of buildings on, for example, an industrial estate, are let to various tenants, with the landlord providing a common waste collection service. This may involve wastes being removed to a central skip on the premises. Usually, the skip will not require a waste management licence[3]. Alternatively, the landlord may collect the tenants' waste and place it in the centralised repository. Presumably the term 'authorised transportation purposes' was put in place partly to deal with this situation.

1   EPA 1990, s 34(4)(a).
2   Burnett-Hall R *Environmental Law*, (1995) Sweet & Maxwell, London, para 11-237.
3   Many smaller skips will be exempt under Sch 3, para 40(1)(c) of the Waste Management Licensing Regulations 1994 (SI 1994/1056): see para 10.65ff.

3.53   However, not all industrial estates are necessarily going to qualify as being only one premises[1]. For example, a large, but 'down-sized' industrial concern may have leased or sold off some of its land to other occupants. In this case, there may be more than one premises. Indeed, it has been suggested that an industrial complex occupied by a number of companies within the same group should not necessarily be regarded as the same premises[2].

1   The term 'premises' is an ordinary English word 'which takes colour and content from the context in which it used' *Maunsell v Olins* [1975] 1 All ER 16 at 19C, per Viscount Dilhorne. A holiday camp containing self-contained chalets all owned by one company has been held to be one premises (*Phonographic Performance Ltd v Pontin's Ltd* [1967] 3 All ER 736).
2   Burnett-Hall R *Environmental Law*, (1995) Sweet & Maxwell, London, para 11-237.

3.54   Authorised transportation purposes includes the time period from when Britain's national territory is entered until the waste has 'landed'[1]. This provision has obvious relevance to transfrontier waste shipments. The point when waste has 'landed' is not clear, but would appear to be at the dockside or prior to passing through customs. However, anything greater than short-term dockside storage would normally require a waste management licence[2].

1   EPA 1990, s 34(4)(b).
2   EPA 1990, s 33: see para 7.26ff. Most waste covered by transfrontier notifications would be special waste. Hence many of the exemptions from waste management licences do not apply. However, storage of 'Green List' wastes, such as waste paper, passing for recovery (see para 5.47ff) might, if the requirements were satisfied, qualify for an exemption under Sch 3 to the Waste Management Licensing Regulations 1994 (SI 1994/1056): see para 10.83ff.

3.55   Before making an arrangement to have waste removed[1], the Code of Practice requires that a party to the duty of care must make a number of checks: '*Anyone intending to transfer waste to a carrier will need to check that the carrier is registered or is exempt from registration*'[2] [author's emphasis]. This can be done by asking to see a copy of the carrier's registration certificate. However, a photocopy of a registration certificate is not valid and does not provide evidence of registration[3]. The Code states that it would be 'sensible' for 'every' vehicle employed by a carrier to have a proper copy of the registration certificate or evidence of exemption[4].

1   Code of Practice, para 3.1.
2   Code of Practice, para 3.7.

3 SI 1991/1624, reg 14(2); see para 6.59 and Code of Practice, para 3.7.
4 Code of Practice, para 4.9.

3.56 Similarly, the Code of Practice indicates that anyone using a waste broker must check the broker's registration[1]. However, brokers are not issued with registration certificates[2], and thus evidence of registration can only be obtained by contacting the Agency directly.

1 Code of Practice, para 3.4
2 See para 6.58.

3.57 The Code makes clear that it is essential that the Agency is contacted prior to using a carrier for the first time[1]: '... the holder should check with the ... Agency ... that the carrier's registration is still valid, *even* if his certificate appears to be current'[2]. In this respect, the Code also cautions that the inclusion of a carrier on the Agency's register is not a recommendation or guarantee of the person's suitability to move the particular waste. The holder of the waste must remain alert to any sign that the waste is not being dealt with properly[3].

1 Code of Practice, para 3.8.
2 Code of Practice, para 3.8.
3 Code of Practice, para 3.6.

3.58 Finally, certain persons are exempt from the need to possess a waste carrier registration[1]. An example is a charitable organisation. The Code states that 'in all cases' when using such persons for the first time, the holder is expected to determine that the exemption under which the waste is to be carried is valid[2].

1 See SI 1994/1056, Sch 4, Pt I, para 12(1); SI 1991/1624, reg 2(1) and Chapter 6.
2 Code of Practice, para 3.12.

3.59 Prior to a person sending or taking waste to a waste management facility, the following checks are illustrated in the Code of Practice. Again, these are presented in the Code as a minimum. The existence of a licence for the facility must be verified[1]. It must also be established that the licence permits the operator to accept the type and quantity of waste involved in the transaction[2]. The Code clearly states that the licence should be examined by the holder of the waste, with the holder also showing a description of the waste to the manager of the site[3]. A similar requirement applies to a holder proposing to deliver waste to a facility which claims to be exempt from the need to possess a waste management licence. In this case, the holder should verify that the waste falls within the scope of the exemption[4] and, if need be, seek advice from the Agency.

1 Code of Practice, para 3.15.
2 Code of Practice, para 3.15.
3 Code of Practice, para 3.16.
4 'It is not taking enough care for a holder to consign waste to a contractor who states that he is exempt but does not give the grounds' (Code of Practice, para 3.17: see also *Environment Agency v Short* [1999] Env LR 300 at 307).

3.60 The Code of Practice makes it clear that the making of these checks is a requirement of either the waste producer, when that person delivers the waste personally, or of a carrier intending to move the waste on behalf of a producer[1]:

'A carrier should *always* check that the next holder he delivers to is an authorised person and that the description of the waste he carries is within the licence or exemption of any waste manager to whom he delivers. ...' [Author's emphasis].

However, when a carrier is only providing the transport as part of a contract between the waste producer and disposal site, the Code makes clear that the checking out should be done by the producer[2].

1   Code of Practice, para 3.18.
2   Code of Practice, para 3.18.

3.61   Finally, the wording of s 34(1)(c) of the EPA 1990 causes clear delineations to be set down in respect of the relationship between the parties to the duty of care. These have crucial effects. Section 34(1)(c) requires that the holder of the waste must take all reasonable steps to ensure that waste is passed *to* an authorised person or *to* a person for authorised transport purposes. This creates a one-way chain of verification, in the sense that the duty is on person A to check up on the credentials of the next person, person B. This means that the waste producer must check up on the carrier and that the carrier must check up on the status of the disposal site. However, in the case of a waste management facility of destination, there is no requirement on the operator to ensure that the carrier delivering the waste is an appropriately authorised person[1].

1   As the Code of Practice notes, 'In the Department's view, it is not an offence under section 34(1) of the EPA 1990 for a recipient to accept waste from an unregistered carrier' (Code of Practice, para 4.3).

3.62   Although this might seem a significant defect in the legislation, it should be noted that, if Person A was, for example, an unregistered waste carrier, that person could not truthfully complete the transfer note required by the Environmental Protection (Duty of Care) Regulations 1991 to document the load[1]. An offence may be committed if details were falsified[2]. The requirements on transfer notes are considered separately at para 3.118 below.

1   For example a carrier registration number is necessary: SI 1991/2839, reg 2(2)(e).
2   See para 12.223.

3.63   The requirements on persons receiving waste are set out in section 4 of the Code of Practice. These will affect both waste carriers and waste management facility operators. Given the one-way nature of the requirements for verifying the legitimacy of other persons in a waste transaction, the Code notes that '[c]hecking back . . . need not be as thorough as checking forward'[1]. However, the Code then suggests a number of items which must be considered. The one way nature of the checking process resultant from s 34(1)(c) of the EPA 1990 would appear to cause a number of the requirements of the Code to be closer to advice than to strict and enforceable guidance.

1   Code of Practice, para 4.2.

3.64   For a person who receives waste for the first time, the Code requires that the recipient should ensure that the person delivering the material is properly registered[1]. Hence 'it is reasonable' to ask for the relevant registration certificate or evidence of exemption[2]. The suitability of the waste's containers should be verified[3], along with the waste's description[4].

1   Code of Practice, para 4.4.
2   Code of Practice, para 4.4.
3   Code of Practice, para 4.5.
4   Code of Practice, para 4.6.

Monitoring waste transfers to authorised persons

3.65   Having covered the minimum requirements for the advance verification of the credentials of the other parties, the Code of Practice then sets out how the continued compliance with the duty of care is to be ensured[1]. Overall, the Code places less emphasis on this stage, suggesting that the main requirements are the periodic monitoring of arrangements, particularly waste descriptions and the credentials of the other parties.

1   Code of Practice, section 5.

3.66   In respect of waste descriptions and transfer notes, the Code states that 'anyone' receiving wastes should make 'at least' a visual check that the description matches the waste[1]. For an operator of a waste management facility it is indicated that 'it would be good practice to go beyond this by fully checking the composition of samples of waste received'[2].

1   Code of Practice, para 5.4.
2   Code of Practice, para 5.4.

3.67   Repeated checks on such matters as carrier registrations and waste management licences are unnecessary when the type of waste, carrier and final destination are the same[1]. However, it is recommended that occasional checks are made to ensure that the composition of the waste remains as described on the transfer note[2].

1   See for example Code of Practice, paras 3.8, and 3.23.
2   Code of Practice, para 3.23.

3.68   Besides ensuring that the parties to the transaction are still authorised[1], the Code suggests four other circumstances when additional checking 'should' be done[2]:

–   when a new transaction is proposed whereby the description of the waste or its destination has changed;
–   where several carriers are involved in collecting waste from the same place, and there is the danger that an unauthorised carrier picks up a load – construction and demolition sites are used by the Code as an example;
–   where the waste carrier transporting the waste has changed; and
–   where there has been a change in the licence conditions of the destination.

In relation to the Code's final requirement above, it is immediately observable that, in many instances, a user of a site is highly unlikely to be aware of changes which have been made to a licence. The only exception will be where changes have been made which affect the range of wastes which can be sent to the site. But even in this case, the most likely person to inform the user would be the licence holder.

1   'As a minimum precaution, the licence . . ., registration or evidence of exemption should be seen and checked at least once a year even if nothing has changed in a series of repeated transfers': Code of Practice, para 3.24(c).
2   Code of Practice, para 3.24.

3.69   The Code provides examples of when a person should become concerned that the waste they are responsible for may be being mismanaged[1]. 'Obvious causes of concern' include:

(a)   wrong or inadequate waste descriptions;
(b)   poor packing so that waste may escape;
(c)   poorly completed transfer notes or false information on such notes;
(d)   unsupported claims of being a registered waste carrier or exempt from licensing;
(e)   failure of waste consigned via a carrier to arrive at the agreed destination;
(f)   damaged or interfered with waste containers.

1   Code of Practice, para 5.5.

3.70   On receipt of an indication that all is not well, a person is advised by the Code to make appropriate enquiries[1]. When these enquires have verified the person's suspicions, the 'first action' should normally be to refuse to utilise the carrier or accept further loads of the waste[2]. However, the Code notes that this action may not always be appropriate. The Code uses as an illustration the case of where a breach of contract may occur on the termination of an arrangement between parties. It appears to suggest that the waste can continue to be moved or accepted in these circumstances[3]. However, if these circumstances arise, the Code suggests that the stringency of waste checking and analysis should be considerably enhanced, as should enquiries to ensure that future loads reach their destinations.

1   Code of Practice, para 5.7.
2   Code of Practice, para 5.8.
3   Code of Practice, para 5.8: to overcome such a problem the Code indicates that new waste contracts might contain termination clauses which enter into force when the duty is breached.

3.71   In addition, where there are concerns about the activities of other parties to a waste transaction, the Code requires the Agency be informed 'if appropriate'[1]. Persons 'should' tell the Agency where they know or suspect that the duty of care is breached, unregistered carriers are being used[2], unlicensed waste management is occurring[3], or where there is evidence that licence conditions are being breached[4].

1   Code of Practice, para 5.9.
2   Or where carriers which are not covered by appropriate exemptions are being used: see para 6.08.
3   Or waste management at sites which do not have legitimate exemptions from the need to possess licences.
4   Code of Practice, para 5.12.

SPECIFIC RESPONSIBILITIES OF PARTIES TO THE DUTY OF CARE

3.72   Subject to the exclusions described at para 3.23, the duty of care applies to all persons involved in waste transactions. These parties are named in s 34(1) of the EPA 1990 and cover persons who import, produce, carry, keep, treat, or dispose of controlled waste or, as a broker, have control of such waste. As has been explained earlier, while the duty applies to all of these parties, the degree of responsibility that can be expected to be exercised by each party varies. It is a function of not only what actions are to be deemed as reasonable in the circumstances, but also the identity of parties in a waste management transaction and their proximity to it.

3.73   Although the specific responsibilities of particular parties will vary, much of the information provided in the Code of Practice is applicable to all of them and hence has already been covered earlier in this chapter. However, the Code[1] sets out additional guidance which 'draws out questions of the allocation of responsibility'[2]. Such allocation is particularly necessary in order to decide what steps under the duty are applicable to a person in any particular capacity.

1   Code of Practice, Annex B.
2   Code of Practice, para B.1.

3.74   Any attempt at delineating the nature of each party's responsibilities raises significant matters of interpretation as to how these individuals are to be identified. The question of correct identification is an issue which affects not only the operation of the duty of care, but also certain other requirements in the EPA 1990 which single out particular entities in waste lifecycles and allocates liability to them[1]. It has also been suggested that such identification is needed to ensure that charges in respect of non-compliance with the duty of care are correctly framed[2].

1   Examples of such instances include waste carrier or waste broker registration purposes, when settling the question of waste definitions (as Chapter 2 has shown, waste is defined primarily by the producer's actions or intent), the identity of potential waste management licensees and so on.
2   See Bates J H *UK Waste Management Law* 2nd edn, (1997) Sweet and Maxwell, para 5.05. However it also seems clear that overlaps in the types of individuals named in EPA 1990, s 34(1) may cause persons to be fulfilling two (or more) functions simultaneously.

3.75   As will be shown, it is not always easy to delineate between the parties to the duty of care. This is due to overlaps between the activities being referred to. The blurred nature of the distinctions is starkly highlighted at construction sites, where there may be considerable confusion as to who is acting as producer, broker, carrier etc[1]. Overall, it would be fair to say that the issue is, on occasion, rather muddled. This situation is not helped by some quite fundamental contradictions between the views expressed by the Department of the Environment in different Circulars[2] and contrasts in the level of detail and advice contained in the first and second editions of the Code of Practice[3]. That this confusion continues to this day is even more surprising given that the basic premises of the duty of care have remained the same within that period, while these difficulties were known well before the Code of Practice was revised in 1996.

1   Given the prominent role of the construction industry in UK waste management, these matters are discussed separately at para 3.111 below.
2   Eg Circulars 19/91 and 11/94.
3   See para 3.113 below.

3.76   The paragraphs below set out some principles by which each party can be identified. Also described are the additional requirements of the Code which are aimed specifically at particular parties. However, it should be emphasised that the foregoing will cover the *additional responsibilities* of a party to the duty. Common responsibilities have been covered earlier in this chapter. It is therefore essential that the remainder of this section is read in a manner which takes this division into account. Accordingly, primary reference must also be made to para 3.32ff above.

Waste importers

3.77   Like the other terms used in s 34(1) of the EPA 1990, the nature of a person who imports waste is left undefined. It will therefore hold its ordinary meaning. However, a person who imports waste has overlaps with others named in s 34(1). Accordingly, the concept of 'importer' appears to impinge upon some of the other roles. For example a person who transports waste across a frontier would be acting as both a carrier and an importer. If a person involved in waste importation is not in possession of such waste, then that individual may be acting as a broker as well as an importer. While s 34(1) requires that the only type of broker covered by the duty is one who exercises 'control' over the waste, there is no such caveat in respect of an importer. Hence an importer can be much further removed from having direct responsibility for the waste than would be the case if such an individual was acting as a broker[1].

1   Brokers are discussed at para 3.101 below.

3.78   However, for many practical applications, the concept of 'importer' is almost superfluous. As noted, many persons importing waste will be acting as carriers, others will be brokers. In this respect, it is perhaps telling that the Code of Practice itself does not make separate provision for the specific duties of waste importers. For these reasons, the term will not be considered further here.

Waste producers

3.79 A key term in the EPA 1990, s 34 is the 'waste producer'[1]. Although left undefined, it is critically important to correctly determine that person's identity, particularly as the Code of Practice places significant emphasis on the responsibilities of producers for their wastes[2].

1 The term 'waste producer' is also vital to other regulations such as the Control of Pollution (Amendment) Act 1989 and the Controlled Waste (Registration of Carriers and Seizure of Vehicles) Regulations 1991 (SI 1991/1624). The requirement to register as a controlled waste carrier under the 1989 Act does not apply to a waste producer, unless that person hauls building and demolition waste (SI 1991/1624, reg 2(1)(b)): see para 6.10. It is also a key phrase in respect of how waste is defined: see Chapter 2.
2 See, for example, Code of Practice, para B.2ff.

3.80 The Code of Practice acknowledges that s 34 of the EPA 1990 does not define the nature of a person who 'produces' waste[1]. It suggests[2] that the definition to be applied is that contained in Regulation 1(3) of the Waste Management Licensing Regulations 1994[3]. The 1994 Regulations define 'producer' as meaning:

'. . . anyone whose activities produce . . . waste or who carries out pre-processing, mixing or other operations resulting in a change in its nature or composition.'

This definition is virtually identical to the definition contained in the amended Directive on Waste[4].

1 Code of Practice, para B.2.
2 Code of Practice, para B.2 and see also the definition on page 62 of the Code.
3 SI 1996/1056: oddly the Code of Practice also points to the definition given in Sch 22, para 88 of the Environment Act 1995. While this definition is identical to that contained in the Waste Management Licensing Regulations 1994, this paragraph was not enacted when the Code came into force.
4 Council Directive of 15 July 1975 on Waste (75/442/EEC) (OJ L194/39 25.7.75) as amended by Council Directive of 18 March 1991 amending Directive 75/442 on Waste (91/156/EEC) (OJ L78/32 26.3.91) Article 1(b).

3.81 The identity of a waste producer was considered in the Scottish case of *Gotech Industrial and Environmental Services Ltd and James Pitcairn v James Friel*[1]. In a wide ranging and useful judgment, Lord Allanbridge considered the nature of the waste producer in respect of the now-repealed Control of Pollution (Special Waste) Regulations 1980[2]. Gotech was a company mainly involved in the transportation of waste, with Pitcairn being one of the directors. Staff from Gotech stripped and removed asbestos from pipework in a boiler house on a construction site. The asbestos was taken away and stored on premises owned by the company, where it was subsequently discovered by the relevant authorities. The company and its director were charged under both the Control of Pollution Act 1974[3] and the Health and Safety at Work, etc Act 1974. The charges under the Control of Pollution Act 1974 included non-compliance with the Special Waste Regulations 1980, as Gotech failed – as a waste 'producer' under the Regulations – to raise a consignment note to cover the transport of the waste.

1 [1995] SCCR 22. It is curious to note that the duty of care Code of Practice does not make mention of this decision.
2 SI 1980/1709: note that in respect of the Special Waste Regulations 1996, the term 'producer' is discontinued, being substituted by 'consignor'. Although s 34 of the EPA 1990 was in fact in force at the time of the case, no charges were laid under this provision.
3 Now replaced by Part II of the EPA 1990.

3.82   The court heard argument that the 'producer' of the waste should be either the main contractor on the construction site or the owner of the site. It was also suggested that the waste was produced when a decision was made by either the owner or by the main contractor that it should be removed. By the time Gotech had arrived to carry out the stripping works, the waste had already been 'produced' in the sense that the other parties had already determined its unwanted or spoiled status.

3.83   The notion that Gotech was not to be viewed as the waste producer did not impress Lord Allanbridge, who stated[1]:

'We find no difficulty in concluding that, when the appellants' employees broke up the lagging to remove it from the pipes and put it in the sacks, they were the persons who were "producing" the waste that required to be disposed of by the appellants.'

For these and other reasons, Gotech and Pitcairn's convictions were upheld.

1   *Gotech Industrial and Environmental Services Ltd and James Pitcairn v James Friel* [1995] SCCR 22 at 29D.

3.84   From the above judgment and from the definition in the Waste Management Licensing Regulations 1994[1], the 'producer' is to be viewed as the person who is the original source of the waste. The definition in the 1994 Regulations also indicates that the responsibility shifts when a waste management facility has processed the waste in a manner which constitutes 'pre-processing, mixing or other operations' which affects the waste's composition or nature. When waste has undergone such operations, the operator of the waste management facility becomes the 'producer'.

1   SI 1994/1056, reg 1(3), see para 2.164.

3.85   Although these two identities for waste producers appear reasonably clear cut, the establishment of rules to identify the nature of a waste producer for the purposes of s 34 of the EPA 1990 sometimes can be rather awkward. Examples of such circumstances include when waste is moved from households which are exempt from the duty of care and at premises where a common waste disposal service is being provided by, for example, a landlord. Furthermore, despite the *Gotech Industrial Services* judgment, the matter is by no means settled at construction or demolition sites.

3.86   As householders are exempt from the duty of care in respect of wastes from their own property (see para 3.23), Circular 19/91 indicates that a local authority collecting waste from a domestic property is to be seen as the 'producer'[1]. Similarly, if a waste disposal contractor is employed by a local authority to undertake domestic refuse collection, the Circular argues that the contractor is the producer for the purposes of the duty of care[2]. By analogy, therefore, it might seem that a person collecting waste by way of providing a skip service to households is acting as a producer.

1   Circular 19/91, para 29.
2   A local authority which has arranged for a contractor to collect domestic wastes is acting as a broker: see Circular 19/91, para 30 and para 3.110.

3.87   But whether the Circular is correct on this matter may be open to some debate. The wide application of this principle would cause somewhat absurd results. In the case of household waste collection, for example, it seems difficult to argue that, for the purposes of s 34 of the EPA 1990 the person collecting the waste is the producer; but that the same person in the same circumstances is acting instead as a waste carrier in respect of the Control of Pollution (Amendment) Act 1989.

3.88   Besides construction and demolition sites[1], similar problems of party identification can occur at other premises. This matter is taken up by Circular 11/94[2]:

> '... managing agents, development companies and janitors providing common services (including waste management), will not normally be acting as waste brokers, because they are the producers of the waste concerned.'

Again, there is scope to question whether this assertion is correct. In the circumstances of the examples just quoted, it would appear that there might be two producers. In other words, the responsibility for the production of the waste is shared between the source of the waste and, for example, that person's landlord who provides a common storage facility for all the tenants on an industrial estate. However, this interpretation would appear to then get into difficulties in deciding the primary responsibilities for the transfer note system under the duty of care. Indeed, these difficulties are so fundamental as to cause doubt to be placed on whether two quite separate entities can both 'produce' the same waste. *Inter alia*, this argument would indicate that both 'producers' names would need to be specified on the relevant transfer note. Alternatively, should each producer draft their own separate transfer note to document any load? How should a person, such as an architect for example, be in a position to assess what steps are applicable and reasonable to take to discharge the duty of care? Besides this, the concept of multi-party producers would seem contrary to the meaning of waste producer contained in the Waste Management Licensing Regulations 1994[3].

1   Discussed separately at para 3.111 below.
2   Circular 11/94, Annex 8, para 8.5.
3   SI 1994/1056, reg 1(3) and also Council Directive of 15 July 1975 on Waste (75/442/EEC) (OJ L194/39 25.7.75) as amended by Council Directive of 18 March 1991 amending Directive 75/442/EEC on Waste (91/156/EEC) (OJ L78/32 26.3.91) Article 1(b). According to the Code of Practice, the definition in reg 1(3) of the Waste Management Licensing Regulations 1994 applies to EPA 1990, s 34 (Code of Practice, para B.2 and see also the Code's page 62): see paras 2.156ff and 2.163ff.

3.89   However, despite the difficulties outlined above, it is important not to lose sight of the fact that, in 95% of waste transactions, the identity of the producer will be clear. Hence common sense will normally suffice.

Waste producers' responsibilities

3.90   A consistent theme of the Code of Practice is the importance to the duty of care of the activities of the waste producer. Annex B of the Code states that waste producers bear the sole responsibility for their waste when they hold it[1]. Accordingly, they are liable for any escape of wastes from their premises[2]. Likewise they are principally answerable for the packing of the waste to prevent its escape while in transit[3]. Producers are also best placed to know what their waste is. Hence the Code notes that they bear the 'main' responsibility for ensuring the accuracy of the written description of the waste as it leaves their premises and that the description contains all the necessary information to ensure safe handling by subsequent parties[4].

1   Code of Practice, para B.3.
2   EPA 1990, s 34(1)(b) and see para 3.45 above.
3   Code of Practice, para B.4.
4   Code of Practice, para B.3: see para 3.129.

3.91   The responsibility of producers for the behaviour of subsequent individuals in a waste transaction will vary. The Code suggests that, if the producer uses a carrier who has independently arranged the destination for the waste, the producer has a lower level of liability than would be the case if the producer arranged both the carriage and subsequent disposal or recovery. Accordingly, the Code indicates that, when a registered waste carrier is used, the producer is not absolved from checking up to ensure that the waste is correctly handled at its final destination[1]. Such checks 'would be a prudent means of protecting his[2] position'[3]. But the nature and level of these enquiries would be lower than if a producer arranges not only the carriage, but also the disposal or recovery of the waste. In the latter case, the Code considers that producers 'share' with the waste manager of the destination responsibility for ensuring that the waste falls within the terms of any licence or exemption[4]. Hence producers should, in these circumstances, always ensure that the waste has reached its final destination[5].

1   Code of Practice, para B.5.
2   Ie the producer's.
3   Code of Practice, para 5.2.
4   Code of Practice, para B.3.
5   Code of Practice, para 5.3.

3.92   There are limits on how much checking up is appropriate. For example, the Code of Practice suggests that a producer would not normally be expected to follow the carrier to the disposal site[1]. But the producer is required to bear responsibility when direct evidence of illegal treatment is known and ignored or when such activities could have been readily foreseen. The Code gives two examples: where a carrier's vehicle reappears far too quickly for the waste to have gained its legitimate destination, or where the producer has evidence that the carrier is involved in illegal dumping of other persons' waste[2].

1   Code of Practice, para B.6.
2   Code of Practice, para B.6.

3.93   However, it should be reiterated that the Code of Practice sets down the minimum requirements. In certain circumstances, a waste producer may wish to exceed these. Clearly, a person who is taking significantly more interest in the waste's subsequent handling over and above the requirements of the Code will be setting up additional levels of protection against any criminal proceedings for a breach of the duty of care.

Waste carriers

3.94   The term 'waste carrier' does not have a definition in the EPA 1990. Hence it will have its ordinary meaning. The Code of Practice indicates that a 'carrier' is[1]:

'... a person who transports controlled waste, within Great Britain, including journeys into and out of Great Britain.'

1   Code of Practice, p 60.

3.95   Like some of the other parties nominated in s 34(1) of the EPA 1990, there may be overlaps between persons who act as carriers and some of the other terms. As noted, persons who import wastes would often act as waste carriers. Similarly, producers transporting their own wastes are also acting as waste carriers. The latter example would indicate that the term is wider than that applying to a registered waste carrier under the Control of Pollution (Amendment) Act 1989[1].

1   See Chapter 6.

Carriers' responsibilities

3.96   A carrier's responsibilities are highlighted in Annex B of the Code of Practice. The Code suggests that the degree of accountability is dependent on the carrier's relationship with the other parties in a transaction. An example given is when a carrier is solely required to provide for the transportation of waste which is already subject to a contract between the producer and operator of the waste management facility. In this case, the carrier's responsibilities are narrow in their scope. Hence the Code indicates that there is no need for the carrier to verify that the wastes to be transported are allowable under the licence[1]. But obviously this would not be the case when the carrier is arranging the final destination of the waste on behalf of the waste producer. In this instance, the verification of whether the operator of the destination is an authorised person[2] will be essential, as will be an assessment of the appropriateness of that person accepting the waste.

1   Code of Practice, para B.11.
2   See para 3.49 above.

3.97   Although the Code envisages the existence of differences in the degree of verification needed to be exercised by a carrier, the Code makes it clear that all carriers should check that there is little possibility that the waste will escape[1]. Equally, the Code notes that '[w]hen accepting *any*[2] waste a carrier should make at least a quick visual inspection to see that it appears to match the description [on the transfer note]'.

1   Code of Practice, para B.8.
2   Author's emphasis.

Persons who keep, treat or dispose of[1] waste

3.98   Persons who keep, treat or dispose of waste should be clearly identifiable as they possess, or should possess, an appropriate waste management licence or an authorisation under Part I of the EPA 1990, or be exempt from the waste management licensing system[2].

1   Note that, unlike s 33 of the EPA 1990, s 34 does not refer to the word 'deposit'. However, s 29(6) indicates that the word 'disposal' encompasses instances when waste is deposited: see para 7.16ff.
2   However, unlike s 33 of the EPA 1990, there is no explicit cross reference between s 34 and the lists of disposal and recovery activities set out in Parts III and IV of Sch 4 to the Waste Management Licensing Regulations 1994 (SI 1994/1056). In contrast to s 34, s 33's activities of depositing, treating, keeping and disposing of waste are explicitly linked to the lists of waste management activities set down in these parts of Schedule 4 (see SI 1994/1056: Sch 4, Pt I, para 9 and see para 7.31ff).

Responsibilities

3.99   The one-way nature[1] of the requirement to ensure that persons to whom wastes are transferred are duly authorised persons[2] somewhat diminishes the responsibilities of recipients of wastes. This is acknowledged in the Code of Practice in respect of unregistered waste carriers[3]. However, recipients of waste must not, of course, permit others to contravene s 33 of the EPA 1990[4], while they are required to prevent the escape of waste in their control and to receive waste which has been duly documented by transfer notes and written descriptions.

1   See para 3.61.
2   EPA 1990, s 34(1)(c)(ii).
3   Code of Practice, paras 4.3 and 7.19.

4   As noted at para 3.41, an example might be where a carrier was allowed to dispose of waste in contravention of the conditions of a waste management licence. This requirement does not apply to sites excluded from Part II of the EPA 1990's controls (by way of s 33(4)(c) and SI 1994/1056, reg 16). The most obvious are hazardous waste incinerators (see para 3.44).

3.100   The Code indicates that recipients of wastes 'should normally' be able to rely on the written description of the waste when it arrives at the disposal or recovery facility. However, being responsible for the facility, the Code identifies the operator as being in a strong position to notice differences in waste descriptions. Hence, they bear a greater responsibility in checking the descriptions against the contents of incoming loads in comparison to some of the other parties bound by the duty of care[1].

1   See Code of Practice, para B.13 and also its para 5.3.

Brokers

3.101   There is no statutory definition of a 'broker' in the EPA 1990. A definition of a broker is contained in *Milford v Hughes*[1], which held that brokers are persons:

'... that contrive, make, and conclude bargains and contracts between merchants and tradesmen for which they have a fee or reward.'

Waste brokers are required to be registered by the Directive on Waste[2], with this requirement being transposed by the Waste Management Licensing Regulations 1994[3]. In those Regulations, brokers are persons who 'arrange (as dealer[4] or broker) for the disposal or recovery of controlled waste on behalf of another person'[5]. Although this definition is not used in s 34 of the EPA 1990, it should be noted that its application is confirmed by the Code of Practice[6].

1   (1846) 16 M & W 174 at 177: see para 6.29.
2   Council Directive of 15 July 1975 on Waste (75/442/EEC) (OJ L194/39 25.7.75) as amended by Council Directive of 18 March 1991 amending Directive 75/442/EEC on Waste (91/156/EEC) (OJ L78/32 26.3.91) Article 12.
3   SI 1994/1056, reg 20, para 12 of Sch 4 and Sch 5, along with, reg 20 of the Transfrontier Shipment of Waste Regulations 1994 (SI 1994/1137: see Chapter 5).
4   The Code of Practice defines the word dealer (p 61): 'a dealer in controlled waste acquires waste and sells it on. He may be a holder of the waste, or he may (as a broker does) make arrangements for its transfer without holding it'. However, this may not be correct in the context of the EPA 1990, s 34. Whether a person can act as a broker and 'acquire' waste seems doubtful. Such a person would instead be encompassed by one of the other terms used in the EPA 1990, s 34(1): see above.
5   SI 1994/1056, reg 20(1). This term is broadly similar to that in Article 12 of the Directive on Waste (as amended by Directive 91/156).
6   See Code of Practice, para A.7.

3.102   However, both the definitions outlined above are too wide for the purposes of s 34 of the EPA 1990. The reason is that s 34 only impinges upon brokers when they exercise 'control' over the waste. Indeed, this limitation leaves the Code of Practice to suggest that a broker is[1]:

'... a person who arranges for the disposal or recovery of controlled waste on behalf of another. He does not handle the waste himself or have it in his physical possession, but he controls what happens to it.'

Hence Circular 19/91 asserts that waste collection authorities and waste disposal authorities are acting as brokers when they award contracts for refuse collection and disposal[2].

1   Code of Practice, para 60.
2   Circular 19/91, para 30.

3.103   While s 34 of the EPA 1990 requires a broker to be a person who has control of the waste[1], it is not entirely clear how far the matter of control should be taken. In a slightly different context, Circular 11/94[2] notes that:

'. . . [a]n establishment or undertaking which acts as a broker has control of the waste in the sense that it arranges for the disposal or recovery on behalf of another and is outside the chain of people who handle waste (the producer, holder, carrier, recovery operator, or disposal operator).'

Similarly, the Circular 19/91[3] gives the following guidance:

'. . . [b]rokers may exercise control over waste, although they might not necessarily hold it. For the purposes of the duty, they can be considered as sharing responsibility for any transfer of such waste that they arrange, in addition to the two parties who effect the transfer.'

1   EPA 1990, s 34(1).
2   Circular 11/94, Annex 8, para 8.4.
3   Circular 19/91, para 6.

3.104   The criteria concerning brokers exercising control over waste allow the definition of broker to extend beyond what would usually be regarded as waste disposal contractors. For example, the Code of Practice states that 'If a consultant arranges a waste transfer to such an extent that he controls what happens to the waste, he is a broker, and shares responsibility with the two holders directly involved for the proper transfer of the waste'[1]. A passage to this effect is repeated in the Waste Management Licensing Circular[2].

1   Code of Practice, para 6.3; see also, para B.12.
2   Circular 11/94, Annex 8, para 8.5.

3.105   While brokers must exercise some control over the waste, persons cannot be acting as brokers where wastes are passed directly to them. In these circumstances, the receipt of the waste would cause such a person to fall into one of the other categories of persons named in s 34(1) of the EPA 1990. They would be acting as persons who carry, treat, keep or dispose of controlled waste. This is because a broker is not viewed as an 'authorised person' under s 34 of the EPA 1990, even when in possession of a valid registration[1].

1   The broker would be registered by way of reg 20 of SI 1994/1056 or by reg 20 of SI 1994/1137: see Chapter 6. The only exception to this principle is the waste collection authority. The collection authority is an authorised person under the EPA 1990, s 34(3)(a). It is perhaps because of this that Circular 19/91 (para 30) is able to state: 'where a collection contractor is employed, either the [collection] authority or the contractor may act as the transferee receiving the description and completing the transfer note'. However, this passage still remains somewhat anomalous for the reason that the actual waste may never be transferred to a collection authority by a contractor. It is most likely to be taken directly to a disposal site run by a third party. Collection authorities do not usually operate their own disposal infrastructure. There is also a considerable overlap between persons who act as importers and brokers for transfrontier waste movements: see para 3.77 above.

Responsibilities

3.106   Brokers have many common responsibilities with other parties to the duty of care. The Code of Practice[1] states that:

'A waste broker arranging the transfer of waste between a producer and a waste manager, to such an extent that he controls what happens to the waste, is taking responsibility for the legality of the arrangement.'

Therefore, brokers must ensure that a registered carrier is employed and, as applicable, that a correctly licensed or appropriately exempt waste management site is used[2]. However, the Code of Practice indicates that a broker is not responsible for the packaging of the waste on the grounds that such a person does not directly handle it[3]. But brokers are responsible for the accuracy of the documentation when it is transferred[4]. They also need to verify, in the manner usually required of the waste producer, that the waste has arrived safely[5].

1   Code of Practice, para B.12.
2   Code of Practice, para 3.19.
3   Code of Practice, para B.12.
4   Code of Practice, para 3.19.
5   Code of Practice, paras 3.19 and 5.3.

3.107   The matter of the completion of written descriptions and transfer notes[1] becomes more difficult when waste brokers are involved, even with single transfers. Although the involvement of brokers creates three duty of care parties[2], the activities of a broker do not need to be documented on any transfer note[3]. As already mentioned, for s 34 of the EPA 1990 to impinge upon a broker, the waste must have entered into the broker's 'control'. But while exercising control over the waste, the broker must be acting neither as transferor or transferee[4]. Being neither transferor or transferee, no transfer of waste will occur to such a person. Accordingly, the broker is not required to complete or sign any transfer note.

1   Discussed at para 3.118.
2   See Circular 19/91, para 19.
3   See the Environmental Protection (Duty of Care) Regulations 1991 and the model transfer note reproduced as Figure 3.1.
4   If they did possess the waste, it would seem that the person would be acting in a capacity other than a broker (eg as a waste carrier).

3.108   The Code of Practice emphasises[1] that a person should only use a registered waste broker[2] or one which is exempt from broker registration[3]. However, unless some other element of the duty of care is contravened, it is not clear what offence is being created by the use of an unregistered broker. There is no such offence under s 34 of the EPA 1990. Similarly, while the Waste Management Licensing Regulations 1994[4] set down an offence in respect of a person operating as an unregistered broker, there is no similar contravention by a person who utilises such an individual.

1   Code of Practice, para 3.4.
2   SI 1994/1056, reg 20; see also the Transfrontier Shipment of Waste Regulations 1994 (SI 1994/1137), reg 20.
3   Brokers exempt from registration are those who are also waste management licence holders or possessors of other relevant authorisations for the disposal or recovery facility they operate: see para 6.32.
4   SI 1995/1056, reg 20.

3.109   However, brokers who arrange for other persons to take waste to a licensed or exempt waste management facility in contravention of s 33 of the EPA 1990, or to a site which does not have a licence, will cause an offence under s 34(1). A broker who secures a waste transfer to somebody who is not an authorised person, such as an unregistered waste carrier, will similarly commit an offence.

3.110   It has already been noted that Circular 19/91 views the waste collection authority and waste disposal authority as acting as brokers when they arrange collection and disposal contracts[1]. The Circular 19/91 then sets out some further responsibilities for these bodies[2]:

'In their capacities as brokers, authorities should take the steps suggested in the Code of Practice to check on the other parties and ensure a proper transfer [of waste].'

The necessity of these bodies to actively check up on the operation of the duty of care system is also highlighted[3]:

'Waste collection and disposal authorities will need to ensure that waste transfers which they arrange have proper descriptions and transfer notes in accordance with the duty and the section 34(5) regulations.'

1   Circular 19/91, para 30.
2   Circular 19/91, para 30.
3   Circular 19/91, para 31.

Producers, brokers, sub-contractors and the construction industry

3.111   One of the more difficult areas in respect of s 34 of the EPA 1990 concerns the apportionment of responsibility for persons involved in construction activities and in demolition. This is due to the plethora of organisations which may be found on any large site. Architects, contract managers, sub-contractors and sub-sub-contractors all may be involved either in the production of waste directly or in the arrangement of its production, carriage, disposal or recovery. Unfortunately, the identification of responsibilities of these individuals in respect of s 34(1) of the EPA 1990 is less than clear. It is also a matter which is left notably vague in the Code of Practice.

3.112   A particular problem is to decide the nature of the capacity under which a person on a construction site is acting. Usually, difficulties will arise in the delineation between a waste producer or a waste broker. Circular 19/91 dwells upon this matter[1] by noting that conflicting views have arisen as to the identity of a waste producer on construction and demolition sites[2]. The Circular then states that the producer at a construction site should be viewed as the person undertaking the works which give rise to the waste[3]. This view would be entirely in accordance with *Gotech Industrial and Environmental Services Ltd and James Pitcairn v James Friel*[4] as discussed at para 3.81 above.

1   Circular 19/91, paras 16 and 17.
2   Circular 19/91, para 16.
3   Circular 19/91, para 17.
4   [1995] SCCR 22.

3.113   Having indicated the identity of the producer, Circular 19/91 then states[1] that at a construction site:

'The client for works, although he may make decisions as a result of which something becomes waste, is not himself producing the waste created by the works. Where there are several contractors and sub-contractors on site, the producer of a particular waste is the particular contractor or sub-contractor who (or whose employees) takes an action which creates waste, or, who begins to treat something as if it were waste[2]. Where a client or contractor makes arrangements for the carriage or disposal of waste, for example by letting a disposal sub-contract to a haulier for waste produced on site by a demolition sub-contractor, then that client or contractor will be acting as a broker in respect of the transfer between two sub-contractors; in such a case all three parties will be under the duty.'

This advice was repeated in a virtually identical form in the first edition of the Code of Practice[3]. However, the second edition of the Code is notable for the omission of this entire paragraph, with no further advice or clarification being provided on this issue.

1   Circular 19/91, para 17.
2   Again, this would be in accordance with Lord Allanbridge's views in *Gotech Industrial and Environmental Services*: see para 3.81 above.
3   At para B3.

3.114   Indeed, it would seem that the Department of the Environment is itself fundamentally confused over this matter. The above quotation from Circular 19/91 would appear to be directly contradicted by Circular 11/94 when it was published in 1994. The latter's discussion of broker registration[1] includes the statement that[2]:

'... on a building site where a main contractor, an architect or a civil engineer arrange for the disposal of controlled waste to an appropriate facility as part of their contract, they are arranging for the disposal on their own behalf given that they are the holder of the waste in question. They are not acting as a broker and do not need to register [as a broker].'

This would imply that these individuals – as holders of the waste – are jointly acting as producers, along with the sub-contractors who actually physically create the construction and demolition wastes. However, as noted at para 3.88 above, the concept of a multi-party producer creates significant difficulties in respect of the other facets of the duty of care.

1   Registration is required by SI 1994/1056, reg 20: see Chapter 6.
2   Circular 11/94, Annex 8, para 8.5.

3.115   But it is easy to understand how the Department of the Environment has got itself into difficulties. The notion expressed in Circular 19/91 that all persons who give instructions to contractors involved in waste 'production' at construction sites are acting as brokers has not insignificant ramifications. This could lead to brokers encompassing architects, main contractors, clients etc who, depending on the type of works, its size and the nature of the contractual arrangement, will have varying degrees of responsibility. Clearly, the Environment Agency's broker register[1] could get inordinately large in these circumstances[2].

1   See para 13.45.
2   Circular 19/91 was published well before the broker registration scheme was enacted in 1994, albeit that the requirement for broker registration was contained in the 1991 amendments made by Directive 91/156 to the Directive on Waste (75/442).

3.116   Given the lack in the revised Code of Practice of any guidance on these matters, one is left only with the requirement that, to be covered by the duty of care, brokers must be acting in a manner such that they are exercising control of the waste[1]. As already noted, the Waste Management Licensing Circular 11/94 indicates that a broker has control of the waste when it arranges the disposal or recovery of it on behalf of another party to the duty of care. Accordingly, many of the individuals responsible for activities at construction sites may or may not be exercising control over the waste. But it would seem that only those in close proximity to, and thus having an element of responsibility for, the waste production – carriage – disposal cycle can be said to be exercising control over it.

1   EPA 1990, s 34(1).

3.117 But the length to which the concept of control extends remains an open question. For example, it may be that a main contractor has no role in supervising sub-sub-contractors in their waste creation activities. The contractual responsibility for the activities of these individuals may be expressed in terms of what these persons are actually constructing, and not extend to the waste materials being taken out. Having no role, the main contractor may not satisfy the requirement of brokers in s 34 of the EPA 1990 as no control would appear to be exercisable in these circumstances. However, it may be that such individuals *should have had control* over the waste, but manifestly failed to exercise any control at all. Perhaps this is the heart of the need for the regulation of wastes emanating from construction and demolition sites. But the scope of the duty at these sites remains unclear. Despite the fact that the purported purpose of the Code of Practice is to provide advice on matters such as this, the Code fails to deliver key guidance in this highly problematic area. Furthermore, the fact that the second edition of the Code says less on this matter than the first reflects lamentably upon its credibility.

DOCUMENTING WASTE TRANSFERS: WRITTEN DESCRIPTIONS AND TRANSFER NOTES

The transfer note system

3.118 Section 34 of the EPA 1990 and the Environmental Protection (Duty of Care) Regulations 1991 establish a system of paperwork involving transfer notes. These have the purpose of permitting regulatory authorities to be able to readily identify all parties in a waste transaction. The requirements on documentation were also seen as a way of assisting parties to the duty of care in ensuring that their wastes were being dealt with correctly[1]:

> 'It is open to holders to ask each other for details from records, especially to check what happened to waste after it was consigned. A holder might draw conclusions and alert the . . . [relevant Agency] to any suspected breach of the duty if such a request was refused.'

As will be seen, the documentary system is only partial in its effect. However, it does provide a significant information source on many, but not all, waste management transactions.

1 Circular 19/91, para 24.

3.119 Only movements involving the transfer of non-special waste[1] are required to be subject to the transfer note system[2]. The movement of special waste is documented by way of the consignment note requirements of the Special Waste Regulations 1996[3].

1 Including non-special waste moved as transfrontier shipments: see para 3.159 below.
2 SI 1991/2839, reg 2(3) as amended by SI 1996/972, reg 23.
3 SI 1996/972: see Chapter 4: SI 1991/2839, reg 2(3) (as amended) states that the requirement to use transfer notes does not apply when the waste is special waste *and* when the consignment note or carrier's round schedule is completed in accordance with the Special Waste Regulations 1996. Accordingly, when faced with non-compliance in respect of the 1996 Regulations, the prosecution may wish to consider whether the Environental Protection (Duty of Care) Regulations 1991 have themselves been complied with. For example, the movement of special waste without either a consignment note or a transfer note would invite charges under both Regulations.

3.120 The arrangements by which transfers of wastes between parties is to be documented under the EPA 1990 is, it is submitted, a little odd. This is because the primary legislation requires that 'written descriptions' of the waste must be transferred[1].

However, the Environmental Protection (Duty of Care) Regulations 1991 require that 'transfer notes' are filled in at the same time that written descriptions are transferred[2]. The written description can be included in the transfer note[3]. But there is a contrast in the way s 34 of the EPA 1990 and the Environmental Protection (Duty of Care) Regulations 1991 approach the question of how a waste is to be described in a written description and in a transfer note[4].

1   EPA 1990, s 34(1)(c)(ii).
2   SI 1991/2839, reg 2(1).
3   See Circular 19/91, para 20.
4   See para 3.131 below.

3.121   In respect of prosecution policy, the duality of the written description/transfer note system may require consideration. For example, the Environmental Protection (Duty of Care) Regulations 1991 require that a transfer note must clearly identify the waste being transacted. If it comprehensively fails to do this, a prosecution for non-compliance with the Regulations can be countenanced[1]. As has been noted at para 3.19 above, a prosecution for an infraction of the 1991 Regulations – as opposed to an action for non-compliance with s 34(1) of the EPA 1990 itself – has lower evidential requirements. There is, for example, no need to establish what actions were 'reasonable in the circumstances' in such an instance. Litigation for breaches of the 1991 Regulations may, therefore, be preferred by regulatory bodies where wastes have been blatantly misdescribed.

1   By way of the EPA 1990, s 34(5) and (6).

3.122   However, in respect of waste descriptions, all the Environmental Protection (Duty of Care) Regulations 1991 require is that the transfer note identifies the waste to which it relates[1]. This can be complied with by way of waste descriptions in very general terms[2]. Circumstances may arise where, although a waste has been misdescribed, the description given satisfies the requirements of the 1991 Regulations[3]. Instead the prosecution may need to look to the more stringent criteria in s 34(1)(c)(ii) of the EPA 1990 in respect of the detail necessary for an adequate written description. In the latter case, the regulatory authority is left with more sophisticated evidential requirements – particularly in establishing what actions were reasonable in the circumstances and applicable to the accused – in order to satisfactorily prove the case.

1   SI 1991/2839, reg 2(2)(a).
2   See para 3.131 below.
3   Under the Environmental Protection (Duty of Care) Regulations 1991, it would seem possible to describe a load of mixed paper, cardboard, wood, empty drums, brick etc as 'demolition waste' when it stemmed from a demolition site. However, the waste description would clearly not be adequate as it does not give the recipient sufficient information to prevent a contravention of s 33 of the EPA 1990. It would not, for example, give a person operating a landfill site licensed only for inert wastes such as bricks, rubble and sub-soils sufficient information to prevent a breach of the condition of the licence when the biodegradable wastes in the load were deposited.

3.123   The Environmental Protection (Duty of Care) Regulations 1991 do not set down which body should complete the transfer note. Neither do they prescribe a statutory form. Instead, the requirement is that the information specified within the Regulations[1] must be included on suitable documentation. This allows invoices, for example, to be adapted and permits transferors or transferees to produce their own documentation. However, for the note to be valid, it must contain the information prescribed by the Regulations[2]. If it does not do so, contravention of the Regulations is an offence[3]. The exact nature of the information to be recorded on a transfer note is fully described at para 3.129ff below.

1   SI 1991/2839, reg 2.
2   SI 1991/2839.
3   EPA 1990, s 34(6): offences are discussed at para 3.16ff above.

3.124   Subject to the requirements of s 34 of the EPA 1990 and the Environmental Protection (Duty of Care) Regulations 1991, the parties involved in a waste movement have discretion as to how individual movements are to be documented. Each load can be covered by separate transfer notes. Alternatively, s 34 of the EPA 1990 makes provision for a simplified documentation system for multiple consignments of the same wastes passing between the same parties[1]. It also appears to allow for one transfer note to describe a transaction which involves the transfer of wastes in stages[2]. These matters are considered at paras 3.152 and 3.156 below.

1   EPA 1990, s 34(4A)(b), as amended by the Deregulation and Contracting Out Act 1994, s 33(1).
2   EPA 1990, s 34(4A)(a), as amended by the Deregulation and Contracting Out Act 1994, s 33(1).

3.125   The Code of Practice contains an example transfer note[1] which is reproduced here as Figure 3.1. It can be seen that only one waste transfer can be documented on this form[2]. Many transactions will involve two transfers[3] and quite valid forms have been produced which show, on the same document, the role of three parties in the two transfers.

1   Code of Practice, page 53: note that some very minor changes have been made between this version and that contained in the first edition of the Code of Practice.
2   Ie transfers between producer to carrier or carrier to disposer.
3   Producer-carrier and carrier-disposer.

3.126   Certain elements of the waste industry tend to utilise the two-party type of note as shown in Figure 3.1. Often, individual notes are set up for each producer/carrier transaction. A second note is used to document all transactions from the carrier to the disposal site[1]. This is permissible under s 34 of the EPA 1990 provided that the transfer notes are completed correctly and that valid waste descriptions are utilised. But this arrangement may prove difficult for the Agency to accurately trace loads of waste deposited at a particular waste management facility. For example, a carrier may have individual transfer notes covering the producer-carrier transaction from, say, ten waste producers. However, for the carrier-disposal site movement, one note may be used[2]. The second note does not need to identify the producers or make any other cross reference to the other earlier notes.

1   This can be done using a multiple load transfer notes as described at para 3.152ff below.
2   Provided that it satisfies the legislation, particularly in respect of waste descriptions which accurately reflect what is being transported.

3.127   Given the absence of a requirement in the Environmental Protection (Duty of Care) Regulations 1991 to make an explicit connection between the documentation describing the first and subsequent transactions, it may prove difficult for the Agency to be absolutely confident that the appropriate paperwork is correct and relates directly the particular shipment under investigation. Such difficulties are exacerbated by the existence of transfer notes covering multiple loads[1] and in respect of transfers occurring as a series of stages[2].

1   See para 3.152.
2   See para 3.156: two parties to the duty could, for example, set up a series of transfer notes to cover a range of permutations of waste descriptions. The written descriptions on these would be intended to cover any possible combination of wastes that could conceivably be produced at the premises. Hence the 'best fit' multiple load transfer note could be produced which purports to describe any load under examination by the Agency. This arrangement, of course, would only succeed if it were possible to find a transfer note which did, in fact, match the waste description, as well as correctly describing the movement as a whole.

Figure 3.1

Duty of Care: Controlled Waste Transfer Note

Section A – Description of Waste

1. Please describe the waste being transferred:

2. How is the waste contained?

    Loose ☐   *Sacks* ☐   *Skip* ☐   *Drum* ☐   *Other* ☐   → *please describe:*

3. What is the quantity of waste (number of sacks, weight etc):

Section B – Current holder of the waste (Transferor)

1. Full Name (BLOCK CAPITALS):

2. Name and address of Company:

3. Which of the following are you? (Please ✓ one or more boxes)

producer of the waste ☐	*holder of waste disposal or* ☐ *waste management licence*	→	*Licence number:* *Issued by:*
importer of the waste ☐	*exempt from requirement to have a waste disposal or* ☐ *waste management licence*	→	*Give reason:*
waste collection authority ☐	*registered waste carrier* ☐	→	*Registration number:* *Issued by:*
waste disposal authority ☐ *(Scotland only)*	*exempt from* ☐ *requirement to register*	→	*Give reason:*

Section C – Person collecting the waste (Transferee)

1. Full Name (BLOCK CAPITALS):

2. Name and address of Company:

3. Which of the following are you? (Please ✓ one or more boxes)

	Authorised for ☐ *transport purposes*	→	*Specify which of those purposes:*
waste collection authority ☐	*holder of waste disposal or* ☐ *waste management licence*	→	*Licence number:* *Issued by:*
waste disposal authority ☐ *(Scotland only)*	*exempt from requirement to have* ☐ *a waste management licence*	→	*Give reason:*
	registered waste carrier ☐	→	*Registration number:* *Issued by:*
	exempt from ☐ *requirement to register*	→	*Give reason:*

Section D

1. Address of place of transfer/collection point:

2. Date of transfer: 3. Time(s) of transfer (for multiple consignments, give 'between' dates):

4. Name and address of broker who arranged this waste transfer (if applicable):

Transferor	**Transferee**
5. Signed:	Signed:
Full name: (BLOCK CAPITALS) Representing:	Full Name: (BLOCK CAPITALS) Representing:

FED 0443 (02/96 DDP)

3.128 Besides the difficulties facing the Agency, the whole purpose of passing written descriptions of the waste between parties is to ensure that the recipient has an accurate picture of the type of waste being received[1]. The provisions in respect of multiple loads and for waste transactions undertaken in stages appear to act against these goals. Accordingly, it seems doubtful that either the regulator or the regulated is well served by the transfer note system in its current form. Indeed, certain of the problem areas appear to be so fundamental as to raise significant questions about the effectiveness and utility of the paperwork system as a whole.

1 See the EPA 1990, s 34(1)(c)(ii): this is also a recurrent theme of the Code of Practice.

Describing the waste

3.129 The Environmental Protection (Duty of Care) Regulations 1991 require that the transfer note must '. . . identify the waste to which it relates . . .'[1]. Section 34 of the EPA 1990 requires that, when waste is transferred, a written description of it passes between the parties[2]. The specific requirements for this written description are set down in EPA 1990, s 34(1)(c)(ii), which states that the description must be sufficient 'as will enable other persons to avoid a contravention of . . . section [33] and to comply with the duty under this subsection as respects the escape of waste'. The second element of this phrase appears slightly strange, because it is difficult to see how a written description will, on its own, prevent waste escaping.

1 SI 1991/2839, reg 2(2)(a).
2 EPA 1990, s 34(1)(c)(ii).

3.130 The Environmental Protection (Duty of Care) Regulations 1991[1] substantiate the provisions on the transfer of written descriptions. The Regulations state that, 'at the same time as the written description is transferred', a transfer note is to be completed and signed by the transferor[2] and by the transferee[3].

1 SI 1991/2839.
2 Defined '. . . as the person . . . who transfers a written description of the waste' (SI 1991/2839, reg 1(2)).
3 Defined as 'the person who receives . . . [the written] description' (SI 1991/2839, reg 1(2)). It may be that it was intended that the original purpose of the written description/transfer note dichotomy was to have two separate documents. This dual system would come into play for the documentation of multiple shipments of the same waste which pass between the same transferor and transferee. The transfer note was to provide one, comprehensive, document to describe the entire shipment at the outset of the transaction. The much more simple, written description was then to pass between parties every time that each load was moved. However, this was no longer an objective by the time the Environmental Protection (Duty of Care) Regulations 1991 and Circular 19/91 were published.

3.131 The question of the degree of detail to be provided in a written description is more problematic[1]. As noted, the concept of written descriptions stems from s 34(1) of the EPA 1990, not from the Environmental Protection (Duty of Care) Regulations 1991. In respect of waste descriptions, all the latter does is require the provision of a description which identifies the waste. Hence if the Environmental Protection (Duty of Care) Regulations 1991 existed on their own, a term such as 'industrial waste' may be sufficient to cover waste from a factory. However, s 34(1)(c)(ii) of the EPA 1990 is drafted in a manner which sets out much more demanding requirements on waste descriptions and some considerable care is required in this respect. This is because s 34(1) contains evaluative criteria which must be applied to judge the adequacy of such a description[2]. Of foremost importance is the provision which states that, when waste is transferred, there must be transferred[3] '. . . such a written description of the waste *as will enable other persons to avoid a contravention of that section*[4] . . .'. This means that the description must enable a person who accepts waste to know that the incoming material is suitable and permitted under the waste management licence when it arrives at the disposal site. It also means that descriptions using terms such as 'diggings', 'muck', 'builders' waste' or 'general factory rubbish' are not sufficiently comprehensive to inform the recipient that the material is acceptable under the licence. However, the appearance of these terms on transfer notes is by no means unknown.

1   For inert materials passing to landfills, the guidance in the Code of Practice appears to be able to be substantiated by regulations pertaining to the landfill tax: see para 3.138 below.
2   EPA 1990, s 34(1)(c)(ii).
3   EPA 1990, s 34(1)(c)(ii).
4   EPA 1990, s 33(1), author's emphasis.

3.132   The Code of Practice provides important advice on the nature of an acceptable written description. A description should contain 'some combination of' the following elements[1]:

(a)   the type of premises or business which is the source of the waste;
(b)   the name of substances or substances which compose the waste;
(c)   the process that produced the waste;
(d)   a chemical or physical analysis.

In deciding the proportion of these four elements which needs to be provided to make up a description, the Code of Practice emphasises that the requirement of s 34(1) of the EPA 1990 is that the description should be sufficient to prevent a recipient mismanaging the waste[2]. It should also satisfy the criterion of s 34(1) of being 'reasonable in the circumstances'. Therefore, for many more innocuous wastes, the Code suggests that a simple description based on items (a) or (b) above will suffice.

1   Code of Practice, para 1.8.
2   Code of Practice, para 1.9.

3.133   In respect of describing the source of the waste, the Code of Practice indicates[1] that, usually, it will be enough to set out the occupation of the waste producer or the use made of that person's premises. But this is only sufficient where the waste has no special handling or disposal requirements.

1   Code of Practice, para 1.11–1.12.

3.134   For the name of the substances which make up the waste, the Code of Practice indicates[1] that physical or chemical terms can be used. Alternatively, the common name for the waste can be utilised where this is equally helpful[2]. However, in the latter case, this is appropriate only where the waste is composed of a single material or a simple mixture of substances.

1   Code of Practice, para 1.13.
2   See, in the context of a description of scrap metal for record-keeping purposes under the Scrap Metal Dealers Act 1964, *Jenkins v A Cohen & Co Ltd* [1971] 2 All ER 1384.

3.135   In respect of a description which makes reference to the process which produced the waste, the Code of Practice suggests[1] that such a reference should be made in the case of 'most' industrial wastes. It is also indicated[2] that a description 'would include details of materials used or processed, the equipment used and the treatment and changes that produced the waste'.

1   Code of Practice, para 1.15.
2   Code of Practice, para 1.14.

3.136 In respect of chemical or physical analytical data on the waste, the Code of Practice notes that[1] in certain cases, the provision of details about the process which produced the waste may not always be sufficient. This is likely to be the case when a number of industrial wastes are mixed or where the industrial activity or process alters the properties of the raw materials which now make up the waste. In this instance an analysis will instead be required[2]. The holder may wish to consult with other persons in the waste transaction to see if an analysis is necessary. The Code of Practice suggests that the holder can either provide the information from existing records or obtain a full analysis from a laboratory.

1　Code of Practice, para 1.16.
2　Code of Practice, para 1.17.

3.137 The section in the Code of Practice on waste descriptions makes reference to a national waste classification scheme[1]. At one time it seemed that this was proposed to be used to describe wastes on transfer notes. The classification scheme was published as two consultation papers in the winter of 1995[2]. However, the system – which in its draft form was significantly different from the list of wastes contained in the European Waste Catalogue[3] – has not, at the time of writing, been finalised and enacted[4].

1　Code of Practice, para 1.8.
2　Department of the Environment (1995) *Development of a National Waste Classification System*, Stage 1: An Alphabetical List of Wastes (November 1995), Stage 2: A System for Classifying Wastes (December 1995): Consultation Drafts.
3　Commission Decision of 20 December 1993 establishing a list of wastes pursuant to Article 1(a) of Council Directive 75/442/EEC on Waste, Decision 94/3/EC (OJ L5/15 7.1.94); see para 2.22 and Appendix II.
4　It seems unlikely that the European Waste Catalogue codes are suitable for providing descriptions on transfer notes. They are often too general in their terminology, and therefore would be unlikely to provide a sufficient level of detail to satisfy the requirement that a recipient of the waste should be in a position to know that the waste can be accepted without a contravention of s 33 of the EPA 1990.

Descriptions for 'inert' wastes

3.138 Besides the contents of the Code of Practice, it may be possible to glean some guidance on the nature of acceptable written descriptions for inert wastes from the landfill tax regulations. For landfills accepting 'inactive or inert' wastes, the nature of a written description is not only set out in the Code of Practice but is substantiated by the requirements of the Landfill Tax (Qualifying Material) Order 1996[1]. The nature of the landfill tax has been described in Chapter 1. Briefly, the deposit of wastes commonly referred to as 'inert or inactive' is subject to the lower landfill tax band of £2/tonne. 'Inert or inactive' materials fall within the definition of 'qualifying material' and these are listed in Table 3.1, below.

1　SI 1996/1528.

3.139 The Landfill Tax (Qualifying Material) Order 1996 states that, when waste is transferred between parties, the lower tax rate is allowable if the transfer is documented by way of a transfer note[1] which utilises the descriptions set down in the second column of Table 3.1[2].

1　SI 1996/1528, arts 5 and 6.
2　SI 1996/1528, art 6(a)(i).

Table 3.1 Landfill Tax (Qualifying Material) Order 1996

SCHEDULE[1]
Descriptions of Inert and Inactive Wastes

Group	Description of material	Conditions
Group 1	Rocks and soils	Naturally occurring
Group 2	Ceramic or concrete materials	
Group 3	Minerals	Processed or prepared, not used
Group 4	Furnace slags	
Group 5	Ash	
Group 6	Low activity inorganic compounds	
Group 7	Calcium sulphate	Disposed of either at site not licensed to take putrescible waste or in containment cell which takes only calcium sulphate
Group 8	Calcium hydroxide and brine	Deposited in brine cavity
Group 9	Water[2]	Containing other qualifying material in suspension

Notes:
(1) Group 1 includes clay, sand, gravel, sandstone, limestone, crushed stone, china clay, construction stone, stone from the demolition of buildings or structures, slate, topsoil, peat, silt and dredgings.
(2) Group 2 comprises only the following:
   (a) glass;
   (b) ceramics;
   (c) concrete.
(3) For the purposes of Note (2) above:
   (a) glass includes fritted enamel, but excludes glass fibre and glass-reinforced plastic;
   (b) ceramics includes bricks, bricks and mortar, tiles, clay ware, pottery, china and refractories;
   (c) concrete includes reinforced concrete, concrete blocks, breeze blocks and aircrete blocks, but excludes concrete plant washings.
(4) Group 3 comprises only the following:
   (a) moulding sands;
   (b) clays;
   (c) mineral absorbents;
   (d) man-made mineral fibres;
   (e) silica;
   (f) mica;
   (g) mineral abrasives.
(5) For the purposes of Note (4) above:
   (a) moulding sands excludes sands containing organic binders;
   (b) clays includes moulding clays and clay absorbents, including Fuller's earth and bentonite;
   (c) man-made mineral fibres includes glass fibres, but excludes glass-reinforced plastic and asbestos.
(6) Group 4 includes:
   (a) vitrified wastes and residues from thermal processing of minerals where, in either case, the residue is both fused and insoluble;
   (b) slag from waste incineration.
(7) Group 5:
   (a) comprises only bottom ash and fly ash from wood, coal or waste combustion; and

Table 3.1   Landfill Tax (Qualifying Material) Order 1996 – *contd*

SCHEDULE[1]

Descriptions of Inert and Inactive Wastes

>   (b)   excludes fly ash from municipal, clinical and hazardous waste incinerators and sewage sludge incinerators.

(8)   Group 6 comprises only titanium dioxide, calcium carbonate, magnesium carbonate, magnesium oxide, magnesium hydroxide, iron oxide, ferric hydroxide, aluminium oxide, aluminium hydroxide and zirconium dioxide.

(9)   Group 7 includes gypsum and calcium sulphate based plasters, but excludes plasterboard.

1   SI 1996/1528, Sch 1.
2   For 'water': the description should include the nature of any material held in suspension. The description for the latter should be that allowable under art 6 of SI 1996/1528.

3.140   Alternatively, the Landfill Tax (Qualifying Material) Order 1996 indicates that equivalent terms contained in the relevant notes to Table 3.1 can also be utilised in transfer notes[1]. Finally, 'some other accurate description' can be used[2]. The latter provision leads back to the most basic requirement of the duty of care in respect of any written description. This is that s 34 of the EPA 1990 requires that the waste description passed over is accurate and will be sufficient to avoid the recipient contravening s 33 of that Act. Regardless of whatever term may be selected from the Landfill Tax (Qualifying Material) Order 1996, this remains the over-riding criteria.

1   SI 1996/1528, art 6(a)(ii).
2   SI 1996/1528, art 6(a)(iii).

Describing the transaction

3.141   Besides requiring information on waste types, the Environmental Protection (Duty of Care) Regulations 1991 require that the transfer note should contain the following information[1]:

–   the quantity of waste;
–   whether the waste is loose or in a container;
–   if the waste is in a container, the kind of container; and
–   the time[2] and place of transfer.

In addition, the name and address of the transferor and transferee[3] must be included, along with a statement of whether the transferor is the producer or importer of the waste[4]. The note must also indicate whether the transfer is for authorised transport purposes[5] and, if so, these should be identified[6].

1   SI 1991/2839, reg 2(2)(a).
2   Note that there is no reference in the Environmental Protection (Duty of Care) Regulations 1991 to the 'date' of transfer. However, the model transfer note in the Code of Practice refers to both the date and time of transfer (see Figure 3.1).
3   Defined in SI 1991/2839, reg 1(2).
4   SI 1991/2839, reg 2(2)(c).
5   See para 3.51.
6   SI 1991/2839, reg 2(2)(d).

3.142   Finally, the note requires that transferors and transferees have to be categorised under one of five headings[1]. The categories make up the list of 'authorised persons' in s 34(3) of the EPA 1990:

- the waste collection authority;
- the holder of a waste management licence;
- a person exempt from the need to possess a waste management licence[2];
- a registered waste carrier; or
- a person who is exempt from the need to possess a carrier registration[3].

If waste is to be kept, treated or disposed of at a licensed waste management facility, the licence number and the name of the licensing authority must be given. Similarly, if the transferor or transferee is a registered waste carrier, the registration number must be given, along with the identity of the registration authority.

1   SI 1991/2839, reg 2(2)(e); in Scotland a sixth heading applies – the Scottish waste disposal authority. However, this seems superfluous since the system of resolutions (see para 1.67) has been replaced by waste management licences.
2   Such persons are exempt under s 33(3) of the EPA 1990: these exemptions are discussed in Chapters 10 and 11.
3   The person must be exempt under s 1(3) of the Control of Pollution (Amendment) Act 1989. This section permits exemptions to be prescribed by way of secondary legislation. Hence the exemptions under SI 1991/1624 (see para 6.08) are: the producer of waste which is not 'building or demolition waste; ferry operators when carrying vehicles containing controlled waste; sea disposal vessels; charities and voluntary organisations; and wholly-owned subsidiaries of British Rail. In the latter case, these must already be registered as brokers and have an application for a carrier registration pending (see SI 1991/1624, reg 2(1) as amended by SI 1994/1056, reg 23: and see para 6.25).

3.143   As these provisions emanate from the Environmental Protection (Duty of Care) Regulations 1991, they leave much less room in respect of compliance. As already noted[1], the criteria in s 34(1) of the EPA 1990 for deciding which actions are applicable to each party and 'reasonable in the circumstances' do not apply to compliance with the Regulations themselves.

1   See para 3.19.

Transfer notes: documenting waste movements of animal by-products, from households and to metal reclamation facilities

3.144   It has already been noted that the duty of care does not pertain to householders[1] and to most persons involved in movements of animal by-product wastes[2]. Besides these activities, the Code of Practice singles out metal reclamation facilities as a subject for separate advice, ostensibly on the grounds that there is a need 'to take account of the distinctive features of scrap metal and the circumstances in which it is recovered'[3]. While animal by-product transactions are generally exempted from the requirements on transfer notes[4], special circumstances affect the other two types of transfer.

1   See para 3.23 above.
2   See para 3.27.
3   Code of Practice, para 7.1.
4   As part of the blanket exemption of animal by-product transactions by way of SI 1992/588, reg 7(3) as amended by SI 1994/1056, reg 24: see para 3.27.

Wastes arising from households

3.145   For householders, the exemption from the duty of care[1] is, as noted, comprehensive in its form, covering the householder's responsibilities not only for 'normal' household waste[2], but also in respect of septic tank wastes and building waste produced by the householder on the premises. This general exemption has certain consequences in respect of how other persons document waste collected from such sources. Of most significance are household waste collection rounds and the provision of skips to householders.

1   See para 3.23.
2   It should be noted that this term only applies to occupiers of domestic properties which are wholly used for living accommodation: see the EPA 1990, s 75(5)(a) and para 2.200ff.

3.146   As the duty of care does not apply to householders, there is no requirement to utilise transfer notes to cover the transfer of the waste from a householder to a carrier[1]. Similarly, there is no need to document the load when householders deliver waste themselves to a disposal site, such as a civic amenity facility. Being exempt from the duty as a householder, the transfer of written descriptions does not apply. A transfer from one person to whom the duty applies to another person also covered by the duty only occurs when, for example, a carrier of household waste delivers this waste to a third party disposal facility. While the lack of need for documentation of householder-contractor transfers is not mentioned in the main part of the Code of Practice, it is explicitly referred to in the section on scrap metal[2].

1   This is because the duty only applies to those persons identified in the EPA 1990, s 34(1), who are subject to the duty and required, *inter alia*, to ensure that the transfer of waste only occurs to an authorised person (EPA 1990, s 34(1)(c)(i)). When this transfer occurs, written description must pass between parties (EPA 1990, s 34(1)(c)(ii)). Householders are not subject to the duty because they are exempted under EPA 1990, s 34(2).
2   Code of Practice, para 7.15.

3.147   One effect of this is that, for example, a company operating both a skip service and a transfer station will not need a transfer note to cover the transaction from a householder to the contractor's own facility. There has been no transfer of waste between persons to whom the duty of care applies. Similarly, a waste collection authority will not need a transfer note to document the initial transaction between a householder and the collection vehicle. However, one note will normally be needed to cover the delivery of the waste from the collection vehicle to the disposal facility.

Transfers involving scrap metal

3.148   The Code of Practice devotes an entire section to the operation of the duty of care in respect of the metal reclamation industry. However, the advice is inevitably constrained by the content of the relevant legislation. Neither the EPA 1990 nor the Environmental Protection (Duty of Care) Regulations 1991 make allowance for treating this industrial sector as a special case. Instead, the Code of Practice's section on scrap metal exploits some of the weaknesses of s 34 of the EPA 1990 in a manner which is also relevant to other elements of the waste management industry. It is, for example, prominently noted in that section of the Code that a scrap metal facility would not contravene s 34 if it accepted waste from an unlicensed waste carrier[1].

1   Code of Practice, para 7.19.

3.149   The provisions for the record-keeping system to cover transactions to and from metal reclamation sites are set down in Section 7 of the Code of Practice. Section 7 makes much of the fact that a significant proportion of the records required to be kept by the Environmental Protection (Duty of Care) Regulations 1991 will already be made by way of the provisions of the Scrap Metal Dealers Act 1964[1]. However, it should be noted that the Scrap Metal Dealers Act 1964 only applies to what are generically known as 'scrap yards' as opposed to facilities involving the dismantling of vehicles[2].

1   Code of Practice, para 7.5ff.
2   See Code of Practice, para 7.14; see also para 1.29 of Department of the Environment *The Licensing of Metal Recycling Sites* (1995) Waste Management Paper 4A, HMSO, London and para 11.29ff.

3.150 In respect of transfer notes for metal reclamation sites, the Code of Practice suggests that the records kept by way of the Scrap Metal Dealers Act 1964 may suffice as a way of recording waste transactions under the duty[1]. However, the Code then states that some modification of that record-keeping system is necessary to fully comply with the Environmental Protection (Duty of Care) Regulations 1991[2]. Additional information is required on how the waste is contained, in what capacity the person who transfers the waste is acting, times of transfer and so on.

1   Code of Practice, para 7.7.
2   Code of Practice, para 7.8.

3.151 Besides these changes, the Scrap Metal Dealers Act 1964 records will also need to be modified so that a duplicate information recording system can be provided, with one sheaf being torn off to pass to the person delivering the waste to the site[1]. The Environmental Protection (Duty of Care) Regulations 1991[2] stipulate that each party to a waste transaction retain a copy of the transfer note. Finally, space must also be given for both copies of the transfer note to be signed by the transferor and transferee[3].

1   Or collecting waste from it: EPA 1990, s 34(1)(c)(ii).
2   SI 1991/2839, reg 3.
3   SI 1991/2839, reg 2(1).

Multiple shipments of the same waste

3.152 Section 34 of the EPA 1990 was amended in November 1994 to provide a clarified, and simplified, documentation system for multiple loads of the same waste from the same source[1]. This was accomplished by s 33 of the Deregulation and Contracting Out Act 1994, which added a new s 34(4A) to the EPA 1990.

1   Previously it was claimed that multiple loads could be documented by a single transfer noted by way of a somewhat tortuous interpretation of the Environmental Protection (Duty of Care) Regulations 1991 (see Circular 19/91, para 21). This used s 6(c) of the Interpretation Act 1978, whereby the singular also means the plural in any statute (unless the statute states to the contrary), to suggest that the requirement that the 'time of transfer' is to be recorded on the transfer note could mean '*times* of transfer'. However, this did not appear to overcome a more fundamental obstacle which stemmed from the wording of the EPA 1990, s 34(1)(c). This stipulated that, when waste is transferred, a written description is also to be transferred. This meant that, under the Environmental Protection (Duty of Care) Regulations 1991, reg 2(1), a transfer note is completed at the same time that a written description is transferred.

3.153 As noted earlier, s 34(1) of the EPA 1990 requires that a written description is transferred when waste passes between parties[1]. In relation to a multiple load of the same waste, the amended subsection states[2] that a succession of transfers 'between the same parties of waste of the same description' is to be treated as a single transfer. This means that a multiple load is to be documented by a written description which is handed over when the first load is transferred. Provided that the waste composition and the identities of the transferors and the transferee remain the same, the written description remains valid for all of the later shipments.

1   EPA 1990, s 34(1)(c)(ii).
2   EPA 1990, s 34(4A)(b).

3.154 In respect of the transfer notes required under the Environmental Protection (Duty of Care) Regulations 1991[1], this amendment has the following effect. Regulation 2(1) requires that 'at the same time a written description of the waste is transferred', a transfer note is completed and signed. As a multiple load can be covered by one written description under s 34(4A) of the EPA 1990, a single transfer note is handed over when the written description passes between transferor and transferee. There is no need for further written descriptions to pass between parties, and so there is no requirement that additional transfer notes are to be furnished.

1   SI 1991/2839, reg 2(1).

3.155   Rather unfortunately, it appears that this 'season ticket' arrangement will last indefinitely. Despite the fact that both the Circular 19/91[1] and the revised Code of Practice[2] state that, 'in the Departments'[3] view', a season ticket lasts only for one year, there is no statutory requirement to this effect[4].

1   Circular 19/91, para 21.
2   Code of Practice, para C.4.
3   Ie the Department of the Environment, Scottish Office and Welsh Office.
4   The absence of such a deadline in the Environmental Protection (Duty of Care) Regulations 1991 tends to support the suspicion that the Regulations originally required that each load was to be documented on an individual basis. The advice provided in the original Circular on the interpretation of the then unamended s 34 of the EPA 1990 in respect of multiple loads should therefore be seen as a last minute change of heart at the Department of the Environment after the Regulations were finalised.

Documenting shipments through a number of parties

3.156   Most waste transactions involve three parties: the producer, the carrier and the disposer. In such transactions there are two transfers[1]. The first is between the producer and the carrier, with the second being between the carrier and disposer[2]. Until the Autumn of 1994, s 34 of the EPA 1990 required that both of these transferor/transferee transactions had to be documented by its own written description and be described on one or more transfer notes[3].

1   Other than when household waste is transferred: see para 3.145.
2   Although the simple producer/carrier/disposer model represents the majority of waste transactions, in certain instances more parties may be involved. For example, a carrier may collect waste which has been loaded on an articulated trailer. Later in the journey a second carrier may rendezvous with the load, change the tractor units over and take charge of the waste to complete the journey. There would therefore be three transfers in this example: producer/carrier 1; carrier 1/carrier 2; carrier 2/disposer. A second example might involve a load being taken to temporary storage and then subsequently removed for disposal. This example could involve four transfers: producer/carrier 1; carrier 1/storage facility; storage facility/carrier 2; carrier 2/disposal site.
3   As required by EPA 1990, s 34(1)(c)(ii) and SI 1991/2839, reg 2(1).

3.157   The Deregulation and Contracting Out Act 1994 provided for a more stream-lined arrangement by way of an amendment to s 34(4) of the EPA 1990[1]. This requires that '. . . the transfer of waste in stages shall be treated as taking place when the first stage of the transfer takes place . . .'. This phrase is both seriously ambiguous and not explained at all in the revised Code of Practice. It may mean that the documentation of the first transfer – the producer/carrier transfer in the example given above – is suffi-cient to cover the subsequent stages. It would therefore seem that no further written descriptions or transfer notes need to pass between parties.

1   Deregulation and Contracting Out Act 1994, s 33(1), which inserted new sub-section 4A(a) after s 34(4) of the EPA 1990.

3.158   Although the written description will remain valid for subsequent transfers, the wording of the amended s 34(4A) of the EPA 1990 would appear to indicate that no details of the subsequent transfers of the load of waste need to be recorded on the transfer note. All that is needed is the documentation of the first transfer only[1]. While this amendment significantly simplifies the paperwork covering the shipment, it totally defeats the objectives of the transfer note system: namely to provide a clear trail of documentation whereby a shipment can be traced through each of the parties back to the producer. As an alternative, it may apply to the movement of a large amount of waste in a series of collections, each spaced over an extended time period. But this kind of circumstance appears covered by the multiple shipment amendment already described[2]. Even more oddly, while the revised Code of Practice refers to the amendment which established these revised requirements[3], it does not deign to explain it at all. Might the authors of the Code not have wished to spell out the true nature of this 'deregulation' initiative at that time?

1 SI 1991/2839, reg 2(1) requires that a transfer note passes between parties each time written descriptions are transferred under the EPA 1990, s 34(1)(c)(ii). But the EPA 1990, s 34(4A)(a) requires that the transfer of waste in stages is to be treated as taking place when the first transfer takes place. Therefore, the requirement for a written description to pass over only occurs at the first transfer of the waste, not at later transfers. Accordingly, no further transfer notes are necessary.
2 See para 3.152.
3 Code of Practice, para A.4.

Transfer notes and transfrontier waste shipments

3.159 There is some overlap between the system for the documentation of international waste movements under Regulation 259/93[1] and the duty of care. This only applies to international transfers of non-special waste between parties[2]. Two types of international waste shipment are affected. Firstly, there are those non-special wastes which are subject to the notification procedure in Regulation 259/93, whereby member states receive a notification document in advance of the shipment for their approval. Substances affected will be mainly a small number of non-special 'Amber List' wastes[3] passing intentionally to recovery[4]. The second type of affected shipment will involve 'Green List' wastes passing to recovery which fall under the Regulation's provisions on simplified transport documentation[5].

1 Council Regulation 259/93 of 1 February 1993 on the Supervision and Control of Shipments of Waste within, into and out of the European Community (OJ L30/1 6.2.93), as amended by Commission Decision of 21 October 1994 adapting, pursuant to Article 42(3), Annexes II, III and IV of Council Regulation No 259/93 on the supervision and control of shipments within, into and out of the European Community (OJ L288/36 9.11.94): see Chapter 5.
2 If the waste transported falls within the definition of special waste, the requirement to use the duty of care documentation does not apply: SI 1991/2839, reg 2(3) as amended by SI 1996/972, reg 23.
3 Most Amber List and all Red List wastes would be special wastes.
4 The nature of the Amber List is described at para 5.49.
5 Regulation 259/93, Article 1(3)(a): see paras 5.47, 5.141ff.

3.160 In respect of the requirement in s 34(1)(c)(ii) of the EPA 1990 that written descriptions are transferred when waste passes between parties, the information provided on Regulation 259/93's notification document is sufficient for international transactions of non-special Amber List waste movements to recovery as well as any movement to disposal. Similarly, that sub-section's requirements are satisfied by the provisions affecting green list wastes under Article 11 of Regulation 259/93. Article 11 requires that green list shipments are to be 'accompanied by' a document containing information on matters including waste descriptions[1].

1 See para 5.141.

3.161 However, matters get more difficult in respect of compliance with the transfer note system under the Environmental Protection (Duty of Care) Regulations 1991[1]. For the documentation of international movements of waste for disposal and for non-special Amber List waste transactions, the fact that there is no specific requirement to utilise both a transfrontier waste notification form and a transfer note should be noted.

This means that information required by the Environmental Protection (Duty of Care) Regulations 1991 which does not feature on the transfrontier notification form[2] can be added to it[3]. Care must be taken in respect of this matter. Otherwise, the Environmental Protection (Duty of Care) Regulations 1991 will not be complied with[4].

1 SI 1991/2839, reg 2(1).
2 The form lacks: details of time of transfer; whether the transfer involves the producer or importer; and the nature of the authorised transportation purposes involved in the shipment.
3 Circular 19/91, para 26 indicates that such an action was applicable in respect of consignments falling within the Special Waste Regulations 1980 (SI 1980/1709). These Regulations were superseded by the Special Waste Regulations 1996 (SI 1996/972). Unlike the more recent Regulations, the 1980 Regulations did not contain a provision which exempted the consignment note from having to contain the information prescribed by the Environmental Protection (Duty of Care) Regulations 1991.
4 Non-compliance with the Environmental Protection (Duty of Care) Regulations 1991 could be used as a reason to object to transfrontier shipments. Both Articles 4(3)(c) and 7(4)(a) of Regulation 259/93 allow objections by member states on the grounds of non-compliance with national laws.

3.162 While it is sensible to adapt the transfrontier waste shipment notification form to conform to the Environmental Protection (Duty of Care) Regulations 1991, it is perhaps easier to utilise transfer notes to comply with the requirements of Regulation 259/93 for the documentation of Green List shipments. This is because the Green List transportation document almost complies with the requirements of the Environmental Protection (Duty of Care) Regulations 1991[1]. However, in order to be fully in accord with Article 11 of Regulation 259/93, the type of waste recovery operation to be used needs to be written on the note. This must be classified by way of the list contained in Annex IIB of the Directive on Waste[2].

1 While this is covered more fully at para 5.141, Article 11 of Regulation 259/93 requires that the name and address of the holder, a description of the waste, its quantity, the name and address of the consignee, the type of recovery operation and the date of shipment are all provided.
2 See para 5.141 and Table 2.3 in Chapter 2.

3.163 It is also important to note that the simplified arrangements for multiple loads[1] and for waste movements undertaken in stages[2] envisaged by s 34 of the EPA 1990 cannot apply to either of these types of transfrontier movement. In respect of the transfrontier waste notification document, Regulation 259/93[3] requires that the movement/tracking form accompanies each shipment. While the nature of a waste 'shipment' may be open to some interpretation[4], this matter is sufficiently clear as to apply to shipments using single vehicles/trailers. Similarly for Green List shipments, the Regulation[5] states that the basic shipping document should accompany each and every load.

1 See para 3.152.
2 See para 3.156.
3 Regulation 259/93, Articles 5(3), 8(3), 15(8), 20(7), 22 and 23(6).
4 See para 5.77ff.
5 Regulation 259/93, Article 1(b).

3.164 Despite what seem to be the unequivocal requirements of Regulation 259/93, the duty of care Code of Practice states that the information on the EC notification form 'should' satisfy the duty of care requirements[1]. No mention is made about the documentation of Green List shipments.

1 Code of Practice, paras C.7 and D.22.

Retention of written descriptions and transfer notes

3.165 The Environmental Protection (Duty of Care) Regulations 1991 require that the transferor and transferee[1] must retain certain documents. For all waste management facilities other than landfills, the period of retention is two years from the date at which the transfer of the controlled waste occurred. Hence the 'season ticket' type of transfer note for multiple loads of the same waste[2] must be kept for two years, with this period commencing with the completion of the last transfer of waste[3].

1 Defined in SI 1991/2839, reg 1(2).
2 See para 3.152 above.
3 SI 1991/2839, reg 3 requires that the notes must be kept for two years commencing from the date of 'the transfer'. This must mean from the end of a series of transactions.

3.166 For landfill sites[1], the period of document retention in the Environmental Protection (Duty of Care) Regulations 1991 has been over-ridden by the Landfill Tax Regulations 1996[2]. This requires that transfer notes relating to waste brought into or removed from a landfill must be retained for six years[3].

1 Under the landfill tax, 'there is a disposal of material by way of landfill if – (a) it is deposited on the surface of land or on a structure set into the surface, or (b) it is deposited under the surface of land' (Finance Act 1996, s 65(1)). However, while this definition includes injection into caverns or mines (Finance Act 1996, s 65(3)), it excludes dredgings and pet cemeteries (Finance Act 1996, ss 43 and s 45). The disposal of wastes from mines and quarries at the site of production is also excluded (Finance Act 1996, s 44), but such material would not fall within the definition of controlled waste: see the EPA 1990, s 75(7)(c) and see para 2.55ff.
2 SI 1996/1527, reg 16.
3 HM Customs and Excise (1997) *Notice LFT 1 A General Guide to the Landfill Tax*, para 13.2 indicates that this period can be reduced on the agreement of HM Customs and Excise.

3.167 The Environmental Protection (Duty of Care) Regulations 1991 state that two items must be kept: 'The transferor and transferee shall keep the written description of the waste *and* the transfer note or copies thereof for a period of two years ...' [author's emphasis][1]. As noted at para 3.19 above, an offence occurs if the Regulations are not complied with[2]. This will relate to the two-year retention period for both the written description and for the transfer note, as both are required to be kept by the Regulations.

1 SI 1991/2839, reg 3.
2 EPA 1990, s 34(5) and (6).

3.168 It has already been noted that the 'season ticket' transfer note appears to last indefinitely[1]. If a party to the duty wishes to use the note to cover a continual transaction of the same waste between the same parties, the note will have to be continuously held by the parties.

1 See para 3.155 above.

Duty to furnish written descriptions and transfer notes

3.169 The Environmental Protection (Duty of Care) Regulations 1991 allow the Agency to serve a notice on a person requiring the production of a written description or transfer note[1]. These procedures are discussed at para 12.182ff.

1 SI 1991/2839, reg 4.

Provision of false or misleading information

3.170 The provision by a person of information which is 'false or misleading in a material particular' in respect of a written description is an offence[1]. The general offence of falsifying information is discussed further at para 12.223ff.

1 EPA 1990, s 44(1)(a) as amended by the Environment Act 1995, s 112 and Sch 19, para 4: commenced by SI 1996/186.

Fraudulent use of a waste management licence

3.171 While not specifically covered by s 34 of the EPA 1990, nor by the Environmental Protection (Duty of Care) Regulations 1991, the EPA 1990 contains a provision in respect of the use of a forged waste management licence[1]. This may be utilised for persons who, by purporting to be licence holders, encourage others to use their facilities and cause s 34 of the EPA 1990 to be contravened. This is discussed at para 12.212.

1 EPA 1990, s 35(7A), as amended by the Environment Act 1995, s 120 and Sch 22, para 66(2).

Chapter 4

The Special Waste Regulations

INTRODUCTION

4.01 The Special Waste Regulations 1996[1] were enacted on 1 September 1996, causing a major change in the manner by which toxic waste is defined and controlled. These Regulations are mainly concerned with defining the nature of special waste and setting out a consignment note tracking system to ensure that the movement of such waste can be followed by the Agency 'from cradle to grave'. They are primarily a response to the Directive on Hazardous Waste[2]. The Regulations emanate from powers contained in s 62 of the EPA 1990[3], which allows the Secretary of State to make special provisions in respect of controlled waste which is 'dangerous or difficult to treat, keep or dispose of'[4].

1 SI 1996/972.
2 Council Directive of 12 December 1991 on Hazardous Waste (91/689/EEC) (OJ L377/20), as amended by Council Directive 94/31/EC of 27 June 1994 amending Directive 91/689/EEC on Hazardous Waste (OJ L168/1 2.7.94).
3 EPA 1990, s 62 was commenced by the Environmental Protection Act 1990 (Commencement No 17) Order 1995 (SI 1995/2152), being amended by Sch 22, para 80 of the Environment Act 1995.
4 EPA 1990, s 62(1). Section 75(9) of the EPA 1990 explicitly confirms that special waste is controlled waste.

4.02 The enactment of the new Regulations was not a particularly happy saga for the Department of the Environment. The Special Waste Regulations 1996 were subject to major amendment one month prior to entering into force[1]. The Circular which accompanied the original Regulations[2] was published in June 1996 only to be subject to significant amendment two months later[3]. Even after amendment, the Regulations still retain a considerable internal complexity, whereby extensive cross-reference to various sub-paragraphs is required. This very compact style of drafting perhaps results in a certain elegance, but the explanation of the Regulations to persons unfamiliar with them – jurors for example – may prove challenging.

1 By the Special Waste (Amendment) Regulations 1996 (SI 1996/2019), with further amendments being made by SI 1997/251. Regular changes will be a feature of these Regulations. As is illustrated at para 4.31 below, the Regulations are coupled to the Chemicals (Hazard Information and Packaging for Supply) Regulations 1994 (SI 1994/3247). Those regulations enact the Dangerous Substances Directive 67/548, which is subject to regular amendment. The Directive has been amended on three occasions since the Special Waste Regulations 1996 were made. This has resulted in a succession of changes to the Hazard Information and Supply Regulations (by SI 1997/1460 and SI 1998/3106), with further modifications proposed in 1999. As the Special Waste Regulations 1996 are currently drafted, these amendments are not relevant to the definition of special waste.
2 Department of the Environment *Environmental Protection Act: Part II The Special Waste Regulations* (1996) Circular 6/96, HMSO, London.
3 Department of the Environment *Environmental Protection Act: Part II The Special Waste (Amendment) Regulations 1996*, (1996), Circular 14/96, HMSO, London. It should be noted that Annex B to Circular 6/96 was superseded in 1999: see Environment Agency *Special Wastes: A Technical Guidance Note on their Definition and Classification*, (1999), Environment Agency, Bristol, para 1.1.7.

4.03 Since waste management facilities were subject to environmental controls in the mid-1970s, there have been three different approaches to the definition and control of toxic waste. The first was by way of the Deposit of Poisonous Waste Act 1972. In March 1981, these provisions were replaced with the Britain's late transposition of the

Directive on Toxic and Dangerous Wastes[1], by the Control of Pollution (Special Waste) Regulations 1980[2].

1   Council Directive 78/319 of 20 March 1978 on Toxic and Dangerous Waste (OJ L84/43 31.3.78).
2   SI 1980/1709.

4.04   Being an early EC environmental Directive, the Toxic and Dangerous Waste Directive allowed each member state considerable discretion in the applicable procedures to control such wastes and, more importantly, in the manner by which hazardous waste was defined. The result was a less than desirable lack of uniformity towards waste definitions across the EC. These differences presented particular difficulties in respect of the early Community legislation on transfrontier waste shipments, which relied on the definition of toxic and dangerous waste in the Directive. While the Transfrontier Directive[1] was aimed at unifying the actual control procedures for such waste movements, its effectiveness was significantly undermined by differences in member states' definition of hazardous waste. Hence regulatory controls pertained to certain 'toxic waste' in one country, but not when it was moved into another. This unsatisfactory state of affairs resulted in the recognition of the need to provide a single, EC hazardous waste definition.

1   Directive 84/631, Council Directive of 6 December 1984 on the Supervision and Control within the European Community of the Transfrontier Shipment of Hazardous Waste (OJ L326/1 13.12.84).

4.05   However, initiatives by the European Commission in respect of the need to unify hazardous waste definitions for transfrontier shipment control purposes were themselves overtaken by the activities of extra-EC international fora, in the form of the Basel Convention[1] and the OECD Decision on transfrontier waste shipments passing to recovery[2]. These wider initiatives did not single out hazardous wastes for controls, but applied instead to all types of waste when they are moved across frontiers.

1   1989 Basel Convention on the Control of Transboundary Movements of Hazardous Wastes and their Disposal, 1 JEL 2 at 255: see para 5.12ff.
2   OECD Decision on the Control of Transfrontier Movements of Waste Destined for Recovery Operations, OECD C(92)39/Final as amended by Decision C(93)74/Final: see para 5.21ff.

4.06   Although there resulted a diminished requirement to define hazardous wastes for transfrontier shipment controls, there remained other policy needs which indicated that some form of unified definition across the EC was desirable. Perhaps the most crucial stemmed from the fact that certain other Directives singled out sites accepting hazardous wastes for additional rules. Examples include the Directive on Hazardous Waste Incineration[1] and the Directive on Environmental Assessment[2], with the latter requiring the more significant sites taking hazardous wastes to be subject to an environmental impact assessment. The landfill site classification scheme in the Landfill Directive is also based on whether hazardous waste is accepted[3]. Clearly, a uniform EC definition of hazardous waste is an essential requirement of the unified application of these Directives across all member states.

1   Council Directive 94/67/EC of 16 December 1994 on the Incineration of Hazardous Waste (OJ L365/34).
2   Council Directive 85/337 on the Assessment of the Effects of Certain Public and Private Projects on the Environment (OJ L175 5.7.85) as amended by Council Directive 97/11/EC amending Directive 85/337/EEC on the Assessment of the Effects of Certain Public and Private Projects on the Environment (OJ L73/5 14.3.95) Article 3.
3   See para 1.23.

4.07   Despite what appeared at one time to be a pressing need to unify hazardous waste definitions, there followed a somewhat lengthy gestation period which culminated in the Directive on Hazardous Wastes[1]. After some further delay, a list of hazardous wastes finally emerged[2]. This was supposedly meant to represent a single, uniform hazardous waste list which was to be used by all member states. However, ambiguity in the drafting of the relevant EC initiatives has allowed member states once again to provide their own interpretations and thus produce less than unified definitions[3]. Consequently, there will be inevitable variations between member states in respect of substances which should or should not be on the hazardous waste list. The result is that the goal of a unified EC hazardous waste definition is closer than it was, but still some way off.

1 Council Directive of 12 December 1991 on Hazardous Waste (91/689/EEC) (OJ L377/20 31.12.91).
2 Council Decision of 22 December 1994 establishing a list of Hazardous Waste pursuant to Article 1(4) of Council Directive 91/689/EEC on Hazardous Waste: 94/904/EC (OJ L356/14 31.12.94).
3 Compare the method of definition of special waste in the Special Waste Regulations 1996 to the meaning of hazardous waste in, for example, s 4(2)(a) of Ireland's Waste Management Act 1996.

THE DEFINITION OF SPECIAL WASTE

EC Law: the Directive on Hazardous Waste

4.08 The Council Directive on Hazardous Waste[1] was agreed on 12 December 1991. The Directive is somewhat unusual in its approach as it does not actually define hazardous waste. Rather, it sets down criteria for such a definition, delegating a Technical Committee – established under Article 18 of the Directive on Waste – to work up a meaningful definition from criteria presented to it[2]. The result of the Technical Committee's work was the hazardous waste list, published as Council Decision 94/904[3].

1 Council Directive of 12 December 1991 on Hazardous Waste (91/689/EEC) (OJ L377/20 31.12.91).
2 Directive 91/689, Article 1(4).
3 Council Decision of 22 December 1994 establishing a list of Hazardous Waste pursuant to Article 1(4) of Council Directive 91/689/EEC on Hazardous Waste: 94/904/EC (OJ L356/14 31.12.94).

4.09 Given that the Technical Committee was unlikely to produce a comprehensive and definitive list of hazardous waste at the first attempt, the Directive permits member states to propose other wastes outside the waste list which are viewed as containing toxic properties[1]. These need to be notified to the Commission and reviewed by the Technical Committee. 'Domestic waste' is, however, explicitly exempted from this process and from the Hazardous Waste Directive as a whole[2].

1 Directive 91/689, Article 1(4).
2 Directive 91/689, Article 1(5).

4.10 For operational purposes, the list of wastes in Council Decision 94/904 is clearly more important than the criteria from which it was derived. For this reason, Annex I of the Hazardous Waste Directive, which formed one of the three sets of criteria behind the hazardous waste list, is not reproduced here. Neither is the somewhat complicated methodology for applying the criteria which is set out in the text of the Directive and its Annexes. However, as considerable significance is placed in British law on the toxicity thresholds contained Annex III of the Directive, this Annex is reproduced as Table 4.1. In addition, while Annex II is not referred to in the British definition of special waste, Volume II of the Agency's technical guidance note on special waste definitions[1] is structured around this Annex and is reproduced here as Table 4.2.

1 Environment Agency *Special Wastes: A Technical Guidance Note on their Definition and Classification*, (1999), Environment Agency, Bristol.

Table 4.1
Annex III of the Directive on Hazardous Waste

Properties of Wastes Which Render Them Hazardous

H1	'Explosive': substances and preparations which may explode under the effect of flame or which are more sensitive to shocks or friction than dinitrobenzene.
H2	'Oxidizing': substances and preparations which exhibit highly exothermic reactions when in contact with other substances, particularly flammable substances.
H3-A	'Highly flammable'

- liquid substances and preparations having a flash point below 21°C (including extremely flammable liquids), or
- substances and preparations which may become hot and finally catch fire in contact with air at ambient temperature without any application of energy, or
- solid substances and preparations which may readily catch fire after brief contact with a source of ignition and which continue to burn or to be consumed after removal of the source of ignition, or
- gaseous substances and preparation which are flammable in air at normal pressure, or
- substances and preparations which, in contact with water or damp air, evolve highly flammable gases in dangerous quantities.

H3-B	'Flammable': liquid substances and preparations having a flash point equal to or greater than 21°C and less than or equal to 55°C.
H4	'Irritant': non-corrosive substances and preparations which, through immediate, prolonged or repeated contact with the skin or mucous membrane, can cause inflammation.
H5	'Harmful': substances and preparations which, if they are inhaled or ingested or if they penetrate the skin, may involve limited health risks.
H6	'Toxic': substances and preparations (including very toxic substances and preparations) which, if they are inhaled or ingested or if they penetrate the skin, may involve serious, acute or chronic health risks and even death.
H7	'Carcinogenic': substances and preparations which, if they are inhaled or if they penetrate the skin, may induce cancer or increase its incidence.
H8	'Corrosive': substances and preparations which may destroy living tissue on contacts.
H9	'Infectious': substances containing viable micro-organisms or their toxins which are known or reliably believed to cause disease in man or other living organisms.
H10	'Teratogenic': substances and preparations which, if they are inhaled or ingested or if they penetrate the skin, may induce non-hereditary congenital malformations or increase their incidence.
H11	'Mutagenic': substances and preparations which, if they are inhaled or ingested or if they penetrate the skin, may induce hereditary genetic defects or increase their incidence.
H12	Substances and preparations which release toxic or very toxic gases in contact with water, air or an acid.
H13	Substances and preparations capable by any means, after disposal, of yielding another substance; eg a leachate, which possesses any of the characteristics listed above.
H14	'Ecotoxic': substances and preparations which present or may present immediate or delayed risks for one or more sectors of the environment.

1 Attribution of the hazard properties 'toxic' (and 'very toxic'), 'harmful', 'corrosive' and 'irritant' is made on the basis of the criteria laid down by Annex VI, Pt 1A and Pt IIB, of Council Directive 67/548/EEC of 27 June 1967 of the approximation of laws, regulations and administrative provisions relating to the classification, packaging and labelling of dangerous substances, in the version as amended by Council Directive 79/831/EEC.
2 With regard to attribution of the properties 'carcinogenic' 'teratogenic' and 'mutagenic', and reflecting the most recent findings, additional criteria are contained in the Guide to the classification and labelling of dangerous substances and preparations of Annex VI (Pt II D) to Directive 67/548/EEC in the version as amended by Commission Directive 83/467/EEC.

Table 4.2
Annex II of the Directive on Hazardous Waste[1]

Constituents of the Wastes in Annex I.B Which Render Them Hazardous When They Have the Properties Described in Annex III[2]

Wastes having as constituents:

C1   beryllium; beryllium compounds;
C2   vanadium compounds;
C3   chromium (VI) compounds;
C4   cobalt compounds;
C5   nickel compounds;
C6   copper compounds;
C7   zinc compounds;
C8   arsenic; arsenic compounds;
C9   selenium; selenium compounds;
C10   silver compounds;
C11   cadmium; cadmium compounds;
C12   tin compounds;
C13   antimony; antimony compounds;
C14   tellurium; tellurium compounds;
C15   barium compounds; excluding barium sulfate;
C16   mercury; mercury compounds;
C17   thallium; thallium compounds;
C18   lead; lead compounds;
C19   inorganic sulphides;
C20   inorganic fluorine compounds, excluding calcium fluoride;
C21   inorganic cyanides;
C22   the following alkaline or alkaline earth metals: lithium, sodium, potassium, calcium, magnesium in uncombined form;
C23   acidic solutions or acids in solid form;
C24   basic solutions or bases in solid form;
C25   asbestos (dust and fibres);
C26   phosphorus: phosphorus compounds, excluding mineral phosphates;
C27   metal carbonyls;
C28   peroxides;
C29   chlorates;
C30   perchlorates;
C31   azides;
C32   PCBs and/or PCTs;
C33   pharmaceutical or veterinary compounds;
C34   biocides and phyto-pharmaceutical substances (eg pesticides, etc);
C35   infectious substances;
C36   creosotes;
C37   isocyanates; thiocyanates;
C38   organic cyanides (eg nitriles, etc);
C39   phenols; phenol compounds;
C40   halogenated solvents;
C41   organic solvents, excluding halogenated solvents;
C42   organohalogen compounds, excluding inert polymerized minerals and other substances referred to in this Annex;
C43   aromatic compounds; polycyclic and heterocyclic organic compounds;
C44   aliphatic amines;
C45   aromatic amines;
C46   ethers;
C47   substances of an explosive character, excluding those listed elsewhere in this Annex;
C48   sulphur organic compounds;
C49   any congener of polychlorinated dibenzo-furan;

Table 4.2 – *contd*
Annex II of the Directive on Hazardous Waste[1]

Constituents of the Wastes in Annex I.B Which Render Them Hazardous When They Have the Properties Described in Annex III[2]

C50 any congener of polychlorinated dibenzo-p-dioxin;
C51 hydrocarbons and their oxygen; nitrogen and/or sulphur compounds not otherwise taken into account in this Annex.

1 Directive 91/689/EEC, (OJ L377/20 31.12.91).
2 Annex III is reproduced here as Table 4.1.

4.11 As can be seen, Annex III (see Table 4.1) sets down a series of properties which render a waste hazardous. Some of these properties are well defined – the concept of 'highly flammable' for example being primarily based on a flashpoint of less than 21°C. However, other properties are much more open-ended. An example is the term 'corrosive', which is defined as '. . . substances and preparations which may destroy living tissue on contacts'[1].

1 Sic.

4.12 It should be noted that Table 4.1 shows the list of hazardous properties as portrayed in Directive 91/689. This includes the original footnotes, which cross refer to the Dangerous Substances Directive 67/548[1]. However, it is important to realise that the Dangerous Substances Directive has been much amended. Other than the Directive's number and title, little remains of the original articles. For example, Annex VI, Part IA was superseded by Directive 92/69[2]. Subsequently both Parts I and II were entirely replaced by Article 1(5) of Directive 93/21[3] and further amendments have been made since then[4].

1 Council Directive of 27 June 1967 on the approximation of laws, regulations and administrative provisions relating to the classification, packaging and labelling of dangerous substances (67/548/EEC) (OJ 196/1 16.8.67).
2 Article 1 of Commission Directive 92/69/EEC of 21 July 1992 adapting to technical progress for the seventeenth time Council Directive 67/548/EEC on the approximation of the laws, regulations and administrative provisions relating to the classification, packaging and labelling of dangerous substances (OJ L383/113 29.12.92), with the Annexes being published separately as OJ 383A, 29.12.92.
3 Article 1(5) of Commission Directive 93/21/EEC of 27 April 1993 adapting to technical progress for the 18th time Council Directive 67/548/EEC on the approximation of the laws, regulations and administrative provisions relating to the classification, packaging and labelling of dangerous substances (OJ L110/20 4.5.93), with the Annexes being published separately as OJ 110A, 4.5.93.
4 The most recent amendments include Directives 96/54/EC (OJ 248/1 30.9.96), 96/56/EC (OJ L236/35 18.9.96) and 97/69/EC (OJ L343/19 12.12.97). But, as discussed at para 4.31, these are not relevant to the present (1999) definition of special waste.

4.13 Originally, the Technical Committee set up under Article 18 of the Directive on Waste was required to produce the hazardous waste list six months before the date of implementation of the Directive[1] – 12 December 1993 – when the Directive would come into force[2] and when its predecessor, the Toxic and Dangerous Waste Directive[3], was to be repealed[4]. However, the date of implementation was subsequently moved back by a second Directive[5] to 27 June 1995.

1 Directive 91/689, Article 1(4).
2 Directive 91/689, Article 10(1).
3 Council Directive of 20 March 1978 on Toxic and Dangerous Waste, (OJ L84/43 31.3.78).
4 Directive 91/689, Article 11.
5 Council Directive 94/31 of 27 June 1994 amending Directive 91/689/EEC on Hazardous Waste (OJ L168/28 2.7.94).

4.14 Given that a list of hazardous wastes needed to be drafted six months before the parent Directive came into force, the waste list emerged on 22 December 1994 as Council Decision 94/904[1].

1 Council Decision of 22 December 1994 establishing a list of Hazardous Waste pursuant to Article 1(4) of Council Directive 91/689/EEC on Hazardous Waste: 94/904/EC (OJ L356/14 31.12.94).

4.15 Wastes on the hazardous waste list contained in Decision 94/904 are shown in Appendix II. Each description of waste is matched by a two, four and six digit code. The latter are taken from the European Waste Catalogue (EWC)[1]. From reading the text of Council Decision 94/904, it will be seen that the status of the two and four digit codes is less than clear[2]: only the six digit codes constitute substances on the hazardous waste list – the two and four digit codes are simply used for the reader's orientation purposes. Although this is clarified in many member states' internal implementing legislation, it is less than clear from the text of the Decision itself.

1 Commission Decision of 20 December 1993 establishing a list of wastes pursuant to Article 1(a) of Council Directive 75/442/EEC on Waste, Decision 94/3/EC (OJ L5/15 7.1.94): see Chapter 2.
2 For example, taking the first three entries shown in Appendix II, it might appear that EWC Code 02 'Waste from Agricultural, Horticultural, Hunting, Fishing and Aquaculture Primary Production, Food Preparation and Processing' is as much a hazardous waste as EWC Code 0201 'Primary Production Waste' and EWC Code 020105 'agrochemical wastes'.

4.16 Given the length and complexity of both the European Waste Catalogue and the hazardous waste list, it seems inevitable that changes will be made from time-to-time. In Autumn 1997, the Department of the Environment issued a consultation paper setting out proposed changes to the hazardous waste list[1]. However, at the time of writing, no proposal has been published in the Official Journal of the European Communities[2]. Any such change will cause the definition of special waste to either expand or contract, with knock-on effects onto other elements of the legislation which single out special waste for additional controls[3].

1 DETR *Proposals for Additions to the European Hazardous Waste List*, (1997) Waste Policy Division, DETR, London, September 1997.
2 At the time of writing (Summer 1999) there is an early proposal to produce a revised joint European Waste Catalogue and Hazardous Waste List.
3 Examples include the definition of hazardous waste incinerators, waste facilities needing environmental assessment, hazardous waste landfill sites under the Landfill Directive, sites subject to exemptions from waste management licensing (see para 10.33), levels of fees and charges for waste management licences, the required level of Certificate of Technical Competence (see para 8.136) necessary to manage a particular waste facility, whether special waste consignment notes or controlled waste transfer notes are needed, and so on.

4.17 A potential difficulty can arise from the text of Article 1 of Council Decision 94/904. Article 1 contains a range of concentration thresholds, and these are reproduced, along with the accompanying text, as Table 4.3. From that Table, it can be seen that a list of hazardous properties are presented, which serve to flesh out some of the vaguer hazard criteria contained in Annex III of the original Hazardous Waste Directive. For example, it was mentioned earlier that the term 'corrosive' in Annex III was not defined in the Directive on Hazardous Waste. However, in Council Decision 94/904, 'corrosive' is held to mean, depending upon the substance concerned, corrosive at either 1% or 5% concentration.

4.18 Article 1 of Decision 94/904 makes clear that these additional thresholds were used *as further criteria* to place a waste on the hazardous waste list[1]. The wording of that Article clearly indicates that the thresholds are *not* presented as a way of screening waste already on the list and defining it as either hazardous or non-hazardous. Rather, the text of Article 1 states that the additional criteria were used to inform the decision-making process which resulted in the list. However, this factor appears to have been open to varied interpretation. The Special Waste Regulations 1996 use these criteria in a manner which would appear, at the very least, at variance to the intention of the Council Decision. As will be shown, the main means by which the Special Waste Regulations 1996 judge a hazardous waste is by way of a multi-stage assessment methodology. For example, if a substance appears on the hazardous waste list, its hazardous nature is evaluated in relation to the list of hazardous properties set down in Annex III of the Directive[2]. Should the substance possess any of the properties shown in Table 4.3[3], these properties are then to be evaluated against the thresholds set down in that Table. Conversely, from the texts of the relevant EC provisions, it would seem that those involved in drafting the Hazardous Waste Directive and Decision 94/904 envisaged a simple, single stage, process involving the assessment only of whether a substance was or was not present on the hazardous waste list itself[4].

1 See the second sentence of the text of Article 1 (Table 4.3).
2 SI 1996/972, reg 2(1) as amended by SI 1996/2019, reg 2, Sch 1, para 3.
3 The category 'irritant' in Table 4.2 equates to property H4 in Table 4.1. Similarly 'harmful' relates to H5, 'toxic' to H6, 'carcinogenic' to H7 and 'corrosive' to H8.
4 See Article 1(4) of the Hazardous Waste Directive and Article 1 of Decision 94/904. In addition, this matter appears clear from the second paragraph of Article 1(4) of the Directive, where it is implied that the names of other wastes need to be notified to the Commission 'with a view to adaptation *of the list*' [author's emphasis]. Clearly, it would seem that only the list can be adapted – not the criteria by which it was derived – and that this can only be done by the addition of additional wastes or by way of their delisting. Similarly, a recital of Directive 94/31/EC refers to a '*binding*' list' [author's emphasis], while the title of Council Decision 94/904 commences with the words 'Council Decision of 22 December 1994 establishing *a list* of hazardous waste ...'. See also, in the context of transfrontier waste movements, Council Regulation 259/93, Annex V, Pt 2 and para 5.164ff.

Table 4.3
Text of Council Decision 94/904 setting up a hazardous waste list

Article 1

'The list of hazardous waste annexed to this Decision is hereby adopted[1].

These wastes are considered to display one or more of the properties of Annex III to Directive 91/689/EEC and, as regards H3 to H8 of the said Annex, one or more of the following[2]:

– flash point <= 55°C
– one or more substances classified as very toxic at a total concentration >= 0.1%
– one or more substances classified as toxic at a total concentration >= 3%
– one or more substances classified as harmful at a total concentration >= 25%
– one or more corrosive substances classified as R35 at a total concentration >= 1%
– one of more corrosive substances classified as R34 at a total concentration >= 5%
– one or more irritant substances classified as R41 at a total concentration >= 10%
– one or more irritant substances classified as R36, R37, R38 at a total concentration >= 20%
– one or more substances known to be carcinogenic (categories 1 or 2) at a total concentration >= 0.1%'.

1 The actual list is reproduced as Appendix II.
2 The R numbers (R35, R36 etc) are taken from the Dangerous Substances Directive 67/548 and refer to the risk phrases contained in Annex III of Commission Directive 93/21/EEC of 27 April 1993 adapting to technical progress for the 18th time Council Directive 67/548/EEC on the approximation of the laws, regulations and administrative provisions relating to the classification, packaging and labelling of dangerous substances (OJ 110A/5ff 4.5.93). The nature of risk phrases is considered at para 4.33 below.

The Special Waste Regulations 1996

4.19 In light of the definition of hazardous waste contained in the Directive on Hazardous Waste and Council Decision 94/904, the Special Waste Regulations 1996[1] set out the meaning of 'special waste' in reg 2. Immediately prior to the enactment of the Regulations in September 1996, reg 2 was entirely replaced by an amendment stemming from the Special Waste (Amendment) Regulations 1996[2].

1   SI 1996/972, reg 1(4).
2   SI 1996/2019, reg 2, Sch 1, para 3.

4.20 The definition of special waste was originally supported by non-statutory guidance in the form of Circular 6/96[1]. In light of the change made to the statutory definition by the Special Waste (Amendment) Regulations 1996, the Circular was itself subject to significant amendments and clarifications[2]. In 1999, Annex B to the Circular – which sets out guidance on the definition of special waste – was superseded by the publication by the Environment Agency of a long-awaited Technical Guidance Note[3].

1   Department of the Environment Circular 6/96 *Environmental Protection Act 1990: Part II Special Waste Regulations 1996*, (1996) HMSO, London.
2   By way of Circular 14/96, Department of the Environment *The Environmental Protection Act, Part II Special Waste (Amendment) Regulations 1996*, (1996) HMSO, London. For example, significant deletions were made to many of the flow diagrams illustrating the assessment process for special waste; throughout one Table giving guidance on concentration thresholds the mathematical sign for 'less than' were changed to 'greater than or equal to'; bonded asbestos and clinical waste sharps were originally stated as being special waste but, in the amended Circular, were stated not to be considered as such; and so on.
3   Environment Agency *Special Wastes: A Technical Guidance Note on their Definition and Classification*, (1999), Environment Agency, Bristol, para 1.1.7.

4.21 A detailed and understandable description of the manner by which special waste is defined in the Special Waste Regulations 1996 is somewhat easier now the Regulations have been subject to amendment. However, considerable cross-reference is still needed to the various Parts of Schedule 2 to the Special Waste Regulations 1996, along with reference to parallel legislation on the labelling of dangerous substances and preparations[1]. In an attempt to provide clarity, the following paragraphs will expand upon the various sub-sections which define special waste in reg 2, each commencing with a summary of the provision as a whole.

1   The Chemicals (Hazard Information and Packaging for Supply) Regulations 1994 (SI 1994/3247) as amended by the Chemicals (Hazard Information and Packaging for Supply) (Amendment) Regulations 1996 (SI 1996/1092). Further amendments have been made (SI 1997/1460 and SI 1998/3106), but these are not currently relevant to the Special Waste Regulations 1996: see para 4.31.

4.22 For many wastes which were previously special waste under the Control of Pollution (Special Waste) Regulations 1980, it should be noted that Circular 6/96 suggests that they are likely to remain so under the new regime[1]. This is apparently because certain of the definitional criteria chosen in the Special Waste Regulations 1996 are intended to be similar in intent to those contained in the earlier regulations[2]. However, as the requirements of EC law are wider than the Control of Pollution (Special Waste) Regulations 1980, other waste streams have fallen within the earlier special waste definition for the first time. An example is waste oil. Hence the total annual quantity of special waste in England and Wales in 1997/98 was reported to be 5.6 million tonnes[3].

1   Circular 6/96, Annex B, para 15.
2   It would appear that this is the rationale behind the limited list of hazardous properties contained in
    SI 1996/972, reg 2(2)(a) (as amended by SI 1996/2019, Sch 1, para 3). Regulation 2(2) is discussed at
    para 4.41 below.
3   Personal Communication (1999) to author from Environment Agency.

4.23   The Special Waste Regulations 1996 set out two principal criteria which are to be used to determine if a waste is a special waste[1]. The first approach[2] addresses those wastes contained in the hazardous waste list contained in the EC Decision 94/904. The second approach[3] is intended to encompass wastes not present on the list but which display one or more of a limited range[4] of properties. In addition to these two approaches, prescription-only medicines are to be viewed as special waste[5].

1   SI 1996/972, reg 2, as amended by SI 1996/2019, reg 2, Sch 1, para 3.
2   SI 1996/972, reg 2(1) as amended by SI 1996/2019, reg 2, Sch 1, para 3.
3   SI 1996/972, reg 2(2)(a) as amended by SI 1996/2019, reg 2, Sch 1, para 3.
4   These properties are shown in Part II of Schedule 2 of the Special Waste Regulations 1996 (see Table
    4.1): 'highly flammable' with a flashpoint below 21°C (H3-A (first indent); 'irritant' (H4); 'harmful'
    (H5); 'toxic' (H6); 'carcinogenic' (H7) and 'corrosive' (H8).
5   SI 1996/972, reg 2(2)(b) as amended by SI 1996/2019, reg 2, Sch 1, para 3. Note that the Agency's
    technical guidance note (Environment Agency *Special Wastes: A Technical Guidance Note on their
    Definition and Classification*, (1999), Environment Agency, Bristol (see para 3.2.1)) structures the
    discussion on the definition of special waste somewhat differently, while asserting that the method of
    presentation follows the Regulations. The discussion below follows the structure of the Regulations
    rather than that contained in the Agency's guidance note.

4.24   It should be noted that the Special Waste Regulations 1996 exclude certain wastes from the definition of special waste. Most types of household waste, for example, are not covered[1]. The nature of these exclusions is discussed at paras 4.53–4.59.

1   See SI 1996/972, reg 2 as amended by SI 1996/2019, reg 2, Sch 1, para 3.

Special wastes on the EC hazardous waste list

4.25   The Special Waste Regulations 1996 reproduce the hazardous waste list contained in Commission Decision 94/904[1] as Part I of Schedule 2 to the Regulations[2]. The Regulations define a special waste as a substance which appears on the list and which displays certain toxic or otherwise detrimental properties. The nature of these properties is based on Annex III of the Hazardous Waste Directive, which is reproduced in the Regulations as Part II of Schedule 2 (see Table 4.1).

1   The Special Waste Regulations 1996 make clear that only those substances which are preceded by a
    six digit code have relevance (SI 1996/972, reg 2(1)(a) as amended by SI 1996/2019, reg 2, Sch 1,
    para 3). The other elements, which are preceded by two or four digit codes, should therefore be
    viewed as headings provided for the benefit of the reader's orientation.
2   The EC List is contained in Appendix II.

4.26   Although the Special Waste Regulations 1996 only set out those wastes which are hazardous in Schedule 2, Part I, it is useful to consider the materials listed in the context of the other entries in the European Waste Catalogue[1]. This allows a much clearer picture to emerge as to which substances are, or are not, potentially special wastes[2].

1   The Catalogue is contained in Commission Decision of 20 December 1993 establishing a List of
    Waste pursuant to Article 1(a) of Council Directive 75/442 on Waste, 94/3/EC (OJ L5/15). It is
    discussed at para 2.22ff. Annex B1 of the amended Circular 6/96 provides useful clarification of the
    terms used in the hazardous waste list and its relationship to the European Waste Catalogue.

2   A copy of the complete European Waste Catalogue, which has all non-hazardous and hazardous
    wastes differentiated, is contained in Appendix II (see also the useful guide contained in Environment
    Agency, *Special Waste: A Technical Guidance Note on their Definition and Classification*, (1999),
    Environment Agency, Bristol, Appendix A).

4.27   The testing methodologies appropriate to determine the hazardous properties
are prescribed by Schedule 2, Part IV of the Special Waste Regulations 1996[1] and are
considered at para 4.46.

1   SI 1996/972 as amended by SI 1996/2019, reg 2, Sch 1, para 7.

4.28   For many wastes, the naming of the material on the hazardous waste list and its
inclusion within the properties set down in Schedule 2 are the only criteria that need to
be considered. This applies particularly where a substance has the following properties: H1, H2, H3-A, H3-B and H9 to H14 (see Table 4.1). For example, a paint waste
containing chlorinated solvents with a flashpoint of less than 55°C would be a special
waste. It would fall within the hazardous waste list's European Waste Catalogue Code
080101[1], having hazardous property H3-B 'Flammable'[2].

1   See Appendix II.
2   See Table 4.1.

4.29   However the definition of special waste becomes more involved for certain
other materials. These fall into two classes. The first is those wastes which are covered
by the hazardous waste list and which exhibit properties H4 to H8 (see Table 4.1). The
second is the wastes whose description cannot be found on the hazardous waste list.
These, more detailed, decision criteria are considered below.

Additional criteria for wastes on the hazardous waste list which exhibit hazardous properties H4 to H8

4.30   As noted earlier, the hazardous properties H4 to H8 – irritant, harmful, toxic,
carcinogenic and corrosive – used in the Hazardous Waste Directive (see Table 4.1) are
somewhat subjective and thus require more practical definition. The Special Waste
Regulations 1996 address this matter by way of the hazard thresholds set down in
Council Decision 94/904 which were used to establish the EC Hazardous Waste List
(see Table 4.3)[1]. These thresholds are contained in Part III to Schedule 2 of the Special
Waste Regulations 1996 in a re-ordered and reworded fashion (see Table 4.4). Regulation 2(3) of the Special Waste Regulations 1996 requires that, in respect of properties H4 to H8 (see Table 4.1), no substance should be regarded as a special waste if it
exhibits these properties only at levels below the thresholds shown in Table 4.4.

1   See Decision 94/904 Article 1 and SI 1996/972, reg 2(3) as amended by SI 1996/2019, reg 2, Sch 1,
    para 3.

4.31   It can be seen that Table 4.4 refers to certain risk phrases, such as R36, R37 and
so on. Part IV of Schedule 2 to the Special Waste Regulations 1996[1] provides clarification on the manner by which these and other terms contained in the Table should be
interpreted. This is done way of cross-references to parallel legislation pertaining to
the labelling of dangerous substances or preparations, as set down in the Chemicals
(Hazard Information and Packaging for Supply) Regulations 1994[2]. When enacted,
these Regulations were commonly referred to as 'CHIP 2'[3] and, since their amendment, as 'CHIP 96'. Although for the purposes of labelling of dangerous substances
CHIP 96 has now to become 'CHIP 99'[4], the amendments to the Chemicals (Hazard
Information and Packaging for Supply) Regulations 1994[5] made since 1996 do not

Table 4.4
Special Waste Regulations 1996[1]

Thresholds[2] for Certain Hazardous Properties

A substance is a special waste if 'in the waste':

- the total concentration of substances classified as irritant and having assigned to them
  any of the risk phrases[3] R36 ('irritating to the eyes'), R37 ('irritating to the respiratory
  system') or R38 ('irritating to the skin') is equal to or greater than 20%;
- the total concentration of substances classified as irritant and having assigned to them
  the risk phrase R41 ('risk of serious damage to the eyes') is equal to or greater than
  10%;
- the total concentration of substances classified as harmful is equal to or greater than
  25%;
- the total concentration of substances classified as very toxic is equal to or greater than
  0.1%;
- the total concentration of substances classified as toxic is equal to or greater than 3%;
- the total concentration of substances classified as carcinogenic and placed by the
  approved classification and labelling guide[4] in category 1 or 2 of that classification is
  equal to or greater than 0.1%;
- the total concentration of substances classified as corrosive and having assigned to
  them the risk phrase R34 ('causes burns') is equal to or greater than 5%; and
- the total concentration of substances classified as corrosive and having assigned to
  them the risk phrase R35 ('causes severe burns') is equal to or greater than 1%.

1   SI 1996/972, Sch 2, Pt III.
2   Where percentages are shown, these are to be taken to be percentages as expressed by weight: see
    SI 1996/972, Sch 2, Pt IV, para 3 as amended by SI 1996/2019, reg 2, Sch 1, para 3.
3   Defined in SI 1996/972, reg 1(4): see para 4.33ff.
4   Defined in SI 1996/972, reg 1(4): see para 4.39ff.

have relevance to the current definition of special waste. The Special Waste Regulations 1996[6] solely refer to the Hazard Information and Packaging Regulations prior to
their amendment in 1997 to 1999. This is to be changed at some point to ensure
compatibility toward the end of 1999[7].

1   As amended by SI 1996/2019, reg 2, Sch 1, para 7.
2   SI 1994/3247 as amended by the Chemicals (Hazard and Information) Packaging (Amendment)
    Regulations 1996 (SI 1996/1092).
3   See, for example, Health and Safety Executive *CHIP 2 for Everyone*, (1995) HSE Books, London.
4   SI 1999/197.
5   SI 1997/1460, SI 1998/3106 and SI 1999/197.
6   See SI 1996/972, reg 1(4), as amended by SI 1996/2019.
7   See answer to Parliamentary question by Colin Burgon MP, *Hansard* 31 March 1999 col 767.

4.32   Given the significance of the CHIP 96 provisions in the definition of special
waste under the Special Waste Regulations 1996, it is necessary to consider the
relevant requirements in some detail. As noted, the CHIP 96 provisions stem from the
Chemicals (Hazard Information and Packaging for Supply) Regulations 1994[1]. These
in turn emanated from the much amended Dangerous Substances Directive[2]. Prior to
the implementation of the Special Waste Regulations 1996, the CHIP provisions did
not have any function in relation to waste substances[3].

1   SI 1994/3247 as amended by SI 1996/1092.
2   Directive 67/548 as amended by Article 1(5) of Commission Directive 93/21/EEC of 27 April 1993
    adapting to technical progress for the 18th time Council Directive 67/548/EEC on the approximation
    of the laws, regulations and administrative provisions relating to the classification, packaging and

labelling of dangerous substances ((OJ L110/20 4.5.93), with the Annexes being published separately as OJ 110A 4.5.93).
3   See SI 1994/3247, reg 3(1)(o).

4.33   The CHIP 96 Regulations have the purpose of describing and labelling all potentially hazardous products and are thus familiar to many persons acting in the industrial context. Indeed, the safety and risk phrases printed on labels as set down in CHIP 96 can be seen on the packaging of everyday household items such as bleach. Schedule 2, Part IV to the Special Waste Regulations 1996 couples the CHIP 96 Regulations to the definition of special waste by way of the terms 'approved supply list', 'risk phrase' and 'approved classification and labelling guide'. These terms are defined in Regulation 1(4) of the Special Waste Regulations 1996[1]. They are utilised in Regulation 2 to determine the nature of the hazardous properties 'irritant', 'harmful', 'toxic', 'carcinogenic' and 'corrosive'[2], which are contained in Schedule 2, Part III to the Special Waste Regulations 1996.

1   Being subject to amendment by way of SI 1996/2019, Sch 1, para 2.
2   In other words, properties H4 to H8 as originally set down in Annex III of the Hazardous Waste Directive.

4.34   The full title of the 'Approved Supply List' is the *Approved Supply List (3rd edition) – Information approved for the classification and labelling of substances and preparations dangerous for supply*[1]. This document is in two volumes, with the first volume setting down an alphabetical list of substances and associated index numbers. Also contained in the volume are lists of risk and safety phrases to be printed on packaging containing such materials. The second volume concerns itself primarily with hazard classification and labelling information on a substance-by-substance basis, being also reproduced as a computer database on two disks. The second volume, along with the disks, contains extensive lists of substances and preparations and the concentration thresholds which make them exhibit particular hazardous properties.

1   Health and Safety Commission (1996) HMSO, London: note that SI 1996/2019, reg 2, Sch 1, para 2 amended the original Special Waste Regulations 1996 to refer to the third, rather than second, edition of the Approved Supply List. The third edition remains valid in the context of special waste even though it has been superseded by a fourth edition for the purposes of labelling dangerous substances.

4.35   As noted, the Approved Supply List contains risk phrases and safety phrases to be printed on labels of particular hazardous substances. For the purposes of the Special Waste Regulations 1996, only the risk phrases are subsumed. Risk phrases are set down in Part III of the Approved Supply List[1]. There are 64 single risk phrases contained in that Part, with each phrase describing the type of hazard expected from a particular substance or preparation. Hence the packaging of sodium hypochlorite – a frequent constituent of household bleach – is required to have a label which includes the words 'contact with acids liberates toxic gases' (risk phrase R34). In addition to the single phrases, there are also a series of combined phrases such as 'irritating to eyes and skin' (risk phrase 36/38).

1   Being defined for the purposes of the Special Waste Regulations 1996 by SI 1996/972, reg 14.

4.36   The Special Waste Regulations 1996 use the Approved Supply List to indicate whether the constituents of a particular waste should be considered as having the properties shown in Part III of Schedule 2 to the Regulations (see Table 4.3 above)[1]. This can be done by looking up the relevant substances on Part V of the List and seeing if they have risk phrases assigned to them. Having used the List for the purposes of orientation with respect to Table 4.3, the hazard thresholds contained within the Table can then to be considered.

1 See SI 1996/972, Sch 2, Pt IV, para 2(i) as amended by SI 1996/2019, reg 2, Sch 1, para 7.

4.37 *Example* The effect of the use of CHIP 96 in conjunction with the Special Waste Regulations 1996 is best illustrated by an example. For this purpose a metal finishing waste containing sulphuric acid at 6% w/w concentration will be utilised. This material is used for descaling steel – a process known as steel pickling. This waste falls within Waste Code 110105 in Part I of Schedule 2[1] (see Appendix II). It has corrosive properties and hence comes under item H8 as shown in Table 4.1[2]. Whether those properties are sufficient to bring the material within the Table contained in Part III of Schedule 2 (see Table 4.3) will depend on an assessment against the CHIP 96 criteria[3]. Sulphuric acid is covered by the Approved Supply List[4], having the substance index number 016-020-00-8. Looking up the index number in Part V of the Approved Supply List[5] indicates that, at concentrations greater than or equal to 15%, it would have a risk phrase R35 – 'Causes Severe Burns'[6].

1 Satisfying SI 1996/972, reg 2(1)(a) as amended by SI 1996/2019, reg 2, Sch 1, para 3.
2 Thus satisfying SI 1996/972, reg 2(1)(b) as amended by SI 1996/2019, reg 2, Sch 1, para 3.
3 SI 1996/972, Sch 2, Pt IV, para 2 as amended by SI 1996/2019, reg 2, Sch 1, para 7.
4 See Part I, page 147 of the *Approved Supply List – Information approved for the classification and labelling of substances and preparations dangerous for supply* 3rd edition, 1996.
5 See the Approved Supply List, Part V, page 53.
6 See the Approved Supply List, Part III, page 171.

4.38 The Special Waste Regulations 1996 then require a comparison of the hazardous properties to be made against the thresholds laid down in Schedule 2, Part III[1] (see Table 4.4). This indicates that the thresholds for the risk phrase R35 should be set at a concentration of greater than or equal to 1%. Given the fact that this waste stream has an acid content of 6%, it is to be regarded as a special waste on this basis.

1 SI 1996/972, reg 2(3) as amended by SI 1996/2019, reg 2, Sch 1, para 3.

Substances on the hazardous waste list but not on the approved supply list

4.39 The Approved Supply List is not comprehensive in its list of substances and preparations. Often there is insufficient information to set down confidently the nature of all risks. This also affects complex proprietary mixtures whose listing would, inter alia, make the List inordinately long. In these circumstances, the CHIP 96 Regulations require the manufacturer or supplier to decide on the required risk and safety phrases to be used on the appropriate label, and reference must be made to the 'Approved Classification and Labelling Guide'[1]. The Guide sets down criteria as to when it is appropriate to use particular risk and safety phrases, based on the revised Annex VI of the Dangerous Substances Directive[2].

1 *The Approved Guide to the Classification and Labelling of Substances and Preparations Dangerous for Supply*, Second Edition, Health and Safety Commission 1994, HMSO, London. While the second edition of the Approved Guide was superseded for labelling purposes by a third edition in 1997, the Special Waste Regulations 1996 currently refer explicitly to the second edition (SI 1996/972, reg 1(4) as amended by SI 1996/2019, reg 2, Sch 1, para 2(a)).
2 Directive 67/548 as amended by Article 1(5) of Commission Directive 93/21/EEC of 27 April 1993 adapting to technical progress for the 18th time Council Directive 67/548/EEC on the approximation of the laws, regulations and administrative provisions relating to the classification, packaging and labelling of dangerous substances (OJ L110/20 4.5.93), with the Annexes being published separately as OJ 110A 4.5.93.

4.40 The Approved Classification and Labelling Guide also has a function in determining whether a material is special waste[1]. It is to be used when a substance is not found on the Approved Supply List described above[2]. In this instance, the hazardous properties shown in Table 4.4 (such as harmfulness, toxicity, carcinogenicity etc) must be assessed against the criteria set down in the Approved Guide[3]. If the application of these criteria suggests that the waste has one of the properties making up the CHIP 96 risk phrases, it is then a special waste.

1 SI 1996/972, reg 2(4) and Sch 2, Pt IV as amended by SI 1996/2019, reg 2, Sch 1, paras 3 and 7.
2 SI 1996/972, Sch 2, Pt IV, para 2 as amended by SI 1996/2019, Sch 1, para 7.
3 SI 1996/972, reg 2(3) and Sch 2, Pt IV, para 2(i) as amended by SI 1996/2019, reg 2, Sch 1, para 7.

4.41 For example, if a waste is to be viewed as 'harmful' at a concentration of greater than or equal to 25% (see Table 4.4) and is thus a special waste under the Special Waste Regulations 1996, it must satisfy the requirements of the CHIP 96 risk phrases set down in the Approved Classification and Labelling Guide of R20 'Harmful by Inhalation', R21 'Harmful in Contact with Skin' and R22 'Harmful if Swallowed'[1]. The scientific criteria which determine these thresholds are set out in the Guide, and are mainly based upon standard toxicity data.

1 See para 48 of the *Approved Guide to the Classification and Labelling of Substances and Preparations Dangerous for Supply* (2nd Edition), 1994, HMSO.

Other special waste not featuring on the hazardous waste list

4.42 The Special Waste Regulations 1996 contain a provision which addresses any waste which is not categorised by the EC hazardous waste list. This is achieved by way of reg 2(2)(a)[1]. According to Circular 6/96, the principal purpose of reg 2(2)(a) is to ensure that wastes which were previously considered to be special waste under the earlier Control of Pollution (Special Waste) Regulations 1980[2] remain special waste under the new regime[3].

1 As amended by SI 1996/2019, reg 2, Sch 1, para 3.
2 SI 1980/1709.
3 Circular 6/96, Annex B, para 4.

4.43 It is important to realise that wastes not found on the hazardous waste list are special wastes only when they exhibit one or more of a restricted range of hazardous properties. The first property is 'highly flammable', with a flashpoint of less than 21°C (the first of the five sub-categories of property H3-A)[1]. For wastes which exhibit the properties H4 to H8 (see Table 4.1), the hazard thresholds criteria shown in Table 4.4 must be applied[2] using the Approved Supply List or Approved Classification and Labelling Guide[3]. These have already been described at paras 4.34 and 4.39 above.

1 SI 1996/972, reg 2(2)(a) as amended by SI 1996/2019, reg 2, Sch 1, para 3.
3 SI 1996/972, reg 2(3) as amended by SI 1996/2019, reg 2, Sch 1, para 3.
4 SI 1996/972, reg 2(4) as amended by SI 1996/2019, reg 2, Sch 1, para 3 and Sch 2, Pt IV.

4.44 The wording of reg 2(2) has important ramifications. As noted, it only makes reference to the hazardous properties H3-A (first indent) and properties H4 to H8. Accordingly, a waste not featuring on the hazardous waste list cannot be special waste on the sole grounds that it only exhibits the properties H1, H2, H3-A (second and subsequent sub-categories), H3-B and H9 to H14. The only exception to this rule is prescription-only medicines.

Medicinal products

4.45   With the exception of waste arising from private households[1], the Special Waste Regulations 1996 require that 'medicinal products'[2] are always special waste[3] when they are defined as prescription-only medicines[4]. In this instance, there is no need to consider any of the other evaluative criteria described above, including whether the medicine is on the hazardous waste list.

1   See para 4.54ff.
2   Having the meaning set down in the Medicines Act 1968, s 130, as amended by paras 3(7) to 3(10) of Sch 1 and Sch 2 of the Animal Health and Welfare Act 1984.
3   SI 1996/972, reg 2(2)(b) as amended by SI 1996/2019, reg 2, Sch 1, para 3.
4   As specified in an Order made under s 58 of the Medicines Act 1968 (as amended by s 1 of the Medicinal Products: Prescription by Nurses etc Act 1992).

Testing methods

4.46   Part IV of Schedule 2 to the Special Waste Regulations 1996[1] sets down certain requirements in respect of testing criteria for the hazardous properties referred to in the Regulations[2]. It states that '[e]xcept in the case of a substance listed in the approved supply list', the testing methods required to determine these properties are those set down in Annex V of Council Directive 67/548, which has now been entirely replaced by Directive 92/69[3], published in the Official Journal of the European Communities as a 235-page separate volume[4].

1   SI 1996/972 as amended by SI 1996/2019, reg 2, Sch 1, para 7: put into effect by SI 1996/972, reg 2(4) (as amended).
2   See Environment Agency *Special Wastes: A Technical Guidance Note on their Definition and Classification*, (1999), Environment Agency, Bristol, para 6.8.1.1ff and Volume III.
3   OJ L196/1 16.8.1967 as amended by Directive 92/69 (Article 1 of Commission Directive 92/69/EEC of 31 July 1992 adapting to technical progress for the 17th time Council Directive 67/548/EEC on the approximation of the laws, regulations and administrative provisions relating to the classification, packaging and labelling of dangerous substances (OJ L383 29.12.1992), with the Annexes being published separately. Note that while further amendments have been made to the Directive since Directive 92/69, the Special Waste Regulations 1996 refer to the testing methods contained in 'Council Directive 67/548/EEC, as amended by Commission Directive 92/69' but not to later changes (see SI 1996/972, Sch 2, Pt IV, para 1, as amended by SI 1996/2019, reg 2, Sch 1, para 7).
4   See OJ L383A 29.12.1992.

4.47   The words '[e]xcept in the case of a substance listed in the approved supply list' seem somewhat ambiguous. What is not made clear is the testing methods to be applied to those substances which actually do feature on the Approved Supply List itself. All Part IV to Schedule 2 of the Special Waste Regulations 1996 seems to refer to is the testing methods needed for those substances *not* featuring on the List. However, the intent of the Regulations appears to be that, as testing has already been extensively used to place a substance on the Approved Supply List, there is no need for further testing in respect of wastes which contain substances on the List. However, this would appear more implicit than explicit from the Special Waste Regulations 1996 themselves.

CHIP 96 and the Special Waste Regulations 1996

4.48   From the above discussion and from reading reg 2 and Schedule 2, Part IV to the Special Waste Regulations 1996, it seems to be the case that there are only two separate instances where the Regulations require the CHIP 96 provisions to be applied. The first of these is in relation to deciding which substances should be subject to the testing methods set down in Annex V of the Dangerous Substances Directive[1].

1   Directive 67/548 as amended by Directive 92/69 (Article 1 of Commission Directive 92/69/EEC of 31 July 1992 adapting to technical progress for the 17th time Council Directive 67/548/EEC on the approximation of the laws, regulations and administrative provisions relating to the classification, packaging and labelling of dangerous substances (OJ L383 29.12.1992), with the Annexes being published separately as OJ L383A 29.12.1992. The requirement is found in SI 1996/972, Sch 2, Pt IV, para 1 as amended by SI 1996/2019, reg 2.

4.49   The second mandatory use of CHIP 96 is in relation to the thresholds for the hazardous properties H4 to H8 contained in Part III of Schedule 2 to the Special Waste Regulations 1996 (see Table 4.4)[1]. The restriction to the properties H4 to H8 – thus excluding H1 to H3 and H9 to H14 – is due to the fact that Part IV of Schedule 2 seems only to refer to Part III of the Schedule, not to Part II.

1   SI 1996/972, Sch 2, Pt IV, para 2 as amended by SI 1996/2019, reg 2.

4.50   Apart from the above two instances, there appears to be no further statutory requirement in the Special Waste Regulations 1996 to utilise CHIP 96. Of particular note is the apparent absence of any provision in the Regulations requiring CHIP 96 to be considered in relation to the assessment of the properties H1 to H3 and H9 to H14 in Schedule 2, Part II (see Table 4.1). Despite this, both Circular 6/96[1] and the Agency's more recent Technical Guidance Note[2] suggest that, for any wastes where it is not immediately clear if they exhibit the hazardous properties H1 to H14, CHIP 96 assessment procedures should be used[3].

1   See, for example, Circular 6/96 Annex B, para 28, Annex B3 and Annex B4, para 4.
2   Environment Agency *Special Wastes: A Technical Guidance Note on their Definition and Classification*, (1999), Environment Agency, Bristol.
3   Note that where the original Circular refers to 'CHIP 2', this should read 'CHIP 96' (see Circular 14/96, p 6).

4.51   However, the use of CHIP 96 appears mandatory in assessing the status of a possible special waste only when explicitly required by the Special Waste Regulations 1996. In other instances, CHIP 96 assessments seem not to be required, and all the guidance achieves in these circumstances is to provides non-statutory advice. Indeed, despite the importance of clear assessment procedures to decide if a waste satisfies the relevant criteria of the Regulations, neither s 62 of the EPA 1990 nor the Special Waste Regulations 1996 confer any statutory status on the Guidance and the advice within it[1].

1   This can be contrasted against the Duty of Care Code of Practice (see paras 3.06ff and 3.12ff) and also the so-called 'statutory guidance' (see para 8.231ff) contained in specified Waste Management Papers and in Circular 11/94 in relation to waste management licences.

4.52   Finally, it should also be appreciated that CHIP 96 only relates to substances and preparations. The term 'substance' is defined in the Chemicals (Hazard Information and Packaging for Supply) Regulations 1994[1], with 'preparations' meaning mixtures or solutions of two or more substances[2]. CHIP 96 does not cover manufactured articles[3], which as waste may be hazardous in their own right. An example might be a nickel-cadmium battery or a fluorescent lighting tube containing mercury. Presumably, the hazards presented by an article should, where possible, be assessed on the basis of its constituents.

1   SI 1994/3247, reg 2(1): ' "substance" means chemical elements and their compounds in the natural state or obtained by any production process, including any additive necessary to preserve the stability of the product and any impurity deriving from the process used, but excluding any solvent which may be separated without affecting the stability of the substance or changing its composition.'
2   SI 1994/3247, reg 2(1).
3   See Environment Agency *Special Wastes: A Technical Guidance Note on their Definition and Classification*, (1999), Environment Agency, Bristol, para 4.2.6.

Radioactive waste[1]

4.53 As noted at para 2.53ff, radioactive waste is not generally subject to the provisions of Part II of the EPA 1990[2]. However, the Secretary of State is permitted to prescribe certain provisions of the EPA 1990 which are viewed as applicable to the handling of such waste. Regulation 3 of the Special Waste Regulations 1996 utilises this power to prescribe that certain radioactive wastes are to be taken to be special wastes. Such wastes must possess properties other than radioactivity which would make the material fall within the definition of special waste[3].

1 Note that certain changes are envisaged by the Department of the Environment: *Consultation Paper – Proposed Amendments to the Special Waste Regulations 1996 and the Waste Management Licensing Regulations 1994*, DETR, London, April 1998.
2 EPA 1990, s 78.
3 SI 1996/972, reg 3 and see Circular 6/96, Annex A, para 8.

Exclusions for household waste

4.54 Under the Special Waste Regulations 1996, 'household waste' cannot be special waste[1]. In the context of the 1996 Regulations, the relevant sub-paragraph[2] states that:

' "household waste" means waste which is household waste for purposes of Part II of the 1990 Act or which is treated as household waste for those purposes by virtue of regulation 2(1) of the Controlled Waste Regulations, other than:

(a) asbestos;
(b) waste from a laboratory;
(c) waste from a hospital, other than waste from a self-contained part of a hospital which is used wholly for the purposes of living accommodation.'

1 SI 1996/972, reg 2(1) and (2).
2 SI 1996/972, reg 1(4) as amended by SI 1996/2019, reg 2, Sch 1, para 2(b).

4.55 This sub-section should be read subject to the following provisions. Firstly, the term 'household waste' is as defined in s 75(5) of the EPA 1990[1]. While this matter is discussed further in Chapter 2, this definition encompasses wastes arising from domestic properties, caravans, residential homes, educational establishments and hospitals and nursing homes. Secondly, 'household waste' is to be viewed in the context of the Controlled Waste Regulations 1992. As explained in greater detail at para 2.200ff, the following wastes are also to be treated as 'household waste', in addition to those set out in s 75 of the EPA 1990. They are waste from:

(a) places of worship;
(b) premises occupied by charities;
(c) any land connected with a domestic property, caravan or residential home;
(d) a private garage;
(e) a moored vessel used for living accommodation;
(f) a campsite;
(g) a penal institution;
(h) a royal palace; and
(i) litter or other refuse collected by a local authority.

1 Confirmed by footnote (a) in the definition: as contained in SI 1996/2019, reg 2, Sch 1, para 2(b).

4.56 Accordingly, the definition of household waste requires that all wastes from the sources stated above are not be viewed as special wastes *unless* they are composed of asbestos[1] or stem from a laboratory or hospital located on one of the types of premises mentioned above. Therefore, with the exception of wastes from hospitals or laboratories, wastes such as oils, paints, pesticides and clinical wastes are deemed to fall within the definition of household waste when they have emanated from the premises listed above[2]. Given the blanket exclusion of household waste from the Special Waste Regulations 1996[3], such wastes are exempt from the Regulations when arising from these sources.

1   Interestingly, Circular 6/96 (Annex B1, para 20 as amended by Circular 14/96, Appendix A) indicates that bonded asbestos – which is the most common form of asbestos in the domestic context, being used for fencing and roofing of garages etc – is not to be considered a special waste. This view has been superseded in respect of wastes with an excess of 0.1% w/w asbestos content (see Environment Agency *Special Wastes: A Technical Guidance Note on their Definition and Classification*, (1999), Environment Agency, Bristol, Vol II, p 36).
2   See Circular 6/96, Annex A, para 3, as amended by para 13 of Circular 14/96.
3   SI 1996/972, reg 2(1) and (2), as amended by SI 1996/2019, reg 2, Sch 1, para 3.

Agricultural waste and waste from mines and quarries

4.57   Wastes from agricultural premises are not controlled wastes under s 75 of the EPA 1990[1]. Despite certain agricultural wastes featuring in the hazardous waste list in Council Decision 94/904 and in Schedule 2 to the Special Waste Regulations 1996, as these materials are not controlled wastes they are not subject to the Special Waste Regulations 1996[2]. An example is European Waste Catalogue Code 020105 'Agrochemical wastes', which would encompass many spent or otherwise surplus pesticides and herbicides arising on farm premises (see Appendix II). Clearly the omission of this type of material from the definition of special waste is an infraction of the Directive on Waste[3], the Hazardous Waste Directive and Council Decision 94/904. But this will continue until the definition of controlled waste under s 75 of the EPA 1990 is modified[4].

1   See paras 2.34, 2.60ff.
2   See Circular 6/96, Annex A, para 9 and Environment Agency *Special Wastes: A Technical Guidance Note for their Definition and Classification*, (1999), Environment Agency, Bristol, para 3.3.5.
3   See Chapter 2.
4   However reference should also be made to para 2.26ff.

4.58   Similarly, waste from quarrying and mining activities is not a controlled waste[1]. Examples of hazardous waste from such sources might be asbestos, oils, PCB-containing transformers and so on. None of these materials would be classified as special wastes.

1   EPA 1990, s 75(7)(c): see para 2.57ff.

Waste explosives

4.59   Like agricultural wastes, explosives as defined by the Explosives Act 1875 cannot be controlled wastes[1]. In spite of the fact that waste explosives have their own Chapter Heading[2] in both the Hazardous Waste List and in Part I of Schedule 2 to the Special Waste Regulations 1996, these materials are not special waste[3].

1   EPA 1990, s 75(2): see Chapter 2.
2   Chapter Heading 1604 – Waste Explosives, Waste Codes 160401 (waste ammunition), 160402 (fireworks waste) and 160403 (other waste explosives).
3   See Environment Agency *Special Wastes: A Technical Guidance Note on their Definition and Classification*, (1999), Environment Agency, Bristol, para 3.3.4 and page 1B.4.

DOCUMENTING SPECIAL WASTE MOVEMENTS

The Consignment Note[1]

4.60   Directive 91/689 requires member states to ensure that the transport of hazardous waste is accompanied by an identification form[2]. The information to be contained in this form[3] is that set out in the, now superseded, Directive on the Transfrontier Shipment of Hazardous Waste[4]. Beyond requiring that transfers of hazardous waste are accompanied by the form, no further provisions relating to the detail of the required waste tracking system are laid down in the Directive. The exact nature of the provisions is therefore left to member states' discretion.

1   Note that changes have been proposed to the consignment note in the consultation paper *Proposed Amendments to the Special Waste Regulations 1996 and the Waste Management Licensing Regulations 1994*, DETR, London, April 1998.
2   Council Directive of 12 December 1991 on Hazardous Waste (91/689/EEC) (OJ L377/20 31.12.91), Article 5(3).
3   Directive 91/689, Article 5(5).
4   Council Directive of 6 December 1984 on the Supervision and Control within the European Community of the Transfrontier Shipment of Hazardous Waste (OJ L326/31 13.12.84), as amended by the Council Directive of 22 July 1985 adapting to technical progress Council Directive 84/631/EEC on the supervision and control within the European Community of the transfrontier shipment of hazardous waste (85/469/EEC) (OJ L272/1 12.10.85); the Council Directive of 12 June 1986 amending Directive 84/631/EEC on the supervision and control within the European Community of the transfrontier shipment of hazardous waste (86/279/EEC) (OJ L181/13 4.7.86); and the Council Directive of 23 December 1986 adapting to technical progress for the second time Council Directive 84/631/EEC on the supervision and control within the European Community of the transfrontier shipment of hazardous waste, (87/112/EEC) (OJ L48/31 17.2.87). Directive 91/689 Article 5(3) refers to Part A of Annex I of Directive 84/631. However, this Part was replaced by Commission Directive 85/469, which set down full details of the required transfrontier waste consignment note. Furthermore, Transfrontier Directive 84/631 was entirely repealed by Regulation 259/93 (see Article 43) in May 1994.

4.61   The Special Waste Regulations 1996 describe in some considerable detail the provisions by which shipments are to be documented. These requirements over-ride the necessity to document waste transactions by way of transfer notes under the duty of care[1]. However, the other requirements of the duty of care[2] apply to special waste movements.

1   See the Environmental Protection (Duty of Care) Regulations 1991 (SI 1991/2839), reg 2 as amended by SI 1996/972, reg 23.
2   EPA 1990, s 34: see Chapter 3.

4.62   The Special Waste Regulations 1996 set out the special waste consignment note in Schedule 1[1]. This is reproduced here as Figure 4.1. The Special Waste Regulations 1996 permit the nature of the information contained in the document to be reproduced 'in a form substantially to the like effect', allowing the modification of the consignment note to incorporate company logos and so on[2]. Companies can print their own consignment notes if they so desire. In England and Wales, approximately 200,000 consignment notes are in circulation annually[3].

1   SI 1996/972, reg 1(4).
2   SI 1996/972, reg 1(4).
3   Environment Agency *1997–98 Annual Report and Accounts*, (1998) Environment Agency, Bristol, p 152; the figure for Scotland is about 60,000: SEPA *Annual Report and Accounts 1997–98*, (1998) SEPA, Stirling, p 59.

4.63   The Special Waste Regulations 1996 generally require that either four or five identical copies of the consignment note are prepared for each transaction. This is so

Figure 4.1

The Special Waste Consignment Note

SPECIAL WASTE REGULATIONS 1996	Consignment Note N° _____
N° of prenotice *(if different)* _____	Sheet of

A   CONSIGNMENT DETAILS   PLEASE TICK IF YOU ARE A TRANSFER STATION ☐
1.   The waste described below is to be removed from (name, address and postcode)
2.   The waste will be taken to (address & postcode)
3.   The consignment(s) will be: one single ☐ a succession ☐ carrier's round ☐ other ☐
4.   Expected removal date of first consignment: last consignment:
5.   Name   On behalf of (company)
     Signature   Date
6.   ☎   7. The waste producer was (if different from 1)

B   DESCRIPTION OF THE WASTE   *No of additional sheet(s)* ☐
1.   The waste is   2. Classification
3.   Physical Form: Liquid ☐ Powder ☐ Sludge ☐   4. Colour
     Solid ☐ Mixed ☐
5.   Total quantity for removal   quantity   units (eg kg/ltrs/tonnes)   Container type,
     number and size:
6.   The chemical/biological components that make
     the waste special are:

Component	Concentration (% or mg/kg)	Component	Concentration (% or mg/kg)

7.   The hazards are:
8.   The process giving rise to waste is:

C   CARRIER'S CERTIFICATE   I certify that I today collected the consignment and that the
details in A1, A2 and B1 above are correct. The Quantity collected in the load is:
Name   On behalf of (company) (name &
                                               address)
Signature   Date   at   hrs.
1.   Carrier registration n°/reason for exemption   2. Vehicle registration n° (or mode of
                                                           transport, if not road)

D   CONSIGNOR'S CERTIFICATE
I certify that the information in B and C above are correct, that the carrier is registered
or exempt and was advised of the appropriate precautionary measures.
Name   On behalf of (company)
Signature   Date

E   CONSIGNEE'S CERTIFICATE
1.   I received this waste on   at   hrs.   2. Quantity received   quantity
                                                         units (eg kg/ltrs/tonnes)
3.   Vehicle registration n°   4. Management Operation
     I certify that waste management licence/authorisation exemption n°   authorises the
     management of the waste described in B.
     Name   On behalf of (company)
     Signature   Date

that enough copies are available for all parties in the special waste movement – consignor, carrier and consignee[1] – to retain copies of the documentation. For movements of single loads of special waste, the remaining two copies are sent at different times to the relevant Agency. The first copy is sent to the Agency in advance of the waste's intended movement – the 'prenotification' stage – with the second copy being dispatched to confirm the arrival of the waste at the consignee's premises. This arrangement thereby allows the tracking of a waste movement 'from cradle to grave', as a failure to receive the second copy of the consignment note should prompt the Agency into making enquiries about the status of the shipment.

1   These terms are defined in SI 1996/972, reg 1(4) and considered at para 4.73 below.

4.64   Besides requiring that the requisite number of copies of the note are prepared and that the note is based on the information contained in Schedule 1, the Special Waste Regulations 1996 do not set down in detail further requirements in respect of the printed consignment note. Instead, this is taken up by Circular 6/96[1], whereby certain non-statutory recommendations are made in relation to the forms.

1   Annex A, para 27ff.

4.65   The Circular 6/96 recommends that each consignment note is produced as a five-copy, self-carboning pad[1]. In order to readily make clear which copy of the document should be passed to which party, Circular 6/96 suggests the following colour scheme and headings for the five leaves of the consignment note[2]:

top copy (white)   'prenotification copy – consignor to send to consignee's Agency office'
2nd copy (yellow)   'copy for consignee to send to own Agency office'
3rd copy (pink)   'consignee copy – keep for site lifetime'
4th copy (orange)   'carrier's copy – keep for 3 years'
5th copy (green)   'consignor's copy – keep for 3 years'.

It is also recommended in the Circular that the guidance contained in its Annex C is printed on the reverse side of the note. This Annex provides a summary of the requirements relating to the form and suggests clarifications in respect of certain elements.

1   Circular 6/96, Annex A, para 27.
2   Circular 6/96, Annex A, para 28.

4.66   It should be noted that, in respect of rounds whereby small quantities of waste are picked up from a succession of sources, the consignment note is supplemented by a printed schedule[1]. This type of collection is termed a 'carrier's round' in the Special Waste Regulations 1996 and is discussed separately at para 4.91 below.

1   SI 1996/972, reg 8.

The Agency's unique coding of consignment notes

4.67   The Agency[1] is required to draw up and supply a unique coding identifier for each consignment note[2]. The coding – termed a 'relevant code' in the Special Waste Regulations 1996[3] – must be reproduced on the consignment notes when they are to be used[4]. The Special Waste Regulations 1996 require a person wishing to utilise a consignment note to apply to the Agency for the coding. Only when the code has been received from the Agency can the consignor enact the notification procedure itself.

1   Ie the Environment Agency in the England and Wales or the Scottish Environment Protection Agency.
2   SI 1996/972, reg 4.
3   SI 1996/972, reg 1(4).
4   See SI 1996/972, reg 5(2)(a).

4.68   The Agency can either charge for the release of the coding in advance or in arrears[1]. The applicant has a two-month period of grace to pay the required amount, with that period starting from when the request was made to the Agency[2]. The Special Waste Regulations 1996 permit the Agency to exercise discretion over whether the code is to be assigned to the applicant in the absence of the advance payment of the required fee[3]. However, Circular 14/96[4] states that the withholding of a code until the fee has been paid is only appropriate when previous fees are overdue. The non-payment of fees is a breach of the Special Waste Regulations 1996, being an offence under reg 18[5].

1   SI 1996/972, reg 4(3) as amended by SI 1996/2019, reg 2, Sch 1, para 4(b).
2   SI 1996/972, reg 14(3) as amended by SI 1996/2019, reg 2, Sch 1, para 6(c).
3   SI 1996/972, reg 4(3) as inserted by SI 1996/2019, reg 2, Sch 1, para 4(b).
4   Circular 14/96, para 15.
5   Described at para 4.183 below.

4.69   The usual charge to be made by the Agency for the release of a unique coding number is £15[1]. However, in the case of a consignment consisting 'entirely' of lead acid batteries, this is reduced to £10[2]. In a small number of other cases, there is no charge at all[3]. These relate to the second or subsequent carrier's rounds where less than 400 kgs of special waste is collected on the same vehicle[4], returning products to the supplier[5] and removal of special waste generated on ships[6]. It should be noted that, while there is no fee to pay in these circumstances, this provision does not absolve the applicant from the need to obtain the code from the Agency in advance of a shipment.

1   SI 1996/972, reg 14(1)(b).
2   SI 1996/972, reg 14(1)(a).
3   SI 1996/972, reg 14(2).
4   SI 1996/972, reg 14(2)(a) as amended by SI 1996/2019, reg 2, Sch 1, para 6(b): see para 4.98.
5   SI 1996/972, reg 14(2)(b): see para 4.123.
6   SI 1996/972, reg 14(2)(c): see para 4.114.

4.70   Circular 6/96 envisages that a block of unique coding numbers can be purchased from the relevant Agency responsible for the intended consignee[1]. This arrangement will apply mainly to persons involved in extensive movements of special waste, such as disposal contractors or operators of large industrial plant. Where surplus fees have been paid which will not be utilised, Circular 6/96 states that they are either to be credited to the purchaser or that a refund must be provided[2]. However, the Circular states that no refunds should be issued for codings which have appeared on prenotification copies of the consignment note sent to the Agency, but not followed up with the actual transaction.

1   Circular 6/96, Annex A, para 47.
2   Circular 6/96, Annex A, para 48.

4.71   Circular 6/96 suggests that the £15 fee set out in the Special Waste Regulations 1996 should be seen very much as an interim measure. The intention is that the Agency will set its own fees under s 41 of the Environment Act 1995[1]. The requirement in the Special Waste Regulations 1996 for payment of fees will then be revoked[2]. However, it should be noted that the Agency cannot unilaterally embark on a new fee structure; any proposed scheme must be submitted to the Secretary of State for approval, having been publicised beforehand[3].

1 Environment Act 1995, s 41(1)(c).
2 Circular 6/96, Annex A, para 50. This is expected to be implemented in 2000, see *Hansard* 31 March 1999 Col 767.
3 Environment Act 1995, s 41(9).

4.72 Although there is one Agency for England and Wales, Circular 6/96 requires that requests for codes and payment of fees are made to the local or area office of the Agency covering the consignee[1]. Despite the Circular being published two months after the Agency was formed, this statement would appear to reflect the earlier arrangements for British waste regulation. In practice, all block purchases of codes in England and Wales must be made through the Agency's Peterborough office. The local offices only issue single, individually-coded, consignment notes.

1 Circular 6/96, Annex A, para 47: but there is nothing in the Special Waste Regulations 1996 to this effect.

The identity of consignors, carriers and consignees

4.73 The Special Waste Regulations 1996 establish separate identities for the parties involved in transactions of the special waste. They are the 'consignor', the 'carrier' and the 'consignee'. A 'consignor' is defined as the person 'who causes[1] that waste to be removed from the premises at which it is being held'[2]. Given that 'a carrier' is separately defined in the Special Waste Regulations 1996 (see below), a consignor would usually mean the waste producer. However, rather than use the term 'producer' in the 1996 Regulations[3], a decision was made to broaden the term. This was deemed necessary[4] in order to make the Special Waste Regulations 1996 have clearer application to individuals involved in reconsigning special waste shipments after intermediate storage at premises such as transfer stations[5].

1 The term 'causing' is discussed at para 7.62ff.
2 SI 1996/972, reg 1(4).
3 Which had been the case under the earlier Control of Pollution (Special Waste) Regulations 1980: SI 1980/1709.
4 Circular 6/96, Annex A, para 25.
5 It should be noted that the definition of the term 'consignor' in the Special Waste Regulations 1996 also appears to encompass brokers or agents. They could be viewed as 'causing' waste to be removed from a premises when they were not acting as carriers themselves.

4.74 A 'carrier' is identified in the Special Waste Regulations 1996[1] as a person 'who collects . . . [special] waste from the premises at which it is being held and transports it to another place'. A 'consignee' is defined as 'the person to whom the waste is transported'[2].

1 See SI 1996/972, reg 1(4).
2 SI 1996/972, reg 1(4).

Responsibilities for the completion of the consignment note

4.75 Circular 6/96 makes it clear that carriers and consignees can fill in the majority of the consignment note on behalf of a consignor[1]. However, the Special Waste Regulations 1996 require that, prior to the waste being collected, the consignor must always sign the relevant part of the document to verify the accuracy of the information given[2].

1 Circular 6/96, Annex A, para 33.
2 See SI 1996/972, regs 5(2)(d)(i), 8(3) and 9(2)(c).

NOTIFICATION PROCEDURES

4.76 As already noted, the Special Waste Regulations 1996 concern themselves extensively with a tracking procedure whereby the Agency is informed in advance of the imminent movement of the waste and again when the waste has arrived at its destination. As the consignor, carrier and consignee are all required to fill in relevant items on the consignment note and retain copies, it should be possible to track down the person responsible if the load goes astray. Similarly, incorrect disposal or recovery can be traced back to those responsible by way of the paperwork received at the site.

4.77 The Special Waste Regulations 1996 contain a variety of different notification procedures, of which the most important relate to the consignment of a single load of waste, the transport of multiple loads, and the collection of small quantities of hazardous waste from a number of producers by the same vehicle in the form of a 'carrier's round'. As is described later in this chapter, further requirements apply to more specialised movements and circumstances.

Consignments consisting of single loads

4.78 Prior to a special waste shipment being commenced, five copies of the consignment note must be prepared[1], and Parts A and B completed. As can be seen from Figure 4.1, these relate to details of the waste, the consignor and so on. The Agency must be approached for the unique coding number[2]. The Agency fee for this coding may need to be paid in advance[3] or within two months of the date of the request[4]. The coding obtained from the Agency must be included at the relevant place on the consignment note.

1 SI 1996/972, reg 5(2)(a).
2 Termed 'relevant code': see SI 1996/972, reg 1(4).
3 SI 1996/972, reg 4(3) as amended by SI 1996/2019, reg 2, Sch 1, para 4(b).
4 SI 1996/972, reg 14(3) as amended by SI 1996/2019, reg 2, Sch 1, para 6(c).

4.79 While the requirements in respect of duty of care transfer notes[1] do not apply to special waste movements[2], the provisions of s 34 of the EPA 1990 still apply. This includes the requirement that written descriptions must be transferred when waste passes between holders[3] and that such descriptions must be sufficient to ensure that s 33 of the EPA 1990 is not contravened[4]. Some guidance on the adequacy of special waste descriptions on consignment notes therefore can be gleaned from the Duty of Care Code of Practice[5].

1 EPA 1990, s 34 and SI 1991/2839: see Chapter 3.
2 SI 1991/2839, reg 2(3) as amended by SI 1996/972, reg 23.
3 EPA 1990, s 34(1)(c)(ii): see para 3.118ff.
4 See para 3.39ff. As discussed at para 4.187, the contravention of the requirements of the Special Waste Regulations 1996 in respect of consignment notes, may also be an offence in respect of the Environmental Protection (Duty of Care) Regulations 1991.
5 Department of the Environment *Environmental Protection Act 1990 Section 34, Waste Management The Duty of Care Code of Practice*, (1996) Second Edition, HMSO.

4.80 Once the coding has been obtained, the first copy of the consignment note can be sent off to the Agency, as prenotification, prior to the waste being moved[1]. This must be furnished to the Agency[2] covering the intended destination of the waste[3]. The waste can then be moved within the prenotification period of between 72 hours after the posting of the note and one month[4] after. It should be noted that the 72-hour notification period excludes any of the hours of a Saturday, Sunday, Good Friday, Christmas

Day, bank holiday or other public holiday[5]. A movement before the requisite 72 hours would be an offence[6]. Offences are discussed at para 4.183 below. The movement of the waste after the one month period would also contravene the Special Waste Regulations 1996 unless effected under a fresh notification.

1 SI 1996/972, reg 12(1).
2 Ie the Environment Agency or Scottish Environment Protection Agency. Agency custom and practice appears to indicate that this should be a local Agency office covering the consignee. However, this is not a requirement of the Special Waste Regulations 1996. Transactions to and from Northern Ireland and Gibraltar are dealt with differently – see para 4.148 below.
3 SI 1996/972, reg 5(2)(b).
4 A 'month' means a calendar month: Interpretation Act 1978, Sch 1.
5 SI 1996/972, reg 12(6).
6 The only exceptions to this principle concern emergencies (see SI 1996/972, reg 18(2) and para 7.154ff) and when a consignment 'cannot lawfully remain where it is for 72 hours' (SI 1996/972, reg 12(3)(b)).

4.81 The prenotification can be done by fax[1] provided that the original of the consignment note is forwarded to the Agency 'forthwith' after the removal of the waste[2]. The latter action must be done, by way of hand delivery or by first class post, within one day of the waste's removal[3]. While it seems that any person can complete parts A and B of the note, the duty to send off the note to the Agency is explicitly placed upon the 'consignor'[4].

1 Or by other electronic means.
2 SI 1996/972, reg 12(4).
3 SI 1996/972, reg 12(5).
4 SI 1996/972, reg 5(2)(b).

4.82 On arrival at the consignor's to collect the waste, the carrier must fill in Part C of the four remaining copies[1]. The consignor is required to complete Part D[2], signing to the effect that the description of the waste is correct and verifying the carrier's details. The consignor then retains one copy of the notification and gives the other three copies to the carrier[3]. The carrier must ensure that the three copies handed over travel with the load[4]. On arrival at the waste management facility, the three copies are presented to the consignee[5].

1 SI 1996/972, reg 5(2)(c).
2 SI 1996/972, reg 5(2)(d)(i).
3 SI 1996/972, reg 5(2)(d).
4 SI 1996/972, reg 5(3)(a).
5 SI 1996/972, reg 5(3)(b).

4.83 Provided the consignee wishes to accept the waste[1], he must complete Part E of all three notes, retain a copy for the consignee's records and return a copy to the carrier[2], who is required to retain a copy of the consignment note[3].

1 The Special Waste Regulations 1996 make provision for cases where the waste is rejected (reg 10); see para 4.132.
2 SI 1996/972, reg 5(4)(d).
3 SI 1996/972, reg 5(5).

4.84 The final copy of the note is sent to whichever Agency[1] covers the destination of the waste[2]. This must be done by first class post or by hand delivery to the Agency within one day of receipt of the waste by the consignee[3].

1 Ie the Environment Agency or Scottish Environment Protection Agency – transactions to and from Northern Ireland and Gibraltar are dealt with differently: see para 4.148 below.
2 SI 1996/972, reg 5(4).
3 SI 1996/972, reg 12(5).

Multiple shipments of special waste

4.85   As noted above, a single shipment is subject to a prenotification stage whereby the Agency is made aware of the impending departure of a load. For multiple shipments, the prenotification stage is only made once, and the subsequent loads can then be removed without the need to inform the Agency in advance. However, the consignor is allowed discretion in this matter, and can ship loads under single notifications if that is the preferred option. This simplified notification system for multiple consignments applies only where more than one load of waste of the 'same description' is taken from the same consignor, at the same premises, to the same consignee at the same destination[1]. Given that carriers are not mentioned in these requirements, a multiple load can be removed by different carriers.

1   SI 1996/972, reg 6(2)(a)(i)–(v).

4.86   While only the first load of waste needs to be prenotified to the relevant Agency, all subsequent transactions must occur within a year of the first load being shipped[1]. If this does not happen, a new consignment note must be raised and the first load prenotified as before.

1   SI 1996/972, reg 6(2)(a)(vi).

4.87   The Special Waste Regulations 1996 contain certain other rules which apply to multiple shipments. The fee of £15[1] is payable for each and every load[2]. As noted earlier, persons involved in moving significant quantities of special waste may have made advance purchases of a block of coding numbers and can assign these to each load prior to its removal. However, where individual codes need to be purchased, an application must be made prior to the 72-hour prenotification period. This can be for a single code to cover the first shipment, with further applications being made in advance on a load-by-load basis. Alternatively, a block purchase can be made on the basis of an estimate of the number of loads in the shipment.

1   £10 in the case of loads composed 'entirely' of lead acid batteries.
2   SI 1996/972, reg 14(1).

4.88   In respect of the second and successive movements of a multiple load, two coding numbers will need to be reproduced on each of the consignment notes. Firstly, the unique code obtained from the Agency for each load must be portrayed[1]. Secondly, the note must also contain a written reference to the coding number obtained at the prenotification stage[2].

1   SI 1996/972, reg 5(2)(a).
2   See the upper lines of the consignment note in Figure 4.1 and see also Circular 6/96, Annex A, para 55.

4.89   For the second and subsequent consignments of a multiple load, only four copies of the notification document are prepared for each load[1]. For multiple loads, it is almost inevitable[2] that the prenotification will contain an estimate of the quantity to be shipped in the forthcoming period of up to one year. Circular 6/96 states that, when the individual loads are collected, a more accurate figure can be written on the note at the time of collection[3].

1   SI 1996/972, reg 7(a).
2   For the reason that waste generation will closely follow industrial production levels in the forthcoming year.
3   Circular 6/96, Annex A, para 53.

4.90   Beyond the difference in the numbers of copies of the consignment note prepared, and the lack of a second prenotification copy, the system for documentation of the actual collection, transport and delivery of each multiple load is the same as already described at para 4.82ff.

Carriers' collection rounds for small quantities of special waste

4.91   Certain types of special waste collection involve a collection vehicle picking up small quantities of waste from a variety of sources in the form of a carrier's round. Examples include waste pharmaceuticals collected from chemists' premises; pick-ups of contaminated paint waste – termed 'gunwashings' – for recycling purposes from vehicle paint shops; waste oil collections and so on.

4.92   To apply the normal special waste notification procedures in these instances would often negatively affect the viability of this valuable type of collection service. The fee of £15 for each collection of waste might often be a significant disincentive for the collection of small quantities of wastes for recycling. This disincentive could result in recyclable substances being disposed of, either with the general factory waste or – worse – by disposal on the premises by such methods as open burning, evaporation, illicit discharge to sewer, etc. For these reasons, the Special Waste Regulations 1996 set out separate documentation procedures which apply when a carrier will be picking up small quantities of special waste from a variety of producers to make into single loads[1].

1   SI 1996/972, reg 8.

The nature of a 'carrier's round'

4.93   For the provisions for the collection of small quantities of special waste to apply, the collection system must fall within the definition of a 'carrier's round' in the Special Waste Regulations 1996. This is defined[1] as meaning:

'. . . a journey made by a carrier during which he collects more than one consignment of special waste and transports all consignments collected to the same consignee who is specified in the consignment note.'

Of particular note is that a legitimate carrier's round is a single journey by a carrier via a series of consignors to a consignee. As was the case for the more usual types of special waste shipments described earlier, the provisions for this type of collection service apply to single rounds or to a succession of shipments for a period of up to 12 months.

1   SI 1996/972, reg 1(4).

4.94   Generally[1], each individual carrier's round is required not to last beyond 24 hours, between the collection at the first consignor and delivery to the consignee[2]. This is presumably to prevent waste being stored on the vehicle for long periods or in significant quantities.

1   The exception relates to carrier's rounds involving the transportation of less than 400 kgs of special waste: see SI 1996/972, reg 8(1)(d), Circular 6/96, para 59; and para 4.98 below.
2   SI 1996/972, reg 8(1)(d): the consultation paper *Proposed Amendments to the Special Waste Regulations 1996 and the Waste Management Licensing Regulations 1994*, DETR, London, April 1998, proposes that this period is extended to 72 hours.

4.95   It is not possible to establish a single, cross-border, carrier's round between England and Scotland. The Special Waste Regulations 1996 require that all premises on a round must be located either within the ambit of the Environment Agency, in England and Wales, or the Scottish Environment Protection Agency, but not both[1]. This provision seems a little hard on carriers operating in the Scottish Borders, who must establish a dual system.

1   SI 1996/972, reg 8(1)(b)(ii).

4.96   It should be noted that the Hazardous Waste Directive[1] and the Special Waste Regulations 1996 contain requirements which preclude the 'mixing' of 'categories' of hazardous waste and the mixing of hazardous waste with non-hazardous waste. This is most likely to occur on carrier's rounds, and the provisions are discussed at para 4.176 below.

1   Directive 91/689 (OJ L377/20).

Fees for carrier's rounds

4.97   Subject to a minor exception in respect of carrier's rounds involving the movement of less than 400 kgs of waste in total, there is the usual Agency fee of £15 to pay to obtain a valid consignment note code number[1]. But unlike the standard special waste notification procedure, this fee covers the total round, not the removal of waste from each individual consignor which contributes to the round. Likewise, a succession of carrier's rounds over a year will usually incur the £15 charge for each trip.

1   But this is reduced to £10 in the case of collections of lead-acid batteries: SI 1996/972, reg 14(1).

4.98   However, in recognition that certain rounds may collect extremely small amounts of waste and that the £15 fee may prove a disincentive for the continuation of this service, the fee can be waived in specified circumstances[1]. This applies only to the second or subsequent collection of waste within the same week[2]. Besides this weekly limit, the circumstances specified in the Special Waste Regulations 1996 are as follows. Firstly, the second and subsequent loads collected in a week must be composed of less than 400 kgs of waste in total[3]. Secondly, the Special Waste Regulations 1996 require that the carrier and consignee are the same person in all the rounds[4], that a single vehicle is used in each round[5] and that a consignor cannot be returned to later in the week in the same round[6]. Should any of these conditions be breached, the £15 fee becomes payable for all the rounds undertaken in the week.

1   SI 1996/972, reg 14(2)(a) as amended by SI 1996/2019, reg 2, Sch 1, para 6(a). Although the fee is waived, the consignor must still obtain the unique consignment note coding from the Agency: SI 1996/972, reg 8(2)(a)(i).
2   SI 1996/972, reg 14(2)(a)(iv).
3   SI 1996/972, reg 14(2)(a)(iii) see also Circular 6/96, Annex A, paras 59 and 63. The definition of 'carrier's round' in SI 1996/972, reg 1(4) clearly indicates that the term encompasses all the pick-ups. Hence the 400 kg limit cannot be construed as a limit on individual collections from each consignor. It refers to the total contents of waste on the collection vehicle.
4   SI 1996/972, reg 14(2)(a)(i).
5   SI 1996/972, reg 14(2)(a) as amended by SI 1996/2019, reg 2, Sch 1, para 6(b).
6   SI 1996/972, reg 14(2)(a)(ii).

4.99   Precisely why there is the 400 kgs weight restriction in the Special Waste Regulations 1996 is not made clear in Circular 6/96, but it is primarily directed towards carrier's rounds involved in the delivery of goods or products, where special waste is also collected as part of the commercial service. An example would involve solvents being delivered to automotive body repair shops with paint-contaminated solvent wastes being collected for recovery.

Documentation procedures

4.100   For the provisions in respect of carrier's rounds to apply, certain requirements on documentation must be satisfied[1].

1   SI 1996/972, reg 8 as amended by SI 1996/2019, reg 2, Sch 1, para 5.

4.101   *Document preparation and prenotification*[1]   For a carrier's round, it is not necessary to produce five copies of the consignment note for each and every member of the round. Rather for the first round, four copies[2] of the consignment note are used to document the round in its entirety[3]. All the names and addresses of the consignors are provided on the one note, using additional sheets as necessary[4]. Along with Parts A and B of the note being completed, the relevant code obtained from the Agency must be entered. The note is then photocopied so that a copy is available for each consignor which makes up the round.

1   Prenotification is not required where a load consisting 'entirely' of lead acid vehicle batteries is to be moved: see SI 1996/972, reg 8(2)(a)(ii) as amended by SI 1996/2019, reg 2, Sch 1, para 5(a).
2   Two copies for the Agency (prenotification and second copy to show arrival at consignee); copies for the consignee and carrier: SI 1996/972, reg 8(2)(a)(ii) and 8(2)(b)(i) as amended by SI 1996/2019, reg 2, Sch 1, para 5(b).
3   Thereafter, for subsequent rounds covering the same wastes and consignor, there is no need for prenotification to the Agency and hence three copies are used: see SI 1996/972, reg 8(2)(b)(i) as amended by SI 1996/2019, reg 2, Sch 1, para 5(b).
4   See Circular 6/96, Annex A, para 57.

4.102   In a carrier's round, the consignment note must be substantiated by a printed schedule[1]. The schedule is used to document the actual transactions of special waste from each consignor to the carrier. It is designed to allow both carrier and consignor flexibility so that collections can occur as and when the waste arises. This would not be possible under the more inflexible requirements of the standard consignment note system described earlier. A copy of the schedule is shown here as Figure 4.2.

1   SI 1996/972, reg 8(2)(b)(iii).

4.103   Like the special waste consignment note itself, the schedule can be modified to allow appropriate company logos, addresses, etc[1]. The Special Waste Regulations 1996 require that four copies of the schedule be prepared[2], along with one copy for each consignor in the round. Circular 6/96 recommends that the individual sheets are self-carboning so that details are duplicated on all copies[3]. The top copy can be perforated, so that entries relating to individual consignors can be torn off after signing for the consignor's records.

1   SI 1996/972, reg 8(2)(b)(iii)
2   See SI 1996/972, reg 8(2)(b)(iii): copies each for the carrier and consignee, with *two* copies for the Agency. Why the Agency needs two copies is not clear, but this is confirmed by Circular 6/96, Annex A, para 57.
3   Circular 6/96, Annex A, para 62.

4.104   Once the consignment note code has been obtained from the Agency, the round can then be commenced after the prenotification period of 72 hours[1] has ended[2], starting when the first copy of the consignment note was forwarded to the relevant Agency as a prenotification[3]. The prenotification can be done by fax or e-mail within the requisite 72-hour period[4]. If such methods are used, the written copy of the prenotification must be sent prior to the load being moved, or 'forthwith'[5] after its departure[6].

Figure 4.2

Carrier's Round Schedule

SPECIAL WASTE REGULATIONS 1996: CARRIER SCHEDULE	Consignment Note N° ____ Sheet of

Name and address of premises from which waste was removed

I certify that today I collected the quantity of waste shown from the address given here and will take it to the address given in A2 on the consignment note

Quantity of waste removed	Carrier's signature and Date

I certify that the waste collected is as detailed above and conforms with the description given in B on the relevant consignment note

Name of Consignor	Signature and Date

Consignment Note N°

Name and address of premises from which waste was removed

I certify that today I collected the quantity of waste shown from the address given here and will take it to the address given in A2 on the consignment note

Quantity of waste removed	Carrier's signature and Date

I certify that the waste collected is as detailed above and conforms with the description given in B on the relevant consignment note

Name of Consignor	Signature and Date

Consignment Note N°

Name and address of premises from which waste was removed

I certify that today I collected the quantity of waste shown from the address given here and will take it to the address given in A2 on the consignment note

Quantity of waste removed	Carrier's signature and Date

I certify that the waste collected is as detailed above and conforms with the description given in B on the relevant consignment note

Name of Consignor	Signature and Date

Consignment Note N°

Name and address of premises from which waste was removed

I certify that today I collected the quantity of waste shown from the address given here and will take it to the address given in A2 on the consignment note

Quantity of waste removed	Carrier's signature and Date

I certify that the waste collected is as detailed above and conforms with the description given in B on the relevant consignment note

Name of Consignor	Signature and Date

Consignment Note N°

Name and address of premises from which waste was removed

I certify that today I collected the quantity of waste shown from the address given here and will take it to the address given in A2 on the consignment note

Quantity of waste removed	Carrier's signature and Date

I certify that the waste collected is as detailed above and conforms with the description given in B on the relevant consignment note

Name of Consignor	Signature and Date

Consignment Note N°

1   SI 1996/972, reg 12(1). The hours of any Saturday, Sunday, Good Friday, Christmas day, bank
    holiday or any other public holiday are excluded from the 72-hour period: see SI 1996/972, reg 12(6).
2   In the rather unlikely event that a waste cannot 'lawfully remain where it is' for the 72-hour period, it
    can be collected earlier: see SI 1996/972, reg 12(3)(b).
3   SI 1996/972, reg 8(2).
4   See SI 1996/972, reg 12(4)(a).
5   SI 1996/972, reg 12(5) indicates that this means on the day of removal.
6   SI 1996/972, reg 12(4)(b).

4.105   Once the consignment note has been correctly completed and the prenotification copy sent to the Agency, the collection of a series of loads is possible for a period
of one calendar year. Indeed, it would seem that the multiple load arrangement makes
best advantage of the statutory provisions on carrier's rounds in the Special Waste
Regulations 1996.

4.106   To work efficiently, carrier's rounds may wish to pick up wastes on an occasional, ad hoc, basis. Accordingly, the Special Waste Regulations 1996 permit further
names to be added to the list of consignors in addition to those already featuring on the
prenotification copy of the consignment note which was sent originally to the Agency.
This is done by forwarding details of the additional consignors to the Agency at least
72 hours[1] in advance of the intended collection[2]. It would seem that this form of prenotification can be done by way of a letter, rather than by using further copies of the
consignment note itself. The Special Waste Regulations 1996 require that 'particulars'
of additional consignors are forwarded[3]. But they do not require reference to be made
to the consignment note coding number obtained from the Agency, which is reproduced on the prenotification copy. It may therefore prove difficult for the Agency to
match these letters to the other documentation.

1   SI 1996/972, reg 12(1); the hours of any Saturday, Sunday, Good Friday, Christmas day, bank holiday
    or any other public holiday are excluded from the 72-hour period: see SI 1996/972, reg 12(6).
2   SI 1996/972, reg 8(1)(a) and (b); see Circular 6/96, Annex A, para 57.
3   See SI 1996/972, reg 8(1)(a).

4.107   *Collection of waste on carrier's rounds*   As noted, the carrier must embark
on the round in possession of three copies of the consignment note and four copies of
the schedule[1]. In addition, one photocopy of the note must be included for each
consignor making up the round. The consignment note must have Parts A, B and C
filled in by the carrier[2], and must portray the unique identification code furnished by
the Agency[3].

1   SI 1996/972, reg 8(2)(b) as amended by SI 1996/2019, reg 2, Sch 1, para 5(b).
2   Presumably this means as much of Part C of the note as can be completed at that time and that the
    remainder is finalised at the end of the round: see SI 1996/972, reg 8(5A) as amended by
    SI 1996/2019, reg 2, Sch 1, para 5(e).
3   SI 1996/972, reg 8(2)(b)(ii).

4.108   When the carrier arrives at the consignor, the details of the consignor, the
amount of waste to be collected, etc, must be recorded on the schedule. The consignor
and carrier must then fill in the other requested information, including the Agency
coding used on the original prenotification copy of the consignment note. They should
both certify that the information is correct[1]. The time at which the record was
completed must be recorded by the carrier[2]. Once the schedule has been completed and
signed, the carrier tears the slip containing this information from the top copy of the
schedule and passes the slip, along with a photocopy of the consignment note, to the
consignor[3]. The carrier is then free to proceed to the next consignor on the round.

1 SI 1996/972, reg 8(3) and reg 8(4)(a).
2 SI 1996/972, reg 8(4)(a) as amended by SI 1996/2019, reg 2, Sch 1, para 5(d).
3 SI 1996/972, reg 8(4)(b) and reg 8(5).

4.109 The three copies of the note, along with the remaining copies of the schedule, must travel with the carrier. Before the removal of waste from the last consignor on the round, the Special Waste Regulations 1996 require the carrier to complete Part C of the original consignment note[1]. Presumably, this is the remainder of Part C which was not filled in prior to arrival at the first consignor[2].

1 SI 1996/972, reg 8(5A) as inserted by SI 1996/2019, reg 2, Sch 1, para 5.
2 As Part C is required to have been filled in already by SI 1996/972, reg 8(2)(b)(ii).

4.110 On arrival at the consignee, the three copies of the consignment note and schedule are passed over[1]. On accepting the waste, the consignee must complete Part E of the three copies of the consignment note handed over by the carrier[2]. The consignee must then return a copy of the note and the schedule to the carrier, retain a copy of these documents, and send the final copy of the note and schedule to the Agency responsible for the consignee's premises[3]. The carrier is required to retain the copy of the note and the schedule handed back by the consignee[4] and to dispatch a copy to the Agency 'forthwith'[5].

1 SI 1996/972, reg 8(6)(c): unless the consignee rejects the load – see para 4.132 below.
2 SI 1996/972, reg 8(7).
3 SI 1996/972, reg 8(7)(d): it will be apparent that this arrangement leaves one copy of the schedule left over. As already noted, reg 8(2)(b)(iii) requires that four copies of the schedule are prepared, along with a further copy for each consignor. While Circular 6/96 indicates that *two* copies of the schedule are sent to the Agency (see Annex A, para 57), this is not required by the Special Waste Regulations 1996. In addition, it is not clear what the Agency is supposed to do with the second copy anyway.
4 SI 1996/972, reg 8(8).
5 SI 1996/972, reg 8(7)(d).

4.111 Where multiple loads are to be collected within the required one-year period, the original code provided by the Agency must be reproduced on the consignment note for each of the successive carrier's rounds[1]. Other than that requirement, the documentation of second and subsequent rounds can continue for the year period in the manner described above.

1 SI 1996/972, reg 8(2)(b)(ii).

4.112 Finally, it should be noted that the Special Waste Regulations 1996 envisage that different types of waste can be collected on the same vehicle[1]. In the case where more than one 'description of waste' is specified on the consignment note, the carrier's round schedule must contain a separate entry for each waste type received from the consignor[2]. Alternatively, the descriptions of waste can be shown together on each entry of the schedule, as long as the quantities of the different types of waste are itemised[3]. The purpose of this amended provision is to permit the transportation of mixed loads, such as paint thinners and oils from automotive repair outlets.

1 But they must not be physically mixed together: see para 4.176 below.
2 SI 1999/972, reg 8(2A) as amended by SI 1996/2019, reg 2, Sch 1, para 5(c).
3 See Circular 14/96, para 17.

4.113 From the above, it will be clear that the correct use of paperwork for documenting a carrier's round is somewhat complex. The provisions of reg 8 of the Special Waste Regulations 1996 are therefore likely to prove demanding upon the administrative system set up by the carrier. A similar observation can be made of the requirements on the Agency to match prenotifications with the copies of the completed note and schedule dispatched from the consignee. Details of consignors may stem from the list attached to the original consignment note or from letters or faxes containing details of additional consignors. Certainly, it would seem to be a tall order for the Agency to undertake this duty effectively for the princely sum of £15[1]. However, it should be noted that much less onus is placed on the consignor in respect of the paperwork.

1 £10 for a carrier's round of lead acid batteries, with there being no prenotification stage for such rounds: SI 1996/972, reg 8(2)(a)(ii) as amended by SI 1996/2019, reg 2, Sch 1, para 5(a).

Removal of special waste from ships in harbour areas[1]

4.114 Two derogations from the normal consignment note procedures apply in respect of the unloading of special waste from ships[2]. These separate procedures are viewed by Circular 6/96[3] as necessary on the grounds that the MARPOL Convention[4] requires that Party States should not subject shipping to undue delay. The 72-hour prenotification period to the Agency is therefore a possible contravention of these principles. Accordingly, streamlined provisions apply, but it is important to note that these only relate to special waste actually generated on a ship. Waste generated elsewhere and moved as cargo would fall within the controls which apply to transfrontier waste movements and hence within the ambit of Council Regulation 259/93[5].

1 These provision supersede the earlier Control of Pollution (Landed Ships' Waste) Regulations 1987 (SI 1987/402) and the Control of Pollution (Landed Ships' Waste) (Amendment) Regulations 1989 (SI 1989/65): see SI 1996/972, reg 26.
2 The term 'ship' is subject to its own definition, meaning 'a vessel of any type whatsoever operating in the marine environment including submersible craft, floating craft and any structure which is a fixed or floating platform' (SI 1996/972, reg 1(4)). It should also be noted that, under the Special Waste Regulations 1996, the term 'premises' is held to include a ship (SI 1996/972, reg 1(4)).
3 Circular 6/96, Annex A, para 67.
4 International Convention for the Prevention of Pollution from Ships 1973 (Marpol 73/78), International Maritime Organization.
5 Council Regulation (EEC) No 259/93 of 1 February 1993 on the supervision and control of shipments of waste within, into and out of the European Community (OJ L30/1 6.2.93) see Chapter 5.

Waste discharged from ships for disposal outside the harbour

4.115 The first derogation pertains to the removal of special waste from a ship for disposal elsewhere than in the harbour area[1]. When such waste is to be removed in these circumstances, there is no need to prenotify the relevant Agency[2], nor is there a requirement to pay the £15 fee[3], although the unique identification coding must be obtained and used.

1 SI 1996/972, reg 6(1)(d).
2 SI 1996/972, reg 7.
3 SI 1996/972, reg 14(2)(c)(i).

4.116 Other than these variations, the other elements in the 'standard' notification procedure apply. These have been described earlier, but briefly four copies of the consignment note must be raised for each load, with the master of the ship being viewed as the consignor[1].

1 SI 1996/972, reg 7(b)(ii).

4.117 When the waste is to be moved, the master of the ship and the carrier arrange the completion of Parts A to D of the consignment note. The master retains a copy and the other copies depart with the carrier. On arrival of the waste with the consignee, the remainder of the note is completed in the normal way[1], with the carrier retaining one copy of the note. The consignee retains a copy and dispatches the other copy to the relevant Agency.

1   Unless the load is rejected; see para 4.132 below.

4.118   For the purposes of defining when a shipment is moved outside a harbour area, the term 'harbour area' is given the same meaning[1] as in the Dangerous Substances in Harbour Areas Regulations 1987[2]. Under those provisions, 'harbour area' means all waters within the jurisdiction of a statutory harbour authority or other proprietor of a harbour, including such infrastructure as berths and land used in connection with the loading or unloading of vessels[3].

1   By SI 1996/972, reg 1(4).
2   SI 1987/37.
3   SI 1987/37, reg 2(1).

Special waste removed for disposal in a harbour area or removed outside the area by pipeline

4.119   There is a separate derogation from the need to prenotify the Agency when special waste is to be removed from a ship into reception facilities within a harbour area[1] or where such waste is to be moved by pipeline from a ship to facilities provided outside the harbour area[2]. In this instance, the required number of copies of the consignment note is reduced to three[3]. There is in these circumstances no waste carrier.

1   SI 1996/972, reg 9(1)(a): see para 4.118 above for definition of harbour area.
2   SI 1996/972, reg 9(1)(b).
3   SI 1996/972, reg 9(2).

4.120   For this type of waste transfer, parts A and B of the consignment note are completed as normal, with the relevant code from the Agency being included[1]. There is, however, no need to pay the relevant fee[2]. Precisely who should prepare the consignment note is unlike other instances left unclear in the Special Waste Regulations 1996. However, the 'operator of the reception facilities'[3] has to complete Part C of the note[4], despite Part C of the consignment note having the title 'Carrier's Certificate'. The ship's master is required to ensure that Part D is completed[5].

1   SI 1996/972, reg 9(2)(a).
2   SI 1996/972, reg 14(2)(c)(ii) and (iii).
3   The term 'reception facilities' is left undefined in the Special Waste Regulations 1996.
4   SI 1996/972, reg 9(2)(b).
5   SI 1996/972, reg 9(2)(c).

4.121   When the waste is transferred, the ship's master then retains a copy of the note[1] and passes the other two copies to the operator of the reception facility[2]. The operator must then complete Part E of the note, keep a copy of it and furnish the other copy to the Agency responsible for the facility[3].

1   SI 1996/972, reg 9(2)(c).
2   SI 1996/972, reg 9(2)(c)(iii).
3   SI 1996/972, reg 9(3).

Miscellaneous derogations from the need to prenotify and/or pay Agency fees

4.122   The Special Waste Regulations 1996 permit certain other derogations from the normal notification procedures. Like the derogation in respect of special waste in harbour areas, most of these relate to a dispensation of the need to prenotify the relevant Agency of the intended movement. However, in contrast to the harbour-related derogations, it would seem that these other procedures are of such little practical utility and consequence that it is surprising that they are contained in the Special Waste Regulations 1996 at all. The circumstances where they apply are so limited that the provisions add unnecessary detail to already complex regulations. Although portrayed as deregulatory in their intent[1], the resultant savings in industrial costs appear close to being negligible. Be that as it may, three further derogations are contained in the Special Waste Regulations 1996.

1 See Circular 6/96, para 7.

Returning products to suppliers/manufacturers

4.123 In certain instances, a person may end up holding raw materials for which there is no use. Hence it may be proposed to re-ship them back to a supplier or to the manufacturer. This raw material may fall within the meaning of controlled waste, particularly if the holder wishes to discard it[1].

1 See para 2.75ff.

4.124 A derogation from the normal consignment note procedures applies in the case of the return to a manufacturer or supplier of special waste which constitutes 'product or material for the purposes of return'[1]. It avoids both the prenotification stage[2] and the need to pay the £15 fee to the relevant Agency[3].

1 SI 1996/972, reg 6(1)(b).
2 SI 1996/972, reg 6(1)(b).
3 SI 1996/972, reg 14(2)(b).

4.125 To fall within the provisions, the material to be returned must have been supplied to the holder by the manufacturer or supplier to which it is proposed that the special waste will be returned[1]. In addition, the consignor[2] must be satisfied that the material did not meet the specification that was expected of the material[3]. The emphasis of the Special Waste Regulations 1996 solely upon the failure of the material to meet the required specification would mean that, for example, surplus but otherwise usable product returned to the manufacturer would still need prenotification[4]. This type of material would be returned for reasons different from those set down in the Special Waste Regulations 1996.

1 SI 1996/972, reg 6(1)(b).
2 The person to whom the material was supplied – SI 1996/972, reg 7(b)(i).
3 SI 1996/972, reg 6(2)(b) and repeated in reg 14(2)(b).
4 The returned product does, of course, need to fall within the definition of controlled waste: see Chapter 2.

4.126 In the circumstances of a return to supplier or manufacturer, the Special Waste Regulations 1996 indicate that the consignee is to be taken as the person to whom the product or material is to be returned[1]. Excepting the prenotification, the documentation of the shipment is done in the same way as described for normal shipments: four copies of the consignment note are prepared, with individual copies passing to consignor, carrier and consignee, and the Agency receiving the final copy on the waste's arrival. Although there is no £15 fee to pay[2], it should be noted that the requirement to obtain and use the Agency's unique coding still remains.

1 SI 1996/972, reg 7(c).
2 SI 1996/972, reg 14(2)(b).

4.127 Finally, it should be noted that the storage of the returned special waste at the site of the manufacturer or supplier may be restricted. While it would not normally require a waste management licence, storage of returned goods which are special waste may be permissible under the exemptions from waste management licences contained in the Waste Management Licensing Regulations 1994[1]. However, this only holds provided the storage is in accordance with the terms set down in the relevant exemptions and that the storage activity is registered with the Agency in advance of the arrival of the waste[2].

1 SI 1994/1056, Sch 3, para 28, as amended by SI 1996/972, reg 25 and Sch 3.
2 See para 10.99ff.

Transportation of special waste between two companies in the same corporate grouping

4.128 The Special Waste Regulations 1996 contain a derogation from the need to prenotify consignments of special waste which are to be transferred between two arms of the same company located at different sites[1]. However, the derogation only applies when both consignor and consignee are bodies corporate and belong to the same group[2].

1 SI 1996/972, reg 6(1)(c).
2 'Group' is defined as meaning the body corporate in question, any holding company or subsidiary and any other body corporate of the holding company. But a body corporate for the Special Waste Regulations 1996 does not mean 'a corporation sole or a Scottish partnership'. However it does include a company incorporated outside Britain. The terms 'holding company' and 'subsidiary' are given the meaning contained in s 736 of the Companies Act 1985 (as substituted by s 144(1) of the Companies Act 1989): SI 1996/972, reg 6(3).

4.129 This derogation is subject to two further restrictions. Firstly, the purpose of the transfer must be temporary storage pending disposal or recovery[1]. According to Circular 6/96, 'this limitation is to prevent waste moving around without prenotification within waste management companies, when destined for final disposal or recovery'[2].

1 SI 1996/972, reg 6(2)(c) and SI 1994/1056, Sch 4, Pt III, para 15 or Sch 4, Pt IV, para 13.
2 Circular 6/96, Annex A, para 66.

4.130 The second restriction is that the derogation from prenotification procedures applies only when the consignee is a holder of a waste management licence, with the licence explicitly authorising the actual storage operation[1]. Alternatively, the shipment is legitimate if the site is excluded or exempted from the need to possess a licence[2]. The latter circumstances apply when the site possesses an appropriate authorisation under Part I of the EPA 1990[3] or falls within the terms of a registered exempt activity under the Waste Management Licensing Regulations 1994[4]. In the case of the latter, it should be noted that many of the exemptions are applicable only to the receipt of waste other than special waste[5]. For this reason, the lawful receipt of special waste may not always be possible.

1 SI 1996/972, reg 6(2)(c)(i).
2 SI 1996/972, reg 6(2)(c)(ii): exclusions and exemptions are discussed at para 10.05.
3 By way of SI 1994/1056, reg 16.
4 SI 1994/1056, reg 17.
5 See para 10.33.

Removal of consignments of lead acid motor vehicle batteries[1]

4.131 Consignments of special waste which consist 'entirely' of lead acid motor vehicle batteries do not need to be prenotified[2]. In addition, the Agency fee for providing the unique coding is reduced from £15 to £10[3]. However, the documentation for the collection, transport and subsequent management of such consignments are all required to be in accordance with the consignment note procedures relating to 'standard' special waste movements[4]. Alternatively, the provisions in respect of carrier's rounds can apply[5].

1 The consultation paper *Proposed Amendments to the Special Waste Regulations 1996 and the Waste Management licensing Regulations 1994*, DETR, London, April 1998 proposes minor changes to these arrangements.
2 SI 1996/972, reg 6(1)(e).
3 SI 1996/972, reg 14(1)(a).
4 See paras 4.78 and 4.85.
5 See para 4.91.

ARRANGEMENTS FOR INSTANCES WHEN A CONSIGNEE REJECTS A LOAD OF SPECIAL WASTE[1]

4.132 A criticism of the Control of Pollution (Special Waste) Regulations 1980[2] was that there was no procedure which could adequately document the rejection of a load of waste by an operator of a waste management facility. Such rejections might happen when the load was improperly described or might be the result of matters such as breakdowns or unforeseen capacity problems at the facility. Under the 1980 Regulations, rejection became difficult for the reason that it was not possible to legally prenotify the re-direction of the waste unless the 72-hour prenotification period had lapsed. Therefore, a quite proper rejection, for example when the acceptance of the load would contravene the conditions of a licence, would result in the illegal transportation of the load away from the site. Conversely, the temporary storage of the waste at the site for the prenotification period might also be an offence as the facility may not be licensed to accepted it.

1 The consultation paper *Proposed Amendments to the Special Waste Regulations 1996 and the Waste Management licensing Regulations 1994*, DETR, London, April 1998 proposes changes to these procedures; see also *Hansard* 31 March 1999 Col 767.
2 SI 1980/1709.

4.133 These matters have been addressed by the Special Waste Regulations 1996[1]. However, it should be noted that these procedures are only triggered when the consignee[2] rejects the load. They do not apply to instances where persons other than the consignee express a wish for a load to be re-routed to a different destination while in transit.

1 SI 1996/972, reg 10.
2 Defined in reg 1(3): see para 4.73.

4.134 When a load of waste is rejected, the consignee does not, for obvious reasons, need to complete Part E of the consignment note in the normal way[1]. The actions to be taken instead depend on whether or not the consignee has been handed the paperwork before making the decision to reject the load.

1 SI 1996/972, reg 10(2).

4.135 If the consignment note has actually been passed to the consignee before the load is rejected, the Special Waste Regulations 1996 require the consignee to write on Part E that the load was rejected[1]. The reasons for rejection must also be included. A copy of the note is then retained by the consignee in the normal way[2]. Similarly, one copy is then sent by the consignee to the Agency[3], with the other being passed back to the carrier[4].

1   SI 1996/972, reg 10(3)(a).
2   SI 1996/972, reg 10(3)(b).
3   SI 1996/972, reg 10(3)(c). (With the relevant schedule if the rejected load relates to a carrier's round.)
4   SI 1996/972, reg 10(3)(d).

4.136   Alternatively, where no copy of the consignment note has been furnished to the consignee, the consignee must ensure that a 'written explanation' of the reasons behind the rejection of the load is furnished 'forthwith' to the Agency which covers the location of the consignee[1].

1   SI 1996/972, reg 10(4).

4.137   Where either the actual consignment note or a written explanation of refusal is to be furnished to the Agency, this must be done within one day of the removal of the waste[1], either by hand delivery or by first class post.

1   SI 1996/972, reg 12(5).

4.138   When a load has been rejected, the Special Waste Regulations 1996 place additional responsibilities on the carrier. Regardless of whether or not the carrier has passed the consignment note to the consignee, the carrier must inform the Agency of the rejection and also seek instructions from the consignor[1].

1   SI 1996/972, reg 10(5)(a).

4.139   On being informed by the carrier of the load's rejection, the consignor is given three options. The waste can be returned to the place from where it was collected[1] or from where it was produced[2]. Alternatively, delivery to a different facility – which must be subject to a 'waste management licence'[3] – can be proposed, provided that the licence is appropriate for the waste in question[4]. It should be noted that the consignment of the waste to a facility which is authorised other than by a waste management licence appears not to be countenanced by the Special Waste Regulations 1996. This omission would therefore exclude the reconsignment of the waste to a plant such as a high temperature incinerator which is subject to an authorisation under Part I of the EPA 1990.

1   SI 1996/972, reg 10(6)(a).
2   SI 1996/972, reg 10(6)(b).
3   Defined in SI 1996/972, reg 1(4) as having the meaning contained in the EPA 1990, s 35(1).
4   SI 1996/972, reg 10(6)(c).

4.140   Having selected one of these three options, the consignor is then required 'forthwith' to inform the Agency and the carrier of his intentions[1]. The carrier then has to take 'all reasonable steps'[2] to ensure that the consignor's instructions are fulfilled[3].

1   SI 1996/972, reg 10(5)(b).
2   See 'taking all reasonable precautions': para 7.145ff.
3   SI 1996/972, reg 10(5)(c).

4.141   Precisely how the details of the rejected load departing from the intended consignee should be recorded is not made clear in the Special Waste Regulations 1996. On the one hand, reg 12(3) requires that in these circumstances, 'a copy of the consignment note ... may' be furnished to the Agency within the initial 72-hour prenotification period. Whether this is a new note or a photocopy of the amended original version is not clear. From reading reg 12(1) it would appear that a fresh consignment note is envisaged for this purpose[1]. However, this requirement is by no means explicit.

1   Due to reg 12(1) cross-referring to reg 5.

4.142   The picture is additionally confused by the fact that reg 12(3) clearly states[1] that the requirement to furnish the Agency with a copy of the note only applies where it is proposed to reconsign the waste to premises subject to a waste management licence. It will have become apparent from the earlier discussion that, besides re-consignment to a site possessing a waste management licence, reg 10(6) envisages two other options: return to the premises of production or, if different, back to the place where the waste was collected. But there is no reference made at all in the Special Waste Regulations 1996 as to how these latter journeys are to be documented. Unlike the case of sending a rejected load to a licensed site, reg 12 is entirely silent in these respects[2].

1   By way of SI 1996/972, reg 12(3)(a) and its reference to reg 10(6)(c).
2   It should also be noted that the consignee's rejection of a load would not normally count as an 'emergency' under reg 18(2) (see para 4.188 below). Similarly, while it is possible to ignore the 72-hour prenotification requirement by way of reg 12(3)(b) – but only where the circumstances that the waste cannot lawfully remain where it is apply – this provision does not exempt the load from the other requirements on documentation.

4.143   In respect of these apparent deficiencies, Circular 6/96 provides some guidance. But this appears to have a rather unstable statutory footing. Firstly, in the case of returns of waste to the producer or to the place where it was collected, the Circular[1] suggests that the carrier's copy of the note should travel with the load. On arrival at the destination, the recipient should make a photocopy of this note for record-keeping purposes. When the waste is to be sent out later from this destination, the Circular states that a fresh set of consignment notes should be used, with another code being obtained from the Agency.

1   Circular 6/96, Annex A, para 77.

4.144   By contrast, for reconsignment to a facility possessing a waste management licence, Circular 6/96 states[1] that the details of the second journey can be written on the original consignment note. This note should be photocopied and sent to the Agency – presumably at the time the waste is redirected – with a second copy being sent to document the waste's arrival at the facility. The Circular indicates that the carrier must apply to the Agency for a new unique identification code for the journey to the facility. In these circumstances, the Circular claims that 'no fee is payable under reg 14'. However, reg 14 – which lists circumstances when the requisite fees are not payable – makes no mention of the circumstances when waste is reconsigned.

1   Circular 6/96, Annex A, para 78.

TRANSFERS OF SPECIAL WASTE BETWEEN AREAS OF JURISDICTION OF THE ENVIRONMENT AGENCY AND SEPA

4.145   For special waste transactions across the English/Scottish border, the procedures for the completion of the consignment notes as described above all apply. The only difference is that the transfer will involve the areas of jurisdiction of both the Environment Agency and the Scottish Environment Protection Agency (SEPA). For a consignment from England or Wales for disposal or recovery in Scotland, SEPA must receive the prenotification copy of the consignment note[1]. Similarly, a consignment from Scotland to England or Wales would require that the prenotification is to the Environment Agency.

1   SI 1996/972, reg 5(2)(a).

4.146   In addition, tracking waste shipments between England and Scotland clearly requires some formal inter-Agency co-operation. The Special Waste Regulations 1996 contain provisions to ensure that both the English and Scottish Agencies are aware of cross-border special waste movements[1]. These relate to instances where one Agency covers the site of the consignor and the other the waste management facility.

1   SI 1996/972, reg 11.

4.147   For England/Scotland transactions, where one of the two Agencies has been sent a copy of the consignment note[1], the receiving Agency has two weeks to copy it and pass it on to their regulatory counterpart[2].

1   Or where an explanation of the rejection of a load has been furnished instead by a consignee – see para 4.136 above.
2   SI 1996/972, reg 11.

TRANSFERS OF WASTE FROM NORTHERN IRELAND AND GIBRALTAR

4.148   Shipments of waste to and from Northern Ireland and Gibraltar are covered by a combination of the Special Waste Regulations 1996[1] and the relevant regulations relating to Northern Ireland[2] and Gibraltar, for the reason that they are viewed as internal transfers within an EC member state[3]. The requirements of Council Regulation 259/93[4] in respect of transfrontier shipments do not apply[5].

1   SI 1996/972, reg 13.
2   Special Waste (Northern Ireland) Regulations 1998, SR 1998/289.
3   See Circular 6/96, Annex A, para 18.
4   Council Regulation (EEC) No 259/93 of 1 February 1993 on the supervision and control of shipments of waste within, into and out of the European Community (OJ L30/1 6.2.93): see Chapter 5.
5   However, where shipments are to pass through, or from, these countries for disposal or recovery outside Great Britain (ie outside England, Scotland and Wales), the requirements of EC Regulation 259/93 apply instead.

4.149   Where waste is imported into Great Britain from either Northern Ireland or Gibraltar, the usual notification procedures described above apply. However, the paperwork trail on the shipment is to be viewed as starting at the point where the waste is imported. The Northern Ireland[1] or Gibraltar notification system ends at the port of departure. Accordingly, for the British part of the transaction, the 'consignor' should be taken to be the 'person importing the special waste'[2] and the port of entry is to be viewed as the premises where the waste is held[3].

1   The Special Waste Regulations 1996 do not apply to Northern Ireland: SI 1996/972, reg 1(2).
2   SI 1996/972, reg 13(1)(a).
3   SI 1996/972, reg 13(1)(b).

4.150   For shipments in the opposite direction (ie from Britain to Northern Ireland or Gibraltar), the consignee becomes the 'person exporting the waste'[1] and that person is considered to receive the waste at the port of exportation[2]. Other than that, the provisions described earlier for documenting special waste movements apply.

1   SI 1996/972, reg 13(2).
2   SI 1996/972, reg 13(2)(b).

REQUIREMENTS ON CONSIGNORS, CARRIERS AND CONSIGNEES TO KEEP RECORDS

4.151   The Directive on Waste[1] already requires that establishments and undertakings holding permits for disposal and recovery should keep records of the wastes accepted[2].

The Directive on Hazardous Waste[3] extends these requirements to others persons involved in hazardous waste transactions. Article 4 of that Directive requires that 'producers' of hazardous waste must keep a record of the 'quantity, nature, origin and, where relevant, the destination, frequency of collection, mode of transport method', along with the disposal or recovery operation utilised[4]. A similar requirement applies to establishments and undertakings transporting hazardous waste.

1 Council Directive of 15 July 1975 on Waste (75/442/EEC) (OJ L194/39 25.7.75) as amended by Council Directive of 18 March 1991 (91/156/EEC) (OJ L78/32 26.3.91).
2 Directive 75/442, Article 14 as amended by Directive 91/156, Article 1.
3 Directive 91/689.
4 Directive 91/689, Article 4(2) as cross referenced to Article 14 of Directive 75/442 (as amended by Directive 91/156).

4.152 The Directive on Hazardous Waste requires that such records should be kept by the disposal or recovery site for at least three years. An equivalent minimum time period for waste carriers is set at 12 months[1].

1 Directive 91/689, Article 4(3).

4.153 These requirements are transposed into British law principally by the Special Waste Regulations 1996[1]. Supplementary requirements on the record keeping of special waste at the premises of consignees are also to be found in amendments made to the Waste Management Licensing Regulations 1994[2]. As will be shown below, in certain cases the timescales contained in the Hazardous Waste Directive for document retention are expanded. The Special Waste Regulations 1996 allow records to be kept in any form[3], thereby permitting computer storage, as well as microfiche etc. However, Circular 6/96 states that these records are additional to the keeping of paper copies[4]. This requirement does not appear to emanate directly from the Special Waste Regulations 1996.

1 SI 1996/972, reg 15.
2 SI 1994/1056, Sch 4, para 14 as amended by SI 1995/288, reg 3(19)–(21) and by SI 1996/972, reg 25 and Sch 3.
3 SI 1996/972, reg 15(8): however there is no equivalent provision in the Waste Management Licensing Regulations 1994 (see SI 1994/1056, Sch 4, para 14 as amended by SI 1995/288, reg 3(19)–(21) and by SI 1996/972, reg 25 and Sch 3).
4 Circular 6/96, para 92.

Record-keeping by consignors

4.154 The Special Waste Regulations 1996 require that registers of consignment notes must be kept 'at each site from which any consignment of special waste has been removed'[1]. Therefore, for a large company it appears not to be allowable to keep all the records at a central location, rather they must be retained at individual plants. Precisely what happens if a premises closes is not made clear. However, all copies need to kept for a period of three years[2]. Where a carrier's round picks up waste from the consignor, the retained copy of the consignment note must be supplemented by a copy of the relevant part of the schedule which was passed to the carrier[3].

1 SI 1996/972, reg 15(1).
2 SI 1996/972, reg 15(4).
3 SI 1996/972, reg 15(1).

Record-keeping by special waste carriers

4.155 The requirements of the Special Waste Regulations 1996 in respect of record-keeping by carriers are generally similar to those applicable to consignors. Each waste carrier must retain for three years[1] the relevant copy of the consignment note for each load of waste transported[2]. Where any special waste has been transported by way of a carrier's round, a copy of the schedule documenting the round also has to be retained[3]. There is, however, no requirement that these documents are kept at any particular location.

1   SI 1996/972, reg 15(4).
2   SI 1996/972, regs 5(5) and 15(2).
3   SI 1996/972, regs 8(8) and 15(2).

Record-keeping by the consignee

4.156   As noted, both the Waste Management Licensing Regulations 1994[1] and the Special Waste Regulations 1996[2] contain requirements on consignees in respect of record-keeping. Both Regulations differentiate between types of consignee and set down separate provisions for each of them. Consignees are defined as holders of either waste management licences or authorisations under Part I of the EPA 1990, as well as operators of waste management activities which are exempt from licensing but registered under Schedule 3 of the Waste Management Licensing Regulations 1994[3].

1   SI 1994/1056, Sch 4, para 14, as amended by SI 1995/288, reg 3(20) and (21) and by SI 1996/972, reg 25 and Sch 3.
2   SI 1996/972, reg 15.
3   SI 1994/1056: Part I authorisations and the system of exemptions are discussed in Chapter 10.

Waste acceptance records

4.157   Under the Waste Management Licensing Regulations 1994[1], recovery or disposal facilities subject to waste management licences or Part 1 authorisations[2] have to keep records of 'the quantity, nature, origin and, where relevant, the destination, frequency of collection, mode of transport and treatment method of any waste which is disposed of or recovered'.

1   SI 1994/1056, Sch 4, para 14(1).
2   But not recovery facilities subject to exemption from waste management licences by way of either SI 1994/1056, reg 17(1) and Sch 3 or the Deposits at Sea (Exemptions) Order 1985 (SI 1985/1699): see para 10.13ff (SI 1994/1056, Sch 4, para 14(2) as amended by SI 1995/288, reg 3(20)). However, it is unlikely that these provisions would themselves permit the deposit of special waste.

4.158   The legislation also contains an additional requirement for recovery and disposal facilities dealing specifically with special waste. The Waste Management Licensing Regulations 1994 require that a record is to be kept 'of the carrying out and supervision of the operation and, in the case of a disposal operation, the after-care of the site'[1]. It would seem that this applies to all recovery and disposal facilities, including the small number of facilities which recover[2] special waste but which are subject to exemptions from licensing[3]. However, the precise purpose and meaning of this requirement is not that clear. Circular 6/96 does not provide an explanation.

1   SI 1994/1056, Sch 4, para 14(1A) as amended by SI 1996/972, reg 25 and Sch 1.
2   The term 'recovery' covers waste storage, and thus transfer stations: see SI 1994/1056, reg 13 and Sch 4, Pt IV, para 13.
3   While SI 1994/1056, Sch 4, para 14(2) and (3) exclude exempt activities from the need to keep the records stipulated under para 14(1), no exclusion applies to the additional information required to be retained by way of para 14(1A).

Retaining registers of consignment notes

4.159 For a site subject to a waste management licence, copies of the consignment notes and carrier's round schedules must be kept by consignees until the licence has been surrendered or revoked[1]. The Special Waste Regulations 1996 also clearly state that these copies must be kept by the consignee 'at each site at which any consignment of special waste has been received'[2]. Accordingly, the consignment notes cannot be held elsewhere, a difficulty which may manifest itself if a particular facility's site office is prone to periodic vandalism. Likewise, significant problems will arise in respect of a closed landfill site which has not been the subject of a licence surrender. As noted at para 8.180, the period between closure and licence surrender may be 50 or more years into the future, but the Special Waste Regulations 1996 envisage the records staying on the premises for that period. Finally, it should be noted that these requirements mean that the premises where mobile plant[3] has been operated must retain the records, rather than the licence holder for the equipment.

1 SI 1996/972, reg 15(5).
2 SI 1996/972, reg 15(3).
3 See para 8.07ff.

4.160 The only time when the records can be moved elsewhere is when the licence is surrendered or revoked entirely[1]. When this occurs, the records are passed on to the Agency, who must retain them for at least three years[2].

1 SI 1996/972, reg 15(5).
2 SI 1996/972, reg 15(5).

4.161 In the case of a waste management facility which is subject to an authorisation under Part I of the EPA 1990, the requisite records also need to be kept until that authorisation is surrendered or revoked[1]. Finally, for any site subject to an exemption from the need to possess a waste management licence, copies of consignment notes and carrier's round schedules need to be kept for three years[2]. For both of these instances, the Special Waste Regulations 1996 require the consignment notes and schedules to be kept only at the site which accepted the waste[3].

1 SI 1996/972, reg 15(6).
2 SI 1996/972, reg 15(6).
3 SI 1996/972, reg 15(3).

Recording special waste deposits

4.162 Article 2 of the Hazardous Waste Directive requires every site where the 'tipping (discharge)' of hazardous waste takes place to ensure that the waste is 'recorded and identified'[1]. This is transposed by reg 16 of the Special Waste Regulations 1996, which requires any person 'who makes a deposit' of special waste 'in or on' any land to record the location of each deposit[2]. These records must take the form of 'a site plan marked with a grid' or 'a site plan with overlays on which deposits are shown in relation to the contours of the site'[3]. The deposits must be described by means of a 'reference to the register of consignment notes' kept by the consignee[4].

1 Directive 91/689, Article 2(1).
2 SI 1996/972, reg 16(1).
3 SI 1996/972, reg 16(2).
4 SI 1996/972, reg 16(3).

4.163 Where special waste is disposed of by pipeline or within the curtilage of the premises of production, no consignment notes will be available. In this case, the

Special Waste Regulations 1996 require that the deposits are described 'by reference to a record of the quantity and composition of the waste and the date of its disposal'[1]. However, the Regulations still indicate that grid plans or overlays are required to show the location of the special wastes[2].

1 SI 1996/972, reg 16(3).
2 See SI 1996/972, reg 16(2).

4.164 Only where liquid waste is discharged into underground strata or disused workings[1] is the requirement on grids or overlays replaced[2]. In this case, the Special Waste Regulations 1996 require that records of each deposit must comprise a written statement of the quantity and composition discharged.

1 There is no definition of 'disused workings' in the Special Waste Regulations 1996, but it would defeat the purpose of the Regulations if such a term could be used in relation to an old quarry or open cast mine.
2 SI 1996/972, reg 16(4).

4.165 All such deposit or discharge records have to be held until the site's waste management licence is surrendered or revoked[1]. However, in contrast to the register of consignment notes (see above), the permissible location where the deposit records can be stored is not defined in the Special Waste Regulations 1996. Hence these records can either be kept at the site or moved to a different location such as the operator's central offices.

1 SI 1996/972, reg 16(1).

4.166 One final unresolved matter is the extent of the need to keep records in relation to sites accepting special waste for disposal other than to landfill. As is noted at para 7.16ff, the meaning of the term 'deposit' in s 33 of the EPA 1990 has been construed widely, to encompass permanent deposits as well as the temporary placing down of waste at facilities such as transfer stations. As reg 16(1) of the Special Waste Regulations 1996 requires any person involved in 'a deposit of special waste in or *on land*'[1] to make the appropriate records, this provision might encompass transfer stations and treatment plants. However, they clearly cannot produce a meaningful grid or overlay marking the deposits. This matter is left unresolved in Circular 6/96.

1 Author's emphasis.

Record-keeping for wastes moved under the Special Waste Regulations 1980

4.167 Many sites pre-dating the enactment of the Special Waste Regulations 1996 will also have records resulting from the operation of the Control of Pollution (Special Waste) Regulations 1980[1]. Like the 1996 Regulations, the records to be kept under the earlier Regulations were registers of consignment notes and records of deposits of special waste[2]. While waste producers and carriers were required to keep the consignment notes for two years[3], operators of waste management sites had to retain the notes until the licence was surrendered or revoked[4]. The latter also had to record the location of deposits of waste in a manner similar to that required by the Special Waste Regulations 1996[5].

1 SI 1980/1709.
2 SI 1980/1709, reg 13.
3 SI 1980/1709, reg 13(4).
4 SI 1980/1709, reg 13(5).
5 SI 1980/1709, reg 14.

4.168 As the Control of Pollution (Special Waste) Regulations 1980 have been revoked[1], the Special Waste Regulations 1996 make provision to ensure that some of the records kept under the previous legislation are still retained[2]. However, the 1996 Regulations only require the retention of the records in respect of the location of the deposits of special waste[3]. There is no equivalent requirement to retain the consignment notes kept under the Control of Pollution (Special Waste) Regulations 1980[4].

1 SI 1996/972, reg 26.
2 SI 1996/972, reg 16(5).
3 SI 1996/972, reg 16(5), which refers to records kept under SI 1980/1709, reg 14.
4 SI 1996/972, reg 16(5) only refers to records kept under reg 14 of the Control of Pollution (Special Waste) Regulations 1980. Consignment notes were, however, required to be kept under reg 13 of the 1980 Regulations.

4.169 For the records of special waste deposits kept under the Control of Pollution (Special Waste) Regulations 1980, the period for which the records are to be retained is the same as applicable for records made under the Special Waste Regulations 1996 (see para 4.156 above)[1]. At the end of that period, they are then handed over to the Agency.

1 SI 1996/972, reg 16(5).

Records of special waste moved under transfrontier shipment notifications

4.170 Article 35 of Council Regulation 259/93[1] requires that all transfrontier shipment documentation must be retained for at least three years. Circular 6/96 suggests[2] that the requirement to retain registers of consignment notes applies to waste which is special waste but which was moved under the notification documents for transfrontier waste shipments. Therefore, the Circular would suggest that, for a consignee, the three year retention period would be extended to the same period as pertaining to special waste consignment notes. However, this requirement does not, in fact, feature in the Special Waste Regulations 1996 themselves.

1 Council Regulation (EEC) No 259/93 of 1 February 1993 on the supervision and control of shipments of waste within, into and out of the European Community (OJ L30/1 6.2.93) and see Chapter 5.
2 Circular 6/96, Annex A, para 19.

4.171 Although reg 13(4) delineates where the requirements of the Special Waste Regulations 1996 apply to transfrontier shipments, reg 15 – which sets up the requirements on registers – explicitly refers only to 'consignment notes'. These are defined by reg 1(4) as meaning copies of the form set out in Schedule 1 to the Special Waste Regulations 1996. This would appear not to include transfrontier notification documents within reg 15. The definition might be extended by way of the provision, at the start of reg 1(4), which states that the definitions therein apply 'unless the context otherwise requires'. Whether this is sufficiently strong to support the contention that the words 'consignment note' can embrace transfrontier waste notification documents seems a rather open question. What is clearer is that the requirement[1] to record deposits of special waste applies to wastes transported under the transfrontier shipment notification system[2]. However, to so apply, the waste transported under the transfrontier notification document must, of course, fall within the definition of special waste[3].

1 SI 1996/972, reg 16.
2 Under Council Regulation 259/93: see Chapter 5.
3 See Circular 6/96, Annex A, para 19 and SI 1996/972, reg 13(4).

Consignors' and carriers' rights of access to consignees' records

4.172 Consignors and waste carriers are permitted access to certain records on special waste held by consignees by way of Schedule 4 of the Waste Management Licensing Regulations 1994[1]. However, this applies principally to records held at disposal or recovery facilities[2] which are subject to waste management licences or to authorisations under Part I of the EPA 1990[3]. It does not apply to recovery facilities which are exempted from the need to possess waste management licences[4].

1 SI 1996/1056, reg 19 and Sch 4, para 14.
2 Which include transfer stations: see SI 1994/1056, reg 1(3) and Sch 4, Pt III, paras 14 and 15 and Pt IV, para 13.
3 The nature of Part I authorisations is explained at para 10.14ff.
4 Being exempted under either the exemptions contained in SI 1994/1056, reg 17(1) or under the Deposits in the Sea (Exemptions) Order 1985: see SI 1994/1056, Sch 4, para 14(2) and (3), as amended by SI 1995/288, reg 3(20) and (21).

4.173 Access is restricted to the information prescribed in the Waste Management Licensing Regulations 1994[1]: 'the quantity, nature, origin and, where relevant, the destination, frequency of collection, mode of transport and treatment method of any waste which is disposed of or recovered'. Only 'previous holders' of special waste are entitled to gain access to these records[2]. Hence a carrier or a consignor is entitled to view these records.

1 SI 1994/1056, Sch 4, para 14(1)(a).
2 SI 1994/1056, Sch 4, para 14(1)(b) as amended by SI 1996/972, reg 25 and Sch 3.

4.174 The denial by a consignee of a request by a previous holder of waste for access to the specified information is an offence[1]. A similar sanction applies where entries are falsified or where false or misleading information is provided[2]. Whether the Agency would wish to become involved in a dispute between waste holders on access to records may be somewhat doubtful, and thus a person refused access may need to consider initiating their own proceedings under the Special Waste Regulations 1996.

1 SI 1994/1056, Sch 4, para 14(4) as amended by SI 1996/972, reg 25, Sch 3.
2 SI 1994/1056, reg 14(6) and (7) as amended by SI 1996/972, reg 25 and Sch 3: false and misleading information is discussed at para 12.209ff.

4.175 This provision does, of course, go much further than the requirements on access to duty of care transfer notes for non-special waste[1]. It stems from Article 4.3 of the Directive on Hazardous Waste[2]. The use of this mechanism might be an invaluable way for waste consignors or carriers to satisfy themselves that their waste is being correctly managed.

1 EPA 1990, s 34: see Chapter 3.
2 Council Directive of 12 December 1991 on Hazardous Waste (91/689/EEC) (OJ L377/20 31.12.91). See Circular 6/96, Annex A, para 96.

RESTRICTIONS ON MIXING SPECIAL WASTE

4.176 The Directive on Hazardous Waste forbids establishments and undertakings involved in collection, disposal, recovery or transportation to mix 'different categories' of hazardous waste or to mix hazardous with non-hazardous waste[1]. The only time that this is possible[2] is at a site which is subject to the requirement for a permit by way of the Directive on Waste[3]. It should be noted that this derogation does not apply to recovery facilities which are subject to the lesser registration system, as opposed to being subject to a permit[4]. Waste producers are, of course, not covered by these restrictions on mixing waste.

1 Directive 91/689, Article 2(2).
2 Directive 91/689, Article 2(3).
3 Directive 75/442 as amended by Directive 91/156: permits are required by way of Articles 9, 10 and 11.
4 The difference between registrations and permits is described more fully at para 10.07ff.

4.177 The requirements of the Directive in respect of 'mixing' are transposed by reg 17 of the Special Waste Regulations 1996[1]. The statement that 'different categories' of special waste and special and non-special waste should not be mixed is repeated. Circular 6/96 confirms[2] that this requirement does not apply to waste producers and that the restriction on mixing categories of waste 'should be interpreted in the broadest sense'. It then provides the caveat that 'Special wastes should not be mixed if this might endanger human health, the process or method of mixing could harm the environment, or prevents the close monitoring of the disposal or recovery of special waste'. The precise purpose and intent of this provision remains less than clear.

1 SI 1996/972, reg 17(1).
2 Circular 6/96, Annex A, para 89.

4.178 The Hazardous Waste Directive itself gives little indication of what is meant by the term 'category of waste' in the context of restrictions on mixing. It would seem that the only time the term is used in EC waste management law is in Annex I of the amended Directive on Waste[1]. However, these categories are so wide as to appear meaningless in this context. The Hazardous Waste Directive may be referring to the different waste types resultant from the compilation of the hazardous waste list or European Waste Catalogue[2]. But the Directive leaves this matter unclear. In *R v Environment Agency, ex p Sellers and Petty*, Harrison J confirmed that there is no obvious definition of 'categories', ruling that setting boundaries on this matter 'is a matter of impression and a matter of fact and degree'[3].

1 Directive 75/442 as amended by Directive 91/156; see Table 2.1 in Chapter 2.
2 Discussed at para 4.15.
3 See the joined cases of *R v Environment Agency and Redland Aggregates Ltd, ex p Gibson, R v Environment Agency and Redland Aggregates Ltd, ex p Leam* and *R v Environment Agency, ex p Sellers and Petty* [1999] Env LR 73 at 108.

4.179 It is less than obvious how this matter is to be resolved. Circular 6/96 notes[1] that the provision does not prevent carriers from picking up different wastes in the same round when the waste is packaged in separate containers. And certainly it would not seem to preclude a tanker collecting the same wastes from a number of premises: waste oil collection is an example[2]. But the matter becomes less certain when obviously different wastes are mixed.

1 Circular 6/96, Annex A, para 91.
2 But all the wastes would need to be special waste: otherwise reg 17(1)(a) of the Special Waste Regulations 1996 would be compromised.

4.180 Like the Directive on Hazardous Waste, the mixing of different categories of waste is permissible under the Special Waste Regulations 1996 at facilities which benefit from a waste management licence or a Part I authorisation under the EPA 1990[1]. However, mixing is also permitted in the Special Waste Regulations 1996 at facilities subject to exemption[2] from the need to possess a waste management licence[3]. Given the provisions of Article 2 of the Hazardous Waste Directive, which specifically only allows categories of waste to be mixed at facilities subject to permits – as distinct from other waste management sites subject to registrations – issued via the Directive on Waste, this provision would seem not to correctly transpose EC law[4].

1   SI 1996/972, reg 17(2)(a).
2   By way of reg 17 of the Waste Management Licensing Regulations 1994, SI 1994/1056: see Chapters 10 and 11.
3   SI 1996/972, reg 17(2)(b); few would be allowed to handle special waste under the terms of exemption, but an obvious example is waste oil.
4   As noted in Chapter 10, the majority of activities which are exempted from waste management licences need registrations under SI 1994/1056, reg 17. The Directive on Waste clearly views 'permits' and 'registrations' as two quite separate and distinct entities (see Directive 75/442 as amended by Directive 91/156, Article 11).

4.181   It has already been noted that the Special Waste Regulations 1996 prevent the mixing of hazardous waste with 'non-hazardous waste'. In *R v Environment Agency, ex p Sellers and Petty*[1] it was held that the latter term refers only to non-hazardous *waste* – not to other materials which are not waste at all. Hence the blending of organic wastes with gas oil prior to combustion in a cement kiln was found not to be precluded by this provision.

1   See the joined cases of *R v Environment Agency and Redland Aggregates Ltd, ex p Gibson, R v Environment Agency and Redland Aggregates Ltd, ex p Leam* and *R v Environment Agency, ex p Sellers and Petty* [1999] Env LR 73 at 109.

4.182   Finally, it should be noted that the restrictions on mixing contained in the Special Waste Regulations 1996 apply to transfrontier waste shipments, which are controlled by way of EC Regulation 259/93[1]. However, the waste moved must fall within the definition of special waste contained in the 1996 Regulations[2].

1   Council Regulation (EEC) No 259/93 of 1 February 1993 on the supervision and control of shipments of waste within, into and out of the European Community (OJ L30/1 6.2.93), and see para 5.198.
2   See Circular 6/96, Annex A, para 19 and SI 1996/972, reg 13(4).

OFFENCES

4.183   Regulation 18 of the Special Waste Regulations 1996 establishes the offence of failing to comply with the requirements of the Regulations[1]. It should be noted that, strictly, *any* breach of regs 1 to 18 of the Special Waste Regulations 1996 is an offence. However, common sense will of course prevail in this matter, with Circular 6/96[2] making an explicit reference to the relevant sections on regulatory proportionality discussed in Circular 11/94[3]. Similarly, the Circular notes that consignment notes should be completed 'as fully as reasonably possible'[4], while minor changes/corrections of details on the documents are also envisaged as acceptable[5].

1   SI 1996/972, reg 18(1). It should be noted that Agency personnel are excluded from the offence provisions contained in reg 18 (see reg 18(1)). Such staff can act in breach of the Special Waste Regulations 1996 and, for example, can transport special waste without any notification documents. However, the wording does not appear to extend this immunity to a third party acting under the instructions of the Agency. The Special Waste Regulations 1996 only refer to persons who are duly authorised as 'a member, officer or employee' of the Agency. While third parties could be duly authorised by the Agency, they are not members, officers or employees of it.
2   Circular 6/96, Annex A, para 82.
3   Circular 11/94, paras 9 to 17: see para 12.34ff.
4   Circular 6/96, Annex A, para 34.
5   Circular 6/96, Annex A, para 37–38.

4.184 In addition to the requirement to fulfil the Special Waste Regulations 1996, the Regulations create separate offences in respect of the provision of false or misleading information or the making of false entries[1]. Similar provisions are contained in s 44 of the EPA 1990[2] and in other associated regulations and, for this reason, a more lengthy discussion of this provision can be found in at para 12.226.

1 SI 1996/972, reg 18(3) and (4).
2 As amended by s 112 and Sch 19 of the Environment Act 1995.

4.185 A person found guilty of any offence in the Special Waste Regulations 1996 is liable to a fine not exceeding level five[1] on summary conviction[2]. On conviction on indictment, a fine, imprisonment of up to two years, or both, can be levied[3]. Given that hazardous waste is being dealt with by the Special Waste Regulations 1996, the level of fine is in immediate contrast to the £20,000 maximum allowable under the EPA 1990[4].

1 Currently £5,000 (Criminal Justice Act 1991).
2 SI 1996/972, reg 18(9)(a).
3 SI 1996/972, reg 18(9)(b).
4 See EPA 1990, s 33 and Chapter 7.

4.186 The Special Waste Regulations 1996 contain the usual provisions relating to the personal liability of directors, managers, secretaries etc and set out when they are to be held culpable for an offence committed by a body corporate due to their consent, connivance or neglect[1]. Bodies corporate managed by their members are also caught by this provision[2]. The Regulations also provide that, where one person commits an offence due to the act or default of another, the second person can be found guilty of the offence, regardless of whether the first person was charged[3].

1 SI 1996/972, reg 18(6).
2 SI 1996/972, reg 18(7): see para 7.156ff.
3 SI 1996/972, reg 18(5): see para 7.173ff.

4.187 Finally, while the requirements for the documentation of waste movements under the Environmental Protection (Duty of Care) Regulations 1991 do not normally apply when special waste is transported[1], this principle is subject to an important caveat. Regulation 2(3) of the Environmental Protection (Duty of Care) Regulations 1991 absolves a waste holder of the requirements of those Regulations only when a correctly completed consignment note[2] is utilised in the manner set down by the Special Waste Regulations 1996. Accordingly, should special waste be moved under an improperly-completed consignment note – or without being accompanied by such a note – offences may occur under both the Environmental Protection (Duty of Care) Regulations 1991[3] and the Special Waste Regulations 1996.

1 SI 1991/2839, reg 2(3) as amended by SI 1996/972, reg 23.
2 Or, if relevant, a carrier's round schedule.
3 Offences in respect of s 34 of the EPA 1990 and the Environmental Protection (Duty of Care) Regulations 1991 are discussed at para 3.18ff.

DEFENCES

4.188 The Special Waste Regulations 1996 contain one principal statutory defence which relates to non-compliance with the provisions due to the occurrence of an emergency[1]. A person charged with an offence must prove[2]:

'... that he was not reasonably able to comply with the provision by reason of an emergency or grave danger and that he took all steps as were reasonably practicable in the circumstances for –

(a) minimising any threat to the public or the environment; and
(b) ensuring that the provision in question was complied with as soon as reasonably practicable after the event.'

It should be noted that all the criteria set down must be applicable for the statutory defence to succeed. As discussed further at para 7.154, the question of the nature of 'an emergency' was considered in *Waste Incineration Services v Dudley Metropolitan Borough Council*[3], with a dictionary definition of the term being applied.

1   SI 1996/972, reg 18(2).
2   Note where the burden of proof lies: this matter is discussed further at para 7.155.
3   [1992] 1 Env LR 29.

4.189   In addition to this statutory defence, it should be noted that a second defence can be used in respect of a person moving waste prior to the expiry of the Agency's 72-hour notification period[1]. Regulation 12(3)(b) allows the waste to be moved when 'the consignment cannot lawfully remain where it is for 72 hours'. Again, the burden of proof to show why the load had to be moved rests with the defendant[2].

1   See paras 4.80 and 4.132 above.
2   See para 7.155.

Chapter 5

Transfrontier waste shipments

INTRODUCTION

5.01 This chapter will describe the regulatory system of the United Kingdom[1] which sets out to control the international waste trade. Although the scale of the trade nationally is quite small by comparison to some of the UK's European neighbours, the issue has been high profile, and received considerable public attention in the late 1980s[2].

1 Both Regulation 259/93 and SI 1994/1137 apply to England, Wales, Scotland and Northern Ireland.
2 See for example 'Major Scheme to Import Waste from USA Leads to Growth in Transfrontier Traffic' *Ends Report* 157 Feb 1988, p 7; 'The Toxic Waste Trade takes a Nasty Turn' *Ends Report* 161 June 1988, pp 9–10; 'Policy Shift on Waste Imports Gathers Pace' *Ends Report* 162 July 1988, p 17.

5.02 By contrast to international waste movements to recovery, waste movements to and from the UK for disposal are very much one way and diminishing. As a consequence of the country's comprehensive waste disposal infrastructure and the explicit policy statement contained in the United Kingdom Management Plan for Exports and Imports of Waste[1] (hereinafter the 'Export/Import Plan'), no waste is exported for disposal from this country. There are also considerable restrictions imposed on wastes stemming from non-European Community countries passing to the UK for disposal[2]. The result is that most of the waste imported into the UK for disposal purposes stems from the Republic of Ireland, where there is no merchant high temperature incineration capacity.

1 Department of the Environment (1996) *United Kingdom Management Plan for Exports and Imports of Waste* HMSO, London; as amended by Department of the Environment (1996) *United Kingdom Management Plan for Exports and Imports of Waste Addendum 1*, HMSO, London.
2 See, for example, 'Ban on Australian Waste sets Precedent' *Ends Report* 209 June 1992, p 23 and see para 5.122.

5.03 The UK is involved in a significant two-way trade in wastes destined for recovery. In general, the range of wastes imported for recovery is much wider than those waste types exported. While significant quantities of imported hazardous wastes are recovered in the UK – mainly solvents and other high calorific wastes destined for reclamation or to be burnt as fuel in cement manufacture – virtually all the exported wastes are materials such as metal scrap, waste paper and other less environmentally significant substances.

5.04 On a global basis, the international trade in wastes remains extensive, being complicated by three factors. The first is the variety and extent of the trade. Many transnational waste movements involve substances of very low potential hazard. They have continued for many years without significant regulatory controls, and mostly without incident[1]. Other waste movements involve substances which are environmentally harmful, have high disposal costs and may be attractive to individuals who wish to dump the materials on an unsuspecting, less-developed country. There have been a number of examples of these practices in the past, particularly involving Africa, Latin America and, increasingly, those states which previously composed the Soviet Bloc.

1 For example, figures for the export of metal scrap from the European Community (1992 figures) were: Indonesia 230 000 tonnes; India 1.2 million tonnes; Malaysia 278 000 tonnes; Mexico 27 000 tonnes; Czechoslovakia 340 000 tonnes. Source: *ENDS Report* 234 July 1994, pp 29–30.

5.05   The second factor, although inter-linked with the first, reflects the geopolitical context of the regulation of the global waste trade. Controlling the international waste trade effectively is perhaps one of the most complex and ambitious attempts at addressing an international environmental issue. The trade of materials to recycling and recovery facilities is, as noted, widespread and economically important to many countries. Effective regulation must therefore, on the one hand, provide sufficient controls to achieve the desired level of regulatory oversight of international waste transactions; but, on the other hand, the control system must not stifle the trade itself.

5.06   Finally, comprehensive global control must be applicable to a variety of governmental systems and political alliances. There are significant differences in many states' attitude to the international waste trade, especially as to the degree to which waste transactions – particularly those involving waste recovery – are desirable. These attitudes are themselves coloured by the often opposing forces of national and international environmental groups and the powerful influence of the recycling industries involved.

5.07   The result is a somewhat bewildering system of inter-locking and, sometimes, overlapping international agreements which attempt to address all of, or some parts of, the global waste trade[1]. Given this varied texture, it is particularly important that individuals involved in proposals to ship any waste materials out of the European Community take extreme care in respect of compliance with the required regulatory measures.

1   Not all countries are parties to the same range of agreements. While the USA is an OECD country, it has yet to sign the Basel Convention. Many highly industrialised states such as Malaysia and Indonesia are not OECD members. These matters become highly important as different transfrontier control procedures apply depending on upon whether or not a state is a member of one or more relevant international treaties.

THE BASEL CONVENTION, THE OECD DECISION AND LOMÉ IV CONVENTION[1]

5.08   The most important international agreement on the global waste trade is the 1989 Basel Convention on the Control of Transboundary Movements of Hazardous Wastes and their Disposal[2]. The Convention was drafted and agreed under the auspices of the United Nations, in the light of a number of dumping scandals affecting less developed countries. Not surprisingly, the Convention had a considerable influence on the form of European Community Regulation 259/93 on the control of international waste movements into, within and out of the Community[3]. The latter Regulation constitutes the formal control framework for waste movements which affect Community member states.

1   See generally Kummer K (1995) *International Management of Hazardous Wastes – The Basel Convention and Related Rules*, Clarendon Press, Oxford.
2   UNEP EP/IG.80/3 22nd March 1989: reprinted in, for example, 1 JEL 2 (1989) pp 255–277.
3   Council Regulation (EEC) No 259/93 of 1 February 1993 on the supervision and control of shipments of waste within, into and out of the European Community OJ L30/1 6.2.93.

5.09   Besides the Basel Convention, other international agreements also had an important influence on the final form of Regulation 259/93. Work undertaken at OECD (Organisation of Economic Co-Operation and Development) level has been a very significant determining factor on the international control system for wastes passing to recovery, and the Lomé IV Convention affects exports of hazardous wastes to African, Caribbean and Pacific (ACP) states.

5.10   The provisions of these transnational agreements will only be summarised below, with the discussion concentrating on the salient points relevant to the United Kingdom. A much more detailed description of Regulation 259/93 – the primary implementation mechanism for the requirements of the international agreements – will be given. This description will also encompass the Transfrontier Shipment of Waste Regulations 1994[1], which substantiate Regulation 259/93 in UK law.

1   SI 1994/1137.

5.11   Given the fact that much of the implementing legislation has the purpose of putting into effect international agreements such as the Basel Convention, reference should be made to relevant agreements where ambiguities in interpretation arise.

Basel Convention

5.12   The Basel Convention on the Control of Transboundary Movements of Hazardous Wastes and their Disposal was agreed on 22 March 1989, with the UK and the European Community becoming parties on 8 May 1994. The Convention obliges party states to ensure that international waste movements do not cause wastes to be managed in an environmentally unsound manner at destination. Wherever practicable, it requires wastes to be disposed of[1] as close to the site of generation as is possible[2]. In general, parties should allow waste to be moved to disposal only if the state of export does not itself have the technical capacity and the necessary facilities to arrange the environmentally sound waste management[3].

1   The meaning of 'disposal' under the Convention is discussed in para 5.18 below.
2   Basel Convention, Article 4(2).
3   Basel Convention, Article 4(9).

5.13   The Basel Convention mainly concerns hazardous wastes[1]. Although both waste[2] and hazardous waste are defined[3], the definition has little immediate relevance to movements between European Community states, as it has been overtaken by the provisions of Regulation 259/93[4]. Besides hazardous wastes, the Convention also applies to 'other wastes'. These are defined as being household waste and residues from the incineration of such wastes[5]. In November 1998, two new annexes to the Convention were adopted[6]. These were formerly known as Lists A and B and set out respectively substances which are and are not to be considered hazardous wastes[7]. Radioactive wastes and wastes derived from shipping which are subject to other international control agreements will continue to be explicitly excluded from the Convention[8].

1   Basel Convention, Article 1.
2   Basel Convention, Article 2(1).
3   Basel Convention, Article 1(a) and (b).
4   Regulation 259/93, Article 2(a): for a discussion of waste definitions in an international context, see Boutoux L and Leone L (1997) *The Legal Definition of Waste and its Impact on Waste Management in Europe*, Office of Official Publications of the European Communities, Luxembourg EUR 17716 EN.
5   Basel Convention, Article 1(2) and Annex II.
6   Decision IV/9 adding Annexes VIII and IX (see para 5.164ff).
7   There remains also a proposed C List, for wastes which are not yet assigned to the A or B Lists, as well as a D List of other wastes 'of particular concern'.
8   Basel Convention, Articles 1(3) and 1(4).

5.14   The Convention allows parties to prohibit the importation of hazardous and other wastes when they are to pass to disposal[1]. Other parties are then required to reinforce this ban by prohibiting the export of waste to that party state[2]. Transboundary movements of hazardous wastes for disposal to or from non-party states are not to be permitted[3], unless subject to bilateral, multilateral or regional agreements with non-party states[4]. All such agreements must be compatible with the underlying principle of the Convention that wastes should be subject to 'environmentally sound management'.

1   Basel Convention, Article 4(1)(a).
2   Basel Convention, Article 4(1)(b).
3   Basel Convention, Article 4(5).
4   Basel Convention, Article 11.

5.15   The Convention requires that all international shipments of hazardous waste destined for disposal are subject to advance approval on the basis of prior informed consent[1]. This is done by way of a notification document which is sent to the affected competent authorities in the states of export, transit and destination. Each state is permitted to veto a proposed shipment, provided that this action is in line with the requirements of the Convention. In tandem with the notification document, a written contract must exist between the notifier and consignee, which specifies the 'environmentally sound management of the waste in question'[2]. Besides the contract, the transit state and state of import can also insist that the transaction is covered by insurance, a bond or a guarantee[3]. Subject to certain specified conditions[4], a 'season ticket' general notification can be used to cover a series of shipments of the same waste for a period of one year[5].

1   Basel Convention, Article 6.
2   Basel Convention, Article 6(3).
3   Basel Convention, Article 6(11).
4   Basel Convention, Article 6(6).
5   Basel Convention, Article 6(8).

5.16   Once the notification document has been approved by all affected parties, it then becomes a consignment note which accompanies the waste in transit. On receipt of the waste, the disposer must inform the state of export that the waste has arrived, and again inform the state of export when the waste has been disposed of[1]. The non-appearance of the completed notification document will therefore alert the relevant competent authorities that the waste has gone astray in transit.

1   Basel Convention, Article 6(9).

5.17   In the event that a shipment gets into difficulties, alternative arrangements for environmentally sound disposal can be undertaken. However, if acceptable disposal cannot be accomplished, the Convention requires the party state of export to have the waste returned[1]. No other party state can obstruct this return movement[2].

1   Basel Convention, Article 8.
2   Basel Convention, Article 8.

5.18   As originally drafted, the Basel Convention's stance on international movements of hazardous waste for recovery was somewhat contradictory. As noted, the Convention is restrictive towards transfrontier waste movements for 'disposal'. Whilst the Convention contains separate lists of disposal and recovery processes[1], the Convention classes both lists as 'disposal' operations[2]. However, despite being restrictive on movements to 'disposal' facilities[3], the Convention then sets out a general presumption in favour of a free trade in wastes passing to recovery[3]:

'Parties shall take appropriate measures to ensure that the transboundary movement of hazardous wastes and other wastes only be allowed if . . . [t]he wastes in question are required as a raw material for recycling or recovery industries in the State of import . . .'

This requirement therefore sits a little uncomfortably with much of the rest of the Convention.

1 These are broadly similar, but not identical, to Annexes IIA and IIB of the Directive on Waste (as amended), see Tables 2.2 and 2.3 of Chapter 2.
2 See Basel Convention, Article 2(4) and Annex IV.
3 Basel Convention, Article 4(9)(b).

5.19 The Convention's less than clear stance on waste movements to recovery has been augmented by detailed procedures agreed through the OECD. The Convention was subsequently modified[1] to address some of these matters, being amended at the Convention's 1995 conference[2] to ban 'hazardous waste' shipments to recovery plants in non-OECD countries at the end of 1997. This amendment has not yet been formally ratified by the required number of party states.

1 *Amendment to the Basel Convention on the Control of Transboundary Movements of Hazardous Waste and their Disposal Concluded at Basel 22 March 1989*, CM 3322, 1996, HMSO.
2 Decision III/1.

5.20 The Basel Convention has also set up a Secretariat which acts as a clearing house to ensure that information on the waste trade, along with each party's regulatory stance to it, is conveyed to the other party states[1]. The Convention introduces a mechanism which allows all parties to meet up periodically[2] and amendments to the Convention can be adopted at this Conference[3].

1 Basel Convention, Article 16.
2 Basel Convention, Article 15.
3 Basel Convention, Article 17.

The OECD Decision

5.21 Work by the OECD[1] on the movement of wastes passing to recovery has greatly influenced the style of international regulation of this important aspect of the waste trade. This work culminated in the production of the OECD Decision on the Control of Transfrontier Movements of Waste Destined for Recovery Operations[2], which was enacted as a multilateral agreement under Article 11 of the Basel Convention. This Decision, which is referred to here and in Regulation 259/93 as the 'OECD Decision', sets down the main requirements for waste passing internationally to recovery. It applies to shipments of wastes to, from and through the 29 nations which presently make up the OECD[3].

1 All European Community states are OECD members. The other states are Australia, Canada, the Czech Republic, Hungary, Iceland, Korea, Japan, Mexico, New Zealand, Norway, Poland, Switzerland, Turkey and the USA. The European Community has observer status. For a discussion of the manner by which OECD states implement the Decision, see OECD (1998) *Final Guidance Document for Distinguishing Waste from Non-Waste* (Env/Epoc/Wmp (98) 1/Rev 1), OECD, Paris.
2 OECD C(92)39/Final as amended by Decision C(93)74/Final 23.7.93; C(94)153 28.7.94 and C(96)231 10.12.96.
3 An exception is Japan, which has not accepted the Decision: see Kammer K (1995) *International Management of Hazardous Wastes – The Basel Convention and Related Rules*, Clardendon Press, Oxford, p 162. It would seem also that Poland and Hungary are not currently bound by the Decision: see Commission Regulation 1547/99 and para 5.140ff below.

5.22 The OECD decision proposes a three-tiered control system for transfrontier waste movements to recovery plants. This hierarchy takes into account the fact that the international trade in many wastes for recovery, such as metal scrap, waste paper, etc is extensive, mature and has often continued with limited environmental impact. These wastes are identified on the Green List, being subject to a lesser range of controls. But other wastes passing to recovery, particularly those that are toxic or otherwise environmentally hazardous, are subject to more stringent controls. These are specified on the Amber or Red Lists, with the latter having the tightest control system. A review mechanism is contained in the Decision to assign more wastes to any of the three Lists as and when required[1]. As the procedures for these wastes are replicated in European law by Regulation 259/93, they are discussed in detail below[2]. In general, Green List wastes passing to recovery can be traded freely and are exempt from any formal notification procedure. However, care must be taken in applying this principle indiscriminately. Individual non-OECD countries can indicate that they regard some, or all, Green List wastes as hazardous and hence falling within the more stringent procedures pertaining to wastes on the Amber and Red Lists. In addition, a number of mainly African, Caribbean and Pacific (ACP) states have banned all Green List shipments[3].

1   OECD Decision C(92)39/Final, Annex 1(II)(7).
2   See para 5.46ff.
3   See para 5.137ff below.

The Lomé Convention

5.23   The Lomé IV Convention requires[1] the prohibition of exports of 'hazardous waste' from the European Community to 70 African, Caribbean and Pacific (ACP) states. It was signed in 1989 and is one of a series of aid and trade agreements between the ACP nations and the European Community[2]. The Lomé IV Convention is designed to last ten years, with a five year review in 1994.

1   Article 39.
2   There have been a succession of Lomé Conventions. These developed upon the European Economic Community's early relationship with ACP states which were previously French colonies. Since the First Lomé Convention was signed in 1975, the number of ACP participants has increased from 46 to 70.

COUNCIL REGULATION 259/93 ON TRANSFRONTIER WASTE SHIPMENTS

5.24   The Council Regulation (EEC) on the Supervision and Control of Shipments of Wastes within, into and out of the European Community was finalised in February 1993[1]. Its purpose was to replace the existing Community control structure for hazardous waste exports and imports, whilst addressing the requirements of the Basel and Lomé Conventions and the OECD Decision on wastes passing internationally to recovery. As the European Community and all the member states have ratified the Basel Convention, the Regulation follows the provisions of the Conventions and the OECD Decision closely. In contrast to the Basel Convention, it applies to all wastes, not only wastes which are viewed as hazardous. The Regulation was implemented in May 1994, when its predecessor, Directive 84/631, was repealed[2], and despite an attempt by the European Parliament to have it annulled[3].

1   Council Regulation (EEC) No 259/93 of 1 February 1993 on the supervision and control of shipments of waste within, into and out of the European Community, OJ L30/1 6.2.93; as amended by Commission Decision 94/721 of 21 October 1994 adapting, pursuant to Article 42(3), Annexes II, III and IV of Council Regulation (EEC) No 259/93 on the supervision and control of shipments within, into and out of the European Community (OJ L288/36 9.11.94); by Commission Decision 96/660 of 14 November 1996 adapting pursuant to Article 42(3), Annex II to Council Regulation (EEC) No 259/93 on the supervision and control of shipments within, into and out of the European Community,

OJ L304/15 27/11/96; by Council Regulation 120/97 of 20 January 1997 amending Regulation No 259/93 on the supervision and control of shipments of waste, within, into and out of the European Community (OJ L22/14 24.1.97); by Commission Decision of 18 May 1998 adapting, pursuant to Article 42(3), Annexes II and III of Council Regulation (EEC) No 259/93 on the supervision and control of shipments within, into and out of the European Community (Decision 98/368/EC: OJ L165/20 10.6.98); and by Commission Regulation (EC) No 2408/98 of 6 November 1998 amending Annex V of Council Regulation 239/93 on the supervision and control of shipments of waste within, into and out of the European Community (OJ L298/19 7.11.98).

2 Council Directive of 6 December 1984 on the Supervision and Control within the European Community of the Transfrontier Shipment of Hazardous Waste, OJ L326/31 13.12.84 (repealed by Regulation 259/93, Article 43).

3 *European Parliament v Council of European Communities* [1994] ECR I-2857.

5.25 For all shipments, except those Green List wastes such as scrap metal, the Regulation sets up a system which allows the country of intended destination to receive sufficient advance information on a proposed international waste movement to make an informed decision on its desirability. Once the waste has been shipped, the consignment note tracking system indicates to the competent authorities of dispatch, transit and destination when the waste was moved, when it arrived, where it went to and that it was either disposed of or recovered. Besides the control documentation, all affected waste movements are subject to commercial contracts[1] and financial guarantees or insurance covering each shipment[2].

1 See para 5.80.
2 See para 5.85.

5.26 The Regulation is complex, setting down provisions pertaining to the variety of transactions possible from differing source countries within and outside the European Community. This complexity is, in part, a reflection of the variety of international treaties. As noted, the requirements also vary depending on whether the waste is to pass to recovery or disposal, and must have regard to an individual party state's stance on the trade.

5.27 The Regulation is much longer than all other examples of Community environmental legislation, containing 44 Articles and five Annexes. It is also not easy to read. A considerable amount of cross referencing exists, some of which then goes on to refer to further Articles. In addition, a number of typographical errors in the English version in the Official Journal do little to assist clarity, and a small number of these appear to alter the sense, or increase the ambiguity, of certain Articles[1].

1 This problem raises the interesting question of where a copy of the definitive text is to be located. In this respect, it is notable that Circular 13/94, where a reproduced version of the text of the Regulation is to be found, notes: 'Minor typographical errors in the OJ text have been corrected without comment, but material changes (eg inserting missing text) are marked with square brackets. These changes are based on the text adopted by the Council in December 1992'.

5.28 Being a regulation, rather than a Council Directive, Regulation 259/93 does not strictly require implementing provisions in order to enter into force in UK law[1]. However, although the Regulation has direct application in member states' law, certain additional provisions have been made to cement it more firmly into the national regulatory system. This has been accomplished by the Transfrontier Shipment of Waste Regulations 1994[2], which addresses such matters as offences, penalties, procedures for approving financial guarantees, etc.

1 See Article 249 of the Treaty establishing the European Community: 'A Regulation shall have general application. It shall be binding in its entirety and directly applicable in all Member States' (formerly Article 189).

2 SI 1994/1137, as amended by SI 1996/593, reg 3, Sch 2, para 11(2), (3) and SI 1996/972, reg 26.

5.29   The Transfrontier Shipment of Waste Regulations are accompanied by Circular 13/94[1]. However, readers should note that this circular has been partially superseded. Somewhat surprisingly, some of it has been replaced by way of a letter from the Department of the Environment to all UK waste regulation bodies[2]. Further minor changes were made more formally by the Export/Import Plan[3].

1   Department of the Environment Circular 13/94, *European Communities Act 1972. Council Regulation (EEC) No 259/93 on the Supervision and Control of Shipments of waste within, into and out of the European Community. The Transfrontier Shipment of Waste Regulations 1994*, HMSO, London.
2   DOE letter dated 26 January 1995 *EC Waste Shipments Regulation (259/93)*: the letter notes (para 2) 'I am copying this letter to the local authority associations, and to trade associations and other bodies with an interest. Bearing in mind that some of the advice below supplements or replaces that contained in DOE Circular 13/94, I would be grateful if you would ensure that this information is circulated widely amongst those organisations with which you have contact on transfrontier shipment of waste issues'.
3   See for example Export/Import Plan, paras 1.4 and 4.23: the Plan is discussed at para 5.37.

5.30   The requirements of Regulation 259/93 can be divided into two categories. Firstly, there are those general provisions which are applicable to virtually all international waste transactions. Secondly, there are the detailed requirements of the Regulation in respect of particular configurations of shipment within, out of, into or through the European Community and whose form is dependent on whether disposal or recovery is to occur and the type of state involved.

Regulatory responsibilities in the UK

5.31   Member states have to designate the competent authority for administering the Regulation[1]. They also have a duty to take measures to ensure compliance with the Regulation[2]. According to Regulation 259/93, such measures 'may' include spot checks on the waste producer, at the frontier, in transit, etc. In addition, the administrative cost of implementing the notification procedures, along with the cost of return, disposal or recovery if a shipment gets into difficulties, may be subject to charges[3].

1   The Regulation does not directly address shipments within a member state (Article 13(1)), but its procedures could be used to set up an internal waste tracking mechanism if a member state so required (Article 13(4)). Whatever the system selected, member states must establish 'appropriate systems for the supervision and control' of internal waste movements (Regulation 259/93, Article 13(2)).
2   Regulation 259/93, Article 30.
3   Regulation 259/93, Article 33.

5.32   Regulation 259/93 extensively refers to the duties of three types of competent authority: 'competent authority of dispatch'; 'competent authority of destination' and 'competent authority of transit'. For exports of waste from the UK, the competent authority of dispatch is the Agency which has jurisdiction for the area from which the waste is dispatched[1]. Usually, this will be the Agency responsible for the waste producer[2]. For imports into the UK, the competent authority is the Agency responsible for the intended destination[3].

1   1994/1137, reg 3 and Regulation 259/93, Article 2(c): arrangements for Northern Ireland are in transition, with the intention to centralise the waste regulation function from the district councils (see para 1.108ff). The remainder of this Chapter will use the term 'Agency' to refer to all UK competent authorities, including the Secretary of State in his role as competent authority of transit.
2   Where wastes have been collected from several sources, it is the regulatory authority with jurisdiction over the location of the collection point: see Circular 13/94, para 34.
3   SI 1994/1137, reg 3.

5.33   For exports of waste from the UK to a European Community destination, the competent authority of destination is the body so designated by that member state. For countries which are outside the European Community but within OECD, the competent authority of destination is that which has been designated by the OECD Secretariat[1]. For movements involving non-OECD countries who are Basel Convention parties, details of the competent authorities can be obtained from the Basel Convention Secretariat[2].

1   The Secretary, Waste Management Policy Group, Organisation of Economic Cooperation and Development, 2 Rue André Pascal, 75775 Paris, Cedex 16 (Tel +33 1 45 28 82 00).
2   Circular 13/94, para 37: Secretariat of the Basel Convention, Geneva Executive Centre, 15 Chemin des Anénomes (Building D), 1219 Chatelaine (GE), Switzerland (Tel +41 22 979 91 11). (Web Site: http://www.unep.ch/Basel/index.html).

5.34   The term 'competent authority for transit' in Regulation 259/93 refers to the regulatory authority through whose area waste is transported. One competent authority per country must be designated as having responsibility for through traffic[1]. For this reason, the Secretary of State – rather than the Agency or SEPA – remains the competent authority for this purpose in the UK[2].

1   Regulation 259/93, Article 36.
2   SI 1994/1137, reg 4.

5.35   The Regulation uses the term 'correspondent' in relation to the national focal point for general enquiries and reporting in each member state[1]. In the UK, the Secretary of State performs this role[2]. The European Community's correspondent is the European Commission[3].

1   Regulation 259/93, Articles 2(f) and 37.
2   SI 1994/1137, reg 5.
3   Regulation 259/93, Article 2(f): DG XI.E.3 – Waste Management Policy, European Commission, Rue de la Loi 200, B-1049 Brussels (Tel +32-2 299 2036).

5.36   Customs offices at entry and exit points can also be designated by member states, with names and addresses forwarded to the Commission for publication. It is open to a member state to require that all movements use such entry and exit points when waste enters or leaves the European Community[1].

1   Regulation 259/93, Article 39.

The UK's Export/Import Plan[1]

5.37   Under Regulation 259/93[2], member states may establish a set of general written principles to prohibit or to limit transfrontier waste movements passing to disposal[3]. There are, however, no equivalent provisions in respect of waste passing to recovery[4]. Whatever measures have been decided upon should be notified to the Commission. The contravention of these general rules is a ground for objection over individual transfrontier shipments to disposal facilities[5]. It would appear that these rules may also fall within the scope of objections on the grounds of the contravention of waste management plans under the Directive on Waste, which competent authorities can use as reasons for objection in respect of proposals for shipments to disposal[6] or to recovery[7].

1   It was proposed in December 1998 to make a further modification to clarify the Export/Import Plan: see *Hansard* written answers 2 December 1998 column 185. However, a later announcement indicated that a general review of the plan is to take place, with a consultation document to be issued in the Autumn of 1999 (see *Hansard* 31 March 1999 Col 758).

2   Regulation 259/93, Article 4(3)(a)(i).
3   Defined as being encompassed by Annex IIA of Directive 75/442 on Waste (Regulation 259/93, Article 2(i)).
4   There is no equivalent to Regulation 259/93, Article 4(2)(c) in Article 7, which sets out grounds for objection for transactions involving recovery.
5   See Regulation 259/93, Article 4(2)(c).
6   Regulation 259/93, Article 4(3)(b).
7   Regulation 259/93, Article 7(4)(a).

5.38   The UK Government has used the opportunity presented by Article 7 of the Directive on Waste[1] to draw up a national plan pertaining to transfrontier waste movements[2]. The statutory basis of this document is the Transfrontier Shipment of Waste Regulations 1994[3]. The operation of the plan is central to the manner by which proposals for notifications to ship waste for disposal and recovery are to be dealt with by the Agency. It is legally binding[4] and the Agency must formally object to any shipment which the plan indicates should not go ahead[5]. The plan also sets out a decision-making framework against which the Agency must judge other notifications[6]. As will be apparent from the remainder of this Chapter, its provisions are a key influence on how proposals to ship waste to or from the UK are to be handled.

1   Council Directive of 15 July 1975 on waste (75/442/EEC), OJ L194/39 25.7.75 (as amended by Council Directive of 18 March 1991 amending Directive 75/442/EEC on Waste (91/156/EEC) (OJ L78/32 26.3.91) and Commission Decision of 24 May 1996 adapting Annexes IIA and IIB to Council Directive 75/442/EEC on Waste (96/350/EC) (OJ L135/32 6.6.96)).
2   Department of the Environment *United Kingdom Management Plan for Exports and Imports of Waste* (1996), HMSO, London.
3   SI 1994/1137, reg 11.
4   Export/Import Plan, paras 1.2, 2,2 and 2.3.
5   SI 1994/1137, reg 11(3) and (4).
6   Export/Import Plan, para 2.4.

5.39   The focus of this plan is the Secretary of State's policies 'in relation to the import and export of waste for recovery or disposal into and out of the United Kingdom'[1]. The Transfrontier Waste Shipment Regulations 1994[2] also require the content of the plan to reflect the 'plan making provisions' of the relevant objectives contained in Article 3(1) of Directive on Waste[3]. The nature of these objectives is set down in the Waste Management Licensing Regulations 1994[4].

1   SI 1994/1137, reg 11(1).
2   SI 1994/1137, reg 11(6).
3   Council Directive of 15 July 1975 on Waste (75/442/EEC), OJ L194/39 25.7.75 (as amended by Council Directive of 18 March 1991 amending Directive 75/442/EEC on Waste (91/156/EEC) (OJ L78/32 26.3.91) and Commission Decision of 24 May 1996 adapting Annexes IIA and IIB to Council Directive 75/442/EEC on Waste (96/350/EC) (OJ L135/32 6.6.96)).
4   SI 1994/1056, Sch 4, para 4(1)(b).

5.40   Once the plan was finalised, the Transfrontier Shipment of Waste Regulations 1994 required it be sent to all competent authorities of dispatch and destination[1]. Copies are available to the public on payment of a fee[2]. A draft of this plan was published in February 1995[3], with the finalised version entering into force in June 1996[4]. The plan was amended at the end of that year, with changes taking effect on 13 January 1997[5].

1   SI 1994/1137, reg 11(5)(a).
2   SI 1994/1137, reg 11(4)(b).
3   *Waste Management Plan for the UK, Imports and Exports of Waste, a Draft for Consultation*, Department of the Environment, 1995.
4   Export/Import Plan, page vii.

5 Department of the Environment *United Kingdom Management Plan for Exports and Imports of Waste. Addendum 1*, (1996) HMSO, London.

The definition of waste under Regulation 259/93

5.41 Regulation 259/93 does not apply just to hazardous wastes, but refers to all waste movements between member states or into or out of the European Community[1]. The definition of waste and its delineation from the concept of 'goods' is set out in Chapter 2 and will not be repeated here. However, because Regulation 259/93 has direct application[2] in Community law, it contains a free-standing definition of waste[3] which is quite independent of the definition currently[4] set out in the Environmental Protection Act 1990[5]. Hence it is appropriate that the nature of this definition should be briefly reviewed. It also should be noted that, in respect of waste imported into Great Britain, the Controlled Waste Regulations 1992[6] hold that such materials are always to be classified as 'industrial waste', regardless of source or composition.

1 Regulation 259/93, Articles 1 and 2(a).
2 Ie without requiring a member state to transpose the provisions into indigenous law: see Article 249 of the amended Treaty on European Community.
3 See para 2.26 and *Euro Tombesi* [1998] Env LR 59 at 87, para 46; *Mayer Parry Recycling Ltd v Environment Agency* [1999] Env LR 489; Case C-192/96 *Beside BV v Minister van Volkshuisvesting* [1999] Env LR 328 at 352, para 27. Possibly for this reason, the Transfrontier Shipment of Waste Regulations 1994 make reference to 'waste', not 'controlled waste'.
4 Note that the existing definition is due for amendment by the Environment Act 1995, Sch 22, para 88. When enacted, this will bring the national waste definition closer to that contained in Regulation 259/93.
5 EPA 1990, s 75: see para 2.31ff.
6 SI 1992/588, reg 5(1) and Sch 3, para 17: the nature of industrial waste is discussed further at para 2.205ff.

5.42 The Regulation determines substances which are 'wastes' through the definition given in Article 1(a) of the Directive on Waste[1]. Article 1(a) of the Directive states:

'"waste" shall mean any substance or object in the categories set out in Annex I[2] which the holder discards or intends or is required to discard'.

What should be noted is that, in both Regulation 259/93 and in the Directive on Waste, this definition is the subject of a number of caveats. It would seem that there are minor differences between the caveats contained in the regulation and those set down in the Directive.

1 Regulation 259/93, Article 2(a); Council Directive of 15 July 1975 on Waste (75/442/EEC), OJ L194/39 25.7.75 (as amended by Council Directive of 18 March 1991 amending Directive 75/442/EEC on Waste (91/156/EEC) (OJ L78/32 26.3.91) and Commission Decision of 24 May 1996 adapting Annexes IIA and IIB to Council Directive 75/442/EEC on Waste (96/350/EC) (OJ L135/32 6.6.96)) Article 1(a): see para 2.20.
2 See Table 2.1 in Chapter 2.

5.43 Exclusions from the general definition of waste in the Regulation itself include waste generated by ships and offshore platforms 'provided that such waste is the subject of a specific binding international instrument'[1], shipments of 'civil aviation waste'[2]; shipments of radioactive waste[3] and shipments of waste into the Community which are covered by the Protocol on Environmental Protection to the Antarctic Treaty[4].

1 Regulation 259/93, Article 1(2)(a).
2 Regulation 259/93, Article 1(2)(b).
3 Regulation 259/93, Article 1(2)(c): as defined by Directive 92/3/Euratom, Article 2 (OJ L35/24 12.2.92).
4 Regulation 259/93, Article 1(2)(e).

5.44 Certain other wastes[1] are also explicitly excluded by Regulation 259/93 'where they are already covered by other relevant legislation'. These include radioactive wastes; wastes resulting from prospecting, extraction, treatment and storage of mineral resources and the working of quarries; animal carcasses, faecal matter and 'other natural, non-dangerous substances used in farming'[2]; waste waters excepting liquid wastes; and decommissioned explosives.

1 Regulation 259/93, Article 1(2)(d), which cross refers to Article 2(1)(b) of the Directive on Waste: note that this causes radioactive waste to be subject to exclusions in both Articles 1(2)(c) and 1(2)(d) of the regulation.
2 Directive on Waste, Article 2(1)(b)(iii).

5.45 The latter waste types are similarly excluded in the Directive on Waste. However, in the context of Regulation 259/93, an interesting question develops in relation to the words which require wastes to be excluded from the Regulation[1] 'where they are already covered by other relevant legislation'. Hence, should this exclusion apply, the waste is not subject to the Regulation's transfrontier control system at all[2]: the context would suggest that the 'other legislation' referred to in Regulation 259/93 as being 'relevant' must be legislation which is directed to the control of transfrontier waste movements. This would appear to be in line with the view taken by the Department of the Environment in Circular 11/94[3]. Referring in that instance to the definition of waste under the Directive on Waste, the Department of the Environment states that something is 'covered' by other legislation 'if the legislation provides an effective means of pursuing the aims of the Directive . . .'[4]. The Department's assertion can be translated by analogy to mean that an item is 'covered' by provisions other than Regulation 259/93 where such provisions successfully promote the aims of that Regulation. Clearly, in comparison to the Directive on Waste and indigenous waste movements, there is a very limited amount of legislation 'covering' international waste shipments. But it is not always clear which legislation does in fact establish transfrontier rules which are equivalent to those in Regulation 259/93. Examples include the Directive on the Processing and Disposal of Animal Waste[5]. However, there remains uncertainty as to what is, in fact, 'covered' by other legislation. This factor would suggest that the definition of waste under Regulation 259/93 is at least different and possibly wider than that contained in the Directive on Waste. It also illustrates the rather uncomfortable boundary between the environmental controls espoused by the Regulation and the animal or plant health controls eminating from Community agricultural directives.

1 Regulation 259/93, Article 1(2)(d).
2 For example, wastes from some quarrying operations are listed in Annex II to the Regulation as being on the Green List (see Appendix III, Table 1). Waste straw, liquid pig manure and faeces are present on the Amber List (see Appendix III, Table 2).
3 Circular 11/94 *Environmental Protection Act 1990: Part II; Waste Management Licensing; The Framework Directive on Waste*, HMSO, London.
4 Circular 11/94, para 1.16.
5 Council Directive of 27 November 1990 laying down Veterinary Rules for the Disposal and Processing of Animal Waste, for its placing on the Market and for the Prevention of Pathogens in Feedstuffs of Animal or Fish Origin and Amending Directive 90/425/EEC. (Directive 90/667/EEC) OJ L363/51 27.12.1990.

The Green, Amber and Red Lists of wastes for passing to recovery

5.46 Regulation 259/93 contains one set of control procedures for wastes passing internationally for disposal and three levels of control for wastes passing to recovery. The arrangements for wastes passing to recovery reflect the requirements of the OECD

Decision already mentioned, and are centred upon the presence of the description of a particular waste in one of three Annexes. The Annexes set out respectively the Green, Amber and Red Lists referred to earlier. However, the Lists contained in Regulation 259/93 were superseded in November 1994[1], since then the Amber List has been superceded[2] and the Green List replaced twice[3].

1   Commission Decision 94/721 of 21 October 1994 adapting, pursuant to Article 42(3), Annexes II, III and IV to Council Regulation (EEC) No 259/93 on the supervision and control of shipments within, into and out of the European Community (OJ L288/36 9.11.94). The Decision became part of Regulation 259/93 by way of Article 42(3).
2   Commission Decision of 18 May 1998 adapting, pursuant to Article 42(3), Annexes II and III to Council Regulation (EEC) No 259/93 on the supervision and control of shipments of waste, into and out of the European Community (OJ L165/20 10.6.98).
3   By Commission Decision 96/660 of 14 November 1996 adapting, pursuant to Article 42(3), Annex II to Council Regulation (EEC) No 259/93 on the supervision and control of shipments within, into and out of the European Community (OJ L304/15 27.11.96) and by Commission Decision 98/368/EC of 18 May 1998 adapting, pursuant to Article 42(3), Annexes II and III to Council Regulation (EEC) No 259/93 on the supervision and control of shipments of waste within, into and out of the European Community (OJ L165/20 10.6.98).

5.47   Annex II of the Regulation contains the 'Green List' of wastes and is concerned with wastes which in common language might be described as 'scrap materials', such as iron and steel, gold, platinum, scrap plastics, paper and cardboard, glass, etc (see Appendix III, Table 1). It should be noted that Annex II starts with an important caveat:

'Regardless of whether or not wastes are included on this list, they may not be moved as green wastes if they are contaminated by other materials to an extent which (a) increases the risks associated with the waste sufficiently to render it appropriate for inclusion in the amber or red lists, or (b) prevents the recovery of the waste in an environmentally sound manner'[1].

1   See also Export/Import Plan, para 4.24ff.

5.48   The Green List describes an interesting list of miscellaneous waste types, including scrap ships 'properly emptied of any cargo and other materials arising from the operation of the vessel which may have been classified as a dangerous substance or waste'. In relation to international movements of scrap motor vehicles, it is required that they are 'drained of liquids'. If they have not been properly drained, they then fall within the more stringent requirements for wastes allocated to the Amber List.

5.49   The 'Amber List' of wastes is contained in Annex III of Regulation 259/93 (see Appendix III, Table 2). Again, this List is headed by a caveat similar to that applicable to the Green List[1]. Wastes on the Amber List are those which are considered to present a more significant hazard. Many ferrous and non-ferrous metal ashes and residues feature on the list, as do scrap lead acid batteries, waste oils, halogenated and non-halogenated solvents, distillation residues, sewage sludge, pig manure, faeces, and 'municipal and household' waste. Annex IV constitutes the 'Red List' of substances (see Appendix III, Table 3). This Annex is much shorter, being concerned principally with wastes where recovery – whilst being conceivable – is technically or financially doubtful and where environmental effects of indiscriminate disposal are potentially considerable. PCB-contaminated materials, asbestos dusts and fibres and leaded anti-knock compound sludges all feature on this List. It would be expected that Amber and Red List substances would usually fall within the British definition of special waste[2].

1   See para 5.47.
2   Export/Import Plan, para 6.51: an obvious example of an exception to this general principle is Household Waste (Code AD160).

5.50   The contents of each of the Lists are not absolute. Countries which are the possible destinations of such shipments can request that a substance which currently appears on the Green List be placed on the Amber or Red Lists[1]. In addition, Green List wastes can fall within the ambit of the higher levels of control applicable to the other Lists for two further reasons. The first is if the wastes shows hazardous properties[2], as defined by Annex III of the Directive on Hazardous Wastes[3]. Secondly, at a member state level, Green List wastes may be subject to the level of control set down for Amber or Red List substances 'in exceptional cases' and 'for environmental or public health reasons'. The latter are not defined, but member states must immediately notify the Commission and inform other member states: the reasons for this decision must be included[4]. All these actions are to be ratified by the expert committee set up under Article 18 of the Directive on Waste.

1   Regulation 259/93, Article 17(3).
2   Regulation 259/93, Article 1(3)(c).
3   Directive 91/689 (Council Directive of 12 December 1991 on Hazardous Waste. OJ L377/30 31.12.91).
4   Regulation 259/93, Article 1(3)(d).

5.51   Article 10 of the Regulation requires that waste which is to pass to recovery but which is not assigned to any of the Lists is to be subject to the procedures appropriate for Red List wastes. In 1997 the Divisional Court considered a judicial review against the Environment Agency on behalf of a number of scrap metal processors, *R v Environment Agency, ex p Dockgrange Ltd, Mayer Parry Ltd and Robinson Group Ltd*[1]. The case involved the importation of waste from scrap fragmentiser plants in continental Europe from which the UK companies recovered metals by way of specialist processing. The unrecoverable residues were to pass to landfill. These particular wastes were not categorised on any of the Lists. The importers considered that these materials should enter the UK as Green List wastes. Whilst a generic description of the wastes was not present on the Green List, descriptions of all of the constituents of the waste, such as aluminium, magnesium, rubber, plastic, small quantities of gold, silver, wood and fabric, were present. By contrast, the Agency felt that fragmentiser waste, whilst not identified as such in the Lists[2], was a discrete waste category in its own right. Being a discrete category, it should be considered under Article 10 of the Regulation as an 'unassigned waste'[3] and therefore should be dealt with as Red List waste and subject to formal notification procedures.

1   [1998] 10 JEL 1, 146.
2   If it was so identified, then there would have been little argument: see *R v Environment Agency, ex p Dockgrange* at 152.
3   Interestingly, a number of other member states apparently were content to view the material as Green List waste.

5.52   The Divisional Court found against the Environment Agency. In respect of Article 10 of Regulation 259/93, Carnwath J considered that both individual components and generic mixtures should be considered in judging whether the wastes were contained on the Lists set out in the Regulation's Annexes[1]. In addition, the Regulation's requirements on Green List waste transactions[2] require that the quantity of each shipment is specified. Carnwath J considered that, where it was possible to correctly judge the quantities of the substances which made up the mixture of wastes set out on the Green list, then the mixture itself should be considered to be covered by the Green List. In this case, the court was convinced that the scrap metal processors could guarantee the proportion of different substances with 95% accuracy[3]. However, if this could not be so guaranteed, then it was felt that the waste should be considered as unassigned. It was also held that the materials which made up the loads could be considered, individually and collectively, as environmentally harmless: again this pointed towards the Green List as the basis of the requisite procedures[4].

1   *R v Environment Agency, ex p Dockgrange* [1998] 10 JEL 1, 146 at 152.
2   Regulation 259/93, Article 11: see para 5.136ff.
3   *R v Environment Agency, ex p Dockgrange* at 152.
4   *R v Environment Agency, ex p Dockgrange* at 153.

5.53   As somewhat of a contrast, the European Court of Justice subsequently considered the question of categorisation on the Lists in respect of partially separated fractions of household waste[1]. These wastes had been imported into Holland from Germany without notification. The waste was composed of eight bales of mainly plastics, with it being claimed that the bales were to be shipped on to a plastic reprocessor in the Far East. The composition of the bales was somewhat variable, with the plastic content varying between 58% to 92% and the remainder being made up of paper and cardboard, wood, metal, glass and textiles from the original household wastes. In one bale, six live rounds of ammunition were discovered.

1   *Beside BV and I M Besselsen v Minister van Volkshuisvesting, Ruimtelijke Ordening en Milieubeheer* [1999] Env LR 328.

5.54   The Dutch competent authority required the importer to ship the waste back to Germany on the grounds that the material fell within the Amber List and should have been notified[1]. The importers claimed that such a requirement was unlawful. The case was forwarded to the European Court by the national court for clarification on three points of law. The main point concerned whether the bales fell within the Amber List's category of 'municipal/household wastes'[2]. A significant proportion of the constituents were plastics as described on the Green List, which were mixed with other substances on the Green List, as well as a small proportion of other materials not covered by that List.

1   Hence it was claimed to constitute 'illegal traffic' under Article 26 of Regulation 259/93: see para 5.188ff.
2   Amber List category AD160 see Table 2 in Appendix III.

5.55   The court made clear that it considered that the origin of the waste was not a decisive consideration when interpreting the Green, Amber and Red Lists[1]. Hence separately collected fractions of household waste – such as glass, plastics, paper etc – could be held to be covered by the Green List. However, it was also held that, if the particular Green List waste was mixed with other wastes from that List – or with Amber List wastes – and 'having regard to the extent to which it was contaminated'[2], it would fall within the Amber List category of 'municipal/household wastes'. Conversely, 'municipal/household waste' does not cease to be on the Amber List – and hence does not fall within the Green List – 'unless it has been collected separately or *properly sorted*'[3].

1   *Beside* [1999] Env LR 328 at 352, para 29.
2   *Beside* [1999] Env LR 328 at 353, para 31.
3   *Beside* [1999] Env LR 328 at 353, para 32 [author's emphasis].

5.56   While matters as to the degree to which the waste is contaminated and the consistency of waste compositions between batches is a common thread of both the *Dockgrange* and *Beside* judgments, the mixing of Green List wastes is approached contrastingly and with opposing results. No doubt further judicial consideration is needed to settle this issue – and one does wonder how Carnwath J would have approached the *Dockgrange* case in the light of the European Court's finding. However, the ideal way to deal with this is to assign the fragmentiser wastes in

Dockgrange to one of the Lists[1]. Overall, it seems undesirable that waste whose composition causes it not to fit into any category of the Lists should instead be 'deconstructed' into its components and – on the basis of the latter – held to be contained in the Green List. Whilst there is degree of protection built into the List in the form of the caveat which states, inter alia, that any wastes which are contaminated should not be considered as being on the Green List[2], there may be practical reasons why this approach is not ideal. In particular, it appears to cause doubt and potential argument between regulator/regulated and – as was evident in *Dockgrange* – undesirable variance in regulatory approach between different member states.

1   This would need to be done by the OECD at first instance. The Lists in Regulation 259/93 cannot be changed unless agreement has been reached by that body: see Article 42(3).
2   See para 5.47.

The definition of recovery and disposal in Regulation 259/93

5.57   The procedures under Regulation 259/93 for international waste movements differ significantly depending on whether wastes are to pass to 'disposal' or to 'recovery'. There is a general requirement for member states to restrict international movements for disposal but to allow, in line with the requirements of the OECD Decision, wastes to pass to recovery facilities in the OECD. Given this very significant and contrasting approach, it is important to consider the meaning of the terms 'disposal' and 'recovery' under the Regulation.

5.58   Regulation 259/93 defines the words 'disposal' and 'recovery' as having the meaning contained in Article 1 of the Directive on Waste[1]. The latter Directive holds that 'disposal' embraces any of the operations shown in Annex IIA[2], with 'recovery' referring to the operations covered by Annex IIB[3]. These two Annexes are reproduced as Tables 2.2 and 2.3 in Chapter 2[4].

1   Council Directive of 15 July 1975 on Waste (75/442/EEC) (OJ L194/39 25.7.75) (as amended by Council Directive of 18 March 1991 amending Directive 75/442/EEC on Waste (91/156/EEC) (OJ L78/32 26.3.91) and Commission Decision of 24 May 1996 adapting Annexes IIA and IIB to Council Directive 75/442/EEC on Waste (96/350/EC) (OJ L135/32 6.6.96)), Articles 1(e) and (f).
2   Directive on Waste Article 1(e) as amended by Article 1 of Directive 91/156.
3   Directive on Waste (as amended), Article 1(f).
4   The Annexes were amended in 1996 to make them follow more closely the Basel Convention: see Commission Decision of 24 May 1996 adapting Annexes IIA and IIB to Council Directive 75/442/EEC on Waste (OJ L135/32 6.6.96). Note there are differences between them and the lists of disposal and recovery operations contained in the British Waste Management Licensing Regulations 1994 (SI 1994/1056, Sch 4, Pts III and IV).

5.59   From the text of the Directive on Waste, it is quite clear that a particular waste management facility should be readily classifiable into either Annex IIA or IIB. The Directive requires permits for Annex IIA activities and sets down minimum requirements for such documents[1]. Recovery installations, as defined in Annex IIB, are subject to significantly different provisions. They either need to possess a permit[2] or they can be exempted from the permit requirement and subject instead to a registration[3]. It is sufficient to note at this stage that the Directive envisages somewhat lesser requirements upon sites subject to a registration than those which apply in respect of permits. But what does appear clear is that a site should be identified as fitting within either one Annex or the other. In particular, it is not appropriate that a site should be seen as embraced by Annex IIA if it accepts one type of waste but Annex IIB if it accepts another. If nothing else, it would defeat the requirements on permits and registrations.

1 Council Directive of 15 July 1975 on Waste (75/442/EEC) (OJ L194/39 25.7.75) (as amended by
   Council Directive of 18 March 1991 amending Directive 75/442/EEC on Waste (91/156/EEC)
   (OJ L78/32 26.3.91) and Commission Decision of 24 May 1996 adapting Annexes IIA and IIB to
   Council Directive 75/442/EEC on Waste (96/350/EC) (OJ L135/32 6.6.96)), Article 9.
2 Council Directive of 15 July 1975 on Waste (75/442/EEC) (OJ L194/39 25.7.75) (as amended by
   Council Directive of 18 March 1991 amending Directive 75/442/EEC on Waste (91/156/EEC)
   (OJ L78/32 26.3.91)), Article 10.
3 Council Directive of 15 July 1975 on Waste (75/442/EEC) (OJ L194/39 25.7.75) (as amended by
   Council Directive of 18 March 1991 amending Directive 75/442/EEC on Waste (91/156/EEC)
   (OJ L78/32 26.3.91)), Article 11. See para 10.07ff.

5.60   The majority of waste management practices are clearly identifiable either as
recovery or disposal operations. However, recovery itself is a relative concept which
has the potential for abuse. In addition, a significant ambiguity arises in relation to
processes involving the combustion of waste and also those which involve intermediate holding points.

'Genuine' recovery

5.61   While it is necessary to identify a recovery operation as one which is listed in
Annex IIB of the Directive on Waste, it is equally important to the workings of the
transfrontier control system that bona fide recovery is to take place at the intended
destination of an international waste movement. Although this might be viewed as a
somewhat self-evident assertion, fraudulent or 'sham' recovery is by no means
unknown in the international waste trade. This is acknowledged in Regulation 259/93
itself, where a ground for a competent authority to object to a shipment is that the ratio
of the recoverable to non-recoverable waste is so low as not to be economically or
environmentally warranted[1].

1 Regulation 259/93, Article 7(4)(a). See para 5.154.

5.62   The UK's Export/Import Plan provides guidance for the Agency on such
considerations[1]. For a shipment to recovery to be allowable, the Agency must address
the following matters:

(a) The Agency must be familiar with the recovery technique being proposed, and the
     characteristics of the waste should be similar to materials routinely consigned to
     recovery processes in the UK[2].
(b) The nature of any contamination in the material to be recovered and the reasons
     for this contamination must be ascertained. The Agency must be satisfied that
     contamination arose as part of an industrial process and was not the result of
     blending with materials which would otherwise require disposal.
(c) The Agency must ascertain the ratio of the material to be recovered to the unre-
     coverable fraction remaining, which should be typical for UK recovery plants[3].
     This matter has significance given that (a) most of the residues will inevitably
     pass to landfill, and (b) that the UK's Plan has a strong presumption against the
     use of landfill as a destination for imported waste[4].
(d) The value of the material recovered must be known. A key test is whether the
     material recovered is of greater value than the disposal cost associated with the
     remaining residues[5].

In making such decisions, the Agency is required to balance both environmental and
economic considerations[6]. Due to the environmental nature of the legal base of the
Regulation[7], the Export/Import Plan holds that the overriding consideration is environmental benefit, particularly where the value of the material recovered is
marginal[8].

1   Export/Import Plan, para 6.4ff.
2   Export/Import Plan, para 6.14ff.
3   Export/Import Plan, para 6.17.
4   Export/Import Plan, para 6.17.
5   Export/Import Plan, para 6.7.
6   Export/Import Plan, para 6.6.
7   Article 130s of the EC Treaty (now Article 175): see also Case C-187/93: *European Parliament v EU Council* [1994] ECR I-2857.
8   Export/Import Plan, para 6.8.

5.63   For imports to Great Britain, the plan requires[1] that any recovery facility must be subject to a waste management licence or Part I authorisation under the EPA 1990. Although importation to a facility which is exempt from licensing under the Waste Management Licensing Regulations 1994[2] is conceivable, it is not generally permissible. Most of the exemptions stipulate that special wastes should not be handled[3]. Hence Amber and Red List shipments, which usually will involve special waste, will not be possible[4].

1   Export/Import Plan, para 6.12.
2   See Chapter 10.
3   See para 10.33.
4   Oddly, the plan also highlights as an additional criterion whether wastes will contain List I substances under the Groundwater Directive (80/68) (Export/Import Plan, para 6.13). However, raising such matters in this context seems a trifle anomalous given that waste management licences should not be granted unless they comply with that Directive: see SI 1994/1056, reg 15 and see para 8.70ff.

Incineration on land and use principally as a fuel

5.64   It is important to delineate between the disposal option of 'incineration' (D10 on the Directive on Waste's Annex IIA List: see Table 2.2 in Chapter 2) and the recovery category of 'Use principally as a fuel or other means to generate energy' (Category R1 on the Annex IIB list: see Table 2.3)[1]. For shipments to and from the UK, this matter is significantly clarified by the Export/Import Plan[2]. The main area of practical controversy involves the establishment of boundaries between the disposal option of incineration and the combustion of waste in cement manufacture. This is a highly significant issue for two reasons:

(a)   the plan places restrictions on wastes being imported for disposal, but lesser constraints on importation of wastes for recovery; and

(b)   the use of wastes as fuels in cement manufacture is relatively new and remains controversial with local communities neighbouring the facilities.

While it is conceivable that an incineration facility could be classed as a recovery process[3], the plan considers that this is dependent upon the 'primary purpose' of the facility[4]. Where the incinerator was 'purpose built' for the dual function of combustion of waste and energy recovery, the Export/Import Plan considers that the unit falls within the scope of waste recovery[5]. However, if the primary purpose of the facility is to destroy wastes, then it falls into the category of waste disposal operation. It would seem that virtually all of the UK's merchant hazardous waste incinerators fall within the latter category[6].

1   A further problem arises in relation to waste storage. This is discussed at para 5.66. In respect of incineration, see Fluck J 'The Term "Waste" in EU Law' (1994) *Eur Env LR* March 1994 79 at 83.
2   Export/Import Plan, Chapters 5 and 6.
3   Export/Import Plan, para 5.42A (Department of the Environment *United Kingdom Management Plan for Exports and Imports of Waste. Addendum 1*, (1996) HMSO, London).
4   Export/Import Plan, para 6.26.
5   Export/Import Plan, para 6.27.

6   However, this is disputed by certain incinerator operators (see *Ends Report* 271 'Incineration Firms Fight to Retain Hazardous Waste Imports', August 1997, pp 10–11).

5.65   In the case of combustion of waste in cement manufacture[1], such facilities are generally to be viewed as accepting wastes for burning as a fuel and hence fitting into the R1 category (see Table 2.3 in Chapter 2). But, as operators of such facilities are often paid to receive these wastes, the Export/Import Plan contains important decision criteria to determine whether a proposed shipment will take advantage of the combustion potential of the materials or involve waste disposal. These matters become particularly pertinent when the calorific value[2] of certain waste materials internationally consigned for 'use as fuel' may be low. Prior to the publication of the plan, an extreme example of this type of problem was a proposal to combust wastes containing organic phosphates in a cement kiln. Although this was proposed under the guise of recovery and 'use as a fuel', the materials were derived from the manufacture of fire retardants. To prevent such abuses, the Export/Import Plan contains two limits on the calorific value of wastes to be recovered by being burnt as a fuel[3]. For cement kilns, a limit of 21 MJ/kg is set down[4]. In the case of other uses of wastes as fuels, the limit is 11 MJ/kg[5].

1   See, for example, House of Commons Environment Committee (1995) *The Burning of Secondary Liquid Fuel in Cement Kilns*, Second Report 1994–95, HMSO, London.
2   Calorific value is a measure of the quantity of heat produced by the complete combustion of a given mass of substance. Examples include toluene: 43 MJ/kg; methanol: 24 MJ/kg; clinical waste (as 100% animal or human tissue): 2.3 MJ/kg; household waste: 7–10 MJ/kg. (Sources: Conway R A and Ross R D *Handbook of Industrial Waste Disposal* (1980) Van Nostrand Reinhold, New York; Royal Commission on Environmental Pollution (1993) *Seventeenth Report. Incineration of Waste*, Cm 2181, HMSO, London, Chapter 5.
3   In contrast, a dividing line of 30 MJ/kg is set for waste oils passing to incineration for the purposes of the Directive on the Incineration of Hazardous Waste (Directive 94/67, OJ L365/34 31.12.94). Plants which solely accept waste oils of a calorific value above that threshold and below a specified PCB or PCP level are exempt from the requirements of that Directive (Directive 94/67, Article 2).
4   Export/Import Plan, para 6.32.
5   Export/Import Plan, para 6.44.

Transactions to intermediate holding points and operations

5.66   From Table 2.3 of Chapter 2, it will be apparent that certain intermediate processing operations, such as blending and repackaging, along with storage, may be classified as disposal and recovery operations under both Regulation 259/93 and the Directive on Waste[1]. On the actual transfrontier shipment consignment note[2], for example, these options are listed as possible destinations for international waste shipments[3].

1   Regulation 259/93, Article 2(k) and (i); Article 1(e) and (f) and Annexes IIA and IIB of the Directive on Waste.
2   See para 5.69ff.
3   See the notes to Box 9 in Figure 5.1.

5.67   The UK's Export/Import Plan places significant restrictions upon proposals to move waste to intermediate holding points. In the case of a transfrontier movement to disposal which involves waste storage, the shipment should only be contemplated where the storage facility is located at the same site as the final disposal operation[1]. Storage prior to final disposal at a different location is not allowed[2]. In respect of off-site storage prior to recovery, the plan is somewhat more accommodating. As long as it is absolutely clear to the Agency that acceptable recovery is subsequently to take place, the shipment is allowable[3].

1   Export/Import Plan, para 5.88.
2   Export/Import Plan, para 5.89.
3   Export/Import Plan, para 6.60.

5.68   Transfrontier waste movements to repackaging or blending operations also are similarly dealt with by the plan, with no restrictions where such operations will occur at the site of allowable final disposal or recovery[1]. Where off-site blending is permissible, the plan takes the stance that waste which is blended for use as a fuel remains defined as waste until combustion[2]. Although blending is described as a disposal operation in Annex IIA of the Directive on Waste, it is not explicitly covered in Annex IIB. However, the Export/Import Plan considers that it is embraced by R11 – 'Use of Wastes obtained from any of the operations numbered R1 to R10' – and R13 – waste storage[3]. Only in special cases[4] does the Export/Import Plan allow importation to off-site blending or repackaging prior to disposal. By contrast, it is generally acceptable to import waste to the UK for the purposes of blending prior to authorised recovery. However, it is essential that the Agency is vigilant in respect of the justification for the blending operation. The plan holds that whilst contamination derived from normal industrial usage of solvents is acceptable when the waste is to pass to recovery[5], where contaminants are to be or have been added during blending in order to dispose of other contaminated waste, the waste is considered as passing to disposal, not recovery[6]. Hence objections should be raised by the Agency unless the proposal is in accordance with the other provisions on the Export/Import Plan for transactions to disposal facilities. In all cases where blending or repackaging prior to disposal is proposed, the consignment note must clearly set out the nature of the final disposal operation. In the case of recovery, the final destination does not necessarily need to be stipulated on the consignment note[7].

1   Export/Import Plan, para 5.79, 5.87.
2   Export/Import Plan, para 6.34.
3   Export/Import Plan, para 6.34 and 6.56.
4   Export/Import Plan, paras 5.67 and 5.77.
5   Export/Import Plan, para 6.42(a).
6   Export/Import Plan, para 6.43.
7   Export/Import Plan, para 6.35.

The Transfrontier Shipment Consignment Note

The Notification and Movement/Tracking Form

5.69   Regulation 259/93 requires the European Commission to draw up a consignment note for wastes passing internationally both to recovery and disposal, along with an appropriate certificate to be filled in once the waste had been actually recovered or disposed of[1]. This certificate is used to indicate that the waste has been disposed of or recovered 'in an environmentally sound manner'[2]. The term 'environmentally sound manner' is not defined.

1   Regulation 259/93, Article 42(1).
2   Regulation 259/93, Article 27(2).

5.70   A copy of the finalised consignment note is shown in Figure 5.1[1]. It can seen that it has two parts: the Notification Form and the Movement/Tracking Form. The Movement/Tracking Form contains the certificate which shows that recovery or disposal has taken place[2]. It is used for all shipments, except transactions involving Green List waste passing to recovery[3].

Figure 5.1

Transfrontier Waste Shipment Notification Form (first page)

EUROPEAN COMMUNITY (a)

TRANSFRONTIER MOVEMENT OF WASTE
Notification Form

COPY FOR:

1. Notifier/exporter (name, address) and registration N° where applicable:
Tel.: Fax:
Contact person:

2. Consignee (name, address) and registration N° where applicable:
Tel.: Fax:
Contact person:

3. Notification concerning (1): N° 000000
A (i) Single movement
(ii) General notification (multiple movements)
B (i) Disposal (no recovery)
(ii) Recovery operation
C* Pre-authorized recovery facility — yes / no
* (Only to be completed if B (ii) applies)

4. Total intended number of shipments

5. Total intended quantity (b) — Kg / liters

6. First shipment not before: — Departure of last shipment not after:

7. Intended carrier(s)* (name, address) and registration N° where applicable:
Tel.: Fax:
Contact person: * (attach list if more than one)

8. Disposal/recovery facility (name, location, address):
Tel.: Fax:
Registration N° where applicable:
and limit of validity:
Contact person:

9. Code N° of disposal/recovery operation (2):
and technology employed:*
* (attach details if necessary)

10. Waste generator/producer (name and address):
Tel.: Fax:
Contact person:
Process and location of generation:*
* (attach details if necessary)

11. Mode(s) of transport (2):

12. Packaging type(s) (2):

13. Name and chemical composition of the waste:

14. Physical characteristics (2):

15. Waste identification code
– in country of export/dispatch:
– in country of import/destination:
International Waste Identification Code (IWIC):
European Waste Catalogue (EWC):
Other (specify):

17. Y number:

18. H number (2):

16. OECD classification (1): amber — red — and number
other*
* (attach details)

19. UN identification number: — UN class (2):
and proper shipping name:

20. Concerned countries (2), code numbers of competent authorities (where applicable), and specific points of entry and exit:

Country of export/dispatch	Transit countries			Country of import/destination

21. Customs offices of entry and/or departure (European-Community):
Entry:
Departure:

22. Number of annexes attached

23. Notifier/exporter's declaration: I certify that the above information is complete and correct to the best of my knowledge. I also certify that legally-enforceable written contractual obligations have been entered into and that any applicable insurance or other financial guarantees are or shall be in force covering the transfrontier movement.
Name: Signature:
Date:

FOR USE BY COMPETENT AUTHORITIES

24. TO BE COMPLETED BY COMPETENT AUTHORITY OF COUNTRY OF IMPORT/DESTINATION
Notification received — Acknowledgment sent
on: — on:
Name of competent authority, stamp and/or signature

25. CONSENT* TO THE MOVEMENT PROVIDED BY COMPETENT AUTHORITY
of: (name of country) **on:**
Name of competent authority, stamp and/or signature
Consent expires on:
Specific conditions (1) — no — yes, **see block 26 overleaf**
* (not required for amber list wastes under OECD Decision)

SPECIMEN

Printed by Wilhelm Köhler, 32423 Minden (Germany)

(1) Enter X in appropriate box(es). (2) See codes on the reverse.
(a) Forms also used by OECD
(b) Indicate one of the two. Competent authorities are allowed to ask for the quantity in kg only.

Figure 5.1 – *contd*

Transfrontier Waste Shipment Notification Form (second page)

List of abbreviations used in the notification form

DISPOSAL / RECOVERY OPERATIONS (Block 9)

DISPOSAL (NO RECOVERY)

D1	Deposit into or onto land, (e. g., landfill, etc.)
D2	Land treatment, (e. g., biodegradation of liquid or sludgy discards in soils, etc.)
D3	Deep injection, (e. g., injection of pumpable discards into wells, salt domes or naturally occuring repositories, etc.)
D4	Surface impoundment, (e. g., placement of liquid or sludge discards into pits, ponds or lagoons, etc.)
D5	Specially engineered landfill, (e. g., placement into lined discrete cells which are capped and isolated from one another and the environment, etc.)
D6	Release into a water body except seas/oceans
D7	Release into seas/oceans including sea-bed insertion
D8	Biological treatment not specified elsewhere in this list which results in final compounds or mixtures which are discarded by means of any of the operations numbered D1 to D12
D9	Physico-chemical treatment not specified elsewhere in this list which results in final compounds or mixtures which are discarded by means of any of the operations numbered D1 to D12 (e. g., evaporation, drying, calcination, etc.)
D10	Incineration on land
D11	Incineration at sea
D12	Permanent storage, (e. g., emplacement of containers in a mine, etc.)
D13	Blending or mixing prior to submission to any of the operations numbered D1 to D12
D14	Repackaging prior to submission to any of the operations numbered D 1 to D12
D15	Storage pending any of the operations numbered D1 to D12

RECOVERY OPERATIONS

R1	Use as a fuel (other than in direct incineration) or other means to generate energy
R2	Solvent reclamation/regeneration
R3	Recycling/reclamation of organic substances which are not used as solvents
R4	Recycling/reclamation of metals and metal compounds
R5	Recycling/reclamation of other inorganic materials
R6	Regeneration of acids or bases
R7	Recovery of components used for pollution abatement
R8	Recovery of components from catalysts
R9	Used oil re-refining or other reuses of previously used oil
R10	Land treatment resulting in benefit to agriculture or ecological improvement
R11	Uses of residual materials obtained from any of the operations numbered R1 to R10
R12	Exchange of wastes for submission to any of the operations numbered R1 to R11
R13	Accumulation of material intended for any operation numbered R1 to R12

NOTE: Disposal ("D") operations are not relevant to the OECD Control System

---

MODES OF TRANSPORT (Block 11)

R = Road

T = Train/Rail

S = Sea

A = Air

W = Inland Waterways

PACKAGING TYPES (Block 12)

1. Drum
2. Wooden barrel
3. Jerrican
4. Box
5. Bag
6. Composite packaging
7. Pressure receptacle
8. Bulk
9. Other (specify)

PHYSICAL CHARACTERISTICS (Block 14)

1. Powdery/powder	5. Liquid
2. Solid	6. Gaseous
3. Viscous/paste	7. Other (specify)
4. Sludgy	

H NUMBER AND UN CLASS (Blocks 18 and 19)

UN Class	H number	Designation
1	H1	Explosive
3	H3	Inflammable liquids
4.1	H4.1	Inflammable solids
4.2	H4.2	Substances or wastes liable to spontaneous combustion
4.3	H4.3	Substances or wastes which, in contact with water, emit inflammable gases
5.1	H5.1	Oxidizing
5.2	H5.2	Organic peroxides
6.1	H6.1	Poisonous (acute)
6.2	H6.2	Infectious substances
8	H8	Corrosives
9	H10	Liberation of toxic gases in contact with air or water
9	H11	Toxic (delayed or chronic)
9	H12	Ecotoxic
9	H13	Capable, by any means, after disposal, of yielding another material, e. g., leachate, which possesses any of the characteristics listed above

---

OECD COUNTRY CODES (Block 20)

Australia :	AU	Finland :	FI	Ireland :	IE	Netherlands :	NL	Sweden :	SE
Austria :	AT	France :	FR	Italy :	IT	New Zealand :	NZ	Switzerland :	CH
Belgium :	BE	Germany :	DE	Japan :	JP	Norway :	NO	Turkey :	TR
Canada :	CA	Greece :	GR	Luxemburg :	LU	Portugal :	PT	United Kingdom :	GB
Denmark :	DK	Iceland :	IS	Mexico :	MX	Spain :	ES	United States :	US

For other countries ISO Standard 3166 abbreviations shall be used.

26. SPECIFIC CONDITIONS ON CONSENTING TO THE MOVEMENT

THE INTERNATIONAL WASTE IDENTIFICATION CODE (IWIC – BLOCK 15), THE OECD CLASSIFICATION LISTS OF WASTES DESTINED FOR RECOVERY OPERATIONS (AMBER, RED – BLOCK 16) AND THE CATEGORIES OF WASTES SUBJECT TO CONTROL (TABLE Y – BLOCK 17), AS WELL AS MORE DETAILED INSTRUCTIONS CAN BE FOUND IN A GUIDANCE MANUAL AVAILABLE FROM OECD.

Figure 5.1 – *contd*

Transfrontier Waste – Movement/Tracking Form (front page)

	TRANSFRONTIER MOVEMENT OF WASTE
EUROPEAN COMMUNITY(a)	**Movement/Tracking Form**

1. Notifier/exporter (name, address) and registration N° where applicable:
Tel.: Fax:
Contact person:

3. Corresponding to Notification N° **000000**

4. Serial number of shipment:

8. Disposal/recovery facility (name, location, address):
Tel.: Fax:
Registration N° where applicable:
and limit of validity:
Contact person:

2. Consignee (name, address) and registration N° where applicable:
Tel.: Fax:
Contact person:

9. Code N° of disposal/recovery operation (2):
and technology employed:

5. 1st Carrier (name, address):
Registration N°: (where applicable)
Tel.: Fax:

6. 2nd Carrier (3) (name, address):
Registration N°: (where applicable)
Tel.: Fax:

7. Last Carrier (name, address):
Registration N°: (where applicable)
Tel.: Fax:

10. Identity of means of transport:
Date of transfer:
Signature of Carrier's Representative:

11. Identity of means of transport:
Date of transfer:
Signature of Carrier's Representative:

12. Identity of means of transport:
Date of transfer:
Signature of Carrier's Representative:

13. Name and chemical composition of the waste:

14. Physical characteristics (2):

15. Waste identification code
– in country of export/dispatch:
– in country of import/destination:
International Waste Identification Code (IWIC):
European Waste Catalogue (EWC):
Other (specify):

17. Actual quantity(b)
Kg
liters

18. Number of packages:

16. OECD classification (1): amber
other* red and number: (attach details)

19. UN identification number:
and proper shipping name:
UN class (2):

20. Special handling instructions:

22. Notifier/exporter's declaration: I certify that the information in blocks 1 to 9 and 13 to 21 above is complete and correct to the best of my knowledge. I also certify that legally-enforceable written contractual obligations have been entered into, that any applicable insurance or other financial guarantees are in force covering the transfrontier movement, and that *

(i) all necessary consents have been received; **or**

(ii) the shipment is directed at a recovery facility within the OECD area and no objection has been received from any of the concerned countries within the 30 day tacit consent period; **or**

(iii) the shipment is directed at a recovery facility pre authorized for that type of waste within the OECD area; such an authorization has not been revoked, and no objection has been received from any of the concerned countries.

Name: Signature:

21. Actual date of shipment:

Date:
* (delete sentences not applicable)

TO BE COMPLETED BY CONSIGNEE / DISPOSAL / RECOVERY FACILITY

23. Shipment received by consignee on: (if not disposal/recovery facility)
accepted (1) rejected*
Quantity received(b): Kg liters
Date: Name: Signature:
* (immediately contact competent authorities)

24. Shipment received at disposal/recovery facility on:
accepted (1) rejected*
Quantity received(b): Kg liters
Date: Name: Signature:
Disposal/recovery to be completed by:
Method of disposal/recovery:
* (immediately contact competent authorities)

25. I certify that the disposal/recovery of the waste described above has been completed *
Date:
Name:
Signature:

* (not required by OECD control system)

(1) Enter X in appropriate box(es). (2) See codes on the reverse. (3) If more than three carriers, attach information as required by blocks 6 and 11.
(a) Forms also used by OECD
(b) Indicate one of the two. Competent authorities are allowed to ask for the quantity in kg only.

COPY FOR:

Figure 5.1 – *contd*

Transfrontier Waste – Movement/Tracking Form (back page)

List of abbreviations used in the movement/tracking form

DISPOSAL / RECOVERY OPERATIONS (Block 9)

DISPOSAL (NO RECOVERY)

D1	Deposit into or onto land, (e. g., landfill, etc.)
D2	Land treatment, (e. g., biodegradation of liquid or sludgy discards in soils, etc.)
D3	Deep injection, (e. g., injection of pumpable discards into wells, salt domes or naturally occuring repositories, etc.)
D4	Surface impoundment, (e. g., placement of liquid or sludge discards into pits, ponds or lagoons, etc.)
D5	Specially engineered landfill, (e. g., placement into lined discrete cells which are capped and isolated from one another and the environment, etc.)
D6	Release into a water body except seas/oceans
D7	Release into seas/oceans including sea-bed insertion
D8	Biological treatment not specified elsewhere in this list which results in final compounds or mixtures which are discarded by means of any of the operations numbered D1 to D12
D9	Physico-chemical treatment not specified elsewhere in this list which results in final compounds or mixtures which are discarded by means of any of the operations numbered D1 to D12 (e. g., evaporation, drying, calcination, etc.)
D10	Incineration on land
D11	Incineration at sea
D12	Permanent storage, (e. g., emplacement of containers in a mine, etc.)
D13	Blending or mixing prior to submission to any of the operations numbered D1 to D12
D14	Repackaging prior to submission to any of the operations numbered D 1 to D12
D15	Storage pending any of the operations numbered D1 to D12

NOTE: Disposal ("D") operations are not relevant to the OECD Control System

RECOVERY OPERATIONS

R1	Use as a fuel (other than in direct incineration) or other means to generate energy
R2	Solvent reclamation/regeneration
R3	Recycling/reclamation of organic substances which are not used as solvents
R4	Recycling/reclamation of metals and metal compounds
R5	Recycling/reclamation of other inorganic materials
R6	Regeneration of acids or bases
R7	Recovery of components used for pollution abatement
R8	Recovery of components from catalysts
R9	Used oil re-refining or other reuses of previously used oil
R10	Land treatment resulting in benefit to agriculture or ecological improvement
R11	Uses of residual materials obtained from any of the operations numbered R1 to R10
R12	Exchange of wastes for submission to any of the operations numbered R1 to R11
R13	Accumulation of material intended for any operation numbered R1 to R12

PHYSICAL CHARACTERISTICS (Block 14)

1. Powdery/powder
2. Solid
3. Viscous/paste
4. Sludgy
5. Liquid
6. Gaseous
7. Other (specify)

OECD COUNTRY CODES (Blocks 26–27–28)

Australia:	AU	Finland:	FI	Ireland:	IE	Netherlands:	NL	Sweden:	SE
Austria:	AT	France:	FR	Italy:	IT	New Zealand:	NZ	Switzerland:	CH
Belgium:	BE	Germany:	DE	Japan:	JP	Norway:	NO	Turkey:	TR
Canada:	CA	Greece:	GR	Luxemburg:	LU	Portugal:	PT	United Kingdom:	GB
Denmark:	DK	Iceland:	IS	Mexico:	MX	Spain:	ES	United States:	US

For other countries ISO Standard 3166 abbreviations shall be used.

FOR USE OF CUSTOMS OFFICES *				
26. COUNTRY OF EXPORT/DISPATCH OR (FOR EC) CUSTOMS OFFICE OF EXIT The waste described overleaf has left the country/Community on: Stamp: Signature:	**27.** STAMPS OF CUSTOM OFFICES OF TRANSIT COUNTRIES			
	Name of country (2):		Name of country (2):	
	Entry	Departure	Entry	Departure
28. COUNTRY OF IMPORT/DESTINATION The waste described overleaf has entered the country on: Stamp: Signature:	Name of country (2):		Name of country (2):	
	Entry	Departure	Entry	Departure

(2) See country codes above.   * Not required by OECD control system

THE INTERNATIONAL WASTE IDENTIFICATION CODE (IWIC – BLOCK 15), THE OECD CLASSIFICATION LISTS OF WASTES DESTINED FOR RECOVERY OPERATIONS (AMBER, RED – BLOCK 16) AND THE CATEGORIES OF WASTES SUBJECT TO CONTROL, AS WELL AS MORE DETAILED INSTRUCTIONS CAN BE FOUND IN A GUIDANCE MANUAL AVAILABLE FROM OECD.

1   Commission Decision 94/774, OJ L310/70 3.12.94.
2   Commission Decision 97/774, Article 1.
3   See para 5.141.

5.71   The consignment note is required to be printed on unforgeable white paper to the specification set down[1] in Commission Decision 94/774. Persons wishing to act as notifiers for the export of waste from the UK have to approach the respective Agency for the notification documents. For exports from another member state to the UK, the form is to be obtained from the competent authority of dispatch of the relevant member state. The same is true for exports from an OECD state to the UK. However, where exceptional circumstances warrant an import to the UK from outside the European Community and the OECD, the Agency covering the proposed consignee is responsible for issuing the consignment note[2].

1   Decision 94/774 OJ L310/70 3.12.94, Article 2.
2   See Circular 13/94, para 50.

5.72   The European Commission has been due to publish a guidance document on the completion of the note for some time. In the interim, regulatory bodies have been advised[1] to use the guidance originally drafted by the OECD[2].

1   See DOE Letter of 26 January 1995 to all waste regulation authorities.
2   OECD (1995) *The OECD Control System for Transfrontier Movements of Wastes destined for Recovery Operations. Guidance Manual* OECD Environment Monographs No 96, OECD, Paris.

5.73   Regulation 259/93 requires the language used on the consignment note[1] to be acceptable to the competent authority of despatch in the case of exports, and to the competent authority of destination in the case of imports[2]. Other competent authorities which are affected by the notification can demand a translation if necessary[3].

1   This includes the contract and financial guarantee: Regulation 259/93, Article 31(1).
2   Regulation 259/93, Article 31(1).
3   Regulation 259/93, Article 31(1).

5.74   Copies of the consignment note and any other relevant documentation are required by the Regulation 259/93 to be preserved for three years[1]. This applies to documentation held by competent authorities, the notifier and the consignee[2]. Circular 13/94 advises that the three-year period commences after the completion of the last shipment covered by the notification[3]. In respect of consignees, these time scales may be overridden by the Special Waste Regulations 1996[4], as Circular 6/96 states that such notes must be retained until the facility's licence is surrendered[5].

1   Regulation 259/93, Article 35.
2   Under the regulation itself, this does not apply to the carrier unless the carrier and the notifier are the same person. But this requirement is imposed separately by the Special Waste Regulations 1996 (SI 1996/972, reg 15(4)).
3   Circular 13/94, para 161.
4   See SI 1996/972, reg 13(4) and regs 15 and 16.
5   Circular 6/96, Annex A, para 19. However, there appears to be some doubt as to the statutory basis of this assertion – see para 4.171.

5.75   The Transfrontier Shipment of Waste Regulations 1994 contains a discretionary power for specified documentation to be forwarded to the Secretary of State[1]. This power was originally put into practice by Circular 13/94, with Her Majesty's Inspectorate of Pollution (HMIP) being nominated. Since the Agency's formation, this arrangement has been discontinued.

1   SI 1994/1137, reg 16 and see Annex 3 of Circular 13/94.

5.76 The Environmental Protection Act 1990 contains provisions on the duty of care which apply to transfrontier waste movements within British jurisdiction[1]. For any non-special waste moved[2], this includes the need to record specified details when waste is transferred between parties, as stipulated by the Environmental Protection (Duty of Care) Regulations 1991[3]. While most of the information required by the 1991 Regulations is satisfied by the consignment note prescribed for Regulation 259/93, the time and place of transfer and whether the waste is loose or in a container is not formally requested on the consignment note. In order to fully comply with the Duty of Care Regulations[4], it would seem that this information must be hand written on the note. While there is this slightly unsatisfactory overlap between the national and Community provisions in respect of the duty of care, the Special Waste Regulations 1996[5] make it clear that the majority[6] of the regulations, including the requirements for special waste notifications, do not apply to transfrontier waste shipments. However, the requirements on registers and retention of documents[7], site records[8] and restrictions on mixing categories of special waste[9] will apply to transfrontier waste movements where the material in question is special waste.

1 EPA 1990, s 34. See para 3.159.
2 The requirements in the Duty of Care Regulations 1991 in respect of the documentation of waste movements do not apply to waste embraced by the definition of special waste (see SI 1991/2839, reg 2(3), as amended by SI 1996/972, reg 23 and see para 3.10).
3 SI 1991/2839, reg 2.
4 SI 1991/2839, reg 2(2).
5 SI 1996/972 as amended by SI 1996/2019, reg 13(4).
6 SI 1996/972, regs 5–12: see Circular 13/94, para 19.
7 SI 1996/972, reg 15. But see para 5.74.
8 SI 1996/972, reg 16. See paras 4.162 and 4.171.
9 SI 1996/972, reg 17. See para 4.176.

Documenting waste shipments

5.77 Regulation 259/93 requires a copy of the standard consignment note to 'accompany' all transfrontier 'shipments'[1]. However, there is no definition of a 'shipment' of waste. For many shipments to the UK this does not matter as they involve articulated trailers which are not off-loaded at the port of entry.

1 Regulation 259/93, Articles 5(3), 8(3), 15(8), 20(7), 22 and 23(6): except movements involving Green List wastes for recovery.

5.78 However, the lack of definition of a 'shipment' becomes more problematic for instances where wastes are transported by sea in bulk and are unloaded at the port of entry onto a number of vehicles. When the waste shipment is at sea, it is accompanied by a copy of the consignment note. This appears to satisfy the requirements of the relevant Articles of the Regulation[1], which require that a copy or specimen of the note 'shall accompany each shipment'. But if the waste is off-loaded into a succession of vehicles at the port of entry, it is not clear if each lorry load should then be viewed as a 'shipment' and accompanied by individual copies of the note, or if the whole shipment to one site is covered by the one note. Unfortunately, Circular 13/94 does not help in this matter, somewhat muddying the waters by making a distinction between 'shipments' and 'consignments'[2]. In respect of consignments, the circular only provides two examples. Where a ship load of waste is to be divided at the port of entry into three parts for disposal at three different disposal sites, it is considered that there are three separate consignments. However, where a ship load is placed on a number of vehicles, and is destined for one site, there is one consignment[3]. The Basel Convention, however, appears to indicate that all individual loads are accompanied by the required movement document[4]. Given the regulatory necessity of having all loads accompanied by appropriate documentation, a competent authority can use its discretionary powers[5] to require that relevant documentation is held in the cabs of all vehicles when being transported by road, or that copies are attached to unaccompanied trailers for sea crossings.

1 Regulation 259/93, Articles 5(3), 8(3), 15(8), 20(7), 22 and 23(6).
2 Circular 13/94, paras 25 and 28.
3 Circular 13/94, para 28.
4 Basel Convention, Article 4(7)(c).
5 Regulation 258/93, Articles 4(2)(d), 7(3), 15(5), 20(5) and 23(4): see para 5.98.

Responsibilities for the consignment note procedures

5.79 Regulation 259/93 places the primary responsibility on the waste producer[1], as 'notifier' to deal with the consignment note procedure. Other parties, such as carriers or brokers[2], can only become notifiers 'where it is not possible' for the producer to take the responsibility[3]. An example of this might be where materials that have been illicitly deposited require disposal. In the infrequent case where those responsible for the waste are not known, the Regulation transfers responsibility for being the notifier to the 'holder'. This is the person who has legal control or possession of the waste[4]. However, although this hierarchy of responsibilities is set out in the Regulation, what often happens in practice is that waste management contractors act as notifiers. The latter practice is encouraged by the presence on the notification form of separate boxes for notifiers and waste producers. It also seems to be countenanced by the OECD Guidance Manual[5]. However, Circular 13/94 is clear that the hierarchical approach for notifiers should be followed and that persons other than the waste producer should act as notifiers only for mixed loads or where there are other genuine reasons why notification by the producer is not possible[6]. This matter is significant for the reason that, under Article 25 of Regulation 259/93, the notifier has primary responsibility for the waste, including its return. This is particularly the case prior to the waste's transfer to a consignee[7].

1 Defined as 'the person whose activities produced the waste (original producer)': Article 2(g)(i). Note that the definition of 'producer' is more restricted in Regulation 259/93 than in Article 1 of the amended Waste Directive (75/442), where this definition is expanded to include 'anyone who carries out pre-processing, mixing or other operations resulting in a change in the nature or composition of this waste'.
2 These bodies must be duly authorised (Regulation 259/93, Article 2(g)(ii)) either in the UK or in another member state. If they are not, they need to register with the respective Agency in the UK (see Circular 13/94, para 27). Registration of carriers and brokers is discussed in Chapter 6.
3 Regulation 259/93, Article 2(g).
4 Regulation 259/93, Article 2(g).
5 See the use of the term 'notifier or exporter' in para 3.1 of OECD (1995) *The OECD Control System for Transfrontier Movements of Wastes Destined for Recovery Operations. Guidance Manual*, OECD, Paris.
6 See Circular 13/94, para 26.
7 Note that the carrier does not bear any such responsibility under Article 25 of the Regulation, unless also acting as notifier or consignee.

Contracts

5.80 Generally, Regulation 259/93 requires that transboundary movements of waste are required to be the subject of formal contracts between notifier and consignee[1]. However, and rather oddly, no contract appears to be required by Regulation 259/93: where waste is imported into the European Community for disposal; where waste has been sent to the European Community from a non-OECD Country for recovery; and where the Community is a transit state. Circular 13/94 advises that these deficiencies should be made up and that contracts should always be required for these transactions[2].

1 Regulation 259/93, Articles 3(6), 6(6), 15(4), 17(4) and 17(7).
2 Circular 13/94, para 55.

5.81 There are, however, two exceptions to the need to use contracts:

(a) when wastes which involve substances on the Green List are moved[1];
(b) when waste is to be shipped internationally within the European Community between two arms of the same company.

In the latter case, the contract is substituted by a declaration 'undertaking to dispose of the waste'[2]. Regulation 259/93 does not elaborate further as to the nature of such a declaration. Given that no mention is made of this arrangement in respect of shipments outside the European Community, it is not clear what mechanism is applicable[3].

1 Reproduced as Annex II of Regulation 259/94 as amended by Commission Decision 94/721 of 21 October 1994 adapting, pursuant to Article 42(3), Annexes II, III and IV of Council Regulation (EEC) No 259/93 on the supervision and control of shipments within, into and out of the European Community (OJ L288/36 9.11.94). It should be noted that the country of destination must concur that the waste is to be viewed as being on the Green List. As is noted at para 5.137 a non-OECD country can re-designate substances onto the Amber and Red Lists if it wishes (Regulation 259/93, Article 17(3)).
2 Regulation 259/93, Article 3(6) and 6(6).
3 Circular 13/94 does not refer to arrangements considered appropriate in these circumstances.

5.82 Where contracts are required, the wording must include the obligation on the notifier to take the waste back if the shipment has not been completed as planned or has been made in violation of the Regulation[1]. The most obvious type of violation is that the composition of the waste was not as described on the notification. The contract must also require the consignee to complete and return the disposal or recovery certificate on the consignment note when the waste has been processed[2]. Where waste is to be sent to repackaging or blending prior to disposal or to recovery, the Export/Import Plan advises that the contract must embrace the final waste management process[3], but the certificate of disposal on the consignment note is to be completed when the repackaging or blending itself has taken place[4].

1 Regulation 259/93, Articles 3(6), 6(6), 15(4) and 17(7).
2 Regulation 259/93, Articles 3(6), 6(6) and 15(4): Regulation 259/93 is a little inconsistent on these requirements in relation to all of the permutations of waste movement. See para 5.80.
3 Export/Import Plan, paras 5.72, 5.83 and 6.39.
4 Export/Import Plan, para 5.73, 5.83 and 6.35.

5.83 Where wastes are shipped out of the European Community, the requirements of the Regulation cannot, by definition, have effect on the consignee. In these circumstances, the contract is to be seen as the primary mechanism by which the consignee is required to return the completed consignment note to the relevant competent authority. In addition, the contract must include a clause which requires that, should a financial guarantee[1] have been released by the consignee sending the competent authority an incorrect disposal certificate, the consignee should bear the costs of arranging the return of the waste and for its 'environmentally sound' disposal or recovery[2]. Circular 13/94 contains a check list of the obligations which 'must' be contained in all contracts[3].

1 See para 5.85.
2 Regulation 259/93, Articles 15(4) and 17(7).

3   See Circular 13/94, para 57 (note that it refers to some shipments which are now prohibited by the Export/Import Plan). Further guidance is set out in OECD (1995) *The OECD Control System for Transfrontier Movements of Wastes Destined for Recovery Operations. Guidance Manual*, OECD, Paris, Appendix E.

5.84   Under the Transfrontier Shipment of Waste Regulations 1994, a notifier who exports waste from the UK commits an offence if a contract has not been entered into[1]. Offences are discussed at para 5.185ff below. Although not explicitly required by the Regulation, Circular 13/94[2] suggests that the Agency should normally possess a copy of the contract. It may therefore require that the contract be attached to the notification.

1   SI 1994/1137, reg 12(7).
2   Circular 13/94, para 54.

Financial guarantees

5.85   Other than shipments of Green List wastes[1], Regulation 259/93 requires all international waste transactions be subject to a financial guarantee or equivalent insurance[2]. In practice, most shipments are subject to a financial guarantee. The requirement for a financial guarantee is above that which requires the existence of contracts between the notifier and consignee to ensure that the notifier takes the waste back. The purpose of the financial guarantee is to require funds to be available to the relevant competent authority when shipments get into difficulties. The funds must cover the cost of returning the waste as well as any other expenditure made in respect of the waste's subsequent disposal or recovery. Circular 13/94 emphasises[3] that the financial guarantee should not contain provision for third party liability or compensation. These matters should be addressed separately from Regulation 259/93, as they are covered by the requirements of national transport conventions and member states' own transportation legislation.

1   In the case of a non-OECD country, the country of destination must concur that the waste is to be viewed as being on the Green List. As is noted at para 5.137, a non-OECD country can re-designate substances onto the Amber and Red Lists if it wishes (Regulation 259/93, Article 17(3)).
2   Regulation 259/93, Article 27(1).
3   Circular 13/94, paras 21 and 66.

5.86   A financial guarantee is required to be returned or otherwise annulled when the signed certificate of disposal or recovery on the Movement/Tracking Form has been sent[1]. The Regulation does not specify the body – notifier, carrier or consignee – which should provide the guarantee.

1   Regulation 259/93, Article 27(2).

Approving the guarantee

5.87   For the UK, the financial guarantee is subject to its own process of advance approval as part of the system of prior informed consent. This approval mechanism is contained in the Transfrontier Shipment of Waste Regulations 1994[1] as, under Regulation 259/93, the inadequacy of the guarantee is not given as a grounds for objection of the shipment.

1   SI 1994/1137, reg 7.

5.88   Except in cases where the UK is acting as only a transit authority, the guarantee is approved when a certificate is issued by the Agency[1] of its adequacy[2]. The Transfrontier Shipment of Waste Regulations 1994[3] require that an application for the certificate is made to whichever Agency has jurisdiction over the notifier for an export, or the consignee for an import. If the Agency is satisfied that the financial guarantee is sufficient to cover of the cost of re-shipment to the notifier, and/or the wastes' alternative disposal or recovery, the certificate must be issued[4].

1　Where the UK is to be a transit country, the Secretary of State is the person who raises the certificate (SI 1994/1137, regs 4 and 7).
2　SI 1994/1137, regs 3(a) and 7.
3　SI 1994/1137, reg 7(2).
4　SI 1994/1137, reg 3 and Regulation 259/93, Article 27.

5.89　It should be noted that *all* financial guarantees require the approval of the Agency. This is the case even when the country of export or destination has already indicated that the guarantee is satisfactory. However, Circular 13/94[1] states that the requirements of other member states on the financial guarantee should be normally acceptable to the UK and that '[i]t would be unfortunate for conflicting and competing requirements in different states to result in a demand for a single shipment to be covered by more than one guarantee'. As the circular points out, there are no mechanisms in Regulation 259/93 for mediating between member states on disputes about the acceptable nature of the guarantee.

1　Circular 13/94, para 76.

5.90　Of particular importance to the correct operation of the financial guarantee is its wording. It should permit any affected competent authorities to have ready access to funds where a waste shipment has entered into difficulties. Circular 13/94 declines to prescribe the nature of the guarantee, listing instead a series of options[1]. Industry operated funds have not generally been favoured by notifiers of transfrontier waste shipments. In practice, most guarantees involve access to banking facilities.

1　Circular 13/94, para 77.

5.91　The size of the guarantee will, of course, vary depending on the nature and form of the waste, transportation costs and the price of alternative disposal or recovery. It will also depend on the number of shipments to be covered[1]. Circular 13/94 sets down a simple formula to illustrate a method of arriving at the level of the financial guarantee[2]:

Size of Guarantee (£) = A1 + A2 + B + C

Where:

A1　= the cost of transport
A2　= the transport cost for the waste's return
B　　= the estimated cost of alternative disposal or recovery
C　　= handling and administrative costs (not included above).

The circular notes that the worst case scenario approach to setting the level of the guarantee provides the maximum level of protection. However, the circular also suggests that 'competent authorities should take a realistic view of the relative risks involved in any particular case . . .'[3].

1　Circular 13/94 recommends that, for multiple shipments, the guarantee either provides funds to cover all of them or that the number of shipments in transit are limited. This can be done by laying down a condition of transport to restrict the number of shipments which can be in transit at any one time. The number of shipments permissible can be set at the level of guarantee proposed (see Circular 13/94, para 85). Transport conditions are discussed at para 5.98.
2　Circular 13/94, para 83.
3　Circular 13/94, para 84.

5.92 Circular 13/94 recommends that a copy of the certificate is attached to the relevant part of the consignment note[1]. Under the Transfrontier Shipment of Waste Regulations 1994, the Agency has defined statutory time periods in which to issue the certificate approving the financial guarantee[2]. These vary according to the type of shipment, its source and intended destination and whether disposal or recovery is proposed. The time periods commence when the application for a certificate is made and, unless an application and the notification are made together, they are independent of any time limit set down for the notification itself[3]. Indeed, the circular suggests that an application can be made for a certificate after the shipment has been otherwise authorised[4].

1 Circular 13/94, para 70.
2 SI 1994/1137, reg 7(4).
3 See Circular 13/94, para 69.
4 Circular 13/94, para 70: however, as noted above, the shipment cannot be moved until the certificate is granted.

5.93 The relevant time periods for issuing the certificate are as follows[1]:

(a) 20 days where the UK is a transit country for waste to pass between member states for disposal in the European Community;
(b) 30 days where the waste stems from a member state and is to be disposed of in the UK;
(c) 30 days where the waste is to pass to recovery in the UK or in another member state;
(d) 60 days where the waste is to be imported into the European Community for disposal and the UK is solely a transit country;
(e) 70 days where the waste is to be imported from outside the European Community into the UK for disposal;
(f) 60 days where the waste is passing through the European Community, with the UK as the member state of export;
(g) 20 days where the waste is passing through the European Community and the UK is solely a transit state.

1 SI 1994/1137, reg 7(4): certain combinations of shipment have been omitted where they are prevented by the Export/Import Plan.

5.94 It should be emphasised that the financial guarantee would only be drawn down where all other methods of returning the shipment or providing alternative recovery or disposal have failed. Normally, the contract between the parties should ensure that any problems with the shipment are appropriately rectified.

Releasing the guarantee

5.95 Once the transfrontier movement is complete, the financial guarantee is to be released when the waste has been disposed of or recovered in an 'environmentally sound manner'[1]. Environmentally sound disposal or recovery is indicated by the consignee returning the Movement/Tracking Form with the certificate of disposal or recovery completed.

1 Regulation 259/93, Article 27: for multiple loads (see para 5.105), the financial guarantee is released when the last load is satisfactorily dealt with.

5.96 'Environmentally sound' disposal or recovery is clearly a rather nebulous concept. It is not defined further in Regulation 259/93 nor in the Transfrontier Shipment of Waste Regulations 1994. According to Circular 13/94[1], for wastes sent to the

UK the 'fundamental requirement' of 'environmentally sound management' is the fact that the site is licensed or authorised to deal with the waste in question[2]. In essence, if the UK destination was not environmentally sound, it would not be licensed by the Agency in the first place.

1   Circular 13/94, para 31.
2   See also the Export/Import Plan, especially Chapters 5 and 6.

5.97   Article 35 of Regulation 259/93 requires that the documentation making up the financial guarantee should be kept for a period of at least three years after the shipment.

Conditions of transport

5.98   Regulation 259/93 allows competent authorities discretion to impose conditions on the transport of waste passing through their area of jurisdiction[1]. They must not, however, be more stringent than conditions applying to internal waste movements. Any conditions must be entered in the appropriate place on the consignment note[2].

1   Regulation 259/93, Articles 4(2)(d), 7(3), 15(5), 20(5) and 23(4).
2   Circular 13/94 notes that the Regulation is inconsistent in respect of the requirement to enter
    conditions of transport on the consignment note (see note 20 to para 87 of the circular). However, it is
    recommended that all conditions are written onto the note.

5.99   These conditions can require that only a specified proportion of a large, multiple shipment is in transit at any one time[1]. This requirement can also be contained in the wording of the financial guarantee. It may also be possible to specify that a copy of the consignment note travels with every vehicle[2]. Any transport conditions are directly enforceable in UK law. A breach of any transport conditions is an offence under the Transfrontier Shipment of Waste Regulations 1994[3].

1   See Circular 13/94, para 85.
2   As discussed earlier, the Regulation is less than clear on this point.
3   SI 1994/1137, reg 12(2): offences are discussed at para 5.185ff below.

Charges and cost recovery

5.100   Regulation 259/93 allows competent authorities to make financial charges against the notifier or, as appropriate, the consignee for the costs of operating the transfrontier control system[1]. Cost recovery applies to both routine administration costs, including expenditure incurred on analysis and inspections, and any costs incurred in obtaining a shipment's return and arranging alternative disposal or recovery.

1   Regulation 259/93, Article 33.

5.101   Circular 13/94 encourages charges to be made for those functions which are based on 'full cost recovery'[1]. This is therefore unique to UK waste regulation, as the level of other charges, such as for waste management licences, carrier and broker registrations, etc, are subject to governmental approval[2]. Given that 'supervisory costs and the costs of analysis and inspections' may vary widely[3], the circular cautions regulatory bodies against adopting a flat rate fee. But how they charge is left entirely to their discretion. The circular does, however, advise that partial refunds are to be provided and that the charges should be modified where a shipment has been refused consent[4]. Where payment is due and has not been made, the circular[5] allows the Agency to refuse to deal with further notifications. However, it also states that unpaid administration costs cannot be recovered from any financial guarantee[6].

1   Circular 13/94, para 166.
2   See paras 6.52 and 9.142ff.
3   Circular 13/94, para 168.
4   Circular 13/94, para 169.
5   Circular 13/94, para 170.
6   Circular 13/94, para 170.

5.102 Besides day-to-day administration charges, Regulation 259/93 allows the recovery of regulatory costs incurred when a shipment has run into difficulties. As noted above, the contract between notifier and consignee should cause its return. Where this cannot occur, all costs arising from the return of the waste, and/or its environmentally sound disposal or recovery, can be charged against the notifier[1]. The first method of recouping these costs will be against the financial guarantee. Where this is not possible, Circular 13/94 indicates that the costs can be recovered separately from the notifier[2]. Only where this turns out to be impracticable should the notifier's member state be requested to provide recompense.

1   Regulation 259/93, Article 33(2) and (4).
2   Circular 13/94, para 171.

5.103 The only time when the notifier is not held responsible for paying for the waste's alternative disposal or recovery is where the consignee has been the cause of the illegal traffic[1]. Again, public costs can be recouped for disposal or recovery from the consignee in these circumstances.

1   Regulation 259/93, Article 33(2); 'illegal traffic' is defined in Article 26: see para 5.188.

Appeals

5.104 It should be appreciated that, unlike the earlier Transfrontier Shipment of Hazardous Waste Regulations 1988[1], there are no appeal provisions to the Secretary of State against the Agency's decision. This applies to objections to a shipment, transport conditions or in relation to the notices requiring the waste's return[2].

1   SI 1988/1562.
2   See para 12.128.

Multiple shipments

5.105 Regulation 259/93 allows for a general notification procedure to be used where waste 'having the same physical or chemical characteristics is shipped periodically to the same consignee following the same route'[1]. All the competent authorities affected by the shipment need to agree in advance to the use of the general notification procedure[2]. A single notification, using one consignment note, can be used[3] to enact the process of prior informed consent for the multiple load[4]. No further prenotification is necessary once the shipment is agreed. However, the general notification procedure can only cover shipments for a period of a year[5].

1   Regulation 259/93, Article 28(1).
2   See Regulation 259/93, Article 28(3).
3   Regulation 259/93, Article 28(4).
4   Regulation 259/93, Article 28(2).
5   Regulation 259/93, Article 28(2)

5.106 After consent has been given for the movement of the multiple shipment, the procedures for the dispatch of the individual loads are essentially similar to those applied to single shipments[1]. Copies of the consignment note are sent off to the affected competent authorities three days prior to the shipment being moved. Each shipment is then accompanied by the consignment note.

1   See paras 5.125ff and 5.151ff.

5.107   The general notification procedure cannot be used if, before the waste is to be moved, a different route is chosen which passes through an additional competent authority[1]. Similarly, if the composition of the waste changes or if conditions imposed by the competent authorities are not respected, the regulation requires that the general notification arrangement 'shall' be cancelled by the competent authorities[2]. This decision must be communicated to the other competent authorities affected by the shipment.

1   Regulation 259/93, Article 28(1).
2   Regulation 259/93, Article 28(3).

Powers for authorities to transmit documents

5.108   The notifier usually transmits the notification by sending the consignment note to the relevant competent authorities[1]. However, Regulation 259/93 allows a competent authority of dispatch to elect to transmit the consignment note itself and to ensure that copies are sent to the other affected competent authorities[2].

1   See paras 5.125ff and 5.151ff.
2   Regulation 259/93, Articles 3(8), 6(8) and 15(11): note there is a significant misprint in Article 15(11) as published in the Official Journal. This is corrected in the version of Regulation 259/93 in Annex 1 of Circular 13/94.

5.109   This arrangement has two advantages. It can be used as a way of ensuring that the notification is done correctly. In addition, the competent authority of dispatch gains an immediate power of veto on shipments to disposal[1]. Should a proposed shipment be vetoed, there is no need to consult any of the other competent authorities about the shipment. The veto can only be undertaken on the basis of the reasons allowed in Regulation 259/93[2]. It should be emphasised that this power of veto is not available for shipments passing to recovery.

1   Regulation 259/93, Articles 3(8) and 15(11).
2   See para 5.129.

5.110   When the Agency wishes to act on behalf of a UK notifier, these requirements are substantiated by the Transfrontier Shipment of Waste Regulations 1994[1]. The Agency must advertise its intention to utilise this power[2]. This is done by a published notice which must describe the notifications to which the decision applies[3]. The Agency therefore has discretion to specify to which notifications the powers should have application.

1   SI 1994/1137, reg 6 as amended by SI 1996/593, reg 11(2).
2   SI 1994/1137, reg 6(1).
3   SI 1994/1137, reg 6(2).

5.111   In the case of the Environment Agency, the notice must be published in the London Gazette[1]. For the Scottish Environment Protection Agency, the Edinburgh Gazette should be utilised[2]. Both Agencies must also publicise the decision 'in such other manner as the [waste regulation] authority consider [sic] appropriate for bringing the matters to which it relates to the attention of persons likely to be affected by them'[3]. The decision comes into effect two weeks after the final notice was published[4]. It can be cancelled by advertising its withdrawal, and cancellation comes into effect two weeks later[5].

1 SI 1994/1137, reg 6(7)(a) as amended by SI 1996/593, reg 11(2).
2 SI 1994/1137, reg 6(7)(b) as amended by SI 1996/593, reg 11(2): for Northern Ireland, publication
   must be in the Belfast Gazette and three local papers (reg 6(7)(c)).
3 SI 1994/1137, reg 6(7) as amended by SI 1996/593, reg 11(2).
4 SI 1994/1137, reg 6(2).
5 SI 1994/1137, reg 6(6).

5.112 Once the decision is effected, the notifier is required to send the entire consignment note to the relevant Agency. No other competent authority needs to be contacted at this stage[1]. If the notification relates to wastes passing internationally for disposal, the Agency can object to it immediately[2]. Although Regulation 259/93 gives a variety of grounds[3], such a proposal will contravene the Export/Import Plan[4]. This power of veto means that there is no need for the Agency to get in touch with the other competent authorities or the consignee. As noted, the power of veto is only to be exercised in respect of consignments of waste to disposal, not to recovery facilities.

1 SI 1994/1137, reg 6(3).
2 SI 1994/1137, reg 6(5).
3 Regulation 259/93, Article 4(3): see paras 5.38ff and 5.129. This Article pertains only to movements
   of waste between member states for disposal. However, the same grounds are applicable for exports
   of waste from the Community for disposal in EFTA states (see Regulation 259/93, Article 15(3)).
4 Export/Import Plan, para 3.1.

5.113 For proposals with respect of recovery, the Agency must forward the consignment note, within three working days of its receipt, to the competent authority of destination, with copies to transit authorities and to the consignee[1]. In practice, this allows the Agency very little time to consider the notification[2]. Once the consignment note has been transmitted, the more usual notification procedures set down in Regulation 259/93 then continue as normal[3].

1 SI 1994/1137, reg 6(4).
2 It can subsequently object to it. But, as Circular 13/94 (para 62) points out, this would lose an
   administrative advantage gained from this more streamlined system.
3 See para 5.152ff below.

Movements of waste to and from Gibraltar, the Isle of Man, the Channel Islands, etc

5.114 States such as Gibraltar, the Channel Islands and the Isle of Man are either Dependent Territories[1] or Crown Dependencies[2] of the UK. With the exception of Gibraltar, all of these, along with the two British Sovereign Bases in Cyprus, fall within the definition of 'third countries'[3] under Regulation 259/93 in respect of international waste transactions for disposal. They only become encompassed by the UK's ratification of the Basel Convention when they have their own legislation in place that fulfils the Convention's requirements[4]. The result is that, at present, shipments to or from these countries are to be subject to the requirements of the Regulation in relation to non-Basel Convention Parties[5]. Shipments between Gibraltar and the UK are viewed as internal movements and not subject to Regulation 259/93 at all[6]. Hence such shipments are to be documented by, as the case may be, duty of care transfer notes[7] or by consignment notes under the Special Waste Regulations 1996[8]. The Channel Islands, Gibraltar and Bermuda are OECD countries and hence shipments in respect of recovery are allowable[9]. According to the Export/Import Plan[10], the Dependent Territories have been invited to be included within the UK's ratification of the Basel Convention. But the decision to take up this option rests with the particular government concerned.

1 The full list of Dependent Territories covers Anguilla, Bermuda, British Antarctic Territory, British Indian Ocean, Cayman Islands, Falkland Islands, Gibraltar, Montserrat, Pitcairn, Henderson, Ducie, Oeno Islands, St Helena, St Helena Dependencies, South Georgia and South Sandwich Islands and Turks and Caicos Islands.
2 Channel Islands and Isle of Man. It is understood that bilateral agreements under the Basel Convention have been established between the UK and the Isle of Man (entered into force 7/8/96) and the states of Jersey (20/5/97).
3 See Circular 13/94, para 96.
4 Circular 13/94, para 96.
5 See paras 5.115 and 5.118.
6 Export/Import Plan, para 1.14.
7 1990 Act, s 34 and SI 1991/2839: see Chapter 3.
8 SI 1996/972 as amended SI 1996/2019: see Chapter 4.
9 Export/Import Plan, para 2.20.
10 Export Import Plan, para 2.21.

INTERNATIONAL MOVEMENTS OF WASTES FOR DISPOSAL[1]

General principles

5.115   At Community level, proposals involving the export of waste out of Europe for disposal elsewhere are subject to a general prohibition in Regulation 259/93[2]. The only exception to this prohibition[3] concerns countries which are members of the European Free Trade Association (EFTA) and which are Basel Convention parties[4]. However, even in respect of these EFTA countries, the ban in Regulation 259/93 on shipments[5] applies where the country prohibits waste imports or where the competent authority of dispatch considers that the waste will not be soundly managed on arrival at an EFTA destination.

1 This section will describe the procedures for the principal type of waste movements affecting the UK. For brevity, transit movements through the European Community and transit movements between member states via third states are excluded. The provisions of Regulation 259/93 in respect of these movements are, however, summarised in Circular 13/94: see for example paras 113, 123, 124.
2 Regulation 259/93, Article 14(1) and, in the case of African, Caribbean and Pacific (ACP) Countries, this is repeated by Article 18.
3 Regulation 259/93, Article 14(1).
4 Norway, Switzerland, Iceland and Liechtenstein.
5 Regulation 259/93, Article 14(2).

5.116   There is also a presumption in Regulation 259/93 against an extensive trade in wastes for disposal[1] between member states. Member states are given the obligation to 'prohibit generally or partially or to object systematically' to shipments of waste[2] and to arrange for the disposal of waste as close to the site of generation as is possible. Overall, the intention is that member states should become self-sufficient in their waste disposal infrastructure[3]: the so-called 'proximity proposal'.

1 Disposal is defined in Annex IIA of Directive 75/442: see para 5.37ff above and Table 2.2 in Chapter 2.
2 Regulation 259/93, Article 4(3)(a)(i).
3 Regulation 259/93, Article 4(3)(a)(i).

5.117   There is one derogation to the general presumption against extensive inter-member state waste trade involving disposal. Movements between member states are allowed for countries where the quantity of *hazardous waste*[1] produced is too small to warrant an indigenous disposal facility. Disputes between member states as to the level of such derogations have to be arbitrated. As a last resort, these may be settled by the

Commission[2], being resolved by the Committee of Experts set up under Article 18 of the amended Directive on Waste[3]. It appears that qualified majority voting applies to such decisions.

1 As defined by Directive 91/689 – see para 4.08: no such derogations apply to non-hazardous wastes.
2 Regulation 259/93, Article 4(3)(a)(iii).
3 Council Directive of 15 July 1975 on Waste (75/442/EEC) (OJ L194/39 25.7.75) (as amended by
   Council Directive of 18 March 1991 amending Directive 75/442/EEC on Waste (91/156/EEC)
   (OJ L78/32 26.3.91) and Commission Decision of 24 May 1996 adapting Annexes IIA and IIB to
   Council Directive 75/442/EEC on Waste (96/350/EC) (OJ L135/32 6.6.96)).

5.118 Under Regulation 259/93, imports of waste into the European Community for disposal are generally prohibited unless they are from: (a) an EFTA Country who is also a Basel Convention party; (b) other countries who are Basel Convention parties; or (c) a country with which the European Community, or the Community in conjunction with its member states, has concluded bilateral agreements under Article 11 of the Basel Convention, or where individual member states had made agreements prior to the regulation coming into force[1].

1 Regulation 259/93, Article 19(1).

5.119 In exceptional cases, Regulation 259/93 allows member states to make further bilateral agreements covering importation into the Community for the disposal of 'specific' waste 'where such waste will not be managed in an environmentally sound manner in the country of dispatch'[1]. Countries wishing to send waste to member states in these circumstances must set out the reasons why they themselves cannot handle the waste[2] and forward such reasons to the relevant competent authority. For non-EFTA countries, this request is quite independent of the actual notification process[3]. It would seem that this is a function undertaken by the country at government level[4], not by the notifier of the proposed shipment. Circular 13/94 emphasises that bilateral agreements can only be made via diplomatic channels[5]. Should the Agency receive a notification from such a state for disposal in the UK, the Secretary of State should be contacted for advice.

1 Regulation 259/93, Article 19(2).
2 Regulation 259/93, Article 19(3).
3 Regulation 259/93, Article 19(3).
4 See the reference to 'countries' in Article 19(3).
5 Circular 13/94, para 98: see also Export/Import Plan, para 5.13.

5.120 Besides the provisions of Regulation 259/93, certain wastes are subject to individual prohibition under other legislation. For example, any amphibole asbestos[1] is prevented from being imported into the UK by the Asbestos (Prohibitions) Regulations 1992[2]. The Animal Products and Poultry Products Order 1980[3], which is administered by the Ministry of Agriculture, also has relevance. It was used in 1988 to prevent domestic waste being imported into the UK from the Netherlands and the US[4]. Section 141[5] of the EPA 1990 allows the Secretary of State to prohibit the import or export of particular types of waste by regulations.

1 Including crocidolite (blue asbestos), amosite (brown asbestos), fibrous actinolite, fibrous
   anthophyllite, fibrous tremolite and any mixture containing these minerals (SI 1992/3067, reg 2(1)).
2 SI 1992/3067, reg 3.
3 SI 1980/14, as amended by SI 1982/948 and SI 1994/2920.
4 *Ends Report* 160 'Domestic Waste Import Plan falls Foul of Animal Health Controls' May 1988.
5 EPA 1990, s 141, as amended by the Environment Act 1995, Sch 22, para 90: see also the EPA 1990,
   s 140, as amended by SI 1999/1108, reg 2.

5.121 The UK's policy in relation to shipments for disposal was expressed originally in the 1990 Environment White Paper[1] and latterly in the Export/Import Plan[2]. The plan sets out the UK's position on waste movements to other member states[3]: 'It is the Government's policy . . . that no waste should be exported from the UK for disposal to *any* other country'. This policy primarily stems from the comprehensive nature of the UK's own waste management infrastructure.

1 *This Common Inheritance: Britain's Environment Strategy* 1990, HMSO, London.
2 Department of the Environment (1996) *United Kingdom Waste Management Plan For Exports and Imports of Waste*, HMSO, London.
3 Export/Import Plan, para 3.1.

5.122 In respect of imports of waste for disposal in the UK, the plan is somewhat more accommodating. However, the overall presumption is that imports of waste for disposal should only occur in exceptional circumstances[1]. It is up to the particular country to make a case; this is not to be done by the notifier[2]. The merits of each case will generally[3] be judged on the grounds that environmentally acceptable alternative disposal could not be reasonably acquired by the country[4], or that an emergency has arisen which has affected the availability of the existing waste management infrastructure[5]. In any case, imports are generally banned in respect of:

(a) landfill[6];
(b) sea disposal[7] and sea incineration[8];
(c) biological, chemical or physical treatment with the subsequent landfill of the residues in the UK[9];
(d) permanent storage[10];
(e) blending, mixing[11] and repackaging[12], excepting where this is done prior to permissible final disposal taking place;
(f) storage[13], unless part of another permissible disposal operation.

1 Export/Import Plan, para 5.1.
2 Export/Import Plan, para 5.24.
3 See Chapter 5 of the Export/Import Plan for specific details.
4 See Export/Import Plan, para 5.8ff.
5 See Export/Import Plan, para 5.51ff.
6 Items D1 and D5 on Table 2.2 in Chapter 2, but also including D2, D3 and D4: Export/Import Plan, para 5.32.
7 Items D6 and D7 on Table 2.2 in Chapter 2: Export/Import Plan, para 5.34.
8 Item D11 on Table 2.2 in Chapter 2: Export/Import Plan, para 5.69.
9 Items D8 and D9 on Table 2.2 in Chapter 2; Export/Import Plan, para 5.37ff.
10 Item D12 on Table 2.2 in Chapter 2: Export/Import Plan, para 5.70.
11 Item D13 on Table 2.2 in Chapter 2: Export/Import Plan, para 5.71ff.
12 Item D14 on Table 2.2 in Chapter 2: Export/Import Plan, para 5.80ff.
13 Item D15 on Table 2.2 in Chapter 2: Export/Import Plan, para 5.88ff.

5.123 The main exception to the general prohibition set out above is in respect of high temperature incineration[1]. The Export/Import Plan makes the distinction between incineration and combustion for energy recovery purposes[2]. It also delineates between 'high temperature incineration'[3] and 'other types of incineration on land'[4]. High temperature incineration is defined as incineration at facilities whose sole purpose is to provide a commercial service for destroying the multiplicity of chemical wastes[5]. Significantly, clinical waste and municipal waste combustion facilities are stated as falling within the plan's concept of 'other types of incineration on land'.

1 Export/Import Plan, para 5.42ff.
2 Export/Import Plan, para 6.26ff: see para 5.64.
3 Export/Import Plan (as amended by Department of the Environment *United Kingdom Management Plan for Exports and Imports of Waste. Addendum 1*, (1996) HMSO, London), para 5.43A.

4   Export/Import Plan (as amended), para 5.67A and 5.68A.
5   Export/Import Plan (as amended), para 5.43A.

5.124   Although there is a general ban on imports from other Community states to other types of incineration, there have been two significant exceptions for high temperature incineration[1]:

(a)   Ireland and Portugal. Both member states are considered to produce too little hazardous waste to justify investment in incineration infrastructure. Hence imports from these countries to UK high temperature incinerators can continue indefinitely[2].

(b)   Other member states to June 1999. In this case, importation for high temperature incineration in the UK was allowable on a reducing basis up to 1999. However, it was subject to a strict quota, which for the year commencing June 1998 is 4700 tonnes[3]. All such transactions had to be completed by 31 May 1999[4].

Otherwise, all imports for incineration from member states or OECD countries outside the European Community are banned, except in cases of emergency[5]. Other states must make a duly motivated request to the competent authority[6].

1   Export/Import Plan, para 5.55.
2   Export/Import Plan, para 5.56.
3   Export/Import Plan, para 5.61.
4   Export/Import Plan, para 1.6.
5   Export/Import Plan, para 5.62 and 5.64.
6   Export/Import Plan, para 5.66. For example, in September 1998 the Agency acceded to a request from South Africa to allow 2,800 tonnes of PCB and pesticide containing wastes to be accepted for incineration in Britain over three years (see Environment Agency Press Release 116/98).

Notification procedures for movements of waste within the European Community for disposal in the UK[1]

5.125   The following paragraphs describe the normal procedures for single notifications which are transmitted by the notifier[2]. The locus of control of individual waste movements between member states for disposal is, as noted, the consignment note[3]. For an import into the UK[4], the note is issued to the notifier by the notifier's competent authority[5], not by the Agency. Alongside the consignment note, all shipments should be covered by a contract[6]. The financial guarantee must be arranged and certified prior to the waste's despatch[7].

1   See Circular 13/94, para 104: for brevity reasons, the procedures which apply in exceptional cases in respect of shipments to the UK from outside the Community are omitted below: see Regulation 259/93, Article 19ff and Circular 13/94, para 120.
2   Multiple load provisions are set down in Regulation 259/93, Article 28: see para 5.105.
3   Using the notification document contained in Commission Decision 94/774 (OJ L310/70 3.12.94).
4   Given the presumption in the Export/Import Plan against exports from the UK for disposal, the relevant procedures in Regulation 259/93 for enacting other types of shipment will not be summarised here.
5   Regulation 259/93, Article 3(3).
6   Regulation 259/93, Article 3(6): see para 5.80.
7   Regulation 259/93, Article 27 and SI 1994/1137, reg 7: see para 5.85.

5.126   When waste is to be moved to the UK, whichever Agency is responsible for the consignee is notified by the receipt of the consignment note[1]. Copies of the note are sent at the same time to the intended disposal site, as well as to the competent authorities covering the notifier and any transit states. Once the notification has been received, the Agency covering the consignee must acknowledge[2] its receipt to the notifier and to the other competent authorities within three working days[3].

1 Regulation 259/93, Article 3(1).
2 Under Regulation 259/93 'acknowledgement' simply means acknowledging receipt of the notification. By contrast, under the earlier legislation – Directive 84/631 – the term meant that the shipment had been authorised.
3 Regulation 259/93, Article 4(1).

5.127 The Agency has to make a decision on the proposed shipment's acceptability within 30 days of acknowledgement. However, unless agreed otherwise between the affected competent authorities, 21 days must be given before approval is sent so that any other competent authority has time to record any objection[1]. Accordingly, the latter have 20 days in which to raise objections[2].

1 Regulation 259/93, Article 4(2)(a).
2 Regulation 259/93, Article 4(2)(b).

5.128 Transport conditions[1] can be placed on the proposed shipment both by the competent authority of dispatch and by transit authorities[2]. Regulation 259/93 requires that these conditions 'may not be more stringent than those laid down in respect of similar shipments occurring wholly within their jurisdiction'[3].

1 See para 5.98 above
2 But not by the competent authority of destination. Oddly, the competent authority of destination can set down conditions in respect of shipments between member states for recovery (see Regulation 259/93, Article 7(3)).
3 Regulation 259/93, Article 4(2)(d).

5.129 Objections must be conveyed in writing to the notifier and competent authorities involved in the shipment. They must be made in accordance with the grounds stipulated in Regulation 259/93. The competent authorities can object if the shipment is against the general rules previously formulated on the permissibility of transfrontier movements for disposal[1]. The authorities of dispatch and destination[2] can object to individual movements if the shipment is contrary 'especially'[3] to Articles 5 and 7 of the Directive on Waste. As noted previously, these Articles concern the 'proximity principle' that disposal infrastructure should be provided 'to enable waste to be disposed of in one of the nearest appropriate installations'[4] and that all waste movements must be in compliance with waste disposal plans[5]. Objections can also be raised where a competent authority is prioritising a particular installation close by for disposing of some other waste[6]. As noted at para 5.37, for the UK the principal set of decision rules is the Export/Import Plan. When a notification has been received, the Agency is required to adhere to this plan by the Transfrontier Shipment of Waste Regulations 1994[7].

1 Regulation 259/93, Article 4(2)(c).
2 But not transit authorities.
3 Regulation 259/93, Article 4(3)(b).
4 Council Directive of 15 July 1975 on Waste (75/442/EEC) (OJ L194/39 25.7.75) (as amended by Council Directive of 18 March 1991 amending Directive 75/442/EEC on Waste (91/156/EEC) (OJ L78/32 26.3.91) and Commission Decision of 24 May 1996 adapting Annexes IIA and IIB to Council Directive 75/442/EEC on Waste (96/350/EC) (OJ L135/32 6.6.96)) Article 5(2).
5 Council Directive of 15 July 1975 on Waste (75/442/EEC) (OJ L194/39 25.7.75) (as amended by Council Directive of 18 March 1991 amending Directive 75/442/EEC on Waste (91/156/EEC) (OJ L78/32 26.3.91) and Commission Decision of 24 May 1996 adapting Annexes IIA and IIB to Council Directive 75/442/EEC on Waste (96/350/EC) (OJ L135/32 6.6.96)) Article 7.
6 Regulation 259/93, Article 4(3)(b)(ii).
7 SI 1994/1137, reg 11.

5.130 The competent authorities of dispatch, transit and destination can also raise objections if[1]:

(a) the shipment is not in accordance with national legislation relating to 'environmental protection, public order, public safety or health protection'; or
(b) if the notifier has been found guilty of illegal trafficking[2]; or
(c) if the shipment is contrary to obligations created by international conventions.

1 Regulation 259/93, Article 4(3)(c).
2 This does not apply to the UK. Regulation 259/93 allows shipments to be refused on these grounds 'in accordance with national legislation'. However, there is no such provision in the UK's national legislation, the Transfrontier Shipment of Waste Regulations 1994, SI 1994/1137. The only instance when it could be invoked is the rather unlikely scenario of the notifier being earlier deregistered by the Agency from being a controlled waste carrier or broker (see Chapter 6) due to abuse of transfrontier waste controls.

5.131 Waste cannot be moved unless the shipment has been formally authorised. If the shipment is enacted without a competent authority's consent, it falls within the definition of 'illegal traffic' under Article 26[1]. If it enters or leaves the UK in these circumstances, an offence is committed under the Transfrontier Shipment of Waste Regulations 1994[1].

1 SI 1994/1137, reg 12(1): offences are discussed at para 5.185 below.

5.132 If no objection is raised by the other competent authorities, the shipment to the UK is authorised by the Agency stamping the consignment note[1] and sending it back. The notifier must also receive from the Agency a copy of the certificate approving the financial guarantee[2]. The shipment cannot be moved until these documents have been received by the notifier[3]. Copies of the consignment note must be sent to the other competent authorities involved[4]. Oddly, it would appear that, unlike the provisions of Regulation 259/93 for shipments for recovery[5], written consent to a shipment for disposal seems not to have a maximum time limit of one year. Single[6] notifications for disposal appear to be valid indefinitely. However, it may be that this defect in the drafting can be dealt with by adding a transport condition[7] to the effect that the notification is time limited.

1 Regulation 259/93, Article 4(5).
2 SI 1994/1137, reg 7: see para 5.88ff.
3 Regulation 259/93, Article 5(1) and SI 1994/1137, reg 7(1).
4 Regulation 259/93, Article 4(2)(a).
5 See Regulation 259/93, Article 7(2).
6 However, if more than one load is moved under the general notification procedures for multiple loads, the regulation is explicit that the general notification only lasts for one year (see Regulation 259/93, Article 28(2)).
7 Regulation 259/93, Article 4(2)(d).

5.133 Three working days prior to the intended departure of the shipment, copies of the consignment note must be sent to all the competent authorities involved in the shipment[1]. The shipment can then be moved, accompanied by the consignment note duly stamped[2], and with the relevant parts on the Movement/Tracking Form completed by the notifier and carrier. The original copy of the note can be replaced by a 'specimen' of it if a competent authority so requests[3].

1 Regulation 259/93, Article 5(2).
2 Regulation 259/93, Article 5(3).
3 Regulation 259/93, Article 5(3).

5.134 Once the waste has reached its destination, the consignee has three working days to send back copies of the consignment note to the notifier and to the competent authorities concerned[1]. All sections must be completed with the exception of the part of the Movement/Tracking Form which relates to the certificate of disposal/recovery. Within 180 days of receipt of the waste for disposal, the consignee must send the note, with the certificate of disposal duly completed, to the notifier and to all the competent authorities[2]. The receipt of the latter causes the financial guarantee to be released[3].

1   Regulation 259/93, Article 5(5).
2   Regulation 259/93, Article 5(6).
3   Regulation 259/93, Article 27(2).

INTERNATIONAL MOVEMENTS OF WASTES FOR RECOVERY[1]

5.135 Given the extensive restrictions placed upon transactions involving international shipments for disposal by the Export/Import Plan, the most significant transfrontier shipments to and from the UK concern wastes passing to recovery[2]. The government's stated policy is to support the continuation of this trade, provided that it involves environmentally acceptable recovery facilities[3]. The procedures on movements to recovery which are set out in Regulation 259/93 are somewhat complex, varying depending primarily on the type of state involved[4], the nature of the waste, and whether it appears on the Green, Amber or Red Lists[5].

1   This section will describe the procedures for the principal type of waste movements affecting the UK. For brevity, transit movements through the European Community and transit movements between member states via third states are excluded. The provisions of Regulation 259/93 in respect of these movement are, however, summarised in Circular 13/94: see for example paras 113, 123, 124.
2   Defined by Directive 75/442, Article 1(f) (see Regulation 259/93, Article 2(k) and Table 2.3 in Chapter 2).
3   Export/Import Plan, para 1.29.
4   EC member state, OECD Country, Basel Convention party or other state.
5   Regulation 259/93, Annexes II, III or IV as amended by Commission Decision of 21 October 1994 adapting, pursuant to Article 42(3), Annexes II, III and IV to Council Regulation (EEC) No 259/93 on the supervision and control of shipments within, into and out of the European Community (OJ L288/36 9.11.94) and by Commission Decision of 18 May 1998 adapting pursuant to Article 42(3), Annexes II and III to Council Regulation (EEC) No 259/93 on the supervision and control of shipments within, into and out of the European Community (Decision 98/368 OJ L165/20 10.6.98): see Tables 1–3 of Appendix III.

Procedures for Green List wastes

5.136 Green List international waste shipments to recovery are excluded from the main provisions of Regulation 259/93. However, Regulation 259/93 categorically states that 'all' of the provisions of the Directive on Waste apply to Green List shipments[1]. Hence such movements within the European Community must pass to recovery facilities that either have permits under Article 10 of the Directive on Waste or are subject to the lesser registration system set out in Article 11 of the Directive[2]. Registered waste carriers and registered brokers should also be used, unless a registration is not required[3].

1   Regulation 259/93, Article 1(3)(b).
2   See Chapters 10 and 11.
3   See Chapter 6.

5.137 The movement of Green List waste within the European Community and between the Community and the 29 OECD nations are reasonably straightforward. However, it may be less easy in respect of non-OECD countries. Firstly, the material must not fall within the concept of hazardous waste as set out in Annex V of

Regulation 259/93[1]. If it does, it cannot be shipped. Secondly, the Commission has been required to contact each non-OECD state[2] to enquire if that country intends to continue to allow trade in these wastes. This was done by the Commission sending a copy of the Green List of wastes and requesting written confirmation that they are 'not subject to control in the country of destination'[3]. Confirmation was also requested that the country will accept these wastes without: (a) requiring the control procedures either appropriate for Amber or Red List wastes going to recovery; or (b) without applying the procedures in the Regulation for wastes going to disposal[4]. Each country had six months in which to reply.

1   Regulation 259/93, Article 16, as amended by Council Regulation (EC) No 120/97 of 20 January 1997 amending Regulation (EC) No 259/93 on the supervision and control of shipments of waste within, into and out of the European Community (OJ L22/14 24.1.97), with Annex V being amended by Commission Regulation (EC) No 2408/98 of 6 November 1998 amending Annex V to Council Regulation (EEC) No 259/93 on the supervision and control of shipments of waste within, into or out of the European Community (OJ L298/19 7.11.98): see para 5.164.
2   Decision of the OECD Council Concerning the Control of Transfrontier Movements of Wastes Destined for Recovery Operations, C(92)39/FINAL 6 April 1992.
3   Regulation 259/93, Article 17(1).
4   Regulation 259/93, Article 17(1).

5.138   Where a non-OECD country of destination has indicated that any Green List waste already 'is subject to control', or where it requests that certain types of Green List wastes are to be subject to the Amber or Red Lists, the details are passed to the expert committee set up under Article 18 of the Directive on Waste[1]. The Commission must then set out which level of controls under Regulation 259/93 – Amber or Red List – are appropriate for that waste.

1   Regulation 259/93, Article 17(3).

5.139   In 1994, the Commission issued a Decision[1] which outlined the responses obtained from some of the non-OECD states. However, this was a provisional list and was repealed in August 1999[2], being replaced by two EC Regulations: 1420/99[3] and 1547/99[4]. Council Regulation 1420/99 entered into force at the end of September 1999. It lists those non-OECD states that do not wish to accept some specified Green List wastes or any of them[5] (see Table 4 in Appendix III). It also identifies those non-OECD states that have not responded to the Commission's earlier requests. In the case of those states, all Green List wastes are to be subject to the procedures in Regulation 259/93 in respect of wastes passing to disposal[6]. The latter are listed in Annex B of the Regulations, which also indicates countries which have requested that specified Green List waste is to be consigned only under disposal controls. This Regulation is likely to be subject to regular review by the Commission[7], the first taking place in March 2000.

1   Commission Decision of 20 July 1994 determining the control procedure under Council Regulation (EEC) No 259/93 as regards certain shipments of waste to certain non-OECD countries (Decision 94/575) (OJ L220/15 25.8.94). It thereby supersedes Annex 6 of the UK Export/Import Plan.
2   See Commission Regulation (EC) No 1547/99, Article 3.
3   Council Regulation (EC) No 1420/99 of 29 April 1999 establishing common rules and procedures to apply to shipments to certain non-OECD countries of certain types of waste (OJ L166/6 1.7.99).
4   Commission Regulation (EC) No 1547/99 of 12 July 1999 determining the control procedures under Council Regulation (EEC) No 259/93 to apply to shipments of certain types of waste to certain countries to which OECD Decision C92(39) final does not apply (OJ L185/1 17.7.99).
5   Regulation 1420/99, Article 1.
6   Regulation 1420/99, Article 2. There is thus some overlap with Regulation 1547/99 Annex C (see para 5.104 and Table 5 in Appendix III).
7   Regulation 1420/99, Article 4. It should also be noted that the peculiarly worded Article 5 requires the entire Regulation to be reviewed 'to bring it into line with Regulation (EC) No 259/93'. Presumably, this is necessary as there is an internal inconsistency between the two Regulations.

5.140   The second Regulation – 1547/99 – affects only those countries to which the OECD Decision[1] does not apply. These countries fall into two classes: non-OECD member states and those OECD countries which have yet to actually implement the OECD Decision. The latter are the new entrant OECD states, such as Poland and Hungary, and this Regulation will no longer apply to them once the country implements the OECD Decision[2]. Regulation 1547/99 entered into force in August 1999. It sets out a variety of controls for Green List wastes in the context of the affected countries, specifying those states which require particular Green List wastes to be dealt with under (see Table 5 in Appendix III):

–   Amber List controls[3];
–   Red List controls[4];
–   procedures applicable for wastes exported from the EC for disposal[5]; and
–   'normal' Green List controls[6].

Hence, for example, excepting specified metal and electronic scrap, scrap ships, slag, specified textiles, wood wastes and bones[7], an export of Green List waste for recovery in China has to be processed under Red List controls. Similar arrangements apply for example to Hungary[8], although the range of wastes subject to Green List controls is less extensive. However, as Hungary has OECD membership, the requirement that Red List controls apply will be lifted when that country has implemented the OECD Decision[9].

1   See para 5.21.
2   Regulation 1547/99, Article 1(5).
3   Regulation 1547/99, Article 1(1) and Annex A. Amber List controls are discussed in para 5.159ff.
4   Regulation 1547/99, Article 1(2) and Annex B. Red List controls are discussed in para 5.159ff.
5   Regulation 1547/99, Article 1(3) and Annex C. While disposal controls are discussed at para 5.125ff, it should be noted that there are slight differences in approach for wastes exported from the EC (see Regulation 259/93, Article 15).
6   Regulation 1547/99, Article 1(4) and Annex D. Green List controls are discussed in para 5.136ff. Note that there is an inconsistency in the drafting of Article 1(4) in comparison to the first paragraph of Annex D. The former confirms that Green Lists controls under Article 1(3) of Regulation 259/93 apply. Annex D states that the wastes listed therein may be moved from the EC 'without recourse to *any* of the control procedures provided for in the Regulation' [author's emphasis]. It is assumed that Article 1(4) has precedence.
7   See Regulation 1547/99, Annex B and D (Table 5 of Appendix III).
8   See Annex B and D (Table 5 of Appendix III).
9   See Regulation 1547/99, Article 1(5).

Documenting Green List movements

5.141   Transfrontier shipments of Green List wastes are subject to only limited documentary control under Regulation 259/93[1]. The requirements, set out in Article 11, hold that any transaction be accompanied by the following information[2]:

(a)   the name and address of holder;
(b)   the 'usual commercial description' of the waste;
(c)   the quantity involved;
(d)   the name and address of the consignee;
(e)   the intended recovery operation[3]; and
(f)   the anticipated date of shipment.

This information must be signed by the holder. Oddly, Article 1(3) appears to partially over-rule Article 11, by only requiring that items (b) to (e) have application to Green List waste shipments.

1   Regulation 259/93, Article 1(3)(a).
2   Regulation 259/93, Article 11(1).
3   Using the descriptions set out in Annex IIB of the Directive on Waste.

5.142 For movements of Green List waste on UK soil, the requirements of Regulation 259/93 are substantiated by the duty of care[1] and the associated Environmental Protection (Duty of Care) Regulations 1991[2]. The latter contain requirements on transfer notes[3]. This duplicates most of the information required by Regulation 259/93, Article 11, although the type of recovery operation also needs to be stipulated. However, in the context of transfrontier shipments, the system for 'season ticket' transfer notes covering multiple shipments of the same waste do not apply[4]. These are over-ridden by the requirement of Article 11 that each shipment 'is accompanied' by the relevant information[5].

1   EPA 1990, s 34: see Chapter 3.
2   SI 1991/2839.
3   SI 1991/2839, reg 2(1): see para 3.118ff.
4   See para 3.159ff.
5   It would seem that for a multiple load, the first load should contain all the information required by the Duty of Care Regulations. Provided that details of the transactions that follow are the same as for the first load, subsequent loads need to be accompanied only by the information set out in Article 11 of the regulation.

5.143 These provisions are also partially reinforced by the Transfrontier Shipment of Waste Regulations 1994[1]. The 1994 Regulations make 'any notifier who ships waste[2] from the United Kingdom' commit an offence unless[3] the waste is 'accompanied by the information' prescribed by Article 11. The fact that the information must also be signed is reiterated in the 1994 Regulations[4].

1   SI 1994/1137.
2   Green List waste.
3   SI 1994/1137, reg 12(8): offences are discussed at para 5.185.
4   SI 1994/1137, reg 12(8).

5.144 Two items should be noted in relation to the requirements of the Transfrontier Shipment of Waste Regulations 1994 on Green List movements. Firstly, the offence provisions only apply to Green List waste shipments leaving the UK and are solely directed towards the 'notifier'. 'Notifier' is defined in Regulation 259/93[1] as the original producer of the waste. Only where it 'is not possible' for the notifier to be the producer is the carrier or broker to be viewed as the notifier[2]. Secondly, the 1994 Regulations make no provision for Green List waste shipments entering the UK[3], referring only to offences committed by persons who ship waste 'from' the UK[4]. The offence is also solely directed to 'notifiers', who in this instance can only be UK-based carriers or brokers[5]. Hence only s 34 of the EPA 1990 and the Duty of Care Regulations 1991 would appear to apply for Green List waste imports.

1   Regulation 259/93, Article 2(g).
2   All expressions in Regulation 259/93 are deemed to have the same meaning in the Transfrontier Shipment of Waste Regulations (SI 1994/1137, reg 2(2)(a)).
3   Although such a movement would be covered by the duty of care and the requirement that the load is documented by appropriate transfer notes (EPA 1990, s 34: see para 3.118), these notes do not fully fulfil Article 11. They do not contain all the information required and, as 'season ticket' notes can be used, they do not meet the requirement that all loads are accompanied by documentation.
4   See SI 1994/1137, reg 12(8).
5   By definition, the producer will be out of the UK's jurisdiction. 'Notifier' is defined in Article 2(g) of the Regulation.

Moving Amber and Red List wastes

5.145 The following paragraphs describe the normal procedures for single notifications to recovery plants[1]. It will be apparent that the procedures have similarities to those relating to movements of waste for disposal. The same notification document is used[2], with contracts and financial guarantees being required. The system of pre-notification of the competent authorities can also be changed, if the authority of dispatch has elected to transmit the notification document itself[3]. But such an arrangement does not, in this instance, give the competent authority an immediate power of veto over the shipment[4].

1   The system for the general notification of multiple loads is described at para 5.105 above: Regulation 259/93, Article 28.
2   Using the consignment note contained in Commission Decision 94/774, (OJ L310/70 3.12.94). See Figure 5.1.
3   Regulation 259/93, Article 6(8).
4   See para 5.108.

5.146   In respect of Amber List shipments, there is one significant difference in the manner by which the notification document is to be treated when it has been received by the competent authority of the proposed destination. This does not, however, apply to Red List waste transactions[1]. For shipments of Amber List wastes within the European Community and shipments from the Community to OECD countries[2], Regulation 259/93 contains a streamlined notification system based on the concept of tacit consent[3]. This means that all competent authorities are informed of the shipment in advance in the usual way. But there is no requirement on the competent authority of destination to formally approve the shipment. The waste can be moved if no reply has been received by the notifier at the end of a specified period. The emphasis, therefore, is on the competent authority to lodge an objection within the time allowed. This is in obvious contrast to international shipments for disposal, where the onus is upon the notifier to receive the competent authority's formal approval prior to the shipment.

1   Regulation 259/93, Article 10 and Article 17(6).
2   Note that Circular 13/94 (para 115) appears to cast doubt on whether OECD states are permitted to use this option, despite the wording of Article 17(4).
3   Regulation 259/93, Article 8.

5.147   Although formal written consent is not necessary for Amber List transactions to recovery in the European Community and in OECD countries, competent authorities are allowed discretion on whether they will provide written consent. Circular 13/94 suggests that, even if a UK competent authority considers that tacit consent should be granted, an early written communication of consent is the most desirable approach to the approval of notification[1].

1   Circular 13/94, para 102.

'Pre-authorised' recovery facilities

5.148   As an additional simplification to the general system of tacit consent, competent authorities covering the destination of Amber List wastes in both the European Community and OECD are allowed to apply a streamlined procedure to the pre-notification process[1]. This is done by the competent authority declaring that objections will not be raised against certain shipments to specific facilities. This allows the recovery plant to be given a 'pre-authorised facility' status[2]. This must be for a stipulated time period[3], with the Commission being informed of the name and address of the recovery plant, the nature of its technologies, types of wastes that are to be covered and the duration of the authorisation[4]. The Commission is required to send this information to the other member states concerned with the shipment and to the OECD Secretariat[5]. Circular 13/94[6] requests that the Secretary of State, as correspondent under Regulation 259/93, is also informed.

1 Regulation 259/93, Article 9(1) and, for OECD states, Article 9(1) in conjunction with Article 17(4).
2 Circular 13/94, para 39.
3 Regulation 259/93, Article 9(1).
4 Regulation 259/93, Article 9(2).
5 Regulation 259/93, Article 9(2).
6 Circular 13/94, para 39.

5.149 The option of 'pre-authorising' a European Community or OECD-based recovery facility is intended to lessen the bureaucratic burden on the notifier. However, the exact nature of the requirements is a little unclear[1]. The main problem concerns the timescale allowed for the competent authorities to deal with the notification. There is some doubt as to whether the 30 day timescale for lodging an objection, as set down in Article 7 of Regulation 259/93, applies in this instance[2]. This is because Article 9 also provides for certain procedures, which appear to over-ride Article 7. Hence Article 9(3) states that the notifier must send the consignment note to the relevant competent authorities and that '[s]uch notification shall arrive prior to the time the shipment is dispatched'. The requisite timescale is not specified, but competent authorities of dispatch and transit are still allowed to raise objections to the load and impose transport conditions. Clearly, if under Article 9(3) the load can be dispatched immediately after the notifications have reached the competent authorities, they are not allowed any time to lodge objections or impose transit conditions.

1 Regulation 269/93, Article 9.
2 Although seven days are set down in Article 9(4), this only applies when a member state's own domestic laws require all contracts to be received by the competent authority. As there are no provisions contained in SI 1994/1137 with respect to the UK, this seven day period does not appear to apply (see Circular 13/94, para 111).

5.150 Given the lack of clarity on the exact nature of the provisions of Article 9, it may be that this option will be little used in practice. For this reason, it will not be considered further in the discussion below.

Amber and Red List shipments within the European Community for recovery

5.151 The UK's Export/Import Plan allows, subject to the procedures set out in the regulation, unrestricted movements of Amber and Red List wastes between the UK and other Community States[1]. Additional information must be given on the consignment note as to the intended disposal method for post-recycling residues, the proportion of recycled material in relation to such residues and the estimated value of the recycled material[2]. A financial guarantee must be drawn up[3] and must be approved by the Agency[4]. An appropriately worded contract must exist between notifier and consignee[5]. The notifier's competent authority issues the notification document[6], which is then sent by the notifier to the consignee's competent authority, with copies passing to the consignee and to any transit authorities.

1 See Export/Import Plan, Chapters 4 and 6 and see Circular 13/94, para 104.
2 Regulation 259/93, Article 6(5).
3 Regulation 259/93, Article 27(2): see para 5.85.
4 SI 1994/1137, reg 7.
5 Regulation 259/93, Article 6(6): see para 5.80.
6 Regulation 259/93, Article 6(3).

5.152 Once the pre-notification has been received by the competent authority of destination, its receipt must be acknowledged within three working days[1]. Copies of the acknowledgement are then sent to the other competent authorities and to the consignee[2].

1   Regulation 259/93, Article 7(1).
2   Regulation 259/93, Article 7(1).

5.153 The competent authorities of dispatch, transit and destination can lay down transport conditions on the proposed movement of Amber or Red List waste. This must be done within 20 days of dispatch of the acknowledgement of notification[1].

1   Regulation 259/93, Article 7(3).

5.154 Objections may be made by the competent authorities of dispatch and destination on grounds similar to those relating to movements of waste for disposal. Briefly[1], the grounds are that (a) the shipment is contrary to a waste disposal plan; (b) the shipment is not in accordance with national laws; (c) the notifier has been found guilty of illegal trafficking[2]; and (d) the shipment is contrary to an international convention[3]. However, there are two important differences. Firstly, the 'proximity principle' does not apply for wastes going to recovery[4]. Hence the existence of a closer plant to that proposed is not a reason for objection. Instead, an objection can be made by the competent authority of dispatch and destination[5]:

> 'if the ratio of the recoverable and non-recoverable waste, the estimated value of the materials to be finally recovered or the cost of the recovery and the cost of the disposal of the non-recoverable fraction do not justify the recovery under economic and environmental considerations.'

This is aimed at preventing fraudulent transactions to recovery and the practice of 'seeding' loads of waste of poor recovery potential with recoverable materials. It is also intended to prevent international transactions where the economics and recovery potential of the load may be highly marginal[6]. However, transit authorities cannot use the latter as a reason for objection. Although they can object on grounds (b), (c) and (d) above, they cannot object on the grounds that the proposed shipment is contrary to their waste management plans[7].

1   See para 5.129.
2   As noted in para 5.130, this does not apply to the UK.
3   Regulation 259/93, Article 7(4)(a).
4   Confirmed by the European Court of Justice in *Chemische Afvalstoffen Dusseldorp BV v Minister Van Volkshuisvesting Ruintelijke Ordening en Milieubeheer* [1999] Env LR 360.
5   Regulation 259/93, Article 7(4)(a): see Export/Import Plan, paras 4.5 and 6.4ff.
6   See para 5.61.
7   Regulation 259/93, Article 7(4)(b).

5.155 Provided that the shipment is composed of wastes found on the Amber List, it can be moved under the system of tacit consent if no objection has been lodged within 30 days[1]. Alternatively, written consent can be given before the end of the 30-day period if all the affected competent authorities wish the shipment to proceed. In contrast to the provisions for wastes passing to disposal, written consent or an objection can be provided by post, or by fax followed by post[2]. Unlike the case of wastes passing to disposal[3], Regulation 259/93 does not make it clear that the consignment note should be stamped when written consent is granted. However, Circular 13/94 states[4] that stamping the note constitutes written consent. Written or tacit consent lasts for a period of a year.

1   Regulation 259/93, Article 8(1).
2   Regulation 259/93, Article 7(2).

3   Regulation 259/93, Article 4.
4   Circular 13/94, para 101.

5.156   Wastes destined for recovery which feature on the Red List, along with those that have not been assigned to the Green, Amber and Red Lists, always require formal written consent[1]. Tacit consent does not apply.

1   Regulation 259/93, Article 10.

5.157   When a shipment of Amber or Red List waste is due to move, the notifier must send copies of the note to all the competent authorities three days before the shipment commences[1]. A copy of the note also needs to accompany the shipment[2].

1   Regulation 259/93, Article 8(2).
2   Regulation 259/93, Article 8(3).

5.158   Once the shipment of Amber or Red List waste has been received for recovery, copies of the consignment note must be completed and sent to the notifier and to the competent authorities within three days[1]. The certificate of recovery must be sent to the notifier within 180 days of receipt[2], with copies forwarded to the other competent authorities. On receipt of the certificate of recovery, the financial guarantee is released[3].

1   Regulation 259/93, Article 8(5).
2   Regulation 259/93, Article 8(6).
3   Regulation 259/93, Article 27(2).

Amber and Red List waste shipments out of the European Community for recovery

Shipments to OECD states for recovery[1]

5.159   The export of waste for recovery in OECD states is allowable under Regulation 259/93[2]. This is, of course, subject to any such country electing under the Regulation to prevent such shipments[3]. In addition, the Regulation[4] and the Export/Import Plan[5] requires the Agency to raise objection if it considers that recovery will not take place in an 'environmentally sound manner'.

1   See Export Import Plan, para 4.7ff and Circular 13/94, paras 115, 116 and 118.
2   See Regulation 259/93, Article 16(1)(a) as amended by Regulation 120/97, Article 1.
3   Regulation 259/93, Article 16(3)(a).
4   Regulation 259/93, Article 16(3)(b).
5   Export/Import Plan, para 4.9.

5.160   For those wastes on the Amber List, the notification procedure detailed above for movements of wastes for recovery within the European Community is applied[1]. The consignment note is obtained from the Agency, completed, and sent by the notifier to the competent authority of the OECD state[2], with copies to the other affected competent authorities. Tacit consent is assumed should no objections be received within 30 days of notification. For any wastes passing to recovery which feature on the Red List, written consent must be received by the competent authorities concerned[3].

1   Regulation 259/93, Article 17(4): see para 5.151 above.
2   Regulation 259/93, Article 6(1) as applied by Article 17(4): see Circular 13/94, para 116.
3   Regulation 259/93, Article 17(6).

5.161   For exports from the European Community there are, of course, no provisions in Regulation 259/93 which require the compliance of the competent authority covering the consignee. Where Amber or Red List wastes pass out of the Community, the customs post must receive a copy of the consignment note. The Regulation states that customs must then forward a copy of the consignment note to the competent authority of 'export'[1]. Circular 13/94 implies that the latter is a drafting error[2] and that it means that the Agency – as competent authority of dispatch – should be sent the copy.

1   Article 17(7).
2   Circular 13/94, para 119: under Article 2 of Regulation 259/93 only the competent authorities of 'dispatch', 'destination' and 'transit' are defined. There is no definition of the 'competent authority of export'.

5.162   After the shipment leaves the European Community, there is no legal obligation under Regulation 259/93 on the consignee to send back copies of the consignment note immediately on receipt of the waste[1]. All that is required is that, under the contract, the note is returned within 180 days with the certificate of recovery completed[2]. Once the certificate has been received by the competent authority, the financial guarantee can be released[3].

1   Although no European Community country is informed of the waste's arrival at the consignee's premises, Article 17(7) requires the competent authority of 'export' (sic) to make enquiries if nothing has been heard from the consignee 42 days after the shipment passed out of the Community. The consignee is under no duty to inform the competent authority of its arrival. This is in contrast to shipments out of the Community to disposal (Article 15(4)(b)) and to shipments to non-OECD states for recovery (Article 17(8): which makes Article 15(4)(b) have application).
2   Article 6(6) as applied by Article 17(4).
3   Article 27(2).

Shipments to non-OECD states for recovery

5.163   Between 1 January and 10 November 1998[1], it was prohibited to consign wastes which appeared on the Amber or Red Lists[2] from the Community to recovery facilities in any non-OECD state[3]. This was regardless of whether they are Basel Convention parties and was an outright ban. However, it was an interim measure, pending changes to the Basel Convention.

1   See Commission Regulation (EC) No 2408/98 of 6 November 1998 amending Annex V to Council Regulation (EEC) No 259/93 on the supervision and control of shipments of waste within, into or out of the European Community (OJ L298/19 7.11.98), Article 3.
2   Export of Green List wastes were possible, providing that the intended recipient nation has not previously lodged general objections in accordance with Article 17.
3   Regulation 259/93, Article 16(1)(b) as amended by Council Regulation 120/97 of 20 January 1997 amended Regulations (EC) No 259/93 on the supervision and control of shipments of waste within, into and out of the European Community (OJ L22/14 24.1.97).

5.164   Since 10 November 1998, this ban has been partially lifted, but only in respect of non-hazardous wastes[1]. The manner by which 'non-hazardous waste' in this context has been defined involves a 'belt and braces' approach of some resultant complexity. Annex V of Regulation 259/93 uses a series of definitions of substances which are – and are not – hazardous wastes in a manner which may be considered akin to a number of increasingly fine sieves. The manner which these operate is explained in the Introductory Notes set out on the first page to the Annex. The first approach in Part 1 of Annex V uses the Basel Convention's Annex VIII and IX[2], which are described in Regulation 259/93 as 'List A' and 'List B'[3]. List A sets out a variety of wastes which are always to be considered as being hazardous (see Appendix III, Table 6). Examples include lead acid batteries, clinical waste and waste oil. List B, by contrast sets out those wastes which are *not* to be considered hazardous (see Appendix III, Table 7). Examples include iron and steel scrap, batteries not containing lead, cadmium or mercury[4], waste electrical goods and circuit boards, plastics, paper, textiles and so on. Annex V makes clear that, should a waste be clearly described on either of these lists, then there is no need to consider any of the subsequent decision methodology set out in Annex V[5].

1 For most purposes this will mean the small number of waste categories which, whilst featuring on the Amber List, do not exhibit hazardous properties. The ban on shipments to non-OECD countries never applied to Green List waste.
2 These Annexes were made part of the Basel Convention in November 1998.
3 Regulation 259/93 Annex V part 1.
4 And which are 'conforming to a specification' (sic).
5 See Regulation 259/93 Annex V (as amended by Commission Regulation 2408/98 Article 1) Introductory Note 2.

5.165 Should a waste not fall within the methodology set out above, the next approach to be used is contained in Part 2 of Annex V. This is a duplicate of the hazardous waste list contained in Decision 94/904/EC[1] and which, for internal movements of hazardous waste in Britain, forms the basis of the Special Waste Regulations 1996[2]. However, in the context of Regulation 259/93, the criteria to be applied to determine if a material is hazardous is restricted to whether or not it is featured on the hazardous waste list. Unlike the way special waste is defined in Britain, there is much less emphasis placed on whether a material is both on the hazardous waste list *and* has the requisite hazardous properties set down in the Hazardous Waste Directive[3] and in Decision 94/904[4]. Indeed, there are only two instances when these properties come into play. These involve when a member state[5] 'in exceptional cases'[6] considers that:

(a) a particular waste should be excluded from the export ban to non-OECD countries due to its non-hazardous nature[7] or

(b) whilst not described by Annex V, a waste should be regarded as hazardous[8] and hence subject to the ban.

1 Council Decision of 22 December 1994 establishing a list of hazardous waste pursuant to Article 1(4) of Council Directive 91/689/EEC on Hazardous Waste (OJ L356/14 31.12.94) Article 1: see para 4.08 and Appendix II.
2 SI 1996/972: see para 4.19.
3 Council Directive of 12 December 1991 on hazardous waste (91/689/EEC: OJ L377/20 31.12.91), Annex III: see para 4.11 and Table 4.1 in Chapter 4.
4 Council Decision of 22 December 1994 establishing a list of hazardous waste pursuant to Article 1(4) of Council Directive 91/689/EEC on Hazardous Waste (OJ L356/14 31.12.94) Article 1: see para 4.17 and Table 4.3 in Chapter 4.
5 Note that the term used is 'member state' not 'competent authority', implying that this decision is a matter of national government, not the Agency.
6 See Regulation 259/93 Annex V Introductory Notes 3 and 4 (as amended by Commission Regulation 2408/98 Article 1).
7 See Regulation 259/93 Annex V Introductory Note 3 (as amended by Commission Regulation 2408/98 Article 1).
8 See Regulation 259/93 Annex V Introductory Note 3 (as amended by Commission Regulation 2408/98 Article 1): see para 5.167 below.

5.166 Should a waste not feature on Regulation 259/93's Annex V Parts 1 or 2, it must be then considered in respect of Part 3. Part 3 is a slightly amended copy of the Amber and Red Lists (see Appendix III, Tables 2 and 3) contained in Annex III and IV of the Regulation. The difference is that used blasting grit, asphalt cement, surfactants, 'liquid pig manure; faeces', sewage sludge and municipal/household wastes[1] are to be regarded as excluded from the Amber List in the context of Annex V and the ban of shipments to non-OECD states. This exclusion means that, unless otherwise identified elsewhere in Annex V, these materials are not subject to Regulation 259/93's export ban.

1 Respectively Amber List waste codes AB 130, AC 020, AC 250, AC 260, AC 270 and AD 160.

5.167 Finally, if a waste is considered to be hazardous but has escaped being identified on Regulation 259/93's Annex V Parts 1–3, the member state must inform the proposed destination country 'prior to taking a decision'[1]. Presumably this gives time for the state destination to make representations. It seems that the member state can unilaterally consider that the material is a hazardous waste, but this decision must be made only in 'exceptional cases' and in respect of the hazardous criteria set down in the Hazardous Waste Directive[2], in Decision 94/904[3] and in respect of the contents of the header to the Green List in Regulation 259/93[4]. The Commission also needs to be informed by the end of the calendar year, who must then circulate the details to other member states and the Basel Convention Secretariat. The details then are to be considered with a view to the amendment of Annex V of Regulation 259/93.

1 Regulation 259/93 Annex V Introductory Note 4 (as amended by Commission Regulation 2408/98 Article 1).
2 Council Directive of 12 December 1991 on hazardous waste (91/689/EEC: OJ L377/20 31.12.91), Annex III: see para 4.11 and Table 4.1 in Chapter 4.
3 Council Decision of 22 December 1994 establishing a list of hazardous waste pursuant to Article 1(4) of Council Directive 91/689/EEC on Hazardous Waste (OJ L356/14 31.12.94) Article 1: see para 4.17 and Table 4.3 in Chapter 4.
4 Regulation 259/93 Annex II: see para 5.47 and Appendix III, Table 1.

5.168 In respect of the forgoing material, one point needs to be emphasised. The fact that a waste is not to be considered as falling into Regulation 259/93 Annex V's definition of hazardous waste – and hence the prohibition on export from the Community to non-OECD countries – does not prejudice the need for it to be classified in accordance with the Green, Amber or Red Lists for other reasons. Classification remains necessary in order to determine the method of notification and the paperwork required for the waste's proposed movement[1]. Prospective shippers must also ensure that the state of destination has not unilaterally banned specified types of waste or required a Green List waste be subject to Amber or Red List controls[2].

1 See para 5.135ff.
2 See para 5.137.

5.169 Regulation 259/93 contains detailed notification procedures for the movement of wastes not subject to the ban to non-OECD countries[1]. The affected shipments will be those which: (a) do not fall within the definition of hazardous waste under the criteria just described; and (b) are not contained on the Green List. However, the limited array of substances remaining[2] has little significance in the UK context. Furthermore, it seems likely that proposals to remove materials such as sewage sludge or household wastes from the UK to a non-OECD country are unlikely to be positively received by the Agency. For these reasons, the procedures will not be subject to further description.

1 Regulation 259/93, Article 17(4)ff.
2 Principally used blasting grit, asphalt cement, surfactants, 'liquid pig manure; faeces', sewage sludge and municipal/household wastes, along with other wastes which member states 'in exceptional cases' consider non-hazardous.

Imports of Amber and Red List waste into the European Community for recovery[1]

5.170 Under Regulation 259/93, the range of countries which are able to send waste to the Community for recovery is different from those that are able to send waste for disposal. Imports are prohibited unless from[2]:

(a) OECD countries[3];
(b) other countries who are Basel Convention parties and/or have concluded bilateral, multilateral or regional agreements with the European Community or with the European Community and its member states; or
(c) countries where agreements have been made prior to the Regulation, where such agreements were in progress when the regulation was adopted or where subsequent agreements have been made in exceptional cases[3].

1 See Circular 13/94, paras 121 and 122.
2 Regulation 259/93, Article 21.
3 These do not need to be Basel Convention parties: the US is an example.

5.171 Where the European Community has finalised bilateral agreements with non-OECD States, Circular 13/94 notes that the UK government is prepared to enter into individual agreements[1]. Where the Agency receives a request from a non-Basel Convention party involving importation to recovery, the Secretary of State must be approached for advice[2].

1 Circular 13/94, para 98.
2 Circular 13/94, para 98.

5.172 The importation of wastes for recovery from non-OECD countries is subject to the rules relating to imported waste destined for disposal in the Community[1]. However the objection criteria to be applied are those which are used in respect of other types of shipment to recovery[2]. The approach of considering such shipments under the disposal procedures can be changed if appropriate multilateral or bilateral agreements have been made. Once they are in place, shipments can be considered under the normal procedures set down for Amber or Red List transactions[3]. In all cases, proposals to import waste into the UK will be judged against the contents of the Export/Import Plan.

1 Regulation 259/93, Article 22(2).
2 Regulation 259/93, Articles 22(2) and 7(4).
3 See also Circular 13/94, para 122.

ENFORCEMENT PROVISIONS

5.173 Although Regulation 259/93 has direct application in UK law, certain of its requirements need amplification by a member state's own legislation. As noted, the Transfrontier Shipment of Waste Regulations 1994[1] fill out the Regulation's provisions and establish legal mechanisms to put certain of the Regulation's more generally worded principles into effect. The remainder of this chapter sets out the nature of these requirements.

1 SI 1994/1137, as amended by SI 1996/593 and SI 1996/972.

Shipments in difficulties and illegal traffic

5.174 As has been noted at para 5.80 above, clauses in the contract between notifier and consignee are required to ensure that wastes are returned if disposal or recovery cannot be undertaken or if a shipment has been made in violation of Regulation 259/93[1]. If the terms of the contract cannot be fulfilled, the costs of returning the waste should be borne by the notifier. If this fails, the financial guarantee can be invoked by the competent authority to effect the waste's return and/or alternative management[2].

1 Regulation 259/93, Articles 3(6) and 6(6).
2 In addition, Article 33 of Regulation 259/93 permits the competent authority to recover any other costs, such as those not covered by the financial guarantee or those incurred due to the non-availability of the guarantee: see Circular 13/94, para 127.

5.175 The obligations to return the waste under both the contact[1] and the financial guarantee cease when the relevant competent authority receives the disposal or recovery certificate[2]. It is possible that a certificate may be made fraudulently. Equally, it is conceivable that waste is shipped without any notification at all. To address these circumstances, Regulation 259/93 allows for the costs of a member state arranging for the waste to be taken back, and/or its recovery or disposal, to be charged against the person who should have acted as notifier. If this is not possible, the notifier's member state can be required to pay[3].

1 Regulation 259/93, Article 25(3).
2 Regulation 259/93, Article 27(2).
3 Regulation 259/93, Article 33(2).

5.176 Two separate articles of Regulation 259/93 define the circumstances when waste is to be returned[1]. The first concerns a waste shipment which has been notified and subsequently dispatched from the UK. If it turns out that the shipment cannot be dealt with as detailed in the consignment note or accompanying contract, the Agency[2] has to ensure that the waste can be disposed of or recovered 'in an alternative and environmentally sound manner'[3]. Usually, this will be paid for under the terms of the contract. But should a competent authority not be satisfied that satisfactory disposal or recovery will occur, the Regulation requires the notifier to bring the waste back to the state of dispatch.

1 Regulation 259/93, Articles 25(1) and 26(2).
2 As competent authority of despatch: SI 1994/1137, reg 3(a).
3 Regulation 259/93, Article 25(1).

5.177 The requirement to have the waste returned becomes more rigid if the notifier is found to be responsible for illegal traffic[1]. In this case, the Agency is required to take action to ensure that the waste is returned to the notifier. The Regulation holds that the waste must be otherwise disposed of or recovered where return is impracticable[2].

1 Regulation 259/93, Article 26(2); 'illegal traffic' is defined in Article 26(1): see para 5.188. Note that there are other offences contained in SI 1994/1137 which do not fall within the definition of 'illegal traffic' under Regulation 259/93.
2 Regulation 259/93, Article 26(2).

5.178 For notifiers based in the UK, these requirements are enacted by Regulation 8 of the Transfrontier Shipment of Waste Regulations 1994[1]. If the Agency is required by Regulation 259/93[2] to ensure that the waste is returned to the UK, this can be effected by serving a statutory notice on the notifier[3]. Non-compliance with the notice is an offence[4].

1 SI 1994/1137.
2 Regulation 259/93, Articles 25(1) or 26(2).
3 SI 1994/1137, reg 8(1): such notices are discussed at para 12.128ff.
4 SI 1994/1137, reg 12(9): see para 12.137ff.

5.179 In cases where a UK consignee is responsible for illegal traffic[1], Regulation 259/93 places a duty on the Agency to ensure that the waste is disposed of[2] by the consignee in an 'environmentally sound manner'[3]. If this is not possible, the Agency should itself arrange for the waste's disposal[4]. These requirements are put into legal form by the Transfrontier Shipment of Waste Regulations 1994[5]. The Agency covering the destination can serve a notice on the consignee[6] to ensure the environmentally sound disposal or recovery of the waste.

1 As defined by Regulation 259/93, Article 26(1): see para 5.188.
2 Recovery is not referred to.
3 Regulation 259/93, Article 26(3).
4 Regulation 259/93, Article 26(3).
5 SI 1994/1137, reg 9.
6 SI 1994/1137, reg 9(1): such notices are discussed at para 12.132.

Procedures for the return of waste

5.180 Unfortunately, Regulation 259/93 does not comprehensively set out the measures applicable for the return of a shipment. While it states that a further notification shall be made to cover the transaction[1], it does not clearly indicate the procedures for the consideration of this matter. It states that no member state should object to such a notification when a 'duly motivated' request has been made by the competent authority of – presumably – the original destination[2]. In addition, the Regulation also requires that, unless the effected competent authorities agree otherwise, the waste must be returned within 90 days or, when the shipment has constituted illegal traffic[3], 30 days[4]. However, no more information is provided.

1 Regulation 259/93, Articles 25(2) and 26(2).
2 Regulation 259/93, Articles 25(2) and 26(2).
3 Defined in Article 26(1): see para 5.188.
4 Regulation 259/93, Articles 25(1) and 26(2).

5.181 Although it may be initially attractive to assume that, in the absence of anything to the contrary, the notification procedures set out in the Regulation in respect of a 'normal' transfrontier movement are to be applied, this does not seem the case[1]. Firstly, most transaction procedures[2] require a member state not to make a decision on a notification until after a period of at least 21 days[3], thereby allowing other competent authorities time to make objections. But this seems inapplicable for a return. It is imperative that the waste should be moved as soon as possible and, particularly, within the timescales required by the Regulation. In any case, member states are forbidden by the Regulation from lodging objections[4]. In addition, a wholly new notification document raised by the competent authority of dispatch – in this case the regulatory body responsible for where the waste has ended up – will result in the consignment note numbering system not being in accordance with that stipulated on any financial guarantee. It therefore seems that a notification for a return is to be effected using a new consignment note[5] completed in a manner which is agreeable between the member states affected by the shipment. Circular 13/94 advises that the second notification document should cross-refer to the original consignment note and should contain a written explanation of the circumstances of the return[6]. The disadvantage of this informal arrangement is that, should it be breached, no offence under the Regulation is automatically committed.

1 See Circular 13/94, para 126.
2 See for example Regulation 259/93, Article 3.
3 Sixty days in the case, for example, of imports to disposal from outside the Community: Regulation 259/93, Article 20(5).

4 Regulation 259/93, Articles 25(2) and 26(2).
5 In *Beside BV and IM Besselsen* [1999] Env LR 328, it was confirmed that any return shipment must be duly notified and that member states should not effect the repatriation of waste without notification.
6 Circular 13/94, para 126.

Powers of customs officers to detain shipments

5.182 The Transfrontier Shipment of Waste Regulations 1994 allow the Agency to request a customs officer[1] to detain a transfrontier waste shipment for up to three working days[2]. The Commissioners of Customs and Excise are given discretion to decide the manner of the detention[3]. Circular 13/94 states that, on such a detention, the customs officer should immediately alert the Agency that the load has been detained and, if different, must also contact whichever Agency has jurisdiction over the port of entry. The Agency then has to take responsibility for the load at the end of the three day period[4]. For the detention to be lawful, it would seem that a notice under the Transfrontier Shipment of Waste Regulations 1994 must have been served by the end of the three day detention period on either the notifier or consignee requiring the waste to be detained[5]. The very short time period would seem to be a significant obstacle to this process, particularly as notices have to be formally served. Although the Agency also has other powers under the Environment Act 1995 to take possession of the waste or to otherwise detain it[6], these are restricted to instances where pollution of the environment or harm to human health is occurring. This may be a somewhat unlikely occurrence for many transfrontier shipments detained by customs.

1 A customs officer is any officer within the meaning of the Customs and Excise Management Act 1979: SI 1994/1137, reg 10(3).
2 SI 1994/1137, reg 10(1).
3 SI 1994/1137, reg 10(2).
4 Circular 13/94, para 129.
5 SI 1994/1137, regs 8 and 9: see para 12.128ff.
6 Environment Act 1995, s 108(4)(g) and (h), s 109: see paras 12.68 and 12.98.

Prohibition of mixing of wastes

5.183 Regulation 259/93 requires[1] that wastes which are subject to individual notifications cannot be mixed during shipment. The Transfrontier Shipment of Waste Regulations 1994[2] make this an offence under UK law. It would appear that the provision on mixing is intended to ensure loads subject to individual consignment notes cannot be physically combined. Such an activity may cause the waste to no longer be identifiable in respect of the consignment note, resulting in difficulties if the waste needs to be returned to the notifier. However, it would seem that 'mixing' would not extend to the transport of small quantities of separately packaged wastes from different sources on one vehicle. As long as each of the containers are identifiable in respect of the separate consignment notes, the prohibition on mixing seems not to be contravened. Furthermore, the prohibition in Regulation 259/93 concerns mixing 'during shipment', allowing mixing prior to shipment and subsequent to its delivery to the consignee.

1 Regulation 259/93, Article 29.
2 SI 1994/1137, reg 12(6).

5.184 A provision of similar construction is contained in the Special Waste Regulations 1996[1] which have application to transfrontier waste movements[2]. In this instance, the 1996 Regulations require 'different categories' of special waste, as well as special and non-special waste, not to be mixed. Like the separate prohibition on mixing contained in Regulation 259/93, there are exceptions: mixing is allowable prior to despatch or after it has arrived at an appropriately authorised facility[3]. Contravention of these requirements is an offence under the 1996 Regulations[4].

1   SI 1996/972, as amended by SI 1996/2019, reg 17.
2   See SI 1996/972, reg 13(4): see para 4.176.
3   See para 4.180.
4   SI 1996/972, reg 18: see para 4.183.

Offences and defences

5.185   The Transfrontier Shipment of Waste Regulations 1994 list a series of offences which relate directly to non-compliance with Regulation 259/93 or with the 1994 Regulations themselves[1]. These are detailed individually below. The 1994 Regulations also provide that, if a person commits an offence due to an act or default of someone else, the latter person can charged whether or not the former is subject to proceedings[2]. Directors, managers, secretaries or other similar offices of bodies corporate can also be charged individually with offences, as well as the body corporate itself[3].

1   SI 1994/1137, reg 12.
2   SI 1994/1137, reg 12(11): see para 7.173ff.
3   SI 1994/1137, reg 13: see para 7.156ff.

5.186   For persons accused of offences under the Transfrontier Shipment of Waste Regulations 1994, there is one common statutory defence, which is supplemented in some cases. The defence common to all the offences requires persons charged to prove that they took 'all reasonable steps and exercised all due diligence' to avoid the commission of the offence[1]. As will be seen below, a second statutory defence specific to certain provisions is also set down.

1   SI 1994/1137, reg 14(1): note the contrast with the statutory defence in s 33 of the EPA 1990, which refers to 'all reasonable precautions' and all due diligence: see para 7.145ff.

5.187   The Transfrontier Shipment of Waste Regulations 1994 hold[1] that a person found guilty of an offence may, on summary conviction, be subject to a fine not exceeding the statutory maximum[2]. On conviction on indictment, imprisonment of up to two years, a fine, or both can be levied[3]. The only exception to this rule is in respect of persons who are found guilty of shipping Green List wastes without appropriate documentation, where only a level 3 fine[3] can be imposed[4].

1   SI 1994/1137, reg 15(1).
2   Currently £5,000: £2,000 in Northern Ireland.
3   Currently £1,000.
4   SI 1994/1137, regs 12(8) and 15(2): see para 5.202.

Causing illegal traffic

5.188   Regulation 259/93 gives member states an explicit responsibility to take 'appropriate legal action' to prohibit and punish 'illegal traffic'[1]. The circumstances which compose illegal traffic under the regulation are quite specific and these are made an offence under the Transfrontier Shipment of Waste Regulations 1994[2]. Illegal traffic is defined in Regulation 259/93[3] as a movement of waste:

(a)   which has been effected without notification to the relevant competent authorities[4]. According to Circular 13/94, this category of illegal traffic would include changing the route of a multiple shipment, shipping misdescribed waste or shipping waste under a time expired notification[5];

(b)   which is without the consent of the competent authorities[6]. This would include moving wastes to recovery before the period allowed for tacit consent had expired[7];

(c)   where the competent authority's consent was the result of 'falsification, misrepresentation or fraud'[8];

(d)   where the consignment note has not been correctly filled in[9];

(e)   where the shipment results in the contravention 'of Community or international rules'[10]. It should be noted that rules of individual member states are not included under this provision. Hence prosecution would be restricted to a contravention of, for example, the Basel Convention or the Directive on Waste.

1   Regulation 259/93, Article 26(5).
2   SI 1994/1137, reg 12(1).
3   Regulation 259/93, Article 26(1).
4   Regulation 259/93, Article 26(1)(a).
5   Circular 13/94, para 138.
6   Regulation 259/93, Article 26(1)(b).
7   Circular 13/94, para 139: tacit consent is explained at para 5.146.
8   Regulation 259/93, Article 26(1)(c).
9   Regulation 259/93, Article 26(1)(d).
10   Regulation 259/93, Article 26(1)(e).

5.189   Besides items (a) to (e) above, Regulation 259/93 also defines 'illegal traffic'[1] as any contravention of Articles 14, 16, 19 and 21. This refers to[2]:

(a)   exports out of the European Community for disposal[3]:

– to any state which is not both an EFTA country and a Basel Convention party;
– to an EFTA country which has banned waste imports or has not given written consent to the waste movement; or
– to an EFTA country when the competent authority of dispatch considers that the waste will not be managed 'in accordance with environmentally sound methods' in the EFTA state;

(b)   exports of Amber or Red List waste out of the European Community for recovery at a non-OECD country[4];

(c)   exports out of the European Community for recovery to any country[5]:

– which has not consented to the shipment;
– which has prohibited imports; or
– where the competent authority of dispatch considers that the waste will not be managed in accordance with 'environmentally sound methods';

(d)   imports into the Community for disposal except from[6]:

– countries which are Basel Convention parties;
– non-Basel Convention parties where the Community or the Community and its member states have agreed bilateral agreements under the Convention; or
– non-Basel Convention parties where bilateral agreements with individual member states were made prior to May 1994 or, after May, where they have been agreed on in exceptional cases;

(e)   imports into the Community for recovery except from[7]:

– OECD countries;
– non-OECD counties which are Basel Convention parties and/or with which the Community or the Community and its member states have concluded bilateral, multilateral or regional agreements; or

- non-OECD countries which had made bilateral agreements with a member state prior to May 1994 or where they have been made after that date in exceptional circumstances.

1 Regulation 259/93, Article 26(1)(f).
2 See also Circular 13/94, para 138 to 143.
3 Regulation 259/93, Article 14.
4 Regulation 259/93, Article 16(1) as amended by Regulation 120/97, Article 1.
5 Regulation 259/93, Article 16(3).
6 Regulation 259/93, Article 19.
7 Regulation 259/93, Article 21.

5.190 Under the Transfrontier Shipment of Waste Regulations 1994, a person who, 'in the UK', contravenes Regulation 259/93 'so that waste is shipped in circumstances which are deemed to be illegal traffic under Article 26' commits an offence[1].

1 SI 1994/1137, reg 12(1).

5.191 A conviction for illegal traffic may have a further consequence in certain member states. Regulation 259/93 permits a competent authority to use the conviction of a consignee or notifier as a ground for objection to further shipments[1]. However, this can only be undertaken where such a refusal is made 'in accordance with national legislation'[2]. As the Transfrontier Shipment of Waste Regulations 1994[3] are silent on this matter, this provision does not seem to have application in the UK. Instead, convictions of UK notifiers and consignees will count as 'prescribed offences' and 'relevant offences'[4]. As discussed elsewhere[5], these offences may jeopardise a person's registration as a controlled waste carrier or broker and affect whether a person is 'fit and proper' to hold a waste management licence.

1 Regulation 259/93, Articles 4(3)(c), 7(4)(a), 15(3), 17(4), 20(3) and 22.
2 Regulation 259/93, Articles 4(3)(c) and 7(4)(a).
3 SI 1994/1137.
4 SI 1994/1137, reg 19 amends the lists of prescribed and relevant offences contained in the Controlled Waste (Registration of Carriers and Seizure of Vehicles Regulations 1991 (SI 1991/1624, Sch 1) and the Waste Management Licensing Regulations 1994 (SI 1994/1056, reg 3).
5 See paras 6.63ff and 8.117.

Non-compliance with transport conditions

5.192 In addition to the offence associated with illegal traffic, there is a second, more general offence in the 1994 Regulations[1]. This relates to any person who 'transports, recovers, disposes of or otherwise handles waste' in the UK in contravention of a transport condition imposed on the shipment. As discussed at para 5.98, conditions of transport can be imposed by any competent authority by setting them down on the consignment note[2].

1 SI 1994/1137, reg 12(2).
2 Regulation 259/93, Articles 4(2)(d), 7(3), 15(5), 20(5) and 23(4).

5.193 Two statutory defences to this offence are contained in the 1994 Regulations. There is the usual provision requiring persons charged to prove that they took all reasonable steps and exercised all due diligence[1]. But as an alternative, it is open to the person to establish 'that he was not reasonably able to comply with the condition concerned[2] by reason of an emergency'[3].

1 SI 1994/1137, reg 14(1): see paras 5.186 and 7.145ff.
2 Ie the condition imposed on the transport.
3 SI 1994/1137, reg 14(2): the nature of an emergency is considered at para 7.154.

Fraudulent completion and failure to return a certificate of disposal

5.194   An offence is committed if a UK consignee fails to return the completed certificate of disposal or recovery within the 180 day time period[1]. Similarly, a person who sends back a certificate 'which is false in a material particular' commits an offence[2]. The statutory defence of taking all reasonable steps and exercising all due diligence applies[3]. But this is supplemented by an alternative, involving the defendant establishing that the certificate could not be furnished because disposal or recovery within the requisite time was prevented by an emergency[4]. However, in addition to providing evidence that an emergency had arisen, the Transfrontier Shipment of Waste Regulations 1994 also require the consignee to show that the waste was disposed of or recovered 'as soon as was reasonably practicable' by him or that 'he is taking all reasonable steps to ensure that the waste is disposed of or recovered as soon as is reasonably practicable'[5].

1   SI 1994/1137, reg 12(3): as required by Regulation 259/93, Articles 5(6), 8(6) and 20(9).
2   1994/1137, reg 12(3): false statements are discussed at para 12.209ff.
3   SI 1994/1137, reg 14(1).
4   SI 1994/1137, reg 14(3)(a): see para 7.154.
5   SI 1994/1137, reg 14(3)(b).

Shipping waste without a certificate approving the financial guarantee

5.195   The Transfrontier Shipment of Waste Regulations 1994 make it an offence for a person to 'ship' waste into or out of the UK unless a certificate has been issued by the Agency signifying its approval of the financial guarantee[1]. Other than Green List passing to recovery, this applies to all loads entering or leaving the UK and is regardless of whether the guarantee has been approved by any of the other competent authorities[2].

1   SI 1994/1137, regs 7(1) and 12(4).
2   See para 5.85ff above.

5.196   As a contrast to other wording of offences such as those set out in s 33 of the EPA 1990[1], the offence relates solely to persons who 'ship' the waste. Clearly, this will directly impinge upon the person undertaking the transport: that person is obviously 'shipping' the waste. In addition, given the purpose of the 1994 Regulations and Regulation 259/93, it seems appropriate to argue that persons who arrange for the waste to be moved – in other words individuals such as the notifier or a broker – may constitute persons who 'ship' the waste.

1   See Chapter 7.

Falsifying information to obtain a financial guarantee

5.197   The provision of information 'which is false in a material particular' with a view to obtaining a certificate approving the guarantee is an offence under the 1994 Regulations[1].

1   SI 1994/1137, reg 12(5): false statements are discussed further at para 12.209ff.

Mixing wastes which are subject to separate notifications

5.198   The prohibition in Regulation 259/93 on the mixing of wastes which are subject to separate notifications[1] is made an offence under the Transfrontier Shipment of Waste Regulations 1994[2].

1   Regulation 259/93, Article 29: see para 5.183.
2   SI 1994/1137, reg 12(6).

Shipping waste from the UK without a contract

5.199 Regulation 259/93 requires that most shipments should be covered by contracts[1]. The 1994 Regulations make it an offence[2] to transport waste without a contract as required by Articles 3(6), 6(6) or 15(4) of the Regulation.

1 See para 5.80 above.
2 SI 1994/1137, reg 12(7).

5.200 It has been noted that Regulation 259/93 is somewhat inconsistent as to the circumstances when contracts are needed. Circular 13/94[1] therefore requires the Agency should always require evidence that a contract exists for all non-Green List waste shipments. However, it should be apparent that the offence in the 1994 Regulations only pertains[2] to transactions affected by Articles 3(6), 6(6) and 15(4). Accordingly, regulatory bodies need to exercise care in respect of the verification of contracts for the few shipments of waste which are: imported for disposal into the European Community; imported for recovery from a non-OECD state; exported out of the Community for recovery; or where the Community is to be a transit state. In these instances, there is no offence under the 1994 Regulations for moving wastes to these destinations without a contract.

1 Circular 13/94, para 55.
2 It should also be noted that exports of waste from the Community for recovery also require a contract under Regulation 259/93 (see Articles 17(4) and 17(7)), albeit less explicitly than in Articles 3(6), 6(6) and 15(4). However, there is no reference to this in the offences set down in the Transfrontier Shipment of Waste Regulations 1994 (reg 12(7)).

5.201 Although it may be tempting to circumvent this problem by making the existence of a valid contract a condition of transport[1], this may be unlawful. A requirement of the relevant articles of Regulation 259/93 is that transport conditions should not be more stringent than those applied to indigenous waste movements[2]. Requiring formal contracts on all transfrontier shipments would appear to breach this provision, as there is no statutory requirement for waste movements within the UK to be covered by written contracts.

1 See para 5.80.
2 Regulation 259/93, Articles 4(2)(d), 7(3), 15(5), 20(5) and 23(4).

Conveying Green List waste without appropriate documentation

5.202 All Green List waste shipments to recovery are required to be 'accompanied' by the requisite documentation[1]. A person who fails to do this commits an offence[2]. The statutory defence of taking all reasonable steps and exercising all due diligence applies[3]. In this instance a person so convicted will face a maximum fine of level 3 on the standard scale[4]. Unlike non-compliance with the duty of care system of transfer notes[5], the offence is not one which is indictable. However, this would also be an offence in respect of the duty of care itself[6].

1 Regulation 259/93, Article 11: see para 5.141.
2 SI 1994/1137, reg 12(8).
3 SI 1994/1137, reg 14(1).
4 Currently £1,000 or, in Northern Ireland, £400.
5 See EPA 1990, s 34(6) and para 3.18ff.
6 EPA 1990, s 34: see Chapter 3.

Obstruction

5.203 The final[1] offence under the Transfrontier Shipment of Waste Regulations 1994 involves obstruction[2]. This specifically relates to the obstruction of Agency officers by consignees when waste is subject to a notice requiring its disposal or recovery[3], or the obstruction of customs officers exercising their powers to detain waste[4]. It does not, however, relate to obstruction of Agency staff by notifiers[5]. A person charged with obstruction has the somewhat bizarre statutory defence that all reasonable steps and all due diligence were exercised to avoid the commission of the offence[6].

1   The 1994 Regulations also contain an offence provision in respect of non-compliance with statutory notices served to effect the return of a transfrontier shipment. This matter is discussed at para 12.128ff.
2   SI 1994/1137, reg 12(10): the nature of 'obstruction' is discussed at para 12.202ff.
3   SI 1994/1137, reg 9: see para 12.132ff.
4   SI 1994/1137, reg 10: see para 5.182.
5   Hence it does not apply where the Agency is exercising its powers under Regulation 8 to effect the return of waste to a notifier.
6   SI 1994/1137, reg 14(1): the relevant provision on obstruction in the Environment Act 1995 is s 110. In s 110 there is no statutory defence.

Chapter 6

Registration of waste carriers and waste brokers

INTRODUCTION

6.01 This chapter describes the provisions contained in the Control of Pollution (Amendment) Act 1989 and in the Waste Management Licensing Regulations 1994[1] for the registration of controlled waste carriers and controlled waste brokers. The requirements of these two enactments are considered together for the reason that many of the statutory requirements are identical. The provisions also allow a person to possess a joint carrier and broker registration.

1 SI 1994/1056, reg 20 and Sch 5.

6.02 The purpose of the Control of Pollution (Amendment) Act 1989 is to put out of business the minority of waste carriers who are perpetual offenders. The Act[1] and associated Regulations[2] require waste carriers who transport controlled waste on behalf of third parties to be subject to formal registration. Registration also applies to all commercial bodies who move building and demolition waste, even that which is produced by themselves. The Act permits registration to be refused or revoked if a carrier has acquired certain prescribed criminal convictions. It sets up an appeal procedure for such decisions, with the regulations[3] prescribing a certificate which shows proof of registration. Finally, the 1989 Act requires evidence of carrier registration to be produced on demand, and permits vehicles to be seized in a very limited set of circumstances. The latter powers, concerning the production of evidence of registration and the seizure of vehicles, are discussed in parallel to other general enforcement powers of the Agency in Chapter 12. The 1989 Act and associated regulations are accompanied by their own circular[4], which sets out non-statutory guidance on interpretation and implementation. For the financial year 1997/98, a total of 79,346 controlled waste carriers were registered with the Environment Agency[5].

1 Control of Pollution (Amendment) Act 1989 as amended by the EPA 1990, Sch 15, para 31 and the Environment Act 1995, Sch 22, para 37.
2 SI 1991/1624 as amended by SI 1992/588, reg 10, SI 1994/1056, reg 23, SI 1994/1137, reg 19, SI 1996/593, reg 3 and Sch 2, para 9, SI 1996/972, reg 22 and SI 1998/605, reg 2.
3 SI 1991/1624, Sch 3.
4 Department of the Environment (1991) *Control of Pollution (Amendment) Act 1989 The Controlled Waste (Registration of Carriers and Seizure of Vehicles) Regulations 1991*, Circular 11/91, HMSO, London.
5 Environment Agency (1998) *Environment Agency Annual Report and Accounts 1997/98*, Environment Agency, Bristol, Appendix 5: figure excludes registrations in Scotland.

6.03 The system for the registration of waste brokers, requires that, subject to certain significant prescribed exclusions, all brokers of controlled waste who arrange for waste to be transported, disposed of or recovered by third parties need to apply for a registration[1]. Registration can be refused or revoked if the broker has been convicted of relevant offences. Although the broker registration process is similar to carrier registration, and an application costs the same amount, no broker registration certificates are required to be issued. For the year 1997/98, there were 1,784 organisations registered with the Environment Agency as brokers[2].

1 SI 1994/1056, reg 20, Sch 4, para 12 and Sch 5, as amended by SI 1998/606, reg 2(3).

2 Environment Agency (1998) *Environment Agency Annual Report and Accounts 1997/98*, Environment Agency, Bristol, Appendix 5: figure excludes registrations in Scotland which are not presented in the respective annual report. However the equivalent figure is about 6,000 carriers and brokers in total.

6.04 This chapter commences with a detailed description of the types of controlled waste carrier who are required to register. A similar discussion on brokers follows. The offence of operating as an unregistered waste carrier or waste broker is then considered. As the actual application procedure, the registration renewal process and the refusal or revocation system are similar in respect of both waste carriers and waste brokers[1], they are considered together in subsequent sections of this chapter. A discussion of the Agencies' duties in the establishment of carrier and broker registers, however, is to be found at para 13.43ff.

1 SI 1991/1624 and SI 1994/1056, Sch 5.

6.05 The provisions of the Control of Pollution (Amendment) Act 1989 predated the enactment of Article 12 of the Directive on Waste[1], which requires establishments and undertakings who collect or transport waste on a professional basis to be registered. In order to ensure full compliance with that Article, additional provisions were introduced in the Waste Management Licensing Regulations 1994[2]. These affect bodies such as charities and the waste collection authorities, which hitherto did not need to register. As these provisions are somewhat different from the main requirements of the 1989 Act, they are described separately at para 6.105 of this chapter. Article 12 of the Directive also requires the registration of waste brokers. This requirement is transposed by the 1994 Regulations, principally by Schedule 5.

1 Council Directive of 15 July 1975 on Waste (75/442/EEC), (OJ L194/39 25.7.75) (subsequently amended by Council Directive of 18 March 1991 amending Directive 75/442/EEC on Waste (91/156/EEC) (OJ L78/32 26.3.91) and by Directive 91/692 (OJ L377/48)).
2 SI 1994/1056, Sch 4, Pt 1, para 12.

THE REGISTRATION OF CONTROLLED WASTE CARRIERS

6.06 The Control of Pollution (Amendment) Act 1989 has, as its origins, a Private Members Bill introduced by Joan Ruddock MP. The Bill was drafted mainly as a response to the problem of wide-scale flytipping of construction industry waste in London. The scale of this issue is well illustrated by the case of Millwall Football Club, which discovered 10,000 tonnes of such wastes dumped on its visitors car park[1]. Given that the average payload of construction industry heavy goods vehicles is between 10 and 20 tonnes, the scale and level of organisation behind such an operation is immediately apparent.

1 Reeds J (1986) 'Catching Flytippers: the Rogues of Rubbish' *Surveyor* 4 September, pp 12–15.

6.07 The 1989 Act came fully into force in 1992[1], being expanded upon by the Controlled Waste (Registration of Carriers and Seizure of Vehicles) Regulations 1991[2]. As will be seen, certain types of controlled waste carrier are excluded from the scope of the 1989 Act. Some of these bodies, such as waste collection authorities and charities, are instead subject to a system of registration which is different and significantly less complex from that contained in the 1989 Act[3].

1 Control of Pollution (Amendment) Act 1989 (Commencement) Order 1991 (SI 1991/1618).
2 SI 1991/1624 as amended by SI 1992/588, reg 10, SI 1994/1056, reg 23, SI 1994/1137, reg 19, SI 1996/593, reg 3 and Sch 2, para 9, SI 1996/972, reg 22 and SI 1998/605, reg 2.
3 SI 1994/1056, reg 14 and Sch 4, Pt I, para 12: see para 6.105.

Exclusions from the need to possess a carrier registration

6.08   Under the 1989 Act, certain classes of person do not need to possess a valid carrier registration[1]. Other types of person are excluded by the Controlled Waste (Registration of Carrier and Seizure of Vehicles) Regulations 1991[2].

1   Control of Pollution (Amendment) Act 1989, s 1(2).
2   SI 1991/1624 as amended by SI 1992/588, reg 10, SI 1994/1056, reg 23, SI 1994/1137, reg 19, SI 1996/593, reg 3 and Sch 2, para 9, SI 1996/972, reg 22 and SI 1998/605, reg 2.

Householders

6.09   Householders are entirely excluded from the legislation by s 1 of the Control of Pollution (Amendment) Act 1989. They are not transporting waste 'in the course of any business ... or otherwise with a view to profit' as is required by s 1(1) of the 1989 Act.

Producers of waste which is not building and demolition waste

6.10   Besides householders, the most important class of individual who is absolved from the need to possess a carrier registration is a person who actually produces controlled waste[1]. However, the waste producer is only exempt when transporting controlled waste which is *not* 'building or demolition waste'[2]. Under the 1991 Regulations, building and demolition waste 'means waste arising from works of construction or demolition, including waste arising from preparatory work thereto'[3]. The word 'construction' is then further defined as an activity which 'includes improvement, repair or alteration'[4]. The reader's attention is drawn to the contrasting use of the verbs, 'means' and 'includes' in these two definitions. How far the boundary of building and demolition waste extends is not clear. It has been suggested[5] that the need for registration may not, for example, extend to decorators taking their empty paint pots back to a depot in a van.

1   SI 1991/1624, reg 2(1)(b).
2   SI 1991/1624, reg 2(1)(b).
3   SI 1991/1624, reg 2(2).
4   Definition added by SI 1992/588, reg 10(1).
5   Bates J H (1992) *UK Waste Law*, Sweet & Maxwell, London, para 9.05.

6.11   Other than building and demolition wastes, persons carrying any other type of controlled waste which they produced themselves are excluded from the 1989 Act[1], mainly due to the need to keep the number of registrations to a manageable level. The inclusion within the ambit of the 1989 Act of producers of building and demolition waste was deemed necessary, as it was the purpose of the original Ruddock Bill to address the anti-social activities of this sector.

1   SI 1991/1624, reg 2(1)(b).

6.12   It should be made clear that, subject to a very small number of exclusions[1], the Control of Pollution (Amendment) Act 1989 applies to all persons transporting building or demolition waste beyond the boundaries of the premises on which the waste was produced. There is no exemption for size of company or type of vehicle. Given that virtually all builders, plumbers etc deal with building and demolition waste[2] virtually all of them should be registered. Indeed, a significant proportion of the 79,000 controlled waste carriers in England and Wales are builders. Whether carrier registration in respect of this type of activity serves any useful purpose is a moot point. Given the number of builders nationwide, it is clear that there is still extensive evasion. It addition, it would seem that small builders are increasingly leaving wastes behind once a job has been completed, requiring householders to arrange for disposal. The disappearance of small builders' vans and pick-ups from landfill sites has been a noticeable and, perhaps, unfortunate consequence of this legislation[3].

1   Bodies such as the waste collection authority and charities are excluded, but require a separate registration under the Waste Management Licensing Regulations: see para 6.105 below.
2   This matter was clarified by the definition of construction added by SI 1992/588, reg 10(1).
3   This trend has been exacerbated further by the landfill tax (see para 1.100ff).

6.13   When involved in the carriage of waste which is not building and demolition waste, the producer does not need to obtain registration. However, neither the Control of Pollution (Amendment) Act 1989 nor the regulations contain a definition of a 'waste producer'. Although the term 'waste producer' is also applicable in other contexts, namely in respect of the duty of care[1] and also in relation to the definition of waste in the Waste Management Licensing Regulations 1994[2], it would seem inappropriate to regard such definitions as common between these, quite separate, items of legislation and the 1989 Act and associated regulations. For example, the 1994 Regulations state that the producer of waste is:

'... anyone whose activities produce ... waste or who carries out pre-processing, mixing or other operations resulting in a change in its nature or composition.'

The Controlled Waste (Registration of Carriers and Seizure of Vehicles) Regulations 1991 hold that, unless building or demolition waste is involved, waste producers do not need to register to haul the waste they produce[3]. If this requirement was to be applied in conjunction with the definition of waste producer contained in the 1994 Regulations, persons operating waste transfer stations would not require registration in respect of outward movements of non-building and demolition waste. Clearly, this interpretation cannot be viewed as congruent with an analysis of the purpose of the 1989 Act nor Article 12 of the Directive on Waste.

1   See para 3.79.
2   SI 1994/1056, reg 1(3): see para 2.156ff.
3   SI 1991/1624, reg 2(1)(b).

Transporters of animal by-products and carcasses

6.14   The Waste Management Licensing Regulations 1994 absolve transporters of animal carcasses and animal by-products from the need to be registered under the Control of Pollution (Amendment) Act 1989[1]. This is not a blanket exclusion, but applies only to those vehicles which satisfy certain terms and conditions[2]. If a vehicle does not satisfy these terms and conditions, a registration under the 1989 Act is required. Accordingly, an offence is committed by an operator of an unregistered vehicle in the latter circumstances.

1   SI 1994/1056, reg 23(3).
2   See para 6.20 below.

6.15   Generally, Circular 11/94 advises that many animal by-products transferred for use in the rendering or other related industries will not fall within the definition of controlled waste: they are 'not a discard of waste but a transfer for normal commercial use'[1]. But in some instances, animal by-products may fall within the definition of controlled waste.

1   Circular 11/94, Annex 4, para 4.91: waste definitions are discussed in Chapter 2.

6.16   Where animal by-product wastes are to be carried, a system has been devised which relies on the fact that the provisions of the Animal By-Products Order 1992[1] broadly cover the requirements of Article 12 of the Directive on Waste[2].

1   SI 1992/3303, as amended by SI 1996/827 and SI 1997/2894. Note that the Animal By-Products Order 1992 has been repealed by the Animal By-Products Order 1999 (SI 1999/646). However as discussed below, the waste legislation still refers to the earlier Order.
2   Council Directive of 15 July 1975 on Waste (75/442/EEC) (OJ L194/39 25.7.75) (as amended by Council Directive of 18 March 1991 amending Directive 75/442/EEC on Waste (91/156/EEC) (OJ L78/32 26.3.91)).

6.17   The exemption from registration for carriers subject to the Animal By-Products Order 1992 only pertains to specified activities involved in the transportation of animal by-products[1]. In addition, the exemption only holds when vehicles are moving wastes which are animal by-products and where that transport is in accordance with Schedule 2 to the Order[2]. The exemption from carrier registration does not, however, hold in relation to third-party carriers of animal by-products[3]. The latter need a controlled waste carrier registration under the Control of Pollution (Amendment) Act 1989. Neither does the exemption hold when authorised carriers of animal by-products move materials such as construction and demolition wastes that they have produced themselves[4].

1   SI 1991/1624, reg 2(1)(i)(i) as amended by SI 1994/1056, reg 23(3).
2   SI 1991/1624, reg 2(1)(i) as amended by SI 1994/1056, reg 23(3).
3   See SI 1991/1624, reg 2(1)(i) as amended by SI 1994/1056, reg 23(3) and see Circular 11/94, Annex 4, para 4.93.
4   SI 1991/1624, reg 2(1)(i) as amended by SI 1994/1056, reg 23(3), only refers to the 'transport of animal by-products'.

6.18   The Animal By-Products Order 1992 implements Council Directive 90/667[1] and establishes veterinary rules in Britain for the processing, disposal and re-sale of animal waste. It does not apply to waste food covered by the Diseases of Animals (Waste Food) Order 1973[2], nor to certain types of materials[3] obtained from animals which have been slaughtered 'in the normal way' when these materials are not used for the manufacture of foodstuffs[4]. An example of a non-foodstuff use of such materials might be in the production of clothing from animal hides.

1   OJ L365/51 27.11.90.
2   SI 1973/1936 as amended by SI 1987/232.
3   Hides, skins, hooves, feathers, wool, horns, hair, blood and similar products: SI 1993/3303, Article 4(2).
4   SI 1993/3033, Article 4(2).

6.19   As noted, animal by-products transported by operators of premises subject to specified[1] Articles of the Animal By-Products Order 1992 do not need a controlled waste carrier registration. Such operators are:

–   renderers which possess an 'approval' from the Ministry of Agriculture, Fisheries and Food (MAFF)[2] or are required to be registered as a premises for the collection and use of animal by-products as petfoods or for 'technical' or pharmaceutical products[3];
–   registered premises involved with the feeding of animal by-products, such as zoos, circuses, fur farms, packs of hounds or maggot farms in the production of fishing bait[4].

In addition, operators of knackers' yards[5] and other sites licensed[6] by MAFF which use any specified animal by-product[7] for the production of materials which have not been fully rendered[8] should have been excluded – and were so originally – by the Waste Management Licensing Regulations 1994[9]. However, the Animal By-Products Order 1992 was both amended in 1997[10] and repealed in 1999[11] and since these changes the cross-referencing to the Order in the 1994 Regulations no longer makes sense. Hence it seems that knacker's yards currently may need a carrier registration when moving controlled wastes.

1   SI 1992/3303, Article 5, 6, 8, 9 and 10: see SI 1991/1624, reg 2(1)(i), as amended by SI 1994/1056, reg 23.
2   SI 1992/3303, Article 8, as exempted by SI 1991/1624, reg 2(1)(i), (ii).
3   SI 1992/3303, Article 9, as exempted by SI 1991/1624, reg 2(1)(i), (ii).
4   SI 1992/3303, Article 10, as exempted by SI 1991/1624, reg 2(1)(i), (ii).
5   Defined in s 34 of the Slaughterhouses Act 1974 (in Scotland, s 6 of the Slaughter of Animals (Scotland) Act 1980): see SI 1991/1624, reg 2(2) as amended by SI 1994/1056, reg 23(4).
6   Which are knacker's yard licences or are licences issued under Articles 5(2)(c) and 6(2)(d) of the Order.
7   As defined in SI 1993/3303, Pts I and II of Sch 1, as amended by SI 1996/827 and SI 1997/2849.
8   SI 1992/3303, Article 5(2)(c) or 6(2)(d), as exempted by SI 1991/1624, reg 2(1)(i)(i) (as amended by SI 1994/1056, reg 23).
9   SI 1994/1056, reg 23(3) and see the reference to Article 5(2)(c) and 6(2)(n) of the Order.
10 SI 1997/2894, reg 2(3).
11 SI 1999/646, art 35 and Sch 6.

6.20   Notwithstanding the apparent anomaly caused by the revocation of the Animal By-Products Order 1992, the existence of the reference to that Order in the Waste Management Licensing Regulations 1994 makes it appropriate to briefly review the requirements. Schedule 2 to the 1992 Order sets down conditions for the transport of animal by-products:

–   vehicles and any containers used for transporting animal remains must not leak and must be adequately covered;
–   vehicles, containers and any covers must be maintained in a clean condition;
–   persons consigning animal carcasses, by-products etc[1] must keep records of each consignment and must ensure that identifying documentation accompanies each load. These records must show the date the animal materials were removed, the quantity, description and source of the animal materials, the intended destination and the name of the haulier;
–   records must be retained by consignor and consignee for two years;
–   renderers, knackers' yards and other registered premises must keep records of the source, quantity and description of the animal by-product and the date it was delivered;
–   knackers' yards and other registered premises must indicate the use to which the material was put;
–   where materials are transported which were hitherto destined for human consumption, they must be marked on the container or other packaging material by appropriately lettered labels.

1   As defined in SI 1992/3303, Sch 1, Pt I.

6.21   The above provisions in relation to waste animal by-products go hand-in-hand with the exclusion of these materials from the requirements of the duty of care under s 34 of the EPA 1990[1] and from the need for premises which 'keep or treat'[2] animal remains from the need to possess waste management licences[3].

1   SI 1994/1056, reg 24(7): see para 3.27.
2   But which are not involved in the 'disposal' of animal by-products.
3   SI 1994/1056, reg 17 and Sch 3, para 23: see para 10.245ff.

Other exclusions from carrier registration

6.22 Under the Control of Pollution (Amendment) Act 1989, certain other waste carriers are explicitly excluded from the requirement to possess a registration:

(a) persons transporting controlled waste 'within the same premises between different places in those premises'[1];
(b) persons importing waste into Britain from a non-UK source up to the point at which it is landed[2]; and
(c) the transport by air or sea of waste from a point of departure in Britain to a place outside Britain[3].

1 Control of Pollution (Amendment) Act 1989, s1(2)(a): the term 'premises' is discussed at para 3.52ff.
2 1989 Act, s 1(2)(b).
3 1989 Act, s 1(2)(c).

6.23 The provisions of the 1989 Act do not apply to the waste collection authority, the Agency[1] or the waste disposal authority[2]. Given the increased emphasis on compulsory competitive tendering for refuse collection, the exemption of the waste collection authority did invite claims of unfairness and dual standards. In addition, this omission was not in accordance with the requirements of the Directive on Waste[3]. The result is that such bodies were included within a simplified registration scheme contained in Schedule 4 to the Waste Management Licensing Regulations 1994[4].

1 As 'waste regulation authority': see the EPA 1990, s 30 as amended by the Environment Act 1995, s 120 and Sch 22, para 62.
2 SI 1991/1624, reg 2(1)(a).
3 Council Directive of 15 July 1975 on Waste (75/442/EEC) (OJ L194/39 25.7.75) (as amended by Council Directive of 18 March 1991 amending Directive 75/442/EEC on Waste (91/156/EEC) (OJ L78/32 26.3.91)) Article 12.
4 SI 1994/1056, Sch 4, Pt 1, para 12: see para 6.105 below.

6.24 Circular 11/91 makes it clear that Local Authority Waste Disposal Companies (LAWDCs) fall within the controls contained in the 1989 Act[1]. They are 'waste disposal contractors' within the meaning of s 30(5) of the EPA 1990.

1 Circular 11/91, Annex 1, para 1.10(a).

6.25 The above exclusions under the Control of Pollution (Amendment) Act 1989 are supplemented by further exemptions which relate to[1]:

(a) any ferry operator, in relation to the carriage on the vessel of vehicles containing controlled waste;
(b) an operator of a vessel[2], aircraft, hovercraft, floating container or 'vehicle in relation to its use' after it has been loaded with waste for the purposes of disposal at sea[3] under ss 5, 6 and 7 of the Food and Environmental Protection Act 1985[4]; and
(c) a charity and a voluntary organisation[5,6].

Certain of these bodies do not require a registration at all. However, charities and voluntary organisations wishing to haul waste on behalf of third parties are subject to the system of registration set down in the Waste Management Licensing Regulations 1994[7].

1 SI 1991/1624, reg 2(1)(c–g).
2 As defined by s 742 of the Merchant Shipping Act 1894.
3 Sea disposal is mainly controlled through licences issued under s 5 of Part II of the Food and Environment Protection Act 1985. Section 6 of the 1985 Act covers licences for the un-utilised option of sea incineration, whilst s 7 allows certain exemptions to be made from the need to possess a sea disposal licence. These exemptions are to be found in the Deposits in the Sea (Exemptions) Order 1985 (SI 1985/1699 as amended by SI 1994/1056, reg 21).

4   Circular 11/91, Annex 1, 1.10(e)(2) indicates that the reference to vehicles '... applies only to the
    transport of controlled waste in circumstances in which the controls imposed by Part II of the 1985
    Act apply. This means, for example, that the transport of controlled waste by road to the place at
    which it is loaded onto a vessel does not fall within the scope of this exemption'.
5   Defined by way of s 48(1) of the Local Government Act 1985 or s 83(2D) of the Local Government
    (Scotland) Act 1973.
6   Any 'wholly owned subsidiary' of the British Railways board is also exempt. But this appears to be
    only temporary. It is exempt only if it is already registered as a broker of controlled waste (under
    SI 1994/1056, Sch 4, para 12 and whilst the application for a carrier registration is pending
    (SI 1991/1624, reg 2(1)(c) as amended by SI 1994/1056, reg 23(2): see also Circular 11/94,
    para 23).
7   SI 1994/1056, Sch 4, Pt 1, para 12(1).

Vehicles under hire to third parties

6.26   Registration as a controlled waste carrier under the Control of Pollution
(Amendment) Act 1989 relates to a person, not to individual vehicles. However, in
some waste transactions, the question of which person should be subject to registration can become complex. In instances where vehicles are hired and driven by the
hirer this is relatively straightforward, but gets more difficult when both vehicle and
driver are sub-contracted to work for another person. Such practices are particularly
common in respect of the movement of construction and demolition waste, where
small haulage companies or self-employed owner drivers may provide significant
amounts of waste carriage. In addition, there is often no formal written contract which
establishes the terms of hire or sub-contract.

6.27   It would seem that, where persons hire vehicles and utilise their own drivers
to carry waste[1], then the hirer should be a registered waste carrier. In this instance,
the activities of the vehicle are left to the whim of the person who has arranged the
hire. It also makes no difference to whether a registration is needed if a vehicle is
hired or is lent to another person[2]. Furthermore, registered waste carriers do not
commit an offence when they have under their immediate control vehicles owned by
other persons, including their drivers, who are not registered. According to
McCowan LJ[3] the fundamental issue in deciding which body should possess a carrier registration concerns the question of correctly deciding the identity of the person who is exercising direct control over the carriage of the waste. Accordingly, a
person who is a registered carrier and is exercising charge of the vehicle, sitting in
the cab with a driver who is not – and whose employer does not – possess a registration is acting as a registered carrier[4]. However, in other instances the relationship
may not be as clear-cut. A more distant relationship may mean that a person who
arranges the carriage of waste by others is acting in the role of a broker[5], with the
person directly responsible for the transportation needing a registration as a controlled waste carrier. Hence a dividing line exists somewhere between, on the one
hand, a registered person sitting in the cab of another vehicle and, on the other hand,
a person acting as a broker and arranging others to undertake the transportation of
waste. Such a dividing line is a matter of degree and dependent upon the facts of
each case[6].

1   Ie construction or demolition waste, and other waste moved behalf of third parties.
2   *Cosmick Transport Services v Bedfordshire County Council* [1996] Env LR 78 at 85/86.
3   *Cosmick Transport Services v Bedfordshire County Council* [1996] Env LR 78 at 85.
4   See *Cosmick Transport Services v Bedfordshire County Council* [1996] Env LR 78.
5   See para 6.28 below and para 3.101ff.
6   See, in the context of the Road Traffic Act 1988, *Hallett Silberman Ltd v Cheshire County Council*
    [1993] RTR 32.

THE REGISTRATION OF CONTROLLED WASTE BROKERS

6.28 Article 12 of the Directive on Waste[1] requires that establishments or undertakings 'which arrange for the disposal or recovery of waste on behalf of others (dealers or brokers)' are either subject to an authorisation or are registered with the competent authorities. This requirement is put into effect by the Waste Management Licensing Regulations 1994[2].

1 Council Directive of 15 July 1975 on Waste (75/442/EEC) (OJ L194/39 25.7.75) (as amended by Council Directive of 18 March 1991 amending Directive 75/442/EEC on Waste (91/156/EEC) (OJ L78/32 26.3.91)).
2 SI 1994/1056, reg 20, Sch 4, para 12 and Sch 5, as amended by SI 1998/606, reg 2(4).

6.29 The relevant part of the 1994 Regulations refers to persons who 'arrange (as dealer or broker) for the disposal or recovery of controlled waste on behalf of another person'[1]. As a convenient short-hand, these individuals will be referred to below as 'waste brokers'. There is no more clarification given in the Regulations as to the identity of waste brokers[2]. In *Milford v Hughes*[3] a dictionary definition of a broker was applied. Brokers were 'those that contrive, make, and conclude bargains and contracts between merchants and tradesmen, for which they have a fee or reward'. As an immediate contrast to the British provisions the legislation for Northern Ireland sets out a definition: ' "Broker" means a person who has control of controlled waste for the purposes of having carried out on behalf of another person ... the importation, carriage, keeping, treatment or disposal of controlled waste'[4].

1 SI 1994/1056, reg 20(1).
2 However, see Department of the Environment (1996) *Waste Management The Duty of Care A Code of Practice*, 2nd edn, HMSO, pages 60–61; and see para 3.101.
3 (1846) 16 M & W 174. See also *Lester v Balfour Williamson Merchant Shippers Ltd* [1953] 1 All ER 1146.
4 Waste and Contaminated Land (Northern Ireland) Order 1997 (SI 1997/2778 NI 19), Article 5(14).

6.30 Members of the waste management industry can also act as brokers when they arrange the disposal or recovery of waste on behalf of others. However, as is outlined in the next section, they only need to register when they are not directly involved in the actual disposal or recovery of the waste, or in its transportation[1]. According to Circular 19/91[2] which accompanies the provisions of the EPA 1990 on the duty of care[3], both the Waste Disposal Authority and Waste Collection Authority may be acting as brokers. However, these bodies are exempt from the principal requirements for registration[4].

1 See SI 1994/1056, reg 20 and Circular 11/94, Annex 8, para 8.12.
2 Circular 19/91, para 30.
3 EPA 1990, s 34: see para 3.102.
4 See para 6.105 below.

6.31 All establishments or undertakings acting as brokers of controlled waste had to be registered by 31 December 1994, otherwise an offence was committed[1]. Establishments and undertakings in this sense are viewed by Circular 11/94[2] as including bodies corporate, partnerships, authorities, societies, trusts, clubs and other organisations[3].

1 SI 1994/1056, reg 20(1).
2 Circular 11/94, Annex 8, para 8.11.
3 See para 10.22.

Exclusions from the need to possess a broker registration

Persons actually carrying out disposal or recovery activities

6.32   Certain types of organisation are exempt from the need to register as a broker. The most important exemption concerns organisations involved in the recovery or disposal of controlled waste for a third party. However, this is only applicable where the organisation is 'authorised' to carry out the disposal or recovery of the waste[1] by one of the following[2]: a waste management licence or authorisation under Part I of the EPA 1990; a discharge consent[3]; a sea disposal licence[4]; a waste recovery operation subject to an exemption under the Waste Management Licensing Regulations 1994[5]; and an exempt recovery operation subject to the Deposits in the Sea (Exemptions) Order 1985[6]. It is not clear exactly what is meant by the term 'authorised'. On the one hand, it might mean generally authorised to dispose of or receive waste. But, on the other hand, it may mean authorised to deal with the particular waste in question. If the latter interpretation is right, should the waste be outside the terms and conditions of the authorisation, the exemption from broker registration will not apply.

1   SI 1994/1056, reg 20(2).
2   SI 1994/1056, reg 20(2).
3   Under Chapter II of Pt III of the Water Resources Act 1991 or, in Scotland, under Pt II of the Control of Pollution Act 1974.
4   Under Pt II of the Food and Environmental Protection Act 1985.
5   As exempt under SI 1994/1056, reg 17(1): exemptions are discussed in Chapters 10 and 11.
6   As exempt under SI 1985/1699, Article 3, as amended by SI 1994/1056, reg 21.

Persons transporting the waste for disposal or recovery

6.33   The second class of person who is not required to register as a waste broker is a registered carrier of controlled waste[1] when that person actually transports the waste to or from any place in Britain[2]. A similar proviso affects the waste collection, disposal and regulation authorities, charities and voluntary organisations which are registered as professional transporters of waste[3,4].

1   SI 1994/1056, reg 20: it is assumed that this refers to a person registered under the Control of Pollution (Amendment) Act 1989, although this is not made explicit in Regulation 20.
2   Ie England, Scotland and Wales only: not Northern Ireland.
3   Ie those registered under Pt I of Schedule 4 of SI 1994/1056: see para 6.105.
4   However, this does not apply to Local Authority Waste Disposal Companies (LAWDCs) constituted under s 30(5) of the 1990 Act. A LAWDC will need to register as a broker under Schedule 5 to the Waste Management Licensing Regulations 1994 if it is acting as a waste broker: see Circular 11/94, Annex 8, para 8.16(c).

Charities, voluntary organisations, the WDA, the WCA and the Agency

6.34   Other charities and voluntary organisations which are involved in waste broking, but who do not act as professional collectors of waste, are excluded from the provisions of Schedule 5[1]. The Agency, the Waste Collection Authority and Waste Disposal Authority are also excluded[2]. They are instead subject to the streamlined registration provisions contained in Schedule 4 to the Waste Management Licensing Regulations 1994, described at para 6.105 below.

1   SI 1994/1056, reg 20(4)(a) and (b).
2   SI 1994/1056, reg 20(4)(c).

OFFENCES

6.35   The Control of Pollution (Amendment) Act 1989 sets out offences in respect of persons acting as unregistered waste carriers. Similarly, the Waste Management

Licensing Regulations 1994 contain provisions in respect of waste brokers. These particulars are discussed below. A person who uses an unregistered waste carrier also commits an offence in respect of the duty of care[1]. An unregistered carrier is not an 'authorised person' under s 34(3)(d) of the EPA 1990. By contrast, a person who utilises an unregistered waste broker does not appear to commit an offence.

1 EPA 1990, s 34: see Chapter 3.

The offence of operating as an unregistered waste carrier

6.36 Section 1 of the Control of Pollution (Amendment) Act 1989 sets out the principal offence[1]:

'. . . [I]t shall be an offence for any person who is not a registered carrier of controlled waste[2], in the course of any business of his or otherwise with a view to profit, to transport any controlled waste to and from any place in Great Britain.'

The word 'person' covers self employed individuals, partnerships and corporate bodies[3]. 'Transport' is defined[4] as including road, rail, air and inland waterway movements. However, transport excludes the movement of waste by pipeline. In respect of the phrase concerning the transportation of controlled waste 'in the course of any business', transportation can be ancillary to the actual business taking place and may not result in an actual profit being realised[5]. In addition, the concept of 'business' is much wider than the notion of a 'trade' and it may not be essential that any payment is made between parties[6]: 'the word [business] means almost anything which is an occupation and not a pleasure'[7].

1 Control of Pollution (Amendment) Act 1989, s 1(1).
2 'Controlled waste' is given the same meaning as in Part II of the EPA 1990 (1989 Act, s 9 as amended by para 31(5) of Sch 15 of the 1990 Act).
3 Interpretation Act 1978, s 5, Sch 1.
4 1989 Act, s 9(1).
5 See *Havering London Borough Council v Stevenson* [1970] 1 WLR 1375.
6 *Rolls v Miller* [1881–5] All ER Rep 915 at 918 G/I.
7 *Rolls v Miller* [1881–5] All ER Rep 915 at 920 E/F.

6.37 Persons convicted of an offence under s 1 of the 1989 Act are subject to a fine not exceeding of level 5[1] on the standard scale[2]. The offence is not one which is indictable.

1 Currently £5,000.
2 SI 1991/1624, reg 1(5).

6.38 The 1989 Act also permits the prosecution of persons other than those directly responsible for an offence[1]. For example, where Person A commits an offence, but the offence is in fact the fault of Person B, Person B also can be charged[2]. Indeed Person B can be charged, regardless of whether proceedings are taken against Person A[3].

1 Control of Pollution (Amendment) Act 1989, s 7(5) and (6).
2 1989 Act, s 7(5).
3 The wording of the 1989 Act in this respect is close to that contained in s 158 of the EPA 1990: see para 7.173.

6.39 The provisions in the 1989 Act relating to offences involving bodies corporate[1] are also similar in content[2] to s 157 of the EPA 1990. They allow both a body corporate and individual directors, managers, secretaries and other similar officers, to be charged with the same offence. This also applies in the case where a body corporate is managed by its members[3]. Given their similarities to s 157 of the EPA 1990, these requirements are discussed further at para 7.156ff.

1   Control of Pollution (Amendment) Act 1989, s 7(6).
2   There are some minor differences in the wording and phraseology.
3   1989 Act, s 7(7).

6.40   Convictions under the Control of Pollution (Amendment) Act 1989 may also affect the ability of a person to possess an operator's licence in respect of heavy goods vehicles. Such licences have to be renewed periodically and can be revoked or suspended[1]. Convictions under the 1989 Act can be taken into account when considering the desirability of a person applying for, or continuing to possess, such a licence[2].

1   Transport Act 1968, s 69.
2   Transport Act 1968, s 69 as amended by the EPA 1990, Sch 15, para 10.

Statutory defences

6.41   Three statutory defences are available for a person charged with the offence of operating as an unregistered carrier contrary to s 1 of the Control of Pollution (Amendment) Act 1989[1]. They are:

(a)   '... that the waste was transported in an emergency of which notice was given, as soon as practicable after it occurred, to the ... [Agency[2]] in whose area the emergency occurred'[3];

(b)   that the person accused of the offence 'neither knew[4] nor had reasonable grounds for suspecting that what was being transported was controlled waste and took all such steps as it was reasonable to take for ascertaining whether it was such waste'[5]; or

(c)   that the person was acting under the instructions of his employer[6].

It should be noted that the burden of proof is upon the defendant to show that the statutory defences have been satisfied[7].

1   Control of Pollution (Amendment) Act 1989, s 1.
2   As waste regulation authority: see the EPA 1990, s 30 as amended by the Environment Act 1995, Sch 22, para 62.
3   1989 Act, s 1(4)(a).
4   See para 7.55ff.
5   1989 Act, s 1(4)(b).
6   1989 Act, s 1(4)(c).
7   See *Tesco v Nattrass* [1971] 2 All ER 127 at 152 E/F and *Naish v Gore* [1971] 3 All ER 737 at 741G: discussed fully at para 7.155.

6.42   Unlike s 33(7) of the EPA 1990, where the word 'emergency' is not defined in the statutory defences, the 1989 Act holds that[1] an 'emergency' means:

'in relation to the transport of any controlled waste, ... any circumstances in which, in order to avoid, remove or reduce any serious danger to the public[2] or serious risk of damage to the environment, it is necessary for the waste to be transported from one place to another without the use of a registered carrier of such waste'[3].

It is curious to note that the words used are 'damage to the environment' and not 'pollution of the environment' which features in the EPA 1990. Similarly, there is no reference to 'harm to human health'[4].

1   Control of Pollution (Amendment) Act 1989, s 3(6).

2 'The public' is normally taken to be third parties, not employees of the company: see for example *DPP v Milbanke Tours Ltd* [1960] 2 All ER 467; *Morrisons Holdings Ltd v IRC* [1966] 1 All ER 789; *IRC v Park Investments Ltd* [1966] 2 All ER 785.
3 The word 'emergency' is discussed further at para 7.154.
4 As contained in s 33 of the EPA 1990.

The offence of operating as an unregistered waste broker

6.43 Subject to any of the exclusions described at para 6.32 above, an unregistered establishment or undertaking acting as a broker will be guilty of an offence[1] and may be subject to a fine not exceeding level five on the standard scale[2]. The offence is not one which is indictable. Both a body corporate and its directors, managers, secretaries etc can be prosecuted for failing to register[3].

1 SI 1994/1056, reg 20(1).
2 SI 1994/1056, reg 20(5): currently £5,000.
3 SI 1994/1056, reg 20(6) and the EPA 1990, s 157: see para 7.156ff.

6.44 By contrast to the principal offence under s 1 of the Control of Pollution (Amendment) Act 1989, the offence of operating as an unregistered waste broker[1] is not subject to any statutory defences. There is therefore, for example, no defence, similar to that contained in the 1989 Act, which would permit an unregistered broker to arrange for waste to be moved in an emergency.

1 SI 1994/1056, reg 20(1).

APPLICATIONS FOR CARRIER OR BROKER REGISTRATION

6.45 The respective Agencies have the duty to establish and maintain registers of controlled waste carriers[1] and waste brokers[2].

1 SI 1991/1624, reg 3(1).
2 SI 1994/1056, Sch 5, para 2: registers are discussed at para 13.43ff.

6.46 A person wishing to register as a controlled waste carrier or broker (or both) should apply to be registered with the Agency which covers the carrier's proposed or actual 'principal place of business'[1]. Circular 11/91 suggests that, where an applicant has more than one place of business, the principal place of business is where the administration of the business occurs and from where control is exercised on any of the divisions of the business[2]. Should the applicant not have a place of business in Great Britain, that person can apply to either the Environment Agency or Scottish Environment Protection Agency for registration[3,4]. Until the Waste and Contaminated Land (Northern Ireland) Order 1997[5] is fully enacted, a carrier based in Northern Ireland but working in Britain must register with either the Environment Agency or the Scottish Environment Protection Agency[6]. Waste brokers involved in other transfrontier waste shipments[7] must either be registered in Britain or with another member state[8].

1 SI 1991/1624, reg 4(1); SI 1994/1056, Sch 5, para 3(1).
2 Circular 11/91, Annex 1, para 1.13; Circular 11/94, Annex 8, para 8.22: see *Palmer v Caledonian Rly Co* [1892] 1 QB 823 at 827.
3 SI 1991/1624, reg 4(1); SI 1994/1056, Sch 5, para 3(1).
4 'Great Britain' constitutes England, Scotland and Wales.
5 SI 1997/2778 (NI 19).
6 See, in respect of WRAs, Circular 11/94, Annex 1, para 1.13; Circular 11/94, Annex 8, para 8.22.
7 See Chapter 5.
8 See Circular 13/94, para 27.

6.47   Multiple applications for registration are not allowed[1] and can result in a refusal to register that person[2].

1   SI 1991/1624, reg 4(2); SI 1994/1056, Sch 5, para 3(2).
2   SI 1991/1624, reg 5(1)(a); SI 1994/1056, Sch 5, para 3(13).

6.48   Once an application has been received, the Agency has two months in which to process the application and to grant a registration[1]. However, this can be extended on the 'agreement' of the applicant and the Agency[2].

1   Control of Pollution (Amendment) Act 1989, s 4(1); SI 1994/1056, Sch 5, para 1(1) and para 6(1)(b).
2   1989 Act, s 4(1); SI 1994/1056, Sch 5, para 1(1).

6.49   The Controlled Waste (Registration of Carriers and Seizure of Vehicles) Regulations 1991 allow the Agency to set out the details which must be contained in a carrier registration application form[1]. Similarly, the Waste Management Licensing Regulations 1994 require the Agency to have available a broker registration form[2]. Both forms must be given out free of charge on request[3]. It should be noted that the statutory application forms contained in the 1991 and 1994 Regulations are no longer to be used[4]. A joint broker/carrier application can also be made on the Agency's form[5].

1   SI 1991/1624, reg 4(6) amended by SI 1998/605, reg 2(2)(a).
2   SI 1994/1056, Sch 5, para 3(6), as amended by SI 1998/606, reg 2(4)(a).
3   SI 1991/1624, reg 4(8).
4   See SI 1998/605, reg 2(2) and SI 1998/606, reg 2(4).
5   SI 1994/1056, Sch 5, Pt I, para 3(8): see Circular 11/94, Annex 8, para 8.27.

6.50   Once the application form has been completed, it must be signed to the effect that the information provided is accurate. Should a person applying for a carrier registration 'without reasonable excuse'[1] fail to provide relevant information to the Agency or provide information which is known to be 'false or misleading[2] in a material particular or recklessly provides information which is false in a material particular', an offence is committed[3]. On summary conviction, a person so doing is liable to a fine not exceeding level 5[4]. Unlike the offence of making false statements contained in the EPA 1990[5], the 1989 Act explicitly places the onus upon a person so charged to show that there was a reasonable excuse for failing to provide the correct information[6]. The 1989 Act also states that the prosecution is not required to show that the person did not have any such excuse[7].

1   See para 12.109ff.
2   The words 'or misleading' were added by the Environment Act 1995, Sch 19, para 3.
3   Control of Pollution (Amendment) Act 1989, s 7(3)(b). For the meaning of words such as 'false' and 'reckless', see para 12.238ff.
4   Currently £5,000.
5   EPA 1990, s 44, as amended by the Environment Act 1995, s 112 and Sch 19, para 4: see para 12.214.
6   1989 Act, s 7(3).
7   1989 Act, s 7(3).

6.51   There appears to be a question over whether the falsification of information as part of a broker application is an offence. The Waste Management Licensing Regulations 1994 refer to s 71(3) of the EPA 1990[1]. However, s 71(3)(b) has been repealed by the Environment Act 1995[2]. The 1995 Act amends s 44 of the EPA 1990[3] which now contains the main provisions relating to persons who provide false information. Section 44 covers only false statements relating to Part II of that Act. The broker registration provisions are not contained in Part II. If anything, broker registration stems from the transposition of the Directive on Waste[4] by virtue of s 2(2) of the European Communities Act 1972. It follows that the power to obtain information under s 73(1)(a) of the EPA 1990 is extended to broker registration by virtue of reg 20(8) of the Waste Management Licensing Regulations 1994. However, on the face of it, there is nothing which specifically addresses false information supplied to obtain a broker registration.

1   SI 1994/1056, reg 20(8).
2   Section 112 and Sch 19.
3   EPA 1990, s 44 as amended by Environment Act 1995, s 112 and Sch 19, para 4.
4   Council Directive of 15 July 1975 on Waste (75/442/EEC) (OJ L194/39 25.7.75 (as amended by Council Directive of 18 March 1991 amending Directive 75/442/EEC on Waste (91/156/EEC) (OJ L78/32 26.3.91)) Article 12.

6.52   A fee must be included with the completed and signed application form. For applications for carrier, broker or joint carrier/broker registration[1,2], this is contained in the annual charges scheme made under s 41 of the Environment Act 1995[3].

1   SI 1991/1624, reg 4(9) as amended by SI 1998/605, reg 2(2)(B); SI 1994/1056, Sch 5, para 11 as amended by SI 1998/606, reg 2(4)(c).
2   Extending an existing carrier registration to cover waste broking, or a broker registration to cover waste carrying, is discussed at para 6.83 below.
3   For the financial year 1999/2000, a fee of £117 has been set by the Environment Agency and SEPA.

6.53   Once the form has been received and the payment cleared, a copy of the application has to be entered onto the register held by the Agency[1]. Unless the Agency proposes to refuse a controlled waste carrier application[2], it must issue a certificate to indicate the acceptance of the application for registration[3]. The controlled waste carrier certificate must contain the information set down in Schedule 3 to the 1991 Regulations (see Figure 6.1). Somewhat perversely, however, there are no provisions for a certificate to be issued in the case of an application for a broker registration. This contrast means that it is much easier for a waste carrier to demonstrate evidence of registration, as this can be done by way of the certificate. Evidence of a broker's registration can only be gained by contacting the respective Agency.

1   SI 1991/1624, reg 4(10); SI 1994/1056, Sch 5, Pt I, para 3(10): registration is discussed at para 13.43ff.
2   See para 6.61 below.
3   SI 1991/1624, reg 6(3)(a).

6.54   For both controlled waste brokers and carriers, the registration period of three years commences with the date of registration[1], unless revoked by the Agency or surrendered by the applicant. Initially, all controlled waste carriers had to apply by 1 April 1992. This period was extended to 1 June 1992 for some builders and hauliers of construction industry waste by the Controlled Waste Regulations 1992[2]. Persons wishing to act as controlled waste brokers had until 1 January 1995 in which to apply, and they could continue operating as brokers past that date whilst their application was pending determination[3]. Persons who are unregistered and who propose to carry or broker controlled waste must now await the determination of their applications and, in the case of waste carriers, the receipt of the certificate.

1   SI 1991/1624, reg 11(2); SI 1994/1056, Sch 5, para 7(1).
2   SI 1992/588, reg 10(2): see Circular 14/92, Annex 6, paras 6.5–6.7.
3   SI 1994/1056, reg 20(4)(d).

6.55   As has been noted, 'a person' is required to register as a controlled waste carrier and, under the Interpretation Act 1978[1], 'a person' includes individuals, partnerships

Figure 6.1   Controlled Waste Carrier Certificate

CERTIFICATE OF REGISTRATION UNDER THE CONTROL OF POLLUTION
(AMENDMENT) ACT 1989

Regulations 6(3), 7(2) and 8(2)

Regulation Authority
Name:
Address:
Post Code:
Tel: Telex: Fax:

The following information is hereby certified by the above-mentioned authority to be
information which at the date of this certificate† is entered in the register which they
maintain under regulation 3 of the Controlled Waste (Registration of Carriers and Seizure of
Vehicles) Regulations 1991—

Name(s) of registered carrier:

Registration number:

Business name (if any):

Address of registered carrier's principal
place of business:

Tel: Telex: Fax:

Date of registration:

Date of expiry of registration*:

Date on which last amendment (if any) was
made to the carrier's entry in the register:

Signature of authorised officer   Date:
of the regulation authority:

† You can check whether there has been any change in the information contained in this
certificate by contacting the regulation authority named above.

* Registration will expire on this date unless—

(*a*)   it is revoked before expiry;

(*b*)   the carrier requests the removal of his name from the register at an earlier time;

(*c*)   an application for renewal is made within the six months ending on the expiry date and
the application is still outstanding, or is the subject of an appeal, on that date;

(*d*)   in the case of a registered partnership, if any of the partners ceases to be registered *or* if
anyone who is not registered becomes a partner.

and bodies corporate. The Waste Management Licensing Regulations 1994 use a
different term in respect of brokers: 'an establishment or undertaking'[2]. The Department of the Environment's view on these terms is that each company within a group of
companies needs to have a separate registration[3]. Hence Circular 11/91 claims that

each company within a group of companies falls within a definition of a 'person' in relation to s 1 of the 1989 Act: 'it will not be possible for a company to rely on the registration of another company in the same group as authority for transporting controlled waste'. Similarly, in relation to waste brokers, Circular 11/94 notes that '[a]s a body corporate, each company in a group of companies is an establishment . . . and each company must separately apply where necessary for registration'[4].

1 Section 5, Sch 1.
2 According to Circular 11/94, Annex 8, para 8.11, 'establishments or undertakings' include a body corporate, a partnership, society, trust, club or other organisation. 'A private individual is not an establishment or undertaking, but a person operating a relevant business will need to register': discussed further at para 10.22.
3 Circular 11/91, Annex 1, para 1.3; Circular 11/94, Annex 8, para 8.11.
4 Circular 11/94, Annex 8, para 8.11.

6.56 In the case of a partnership, all of the partners need to be registered[1], with all their names being recorded in the register under one entry[2]. One fee is to be paid for a partnership's waste carrier registration and one carrier registration number is issued[3].

1 SI 1991/1624, reg 4(4); SI 1994/1056, Sch 5, para 3(5).
2 SI 1991/1624, reg 6(2); SI 1994/1056, Sch 5, para 4(2).
3 SI 1991/1624, reg 6(2); SI 1994/1056, Sch 5, para 4(2).

6.57 When a certificate for a carrier registration is issued, it must be accompanied by a copy of the entry made in the Agency's register[1]. Circular 11/91 suggests that the following information should also be passed by the Agency to the successful applicant[2]:

– the requirement that the carrier must notify the Agency of any change of circumstances affecting the contents of the register;
– that the certificate is required to be returned if the carrier surrenders the registration, when the registration is revoked or when the details on it have been altered and a new version issued;
– that the certificate is to be used to establish proof of registration and that it may be required to be produced within seven days if requested[3];
– unless done previously, the procedure and charges for the provision of copies of the certificate;
– if applicable, the specific provisions relating to changes in the composition of the partnerships.

1 SI 1991/1624, reg 6(3)(b).
2 Circular 11/91, Annex 1, para 1.54.
3 Discussed further at para 12.147ff.

6.58 For brokers, the successful applicant is required to be sent only a copy of the entry on the register[1]. Circular 11/94 suggests that, along with the entry, the broker should be advised that the Agency needs to be kept informed of any changes in the broker's circumstances which may affect the information contained in the register. In addition, if the broker is acting as a partnership, the broker needs to be informed of the specific requirements pertaining to partnerships[2]. These are discussed at para 6.80.

1 SI 1994/1056, Sch 5, para 4(3).
2 Circular 11/94, Annex 8, para 8.61.

6.59 Once registered, a carrier or broker registration applies nationally. For controlled waste carriers, proof of registration is provided by the certificates issued[1]. Further copies of the waste carrier certificates can be obtained on request from the

Agency[2], which is entitled to make a 'reasonable charge' for them[3]. Such copies need to be marked to the effect that they are duplicates[4]. Provided that they contain the prescribed information, copies can be reproduced by the Agency in a different form or size[5]. For example they can be reproduced in a format similar to credit cards. However, photocopies of the certificates are not a valid proof of registration[6].

1   SI 1991/1624, reg 6(3).
2   SI 1991/1624, reg 9(1).
3   SI 1991/1624, reg 9(1).
4   SI 1991/1624, reg 9(2).
5   Circular 11/91, Annex 1, para 1.65.
6   See SI 1991/1624, reg 14(2): see also SI 1991/1624, reg 9, Circular 11/91, Annex 1, para 1.85 and Department of the Environment (1996) *Waste Management The Duty of Care A Code of Practice* (2nd edn), HMSO, London, para 3.7.

6.60   A national database is kept of registered waste carriers: the Co-ordinated Local Authority Database of Waste Carriers (CLADWAC), which was originally co-ordinated by the London Waste Regulation Authority. This permits any Agency office that is equipped with a suitable computer terminal to check if a person is a registered carrier. Broker details are also now found on CLADWAC.

GROUNDS FOR REFUSAL OF AN APPLICATION TO REGISTER

6.61   The Control of Pollution (Amendment) Act 1989 sets out the grounds under which the Agency can refuse an application for a carrier registration[1]. These are augmented by further provisions in the Controlled Waste (Registration of Carriers and Seizure of Vehicles) Regulations 1991[2]. Similar requirements in relation to waste brokers are contained in Schedule 5 to the Waste Management Licensing Regulations 1994. An application for a registration can be refused 'if, and only if'[3]:

(a)   there has been a contravention of the application procedures[4]; or
(b)   the applicant 'or any other relevant person' has been convicted of a specified offence[5] and, 'in the opinion of' the Agency[6], it is undesirable for the applicant to be authorised to transport controlled waste or to arrange (as a dealer or broker) for controlled waste to be disposed of or recovered on behalf of others[7].

1   1989 Act, s 5.
2   SI 1991/1624, reg 5.
3   SI 1991/1624, reg 5(1); SI 1994/1056, Sch 5, para 13.
4   See SI 1991/1624, reg 4; SI 1994/1056, Sch 5, para 3: described at para 6.46ff above.
5   The nature of the offences is different for controlled waste carriers and waste brokers and is discussed at para 6.63 below.
6   The respective Agency acting as Waste Regulation Authority.
7   See SI 1991/1624, reg 5(1)(b); SI 1994/1056, Sch 5, para 3(13)(b).

6.62   The convictions which may preclude a carrier's or broker's continued involvement with controlled waste are, in the case of waste carriers, referred to as 'prescribed offences'[1]; in the case of brokers, as 'relevant offences'[2].

1   SI 1991/1624, reg 1(2) and Sch 1.
2   SI 1994/1056, Sch 5, para 3(13)(b) and para 1(1).

6.63   Table 6.1 lists the 'prescribed offences' under the Control of Pollution (Amendment) Act 1989. They are found in the Controlled Waste (Registration of Carriers and Seizure of Vehicles) Regulations 1991[1]. 'Relevant offences' must be considered in relation to waste brokers[2], being set down in the Waste Management Licensing Regulations 1994[3]. 'Relevant offences' are, with one exception[4], the same as those which may be considered when a person's 'fit and proper' status is evaluated in relation to the posses-sion of a waste management licence under s 74 of the EPA 1990[5]. Whilst the Water Resources Act 1991 is not listed as a prescribed offence[6], in the 1991 Regulations convictions under this Act are prescribed offences by way of the Water Consolidation (Consequential Provisions) Act 1991[7]. Oddly, convictions in respect of the Clean Air Act 1993 are relevant offences in relation to waste brokers (and waste management licences), but seem not to be prescribed offences in respect of controlled waste carriers.

1   SI 1991/1624, reg 1(2) as amended by SI 1994/1137, reg 19, SI 1996/972, reg 22.
2   SI 1994/1056, Sch 5, para 1(1).
3   SI 1994/1056, reg 3 as amended by SI 1994/1137, reg 19(3) and SI 1996/972, reg 25 and Sch 3.
4   Offences in respect of the landfill tax are 'relevant offences' for the purposes of whether a person is 'fit and proper' under s 75 of the EPA 1990. However, they do not apply in the context of waste brokers (see SI 1997/351, reg 2).
5   See para 8.117 and Table 8.2 in Chapter 8.
6   See SI 1991/1624, Sch 1: this is in immediate contrast to the relevant offences listed in SI 1994/1056, reg 3.
7   See the Water Consolidation (Consequential Provisions) Act 1991, Sch 2, para 1(1) and see *ENDS Report* 236 September 1994, pp 40–41; see also the Interpretation Act 1978, s 16.

Table 6.1

Prescribed Offences under the Controlled Waste (Registration of Carriers and Seizure of Vehicles) Regulations 1991[1]

Section 22 of the Public Health (Scotland) Act
Section 95(1) of the Public Health Act 1936
Section 60 of the Transport Act 1968
Sections 3, 5(6), 16(4), 18(2), 31(1), 34(5), 78, 92(6) and 93(3) of the Control of
    Pollution Act 1974
Section 3 of the Refuse Disposal (Amenity) Act 1978
The Control of Pollution (Special Waste) Regulations 1980[2]
Section 9(1) of the Food and Environment Protection Act 1985
The Transfrontier Shipment of Hazardous Waste Regulations 1988
The Merchant Shipping (Prevention of Pollution by Garbage) Regulations 1988[3]
Sections 1, 5, 6(9) and 7(3) of the Control of Pollution (Amendment) Act 1989
Sections 107, 118(4) and 175(1) of the Water Act 1989
Sections 23(1), 33, 34(6), 44, 47(6), 57(5), 59(5), 63(2), 69(9), 70(4), 71(3) and 80(4) of
    the Environmental Protection Act 1990.
The Transfrontier Shipment of Waste Regulations 1994[4]
Sections 85, 202 or 206 of the Water Resources Act 1991[5]
The Special Waste Regulations 1996[6]

1   SI 1991/1624, reg 1(2) and Sch 1.
2   SI 1981/1709.
3   Note that these Regulations have been revoked (see SI 1998/1377 reg 1(2)). The replacement regulations are not referred to in the list of prescribed offences in SI 1991/1624.
4   SI 1991/1624, Sch 1 as amended by SI 1994/1137, reg 19(1).
5   Whilst not explicitly mentioned in SI 1991/1624, these sections of the 1991 Act appear to be included by way of para 1(1) of Sch 2 of the Water Consolidation (Consequential Provisions) Act 1991: see *ENDS Report* 236 September 1994, pp 40–41; see also the Interpretation Act 1978, s 16.
6   SI 1991/1624, Sch 1 as amended by SI 1996/972, reg 22.

6.64   It should be noted that assault of Agency staff and breaches of injunctions do not count as either prescribed or relevant offences. Although a conviction for obstruc-tion under s 69(9) of the EPA 1990 is set down as being both a prescribed and a relevant offence (see Table 6.1), s 69 of the EPA 1990 has been repealed by the Envi-ronment Act 1995[1]. Whilst the 1995 Act contains its own provisions on obstruction in s 110, which apply across all of the Agency's functions, convictions under that section are neither prescribed nor relevant offences.

1   Section 120(1) and Sch 22, para 85.

6.65   The prescribed or relevant offences committed by 'another relevant person' can also constitute grounds for refusal of registration. The circumstances where such offences can be considered are where[1]:

(a) a person has been convicted of a prescribed (or, as the case may be, relevant) offence when under the employment of the applicant or another registered carrier[2];

(b) a person received convictions and was involved in a partnership where one of the members was either the applicant or a registered carrier (or, as the case may be, a broker);

(c) a body corporate was convicted of the offence at a time the applicant was 'a director, manager, secretary or other similar officer'[3] of that body corporate;

(d) the applicant is a body corporate and a director, manager, etc was convicted of a prescribed offence, or where such a person was an officer of a different body corporate which had received convictions for prescribed offences.

It appears that the conviction of 'another relevant person' when that person was acting as an *individual*[4] is not caught by the above criteria. These circumstances are essentially similar to s 74(7) of the EPA 1990. The latter relates to the possession of relevant offences and the notion of whether a person is 'fit and proper' to hold a waste management licence and hence are described at para 8.122ff.

1   Control of Pollution (Amendment) Act 1989, s 3(5); SI 1994/1056, Sch 5, para 1(3).
2   A person acting in the course of employment by an unregistered waste carrier (or, as the case may be, broker) appears not to be affected.
3   The meaning of this phrase is discussed at para 7.156ff.
4   Ie not within a partnership or as part of a body corporate.

6.66   In relation to offences committed by a business or by a partnership, the Agency must have regard to whether, where previous convictions relating to prescribed offences occurred, the individual now applying had been party to the events leading up to the earlier convictions of a body corporate or partnership[1].

1   Control of Pollution (Amendment) Act 1989, s 3(6); SI 1994/1056, Sch 5, para 1(2): see also Circular 11/91, Annex 1, para 1.37 and Circular 11/94, Annex 8, para 8.40.

6.67   Should the Agency decide to refuse an application, the applicant has to be informed to that effect by way of a notice. The reasons for refusal should accompany the notice[1], which can be served by hand or by post[2]. The person also should be informed of the right to appeal, how an appeal may be lodged and of the 28-day appeal period[3]. The applicant cannot haul or broker controlled waste until the appeal has been heard. No fees are due to be refunded if registration is refused[4].

1   SI 1991/1624, reg 5(2); SI 1994/1056, Sch 5, para 3(14).
2   SI 1991/1624, reg 26, SI 1994/1056, reg 1(7) as amended by SI 1995/288, reg 3(2) and the EPA 1990, s 160.
3   Circular 11/91, Annex 1, para 1.44; Circular 11/94, Annex 8, para 8.53.
4   Circular 11/91, Annex 1, para 1.24; Circular 11/94, Annex 8, para 8.35.

6.68   If the applicant fails correctly to adhere to the application process[1], both Circulars 11/91 and 11/94 emphasise the need for the Agency to be pragmatic. Hence the Agency should suggest to the applicant that information has been missed off the form or that the correct payment has not been made. Only when an applicant has not responded to such prompting should the Agency consider refusing the application[2].

1   Ie fails to satisfy the requirements of reg 5(1)(a) of SI 1991/1624 or of para 3(13)(a) of Pt I of Sch 5
     of SI 1994/1056.
2   Circular 11/91, Annex 1, para 1.31; Circular 11/94, Annex 8, para 8.42.

6.69   As noted, the most important reason for refusing a registration is that the applicant or another relevant person has received convictions in relation to prescribed or
relevant offences[1]. The Rehabilitation of Offenders Act 1974 applies in respect of any
of these offences. Convictions become 'spent' after a specified duration, which varies
depending upon the severity of the offence. The time periods contained in the Rehabilitation of Offenders Act 1974 are shown in both Circular 11/91 and Circular 11/94[2],
but in summary the most relevant to waste regulation are:

–   seven years for a prison sentence of six months or less;
–   five years for a fine or community services order;
–   one year for a conditional discharge; and
–   six months for an absolute discharge.

For the purposes of completing the application form, the key date with respect to spent
convictions is when the person filled in the form and signed it[3]. However, when the
Agency considers the offences, they must not be spent at the time the decision on
registration is being made[4]. Indeed, when an appeal has been lodged, only offences
which are not spent at the date of the appeal decision being made can be considered.
Obviously, if the conviction is spent, it cannot be used as a reason to refuse the application.

1   SI 1991/1624, reg 5(1)(b); SI 1994/1056, Sch 5, para 3(13)(b).
2   Circular 11/91, Table 1.3; Circular 11/94, Table 8.2.
3   Circular 11/91, Annex 1, para 1.34.
4   Circular 11/91, Annex 1, para 1.34; Circular 11/94, Annex 8, para 8.45.

6.70   The Rehabilitation of Offenders Act 1974 does not apply to bodies corporate.
Therefore all relevant convictions by bodies corporate must be recorded on the application form, no matter how long ago they occurred. However, Circulars 11/91 and
11/94 advise the Agency to have regard to the time periods set out in the 1974 Act
when considering their significance[1].

1   Circular 11/91, Annex 1, para 1.42; Circular 11/94, Annex 8, para 8.51.

6.71   Both Circulars make it clear that the Agency has discretion to decide if a person
subject to previous convictions should be registered as a carrier or broker. They also
emphasise that the onus is on the applicant to provide the information necessary to
satisfy the regulation authority that it is desirable for the person to be authorised to
transport controlled waste or to act as a broker[1]. In this respect, an applicant affected
by prescribed or relevant offences should complete as fully as possible the relevant
section on the application form regarding mitigating circumstances. The Agency must
ensure that these matters are given a full and fair consideration, particularly where a
person's livelihood may be at stake[2].

1   Circular 11/91, Annex 1, para 1.28; Circular 11/94, Annex 8, para 8.38.
2   See *R v Barnsley Metropolitan Borough Council, ex p Hook* [1976] 3 All ER 452; *Cinnamond v
     British Airports Authority* [1980] 2 All ER 368; *Lloyd v McMahon* [1987] 1 All ER 1118.

6.72   Although the Agency has discretion to refuse an application, it must follow the
series of steps set out in the relevant circulars when deciding if refusal should take
place[1]. The most obvious question to be considered is whether the offence was carried
out by the applicant who is now applying for registration. Secondly, if the offence was

not committed by the applicant, whether it was committed by 'another relevant person'[2].

1   See Circular 11/91, Annex 1, paras 1.38 to 1.43 and Circular 11/94, Annex 8, paras 8.47 to 8.52.
2   Ie (a) by a person under the applicant's employment, (b) by one of the applicant's partners, (c) at a time when the applicant was a director, manager, etc of a body corporate or (d) by the applicant who, at that time, was a member of the business which committed an offence and who was party to the offence: see Circular 11/91, Annex 1, para 1.39; Circular 11/94, Annex 8, para 8.48.

6.73   The Agency must then consider the gravity of the relevant offences and their number[1]. Generally, the information provided by the applicant on the application form should be sufficient for this purpose. However, Circulars 11/91 and 11/94 indicate that the Agency is entitled to ask for more information by serving a notice under s 71(2) of the EPA 1990 on the applicant[2,3].

1   Circular 11/91, Annex 1, para 1.43; Circular 11/94, Annex 8, para 8.52.
2   Circular 11/91, Annex 1, para 1.43; Circular 11/94, Annex 8, para 8.52.
3   A s 71 notice is given application to the Control of Pollution (Amendment) Act 1989 by the latter's s 7(1) (as amended by the EPA 1990, Sch 15 and by the Environment Act 1995, Sch 22, para 37(5)); similarly, s 71 notices can be used in relation to waste brokers by way of reg 20(8) of SI 1994/1056: s 71 notices are discussed at para 12.174ff.

6.74   Both circulars advise that an isolated conviction should not be seen as a reason to refuse registration where there are mitigating circumstances[1]. In terms of numbers of convictions, regard should be had to whether there has been any repetition of the offence by other persons in the applicant's business and also of the action taken by the applicant to prevent its recurrence. If the offences have been committed by more than one person within the organisation, the applicant's and other relevant company officers' position in the business at that time should be considered.

1   Circular 11/91, Annex 1, para 1.43(a); Circular 11/94, Annex 8, para 8.52(a).

6.75   In the case of convictions by 'another relevant person', both circulars[1] state that the type of applicant and the position of the 'other relevant person' in the applicants' business may be important. For example, if the applicant is a body corporate, and if the 'other relevant person' holds a position of authority in that business, such an offence 'may be considered to be of significance commensurate with any which the applicant himself might have committed'.

1   Circular 11/91, Annex 1, para 1.43(d); Circular 11/94, Annex 8, para 8.52(c).

6.76   Certain of the prescribed or relevant offences may not involve the transport, keeping or disposal of controlled waste. An example might be a farmer who wishes to transport controlled waste who previously had convictions under the Water Resources Act 1991 due to unconnected activities which polluted a watercourse. Accordingly, the circulars advise[1] that particular regard should be made to offences involving the unlawful deposit, treatment, keeping, disposal or transport of controlled wastes, along with breaches of the duty of care[2]. Further regard also should be had to whether 'serious' pollution of the environment, harm to human health or 'serious' detriment to the amenity of the locality occurred when the relevant offences were committed[3] or whether special waste had been involved[4].

1   Circular 11/91, Annex 1, para 1.43(e); Circular 11/94, Annex 8, para 8.52(e).
2   EPA 1990, s 34: see Chapter 3.
3   Circular 11/91, Annex 1, para 1.43(g); Circular 11/94, Annex 8, para 8.52(g).
4   Circular 11/91, Annex 1, para 1.43(f); Circular 11/94, Annex 8, para 8.82(f).

6.77 The final criteria for judging the significance of offences is the penalty imposed for the commission of the offence[1]. However, as the circulars acknowledge, the level of fine imposed is often tempered by the Court's determination of the offender's ability to pay. But more serious offences are flagged by the fact that a community service order or a prison sentence was imposed.

1 Circular 11/91, Annex 1, para 1.43(h); Circular 11/94, Annex 8, para 8.52(h).

CHANGING REGISTRATION DETAILS

6.78 Certain minor amendments to the registration details can be made without needing to go through the formal application process again. However, amendments such as the addition of new members to a partnership or the conversion of an existing carrier registration to a joint carrier and broker registration (or the expansion of a broker registration to include carrier registration) will need to follow the application process which has been described above.

Making general changes

6.79 Once registered, the details contained on the Agency's register must be kept up to date. Accordingly, the person registered must notify the Agency of any change of circumstances affecting the information held on the register[1].

1 SI 1991/1624, reg 8(1); SI 1994/1056, Sch 5, para 4(6).

6.80 The requirements upon partnerships are particularly stringent, especially where a new partner joins a partnership which is already registered. If the new partner fails to register with the relevant Agency, the partnership's registration 'shall cease to have effect'[1]. Consequently, the Agency must be informed in advance of the changes by the prospective partner applying separately. A new entrant into an existing partnership may make an application for registration as a partner to the Agency which currently holds the registration details[2]. Both Circular 11/91 and Circular 11/94 suggest that a new entrant to an already registered partnership has to pay a separate application fee[3]. If a new partner successfully applies to join an existing registered partnership, the registration period of the original partnership is unaffected[4]: it is not extended to three years from the date the person joined. In addition, the registration of a partnership is not transferable. A partner who joins another partnership which also carries or brokers controlled waste must make a new application[5].

1 SI 1991/1624, reg 11(6); SI 1994/1056, Sch 5, para 7(9).
2 SI 1991/1624, reg 4(5); SI 1994/1056, Sch 5, para 3(5).
3 Circular 11/91, Annex 1, para 1.24; Circular 11/94, Annex 8, para 8.35.
4 SI 1991/1624, reg 11(7); SI 1994/1056, Sch 5, para 7(10).
5 Circular 11/91, Annex 1, para 1.78(d); Circular 11/94, Annex 8, para 8.94(d).

6.81 The Agency must amend the register when it has been advised of any relevant changes, noting the date of the amendment and, if needed, arrange for a new carrier registration certificate and copy of the register's details to be sent out[1]. No charge should be made by the Agency for the supply of this information and, in the case of a controlled waste carrier certificate, for the new certificate[2].

1 SI 1991/1624, reg 8(2); SI 1994/1056, Sch 5, para 4(7).
2 SI 1991/1624, reg 8(2)(iv); SI 1994/1056, Sch 5, para 4(7)(iii).

6.82   Should a carrier's principal place of business be transferred from the area of one Agency to that of the other within the three year registration period, the registration stays with the first Agency[1]. Only when the registration is up for renewal does an application to the second Agency need to be made.

1   Circular 11/91, Annex 1, para 1.20; Circular 11/94, Annex 8, para 8.31.

Expanding an existing registration to permit a carrier to act as a broker (or vice versa)

6.83   An existing registration as a controlled waste carrier can be expanded to allow a person to also act as a waste broker. An application is made to the respective Agency on their own form[1], which must be provided to the applicant free of charge[2]. The requisite fee must accompany the application when it is sent off to the Agency[3]. The application is then considered in respect of the requirements of Schedule 5 to the Waste Management Licensing Regulations 1994, which have been discussed at para 6.61 above.

1   SI 1994/1056, Sch 5, Pt 1, paras 3(6) as amended by SI 1998/606, reg 2(4)(a).
2   SI 1994/1056, Sch 5, Pt 1, para 3(10).
3   SI 1994/1056, Sch 5, Pt 1, para 3(11) as amended by SI 1998/606, reg 2(4)(c): for the financial year 1999/2000, the fee was £31.

6.84   Similarly, a broker registration can be modified to permit the registered organisation to carry controlled waste. The application form supplied by the Agency must be completed[1], and sent to the relevant Agency, accompanied by the required payment[2]. The application is then considered in relation to the requirements of Regulation 5 of the 1991 Regulations: see para 6.61 above.

1   SI 1991/1624, reg 4(6) as amended by SI 1998/605, reg 2(2)(a).
2   SI 1991/1624, reg 4(9) as amended by SI 1998/605, reg 2(2)(b). Oddly, while the 1999/2000 Charging Scheme allows for a carrier registration to be upgraded to a combined carrier and broker registration for £31, there is no equivalent provision in respect of registered brokers who wish to act as waste carriers. It would seem that the full carrier registration charge of £117 is applicable in this circumstance.

6.85   Although registration lasts for three years unless renewed, the successful applicant for an expanded registration has a choice on how long the additional component of the registration can continue. It can either cease when the initial registration requires renewal or it can continue to the end of the three year period which commenced when the expanded registration was granted. Therefore, if a carrier has been registered for a year, a successful application for additional broker registration can last until the carrier registration is to be renewed, or the carrier registration can be renewed at the end of the three year period and the broker registration renewed subsequently at the end of the following year. The person has a choice in this matter, but a desire for the broker and carrier registration to cease together must be expressed at the time of the application to expand the registration[1].

1   SI 1994/1056, Sch 5, para 7(2); see Circular 11/94, Annex 8, para 8.86.

REGISTRATION RENEWALS

6.86   Towards the end of the three year registration period, the registration must be renewed. Renewal is effected using the Agency's carrier or broker registration forms[1].

Joint applications for carrier and waste broker registration can be made on such forms[2]. A re-registration fee has been set by the Agency for renewals, including for the joint carrier/broker registration[3].

1   SI 1991/1624, reg 4(6) (as amended by SI 1998/605, reg 2(2)); SI 1994/1056, Sch 5 para 3(7) (as amended by SI 1998/606, reg 2(4)(l)).
2   SI 1994/1056, Sch 5, para 3(9).
3   SI 1991/1624, reg 4(9); SI 1994/1056, Sch 5, para 3(11)(b): the fee is contained in the annual charging scheme made under s 41 of the Environment Act 1995. The charge for the financial year 1999/2000 is £80 from October 1999.

6.87   The Agency must, 'no later than six months before . . . expiry'[1], serve notice on all affected registered carriers and brokers that registration will cease on a specified date. When the Agency serves notice, the carrier or broker has to be informed of the fact that the registration will continue once an application for renewal has been received[2]. A copy of the registration renewal form should be included with the notice, along with the current details that are held on the register[3]. However, both circulars emphasise that the contacting of registered carriers or brokers is simply a reminder process. The onus is upon the recipient to remember that the three year period is close to expiry[4].

1   SI 1991/1624, reg 11(3); SI 1994/1056, Sch 5, para 7(5).
2   SI 1991/1624, reg 11(3)(a) and reg 11(4); SI 1994/1056, Sch 5, para 7(5) and 7(6).
3   SI 1991/1624, reg 11(3); SI 1994/1056, Sch 5, para 7(5).
4   Circular 11/91, Annex 1, para 1.73; Circular 11/94, Annex 8, para 8.89.

6.88   Provided an application for re-registration is made within the six-month period prior to expiry, a registered waste carrier or broker is allowed to continue operating until the application is determined[1].

1   SI 1991/1624, reg 11(4); SI 1994/1056, Sch 5, para 7(6).

6.89   If a carrier or broker applies for renewal before the three-year period is up, then the new registration period of three years commences when the existing registration ceases[1]. It does not commence on the date when the application is processed or the certificate is sent off. However, if the carrier or broker exceeds the three-year period and does not put in a renewal, a completely new application must be made and they cannot haul or broker controlled waste again until the registration has been granted.

1   SI 1991/1624, reg 11(8); SI 1994/1056, Sch 5, para 7(11).

6.90   The Agency has two months in which to deal with renewals and it appears that, unlike an initial registration, this cannot be extended by way of mutual consent[1]. Once processed, a new certificate and a copy of the re-registered carrier's details contained in the register have to be sent off[2]. A new expiry date must be entered on the register, along with any other changes made[3]. The date the amendments were made must be recorded[4].

1   Control of Pollution (Amendment) Act 1989, s 4(1); SI 1994/1056, Sch 5, para 1(1).
2   SI 1991/1624, reg 7(2); SI 1994/1056, Sch 5, para 4(5).
3   SI 1991/1624, reg 7(1); SI 1994/1056, Sch 5, para 4(4).
4   SI 1991/1624, reg 7(1)(c); SI 1994/1056, Sch 5, para 4(4)(c).

6.91   The grounds for refusing an application for a renewal of registration are the same as those which pertain to applications for initial registration[1]. These have been discussed above at para 6.61.

1   SI 1991/1624, reg 5(1); SI 1994/1056, Sch 5, para 3(13).

REVOCATION OF REGISTRATION

6.92 A registered waste carrier or broker can lose registration by a process of formal revocation. Like the refusal of an application to register, revocation can be undertaken 'if, and only if'[1] two conditions are satisfied. They are that:

(a) the person or 'another relevant person' has been convicted of, as the case may be, a prescribed offence or a relevant offence[2]; and

(b) where, 'in the opinion of' the Agency[3], it is considered undesirable for the registered carrier to continue to transport controlled waste[4] or for the registered broker to arrange for waste to be disposed of or recovered by third parties[5].

1 SI 1991/1624, reg 10(1); SI 1994/1056, Sch 5, para 5(1).
2 As noted earlier at para 6.63 there is a subtle difference between these.
3 As Waste Regulation Authority: see the EPA 1990, s 30 (as amended by the Environment Act 1995, Sch 22, para 62).
4 SI 1991/1624, reg 10.
5 SI 1994/1056, Sch 5, para 5(1)(b).

6.93 A further caveat concerns the instance in which an individual previously was a member of a body corporate that had received convictions for prescribed or relevant offences. The offences become of consequence if the individual was party to them[1] and the Agency must have regard to them when making its decision.

1 Control of Pollution (Amendment) Act 1989, s 3(6); SI 1994/1056, Sch 5, para 1(2).

6.94 The procedures to be followed by the Agency to cause revocation are essentially similar to those set out for refusal of registration[1]. However, before revoking the registration, the Agency should invite the affected person to provide any additional information, for example mitigating circumstances, which the Agency should take into account in making its decision[2].

1 Circular 11/91, Annex 1, para 1.29; Circular 11/94, Annex 8, para 8.39.
2 Circular 11/91, Annex 1, para 1.61; Circular 11/94, Annex 8, para 8.67.

6.95 Both circulars acknowledge the fact that carriers' or brokers' conviction for prescribed or relevant offences may come to light by way of means other than them directly informing the Agency[1]. In such cases, the Agency should notify the carrier or broker of the information and 'provide him with details of the conviction' (sic). Affected carriers or brokers should be 'invited' to confirm the accuracy of the information and to fill in any relevant information which is not in the possession of the Agency. They should also be asked to confirm if it is they or another relevant person who has been convicted of prescribed offences. Finally, if the Agency's information is confirmed, any additional information which the Agency should take into account in making its decision on whether it is appropriate that registration should continue must be provided[2].

1 Circular 11/91, Annex 1, para 1.63; Circular 11/94, Annex 8, para 8.69.
2 Circular 11/91, Annex 1, para 1.63; Circular 11/94, Annex 8, para 8.69.

6.96 As is the case with refusals to register, a registered carrier or broker must be told of the decision to revoke by way of a notice[1]. The reasoning must be included[2], along with the person's rights of appeal, etc. No fees are due to be refunded[3]. The notice can be served by hand or by post[4].

1 SI 1991/1624, reg 10(2); SI 1994/1056, Sch 5, para 5(2).
2 SI 1991/1624, reg 10(2); SI 1994/1056, Sch 5, para 5(2).

3   Circular 11/91, Annex 1, para 1.24; Circular 11/94, Annex 8, para 8.35.
4   SI 1991/1624, reg 24 and the EPA 1990, s 160; SI 1994/1056, reg 1(7) as amended by SI 1995/288, reg 3(2).

6.97   Where an appeal is lodged[1], the carrier or broker is permitted to continue in business until the appeal is determined[2]. The carrier or broker must be informed of this fact in conjunction with the appeal notice[3]. The appeal period is 28 days from the date of revocation. If this period expires with no appeal having been lodged, the registration is deemed to have been revoked[4].

1   See para 6.99.
2   Control of Pollution (Amendment) Act 1989, s 4(7); SI 1994/1056, Sch 5, para 7(8)(b).
3   Circular 11/91, Annex 1, para 1.68; Circular 11/94, Annex 8, para 8.72.
4   SI 1991/1624, reg 11(5)(a); SI 1994/1056, Sch 5, para 6(6)(c).

6.98   If a carrier registration is revoked and no appeal is lodged, or if the appeal is not determined in the carrier's favour, the registration certificate and any copies must be returned to the Agency[1]. However, it appears that a person flouting such a requirement does not actually commit an offence. As controlled waste brokers are not issued with registration certificates, there is no similar requirement in Schedule 5 to the Waste Management Licensing Regulations 1994.

1   SI 1991/1624, reg 13.

APPEALS

6.99   Appeals to the Secretary of State can be lodged when an application has been refused or registration revoked[1] or if an application has not been dealt with by the Agency within two months of receipt[2]. The two-month period can be extended by mutual consent in the case of an initial application for registration. However, such an extension is not possible in relation to an application for a renewal of registration[3]. Where an application is refused or a registration revoked, the applicant has 28 days from the date on which the Agency's notice was received in which to lodge an appeal[4].

1   Control of Pollution (Amendment) Act 1989, s 4(1) and(2); SI 1994/1056, Sch 5, para 6(1) and (2).
2   1989 Act, s 4(1); SI 1994/1056, Sch 5, para 6(1)(b).
3   SI 1991/1624, reg 4(1); SI 1994/1056, Sch 5, para 1(1).
4   SI 1991/1624, reg 16; SI 1994/1056, Sch 5, para 6(6).

6.100   The lodging of an appeal against the revocation of a registration or the refusal of an application for a renewal results in the continuation of the registration until the appeal is decided[1]. Conversely, a first time applicant who is refused registration is not allowed to carry or broker waste until the appeal is discharged.

1   Control of Pollution (Amendment) Act 1989, s 4(7); SI 1991/1624, reg 11(1)(b); SI 1994/1056, Sch 5, paras 7(7) and 7(8).

6.101   Appeals to the Secretary of State must be made in writing[1] and have to be accompanied by a number of documents. These include[2]:

- a statement of the grounds for appeal;
- a copy of the application when a registration has been refused or a copy of the entry on the register where a registration has been revoked;
- copies of relevant correspondence;

– the notice of refusal or revocation from the Agency; and
– a statement indicating if the appellant wishes the appeal to be conducted by written representations or by a hearing.

Copies of the statements of the grounds for the appeal and of whether written representations or a hearing are preferred should also be sent to the Agency concerned[3].

1 SI 1991/1624, reg 15(2): however, this appears to apply to waste carriers only and there is no explicit requirement for the notice to be in writing for waste brokers.
2 SI 1991/1624, reg 15(2); SI 1994/1056, Sch 5, para 6(4).
3 SI 1991/1624, reg 15(3); SI 1994/1056, Sch 5, para 6(5).

6.102   For controlled waste carrier or broker appeals[1], the Secretary of State can appoint a person to determine the appeal on his behalf or can refer any part of the appeal to such a person[2]. The person must be appointed according to the requirements of Schedule 20 to the Environment Act 1995[3] and when appointed must operate in accordance with those provisions. Typically, most carrier appeals in England and Wales are delegated to the Planning Inspectorate in Bristol.

1 Control of Pollution (Amendment) Act 1989, s 4(9) (as amended by the Environment Act 1995, s 120(1) and Sch 22, para 37(3); SI 1994/1056, Sch 5, para 6(13) as amended by SI 1996/593, reg 3, Sch 2, para 10(6)(b)).
2 Environment Act 1995, s 114 and 1989 Act s 4(9) as amended by the Environment Act 1995, Sch 22, para 37(3).
3 Environment Act 1995, s 114.

6.103   Both the appellant and the Agency can request that the appeal is dealt with by written representations or by a hearing[1], with the legislation requiring such a request to be granted. The Secretary of State is also given the power to require a hearing. A person who holds a hearing is appointed by the Secretary of State. Once appointed, the person conducts the hearing and is required to make a written report to the Secretary of State[2].

1 SI 1991/1624, reg 17(1); SI 1994/1056, Sch 5, para 6(7).
2 SI 1991/1624, reg 17(2); SI 1994/1056, Sch 5, para 6(8).

6.104   Once the appeal is determined, the Secretary of State can direct the Agency to register the carrier, can dismiss the appeal or can cancel the registration[1]. For both carriers and brokers, the Agency has the duty to comply with the Secretary of State's decision[2]. The appellant and Agency must be informed of the decision in writing[3]. The reasons for the decision have to be included, along with a copy of the written report made to the Secretary of State of any hearing.

1 Control of Pollution (Amendment) Act 1989, s 4(3); SI 1994/1056, Sch 5, para 6(9).
2 1989 Act, s 4(5); SI 1994/1056, Sch 5, para 6(12).
3 SI 1991/1624, reg 18; SI 1994/1056, Sch 5, para 6(10).

THE REGISTRATION OF THE WASTE COLLECTION AUTHORITY, CHARITIES, VOLUNTARY ORGANISATIONS AND OTHER BODIES

6.105   Certain bodies were deliberately excluded from the requirements of the Control of Pollution (Registration of Waste Carriers and Seizure of Vehicles) Regulations 1991[1]. Some, such as the producer of waste other than building and demolition waste, are excluded entirely. Others are subject to a different registration system which is a simplified version of that emanating from the Control of Pollution (Amendment) Act 1989. This is to be found in paragraph 12 of Schedule 4 to the Waste Management

Licensing Regulations 1994. As the provisions of this system are not common to the usual carrier and broker registration scheme, they will be dealt with separately below.

1   SI 1991/1624, reg 2(1)(a).

Collectors and transporters of waste on a professional basis

6.106   Bodies subject to the lesser system of registration under Schedule 4 to the 1994 Regulations are[1] the waste disposal and collection authorities, the Agency[2], charities and voluntary organisations[3,4].

1   SI 1994/1056, Sch 4, Pt I, para 12(1); SI 1991/1624, reg 2(1)(a), (c) and (g).
2   As Waste Regulation Authority: see s 30 of the EPA 1990 (as amended by the Environment Act 1995, Sch 22, para 62).
3   Defined as being encompassed by s 48(11) of the Local Government Act 1985 (or s 83(2D) of the Local Government (Scotland) Act 1973 (SI 1991/1624, reg 2(1)(g)).
4   The final body covered by such provisions is any 'wholly owned subsidiary' of the British Railways Board which has applied in accordance with the Controlled Waste Carriers (Registration and Seizure of Vehicles) Regulations 1991 for registration as a carrier of controlled waste (SI 1994/1056, Sch 4, Pt 1, para 12(1); SI 1991/1624, reg 2(1)(c) as amended by SI 1994/1056, reg 23(2)). However, this provision is only relevant whilst the application is pending. Once registration under the Control of Pollution (Amendment) Act 1989 has been achieved, a registration under Schedule 4 is no longer necessary.

6.107   If these bodies are not registered in accordance with paragraph 12 of Part I to Schedule 4, they commit an offence if they 'collect or transport[1] waste[2] on a professional basis'[3]. It should be noted that there is no requirement, analogous to that under the Control of Pollution (Amendment) Act 1989, for these bodies to be registered when moving building or demolition waste produced by them. Registration is only required when these wastes are moved on the above-mentioned 'professional basis'.

1   The words 'collect' and 'transport' are given the same meaning as in Article 12 of the Directive on Waste (Council Directive of 15 July 1975 on Waste (75/442/EEC) (OJ L194/39 25.7.75) (as amended by Council Directive of 18 March 1991 amending Directive 75/442/EEC on Waste (91/156/EEC) (OJ L78/32 26.3.91)) and by Directive 91/692 (OJ L377/48)): SI 1994/1056, Pt I, Sch 4, para 12(11).
2   Not '*controlled* waste'.
3   SI 1994/1056, Pt I, Sch 4, para 12(1).

6.108   Circular 11/94 suggests that the purpose of the phrase 'to collect or transport waste on a professional basis' is to 'exclude [from registration] organisations for whom the transport of waste is solely incidental to their main business, and is not a significant part of their business'[1]. Accordingly, it would appear from the circular that a voluntary organisation established principally to recycle materials such as waste paper would need a registration. But a scout group who, along with a number of other unrelated activities, collects waste paper as one of a number of ways of raising funds is not transporting waste on a professional basis.

1   Circular 11/94, Annex 1, para 1.74(c).

6.109   In addition, the Waste Management Licensing Regulations 1994 hold that there is no need for bodies potentially subject to these provisions to register when they are involved in collection and transportation activities which are in accordance with the terms and conditions of 'a permit'[1]. The nature of such a 'permit' can be a waste management licence, a disposal licence, an authorisation under Part I of the EPA 1990, a resolution, a licence under Part II of the Food and Environment Protection Act 1985 or a consent granted under either Chapter II of Part III of the Water Resources Act 1991 or under Part II of the Control of Pollution Act 1974[2]. Beyond the fact that a similar wording is found in Article 12 of the Directive on Waste, the precise intention of this provision is less than clear, particularly in relation to waste management licences and Part I authorisations. Neither lay down requirements in respect of waste carriage. Although the requirements are repeated in Circular 11/94[3], no further clarification is given.

1   SI 1994/1056, Sch 4, Pt I, para 12(3).
2   SI 1994/1056, Sch 4, Pt I, para 1: note that exempt activities registered under SI 1994/1056, regs 17 and 18 are not mentioned; exempt activities are discussed in Chapters 10 and 11.
3   Circular 11/94, Annex 1, para 1.79.

6.110   A person found guilty of an offence of failing to be registered under paragraph 12(1) of Part 1 to Schedule 4 may be subject to a fine of up to level 2[1] on the standard scale[2]. However, it seems that such a body is unlikely to ever be convicted. Firstly, Circular 11/94 cautions the Agency from taking enforcement action[3]:

'A failure to register under paragraph 12 of Schedule 4, where this is the only breach of the Regulations, does not itself threaten pollution or harm to the environment. Authorities should not expect to take enforcement action for such technical breaches, until and unless the establishment or undertaking concerned fails to cooperate with the reasonable actions open to the authority to secure a registration.'

The second reason why prosecution is unlikely stems – despite what is implied by the final line of the Circular just quoted[4] – from the fact that Paragraph 12(7) of Part I to Schedule 4 requires the Agency to register the activity if it receives notice of it in writing 'or otherwise becomes aware of those particulars'[5]. Clearly, the Agency will become aware of an unregistered activity when it discovers it. It then has the statutory duty to register it, regardless of whether an application is made or not[6].

1   Currently £500.
2   SI 1994/1056, Sch 4, Pt 1, para 8.
3   Circular 11/94, Annex 1, para 1.75.
4   This near-contradiction appears to be acknowledged by para 1.76 of Annex 1 of Circular 11/94.
5   SI 1994/1056, Sch 4, Pt 1, para 12(7).
6   A similar wording is used in SI 1994/1056, reg 18(4) in relation to the need to register exemptions from waste management licences: see para 10.24ff.

Brokers of waste

6.111   The Waste Disposal Authority and Waste Collection Authority, along with the Agency[1], charities and voluntary organisations, are exempt from the general requirement to register their brokerage activities in accordance with Schedule 5 to the Waste Management Licensing Regulations 1994[2]. Instead, if they wish to arrange the brokerage of 'waste'[3] on behalf of others[4], they must register under the simplified registration system set out in Schedule 4, paragraph 12 of the 1994 Regulations[5].

1   As Waste Regulation Authority: see the EPA 1990, s 30.
2   SI 1994/1056, reg 20(3).
3   Not '*controlled* waste'.
4   See para 6.29 for a definition of a broker.
5   SI 1994/1056, Sch 4, Pt I, para 12(2).

6.112   Should they not be so registered, an offence is committed if the activities of these organisations are encompassed by the definition of a controlled waste broker[1]. Like those waste carriers which fall within these requirements and which have been discussed at para 6.110 above, the commission of an offence under these provisions is likely to result in a maximum fine of level 2 on the standard scale[2]. The offence is not one which is indictable.

1 SI 1994/1056, Sch 4, Pt I, para 12(2).
2 SI 1994/1056, Sch 4, Pt I, reg 12(8).

6.113 For reasons similar to those described at para 6.110 above[1], it appears that these bodies are unlikely to face prosecution for operating as unregistered brokers.

1 See SI 1994/1056, Sch 4, Pt 1, para 12(7).

The transporter and broker registration process

6.114 The waste collection and disposal authorities, the Agency and charities and voluntary organisations are required to register with the Agency which covers their principal place of business if they wish to be involved with the carriage of waste or its brokerage[1].

1 SI 1994/1056, Pt I, Sch 4, para 12(4): if there is no such place in Great Britain, an application for a registration can be made to any waste regulation authority: SI 1994/1056, Pt I, Sch 4, para 12(4).

6.115 No fee is payable for a registration, no application form is used and no registration certificate is issued. The registration of these bodies continues indefinitely and cannot be revoked. The requirements in relation to the contents of the registers are described at para 13.54ff.

Chapter 7

Enforcement against unauthorised waste management activities: s 33 of the EPA 1990

INTRODUCTION

7.01 This chapter considers the main enforcement provision of the EPA 1990, namely s 33. That section constitutes the principal regulatory power in Part II of the Act, being designed to ensure that environmentally acceptable activities continue at licensed sites and that unauthorised waste management practices are prevented.

7.02 A number of words and phrases contained in s 33 of the EPA 1990 raise key points of law. In addition, s 33 prompts important questions concerning corporate responsibilities in relation to waste management activities, the processes through which criminal liability may attach and the defences available both to companies and their directors and officers.

SECTION 33 OF THE EPA 1990: THE MAIN PROVISIONS

7.03 Section 33(1) requires that a person[1] shall not:

'(a) deposit controlled waste, or knowingly cause or knowingly permit controlled waste to be deposited in or on any land unless a waste management licence authorising the deposit is in force and the deposit is in accordance with the licence;

(b) treat, keep or dispose of controlled waste, or knowingly cause or knowingly permit controlled waste to be treated, kept or disposed of –
   (i) in or on any land, or
   (ii) by means of any mobile plant,
   except under and in accordance with a waste management licence;

(c) treat, keep or dispose of controlled waste in a manner likely to cause pollution of the environment or harm to human health'.

Contravention of this section results in an offence being committed[2].

1 Interpretation Act 1978, s 5 and Sch 1 state that 'a person' includes a body of persons corporate and unincorporate.
2 EPA 1990, s 33(6).

7.04 The principal offence in s 33(1) of the EPA 1990 is subject to two significant provisos, which are contained in s 33(2) and s 33(3). Firstly, under s 33(2), s 33(1) does not apply 'in relation to household waste[1] from a domestic property'[2] which is treated, kept or disposed of within the curtilage of the dwelling. This exclusion therefore permits the continuation of such practices as bonfires on domestic properties, household waste composting[3] and so on. However, this provision does not apply in the case of household waste which is composed of mineral or synthetic oil or grease, asbestos and clinical waste[4]. Should such undesirable materials be deposited within the curtilage of a domestic dwelling, an offence under s 33 will be committed[5].

1 Defined by the EPA 1990, s 75(5) and by the Controlled Waste Regulations 1992 (SI 1992/588): see para 2.200.

2   Note that the word 'domestic property' restricts the definition of household waste contained in s 75 of the EPA 1990 to s 75(5)(a) only (see paras 2.220ff and 3.24). The offence provision in s 33(1) continues to apply to household waste produced from caravans, residential homes, educational establishments and hospitals and nursing homes (as described in s 75(5)(b) to (e)). An additional reinforcement to this requirement is contained in SI 1994/1056 (Sch 4, para 9(6)), which makes clear that the exclusion under s 33(2) does not relate to household waste being managed by any 'establishment or undertaking' (the latter concept is explained at para 10.22), as opposed to a person acting as a private individual.
3   Although it might be argued that materials passing to compost heaps are not waste as the householder is not discarding them: waste definitions are discussed in Chapter 2.
4   SI 1992/588, reg 3(1): see para 2.200ff.
5   See also Circular 14/92, Annex 1, para 1.21.

7.05   The second instance where s 33(1) does not apply is in respect of waste management activities which have been excluded or exempted[1] by regulations made by the Secretary of State[2]. In exercising this power, the Secretary of State is required[3] to have regard to the expediency of excluding from regulatory control deposits of waste which are so small or 'of such a temporary nature', where treatment and disposal methods are innocuous or where adequate controls are provided by other enactments. Such provisions are contained in regs 16 and 17 of the Waste Management Licensing Regulations 1994[4].

1   The distinction between exclusions and exemptions is discussed at para 10.05.
2   EPA 1990, s 33(3).
3   EPA 1990, s 33(4).
4   SI 1994/1056 as amended by SI 1995/288 and SI 1996/972: see Chapters 10 and 11.

7.06   An important element of s 33 of the EPA 1990 is s 33(5), which is aimed at clarifying the responsibilities of persons who act as the controllers of motor vehicles[1]. When waste is deposited from a motor vehicle in contravention of s 33(1), the person 'who controls or is in a position to control the use of the vehicle' is to be treated as knowingly causing the deposit 'whether or not he gave any instructions for this to be done'[2]. According to Circular 11/94[3], this provision:

'... places the onus on the owner or manager of vehicles used to transport controlled waste to ensure that his employees, or those to whom he might lend his vehicles, do not fly-tip waste. This provision only applies to those who control, or are in a position to control, the use of the vehicle. It does not therefore affect those who for example only hire out vehicles.'

Section 33(5) of the EPA 1990 therefore seeks to overcome the not infrequent claim by company managers that their drivers were on a 'frolic of their own' and that the manager could not be held responsible for the unlawful activities[4].

1   Note that, unlike the Control of Pollution (Amendment) Act 1989 (s 9(1): see para 12.154ff), the EPA 1990 does not provide a definition of a 'vehicle'.
2   EPA 1990, s 33(5).
3   Circular 11/94, Annex 4, para 4.12.
4   See, for example, *Rose v Plenty* [1976] 1 All ER 97 and *Cleveland County Council v Brian Edward George Gibben* (29 July 1985, unreported) QBD.

7.07   It should be noted that, although s 33(5) of the EPA 1990 appears primarily aimed at providing the Agency with a more effective grasp on the perpetrators of fly-tipping, the sub-section also applies to waste deposited by vehicles at licensed waste management facilities. It therefore illustrates the need for waste disposal contractors to ensure that their procedures are adequate to satisfy the appropriate statutory defences in s 33(7)[1].

1   See para 7.144ff.

7.08   Section 33(6) of the EPA 1990 makes it an offence to contravene any condition of a waste management licence. This is a free standing offence unconnected to the question of whether any waste was being deposited at that time. It may also constitute an offence involving strict liability[1]. It should be noted that, in contrast to the phraseology of s 33(1), there are no caveats which, for example, require that a person must have 'knowingly contravened' a condition of a licence or 'knowingly caused or knowingly permitted the contravention of a licence'[2].

1   See para 7.115ff.
2   Despite somewhat similar wording, this is, for example, in contrast to the legislation on the licensing of sex establishments: see Sch 3, para 20(1)(c) of the Local Government (Miscellaneous Provisions) Act 1982 and see Lord Bridge in *Westminster City v Croyalgrange Ltd* ([1986] 2 All ER 353 at 357A), discussed at para 7.57.

7.09   Section 33(6) was probably the most significant advance upon the earlier legislation under the Control of Pollution Act 1974. Prior to May 1994, the wording of s 3 of the Control of Pollution Act 1974 caused the principal offence provision not to apply in the case where there occurred breaches of waste disposal licence conditions which were unconnected to those which directly related to the waste deposited[1]. Examples of such conditions might concern site security arrangements or environmental monitoring boreholes.

1   See *Leigh Land Reclamation v Walsall Metropolitan Borough Council* (1990) 155 JP 547: see paras 7.17ff and 7.140ff.

7.10   Three statutory defences are available to a person charged under s 33. They are[1] that the person charged with an offence must prove:

'(a)   that he took all reasonable precautions and exercised all due diligence to avoid the commission of the offence; or

(b)   that he acted under instructions from his employer and neither knew nor had reason to suppose that the acts done by him constituted a contravention of subsection (1)[2] above; or

(c)   that the acts alleged to constitute the contravention were done in an emergency in order to avoid danger to human health in a case where –

(i)   he took all such steps as were reasonably practicable in the circumstances for minimising pollution of the environment and harm to human health; and

(ii)   particulars of acts were furnished to the waste regulation authority as soon as reasonably practicable after they were done.'

These important provisions are discussed further at para 7.144 below.

1   EPA 1990, s 33(7), as amended by the Environment Act 1995, s 120, Sch 22, para 64.
2   Ie the EPA 1990, s 33(1).

7.11   Penalties for the contravention of s 33(1) and s 33(6) are set out in s 33(8) and s 33(9). Unless special waste is involved, a person who commits an offence is liable[1]:

(a)   on summary conviction, to imprisonment for a term not exceeding six months or a fine not exceeding £20,000 or both; and

(b)   on conviction on indictment, to imprisonment for a term not exceeding two years, or a fine, or both.

The penalties in cases involving special waste[2] are similar, although the length of the maximum term of imprisonment on conviction on indictment is increased from two to five years[3].

1   EPA 1990, s 33(8).
2   Defined by SI 1996/972 as amended by SI 1996/2019; see Chapter 4.
3   EPA 1990, s 33(9).

7.12   It will be apparent that there is some overlap between s 33 and the duty of care under s 34 of the EPA 1990[1], and certain conduct may result in offences being committed under both sections. At summary conviction, the fine under s 33 is much higher than that under s 34, with the latter being set at the statutory maximum[2]. In addition, imprisonment is not available under s 34 at summary trial. While convictions under either section affect a person's ability to retain a controlled waste carrier or broker[3] registration or to remain a 'fit and proper person'[4], only convictions under s 33 affect a person's ability to hold a heavy goods vehicle operators' licence under the Transport Act 1968[5]. The latter does not apply to convictions under s 34. These factors may influence prosecution policy, particularly where the offence is a serious one which should reflect the higher penalties contained in s 33.

1   See Chapter 3.
2   Currently £5,000.
3   See para 6.62.
4   See para 8.117ff.
5   Transport Act 1968, s 69, as amended by the EPA 1990, Sch 15, para 10.

7.13   Section 158 of the EPA 1990 is designed to address instances when offences were committed by a person which were the result of the act or default of someone else. Section 158 allows the second person to be prosecuted, whether or not the person who created the offence is subject to proceedings. Hence the Agency can charge both an employee and an employer or it can simply charge the employer, and not bother with the employee[1].

1   Employers' and directors' liability is discussed at paras 7.117ff, 7.135ff and 7.156ff.

KEY TERMS AND CONCEPTS IN S 33 OF THE EPA 1990

7.14   Certain terms within s 33(1) require careful interpretation. Of particular importance are the verbs 'deposit', 'treat', 'keep' and 'dispose of'. The provisions are also subject to significant limitations and qualifications laid down in Schedule 4 to the Waste Management Licensing Regulations 1994. The meaning of the phrases 'pollution of the environment'[1] and 'harm to human health' contained in s 33(1)(c) are also of importance. However, the latter two phrases are also integral with other criteria under which waste management licence applications are evaluated, and for that reason, are discussed at para 8.40ff. The nature of persons who 'knowingly cause' and 'knowingly permit' invites detailed interpretation, as does the question of whether strict liability applies to other elements of s 33(1) and (6). These matters are discussed below.

1   Defined in the EPA 1990, s 29.

7.15   A distinction is made in s 33 of the EPA 1990 between activities that involve the deposit of waste[1] and other types of waste disposal activity involving treating, keeping or disposing of controlled waste[2]. It seems that, at the time of the passage of the legislation through Parliament, the intention was for s 33(1)(a) to address fly-tipping, and that s 33(1)(b) was to be directed at actual waste management facilities (whether licensed or not)[3]. However, the manner by which these sub-sections were finally drafted leaves considerable overlap. An unlicensed landfill, for example, can be a place where controlled waste is deposited[4] or a place where controlled waste is disposed of[5]. In the case of a licensed facility, the overlap is more obvious. The wording of both s 33(1)(a) and (b) refers to the deposit, or the treatment, keeping or disposal, of waste being made 'in accordance with' a waste management licence. For example, a person who brings waste which is outside the ambit of the conditions of the licence onto a facility is caught by both sections. When the waste is tipped out it is *deposited*[6]. However, it has also been brought onto the site for the purposes of *disposal*[7]. The existence of these overlaps highlights the need for a careful interpretation of the terms and an appreciation of their boundaries.

1   EPA 1990, s 33(1)(a).
2   EPA 1990, s 33(1)(b).
3   See Official Report Sub-Committee H, Column 420, para 3.
4   EPA 1990, s 33(1)(a).
5   EPA 1990, s 33(1)(b).
6   EPA 1990, s 33(1)(a).
7   EPA 1990, s 33(1)(b).

'Depositing' and 'disposing of' controlled waste

7.16   It has been noted that s 33 of the EPA 1990 makes it an offence, *inter alia*, to 'deposit'[1] controlled waste and to 'dispose of'[2] such waste unless in accordance with the conditions of a waste management licence. The concept of 'depositing' waste also featured in the principal offence provision of the Control of Pollution Act 1974[3], with the wording bearing similarity to that repeated in the EPA 1990. The EPA 1990 also uses the terms 'dispose of' and 'disposed of'[4], which has similarity to the Control of Pollution Act 1974's term 'disposing of'[5]. However, as is suggested below, given the purpose of both statutes, the terms 'disposing of', 'disposed of' and 'dispose of' should be viewed as synonymous.

1   EPA 1990, s 33(1)(a).
2   EPA 1990, s 33(1)(b).
3   Control of Pollution Act 1974, s 3(1)(a).
4   EPA 1990, s 33(1)(b).
5   Control of Pollution Act 1974, s 3(1)(b).

7.17   In the past, the notion of a 'deposit' of controlled waste has proved problematic, being the subject of two conflicting judgments at the Divisional Court. These both related to its use in the Control of Pollution Act 1974. The first was *Leigh Land Reclamation v Walsall Metropolitan Borough Council*[1], in which Bingham LJ held that[2]:

'... the meaning of 'deposit' takes its colour from the context in which the word is used. This statute[3] is concerned, primarily at least, with the manner in which waste is disposed of. Its provisions, and the conditions of the licence, are directed towards the mode of final disposal and not to the intermediate processes. For the purposes of this Act, waste is, in my view, to be regarded as deposited when it is dumped on the site with no realistic prospect of further examination or inspection to reject goods of which deposit is not allowed under the licence.'

The ramifications of this judgment were considerable, particularly as it meant that transfer stations[4] could not be addressed by the offence provision of the Control of Pollution Act 1974[5] as no 'deposit' (in Bingham LJ's sense) would ever occur. Similarly, at licensed landfill sites, an inspector had to witness unsuitable wastes being bonded with the mass of the fill in order to obtain sufficient evidence that the material was deposited. Clearly, this hindered any requirement that the waste was removed immediately for environmental or public health reasons. Accordingly, many commentators considered that *Leigh Land* was wrongly decided and was an over-restrictive influence against effective environmental protection.

1   (1990) 155 JP 547, see also Laurence D (1992) 'The Meaning of "Deposit" under COPA and the EPA', *Waste Management* May 1992, pp 13–17.
2   *Leigh Land* at 559E/F.
3   Ie the Control of Pollution Act 1974.
4   Where waste is, by definition, temporarily placed down.
5   Control of Pollution Act 1974: s 3(1)(a).

7.18   In November 1992, the Divisional Court heard two joined cases which turned upon Bingham LJ's interpretation of the word 'deposit'. These were *R v Metropolitan Stipendiary Magistrate, ex p London Waste Regulation Authority* and *Berkshire County Council v Scott*[1]. Both concerned unlicensed transfer stations. The former case involved information issued in relation to s 3(1)(b) of the Control of Pollution Act 1974, which made it an offence to use plant or equipment to 'dispose of' waste without a waste disposal licence. The *Berkshire* case concerned a statutory notice[2], which required an occupier to remove a large quantity of waste 'deposited' on unlicensed land. In both instances, the lower courts had felt bound to follow Bingham LJ in *Leigh Land*. They therefore held that the words 'disposed of' and 'deposit' in the Control of Pollution Act 1974 should be interpreted as only involving final disposals or deposits – not temporary ones.

1   [1993] 3 All ER 113; see also Laurence D (1993) 'Divisional Court Settles the Meaning of "Deposit"' *Wastes Management*, February 1993 pp 8–9.
2   The power to issue such notices was contained in s 16 of the Control of Pollution Act 1974. This provision has been continued by s 59 of the EPA 1990: see para 12.101ff.

7.19   In the Divisional Court, Watkins LJ reviewed Bingham LJ's judgment, coming to the conclusion that it was wrongly decided. Watkins LJ considered the case of a large pile of rubbish which had been temporarily deposited with the eventual intention to move it on elsewhere. If this did not create an offence 'we cannot discern any basis on which the court should hold that Parliament intended to create such a lacuna in the environmental protection afforded by statute'[1].

1   *Berkshire County Council* at 121A.

7.20   Watkins LJ also disagreed with the contention that the words 'dispose of' should be restricted to final disposals only, noting[1]:

'Why should this be so? An article may be regarded as disposed of if it is destroyed or if it is passed on from one person to another; the ordinary sense of the term, certainly in a context such as that of this Act[2], rests in the notion of getting rid of something. It has, in our judgement, no more to do with finding a "final resting place" than has the word "deposit" in s 3(1)(a).'

Instead, it was concluded that[3]:

'For all these reasons, we feel compelled to conclude in principle that s 3(1)[4] is not concerned only with final deposits or disposals. To hold otherwise would, we think, involve an unnecessary erosion of the efficacy of the Act which, in our judgement, is as much concerned with the environmental damage that may be caused at a waste transfer station as with the effects created on or by a site where waste reaches its "final resting place". Since we cannot escape the conclusion that the decision in the *Leigh* case was to the contrary, we are driven to hold, with respect, that it was wrongly decided. The result does not, in our view, widen the application of the Act to any unacceptable extent: on the contrary we think it vindicates its purpose.'

1   *Berkshire County Council* at 121B.
2   Control of Pollution Act 1974.
3   *Berkshire County Council* at 121H.
4   Of the Control of Pollution Act 1974.

7.21   Although this judgment concerned the Control of Pollution Act 1974, it was upheld in respect of the EPA 1990 in *Thames Waste Management v Surrey County Council*[1]:

'To my mind, although clearly "deposit" is a putting down, it has also, as Waite LJ[2] made plain, to be construed, unless the context otherwise required, in a broad sense'.

In addition, both the Control of Pollution Act 1974 and the EPA 1990 are the principal vehicle by which the Directive on Waste[3] is transposed in British law. And in this respect[4], the subsidiary Waste Management Licensing Regulations 1994 have an essential function in ensuring the full implementation of the amendments made to the original Directive by Directive 91/156[5]. It would seem self-evident that the requirements of the Directive relate as much to temporary deposits of waste as to those which are permanent. An example is the list of disposal and recovery activities listed in Annexes IIA and IIB of the Directive, which are also contained in Schedule 4 to the Waste Management Licensing Regulations 1994[6]. Items D15 and R13 of the Annexes IIA and IIB[7] both relate to temporary waste storage operations away from the site of production.

1   [1997] Env LR 148 at 155/156: see also *R v Leighton and Town and Country Refuse Collection Ltd* [1997] Env LR 411 and *R v Smith* [1999] Env LR 433.
2   In *Scott v Westminster City Council* (1995) 93 LGR 370, where it was held that the word 'deposit' was a term of wide connotation apt to describe the placing of one object on another. Unless the context required otherwise, it should be interpreted in the broad sense (see also *Craddock v Green* (1982) 81 LGR 235).
3   Council Directive of 15 July 1975 on Waste (75/442/EEC) (OJ L194/39 25.7.75) (as amended by Council Directive of 18 March 1991 amending Directive 75/442/EEC on Waste (91/156/EEC) (OJ L78/32 26.3.91) and Commission Decision of 24 May 1996 adapting Annexes IIA and IIB to Council Directive 75/442/EEC on Waste (96/350/EC) (OJ L135/32 6.6.96)): see para 2.19.
4   See Circular 11/94, para 7.
5   Council Directive of 18 March 1991 amending Directive 75/442/EEC on Waste (91/156/EEC) (OJ L78/32 26.3.91).
6   See Tables 2.2, 2.3, 2.5 and 2.6 in Chapter 2. Note that there are now minor differences between the Annexes of the Directive and Parts III and IV of Sch 4 of SI 1994/1056 due to amendments resultant from Commission Decision of 24 May 1996 adapting Annexes IIA and IIB to Council Directive 75/442/EEC on Waste (96/350/EC) (OJ L135/32 6.6.96).
7   Prior to the Directive being amended, the wordings were the same as Item 15 of Part III and Item 13 of Part IV of Sch 4 to the Waste Management Licensing Regulations 1994.

7.22   In addition, and as was acknowledged in *R v Metropolitan Stipendiary Magistrate* and *Berkshire County Council*[1], s 4(3) of the Control of Pollution Act 1974 appeared to have been overlooked by the earlier judgment of Bingham LJ. That subsection referred[2] to deposits of a 'temporary nature' which can be excluded from the offence provisions of the Control of Pollution Act 1974 by secondary legislation. A similar requirement exists in the EPA 1990: s 33(4)(a). As Watkins LJ points out[3], the existence of the notion of a temporary deposit in the wording of the Control of Pollution Act 1974 'seems to us to add a further, a conclusive, obstacle to the respondents'[4] submissions'.

1   *Berkshire County Council* at 121C.
2   Control of Pollution Act 1974, s 4(3)(a).
3   *Berkshire County Council* at 121C.
4   Ie the operators of the two illegal transfer stations.

7.23 Finally, the judgment raises the interesting legal point of the Divisional Court over-ruling itself. Watkins LJ notes[1] that there is no rule of *stare decisis*[2] between different Divisional Courts. Whether a Divisional Court was bound by its previous decisions was reviewed in *R v Greater Manchester Coroner, ex p Tal and Another*[3]. Goff LJ found that[4]: 'we do not consider that there is any authority which decides that a Divisional Court in such a case is not free to depart from a previous decision of another Divisional Court'. However, as Watkins LJ noted in *Berkshire County Council*[5], to so depart, the later court must be satisfied that one of its previous decisions was erroneous.

1   *Berkshire County Council* at 120G.
2   The need for a judgment to follow earlier cases which had been decided in a particular manner.
3   [1984] 3 All ER 240: see also *Colchester Estates (Cardiff) v Carlton Industries plc* [1984] 2 All ER 601 and *Re Smith (a bankrupt), ex p Braintree District Council v the Bankrupt* [1988] 3 All ER 203.
4   [1984] 3 All ER 240 at 247A.
5   *Berkshire County Council* at 120H.

7.24 In conclusion, it appears that the words 'deposit' and 'dispose of' in s 33 of the EPA 1990 should be considered broadly[1]. They refer both to temporary and permanent resting places. Once inappropriate waste has been deposited at either a licensed or unlicensed site, the only recourse a person who put it there should have is to the statutory defences set down by Parliament in s 33(7). The most important of these is that the person 'took all reasonable precautions and exercised all due diligence to avoid the commission of the offence'[2]. Accordingly, this test should be sufficient for a licence holder charged, in the manner of *Leigh Land*, after inappropriate waste was deposited. Clearly, if the waste checking system has been at a sufficiently vigilant level, the material will be immediately removed and the statutory defence satisfied. But if, for example, the unauthorised waste is buried by a landfill's machine driver after deficient checking, then the statutory defence appears to fall. There seems to be no need for any rarefied debate on the judicial meaning of 'deposit' in these circumstances.

1   See also *Thames Waste Management v Surrey County Council* [1997] Env LR 148 at 155/156; *R v Leighton and Town and Country Refuse Collection Ltd* [1997] Env LR 411 at 420 and 423; and *R v Smith* [1999] Env LR 433.
2   EPA 1990, s 33(7)(a): see para 7.145ff.

'Treating' controlled waste

7.25 The offence provision of s 33 of the EPA 1990 also has specific application to persons who 'treat' waste[1], with the word being defined in s 29(6). Subject to any regulations made by the Secretary of State under s 29(7),

> '. . . waste is "treated" when it is subjected to any process, including making it reusable or reclaiming substances[2] from it and "recycle" (and cognate expressions) shall be construed accordingly.'

Although the word 'process' is defined by Part I of the EPA 1990[3], that definition is not of relevance to waste management controls, which are set out in Part II. The Secretary of State has the power under s 29(7) to prescribe activities which involve treatment, but none have been so prescribed. However, some guidance is given in *Nurse v Morganite Crucible Ltd*[4], albeit that the House of Lords felt that the term 'process' constitutes '. . . a word of very wide general meaning and must take colour from its context'[5] and that 'it is possible that it has different meanings in different contexts'[6]. *Nurse* related to the Factories Act 1961 and the Asbestos Regulations 1969. Due to the common and frequent use of the term within the Factories Act 1961 and the Asbestos Regulations 1969, Lord Griffiths was reluctant to set down a hard and fast definition.

However, in terms of the Asbestos Regulations 1969, the word process was held to mean 'any operation or series of operations being an activity of more than minimal duration'[7]. It was therefore found to include demolition[8].

1   EPA 1990, s 33(1)(b).
2   'Substance' is defined in s 29(11) as meaning 'any natural or artificial substance, whether in solid or liquid form or in the form of a gas or vapour'.
3   EPA 1990, s 1(5).
4   [1989] 1 All ER 113 (*R v AI Industrial Products plc* [1987] 2 All ER 368 overruled).
5   *Nurse* at 117E.
6   *Nurse* at 119J: in the context of capital allowances for industrial buildings, cleaning equipment used in conjunction with plant hire was held not to be 'a process' (*Vibroplant Ltd v Holland (Inspector of Taxes)* [1981] 1 All ER 526). But that finding was considered irrelevant in the context of health and safety legislation in *Nurse* (see *Nurse* at 119G).
7   *Nurse* at 120A.
8   Separately, in *Sheffield City Council v A D H Demolition Ltd* (1983) 82 LGR 177, despite demolition being a one-off activity, it was held to constitute a process, with burning of rubbish contrary to the Clean Air Act 1968 being part of that process.

'Keeping' controlled waste

7.26   There is no definition of the word 'keep' in Part II of the EPA 1990. This omission is a little unfortunate, leaving the scope of the term somewhat uncertain. Often questions of whether a person 'kept' waste will be decided on the ordinary English usage of the term[1] and the facts of the case. But from case law in other fields, it would seem necessary that the activity must involve more than transient storage for a person to be held to 'keep' controlled waste. Some support for this matter is also gained from a consideration of the scope of the regulations implementing the EPA 1990 and from customary practices of the waste management industry itself.

1   See *R v Leighton and Town and Country Refuse Collection Ltd* [1997] Env LR 411 at 420.

7.27   A useful judicial starting point is *Biggs v Mitchell*[1], a case involving the temporary storage of gunpowder in a railway warehouse prior to dispatch to a number of destinations elsewhere. As the law stood, 50 lbs could be held on a premises without the requisite authorisation. However the warehouse was found to contain a number of separate packages giving a collective weight of 300 lbs. Examining the purposes of the trade in gunpowder at that time, Crompton J noted that there appeared to be no provision in the relevant legislation which addressed the frequent occurrence of the temporary storage of gunpowder in a similar manner to that occurring in the warehouse. Accordingly, it was found that this method of storage did not fall within the offence of 'keeping' gunpowder. Perhaps not surprisingly, the judge averred from indicating how long a package could be delayed at a temporary resting place for the act to constitute 'keeping', beyond feeling that this would happen when storage was for 'an unreasonable time'.

1   (1862) 2 B & S 522 (English Reports at 1167).

7.28   Similarly, in the Canadian case of *Blue v Pearl Assurance Co Ltd*[1], the keeping of a small[2] quantity of fuel overnight in a garage was held not to constitute the keeping of petrol. The petrol did not remain in the garage continuously, but on at least one occasion was held there overnight by mistake[3]. This was held not to constitute 'keeping'.

1   [1940] 3 WWR 13.
2   It would seem also that the quantity involved – half a gallon – may have been significant in the court's decision.
3   *Blue* at 19/20.

7.29 These positions are also substantiated by the case of *Dudley v Holland*[1], where vehicles were temporarily placed on the public highway while a car showroom was being re-arranged. One of the vehicles was found not to possess a motor excise licence. In this instance, the then Vehicles (Excise) Act 1962 contained the dual offence of unlawfully 'using' or 'keeping' vehicles. It was held that these concepts were aimed at different circumstances[2]. Lord Parker held[3]:

'. . . I approach the word 'keeps' in what seems to me the ordinary meaning of some continuing process; not a mere isolated moment, but a keeping of the car there, at any rate for some interval of time. It is no doubt a matter of degree and fact in every case.'

1 [1963] 3 All ER 732.
2 See *Dudley* at 734E: which has a certain parallel to the EPA 1990's construction of s 33 and the range of offences involving waste being 'deposited', 'kept', 'treated' or 'disposed of' (see para 7.103ff below).
3 *Dudley* at 734G/H.

7.30 From these three, somewhat disparate, judgments, it can be seen that the concept of 'keeping' probably involves something more than transient storage of short duration. This position does, to some degree, hold credence for the EPA 1990 and associated regulations. For example, long distance waste haulage is by no means uncommon and this may involve wastes remaining on vehicles overnight. This may particularly be the case for special wastes and for those moved as transfrontier shipments. Drivers may need to rest in order to stay within permitted tachograph hours and may, due to delay, arrive at the intended destination after closure. Short-term, overnight storage seems inevitable in these circumstances. Although there are an extensive series of exemptions set out in the Waste Management Licensing Regulations 1994[1], none seems to comprehensively address this type of circumstance[2]. This apparent omission either suggests that holding wastes overnight at lorry parks is unlawful or that, as was the case in *Biggs v Mitchell*, this practice is not an offence due to the nature of 'keeping' waste under s 33 of the EPA 1990. Finally, the Special Waste Regulations 1996[3] appear to countenance transitory storage on vehicles. They make provisions for so-called 'carrier's rounds' for collections of small quantities of special wastes. These are explicitly restricted to a duration of 24 hours[4]. In the absence of any provision to the contrary, such a requirement would be satisfied if a round started in the early afternoon, being completed by lunchtime the following day. Again, overnight storage is inevitable in such a timescale. In the end, only an appropriate precedent will decide the nature of the correct view, but it does seem that 'keeping' controlled waste involves something more that transitory storage.

1 SI 1994/1056, Sch 3: see Chapters 10 and 11.
2 For example, whilst Sch 3, para 40 allows for temporary secure storage, it only pertains to solid waste and does not apply at all to special waste (see para 10.65ff).
3 SI 1996/972 as amended by SI 1996/2019.
4 SI 1996/972, reg 8(1)(d).

The Waste Management Licensing Regulations 1994: depositing, treating, keeping and disposing of waste

7.31 As has been discussed in Chapter 2[1], the Waste Management Licensing Regulations 1994 attempt to closely connect the provisions of the Directive on Waste to Part II of the EPA 1990[2]. Of significance to this chapter are the lists of operations which are classed as disposal or recovery activities under the Directive[3]. While it may be correct to assert that the Annexes in the Directive were intended to illustrate indicative types of recovery and disposal operations[4], this is not how they were considered in the context of the Waste Management Licensing Regulations 1994. Instead, the Regulations make them explicitly connect to s 33 of the EPA 1990 and to the concepts of 'depositing', 'treating', 'keeping' and 'disposing of' waste[5]. As shown below, the practical benefit of these cross-connections to effective waste regulation is, it is submitted, not immediately obvious. Their effects are somewhat complex and, indeed, neither entirely logical nor unambiguous[6]. However, the ramifications of these provisions seem significant, as the Waste Management Licensing Regulations 1994 place constraints upon the scope of application of the different sub-sections of the principal offence provision of s 33(1) of the EPA 1990.

1   See para 2.35ff.
2   See SI 1994/1056, reg 19 and Sch 4; Circular 11/94, paras 5–8 and Annex 1.
3   See Tables 2.2 and 2.3 in Chapter 2. Note that there are now minor differences between the Annexes of the Directive and Parts III and IV of Sch 4 of SI 1994/1056 due to amendments resulting from Commission Decision of 24 May 1996 adapting Annexes IIA and IIB to Council Directive 75/442/EEC on Waste (96/350/EC) (OJ L135/32 6.6.96), which are set out in Sch 4 to the Waste Management Licensing Regulations 1994 (see Tables 2.5 and 2.6).
4   See para 51 of the Opinion of Advocate General Jacobs in *Euro Tombesi* [1998] Env LR 59 at 74.
5   SI 1994/1056, Sch 4, para 9(3)–(5).
6   As will become evident from the discussion below, a clear description of their application is not an easy task.

7.32   Regulation 1(3) of the Waste Management Licensing Regulations 1994 defines the words 'disposal' and 'recovery'. These definitions are taken to hold 'unless the context otherwise requires'. The word 'disposal' in the Waste Management Licensing Regulations 1994 is held to 'mean'[1] those operations in Part III of Schedule 4 (see Table 2.5). Similarly, the Regulations hold that a reference to waste being 'disposed of' should be viewed as involving waste being submitted to one of those operations listed. Likewise, the Waste Mangement Licensing Regulations 1994 hold that the word 'recovery' is to be taken to 'mean' those operations listed in Part IV of Schedule 4 (see Table 2.6), while any references to 'waste being recovered' should be seen as meaning the submission of waste to one of those operations. In essence, therefore, reg 1(3) makes clear that the Waste Management Licensing Regulations 1994 do not embrace disposal or recovery activities outside Parts III and IV of Schedule 4 when the words 'disposal', 'disposed of', 'recovery' or 'recovered' are used.

1   In other words is 'restricted solely to'.

7.33   However, the first line of reg 1(3) states that the above definitions shall apply 'In these Regulations'. They do not, therefore, apply to any other regulations nor to the EPA 1990, unless the Waste Mangement Licensing Regulations 1994 explicitly require that the specified enactment should do so. In the latter respect, reg 19 and Schedule 4 to the Waste Management Licensing Regulations 1994 have important ramifications, as they further cement the relationship between the Directive on Waste and the EPA 1990. What appears to have been intended[1] is to ensure that waste management licences solely pertain to the activities listed in Parts III and IV of the Schedule (see Tables 2.5 and 2.6). This may reflect the then Conservative government's deregulatory agenda, in particular the conceptual approach that national legislation which implemented Community law only covered the essential requirements but did not embellish them. However, in respect of the Waste Management Licensing Regulations 1994 this objective seems only to be partially accomplished, with the main result being an apparent muddle.

1   See Circular 11/94, Annex 1, para 1.11; see also Annex 4, para 4.8.

7.34 Schedule 4 to the Waste Management Licensing Regulations 1994 stipulates that[1], in relation to s 33(1)(a) of the EPA 1990, any reference to the deposit of waste on land 'shall include a reference' to any operation listed in Parts III and IV of Schedule 4 (see Tables 2.5 and 2.6). Therefore waste management activities outside those Parts can be addressed by the offence of 'depositing' waste under s 33(1)(a) of the EPA 1990. In the case of s 33(1)(b), the approach is different. The Schedule states[2] that any reference to the treatment, keeping or disposal of controlled waste 'shall be taken to be' a reference to submitting wastes to the operations listed in Parts III and IV of Schedule 4. For the activities embraced by s 33(1)(b), therefore, the waste management operation must always feature on the lists shown in Tables 2.5 and 2.6.

1   SI 1994/1056, Sch 4, para 9(3).
2   SI 1994/1056, Sch 4, para 9(4).

7.35 In addition, the Schedule also contains a further significant requirement in respect of s 33(1)(b) and the reference to submitting wastes to activities involving their treatment, keeping and disposal. Besides paragraph 9(4) requiring that any reference to these three waste management activities in s 33(1)(b) is restricted to the operations listed in Parts III and IV, it ends with the words 'other than an operation mentioned in sub-paragraph (3)[1] above'. The purpose of this phrase, along with its practical effect, is particularly hard to delineate. As already explained, the sub-paragraph being referred to here (Sch 4, para 9(3)) contains the requirements in respect of 'depositing' controlled waste in s 33(1)(a). It appears from Circular 11/94[2] that this exclusion clause causes only those operations which do not involve the deposit of waste to be covered by para 9(4). In other words, it seems to be the intention that, where an activity involves both the deposit of waste and, for example, the disposal[3] of waste, then s 33(1)(b) does not apply. Conversely, when the disposal[4] operation does not involve deposit, only those activities shown in Parts III and IV of the Schedule are subject to s 33(1)(b)[5].

1   Ie para 9(3) to Sch 4 and its reference to s 33(1)(a).
2   See Circular 11/94, Annex 4, para 4.7.
3   Equally the treatment or keeping.
4   Or keeping or treatment.
5   Clearly, how the word 'deposit' is to be construed is also crucial in this matter (see para 7.16), but it would seem that Sch 4, para 9(4) is causing the definition of 'disposal' in s 29(6) to be clearly split into deposit-related and non-deposit related disposal activities.

7.36 Finally, having made reference to s 33(1)(a) and (b) of the EPA 1990, Schedule 4 to the Waste Management Licensing Regulations 1994 then refers to s 33(1)(c) and hence to the offence of treating, keeping or disposing of waste in a manner which causes environmental pollution. The Schedule holds that any reference to the treatment, keeping or disposal[1] 'shall include' a reference to submitting waste to the activities set out in Tables 2.5 and 2.6[2]. The use of the word 'include' indicates a similar approach to that relating to s 33(1)(a). It therefore applies to all waste management activities which result in environmental pollution, not only those which feature in Parts III and IV (see Tables 2.5 and 2.6). Again, this is in contrast to the approach applied to s 33(1)(b) of the EPA 1990.

1   Or, in the case of mobile plant, the treatment or disposal.
2   SI 1994/1056, Sch 4, para 9(5).

7.37 In summary, therefore, it is apparent that, for s 33(1)(a)[1] and s 33(1)(c)[2] of the EPA 1990, the lists of waste management activities which form Parts III and IV of Schedule 4 are not all inclusive. Other recovery or disposal operations outside the list shown in Tables 2.5 and 2.6 can be addressed by those sub-sections. A pertinent example of an activity which does not feature is waste storage at the place of waste production, which is excluded from both Parts[3].

1 SI 1994/1056, Sch 4, para 9(3).
2 SI 1994/1056, Sch 4, para 9(5).
3 See items D15 and R13 in Tables 2.5 and 2.6 in Chapter 2.

7.38 But as an immediate, and potentially important, contrast in respect of s 33(1)(b), the use of word 'means' in Schedule 4 instead of the word 'includes'[1] requires that no other recovery or disposal activity beyond the scope of the lists in Parts III and IV can be addressed. Among other matters, this means that waste producers cannot be charged under s 33(1)(b) with unlawfully 'keeping' wastes on their premises where no licence is in force[2]. To successfully take an action against waste located at the site of production, it would be necessary for the Agency to show that the waste had been deposited there[3] or that the waste constituted an environmental hazard[4].

1 SI 1994/1056, Sch 4, para 9(4).
2 While non-special waste can be held on the premises without a licence under the exemption contained in SI 1994/1056, Sch 3, para 41(1), the limits on special waste are tightly defined. For example, only 23,000 litres of liquid special waste can be held without a licence being required (SI 1994/1056, Sch 3, para 41(2)): see para 10.56.
3 EPA 1990, s 33(1)(a).
4 EPA 1990, s 33(1)(c). A second example of an activity excluded from Pt IV to Sch 4 of SI 1994/1056 is the blending of wastes: see Department of the Environment (1996) *United Kingdom Plan for the Exports and Imports of Waste*, HMSO, London, para 6.34.

7.39 The example of waste being held at the producer's premises also illustrates the rather bizarre logic of the provisions in Schedule 4. While a person cannot be prosecuted under s 33(1)(b) for 'keeping' unlawful waste at the site of production without a licence, under s 35 of the EPA 1990 that person can be granted a licence which explicitly authorises the keeping of waste. Section 35 is one of the key sections in Part II of the EPA 1990, for the reason that it sets down the main requirements for the granting of waste management licences[1]. Besides making reference to s 33, Schedule 4 to the Waste Management Licensing Regulations 1994[2] states that, where references are made to 'treatment, keeping or disposal[3] in s 35 of the EPA 1990, such references shall 'include' references to the activities shown in Tables 2.5 and 2.6. The use of the word 'includes' in this provision means that it is therefore possible to have licensed facilities of types not listed in the Tables. That this is the case is also illustrated by the Waste Management Licensing (Charges) Scheme 1999–2000[4], whereby a licence permitting a producer to 'keep' waste is subject to an annual subsistence charge[5].

1 See paras 8.05, 8.225ff.
2 SI 1994/1056, Sch 4, para 9(5).
3 Or, in the case of mobile plant, the 'treatment or disposal'.
4 See para 9.142ff.
5 See Part A of Table 2 of Annex 1 of the Waste Management Licensing (Charges) Scheme 1999–2000.

7.40 But although s 35 of the EPA 1990 countenances the keeping of waste at the site of its production under a licence, it seems that the keeping of waste in these circumstances in breach of the conditions of a waste management licence cannot be an offence under s 33(1)(b) itself. This is a consequence of Schedule 4's limitation on s 33(1)(b) to only those activities covered in Tables 2.5 and 2.6. However, and rather perversely, the breach of a condition in such circumstances remains an offence under s 33(6). By contrast to the offence provision of s 33(1), s 33(6) is not subject to any constraint from Schedule 4, para 9. In effect, all para 9 appears to be doing in respect of s 33(1)(b) is to remove the area of overlap between that sub-section and s 33(6). But it should also be pointed out that a person storing waste at the site of production in contravention of a licence may also be subject to s 33(1)(a) in respect of the deposit of waste contrary to the licence. Schedule 4 does not seem to place any constraints in the latter respect.

7.41 Usually, some explanation of the relevant provisions is to be found in Circular 11/94. However, the Circular deals with the matters raised by para 9 to Schedule 4 in a highly cursory manner, which is particularly unfortunate given the centrality of s 33 of the EPA 1990 to the entire waste regulation system. The Circular[1] sets out the following interpretation of what Schedule 4, paras 9(3)–(4) are seeking to achieve:

'Taken together, these provisions leave s 33(1) applying waste management licensing as follows:

(a) s 33(1)(a) applies to any deposit of Directive waste, whether temporary or permanent and is not limited to directive disposal and recovery operations;

(b) s 33(1)(b) applies to Directive disposal and recovery operations.

That is the scope of licensing is limited to the deposit, Directive disposal or Directive recovery of Directive waste.'

Such a view also appears to be confirmed elsewhere in the Circular[2].

1 Annex 4, para 4.8.
2 Circular 11/94, Annex 1, para 1.11.

7.42 However, this statement neither provides an adequate explanation of the provisions nor appears to be wholly correct. Although the paragraph just quoted constitutes a reasonably accurate summation of the breadth of s 33(1) of the EPA 1990, it has been noted that waste management licences stem principally from s 35. As alluded to above, Schedule 4, para 9(5) allows licences to be issued under s 35 to a range of facilities which are broader than those defined in Parts III or IV to Schedule 4 (see Tables 2.5 and 2.6). But the enforcement of certain of these licences will be subject to the odd series of restrictions already described. Unfortunately, the Circular does not elaborate further, particularly in relation to the reference in para 9(4) to Schedule 4. This is unfortunate as the latter appears to exclude s 33(1)(b) of the EPA 1990 entirely from having application at instances when wastes are 'deposited'.

7.43 None of these matters are trivial, particularly as effective regulation requires prosecuting authorities to be confident that offenders are being correctly charged. The uncertainties described above clearly work against this principle. That the entire matter is unsatisfactory is illustrated by Burnett-Hall's analysis[1] of these provisions, which points to a rather different conclusion. This is that the effect of Schedule 4 to the Waste Management Licensing Regulations 1994 is to cause waste management licences not to be required at all for any waste stored on the premises of production. As Burnett-Hall acknowledges, elsewhere in the Waste Management Licensing Regulations 1994 provisions on statutory exemptions from waste management licences are included, which, *inter alia*, cover storage at the site where the waste was produced[2]. But he appears to regard the presence of the latter provisions, while being somewhat odd, as being superfluous in the context of Schedule 4 to the Waste Management Licensing Regulations 1994.

1 'Waste Controls and Development Projects' *The Law and the Wastes Industry*, IWM Proceedings, December 1997, p 13.
2 SI 1994/1056, Sch 3, para 41: see para 10.55ff.

7.44 Which of the above analyses are correct will only be determined by judicial decision. However, the fact that Burnett-Hall is able to reach a markedly different conclusion clearly illustrates the uncertainty created by Schedule 4 to the Waste Management Licensing Regulations 1994. Indeed, it may be correct to assert that, out of all the provisions in the EPA 1990 and associated regulations, para 9 to Schedule 4 is one of the prime candidates for significant amendment.

The meaning of 'land' in s 33 of the EPA 1990

7.45 The word 'land' is defined in s 29(8) of the EPA 1990:

'... "land" includes land covered by waters where the land is above the low water mark of ordinary spring tides and references to land on which controlled waste is treated, kept or deposited are references to the surface of the land (including any structure set into the surface).'

Curiously, this sub-section uses the phrase 'treated, kept or *deposited*' [author's emphasis], not 'treated, kept or disposed of'.

7.46 The word 'land' in s 29(8) of the EPA 1990, clearly means more than the natural surface of land and, as noted, includes structures 'set into it'. The definition also uses the word 'includes', so that other items can be seen as 'land' when appropriate within the context of the statute. Given that structures are mentioned as constituting 'land' within this meaning, it seems that, by analogy, depositing waste into a skip or other container should be taken to be a deposit 'on land'. It would clearly be anomalous that the placing of waste into a concrete bay should be taken to be a deposit 'on land', but the placing of the same material into a metal skip should not[1].

1 Such a distinction would, if nothing else, defeat the purpose of the EPA 1990 and the Directive on Waste, particularly where transfer stations are concerned: see, for example, Items 14 and 15 of Part III of Sch 4 of SI 1994/1056 and see Table 2.5 in Chapter 2.

7.47 That the definition of 'land' in the Interpretation Act 1978 is also of relevance was confirmed by *Gotech Industrial and Environmental Services v James Friel*[1]. Under Schedule 1 to the Interpretation Act 1978, the word land 'includes buildings and other structures, land covered with water, and any estate, interest, easement, servitude or right in or over land'. In the light of *Gotech*, this paragraph should be read in parallel to the definition of land in the EPA 1990: clearly the definitions are close and there is no contrary meaning between them.

1 (1995) SCCR 22.

7.48 The fact that s 29 of the EPA 1990 holds that land 'includes' water within the low water mark indicates that it extends to many inland watercourses. This results in s 33 of the EPA 1990 potentially overlapping with the offence provisions of the Water Resources Act 1991[1] when a person deposits waste into controlled waters. But, given that the Food and Environment Protection Act 1985[2] has the purpose of covering sea disposal activities, it would seem that 'land' does not extend further below the low water mark[3].

1 Water Resources Act 1991, s 85: indeed watercourses may not actually have water in them to be subject to the Water Resources Act 1991: see *R v Dovermoss* (1995) 159 JP 448.
2 See para 1.74.
3 This would appear confirmed by Circular 11/94, Annex 3, para 3.5.

7.49   Since the formation of the Agency, the main boundary for waste regulation will be between the area of jurisdiction of 'land', which is under the control of the Agency, and the 'sea' which is under the control of the Ministry of Agriculture, Fisheries and Food (MAFF)[1] via the Food and Environment Protection Act 1985. The definition of 'sea' in the Food and Environment Protection Act 1985[2] is interesting as it overlaps with the EPA 1990's concept of 'land':

'. . . "sea" includes any area submerged at mean high water springs and also includes, so far as the tide flows at mean high water springs, an estuary or arm of the sea and the waters of any channel, creek, bay or river.'

The overlap in definitions causes the area of land between the low spring tides and high tide spring tides to be both 'land' and 'sea'[3].

1   In Scotland, the Secretary of State for Scotland.
2   Food and Environment Protection Act 1985, s 24.
3   This is acknowledged in Circular 11/94, Annex 3, para 3.3.

7.50   This overlap between the Agency and the MAFF is resolved by reg 16 of the Waste Management Licensing Regulations 1994. This requires that s 33 of the EPA 1990 does not apply when a facility is 'the subject of' a licence from the Ministry under the Food and Environment Protection Act 1985 or where the activity falls within the Deposits in the Sea (Exemptions) Order 1985[1], which exempts the activity from the need for a licence. While space precludes the reproduction of the full list of exemptions under the Order, what should be noted is that very few waste management activities on the foreshore are exempt from the licensing provisions of the Food and Environment Protection Act 1985. The most significant exemption involves[2]:

'Deposit of any article or substance in the maintenance of harbour, coast protection (other than beach replenishment), drainage or flood control works, if made on the site of the works;'

However, it would seem that, where the facility is neither the subject of a licence under the Food and Environment Protection Act 1985 nor covered by an exemption, s 33 of the EPA 1990 would appear to have application to prevent the unauthorised disposal of waste within the area up to the low water mark.

1   SI 1985/1699 as amended by SI 1994/1056, reg 21.
2   SI 1985/1699, Sch 1, para 20.

7.51   Circular 11/94 considers cases where there may be overlap in jurisdiction between MAFF and the Agency. The Circular notes that it is possible that a waste management operation may straddle the high water mark[1]. In this case, the Agency must consult MAFF (and vice versa) and licences will be needed under both the Food and Environment Protection Act 1985 and EPA 1990. In respect of unauthorised waste management activities on the foreshore, the following advice is given[2]:

'. . . the main activities currently carried out on the foreshore which may be affected, are the disposal of minestone waste and the use of dredged spoil materials beneficially in coastal defence schemes, beach and mudflat nourishment, or the creation of marine and intertidal habitats. These all require to be licensed under the 1985 Act[3]. Where unauthorised disposal takes place on the foreshore which is not subject to a 1985 Act licence, then it will be for MAFF or the Scottish Office as appropriate to take any necessary enforcement action under the 1985 Act'.

The precise statutory basis of the latter assertion is not clear. As noted, the Waste Management Licensing Regulations 1994[4] seems only to disapply s 33 of the EPA

1990 in cases where a licence or exemption under the Food and Environment Protection Act 1985 is in place. Clearly, this appears not to pertain at places where wastes are being disposed of in an unauthorised manner on the foreshore.

1 Circular 11/94, Annex 3, para 3.6.
2 Circular 11/94, Annex 3, para 3.5.
3 The Food and Environment Protection Act 1985.
4 SI 1994/1056, reg 16(1)(d).

The meaning of 'knowingly causing and knowingly permitting'

7.52   The offence provision of s 33(1) of the EPA 1990 uses the phrase 'knowingly cause or knowingly permit'. The words 'cause or knowingly permit' are familiar to environmental law and have a long lineage, dating back to the Salmon Fisheries Act 1861. They are continued in aquatic pollution law, for example, by s 85 of the Water Resources Act 1991. Similar words feature in a number of other statutes, including road traffic law[1], sex shop licensing[2] and ancient monument protection[3].

1 Road Traffic Act 1988 and subsidiary regulations.
2 Local Government (Miscellaneous Provisions) Act 1982, Sch 3, para 20.
3 Ancient Monuments and Archaeological Areas Act 1979, s 2(1).

7.53   Although such terms feature in other legislation, their interpretation for the purposes of s 33 of the EPA 1990 is less than straightforward. In comparison to recent water pollution legislation, for example, few judicial decisions are available which have relevance to waste management. It may also be incorrect to directly translate into the EPA 1990 the principles set down in cases relating to water pollution law. By contrast, the word 'causing' is prefixed by the word 'knowingly' in s 33(1) of the EPA 1990 and there are quite different statutory defences. Similarly, there are also significant differences in the wording used in road traffic or sex shop licensing legislation. Again, such distinctions require that caution is to be applied when using case law drawn from unrelated legislation to interpret s 33 of the EPA 1990.

7.54   In examining the interpretation of the legislation, it is important also to remember that the courts will look to a meaning which best suits the purpose of the EPA 1990, rather than one which stems solely from case law derived from the application of other statutes. It may also be necessary that such a consideration embraces the aims and objectives of Directive on Waste[1]. The following sections will consider, in turn, matters of knowledge, causation and permission. These threads will then be drawn together through a consideration of the limited existing case law which has direct relevance to s 33 of the EPA 1990.

1 Council Directive of 15 July 1975 on Waste (75/442/EEC) (OJ L194/39 25.7.75) (as amended by Council Directive of 18 March 1991 amending Directive 75/442/EEC on Waste (91/156/EEC) (OJ L78/32 26.3.91) and Commission Decision of 24 May 1996 adapting Annexes IIA and IIB to Council Directive 75/442/EEC on Waste (96/350/EC) (OJ L135/32 6.6.96)), in particular Article 4.

'Knowingly'

7.55   The use of the word 'knowingly' in s 33(1) of the EPA 1990 would seem in general to require that an offence is established only where there is *mens rea*, a criminal intention on behalf of the accused or some other knowledge of an act which was wrong. *Mens rea* can also include thoughtlessness, which may include a reckless disregard of the nature and consequences of a particular act[1]. The question of whether *mens rea* is required in respect of statutes which use the word 'cause' or 'permit' or other analogous phrases[2] seems to have bedevilled case law for much of this century[3].

Without the requirement for mens rea, any offence would be one of strict liability[4]. As a general principle[5], the courts have been unwilling to hold persons liable for offences which were committed without any form of intent, blame or recklessness. But there are exceptions to this particularly in 'public interest' statutes[6]. In many of the water pollution judgments, for example, certain offences have been held to involve strict liability, and therefore that legislation does not require knowledge in respect of causing[7]. By contrast, in s 33 of the EPA 1990, strict liability does not apply in respect of 'causing' or 'permitting'[8]: some form of knowledge is necessary. However, the precise nature of what the accused must be shown to know is a difficult matter, particularly in respect of companies, and this matter will be revisited later[9]. Furthermore, having got as far as establishing the accused's knowledge, the prosecution's case must then not be disturbed by the defence satisfying any of the statutory defences in s 33(7)[10], such as that all due diligence and reasonable precautions were exercised to prevent the occurrence of the offence.

1 *Sweet v Parsley* [1969] 1 All ER 347, per Lord Diplock at 360I.
2 Eg to 'suffer'.
3 See for example *Sherras v de Rutzen* [1895-9] All ER Rep 1167.
4 It has been noted that the words 'strict liability' and 'absolute liability', although not necessarily holding similar meanings, have tended to be used interchangeably in certain judgments which consider mens rea and these type of offences: see Parpworth J 'The Offence of Causing Water Pollution: a New South Wales Perspective' (1997) 9 JEL 1 59 at 72.
5 See Lord Reid in *Tesco Supermarkets Ltd v Nattrass* [1971] 2 All ER 127 at 130H to 131E.
6 See, for example, *Sherras v de Rutzen* [1985-9] 1 All ER Rep 1167; *Sweet v Parsley* [1969] 1 All ER 347; *Alphacell Ltd v Woodward* [1972] 2 All ER 475; see also *Korten v West Sussex County Council* (1903) 88 LT 466 at 470, 471.
7 It has also been suggested that the use of the word 'knowingly' before 'permit' is somewhat tautological (see *Sweet v Parsley* at 361D/E; *Alphacell v Woodward* at 483J and 491E). It is difficult to permit an act without knowledge, while shutting one's eyes to the obvious constitutes permission (see para 7.78ff below).
8 Whether it applies to persons who 'deposit' or 'treat, keep or dispose of' waste – as opposed to persons who 'knowingly cause' or 'knowingly permit' these actions – is considered at para 7.117ff below.
9 See paras 7.117ff and 7.135ff.
10 See para 7.144ff.

7.56 A phrase which has some similarity to the triumvirate contained in s 33(1)(a) of the EPA 1990 of depositing waste, knowingly causing the deposit of waste or knowingly permitting the deposit of wastes[1] can be found in the Local Government (Miscellaneous Provisions) Act 1982[2]. The latter is directed against persons who knowingly use, knowingly cause or permit the use of a premises as a sex establishment. Such premises must be licensed and the licensee responsible must abide by the terms and conditions of the licence.

1 Or, indeed, treat, keep or dispose of controlled waste, or knowingly cause or knowingly permit controlled waste to be treated, kept or disposed of (EPA 1990 s 33(1)(b)).
2 Local Government (Miscellaneous Provisions) Act 1982, Sch 3, para 20.

7.57 The relevant sections of the Local Government (Miscellaneous Provisions) Act 1982 were considered in the House of Lords decision of *Westminster City Council v Croyalgrange Ltd*[1]. Lord Bridge set down five tests which must be satisfied by the prosecution in order to a create an offence under that Act[2]. These are repeated below for the reason that analogies can be drawn with the offence provisions of s 33 of the EPA 1990, particularly in respect of persons who knowingly cause waste to be handled on land contrary to s 33. Lord Bridge stated that, in relation to the Local Government (Miscellaneous Provisions) Act 1982, the prosecution must establish that[3]:

(1) the local authority had made a resolution that sex shop licensing should apply in their area;
(2) premises where the alleged offence took place was used as a sex establishment;
(3) the defendant used the premises as a sex establishment or caused or permitted its use;
(4) no licence for the use had been granted and the requirement for the possession of a licence had not been waived; and
(5) where applications had been made before Schedule 3 to the Local Government (Miscellaneous Provisions) Act 1982 had come into force and were awaiting determination, no application had been made in respect of the particular premises.

Lord Bridge then noted[4]:

'If all these facts are proved and nothing more, I can see no reason in logic or justice why the court should not hold that a sufficient prima facie case has been established on the basis that the defendant's knowledge of the true position in regard of the licensing of the use of the premises can be properly inferred.'

1 [1986] 2 All ER 353: it should be noted that, when a sex shop licence is contravened, a person is only guilty when he or she, 'without reasonable excuse knowingly contravenes, or without reasonable excuse knowingly permits the contravention of' a term, condition or restriction of a licence (Local Government (Miscellaneous Provisions) Act 1982, Sch 3, para 20(1)(c)). This is in immediate contrast to s 33(1) and s 33(6) of the EPA 1990 where there is no requirement that a person must, for example, 'knowingly deposit' controlled waste (s 33(1)(a)) or 'knowingly contravene' any condition of a waste management licence (s 33(6)) to commit an offence. Similarly, the caveats in the Local Government (Miscellaneous Provisions) Act 1982 concerning 'reasonable excuse' are set out in slightly different form in the statutory defences of the EPA 1990 in s 33(7).
2 Local Government (Miscellaneous Provisions) Act 1982, Sch 3, para 20(1)(a).
3 *Croyalgrange* at 358C.
4 *Croyalgrange* at 358E.

7.58 Having got that far, Lord Bridge considered that a second stage then came into play in respect of the question of knowledge[1]. That stage was designed to embrace such matters as whether there was a genuine but mistaken belief that the sex shop was in fact licensed. Clearly, if this fact could be established, the accused should be acquitted. But in this respect, Lord Bridge placed an onus on the defendant to provide evidence to demonstrate such lack of knowledge. He considered that it was not solely for the prosecution to establish that a person knew that a sex establishment did not possess a licence. This matter was illustrated by Lord Bridge by way of reference to the earlier House of Lords decision of *Sweet v Parsley*[2]:

'If authority to support this analysis is required, I find it in the speech of Lord Diplock[3] . . . where he said:

"*Woolmington's* case[4] . . . affirmed the principle that the onus lies on the prosecution in a criminal trial to prove all the elements of the offence with which the accused is charged. It does not purport to lay down how the onus can be discharged as respects any particular elements of the offence. This, under our system of criminal procedure, is left to the common sense of the jury. . . . The jury is entitled to presume that the accused acted with knowledge of the facts, unless there is some evidence to the contrary originating from the accused who alone can know on what belief he acted and on what ground the belief, if mistaken, was held. What *Woolmington's* case did decide is that, where there is any such evidence, the jury, after considering it and also any relevant evidence called by the prosecution on the issue of the existence of the mistaken belief, should acquit the accused unless they feel sure that he did not hold the belief . . ."[5]'

1 *Croyalgrange* at 358F/G.
2 *Croyalgrange* at 358J to 359A.
3 *Sweet v Parsley* [1969] 1 All ER 347 at 362–363.
4 *Woolmington v DPP* [1935] All ER Rep 1.
5 See also, for example, *DPP v Morgan* [1975] 2 All ER 347 and *Reynolds v G H Austin Ltd* [1951] 2 KB 135.

7.59 By analogy to the EPA 1990, it therefore seems possible to reduce Lord Bridge's five tests in *Croyalgrange* to three tests by removing those elements in the Local Government (Miscellaneous Provisions) Act 1982 which are not relevant to s 33 of the EPA 1990. Accordingly, the tests then concern the need for the prosecution to show:

(1) that controlled waste was deposited (or as the case may be kept, treated, or disposed of) at the premises where the alleged offence took place;

(2) that the defendant caused (or, as the case may be, permitted) controlled waste to be deposited, kept, treated or disposed of;

(3) that no licence for the use of the land for waste disposal purposes had been granted or, as the case may be, that the activity in question was not authorised by the licence.

The matter then will turn on the question of the defendant's knowledge, with the defence introducing evidence to indicate that knowledge was absent.

7.60 Lord Brightman took a slightly different approach in *Croyalgrange*, but also considered that[1], if the defendant chooses not to give evidence of his or her absence of knowledge, and where there is no other evidence to support the person's absence of knowledge, 'the court may properly infer without direct evidence that the defendant did indeed possess the requisite knowledge'. This principle is now, of course, substantiated by the fact that the court can make general inferences in respect of instances where defendants exercise their right to silence and decline to give evidence.

1 *Croyalgrange* at 359F.

7.61 Moreover, evidence that the defendant had deliberately refrained from inquiring[1] or that the person had shut their eyes to the obvious may be sufficient to indicate that the person did know what was going on[2]. Again, Lord Brightman's requirement that it is up to the defence to produce evidence to the contrary comes into play at this instance. The most obvious source of that evidence is the defendant's own testimony[3].

1 Indeed, in *R v Shorrock* [1993] 3 All ER 917 at 925F/G a person's knowledge would seem to be established 'if either he knew or ought to have known, in the sense that the means of knowledge was available to him' (see also *Leakey v National Trust for Places of Historic Interest or Natural Beauty* [1980] 1 All ER 17 and *Fransman v Sexton* [1965] Crim LR 556).
2 See *Croyalgrange* per Lord Bridge at 359C: see also para 7.78 in respect of permitting.
3 One final issue arises from *Croyalgrange*. Paragraph 20(1)(a) of Sch 3 to the Local Government (Miscellaneous Provisions) Act 1982 creates an offence when a person '*knowingly uses*, knowingly causes or permits the use of' a premises as a sex establishment without or in contravention of the terms and conditions of a licence. The words 'knowingly uses' were considered by Lord Bridge. Because the words would be tautological otherwise, Lord Bridge held (*Croyalgrange* at 357F) that the knowledge being referred to was the knowledge that the premises was used as a sex shop *and* knowledge that a licence was required (or even that the terms and conditions of the licence were being breached). That this interpretation does not apply to the EPA 1990 is made clear in *Ashcroft v Cambro Waste Products Ltd* [1981] 3 All ER 699 and, subsequently, in *R v Environment Agency, ex p Shanks & McEwan (Teesside) Ltd* [1997] JPL 824 at 831, with the latter explicitly referring to *Croyalgrange* (discussed at para 7.94ff). Finally, there is one other salient point of construction which

distinguishes s 33 of the EPA 1990 from Local Government (Miscellaneous Provisions) Act 1982, Sch 3, para 20. This is that s 33 makes it an offence to deposit waste, or knowingly cause or knowingly permit waste to be deposited. Unlike the Local Government (Miscellaneous Provisions) Act 1982, it does not involve any offence involving *knowingly depositing*, knowingly causing or knowingly permitting waste to be deposited (see para 7.109ff).

'Causing'

7.62 The question of causation has proved somewhat problematic in environmental law. As will be discussed below, case law shows that an essential part of establishing causation is to rely upon its common sense meaning and, primarily, questions of fact. In certain cases, some form of identifiable act by the person charged with an offence involving 'causing' can be established. Alternatively, a combination of acts of different parties can cause an offence. In all cases, persons charged with causing must be in some position by which the outcome of the event was within their influence. Finally, inaction by a defendant may cause an event to happen, but such inaction must have lead to the event and be significantly responsible for it.

7.63 Two dictionaries[1] give the words 'to cause' the following meanings:

'. . . to be the cause of, bring about'[1].

'. . . to be the cause of, produce, make happen'[2].

Although, as noted, the word 'cause' appears in a number of other statutes, a very significant body of case law has arisen in the water pollution field. Whilst these judgments do not always assist in respect of the EPA 1990 and questions of knowledge, they are sufficient to provide a description of how the word 'cause' in s 33 of the EPA 1990 is to be interpreted, particularly as such an interpretation is centred on the ordinary meaning of the word. However, it should be emphasised that the presence of the prefix 'knowingly' in s 33 of the EPA 1990 places significant limitations on the strict liability approach which has developed in the water pollution context[3].

1 *Collins Concise Dictionary 1997.*
2 *Oxford Concise Dictionary 1995.*
3 See para 7.109ff.

7.64 In *A-G's Reference (No 1 of 1994)*[1] Lord Taylor of Gosforth set down five steps which need to be addressed in considering causation[2]:

'(1) It is a question of fact in each case whether a defendant "caused" the polluting matter to enter controlled waters.

(2) The word "knowingly" is not to be implied as qualifying the word "causes" in section 107(1)(a)[3].

(3) The word "causes" is to be given its plain commonsense meaning and is not to be refined by introducing concepts such as causa causans, effective cause, novus actus, proximate or principle cause.

(4) The word "causes" involves some active participation in the operation or chain of operations resulting in the pollution of controlled waters.

(5) "Mere tacit standing by and looking on" . . . is insufficient to amount to causing.'

In respect of the final point, it may well be that, while a defendant did not cause an act because nothing was actually done at all, the person may be found to have 'knowingly permitted' it[4]. This differentiation has obvious application to s 33 of the EPA 1990 as a result of *Empress Car Co (Abertillery) Ltd v National Rivers Authority*, where the House of Lords held[5]:

'Putting the matter shortly, if the charge is "causing", the prosecution must prove that the pollution was caused by something which the defendant did, rather than merely failed to prevent. It is, however, very important to notice that this require-ment is not because of anything inherent in the notion of "causing". It is because of the structure of the subsection[6] which imposes liability under two separate heads: the first limb simply for doing something which causes the pollution and the second for knowingly failing to prevent the pollution. The notion of causing is present in both limbs: under the first limb, what the defendant did must have caused the pollu-tion and under the second limb, his omission must have caused it. . . . Liability under the first limb . . . therefore requires that the defendant must have done something.'

This important distinction naturally has relevance to the framing of appropriate charges.

1 [1995] 1 WLR 599.
2 *A-G's Reference* at 612H to 613A.
3 Ie the Water Act 1989, s 107(1)(a). This step is irrelevant to the EPA 1990 because it refers to causation in water pollution law being a strict liability offence. Being prefixed in the EPA 1990 by the word 'knowingly', this proposition does not apply in relation to s 33 of that Act.
4 *Empress Car Co (Abertillery) Ltd v National Rivers Authority* [1998] 1 All ER 481 at 485H, 492F/G, 493F.
5 *Empress Car Co (Abertillery) Ltd v National Rivers Authority* [1998] 1 All ER 481 at 485B/C.
6 In this instance, the Water Resources Act 1991, s 85(1) which juxtaposes 'cause' with 'knowingly permit'.

7.65 One of the leading cases on the interpretation of the words 'to cause' in water pollution law is the 1972 House of Lords decision of *Alphacell Ltd v Woodward*[1]. Like Lord Taylor 22 years later in *A-G's Reference No 1*, Lord Wilberforce in *Alphacell* took the view that 'causing' must be given its common sense meaning[2]. He viewed the fact that Alphacell Ltd had constructed and maintained settling tanks, the pumps of which became blocked with leaves, as the events which clearly caused pollution when the tanks overflowed[3]. Lord Salmon concurred[4]:

'I consider, however, that what or who has caused a certain event to occur is essen-tially a question of fact which can be best answered by ordinary common sense rather than abstract metaphysical theory.

It seems to me that, giving the word "cause" its ordinary and natural meaning, anyone may cause something to happen, intentionally or negligently or inadver-tently without negligence and without intention. For example, a man may deliber-ately smash a porcelain vase; he may handle it so negligently that he drops and smashes it; or he may without negligence slip or stumble against it and smash it. In each of these examples, no less in the last than the other two, he has caused the destruction of the vase.'

1 [1972] 2 All ER 475.
2 *Alphacell* at 479B; such a view has been re-affirmed with approval in, for example, *Wrothwell Ltd v Yorkshire Water Authority* [1984] Crim LR 43; *Lockhart v National Coal Board* [1981] SLT 161 at 171; *National Rivers Authority (Southern Region) v Alfred McAlpine Homes (East) Ltd* [1994] Env LR 198 at 201; *National Rivers Authority v Wright Engineering Co Ltd* [1994] Env LR 186 at 189; *National Rivers Authority v Yorkshire Water Services Ltd* [1994] Env LR 177 at 182, DC; *CPC (UK) Ltd v National Rivers Authority* [1995] 7 JEL 1, 169; *A-G's Reference (No 1 of 1994)* [1995] 1 WLR 599 at 615A/B; *Empress Car Co (Abertillery) Ltd v National Rivers Authority* [1998] 1 All ER 481 at 486E. See also *Leyland Shipping Co v Norwich Union Fire Insurance Society Ltd* [1918–19] All ER Rep 443 at 449I and *Yorkshire Dale Steamship Co Ltd v Minister of War Transport, The Coxwold* [1942] 2 All ER 6 at 12A/C and 15A.
3 This view in *Alphacell* was supported by Viscount Dilhorne (at 482G), Lord Pearson (at 488E), Lord Cross (at 489G) and Lord Salmon (at 490D).
4 *Alphacell* at 490A.

7.66   In certain water pollution judgments[1], there has been an attempt to adduce from the evidence 'a positive and deliberate act' which caused the offence to manifest itself. However, although the identification of such an act may be a helpful conceptual way of viewing the evidence in order to determine causation[2], in law it is not an essential ingredient. Indeed, *Empress Cars* regards this is a source of potential distraction from the real issue. The judgment involved water pollution caused by the opening of a valve on a defectively bunded fuel tank by an unknown third party. On behalf of the car company it was unsuccessfully argued that the third party – as opposed to the company who stored the fuel on its land and failed to adequately bund the tank or secure the premises from trespassers – 'caused' the pollution. In water pollution law, it is fundamental to the interpretation of causation that the words 'to cause' should be viewed in their ordinary sense and should not be subject to further refinements[3]. Accordingly, to establish that a person caused something 'it is sufficient that his activity has been a cause, it does not require to be the cause'[4]: '. . . because to say that something else caused the pollution (like brambles clogging the pumps or vandalism by third parties) is not inconsistent with the defendant having caused it as well'[5]. Anything beyond absolute passivity may constitute a cause, including the maintenance of a system, the carrying on of an enterprise, the management of a going concern or the arranging of its cessation and closure[6]: '. . . maintaining tanks, lagoons or sewage systems full of noxious liquid is doing something, even if the immediate cause of the pollution was lack of maintenance, a natural event or the act of a third party'[7]. Moreover, matters of foreseeability, negligence or intention are not relevant to the consideration of causation[8].

1 Eg *Price v Cromack* [1975] 2 All ER 113; *Wychavon District Council v National Rivers Authority* [1993] 2 All ER 440.
2 Despite that *Empress Cars* appears to somewhat disapprove of this approach, it appears in the subsequent water pollution judgment of *Environment Agency v Brock plc* [1998] Env LR 607 at 613.
3 See *National Rivers Authority v Yorkshire Water Services* [1995] 1 All ER 225 at 232A, *A-G's Reference (No 1 of 1994)* [1995] 1 WLR 599, at 615A.
4 *Empress Car Co (Abertillery) Ltd v National Rivers Authority* [1998] 1 All ER 481 at 493F.
5 *Empress Cars* at 492H.
6 *Empress Cars* at 494B.
7 *Empress Cars* at 492G; but obviously there remains a question as to whether the act was so remote as to not be a cause at all.
8 *Empress Cars* at 493 F/G: note that, in the context of s 85(1) of the Water Resources Act 1991, the House of Lords also indicated that knowledge is also a factor which does not need to be established. However, s 33 of the EPA 1990 uses the term 'knowingly cause'. But as discussed at para 7.61, shutting one's eyes to the obvious is viewed as implicit 'knowledge'.

7.67   In the light of *Alphacell v Woodward* and particularly since *Empress Cars*, when a defendant is responsible for a premises where an unauthorised aquatic discharge took place, then that person is strictly liable under the provisions of water pollution law. Hence in *CPC (UK) Ltd v National Rivers Authority*[1] it was held that a sub-contractor's installation of defective pipework was not the *principal* cause of water pollution when a leak emerged a number of months after installation. CPC (UK), the company on whose premises the defective pipework was installed, were therefore found guilty[2], despite the fact that they did not own the plant when the pipes were installed. This judgment follows the approach of the ordinary meaning of causation, in the sense that the pollution incident would not have occurred if industrial activities by CPC (UK) were not being undertaken on the site. It therefore follows the 'public interest' dicta laid down in *Alphacell v Woodward*[3] that it is appropriate that persons who pollute rivers should be subject to penalties and that mitigating circumstances become relevant only at the time of sentencing[4]. However, it should be noted that whilst causing water pollution is a strict liability offence under the Water Resources Act 1991, there are limits[5]:

'While liability under s 85(1) is strict and therefore includes liability for certain deliberate acts by third parties and (by parity of reasoning) natural events, it is not absolute liability in the sense that all that has to be shown is that the polluting matter escaped from the defendant's land, irrespective of how this happened. It must still be possible to say that the defendant caused the pollution.'

1   [1995] 7 JEL 1, 69.
2   See also *Environment Agency v Brock plc* [1998] Env LR 607 at 614.
3   See for example Lord Salmon in *Alphacell* at 491A–D.
4   See for example, in a different field, *R v J O Sims Ltd* [1993] Env LR 323.
5   *Empress Cars* at 490E.

7.68   The much earlier case of *Yorkshire West Riding Council v Holmfirth Urban Sanitary Authority*[1] indicates that causation can involve the failure to take a particular course of action. The defendants, a council sewage authority, reconstructed a length of ancient sewer. Gravity being what it is, this resulted in sewage flowing into the River Holme in a considerably enhanced fashion. However, the defendants did not actually place any extra sewage down the pipe nor did they install a new outfall point. The latter was in place already. All they did was improve the infrastructure which connected the source of the sewage to the outfall. The council was found to have caused and permitted the pollution by way of their improvement activities. Lopes LJ noted that[2]:

'. . . it is quite possible that by having done nothing on an occasion when they ought to have done something, they[3] may have caused that to happen which was intended to be prevented by this section[4].'

It is submitted that this decision clearly follows the ordinary meaning of causation. The cause was the local authority's reconstruction of the sewer. Unless it could be shown that they should be viewed as exemplifying 'absolute passivity' – whereby the defendant cannot be said to have done anything at all[5] – the local authority would almost inevitably commit the offence.

1   [1894] 2 QB 842; note that the headnote in this case is somewhat confusing as it refers to 'permitting', but from reading the case it appears that the council was served with an information which stated that it both caused and knowingly permitted sewage to enter the watercourse. It also appeared that the discharge continued for at least a year, and possibly up to the Court of Appeal's ruling.
2   *Holmfirth* at 850.
3   Ie the Sanitary Authority as defendants.
4   Rivers Pollution Prevention Act 1876, s 3.
5   *Empress Cars* at 492F/G and 493F: but even then, there is the alternative possibility that they 'knowingly permitted' the offence (see para 7.78ff).

7.69   Besides the fact that making improvements or changes to the configuration of some equipment can be held to be a cause, failing to maintain equipment has also been held to attribute causation to those responsible[1]. Again, this assertion goes hand-in-hand with the need to approach causation through common sense. Furthermore, the act which caused the pollution does not need to be proximate to the pollution event. In *Lockhart v National Coal Board*[2], despite pumps of a coal mine being identified as the cause of pollution when they were switched off in 1977, the Coal Board were found to have caused the pollution when polluting matter flooded from the mine in 1979[3]. In addition, the fact that the Coal Board no longer had rights of access to the mine was not considered a matter of significance. In considering causation, the High Court of the Justiciary held[4]:

'Nor is it an answer that the respondent was not in a legal position to do anything about pumping out the water after the mining operations had ceased and the lease had expired. That was something for which the respondent was responsible for in entering upon such a lease.'

The latter finding may be of significance in respect of the EPA 1990 and the enforcement of waste management licence conditions which pertain to land outside the licensee's occupation[5].

1 See *A-G's Reference (No 1 of 1994)* [1995] 1 WLR 599 at 614H and *Lockhart v National Coal Board* 1981 SLT 161.
2 1981 SLT 161 at 171.
3 In this respect, *Lockhart* has certain parallels with the circumstances of many landfills, where the effects of unauthorised activities may not be felt until many years later.
4 *Lockhart* at 172.
5 See the EPA 1990, ss 35(4) 35A, 36A, 37A and 38(9A)–(9C) (as amended by the Environment Act 1995, Sch 22, paras 67, 69, 71 and 72): see paras 8.23ff, 8.244ff, 9.09, 9.32 and 9.54.

7.70   In *National Rivers Authority v Yorkshire Water Services Ltd*, whether Yorkshire Water could be classed as a passive onlooker was considered by the Divisional Court and later in the House of Lords. In the Divisional Court, Buckley J[1] held that the operation of a sewage works by Yorkshire Water, from which a slug of contaminated effluent was discharged to a river, was a sufficient cause to convict the water company. This was despite an unknown third party discharging the polluting matter into the sewer system which fed the works. This material passed through the works – which operated on the basis of a gravity feed and the illicitly discharged matter did not receive the physical assistance of the works' operator – and was discharged into a watercourse by the works' outfall. Buckley J held that this instance was similar to *Alphacell*[2] and that Yorkshire Water had caused the pollution. On appeal by Yorkshire Water, the House of Lords took a somewhat different approach to the facts of this case[3]. Their Lordships were concerned principally with an interpretation of the relevant statutory defences, and on this basis, Yorkshire Water was acquitted. However, Lord Mackay of Clashfern[4] upheld Lord Wilberforce's view in *Alphacell*[5] that 'causing' must be given its common sense meaning. Accordingly, Lord Mackay stated that the sewage collection infrastructure set up by Yorkshire Water, the illicit discharge and the operation of the sewage treatment works 'does not preclude' the conclusion that Yorkshire Water Services caused the discharge. It was for the magistrates or jury to decide on the basis of the facts of the case before them.

1 [1994] Env LR 177.
2 *Yorkshire Water Services* (DC) at 182.
3 *National Rivers Authority v Yorkshire Water Services Ltd* [1995] 1 All ER 225.
4 *Yorkshire Water Services* (HL) at 232.
5 See *Alphacell* [1972] 2 All ER 475 at 479B/C.

7.71   The approach of Lord Mackay in *Yorkshire Water Services* received subsequent approval by the House of Lords in *Empress Cars*, where it was noted that there may be a number of correct answers to the question of 'who caused pollution?'. But the conceptual basis of this type of question in establishing a pollution offence was viewed as inappropriate. The question should be re-focused upon whether or not the particular defendant caused pollution[1]:

'The fact that for different purposes or even for the same purpose one could also say that that someone or something else caused the pollution is not inconsistent with the defendant having caused it'.

1 *Empress Car Company (Abertillery) Ltd v National Rivers Authority* [1998] 1 All ER 481 at 487J.

7.72 Since the *Empress Cars* decision, the scope of a defendant to be classed as a passive onlooker to a pollution incident – as opposed to being a cause – has been greatly restricted. This has lead to certain earlier water pollution judgments being overruled[1]. In addition, *Empress Cars* has significantly eased the burden on the prosecution where there is more than one party involved. Previously, it had been held that third parties broke the chain of causation in a manner that often precluded the defendant from being liable[2]. But in *Empress Cars*, it was rightly held that vandals who tamper with potentially insecure liquid storage tanks do not disrupt the chain of causation. *Empress Cars* followed the principles of *CPC (UK) Ltd*, emphasising the strict liability nature of the Water Resources Act 1991. Following *CPC (UK) Ltd*, the very action of a person gathering potentially polluting matter on land was held to be the cause if it subsequently escaped[3]. Accordingly, the strict liability approach may stretch a considerable distance, extending to a company who had, for example, arranged a properly constructed and bunded fuel storage facility which was aimed at precluding spillages when oil was delivered. While the company would remain liable for the pollution of any watercourse due to the negligent operation by a third party of an oil delivery vehicle, the mitigating circumstances concerning the tank's construction and the fault of others should be taken into account in sentencing[4], not by way of legal interpretation.

1 This includes *Price v Cromack* [1975] 2 All ER 113; *Wychavon District Council v National Rivers Authority* [1993] 2 All ER 440: both overruled by *Empress Car Co (Abertillery) Ltd v National Rivers Authority* [1998] 1 All ER 481 at 485H/J.
2 See for example *Impress (Worcester) Ltd v Rees* [1971] 2 All ER 357; *National Rivers Authority v Wright Engineering Co Ltd* [1994] Env LR 186.
3 See *Empress Car Co (Abertillery) Ltd v National Rivers Authority* [1998] 1 All ER 481 at 490D, 492E.
4 Or, indeed, as to whether the person should be charged with the offence at all.

7.73 *Multiple Causes* The water pollution judgment of *CPC (UK) Ltd v National Rivers Authority*[1] is also useful, as Evans LJ addressed the question of joint responsibility by two or more bodies whose acts collectively resulted in pollution. In respect of a defective pipe installed by sub-contractors, he held[2] that:

'. . . the fact that the appellants were unaware of the existence of the defect and could not be criticised for failing to discover it, meant that the defect was latent rather than patent, so far as they were concerned, but this was not relevant in law, because the statute does not require either fault or knowledge[3] to be proved against them. If they did cause the pollution, then it was equally irrelevant that some other person might be held to have "caused" it also. . . . The Acts[4] do not require proof that their acts were "the cause" or "the sole cause" of the escape, but whether they, the defendants, caused it by reason of those acts.'

The fact that the defendants did not actually own the factory at the time that the pipework was installed was also found to be not relevant. Once the court was satisfied that the defendants had caused the escape[5]:

'. . . then whatever part had been played in the history of events by their predecessor's sub-contractors was irrelevant to their guilt as a matter of law.'

From this decision, it is submitted that in respect of the EPA 1990, when an operation is under the control of the defendant, that person is liable under s 33(1) of the EPA 1990 provided that person's knowledge can be established[6]. Once this is established, the EPA 1990 then leaves the defendant to invoke the statutory defences in s 33(7). Of particular relevance to a case analogous to the facts of the *CPC (UK)* will be the defence contained in s 33(7)(a), that the person charged took all reasonable precautions and exercised all due diligence to avoid the commission of the offence.

1 [1995] 7 JEL 1 69; see also *Empress Car Co (Abertillery) v National Rivers Authority* [1997] JPL 908 at 909.
2 *CPC (UK) Ltd* at 72.
3 Contrast with 'knowingly cause' in the EPA 1990, s 33(1).
4 Water Resources Act 1991 and the Salmon and Freshwater Fisheries Act 1975.
5 *CPC (UK) Ltd* at 72/73; see also *Environment Agency v Brock plc* [1998] Env LR 607 at 611ff.
6 See paras 7.55ff and 7.117ff.

7.74 Indeed, it may be the case that no single party actually caused the pollution, but that the combination of their individual acts was the source of causation. In *A-G's Reference (No 1 of 1994)*[1], three parties were found to have been responsible for causing a serious water pollution incident. They were the waste disposal company that discharged unsuitable material to a sewer, the borough council sewerage agent who failed to maintain the sewerage infrastructure so that the discharge overflowed into a watercourse, and the water company which had responsibility for the discharge consent covering the overflow.

1 [1995] 1 WLR 599.

7.75 *Causation by Employees* In water pollution law, employers seem to be held to be strictly liable for their employees' actions[1]. But given that it seems that it was the intention of the Department of the Environment to differentiate between 'cause' in the sense of the water pollution judgments referred to here and 'knowingly cause' in s 33 of the EPA 1990, it may be questionable whether such principles have an automatic bearing on the interpretation of s 33. By contrast to water pollution law, there is (a) the question of the accused's knowledge[2], and (b) the statutory defences laid down in s 33(7), such as the taking of 'reasonable precautions' and exercising 'due diligence'[3].

1 See *National Rivers Authority (Southern Region) v Alfred McAlpine Homes (East) Ltd* [1994] Env LR 198. Note that this judgment has been held to have a bearing on the EPA 1990, s 33: see *R v Environment Agency, ex p Shanks and McEwan (Teesside) Ltd* [1997] JPL 824 and para 7.94ff.
2 See paras 7.55ff, 7.117ff and, for example, *Lovelace v DPP* [1954] 3 All ER 481; *Smith of Maddiston Ltd v Macnab* 1975 SLT 86 at 89.
3 See para 7.145ff and, for example, *Sopp v Long* [1970] 1 QB 518.

7.76 *Extraordinary Events, 'Acts of God', Terrorists, etc* In a very restricted number of instances, an intervening event may occur which is 'so far out of the ordinary course of things that in the circumstances any active operations of the defendant fade into the background'[1]. But the emphasis is upon an event which is an extraordinary one. The activities of vandals, natural forces and persons illicitly pouring chemicals into the sewers were not so considered by Lord Hoffmann in *Empress Cars*. The only example of an event which he classed as extraordinary was a terrorist attack which resulted in a pollution incident[2]. However, Lord Clyde[3] appears to concede that natural forces, acts of God and third parties may at least need to be taken into account[4]. But even when there are concurrent causes, foreseeability does not need to be addressed[5] since liability will follow unless the intervening event is of such an 'unnatural, extraordinary or unusual character' that whatever the defendant did was only part of background events.

1 *Empress Car Co (Abertillery) Ltd v National Rivers Authority* [1998] 1 All ER 481 at 493H.
2 *Empress Cars* at 491H/J.
3 The other three Law Lords simply agreed with Lord Hoffmann.
4 *Empress Cars* at 493E: see also *Environment Agency v Brock plc* [1998] Env LR 607 at 613.
5 *Empress Cars* at 494D.

7.77 The question of the relationship between causes and so-called 'acts of God' was considered much earlier in *Southern Water Authority v Phillip Maurice Pegrum and*

Jeffrey Maurice Pegrum[1]. In *Pegrum*, a pig breeding sheds' effluent storage lagoon overflowed into a neighbouring watercourse. A combination of unusually heavy rain and a blocked drain were claimed to be acts of God and hence it was asserted that the latter, rather than the defendants, caused the pollution. It was found that the rainfall was by no means extraordinary for the time of year. In addition, the blocked drain was not considered to be an act of God on the facts of this case[2]:

'. . . if the respondents [the Pegrums] were negligent in not providing or maintaining drains adequate to deal with this amount of rainfall, then they could not as a matter of law rely on the act of God defence, for then their negligence would be *the* (or at any rate *a*) cause of the pollution'.

Post-*Empress Cars*, there seems to be little merit in trying to contest a *Pegrum* type of case. As was the case in *CPC UK Ltd*, that the defendants established their pig breeding facility was sufficient to be the cause when polluted matter escaped from it.

1 (1989) 153 JP 581; *Pegrum* is also useful as it may have a potential application in instances where the statutory defence of s 33(7) in the EPA 1990 of taking all reasonable precautions is invoked in a relation to acts of God. Henry J held that an act of God (at 587A/B) '. . . is an operation of natural forces so unpredictable as to excuse the defendants all liability for its consequences'. An example of such acts in relation to waste management might be where it was claimed that landfill site licence conditions were breached due to bad weather (see also *Greenock Corpn v Caledonian Rly Co* [1916–17] All ER Rep 426).
2 *Pegrum* at 587F.

Permitting

7.78 The *Collins Concise Dictionary*[1] provides that the words 'to permit' involve the granting of permission to do an act or to consent to an act or to tolerate it. Similarly, the *Concise Oxford Dictionary*[2] holds that 'to permit' means giving permission or consent, authorising or giving an opportunity. It has been held that, depending on the context, ' "permitting" has a narrow meaning of assenting or agreeing to or a wider meaning of not taking reasonable steps to prevent something which is in one's power'[3]. Unlike the instance of 'causing' water pollution, there are few, if any, precedents on the issue of knowingly permitting discharges into the aquatic environment[4]. Consequently, the position on the correct interpretation of the phrase is much less settled in water pollution law. Road traffic law appears to be the best source of guidance on how the phrase should be approached in general terms.

1 1997 edn.
2 1995 edn.
3 *Vehicle Inspectorate v Nuttall* [1999] 1 WLR 629 at 635C/D.
4 Although a number of judgments on 'causing' pollution do reflect upon the difference between causing and knowingly permitting: see eg *Alphacell v Woodward* [1972] 2 All ER 475.

7.79 In *Alphacell v Woodward*, Lord Wilberforce provided[1] a distinction between the words 'causing' and 'knowingly permitting' in s 2(1) of the Rivers (Prevention of Pollution) Act 1951[2]. Knowingly permitting an act which causes pollution should be seen as an action:

'. . . which involves a failure to prevent the pollution, which failure, however, must be accompanied by knowledge.'

1 *Alphacell v Woodward* at 479B.
2 Now s 85 of the Water Resources Act 1991.

7.80 In the road traffic case of *Goodbarne v Buck*[1], MacKinnon LJ provides guidance on the circumstances where a person 'permits' a vehicle to be used[2]:

'In order to make a person liable for permitting another person to use a motor vehicle, it is obvious that he must be in a position to forbid the other person to use the motor vehicle.'

The person who is able to grant such a permission is not necessarily the owner or keeper of the vehicle, but anybody who is in a position to grant permission to another person[3].

1   [1940] 1 All ER 613.
2   *Goodbarne* at 616D.
3   See *Lloyd v Singleton* [1953] 1 All ER 291; but it seems doubtful that a person who somehow gives himself leave to do an act can be held to be 'knowingly permitting'. While *Keene v Muncaster* [1980] RTR 377 might be viewed as specific to a statute unrelated to the EPA 1990, it would appear that this principle has also been upheld in *Waddell v Winter* (1967) 202 Estates Gazette 1225 in relation to caravan sites.

7.81   The dicta that a person cannot permit something which that person is unable to forbid was reaffirmed by *Tophams Ltd v Earl of Sefton*[1]. Lord Hodson stated that one cannot permit that which one does not control[2], whilst Lord Guest held[3] that the ordinary meaning of 'to permit' is to give leave for an act to be done which the person permitting it has the power to prevent[4].

1   [1966] 1 All ER 1039.
2   *Tophams* at 1043C.
3   *Tophams* at 1045B.
4   See *Tophams* per Lord Upjohn at 1049E; *Sweet v Parsley* [1969] 1 All ER 347 at 363H and *Earl of Leicester v Well-next-the-Sea UDC* [1972] 3 All ER 77. See also *Rochford RDC v Port of London Authority* [1914] 2 KB 916 at 921 and *Watkins v O'Shaughnessy* [1939] 1 All ER 385 at 387A and 389E.

7.82   Although it does not refer to *Goodbarne v Buck*, *McLeod (Houston) v Buchanan*[1] indicates that in some instances a person by their omission permits a third party to do an act. Comparing the words 'to cause' and 'to permit' in the Road Traffic Act 1930[2], Lord Wright[3] stated that:

'To permit is a looser and vaguer term. It may denote an express permission, general or particular, as distinguished from a mandate. The other person is not told to use a vehicle in the particular way, but he is told that he may do so if he desires. However, the word also includes cases in which permission is merely inferred. If the other person is given the control of the vehicle, permission may be inferred if the vehicle is left at the other person's disposal in such circumstances as to carry with it a reasonable implication of a discretion or liberty to use it in the manner in which it was used. In order to prove permission, it is not necessary to show knowledge of similar user [sic] in the past, or actual notice that the vehicle might be, or was likely to be, so used, or that the accused was guilty of a reckless disregard of the probabilities of the case, or a wilful closing of his eyes. He may not have thought at all of his duties under this section.'[4]

1   [1940] 2 All ER 179.
2   Now the Road Traffic Act 1988.
3   *McLeod* at 187A.
4   See also *McLeod* per Lord Russell of Killowen at 185E/F.

7.83   Similarly, in *James & Son Ltd v Smee*[1], it was held that, in contrast to the word 'using', the word 'permitting' in reg 75 of the Motor Vehicles (Construction and Use) Regulations 1951 required an assessment of the accused's state of mind[2]. Parker J held that[3]:

'Knowledge, moreover, in this connection includes the state of mind of a man who shuts his eyes to the obvious or allows his servant to do something in the circumstances where a contravention is likely not caring whether a contravention takes place or not.'[4]

1 [1954] 3 All ER 273.
2 Ie that the offence implies *'knowingly* permitting'; see also, for example, *Re Caughey, ex p Ford* (1876) 1 Ch D 521 at 527.
3 *Smee* at 278G/H.
4 See also, for example, *McLeod (or Houston) v Buchanan* [1940] 1 All ER 179 at 185; *Mallon v Allon* [1963] 3 All ER 843 at 847C/D; *Smith of Maddiston Ltd v Macnab* 1975 SLT 86 at 89; *R v Shorrock* [1993] 3 All ER 917; *Johnson v Youden* [1950] 1 All ER 300; and *Robinson v DPP* [1991] RTR 315.

7.84 The above proposition seems to accord with *Berton v Alliance Economic Investment Co*[1], where the word 'permit' was held by Atkin LJ to have two faces[2]:

'To my mind the word 'permit' means one of two things, either to give leave for an act which without that leave could not be legally done, or to abstain from taking reasonable steps to prevent the act where it is within a man's power to prevent it.'[3]

However, there are limits as to how far steps should be taken to prevent an act occurring. While these may include the instigation of legal proceedings[4], the phrase does imply that there are finite limits on what action is required[5].

1 [1922] 1 KB 742 at 759.
2 *Berton* at 759.
3 See *McPhail v Allan & Dey Ltd* 1980 SLT 136 at 138; see also *Webb v Maidstone and District Motor Services Ltd* (1934) 78 Sol Jo 336 at 337; *Korten v West Sussex County Council* (1903) 88 LT 466 at 472; and generally *Evans v Dell* [1937] 1 All ER 349 and *Roper v Taylor's Central Garages (Exeter) Ltd* [1951] TLR 284.
4 *Berton v Alliance Economic Investments Co Ltd* [1922] 1 KB 742 at 761; *Atkin v Rose* [1923] 1 Ch 522 at 533; *Barton v Reed* [1932] 1 Ch 362 at 376.
5 See Atkin LJ's reference to 'reasonable steps' in *Berton v Alliance Economic Investments Co Ltd* [1922] 1 KB 742 at 761: this principle may be satisfied if advice is obtained that legal proceedings are not likely to be successful; see also *Commercial General Administration Ltd v Thomsett* (1979) 250 Estates Gazette 547. In general, it would seem that the converse of permitting is forbidding. But forbidding does not extend to physically preventing some action.

7.85 These positions are very much in accordance to the recent House of Lords judgment of *Vehicle Inspectorate v Nuttall*[1]. This judgment involved tachograph offences and focused on whether an owner of a coach company could be held liable for having 'permitted' offences on behalf of his drivers by failing to verify their compliance with the legislation. It was held that 'permitted' in this context held a wide meaning, including failing to take reasonable steps to prevent something. Consequently '... there is no place [for such matters as] subjective foresight of the prospect, or risk, of a contravention being committed'[2]. A failure to take reasonable steps, however, must be deliberate and the offence is certainly not one of strict liability[3]. Hence the court held that, if it can be shown that a sufficient regime of verification was in existence, then this would fall within the concept of taking reasonable steps to prevent the contravention. Conversely, '... if the defendant's state of mind is one of not caring whether a contravention ... took place that would be generally sufficient to establish recklessness and that ... is the necessary mental element ...'[4]. Overall, the '... offence of permitting is a crime of omission which arises from the duty to act and involves a failure to perform that duty'[5].

1 [1999] 1 WLR 629.
2 *Vehicle Inspectorate v Nuttall* at 631G.
3 *Vehicle Inspectorate v Nuttall* at 635F.
4 *Vehicle Inspectorate v Nuttall* at 636D/E.
5 *Vehicle Inspectorate v Nuttall* at 639G.

7.86 Precisely how far a company can be held liable for 'knowingly permitting' an act due to its disinterest in the activities of employees remains a difficult issue. Much will depend upon the question of whether s 33 of the EPA 1990 imposes vicarious liability on a company[1]. If it does not, from *Hill & Sons (Botley and Denmead) Ltd v Hampshire Chief Constable*[2], it would appear that negligence of a company in this respect may not be sufficient, particularly when established procedures have been followed[3]. The test is, it would seem, whether there has been a 'reckless' disregard of the activities of employees by the company or by persons who can be identified as the guiding mind[4] of the company[5].

1   See paras 7.109ff, 7.117ff and 7.145ff.
2   [1972] RTR 29.
3   See also *Fransman v Sexton* [1965] Crim LR 556.
4   See para 7.147ff.
5   See *Vehicle Inspectorate v Nuttall* [1999] 1 WLR 629 and also *Gray's Haulage Co Ltd v Arnold* [1966] 1 All ER 896 at 898.

Knowingly permitting and knowingly causing: what needs to be known?

7.87 The above sections have analysed matters of causation, permission and knowledge. However, the question of knowledge has been considered in general terms. By its use of the word 'knowingly', s 33 of the EPA 1990 obviously requires something to be known, but what? This section will consider this matter in the light of the three available judgments which have direct relevance to the EPA 1990.

Knowingly permitting

7.88 Two Divisional Court decisions exist which are immediately applicable to the concept of 'knowingly permitting' in s 33(1) of the EPA 1990. The cases are *Ashcroft v Cambro Waste Products Ltd*[1] and *Kent County Council v Beaney*[2].

1   [1981] 3 All ER 699.
2   [1993] Env LR 225.

7.89 In *Ashcroft v Cambro Waste Products Ltd*[1], the company was charged under the Control of Pollution Act 1974[2] with knowingly permitting the deposit of controlled waste in contravention of the conditions of a waste disposal licence. It was alleged that the company failed to provide adequate cover for deposited oily wastes and blue asbestos[3]. The company's defence contended that the offence in the Control of Pollution Act 1974 contemplated that the prosecution should show not only that the company knowingly permitting the deposit of waste in breach of the condition, but also that it knowingly permitted the breach of the actual licence condition. That contention was not upheld by Boreham J, who stated that it was sufficient for the prosecution to show that the company knowingly permitted the deposit of the waste. In addition, the knowledge of the site foreman that the waste had been deposited was sufficient to convict the company. That *Ashcroft* constituted the correct approach to the construction of s 33 of the EPA 1990 was subsequently affirmed in *R v Environment Agency, ex p Shanks & McEwan (Teesside) Ltd*[4].

1   [1981] 3 All ER 699.
2   Control of Pollution Act 1974, s 3.
3   This case was before the judgment of *Leigh Land Reclamation v Walsall Metropolitan Borough Council* (1990) 155 JP 547. Although *Leigh Land* does not refer to it, if the *Ashcroft* decision had been made after that case, the deficiencies in the Controll of Pollution Act 1974, which *Leigh Land* highlighted, may well have resulted in Cambro Waste Products acquittal.
4   [1997] JPL 824 at 829/830.

7.90   The Divisional Court also held[1] that only once a case had been made out that a defendant knowingly permitted the deposit of controlled waste could the defence look to the statutory defences as set out in the relevant statute[2].

1   *Ashcroft* at 702C/D.
2   In this case, the Control of Pollution Act 1974, s 4(3)(c). It has been suggested elsewhere in Jarvis J & Fordham M (1993) *Lender Liability*, Cameron May, London, pp 102–107 that *Westminster City Council v Croyalgrange* is in immediate contrast to this decision. In *Croyalgrange*, both knowledge of an unlawful use of a premises as a sex shop and knowledge of the breach of the terms and conditions of the licence needed to be established. But in *Ashcroft* only the knowledge of the waste being deposited was required. However, as noted earlier, the offence under the Local Government (Miscellaneous Provisions) Act 1982 is worded differently to that contained in either the Control of Pollution Act 1974 (s 3) or EPA 1990 (s 33). Besides knowingly causing and permitting, the Local Government (Miscellaneous Provisions) Act 1982 makes it an offence to 'knowingly use' a premises as a sex establishment. This is an immediate distinction to s 33 of the EPA 1990 where only the words 'causing' and 'permitting' are qualified by the word 'knowingly' – there is no offence of *knowingly* depositing waste, nor, with respect to s 33(6), *knowingly* breaching licence conditions

7.91   While *Ashcroft* related to a licensed waste management facility, *Kent County Council v Beaney*[1] referred to the tipping of waste on land which did not have the benefit of a waste disposal licence[2]. Mr Beaney occupied a farm on which he allowed others to tip controlled wastes, ostensibly for landraising purposes. Fires were observed to be burning at the site and skips were seen to be tipped. All the tipping activities were done by third parties. Mr Beaney was charged with knowingly permitting controlled waste to be deposited.

1   [1993] Env LR 225.
2   *Beaney* also pertained to the Control of Pollution Act 1974.

7.92   The magistrates' verdict was that there was no case to answer. There was no evidence that Mr Beaney had knowingly permitted the disposal operations on his land. They felt that a particularly telling point was the fact that the regulatory authority's inspector did not ask him in an interview if he knew what was going on. However, the Divisional Court noted that the activities were close to the defendant's farmhouse, a considerable number of deposits of waste had occurred and skip vehicles were involved. After Mr Beaney's interview with the inspector, the two of them had walked around the site. These factors were supplemented by the fact that he had mentioned landraising with hardcore at the interview. Mann LJ held that both the proximity of the farmhouse to the operations and the frequency by which waste was deposited[1]:

'. . . must give rise to the inference that Mr Beaney both knew what was occurring and that he was permitting it to occur.'

Accordingly, the court felt that it was up to the defence to displace this 'provisional inference' by way of evidence. The case was therefore remitted back to the magistrates for re-hearing.

1   *Beaney* at 228.

Knowingly causing

7.93   Under the Control of Pollution Act 1974, the principal offence provision used the phrase 'cause and knowingly permit'[1], not 'knowingly cause or knowingly permit' as found in s 33(1)(a) and (b) of the EPA 1990. Correspondence between the government and the then Labour Opposition spokesperson on waste indicated that the government's intention by the insertion of the word 'knowingly' before the word 'cause' in the Environmental Protection Bill was to prevent the courts being subject to lengthy discourses on whether it was necessary to identify criminal intention on behalf of the accused or the accused's knowledge that an act is wrong[2], thereby making it clear that strict liability is not to apply in respect of causing. However, as will be discussed below, more recent case law seems to be taking quite a different tack.

1   Control of Pollution Act 1974, s 3(1).
2   Cf *Sweet v Parsley* [1969] 1 All ER 347: in other words to clearly differentiate between the definition of 'cause' in water pollution law and its meaning under the EPA 1990.

7.94   The principal judgment on 'knowingly causing' under s 33 of the EPA 1990 is *R v Environment Agency, ex p Shanks & McEwan (Teesside) Ltd*[1]. The case involved a licensed liquid waste treatment plant operated by Shanks & McEwan. A tanker containing oil wastes, which was owned by a third party, arrived at the site. Rather than deliver the wastes into one of the tanks at the plant, the driver was directed to off-load the material into a bunded area, due to one of the tanks being out of commission. Unfortunately, this activity was not only contrary to the procedures required by the licence, but was also observed by two inspectors from the Environment Agency.

1   [1997] JPL 824.

7.95   Shanks & McEwan was charged with 'knowingly causing' controlled waste to be 'deposited' contrary to s 33(6) of the EPA 1990. As noted at para 7.08, s 33(6) makes it an offence to contravene s 33(1). It also contains a separate offence in relation to the breach the conditions of a waste management licence. In this instance, the Environment Agency's information referred to a contravention of s 33(1)(a) – knowingly causing the deposit of waste otherwise than in accordance with the licence. The information did not utilise the separate offence provision of s 33(6), which specifically refers to the breach of a licence condition and which, as noted earlier, does not have qualifications concerning knowledge, causation or permission. If it had, the case may not have needed to be subject to the consideration of the Divisional Court.

7.96   Whilst this matter probably hampered the prosecution in establishing its case, it also seems that the defence was somewhat fettered by the manner by which they had set out to rebut the prosecution's case in the magistrates' court. The whole defence revolved around the question of attribution of causation upon the company, particularly in the light of s 33(1) of the EPA 1990, which requires that causation be accompanied by knowledge. In essence, it was argued that the company did not *knowingly* cause the events which resulted in a breach of the licence. This strategy placed less reliance on the statutory defences in s 33(7) of the EPA 1990, particularly in respect of whether due diligence had been exercised by the company[1]. Hence there was no defence argued in the manner of *Tesco Supermarkets Ltd v Nattrass*[2], to the effect that, while an underling had slipped up and breached procedures, liability should not rest upon the body corporate. Again, it may be that, if this tack had been followed, the case would not have been before the Divisional Court.

1   From the magistrates' finding, it would appear that there was an attempt to argue that the deposit was the result of an emergency. But for self-evident reasons – see para 7.153ff – this was not found by the magistrates to be the case.
2   [1971] 2 All ER 127: see para 7.148ff.

7.97   The manner by which the Divisional Court approached the crucial matter of knowledge and the liability of a company when an employee has caused a contravention of s 33(1) constituted a vigorous assertion of what is close to strict liability. The court clearly emphasises that this is the appropriate view of s 33 of the EPA 1990, due to the presence of the statutory defences built into the EPA 1990 in s 33(7)[1]. The *Shanks & McEwan* judgment therefore could be said to throw up a much more robust approach in these more environmentally conscious times. Alternatively, it may be that the court went too far and that subsequent decisions may place much more emphasis on the matters subject to detailed analysis earlier in this chapter.

1   *Shanks & McEwan (Teesside)* at 829, 830 and 833. This case can be distinguished from, for example, *John Henshall (Quarries) Ltd v Harvey* [1965] 1 All ER 725, where the failure of a weighbridge clerk did not impute liability on the company when an overweight vehicle was let out on the public highway.

7.98   The first significant aspect of the judgment is the upholding of the approach of *Ashcroft v Cambro Waste Products*[1]. Like that earlier judgment, Mance J did not accept that, for an offence under s 33 of the EPA 1990 to be committed, the company must (a) know that a deposit of waste had occurred, and (b) know that a licence condition had been breached. When waste was deposited in a manner not authorised by the licence, it was sufficient to show only knowledge of the deposit of waste[2].

1   [1981] 3 All ER 699.
2   *Shanks & McEwan (Teesside)* at 831/832, 833.

7.99   In respect of the appearance of the qualification 'knowingly' in front of 'cause' in s 33(1) of the EPA 1990, the court held that this was included to ensure that s 33(1) only applied to acts involving controlled waste which were intentional[1]. Mance J states[2]:

'So far as it is necessary to seek any explanation for the insertion of the word "knowingly" before "cause" in the 1990 Act, when it did not appear there in the 1974 Act[3], one likely explanation is that it was considered appropriate to assimilate the operation of section 33(1) in cases of permission and causation, where the person responsible for the deposit may be less immediately involved than the person actually undertaking the deposit. On this basis, section 33(1)(a) makes clear that in both cases a defendant must know that controlled waste is to be deposited in or on any land. Once he knows this, the strict obligation imported by the rest of section 33(1)(a) comes into play. The initial case of a person actually depositing controlled waste in or any land remains free of any expressed requirement of knowledge. Normally, no doubt, such a person would know what he was doing. Even if he was, for some reason, under a misapprehension, he could in appropriate circumstances establish a defence under s 33(7)(a).'

1   *Shanks & McEwan (Teesside)* at 830.
2   *Shanks & McEwan (Teesside)* at 831.
3   Control of Pollution Act 1974.

7.100   The court then considered the matter of whether or not Shanks & McEwan, as the company, knew of the deposit of waste which caused a condition to be breached. In this respect, the approach in *Ashcroft* was again followed, whereby the knowledge of a key – but not senior – operative was considered sufficient to ascribe knowledge to the company as a whole[1]. But in relation to the need to consider vicarious liability – which would involve a consideration of the knowledge of persons close to the directing mind of the company[2] – this matter was short-circuited. Instead, the court chose to consider the nature of exactly *what* facts a company needs to be proven to know in instances such as this. The conclusion of the court was that it was sufficient for a company to know that wastes were being generally deposited at the facility[3]. Knowledge of any particular deposit was not essential. The very fact that the treatment plant was open for business was enough to ascribe knowledge to the company[4]. As Mance J puts it[5]:

'The issue of principle before us is simply whether a company may under section 33(1)(a) be said to have knowingly caused a deposit by operating a business inviting such deposits to be made in or on its land. The answer to this, in my judgment, is that, if section 33(1)(a) does require knowing causation of the deposit in or on land at … [the treatment plant at the date of alleged offence] on the part of senior management, then it is sufficient that the appellant company's senior management knowingly operated and held out the site … for the reception and deposit in or on it of just such controlled waste. It is unnecessary to show more specific knowledge regarding particular loads on the part of senior management. It is *a fortiori* unnecessary to show any knowledge of this or any deposit being made into the bund. Although the language of the information identifies the bund, the statute only requires knowledge of the deposit "in or on the land", that is the premises [of the treatment plant]'.

1   *Shanks & McEwan (Teesside)* at 831.
2   See paras 7.109ff, 7.117ff and 7.147ff.
3   *Shanks & McEwan (Teesside)* at 831.
4   Similarly, it was held (at 831) that 'knowingly permit' should also be so construed: 'In relation to the phrase 'knowingly permit', permission is likely to be given in general terms for an activity, rather than on a load by load basis'. Hence 'as far as the involvement of senior management is concerned', the prosecution in *Shanks & McEwan (Teesside)* could also have been brought on grounds of knowingly permit, besides knowingly cause: see also *Korten v West Sussex County Council* (1903) 88 LT 466 at 469, where a company managing director was held liable for 'permitting' his company to issue a false trade description.
5   *Shanks & McEwan (Teesside)* at 832.

7.101   The court then further cemented its strict liability approach by alluding approvingly to the earlier water pollution case of *National Rivers Authority (Southern Region) v Alfred McAlpine Homes (East) Ltd*[1]. It held that[2], even if it is not correct to assert that the company's general knowledge of its own business is sufficient to embrace individual deposits of waste on its land, this would be a 'powerful reason' to extend the requirement of attribution on the company for the acts of its employees. Again, the existence of the 'due diligence' defence in s 33(7) of the EPA 1990 is pointed to as an appropriate safeguard against wrongful conviction[3].

1   [1994] Env LR 198: see para 7.75.
2   *Shanks & McEwan (Teesside)* at 833.
3   *Shanks & McEwan (Teesside)* at 833.

7.102   Finally, the only other judgment concerning 'knowingly causing' is *Environment Agency v Singer*[1]. Although the appeal by the Agency was unsuccessful for other reasons, Kennedy LJ did briefly reflect[2] on 'knowingly causing' in the circumstances where a licensee of a transfer station failed to secure the premises to prevent – so it was claimed – the unauthorised entry of others who were scavenging wastes. Although not charged, the latter were alleged to be disposing of wastes contrary to s 33(1) of the EPA 1990. Hence the prosecution claim that the defendant 'knowingly caused' this disposal activity. The Divisional Court stated that the fact that such persons 'habitually' came onto the land for the purposes of scavenging and that nothing was done about it may be sufficient to successfully allege that the licensee 'knowingly caused' the disposal activity. However, it may be that this remark was made *obiter* and that, more obviously, this circumstance might be better addressed through the offence of 'knowingly permitting'.

1   [1998] Env LR 380.
2   *Singer* at 383/384.

Correctly framing and proving charges under s 33

7.103 In *Shanks & McEwan (Teesside)* the Agency made life difficult for itself by its selection of the wording of the information. In respect of the oily waste delivery which contravened the licence conditions, the Agency laid charges alleging contravention of s 33(1)(a) of the EPA 1990, rather than contravention of s 33(6). Given that s 33 of the EPA 1990 potentially contains 16 separately-worded offences[1], it is not surprising that it is sometimes difficult to decide on the nature of appropriate charges. This difficulty is compounded by overlaps between the offence provisions, coupled with significant differences in wordings which affect such matters as applicability and evidential requirements. Although this matter has been simplified by *R v Leighton and Town and Country Refuse Collection Ltd*[2], it remains a difficult issue, which can be subdivided into five potential problem areas. What should become apparent is that the liability of a licensee under s 33 of the EPA 1990 is much clearer as a result of case law. By contrast, liability issues affecting other parties in waste management – such as a waste producer – still remain for judicial determination.

1 Three offences in s 33(1)(a) – to deposit, knowingly cause or knowingly permit waste to be deposited; nine offences in s 33(1)(b) – to treat, keep or dispose of waste, to knowingly cause waste to be treated, kept or disposed of, to knowingly permit waste to be kept, treated or disposed of; three in s 33(1)(c) – to treat, keep or dispose of waste in a manner which causes pollution or harm; one offence in s 33(6) – to breach the conditions of a licence.
2 *R v Leighton and Town and Country Refuse Collection Ltd* [1997] Env LR 411. See para 7.104ff.

Avoiding duplicity

7.104 *R v Leighton and Town and Country Refuse Collection Ltd*[1] concerned a case taken by the Environment Agency against a company operating a waste transfer station and against its managing director, who was also a 99% shareholder in the enterprise. The transfer station was subject to a waste management licence, but there was also an unlicensed landfill in close proximity. Charges were brought in respect of non-compliance with the transfer station's licence conditions and also unauthorised tipping at the landfill. The evidence appears to straddle the implementation of the EPA 1990, and hence an information was served on the company in respect of contravening s 33 of that Act, as well as non-compliance with s 3 of the earlier Control of Pollution Act 1974. The managing director was also charged with consenting to the offences or causing them by his connivance or neglect[2]. At the lower court, the company – on the basis of its insolvency – was subject to a conditional discharge, with the director being required to pay a £14,000 fine and £25,000 costs. The case passed to the Court of Appeal on a number of grounds, one of which was that the informations were bad for duplicity.

1 *R v Leighton and Town and Country Refuse Collection Ltd* [1997] Env LR 411.
2 Control of Pollution Act 1974, s 87(1) and the EPA 1990, s 157: see para 7.156ff.

7.105 The basis of the claim by the appellant concerning duplicity was that each information alleged three offences. This was because each count made reference, in the case of the Control of Pollution Act 1974, to 'depositing', 'causing' or 'knowingly permitting' waste to be deposited and, in respect of the EPA 1990, 'treating', 'keeping' or 'disposing of' waste[1]. Hence a significant element of the appeal concerned whether the statutes contained a limited array of single offences which may be committed in a number of ways or whether, in the case of the EPA 1990 for example, each of the 16 elements was itself a single offence. Whilst the fact that overlaps in the offence provisions of s 33 of the EPA 1990 exist had been accepted to by the High Court earlier[2], the method of framing the charges in this instance brought the question of possible duplicity into immediate focus.

1   A similar claim was made in respect of the directors' liability charges: the words 'consenting', 'conniving' or 'neglecting' (see para 7.156ff) were all contained in each charge.
2   The existence of overlaps between the EPA 1990, s 33(1) and s 33(6) is acknowledged in both *Thames Waste Management v Surrey County Council* [1997] Env LR 148 at 155, where Rose LJ notes that charges can be made under either section in such circumstances; similarly, in *R v Environment Agency, ex p Shanks & McEwan (Teesside) Ltd* [1997] JPL 824 at 828, Mance J points to the fact that these are overlapping, but differently constructed offence provisions; see also *London Waste Regulation Authority v Drinkwater Sabey Ltd* [1997] Env LR 137 at 143.

7.106   In the Court of Appeal, Auld LJ held that the formulations contained in the two statutes, as in other enactments such as road traffic and water pollution law, refer to different acts requiring different proof[1]. They do not constitute different offences which should be set out in separate indictments. The wording of each of the sub-sections of the EPA 1990[2] each create one offence which can be committed in a number of different ways. Hence, '[i]n our view, ... [s 33(1) of the EPA 1990] creates, in paragraphs (a), (b) and (c), three separate offences, each of which may be committed by any one of the different acts specified'[3].

1   *R v Leighton and Town and Country Refuse Collection Ltd* [1997] Env LR 411 at 416.
2   Ie s 33(1)(a), s 33(1)(b) or s 33(1)(c).
3   *R v Leighton* at 418: however, this does not, of course, mean that all elements of the EPA 1990, s 33(1) can be bundled together as one charge. This would be bad for duplicity: see *R v Leighton* and also *R v Environment Agency, ex p Shanks & McEwan (Teesside) Ltd* [1997] JPL 824 at 828.

7.107   However, the Court of Appeal added one caveat[1]:

'Accordingly, in each case it was in principle permissible for the prosecution to charge a single offence stating the various acts of commission in the alternative[2]. To have required it to charge each alternative in a separate count would have resulted in a prolix and unmanageable indictment. We say "in principle" only to make the point that if, in any instance, the prosecution is confident before trial that it can prove the precise mode of committing the offence and/or that it cannot prove one or more of the others, it should specify the particular mode upon which it relies and leave it at that. There would be no point in including alternatives provided by the statute for which there was no evidential support.'

1   *R v Leighton and Town and Country Refuse Collection Ltd* [1997] Env LR 411 at 419.
2   Earlier in the judgment (at 417), the court made reference to r 7 of the Indictment Rules 1971, SI 1971/1253 which allows persons to be charged in the alternative in defined circumstances.

7.108   Where informations are laid in the alternative, the court is left to decide under which provision the defendant should be convicted[1]. Whilst the general principle of laying charges in the alternative has been upheld unanimously by the House of Lords in *R v Bellman*[2], Lord Griffiths gives the following warning[3]:

'The very fact that offences are being charged in the alternative obviously weakens the prosecution case and enables the defence to invite the jury to say that as the prosecution cannot make their mind up which crime the accused committed they, the jury, cannot be sure of his guilt. But equally, I have no doubt that in certain circumstances justice requires that an accused should face mutually contradictory counts.'

Hence the finding in *R v Leighton*[4] that the prosecution should generally be as specific wherever possible in the framing of charges. Moreover, charging in the alternative poses an additional burden on the court, particularly in the case of a trial judge whose summing up must ensure that the jury is directed as to the evidential nature of each alternative[5].

1   See for example, in respect of road traffic law, *Ross Hillman Ltd v Bond* [1974] RTR 279 at 290E; see also *R v Bellman* [1989] 1 All ER 22 and *R v Newcastle-upon-Tyne Justices, ex p John Bryce (Contractors) Ltd* [1976] 2 All ER 611 at 612H/J.
2   [1989] 1 All ER 22.
3   *Bellman* at 26(e).
4   *R v Leighton and Town and Country Refuse Collection Ltd* [1997] Env LR 411 at 419.
5   *R v Leighton* at 420.

Strict liability in s 33(1) of the EPA 1990

7.109   One very significant area of uncertainty in interpreting s 33 of the EPA 1990, in the framing of correct charges and, additionally, in terms of evidential requirements, concerns the question of *mens rea*. This is apparent from the absence of any prefix in s 33(6) and in certain elements of s 33(1) concerning knowledge[1]. On the one hand, it seems settled law that the lack of any qualification on *mens rea* in a statute does not necessarily imply that *mens rea* does not need to be established[2]. But on the other hand, it may be that the absence of such qualification causes the provision to fall into the class of provisions which have been loosely described as 'public nuisances'[3] for which proof of *mens rea* is not necessary. The distinction between this type of offence and more 'normal' criminal provisions is explained by Lord Diplock in *Sweet v Parsley*[4]:

> 'Where penal provisions are of general application to the conduct of ordinary citizens in the course of their every day life, the presumption is that the standard of care requiring them in informing themselves of the facts which would make their conduct unlawful, is that of the familiar common law duty of care. But where the subject matter of a statute is the regulation of particular activity involving potential danger to public health, safety or morals, in which citizens have a choice whether they participate or not, the court may feel driven to infer an intention of Parliament to impose, by penal sanctions, a higher duty of care on those who choose to participate and to place on them an obligation to take whatever measures may be necessary to prevent the prohibited act, without regard to those considerations of cost or business practicability which play a part in the determination of what would be required of them in order to fulfil the ordinary common law duty of care.'

1   'Deposit', 'treat', 'keep' and 'dispose of' in the EPA 1990, s 33(1)(a) and (b), in relation to the breach of a licence condition under s 33(6), or in respect of s 33(1)(c).
2   See for example *Sweet v Parsley* [1969] 1 All ER 347 at 350D, 353I, 356E.
3   *Sherras v de Rutzen* [1895-1899] All ER Rep 1167; *Alphacell v Woodward* [1972] 2 All ER 475 at 486A/B.
4   [1969] 1 All ER 347 at 362B.

7.110   Hence it may be that those elements of s 33 of the EPA 1990 which are not prefixed by the word 'knowingly' do not contain the implicit requirement on prosecuting authorities to establish *mens rea*. Furthermore, while this question has yet to be properly settled, the argument that s 33(6) of the EPA 1990 should be seen as creating strict liability offences is supported by analogy to statutory controls on pollution of the aquatic environment. In this instance, discharge consents seem to have similarities to waste management licences in that they authorise any aquatic discharge and make authorisation subject to particular conditions.

7.111   The question of the contravention of the conditions of such a consent was considered in *Taylor Woodrow Property Management Ltd v National Rivers Authority*[1]. Taylor Woodrow was prosecuted under s 85(6) of the Water Resources Act 1991 after a release of oil into a watercourse. The discharge of oil breached the consent of the outfall of a surface water discharge system built and maintained by Taylor Woodrow. Although the drainage system served an industrial estate, the units of which had been sold to third parties, Taylor Woodrow retained the discharge consent. Certainly, it was a third party, not Taylor Woodrow, whose actions had resulted in the discharge.

1   [1995] Env LR 52.

7.112   Prior to setting out the outcome of *Taylor Woodrow*, it should be noted that s 85(6) of the Water Resources Act 1991 has a similarity in construction to s 33(6) of the EPA 1990. It states that:

'... a person who contravenes this section or the conditions of any consent ... shall be guilty of an offence ...'.

There is, however, no equivalent statutory defence involving matters such as 'due diligence' or 'reasonable precautions' as set down in the s 33(7) of the EPA 1990[1]. Furthermore, in the Water Resources Act 1991, the word 'contravention' is defined[2], whereas in the EPA 1990 it is undefined and therefore holds its ordinary meaning.

1   See the Water Resources Act 1991, s 89 (as amended by the Environment Act 1995, ss 60 and 120, Sch 22, para 128).
2   Water Resources Act 1991, s 221: the word 'contravention' includes a failure to comply.

7.113   At the Divisional Court, it was submitted on behalf of Taylor Woodrow that there would be an offence under s 85(6) of the Water Resources Act 1991 only if the discharge had been made by the company itself. Steyn LJ disagreed[1]:

'In these circumstances, I regard it as unrealistic to argue that Taylor Woodrow are not criminally liable because they did not commit a positive act or discharge. On the finding of the stipendiary magistrate, the answer is that they failed to comply with a positive obligation contained in a condition lawfully applicable.

For my part, I would say that the submission flies not only in the face of the plain meaning of section 85(6) read with 88(2) and Schedule 10, but that it is also at variance with the objective of the relevant part of the Act. The Act clearly contemplated an effective and workable system of consents, subject to conditions. And it was certainly intended that the regime constituted by conditional consents was to be comprehensive and without gaps.'

1   *Taylor Woodrow* at 58/59.

7.114   In the light of *Taylor Woodrow*, it may appear that there is good reason to suppose that the s 33(6) of the EPA 1990 involves a strict liability offence. As noted, *Taylor Woodrow* suggests that the holder of the consent is still liable for an offence which is created when another person's actions result in the conditions of a consent being breached. Again, this appears to be highly applicable to holders of waste management licences. An instance might be where a licence condition defining the nature of acceptable waste was breached by a waste delivery vehicle controlled by a third party. In such cases, a rapid response in accordance with defined procedures would cause the licensee to be in a position to demonstrate the statutory defence under s 33(7) of the EPA 1990 of taking all reasonable precautions and exercising due diligence. A lax response would result in the licensee's guilt. There seems to be little injustice in either of these positions.

7.115   By contrast to the other sub-sections of s 33(1) of the EPA 1990, s 33(1)(c) – which makes it an offence for a person to treat, keep or dispose of waste in a manner likely to cause pollution of the environment or harm to human health – is not qualified in any way by the terms 'knowingly causing or knowingly permitting'. Hence, from the face of the statute, it appears to be a strict liability offence, with any defendant being left with the only option of satisfying one of the statutory defences in s 33(7).

7.116 As well as the other elements of s 33(1), whether strict liability is contained in s 33(1)(c) remains undetermined by precedent. However, in the light of the general approach of the Divisional Court in *Shanks and McEwan (Teesside)*[1], it seems likely. Certainly regard must be had to the context and intent of the provisions of s 33(1)(c). These would suggest that the matters being addressed are those which are so serious as to warrant the creation of strict liability. Such an assertion would be consistent with the view of water pollution offences taken by the courts[2].

1 [1997] JPL 824. See para 7.94ff.
2 See *Alphacell Ltd v Woodward* [1972] 2 All ER 475, *Southern Water Authority v Phillip Maurice Pegrum and Jeffrey Maurice Pegrum* (1989) 153 JP 581; *Wrothwell Ltd v Yorkshire Water Authority* [1984] Crim LR 43; *Wychavon District Council v National Rivers Authority* [1993] 2 All ER 440; *National Rivers Authority (Southern Region) v Alfred McAlpine Homes (East) Ltd* [1994] Env LR 198; *National Rivers Authority v Yorkshire Water Services Ltd* [1994] Env LR 177 at 182 (DC); *National Rivers Authority v Yorkshire Water Services Ltd* [1995] 1 All ER 225, HL; *CPC (UK) Ltd v National Rivers Authority* [1995] 7 JEL 1 69; *Empress Car Co (Abertillery) v National Rivers Authority* [1998] 1 All ER 481; and see also *Taylor Woodrow Property Management v National Rivers Authority* [1995] Env LR 52, where it was held that the breach of a consent condition is an strict liability offence, and *R v J O Sims Ltd* [1993] 1 Env LR 323 in relation to causing and permitting damage to a scheduled ancient monument.

Section 33 of the EPA 1990: the 'knowledge' elements

7.117 While the above analysis would suggest that – subject to the statutory defences contained in s 33(7) of the EPA 1990 – some elements of s 33 contain strict liability provisions, this does not apply to those parts which are prefixed by the word 'knowingly'. This contrast invites analysis, particularly from the perspective of the variety of roles of persons in waste management who are likely to commit offences. It may be that the provisions which are not prefixed by the word 'knowingly' are aimed at persons who are inevitably located in close proximity to the offence. In other words they are designed to address those individuals who actually undertake the immediate act which results in s 33 of the EPA 1990 being contravened. By definition, the doing of the particular act will mean that they, or their employees, will know of it[1]. Often waste disposal contractors of one sort or another will be involved, bodies who are, or should be, well aware of their responsibilities.

1 See paras 7.89ff and 7.94ff.

7.118 It will be recalled that, in *Shanks & McEwan (Teesside)*[1], a relatively junior employee breached both internal procedures and the waste management licence by directing wastes to be off-loaded in an unauthorised manner. In order to convict that person's employer of the offence of knowingly causing the deposit of waste in contravention of the licence[2], it was held that the only knowledge necessary of the waste management company was that the particular treatment plant was open for general waste management activities. The Environment Agency was not required to show that the company itself possessed knowledge of the detail of the activity which resulted in the licence conditions being breached. A similar finding was also made in *Ashcroft v Cambro Waste Products Ltd*[3], when the knowledge of a landfill site foreman was considered sufficient, under the Control of Pollution Act 1974, to convict an employer.

1 *R v Environment Agency, ex p Shanks & McEwan (Teesside) Ltd* [1997] JPL 824.
2 EPA 1990, s 33(1)(a).
3 [1981] 3 All ER 699: see para 7.89.

7.119 It may well be that the *Shanks & McEwan (Teesside)* and *Ashcroft* decisions hold most readily in the context of commercial waste management companies who will, by definition, know whether or not waste management activities are occurring at a particular site. Indeed, to hold that they may not be liable for the acts of their employees seems to significantly undermine the purpose of the statute and Community law – namely to cause the effective regulation of the waste management industry. In any event, like any other person subject to prosecution under s 33 of the EPA 1990, a waste company may seek protection from the statutory defences under s 33(7). Furthermore, the courts retain their considerable discretion on the nature of effective penalties.

7.120 In the case of other industrial activities, particularly companies who produce – as opposed to those who commercially manage – controlled waste, there remains the question of what needs to be known for the company – as well as any employee – to be guilty of an offence. Many of these will not be so knowledgeable of their responsibilities, frequently delegating the specialist management of wastes to the contractors already referred to. It may be that s 33 was drafted with this distinction in mind[1]. This analysis would suggest that the terms 'knowing cause' or 'knowingly permit' were originally designed, *inter alia*, to embrace the offences of the latter, less experienced and less knowledgeable individuals. Hence it may be that the provisions of the EPA 1990, by their use of the word 'knowingly', contain a greater level of protection to such persons, particularly as otherwise they might commit offences without intent or blame.

1   The division between the two classes of individuals set out here does have a certain parallel with the two types of body identified in the quotation used at para 7.109 from Lord Diplock in *Sweet v Parsley*.

7.121 An example might involve a subsidiary of a major company, whose employees placed unsuitable waste in a skip which was subsequently deposited at a waste management facility in breach of licence conditions. While the employees are likely to be caught by the concept of 'knowingly causing' waste to be deposited in breach of the licence under s 33(1) of the EPA 1990, might their employer also be liable? What seems a little unclear is whether the approach to strict liability contained in *Shanks & McEwan (Teesside)* will always pertain in such instances. The employer may be totally ignorant that waste is being deposited at any particular location[1]. The responsibility for waste management, particularly in a large company, may be delegated. Although an assessment of liability will partially rest on the statutory defences[2], the knowledge pre-requisites of s 33(1) of the EPA 1990 should at least be considered.

1   However, if employers can be found to have shut their eyes to the obvious, knowledge can still be imputed: see para 7.57ff and *John Henshall (Quarries) Ltd v Harvey* [1965] 1 All ER 725 at 728H.
2   See para 7.144ff.

7.122 In this respect, *Shanks & McEwan (Midlands) Ltd v Wrexham Maelor Borough Council*[1] raises an important issue concerning the relationship between the offence provisions of s 33(1) of the EPA 1990 and that of s 33(6). It also appears to confirm the view that s 33(6) may only apply to licence holders and other waste management contractors whose very acts are the immediate cause of a breach of licence conditions. It would seem necessary to charge other persons who are in less close proximity to the breach with one of the other offences in s 33(1). The *Shanks & McEwan (Midlands)* case arose from the inadequate daily covering of wastes at a landfill owned by a large waste management contractor. It is a little unusual as it concerns the relationship between two subsidiary companies within the same corporate grouping, with this split seeming to cause a muddle as to who should be the correct recipient of a summons for the alleged offence. However, it would seem that this judgment has wider significance, particularly in respect of the correct charging of persons who are involved in licence condition contraventions but who did not themselves actually undertake the act which resulted in the breach.

1   (1996) Times, 10 April.

7.123   In this case, the licence itself was in the name of Shanks & McEwan (Midlands) Ltd, while the actual occupier of the site and operator of the facility was Shanks & McEwan (Northern) Ltd. Shanks & McEwan (Midlands) was charged in respect of non-compliance with the cover condition. The allegation was that the latter contravened s 33(6) of the EPA 1990 by contravening a condition of their waste management licence. This was despite the fact that the licensee, Shanks & McEwan (Northern), had been issued with an earlier statutory notice[1] which sought to require compliance with licence.

1   This would have been served under either ss 38 or 42 of the EPA 1990: see Chapter 9.

7.124   On behalf of Shanks & McEwan (Midlands) Ltd, it was argued that the manner by which the licence was drafted caused the responsibility for compliance with the conditions to be split between the two companies. This interpretation emanated from the wording of the conditions, one of which referred to 'holders of the site licence' and required compliance with the licence in general terms. The other condition – which was the only one alleged to have been contravened in the information – was more specific, referring explicitly to the daily covering of waste. Hence Leggatt LJ was persuaded that the general condition applied to Shanks & McEwan (Midlands) Ltd as licence holder, but the specific condition on the covering of waste pertained to Shanks & McEwan (Northern) Ltd as site operator[1].

1   From usual custom and practice within waste regulation authorities, there seems little doubt that this duality was not what was intended by those who wrote the licence.

7.125   The fact that it was Shanks & McEwan (Midlands) – as opposed to Shanks & McEwan (Northern) – who faced charges in respect of the breach of the condition requiring daily cover caused the company to be acquitted. This partly stemmed from the acceptance by the Divisional Court of the dichotomy alleged to be contained in the licence. But in addition, it was argued that s 33(6) of the EPA 1990 was limited in its range and did not extend to persons somewhat removed from the actual site operations. Again, this was accepted by Leggatt LJ, who summed up the matter in the following way:

'At the end of the argumentation the question is whether a person contravenes any condition of the licence if he does nothing or omits nothing that is required of him with the result that a contravention occurs. However, the Act does not speak merely of the occurrence of a contravention. It says[1]:

"(6) A person who contravenes subsection (1) above or any condition of a waste management licence commits an offence."

It appears to me that it contemplates that an act may be done which constitutes a failure of compliance with a condition, with the result that the person concerned is guilty of an offence under that subsection. It is not sufficient merely that there should be a contravention of a licence so as to make the licence holder, who is or may be oblivious of the contravention, guilty of an offence of contravening a condition of the licence. That conclusion is consistent with the first part of subsection (6), which refers to a person who contravenes subsection (1).

When one refers back to subsection (1) of s 33 one finds that the essential contrast under sub-section (1)(b) is between keeping or disposing of controlled waste or knowingly causing or knowingly permitting controlled waste to be kept or disposed of. In either case to be guilty a person would have to know of the occurrence of the offence alleged whereas if the construction contended for by the Appellants[2] were correct, in relation to a condition, there could be a contravention of which they were wholly ignorant and yet they would still be guilty of an offence.

That does not seem to be what is contemplated by the statute, and I am accordingly confirmed in the view that, for a person to contravene any condition of a waste management licence, it is necessary for that person to be the person by whom the offence is committed.'

1   EPA 1990, s 33(6).
2   Ie Shanks & McEwan (Midlands) Ltd.

7.126   Although this finding is expressed in language which, given its importance, could have merited additional clarity[1], it seems to mean the following. Although the court did not address the matter of *mens rea* directly, it would appear to be the view that persons who are somewhat removed from the act which caused the licence to be contravened should in general be charged under s 33(1) of the EPA 1990. Typically, this will be in respect of 'knowingly causing' or 'knowingly permitting'. Certainly, the court seems to be saying – but only implicitly – that s 33(6) contains a strict liability offence which pertains only to persons who actually did the deed which resulted in the licence being contravened.

1   It is also notable that it appears that no precedents were placed before the court by either party to the case.

7.127   Ascribing knowledge to a company – as opposed to its employees – is also difficult when considering whether a company's liability under s 33 of the EPA 1990 is fixed by the acts of one or more of its employees. On the one hand, *Empress Cars*[1] makes clear that causation can itself be readily attributed. But on the other hand – and in contrast to water pollution law – the use of the term 'knowingly' in s 33 of the EPA 1990 appears to require that the knowledge of the employer must be clearly established. Furthermore, even when the requisite knowledge is proven, the company may still have recourse to the statutory defences in s 33(7) of the EPA 1990. While *Shanks and McEwan (Teesside)* has clarified this matter in respect of waste management companies[2], the issue of deciding the liability of other types of organisation in respect of the knowledge requirement of s 33 is not an easy area of law. It boils down to dual analysis of how a company is constituted and how it goes about the supervision of its employees. Both factors are necessary in light of the 'knowingly' element of s 33(1) and also in respect of statutory defences in s 33(7).

1   *Empress Car Co (Abertilliary) Ltd v National Rivers Authority* [1998] 1 All ER 481: see paras 7.64 and 7.72ff.
2   See para 7.94ff.

7.128   Lord Denning's description of the relationship of the various individuals within a company is well known[1]:

'A company may in many ways be likened to a human body. They have a brain and a nerve centre which controls what they do. They also have hands which hold the tools and act in accordance with directions from the centre. Some of the people in the company are mere servants and agents who are nothing more than hands to do the work and cannot be said to represent the mind or will. Others are directors and managers who represent the directing mind and will of the company, and control what they do. The state of mind of these managers is the state of mind of the company and is treated by the law as such.'

This approach is significant as, unlike in certain European jurisdictions, companies in Britain are not automatically liable under criminal law for the acts of employees. Given that s 33 of the EPA 1990 often explicitly requires a court to consider whether each and every person accused has knowledge of a particular act which resulted in an offence, where both a company and an individual is charged, both need to have the requisite knowledge. The uncertainty stems from what needs to be known. Certainly, the knowledge of the employee does not automatically result in an employer having knowledge. As Lord Denning notes above, matters of corporate knowledge have been held to be dependent upon the state of mind of those who represent the directing mind and will of the company.

1   *H L Bolton (Engineering) Co Ltd v T J Graham & Sons Ltd* [1956] 3 All ER 624 at 630D/E.

7.129   In the trading standards case of *Tesco Supermarkets v Natrass*, Lord Reid held[1]:

'Normally the board of directors, the managing director and perhaps other superior officers of a company carry out the functions and speak and act as the company. Their subordinates do not. They carry out orders from above and it can make no difference that they are given some measure of discretion. But the board of directors may delegate some part of their functions of management giving to their delegate full discretion to act independently of instructions from them. I see no difficulty in holding that they thereby put such a delegate in their place so that within the scope of the delegation he can act as the company.'

Similarly in *R v Andrews Weatherfoil Ltd*[2], it was held that:

'It is necessary to establish whether the natural person or persons in question have the status and authority which in law make their acts in the matter under considera-tion the acts of the company so that the natural person is to be treated as the company itself'.

1   *Tesco* at 132G.
2   [1972] 1 All ER 65 at 70B. See also *R v HM Coroner for East Kent, ex p Spooner* (1987) 88 CR App Rep 10 at 16.

7.130   The degree and make-up of delegation will be unique to each commercial entity[1]. On the one hand, there may be 100% delegation in the manner described by Lord Parker in *John Henshall (Quarries) Ltd v Harvey*[2]:

'If a master completely hands over the effective management of a business to some-body else, then as it is often said he cannot get out of his responsibility by such dele-gation. In those circumstances he is fixed with the knowledge of his delegate'.

But in other cases, delegation will be spread in varying degrees within the commercial entity. It would seem that the location of persons who will be in a position to have the requisite knowledge on behalf of a company is not always easy to track down. But, if the *Tesco Supermarkets* view of corporate liability is to apply to s 33 of the EPA 1990, it seems essential for a successful prosecution of a body corporate that they are so isolated. Viscount Dilhorne in *Tesco* considered the extract already quoted above from Lord Denning[3] and held[4]:

'These passages, I think, clearly indicate that one has in relation to a company to determine who is or who are, for it may be more than one, in actual control of the operations of the company, and the answer to be given to that question may vary from company to company depending on its organisation.'

Similarly while s 157 of the EPA 1990 identifies the nature of senior corporate governance for the purposes of directors' liability[5], provisions such as this only give an indication of the type of people who represent the 'mind' of a company. The constitution of the company as a whole must be taken into account[6]. In *Tesco*, Lord Morris considered the provision in the Trade Descriptions Act 1968 on directors' liability – which is equivalent to s 157 of the EPA 1990[7] – and held that it was 'an indication . . . (which need not necessarily be an all-embracing indication)' of who is responsible for corporate governance. In *El Ajou v Dollar Land Holdings plc*[8], Nourse LJ stated that:

'It is important to emphasise that management and control is not something to be considered generally or in the round. It is necessary to identify the natural person or persons having management and control in relation to the act or omission in point[9]. . . . Decided cases show that, in regard to the requisite status and authority, the formal position, as regulated by the company's articles of association, service contracts and so forth, though highly relevant, may not be decisive'[10].

Overall, it would seem that the identification of the directing mind is a constitutional question for each organisation[11].

1 See for example *Tesco* at 146A/B and at 148F.
2 [1965] 1 All ER 725 at 729E: see also *Magna Plant v Mitchell* [1966] Crim LR 394 (note that a more lengthy extract than that actually contained in the court report is to be found in *Tesco* at 134E).
3 As well as the analysis of the nature of the state of mind of a company in *Lennard's Carrying Co Ltd v Asiatic Petroleum Co Ltd* [1914–15] All ER Rep 280 at 283.
4 *Tesco* at 146A; se also *Moore v I Bresler Ltd* [1944] 2 All ER 515.
5 See para 7.156ff.
6 *Tesco* per Lord Pearson at 148F. See also *Admiralty v SS Divina, The Truculent (Owners)*, [1951] 2 All ER 968 at 979C.
7 See para 7.156.
8 [1994] 2 All ER 685 at 696A/C.
9 See also *Meridian Global Fund Management Asia Ltd v Securities Commission* [1995] 2 AC 500.
10 See also *El Ajou v Dollar Land Holdings plc* [1994] 2 All ER 685 per Rose LJ at 699H/J.
11 Per Hoffmann LJ in *El Ajou* at 705F. See also *Arthur Guinness & Co (Dublin) Ltd v Owners of the Motor Vessel Freshfield, The Lady Gwendolen* [1965] 2 All ER 283.

7.131 In the case of a sole trader, the mind of the company will be that individual. If a small company delegates full responsibility to a manager, the manager will speak as the company, as that person is acting in the place of the employer. However, when there is a situation such as with Tesco Supermarkets, where there are hundreds of branches, it was not considered that the individual branch managers represented the mind and will of the company. But this was due to the constitution of the company, where there was considerable intermediate management and supervision of branch managers by way of inspectors, regional controllers and regional managers[1]. In other circumstances, it seems clear that where a person is delegated full discretion to act independently of the directors, then such a person is acting as the company[2].

1 See *Tesco* at 135G, 137J and at 150C/E.
2 *Tesco* per Lord Reid at 132G/H: see, in the case of whether persons employed by another are to be viewed as employees or independent contractors, *Performing Rights Society Ltd v Mitchell and Booker (Palais de Danse) Ltd* [1924] 1 KB 762.

7.132   In some cases, it is possible to ascertain the intention of the company by way of its actions. In *H L Bolton (Engineering) Co Ltd v T J Graham & Sons Ltd*[1], the three directors met informally without having formal board meetings or taking minutes. In that case, circumstantial evidence sufficed. At their request, an architect had drawn up plans for land occupied by tenants. This was viewed by the court as a clear indication that the company intended to seek repossession of a particular piece of land. Similarly, written instructions from directors to employees have been held as showing the company's state of mind[2].

1   [1956] 3 All ER 624 at 630H/I.
2   *Camden London Borough Council v Fine Fare Ltd* [1987] BTLC 317.

7.133   The above discussion has indicated that, for knowledge to be imputed on a company, the knowledge must be in the hands of a key decisionmaker. This may be a difficult matter for the prosecution to address. While articles of association are helpful in respect of companies, they are, as noted, only indicative. In other cases, interviews with decision-makers will be necessary. But again, care is needed. In *Woodhouse v Walsall Metropolitan Borough Council*[1], a manager of a waste treatment plant was held not to constitute the directing mind and will of his employer in the context of the directors' (etc) liability provision of the Control of Pollution Act 1974[2]. This was despite his own claim that he spoke for the company and also from evidence of internal company structures. In other instances, this line of inquiry might be stymied by persons exercising rights to silence. However, as noted at para 7.57ff in respect of *Westminster City Council v Croyalgrange*[3], at least some onus is placed on a company to show that it did not, in fact, have knowledge. In addition, the fact that someone declines to give evidence in proceedings is now admissible and inferences can be taken from it. Finally, it should also be appreciated that it does not necessarily hold that the knowledge of one key individual always causes the company to be found to know. An example might be when a director did an act 'behind the back' of the company and the other directors[4]. Given this context, it may be that in this increasingly environmentally-conscious age, the alternative strict liability approach of *Shanks & McEwan (Teesside)* and *Ashcroft* will prevail[5]. However, it would seem necessary that this matter be judicially considered further. Three reasons make this desirable: (1) the decisions of *Ashcroft* and *Shanks & McEwan (Teesside)*, although setting a low threshold on *what* needs to be known, relate only to the activities of waste management companies. Section 33(1) of the EPA 1990 also pertains to bodies less directly concerned with waste management, embracing any company who produces waste[6]; (2) the very existence of decisions such as *Tesco Supermarkets Ltd v Nattrass*, which sets a high threshold on *who* must have the knowledge; and (3) the insertion of the word 'knowingly' before 'cause' in s 33(1) of the EPA 1990, which creates such an obvious contrast to water pollution law.

1   [1993] Env LR 30: discussed at para 7.159ff.
2   Control of Pollution Act 1974, s 87(1); equivalent to s 157 of the EPA 1990 – see para 7.156ff.
3   [1986] 2 All ER 353.
4   See *El Ajou v Dollar Land Holdings plc* [1994] 2 All ER 685.
5   See also *National Rivers Authority (Southern Region) v McAlpine Homes (East) Ltd* [1994] Env LR 198 (see para 7.75) and see, for example, in the context of defective building construction, *Gammon (Hong Kong) Ltd v A-G of Hong Kong* [1984] 2 All ER 503. But other statutes where strict liability applies seem distinguishable from the EPA 1990 for the reason that, in the absence of an underling causing an employer to be liable, the particular law would not be workable: see for example, *Tesco Stores Ltd v Brent London Borough Council* [1993] 2 All ER 718 (video sold to a minor); *Lindley v George W Horner & Co Ltd* [1950] 1 All ER 234 and *Lamb v Sunderland and District Creamery Ltd* [1951] 1 All ER 923 (food safety); *Director General of Fair Trading v Pioneer Concrete (UK) Ltd* [1995] 1 AC 456 (restrictive practices); and see, generally, *Meridian Global Funds Management Asia Ltd v Securities Commission* [1995] 2 AC 500.
6   Including, *inter alia*, supermarkets such as Tesco Stores.

7.134 Finally, it should also be appreciated that, while both the employer and employee can be charged separately with the same offence, the circumstances in which each finds itself will be usually quite different. This factor will apply as much to matters of knowledge as it does to the possible statutory defences in s 33(7) of the EPA 1990. While it is obvious that only an employee can invoke the defence of acting under instructions of an employer[1], it is open to both to show that they took all reasonable precautions and exercised all due diligence[2]. Given the quite different circumstances of the employee and employer, the nature of the required precautions and diligence may well be quite different for each of these individuals. A similar comment also applies to sentencing.

1   EPA 1990, s 33(7)(b): see para 7.152.
2   EPA 1990, s 33(7)(a): see para 7.145ff.

Who is involved when waste is deposited, treated, kept or disposed of?

7.135 Given that the above analysis has suggested that a strict liability regime may hold to those persons who hold waste management licences and contravene s 33 of the EPA 1990, it would seem that waste contractors acting as employers can be charged with 'depositing' waste, in the same fashion as can their drivers. As already noted, the *Shanks and McEwan (Teesside)* judgment clearly indicates that a waste management company is potentially liable – subject to the statutory defences in s 33(7) of the EPA 1990 – when an employee breaches s 33[1]. But despite *R v Leighton*'s assertion that information can be laid in the alternative[2], it remains important to consider whether employers can in this context actually 'deposit' waste under the EPA 1990, or whether their actions always involve matters of permission or causation with their concomitant additional burden of proof in respect of knowledge[3].

1   See para 7.94ff.
2   See also *R v Leighton and Town & Country Refuse Ltd* [1997] Env LR 411 at 419: see para 7.104ff.
3   But note that, in cases where motor vehicles are involved in waste 'deposits', s 33(5) requires that controller of the vehicle to have 'knowingly caused' the deposit, regardless of whether instructions to that effect were issued (see para 7.06). However, see also the analysis of s 33(5) in *Shanks & McEwan (Teesside)* [1997] JPL 824 at 833/834.

7.136 From the face of s 33(1)(a) of the EPA 1990, it is not clear whether or not a driver *and* an employer can be convicted of *depositing* waste, or whether it should be alleged that the driver is 'depositing' waste and the employer is either 'knowingly causing' (or even 'knowingly permitting') the deposit. However, if it is held that only the driver 'deposits' waste, then this does not appear to fall in line with the construction and purpose of s 33(1)(b). No driver is ever likely to 'treat' or 'keep' waste – this is likely to be the function of the organisation as a whole.

7.137 It also seems appropriate to look to analogies with road traffic law in these respects. As noted earlier, the offence provisions of many road traffic statutes frequently refer to the 'user' of the vehicle, along with persons who 'cause or permit' the vehicle's use. The result is offences of similar construction to s 33(1)(a) or s 33(1)(b) of the EPA 1990[1]. In respect of driver/employee culpability, the road traffic case of *James & Son Ltd v Smee*[2] held that: 'It cannot be said that only the servant uses and that the master merely causes or permits such use'. This was affirmed in *Ross Hillman v Bond*[3] in relation to the Road Traffic Act 1972[4], where it was found that '. . . a master "uses" the vehicle which his servant is driving on the master's business'[5]. In the case of 'users' of vehicles, the offence in road traffic law is strict liability, whilst 'causing' or 'permitting' vehicles to be used is seen as requiring the establishment of *mens rea*[6]. Finally, in *Hallett Silberman v Cheshire County Council*[7] it was confirmed that overlaps will exist in these provisions and that persons, particularly employers, will both use a vehicle – as will any driver – but also may simultaneously 'cause or permit' its use:

'No doubt by separately proscribing particular acts which amount to causing or permitting the use of a vehicle, Parliament imposed some limits on the persons whose activities were to be regarded as amounting to the use of a vehicle but, as in the case of an employer, a person can at the same time be a person who uses and a person who causes or permits another to use. Nor does it follow that two persons may not in relation to a particular use both be persons who use.'

1 See *R v Leighton and Town & Country Refuse Ltd* [1997] Env LR 411 at 416.
2 [1954] 3 All ER 273 at 277H.
3 [1974] RTR 279: see also *Hallett Silberman v Cheshire County Council* [1993] RTR 32, where the hirer of a tractor unit and a self-employed driver were both held to be 'using' the vehicle.
4 Now the Road Traffic Act 1988.
5 *Ross Hillman v Bond* at 290C/D; owners of vehicles on hire to a third party have been held not to be 'using' the vehicle: *Windle v Dunning & Son Ltd* [1968] 2 All ER 46. Depending upon the facts, it is possible that they can be convicted of *causing* the vehicle to be used. In addition, when a third party is permitted to drive a motor vehicle, the person who granted the permission cannot be convicted of 'using' the vehicle unless there is a master-servant relationship (*Crawford v Haughton* [1972] 1 All ER 535): but see criticisms in *Hallett Silberman v Cheshire County Council* at 38H/J.
6 See for example, *James and Son Ltd v Smee* [1954] 3 All ER 273 at 278A; *Ross Hillman v Bond* at 290C.
7 [1993] RTR 32 at 40F/G.

7.138 By way of an analogy to the above judgments, it may well be that a employer can be held to 'deposit' waste contrary to s 33(1)(a) of the EPA 1990. At the same time, that person may well have also 'knowingly caused' or 'knowingly permitted' the waste to be deposited. If this is right, the prosecution does not need to establish the employer's knowledge, it can look to the unqualified offence of depositing waste. Once it has been established that the employer was responsible for the deposit of the waste[1], all the employer is left with is to rely on the statutory defences in s 33(7) of the EPA 1990.

1 See the parallels with 'using' motor vehicles, as described earlier and see also *Hallett Silberman v Cheshire County Council* at 41J to 42C.

7.139 If s 33(1)(a) or (b) of the EPA 1990 is to be construed in this manner, a further issue must be considered. This relates to s 33(5) which holds that, when waste is deposited from a motor vehicle, the controller of the vehicle shall be held to have *knowingly caused* the deposit regardless of whether that person issued instructions for the deposit to be made. This requirement would indicate that two elements of s 33(1)(a) are being contravened when a driver deposits waste from a vehicle. Both the driver and the employer 'deposit' the waste and also 'knowingly cause' its deposit[1]. Whether both bodies would be convicted is a different matter. Once more, much would depend on whether the employer could satisfy the statutory defences of s 33(7) of the EPA 1990[2].

1 See *Hallett Silberman v Cheshire County Council*: however, it seems unlikely that, notwithstanding the reference in s 33(5) solely to 'knowingly causing', drivers could 'knowingly permit' their own deposits: see *Keene v Muncaster* [1980] RTR 377 and *Waddell v Winter* (1967) 202 Estates Gazette 1225; see also *Shanks & McEwan (Teesside)* [1997] JPL 824 at 833/834.
2 See para 7.144.

A restriction on the scope of s 33(1) of the EPA 1990

7.140 While *Shanks & McEwan (Midlands)* has alluded to the fact that s 33(6) of the EPA 1990 is restricted in its embrace, it should be also noted that s 33(1) also has a specific and significant limitation. Whilst Bingham LJ's consideration of the word 'deposit' in *Leigh Land Reclamation Ltd v Walsall Metropolitan Borough Council*[1] was subsequently reversed, his second finding relating to breaches of licence conditions which are unrelated to the actual deposit of waste still appears to be of significance. Although it concerns to the earlier Control of Pollution Act 1974, it would appear to place limits upon the scope of s 33(1) when licence conditions are breached. Section 33(1) makes it an offence, *inter alia*, to 'deposit controlled waste . . . unless . . . the deposit is in accordance with the licence' and to 'treat, keep or dispose of controlled waste . . . except under and in accordance with a waste management licence'. What should be noted is that some active operation is being referred to, which involves waste being deposited, or kept, or treated or disposed of. This means that only the conditions of a licence which relate to such an operation can be enforced through s 33(1). Other conditions which are unconnected to the deposit, treatment, etc of waste must be enforced though s 33(6). An example of the latter might be conditions which requires landfill gas to be monitored or a site notice to be displayed at the entrance.

1   (1990) 155 JP 547: see para 7.17ff.

7.141   In *Leigh Land* it was argued by the prosecution that, once a licence condition was breached, any further deposit of waste on the site would result in an offence being committed. Whether or not the nature of the waste subsequently being deposited was within the terms of the licence was immaterial. The fact that waste was being deposited at all was sufficient. This argument was not upheld by Bingham LJ[1]:

> 'These deposits of plastic off-cuts, filter cakes, office waste and wood and vegetation, on which the informations were founded, were of authorised materials and no criticism is made of the manner in which they were deposited. To hold that those deposits were not made in accordance with the conditions of the licence because there was some improper deposit previously or because . . . there was no sign board or no eating facilities in the site office would strain the language of this statute beyond the limits acceptable in a criminal statute . . .'

Accordingly, for s 33(1) to be used to deal with non-compliance with licence conditions, the non-compliance must directly relate to the waste which is deposited or, as the case may be, which is kept, treated or disposed of[2]. Non-compliance of conditions other than these should be addressed by the separate offence provision contained in s 33(6) of the EPA 1990.

1   *Leigh Land* at 556F/G.
2   See also *R v Leighton and Town & Country Refuse Ltd* [1997] Env LR 411 at 427.

7.142   This interpretation was considered subsequently in *Thames Waste Management Ltd v Surrey County Council*[1], in respect of non-compliance with a condition which required wastes at a landfill to be subject to daily cover. In this instance, *Leigh Land* was distinguished[2]. In *Leigh Land* there was, as noted, no criticism of the nature of the waste being deposited at the site. The issue lay in activities unconnected to the wastes which were identified in the informations as being deposited. However, in *Thames Waste Management*, the manner by which the waste specified in the informations as being deposited was clearly contrary to the licence as the waste was not covered properly. It was also held that circumstances such as these cause an overlap in offences between s 33(1) and s 33(6), the prosecution can validly serve informations under either sections.

1   [1997] Env LR 148.
2   *Thames Waste Management* at 155.

7.143   However, there are obvious limits to the area of overlap between s 33(1) and s 33(6). Other conditions may be totally unconnected with waste being deposited or to a lesser extent kept or disposed of. In *Leigh Land*, Bingham LJ made mention of site notice boards and the site office. Other instances may concern environmental monitoring and general environmental control such as leachate management at landfills or the cleaning of interceptors at scrapyards and waste treatment plants. Certainly, once a landfill site has been filled, conditions will require enforcement which inevitably are unconnected with any active disposal operation. However, these are generally the sole responsibility of the site operator. Hence, as was alluded to in *Shanks & McEwan (Midlands)*, such conditions should be enforced through s 33(6) of the EPA 1990.

SECTION 33 OF THE EPA 1990: THE STATUTORY DEFENCES

7.144   The foregoing material has emphasised the importance of the statutory defences set out in s 33(7) of the EPA 1990[1]. The primary function of the defences is to avoid the creation of absolute offences, whereby persons are punished regardless of guilt or blame. It will be apparent that they have particular significance in the context of companies, where significant delegation of responsibility to underlings is inevitable. Such protection becomes crucial to waste management companies, where convictions under the EPA 1990 are both relevant offences under that Act[2] and prescribed offences under the Controlled Waste (Registration of Carriers and Seizure of Vehicles) Regulations 1991[3]. Such convictions may mean that an organisation may no longer be considered suitable to act as a controlled waste carrier/broker or, as the case may be, to hold waste management licences.

1   As amended by the Environment Act 1995, s 120, Sch 22, para 64: the text of s 33(7) of the EPA 1990 is contained at para 7.10 above. See also *R v Smith* [1999] Env LR 433.
2   See para 8.117ff.
3   See para 6.63.

Taking reasonable precautions and exercising due diligence

7.145   In respect of the first statutory defence in s 33(7)(a) of the EPA 1990, what amounts to all reasonable precautions, and the nature of all due diligence, will turn primarily on the facts of the case[1]. It would seem that the question of whether the precautions were 'reasonable' is subjective, in the sense of whether it was reasonable for the persons accused to take whatever precautions they took[2]. Matters of foreseeability are relevant in establishing the statutory defence[3]. Indeed, the concept of 'due diligence' itself may well be analogous to the common phrase of taking 'reasonable care'[4]. Furthermore, the concept should be viewed as dynamic in its nature, in the sense that what constitutes due diligence will change with time: people should learn from previous mistakes[5]. Due diligence has been held to be the opposite of negligence, with negligence connoting a lack of care[6]. Due diligence therefore implies establishing an effective management system to avoid the commission of criminal offences[7].

1   See *Riverstone Meat Co Pty Ltd v Lancashire Shipping Co Ltd* [1960] 1 All ER 193 at 201D & G and 223H/I; see also *Tesco Supermarkets Ltd v Nattrass* [1971] 2 All ER 127 and *Environment Agency v Short* [1999] Env LR 300.
2   See *Austin Rover Group v HM Inspector of Factories* [1989] 3 WLR 520 at 534C, albeit that a differently worded defence – from the Health and Safety at Work etc Act 1974 – is being referred to.
3   *Austin Rover Group v HM Inspector of Factories* [1989] 3 WLR 520 at 525G, 526F.
4   *Riverstone Meat Co Pty Ltd v Lancashire Shipping Co Ltd* [1960] 1 All ER 193 at 203H/I, 219H, 223G.
5   See *Riverstone Meat Co Pty Ltd v Lancashire Shipping Co Ltd* [1960] 1 All ER 193 at 226E.
6   *Tesco Supermarkets Ltd v Nattrass* [1971] 2 All ER 127 at 156D.

7 See also *Texas Homecare v Stockport Metropolitan Borough Council* [1987] Crim LR 709, *Barker v Hargreaves* [1981] RTR 197 and *Walkers Snack Foods v Coventry City Council* [1998] 3 All ER 163.

7.146 In general, if s 33(7) of the EPA 1990 is read in conjunction with the other requirements of the EPA 1990 and the duty of care[1], it becomes apparent that the threshold of due diligence should be viewed as quite a high one. The duty applies to all parties in waste transfers and hence to every company that produces waste. It may therefore be difficult to rebut the argument that a fundamental ignorance of the need to fulfil the basic requirements of the duty of care cannot be squared against the need to take reasonable precautions or exercise the requisite due diligence. A failure of the basic tenets of the duty[2] seems unlikely to satisfy this statutory defence.

1 EPA 1990, s 34, and in particular see Department of the Environment *Waste Management The Duty of Care A Code of Practice*, (1996) Second Edition, HMSO, London; see also para 3.06ff.
2 For example, to ensure that registered waste carriers are used, or that the waste is adequately described (see para 3.129ff) on a transfer note and that the materials that make up a load of waste are suitable for the intended site.

7.147 Individuals, their company, its directors and other similarly senior staff are all open to prosecution for offences under the EPA 1990. Obviously, a company can only suffer prosecution due to the acts of one or more employees. However, the question of whether an act of an employee will cause an employer to be liable is a potentially diffi-cult area of law. It is by no means always the case that employers are always respon-sible for employee's acts and that criminal liability will follow. Furthermore, it is certainly not the case that individual directors and other senior managers will be personally liable for such acts. While corporate liability is discussed below, the ques-tion of directors' liability follows.

7.148 The leading judgment on the imputation of knowledge from an employee to an employer is *Tesco Supermarkets Ltd v Nattrass*[1]. While the construction of the statu-tory defences in trading standards law as considered in *Tesco v Nattrass* is substan-tially different to that of the EPA 1990[2], the House of Lords set out a series of important general principles in respect of the liability of companies. The context of statutory provisions on trading standards or environmental protection is well expressed by Lord Diplock[3]:

'Where, in the way that business is now conducted, they are likely to be acts or omissions of employees of that party and subject to his orders, the most effective method of deterrence is to place upon the employer the responsibility of doing everything which lies within his power to prevent his employees from doing anything which will result in the commission of an offence.

This, I apprehend, is the rational and moral justification for creating in the field of consumer protection, as also in the field of public health and safety, offences of "strict liability" for which an employer or principal, in the course of whose business the offences were committed, is criminally liable, notwithstanding that they are due to acts and omissions of his servants or agents which were done without his knowl-edge or consent or even were contrary to his orders.'

However, this does not mean that a body corporate will always be held liable regard-less of matters of blame or knowledge. Lord Diplock continues[4]:

'But this rational and moral justification does not extend to penalising an employer or principal who has done everything that he can reasonably be expected to do by supervision or inspection, by improvement of his business methods or by exhorting those whom he may be expected to control or influence, to prevent the commission of the offence . . .⁵. What the employer or principal can be reasonably be expected to do to prevent the commission of an offence will depend on the gravity of the injury which it is sought to prevent and the nature of the business in the course of which such offences are committed.'⁶

1   [1971] 2 All ER 127: see also, for example, *R v P&O European Ferries (Dover) Ltd* (1990) 93 Cr App Rep 72.
2   It is important to appreciate that of critical significance to the outcome of the *Tesco* case was the wording of the statutory defence contained in the Trade Descriptions Act 1968, which is worded significantly differently to s 33(7)(a) of the EPA 1990: s 24 of the Trade Description Act 1968 allows a person charged with an offence to prove that the commission of the offence was 'due to a mistake or to reliance on information supplied to him or the act or default of another person, an accident or some other cause beyond his control; *and* (b) that he took all reasonable precautions and exercised all due diligence to avoid commission of such an offence by himself or any person under their control' [author's emphasis]. In s 33(7)(a) of the EPA 1990, there is no reference to 'another person' – a fact that helped to acquit Tesco Supermarkets. A different statutory defence in the Video Recordings Act 1984 resulted in the conviction of the supermarket chain of selling an 18 certificate film to a minor: see *Tesco Stores Ltd v Brent London Borough Council* [1993] 2 All ER 718.
3   *Tesco v Nattrass* at 151D: note that a larger extract than shown here is used approvingly by Boreham J in *Ashcroft v Cambro Waste Products Ltd* [1981] 3 All ER 699 at 700J, clearly suggesting that certain waste management offences fall within ambit of strict liability offences as envisaged by Lord Diplock.
4   *Tesco v Nattrass* at 151F.
5   At this point Lord Diplock makes reference to *Lim Chin Aik v R* [1963] AC 160 at 170 and *Sweet v Parsley* [1970] AC 132 at 163, [1969] 1 All ER 347 at 362.
6   [1971] 2 All ER 127: discussed below. See also *Seaboard Offshore Ltd v Secretary of State for Transport, The Safe Carrier* [1993] 3 All ER 25. In *R v British Steel plc* [1995] 1 WLR 1356 it was held that, in contrast to the wording of the Health and Safety at Work etc Act 1974, the presence of a 'due diligence' defence in trading standards law was a powerful indication that the purpose of trading standards offences was to penalise those at fault, not those who were in no way to blame.

7.149   In respect of companies, while responsibility can be delegated, corporate liability for the actions of the delegatee cannot. To avoid a company being found liable for the acts of an employee under s 33(7) of the EPA 1990 on the grounds of failure to exercise all due diligence and take reasonable precautions, the defence must clearly show that adequate systems of supervision were in place to ensure that, whenever practicable, employees' actions were kept under control. There is, not surprisingly, more to this than setting up a paper system of procedures. As Lord Reid notes in *Tesco Supermarkets v Nattrass*¹:

'But if justices were to accept as sufficient a paper scheme and perfunctory efforts to enforce it they would not be doing their duty – that would not be "due diligence" on the part of the employer.'²

Similarly Viscount Dilhorne held, in relation to an employer³:

'That an employer, whether a company or an individual, may reasonably appoint someone to secure that the obligations imposed by the [Trade Descriptions] Act are observed cannot be doubted. Only by doing so can an employer who owns and runs a number of shops or a big store hope to secure that the Act is complied with, but the appointment by him of someone to discharge the duties imposed by the Act in no way relieves him from having to show that he has taken all reasonable precautions and has exercised all due diligence if he seeks to establish the statutory defence. He cannot excuse himself if the person appointed fails to do what he is supposed to do unless he can show that he himself has taken such precautions and exercised such diligence. Whether or not he has done so is a question of fact and while it may be that the appointment of a competent person amounts in the circumstances of a particular case to the taking of all reasonable precautions, if he does nothing after making the appointment to see that proper steps are in fact being taken to comply with the Act, it cannot be said that he exercised all due diligence.'

The latter sentiment seems particularly apt in the context of the trend of many companies in respect of regulatory compliance. Increasingly managers are being employed with designated briefs on environmental matters and companies are establishing internal performance review systems, including environmental audits and compliance monitoring.

1   *Tesco v Nattrass* at 135E.
2   Albeit that, whilst *Durham County Council v Peter Connors Industrial Services* [1992] Crim LR 743, DC involved statutory defences different to those appearing in s 33 of the EPA 1990, this general point seems to have been very much in the court's mind; see also Laurence D (1992) 'Company Loses its Battle in Divisional Court' *Wastes Management* Sept 1992, pp 28–29.
3   *Tesco v Nattrass* at 145B/C.

7.150   Once a system has been set up whereby the employer can show that due diligence and all reasonable precautions are being exercised, the statutory defence is proven. As Lord Diplock put it in *Tesco v Nattrass*[1]:

'If the principal has taken all reasonable precautions in the selection and training of servants to perform supervisory duties and has laid down an effective system of supervision and used due diligence to see that it is observed, he is entitled to rely on a default by a superior servant in his supervisory duties as a defence . . ., as well as, or instead of, on an act or default of an inferior servant who has no supervisory duties under his contract of employment. Thus, the supervisory servant may have failed to give adequate instructions to the inferior servant or may have failed to take reasonable steps to see that his instructions were obeyed. In the former case the supervisory servant may alone be to blame. In the latter case both may be to blame. Or it may be . . . that the commission of the offence is due to a combination of separate acts or omissions by two more inferior servants none of which taken by itself would have resulted in the commission on an offence.'

However, it should be emphasised that the latter circumstances apply, if and only if, due diligence and reasonable precautions on behalf of the employer have been established.

1   *Tesco v Nattrass* at 154C/D.

7.151   From the above, it is thus submitted that, when a company is faced with a prosecution for 'knowingly permitting' or 'knowingly causing' contrary to s 33 of the EPA 1990, there is a double emphasis upon the internal management and reporting system. Firstly, as noted earlier, the company needs to address the 'knowingly' element. It needs to be able to show to the court[1] that it had a sufficiently robust system to make sure that knowledge came upward in the company to those who represent it. If it cannot provide evidence that such as system was robust, then it appears open for the prosecution to claim that the company 'looked the other way'[2]. Once it is clearly indicated that the company could not possibly – and genuinely – have known about the incident, then acquittal appears certain[3]. The second stage involving the statutory defence only comes into play after it has been shown that an employer did have the requisite knowledge. Then the internal management system must have been robust enough to demonstrate that the 'all due diligence' and 'all reasonable precautions' tests have been satisfied in respect of statutory defences.

1   Note that, as set out at para 7.57ff, if the approach taken in *Croyalgrange* [1986] 2 All ER 353 is followed, the burden to establish this matter rests at least partly on the defence.
2   Cf Lord Bridge in *Croyalgrange* at 359C and see para 7.57ff.

3   But in the light of *R v Environment Agency ex p Shanks & McEwan (Teesside) Ltd*, waste
    management companies in particular seem under a vigorous form of strict liability.

Acting under instructions of an employer

7.152   The second statutory defence in s 33(7) of the EPA 1990[1] is primarily aimed at
persons who are drivers of waste delivery vehicles or lowly plant operatives. The sub-
section includes the phrase that the person 'neither knew nor had reason to suppose'
that the acts contravened s 33(1)[2]. An essentially similar phrase was contained in the
Control of Pollution Act 1974[3]: 'did not know and had no reason to suppose'. In *Kent
County Council v Rackham*[4], the latter phrase was held, not surprisingly, to follow its
ordinary meaning. French J found that the word 'suppose' should have a meaning
closer to 'suspect' than 'believe'. Matters concerning questions of knowledge are
covered at para 7.55ff.

1   Sub-section (b).
2   Interestingly, there is no cross reference from the EPA 1990, s 33(7)(b) to offences under s 33(6).
3   Section 3(4)(a)(ii).
4   (4 February, 1991 unreported), QBD.

Emergencies

7.153   The third statutory defence in s 33(7) of the EPA 1990 was subject to amendment by the Environment Act 1995[1] and is now somewhat more difficult to dissect[2]. It
appears to be constructed to require that, regardless of what the acts were, they had to
be done in an 'emergency in order to avoid danger to human health'. The nature of the
emergency seems therefore restricted, relating only to human health protection. If
there is no danger to human health, then it would seem that this statutory defence falls
without getting any further. However, if it is satisfied to this point, the defence is also
then subject to two additional caveats. '[S]uch steps as were reasonably practicable in
the circumstances' must have been taken by the person accused of breaching the EPA
1990, s 33 with the objective of minimising pollution of the environment and harm to
human health[3]. Secondly, the sub-section also requires that the Agency is informed 'as
soon as reasonably practicable' afterwards. Again, if these matters are not satisfied, the
statutory defence falls.

1   Environment Act 1995, s 120, Sch 22, para 64.
2   The full wording is contained at para 7.10.
3   The nature of 'pollution of the environment and harm to human health' is discussed at para 8.40ff.

7.154   The definition of an emergency was considered in *Waste Incineration Services
Ltd v Dudley Metropolitan Borough Council*[1] in respect of the Control of Pollution Act
1974[2]. *Waste Incineration Services* concerned the breach of a condition of waste
disposal licence which forbade bank holiday operation. On the basis of the facts of the
case – particularly that the waste could instead have been stored temporarily elsewhere
at the site of production – it was held that no emergency existed at the time the condition was contravened. Nolan LJ held that the term 'emergency' must bear its ordinary
meaning[3]. Accordingly the dictionary definition – that an emergency meant 'a state of
things unexpectedly arising and urgently demanding attention' – was sufficient.
Whether an emergency arose was viewed by the court as a question of fact, not law[4].

1   [1992] 1 Env LR 29.
2   Control of Pollution Act 1974 s 3(4), the wording which is very close to s 33(7)(c) of the EPA 1990.
3   *Waste Incineration Services* at 33.
4   *Waste Incineration Services* at 33: see also *Larchbank v British Petrol (Owners)* [1943] AC 299 at
    304 and 307.

Statutory defences: the burden of proof[1]

7.155 It is for the defence to satisfy the statutory defences. A provision similar to s 33(7)(a) of the EPA 1990 can be found the Trade Descriptions Act 1968[2]. The latter was considered in *Tesco Supermarkets Ltd v Nattrass*[3], where Nolan LJ held that, in relation to a person charged under that Act[4]:

'. . . the onus of proving that he was not to blame lies on him. It is reasonable that this should be so since the facts which constitute the defence lie within his knowledge and not within that of the prosecution.'

Similarly in another trade descriptions case, *Naish v Gore*[5], Lord Widgery held that:

'It is for the defendant to prove that he took all reasonable precautions, and if he has taken none, that means he must prove that none could reasonably have been taken.'[6]

While the onus is placed on the defence in this matter, the burden of proof is lower. It is based on an evaluation of the evidence on the criteria of the balance of probabilities, as opposed to the establishment of the evidence beyond reasonable doubt[7].

1 See also para 10.51ff.
2 Trade Descriptions Act 1968, s 24(1).
3 [1971] 2 All ER 127.
4 *Tesco v Nattrass* at 152E/F.
5 [1971] 3 All ER 737, at 741G: see, in respect of sampling, *Rotherham Metropolitan Borough Council v Raysun (UK) Ltd* 153 JP 37. See also *Sherratt v Geralds the American Jewellers Ltd* (1970) 68 LGR 256; *Simmons v Potter* [1975] RTR 347; and *Texas Homecare Ltd v Stockport Metropolitan Borough Council* [1987] Crim LR 709. In respect of an employee not receiving instructions from an employer, see *Lynch v Tudhope* 1983 SCCR 337.
6 See, in the field of health and safety, *Austin Rover Group v HM Inspectorate of Factories* [1989] 3 WLR 520 at 526F and 534F.
7 See *R v Carr-Briant* [1943] 2 All ER 156, at 158H/159A; *R v Dunbar* [1957] 2 All ER 737 at 740B; *R v Hudson* [1965] 1 All ER 721 at 724B; and see also *Waste Incineration Services Ltd v Dudley Metropolitan Borough Council* [1992] 1 Env LR 29 at 33.

DIRECTORS' LIABILITY

7.156 Section 157 of the EPA 1990 makes those responsible for the operation of a company personally liable for its misdeeds. It is therefore possible to separately prosecute a company and its officers for offences under Part II of the EPA 1990. In relation to companies, two aspects must be settled for s 157(1) of the EPA 1990 to have application. Firstly, those individuals charged must fall with the categories of 'any director, manager, secretary or other similar officer of the body corporate or a person who was purporting to act in any such capacity'. Secondly, the events which resulted in the company committing the offence must be proven to have been committed with 'the consent or connivance of, or to have been attributable to any neglect' by those responsible for the company. Hence the two questions required to be addressed in any proceedings where s 157 of the EPA 1990 is invoked is (a) was the accused acting in a position in the company which is subject to s 157 and, if the answer to (a) is affirmative, (b) were those actions due to the person's consent, connivance or neglect? Obviously, the existence of the second arm of s 157 sets up an additional burden of proof on the prosecution over and above that which was necessary to demonstrate that the company itself committed an offence.

'Directors, managers, secretaries and other similar officers'

7.157 Phrases similar to s 157 of the EPA 1990 occur in other statutes including the Trade Descriptions Act 1968[1], the Companies Act 1948[2], the Fair Trading Act 1973[3], the Theft Act 1968[4] and the Fire Precautions Act 1971[5]. In relation to the equivalent provision to s 157 of the EPA 1990 in the Fire Precautions Act 1971, Simon Brown J held in *R v Boal*[6] that its purpose is to[7]:

'. . . fix with criminal liability only those who are in a position of real authority, the decision-makers within the company who have both the power and responsibility to decide corporate policy and strategy. It is to catch those responsible for putting proper procedures in place; it is not meant to strike at underlings.'

1   Section 20(1).
2   Section 441.
3   Section 132.
4   Section 18.
5   Section 23.
6   [1992] 3 All ER 177.
7   *Boal* at 181J.

7.158   It is necessary, therefore, to determine the boundary between the real decision-makers and their underlings. The nature of 'directors' is relatively straightforward[1] as it is those identified in the articles of association of any company. As discussed below, persons who have job titles such as 'technical director' may not be sufficiently senior to be embraced with the meaning of 'director' under s 157(1) of the EPA 1990. In a manner similar to directors, the term 'secretary' in s 157 refers only to the company secretary, who will be similarly identified in a firm's articles. Details of directors and secretaries can be obtained from Companies House. The nature of 'officers' and 'managers' is less obvious from the face of statute. From *Registrar of Restrictive Trading Agreements v W H Smith & Son Ltd*[2], it would seem that the terms 'officers' and 'managers' overlap.

1   See *Gibson v Barton* (1875) LR 10 QB 329 at 336.
2   [1969] 3 All ER 1065 at 1069H/I.

7.159   The decision in *R v Boal* was considered approvingly in *Woodhouse v Walsall Metropolitan Borough Council*[1] in relation to s 87(1) of the Control of Pollution Act 1974. Section 157(1) of the EPA 1990 is the direct replacement to s 87(1). Mr Woodhouse, the general manager of Caird Environmental's Minworth waste treatment plant, was found not to be sufficiently senior in the company to be caught by s 87(1) of the Control of Pollution Act 1974. Despite being in charge of the facility, he had neither the power nor the responsibility to decide corporate policy and strategy[2].

1   [1993] Env LR 30.
2   See also *Gibson v Barton* (1875) LR 10 QB 329 at 336ff.

7.160   In *Woodhouse*, McCowan LJ notes[1] that, despite the claim by the accused at interview that he did have the authority to speak on behalf of the company, there was no evidence presented to suggest that he did, in fact, have such authority. This would appear to suggest that corroboration, through the articles of association of the company[2] or by way of a statement from an appointed spokesman or a board member of the company, is needed to enable the prosecution to assert the true picture.

1   *Woodhouse* at 33.
2   See *Gibson v Barton* (1875) LR 10 QB 329 at 337.

7.161   The finding that s 157(1) of the EPA 1990 does not extend to underlings other than very senior managers means that, for example, certain persons classed as 'technical competent managers' under the Certificate of Technical Competence (COTC) scheme contained in the Waste Management Licensing Regulations 1994[1], will not normally be viewed as sufficiently senior to fall within s 157(1). This will apply to many persons employed by the larger waste management companies who have the job title 'site manager' or even 'area manager'.

1   SI 1994/1056, reg 4 as amended by SI 1996/634, reg 2(2) and SI 1997/2203, reg 2: see para 8.136ff.

7.162   It should be noted that the term 'manager or other similar officer' in s 157 of the EPA 1990 covers a range of persons who exercise real power within a company. For this reason, the Director of Roads in Strathclyde Regional Council, for example, was held to fall within a provision equivalent to s 157 of the EPA 1990 in respect of a serious workplace accident[1].

1   *Armour v Skeen* 1977 SLT 71 at 74/75.

7.163   In certain cases, it may be that a person of status different from that formally identified in the company structure is in fact the key decision-maker. This may happen in relation to companies in receivership and also in respect of individuals who, for one reason or other, are exercising the real power 'behind the scenes'.

7.164   Given the wide-ranging powers of receivers and administrators in the running of companies, it is not surprising that they may be caught by s 157 of the EPA 1990. It is possible that many fall within the phrase 'other similar officer of the body corporate' in s 157[1]. In *Registrar of Restrictive Trading Agreements v W H Smith & Son Ltd*[2] it was held that an 'officer' is 'a person who is managing in a governing role the affairs of the company itself'[3]. Receivers and administrators will be caught if they end up undertaking significant functions involving corporate governance[4]. Section 157(1) of the EPA 1990 also relates to 'shadow directors' who, while not appearing on the articles of association of the company, act as key decision-makers[5].

1   See *Re X Co Ltd* [1907] 2 Ch 92 at 96.
2   [1969] 3 All ER 1065.
3   See also *Re Home Treat Ltd* [1991] BCC 165 at 171.
4   Compare *Re B Johnson & Co (Builders) Ltd* [1955] 2 All ER 775 to *Re Tasbian Ltd (No 3)* [1992] BCC 358.
5   See, for example, *El Ajou v Dollar Land Holdings plc* [1994] 2 All ER 685.

7.165   Section 157(1) of the EPA 1990 also refers to persons who are 'purporting to act' in the capacity of directors, managers etc. The purpose of this phrase is to ensure that s 157 does not only apply to persons who have been formally and validly appointed to the company. It causes liability to extend to key decision-makers whose appointment under a company's articles is defective[1].

1   This formula of wording corrected the defect in earlier legislation as expressed in *Dean v Hiesler* [1942] 2 All ER 340: see also *Gibson v Barton* [1875] LR 10 QB 329.

7.166   Finally s 157(2) of the EPA 1990 serves to extend the scope of application of s 157(1) in respect of instances where bodies corporate are run by their members. It holds that the actions or default of a member 'in connection with his functions of management' are to be classed as that of directors in s 157(1). This sub-section is often cited as having application in small companies. However, a person who has controlling shares in a privately owned company will usually also be acting as a director and hence subject to s 157(1) anyway. It may be that this sub-section also embraces elected members of local authorities who, while not formally being identified in s 157(1), may constitute the locus of control in such state bodies. The chairperson of a particular committee of the local authority might be an example of such an individual[1]. However, as discussed below in respect of directors' responsibilities, whether s 157 applies is a matter which is totally dependent upon that person's role in the organisation's corporate decisionmaking. Only those elected members who have a very 'hands on' approach to local government are likely to be subject to s 157.

1   Officers of the local authority will be caught by s 157(1): see *Armour v Skeen* 1977 SLT 71.

'Consent, connivance and neglect'

7.167   Having identified those persons to whom s 157 of the EPA 1990 is directed, it is then necessary to consider the nature of the acts they should or, as the case may be, should not do to avoid personal liability[1]. Given the practical breadth of the job descriptions and the variety of roles of persons identified in s 157(1), it difficult to set down general rules. However, the duties of directors are somewhat clearer and hence will be discussed below. It may well be that the basic principles which apply to directors also apply in general terms to other individuals of sufficient seniority to be subject to s 157.

1   *R v Leighton and Town and Country Refuse Ltd* [1997] Env LR 411 at 420 affirms that, where a prosecutor is unsure of which words 'consent', 'connivance' or 'neglect' are most appropriate, two or more can included together in an indictment without the risk of duplicity: see para 7.104ff.

7.168   The precise duties of directors will depend upon the nature and size of the business, and also the manner by which the business operates[1]. The latter will vary considerably, even between companies of similar size and market. Some companies may have extensive delegation, while in others directors may be much more 'hands on'. In considering the nature of a director's responsibilities 'it is necessary to consider not only the nature of a company's business, but also the manner in which the work of the company is in fact distributed between the directors and the other officials of the company'[2]. This view was separately confirmed in *Armour v Skeen*, where it was noted that each case will depend on its particular facts[3]. Within such a consideration, it is essential that the division of distribution is reasonable in order to avoid liability.

1   *Re City Equitable Fire Insurance Co Ltd* [1925] 1 Ch 407 at 426/427.
2   *City Equitable* at 427.
3   *Armour v Skeen* 1977 SLT 71 at 74/75.

7.169   In respect of a director's responsibilities, that individual must take 'reasonable care', a requirement which is to be measured on the degree of care an ordinary person might be expected to take in such circumstances. A director is thus not required to exhibit in the performance of duties a greater degree of skill than might be reasonably expected of that person[1]. A director is not expected to know of the minutiae of the company's business. However, when signatures are required on documents, directors must be reasonably diligent in ensuring that they know what they are signing. The nature of the responsibility will vary, depending upon the complexity of the document[2]. In respect of duties which may be 'properly' delegated to others, a director should, in the absence of suspicion[3], be justified in expecting that the delegated duties are being performed honestly[4]. Directors must exercise supervision of delegatees in a manner which ensures that they cannot be held to be responsible for an offence due to neglect[5], but they are not required to actively supervise the activities of the other directors[6]. In either case, they still need to exercise reasonable care[7].

1   *City Equitable* at 428.
2   See *Re D'Jan of London Ltd* [1993] BCC 646, where a simple insurance claim form, which contained material inaccuracies, was signed by a director without being read.
3   If there is suspicion, then this would not seem to hold: see *Huckerby v Elliott* [1970] 1 All ER 189 at 194D.
4   *City Equitable* at 429.

5   See the EPA 1990, s 157(1).
6   *Huckerby v Elliott* at 194B.
7   See *Hirschler v Birch* (1986) 151 JP 396, where a company run by two directors bought car brake
    lights when (a) it was their first venture in that area of commerce, and (b) when it was known that the
    lights had already been outlawed in some EC member states. The director not directly involved in the
    transaction should at least have inquired of the other director as to the legality of the enterprise.

7.170   Having set out the general context of the activities of persons subject to s 157 of the EPA 1990, it is appropriate to consider matters which constitute 'consent', 'connivance' and 'neglect'. In respect of matters involving 'consent' it has been held that a director consents to something when he is well aware of what is going on and agrees to it[1]. Consent means something more than passive acquiescence, involving a positive demonstrable affirmative act, which can be made orally or in writing, or may be surmised from conduct[2]. In the case of connivance, a working definition might involve a director who is aware of what is going on, but where agreement is tacit, not actively encouraging it but letting it continue and doing nothing about it[3].

1   *Huckerby v Elliott* at 194F/G.
2   *Bell v Alfred Franks Ltd* [1980] 1 WLR 340 at 347B, 348B and 350A, where it was also held that
    connivance involved knowledge of what was going on.
3   *Huckerby v Elliott* at 194G/H: see also *Phillips v Phillips* [1844] 1 Rob Eccl 144.

7.171   In *Re Hughes, Rea v Black*[1], it was held that 'neglect' applies only where a person, acting consciously, omits to do an act which should have been done[2]. It may also be that neglect occurs when a person is 'recklessly careless' about whether or not their duties are being fulfilled[3]. Returning to the fundamental point, whether someone can be held to have acted negligently can only be established from considering the nature of the person's duties which were alleged to have been neglected[4].

1   [1943] 2 All ER 269, at 271H.
2   See *Hirschler v Birch* (1986) 151 JP 396.
3   *City Equitable* at 525.
4   *City Equitable* at 427: see also *Crickitt v Kursaal Casino Ltd (No 2)* [1968] 1 All ER 139 at 147A.

7.172   It also needs to be appreciated that the statutory defences in s 33(7) of the EPA 1990 apply in this instance as to any other case where persons are charged under s 33 of the EPA 1990. As with the majority of offences likely to be committed in respect of s 33, the defence of exercising all reasonable precautions and exercising all due diligence will be that which is most often likely to be invoked in respect of directors and managers subject to individual charges. Clearly, there will be overlaps between what is required to be established in respect of the offence and the statutory defence. This will particularly be the case where a director is claimed to be liable under s 157 of the EPA 1990 due to neglect. Given that due diligence and neglect are almost opposites, it seems difficult to hold that a person who has been found to have neglected their duties can be held to have exercised all reasonable precautions and taken all due diligence. Hence the statutory defence appears somewhat superfluous in this context[1].

1   Although note that the burden of proof will be contrasting. Neglect must be proved by the prosecution
    on the grounds of 'beyond reasonable doubt'; due diligence must be established by the defence on the
    criteria of the 'balance of probabilities': see para 7.155.

OFFENCES CAUSED BY THE ACT OR DEFAULT OF ANOTHER PERSON

7.173   Section 158 of the EPA 1990 holds that where an offence has been committed by someone 'due to the act or default of some other person', the latter person may be convicted of the offence. This is notwithstanding whether any proceedings were taken against the person who actually committed the offence. Similar provisions are also contained in the Control of Pollution (Amendment) Act 1989[1] in respect of offences relating to controlled waste carriers and also in particular items of relevant secondary legislation[2]. The provision, inter alia, facilitates employers being prosecuted for acts of their employees. It also would, for example, be relevant to proceedings against a waste producer who placed unsuitable wastes in a skip. The skip was then transported to a licensed site by a waste carrier, with the contents being deposited in breach of the waste management licence.

1　Control of Pollution (Amendment) Act 1989, s 7(5).
2　See SI 1994/1056, Sch 3, para 14(8) (as amended by SI 1996/972, Sch 3,and in conjunction with SI 1996/972, reg 18(5)): record-keeping; SI 1994/1137, reg 12(11): transfrontier waste shipments; SI 1996/972, reg 18(5): special waste.

7.174　Words similar to s 158 of the EPA 1990 are to be found in a range of other statutes. Questions of interpretation arise from the use of the phrase 'act or default'. While the matter of whether a person's 'act' resulted in someone else contravening the EPA 1990 or similar provisions will be mainly a question of fact[1], the matter of whether a 'default' resulted in a particular outcome is somewhat more difficult. Generally like neglect[2], a default must be a wilful act, albeit that the courts have held that the outcome of such an act may have been unintentional or have arisen out of forgetfulness. But there must be a causative link between whatever happened which resulted in the offence and the accused person's actions (or lack of them)[3]. In *Re Young and Harston's Contract*[4] it was held that 'Default is a purely relative term, just like negligence. It means nothing more, nothing less, than not doing what is reasonable under the circumstances – not doing something which you ought to do . . .'. Similarly, in *Re Bayley-Worthington and Cohen's Contract*[5], default was held to entail[6] '. . . either not doing what you ought or doing what you ought not[7], having regard to your relations with the other parties concerned . . . In other words, it involves a breach in some duty you owe to another or others'. The latter judgment also clarified the finding in *Harston's Contract* concerning what is to be viewed as 'reasonable'. It does not require the court to be shown that unreasonable conduct had occurred. Much later, the House of Lords considered a provision similar to s 158 of the EPA 1990 in *Tesco Supermarkets Ltd v Nattrass*[8]. Lord Diplock held that:

> '[i]n the expression "act or default" . . . the word "act" is wide enough to include any physical act of the other person which is causative of the offence. But the use of the word "default" instead of the neutral expression "omission" connotes a failure to act which constitutes a breach of the legal duty to act. A legal duty may arise independently of any contract or it may be a duty owed to another person arising out of a contract with him.'[9]

1　See para 7.62ff for a discussion of causation.
2　See para 7.171.
3　See also *Noss Farm Products Ltd v Lilico* [1945] 2 All ER 609; *Lester v Balfour Williamson Merchant Shippers Ltd* [1953] 1 All ER 1146.
4　[1885] 31 Ch D 168 at 174.
5　(1909) 1 Ch 648.
6　*Re Bayley-Worthington and Cohen's Contract* 1 Ch 648 at 656. See also *Lamb v Sunderland and District Creamery Ltd* [1951] 1 All ER 923.
7　See also *Neath RDC v Williams* [1951] 1 KB 115 at 127.
8　[1971] 2 All ER 127.
9　*Tesco Supermarkets Ltd v Nattrass* [1971] 2 All ER 127 at 152J/153F.

Chapter 8

The granting of waste management licences

INTRODUCTION

8.01 This chapter will describe the requirements of the EPA 1990 which relate to waste management licence applications. It should be read in conjunction with Chapter 7 which describes the criminal sanctions for non-compliance with the licence. Administrative sanctions, along with other powers to control licences after they are issued, are the subject of Chapter 9.

8.02 For the financial year 1997/98, there were 7,353[1] licensed waste management sites in existence in England and Wales. However, few of these have been the subject of a full waste management licence application under the provisions set down in the Part II of the EPA 1990 and described in this chapter. Most were originally licensed under the Control of Pollution Act 1974 and became subject to waste management licences by way of the transitional provisions under the EPA 1990[2]. These provisions eliminated the need for holders of licences which existed before 1 May 1994 to make a full application under the EPA 1990's much more stringent requirements. One effect of these transitional provisions is that a significant proportion of the contents of this chapter has yet to apply to Britain's older waste management facilities.

1 Environment Agency (1998) *1997–1998 Annual Report and Accounts*, Environment Agency, Bristol, Appendix 5: the equivalent figure for Scotland is 944: SEPA (1998) *Annual Report and Accounts 1997–1998* SEPA, Stirling p 59.
2 Section 77 and Commencement Order 15 SI 1994/1096: see para 9.82ff.

8.03 Of the total number of licensed disposal and recovery facilities in England and Wales, about 1,600[1] of these are scrapyards and vehicle dismantlers. Whilst Chapter 11 deals with the exemptions appropriate for such sites, they apply to only a small proportion of such facilities. The remainder must be covered by waste management licences and are subject, in varying degrees, to the following provisions.

1 'Agency to clamp down on scrap yards', *Ends Report* 286, November 1998 p 16.

8.04 The EPA 1990 requires that management licences continue in force until they are surrendered by the holder under the procedure set down in s 39[1]. Non-compliance with their conditions is an offence under s 33 of the EPA 1990[2]. Once issued, licences can be subsequently modified, suspended or partially revoked[3]. Alternatively, they can be revoked entirely under s 38[4] or s 42[5] as a consequence of the miscreant behaviour of the licensee. A licence is not transferable[6] unless such a transfer is effected by the Agency in accordance with s 40[7]. In the case of licence surrender or transfer, an essential prerequisite is the consent of the Agency.

1 EPA 1990, s 35(9): see para 9.93.
2 EPA 1990, s 33(6): see Chapter 7.
3 See paras 9.03, 9.17 and 9.40.
4 EPA 1990, s 35(11) makes this explicit in respect of revocation under s 38; oddly there is no equivalent cross reference in s 35(11) to revocation under s 42. Revocation under s 38 is discussed at para 9.22ff.
5 See para 9.26.
6 EPA 1990, s 35(10).
7 See para 9.114ff.

LICENCE APPLICATIONS

Types of waste management licence

8.05   The 1990 Act envisages two types of waste management licence[1]: a 'site licence' and a 'mobile plant licence'.

1   EPA 1990, s 35(1) and (12).

8.06   A site licence is by far the most common, being defined as a licence 'authorising the treatment, keeping or disposal of waste in or on land'. In practice, this will embrace all waste disposal and recovery facilities other than those which are mobile plant or are excluded or exempted from licensing[1]. Given the requirements of Article 9 of the Directive on Waste[2] in respect of the duty on member states to ensure that all waste management facilities obtain permits, the terms 'treatment, keeping or disposal' should be interpreted broadly and in a manner that furthers the aims of the directive. In addition, the EPA 1990 makes it clear that 'treatment' of waste includes 'making it re-usable or reclaiming substances from it ...'[3]. 'Keeping' is undefined in the EPA 1990 and has its ordinary meaning[4]. The word 'disposal' is not defined in the primary legislation, but, in relation to the Control of Pollution Act 1974, was subject to a detailed interpretation in the joined cases of *R v London Stipendiary Magistrate, ex p London Waste Regulation Authority* and *Berkshire County Council v Scott*[5]. Disposal was held to cover both temporary and final disposal[6,7].

1   See Chapters 10 and 11.
2   Council Directive of 15 July 1975 on Waste (75/442/EEC) (OJ L194/39 25.7.75) (as amended by Council Directive of 18 March 1991 amending Directive 75/442/EEC on Waste (91/156/EEC) (OJ L78/32 26.3.91)). See para 12.04ff.
3   EPA 1990, s 29(6).
4   See para 7.26ff.
5   [1993] 3 All ER 113: see para 7.16ff.
6   Although the EPA 1990 makes it an offence to 'deposit' controlled waste in the absence of a licence, unlike the earlier Control of Pollution Act 1974 (s 3), it does not countenance licences which explicitly authorise the deposit of waste. Instead, the term 'deposit of waste' is encompassed by the word 'disposal' (EPA 1990, s 29(6)).
7   The term 'treatment, keeping and disposal' form the basis of the categorisation of facilities under the Waste Management Licensing (Charges) Scheme 1999–2000: see para 9.142.

8.07   A mobile plant licence, as its name suggests, authorises the 'treatment or disposal of waste' by means of mobile plant. The Secretary of State has the power to prescribe the nature of mobile plant under s 29(10) of the EPA 1990. This has resulted in mobile plant being defined in the Waste Management Licensing Regulations 1994[1]. Six types of mobile plant are currently prescribed and these apply only if such a plant is[2]:

'... designed to move or be moved by any means from place to place with a view to being used at each such place or, if not so designed, is readily capable of so moving or being so moved ...'

1   SI 1994/1056, reg 12 as amended by reg 3(3) of SI 1995/288 and SI 1996/634.
2   SI 1994/1056, reg 12(1) as amended by SI 1995/288, reg 3(3) and SI 1996/634, reg 2(4).

8.08   The six types of mobile plant prescribed are[1]:

–   plant[2] designed to incinerate waste[3] including animal remains, at a rate not exceeding 50 kgs per hour[4], which does not process clinical waste[5], sewage sludge, sewage screenings or municipal waste[6];

- plant for the recovery of waste oil from electrical equipment which uses 'filtration and or heat treatment'[7];
- plant for the destruction by dechlorination of PCBs or PCTs[8];
- waste vitrification plant[9];
- microwave treatment plant for clinical waste[10]; or
- waste soil treatment plant[11].

1 SI 1994/1056, reg 12 as amended by SI 1995/288, reg 3(3) and SI 1996/634, reg 2(4).
2 As defined in SI 1991/472, Sch 1, Section 5.1 (as amended by SI 1992/614, reg 2, Sch 1, para 9).
3 Defined as meaning solid or liquid wastes or gaseous wastes (other than gas produced by biological degradation of waste): SI 1991/472, Sch 1, Section 5.1 (as amended by SI 1994/1271, reg 3, Sch 1, para 8 and SI 1998/767, reg 2(2)(b)).
4 Ie an incinerator which is exempt from Part 1 of the EPA 1990 which is neither subject to a Part A or Part B authorisation
5 Defined in SI 1992/588, reg 11(2) but for the purposes of the definition of an exempt incinerator under SI 1991/472 (Sch 1, Section 5.1), the term 'clinical waste' does not include waste which is 'wholly' animal remains.
6 'A municipal waste incinerator' is as defined by Article 1 of Directive 89/369/EEC on the prevention of air pollution from municipal waste incineration plants (see SI 1991/472, Sch 1, Section 5.1). Circular 11/94 (Annex 4, para 4.10, n 34) states that: '"Municipal waste" therefore means in this context domestic refuse, as well as commercial or trade refuse and other waste which, because of its nature or composition, is similar to domestic refuse.'.
7 SI 1994/1056, reg 12(1)(b)(i) as amended by SI 1995/288, reg 3(3).
8 SI 1994/1056, reg 12(1)(b)(ii) as amended by SI 1995/288, reg 3(3).
9 SI 1994/1056, reg 12(1)(c) as amended by SI 1995/288, reg 3(3).
10 SI 1994/1056, reg 12(1)(d) as amended by SI 1995/288, reg 3(3); clinical waste has the same definition (SI 1994/1056 reg 12(2) as amended by SI 1995/288, reg 3(3)) as in the Controlled Waste Regulations (SI 1992/588, reg 1(2)): see para 2.210.
11 SI 1994/1056, reg 12(1)(e) (as amended by SI 1995/288, reg 3(3) and SI 1996/634, reg 2(4)).

8.09 The definition of mobile plant is to be regularly reviewed to encompass new innovations[1]. Hence, since 1994, it has been modified twice[2].

1 Circular 11/94, Annex 4, para 4.10.
2 By SI 1995/288, reg 3(3) and SI 1996/634, reg 2(4).

8.10 Excepting mobile plant, only the 'person in occupation' of the relevant land can hold a site licence[1,2]. For mobile plant, the licence holder is restricted to the person who 'operates' the plant[3]. Presumably, a prospective purchaser of land can apply for a site licence, but such a person would need to be able to demonstrate occupation – by, for example, the possession of title – prior to the licence being validly issued.

1 EPA 1990, s 35(2)(a).
2 The word 'occupier' is explored at para 12.108.
3 EPA 1990, s 35(2)(b).

The application process

8.11 Usually, an application for a waste management licence is made to the Agency in whose area the proposed site is to be situated[1]. The application system for a mobile plant licence is slightly different, in that the application is made to whichever Agency covers the operator's principal place of business[2]. Circular 11/94 suggests that a principal place of business 'is the place at which the applicant conducts the administration of his business and from which the various divisions of his business are controlled'[3,4].

1 EPA 1990, s 36(1)(a).
2 EPA 1990, s 36(1)(b).
3 Circular 11/94 Annex 4, para 4.33.

4   It is the duty of the Agency *who grants* the licence to ensure that the activities at the site do not cause harm to human health or pollution of the environment and are in compliance with conditions (EPA 1990, s 38(1). Accordingly, if a mobile plant is licensed in Scotland, but operated in England or Wales, some close co-operation is required between the Environment Agency and the Scottish Environment Protection Agency.

8.12   An application for a waste management licence must be made in writing[1] on the Agency's form and be accompanied by the prescribed fee[2]. The fees which accompany licence applications are set down in the Waste Management Licensing (Charges) Scheme which is current for the financial year in which the application is to be made. The Scheme is obtained directly from the Agency and emanates from s 41 of the Environment Act 1995, which permits the Agency to set statutory charges in specified circumstances. It is discussed at para 9.142. But as the Scheme changes annually, reference needs to be made to the up-to-date version for precise details of application fees[3].

1   SI 1994/1056, reg 2(1).
2   EPA 1990, s 36(1), as amended by the Environment Act 1995, s 120 and Sch 22, para 68(2): commenced by SI 1996/186 and SI 1998/604.
3   There are also differences between the Scheme in England and Wales as compared to Scotland.

8.13   The application must be accompanied by other information which the Agency 'reasonably requires'[1]. In a case where an applicant fails to provide sufficient information, the Agency is allowed to refuse to proceed with its consideration of the application[2]. The application can either be rejected or held in abeyance until the required information is forthcoming.

1   EPA 1990, s 36(1), as amended by the Environment Act 1995, s 120 and Sch 22, para 68(2).
2   EPA 1990, s 36(1A), as amended by the Environment Act 1995, Sch 22, para 68(2).

8.14   The Agency has a four-month determination period for a licence application[1], although this is extendable by agreement between parties. This period, which is double that allowed under the earlier Control of Pollution Act 1974, is intended to reflect the increased level of complexity in licence application made under the EPA 1990, particularly in respect of whether an applicant is to be viewed as a 'fit and proper person'[2].

1   EPA 1990, s 36(9).
2   EPA 1990, s 74: see para 8.112ff.

8.15   At the end of the four-months' determination period, should an applicant have neither agreed to an extension of this period nor been informed of a decision, the application is deemed as refused[1]. Where an application has been formally turned down or has been subject to deemed refusal, the applicant can appeal to the Secretary of State[2]. Given the importance of the determination period set down in the EPA 1990, Circular 11/94 advises regulatory bodies to formally acknowledge the date of receipt of the licence application[3]. This action will clearly indicate to all parties the commencement of the four-month determination period. However, no appeal is allowed when the Agency has refused[4] to proceed with the application due to applicant's failure to provide any additional information required[5]. The four-month determination period recommences when the additional information has been received[6].

1   EPA 1990, s 36(9).
2   EPA 1990, s 43(1). Appeals are discussed at para 9.126ff.
3   Circular 11/94, Annex 10, para 10.19.
4   EPA 1990, s 36(1A), as amended by the Environment Act 1995, s 120, Sch 22, para 68(2).
5   EPA 1990, s 36(9A)(a), as amended by the Environment Act 1995, s 120, Sch 22, para 68(5).
6   EPA 1990, s 36(9A)(b), as amended by the Environment Act 1995, s 120, Sch 22, para 68(5).

8.16 In respect of a licence application, the EPA 1990 holds that provision of information which is 'false or misleading' or is false and made 'recklessly' is an offence[1].

1   EPA 1990, s 44(1)(b), as amended by the Environment Act 1995, s 112 and Sch 19, para 4: see paras 12.214 and 12.238.

Statutory consultees in licence applications

8.17 One component of the licence application process involves the Agency contacting specified statutory consultees whose interests may be affected by the proposal. The Agency must refer the proposal to the 'appropriate planning authority'[1] and Health and Safety Executive[2]. The latter body was reinstated as a consultee by an amendment to the Environmental Protection Bill at the House of Lords Committee Stage.

1   Defined in the EPA 1990, s 36(11) (as amended by the Environment Act 1995, Sch 22, para 68(6)) as the county council in England except in the following cases: London metropolitan districts, where unitary authorities have been created or where National Park Authorities oversee development control. In Wales, it is the 22 unitary authorities, either the county or county borough council. Similarly in Scotland it is the responsibility of the unitary authority.
2   EPA 1990, s 36(4) as amended by the Environment Act 1995, s 120.

8.18 Section 36(4) of the EPA 1990 states that such bodies must be consulted '[w]here the waste regulation authority proposes to issue a licence'. This wording allows the Agency to reject a licence application without consulting such a bodies. Examples of such occasions might be where the applicant was not a 'fit or proper person'[1] or where what was proposed by the applicant was so inadequate that it would obviously cause pollution of the environment when put into practice.

1   See para 8.112ff below.

8.19 The range of consultees in the EPA 1990 is extended where an application involves land notified under s 28(1) of the Wildlife and Countryside Act 1981. If the Agency proposes to issue a licence, the application must also be referred to the 'appropriate nature conservation body'[1]. Again, the Agency should 'consider any representations' made by the appropriate body[2]. The Environment Act 1995 also contains a duty[3] on the Agency to consult conservation bodies[4] in respect of any proposal which may affect any land subject to earlier notification from such bodies[5].

1   The Nature Conservancy Council in England, the Countryside Council for Wales or Scottish Natural Heritage (the latter body was incorporated into the EPA 1990 by way of an amendment contained in the Natural Heritage (Scotland) Act 1991, s 4, Sch 2, paras 10(1) and (2).
2   EPA 1990, s 36(7).
3   Environment Act 1995, s 8(3); (in Scotland s 35 of the Environment Act).
4   The Nature Conservancy Council, Countryside Council for Wales, National Park or Broads Authority or, in Scotland, Scottish Natural Heritage.
5   As notified under ss 8(1) and 8(2) of the Environment Act 1995, or in Scotland, s 35(1) or (3).

8.20 Finally, neighbouring landowners must be consulted if the licence is to require works to be undertaken on their land[1]. The nature of this requirement and the consultation process itself is discussed at para 8.23 below.

1   EPA 1990, ss 35A and 36A, as amended by the Environment Act 1995, Sch 22, para 67 and 69.

8.21 A 28-day period for consultations with the local planning authority, Health and Safety Executive or, where required, the appropriate nature conservation body is set down[1]. Oddly, the EPA 1990 requires that this time period is triggered by the date of receipt of the application by the Agency, not the date of receipt by the consultee. However, it can be extended, provided that the Agency and consultee agree to that effect in writing.

1   EPA 1990, s 36(10) as amended by the Environment Act 1995, s 120, Sch 22, para 68(2).

8.22   Under s 36 of the EPA 1990, the Agency has a duty to 'consider any representations about the proposal' which are made by the planning authority or Health and Safety Executive on consultation[1]. A similar requirement affects consultees with nature conservation interests[2]. Clearly, the duty to 'consider' the representations is much less strong than would be the case, for example, if the relevant section said 'change the proposed licence in the light of such representations'. In addition, the earlier arrangements prior to the formation of the Agency[3] allowed for an appeal to the Secretary of State to be lodged where there was disagreement between the National Rivers Authority and the Waste Regulation Authority. However, since it was amended by the Environment Act 1995[4], the EPA 1990 no longer contains an arrangement for a disgruntled consultee to lodge an appeal.

1   EPA 1990, s 36(4)(b).
2   EPA 1990, s 36(7)(b).
3   And hence prior to the deletion of s 36(5) by Sch 22, para 68(4) of the Environment Act 1995.
4   Environment Act 1995, Sch 22, para 68(4).

Consultation and compensation where licence conditions will affect neighbouring landowners

8.23   On some occasions, the Agency may wish to propose licence conditions which require a licensee to do works on a third party's land. For example, environmental monitoring boreholes may need to be installed around the periphery of a landfill situated in an old quarry, where the area of ownership of the licensee only extends to the quarry's edge. Such boreholes will need to be maintained throughout the duration of the licence and be regularly monitored by the licensee. The Agency has the power to impose such a requirement[1], with the affected landowner being required by the EPA 1990 to consent to such works. However, that person has to be consulted about the nature of such conditions in advance and, later on, be granted appropriate compensation from the licensee.

1   EPA 1990, s 35(4): see para 8.244.

8.24   The requirements on consultation and compensation were finally introduced in 1999[1] by amendments to the EPA 1990[2], being coupled to further provisions which apply when licences are suspended[3] or modified[4]. The changes to the primary legislation allow the Secretary of State to make regulations in respect of compensation[5] and resulted in the Waste Management Licences (Consultation and Compensation) Regulations 1999[6].

1   They were originally to be implemented in 1996, see DOE Press Release 651 20/12/95. These requirements do not seem to apply to persons affected by any condition of existing waste management licences issued prior to the commencement of this provision.
2   EPA 1990, ss 35A and 36A, as amended by the Environment Act 1995, s 120, Sch 22, paras 67 and 69 (commenced by SI 1999/803, Article 3): see also Cooke E (1995) 'Compensation for Landowners but no Teeth for Licence Holders', *Wastes Management*, October 1995, p 52.
3   EPA 1990, ss 35A(1)(a)(ii), 38(9A)–(9C), as amended by the Environment Act 1995, s 120, Sch 22, paras 67 and 72: see para 9.54.
4   EPA 1990, s 37A, as amended by the Environment Act 1995, s 120, Sch 22, para 71: see para 9.09.
5   EPA 1990, s 35A(3) and (4).
6   SI 1999/481.

8.25   The amendments to the primary legislation establish the following procedures. Where it is proposed that a waste management licence is to be issued containing conditions which affect the rights of neighbouring 'owners[1], lessees or occupiers'[2], these persons must be consulted prior to the licence being issued. The Agency must send the affected person a notice[3] setting out the condition, the nature of the works and 'other things which that condition might require the holder of the licence to do' and a date by which representations must be received[4]. Unlike the statutory consultees, where a 28-day consultation period is set down[5], a three-month long consultation period is prescribed in relation to any condition resultant from a licence application[6]. The Agency must 'consider' any representations made by the recipient of the notice[7] but, to be valid, representations must be received within the timescale required by the notice[8].

1   Defined in the EPA 1990, s 36A(8).
2   EPA 1990, s 36A, as amended by the Environment Act 1995, s 120, Sch 22, para 69.
3   EPA 1990, s 36A(2).
4   EPA 1990, s 36A(4).
5   EPA 1990, s 36(10).
6   SI 1999/481, reg 3(a).
7   EPA 1990, s 36A(6).
8   EPA 1990, s 36A(7).

8.26   Should this type of condition be contained in a waste management licence, compensation is payable from the licensee to the affected party in respect of 'loss or damage' in the following circumstances[1]:

(a)   depreciation of the value of the affected land and other land indirectly affected;
(b)   other loss or damage not related to depreciation of land value but which – if it had been subject to compulsory purchase under the Acquisition of Land Act 1981[2] – the person would have been entitled to receive compensation in respect of disturbance;
(c)   damage to or 'injurious affection of' any other related land interest; and
(d)   losses in respect of any work carried out by the landowner 'which is rendered abortive' by the licence requiring access to the land.

A compensation claim must be lodged either within 12 months of the right of access being required by the licence or within six months of the licensee requiring access to the land[3]. In either case, the entitlement to compensation starts as soon as the licence requires the right of access to be granted[4] or, when the licence has been subject to an appeal to the Secretary of State[5], the date of determination of the appeal[6]. An application is made directly to the licence holder[7], setting out[8]:

(a)   a copy of the 'grant of rights' – presumably the third party's permission for access – and any relevant plans;
(b)   a description of the landowner's interest in the land;
(c)   a statement of the amount of compensation required, itemised in accordance with the list of specified circumstances whereby compensation arises[9] and showing the basis of the figure claimed; and
(d)   a copy of the appeal notice in respect of any licence as issued by the Secretary of State.

1   SI 1999/481, reg 4.
2   In Scotland, the Acquisition of Land (Authorisation Procedure) (Scotland) Act 1947.
3   SI 1999/481, reg 6.
4   SI 1999/481, reg 5(1).
5   See para 9.126ff.
6   SI 1999/481, reg 5(2).

7 SI 1999/481, reg 6(2).
8 SI 1999/481, reg 6(3).
9 As listed earlier in this paragraph.

8.27 Compensation claims are assessed[1] in accordance with the rules set out in the Land Compensation Act 1961[2] which are normally applied to land affected by the activities of organisations such as the utilities. Compensation claims can embrace the cost of drawing up the claim[3], as well as valuation and other legal expenses[4], with additional provisions affecting land subject to mortgages[5]. However, the licensee is protected from having to pay additional compensation caused by the landowner making improvements to the affected land with a view to enhancing its value in order to inflate the claim[6].

1 SI 1999/481, reg 7(2).
2 In Scotland, the Land Compensation (Scotland) Act 1963.
3 SI 1999/481, reg 7(4).
4 SI 1999/481, reg 7(6).
5 SI 1999/481, reg 7(5) and 8(1).
6 SI 1999/481, reg 7(3).

8.28 Disputes as to the amount of compensation appropriate are to be settled by the Lands Tribunal[1], with the procedures in the Land Compensation Act 1961[2] applying[3]. In all cases, payment is to be made at a date agreed between claimant and licensee or as set down by the Lands Tribunal or a court 'as soon as reasonably practicable' after the amount has been finally determined[4].

1 SI 1999/481, reg 8(3).
2 Land Compensation Act 1961, ss 2 and 4; in Scotland, the Land Compensation (Scotland) Act 1963, ss 9 and 11.
3 SI 1999/481, reg 8(4).
4 SI 1999/481, reg 8(2).

Criteria for determining waste management licence applications

8.29 For an application to succeed, usually there is also a need for valid planning permission to be in force on the land[1]. The primary requirement to be satisfied then is s 36 of the EPA 1990. Section 36 of the EPA 1990 requires the Agency to reject an application for a waste management licence if[2]:

(a) it is satisfied that the applicant is not a fit and proper person; or that
(b) rejection is necessary for the purposes of preventing pollution of the environment, harm to human health or serious detriment to the amenities of the locality[3].

Certain of these criteria, whilst defined in the EPA 1990, are further embellished in the Waste Management Licensing Regulations 1994. Examples are the provisions on groundwater[4] and on the 'relevant objectives' of the Directive on Waste[5]. The criteria in the EPA 1990 may also be affected by the terms of reference of the Agency itself, as set down in the Environment Act 1995.

1 EPA 1990, s 36(2).
2 EPA 1990, s 36(3).
3 The ability of the Agency to utilise the concept of serious detriment of the locality is somewhat constrained: see para 8.49 below.
4 SI 1994/1056, reg 15.
5 SI 1994/1056, Sch 4, Pt I.

8.30 One result of this variety of influences on licence application decision criteria is that it is difficult to readily set out the provisions as a simple, succinct, staged progression. Cross-referral between the primary and secondary legislation is inevitable. Some of the secondary legislation contains very detailed provisions, whilst the requirements of the criteria of 'fit and proper person' rely extensively on Department of the Environment guidance and discretionary application by the Agency. Not all the requirements are relevant to every waste management licence application, which adds to the complexity. The account of these provisions below is structured to allow accessibility. However, some cross-referral between topics is an inevitable consequence of the structure of the legislation.

Planning permission

8.31   Waste management licences usually operate in tandem with planning permission. Planning permission is granted in respect of land and hence would transfer with title to a subsequent landowner. By contrast, a waste management licence is issued to a person and cannot be transferred unless approved by the Agency[1]. Broadly, the development control system should concern itself solely with the land use aspects of a particular application for a waste facility. The waste management licence should focus much more upon the detailed site works and management necessary to prevent adverse environmental or human health impacts. Where the precise boundary lies remains, however, rather vague[2]. In addition, the boundary itself shifts depending upon the date when planning permission was granted, or whether a certificate of lawful, or established, use has been issued in the stead of such permission[3].

1   EPA 1990, s 40: see para 9.114.
2   See Circular 11/94, Annex 1, paras 1.50ff; Department of the Environment (1994) *Planning Policy Guidance: Planning and Pollution Control* (PPG 23), HMSO, London, WMP 4, paras 1.17ff and *Gateshead Metropolitan Borough Council v Secretary of State for the Environment and Northumbrian Water Group plc* [1993] 6 JEL 1 pp 93–101, *Gateshead Metropolitan Borough Council v Secretary of State for the Environment and Northumbrian Water Group* [1995] Env LR 37, CA, *R v Bolton Metropolitan Borough Council, ex p Kirkham* (DC) [1998] Env LR 560; on appeal [1998] Env LR 719, CA.
3   SI 1994/1056, para 4, Pt 1, Sch 4: see para 8.49 below.

8.32   A waste management licence can only be granted where there exists a planning permission 'in force in relation to that use of the land'[1]. Alternatively, a licence can be issued in circumstances where no planning permission was required or where the existence of a valid certificate of established use under s 192 of the Town and Country Planning Act 1990[2,3] or a certificate of lawful use[4] legitimises the development. Licences granted where a planning permission was required but not granted (or where an appropriate certificate was required) are invalid.

1   EPA 1990, s 36(2)(a): according to PPG 23, an outline planning permission is not sufficient for a waste management facility. In all cases, a full planning permission is needed (see PPG 23, para 3.20).
2   In Scotland, s 90 of the Town and Country Planning (Scotland) Act 1972.
3   EPA 1990, s 36(2)(b).
4   See s 191(7)(c) of the Town and Country Planning Act 1990: as amended by s 10(1) of the Planning and Compensation Act 1991.

8.33   It is not the purpose of this book to explore the development control aspects of waste management facilities in any detail. However a brief discussion provides a useful context of the relationship between planning permission and waste management licences. Generally, the development control aspects are 'county matters'[1] in England and hence the county council will have jurisdiction. In other instances, metropolitan boroughs or unitary authorities have responsibility.

1   See *R v Berkshire County Council, ex p Wokingham District Council* [1997] Env LR 545.

8.34   Increasingly, development control in England and Wales has become 'plan lead', with the primary criteria for judging the appropriateness of a new land use activity being whether it conforms to the local plan published by the planning authority. Development plans are required by Part II of the Town and Country Planning Act 1990[1,2]. In England[3], the production of a plan covering the strategic aspects of waste management is usually a county council function, being published either together with a plan for minerals working or separate to it. In the case of the metropolitan boroughs, or where unitary authorities have been created, these matters are considered within the local authority's unitary development plan. Only in limited cases can departures be made from that plan.

1   In Scotland, Pt I of the Town and Country Planning (Scotland) Act 1972.
2   Where appropriate, they must reflect the relevant objectives set down in SI 1994/1056, Sch 4, paras 2, 3, 4 and 7.
3   In Wales, it is a function of the 22 unitary authorities: the county council or county borough.

8.35   In addition to the local plan, the Town and Country Planning Act 1990 requires a local authority to have regard to national policies in the development control process. Perhaps the most important policy document in this context is Planning Policy Guidance note (PPG) 23[1]. The White Paper on the National Waste Strategy makes it clear that the content of the Strategy is a material consideration to decision-making on planning permission for waste management facilities[2].

1   Department of the Environment (1994) *Planning Policy Guidance: Planning and Polution Control*, HMSO, London: due to be revised (see Department of the Environment (1996) *Revision of Planning Policy Guidance Note 23 'Planning and Pollution Control on Waste Issues'*, Consultation Draft, DOE, London) and partially superseded by a revised PPG 10 (see Department of the Environment, Transport and the Regions (1998) *Planning Policy Guidance: Planning and Waste Management* (PPG 10), Consultation Draft, DETR, London).
2   Department of the Environment (1995) *Making Waste Work: A Strategy for Sustainable Waste Management in England and Wales*, Cm 3040, London, HMSO, para 4.12. See para 1.09.

8.36   For a planning application to succeed, it must also satisfy a series of more localised criteria which ensure that the particular activity is compatible with the other land users who are in proximity to it[1]. Planning Policy Guidance Note 23[2] sets out considerations which are material to the development control aspects of waste management facilities. These include[3]:

–   the availability of land for the waste management activity, taking into account its proximity to other development or land use;
–   the sensitivity of the area, as reflected in landscape, agricultural land quality, nature conservation or archaeological designations, if evidence suggests that there is a risk of such features being affected by pollution;
–   any loss of amenity which the activity might cause;
–   any environmental benefits emanating from the proposal, such as regeneration of derelict land, or transport improvements;
–   the design of the site and the visual impact of the development, including such matters as its impact on the road network and the surrounding environment;
–   the condition of the site itself, where it is known or likely to be contaminated, and any potential for remediation;
–   the proposed after use of the site, and feasibility of achieving restoration to the required standard;
–   the potential use of mineral workings as landfill;
–   the hours of operation required by the development where these may have an impact on neighbouring land use;

- the possibility that nuisance might be caused, for example, by birds, vermin or over blown litter; and
- transport requirements, including the scope of transporting waste to the site by rail or water.

1 See for example *Envirocor v Secretary of State for the Environment and British Cocoa Mills (Hull) Ltd* [1996] JEL Vol 8 No 2 p 354 and Stephen Tromans' evaluation of the judgment at p 362.
2 Department of the Environment (1994) *Planning Policy Guidance: Planning and Pollution Control* (PPG 23), HMSO, London.
3 PPG 23, para 3.1; see also para 1.33.

8.37 It should also be noted that the Waste Management Licensing Regulations 1994 also contain provisions which may affect development control decisions and the content of planning permissions. The decision-making process must ensure that the 'relevant objectives' of the Directive on Waste are fulfilled[1].

1 SI 1994/1056, Sch 4, paras 1–4, 7: see para 8.50 below, and see *R v Bolton Metropolitan Borough Council, ex p Kirkham* [1998] Env LR 560; on appeal [1998] Env LR 719, CA.

8.38 Finally, certain applications for planning permission for waste management activities will need to be accompanied by a written environmental statement as required by the Town and Country Planning (Environmental Impact Assessment) (England and Wales) Regulations 1999[1]. Such statements are mandatory in the case of the types of development listed in Schedule 1 to the 1999 Regulations: waste 'disposal' facilities involving (a) installations for the incineration, chemical treatment[2] and landfill of hazardous[3] waste; and (b) incinerators and chemical treatment facilities of over 100 tonnes per day capacity for non-hazardous wastes. In addition, a material change of use of land involving the incineration, chemical treatment or landfill of hazardous waste also requires an environmental statement[4].

1 SI 1999/293: in Scotland, the Environmental Impact Assessment (Scotland) Regulations (SSI 1991/1): see also Department of the Environment Circular 02/99 *Environmental Impact Assessment.*
2 As defined in Heading D9 of Annex IIA to the Directive on Waste (see Table 2.2 in Chapter 2).
3 'Hazardous waste' is as defined in the Directive on Hazardous Waste (91/689/EEC) – see Chapter 4. Note that the Regulations no longer refer to 'special waste'.
4 SI 1999/293, reg 31.

8.39 The local planning authority is left with discretion to require an environmental statement in the case of other waste management activities. These are listed in Schedule 2 to the Town and Country Planning (Environmental Impact Assessment) (England and Wales) Regulations 1999, which describes other installations where an environmental statement may be required for the 'disposal'[1] of waste. These include all other incinerators, other disposal installations exceeding 0.5 hectare, disposal installations situated within 100m of any 'controlled water', sludge deposition sites in excess of 0.5 hectare, scrap yards and vehicle dismantlers within 100m of any controlled water and knackers yards. Generally, these activities should be the subject of an environmental statement where the project is '... likely to have significant effects on the environment by virtue of factors such as its nature, size or location'[2]. Circular 02/99 advises that a Schedule 2 waste disposal installation of a capacity in excess of 50,000 tonnes per year 'is more likely to' be a candidate for an environmental statement[3].

1 An interesting question develops as to which waste management activities constitute 'disposal' under the 1999 Regulations: see para 8.94ff.
2 SI 1999/293, reg 2(1).
3 Circular 02/99, Annex A, para A36.

Pollution of the environment and harm to human health

8.40 Besides the need for a valid planning permission, the EPA 1990 requires the Agency to reject an application for a waste management licence if rejection is necessary for the purposes of preventing pollution of the environment or harm to human health[1]. As will be seen, the EPA 1990 is somewhat sketchy on what is envisaged by 'harm to human health'. However, 'pollution of the environment' is subject to a detailed exposition.

1 EPA 1990, s 36(3).

8.41 Under s 29(2) of the EPA 1990, the 'environment' is held to constitute 'all, or any, of the following media, namely land, water and air'. 'Pollution of the environment' is stated[1] as meaning 'pollution of the environment due to the release or escape (into any environmental medium)' of substances[2] 'constituting or resulting from the waste' and capable, by reason of concentrations and quantity, of causing 'harm' to man or any other living organisms supported by the environment. It should be noted that it is essential to the definition that the escape being referred to must be from land on which controlled waste is kept, treated or deposited or from 'fixed plant[3] by means of which controlled waste is treated, kept or disposed of'.

1 EPA 1990, s 29(3) .
2 Defined in s 29(11) as meaning 'any natural or artificial substance, whether in solid or liquid form or in the form of a gas or vapour'.
3 Precisely why the words 'fixed plant' are inserted into this sub-section is not immediately clear. Pollution from *mobile* plant is incorporated within the definition of 'pollution of the environment' in s 29(3) by way of s 29(4) of the EPA 1990.

8.42 From the above, it will be clear that there are a number of steps in the EPA 1990 which are necessary to establish 'pollution of the environment'. Within this evaluation, an interpretation which best fits the purpose of the Directive on Waste[1] must be applied, by way of the provisions in the Waste Management Licensing Regulations 1994 on 'relevant objectives'[2]. However, within the confines of the EPA 1990 itself, the first step to understanding the concept of pollution of the environment is self-evident. The environment must be shown to have been polluted. In the water pollution case of *R v Dovermoss*[3], it was held that, in relation to the definition of 'polluting matter', the terms 'pollute', 'pollutant' and 'pollution' are ordinary English words and that guidance on their meaning can be obtained from the Oxford English Dictionary. 'Pollution' in that Dictionary means 'to make physically impure, foul or filthy: to dirty, stain, taint or befoul'[4].

1 Council Directive of 15 July 1975 on Waste (75/442/EEC) (OJ L194/39 25.7.75) (subsequently amended by Council Directive of 18 March 1991 amending Directive 75/442/EEC on Waste (91/156/EEC) (OJ L78/32 26.3.91)).
2 SI 1994/1056, Sch 4: see para 8.50.
3 (1995) 159 JP 448.
4 For a definition of pollution in the context of groundwater, reference should be made to Directive 80/68 on groundwater and para 8.70ff below.

8.43 The second step envisaged by the EPA 1990 in establishing 'pollution of the environment' requires the identification of the occurrence of a release or escape. Thirdly, the substances involved in the release or escape must have emanated from land where waste was treated, kept or disposed of or from fixed plant involved in those operations. Finally, the substances or articles which did escape have to be identified as 'capable' of causing 'harm' to man or any other living organism.

8.44 In the context of the phrase 'pollution of the environment', the word 'harm' is also defined[1]:

' "harm" means harm to the health of living organisms or other interference with the ecological systems of which they form part and in the case of man includes offence to any of his senses or harm to his property'[2].

The words 'offence to any of his senses' in the definition of 'harm' appears to include smells and may be potentially extendable to aesthetic factors such as visual intrusion. Such factors have relevance in relation to the 'relevant objectives' of the Directive on Waste[3]. There are therefore overlaps with the concept of statutory nuisance contained in Part III of the EPA 1990[4].

1 EPA 1990, s 29(5).
2 The word 'harmless' is also given a corresponding meaning in s 29(5).
3 Relevant objectives are discussed at para 8.50.
4 See Department of the Environment (1994) *Licensing of Waste Management Facilities*, (3rd Ed), Waste Management Paper 4, HMSO, London, para 1.31.

8.45 Pollution of the environment in s 29 of the EPA 1990 is therefore a very wide-ranging concept. For example, it can include gas emanating from land in which waste has been deposited, or from where waste is treated, kept or disposed of. However, such gases must constitute the waste or result from it[1]. Indeed, Waste Management Paper 4 suggests that the concept of 'the environment' should be interpreted broadly[2]:

'In assessing pollution, WRAs[3] should have regard to the wider environment. They should, for example, consider the impacts of emissions on global climate change as well as on local air, water, soil, flora and fauna'[4].

1 This has, for example, some considerable relevance to controls over the disposal of chlorofluorocarbons (CFCs) from surplus refrigeration units and the need to ensure that all such gases are removed in a controlled manner to allow their later disposal. The relationship between s 33 and the CFC issue is set out in Circular 11/94, Annex 4, paras 4.95–4.103.
2 Waste Management Paper 4, para 1.6.
3 Ie the Environment Agency or Scottish Environment Protection Agency.
4 This would appear to embrace the widening of the term which is resultant from the notion of 'relevant objectives': see SI 1994/1056, Sch 4, Pt I and para 8.50ff below.

8.46 Finally, it should be noted that the wording used refers to substances or objects resulting from the waste which are 'capable' of causing harm to man or other living organisms. There is therefore no need to show that actual harm has occurred. What matters are factors of risk. In the case of *R v Board of Trustees of the Science Museum*[1], the concept of risk was considered in respect of the Health and Safety at Work etc Act 1974 and the emission of legionella bacteria from an air conditioning plant. Lord Justice Steyn held that the word 'risk'[2]:

'. . . conveys the idea of possibility of danger. Indeed, a degree of verbal manipulation is needed to introduce the idea of actual danger . . .'

In a slightly different context[3], it was held[4] that it is not necessary to carry out an arithmetic assessment of risk in deciding whether a 'bad neighbour'[5] land use should continue.

1 [1993] 3 All ER 853.
2 [1993] 3 All ER 853 at 858J/859A.
3 Town and country planning.
4 *Barker and Bristow Ltd and Wirral Waste Management Ltd v Secretary of State for the Environment* [1994] Env LR 226.
5 An extension to a landfill.

8.47   In respect of the possible implications of a waste management facility upon groundwater, a major influence on the criteria of pollution of the environment will be whether the requirements of reg 15 of the Waste Management Licensing Regulations 1994 are satisfied. Regulation 15, which implements the Groundwater Directive[1], is discussed at para 8.70ff below.

1   Council Directive of 17 December 1979 on the protection of groundwater against pollution caused by certain dangerous substances (Directive 80/68/EEC) (OJ L20/43 26.1.80).

8.48   By contrast to the phrase 'pollution of the environment', the concept of 'harm to human health' is not defined. Section 29(5) of the EPA 1990 – which defines 'harm' – specifically relates only to the definition used in s 29(3) of 'pollution of the environment'. Accordingly, harm to human health must have its ordinary meaning. But such an interpretation is also coloured by the requirement to uphold the 'relevant objectives' of the Directive on Waste[1]. Like 'pollution of the environment', an element of risk management will be contained in deciding whether or not the granting of a waste management licence will cause harm to human health.

1   Council Directive of 15 July 1975 on Waste (75/442/EEC) (OJ L194/39 25.7.75) (as amended by Council Directive of 18 March 1991 amending Directive 75/442/EEC on Waste (91/156/EEC) (OJ L78/32 26.3.91)); relevant objectives are discussed at para 8.50ff.

Serious detriment to the amenities of the locality[1]

8.49   The EPA 1990 also requires the Agency not to reject a licence unless serious detriment to the amenities of the locality may arise. However, the application of this decision criteria is significantly restricted. It can only be assessed in relation to waste management licence applications which concern sites where no planning permission is in force[2]. But the meaning of the words 'planning permission' in this sub-section has been changed by the Waste Management Licensing Regulations 1994[3] to mean only a permission granted after 30 April 1994. The result is that the serious detriment criteria can be invoked where a planning permission was issued before that date. Similarly, it must be considered where a certificate of lawful or established use exists or where a planning permission is otherwise not required[4]. The criteria of serious detriment to the amenities of the locality are subject to a critical influence by the 'relevant objectives'[5].

1   It is interesting to note the contrast between the wording of s 33(1)(c) and s 36(3). In the latter case, there are three criteria: pollution of the environment, harm to human health and, where applicable, serious detriment to the amenities of the locality. However, in the offence provision contained in s 33(1)(c), 'serious detriment to the amenity' is not mentioned. It seems possible that, in s 33, the term 'pollution of the environment' has a wider meaning than in s 36, in order to embrace the absence of the serious detriment to amenities criteria. This will be particularly the case due to the provisions of the EPA 1990 being required to accord to the 'relevant objectives' (see SI 1994/1056, Sch 4 and para 8.50ff) of the Directive on Waste.
2   EPA 1990, s 36(3).
3   SI 1994/1056, Sch 4, para 9(7).
4   Many scrapyards and vehicle dismantlers' premises are subject to such certificates.
5   See para 8.50ff.

Relevant objectives

8.50   The Waste Management Licensing Regulations 1994 exert an influence on the criteria set down in s 36(3) of the EPA 1990 under which licence applications are judged. The Agency has a duty to ensure that the 'relevant objectives' of the Directive on Waste are followed. This provision is general to a range of specified functions of the Agency[1], including the licence application process[2]. Given that the objectives apply across a number of the Agency's powers, they are discussed in more detail at para 12.13ff, but in summary, two provisions warrant mention. The first, which is a verbatim transposition of the kernel of Article 4 of the Directive on Waste[3], sets out additional provisions which affect the criteria against which licences for disposal and recovery facilities are considered[4]. The second relates[5] to Article 5 of the Directive[6]. However, in respect of the Agency's licensing function, it is of less significance, affecting mainly disposal activities which were granted planning permissions prior to May 1994. As will be discussed, it also lacks any formal mechanism for implementation by the Agency.

1 See SI 1994/1056, Sch 4, paras 2, 3 and 4, as amended by SI 1998/2746, reg 17.
2 SI 1994/1056, Sch 4, para 3(1).
3 Council Directive of 15 July 1975 on Waste (75/442/EEC) (OJ L194/39 25.7.75) (as amended by Council Directive of 18 March 1991 amending Directive 75/442/EEC on Waste (91/156/EEC) (OJ L78/32 26.3.91)).
4 SI 1994/1056, Sch 4, para 4(1).
5 SI 1994/1056, Sch 4, para 4(2).
6 There is a third provision (SI 1994/1056, Sch 4, para 4(3)), but this pertains to the compilation of waste management and other plans. This is beyond the scope of this volume.

8.51 Planning Policy Guidance (PPG) 23[1] attempts to explain relevant objectives as part of an exposition of the wider issue concerning divisions of responsibilities between planning and pollution control in general. However, more detailed guidance can be found in Circular 11/94, Annex 1.

1 Department of the Environment (1994) *Planning Policy Guidance Note 23: Planning and Pollution Control*, 1994, HMSO: see paras 5.3 to 5.8 and Annex 6.

8.52 It would seem that the intention of the Department of the Environment for the provisions on 'relevant objectives' was, as their title suggests, to set goals towards which pollution control bodies must strive. As is discussed at para 12.16, they are claimed not to be decision criteria per se. Moreover, when they apply to a statutory function of the Agency, they are intended to provide an underpinning to the interpretation of that function. In other words, the statutory function must be implemented in a manner which follows the objectives' requirements. Therefore, relevant objectives must be considered when the EPA 1990's own criteria for judging licence applications are being fulfilled[1]: particularly the need to prevent pollution of the environment or harm to human health.

1 EPA 1990, s 36(3): see para 8.29ff above.

8.53 The objectives also overlap onto other environmental legislation and, particularly, development control. The Waste Management Licensing Regulations 1994 attempted to prevent duplication between the functions of the Agency and other statutory authorities. However, as discussed below, this boundary has become somewhat eroded. Finally, the objectives also enhance the Agency's powers in respect of circumstances where the relevant objectives are not fully embraced by the statutory jurisdiction of other regulatory bodies. The latter issue has particular relevance to certain waste management licence applications which relate to sites with extant planning permissions.

8.54 The Agency has been granted these enhanced powers in order to ensure that the relevant objectives have retrospective application to facilities which had been granted a planning permission prior to 1 May 1994 or in cases where a planning permission is not required[1]. The British planning system does not address the requirement of retrospective application particularly well. While the most obvious vehicle to ensure that the relevant objectives are fulfilled is by changing the conditions of a facility's existing planning permission, such an action is likely to invoke claims for compensation. Certificates of lawful or established use are also not subject to change or being made conditional later. Hence a separate method of implementing the objectives on existing waste management sites had to be found. Given that all permits issued by the Agency and other pollution control bodies are by their nature reviewable, such permits have been selected as the mechanism for enacting the required relevant objectives. Indeed, Circular 11/94 claims[2] that provision has been made in the Waste Management Licensing Regulations 1994 for pollution control bodies to be able to meet 'all' the relevant objectives where waste management facilities had received planning permissions prior to 1 May 1994[3]. As will be shown, this assertion seems to be not strictly correct.

1   For example where certificates of lawful or established use have been issued.
2   Circular 11/94, Annex 1, para 1.58.
3   Or where no planning permission is required, including instances where certificates of established or lawful use have been issued.

8.55   *Relevant objectives: disposal and recovery activities*   In respect of disposal and recovery activities[1], the Waste Management Licensing Regulations 1994 place a duty on the Agency to ensure[2]:

'. . .that waste is recovered or disposed of without endangering human health and without using processes or methods which could harm the environment and in particular without –

  (i)   risk to water, air, soil, plants or animals; or
  (ii) causing nuisance through noise or odours; or
  (iii) adversely affecting the countryside or places of special interest.'

1   'Disposal' and 'recovery' are defined by reg 1(3) as falling within the lists contained in Sch 4 to the Waste Management Licensing Regulations 1994 (see Tables 2.5 and 2.6 in Chapter 2).
2   SI 1994/1056, Sch 4, Pt I, para 4(1)(a): a copy of the kernel of Article 4 of the Directive on Waste.

8.56   Originally matters seemed relatively straightforward in respect of the relevant objectives listed in (i) above[1]. It was solely for the Agency to ensure that waste management licence applications only succeed when the proposals are without risk to water, air, soil, plants or animals. This emphasis arose due to the Waste Management Licensing Regulations 1994[2] explicitly forbidding a planning authority from dealing with specified matters when a pollution control body has appropriate statutory powers. Although this reading would appear to be confirmed by Circular 11/94[3,4], it would seem that the duty in (i) above now also applies in the context of development control[5]. For a waste management licence application, it would seem that these objectives are to be embraced by the criteria set down in s 36(3) of the EPA 1990, namely that a licence should not be issued where pollution of the environment or harm to human health may result.

1   SI 1994/1056, Sch 4, para 4(1)(a)(i).
2   SI 1994/1056, Sch 4, para 2(2).
3   See Circular 11/94, paras 1.53 and 1.54.
4   The question of how any activity can be licensed 'without risk' to the matters listed is considered further at para 12.18.
5   See *R v Bolton Metropolitan Borough Council, ex p Kirkham* [1998] Env LR 560; on appeal [1998] Env LR 719, CA.

8.57 In the case of item (ii) above and the duty to ensure that disposal and recovery operations do not cause nuisance through noise and odours[1], it might be thought that the exclusion relating to the planning authority contained in the Waste Management Licensing Regulations 1994 would apply[2]. This would appear to push the responsibility for considering the specified nuisance issues firmly in the direction of the Agency[3]. However, this not the impression given by Circular 11/94[4], which indicates that, in the case of development which was not granted planning permission prior to 1 May 1994, matters in respect of noise[5] are the concern of the planning authority. Given the judicial erosion of the exclusivity of item (i) in respect of development control, it may now be that both the Agency and the planning authorities need to consider these matters within their own, slightly differently focused, statutory remits. Furthermore, if the definition of harm in the EPA 1990[6] includes 'an offence to any of [a person's] senses', it seems difficult to avoid the conclusion that odour and noise are at least partially within the Agency's domain of responsibility.

1   SI 1994/1056, Sch 4, Pt I, para 4(1)(a)(ii).
2   SI 1994/1056, Sch 4, para 2(2).
3   This is consistent with both s 33(6)'s concept of harm to human health and with s 29(5) of the EPA 1990 defining the word 'harm' as including giving offence to a person's senses.
4   Circular 11/94, Annex 1, para 1.54(a).
5   Odours are not mentioned.
6   EPA 1990, s 29(5), see para 8.44.

8.58 Certainly, it seems clear that questions of noise can be considered by the Agency where planning permission was granted prior to 1 May 1994 or in instances when no permission was required for the development now subject to the licence application. In such circumstances, these matters would be embraced within the Agency's determination of whether an application would involve a serious detriment to the amenities of a locality, as set down by s 36(3)(c) of the EPA 1990[1].

1   See SI 1994/1056, Sch 4, para 9(7): s 36(3)(c) is discussed at para 8.49 above.

8.59 The responsibility for the relevant objectives which require that no waste management facility should adversely affect the countryside or places of special interest[1] (item (iii) above) rests, depending upon circumstances, with the Agency or the local planning authority. Normally, it would be the expectation that matters involving issues such as countryside protection would be the domain of development control. Circular 11/94 indicates[2] that, except where no planning permission was required for development[3] or when planning permission had been granted prior to 1 May 1994, the relevant objectives are to be fulfilled through the planning system. This assertion reflects the boundary set down by s 36(3) of the EPA 1990. As noted at para 8.49 above, the Agency can only use the criteria of serious detriment to the amenities of the locality when considering a licence application which relates to a site which either was granted a planning permission prior to 1 May 1994 or where planning permission is not required[4].

1   SI 1994/1056, Sch 4, para 4(1)(a)(iii).
2   Circular 11/94, Annex 1, para 1.54.
3   This includes where a certificate of lawful use or established use was provided.
4   See SI 1994/1056, Sch 4, Pt I, para 9(7).

8.60 In the circumstances which allow the serious detriment to amenity criteria to be used, the Agency must[1] follow the objective of considering the need to protect the countryside and places of special interest. The fact that conditions of a waste management licence can be used to substantiate existing land use controls is likely to prove a useful and powerful tool in relation to older sites. Such facilities may suffer from a poorly detailed planning permission or may be subject to certificates of lawful or established use. The need to follow relevant objectives when considering applications for scrapyards and vehicle dismantlers which possess certificates of lawful or established use becomes important[2]. In a minority of cases such as old quarries, examples of conditions being imposed in the name of preventing adverse effects on the countryside[3] might include detailed requirements for restoration, landscaping and screening, improved access, and so on. It may also be possible to turn down a licence application on the grounds that the access to a site was very bad and would be seriously detrimental to neighbouring land users.

1 See *R v Environment Agency and Redland Aggregates Ltd, ex p Gibson* [1999] Env LR 73.
2 See Department of the Environment (1995) *The Licensing of Metal Recycling Sites*, Waste Management Paper 4A, HMSO, London, para 2.5.
3 SI 1994/1056, Sch 4, Pt I, para 4(1)(a)(iii).

8.61 Respondents to the waste management licence consultation will no doubt provide significant input into the process of determining the best way to apply the relevant objectives in such circumstances. However, since the passing of the Environment Act 1995, it would appear that the Agency's decision may be coloured by its own specific duty under s 7. Section 7 of the 1995 Act requires the Agency to have regard to the need to protect and conserve buildings and items of archaeological or historic interest[1]; to take into account effects of proposals on beauty or amenity or in respect of buildings, flora, fauna, etc[2] and to have regard to the effect of proposals on the economic or social well-being of communities in rural areas[3]. These provisions may extend or otherwise strengthen the statutory basis under which particular actions relating to the relevant objectives are undertaken.

1 Environment Act 1995, s 7(1)(c)(i).
2 Environment Act 1995, s 7(1)(c)(ii).
3 Environment Act 1995, s 7(1)(c)(iii).

8.62 *Relevant objectives: disposal activities* The second category of relevant objective relates to applications[1] involving the *disposal*[2] of waste. In relation to such sites, the requirements of Article 5 of the Directive on Waste are transposed nearly verbatim as additional relevant objectives in the Waste Management Licensing Regulations 1994[3]. Proposed disposal facilities must be in accordance with the following criteria[4]:

'(a) establishing an integrated and adequate network of waste disposal installations, taking account of the best available technology not involving excessive costs; and
(b) ensuring that the network referred to at paragraph (a) above enables –
    (i) the European Community as a whole to become self-sufficient in waste disposal, and the member states individually to move towards that aim, taking into account geographical circumstances or the need for specialised installations for certain types of waste; and
    (ii) waste to be disposed of in one of the nearest appropriate installations, by means of the most appropriate methods and technologies in order to ensure a high level of protection for the environment and public health.'

1 As well as other specified Agency functions: see SI 1994/1056, Sch 4, para 3(1) and see para 12.22.
2 Defined by SI 19994/1056, reg 1(3) as those processes featuring in Part III to Sch 4. These should be viewed as distinct from 'waste recovery operations' as defined by Part IV to Sch 4. These are shown as Tables 2.5 and 2.6 in Chapter 2.
3 SI 1994/1056, Sch 4, Pt I, para 4(2).
4 SI 1994/1056, Sch 4, Pt I, para 4(2).

8.63 Circular 11/94 advises that the development control system will be responsible for the implementation of the above requirements for all new developments subject to planning permission after 1 May 1994[1]. Rather than require a full consideration at the time of each and every application, the circular suggests that it is preferable that they are addressed within the development plan[2].

1 Circular 11/94, Annex 1, paras 1.30 and 1.54.
2 Circular 11/94, Annex 1, para 1.31: see also PPG 23, para 2.23 and Annex 6.

8.64 However, in relation to licence applications which concern proposed facilities which were granted planning permission prior to 1 May 1994, along with instances where such permission is not required, it would appear that the Agency is intended to have responsibility for the implementation of this provision. However, although confirming that 'all' the relevant objectives are to be addressed by the Agency and other pollution control bodies in these circumstances[1], Circular 11/94 is notably vague about how the Agency should address these responsibilities through specific powers. Certainly, it seems hard to envisage how all of these requirements can be enacted by way of s 36(3) of the EPA 1990, even when that sub-section is extended[2] to permit the Agency to consider the question of whether the proposal is seriously detrimental to the amenities of the locality.

1 Circular 11/94, Annex 1, para 1.58.
2 SI 1994/1056, Sch 4, Pt I, para 9(7).

The Agency's statutory functions under the Environment Act 1995

8.65 Since the formation of the Agency in 1996, the requirements against which waste management licence applications are to be evaluated would appear to have been extended. The Environment Act 1995 contains a series of provisions which set out the function and purpose of the Agency as a whole. Such provisions, not surprisingly, need to be met when the Agency is undertaking all of its statutory duties but have particular significance in the consideration of licence applications. The precise influence of these functions on the *vires* of waste licence applications will only appear in the long term.

8.66 Perhaps the most significant requirement of the Environment Act 1995 in respect of waste management licences is the need for the Agency to address the question of sustainability. The 1995 Act holds that the 'principal aim of the Agency' is to discharge its functions in a manner which protects and enhances the environment to 'make the contribution' towards fulfilling the objective of 'sustainable development'[1]. The term 'sustainable development' is not defined in the Act. However, it is commonly held to mean[2]:

'... development that meets the needs of the present without compromising the ability of future generations to meet their own needs.'[3]

The provision on sustainable development is substantiated by statutory guidance made under s 4 of the Environment Act 1995[4]. Of particular potential significance is the following passage from that guidance[5]:

'Because it needs to take a **long term perspective** in considering sustainable development the Agency should seek to take properly into account any longer term implications and effects, particularly those which appear likely to be irreversible, reversible only at high cost over a long timescale or which would raise issues of inter-generational equity.'

389

1 Environment Act 1995, s 4(1): somewhat oddly, this requirement does not apply to SEPA, which is simply required to follow the Secretary of State's guidance on sustainable development: 1995 Act s 31.
2 See for example Department of the Environment (1995) *Making Waste Work. A Strategy for Sustainable Waste Management in England and Wales*, CMND 3040, HMSO, London, para 1.5.
3 See World Commission on Economic Development (1987) *Our Common Future*, Oxford University Press (widely referred to as the 'Bruntland Report').
4 Department of the Environment (1996) *The Environment Agency and Sustainable Development*, Department of the Environment, London.
5 Department of the Environment (1996) *The Environment Agency and Sustainable Development*, Department of the Environment, London, para 10(ii).

8.67 Certain waste management activities may have implications which could negatively affect future generations. For example, the very concept of waste 'disposal' involves the post-consumption abandonment of resources which may be subject to long term scarcity. Furthermore, it may be that the necessity for the Agency to follow sustainable development may be particularly relevant to landfill sites. Biodegradation processes may continue for 100 years or more, and while the present generation has accrued the benefits of the site as an outlet for their wastes, future generations may need to pay for long term environmental monitoring costs and possible remedial site works. Some of these matters are themselves addressed by the EPA 1990. Licence conditions continue to apply until evidence is presented that a site no longer has significant environmental implications[1] and applicants must satisfy the EPA's requirements on financial provision[2]. But the very long-term timescales involved with landfills may not necessary provide an adequate guarantee that costs will not be imposed on future generations. Partly as a response to the long term nature of biodegradation, there have been proposals for 'sustainable landfills' and 'flushing bioreactors'[3], whereby biodegradation is enhanced so that it will occur over much shorter time periods.

1 By way of the procedures on licence surrender: EPA 1990, s 39: see para 9.93ff.
2 EPA 1990, s 74.
3 See for example Department of the Environment (1995) *Landfill Design, Construction and Operational Practice*, Waste Management Paper 26B, HMSO, London, para 1.26 to 1.31, Appendix D.

8.68 It will prove interesting to see how the objective of the Agency to work towards following sustainable principles would be dealt with in any court proceedings, particularly those relating to judicial reviews of decisions to issue landfill licences. However, the view may be taken that they are target duties not enforceable by individuals.

8.69 Besides the requirements with respect to sustainability, the Agency also has a statutory duty[1] which applies to the manner by which it exercises its pollution control powers[2]:

'The Agency's pollution control powers shall be exercisable for the purpose of preventing or minimising, or remedying or mitigating the effects of, pollution of the environment.'

This does not appear to do more than reiterate the requirements of the EPA 1990, that a waste management licence is not issued where pollution of the environment or harm to human health cannot be prevented[3]. However, the preventive approach is being clearly stressed. In respect of water resources, the Agency also has the additional duty under the Environment Act 1995 to conserve or augment such resources and to secure their proper use[4]. This power may strengthen the Agency's role in the protection of surface waters and groundwater in proximity to waste management facilities[5].

1 Environment Act 1995, s 5(1).
2 Defined as including Part II of the EPA 1990, along with the Control of Pollution (Amendment) Act 1989: 1995 Act, s 5(5).
3 EPA 1990, s 36(3).
4 Environment Act 1995 Act, s 6(2).
5 Provisions specific to groundwater in SI 1994/1056, reg 15 are discussed at para 8.70 below.

REGULATION 15, THE GROUNDWATER DIRECTIVE (80/68) AND WASTE MANAGEMENT LICENCE APPLICATIONS

8.70 Regulation 15 of the Waste Management Licensing Regulations 1994 partially implements the Groundwater Directive[1]. The Directive entered into force in December 1981[2], placing restrictions on a wide range of potentially polluting substances from entering groundwater. The Directive states that *all* relevant discharges to groundwater should have complied with its requirements by December 1985[3]. Implementation in the UK has proved troublesome, mainly due to the cynically disingenuous advice provided in Circular 4/82[4], which is exemplified by the statement that[5] '. . . this Directive is very much in line with existing UK practice . . . It will serve in the main to underline and reinforce, rather than alter, current policy and procedures . . .'. Twelve years later, Circular 11/94 glosses over a not inconsiderable turnabout[6]: '. . . the Departments[7] now accept that the Directive requires us to apply the approach in the Directive by more formal legal means'. On top of all of the other changes contained in Part II of the EPA 1990 which were introduced in May 1994, the requirements of reg 15 are extremely wide ranging and it is likely that not all of its ramifications have yet to be felt at a number of a waste management facilities[8].

1 Council Directive of 17 December 1979 on the protection of groundwater against pollution caused by certain dangerous substances (Directive 80/68/EEC) (OJ L20/43 26.1.80).
2 Directive 80/68, Article 21.
3 Directive 80/68, Articles 14 and 21.
4 *EC Directive on the Protection of Groundwater against Pollution Caused by Certain Dangerous Substances 80/68/EEC*, Circular 4/82, HMSO, London.
5 Circular 4/82, para 3.
6 Circular 11/94, Annex 7, para 7.1.
7 The Department of the Environment in England, the Welsh and Scottish Offices.
8 In 1998 a further Statutory Instrument was made to further transpose the requirements of the Groundwater Directive at facilities other than those for which a waste management licence is 'required' (see SI 1998/2746, reg 2(1)(d)). Note that the key word is 'required' not 'granted'. This will apply mainly to waste management activities exempted or excluded (see para 10.20ff) from Part II of the EPA 1990, as well as in respect of non-controlled waste management (see paras 2.34 and 2.48) such as sheep dip disposal.

8.71 Advice on the implementation of the Directive currently stems from two separate circulars. As noted above, the original circular was 4/82, which was then supplemented by Circular 20/90[1]. However, Circular 4/82 is now cancelled in so far as it relates to England[2]. Further advice is now to be found in Annex 7 of Circular 11/94[3].

1 *EC Directive on the Protection of Groundwater against Pollution Caused by Certain Dangerous Substances 80/68/EEC: Classification of Listed Substances*, Circular 20/90, HMSO, London.
2 See Planning Policy Guidance Note (PPG) 23, Section 6, para 6.1.
3 See also Environment Agency (1999) *The EC Groundwater Directive 80/68/EEC and the Waste Management Licensing Regulations, 1994. Interim Internal Guidance on the Interpretation of the Waste Management Licensing Regulations, 1994 (The Protection of Groundwater). Draft for Consultation*, January 1999, Environment Agency, Bristol.

8.72 The majority of the paragraphs which make up reg 15 mainly concern requirements relating to applications for new waste management licences. However, once issued, such licences need to be kept under review in respect of compliance with reg 15[1]. Furthermore, all licences which were transferred from the Control of Pollution Act 1974's waste disposal licensing system also needed to have their groundwater implications re-assessed[2]. It is fair to say that reg 15's requirements for the appraisal of licence applications vis-à-vis the Groundwater Directive are considerably clearer and more embellished than those provisions which relate to existing sites.

1   SI 1994/1056, reg 15(9): see para 9.65ff.
2   SI 1994/1056, reg 15(10): see para 9.68.

8.73   Regulation 15 does not require that the groundwater implications of old, unlicensed landfill sites are investigated. However, such an obligation is clearly contained in Directive 80/68, and would appear to be embraced by the Groundwater Regulations 1998[1].

1   SI 1998/2746; see in particular reg 14: as explained in the Preface, contaminated land issues are beyond the scope of this book.

List I and List II substances

8.74   The Groundwater Directive requires that groundwater is protected from two sets of polluting substances, which are set out in the Directive's Lists I and II (see Table 8.1). List I substances should not be discharged into groundwater[1], while List II substances need to have their rate of introduction into groundwater limited in order to avoid groundwater pollution[2,3].

1   Directive 80/68, Article 3(a).
2   Directive 80/68, Article 3(b)
3   Circular 11/94 (Annex 7, para 7.6) confirms that the pesticides bromoxynil, bromoxynil octanoate and chloropyrifos are List I substances.

Table 8.1

Groundwater Directive (80/68/EEC)
List I of Families and Groups of Substances
List I contains the individual substances which belong to the families and groups of substances enumerated below, with the exception of those which are considered inappropriate to list I on the basis of a low risk of toxicity, persistence and bioaccumulation. Such substances which with regard to toxicity, persistence and bioaccumulation are appropriate to list II are to be classed in list II.
1. Organohologen compounds and substances which may form such compounds in the aquatic environment
2. Organophosphorus compounds
3. Organotin compounds
4. Substances which possess carcinogenic mutagenic or teratogenic properties in or via the aquatic environment[1]
5. Mercury and its compounds
6. Cadmium and its compounds
7. Mineral oils and hydrocarbons
8. Cyanides.

Note
1   Where certain substances in list II are carcinogenic, mutagenic or teratogenic, they are included in category 4 of this list.

Table 8.1 – *contd*

Groundwater Directive (80/68/EEC)

List II of Families and Groups of Substances

List II contains the individual substances and the categories of substances belonging to the families and groups of substances listed below which could have a harmful effect on groundwater.

1. The following metalloids and metals and their compounds:

1. Zinc	11. Tin
2. Copper	12. Barium
3. Nickel	13. Beryllium
4. Chrome	14. Boron
5. Lead	15. Uranium
6. Selenium	16. Vanadium
7. Arsenic	17. Cobalt
8. Antimony	18. Thallium
9. Molybdenum	19. Tellurium
10. Titanium	20. Silver.

2. Biocides and their derivatives not appearing in list I.

3. Substances which have a deleterious effect on the taste and/or odour of groundwater, and compounds liable to cause the formation of such substances in such water and to render it unfit for human consumption.

4. Toxic or persistent organic compounds of silicon, and substances which may cause the formation of such compounds in water, excluding those which are biologically harmless or are rapidly converted in water into harmless substances.

5. Inorganic compounds of phosphorus and elemental phosphorus.

6. Fluorides.

7. Ammonia and nitrites.

8.75 It should be noted that, for all substances appearing on List I, there is a caveat. This is that certain of the substances on List I are to be excluded from the Directive's requirements when they have 'a low risk of toxicity, persistence and bioaccumulation'[1]. By contrast, there is no similar approach in the Directive for excluding any of the substances which figure on List II. In any case, leachate from household waste landfills is likely to contain List I substances[2] at low concentrations[3]. Similarly, List I substances such as hydrocarbons may emanate from less well-managed scrapyards or vehicle dismantlers or from leaking fuel storage tanks.

1   See Directive 80/68's Annex and Circular 20/90, Appendix 1, para 7.
2   See, for example, Vallance R and Savory D (1995) 'Regulation 15: Groundwater and Landfill' *Proceedings of the Institute of Wastes Management*, July 1995, pp 30–32, and Robinson HD (1996) *A Review of the Composition of Leachates from Domestic Wastes in Landfill Sites*, Wastes Technical Division, Environment Agency, Bristol. Leachate from household waste landfills will inevitably fall within List II due to the presence of ammonia.
3   Leachates from landfills involved in the co-disposal of large quantities of wastes containing List I substances may contain significantly greater concentrations.

8.76 The Directive makes different provisions in respect of direct and indirect discharges of List I and List II substances, and these are transposed by reg 15[1]. A direct discharge is one which involves 'the introduction into groundwater of substances in Lists I and II without percolation into the ground or subsoil'[2]. Such a discharge will occur only when the receiving body of water is in direct hydraulic continuity with the deposited waste. An example might be a quarry which is flooded due to the presence of a water table at a height in excess of the quarry's base. An indirect discharge is defined as 'the introduction into groundwater of substances in Lists I and II after percolation through the ground or subsoil'[3]. The latter type of discharge will occur when List I or List II substances pass through an unsaturated sub-surface prior to entering into groundwater. An example might involve a a dry quarry, the base of which is permeable and several metres higher than the water table.

1   Regulation 15(12) requires that all expressions contained in reg 15 have the same meaning as in the Directive.
2   Directive 80/68, Article 1(2)(b).
3   Directive 80/68, Article 1(2)(c).

8.77   Indirect discharges will be the most common issue needing consideration in relation to most waste management facilities[1]. Sites located in areas with high water tables are much less suitable as landfills for technical and environmental reasons, particularly where non-inert wastes are to be deposited.

1   Interestingly, the Agency considers the small but inevitable percolation of leachate through a landfill liner to be an indirect discharge: see Environmental Agency (1999) *The EC Groundwater Directive (80/68/EEC) and the Waste Management Licensing Regulations, 1994. Interim Internal Guidance on the Interpretation and Application of Regulation 15 of the Waste Management Licensing Regulations 1994 (The Protection of Groundwater) Draft for Consultation*, Environment Agency, Bristol, para 1.7.

8.78   It should be made clear that, subject to a very limited set of exclusions, the Directive relates to all activities which may cause the direct release into groundwater of List I and List II substances[1]. The requirements on indirect discharges of List I and List II substances are restricted to those stemming from 'disposal or tipping for the purposes of disposal'[2]. However, the Directive also provides for the control of indirect discharges of List I substances from other sources[3]. The Directive, and reg 15, therefore applies to a wider range of sites than just landfills. As will be illustrated later[4], storage tanks for wastes and fuels appear to be covered, as well as recovery facilities such as scrapyards and car dismantlers.

1   Directive 80/68, Article 4(1), First Indent.
2   Directive 80/68, Article 4(1), Second Indent.
3   Directive 80/68, Article 4(1), Third Indent.
4   See para 8.55ff below.

The definition of groundwater

8.79   Groundwater is defined in the Directive[1] as 'all water which is below the surface of the ground in the saturation zone and in direct contact with the ground or soil'. Circular 11/94 confirms that it is this more narrow definition, rather than that contained in s 104 of the Water Resources Act 1991[2], which is to be used for the purposes of reg 15 of the Waste Management Licensing Regulations 1994[3].

1   Directive 80/68, Article 1(2)(a).
2   Part II of the Control of Pollution Act 1974 in Scotland.
3   Circular 11/94, Annex 7, para 7.4.

8.80   It should be made clear that the Directive does not only seek to protect water that is potentially usable for drinking water purposes. In prohibiting the discharge of List I substances, Article 4(2) requires this principle to apply except where groundwater is 'permanently unsuitable for other uses, especially domestic or agricultural'.

This is supplemented by a requirement that all technical precautions must be utilised to prevent List I substances passing from such unsuitable groundwater into other aquatic systems or causing harm to other ecosystems. These are pretty stringent criteria. Groundwater which fails to meet the standards of, for example, the Drinking Water Directive[1] could be made potable by treatment and therefore cannot be classed as permanently unsuitable. Even water which is unpotable may still have other possible uses, such as as industrial cooling water[2]. Accordingly, the Directive and reg 15 appears to have wide application. However, it is not clear if this extends to groundwaters which are saline by their nature due to their proximity to coastal or estuarine areas.

1   Directive on the Quality of of Water Intended for Human Consumption (80/778/EEC) (OJ L229 30.8.80).
2   Note that Articles 9 and 10 of Directive 80/68 specifically address the need to safeguard 'thermal water'.

De minimis discharges

8.81   Article 2 sets down three instances when the Groundwater Directive does not apply. For waste management facilities, only Article 2(b) has possible relevance. This is that the Directive does not apply to[1]:

> '... discharges which are found by the competent authority of the Member State concerned to contain substances in Lists I and II in a quantity and concentration so small as to obviate any present or future danger of deterioration in the quality of the receiving groundwater.'

However, this exclusion does not apply to any waste management facility which has the potential to discharge List I and List II substances. Indeed, this may be why it is not replicated in reg 15 itself. Circular 11/94 points to the exclusion, citing the case of *EC Commission v Germany*[2] as providing guidance on how this principle should be interpreted[3].

1   Directive 80/68, Article 2(b).
2   [1991] ECR I-825.
3   Circular 11/94, paras 7.7–7.9.

8.82   *Commission v Germany* involved a somewhat complex judgment as to whether German law fully transposed the requirements of the Directive. Much of the judgment is therefore concerned with a detailed comparison between the relevant national legislation and the Directive, with the European Court of Justice deciding that neither the contents of Germany's provisions nor the form of transposition complied with Community law. However, the judgment also includes a number of profound observations in respect of the interpretation of the Directive itself. The most significant finding relates to the application of the de minimis principle in Article 2(b). There has been a tendency to view this Article as a convenient total exclusion from the requirements of the Directive. Hence it might be attractive to argue that the inevitable, but very small, discharge of leachate through a state-of-the-art landfill containment system is excluded by this Article. That this is an inappropriate view of the Directive is clearly stated in *EC Commission v Germany*.

8.83   The European Court held that Article 2(b) refers not to the discharge of List I and List II substances themselves, but only to solutions containing such substances[1]. Hence that Article certainly does not exclude from the Directive the direct or indirect discharge of the actual substances listed. Examples might include the discharge of hydrocarbons or organohalogen compounds such as a pesticide. Secondly, and perhaps more importantly, the Court placed a very restricted view of the scope of application of the exclusion contained in Article 2(b). The only time when the exclusion applies is when it is patently obvious that a discharge of List I or List II substances is so trivial as to be immediately discounted[2]:

'Substances in Lists I or II contained in such discharges must be present in quantities sufficiently small as to obviate *prima facie*, without there even being a need for an evaluation, all risk of pollution of the groundwater. That is why Article 2(b) of the directive refers not to an evaluation by the competent authority of a member state but to a simple finding . . . Thus the meaning of that provision is that if the quantity of substances in List I (or II) contained in discharges of other substances is such that the risk of pollution cannot be automatically excluded, the directive is applicable, and in that case Article 2(b) cannot . . . be taken in conjunction with the other provisions of the directive in order to interpret them.'

This restrictive view would seem to emanate from not only the wording of the relevant Article, but also from the Directive's recitals. Recital 6 states that the Directive should not apply to:

'. . . discharges containing substances in Lists I or II in very small quantities and concentrations, on account of the low risk of pollution and the difficulty of controlling the discharge of such effluent.'

Similarly, Recital 9 requires that all direct discharges of List I substances are 'automatically' prohibited, thereby implying that no prior investigation is needed.

1   *EC Commission v Germany* [1991] ECR I-825, para 16.
2   *EC Commission v Germany* [1991] ECR I-825, paras 17–18.

8.84   Accordingly, Circular 11/94 states that the exception in the Directive for solutions containing List I and List II discharges in small quantities and low concentrations[1]:

'. . . should be interpreted as applying to the disposal of waste only where the nature of the waste is such that any leachate from that waste can pose no danger of deterioration in the quality of the receiving groundwater.'

This means that a very significant number of sites, particularly landfills, are subject to the provisions of reg 15. The exception would seem to be where there is no possibility that any List I or List II substances are contained in the wastes being accepted at a facility: an example might be a site involved in the deposition of inert wastes, such as sub-soils or brick rubble[2].

1   Circular 11/94, Annex 7, para 7.9.
2   Provided, of course, that there was no possibility that contaminated material would be consigned.

Waste management facilities subject to the Groundwater Directive

8.85   The extent of the provisions' application to different types of waste management facility is not immediately clear from either the Directive or reg 15. While the question of the definition of groundwater and de minimis discharges has been addressed above, two other matters require comment. The first concerns the focus of the Directive on 'discharges'. The second concerns only indirect discharges and the somewhat ambiguous wording of Articles 4 and 5, which points to particular waste management facilities being covered but does not clearly define them.

'Discharges' subject to the Directive

8.86 From its title and the wording of the citations and Articles, it is clear that the Directive concerns itself with the need to protect groundwater from pollution. Hence List I substances entering usable groundwater are prohibited and List II substances must have their introduction limited so that water pollution does not result[1]. This is to be achieved by a series of provisions which explicitly relate to direct and indirect discharges[2]. It follows that, if there is no possibility of a direct or indirect discharge, then the requirements of the Directive do not apply[3].

1 Directive 80/68, Article 3.
2 Directive 80/68, Article 4ff.
3 In the case of an engineered containment system at a landfill, there is always the possibility of leakage. A very low permeability liner will, by definition, always result in some, but very small, leachate movement through it. Likewise, leakage would be greater if the system was installed in a defective manner.

8.87 This would appear to have been the ultimate finding in *R v Vale of Glamorgan Borough Council, ex p James*[1]. This case involved a judicial review of a decision to grant a licence for a landfill at the Barry Docks. A third party objector applied for judicial review on a number of grounds, one of which concerned non-compliance with reg 15 of the Waste Management Licensing Regulations 1994.

1 [1996] JPL 832.

8.88 It is important to the judgment to appreciate the circumstances of the proposed landfill. It was proposed to line two disused docks with a synthetic liner of low permeability. Contaminated land derived from other parts of the docks' redevelopment was then to be deposited in the site. Groundwater levels in that area were much higher than the base of the proposed landfill site. This would mean that, if the docks were left to their own devices, they would fill with water. In order to ensure that contaminated materials did not leach from any wastes deposited in the site, it was proposed to maintain a very low leachate level in the landfill by way of pumping. This low level would therefore ensure that the surrounding groundwater would be more likely to slowly seep through the liner and into the landfill. The pumping operation would mean that water might enter the site, but that any contaminated leachate would not pass out through the liner. On behalf of the objector to the scheme it was claimed that the water entering the site was groundwater under the Directive and that the requirements of the Directive would be contravened by the proposal. In particular, the arrangement would cause a direct discharge of List I substances into the groundwater and thus contravene Article 3.

8.89 Hirst LJ held that reg 15, and hence the Groundwater Directive, did not apply to such circumstances[1]:

'I have grave doubts whether water pumped into the system is groundwater for the purposes of the Groundwater Directive, see art 2. I very much doubt whether water entering a site which has substances in it is covered by the phrase "the introduction into groundwater of substances"[2]. It is wholly unclear whether there is going to be percolation through ground or sub soil . . .'.

1 *R v Vale of Glamorgan Borough Council, ex p James* [1996] JPL 832 at 836.
2 See Directive 80/68, Article 3(a) and (b).

8.90 The arrangement whereby the leachate level in a landfill is kept lower than surrounding groundwater is by no means unique to the proposal at the Barry Docks. Accordingly, *R v Vale of Glamorgan Borough Council* will have application at a number of sites in the country. However, for a site to be embraced by this judgment it seems essential that, whilst water can leak in, no leachate can ever leak out into unpolluted groundwater.

Types of waste management facilities

8.91 The Groundwater Directive's provisions in respect of direct discharges are pretty clear in their application: all direct discharges of List I substances are 'prohibited'[1] and all direct discharges of List II substances are subject to a 'prior investigation'[2]. These provisions therefore apply to any industrial activity, including all waste management sites.

1 Directive 80/68, Article 4(1), First Indent.
2 Directive 80/68, Article 5(1).

8.92 However, matters are less clear in respect of indirect discharges. Both the Directive and reg 15 refer to the necessity for indirect discharges of List I and List II substances to be subject to a prior investigation where 'disposal or tipping for the purposes of disposal' takes place[1]. Such discharges must then be either prohibited or granted authorisation. In the case of other, but unspecified, 'activities on or in the ground', the Directive requires that a member state must take 'all appropriate measures' to prevent indirect discharges of List I substances[2]. The latter appears to be a catch-all provision for those activities not covered by the sub-article embracing 'disposal or tipping for the purposes of disposal'[3]. There seems to be, in the latter case, no explicit requirement for authorisation, leaving member states with discretion over applicable measures[4].

1 Directive 80/68, Articles 4(1) and 5(1); SI 1995/1056, reg 15(1)(a) and (b).
2 Directive 80/68, Article 4(1), Third Indent and Article 5(2).
3 Directive 80/58, Article 4(1), Third Indent: confirmed by *EC Commission v Germany* [1991] ECR I-825, para 54.
4 SI 1994/1056, reg 15 does not refer to any indirect discharges other than those involving 'disposal or tipping for the purposes of disposal'.

8.93 Given the contrasting requirements between these two obligations, it seems important to decide which particular types of waste management infrastructure they apply to. This is also necessary as reg 15 applies explicitly only to indirect discharges of List I and List II substances from 'disposal or tipping for the purposes of disposal'[1], but not to the other activities. Unfortunately, the latter term is defined neither in the Directive nor in reg 15[2]. Furthermore, Circular 11/94 does not provide guidance. However, some indication can be obtained from the context of the Directive itself, whilst further clues can be found in the proceedings of *EC Commission v Germany*.

1 SI 1994/1056, reg 15(1)(a) and (b).
2 However, SI 1994/1056, reg 15(12) requires that expressions used in reg 15 have the same meaning as in the Directive.

8.94 Throughout the Waste Management Licensing Regulations 1994, the word 'disposal' is held to mean, 'unless the context otherwise requires', those operations listed in Part III of Schedule 4 to the 1994 Regulations[1]. This list is a near duplicate of Annex IIA of Directive on Waste[2] and is reproduced in Chapter 2 as Table 2.5. It will be seen that landfills are included, along with treatment plants, incinerators[3] and the storage of waste prior to disposal[4]. From the meaning of 'disposal' contained in Annex IIA, it is not immediately apparent that indirect discharges of List I and List II substances from recovery operations[5] are encompassed by reg 15 and the Groundwater Directive. Being classed in reg 1(3) as recovery operations, they represent, under the Waste Management Licensing Regulations 1994, a quite distinct category to disposal operations.

1   SI 1994/1056, reg 1(3).
2   Council Directive of 15 July 1975 on Waste (75/442/EEC) (OJ L194/39 25.7.75) (as amended by Council Directive of 18 March 1991 amending Directive 75/442/EEC on Waste (91/156/EEC) OJ L78/32 26.3.91)).
3   Confirmed as within the ambit of the Groundwater Directive by Article 8(4) of Directive 94/67 of 16 December 1994 on Hazardous Waste Incineration (OJ L365/34 31.12.94).
4   Except storage on the premises of the waste producer.
5   See SI 1994/1056, reg 1(3), Table 2.6 and also Part IV to Sch 4 and Annex IIB of the Directive on Waste.

8.95   While there is no formal definition of the word 'disposal' in the Groundwater Directive, it should be pointed out that the Directive was drafted after the Directive on Waste[1] was originally finalised, but prior to its later amendment by Directive 91/156[2]. In its unamended form, the definition of the word 'disposal' in the Directive on Waste encompassed 'the transformation operations necessary for its[3] re-use, recovery or re-cycling'[4]. Therefore, it would seem that, in order to accurately interpret the Groundwater Directive, it may be appropriate to define disposal in accordance with the definition contained in the Directive on Waste in its unamended form[5,6].

1   Council Directive of 15 July 1975 on Waste (75/442/EEC) (OJ L194/39 25.7.75).
2   Council Directive of 18 March 1991 amending Directive 75/442/EEC on Waste (91/156/EEC) (OJ L78/32 26.3.91).
3   Ie the wastes'.
4   Unamended Directive 75/442 Article 1(b) – see also *Vessoso and Zanetti v Ministère Public of Italy:* C-206/88 [1990] ECR I-1461 and para 2.78ff.
5   See also Harrison J's comments on the definition of 'disposal' in respect of Annex I of Directive 84/360 (OJ L188/20 1984) in *R v Environment Agency and Redland Aggregates Ltd, ex p Gibson* [1999] Env LR 73 at 94.
6   A similar question arises in respect of the definition of 'disposal' in Directive 97/11/EC (OJ L73/5 14.3.97) on the assessment of the effects of certain public and private prospects on the environment (the 'EIA Directive').

8.96   An over-restrictive interpretation also might have odd effects. For example, if the definition of a 'disposal' activity in the Waste Management Licensing Regulations 1994 is used in the context of reg 15, any indirect discharge from waste stored under a waste management licence at the site of the waste producer would be excluded[1]. Paragraph 15 of the list of disposal operations in Schedule 4 to the Regulations excludes temporary storage, pending collection, on the site where the waste is produced[2]. It would seem anomalous to the scope of application of the Groundwater Directive that off-site waste storage would be covered by the Directive, but the storage of the same material where it was produced would not.

1   Storage of special waste above certain thresholds is licensable; see para 10.56.
2   See Item 15 on Table 2.5 in Chapter 2.

8.97   The public policy aspects of this matter also need to be considered. Significant numbers of scrapyards and car dismantlers have for many years regularly discharged List I substances, such as mineral oils and hydrocarbons, into the ground beneath the site, along with List II substances such as lead, copper, zinc etc. Many other waste recovery plants have a similar potential to be highly polluting. It would therefore be anomalous to include a disposal facility, such as a hazardous waste treatment plant which deals with List I substances, within the ambit of the Directive but to exclude a recovery plant which handles similar types of waste. Often such plants may be in direct commercial competition with each other, and both may, for example, have storage tanks which are just as susceptible to spillages and leaks.

8.98 In *Commission v Germany* the German laws current at that time were subject to criticism because they[1]:

'. . . concern only certain types of disposal or tipping for the purpose of disposal and in no way guarantee that every type of disposal or tipping for the purposes of disposal capable of leading to indirect discharge of List I substances is covered . . .'.

Beyond that statement, the Court did not clarify what it viewed 'every type of tipping or disposal' as entailing. However, what seems clear is that the term should be applied to disposal activities comprehensively and not selectively.

1   *EC Commission v Germany* [1991] ECR I-825, para 29.

8.99 Finally, the Groundwater Regulations 1998[1] are intended to transpose the Groundwater Directive in respect of activities other than those where waste management licences are 'required'[2]. The fact that all licensed facilities – whether involving either disposal or recovery – are excluded from the Regulations would indicate they all must fall within the ambit of reg 15. To hold that waste recovery activities do not fall within reg 15 would be to acknowledge a major lacuna in Britain's transposition of the Directive.

1   SI 1998/2746.
2   See SI 1998/2746, reg 2(1)(d).

8.100   The above analysis would suggest that there are interpretative and practical justifications to hold that, despite the restrictive meaning given to the word 'disposal' in reg 1(3) of the Waste Management Licensing Regulations 1994, the term in the context of reg 15 should be interpreted broadly[1]. Such an interpretation is an instance where the words 'unless the context otherwise requires', which are contained within reg 1(3), would appear to apply.

1   Oddly, the fact that the Groundwater Directive applies to recovery facilities is acknowledged in respect of transfrontier waste shipments (see para 5.37ff) in Department of the Environment (1996) *United Kingdom Management Plan for Exports and Imports of Waste*, HMSO, London, paras 6.12 and 6.53.

Applications for waste management licences

8.101   Where the Agency receives an application for a waste management licence which will entail a possible direct discharge of List I and List II substances into groundwater, reg 15 of the Waste Management Licensing Regulations 1994 requires that 'a prior investigation' of the proposed activities must be undertaken[1]. By the absence of any requirement in reg 15 to the contrary, this applies to any waste management facility which has the potential to directly discharge List I and List II substances into groundwater.

1   SI 1994/1056, reg 15(1)(c) and (d).

8.102   For the reasons set out at para 8.92 above, there is less clarity in the drafting of the provisions concerning indirect discharges. An investigation is only necessary in the case of facilities which involve 'any disposal or tipping for the purpose of disposal' of List I or List II substances which may cause an indirect discharge[1]. The Agency must therefore decide whether the waste management licence application is one which involves such activities.

1 SI 1994/1056, reg 15(1)(a) and (b).

8.103 The requirements of reg 15 in respect of when the 'prior investigation' should be undertaken[1] do not seem to be fully in accordance with the custom and practice for waste management licence applications. The regulation requires that an investigation is done '[w]hen the waste regulation authority[2] proposes to issue a waste management licence . . .'. However, Circular 11/94 indicates that[3]:

'. . . [t]he information on which these investigations and conclusions can be based would normally be required by the WRA[2] of an applicant for a licence to dispose of waste on or on the ground.'

Accordingly, the investigation can be undertaken prior to the submission of the application. Should the applicant not provide the full information, the wording of reg 15(1) would indicate that this information can be asked for, and submitted, later. What seems clear is the fact that the initial application should not be rejected solely on the grounds that it does not satisfy the information requirements of reg 15. An opportunity should be given to the applicant to undertake the required investigation[4].

1 SI 1994/1056, reg 15(1).
2 Ie the Environment Agency or the Scottish Environment Protection Agency.
3 Circular 11/94, Annex 7, para 7.12.
4 Usually, the Agency would attempt to glean the missing information from the applicant rather than immediately reject the application on the grounds that it is deficient.

8.104 The nature of the 'prior investigation' referred to in reg 15(1) is set down in reg 15(2). It should 'include'[1] an examination of:

– the hydrogeological conditions of the area concerned;
– the possible purifying powers of the soil and sub-soil;
– the risk of pollution and alteration of the quality of the groundwater from this discharge.

In addition, the investigation should 'establish whether the discharge of substances into groundwater is a satisfactory solution from the point of view of the environment'[2].

1 And hence can address other matters of relevance to the Directive.
2 SI 1994/1056, reg 15(2).

8.105 Regulation 15 explicitly requires that no waste management licence should be issued to facilities where direct or indirect discharges of List I and List II substances may occur 'until the waste regulation authority[1] has checked that the groundwater, and in particular its quality, will undergo the requisite surveillance'[2]. This rather opaque requirement is a near-verbatim transposition of Article 8 of the Groundwater Directive. Precisely what is meant is not immediately apparent, and Circular 11/94 blithely points to Appendix C of Waste Management Paper No 4 as the source of appropriate minimum monitoring requirements for groundwaters[3].

1 The Environment Agency or Scottish Environment Protection Agency.
2 SI 1994/1056, reg 15(3); this is repeated in an unexpanded form in SI 1998/2746, reg 8.
3 Circular 11/94, Annex 7, para 7.13.

8.106   Where the results of the investigation indicate that either direct and indirect discharges of List I substances into groundwater will occur, the Agency can only issue a licence if the study has produced sufficient evidence to satisfy the criteria set down in reg 15(4)(a). Once this has been confirmed, reg 15(6) and (7) require that specified items must be included in any licence when issued (see para 8.247ff below).

8.107   Regulation 15(4)(a) only allows a site involved with the discharge of List I substances to be subject to licensing on strict grounds. Licensing is only permissible where the direct or indirect List I discharges will enter groundwater which satisfies the test of being permanently unsuitable for other uses[1]. In this case, the Agency also has to be satisfied that the presence of the List I substance will not, once discharged, 'impede exploitation of ground (sic) resources'[2]. It is not immediately obvious in either the Directive or reg 15 what 'ground resources' constitute. However, Circular 11/94 indicates that this term should be interpreted as requiring that 'mineral exploitation' is not impeded[3]. Finally, reg 15 requires the licence to be granted only when Agency is convinced that 'all technical precautions will be taken' to ensure that no List I substance is able to migrate from permanently unsuitable groundwater into other aquatic systems or to harm other ecosystems[4].

1   See para 8.80 above.
2   SI 1994/1056, reg 15(4)(a)(i).
3   Circular 11/94, Annex 7, para 7.14.
4   SI 1994/1056, reg 15(4)(a)(ii).

8.108   It should be noted that reg 15(4)(a) requires that the Agency can only be so satisfied 'in the light of the investigation'. This appears to suggest that such an investigation is to be done in all cases. Accordingly, it would seem that the Agency cannot issue the licence without requiring such an investigation. In the light of the Environmental Information Regulations 1992[1], it might be wise for the Agency to be in a position to be able to demonstrate to any third party inquirer that such an investigation was done.

1   SI 1992/3240.

8.109   Should the investigation fail to produce evidence which satisfies the Agency that the groundwater is unsuitable for other uses, reg 15 allows the waste management licence to be issued only if it contains conditions which reflect 'all technical precautions necessary' to prevent the direct and indirect discharges of List I substances into groundwater[1]. Whether this strictly follows the wording of the Directive is somewhat questionable. Article 4 does, as already noted, require member states to 'prohibit' direct discharges[2] and, in the Directive, the requirement that all technical precautions are applied only relates to indirect discharges[3].

1   SI 1994/1056, reg 15(4)(b)
2   Directive 80/68, Article 4(1), First Indent.
3   Directive 80/68, Article 4(1), Second and Third Indents.

8.110   The requirements on licence applications which involve the direct and indirect discharges of List II substances are less complex than those for List I substances. Where a licence is to be issued, it should contain 'in the light of the investigation' conditions which ensure that 'all technical precautions' are observed for preventing List II substances causing 'groundwater pollution'[1]. Although the word 'pollution' is not defined in reg 15, it is defined in the Directive as 'the discharge by man, directly or indirectly, of substances or energy into groundwater, the results of which are such as to endanger human health or water supplies, harm living resources and the aquatic ecosystem or interfere with other legitimate uses of water'[2].

1   SI 1994/1056, reg 15(5).
2   Directive 80/68, Article 1(2)(d).

8.111   Regulation 15 also sets out requirements on the nature of waste management licence conditions which are necessary in respect of List I and List II discharges[1]. These are discussed alongside the other statutory requirements on licence conditions at para 8.247ff below.

1   SI 1994/1056, reg 15(6) and (7).

FIT AND PROPER PERSON

8.112   One of the major concerns about British waste facilities in the formative years up to the enactment of the EPA 1990 was the quality of the management of much of the waste disposal and recovery infrastructure[1]. A person could still legitimately apply for licences and operate major facilities in spite of numerous criminal convictions. Such a person's technical competence could be rudimentary to non-existent. In addition, a number of sites were significantly under-capitalised and unable to fund the long-term liabilities inherent in site restoration and post-closure environmental monitoring. As a consequence, the EPA 1990 sets out to effect significant structural change in these respects. As will be seen, the transition period in respect of certain of these elements will continue into the next century.

1   See House of Lords Select Committee on Science and Technology (1981) *Hazardous Waste Disposal*, Vols I–III, HMSO, London; House of Commons Environment Committee (1989) *Toxic Waste*, Vols I–III, HMSO, London; House of Commons Welsh Affairs Committee (1990) *Toxic Waste Disposal in Wales*, HMSO, London; Royal Commission on Environmental Pollution (1985) *Managing Waste: The Duty of Care*, HMSO, London; The Hazardous Waste Inspectorate (1985) *First Report Hazardous Waste Management – An Overview*, Department of the Environment, London; The Hazardous Waste Inspectorate (1986) *Second Report, Hazardous Waste Management '. . . Ramshackle & Antediluvian'?*, Department of the Environment, London; Department of the Environment (1988) *The Hazardous Waste Inspectorate Third Report*. HMSO, London.

8.113   The EPA 1990 requires[1] that an applicant for a waste management licence must be a 'fit and proper person'[2]. The 'fit and proper' criteria is also assessed when licences are transferred[3]. Once granted, the failure of the licence holder to satisfy certain parts of the 'fit and proper' test may result in a licence being revoked or suspended[4].

1   EPA 1990, s 36(3).
2   Sites which had the benefit of a waste disposal licence under the Control of Pollution Act 1974 and transferred to a waste management licence in May 1994 are treated differently: transitional provisions are discussed at para 9.82ff.
3   EPA 1990, s 40: see para 9.114ff.
4   EPA 1990, s 38(1) and (2) or s 38(6): see para 9.44.

8.114   The full requirements of a 'fit and proper person' are set down in s 74 of the EPA 1990. The Agency is required to have regard to any guidance issued by the Secretary of State in assessing any matters concerning s 74 of the EPA 1990[1]. This is over and above the general duty set out in s 35(8), which requires the Agency to have regard to such guidance 'in relation to licences'. The fit and proper test is of obvious relevance in both instances, as is Chapter 3 of Waste Management Paper No 4 (WMP 4), which contains relevant guidance[2].

1   EPA 1990, s 74(5).
2   Department of the Environment (1994) *Licensing Waste Management Facilities*, 3rd edn, HMSO, London. This advice is, in the case of scrapyards and vehicle dismantlers, supplemented by Waste Management Paper 4A (Department of the Environment (1995) *The Licensing of Metal Recycling Sites*, HMSO, London).

8.115   The EPA 1990 requires that decisions over whether a person is 'fit and proper' are determined in respect of one central criteria. Section 74(2) states that a person's fit and proper status should be judged 'by reference to the carrying on by him of the activities which are or are to be authorised by the licence and the fulfilment of the requirements of the licence'[1]. Matters outside this framework are irrelevant for the purposes of s 74. Although the sub-section fails to state that the matters referred to are exclusive, its purpose is to exclude extraneous considerations from the 'fit and proper' test. But it should be noted that s 74 does *not* then go on to list the factors which make someone fit and proper – what is set out in the following sub-section[2] are three instances when a person is *not* fit and proper. As a matter of statutory interpretation, the three instances listed in s 74(3) may be seen to be quite separate from the fundamental decision criteria contained in the earlier s 74(2).

1   EPA 1990, s 74(2).
2   EPA 1990, s 74(3).

8.116   The three criteria which make a person[1] *not* fit and proper concern whether[2]:

(a)   the person or another relevant person[3] has been convicted of a relevant offence;
(b)   the management of the activities which are or are to be authorised by the licence are not or will not be in the hands of a 'technically competent person'; or
(c)   the person who holds or is to hold the licence 'has no intention of making or is in no position to make financial provision adequate to discharge the obligations arising from the licence'.

1   A person 'includes a body of persons corporate or unincorporate': Interpretation Act 1978, s 5 and Sch 1.
2   EPA 1990, s 74(3).
3   The nature of 'another relevant person' is considered at para 8.122.

Relevant offences

8.117   The EPA 1990 allows the Agency to reject a licence application on the ground that the applicant or an associate has been convicted of relevant offences[1]. Relevant offences can be prescribed by the Secretary of State[2]. They are set out in the Waste Management Licensing Regulations 1994[3] (see Table 8.2), being supplemented in 1997 by offences in respect of the contravention of the provisions on the landfill tax[4]. Perhaps inadvertently, the implementation of the Environment Act 1995 seems to have caused the removal of two of the relevant offences. Sections 69(9) and 70(4) in the EPA 1990 set down offences in respect of powers of entry and such matters as obstruction. However, both sections were entirely deleted, being replaced by the Environment Act 1995's own provisions[5]. It would seem that the list of offences in the Waste Management Licensing Regulations 1994 has not been adjusted to accommodate these changes.

1 EPA 1990, s 36(3).
2 EPA 1990, s 74(6).
3 SI 1994/1056, reg 3 as amended by SI 1994/1137, reg 19(3) and SI 1996/972, reg 25 and Sch 3.
4 SI 1997/351, reg 2, which prescribes as a relevant offence the contravention of para 15(1),(3),(4) or (5) of Sch 5 of the Finance Act 1996.
5 Environment Act 1995, ss 108, 109, 110: see para 12.46ff.

8.118 The Agency can exercise its discretion in assessing whether any relevant offences are severe enough to jeopardise the person's fit and proper status[1]. This is viewed as a significant responsibility[2]:

> 'In all cases, the WRA[3] should bear in mind that determining that anyone is not a fit and proper person may seriously affect his livelihood.'

The assessment mechanism for relevant offences bears a similarity to that applied to waste carriers under the Control of Pollution (Amendment) Act 1989[4]. However, unlike the latter Act, guidance on how these offences should be considered is not set down in a circular but in WMP 4. As was the case with provisions on controlled waste carriers, any offence against the enactments shown in Table 8.2 may be counted as a relevant offence. It is possible, therefore, that such an offence may have been accrued from an activity completely separate from waste management. If this is the case, the offence, on its own, should be viewed as holding limited weight vis-à-vis a person's fit and proper status[5].

1 EPA 1990, s 74(4).
2 WMP 4, para 3.2.
3 Ie the Environment Agency and the Scottish Environment Protection Agency: EPA 1990, s 30 as amended by the Environment Act 1995, Sch 22, para 62(2).
4 See Chapter 6.
5 See WMP 4, Box 3.3 and see the wording of s 74(2).

8.119 WMP 4 stresses that the onus is upon the applicant or other relevant person[1] to provide sufficient information to show that any relevant offences should not affect the person's 'fit and proper' status[2]. Of particular importance are mitigating circumstances and steps taken by the individual to prevent the repetition of the offence. The Agency is required to consider such representations prior to making a decision[3]. Furthermore, as part of the decision on whether the offences affect the person's 'fit and proper' status, the Agency should consider the following factors[4]:

(1) whether it is the applicant or other relevant person who has been convicted;
(2) the number of offences committed. Regard should be had to instances where officers of a body corporate and the body corporate itself receive convictions for the same offence[5]. An isolated conviction with mitigating circumstances should not mean a person is not fit and proper[6]. Repetition of offences is a consideration and any steps taken to prevent the repetition of an offence is seen to be a material factor[7];
(3) the nature and gravity of such offences. Any offences should be assessed solely in relation to the criteria set down by s 74(2): namely that the fit and proper assessment is restricted to an evaluation of the ability of the person to carry on the activities to be authorised by the licence and to fulfil the requirements of the licence. Accordingly, the Agency should focus upon those offences involving the unlawful deposit, treatment, keeping, disposal or transport of controlled waste or the contravention of the duty of care[8].

In assessing the gravity of the offence, particular regard should be had to any offence which involved the unlawful treatment, keeping or disposal of special waste[9].

Similarly, significance should be given to offences causing 'serious' pollution of the environment, harm to human health or serious detriment to the amenity of the locality[10]. Finally, the penalty imposed at conviction should be taken into account. Although fines are recognised as an unreliable indicator of the gravity of the offence, imprisonment should be seen to be of 'particular significance' in the evaluation of the desirability that a person should hold a waste management licence[11].

1   The definition of 'another relevant person' is covered at para 8.122 below.
2   WMP 4, para 3.26.
3   WMP 4, para 3.26: see also *R v Barnsley Metropolitan Borough Council ex p Hook* [1976] 3 All ER 452; *Cinnamond v British Airports Authority* [1980] 2 All ER 368; *Lloyd v McMahon* [1987] 1 All ER 1118.
4   WMP 4, para 3.27.
5   WMP 4, para 3.30.
6   WMP 4, Box 3.2.
7   WMP 4, Box 3.2.
8   WMP 4, Box 3.3.
9   WMP 4, Box 3.4.
10   WMP 4, Box 3.4.
11   WMP 4, Box 3.4.

Table 8.2

Relevant Offences[1]

Regulation 3 of the Waste Management Licensing Regulations 1994

Enactment	**Section/Paragraph**
Public Health (Scotland) Act 1897	s 22
Public Health Act 1936	s 95(1)
Control of Pollution Act 1974	ss 3, 5(6), 16(4), 18(2), 31(1), 32(1), 34(5), 78, 92(6), 93(3)
Refuse Disposal (Amenity) Act 1978	s 2
Food and Environment Protection Act 1985	s 9(1)
Control of Pollution (Amendment) Act 1989	ss 1, 5, 6(9), 7(3)
Water Act 1989	ss 107, 118(4), 175(1)
Environmental Protection Act 1990	ss 23(1), 33, 34(6), 44, 47(6), 57(5), 59(5), 63(2), 69(9), 70(4), 71(3), 80(4)
Water Resources Act 1991	ss 85, 202, 206
Clean Air Act 1993	s 33
Finance Act 1996	Sch 5, para 15(1),(3),(4) or (5)

Regulation
Control of Pollution (Special Waste) Regulations 1980[2]
Control of Pollution (Special Waste) Regulations 1996[3]
Transfrontier Shipment of Hazardous Waste Regulations 1988[4]
Transfrontier Shipment of Hazardous Waste Regulations 1994[5]
Merchant Shipping (Prevention of Pollution by Garbage) Regulations 1988[6]

1   SI 1994/1056, reg 3 (as amended by SI 1994/1137, reg 19(3), by SI 1996/972, reg 25 and Sch 3 and SI 1997/351, reg 2).
2   SI 1980/1709.
3   SI 1996/972 as amended by SI 1996/2019.
4   SI 1988/1562.
5   SI 1994/1137.
6   SI 1988/2292; however, these regulations have been revoked by SI 1998/1377, reg 1(2). It should be noted that the new regulations have not been added on to the list of relevant offences in SI 1994/1056.

8.120 In making the above assessment, convictions overturned on appeal may not be considered[1]. The Waste Management Paper states that convictions which are subject to an appeal which has not yet been heard should result in the Agency considering delaying a decision on the licence application (or application for a transfer) until the appeal has been heard[2]. It also suggests that the Agency should endeavour to require the applicant to agree that the four month decision period for the application[3] is appropriately extended[4]. However, the context would indicate that this applies only when the conviction is so significant that it would, if upheld, result in the person not being 'fit and proper'.

1 WMP 4, para 3.21.
2 WMP 4, para 3.22.
3 EPA 1990, s 36(9).
4 WMP 4, para 3.22.

8.121 The Agency cannot take into account offences by individuals which are 'spent' under the Rehabilitation of Offenders Act 1974[1]. Offences committed by bodies corporate do not become spent, and accordingly they must be disclosed. However, the Agency should not pay heed to them if they are outside the time periods set down in the Rehabilitation of Offenders Act 1974[2].

1 WMP 4, para 3.31.
2 WMP 4, para 3.33.

Offences committed by 'another relevant person'

8.122 As noted above, when licences are applied for relevant offences must be considered both in relation to the prospective licence holder and also to other 'relevant persons'[1]. Whether another person should be treated as having been convicted of a relevant offence in s 74(3)(a) of the EPA 1990, is dependant upon three tests[2].

1 The concept of 'other relevant person' does not apply to a decision to revoke a licence. Such a decision is made wholly on the grounds set down in the EPA 1990, s 38(1)(a) and without reference to s 74. Section 38 refers only to the licence holders and does not make reference to 'another relevant person'. Whether the lack of explicit reference to s 74 allows the Agency to still consider that section is not clear. If it does not, then a person with a string of relevant offences appears able to join with a licence holder *after* the licence has been issued without affecting the licence holder's fit and proper status. This situation could not occur when the licence is applied for (or when a licence has to be transferred) as, in these instances, reference must be made to s 74 in determining the applicant's (or transferee's) fit and proper status.
2 EPA 1990, s 74(7).

8.123 Firstly, an offence by another relevant person should be viewed as relevant if that person has been convicted in the course of employment by the licence holder (or proposed licence holder). Alternatively, the offence is relevant if the person had received a conviction in the course of carrying on a partnership where one of the members was the proposed licence holder[1].

1 EPA 1990, s 74(7)(a).

8.124 Secondly, another relevant person should be treated as having been convicted of a relevant offence if that person was a body corporate which had been convicted of a relevant offence[1], when the proposed licence holder was a 'director, manager, secretary or other similar officer'[2].

1 EPA 1990, s 74(7)(b).
2 These terms are subject to restrictive definitions: see para 7.156ff.

8.125   Finally, another relevant person is to be treated as having been convicted of a relevant offence if the proposed holder of the licence is a body corporate and where a person who is 'a director, manager, secretary or other similar officer'[1] of that body corporate has been convicted of a relevant offence. Alternatively, a conviction would be relevant in these circumstances where the relevant person was a director, manager (etc) of another body corporate at the time when that body had been convicted[2].

1   See para 7.156ff.
2   EPA 1990, s 74(7)(c).

8.126   The essential difference between the second and third tests outlined above is that the second test applies in the case where an individual is to personally hold a waste management licence, while the third test involves a body corporate holding the licence. In the case of the second test, this means that, for example, if Company A had been convicted of a relevant offence when Individual 1 was in a senior management position, Individual 1 may not be fit and proper to personally hold a licence having left Company A. It should be noted that Individual 1 does not need to have personally received a conviction: it is sufficient that Company A had done so. The third test outlined above applies to the circumstances where, for example, Company B was applying for a licence and Individual 2 was a director, manager etc. Should Individual 2 have personally received a conviction in previous employment, or where Individual 2 was a director, manager, etc of Company C when Company C (though not Individual 2) was convicted of a relevant offence, the presence of Individual 2 in Company B as a manager, director, etc may jeopardise Company B's fit and proper status.

8.127   However, the formulations in s 74(7) of the EPA 1990 do not appear to address all possible permutations where an associate of a proposed licensee may have received convictions for relevant offences or have been primarily responsible for the conviction of a previous employer. There are circumstances where a person, whilst holding a key position in relation to the control of a proposed facility, does not fall within the definition of 'another relevant person'. This deficit stems partly from the meaning of the phrase contained in s 74(7) of 'director, manager, secretary or other similar officer'[1]. In particular, the breadth of the meaning of the word 'manager' in this context should be interpreted much more narrowly than its ordinary, common English meaning[2]. In this context, it must refer to someone representing the directing mind and will of the corporate body[3]. As discussed at para 8.173, the word 'manager' in this instance is not synonymous with 'manager' as is used in the Waste Management Licensing Regulations 1994[4] in relation to certificates of technical competence.

1   EPA 1990, s 74(7)(b) and (c).
2   See *R v Boal* [1992] 3 All ER 177; *Woodhouse v Walsall Metropolitan Borough Council* [1993] Env LR 30; WMP 4 Para 3.25 and para 7.156ff, where s 157 of the EPA 1990 is discussed.
3   See, for example, *Tesco Supermarkets v Nattrass* [1971] 2 All ER 127.
4   SI 1994/1056, reg 5.

8.128   Most often the restricted interpretation of the term 'director, manager, secretary or other similar officer' will affect persons who are acting as employees of a proposed licence holder and who are not sufficiently senior to be viewed as directors or managers. Despite convictions for relevant offences in previous employment, they will be excluded from the definition of 'another relevant person'. An example would be an individual who, in earlier employment, discharged day-to-day control of a site or indeed an entire enterprise, but was neither a director or manager of that enterprise, nor a member of any controlling partnership. The conviction of the person's employer would not make the individual 'another relevant person' in these circumstances[1]. This may be in spite of the fact that the person bore the principal responsibility for the erstwhile employer being convicted.

1   Unless, of course, such a person had received a conviction for the offence along with their employer.

8.129   However, the reference to directors, managers, secretaries, etc is not the sole reason why the drafting of s 74(7) of the EPA 1990 is less than satisfactory. Other anomalies seem to exist. A person who had been convicted of relevant offences but at that time was acting as a sole trader[1] would not constitute 'another relevant person' when acting as an employee of the licence applicant. That person would only become 'another relevant person' if he or she was acting in the capacity of a director, manager, etc of a body corporate responsible for the licence application[2]. It would also seem that, when a partnership unconnected to the licence applicant[3] had received convictions for relevant offences, an ex-partner wishing to join with a licence applicant would not constitute 'another relevant person'. The existence of these anomalies appears confirmed by the application of the staged summary of s 74(7), which is set down in Box 3.1 of WMP 4.

1   Ie not as a body corporate or in a partnership.
2   EPA 1990, s 74(7)(c).
3   EPA 1990, s 74(7)(a) refers only to partnerships where a partner is the proposed licence holder, not to partnerships in general.

Technical competence

8.130   The second component of the fit and proper person equation in s 74 of the EPA 1990 for a licence application concerns whether '. . . the management of the activities . . . which are to be authorised by the licence . . . will not be in the hands of a technically competent person'[1]. The detail which makes up this criterion is complex. The following discussion will evaluate the procedures for applications for waste management licences.

1   EPA 1990, s 74(3)(b).

Technically competent management

8.131   The term 'management' in s 74(3)(b) of the EPA 1990 should be seen to be quite different from the word 'manager' as found in s 74(7) and in s 157. It holds its ordinary meaning and is not to be viewed solely as involving those persons who make policy or other strategic decisions at the heart of a company[1]. WMP 4 emphasises that the phrase used in s 74(3)(b) – 'management of the activities which are or are to be authorised by the licence' – requires that this is carried out by a technically competent person who is 'in a position to control the day-to-day activities authorised by the licence and carried out at the licensed site'[2].

1   See also WMP 4, para 3.37.
2   WMP 4, para 3.37.

8.132   Accordingly, technically competent management can only occur where the technically competent person is actually in contact with a site (or a very limited number of sites) for a significant amount of time each day. Although there is little guidance in WMP 4 on this matter, the purpose of the provision is to ensure that waste sites are overseen properly. It is submitted that the only way that this can occur is by the staff designated as technically competent having regular 'hands on' contact with the sites. What seems quite clear is that the requirement for technically competent management cannot be discharged by persons in, for example, a head office physically remote from the site and where visits to the site are infrequent. Although there appears to be uncertainty in this matter[1], it should be recalled that a failure to apply technically competent management does not in itself result in a criminal conviction. Rather it may result in a licence application being refused or the licence being suspended or revoked after issuing. Given the fact that such actions are subject to appeal to the Secretary of State[2], the latter's appeal decisions will, in time, provide an indication of the level of the physical proximity required between those individuals identified as technically competent and the sites for which they are responsible.

1   An earlier draft of WMP 4 was much more specific in relation to these points. Whilst the Agency has published draft guidance on this matter in 1998 – *Agency Assessment of Technical Competence at Waste Management Sites*, Environment Agency, Warrington and in 1999 – *Consultation Paper Statement of Arrangements Regarding the Provision of Technical Competence by Operators of Licensed Waste Management Facilities*, Environment Agency, Warrington – such material, when finalised, would have limited legal status.
2   EPA 1990, s 43; see para 9.126ff.

8.133   In any statute, the singular also means the plural and vice versa unless the context states to the contrary[1]. Accordingly, the EPA 1990 allows the management of a site to be in the hands of a technically competent person or persons. Hence a number of individuals can make up the technically competent management for a site. WMP 4 provides two examples of how this is expected to work in practice[2]:

'It means . . . that for a large and complex site where operational management may be divided functionally, several specialists can be identified as providing the technically competent management. Alternatively, the company structure may mean that day-to-day management is not delegated down to the site but is exercised at a somewhat higher level. This could mean that more than one site was under the day-to-day control of the same individual or group of individuals.'

1   Interpretation Act 1978, s 6.
2   WMP 4, para 3.39.

8.134   Technically competent management is both assessed at the time of the licence application and kept under continual review by the Agency. WMP 4 recommends that the licence holder should be required to submit lists of such competent persons and to keep the lists updated. A condition of licence can be used for this purpose[1].

1   WMP 4, para 3.47.

8.135   Should key personnel change, the criteria of technical competence may fail. In addition, should the operation of a licensed site change – perhaps due to a modification of the licence – then a more stringent regime of technical competence may be needed. This is a function of how technical competence is defined, and accordingly it is appropriate to consider this matter below.

Certificates of technical competence

8.136   The Waste Management Licensing Regulations 1994 contains a table[1] (see Table 8.3) which describes eleven types of waste management facility where managers are required to possess formal qualifications. A system of certification is used as a way of indicating technically competent management[2,3]. Certification is the domain of the Waste Management Industry Training Board (WAMITAB), which at present has the sole right to issue Certificates of Technical Competence (COTCs). Types of facility other than those shown on the Table require technically competent management to be assessed by the Agency on an individual basis[4].

1   SI 1994/1056, reg 4(1) as amended by SI 1997/2203, reg 2.
2   This requirement also applies to the case of older sites which were subject to waste disposal licences and which have had their waste management licences significantly modified since May 1994. It is also open to reappraisal where, since 1 May 1994, personnel have changed substantially: see para 9.85ff.
3   SI 1994/1056, reg 4 as amended by SI 1996/634, reg 2(2) and SI 1997/2203, reg 2.
4   See para 8.170ff.

8.137   The Waste Management Licensing Regulations 1994 hold that a person is technically competent in relation to the type of facility specified in the Table 'if and only if' the person holds a relevant COTC[1]. In an attempt to reflect the diversity of competencies necessary for different waste management facilities, the certificates vary between 'levels' and 'types' of facility. The levels used are 3 and 4, which correspond to standards set down by the National Vocational Qualification (NVQ) scheme[2]. Table 8.3 shows the range of certificates currently available.

1   SI 1994/1056, reg 4(1): subject to transitional provisions: see para 8.144ff below.
2   In Scotland the Scottish Vocational Qualification scheme.

Table 8.3

Regulation 4 of the Waste Management Licensing Regulations 1994[1]

Certificates of Technical Competence

Type of Facility	**COTC**
Landfill Sites A landfill site which receives special waste.	Managing Landfill Operations: special waste (Level 4)
A landfill site which receives biodegradable waste or which for some other reason requires substantial engineering works to protect the environment but which in either case does not receive special waste.	1. Managing Landfill Operations: biodegradable waste (Level 4); or 2. Managing Landfill Operations: special waste (Level 4)
Any other type of landfill site with a total capacity exceeding 50,000 cubic metres.	1. Landfill Operations: inert waste (Level 3); or 2. Managing Landfill Operations: biodegradable waste (Level 4); or 3. Managing Landfill Operations: special waste (Level 4).
Incineration A site on which waste is burned in an incinerator designed to incinerate waste at a rate of more than 50kgs per hour but less than 1 tonne per hour.	Managing Incinerator Operations: special waste (Level 4).
Waste Treatment Plant A waste treatment plant where clinical or special waste is subjected to a chemical or physical process.	1. Managing Treatment Operations: clinical or special waste (Level 4) or 2. *Managing Treatment Operations: special waste (Level 4)*[2]

Table 8.3 – *contd*

Regulation 4 of the Waste Management Licensing Regulations 1994

Certificates of Technical Competence

Type of Facility	COTC
A waste treatment plant where biodegradable waste, but no clinical or special waste, is subjected to a chemical or physical process.	1. Managing Treatment Operations: biodegradable waste (Level 4); or 2. Managing Treatment Operations: clinical or special waste (Level 4) 3. *Managing Treatment Operations: special waste (Level 4)*[2]
A waste treatment plant where waste, none of which is biodegradable, clinical or special waste, is subjected to a chemical or physical process.	1. Treatment Operations: inert waste (Level 3); or 2. Managing Treatment Operations: biodegradable waste (Level 4); or 3. Managing Treatment Operations: clinical or special waste (Level 4) 4. *Managing Treatment Operations: special waste (Level 4)*[2]
Transfer Station A transfer station where: (a) clinical or special waste, is dealt with; and (b) the total quantity of waste at the station at any time exceeds 5 cubic metres.	1. Managing Transfer Operations: clinical or special waste (Level 4); or 2. *Managing Transfer Operations: special waste (Level 4)*[2]
A transfer station where: (a) biodegradable waste, but no clinical or special waste, is dealt with; and (b) the total quantity of waste at the station at any time exceeds 5 cubic metres.	1. Managing Transfer Operations: biodegradable waste (Level 4); or 2. Managing Transfer Operations: clinical or special waste (Level 4); or 3. *Managing Transfer Operations: special waste (Level 4)*[2]
Any other type of waste transfer station where the total quantity of waste at the station at any time exceeds 50 cubic metres.	1. Transfer operations: inert waste (Level 3); or 2. Managing Transfer Operations biodegradable waste (Level 4); or 3. Managing Transfer Operations: clinical or special waste (Level 4); or 4. *Managing Transfer Operations: special waste (Level 4)*[2]
Civic Amenity Sites A Civic Amenity Site.	1. Civic Amenity Site Operations (Level 3); or 2. Managing Transfer Operations: biodegradable waste (Level 4); or 3. Managing Transfer Operations: clinical or special waste (Level 4); or 4. *Managing Transfer Operations: special waste (Level 4)*[2]

1   SI 1994/1056, reg 4 as amended by SI 1997/2203, reg 2.

2   COTCs which are shown in italics relate to the earlier divisions (SI 1994/1056, reg 4 as amended by
    SI 1996/634) prior to the Table being replaced by SI 1997/2203. From 9 October 1997, these
    certificates are no longer awarded.

8.138   A significant number of terms contained in reg 4 and Table 8.3 are left undefined. Such terms therefore hold their ordinary meanings. However, for the purposes
of reg 4 only, 'civic amenity site', 'clinical waste' and 'transfer station' are given definitions[1]. It is also clarified that a 'landfill site' does not include a pet cemetery[2].

1   SI 1994/1056, reg 4(3): a 'civic amenity site' is held to mean a place provided under either s 1 of the
    Refuse Disposal Amenity Act 1978 or s 51(1)(b) of the EPA 1990. Note that the term is defined
    slightly differently in respect of England and Wales in the Waste Management Licensing (Charges)
    Scheme 1999/2000 – see paragraph 1(2) – in that, when operated by LAWDCs, such sites are
    excluded. 'Clinical waste' is given the meaning contained in reg 1(2) of the Controlled Waste
    Regulations 1992 (see para 2.210). A 'transfer station' is defined as 'a facility where waste is
    unloaded in order to permit its preparation for further transport for treatment, keeping or disposal
    elsewhere'.
2   SI 1994/1056, reg 3(3) as amended by SI 1996/634, reg 2(2)(b).

8.139   It is important to understand the manner by which the concepts of 'type' and
'level' of facility operate in reg 4. Table 8.3 allows, for example, a holder of a COTC
for special waste landfill management to manage, besides a landfill accepting special
waste, other landfills which takes biodegradable or inert wastes. However, the holder
of a biodegradable waste landfill management certificate cannot manage a special
waste landfill, but can manage a large inert waste landfill. These restrictions also place
limits on the ability of COTC holders to transfer between 'types' of facility. For
example, a holder of a COTC for incineration is not entitled to manage a waste treatment plant.

8.140   It should be pointed out that, unless the Table indicates otherwise, there are no
de minimis quantities. Hence it would seem that a manager of a site licensed to accept
any biodegradable waste is required to obtain a COTC appropriate for the management of a biodegradable waste facility. If they are licensed to accept wood, landfill
sites which primarily accept construction industry materials such as rubble and sub-
soils will need a biodegradable waste landfill COTC.

8.141   When the COTC scheme was first mooted in the early 1990s, many commentators expressed the view that the nine types of COTC being proposed were too few
and too broad, often failing to reflect the diversity of waste management facilities and
the quite different skills necessary for their operation. In particular, under the original
scheme there were obvious anomalies which were very difficult to justify practically.
For example, an operator of a skip transfer station was required to possess a COTC
that embraced competencies needed for the management of a facility involving special
waste. Managing the latter type of operation requires obviously different skills, technical background and training.

8.142   These anomalies were partly addressed for waste treatment plants by changes
made in 1996[1]. However, major changes for transfer stations and civic amenity sites
did not occur until 1997[2]. It would seem that these deficiencies affected the level of
interest and confidence in the COTC scheme, particularly in respect of operators of
smaller waste management facilities. Whilst these changes were to be welcomed, they
are obviously disruptive to individuals working towards obtaining a COTC. In respect
of changes made in 1996 to the requirements for waste treatment plants, additional

transitional provisions had to be drafted so that certain affected individuals with a particular COTC could continue in their current position[3]. However, the delay in making further changes is likely to prove problematic now that the principal deadline of August 1999 for persons to hold full COTCs has been passed[4].

1   SI 1996/634, reg 2(2)(a).
2   By SI 1997/2203, reg 2.
3   See para 8.162 below: however, the more extensive changes made in 1997 did not warrant the drafting of further transitional provisions.
4   See para 8.153ff.

8.143   In relation to incinerator sites, only one level of COTC is set down for plants with a capacity of between 50kgs per hour and one tonne per hour[1]. However, in a rather opaque paragraph that does not appear to be substantiated by the Waste Management Licensing Regulations 1994, WMP 4 notes[2]:

> 'The handling and management of waste incidental to the operation of an incinerator designed to burn waste at a rate of less than one tonne per hour is included in the category of "waste treatment plant".'

This appears to suggest that most small incinerators – which by definition contain a storage and materials handling element – need staff with COTCs in both incineration and waste treatment. This seems to be even more peculiar in that, as WMP 4 rightly acknowledges, the air pollution aspects of such incinerators are excluded from controls by waste management licences[3]. Accordingly, WMP 4 goes on to note[4] that, in relation to small incinerators, '[t]echnical competence for a licence can therefore only be judged in relation to other aspects including the incidental handling and management of the waste'. If, as might be expected, these aspects are fully considered in the COTC for incineration, then the waste treatment COTC is surely superfluous in this context.

1   Incinerators of less than 50kgs are exempt from needing a waste management licence under the Waste Management Licensing Regulations 1994, reg 17 and Sch 3, whilst facilities with a capacity of over 1 tonne per hour fall under the IPC Regime and are excluded from waste management licensing by reg 16 for that reason: see para 10.14. In neither of these cases is a COTC needed.
2   WMP 4, para 3.49.
3   SI 1994/1056, reg 16.
4   WMP 4, para 3.50.

Technical competent management – transitional provisions

8.144   Although COTCs are required of managers in the manner set out above, the COTC system required time to be phased in. It involves extensive 'on the job' assessment and independent verification. Hence the legislation allows for a person to qualify for deemed technical competence in the transitional phase over which the COTC scheme establishes itself. However, this only applies for a set period of time and mainly affects persons who can be identified as having worked as a 'manager'[1] in an appropriate position in the waste industry for some time prior to the date the particular provision entered into force. Persons new to the waste industry must obtain a full COTC when they wish to act as managers of landfills[2], but there is now permitted a certain amount of leeway in respect of other waste management facilities[3]. Overall, it would seem that a considerable premium is at present being placed on those individuals with sufficient relevant experience to qualify under the transitional arrangements. In addition it seems clear that significant numbers of waste industry staff have not obtained their COTCs by the requisite date in August 1999[4]. Although the Agency is being pragmatic about this deadline[5], precisely how the

Agency or national government is to deal with longer term non-compliance will prove interesting.

1　See para 8.173.
2　SI 1996/634, reg 4(2).
3　See SI 1996/634, reg 4: discussed at para 8.168.
4　See Environment Agency (1998) *The State of Technical Competence in the Waste Industry*, Environment Agency, Bristol.
5　See Environment Agency (1999) *Consultation Paper Statement of Arrangements Regarding the Provision of Technical Competence by Operators of Licensed Waste Management Facilities*, Environment Agency, Warrington.

8.145　Other transitional arrangements introduced since 1994 also reflect the succession of amendments made to the legislation since that date. While these amendments did not change the requirements for COTCs in the Waste Management Licensing Regulations 1994 directly, they cause significant indirect affects. And in this respect, the arrangements are getting increasingly complicated. Many of the changes made elsewhere in the legislation altered the scope of facilities which required technically competent management. For example, the revised, and broader, definition of special waste enacted in 1996 caused managers of certain types of facility to require a more sophisticated level of demonstrable formal competence than hitherto. This affected, for example, persons managing facilities involved in the receipt of waste oil, a substance which was not usually special waste under the earlier regime[1]. Prior to the definitional change, a relevant Level 3 COTC was necessary, but the widening of the special waste definition required the more demanding Level 4 certificate to apply. Although the transitional arrangements usually only last for five years, the widening of the range of facilities subject to these qualifications has occurred at a variety of dates since 1994: hence a variety of cut-off dates have needed to be prescribed, as discussed below.

1　Special waste is discussed in Chapter 4.

8.146　The relevant legislation sets out two avenues to persons with relevant experience which avoid the immediate need to undergo a full assessment of technical competence. These stem not only from the Waste Management Licensing Regulations 1994[1], but also from the Waste Management Licensing (Amendment etc) Regulations 1995[2] and the Special Waste Regulations 1996[3].

1　SI 1994/1056, reg 5.
2　SI 1995/288, reg 4 as amended by SI 1995/1950, reg 3 and SI 1996/634, reg 3.
3　SI 1996/972, reg 20.

8.147　The first transitional provision affects persons under the age of 55[1], who must have made an application[2] to WAMITAB for a certificate of technical competence before a particular prescribed date. They also must be able to show that they were managers of the particular type of facility over the period set out in the regulations. Applications made to WAMITAB after the prescribed date clearly are not valid, with any certificates produced as a result of such applications being unlawful and void. A person who missed the relevant deadline will need to undertake a full COTC assessment.

1　The relevant dates are discussed at para 8.153ff below.
2　It should be noted that the regulations do not state that such a certificate needs to have been granted, just that an application has been made.

8.148　The fact that an application has been made to WAMITAB by the due date means that the person is considered technically competent up to the date contained in the relevant statute. It allows sufficient time to acquire a COTC[1]. Usually, the application also allows a person to manage another waste management facility, but this is restricted to those sites which do not require a higher level of competence or are not of a different type[2] of facility to the site which the person has had previous experience of managing.

1   WMP 4, para 3.52.
2   As defined by Table 1 of reg 4 of SI 1994/1056, as amended by SI 1997/2203, reg 2. See Table 8.3.

8.149   WAMITAB has arranged that persons who have relevant experience as managers can receive a provisional Certificate of Technical Competence ('pCOTC'). However, it should be re-iterated that the regulations[1] only require that an application has been made to WAMITAB[2]. It is irrelevant whether WAMITAB actually grants a pCOTC or not.

1   See SI 1994/1056, reg 5 and SI 1995/288, reg 4.
2   And, of course, that the person can show that they have, in fact, managed an appropriate site over the required period.

8.150   The second way by which a person can manage other waste management facilities without holding a full COTC concerns persons who have reached an age of 55 or more on the date set out in the relevant regulations. They must have had at least five years' experience as the manager[1] of one or more licensed sites[2] over the period of the last ten years. Such a person is deemed technically competent until 10 August 2004[3]. However, qualifying individuals are only allowed to act as the manager of a facility of a similar type (see Table 8.3) to that which they managed in the past. The management of a facility of a different type or higher level would require the possession of a relevant COTC.

1   See para 8.173 below.
2   Or sites covered by resolutions under s 5 of the Control of Pollution Act 1974 or s 54 of the EPA 1990: SI 1994/1056, reg 5(3).
3   SI 1994/1056, reg 5(2).

8.151   For persons over 55 who satisfy the test of relevant experience, there is no formal requirement in the regulations to make an application to WAMITAB. However, WAMITAB has available a Certificate of Qualifying Experience (CQE) for such persons. The possession of a CQE would be a ready way of demonstrating that they are deemed competent by way of age and experience. In the absence of a CQE, it is left to the Agency to make an assessment of the person's competence, with the applicant supplying a statement of experience supported by a curriculum vitae. The names of two referees who are able to vouch for the statement should also be included[1].

1   WMP 4, para 3.52.

8.152   The following sections set out the particular types of transitional exemption and describe the relevant dates. It should be noted that certain categories overlap, particularly in respect of special waste and waste treatment facilities.

8.153   *Managers of waste management facilities prior to 10 August 1994*
Persons under the age of 55 on 10 August 1994 who acted as the manager of a waste management facility described by Table 1 of the 1994 Regulations (see Table 8.3 above) could make an application to WAMITAB for a COTC and thereby obtain transitional exemption. To qualify, they must have been acting as managers of the facility

in the calendar year up to 10 August 1994, and the application must have been made before that date[1]. Such an application allows the person to be considered technically competent until 10 August 1999. The provision is restricted to managers of sites subject to waste disposal licences[2], waste management licences or resolutions[3]. The latter[4] can either have been granted under the earlier Control of Pollution Act 1974 or, in Scotland, under s 54 of the EPA 1990[5]. It should be noted that these provisions have been extended for managers of sites subject to resolutions[6].

1 SI 1994/1056, reg 5(1).
2 Granted under the Control of Pollution Act 1974.
3 SI 1994/1056, reg 5(3).
4 A 'resolution' was the term used for permits granted for facilities operated by local authorities under the Control of Pollution Act 1974 (s 11). Resolutions applied instead of licences to the then publicly owned waste management infrastructure. Although discontinued by the EPA 1990 in respect of England and Wales, they continued to have application to public waste management facilities in Scotland until 1996 (see Environment Act 1995, Sch 23, para 18).
5 The latter will only apply between 1 May 1994 – when the EPA 1990 was enacted – to 10 August 1994.
6 See para 8.155 below.

8.154 A person who had reached the age of 55 on 10 August 1994 is also entitled to continue to act as the manager of particular types of waste management facility[1]. However, the individual must have accrued at least five years' experience in the management of a licensed site[2] in the ten years prior to that date. Such a person is deemed technically competent until 10 August 2004[3].

1 SI 1994/1056, reg 5(2) as amended by SI 1996/634, reg 2(3)(b).
2 Or sites covered by resolutions under s 5 of the Control of Pollution Act 1974 or s 54 of the EPA 1990: SI 1994/1056, reg 5(3).
3 SI 1994/1056, reg 5(2) as amended by SI 1996/634, reg 2(3)(b).

8.155 *Extended provisions for managers of sites subject to resolutions* In contrast to the transitional arrangements relating to a private sector site discussed above, the deadlines for applying to WAMITAB were extended in respect of managers of sites subject to resolutions granted in England and Wales[1] under the Control of Pollution Act 1974[2]. A similar extension applies in Scotland in respect of resolutions granted under the EPA 1990[3]. Accordingly, provided that such persons had applied to WAMITAB before 1 October 1996, they can continue to manage a site until 1 October 2001 without the need to possess a full COTC[4]. In England and Wales, it would seem that the requirements are that, in a 12-month period up to 1 October 1996, the person managed a facility of a type relevant to the particular level of competence[5]. In Scotland, the provisions are slightly different in that a person can have managed a site subject to a resolution in the 15 months prior to October 1996[6].

1 However these provisions do not apply in respect of technical competence in Scotland (SI 1994/1056, reg 5(7), as amended by SI 1996/634, reg 2(3)).
2 Note that this provision does not apply to resolutions granted in Scotland in respect of s 54 of the EPA 1990: see SI 1994/1056, reg 5(4), as amended by SI 1996/634, reg 2(3).
3 SI 1996/916, reg 2.
4 The system of resolutions in Scotland was cancelled in 1996 (Environment Act 1995, Sch 23, para 18). The Regulations contain supplementary provisions which ensure that persons managing such a site in the 12 months prior to 1 October 1996 are classed as technically competent for the management of that facility only (SI 1996/916, reg 2(3)). Although there is no need to apply to WAMITAB to secure this privilege, the person is not allowed to manage any other facility.
5 SI 1994/1056, reg 5(1) and reg 5(4) (as amended by SI 1996/634, reg 2(3). Whilst there were no resolutions in existence in England and Wales between 1 October 1995 and 1 October 1996 this would allow someone who managed a site subject to resolution in Scotland to work in England and Wales.

6   SI 1996/916, reg 2(1): in Scotland, persons who managed sites subject to resolutions which started accepting special waste when that definition was changed in 1996 could benefit from further transitional arrangements (see SI 1997/257). To qualify, affected individuals had to apply to WAMITAB by 1 September 1996.

8.156   Persons who are 55 or over and who operated facilities subject to resolutions can also benefit from this extension. In this case, the person must be at least 55 on 1 October 1996, with the requirements for possession of an appropriate COTC lifted until 1 October 2006[1].

1   SI 1994/1056, reg 5(2) and (4), as amended in respect of England and Wales by SI 1996/634, reg 2(3)(c); in Scotland, SI 1996/916, reg 2(2).

8.157   *Managers of facilities subject to Part 1 of the EPA 1990*   Changes introduced by the Waste Management Licensing (Amendment etc) Regulations 1995[1] allow certain other individuals with appropriate waste management experience to be deemed technically competent. This applies only until 10 August 1999[2] and provides time for the manager to gain a full COTC from WAMITAB. To benefit from the provision the person must have been acting as a manager of a relevant facility sometime between 10 August 1993 and 10 July 1995, and have applied to WAMITAB for a COTC before the July deadline. The other proviso is that the facility must correspond to the category in Table 8.3 which the person wishes to manage after making the application[3].

1   SI 1995/288, reg 4, as amended by SI 1995/1950 and SI 1996/634.
2   SI 1995/288, reg 4(1).
3   SI 1995/288, reg 4(1).

8.158   Two types of individual are affected. The first[1] is a person who was the manager of a recovery or disposal activity which was subject to a Part A authorisation under the EPA 1990[2]. An example of such a facility would be a hazardous or municipal waste incinerator or a solvent or other chemical waste recovery plant. However, should such persons be managing facilities involved in biological or physico-chemical treatment, they may be able to utilise other extended transitional provisions: see para 8.162 below. The second type of person covered is a manager of an activity which 'involved the disposal of waste'[3] at an incinerator which was covered by a Part B authorisation[4].

1   SI 1995/288, reg 4(2)(a).
2   Issued under s 2(4) of the EPA 1990: Part A and Part B authorisations are discussed in paras 1.68ff and 10.14.
3   Oddly, this excludes incinerators with heat recovery capacity which, rather than being classed as a disposal activity under the Waste Management Licensing Regulations 1994, would fall within the definition of waste recovery facilities under SI 1994/1056, Sch 4, Pt IV, para 9. See Table 2.6 in Chapter 2.
4   Issued under s 2(4) of the EPA 1990 and falling within paragraph (a) of Part B of Section 5.1 of Sch 1 of SI 1991/472 (as amended by SI 1992/614, reg 2, Sch 1, para 9 and SI 1994/1271, reg 4(3), Sch 3, para 8 and SI 1998/767, reg 2(2)(b): SI 1995/288, reg 4(2)(b).

8.159   *Managers of facilities no longer exempt from licensing*   A transitional provision also applied[1] to a person who acted as the manager, between 1 May 1994 and 31 July 1995, of a site which did not require a licence under the Control of Pollution Act 1974, but which required licensing under the EPA 1990[2]. The sites affected in this manner were temporarily exempt[3] from the provisions of the EPA 1990 until 31 July 1995 to cover the period involved in making a waste management licence application[4].

The exemption then continued beyond 31 July 1995 once the application had been submitted and was awaiting determination. It was also automatically extended until any appeal on the determination was heard[5].

1   SI 1995/288, reg 4(3).
2   As Chapter 10 shows, the exemptions contained in the Waste Management Licensing Regulations 1994 are highly prescribed. The Control of Pollution Act 1974 prescribed exemptions in the Collection and Disposal of Waste Regulations 1988 (SI 1988/819, Sch 6). The latter exemptions were much less detailed, and did not contain many quantity limits. Accordingly, certain sites which were exempt – particularly those of some considerable size – under the 1988 Regulations required a waste management licence under the new regime.
3   See SI 1994/1056, reg 17 and Sch 3, para 43, as amended by SI 1995/1950, reg 2 and SI 1996/634, reg 2(6).
4   SI 1995/288, reg 4(3).
5   SI 1994/1056, Sch 3, para 43(3).

8.160   The temporary exemption of such sites from the EPA 1990 until 31 July 1995[1] meant that an application to WAMITAB had to be made by an affected manager by that date[2]. To qualify, a person had to be a manager of such a site between August 1993 and July 1995. As was the case with similar provisions under the Waste Management Licensing Regulations 1994, this deemed provision lasts until 10 August 1999[3]: after that date, a full COTC is needed. Unlike the other transitional provisions, a person can only continue to act as the manager of the facility subject to the earlier exemption[4] – the fact that an application was made to WAMITAB does not confer any rights to act as a technically competent manager of any other waste management facility.

1   SI 1994/1056, Sch 3, para 43(2)(b), as amended by SI 1995/1950, reg 2.
2   SI 1995/288, reg 4(4)(a).
3   SI 1995/288, reg 4(4)(a).
4   SI 1995/288, reg 4(3).

8.161   In the case of waste treatment plant involved in biological or physico-chemical treatment, the period of exemption from waste management licensing was extended to 30 September 1996[1]. There are concomitant provisions in respect of technically competent management[2].

1   SI 1994/1056, Sch 3, para 43(2)(a), as amended by SI 1995/1950, reg 2 and SI 1996/634, reg 2(6).
2   See para 8.162 below.

8.162   *Managers of waste treatment plants*   Persons wishing to act as technically competent managers of specified waste treatment plants may be affected by the EPA 1990 and associated regulations in five ways:

(a) the plant may have been licensed under the Control of Pollution Act 1974 and the person applied to WAMITAB prior to 10 August 1994[1];
(b) the facility may have been subject to an IPC authorisation and an application to WAMITAB was made prior to 10 July 1995[2];
(c) the facility may not have required licensing prior to the enactment of the EPA 1990, with the manager's application to WAMITAB being received by 31 July 1995[3];
(d) managers of facilities treating clinical and biodegradable wastes were affected by the change in the requirements for the requisite level of COTC when the Waste Management Licensing Regulations 1994 were amended in 1996[4];
(e) some managers may be able to benefit from the transitional provisions which specifically affect 'physico-chemical' and 'biological' waste treatment plants[5].

The first three categories have already been described above. The final two potential effects on managers of waste treatment plants will be considered below.

1 SI 1994/1056, reg 5(1): see para 8.153 above.
2 SI 1995/288, reg 4(1): see para 8.157 above.
3 SI 1995/288, reg 4(4)(a): see para 8.159.
4 SI 1994/1056, reg 4 as amended by SI 1996/634, reg 2(2)(a). Note that these amendments were replaced entirely by SI 1997/2203, reg 2, but no additional transitional provisions were provided.
5 SI 1995/288, reg 4(5) as amended by SI 1995/1950, reg 3.

8.163 As discussed earlier, the Table in the Waste Management Licensing Regulations 1994 (see Table 8.3) which forms the backbone of the COTC system was amended in 1996. The level of COTC required for persons operating waste treatment plants accepting biodegradable or clinical wastes which undergo chemical or physical processing was enhanced. Prior to the amendment, a manager of such plants only needed a Level 3 COTC, but this has been changed to require a tougher Level 4 certificate[1]. The Waste Management Regulations 1996[2] contains transitional arrangements which pertain to persons who had already made applications to WAMITAB in respect of such plants and who found that the requirements had been stiffened by the changes. Persons who originally correctly applied for a Level 3 COTC in respect of inert waste treatment plants have been given an opportunity to be allowed to gain their Level 4 COTC. They can continue to act as the technically competent management without the need for a Level 4 special waste treatment COTC[3] in the interim[4]. This affects individuals who applied either by 10 August 1994[5] or, later, by 1 April 1996[6]. Persons affected by this provision are permitted to notify WAMITAB that this transitional arrangement is not to apply[7], but on the granting of the Level 3 COTC, they cannot, for obvious reasons, provide the technically competent management of biodegradable and clinical waste treatment facilities.

1 Table 8.3 originally had special waste treatment requiring a Level 4 certificate and any other form of treatment requiring a certificate for 'Treatment Operations: Inert Waste' at Level 3: note that the table was entirely replaced by SI 1997/2203, reg 2.
2 SI 1996/634, reg 5.
3 See Table 8.3.
4 SI 1996/634, reg 5.
5 SI 1994/1056, reg 5(1) and SI 1996/634, reg 5(1).
6 SI 1995/288, reg 4(4) and(5) (as amended by SI 1995/1950, reg 3 and SI 1996/634, reg 5(3)), which does not appear to address the change made to SI 1995/1950 in respect of the reference to 31 March 1996 being changed to 31 September 1996.
7 SI 1996/634, reg 5(2) and (4).

8.164 The transitional provisions were also separately extended in respect of biological[1] and 'physico-chemical' waste treatment plants[2]. Between 1995 and 1996, there was much uncertainty as to whether a large number of treatment plants at factory premises would need licensing[3] and, while this matter is still not entirely clarified by the Department of the Environment, transitional provisions were enacted to delay the need for such sites to possess waste management licences and for their managers to be required to apply for COTCs. Therefore, treatment plants required a licence only after 30 September 1996[4], being hitherto exempt under Schedule 3 to the Waste Management Licensing Regulations 1994[5].

1 Defined as falling within SI 1994/1056, Sch 4, Pt III, para 8 (see Table 2.5 in Chapter 2): SI 1995/288, reg 4(5), as amended by SI 1995/1950, reg 5.
2 Defined as falling within SI 1994/1056, Sch 4, Pt III, para 9 (see Table 2.6 in Chapter 2).
3 See para 2.62ff.
4 SI 1994/1056, Sch 3, para 43(2), as amended by SI 1995/288, reg 2 and SI 1996/634, reg 2(6).
5 SI 1994/1056, Sch 3, para 43.

8.165 Transitional provisions were also made in respect of technically competent management, being contained in amendments made to the Waste Management Licensing (Amendment etc) Regulations 1995[1]. In order to qualify, a person must have managed a biological or physico-chemical treatment plant in the period 1 May 1994 to 30 September 1996[2]. The plant must not have been required to be licensed prior to that date. Finally, the manager must have lodged the application for a COTC with WAMITAB by the September 1996 deadline[3].

1 SI 1995/288, reg 4, as amended by SI 1995/1950, reg 3 and SI 1996/634, reg 3.
2 SI 1995/288, reg 4(5), as amended by SI 1995/1950, reg 3 and SI 1996/634, reg 3(a).
3 SI 1995/288, reg 4(5), as amended by SI 1995/1950, reg 3 and SI 1996/634, reg 3(b).

8.166 *Managers of facilities first subject to the Special Waste Regulations in 1996* The Special Waste Regulations 1996[1] contain provisions on technically competent management which accommodate the widening of the definition of special waste caused by the superseding of the earlier Control of Pollution (Special Waste) Regulations 1980[2]. These apply to persons who found themselves operating a special waste management facility which was not previously defined as such under the superseded definition of special waste. To qualify, such persons must either already hold a COTC for non-special waste treatment[3] or have applied to WAMITAB and be awaiting the granting of the COTC[4,5]. Persons who already possess a Level 3 COTC but who now find themselves managing a special waste facility have until 10 August 2000 to obtain the requisite Level 4 special waste COTC[6]. Similarly, persons who have applied to WAMITAB but not received their COTC have to that date to undergo the full special waste COTC assessment[7]. In order to qualify, the person must have managed the facility before 1 September 1996, and the facility must have been subject to a waste management licence[8]. The second requirement is that the person must have applied to WAMITAB for a Level 4 COTC prior to 1 March 1997[9].

1 SI 1996/972, regs 20 and 20A as amended by SI 1997/251, reg 2.
2 SI 1980/1709.
3 SI 1996/972, reg 20(1)(b)(i).
4 SI 1996/972, reg 20(1)(b)(ii): by way of either SI 1994/1056, reg 5(1) or SI 1995/288, reg 4(1) or (3).
5 Note that SI 1996/972, reg 20 originally referred to persons who were deemed to be technically competent by way of SI 1994/1056, reg 5. However, SI 1997/251, reg 2(a) reduced the reference to reg 5 to reg 5(1) only.
6 SI 1996/972, reg 20(2)(a).
7 SI 1996/972, reg 20(2)(b).
8 SI 1996/972, reg 20(3)(b): presumably managers of facilities which were hitherto excluded or exempt from requiring licences gain their transitional rights from the other provisions described at paras 8.157–8.162 above.
9 SI 1996/972, reg 20(3)(a): in the case of the small number of managers in Scotland who operated sites subject to resolutions which, when the definition of special waste was changed, handled special waste for the first time, the deadline for applying for a COTC was extended to 1 September 1997 (SI 1997/2203, reg 2(4)).

8.167 As the Special Waste Regulations 1996 were originally drafted, persons over 55 years of age were required to apply for a COTC. This error was corrected in February 1997 by the Special Waste (Amendment) Regulations 1997[1]. Now the position of persons who originally qualified for deemed technical competence due to relevant experience and being aged over 55 on 10 August 1994 is unaffected by any change in the definition of special waste[2]. They can therefore continue to act as technically competent managers of special waste facilities to August 2004[3].

1 SI 1997/251, reg 2.
2 By way of SI 1994/1056, reg 5(2) and SI 1996/972, reg 20A (as amended by SI 1997/251, reg 2).
3 SI 1994/1056, reg 5(2).

Agency evaluation of competence

8.168 Two circumstances are provided for in the regulations which permit the Agency to make its own evaluation of technical competence. The first is aimed at addressing problems caused by a national shortage in both holders and applicants for COTCs. It applies only to managers of facilities other than landfills. The second relates to all the facilities, such as scrapyards and vehicle dismantlers, where managers do not need to demonstrate technical competence by applying to WAMITAB for a COTC. In this case, the Agency must make its own assessment. It has been estimated that this provision applies to about 30% of the licenced management infrastructure in England and Wales[1].

1   See Environment Agency (1998) *State of Technical Competence in the Waste Industry*, Environment Agency, Bristol, p 5.

8.169 *Sites requiring COTCs*   In 1996, the Agency was granted discretion[1] to waive certain of the requirements of technical competence set out in the Waste Management Licensing Regulations 1994. These provisions would affect persons who wish to act as managers of specified waste disposal or recovery facilities, but are prevented for the reason that they do not possess the required practical experience within the timespan set out in the regulations. However, this provision only relates to the waste management facilities set out in Table 8.3 which are not landfills[2]. Secondly, it only applies to persons wishing to act as managers of a site which is subject to a waste management licence application[3]. In addition, the persons must already have applied for a COTC from WAMITAB[4]. Notwithstanding that the usual requirements of technical competence under the Waste Management Licensing Regulations 1994[5] are not satisfied, the Agency is given discretion to permit the person to act as a technically competent manager[6]. However, that person can only manage the particular facility subject to the licence application. Furthermore, the person must obtain a full COTC within two years, commencing on the date of the granting of the licence[7]. It would seem that, unless the COTC is obtained, the site would not longer by viewed as being under technically competent management and could be subject to partial licence revocation or licence suspension[8].

1   SI 1996/634, reg 4.
2   SI 1996/634, reg 4(2).
3   SI 1996/634, reg 4(1)(b).
4   SI 1996/634, reg 4(1)(a).
5   SI 1994/1056, reg 4: see para 8.137ff above.
6   SI 1996/634, reg 4(1)(d).
7   See SI 1996/634, reg 4(1).
8   EPA 1990, s 38(2) and (6)(a): see Chapter 9.

8.170 *Sites outside the COTC scheme*   The system of COTCs does not embrace all waste management facilities. Scrapyards and vehicle dismantlers are explicitly excluded by the Waste Management Licensing Regulations 1994[1]. Other activities are implicitly excluded for the reason that they do not appear on Table 1 of reg 4 (reproduced here as Table 8.3). The most obvious omission is landfills of less than 50,000m³ input that do not accept special waste, biodegradable waste or involve significant engineering works.

1   SI 1994/1056, reg 4(2).

8.171 Sites which fall outside the COTC scheme need to have their management competence assessed directly by the Agency. Waste Management Paper No 4 (WMP 4) provides guidance on how this should be done[1], with Waste Management

Paper No 4A providing additional guidance in respect of metal recycling facilities[2]. In accordance with the general guidance contained in WMP 4, two tests should be applied[3]. The Agency should assess the applicant's 'appreciation and understanding of waste management law and practice' and the person's 'type and level of experience in waste management'[4]. Such an assessment should be based upon the evidence supplied by the applicant. According to WMP 4, formal qualifications are not necessarily needed, although the possession of appropriate certificates is to be viewed as evidence of knowledge or understanding. Knowledge of relevant Waste Management Papers and the legislative background to licensing is viewed as a way of establishing appropriate competence. Similarly, whether the person can draft their own working plan to accompany a licence and can competently explain to the Agency how the site will be operated 'is likely to be of a sufficient level of understanding to be technically competent'[5].

1   Department of the Environment (1994) *Licensing of Waste Management Facilities* Waste Management Paper No 4, 3rd edn, HMSO, London, para 3.56 et seq. The Agency is finalising its own internal guidance documents to ensure a consistent national approach by its staff: see Environment Agency (1999) *Consultation Paper Statement of Arrangements Regarding the Provision of Technical Competence by Operators of Licensed Waste Management Facilities*, Environment Agency, Warrington.
2   Department of the Environment (1995) *Licensing of Metal Recycling Sites*, Waste Management Paper No 4A, HMSO, London, pp 35–41.
3   This guidance is repeated and somewhat expanded in respect of metal recycling facilities in WMP 4A. In certain cases, the latter WMP may provide additional guidance which might be useful in the context of assessing the competence of other, non-COTC facility operators.
4   WMP 4, para 3.56.
5   WMP 4, para 3.66.

8.172   For those licensed waste management facilities not within the COTC scheme[1], there is no certificate to obtain. WMP 4 suggests that the Agency should regard the person's experience as sufficient if there is evidence that appropriate expertise has been gained by at least five years' relevant experience at supervisory level in the last ten years[2]. Wherever possible, independent corroboration on this matter should be sought. A statement of experience is viewed by the Agency as the best way of demonstrating competence. This statement should contain the names and addresses of employers, details of disposal facilities managed, along with relevant dates. Two referees should normally be used[3]. Unlike the case for persons of over 55 years of age who are managers of sites subject to the COTC scheme, the WMP makes no distinction in respect of the age of persons who have appropriate prior experience in the year up to August 1994[4]. The only guidance provided on the assessment of relevant experience has been summarised in the previous paragraph. Accordingly, it appears that this assessment should be followed in the appraisal of all non-COTC site managers, regardless of their age.

1   As defined in reg 4 of the 1994 Regulations and shown in Table 8.3.
2   WMP 4, para 3.67.
3   WMP 4, para 3.67.
4   In respect of persons over 55 years of age, it should be noted that the Waste Management Licensing Regulations 1994 only refer to managers of sites listed in the Regulation's Table 1 (see Table 8.3), not to those involved in any other type of facility (see SI 1994/1056, reg 5(2)).

The definition of a 'manager' in relation to technical competence

8.173   An interesting question arises over the breadth of the word 'manager' in respect of the requirement for technical competent management[1]. As noted in Chapter 7, the words 'director, manager, secretary or other similar officer' occur together in s 157 of the EPA 1990 in relation to offences of bodies corporate. The terms also figure in s 74(7), in relation to the concept of 'other relevant person' and the concept of fit and proper person. Generally[2], the word 'manager' in these contexts is taken to be someone close to the 'heart and mind' of the company: in other words someone who controls a company's corporate affairs, makes company policy, financial decisions and so on[3]. Certainly, in relation to s 157, the legal meaning of 'manager' is quite distinct from the common English use of the term.

1   SI 1994/1056, reg 5, SI 1995/288, reg 4, SI 1996/972, reg 20.
2   See para 7.156ff.
3   See, for example, *R v Boal* [1992] 3 All ER 177 and *Woodhouse v Walsall Metropolitan Borough Council* [1993] Env LR 30.

8.174   The question then arises over whether the word 'manager' in reg 5 should be interpreted narrowly in the light of s 157 or in accordance with its more general usage in the English language. Clearly, if the interpretation of a 'manager' appropriate to s 157 is applied in this instance, those persons that are deemed technically competent due to their previous experience are likely to be very limited in number. They will be the upper echelons only of many companies. However, the requirement for technical competence in Part II of the EPA 1990 is for individual waste management sites to be subject to technically competent management: ie that the person directly in charge of the site is technically competent. Hence a highly restricted definition of the word 'manager' would appear to impede the purpose of the statute.

8.175   Besides an evaluation of the purpose of the statute, it should also be noted that, unlike in s 157 of the EPA 1990, the word 'manager' in reg 5 of the Waste Management Licensing Regulations 1994 stands on its own with no mention being made of directors, secretaries etc. *R v Boal*[1] confirms that the interpretation of the term 'manager' is dependent upon its context. In *Boal*, Brown J notes that Lord Denning appears to take a conflicting view of the word 'officer' in *Registrar of Restrictive Trading Agreements v W H Smith & Sons Ltd*[2] as he did when deciding the case of *Re a Company*[3]. However, Brown J appears to accept this view on the grounds that it indicates that the two Denning judgments recognise 'that the words "officer" and "manager" take on different meanings depending upon the context in which they are used'[4].

1   [1992] 3 All ER 177, at 181G.
2   [1969] 3 All ER 1065.
3   [1980] 1 All ER 284.
4   *R v Boal* [1992] 3 All ER 177, at 181G.

8.176   Accordingly, both of these arguments suggest that the word 'manager' in reg 5 of the Waste Management Licensing Regulations 1994 is to be taken to have a meaning akin to its common usage. It is not to be subject to the restrictive definition applied where it appears in s 157 of the EPA 1990[1].

1   Or in s 74(7).

Financial provision

8.177   The third element of s 74 of the EPA 1990's concept of fit and proper person requires licence applicants to be in a position to make financial provision adequate to fulfil the requirements of the licence. Although a range of matters are embraced under the general heading of financial provision, the overall objective remains common. This is to ensure that all the financial liabilities of a waste management facility remain with the licensee, thereby preventing public money becoming involved in such matters as site clean-up or long-term environmental monitoring. In this respect, it would seem that the financial provision concept goes hand-in-hand with the notion of 'sustainability', namely the need to prevent the activities of this generation placing costs upon future generations[1]. As is noted at para 8.66 the Environment Act 1995 requires the Environment Agency[2] to embrace the need to promote sustainability when discharging its functions[3].

1   See Department of the Environment (1995) *Making Waste Work: A Strategy for Sustainable Waste Management in England and Wales* Cm 3040, HMSO, London, para 1.5.
2   This requirement does not apply as explicitly to SEPA.
3   Environment Act 1995, s 4(1).

8.178   Waste Management Paper (WMP) No 4[1] provides statutory guidance on how financial provision should be assessed[2]. The Agency is required to have regard to the guidance contained in the WMP by s 74(5) and, to a lesser extent, s 35(8) of the EPA 1990[3]. The Paper does not, however, describe or assess the financial provision mechanisms themselves particularly well and has received criticism on this account.

1   Department of the Environment (1994) *Licensing of Waste Management Facilities*, Waste Management Paper No 4, 3rd edn, HMSO, London, Chapter 3; oddly, the subsequent Paper on the licensing of scrapyards and vehicle dismantlers (Department of the Environment (1995) *Licensing of Metal Recycling Sites*, Waste Management Paper No 4A, HMSO, London) provides no additional guidance on how financial provision is to be addressed in respect of that sector.
2   See WMP, 4 para 1.4.
3   The concept of statutory guidance is considered at para 8.231.

8.179   In respect of each licence application, the exact nature of the requisite financial provision will depend considerably on the type of site and the economic circumstances of the operator. Each waste management facility is likely to be subject to quite different potential financial liabilities. Both planned expenditure, such as decommissioning and restoration, and provision for unexpected events[1] may need to be considered. A factor also of significance in the selection of an appropriate financial provision mechanism is the need to address circumstances where a licensee starts having difficulty to meet liabilities due to lack of cash flow and, ultimately, insolvency[2].

1   For example, leakage from a landfill liner causing damage to groundwater: see WMP 4, para 3.92.
2   Indeed, insolvency may be a result of Agency enforcement action. The EPA 1990 allows licences to be revoked or suspended: see paras 9.17 and 9.40. If correctly established, the existence of adequate financial provision should mean that the ability to deploy these enforcement tools is not fettered by the need to consider whether the operator may become insolvent, leaving clean-up to be funded from public money.

8.180   Landfill sites prove particularly challenging to the Agency in the assessment of proposals for financial provision. There is a need for continued maintenance and monitoring many years after closure, mainly to ensure that leachate or landfill gas will not cause pollution or threaten public safety. Whilst WMP 4 suggests a post-closure maintenance and monitoring period of 30 years or more[1], terms of up to 500 years have been put forward as the possible period over which landfill gas or leachate generation will finally cease at certain household waste landfills[2]. It is also difficult to close a landfill halfway through the filling process without significant engineering and, even then, long-term monitoring and pollution prevention measures must still be provided.

1   WMP 4, para 3.103.
2   RC Harris, K Knox and N Walker 'A Strategy for the Development of Sustainable Landfill Design', *Proceedings of the Institute of Waste Management*, January 1994, pp 26–29.

8.181   Like the other two components of fit and proper person, the question of financial provision in the EPA 1990 must be considered in respect of the criteria set out in s 74. For a waste management licence application, the proposals put forward by a licence applicant are to be '. . . determined by reference to the carrying on by him of the activities which . . . are to be authorised by the licence and the fulfilment of the requirements of the licence'[1]. Section 74(3)(c) then sets down the circumstances under which a person will not be considered to be fit and proper due to inadequate financial provision. An applicant is not fit and proper if that person 'has not made and either has no intention of making or is in no position to make financial provision adequate to discharge the obligations arising from the licence'[2]. This means that financial provision may not need to be in place at the time of the licence application. But the Agency must be convinced that there is an intention to put it into place and/or that the applicant is in a position to put it into place. This intention will then be formalised and put into practice by appropriate licence conditions.

1   EPA 1990, s 74(2).
2   EPA 1990, s 74(3)(c).

8.182   It also should be noted that financial provision is assessed against the criteria of whether provision is made which is adequate to discharge the obligations arising from the licence. Hence Waste Management Paper 4 warns that financial provision 'should **not** be used to attempt to provide unlimited cover for unspecified future liabilities, or to deal with matters such as compensation where the normal mechanisms would apply'[1]. Any assessment of financial provision, the WMP stresses, should be made solely in relation to the criteria set down in s 74(2), namely in relation to the carrying on of the activities authorised by the licence and the fulfilment of its requirements. Accordingly, 'financial standing is not to be considered in general terms, but only as it is relevant to the obligations of the particular licence applied for'[2].

1   WMP 4, para 3.70.
2   WMP 4, para 3.81.

8.183   WMP 4 requires that the level of financial provision for any licence application should be evaluated on a case by case basis, which requires adjustment according to the site's capacity to cause pollution of the environment or harm to human health[1]. It is envisaged that financial provision is assessed by way of a two stage appraisal[2]. The applicant must be able to demonstrate basic financial competence initially. But only after a draft licence is made available to the applicant can s 74(3)(c) of the EPA 1990 be completely addressed. It is difficult for applicants to demonstrate financial provision unless and until they have had an opportunity to evaluate the implications of the contents of the proposed licence[3].

1   WMP 4, para 3.70.
2   See WMP 4, paras 3.81, 3.89. 3.91 etc.
3   WMP 4, para 3.71.

8.184   According to the Waste Management Paper, the only exception to the need to consider an applicant's proposals for financial provision concerns local authority site operators in Scotland[1]:

'The financial operations of local authorities are supported by taxation: so Scottish local authorities who operate their own waste management sites can always be deemed capable of meeting the criteria of financial provision'.

Whilst not explicitly referred to in the Paper, this sentiment could apply by analogy to local authorities in England and Wales, in respect of licensed infrastructure such as highways depots where controlled waste is stored. However, whether the statement in the Paper accords with the more recent acceptance of the notion of sustainability[2] appears to be an open question. The requirement that any restoration or post-closure remedial work is to be funded by future taxpayers does not appear to sit comfortably with this principle.

1   WMP 4, para 3.74.
2   See para 8.66ff above.

General financial appraisal

8.185   WMP 4 recommends that the Agency should initially only seek 'a general statement about how the applicant proposes to make financial provision'[1] as part of the material submitted with the licence application. However, it would seem that an application should not be rejected at this stage. The decision by the Agency on whether provision is adequate should be deferred 'until a detailed proposal is made to them'[2], presumably in the light of the draft licence conditions.

1   WMP 4, para 3.72.
2   WMP 4, para 3.72.

8.186   All applications are required to provide the limited amount of information as set down in paras 3.81 to 3.90 in the WMP[1]. A summary of these paragraphs will be found below. Precisely how much information is submitted, and at what stage it should be submitted, is not fully covered in the WMP. Indeed, the WMP seems to be a trifle muddled in places in these respects. In addition, much of the general guidance on how overall financial standing of the applicant should be addressed is elementary, distinctly vague or both. However, as the advice in the Paper constitutes 'statutory guidance' to the Agency[2], it seems important that regard is had to it.

1   WMP 4, para 3.75.
2   See WMP 4, para 1.4 and para 8.231ff.

8.187   *All*[1] licence applicants are required to submit a business plan for the development and operation of the facility. This should be capable of 'demonstrating how the applicant will be financing the licence requirements arising from that development and operation'[2]. Such a plan should be assessed by the Agency not in relation to its profitability[3], but rather on the basis that 'such plans would provide the main source of information on the ability of the applicant to fulfil the obligations to be imposed by the licence'[4]. The financial provision criteria should act to ensure that adequate capital is available when a facility is operational. A guaranteed supply of capital is most likely to ensure that sites continue to be operated to acceptable standards, with finance being readily available to address the unexpected. In assessing the application, the Agency will need to determine that the applicant's 'investment plans are soundly based and realistic in relation to the development proposed'[5]. Likewise, '[n]o realistic applicant for a licence should have difficulty in providing evidence to the . . . [Agency] that he is either of sufficient substance or has made appropriate plans to obtain external funding, to meet the immediate obligations of the licence'[6].

1   WMP 4, para 3.75.
2   WMP 4, para 3.82.
3   WMP 4, para 3.82.
4   WMP 4, para 3.82: however, despite this guidance, it seems apparent that a major criteria for judging the viability of a scheme is its profitability. Should the scheme not be profitable, then it is difficult to see how a licence holder (particularly a smaller company) can be certain to sustain 'the fulfilment of the requirements of the licence' as required by s 74(2) of the EPA 1990.
5   WMP 4, para 3.81.
6   WMP 4, para 3.88.

8.188 Once the licence has been drafted, the second stage of the financial provision appraisal can be commenced. This will require a rather more detailed examination of the financial standing of the proposal. The Agency must 'form a view about the ability of the applicant to invest properly in any waste management proposal so as to ensure, as far as possible, that there is safe and responsible management in accord with the proposed licence conditions'[1]. However, the Agency is cautioned about going too far and should not 'explore in detail the exact amount of expenditure proposed for each aspect of [landfill] site preparation'[2] nor 'explore in detail the exact amount of expenditure on each item of [waste treatment] machinery or to get more than a broad idea on how equipment failures and repair needs are to be met'[3].

1 WMP 4, para 3.87.
2 WMP 4, para 3.85.
3 WMP 4, para 3.87.

8.189 In certain cases, there is no need to provide for a specific financial provision beyond a general indication of the existence of adequate funds. This applies particularly for waste disposal facilities which are not landfills[1]. Only when the Agency is not satisfied that the information provided is sufficient should further mechanisms be sought[2]. However, this will only apply where a site will not manifest significant future liabilities[3].

1 WMP 4, paras 3.75, 3.81–3.91, 3.120.
2 WMP 4, para 3.75 and 3.89.
3 WMP 4, para 3.122.

Mechanisms to ensure future financial provision

8.190 It would seem that the Agency generally requires specific mechanisms in respect of financial provision where a licensee's capitalisation is low or where long term liabilities may occur. Hence, cash deposits or bonds are being demanded to cover matters such as site clearance after insolvency for smaller transfer stations or scrapyards. For landfills, bonds or escrow accounts[1] appear to be the norm, in order to address 'routine' expenditure such as restoration and post-closure monitoring, and also unplanned events such as landfill gas migration or liner failure. Not surprisingly, the imposition of the latter type of mechanism has met with opposition from within the waste management industry. It has been argued that financial provision can be satisfied in respect of major public limited companies by an appraisal of their recent accounts. The size and diversity of certain of the major companies, and the relatively small nature of any liability in comparison to the turnover of the group as whole, is advanced as providing sufficient safeguards to satisfy s 74 of the EPA 1990. These factors are claimed to be sufficient to prevent any such company from being in a situation where it 'is in no position to make financial provision adequate to discharge the obligations arising from the licence'[2]. However, this view is, not surprisingly, disputed by the Agency, particularly in the context of landfill operations where financial provision may need to last for generations. Within this equation, the Agency is obviously concerned about company takeovers (particularly non-UK multinationals where assets may be beyond the reach of the British courts), which may upset a presently healthy balance sheet.

1 These are discussed at paras 8.200 and 8.205 below.
2 EPA 1990, s 74(3)(c).

8.191 The Agency's policy in respect of the need to require specific financial provision mechanisms finds sustenance in the Waste Management Paper itself, which sets out additional requirements for the appraisal of financial provision for landfill sites. They should be considered in relation to 'all' waste management licence applications for landfills[1], which will need to have been evaluated under the procedures set out in paragraphs 3.103 to 3.118 of the WMP. The reason why landfill sites are singled out is that, in the post-closure period, the landfill will not be generating income but will still require expenditure.

1   WMP 4, para 3.75. The exception in WMP 4 is given as a landfill operated by Scottish local authorities: see WMP 4, para 3.74 and para 8.184 above.

8.192   The Waste Management Paper is also quite specific that the Agency should, where necessary, require the applicant to make adequate provision to cover corrective remedial action in the event of 'some specified occurrence'[1]. An example given in the WMP of such an occurrence is the failure of a containment system leading to pollution of a watercourse[2]. The Agency is required to be satisfied, as part of the evaluation of the application 'that the applicant has made financial provision to cover these specific risks, and [the Agency] *will usually* wish to make the maintenance of such provision a specific licence condition'[3].

1   WMP 4, para 3.92.
2   WMP 4, para 3.92.
3   WMP 4, para 3.93: author's emphasis.

8.193   At the point where the nature of the required financial provision mechanisms are themselves to be discussed, the Waste Management Paper significantly runs out of steam, becoming increasingly vague and less than helpful[1]. However, the Institute of Wastes Management has collated a report on financial provision which provides a much better discussion of the merits of the available mechanisms[2].

1   For example, escrow accounts, mutual funds, bonds etc are, for some reason, only discussed in a section of the WMP in relation to the post-closure period of landfills (WMP 4, paras 3.103 to 3.118), implying somewhat misleadingly that they have little application in other instances.
2   Institute of Wastes Management (1996) *Position Paper on Financial Provisions for the Prolonged Aftercare of Landfills*, Institute of Wastes Management, Northampton.

8.194   A number of financial provision mechanisms have been identified. They include:

–   trust funds
–   escrow accounts
–   cash 'up front'
–   bonds and guarantees
–   insurance
–   captives
–   accounting provisions.

These mechanisms are discussed in detail below. They provide a variety of short-term and more longer-term solutions. Short-term solutions include the establishment of bonds, financial guarantees and insurance policies. These type of mechanism are well known to the providers of finance. However, it would seem that they may not operate effectively over very long periods. Longer-term solutions might involve such matters as mutual funds or escrow accounts. Increasingly, particular options are being applied to more complex situations in combination.

8.195   In virtually all of these cases, the terms of the particular mechanism are governed by legal agreements. The WMP emphasises that the Agency, the applicant and any provider of third party cover need to be clear as to the exact nature of the terms and conditions of such cover, particularly in relation to the event that triggers the payment, the works or other measures provided for and the appropriate amount of cover[1].

1   WMP 4, para 3.94.

8.196   Although the Agency is permitted considerable discretion as to which of these mechanisms are appropriate, there are limits to the degree of discretion available. In particular, it would be inappropriate to make a commitment to one financial provision mechanism to the exclusion of others. The Agency would be inappropriately fettering its own discretion. The Agency needs be open to approaches by licence applicants with suggestions of how financial provision should be addressed. It is important that the Agency determines each of these on a case by case basis, or at least leaves room to do so. In any case, not all site operators will be able to make the same type of financial provision. Whether certain types of mechanism are available will depend upon the ability of third parties to market suitable products, which also may not be available to smaller, less well funded operators. Other mechanisms may involve operators co-operating and forming 'pools' of suitable funds. Again, not all operators will wish – or will be allowed – to be part of the pool. Finally, the application of financial provision in an environmental context is very new. Hence financial institutions, the normal providers of appropriate mechanisms, are still coming to grips with the demand for these new products. Innovation in these respects is to be expected over the next few years. Rigid rules may inadvertently discourage better solutions to those which are currently available.

8.197   In these respects, the statement on financial provision in the Agency's 1996/97 Annual Report provided an indication of its policy[1]:

> 'The Agency's interim position is that escrow (a fund held by a third party) is the most satisfactory way of ensuring that money will be available when it is needed. The Agency recognises that methods such as bonds, trust funds and mutual insurance schemes are available. In developing these methods further, the private sector has the Agency's active co-operation.'

In all cases, the requirements for financial provision will need to be set out in one or more conditions of the waste management licence. The Agency is left with the not inconsiderable duty of the assessment of long-term costs, particularly in the context of possible unplanned events which, while not likely, may result in significant environmental damage. Given that the EPA 1990 prevents the question of financial provision being re-appraised after a licence has been issued[2], it is vital that such calculations are correctly done at the outset.

1   Environment Agency (1997) *Environment Agency Annual Report and Accounts 1996–97*,
    Environment Agency, Bristol, p 56. Financial provision is not discussed in the 1997–98 Report.
2   Discussed at para 9.70ff.

8.198   *Trust funds*   Trust funds are controlled by independent trustees who are required to use the fund to further those named beneficiaries. How the accumulated monies are to be used is set out in the documentation governing the trust. Payment is at the trustees' discretion, subject to the terms and conditions by which the trust was established, and the requirements of trust law. As the money is only accessible in the manner set out in the terms of the trust, the fund appears to be protected from actions by creditors when a contributor has suffered insolvency.

8.199 Trust funds can be set up between a pool of operators and hence they have a certain similarity to pension funds. In this form, they are attractive as they offer a degree of self-policing between the members in order to safeguard the fund's long-term existence. However, contributors running badly operated sites may be required by the other trustees to withdraw and hence this possibility may defeat one of the fundamental objectives of financial provision. Trust funds are attractive to operators, as they can be sustained by way of judicious investment on the financial markets.

8.200 *Escrow accounts*[1] Escrow accounts are bank accounts under the legal control of a third party, usually a bank. The bank will control the account in the manner set down by legal agreement between the licensee, Agency and bank itself. Funds can be released from the account as and when specified events trigger the provisions of the legal agreement.

1 See McNair D (1994) 'Fit and Proper Person: Assessment of Adequate Financial Provision' *Waste Planning*, Sept 1994, pp 34–37.

8.201 Usually escrow accounts at waste management facilities accumulate by way of a levy on waste delivered. Payment continues into the account until various ceilings in the legal agreement are reached. These are calculated on the basis of the expected payouts of the account for defined events. For example, an escrow account may be set up for a landfill to cover site restoration, post-closure maintenance[1], and remediation of one-off unexpected events[2]. On site closure, the account pays out for the restoration costs. The remaining sum in the account then covers post-closure monitoring and unexpected events, paying out in the manner set down in the legal agreement. Should the operator fail to undertake the works specified, the legal agreement setting up the account allows the regulatory authority to have access to the funds in the account and to use them for that purpose.

1 Eg leachate pumping, landfill gas extraction, maintenance of capping works and environmental monitoring.
2 In some versions these may be split into separate accounts, so that monies for particular elements are 'ring fenced' and remain unaffected by payment from the other accounts.

8.202 By definition, escrow accounts will take a while for the deposited sums to reach a level which would be suitable to address more immediate liabilities. Hence it may be desirable that they are deployed in conjunction with one of the other financial provision mechanisms described in this section. For example, a bond may be used to cover the liabilities of the first few years of a landfill, with the escrow taking over when a defined level of funds has accrued.

8.203 Escrow accounts are conceptually simple to operate. However, their effectiveness is dependent on the correct assessment of the maximum amount of funds to be contained in the account and on the wording of the relevant legal agreement. They offer a significant disadvantage to licensees, as they tie up inordinate amounts of unproductive capital. In addition, there appears to be doubt about whether they offer sufficient protection of funds from actions by creditors after insolvency.

8.204 *Cash 'up front'* An option, which seems particularly applicable for small traders, is the lodging of a defined sum of money directly with the Agency. Being located in the Agency's account, there is no problem of ready availability. Generally, this is preferred only where a person does not have access to any of the other financial provision mechanisms or where their cost is prohibitive. An obvious disadvantage to a licensee is that this arrangement ties up significant capital in the long-term. For that reason alone, the sums will remain relatively small, being enough to cover such matters as the site clearance of a skip transfer station or similar facility.

8.205   *Bonds*   In the past, bonds have tended to be seen as falling within the category of short-term funding mechanisms. They involve a bondsman who is protected by a guarantor, with the terms of access of the bond being governed by legal agreement. If the bond is required to be paid out, the money is recovered from the guarantor – usually the parent company of the landfill operator. Bonds are well known concepts in civil engineering contracts and are generally granted on a short-term (such as three year) renewable basis. For waste management facilities, they represent a suitable way to make provision for the cost of dismantling or for one-off unexpected events. They are not protected against insolvency and tie up money which would be otherwise available in a company.

8.206   Most recently the concept of a 'rolling bond' has been promulgated as a way of ensuring medium- to long-term financial provision at waste management facilities. At a pre-defined interval prior to the expiry of the bond, the licensee is required by legal agreement to take out a second bond for a further fixed term. Failure in this respect would result in the contents of the first bond being paid directly to the Agency or cause such monies to be paid into another financial provision mechanism such as an escrow account.

8.207   *Guarantees*   Financial guarantees have some similarities to bonds, being familiar in the context of transfrontier waste shipments[1]. They are set up in conjunction with a bank and the relevant legal agreement is worded to allow the regulatory authority direct access on the occurrence of defined events. While the company setting up the guarantee has assets, they are durable, but there is no protection against insolvency.

1   See para 5.85ff.

8.208   An alternative to financial guarantees or bonds involves the dispensation of the third party by way of a parent company guarantee or a guarantee put up by named individuals, such as individual directors. However, the lack of third party involvement has obvious disadvantages. Moreover, they are dependent on the continued financial standing of the guarantor and therefore there is no protection in respect of insolvency.

8.209   *Insurance*   Insurance is only suitable to cover unpredictable events. If an event was predictable, it seems doubtful for obvious reasons that a third party would wish to market suitable cover. Hence insurance is not appropriate for restoration or long-term monitoring costs. However, it could be used to cover the mitigation of unexpected events such as landfill gas or leachate migration. Insurance has the advantage of being protected against insolvency. But it is usually of short-term duration, although products offering cover for periods of up to ten years are appearing[1]. The continuation of insurance is usually at the discretion of the insurer. Hence there is no guarantee to the Agency that cover will exist in the long-term.

1   It seems conceivable that a product could be developed which paid out a capital sum at the end of a defined period in the absence of a claim – somewhat like an endowment policy.

8.210   *Captives*   These are insurance companies owned by contributors. Local authority insurance in Britian has been arranged through such a company. A number of different types of captive exist, being generally funded either as stock companies (whereby members inject capital to ensure claims are upheld) or as mutuals (where members solely pay premiums and any shortfall is covered by increased premiums).

8.211 Captives can have single ownership, but these may lack financial strength. Group captives are more robust, but may suffer from a lack of management consensus due to the different priorities of their members. Mutuals can suffer from under-funding as they are totally reliant on premiums to off-set claims. The local authority Municipal Mutual Insurance Company got into difficulties in this respect.

8.212 The attraction of captives to the regulator is that they may be self-policing and, because they have to be independent of their members, they offer some safeguards against insolvency. An advantage to the regulated is that the captive's assets can be re-invested. Hence they do not tie up significant funds unproductively.

8.213 *Accounting provisions* Making provisions in accounts for particular liabilities is a well known accounting practice. Indeed, failure to make such a provision when liabilities exist may affect the legality of the accounts of public companies. The concept has the advantage that the estimation of liabilities is checked by auditors and hence third party verification will provide a certain level of in-built safeguards. Provisions in accounts can be topped up as and when liabilities arise or money is paid out. Accordingly, they may be somewhat more flexible than some of the other financial provision mechanisms which are set by legal agreements at fixed maximum sums.

8.214 However, provisions in accounts offer disadvantages to operators as they are off-set against profits, and are therefore totally dependent on favourable trading conditions. Accounting provisions will not be protected from insolvency and hence may not give any form of long term guarantee. Small companies may not have their accounts audited and hence provisions in accounts may be less than attractive to the Agency in this context.

8.215 *Overdraft facilities* An overdraft facility is seen in the Waste Management Paper as a financial provision option[1]. This is held as something which 'might be possible' in respect of expected claims, particularly in relation to smaller operators[2]. The WMP blandly notes that the existence of such an entity can be ensured by a banker's letter. It is difficult to see how this mechanism could be effective, but a system of rolling credit facilities might work for a smaller operator with limited environmental liabilities.

1   WMP 4, para 3.95.
2   WMP 4, para 3.102.

WASTE MANAGEMENT LICENCES

8.216 The form and content of waste management licences is a function of the statutory provisions, Department of the Environment guidance and custom and practice which has been developed by regulatory bodies since 1976. The key legislation is, unsurprisingly, the EPA 1990 together with the Waste Management Licensing Regulations 1994[1]. Both the primary and secondary legislation have been subject to significant amendment or supplementation by, respectively, the Environment Act 1995 and by a succession of statutory instruments[2]. Besides the legislation, the content of licences is heavily influenced by the more up-to-date Waste Management Papers (WMP), of which WMP 4[3] and WMP 4A[4] are the most relevant. Additional guidance is also to be found in Circular 11/94[5] and, in respect of the relationship with development control, in Planning Policy Guidance Note (PPG) No 23[6]. This section will review the main provisions, particularly those set out in the primary and secondary legislation.

1 SI 1994/1056.
2 SIs 1994/1137, 1995/288, 1995/1950, 1996/508, 1996/593, 1996/634, 1996/972, 1997/351, 1997/2203, 1998/606 (in Scotland, also SI 1996/973, SI 1996/916 and SI 1997/257).
3 Department of the Environment (1994) *Licensing of Waste Management Facilities*, Waste Management Paper No 4, 3rd edn, HMSO, London.
4 Department of the Environment (1995) *Licensing of Metal Recycling Sites* Waste Management Paper 4A, HMSO, London.
5 Department of the Environment (1994) *Environmental Protection Act 1990: Part II Waste Management Licensing The Framework Directive on Waste*, Circular 11/94, HMSO, London.
6 Department of the Environment (1994) *Planning Policy Guidance: Planning and Pollution Control* HMSO, London.

Waste management licences and working plans

8.217 Waste management licences authorise one or more of the following categories of activity[1]: the treating, keeping or disposal of controlled waste. A licence can be made subject to a variety of conditions which promote particular environmental control objectives. These must be attained in order to reduce to acceptable levels adverse impacts of site operations upon the environment and human health[2]. Many waste management licences contain between 30 and 50 such conditions.

1 EPA 1990, s 35(1).
2 See WMP 4, Chaps 2, 4 and 5.

8.218 Besides the conditions, a licence also contains material submitted by a licence applicant. Such material may have been an adjunct of the licence application. Alternatively, it may have been supplemented by further information submitted after the licence is issued and as site operations progress. All of this information – which makes up the 'working plan' of the licence – forms a detailed statement of how the site is to be operated. It will contain appropriate scale drawings, along with explanatory material in the form of written text.

8.219 A licence therefore comprises two sets of documents, which should be viewed as quite distinct[1]:

'The licence conditions are stipulated by the waste regulation authority[2]: they set the performance standards to which the site must be operated. The working plan is the operator's document: it sets out, among other things, the way in which the operator proposes to meet those standards.'

1 WMP 4, para 2.17.
2 Ie the Environment Agency and the Scottish Environment Protection Agency.

8.220 Accordingly, for example, a licence condition may require that a site road is provided to a specification sufficient for it to be suitable for heavy traffic. The working plan will show the location of the road and detail its construction. Similarly, a condition may require that incoming wastes are checked to ensure that they comply with the permissible range of substances set down. The working plan will describe how this is to be achieved.

8.221 The working plan is itself made part of the licence usually by way of one or more appropriately worded licence conditions. Hence the failure of an operator to carry out a particular element of a working plan would be seen as a breach of the relevant licence condition. An offence under s 33(6) of the EPA 1990 would therefore be committed[1].

1   See Chapter 7.

8.222 It is difficult to offer a general view of the nature of licence conditions and the expected content of working plans[1]. Both are highly dependent on the type of site and the actual circumstances of the operation in question. Further advice is contained in the Waste Management Paper (WMP) series[2]. However, in essence, all licence conditions should satisfy the tests set down in WMP 4[3]. They therefore should be:

– necessary;
– enforceable;
– unambiguous; and
– comprehensive.

In 1998, the Agency published model licence conditions with the objective of attaining national consistency in licensing practice[4].

1   Case law is now beginning to emerge on terms within licences: see *Durham County Council v Thomas Swan & Co Ltd* [1995] Env LR 72 (a rather unfortunate definition of an 'empty' drum) and *R v David Smith* [1999] Env LR 433 (definition of when waste is 'accepted' at a licensed site).
2   See WMPs 4 and 4A, along with WMP 26B, 26C, 26D.
3   WMP 4, para 2.4.
4   These are being updated: see Environment Agency (1999) *Library of Licence Conditions and Working Plan Specifications*, Environment Agency, Warrington. It should be noted that these are revised regularly and are primarily aimed at guidance to Agency staff. There are also similar volumes for metal recycling facility licences and mobile plant licences.

8.223 Both licence conditions and working plans should be viewed as perpetually evolving and subject to regular amendment. Licence conditions are somewhat different to, for example, conditions of planning permissions, in that the latter cannot be changed unless compensation is granted. As the next chapter explains, licence conditions can be changed both by the Agency and by way of an application from the operator[1]. The Agency is required to review waste management licences periodically to ensure that they satisfy the criteria of necessity, enforceability, etc, and also 'in the light of changed environmental knowledge and consequent changes in environmental policy'[2]. For example, Circular 11/94 required all licences to be reviewed in respect of the groundwater protection requirements of the Waste Management Licensing Regulations 1994[3] by 31 April 1995. Similarly, Waste Management Paper 4A required that scrapyard and vehicle dismantler licences were all reviewed by 31 March 1996 and that existing licences be modified to reflect its guidance by 1 January 1999 at the latest[4].

1   EPA 1990, s 37: see para 9.03ff.
2   WMP 4, para 1.33.
3   SI 1994/1056, reg 15: see para 9.65ff.
4   WMP 4A, para 1.43.

8.224 Although the licence/working plan dichotomy has been in place since 1976[1] and is clearly cemented in a number of Department of the Environment guidance documents and appeal decisions[2], it should be noted that it does not have a statutory foundation in any of the legislation. There is, for example, no mention of it in the EPA 1990. Neither does the concept of working plans feature in the Waste Management

Licensing Regulations 1994, except that the provisions on public registers require that they are contained in the Agency's register[3].

1   See Department of the Environment (1976) *Waste Management Paper No 4 The Licensing of Waste Disposal Sites*, 1st edn, HMSO, London, para 5.6.
2   Appeals are discussed at para 9.126ff.
3   SI 1994/1056, reg 10(1)(a): see para 13.15.

The content of waste management licences

General licence conditions

8.225   The EPA 1990 requires that a waste management licence can be granted 'on such terms and subject to such conditions' as appear appropriate to the Agency[1]. In this matter, the Agency has considerable discretion. Section 35(3) of the EPA 1990 allows conditions of a licence to relate to the activities authorised by the licence and the precautions to be taken and works to be carried out in relation to those activities. The licence can also include conditions pertaining to the development stage of the site and also to its post-closure period[2].

1   EPA 1990, s 35(3).
2   EPA 1990, s 35(3).

8.226   However, whilst the Agency has wide discretion, this is fettered by the Waste Management Licensing Regulations 1994[1] and by guidance issued by the Department of the Environment. The 1994 Regulations require that no conditions can be included in a waste management licence which have the purpose 'only' of securing the health of persons at work[2]. The significance of the word 'only' needs to be emphasised, as it clearly allows conditions which have a joint environmental *and* health and safety purpose to be included within a waste management licence[3].

1   SI 1994/1056.
2   SI 1994/1056, reg 13.
3   See WMP 4, para 1.30.

8.227   As part of the process of interweaving the Waste Management Licensing Regulations 1994 with the Directive on Waste, all licences for disposal activities[1] must contain conditions which cover[2] the following matters[3]:

(a)   the types and quantity of waste;
(b)   the 'technical requirements';
(c)   the security precautions to be taken;
(d)   the disposal site; and
(e)   the treatment method.

The above five phrases have been extracted directly from Article 9 of the Directive on Waste[4]. However, it will be evident that the precise requirements of certain of these phrases is not immediately obvious. In the Scottish decision of *In Petition of John Guthrie*[5], it was held that a licence which did not specify the quantity of waste was void.

1   As defined in Annex IIA of the Directive and Sch 4, Part III of the Waste Management Licensing Regulations 1994: see Table 2.5 in Chapter 2.
2   See *In Petition of John Guthrie* [1998] Env LR 128 at 136.
3   SI 1994/1056, Sch 4, Pt 1, para 6: see also WMP 4, para 2.2.
4   Council Directive of 15 July 1975 on Waste (75/442/EEC) (OJ L194/39 25.7.75) (as amended by Council Directive of 18 March 1991 amending Directive 75/442/EEC on Waste (91/156/EEC) (OJ L78/32 26.3.91)).
5   [1998] Env LR 128 at 137.

8.228 The EPA 1990 requires that a waste management licence is a licence which authorises the treatment, keeping or disposal of a 'specified description' of controlled waste[1]. This indicates that the licence should clearly state the nature of the wastes that are acceptable at the site. This is also necessary for other reasons. The duty of care Code of Practice[2] requires that parties in waste transactions should ensure that a waste management facility is licensed to take the waste they produce or handle. Secondly, licences are public documents and it is desirable that members of the public should know the nature of wastes accepted at a site. Accordingly, the list of waste types should be explicit in every licence and comprehensible to outsiders.

1 EPA 1990, s 35(1).
2 Department of the Environment (1996) *Waste Management The Duty of Care A Code of Practice*, 2nd edn, HMSO, London: see Chapter 3.

8.229 It should be noted that Circular 6/96 cautions against the inappropriate use of references to the term 'special waste' in licence conditions[1]. An example might be when the term is being used as a central decision criteria for waste acceptance, such as a condition which specifies particular waste types but is subject to the caveat that none of these materials are special wastes. The circular appears to be pointing to the consequences of any review at European Community level of the criteria by which special wastes are defined. Any changes may cause a greater or lesser array of substances to be accepted under this type of condition. Such a change inevitably would not take into account site-specific requirements and may have unpredictable effects.

1 Department of the Environment (1996) *Environmental Protection Act: Part II Special Waste Regulations 1996*, Circular 6/96, HMSO, London, Annex A, para 16.

8.230 The Secretary of State has powers which can affect the content of waste management licences. Licence conditions can be dictated by way of regulations[1]: 'It is intended to use this power to implement specific requirements of EC or other international obligations; and to clarify demarcations between waste management licences and other regulatory regimes'[2]. Evidence of the use of this power can be found in parts of the Waste Management Licensing Regulations 1994[3]. The Secretary of State can also direct which 'terms and conditions' should or should not be included in any particular licence at the time of a licence application[4]. The Agency must give effect to any such direction. As yet, this power does not appear to have been exercised.

1 EPA 1990, s 35(6).
2 Circular 11/94, Annex 4, para 4.27.
3 See for example SI 1994/1056, regs 13, 14, 15(6) and (7).
4 EPA 1990, s 35(7) and see Circular 11/94, Annex 4, para 4.30.

8.231 Section 35 of the EPA 1990 places a duty on the Agency to 'have regard to' any guidance issued by the Secretary of State 'with respect to the discharge of their functions in relation to licences'[1]. A similar requirement exists in s 74, which sets down the manner of the assessment of the credentials of licencees and their associates in respect of whether they are fit and proper persons[2]. This requirement originally stemmed from a perceived need to enhance the status of certain waste management papers to ensure that the guidance is always acted upon[3]. Whether the resultant provisions actually achieve this objective is an interesting question. The guidance mentioned in s 35 and s 74 is labelled 'statutory guidance' in Circular 11/94[4]. Waste Management Papers No 4[5], 4A[6] and 26A[7] constitute such guidance[8]. Some of Circular 11/94 is also to be so viewed[9]: 'those parts of this Circular that guide WRAs[10] in the discharge of these functions[11] are also issued by the Secretary of State under sections 35(8) and 74(5)'.

1 EPA 1990, s 35(8).
2 EPA 1990, s 74(5): fit and proper person is discussed at para 8.112ff below.
3 See para 2.24 of Department of the Environment (1989) *Government's reply to the 2nd Report of the Environmental Committee: Toxic Waste*, Cm 679, HMSO, London.
4 Circular 11/94, para 19.
5 Department of the Environment (1994) *Licensing of Waste Management Facilities*, Waste Management Paper 4, HMSO, London.
6 Department of the Environment (1995) *Licensing of Metal Recycling Sites*, Waste Management Paper 4A, HMSO, London.
7 Department of the Environment (1993) *Landfill Completion*, Waste Management Paper 26A, HMSO, London.
8 Circular 11/94, para 19; WMP 4, para 1.4; WMP 4A, para 1.9; WMP 26A, page 1.
9 Circular 11/94, para 19.
10 Now the English and Scottish Agencies.
11 Ie in relation to licences and in making determinations of whether a person is a fit and proper.

8.232 The concept of 'statutory guidance' does beg the question as to the status of other guidance issued by the Secretary of State. Clearly, if the Agency only needs to have regard to specified elements of Circular 11/94 and WMPs 4, 4A and 26A, the status of the other parts may be called into question. However, that this other 'non-statutory guidance' does not need to be considered would seem to be confirmed by, for example, Waste Management Paper 26B[1], where regulatory bodies are explicitly informed that they can substitute their own views[2]. However, in respect of statutory guidance, it would seem that the enhanced status of certain elements of the general guidance makes its disregard by the Agency more difficult, particularly in the context of rights of licence applicants to appeal[3] or in respect of judicial review proceedings[4].

1 WMP 26B, para 1.12.
2 But see, for example, *R v North Derbyshire Health Authority, ex p Fisher* (1997) 38 BMLR 76 at 80–81.
3 See para 9.126.
4 But see *In Petition of John Guthrie* [1998] Env LR 128 at 136.

8.233 Finally, *R v Derbyshire County Council, ex p North East Derbyshire District Council*[1] held that conditions of a waste disposal licence[2] can only relate to the area where disposal activities take place, not to other areas. In respect of the Control of Pollution Act 1974, Bridge LJ states[3]:

> 'If one reads section 3(1) and section 5[4] together, it is quite clear that the only land to which the disposal licence as such relates is the actual land where the waste material is to be deposited. Areas ancillary which may be in one sense included in the site, such as land to be traversed by an access road, are not part of the land to which the disposal licence relates.'

This statement is a little odd, and perhaps it may be that the requirements for effective environmental protection have moved on since then. It is quite usual and necessary to have conditions on a licence which require works or actions to be carried out outside the area set down on a plan as being covered by the disposal licence. Often it is not possible for the area covered by the licence[5] to extend to all areas which the conditions of the licence seek to control. As already noted, the licence is granted only to the *occupier*[6] of the land, but conditions are needed to ensure that, for example, the public highway is kept clean and, by definition, the licence holder is not in occupation of the public highway. Similarly, conditions may require gas monitoring boreholes to be installed in neighbouring property. This seems precisely the reason for s 35(4) of the EPA 1990 which, as discussed at para 8.244 below, allows conditions to require the licence holder to have access to a third party's land[7].

1   (1979) 77 LGR 389.
2   The case involved a site licensed under the Control of Pollution Act 1974.
3   (1979) 77 LGR 389, at 396.
4   Control of Pollution Act.
5   Ie within the area of the so-called 'red line' which defines the boundary of the licensed area.
6   EPA 1990, s 35(2)(a).
7   The predecessor to s 35(4) in the EPA 1990, s 6(2) of the Control of Pollution Act 1974, was worded
    somewhat similarly. Oddly, the existence of s 6(2) is acknowledged in *R v Derbyshire County Council*
    by Bridge LJ immediately after the quotation reproduced above, suggesting some contradiction in his
    argument.

Licence conditions and record keeping

8.234   Under Schedule 4 to the Waste Management Licensing Regulations 1994[1], all
establishments and undertakings[2] involved in licensed disposal and recovery[3] operations must keep certain records. Such a requirement stems from Article 14 of the Waste
Directive[4]. This information must be made available to the competent authority[5] on
request[6]. The information to be kept is[7]:

'.. a record of the quantity, nature, origin and, where relevant, the destination,
frequency of collection, mode of transport and treatment method of any waste
which is disposed of or recovered; ...'

1   SI 1994/1056, Sch 4, Pt 1, para 14(1) as amended by SI 1995/288, reg 3(19).
2   Defined in Circular 11/94, Annex 5, para 5.10 and Circular 6/95, Annex 1, para 1.4: discussed at para
    10.22.
3   Defined in SI 1994/1056, reg 1(3) and Sch 4, Pt III and Pt IV; see Tables 2.5 and 2.6 in Chapter 2.
4   Council Directive of 15 July 1975 on Waste (75/442/EEC) (OJ L194/39 25.7.75) (subsequently
    amended by Council Directive of 18 March 1991 amending Directive 75/442/EEC on Waste
    (91/156/EEC) (OJ L78/32 26.3.91)) as amended by Directive 91/156.
5   SI 1994/1056, Sch 4, Pt 1, para 14(1)(b) as amended by SI 1996/972, reg 25 and Sch 3.
6   With the exclusion of sea disposal sites subject to the Deposits at Sea (Exemptions) Order 1985 (SI
    1985/1699: see para 10.19), these requirements apply to recovery and disposal facilities covered by
    other legislation, including authorisations under Part 1 of the EPA 1990.
7   SI 1994/1056, Sch 4, Pt 1, para 14(1)(a).

8.235   Circular 11/94[1] states that these requirements should be included as a waste
management licence condition. Similarly, Waste Management Paper No 4[2] requires
that such a condition should ensure that 'relevant, appropriate and meaningful' records
are kept to fulfil these requirements. What does not appear to be that clear is the relationship between the records required by a waste management licence and those
necessary under the duty of care[3]. However, it seems important that there is neither
duplication of record keeping nor omissions which do not comply with the relevant
legislation.

1   Circular 11/94, Annex 1, para 1.90.
2   WMP 4, para 4.43.
3   EPA 1990, s 34: see Chapter 3.

8.236   In this regard, Circular 11/94[1] states that information about the 'quantity,
nature and *origin*[2] of waste, as well as the frequency of collection and mode of transport . . . should be included on the transfer note' required by the duty of care. However,
this seems to beg the question as to the meaning of the word 'origin'. If this term is to
be interpreted in conjunction with the statutory provisions of the duty of care[3], the
'origin' of the waste is to be seen as the previous holder of the waste. This might be the
carrier that delivered the waste to the site. In that context, the 'origin' is not to be taken
to be the waste producer. If this interpretation is followed, there does seem an element
of doubt as to whether the intention of the Directive is being satisfied. It seems

unlikely to be fulfilled when only details of intermediaries in waste transactions are being recorded.

1 Circular 11/94, Annex 1, para 1.89.
2 Author's emphasis.
3 EPA 1990, s 34 and see *Waste Management. The Duty of Care. A Code of Practice* (1996), 2nd edn, HMSO, London and Chapter 3.

8.237 Although Circular 11/94's guidance appears a little less than full in the above respects, the circular[1] does acknowledge that the records required by the duty of care are insufficient in other respects to fully satisfy the record-keeping provisions of the 1994 Regulations. There remains the need to record the method of treatment and, where waste is subsequently sent on for recovery or disposal elsewhere, the destination of each consignment. Certainly, these requirements must be enacted by licence conditions.

1 Circular 11/94, Annex 1, para 1.89.

8.238 Until 1996, these requirements on record-keeping were enforced by s 33 of the EPA 1990 and the offence of breaching licence conditions[1]. The Waste Management Licensing Regulations 1994 themselves lacked their own offence provision in respect of a person's non-compliance with the record-keeping requirements of Schedule 4, para 14. However, the regulations were amended by the Special Waste Regulations 1996[2] so that a person who fails to comply with the record-keeping requirements commits an offence[3]. One statutory defence is allowed, which involves the failure to keep records due to an emergency[4]. On summary proceedings, a person convicted of the offence is liable to a fine not exceeding Level 5 on the standard scale[5]; on indictment the penalty is a custodial sentence of no more than two years or a fine, or both[6]. There are the usual provisions in respect of falsifying records[7], offences by directors and managers (etc) of bodies corporate[8] and in relation to acts of third parties[9]. Precisely why it was necessary to amend this part of Schedule 4 to cause duplication with the other offence provisions in s 33 of the EPA 1990 is not immediately clear[10].

1 EPA 1990, s 33(6): see Chapter 7.
2 SI 1996/972, reg 25 and Sch 3.
3 SI 1994/1056, Sch 4, para 14(4) (as amended by SI 1996/972, reg 25 and Sch 3).
4 SI 1994/1056, Sch 4, para 14(5) (as amended by SI 1996/972, reg 25 and Sch 3), which cross-refers to the statutory defence in the Special Waste Regulations 1996 (SI 1996/972, reg 18): see para 7.154ff.
5 Currently £5,000.
6 SI 1994/1056, Sch 4, para 14(8) (as amended by SI 1996/972, reg 25 and Sch 3), which cross-refers to the Special Waste Regulations 1996 (SI 1996/972), reg 18(9).
7 SI 1994/1056, Sch 4, para 14(6) and (7) (as amended by SI 1996/972, reg 25 and Sch 3): see para 12.218ff.
8 SI 1994/1056, Sch 4, para 14(8) (as amended by SI 1996/972, reg 25 and Sch 3), which cross-refers to the Special Waste Regulations 1996 (SI 1996/972), reg 18(6), (7) and (8): see para 7.156ff.
9 SI 1994/1056, Sch 4, para 14(8) (as amended by SI 1996/972, reg 25 and Sch 3), which cross-refers to the Special Waste Regulations 1996 (SI 1996/972), reg 18(5).
10 Besides waste management licences, these requirements also apply to waste management facilities which are controlled by other legislation. Examples might be waste management sites subject to integrated pollution control authorisations, or sea disposal facilities. It may be that the regulatory system pertaining to these activities needed to be substantiated by specific offence provisions.

Licence conditions relating to non-controlled waste

8.239 Section 35 of the EPA 1990 allows conditions of a waste management licence to be imposed on the handling of waste other than controlled waste at licensed facilities[1]. The only waste material that cannot be so addressed is waste within the meaning of the Radioactive Substances Act 1993[2] unless it either has other properties which make the material special waste[3] or has been prescribed by regulations made under s 78[4]. Excepting the latter materials, s 35 appears to allow the Agency to exercise comprehensive controls on licensed facilities that deal with both controlled and non-controlled wastes[5].

1 EPA 1990, s 35(5).
2 EPA 1990, s 78 (as amended by the Radioactive Substances Act 1993, Sch 3).
3 Special waste is defined in SI 1996/972 as amended by SI 1996/2019: see Chapter 4.
4 SI 1996/972, reg 3 prescribes radioactive waste, which for reasons other than radioactivity would be special waste, as special waste. See Circular 6/96, Annex A, para 8.
5 Those materials which make up waste other than controlled waste in s 35(5) should be viewed as a class of substances whose definition is independent of any description of non-controlled waste made by way of regulations under s 63(1): see Circular 11/94, Annex 4, para 4.26.

8.240 This provision is likely to prove particularly useful to the Agency at licensed facilities such as transfer stations which also store agricultural waste or wastes from mining and quarrying. Section 33(6) of the EPA 1990 makes the breach of any condition of a waste management licence an offence[1]. An example of where the handling of non-controlled waste which may cause licence conditions to be contravened might be where agricultural wastes were accepted at a site in excess of the quantities set down in the waste management licence[2].

1 See Chapter 7.
2 Somewhat bizarrely, however, if the same agricultural waste was deposited outside the area covered by the licence, no offence would be committed. Section 33(6) would be inapplicable in these circumstances for the reason that no licence conditions were involved. Section 33(1) explicitly refers to controlled wastes and, as para 2.60ff has shown, agricultural wastes do not fall currently within that definition.

8.241 In his judgment in *London Waste Regulation Authority v Drinkwater Sabey*[1], Smith J briefly considered the purpose of s 35(5) of the EPA 1990. The judgment principally concerned the relationship between the provisions in the Act to exempt certain, often small scale, recovery activities from licensing[2] and whether such an exemption could apply when the activity was taking place on a site which possessed a waste management licence. It was held that the licence conditions could not touch the exempted activity[3]. However, Smith J's remarks about the meaning of s 35(5) cannot pass without comment, mainly due to what appears to be a misunderstanding of that sub-section. He states[4] that s 35(5):

'... allows conditions to be imposed which relate to other forms of controlled waste, such a special waste or clinical waste, for which authorisation by licence is required and that it is not intended to provide that conditions may be imposed in respect of activities for which no licence is required at all.'

Although the context of the judgment is referring to the system of formal exemption provisions, the statement would be equally applicable where non-controlled waste is being dealt with.

1 [1997] Env LR 137.
2 By way of s 33(3) of the EPA 1990 and SI 1994/1056, reg 17 and Sch 3: see Chapters 10 and 11.
3 See para 10.47ff.
4 *London Waste Regulation Authority v Drinkwater Sabey Ltd* [1997] Env LR 137 at 144.

8.242 However, if Smith J's view of s 35(5) is correct, that sub-section appears to serve no purpose. In addition, it is very hard to see how s 35(5)'s reference to 'waste other than controlled waste' can be construed in the manner set out in the judgment.

The reference to special waste or clinical waste seems to misunderstand the meaning of 'controlled waste', failing to recognise that these materials fall within that definition[1]. Overall, the reference to s 35(5) in this manner seems to have been an *obiter* remark and not one that should be viewed as binding upon other courts.

1   See in the case of special waste, the EPA 1990, s 62(1) and SI 1996/972, reg 2 (as amended by SI 1996/2019, reg 2 and Sch 1), and for clinical waste, SI 1992/588, reg 1(2).

8.243   Besides non-controlled wastes, licence conditions can also address recovered wastes which are awaiting sale in scrapyards and other recovery facilities. Such conditions are appropriate so that a licence can comprehensively exercise control on all stored materials. Many materials awaiting sale in these circumstances will remain waste, particularly those that have only been subject to intermediate processing[1].

1   See *Euro Tombesi* (Cases C-304/94, 330/94, C-342/94 and C-224/95: [1998] Env LR 59, *Kent County Council v Queenborough Rolling Mill Co Ltd* [1990] 89 LGR 306, and paras 2.86 and 2.173.

Licence conditions affecting land owned by third parties

8.244   Section 35(4) of the EPA 1990 allows the obligations of licence conditions to be imposed not only upon licensees but also on third parties:

'Conditions may require the holder of a licence to carry out works or do other things notwithstanding that he is not entitled to carry out the works or do the thing and any person whose consent would be required shall grant, or join in granting, the holder of the licence such rights in relation to the land as will enable the holder of the licence to comply with any requirements imposed on him by the licence.'

This provision allows licence conditions to extend to require the licence holder to undertake works on a third party's land[1] and is intended to ensure that access to neighbouring land is permitted for the life of the waste management facility[2]. The third party is required to consent to such works, with compensation being payable[3].

1   In *R v Derbyshire County Council, ex p North East Derbyshire District Council* ((1979) 77 LGR 389) it was held that a licence condition which required a site access road is valid even if such a road would require a planning permission and no such permission had been granted. Note that this case revolved around the meaning of s 6 of the Control of Pollution Act 1974 and that s 35(4) of the EPA 1990 is a somewhat embellished version of that section.
2   In the water pollution case of *Lockhart v National Coal Board* 1981 SLT 161 at 172, the fact that the Coal Board were no longer leaseholders of land from which mine drainage caused pollution was not a reason which prevented the Board from being liable for the pollution. It was up to the Board to address any liability in the continuation of the lease. This case would seem to parallel circumstances where conditions require a waste management licence to do works on other people's land.
3   The arrangements for consultation and compensation are discussed at para 8.23ff.

8.245   Circular 11/94 provides some guidance on the breadth of this power and the circumstances in which it is to be utilised[1]:

'It is envisaged that the main need of this power will arise where it becomes necessary to modify an existing licence to require additional sampling and monitoring points outside the boundary of land owned by the licensee; and under those circumstances, the owner of the adjacent land will be obliged to grant permission for the necessary facilities to be installed and for access to supervise their operation. It is not desirable to rely on this power more often than strictly necessary; and, in particular, WRAs[2] and applicants for licences should make every effort to avoid the need for such conditions in new licences.'

It therefore appears that the Circular views this provision as one which a neighbour cannot obstruct. Although there is no specific offence in respect of a person who denies a licence holder access, it may well be that such a person falls foul of s 33 of the EPA 1990 in that that person is contravening a condition of a waste management licence. Precisely what the courts will make of such a prosecution appears to be an open question.

1 Circular 11/94, Annex 4, para 4.25.
2 Now the Environment Agency and the Scottish Environment Protection Agency.

Licence conditions and groundwater and surface water protection

8.246 It will be clear from the earlier discussion of reg 15 of the Waste Management Licensing Regulations 1994, that somewhat complicated provisions apply in respect of groundwater. These emanate from the Groundwater Directive[1], which also sets down requirements which must be addressed in the conditions of affected waste management licences. In addition, there appears to be a slightly odd interaction between the EPA 1990 and the Water Resources Act 1991 which may also need to be considered in any affected licence. These requirements are discussed in turn below.

1 Council Directive of 17 December 1979 on the Protection of Groundwater against Pollution Caused by Certain Dangerous Substances (Directive 80/68/EEC) (OJ L20/43 26.1.80).

8.247 *Regulation 15 and licence conditions on groundwater* Regulations 15(6) and 15(7) of the Waste Management Licensing Regulations 1994 set down certain matters which must be included in a licence if one is to be granted. These requirements will only apply when a discharge may occur into groundwater which is subject to reg 15 and the Groundwater Directive[1]. As with the other requirements of reg 15, a differentiation is made between List I and List II substances[2] and between their direct and indirect discharges[3].

1 See para 8.79.
2 See para 8.74.
3 See para 8.76.

8.248 For licences which cover facilities involved with indirect discharges, the terms used in reg 15(6) appear to be, subject only to minor alterations, copies of the contents of Article 10 of the Groundwater Directive. Accordingly, if a licence is to be issued where List I and List II substances are to be indirectly discharged, the licence must only be granted in accordance with conditions which specify:

(a) the place where 'any disposal or tipping'[1] may lead to an indirect discharge of List I or List II substances into groundwater;
(b) the method of disposal or tipping used;
(c) the essential precautions to be taken. In this respect, particular attention must be paid to:

   (i) the nature and concentration of the substances present in the matter to be disposed of or tipped;
   (ii) the characteristics of the receiving environment; and
   (iii) the proximity of water catchment areas, particularly those for 'drinking, thermal and mineral water';

(d) the maximum permissible quantity 'during one or more specified periods of time' of matter containing, or comprising, List I or List II substances to be disposed of or tipped. This must include 'appropriate requirements' for concentration limits for such substance;

(e) the technical precautions required to ensure that any discharges of List I substances are prevented and which ensure that groundwater pollution by List II substances does not occur; and

(f) the measures for monitoring groundwater, including its quality, 'if necessary'.

1 See para 8.91ff.

8.249 The requirements are slightly different for waste management licences which may involve the need to prevent direct discharges. Should the requirements discussed at para 8.74 above in respect of direct discharges be satisfied, the licence must contain conditions which specify[1]:

(a) the place where the List I or List II substances are discharged into groundwater;

(b) 'the method of discharge which may be used';

(c) the essential precautions to be taken, with particular attention paid to:

  (i) the nature and concentration of the substances 'present in the effluents';

  (ii) the characteristics of the receiving environment; and

  (iii) the proximity of water catchment areas, particular those used for 'drinking, thermal or mineral water';

(d) the maximum quantity of List I and List II substances permissible in an effluent during specified time periods, along with the appropriate requirements as to the concentration of those substances;

(e) the arrangements enabling effluents discharged into groundwater to be monitored;

(f) 'if necessary' the measures for monitoring groundwater, especially its quality.

In a similar manner to the provisions on indirect discharges of List I and List II substances, the wording, which stems from reg 15(7), is a close, but not quite exact, copy of Article 9 of the Groundwater Directive.

1 SI 1994/1056, reg 15(7).

8.250 It may have become apparent that the word 'effluent' is used in reg 15(7). This is the term also used in Article 9 of the Directive. Where landfills are concerned, effluent should be taken as relating to material which is commonly known as leachate[1]. For other sites, such as liquid waste storage, the term will cover spillages and leaks. In all cases where direct discharges may be foreseeable, reg 15 requires the permissible level of 'effluent' to be made subject to maximum thresholds in the licence[2]. However, in practice such limits are difficult to attain, for the reason that thresholds are not easy to determine. And, as far as landfills are concerned, should the limit be exceeded there is little that a licence holder can do about it at the point of discharge. For example, a significant leak in a containment system of a landfill, which is submerged under thousands of tonnes of waste, is difficult – if not impossible – to patch. All that can be done is to minimise the consequences of the leak. It is likely that such action may not, in itself, return the level of discharge to below the threshold stipulated by the relevant licence condition. In addition, there are obvious practical difficulties in monitoring the discharge at the point at which it occurs, particularly directly beneath the site.

1 Leachate is the result of rainfall and biodegradation products which are contained within or pass out of the deposited waste mass.

2 SI 1994/1056, reg 15(7).

8.251 However, the imposition of permissible discharge levels may be necessary to satisfy reg 15[1] and the Groundwater Directive[2]. In addition, para 8.253 below discusses the fact that, whilst groundwater pollution may be an offence under s 85 of the Water

Resources Act 1991, s 88 of that Act provides for the defence that the discharge was made under and in accordance with any waste management licence. Hence, despite the obvious practical difficulties in setting limits, such requirements would seem to need to be included as a licence condition. Otherwise, it would appear that neither reg 15 nor the Directive will be complied with.

1   SI 1995/1056, reg 15(7).
2   Directive 80/68, Article 9.

8.252   Where any waste management licence is granted which authorises the indirect or direct discharge of List I and List II substances, reg 15 requires that any authorisation must only be granted for 'a limited period only'[1]. Precisely how this should be articulated as a licence condition is not clear. As somewhat of a contradiction, Circular 11/94 states that '[t]he obligations imposed by the waste management licence, however, should not be subject to a time limit, they would only come to an end if the surrender of the licence were accepted, or if it were revoked . . .'[2]. The latter sentiment does, of course, follow the EPA 1990's concept that licences remain in force until any environmental liabilities have ceased[3]. However, reg 15's clear statement that a time limit needs to be set would appear to warrant some form of response.

1   SI 1994/1056, reg 15(8).
2   Circular 11/94, Annex 7, para 7.18.
3   See, for example, the provisions on licence surrender (EPA 1990, s 39): see para 9.93ff.

8.253   *Conditions reflecting the Water Resources Act 1991*   Unless subject to a formal consent from the Agency, the discharge of substances into surface or groundwater is an offence under s 85 of the Water Resources Act 1991. However, this is subject to certain statutory defences set out in s 88(1) of that Act, one of which concerns the defence that the discharge was made 'under and in accordance with' a waste management licence.

8.254   It seems possible to envisage circumstances whereby a waste management site operator has caused significant pollution of groundwater or surface water, but has complied fully with the licence. If nothing else, the site might thus be immune from prosecution under the Water Resources Act 1991. This could be the case if the conditions of the licence do not explicitly forbid the particular occurrence that caused the pollution[1]. Furthermore, guidance from the Department of the Environment has tended to discourage licence conditions which address environmental matters that are subject to other parallel legislation[2].

1   At first sight, this might sound a somewhat strange assertion. However, many licences are composed of conditions which require works to be undertaken which, if undertaken correctly, should prevent pollution. Hence non-compliance with the licence occurs when the works are not done, not when the pollution arises.
2   See WMP 4, para 1.27ff, for example, and also *A-G's Reference (No 2 of 1988)* (1989) 89 Cr App Rep 314: discussed at para 8.256.

8.255   Somewhat oddly, the interrelationship between the EPA 1990 and the Water Resources Act 1991 does not seem to be considered in any of the guidance. However, it may be that licence conditions should be drafted which explicitly outlaw undesirable surface and groundwater discharges. If nothing else, the absence of such provisions might cause the Agency's credibility to be brought into disrepute. Furthermore, such conditions would seem essential in order to correctly ensure the enforcement of transposed Community law, particularly the Directive on Waste[1] and the Groundwater Directive[2].

1   Council Directive of 15 July 1975 on Waste (75/442/EEC) (OJ L194/39 25.7.75) (subsequently
    amended by Council Directive of 18 March 1991 amending Directive 75/442/EEC on Waste
    (91/156/EEC) (OJ L78/32 26.3.91)).
2   Council Directive 80/68 of 17 December 1979 on the Protection of Groundwater against Pollution
    Caused by Certain Dangerous Substances (OJ L20/43 26.1.80).

Licence conditions and nuisance

8.256   Prior to the implementation of the EPA 1990, the scope of waste disposal
licence conditions which made reference to the prevention of nuisance was restricted
by the case of *A-G's Reference (No 2 of 1988)*[1]. However, it may be that this judgment
no longer applies, albeit that this matter has yet to be considered in court.

1   [1989] 89 Cr App Rep 314.

8.257   In the *A-G's Reference*, the vires of waste disposal licensing under the Control
of Pollution Act 1974 was reviewed with a view to deciding if a rather open-ended
condition on nuisance was allowable. Parker LJ noted that s 9(1) of the Control of
Pollution Act 1974 set down the duties of the then Waste Disposal Authority[1]. A duty
was to take the steps needed to ensure that the activities overseen by the licence did not
cause pollution of water, danger to public health or become seriously detrimental to
the amenity of the locality. In relation to the latter elements, Parker LJ noted[2]:

> 'Can it [the regulatory authority] go further? Can it prohibit the creation of a
> nuisance of whatever kind, whether public or private, notwithstanding that many
> such nuisances would not pollute water, create a danger to public health or cause
> serious detriment to the amenities of the locality? We have no doubt that it could not
> impose a condition preventing a private nuisance and thus convert a purely civil
> wrong into an indictable offence. A prohibition against public nuisances is however
> very different, because a public nuisance is already an indictable misdemeanour and
> there appears to be no obvious objection to the waste disposal authority imposing a
> condition against the commission of crimes.'

1   Not to be confused with the term 'Waste Disposal Authority' as used in the EPA 1990.
2   (1989) 89 Cr App Rep 314 at 322.

8.258   Parker LJ then reviewed the other provisions which are aimed at addressing
public nuisances[1], coming to the conclusion that[2]:

> '. . . we cannot accept that the power to impose conditions, wide though it is in its
> terms, is wide enough to allow a condition prohibiting public nuisances of any and
> all kinds whether or not they pollute water, endanger public health or constitute a
> serious detriment to the amenities of the locality in which the licensed activities
> are carried on. This does not mean that the licence holder is free to commit what-
> ever nuisance he likes. If he does commit such nuisances he may be proceeded
> against at common law or by the particular authority charged with dealing with the
> particular type of procedure [ie Public Health Act 1936, Alkali, etc Works Regu-
> lation Act 1906, etc]. In addition, if nuisance falls within section 7(4) of the [1974]
> Act and cannot be remedied by condition, then the licence can be revoked. Fur-
> thermore, it does not mean that a waste disposal authority cannot impose condi-
> tions necessary in order to prevent the three evils [water pollution, danger to
> public health, serious detriment to the amenity of the locality] which fall within its
> sphere.'

1   Then Part III of the Control of Pollution Act 1974, s 92 of the Public Health Act 1936 and s 1 of the
    Alkali, etc, Works Regulation Act 1906.
2   At 323.

8.259 With the replacement of the Control of Pollution Act by the EPA 1990, the 'three evils' – to use Parker LJ's phrase – have become embellished. Besides the question of whether a proposed licence holder is a fit and proper person, the grounds for refusing an application for a waste management licence concern the need to prevent pollution of the environment, harm to human health and, where applicable[1], serious detriment to the amenities of the locality[2]. These requirements have been covered earlier in this chapter and are somewhat broader than their equivalent in the Control of Pollution Act 1974. In particular, 'pollution of the environment' is defined[3] as meaning pollution due to the escape of substances which are capable of causing harm. The word 'harm' is defined in respect of man and includes giving 'offence to any of his senses or harm to his property'[4]. Clearly odour gives offence to a person's senses and hence is encompassed by s 29(5) of the EPA 1990.

1 See para 8.49.
2 EPA 1990, s 36(3).
3 EPA 1990, s 29(3).
4 EPA 1990, s 29(5).

8.260 In addition, the 'relevant objectives' set out in the Waste Management Licensing Regulations 1994 refer explicitly to nuisance caused by noise or odours[1]. Schedule 4, Part I, para 2(1) places a duty on all specified regulatory bodies to discharge their 'specified functions' in accordance with the objectives. For the Agency, a specified function is that contained within Part II of the EPA 1990[2].

1 SI 1994/1056, Sch 4, Pt I, para 4(1)(a)(ii).
2 SI 1994/1056, Sch 4, Pt I, para 3(1), Table 5.

8.261 Accordingly, it seems that these provisions are now so much wider than that envisaged by the *A-G's Reference* that the latter case no longer appears to have relevance. Indeed, it should also be noted that the relevant objectives contained in Schedule 4, paragraph 4(1) do not make a distinction between public or private nuisances. They refer solely to the word 'nuisance'. However, perhaps with the *A-G's Reference* in mind, the authors of Waste Management Paper 4 still maintain that '[c]onditions in licences relating in a general way to nuisance should be avoided'[1]. This would seem to be a little hard to justify given the Agency's 'relevant objectives'. A second reason behind this statement in the Waste Management Paper may be that matters such as odour should instead be dealt with by Part III of the EPA 1990 and the provisions therein on statutory nuisances. However, Part III is enforced by the local authorities. Such authorities are not granted any explicit role in the Waste Management Licensing Regulations 1994 in implementing the relevant objectives. This includes the objective of preventing nuisance through noise or odour[2].

1 WMP 4, para 1.31.
2 See SI 1994/1056, Pt I, Table 5.

Conditions relating to waste oil storage and recovery

8.262 The Waste Management Licensing Regulations 1994 contain provisions which are specific to the content of any waste management licence which authorises the regeneration of waste oil[1]. It would appear that they seek to transpose a limited number of elements of the Waste Oils Directive[2]. Licences for oil recovery plants must include conditions which ensure[3] that 'base oils derived from regeneration' do not constitute a 'toxic and dangerous waste'. In addition, conditions must ensure that all regenerated oils do not contain PCBs or PCTs 'at all or do not contain them in concentrations beyond a specified maximum limit which in no case is to exceed 50 parts per million'.

1   SI 1994/1056, reg 14: waste oil is held to mean '... any mineral-based lubricating or industrial oil which has become unfit for the use for which it was originally intended and, in particular, used combustion engine oil, gearbox oil, mineral lubricating oil, oil for turbines and hydraulic oil' (SI 1994/1056, reg 1(3): a verbatim transposition of the definition set out in Article 1 of the Waste Oils Directive (Council Directive of the 16 June 1975 on the Disposal of Waste Oils (OJ L194/23 25.7.95), as amended by Council Directive of 22 December 1986 amended Directive 75/439/EEC on the Disposal of Waste Oils (OJ L42/43 12.2.87), Article 1.
2   Council Directive of the 16 June 1975 on the Disposal of Waste Oils (OJ L194/23 25.7.95), as amended by Council Directive of 22 December 1986 amended Directive 75/439/EEC on the Disposal of Waste Oils (OJ L42/4312.2.87), Article 10(3).
3   SI 1994/1056, reg 14(1).

8.263   In the case where a waste management licence authorises the keeping[1] of waste oil, conditions must ensure that this oil is not mixed with 'toxic and dangerous waste' or PCBs or PCTs[2]. This requirement transposes Article 10(1) of the Waste Oils Directive.

1   In other words, storage, see para 7.26ff.
2   SI 1994/1056, reg 14(2).

8.264   The reference in reg 14 of the Waste Management Licensing Regulations 1994 to 'toxic and dangerous waste', which is confirmed as being defined as having the meaning contained in Directive 78/319[1], is a little odd. That Directive[2] has been repealed. At the time the 1994 Regulations were enacted, the definition was scheduled for repeal on 12 December 1993. In June 1994 this deadline was extended, with the definition being eventually repealed on 27 June 1995[3]. However, the Regulations have not been amended to take on board the demise of the Directive[4].

1   SI 1994/1056, reg 14(3).
2   Council Directive of 20 March 1978 on Toxic and Dangerous Waste (78/319/EEC), 1978, (OJ L84/43).
3   Council Directive of 12 December 1991 on Hazardous Waste (OJ L377/20 31.12.91), Article 11 (as amended by Directive 94/31/EC (OJ L168/28 2.7.94)), Article 1.
4   Equally, neither has the Waste Oils Directive been amended and it still refers to Directive 78/319.

Chapter 9

The subsistence of waste management licences

INTRODUCTION

9.01   The previous chapter considered the powers of the EPA 1990 in respect of licence applications and the form and content of waste management licences. The compliance by a licensee to the criteria under which a licence was granted must be kept under review by the Agency after the licence has been issued. For example, the Agency has a duty to ensure that a licensed waste management facility does not cause pollution of the environment, harm to human health or serious detriment to the amenity of the locality[1]. It has the duty to ensure that the conditions of the licence are complied with[2]. The site's environmental performance must continue to conform with the relevant objectives of the Directive on Waste[3] and the provisions pertaining to groundwater protection[4].

1   EPA 1990, s 42(1)(a): see para 9.63.
2   EPA 1990, s 42(1)(b): see para 9.63.
3   SI 1994/1056, Sch 4, Pt 1, paras 2, 3 and 4: see para 9.88ff.
4   SI 1994/1056, reg 15: see para 9.65.

9.02   While the main criminal provisions relating to the breach of waste management licences have been covered in Chapter 7, this chapter reviews the other mechanisms available to ensure that environmentally acceptable and appropriate activities continue at licensed sites. The chapter therefore describes the powers bestowed on the Agency in relation to the modification, revocation and suspension of waste management licences, and those elements of the legislation which bequeath specific duties on the Agency in respect of licences. The latter includes the need to ensure continued compliance with the relevant objectives and the Groundwater Directive[1], along with discussion of the ability of the Agency to monitor whether licensees continue to be 'fit and proper persons'. The procedures required to transfer or surrender a waste management licence are then reviewed. Appeals against the exercise of such powers, all of which are determined by the Secretary of State, are considered. The chapter ends with a discussion of the regime of charges to which all waste management licences are subject.

1   SI 1994/1056, reg 15.

LICENCE MODIFICATION

9.03   Once granted, a waste management licence will be subject to a series of modifications over the life of the site. Such changes can be either at the Agency's or licence holder's behest and reflect the ever-changing nature of the environmental regulation of waste management facilities. Waste Management Paper 4[1] requires the Agency to 'regularly review licences to ensure that the conditions remain appropriate and effective'. A licence modification may be a function, for example, of the Agency's desire to enhance its regulatory grip on a particular site. A proposal for a modification may also reflect a licence holder's wish to make changes to a facility's mode of operation. In the case of very large, complex, waste management facilities, changes to the licence may occur regularly throughout a facility's existence. At some point in the facility's life, the Agency may wish to modify the licence extensively by replacing all the conditions with new ones. This will particularly be the case for those older waste management facilities whose licences transferred from the regime under the Control of Pollution Act 1974[2]. The necessity to modify licences to fully embrace the relevant objectives of the Directive on Waste[3] and the provisions on groundwater protection[4] is also a consideration.

1   Department of the Environment (1994) *Licensing of Waste Management Facilities*, Waste Management Paper No 4, 3rd edn, HMSO, London, para 2.35.
2   For example, Circular 11/94 (Annex 4, para 4.39) states that all licences should have taken on board the new provisions contained in the Waste Management Licensing Regulations 1994 by 31 April 1995; similarly, unless pollution is being caused, scrapyards and vehicle dismantlers have until 1 January 1999 to address the requirement of the Waste Management Paper 4A (see WMP 4A, para 1.43).
3   See SI 1994/1056, Sch 4, Pt 1, paras 2, 3, and 4 and see para 9.88ff.
4   SI 1994/1056, reg 15: see para 9.65ff.

9.04   In parallel to alterations in the conditions of the waste management licence, it is envisaged that a facility's working plan will change regularly[1]. Unless these changes impinge upon the wording of specific conditions, such changes should be permitted without the need to modify the licence[2].

1   WMP 4, para 2.16.
2   WMP 4, para 2.28.

9.05   A waste management licence can be modified under two sub-sections of s 37 of the EPA 1990. Firstly, it can be modified by the Agency as long as the modification does not require unreasonable expense on the part of the holder[1]. The Agency has discretion in this matter[2]. In the second case, the Agency has a statutory duty to modify the licence[3]. The circumstances when this duty arises are 'for the purpose of ensuring that the activities authorised by the licence do not cause pollution of the environment or harm to human health or become seriously detrimental to the amenities of the locality affected by the activities'[4]. While there is a duty on the Agency to make the modification, the nature of the modification itself is left 'to the extent which in the opinion of the authority is required'[5]. The provision in s 37(1) relating to not causing unreasonable expense on the licence holder does not apply in this instance. However, modification under this power must be founded on at least one of the three stipulated criteria: environmental pollution, harm to human health or amenity detriment[6].

1   EPA 1990, s 37(1)(a).
2   See the word 'may' in s 37(1): however, conditions *solely* aimed at securing health and safety at work objectives are not allowed (SI 1994/1056, reg 13).
3   EPA 1990, s 37(2).
4   EPA 1990, s 37(2)(a).
5   EPA 1990, s 37(2)(a).
6   A similar wording to s 37(1) and (2) of the EPA 1990 was contained in s 7(1)(a) and (b) of the Control of Pollution Act 1974. The significance of the contrasting construction of the latter sub-sections is considered in *A-G's Reference (No 2 of 1988)* (1989) 89 Cr App Rep 314 at 321.

9.06   The EPA 1990 also allows a licence to be modified by way of an application from the holder[1]. The application must be accompanied by the prescribed fee set down in the Waste Management Licensing (Charges) Scheme for the current financial year[2]. The determination period of such an application is set at two months[3], commencing on the date of receipt of the application by the Agency. The Agency is allowed to seek the agreement of the applicant for an extension of this period if necessary. Unless this agreement has been confirmed in writing between the applicant and the Agency, the Agency is deemed to have rejected the application if no decision has been forthcoming by the end of this period.

1 EPA 1990, s 37(1)(b) as amended by the Environment Act 1995, Sch 22, para 70(1).
2 EPA 1990, s 37(1)(b) as amended by the Environment Act 1995, Sch 22, para 70(1): charges are
   discussed at para 9.142 below.
3 EPA 1990, s 37(6).

9.07 Like licence applications, proposals for modifications are evaluated by statutory consultees[1]. However, should the Agency be minded to refuse an application for a licence modification, there appears no duty to contact the consultees. If the Agency considers that a modification is needed 'by reason of an emergency' it can postpone the consultation process[2]. The duration of the postponement is left unspecified.

1 EPA 1990, s 37(5) as amended by the Environment Act 1995, Sch 22, para 70(2).
2 EPA 1990, s 37(5)(a).

9.08 The consultation process itself is similar to that set down for a waste management licence application[1]. Accordingly, the 'appropriate planning authority'[2] and the Health and Safety Executive must be consulted, and their representations need to be 'considered'. Where their interest is affected[3], the 'appropriate nature conservation body'[4] needs to be contacted[5]. Since the EPA 1990 was amended, the consultees now have 28 days from the date of receipt of the modification in which to reply[6]. This can be extended by agreement.

1 EPA 1990, s 37(5) as amended by the Environment Act 1995, Sch 22, para 70(2).
2 Defined in the EPA 1990, s 36(11) (as amended by the Environment Act 1995, Sch 22, para 68(6)):
   see para 8.17.
3 Under the Wildlife and Countryside Act 1981, s 28(1).
4 See para 8.19.
5 EPA 1990, s 37(5) (as amended by the Environment Act 1995, Sch 22, para 70(2)) and s 36(7).
6 EPA 1990, s 37(5) (as amended by the Environment Act 1995, Sch 22, para 70(2)) in conjunction
   with s 36(10) (as amended by the Environment Act 1995, Sch 22, para 68(6)).

9.09 Besides the statutory consultees, neighbouring landowners, lessees and occupiers need to be consulted where a licence modification will result in a requirement on the licensee to access their land[1]. Under s 35(4) of the EPA 1990, neighbours are required to acquiesce to such a requirement[2], with compensation being payable by way of the EPA 1990, s 35A[3] and the Waste Management Licences (Consultation and Compensation) Regulations 1999[4]. The EPA 1990 restricts the need for consultation to conditions which on modification establish a new right of access[5]. The consultation period in respect of a licence modification in these circumstances is six weeks[6], but this can be postponed when an emergency warrants immediate action[7]. The procedures by which third parties are notified[8] are broadly similar to those relating to licence conditions resultant from licence applications. Hence they have been described in para 8.23ff, alongside the method by which compensation is determined.

1 EPA 1990, s 37A, as amended by the Environment Act 1995, s 120, Sch 22, para 71 (commenced by
   SI 1999/803).
2 See para 8.244.
3 EPA 1990, s 35A, as amended by the Environment Act 1995, s 120, Sch 22, para 67.
4 SI 1999/481.
5 EPA 1990, s 37A(1)(b) and s 37A(2).
6 SI 1999/481, reg 3(b).
7 EPA 1990, s 37A(9).
8 EPA 1990, s 37A(3)–(9).

9.10 By contrast to the procedures set down in s 36 in relation to licence applications, the Agency is left with discretion to decide whether to 'consider any representations as respects a modification which, in the opinion of the waste regulation authority, will not effect any authority' which is a consultee[1]. This seems to imply that, for example, any response by a local planning authority can be ignored if the Agency feels that the response is not relevant to development control matters and/or is otherwise unnecessary.

1   EPA 1990, s 37(5)(b).

9.11   Note that there do not appear to be any specified grounds in the EPA 1990 for rejecting an application for a licence modification. The requirements for consultation are set down in s 37(5), which require that the procedures relating to the granting of a licence are utilised in the modification process[1]. However, even since this sub-section was amended by the Environment Act 1995, there is no cross referral to s 36(3), which lays down grounds for rejection of a licence application[2]. In the absence of any criteria being set down in the statute, it is submitted that the grounds for rejection must be the same as those available in relation to the granting of a waste management licence. As is described in Chapter 8, these relate to pollution of the environment, harm to human health, amenity detriment and associated elements. It seems also possible that a modification can relate to the criteria set down in s 74, of whether the licence holder[3] is a fit and proper person[4].

1   EPA 1990, s 36(4), (7), and (10) as amended by the Environment Act 1995, Sch 22, para 70(2).
2   There also were no explicit grounds for rejecting waste disposal licence modification under the Control of Pollution Act 1974 either: see 1974 Act, s 7.
3   Or, indeed, 'another relevant person': see the EPA 1990, s 74(7).
4   See the EPA 1990, s 36(3): this is discussed later at para 9.70ff.

9.12   Once the consultation process has been satisfactorily concluded, a licence modification is enacted by serving a notice on the holder of the waste management licence. Such a notice must state the time at which the modification has effect[1]. The notice can be served on the licence holder by way of the procedures set down in s 160 of the EPA 1990 and be served by post[2].

1   EPA 1990, s 37(4).
2   See para 12.185ff.

9.13   The Secretary of State has the power, under s 37(3) of the EPA 1990, to direct the Agency to modify the conditions of a waste management licence. This power has not been used up to now and Circular 11/94[1] states that it will be invoked only in exceptional circumstances[2]. However, it is worth noting that the Agency may be unable to change any such condition imposed by the Secretary of State. Given the duty on the Agency to give effect to such a direction, it appears that only the Minister can alter any effected conditions later. There is, however, no ready mechanism available by which an application can be made to the Secretary of State for such a change[3].

1   Circular 11/94, Annex 4, para 4.40.
2   It should not be confused with the requirement under s 43(3) of the EPA 1990 that the Agency should give effect to any decision made by the Secretary of State to modify a licence after appeal.
3   This would seem to contrast to s 122 of the Environment Act 1995, which allows the Secretary of State to make directions with respect of Community provisions. In this instance, provision is contained in that section for such a direction to be varied.

9.14   If the application to modify the conditions of a waste management licence is rejected, or if the licence holder is unhappy about a modification imposed by the Agency, an appeal to the Secretary of State can be made[1]. The Agency's modification is usually held in abeyance while the appeal is being determined[2].

1   EPA 1990, s 43(1)(a) and (c).
2   See para 9.126ff.

9.15 The EPA 1990 contains provisions which allow the Agency to make a modification instantaneous and regardless of whether an appeal is lodged. But such an action must be justified on specified grounds, namely where:

'. . . in the opinion of the [regulation] authority it is necessary for the purpose of preventing or, where this is not practicable, minimising pollution of the environment or harm to human health . . .'[1].

However, if the Secretary of State or other person adjudicating the appeal finds that the Agency acted unreasonably, the holder of the licence is entitled to recover compensation[2]. Any dispute over whether compensation is payable – or the amount of such compensation – has to be settled by an independent arbitrator[3].

1 EPA 1990, s 43(6) – note that it is not possible to modify with immediate effect a licence due to a site being a serious detriment to amenities.
2 EPA 1990, s 43(7): see para 9.139 below.
3 EPA 1990, s 43(7).

9.16 A similar arrangement existed under the Control of Pollution Act 1974[1]. It was quite clear that regulatory bodies were very reluctant to use this immediate modification provision, as they were concerned about the possibility of having to pay compensation. This appeared to stem partly from a lack of trust in the Department of the Environment following from a small number of what were perceived as bizarre or unhelpful appeal decisions. Given that, at that time, appeals were taking up to two to three years to determine, the amount of potential compensation payable might be considerable.

1 Control of Pollution Act 1974, s 10(3).

LICENCE REVOCATION

9.17 There are a number of grounds for revoking waste management licences:

– where the licence holder is no longer a fit and proper person due to:

   (a) that person's conviction of one or more relevant offences[1]; or
   (b) the facility being no longer managed by a technically competent person[2];

– when the activities authorised by the waste management licence are likely to cause pollution of the environment, harm to human health or be serious detrimental to the amenities of the locality[3];
– when the licence conditions have not been complied with or are unlikely to be complied with[4];
– due to a licensee's non-payment of subsistence fees[5].

1 EPA 1990, s 38(1)(a).
2 EPA 1990, s 38(2).
3 EPA 1990, s 38(1)(b).
4 EPA 1990, s 42(5) as amended by the Environment Act 1995, Sch 22, para 76(4).
5 Environment Act 1995, s 41(5) and SI 1996/508.

9.18 A waste management licence can be revoked entirely. Alternatively, the licence can be partially revoked by placing restrictions on specified waste management activities authorised by the licence. Partial revocation is defined in the EPA 1990 as the revocation of the licence 'so far as it authorises the carrying on of the activities specified in the licence or such of them as the authority specifies in revoking the licence'[1]. The 'activities specified in the licence' are those referred to in s 35(1) of the

EPA 1990, which defines a waste management licence as one which the Agency grants 'authorising the treatment, keeping or disposal' of waste in or on land. This would appear confirmed by the manner in which the Waste Management Licensing (Charges) Scheme 1999/2000 is structured[2]. Partial revocation therefore allows non-operational matters pertaining to the licence to continue to be enforced. An example might be landfill gas monitoring.

1   EPA 1990, s 38(3) and s 42(6)(a): s 41(6) of the Environment Act 1995 uses a similar wording 'to the extent that it authorises the carrying on of an authorised activity'.
2   See the table headings in the Waste Management Licensing (Charges) Scheme 1999–2000, Annex 1, Tables 1–3.

9.19   If a licence is partially revoked under the EPA 1990, 'it shall cease to have effect to authorise the carrying on of the activities specified in the licence or, as the case may be, the activities specified by the authority in revoking the licence ...'[1]. However, the EPA 1990 makes it clear[2] that partial revocation shall not affect any requirements imposed by the licence which the Agency specifies as continuing to bind the holder. This allows the Agency some discretion to indicate which operations should continue on the site, quite apart from the relevant licence's permitted activities or conditions. Revocation is enacted using a statutory notice. With respect to the drafting of such notices, Circular 11/94 warns that the Agency[3]:

'. . . should take care that the notice specifies clearly what activities are affected by the notice and what requirements and obligations remain in place'.

For example, whilst a partial revocation may ban the deposit of specified wastes at a landfill site, the Agency seems able to indicate on the notice that other wastes such as clays can continue to be imported into the site to finish off the capping of a filled cell. However, in the case of the partial revocation of a licence due to non-payment of subsistence charges, the Environment Act 1995 does not permit the Agency to be selective as to which activities are or are not revoked[4].

1   EPA 1990, s 38(5), which in the case of s 42 is referred to in s 42(7) (as amended by the Environment Act 1995, Sch 22, para 76(8)).
2   EPA 1990, s 38(5).
3   Circular 11/94, Annex 4, para 4.47.
4   See Environment Act 1995, s 41(6).

9.20   In cases where the facility is not being managed by a technically competent individual, or where annual subsistence charges have not been paid, the Agency is only allowed to partially revoke the licence[1]. In other cases it has discretion. However, a full revocation of a waste management licence will be inappropriate in many circumstances. It will absolve the licensee of any remaining requirements of the licence. An example might be long-term environmental protection measures, such as the monitoring for gas and leachate at a landfill site. It would also exempt the licence holder from the need to attain a certificate of completion under the EPA 1990's provisions on licence surrender[2]. Hence a partial revocation will be the more usual outcome.

1   EPA 1990, s 38(2) and (3); the Environment Act 1995, s 41(6).
2   EPA 1990, s 39: discussed at para 9.93 below.

9.21   Finally, s 38(7) and s 42(8) of the EPA 1990 provide the Secretary of State with powers to direct that a licence is fully or partially revoked. The Agency has the duty to give effect to such a direction.

Revocation due to convictions for relevant offences

9.22   Full or partial licence revocation can be contemplated if the holder has accrued significant convictions for relevant offences. The nature of such offences is set down in reg 3 of the Waste Management Licensing Regulations 1994[1], being supplemented in respect of convictions in relation to landfill tax avoidance in 1997[2]. These are described in Chapter 8[3]. However, the wording of s 38 is such that it is only 'the *holder* of the licence' who ceases to be fit and proper 'by reason of *his* having been convicted' of a relevant offence[4]. The emphasis is intended to highlight a contrast to s 74 of the EPA 1990: it would seem that revocation under s 38 is focused solely on the holder's conviction and not on those of the holder's staff. Whilst the latter's convictions may prevent a waste management licence being issued[5], the subsequent conviction of the licence holder's managers, directors, etc after the licence is issued would not seem to be a grounds for the licence being revoked under s 38(1) of the EPA 1990.

1   SI 1994/1056, reg 3 as amended by SI 1994/1137, reg 19(3) and SI 1996/972, reg 25 and Sch 3.
2   By SI 1997/351.
3   See para 8.117ff.
4   EPA 1990, s 38(1)(a) – author's emphasis.
5   Such individuals may be regarded as 'another relevant person' in s 74(7): see para 8.122.

9.23   Waste Management Paper 4[1] suggests that a full or partial revocation is to be instigated as soon as a licence holder has been convicted of a significant number of relevant offences[2]. There is no need to await for the outcome of any appeal against the conviction. This is justified on the basis that the licence holder can also appeal to the Secretary of State against the licence revocation and that the Secretary will consider the outcome of the appeal against criminal conviction when the appeal against licence revocation is being heard. Section 43(4) of the EPA 1990 requires that the revocation is lifted once the appeal to the Secretary of State has been lodged and prior to it being determined[3].

1   WMP 4, para 3.24.
2   See para 8.117.
3   While s 43(6) allows immediate revocation on grounds such as pollution of the environment, it would be an exceptional case where a licensee who recently acquired significant relevant offences could be subject to immediate licence revocation under this power.

Revocation due to failure to employ technically competent management

9.24   Section 38 of the EPA 1990 allows a waste management licence to be partially revoked[1] if the 'management' is no longer in the hands of a technically competent person[2]. The nature of 'a technically competent person' is discussed at para 8.130ff. An example might be where a number of holders of certificates of technical competence resigned from the employ of the licence holder. Alternatively, it may be the case that a licensee has persons who are defined as technically competent spread so 'thinly' between waste management facilities that they are incapable of properly exercising their management function.

1   EPA 1990, s 38(2) and (3) does not permit a full revocation.
2   EPA 1990, s 38(2).

Revocation due to threat of pollution

9.25   A licence can be revoked where the continuation of the activities authorised by the licence would cause[1] pollution of the environment or harm to human health[2] or would be seriously detrimental to the amenities of the locality[3]. However, the wording of the EPA 1990 suggests that such an action is very much a last resort. Such a revocation can only be enacted if the pollution, harm or detriment cannot be avoided by modifying the conditions of the licence[4].

1   EPA 1990, s 38(1)(b). See para 7.62ff.
2   See para 8.40ff.
3   See para 8.49.
4   EPA 1990, s 38(1)(c); a licence can also be suspended on these grounds: see para 9.40ff.

Revocation due to failure to comply with licence conditions

9.26   Should a licence holder either fail to comply with the conditions or seem likely to so fail, s 42 of the EPA 1990 allows the Agency to serve a notice requiring compliance[1]. If the Agency is not satisfied that the relevant conditions have been complied with by the time stipulated, the licence can be revoked partially[2] or totally[3].

1   EPA 1990, s 42(5)(a) as amended by the Environment Act 1995, Sch 22, para 76(4) and (5).
2   EPA 1990, s 42(6)(a).
3   EPA 1990, s 42(6)(b). The licence can also be suspended in these circumstances: this is discussed at para 9.48 below.

9.27   A facility subject to its licence being partially or fully revoked for non-compliance with the conditions of the licence may also be causing an offence in respect of s 33(6) of the EPA 1990[1]. But it is of note that a licence revocation is 'without prejudice to any proceedings under section 33(6)'[2]. Accordingly, it would be possible to take legal action under s 33 and to enact a full or (more usually) partial revocation under s 42. Given the delays inherent in legal proceedings, this appears entirely appropriate. There may be a need to address a problem on a site quickly and to subsequently commence proceedings in respect of the licence holder's failures. Alternatively, it may be appropriate to revoke a licence and not to pursue legal proceedings.

1   See Chapter 7.
2   EPA 1990, s 42(5).

Revocation due to non-payment of subsistence charges

9.28   Finally, partial revocation can occur if the holder has not paid the appropriate subsistence charge[1]. The licence is to be revoked in this case under the Environment Act 1995, with revocation being to the extent that the licence authorises the carrying on of an authorised activity. As noted earlier, there is no mechanism for the Agency to select particular activities to be revoked[2]. In addition, unlike licence revocation under s 38 and s 42 of the EPA 1990, the licence holder is not entitled to appeal.

1   Environment Act 1995, s 41(6): the licence can also be suspended on these grounds.
2   Compare s 41(6) of the Environment Act 1995 to s 38(3) of the EPA 1990.

The licence revocation process

9.29   The licence revocation process is effected by way of a notice served on the licence holder[1]. The notice can be served on the licence holder in person or by post[2].

1   EPA 1990, s 38(12) and s 42(5)(a) as amended by the Environment Act 1995, Sch 22, para 76(5); SI 1996/508, reg 3(a).
2   For s 38 and s 42, service is by the provisions of s 160 of the EPA 1990; for s 41 of the Environment Act 1995, by s 123 and by SI 1995/508: see para 12.185ff.

9.30   The provisions on the content of the notices differs between the sub-sections of the EPA 1990. All that is explicitly required, by the statute, to be in a s 38 notice is the the time at which the revocation is to take effect[1]. For licences to be revoked under s 42 for non-compliance with licence conditions, the notice served on the licence holder[2] must state that the Agency is of the opinion that non-compliance is taking place or is likely to take place[3]. It must also specify the matters which make up the actual or expected non-compliance[4] and the steps necessary to make an appropriate remedy[5]. Finally, the period under which those steps are to be taken must be stipulated[6], along with the time at which the revocation is to occur[7]. Where notices under s 38 or s 42 are for the purpose of preventing pollution or harm to human health and are to have immediate application[8], a statement to that effect must be included in the notice[9].

1 EPA 1990, s 38(12).
2 EPA 1990, s 42(5)(a) as amended by the Environment Act 1995, Sch 22, para 76(5).
3 EPA 1990, s 42(5)(a)(i) as amended by the Environment Act 1995, Sch 22, para 76(5).
4 EPA 1990, s 42(5)(a)(ii) as amended by the Environment Act 1995, Sch 22, para 76(5).
5 EPA 1990, s 42(5)(a)(iii) as amended by the Environment Act 1995, Sch 22, para 76(5).
6 EPA 1990, s 42(5)(a)(iv) as amended by the Environment Act 1995, Sch 22, para 76(5).
7 EPA 1990, s 42(7) (as amended by the Environment Act 1995, Sch 22, para 76(8)) and s 38(12).
8 Ie not being lifted on appeal to the Secretary of State.
9 EPA 1990, s 43(6).

9.31 However, once the compliance deadline contained in that notice has passed, there is no requirement in the statute to inform the licence holder that the revocation has taken place. In contrast to the provisions in the Environment Act 1995 on non-payment of charges[1], all that is necessary in the EPA 1990 is the initial notice concerning non-compliance with licence conditions.

1 See para 9.33.

9.32 In cases where the notice requires that works are to be done on land owned by third parties, such persons need to be consulted by way of a further notice from the Agency[1]. The neighbour must permit access[2] but must be compensated by the licensee[3]. The provisions on the service of notice[4] and compensation[5] are similar to those which apply when a licence is granted[6] or modified. The consultation period is set at three months[7], but the service of the notice and/or the consideration of representations from affected landowners can be postponed in the case of an emergency[8]. The fact that a three-month consultation period is prescribed[9], coupled with the concept of an 'emergency' being a quite specific entity[10], will probably mean that notices in these circumstances will be little used in practice, significantly weakening the utility of the provisions on notices where works need to be done outside the boundary of a licensed waste management facility.

1 EPA 1990, s 38(9A)–(9C), as amended by the Environment Act 1995, s 120, Sch 22, para 72(1).
2 EPA 1990, s 38(9A).
3 EPA 1990, s 35A(1)(a)(ii), as amended by the Environment Act 1995, s 120, Sch 22, para 67.
4 EPA 1990, s 38(9B) and the EPA 1990, s 36A.
5 EPA 1990, s 35A and SI 1999/481: note that the EPA 1990, s 35A refers only to licence suspension and revocation under s 38 (see also SI 1999/481, reg 3(a)), making no reference to notices served under s 42 of the EPA 1990.
6 See para 8.23ff.
7 SI 1999/481, reg 3(a).
8 EPA 1990, s 38(9C).
9 Indeed, there is an odd contrast to the six-week period set down in respect of licence modification: see SI 1999/481, reg 3(b).
10 See para 7.154.

9.33 For licence revocation for the non-payment of charges under the Environment Act 1995, the procedures for revocation are set down in a separate statutory instrument[1]. In contrast to the procedures in the EPA 1990 for revocation, the Environment Act 1995 sets out a two-stage process. The Agency may serve a written notice on the holder[2], giving 28 days from date of service in which to pay the overdue amount[3]. The notice must also state to the effect that revocation will occur unless the outstanding debt is settled[4], as well as indicating the 'effect of' licence revocation[5].

1   SI 1996/508.
2   SI 1996/508, reg 3(a): the notice must be served in accordance with s 123 of the Environment Act 1995.
3   SI 1996/508, reg 3(b).
4   SI 1996/508, reg 4(a).
5   SI 1996/508, reg 4(b).

9.34   Should the 28-day period pass without the Agency receiving payment, a separate revocation notice is then to be served[1]. The second notice must set out the reasons for the revocation and the time and date at which it will take effect[2].

1   SI 1996/508, reg 5(1): the notice must be served in accordance with s 123 of the Environment Act 1995.
2   SI 1996/508, reg 5(2)(a).

9.35   The licence holder can appeal against a licence revocation except when a licence is revoked for non-payment of charges[1]. The revocation may be held in abeyance awaiting the determination of the appeal[2]. Where the option of immediate revocation is selected by the Agency[3], compensation is payable if, at appeal, the Secretary of State finds that Agency made an unreasonable decision[4].

1   EPA 1990, s 43(1)(e).
2   EPA 1990, s 43(4).
3   EPA 1990, s 43(6).
4   EPA 1990, s 43(7).

9.36   The Agency is also allowed to submit a request to the High Court for an injunction where it is evident that licence revocation is an ineffectual remedy[1]. However, this power is only available in the case of revocations under s 42 for breach of licence conditions[2]. It neither applies in respect of non-payment of subsistence charges nor, oddly, in the case of the power to revoke a licence under s 38 of the EPA 1990[3].

1   EPA 1990, s 42(6A) (as amended by the Environment Act 1995, Sch 22, para 76(7)): injunctions are considered at para 12.85ff.
2   Such a power also is available in respect of licence suspension under the EPA 1990, s 38(13) (as amended by the Environment Act 1995, Sch 22, para 72(2)).
3   EPA 1990, s 38(13) (as amended by the Environment Act 1995, Sch 22, para 72(2)) only refers to licence suspension under s 38(9), (10) and (11), not to licence revocation under s 38(3) or (4).

The problem of reinstating partially revoked licences

9.37   There is some uncertainty as to how licences are to be reinstated after partial revocation. The relevant sub-section in the EPA 1990[1] states that a licence can be revoked 'so far as it authorises the carrying on of the *activities* specified in the licence'. The provisions of the Environment Act 1995 on unpaid subsistence charge recovery are similar, referring to 'authorised activities'. However, neither Act sets out explicitly a mechanism to reinstate the revoked activities when the particular compliance notice has been satisfied. This is in contrast to the provisions on licence suspension, which make it clear that suspension is envisaged to cease at a defined point[2]. In the absence of appropriate provisions, it might be attractive to surmise that the main way to reinstate a partially revoked licence is by a way of the licence modification[3]. However, the only items which can be modified under the EPA 1990 are the 'conditions'[4]. There is no reference made to modifying the activities specified by the licence[5].

1 EPA 1990, s 38(3), which also has application to revocation under s 42 by s 42(7) (as amended by the Environment Act 1995, Sch 22, para 76(8)).
2 See the EPA 1990, s 38(12) and see also in respect of the the Environment Act 1995, and s 41's suspension sanction for the non-payment of charges, SI 1996/508, reg 5(2)(b).
3 EPA 1990, s 37.
4 EPA 1990, s 37(1).
5 Activities are seen as quite distinct from licence conditions: see the EPA 1990, s 35(1). See also Waste Management Licensing (Charges) Scheme 1999–2000, Tables 1–3.

9.38 The alternative view that partial revocation is permanent is also unattractive. If partial revocation is to be considered as one-way, then a partially revoked licence can only be reinstated by a new licence application. Besides the cost of the application, the full requirements of waste management licensing will fall on the applicant. This will include a complete assessment of the applicant's fit and proper status[1], which is likely to create some considerable difficulties if the site was one that was licensed under the Control of Pollution Act 1974 and which transferred to the EPA 1990's regime by way of the transitional provisions contained in s 77[2]. A new application will also mean that the land will then have the benefit of two licences: the licence that was partially revoked and the new licence.

1 EPA 1990, s 74: see para 8.112ff.
2 See para 9.82 below.

9.39 Given the lack of a formal mechanism, a pragmatic solution has been to assume that the legislation contains an implicit right to reinstate an activity subject to partial revocation. It seems rather pointless to partially revoke a licence pending compliance with specified conditions but, once compliance has been achieved, subsequently to prevent the waste management activity continuing. If nothing else, this interpretation would appear to remove the main incentive on the licensee to comply. Hence partial revocation is to be viewed as holding until the matters set out in the notice have been addressed. Once addressed, the notice should be considered as no longer having effect.

LICENCE SUSPENSION

9.40 There are four grounds for suspending a waste management licence:

- the site is no longer managed by a technically competent person[1];
- serious pollution of the environment or serious harm to human health is likely if the waste management activities at the facility continue[2];
- the licence holder continues not to abide with one or more of the conditions of the licence[3];
- the licensee has failed to pay the annual subsistence charge[4].

1 EPA 1990, s 38(6)(a).
2 EPA 1990, s 38(6)(b) and (c).
3 EPA 1990, s 42(6)(c).
4 Environment Act 1995, s 41(6).

9.41 Waste management licences can be suspended under two separate sections of the EPA 1990[1], as well as, in respect of the non-payment of subsistence charges under s 41 of the Environment Act 1995. Licence suspension should be seen as distinct from licence modification or licence revocation for the reason that suspension always comes into immediate effect. Despite there being an appeal provision in the EPA 1990[2], the suspension of the licence is not lifted pending the determination of the appeal[3]. In addition, the licence holder will commit a criminal offence if measures required by the

Agency when the licence is suspended under the EPA 1990 have not been completed[4]. Suspension is therefore a somewhat more draconian power than licence modification or revocation. Like revocation, it is the activities specified in the licence – not any licence conditions – which can be suspended entirely or partially[5].

1 EPA 1990, s 38(6) and s 42(6)(c).
2 There is no appeal in respect of s 41 of the Environment Act 1995.
3 EPA 1990, s 43(5).
4 EPA 1990, s 38(10) and (11): made applicable to s 42 by s 42(7) (as amended by the Environment Act 1995, Sch 22, para 76(8)): see para 9.56 below.
5 EPA 1990, s 38(8) and s 42(7) (as amended by the Environment Act 1995, Sch 22, para 76(8)); the Environment Act 1995, s 41(6).

9.42 A licence suspended under the EPA 1990 will 'be of no effect to authorise the carrying on of the activities specified in the licence or ... the activities specified by the authority in suspending the licence'[1]. There is no equivalent clarification in the Environment Act 1995 under s 41(6). Suspension under s 42 of the EPA 1990 for non-compliance with the licence conditions does not prejudice, in any way, the possibility of criminal charges under s 33(6) of the Act for breach of conditions of the licence[2].

1 EPA 1990, s 38(8) which, in the case of a suspension under s 42(6)(c), is cross referenced to s 38(8) by s 42(7) (as amended by the Environment Act 1995, Sch 22, para 76(8)).
2 See the EPA 1990, s 42(5).

9.43 The Secretary of State retains a power to direct the Agency to suspend a licence[1], in a similar manner to that available to revoke a licence[2]. The Agency must give effect to such a direction.

1 EPA 1990, s 38(7) and s 42(8).
2 See para 9.21.

Suspension due to failure to ensure technically competent management

9.44 A waste management licence can have all or some of its authorised activities suspended when the holder of the licence ceases to be a fit and proper person[1]. But the 'fit and proper' test is restricted only to where the 'management of the activities authorised by the licence' have ceased to be in the hands of a technically competent person[2].

1 EPA 1990, s 38(6)(a).
2 See para 9.24.

Suspension due to serious pollution of the environment and serious harm to human health

9.45 The second grounds upon which a licence can be suspended is if it appears to the Agency that 'serious' pollution of the environment or 'serious' harm to human health has resulted from, or is about to be caused by (a) the activities to which the licence relates or (b) the happening or the threatened happening of an event affecting those activities[1]. However, suspension in this context can only be effected if the waste management activities at the site 'will' continue to cause, or will cause, serious pollution of the environment or serious harm to human health[2]. The use of the word 'will' in this context would suggest that the Agency needs to be pretty sure of its grounds for suspension.

1 EPA 1990, s 38(6)(b).
2 EPA 1990, s 38(6)(c).

9.46 The words 'serious pollution of the environment' are not used elsewhere in Part II of the EPA 1990[1]. The use of the prefix 'serious' provides a certain contrast to the wording of other sections of Part II of the EPA 1990. For example, the EPA 1990 requires a licence not to be granted where 'pollution of the environment' might occur[2]. A licence can be revoked under s 38 where 'pollution of the environment' might manifest itself[3]. It is also a duty of the Agency to take the steps needed to ensure that licensed activities do not cause 'pollution of the environment'[4]. In none of these cases is the word 'serious' used. It is only used in the circumstance of a licence suspension. This suggests, *inter alia*, that a more stringent test is to be applied in suspending a licence than is needed in revoking it or, indeed, in granting it in the first place.

1 Originally, this phrase was also contained in s 69(3)(a), relating to powers of entry, but this was deleted by the Environment Act 1995, Sch 22, para 85. It is, however, used in Pt 1 of the EPA 1990: see for example s 14.
2 EPA 1990, s 36(3)(a).
3 EPA 1990, s 38(1).
4 EPA 1990, s 42(1).

9.47 At the time the Environmental Protection Bill was subject to Parliamentary scrutiny, an explanation of 'serious pollution' was provided by David Trippier, the then Junior Environment Minister. In a letter to an MP on the House of Commons' Committee, he stated that the more stringent test for licence suspension was needed for the following reason:

'Where any pollution at any level is involved, the authority may exercise their discretion to refuse or revoke licences. These provisions are subject to appeal if the authority have (sic) drawn unreasonably tightly the limit of what they consider acceptable. ... It [suspension] is intended for use in emergency and may take immediate effect, not stopped by any appeal, in stopping the operations authorised by the licence. This is more drastic than normal revocation, and we have therefore included the stiffer test of "serious" pollution or harm so that a threshold exists before authorities wade in with their suspension powers. There is no question of this test preventing *urgent* action to prevent pollution or threats to public health.'

However, the Agency can already revoke or modify a licence immediately under s 43(6), if 'in the opinion of the authority it is necessary for the purpose of preventing or, where that is not practicable, minimising pollution of the environment or harm to human health. . .'. Hence, this already provides an option for revoking or modifying a licence which can have immediate effect, regardless of appeal. There is no element within these provisions which requires the pollution to be 'serious'.

Suspension due to failure to comply with licence conditions

9.48 A licence can also be suspended if the holder fails to abide with a notice that requires compliance with licence conditions[1]. Since the EPA 1990 was amended, this can be due to actual non-compliance with the conditions or when, in the opinion of the Agency, such non-compliance is anticipated[2].

1 EPA 1990, s 42(6)(c).
2 EPA 1990, s 42(5) as amended by the Environment Act 1995, Sch 22, para 76(4).

Suspension due to failure to pay subsistence charges

9.49 Section 41(6) of the Environment Act 1995 allows the Agency to suspend a licence when the annual licensing charges[1] have not been paid. The process for such action is contained in the Environmental Licences (Suspension and Revocation) Regulations 1996[2].

1   These are set out in the Waste Management Licensing (Charges) Scheme, published annually by the Agency: see para 9.142 below.
2   SI 1996/508.

The licence suspension process

9.50 Like licence revocation, licence suspension is effected by a notice which threatens impending suspension unless certain actions are attended to. Circular 11/94[1] advises that the notice should clearly indicate which activities are suspended and which are not. Unlike the notice in respect of suspension for non-payment of Agency charges[2], the EPA 1990 does not make provision for a second notice to confirm to a licensee that the licence is suspended.

1   Annex 4, para 4.47.
2   See SI 1996/508, reg 5.

9.51 The date of suspension and its duration needs to be included in the notice served on the licence holder[1]. The duration of the suspension can be defined either as lasting until a specified date or as being lifted when a particular item of work is completed[2]. The remainder of the contents of the notice is essentially similar to that necessary to enact a licence revocation[3]. The notice is to be served on the licence holder by way of the procedures set down in s 160 of the EPA 1990[4].

1   EPA 1990, s 38(12); s 42(5) and (7) (as amended by the Environment Act 1995, Sch 22, para 76(8)).
2   EPA 1990, s 38(12): applicable to suspension under s 42 by s 42(7) (as amended by the Environment Act 1995, Sch 22, para 76(8)).
3   See para 9.29ff.
4   See para 12.185ff.

9.52 The content of notices for suspension due to non-payment of subsistence charges are set down in the Environmental Licences (Suspension and Revocation) Regulations 1996[1]. The content of the notice is also common to licence revocation under these powers[2], although a suspension notice must also set out the circumstances under which licence suspension is to be lifted[3].

1   SI 1996/508.
2   See para 9.33 above.
3   SI 1996/508, reg 5(2)(b).

9.53 Licence suspension under the EPA 1990 cannot only be used as a way of getting undesirable activities to cease at a waste management facility. It can also require works to be done. This applies both to licences suspended under s 38[1] and s 42[2, 3]. The Agency is permitted, either at the time of suspension or while the licence is suspended, to require the holder to take measures to 'deal with or avert the pollution or harm'[4]. Such measures are those 'which the [waste regulation] authority considers necessary'. The Agency's requirements are indicated either on the original notice served on the licence holder or in a subsequent notice[5]. Either document must state when such a requirement is to have effect and specify the nature of the works to be done to cause suspension to cease.

1   Due to serious pollution of the environment or serious harm to human health being likely to arise: EPA 1990, s 38(6).
2   In the case of non-compliance with licence conditions: by way of s 42(7) (as amended by the Environment Act 1995, Sch 22, para 76(8)).
3   Interestingly, prior to s 42(7) being amended, a printing error in certain versions of the EPA 1990 had resulted in s 38(*12*) being one of the sections referred to in s 42(7). Other versions contained the

correct cross reference to s 38(*11*). Not all copies of the Act contained an errata slip from HMSO (this matter was confirmed in correspondence from HMSO to Lancashire County Council dated 14 October 1994).
4   EPA 1990, s 38(9).
5   EPA 990, s 38(12).

9.54   As was the case with revocation notices, if suspension notices require licensees to undertake works on third parties' land, such persons must consent to give access[1]. They need to be consulted beforehand by way of a notice from the Agency[2], with the consultation period being set at three months[3]. However, the requirements on the issuing of the notice and/or the consideration of representations can be temporarily lifted in the case of an 'emergency'[4]. Compensation is payable by the licensee to the affected neighbours[5].

1   EPA 1990, s 38(9A), as amended by the Environment Act 1995, s 120, Sch 22, para 72(1).
2   EPA 1990, s 38(9B) and s 36A: the requirements are broadly similar to notices served on neighbouring landowners in respect of conditions in proposed licences: see paras 8.23ff and 8.244ff.
3   SI 1999/481, reg 3(a).
4   EPA 1990, s 38(9C): the use of the word 'emergency', coupled with the three-month consultation period, has the disadvantages discussed at para 9.32.
5   EPA 1990, s 35A(1)(a)(ii) and SI 1999/481: compensation claims are discussed at para 8.26.

9.55   Licences suspended under the EPA 1990 are subject to possible appeal to the Secretary of State[1]. However, in contrast to licence modification and revocation, the Agency's decision is not lifted pending an appeal[2]. But there is still the possibility of the Agency paying compensation if the Department of the Environment deems that it acted unreasonably[3].

1   EPA 1990, s 43(1)(d): see para 9.126ff.
2   EPA 1990, s 43(5).
3   EPA 1990, s 43(7).

Sanctions for non-compliance with suspension notices

9.56   As is the case with licence revocation, the most obvious sanction is prosecution under s 33 of the EPA 1990[1] on the grounds that licence revocation or suspension has caused waste management activities to no longer be authorised by the licence. However, there will be circumstances where the Agency can require a licensee to undertake a particular action. This is particularly the case in respect of suspension notices, which can require a person to take the measures which are defined in the notice[2]. Non-compliance with the notice therefore has its own sanctions in the EPA 1990.

1   See Chapter 7.
2   EPA 1990, s 38(9) and s 42(7) as amended by the Environment Act 1995, Sch 22, para 76(8).

9.57   If the Agency's requirements of the notice are not met an offence is committed. Where no special waste is involved, a person who fails to comply 'without reasonable excuse'[1] may be fined up to the statutory maximum on summary conviction[2, 3]. On conviction on indictment, an unlimited fine may be imposed, or imprisonment of up to two years, or both[4]. Where special waste[5] is involved, a fine up to the statutory maximum, or six months imprisonment, may be levied on summary conviction. On conviction on indictment, the maximum period of imprisonment is extended to five years. This can be made in conjunction with a fine or as an alternative to one[6]. In addition, the Agency also has the option of approaching the High Court for an injunction where the notice is proving an ineffectual remedy[7].

1   See para 12.109.
2   Currently £5,000.
3   EPA 1990, s 38(10)(a).

4   EPA 1990, s 38(10)(b).
5   See Chapter 4.
6   EPA 1990, s 38(11).
7   EPA 1990, s 38(13) (as amended by the Environment Act 1995, Sch 22, para 72(2)) and s 42(6A) (as amended by the Environment Act 1995, Sch 22, para 76(7)). Injunctions are discussed at para 12.85ff.

9.58   It will be apparent that the EPA 1990 makes a differentiation between special and non-special wastes in these offences. As such a distinction affects the possible penalties, it may require careful consideration by an enforcing authority. It is notable that s 38(10) of the EPA 1990 states that a person shall be liable to conviction 'otherwise than in relation to special waste'. This refers not only to offences involving any waste which is not special waste, but also applies where a suspension requires works not immediately connected to the deposit of waste to be done at a site. For example, a licence may be suspended for the reason that the site security fence was deficient or that a landfill gas migration prevention trench had become blocked. Clearly, in neither of these cases is special waste involved, and this would accordingly rule out an offence being created under s 38(11).

9.59   Conversely, in order to benefit from the potentially higher penalties involved with special waste, the Agency must satisfy an additional burden of proof. It must be in a position to demonstrate that special waste has in fact been involved. This is not necessarily always easy[1]. In the more marginal of cases, it may therefore be appropriate for the Agency to play safe and to use a notice drafted under s 38(10) of the EPA 1990, as opposed to s 38(11).

1   See para 4.21ff.

9.60   A second, and perhaps more significant, question arises from the relationship between the offence provisions in s 38(10) and s 38(11) of the EPA 1990, and any appeal against the notice made by the licence holder to the Secretary of State[1]. As already noted, in the case of licence suspension, the lodging of the appeal does not cause the Agency's decision to be lifted[2]. It seems conceivable that a licence holder may be subject to legal proceedings for non-compliance with the notice and will wish to exercise the right of appeal in parallel. Given that delays in determining appeals have been the norm since the EPA 1990 was implemented, it also seems equally conceivable that the licence holder may receive a conviction before the appeal is determined. Equally, it may well be that the result of the appeal is the quashing of the original notice. Unfortunately the statute does not appear to resolve this matter.

1   Under the EPA 1990, s 43.
2   EPA 1990, s 43(5).

9.61   One answer might be for the Agency to hold back on the proceedings until the appeal has been determined. But this action significantly lessens the deterrent power of the provisions in the EPA 1990 in relation to non-compliance with the notice and may encourage 'strategic' appeals. Furthermore, the time being taken to adjudicate appeals may mean that the offence is so old that the courts may be reluctant to convict or sentence heavily.

DUTIES OF THE AGENCY IN RESPECT OF WASTE MANAGEMENT LICENCES

9.62   A detailed discussion of the Agency's general statutory duties which are common to both licensed and unlicensed waste management facilities is to be found in

Chapter 12. That chapter considers the Agency's inspection function in more detail and, for example, evaluates the provisions of the EPA 1990 which can be used to require waste to be removed from a site or to have its effects mitigated[1]. By contrast, those duties which are specific to licensed sites will be discussed here. As will be seen, the Agency has considerable discretion as to how its licensing function is to be carried out and the manner by which the statutory enforcement mechanisms described elsewhere in this chapter are to be used. However, in certain cases, the EPA 1990 and associated subsidiary legislation is more specific. This section will also embrace those provisions, particularly as they often require licences to be appropriately modified.

1   EPA 1990, s 59: see para 12.101ff.

The policing of licence conditions

9.63   The EPA 1990 sets down statutory duties for the Agency in respect of waste management licences. Section 42(1) requires the Agency 'to take the steps needed' to ensure that the activities authorised by the licence do not cause pollution of the environment, harm to human health or become seriously detrimental to the amenities of the locality affected by the activities[1]. In addition, the Agency must take similar steps to ensure compliance with all conditions of a waste management licence[2].

1   EPA 1990, s 42(1).
2   EPA 1990, s 42(1)(b).

9.64   The Agency retains discretion as to how to exercise the requirement of ensuring compliance with waste management licence conditions[1]. However, inspection frequencies are set down in Waste Management Paper 4[2] and these are embraced by the EPA 1990's concept of 'statutory guidance'[3]. In relation to the EPA 1990's requirement to ensure that pollution of the environment, harm to human health or serious detriment of the amenities of the locality do not arise from the site's operation, the requirements on the Agency become more formal. They also take a peculiarly circular journey through the EPA 1990. When pollution, harm or detriment to amenities arise, the Agency is required to either revoke the licence 'entirely' or to modify its conditions[4]. The modification has to be 'to the extent which in the opinion of the ... [Agency] is required' to ensure that the pollution, harm or detriment does not occur[5]. If the revocation route is taken[6], s 38 permits full or partial revocation on the grounds that the activities 'would' cause pollution, harm or detriment to amenity[7]. In addition, that section only allows the Agency to revoke when the pollution, harm or detriment cannot be avoided by modifying the conditions of the licence[8].

1   See the use of the word 'may' in s 42(5) of the EPA 1990.
2   WMP 4, p 62: as discussed at para 12.30, these provisions are due for change.
3   See WMP 4, para 1.4; the EPA 1990, s 38(8); and see para 8.231ff.
4   EPA 1990, s 37(2).
5   EPA 1990, s 37(2)(a).
6   And despite the requirement of s 37(2) that revocation is done 'entirely'.
7   EPA 1990, s 38(1)(b).
8   EPA 1990, s 38(1)(c).

Regulation 15: keeping groundwater discharges under review

9.65   As discussed at para 8.70, reg 15 of the Waste Management Licensing Regulations 1994[1] transposes the Groundwater Directive[2] in respect of licensed waste management facilities. Article 11 of the Directive requires that authorisations for the discharge of substances into groundwater are granted only for limited periods and are reviewed at least every four years, after which they must be renewed, amended or withdrawn. This provision is taken up by reg 15(9), which places the duty on the Agency to ensure that all waste management licences are reviewed within the required period. Given the content of both the Directive and reg 15[3], only facilities with the potential to discharge List I and List II[4] substances into relevant groundwater[5] need to be considered. However, should the proposition set out at para 8.91 – that waste recovery facilities are also encompassed by the Groundwater Directive – prove correct, the requirement for review would seem to apply to many scrapyards and vehicle dismantlers as it does to any other type of affected site.

1   SI 1994/1056, reg 15.
2   Council Directive of 17 December 1979 on the protection of groundwater against pollution caused by certain dangerous substances (Directive 80/68/EEC) (OJ L20/43 26.1.80).
3   See para 8.70ff.
4   See para 8.74ff.
5   See para 8.79ff.

9.66   Regulation 15 is notably curt in setting down the nature of the required reviews[1]. It seems to envisage reviews being of two types. Regulation 15 sets out slightly more explicitly the Agency's duties in respect of reviews of licences which existed prior to the enactment of the EPA 1990 in 1994[2]. However, no information is provided on the nature of subsequent reviews[3]. All Circular 11/94 adds is: 'These reviews should of course be directed towards the groundwater protection aspects of the licence, and need to be thorough enough to provide a basis for any necessary modifications to the licence conditions'[4]. Presumably, in the absence of relevant statutory provisions, the Agency can use its discretion as to the form of the reviews[5]. What does seem clear is that reviews must take place on all relevant licences and that the Agency must be in a position to indicate compliance with both the Groundwater Directive's timescales and technical requirements.

1   SI 1994/1056, reg 15(9) indicates only that reviews are done in the requisite time interval.
2   See SI 1994/1056, reg 15(10) and (11).
3   SI 1994/1056, reg 15(9).
4   Circular 11/94, Annex 7, para 7.18.
5   See Environment Agency (1999) *The EC Groundwater Directive (80/68/EEC) and the Waste Management Licensing Regulations, 1994. Interim Internal Guidance on the Interpretation and Application of Regulation 15 of the Waste Management Licensing Regulations, 1994 (The Protection of Groundwater)*, Draft for Consultation, January 1999, Environment Agency, Bristol.

9.67   The application of reg 15 upon sites which possessed waste disposal licences prior to 1 May 1994 is briefly set out in the Waste Management Licensing Regulations 1994[1]. The Agency was required to review all waste management licences current on 1 May 1994 which authorise any activity involving the direct discharge[2], or the indirect discharge by tipping and disposal[3], of List I and List II substances[4]. This is extended by reg 15(11), which is claimed by Circular 11/94[5] to require the review of all waste disposal licences granted or applied for under the Control of Pollution Act 1974[6].

1   SI 1994/1056, reg 15(10).
2   See para 8.76.
3   See para 8.91ff.
4   See para 8.74.
5   Circular 11/94, Annex 7, para 7.19.
6   As not all sites became covered by waste management licences in May 1994: scrapyards, car dismantlers, applications lodged but outstanding on 1 May 1994, licences under appeal etc, are all examples: see Commencement Order 15 (SI 1994/1096).

9.68   In undertaking a review of a facility which possessed a licence under the Control of Pollution Act 1974, the Agency must use its powers of modification and revocation under s 37 and s 38 of the EPA 1990 'to give effect to Council Directive 80/68/EEC'[1]. No further requirements are set down[2]. The absence of detailed requirements, beyond the need to give effect to the Groundwater Directive, is in immediate contrast to the nine subsections of reg 15 which set out how waste management licence applications should be dealt with. This deficit is only partially filled by Circular 11/94, which states that the Agency will[3]:

'... need to consider whether the conditions imposed at existing operational waste disposal sites achieve the level of groundwater protection required under the Directive and, if not, take whatever steps might be necessary. ... [T]he commonest requirements will be variations in the licence conditions to secure: adequate monitoring of the groundwater, containment of the waste deposited in new phases of site construction; prohibition of the deposit of all wastes containing List 1 substances where that would lead to a discharge of these substances into groundwater; and the prohibition of the deposit of wastes where their composition or expected degradation products are such that this would lead to pollution of the groundwater by List II substances. In both the latter cases, of course, the continued deposit of such wastes may be permitted where all the technical precautions necessary to prevent such discharge or pollution are observed.'

1   Ie the Groundwater Directive: SI 1994/1056, reg 15(10).
2   It is quite clear that regs 15(1) to 15(9) apply only to waste management licences at the time of their issuing.
3   Circular 11/94, Annex 7, para 7.21.

9.69   However, slightly peculiar issues emerge which affect the exact nature of the Agency's duties in respect of the reviews of the sites which were subject to licences under the Control of Pollution Act 1974. Although reg 15 contains the requirement to undertake a review of the groundwater implications of all sites which possessed waste management licences on 1 May 1994[1], it seems that there were, in fact, no such licences in existence on that date. Commencement Order 15[2] makes all waste disposal licences issued under the Control of Pollution Act 1974 which existed on 1 May 1994 change to waste management licences the day after, ie on 2 May 1994. Secondly, reg 15(11) applies the provisions of reg 15 to the granting and review 'by disposal authorities of disposal licences under Part 1 of the Control of Pollution Act 1974' as it applies the granting or review by 'waste regulation authorities of waste management licences'. However, this does not appear to require the granting and review of waste *disposal* licences by *waste regulation authorities*. This reading, if correct, seems to throw into confusion the nature of the duties of the Agency for these older licences. Nevertheless, Circular 11/94 is adamant that all relevant licences should have been reviewed for compliance with the Groundwater Directive by 31 April 1995[3].

1   SI 1994/1056, reg 15(10).
2   SI 1994/1096, para 3(3).
3   Circular 11/94, Annex 4, para 4.39; the need to review the groundwater aspects of a facility in respect of reg 15 is not necessarily triggered by an application for a licence modification: see *In Petition of John Guthrie* [1998] Env LR 128 at 137/138.

Keeping financial provision under review after the licence is issued

9.70   The discussion at para 8.181ff on financial provision indicates that licence applicants[1] or transferees[2] satisfy the requirements of s 74 of the EPA 1990 when they have made financial provision adequate to discharge the obligations arising from the licence[3]. As has been described, an assessment by the Agency breaks down into two basic elements. In summary, the first matter to be considered is the general financial standing of the applicant or transferee. The second concerns whether the Agency may wish to look for some particular financial provision mechanism, such a bond or escrow account, to ensure that defined liabilities are adequately funded in the long term. The latter, which is discretionary, can be required by one or more appropriately worded licence conditions.

1   EPA 1990, s 36(3).
2   EPA 1990, s 40(4): see para 9.114ff.
3   EPA 1990, s 74(3)(c).

9.71   In instances other than when licences are applied for or are to be transferred, a significant practical problem is created by the wording of the EPA 1990. The Agency appears greatly constrained in its ability to ensure that financial provision is kept up through the life of the site, particularly when the financial circumstances of the licensee take a significant downturn. It seems to be accepted that the wording of the EPA 1990 prevents the financial provision element being reappraised later at the Agency's discretion[1].

1   See WMP 4, para 3.78.

9.72   The EPA 1990 makes it explicit that the conviction of a licence holder for relevant offences[1], or the failure of that person to ensure technically competent management[2], may preclude a licensee continuing to be a fit and proper person. The licence can be revoked or suspended in these circumstances. However, the Act is much less clear as to whether changes in the licensee's financial standing are also grounds for such actions.

1   EPA 1990, s 38(1)(a).
2   EPA 1990, s 38(2) and s 38(6)(a).

9.73   Certainly, it seems that action by the Agency is possible in respect of those elements of financial provision which are formal requirements of particular licence conditions[1]. A failure to renew a bond or to place money in an escrow account may result in breach of the relevant condition. In this case, the licensee is open to prosecution[2] under s 33 of the EPA 1990[3], as well as the partial revocation of the licence[4] or its suspension[5]. This may be supplemented by the specific penalties contained in the legal agreement covering the particular financial provision mechanism and, depending upon its wording, possible action by the Agency for breach of contract.

1   WMP 4, paras 3.78 to 3.79.
2   However, when a third party such as an insurer declines to continue to provide cover, WMP 4 warns the Agency against seeking enforcement action as the first step in ensuring compliance with a condition requiring continuity of cover. Rather, the Agency 'should first seek to agree with the licensee what alternative form of cover might be provided' (WMP 4, para 3.80).
3   See Chapter 7.
4   EPA 1990, s 42(6).
5   EPA 1990, s 42(7) as amended by the Environment Act 1995, Sch 22, para 76(8).

9.74   However, matters become less clear in respect of the elements of the financial provision assessment which are unconnected to particular conditions. There is the matter of the financial 'health' of the licensee as a whole[1]. In addition, whatever financial provision mechanism originally put in place may turn out later to be inadequate for the purpose.

1   WMP 4 (para 3.82) advises that conditions on financial provision on this broader aspect are inappropriate.

9.75   These circumstances are not explicitly dealt with by the provisions on licence revocation or suspension[1]. Having said that, there does appear to be an interesting question over whether the entire financial provision test might apply to licence *holders*, besides licence applicants or transferees. This is a direct result of the wording of s 74 of the EPA 1990, which in these respects is somewhat contradictory. On the one hand, s 74(1) indicates that the contents of s 74 are only relevant to instances when another section of the Act explicitly requires an assessment of a person's fit and proper nature. As noted, the wording of the EPA 1990 is such that this will only be at licence application[2] or transfer[3] stage. However, s 74(3)(c) also states that the requirement for fit and proper person is not satisfied if adequate financial provision has not been made by the person 'who holds or is to hold' the waste management licence. By definition, a person who 'is to hold' a waste management licence is an applicant for a licence or for a licence transfer. But the reference to a person 'who holds' a waste management licence must surely apply to the licensee after the licence has been issued. The very existence of the words 'who holds' must have some purpose in the statute.

1   EPA 1990, s 38.
2   EPA 1990, s 36(3).
3   EPA 1990, s 40(4).

9.76   Faced with these somewhat contradictory requirements, it may be that the Agency has some leeway in considering financial provision outside the bounds of s 74 and the explicit references to that section which are contained elsewhere in Part II of the EPA 1990. There appear to be two options, although their utility is somewhat speculative. Firstly, should a person no longer be able to meet the requirements of the licence, the site may present a possible risk of pollution of the environment or harm to human health. For example, if the Agency has clear evidence that a landfill is not backed by sufficient funds for capping and restoration works which, *inter alia*, are essential to prevent rainwater ingress, then it seems possible to look to the powers of partial licence revocation[1] or, particularly, suspension[2]. As discussed at para 9.53, licence suspension can operate in conjunction with a notice served on the licensee requiring specified measures to be taken to deal with or avert pollution or harm to human health[3]. It may be possible to use such a notice to require that a bond or a lump sum is lodged with the Agency to cover any eventuality resulting from a failure to comply with the requisite environmental controls. However, the Agency needs to have strong grounds to follow this route. Licence suspension and the statutory works notice is only possible where 'serious' pollution or harm is likely[4]. In addition, any notice requiring additional financial provision must emanate directly from the need to avert pollution or harm[5]. Finally, as suspension is enacted with immediate effect, the Agency may have to pay compensation if an appeal to the Secretary of State by the licensee is subsequently successful[6].

1   EPA 1990, s 38(1)(b): see para 9.18ff.
2   EPA 1990, s 38(6)(b): see para 9.40ff.
3   EPA 1990, s 38(9)
4   EPA 1990, s 38(6): see para 9.45ff.
5   See EPA 1990, s 38(9) and para 9.45.
6   See EPA 1990, s 43(7) and para 9.126ff.

9.77   The second way to address this matter seems also to be untested. When the Agency becomes concerned about a licensee's ability to make adequate financial provision, it may be possible to use the powers contained in s 37(1)(a) to modify the licence[1]. It has already been noted at para 9.11 that s 37(1)(a) of the EPA 1990 does not set out any grounds under which licence modifications should occur[2]. While s 74 does

469

not explicitly apply for this reason[3], it may do so implicitly. Given that no grounds are set down under which modifications are to be considered, it seems that the Agency may search elsewhere in the Act for equivalent provisions. The most obvious are those which apply when a licence application is made. In this case they are[4]: pollution of the environment, harm to human health, serious detriment to the amenities of the locality, and fit and proper person. The latter can, of course, embrace financial provision.

1   EPA 1990, s 37(1) also requires the Agency to demonstrate that the modification will not cause the licensee 'unreasonable' expense: para 9.05.
2   Or indeed under which applications for modifications should be judged.
3   As s 74(1) only gives application to s 74 when a section of the Act explicitly requires that an assessment be done on whether a person is fit and proper.
4   EPA 1990, s 36(3): see paras 8.40ff, 8.49 and 8.112ff.

9.78   Certainly it seems legitimate to impose enhanced financial provision by licence modification when a licence holder wishes to upgrade a site in a manner which greatly increases its potential environmental impact. An example might be a proposal to change a landfill from taking only inert waste to one which accepts household waste. In these circumstances, it certainly seems justifiable to add licence conditions which require that a bond or escrow account is established in order to address any increased environmental risk.

9.79   However, can the Agency use licence modification to address a failure of a licensee in respect of financial provision? For example, while a company may have demonstrated considerable financial strength at the time of licence application, this may have waned significantly since then. The answer to this question is less certain, but it may be possible to add a licence condition to require additional financial provision to be made in such circumstances. An example might be to require the replacement of a parent company guarantee by a bond which addresses specified liabilities.

9.80   Although the latter proposal seems to be untried, the EPA 1990 and associated guidance[1] clearly envisages that a licence modification is to be used to permit the Agency to tighten its overall regulatory grip on a licensee. For example, it is legitimate to modify a licence to reflect changing technology or require additional works caused by environmental impacts which were hitherto not appreciated when the site was originally licensed. Given the contents of s 74(3) of the EPA 1990, which points to licence holders as well as licence applicants needing to make financial provision[2], it might be difficult to justify that the mechanism of modification was not available in these instances. A particularly pertinent circumstance would be where the mitigation of unforeseen events by the licensee has, for example, prematurely emptied an escrow account of funds.

1   See for example WMP 4, para 2.35.
2   EPA 1990, s 74(3)(c).

9.81   In respect of these proposals, it would be interesting to see what decision was reached by the Secretary of State on appeal against such a licence modification. Indeed, even if the financial provision issue was disallowed on appeal, the argument described in this section in respect of s 74(3)(c) of the EPA 1990 and licence modification might, perhaps, be grounds for applying to have the Secretary of State's decision overturned by way of judicial review. Besides the possibility that such a modification may be overturned on appeal, the Agency should also be aware that the condition may be struck out as *ultra vires* when court proceedings for the non-compliance are instigated. Such a collateral challenge can occur[1] despite the fact that no appeal was lodged by the licence holder within the six-month time limit set down in the Waste Management Licensing Regulations 1994[2].

1   See for example *A-G's Reference (No 2 of 1988)* (1989) 89 Cr App Rep 314.
2   SI 1994/1056, reg 7(1)(a).

Fit and proper person and sites licensed under the 1974 Act

9.82   While matters concerning financial provision in respect of licences already issued may result in questions which are difficult to resolve, waste management facilities which were hitherto licensed under the Control of Pollution Act 1974 are treated by the legislation as a special case. Such licences were subject to the transitional provisions in s 77(2) of the EPA 1990. Section 77(2) requires that all such licences 'shall, on and after the relevant appointed day for licences, be treated as a site licence ...' for the purposes of the EPA 1990. Other than scrapyards and vehicle dismantlers, the relevant appointed day for these licences was 1 May 1994[1].

1   SI 1994/1096, reg 2.

9.83   By definition, for a person to hold a site licence[1] under the EPA 1990, the licensee must be a fit and proper person. Accordingly, all holders of waste disposal licences which transferred to waste management licences on 1 May 1994 are deemed to be fit and proper persons. This means that the three arms of the fit and proper test were automatically satisfied at that date – in other words, on 1 May 1994 the licence holder does not have any[2] convictions for relevant offences[3], is technically competent[4] and has sufficient financial provision to fulfil the obligations required by the licence[5, 6].

1   Site licences and mobile plant licences together constitute waste management licences: see the EPA 1990, s 35(12) and para 8.05.
2   Or, perhaps, sufficient: see para 9.84 below.
3   EPA 1990, s 74(3)(a).
4   EPA 1990, s 74(3)(b).
5   EPA 1990, s 74(3)(c).
6   See also Circular 11/94, paras 4.49 and 4.75.

9.84   However, like much of the EPA 1990, the provisions which deem such licensees to be fit and proper persons warrant analysis. For persons who held waste disposal licences under the Control of Pollution Act 1994, any convictions obtained prior to 1 May 1994 do not count as sufficient to jeopardise the first requirement of the fit and proper person test. Although there appeared to be an interesting question on the status of convictions which were gathered prior to 1 May 1994, virtually all will now be 'spent' within the meaning of the Rehabilitation of Offenders Act 1974[1]. It seemed possible to argue that previous convictions prior to 1 May 1994 did not, on their own, jeopardise a waste disposal licence holder's status when the licence is transferred into the new regime. However, they might have counted when that person gained further convictions.

1   It should be noted that the provisions on prescribed offences in respect of the Control of Pollution (Amendment) Act 1989 (see Chapter 6) and controlled waste carrier registration have always been regarded as having retroactive application.

9.85   The second arm of the fit and proper person test is more significant. Under the transitional provisions of s 77(2) of the EPA 1990, any 'disposal licence'[1, 2] became a site licence on 1 May 1994. Accordingly, the licence holder is deemed to be a fit and proper person and hence any manager of such a facility is deemed to be technically competent.

1 As issued under the Control of Pollution Act 1974, s 5.
2 Note that sites run by local authorities which were subject to resolutions under s 11 of the Control of Pollution Act 1974 are not covered by this provision, as a resolution is not a 'disposal licence'. The assumption made when the EPA 1990 was finalised was that all such resolutions should have been upgraded to waste disposal licences via the formation of Local Authority Waste Disposal Companies (see para 1.36). In a minority of cases in England and Wales, this did not happen until after 1 May 1994. In Scotland, resolutions became waste management licences on 1 April 1996 (see Environment Act 1995, Sch 23, para 18).

9.86   However, should a significant number of people who comprise the licence holder's technically competent management depart from the employ of the licensee after 1 May 1994, the latter's deemed fit and proper status may be jeopardised[1]. Furthermore, the manager of a site which was transferred from a waste disposal licence under the Control of Pollution Act 1974 is not to be regarded as technically competent for the management of any other site. For those sites encompassed by the Certificate of Technical Competence (COTC) scheme, that person can only exercise technically competent management of another facility if that person had applied to WAMITAB by the due date, usually[2] August 1994. Alternatively, the person needed to be over 55 years of age on that date and have appropriate relevant experience. Persons who failed to apply to WAMITAB had to obtain a full COTC. A manager of a site outside the COTC scheme can only manage another similar site at the discretion of the Agency[3].

1 See Circular 11/94, Annex 4, para 4.49 and WMP 4, para 3.8ff.
2 See para 8.153ff.
3 Fully discussed at para 8.170ff.

9.87   Finally, there is the question of financial provision. When a waste disposal licence became a site licence under the transitional provisions, financial provision was to be considered adequate to discharge the obligations arising from the new waste management licence. The discussion earlier has pointed to the fact that financial provision is normally assessed only at the time a licence is applied for or transferred. It therefore does not appear that it can be reassessed in the case of a waste management licence which transferred from a waste disposal licence under the transitional provisions. However, it may be that the provisions of s 77(2) of the EPA 1990 cause the level of financial provision at 1 May 1994 to be viewed as adequate on the basis of the licensee's circumstances at that date[1]. Accordingly, in the manner discussed at para 9.77 above, it may be that the powers to modify licence conditions[2] can be used, if it becomes clear to the Agency that the level of financial provision has fallen significantly below that observable on 1 May 1994. Furthermore, it seems entirely appropriate that, when a licence holder applies for a licence modification to accommodate significant changes to the site, such as the acceptance of a wider range of wastes, financial provision requirements with respect of such matters as unexpected events and post-closure are made conditions of the licence.

1 It should be recalled that financial provision contains two principal elements: the overall financial standing of a licence applicant and, if necessary, the imposition of a particular mechanism to ensure provision in respect of specified liabilities. See para 8.185ff.
2 EPA 1990, s 37.

Ensuring compliance with relevant objectives and the Directive on Waste

9.88   As is explained in more detail elsewhere[1], the Agency is under a duty[2] to ensure that the relevant objectives of the Directive on Waste[3] are upheld when carrying out its statutory functions at waste management facilities. There is also an additional duty to ensure compliance with other, more specific, items of Community legislation which are also transposed by the Waste Management Licensing Regulations 1994[4]. These provisions will have detailed consideration at the time of a licence application. However, the operation of licensed waste management facilities with respect to such requirements must be kept under review. Where necessary, the Agency is required to use its powers of licence modification, suspension and revocation to ensure compliance. While the available powers are considered elsewhere in this chapter, one aspect is particularly significant and this concerns the application of the Waste Management Licensing Regulations 1994 to sites originally licensed under the Control of Pollution Act 1974.

1   See para 12.13ff.
2   SI 1994/1056, Sch 4, Pt I, para 2.
3   Council Directive of 15 July 1975 on Waste (75/442/EEC) (OJ L194/39 25.7.75) (as amended by Council Directive of 18 March 1991 amending Directive 75/442/EEC on Waste (91/156/EEC) (OJ L78/32 26.3.91)).
4   SI 1994/1056, regs 13, 14 and 15, Sch 4, Pt I, paras 4, 6 and 14: see Circular 11/94, Annex 4, para 4.39.

9.89   As has been touched upon in respect of financial provision[1] and groundwater protection[2], waste management facilities which were licensed through the Control of Pollution Act 1974 became site licences under the EPA 1990 by way of the transitional provisions contained in s 77 of that Act[3]. The conversion from a waste disposal licence under the earlier legislation to a site licence occurred automatically, without any review being needed to ensure that the facilities complied with the requirements of the EPA 1990 which would normally apply to a licence application. However, once the licences were converted, waste regulation bodies were required to reconsider whether each of these licences fully conformed to Community law and utilise the power to modify them as appropriate[4]. The required criteria are contained in the Waste Management Licensing Regulations 1994[5].

1   See para 9.87.
2   See para 9.65ff.
3   See also SI 1994/1096.
4   Circular 11/94, Annex 4, para 4.39.
5   SI 1994/1056, regs 13, 14 and 15, Sch 4, Pt I, paras 4, 6 and 14: see Circular 11/94, Annex 4, para 4.39.

9.90   The Waste Management Licensing Regulations 1994 cause the Agency to ensure that any licensed facility follows the relevant objectives of the Directive on Waste. They have to make certain that it does not endanger human health or harm the environment and is operated without[1]:

'(i)   risk to water, air, soil, plants or animals; or
(ii)   causing nuisance through noise or odours;
(iii)   adversely affecting the countryside or places of special interest.'

When licences for disposal[2] activities are reviewed, they should be modified to contain conditions which cover[3]:

'(a)   the types and quantities of waste,
(b)   the technical requirements,
(c)   the security precautions to be taken,
(d)   the disposal site, and
(e)   the treatment method.'

In addition, all licences must comply with specified requirements on record keeping[4]. They must avoid conditions specific to health and safety issues[5] and, if they are involved in the processing or storage of waste oils, should comply with the relevant requirements[6]. Such reviews were supposedly to be finished by 31 April 1995[7]. A licence which failed on modification to reflect the requirement that waste quantities should be specified has been held to be void[8].

1   SI 1994/1056, Sch 4, Pt I, para 4(1): see paras 8.55 and 12.15ff.
2   'Disposal' is defined in SI 1994/1056, reg 1(3) as those activities set down in Part III to Sch 4 (see Chapter 2, Table 2.5).
3   SI 1994/1056, Sch 4, Pt 1, para 6: see para 8.277ff.
4   SI 1994/1056, Sch 4, Pt 1, para 14: see para 8.234, WMP 4, para 4.43 and Circular 11/94, Annex 1, para 1.90.
5   SI 1994/1056, reg 13.
6   SI 1994/1056, reg 14: see para 8.262ff.
7   Circular 11/94, Annex 4, para 4.39.
8   See *In Petition of John Guthrie* [1998] Env LR 128.

9.91   Once the licences have been reviewed and appropriately amended to conform to Community law, the environmental performance of the affected sites in those respects needs to be continuously monitored. Circular 11/94 makes it clear[1] that, whenever any review of a licence is undertaken 'for whatever reason', the matter of compliance with the relevant objectives of the Directive on Waste and the Waste Management Licensing Regulations 1994 must be addressed.

1   Circular 11/94, Annex 1, para 1.57.

9.92   As discussed at para 8.60, conditions of a waste management licence can be introduced to substantiate existing land use controls at those older sites which transferred from the licensing regime of the Control of Pollution Act 1974. Poorly detailed planning permissions and certificates of lawful or established use can be substantiated by licence modifications in the name of preventing adverse effects on the countryside[1]. For example, additional requirements for such matters as landscaping and restoration or improved access can be imposed. In a minority of cases, a licence could be revoked[2] on these grounds due to its intolerable impact on a local community.

1   SI 1994/1056, Sch 4, Pt I, para 4(1)(a)(iii).
2   Under the EPA 1990, s 38(1)(b).

SURRENDER OF WASTE MANAGEMENT LICENCES

Enacting licence surrender

9.93   As noted in the previous chapter, there are two types of waste management licence[1]: a site licence and a mobile plant licence. Whilst a mobile plant licence can be surrendered to the Agency who granted it at any time, a site licence cannot be given up unless the Agency accepts the surrender[2]. This surrender is formalised by the Agency issuing a 'certificate of completion' to the licence holder[3].

1   EPA 1990, s 35(12): see para 8.05.
2   EPA 1990, s 39(1).
3   EPA 1990, s 39(9).

9.94   The justification for the Agency having to approve the surrender of a site licence stems from the long-term environmental impacts of many waste management activities. These impacts can extend well beyond the time period in which the site is 'active' and receiving or processing controlled wastes. For example, landfill site biodegradation is slow and may extend over generations. The extensive spillage of oil and other fluids at motor vehicle dismantlers may not, due to the slow nature of sub-surface seepage, cause pollution immediately, but many years after the event. For these and other reasons, environmental monitoring and other pollution control measures may be needed over long time periods. By definition, the primary method to ensure licence holders undertake such measures is by the conditions of the facility's site licence. It is therefore appropriate that the Agency should determine the point at which the holder should be absolved of such duties. The licence surrender can only occur when the licence holder has demonstrated that the condition of the site is such that no pollution or harm to human health can be expected from it. However, the licensing concept of the EPA 1990 is by no means watertight in these respects. For example, if a sole trader licensee dies, it is not clear upon whom the liabilities arising from the licence should then rest. Perhaps a more significant problem concerns bodies corporate in liquidation – a matter discussed further at para 9.104.

9.95 Section 39 of the EPA 1990[1] sets down the procedures for considering an application to surrender a site licence and the issuing of certificates of completion. Until 1998, the Secretary of State was empowered to prescribe the nature of the information required in relation to such an application[2]. The information so prescribed was contained in reg 2 and Schedule 1 to the Waste Management Licensing Regulations 1994. However, the power to prescribe this information has been excised from the EPA 1990 by the Environment Act 1995[3]. While the requirements remain in the Waste Management Licensing Regulations 1994[4], they would seem to have no statutory basis.

1   As amended by the Environment Act 1995, Sch 22, para 73.
2   EPA 1990, s 39(3) (as amended by the Environment Act 1995, Sch 22, para 73(2) (commenced by SI 1996/186, reg 3 and SI 1998/604, reg 2).
3   Environment Act 1995, s 120(1), Sch 22, para 73(2).
4   SI 1994/1056, reg 2 and Sch 1.

9.96 A licence holder who wishes to surrender a site licence must apply to the Agency. The application must be made in writing[1] and must be accompanied[2] by a surrender fee which is set down in the Waste Management Licensing (Charges) Scheme current for that year[3]. Since the change made to s 39 of the EPA 1990 by the Environment Act 1995, an application must be made on the Agency's own forms[4], with the information forming a 'completion report' on the site[5].

1   SI 1994/1056, reg 2(2).
2   EPA 1990, s 39(3) as amended by the Environment Act 1995, Sch 22, para 73(2).
3   See for example Waste Management Licensing (Charges) Scheme 1999–2000, Tables 1–4: see para 9.142.
4   EPA 1990, s 39(3) as amended by the Environment Act 1995, s 120, Sch 22, para 73(2).
5   Department of the Environment (1993) *Landfill Completion*, Waste Management Paper No 26A, HMSO, Chapter 5.

9.97 For waste management facilities which are neither landfills nor metal recycling facilities, guidance on the nature of the information needed to support an application for a certificate of completion is set out Waste Management Paper 4 (WMP 4)[1], Waste Management Paper 26A[2] covers the information required for the surrender of landfill licences, with scrapyard and vehicle dismantling licences being discussed in WMP 4A[3]. The relevant parts of these WMPs are regarded as 'statutory guidance' under s 35(8) of the EPA 1990[4]. In respect of landfills, WMP 4[5] notes that the collation of much of the monitoring data needed to support the application should have occurred throughout the life of the site. Hence that '[t]he completion report should be the culmination of that monitoring, rather than an isolated event'.

1   Department of the Environment (1994) *The Licensing of Waste Management Facilities*, 3rd edn, 1994, HMSO, London.

2   Department of the Environment (1993) *Landfill Completion*, 1st edn, 1994, HMSO, London.
3   Department of the Environment (1995) *The Licensing of Metal Recycling Sites*, Waste Management Paper No 4A, HMSO, London, pp 57–59.
4   WMP 4, page 1; WMP 26A, page 1; WMP 4A, para 1.9: see para 8.231.
5   WMP 4, para 7.21: see also WMP 26A, para 1.13.

9.98   On receipt of a surrender application, the Waste Management Licensing Regulations 1994 place a duty on the Agency to inspect the relevant land[1]. The Agency may also request that the licence holder provide any further information or evidence necessary[2]. The criteria to be considered when the Agency is to determine an application to surrender a licence is set down in s 39(5) of the EPA 1990:

> 'The [Waste Regulation] authority shall determine whether it is likely or unlikely that the condition of the land, so far as that condition is the result of the use of the land for the treatment, keeping or disposal of waste (whether or not in pursuance of the licence), will cause pollution of the environment or harm to human health'[3].

Circular 11/94[4] suggests that such a test should be made on the basis of 'the balance of probabilities'.

1   EPA 1990, s 39(4)(a).
2   EPA 1990, s 39(4)(b).
3   EPA 1990, s 39(5): pollution of the environment and harm to human health are defined in s 29(3) and (5): see para 8.40.
4   Circular 11/94, Annex 4, para 4.52.

9.99   WMP 4 points out[1] that the criteria contained in s 39(5) allow the surrender of a licence pertaining to a contaminated site if the contamination is insufficient to cause pollution of the environment or harm to human health. It does not, therefore, require a total clean-up. In the process of making a decision on licence surrender, WMP 4 also reminds the Agency[2] to focus on contamination stemming from the activities involving the management of controlled waste, and that '[w]here possible the WRA[3] ... should discount contamination from earlier uses, unless they were in connection with the management of waste'[4]. However, this does not mean that the report is focused only on the contamination arising from when the site had the benefit of the site licence. Other activities prior to licensing can be considered, but to be relevant these must have involved controlled waste[5]. In respect of scrapyards and car dismantlers, WMP 4A goes further[6]: 'The presumption should be that, unless there is evidence to the contrary, the use that preceded the waste management or metal recycling licence was NOT itself waste management'.

1   WMP 4, para 7.5.
2   WMP 4, para 7.9.
3   Waste Regulation Authority: now the respective Agency.
4   See also WMP 4A, para 7.6–7.8; see also WMP 4A, para 7.7.
5   WMP 4, para 7.15.
6   WMP 4A, para 7.8.

9.100   For landfills, WMP 26A[1] proposes that 'completion', and hence the point where a certificate of completion can be issued:

> '... is defined as that point at which a landfill has stabilised physically, chemically and biologically to such a degree that the undisturbed contents of the site are unlikely to cause pollution of the environment or harm to human health.'

For other waste management facilities, WMP 4 suggests[2] that completion should be viewed as having occurred when the site is physically stable, 'largely free' of contamination caused by wastes, clear of deposited wastes and residues from any treatment processes and free of continuing discharges which require active site management[3].

1 WMP 26A, para 2.1.
2 WMP 4, para 7.8.
3 See, for metal recycling facilities, WMP 4A, para 7.4.

9.101 The EPA 1990 gives the Agency three months from receipt of the application to make a decision regarding licence surrender[1]. This period can be extended by written agreement between the applicant and the Agency. Subject to any such agreement, if after the end of the three-month period the Agency has neither issued the certificate of completion, nor given notice to the licence holder that the application has not been accepted the application is deemed to have been rejected. In such instances, as well as when there has been a formal rejection by the Agency, the licence holder can appeal to the Secretary of State[2].

1 EPA 1990, s 39(10).
2 EPA 1990, s 43(1)(f): see para 9.126.

9.102 When the Agency proposes to accept the surrender of a site licence, the matter must be referred to the 'appropriate planning authority'[1]. Conversely, the Agency can reject an application unilaterally if it so wishes. The planning authority has 28 days[2] from the date of receipt of the Agency's consultation in which to respond[3], unless both parties agree otherwise in writing. The Agency must consider any representations from the planning authority made within the appropriate time frame[4].

1 EPA 1990, s 39(7) (as amended by the Environment Act 1995, Sch 22, para 73(3)): the phrase 'appropriate planning authority' is defined in the EPA 1990, s 39(12) (as amended by the Environment Act 1995, Sch 22, para 73(6)): see para 8.17.
2 Amended from 21 days: the EPA 1990, s 36(10) (as amended by the Environment Act 1995, Sch 22, para 68(6)).
3 EPA 1990, s 39(11) as amended by the Environment Act 1995, Sch 22, para 73(5).
4 EPA 1990, s 39(7)(b) as amended by the Environment Act 1995, Sch 22, para 73(3).

9.103 If the Agency is satisfied that the evidence provided by the licence holder is sufficient, the application to surrender should be accepted. The Agency is required to issue a notice of determination, and a 'certificate of completion' must accompany the notice[1]. The certificate must state that the Agency is satisfied that the condition of the land is unlikely, from the use of the land for the treatment, keeping or disposal of waste, to cause pollution of the environment or harm to human health. The licence ceases to have effect when the certificate is issued[2]. WMP 4 contains the reminder that the issue of such a certificate 'does not imply that the land is suitable for development, or for any particular use'[3], all it implies is that harm to human health or pollution of the environment is considered to be unlikely to arise from the use of the site for waste disposal activities.

1 EPA 1990, s 39(9).
2 EPA 1990, s 39(9).
3 WMP 4, para 7.7; see also WMP 4A, para 7.18.

Licence surrender and insolvent companies

9.104 An area of potential difficulty in respect of licence surrender concerns companies which become insolvent. While the concept of financial provision[1] is intended to ensure that the obligations of a licensee are adequate for the purpose of the long-term subsistence of a waste management licence, it seems inevitable – particularly with the considerable post-closure after-care periods involving landfills[2] – that some licensees may well get into financial difficulties. Indeed, it also is conceivable that a licensee may declare bankruptcy as a way of attempting to circumvent the obligations of the licence.

1 See para 8.177ff.
2 See para 8.180.

9.105 In *Re Mineral Resources Ltd*[1], a liquidator of a landfill company attempted to 'disclaim' a waste management licence as 'onerous property' under s 178 of the Insolvency Act 1986. Originally, the liquidator had sought to arrange the transfer of the licence, but this had fallen through. On application by the Agency, the Divisional Court decided that the provisions of the EPA 1990 held precedence above those of creditors, on the principal grounds that public policy should not allow persons to 'walk away' from their liabilities under the EPA 1990 and that in the event of inconsistent statutory provisions, the later Act in time prevailed. This was despite finding that the licence fell within the definition of 'property' in the Insolvency Act 1986[2].

1 [1999] 1 All ER 746. This judgment is also referred to elsewhere as *Environment Agency v Stout* [1999] Env LR 407.
2 Insolvency Act 1986, s 436.

9.106 In *Re Mineral Resources Ltd*, Neuberger J highlighted a direct conflict between the Insolvency Act 1986, which allowed 'property' to be subject to disclaimer, and the EPA 1990 which required that waste management licences continued in force until formally surrendered[1]. However, in holding that the EPA 1990 was more recent and that it had tightened the earlier provisions of the Control of Pollution Act 1974[2], it was said that although both the EPA 1990 and the Insolvency Act 1986 had been respectively made to fulfil the public interests of environmental protection and the effective management of insolvent companies, the provisions on insolvency '. . . are of a less wide ranging and important nature, both in the domestic sense and in the international sense . . .'[3]. Consequently, it was held that '. . . the interests in the protection of the environment should prevail over the interest in fair and orderly winding up of companies'[4].

1 *Re Mineral Resources Ltd* [1999] 1 All ER 746 at 757A.
2 *Re Mineral Resources Ltd* [1999] 1 All ER 746 at 757C.
3 *Re Mineral Resources Ltd* [1999] 1 All ER 746 at 757G.
4 *Re Mineral Resources Ltd* [1999] 1 All ER 746 at 757H.

9.107 The *Re Mineral Resources* judgment raised concerns with insolvency practitioners, for the reason that they may be precluded from winding up a company or may themselves be potentially liable[1] under s 33 of the EPA 1990. Not surprisingly, the judgment was quickly followed by three others: *In re Wilmott Trading Ltd*[2], *In re Wilmott Trading Ltd (No 2)*[3] and *Official Receiver as Liquidator of Celtic Extraction Ltd and Bluestone Chemicals Ltd v Environmental*[4] *Agency*[5]. Like *Re Mineral Resources* itself, all three of these judgments had their origins as decisions of Neuberger J. The *Wilmott Trading* cases involved the liquidation of a scrap metal company. In the light of *Re Mineral Resources*, the first case concerned whether the existence of the waste management licence for the facility precluded the company being dissolved. Although the Divisional Court held that the licence was not a bar to company dissolution, the matter of where the obligations of the licence then lay was an issue which the court was reluctant to rule upon.

1 Despite Neuberger J's lengthy analysis of the consequences on insolvency practitioners in *Re Mineral Resources Ltd* [1999] 1 All ER 746 at 762A/C.
2 (1999) Times, 28 April.

3 [1999] 25 LS Gaz R 29.
4 Sic.
5 (14 July 1999, unreported), Ch Div.

9.108 The latter issue was developed upon in *In re Wilmott Trading (No 2)*, where it was held that – post-dissolution of a company – a waste management licence did not fall within the category of *bona vacantia*[1] under s 654 of the Companies Act 1985. Hence its obligations did not fall on the Crown and the Treasury Solicitor.

1 Unclaimed goods.

9.109 It should be apparent that these cases left the position of the waste management licence for the affected facilities extremely uncertain, particularly in the light of the formal licence transfer mechanism and other enforcement powers of the EPA 1990. However, this matter was quickly settled – but not in a way which furthered the aims of the EPA 1990 – in *Official Receiver as Liquidator of Celtic Extraction Ltd and Bluestone Chemicals Ltd v Environmental Agency*[1]. This case was heard by the Court of Appeal as an appeal against separate orders made by Neuberger J which stated that, in the light of his decision in *Re Mineral Resources*, the Official Receiver could not disclaim two waste management licences. Celtic Extraction Ltd was the licensee of a landfill and Bluestone Chemicals was involved in the storage and treatment of chemical wastes. Both were in the hands of liquidators. In the former case, the Official Receiver made investments to comply with the site's waste management licence and the company no longer had any assets. Bluestone Chemicals by contrast had debts of over £1m.

5 (14 July 1999, unreported), Ch Div.

9.110 The Court of Appeal revisited the basis of the *Re Mineral Resources* judgment[1] as to whether a waste management licence fell within the definition of 'property' in s 436 of the Insolvency Act 1986. Unless it did, it could not be disclaimed by a liquidator as 'onerous property' under s 178 of the Insolvency Act 1986[2].

1 Note that the court did not rule on the *Wilmott Trading* cases as it was not directly concerned with the points made.
2 *Celtic Extraction and Bluestone Chemicals* at para 23 of the judgment.

9.111 Like *Re Mineral Resources*, it was decided by the Court of Appeal that a licence is property under the Insolvency Act 1986, noting that precedent had given the term an extremely wide meaning. It either fell within the core meaning of 'property' or within the concept of an 'interest . . . incidental to property' as contained in the definition set out in s 436 of the Insolvency Act 1986.

9.112 The Court of Appeal then considered the matter of whether the licence could be disclaimed as onerous property under s 178 of the Insolvency Act 1986. As in *Re Mineral Resources*, the court considered whether there was an inconsistency between the Insolvency Act 1986 and the EPA 1990. Of significance to its ruling that public policy objectives did not, in fact, favour the EPA 1990 were two main issues. It was noted that if there was a dissolution of a company or the death of a licence holder, the licence would appear to be placed into a kind of legal limbo where its obligations no longer applied[1]. The presence of this anomaly went against the notion that the EPA 1990 always required waste management licences to continue irrespective of the circumstances of the licensee. More importantly, the Court of Appeal noted that Parliament had provided wordings in some other statutes to address instances where there might otherwise be a clash with the Insolvency Act 1986. Examples given were s 36 of the Coal Industry Act 1994, s 9 of the Police Pensions Act and s 91 of the Pensions Act 1995[2]. All these provisions expressly precluded stipulated assets being regarded as 'property' under the Insolvency Act 1986. It followed that, in the absence of any equivalent provision in the EPA 1990, there was no implicit public policy objective to be read into the latter which held it to stand above the Insolvency Act 1986. Hence the Court of Appeal found that a waste management licence could be disclaimed by the liquidator and that the case of *Re Mineral Resources* should be overruled.

1 *Celtic Extraction and Bluestone Chemicals* at paras 39–40, 44 of the judgment.
2 *Celtic Extraction and Bluestone Chemicals* at para 43 of the judgment.

9.113 Inevitably, the *Celtic Extraction and Bluestone Chemicals* judgment means that a change in the primary legislation is necessary to ensure that the long term purpose of the EPA 1990 is fulfilled and that liabilities of insolvent licensees do not pass onto the public purse. However, any such change in the legislation will need to seek an equitable path between this policy objective and the reality that a tightening of the EPA 1990 may preclude liquidators becoming involved with insolvent waste management companies at all. While Neuberger J made a valiant attempt at squaring these conflicting objectives in *Re Mineral Resources*[1], it would seem that his analysis did not provide adequate comfort to the insolvency industry[2]. Even though the Land-fill Directive clearly requires operators to make provision for post-closure liabilities[3], it may prove a difficult task to change the EPA 1990 in a manner which does not nega-tively affect insolvency practitioners.

1 *Re Mineral Resources Ltd* [1999] 1 All ER 746 at 762A–767A.
2 For example, while the provisions of the EPA 1990 on directors' liability (see para 7.156ff) were acknowledged as impinging upon insolvency practitioners, it was felt that the wording offers protection to a 'conscientious honest liquidator'(see *Re Mineral Resources* at 763C/D). However, there was no mention of the liquidator's liabilities under s 33 of the EPA 1990 (see Chapter 7), albeit that there may be some comfort in the statutory defences in s 33 in these circumstances (see para 7.145ff).
3 See Council Directive 99/31/EC of 26 April 1999 on the landfill of waste (OJ L182/1 16.7.1999) recital 28 and Article 13 (the Directive is briefly discussed at para 1.13).

LICENCE TRANSFER

Enacting licence transfer

9.114 Licences are transferred under the provisions of s 40 of the EPA 1990. Transfer is allowable even if the licence is suspended or partially revoked[1]. Both the holder of the licence and proposed transferee should make a joint application to the Agency which granted the licence[2]. In the case of an application for a transfer of a licence for mobile plant, the wording of s 40(2) means that the Agency which covers the original principal place of business retains the responsibility for the continued oversight of the plant.

1 EPA 1990, s 40(1).
2 EPA 1990, s 40(2).

9.115 Since 1998, an application for a licence transfer is to be made on the Agency's own forms[1]. It must be accompanied by the fee set down in the annual Waste Manage-ment Licensing (Charges) Scheme[2]. While the details of the information required for a transfer are set out in the Waste Management Licensing Regulations 1994[3], the Secre-tary of State's power to make these provisions has been removed from the EPA 1990[4]. As is the case with licence applications, the submission of false information in a licence transfer is an offence[5].

1   EPA 1990, s 40(3) (as amended by the Environment Act 1995, Sch 22, para 74 (commenced by
    SI 1998/604, reg 2)).
2   Waste Management Licensing (Charges) Scheme, published annually in England and Wales by the
    Environment Agency and by SEPA in Scotland.
3   SI 1994/1056, reg 2 and Sch 2.
4   EPA 1990, s 40(3) as amended by the Environment Act 1995, Sch 22, para 74.
5   EPA 1990, s 44(1)(b) (as amended by the Environment Act 1995, Sch 19, para 4): see para 12.209ff.

9.116   On receipt of an application for a licence transfer, the Agency must assess
whether the proposed transferee is a fit and proper person[1]. The requirements for fit
and proper status are set down in s 74 of the EPA 1990. For a licence transfer, the
assessment is the same as would be the case for an application for a waste management
licence under the EPA 1990[2].

1   EPA 1990, s 40(4).
2   See para 8.112ff.

9.117   The determination period for a transfer is two months, unless the three parties
agree otherwise[1]. If no such agreement has been made, and the Agency has neither
enacted the transfer nor opposed the application, the transfer is deemed to have been
rejected. The transferee can then appeal to the Secretary of State[2]. Circular 11/94[3]
advises the Agency to formally acknowledge the date of receipt of the application so
that all parties will be aware of the commencement of the statutory determination
period.

1   EPA 1990, s 40(6)
2   EPA 1990, s 43(1)(g): appeals are discussed at para 9.126.
3   Circular 11/94, Annex 10, para 10.19.

9.118   Transfer is effected by the Agency endorsing the licence with the name and
other particulars of the transferee as the holder of the licence. The transfer then occurs
from the date agreed with the applicants and specified in any such endorsement of the
licence[1].

1   EPA 1990, s 40(5).

9.119   The Agency needs to exercise care to ensure that the transferee does actually
have the right of occupation of the land at the time the licence is formally transferred[1].
Otherwise, the transfer may be used by the original holder as a way of circumventing
the procedures of licence surrender and hence that person's liabilities under the
licence. One way to avoid the latter problem might be to arrange that the licence will
only be transferred at the time that the deed or lease on the land subject to the licence
passes between parties. Such a mechanism appears justifiable on the grounds of the
need to satisfy the requirement of s 40(4) that the transferee is a fit and proper person.
Perhaps the most important requirement[2] is that the licence holder must be in a position to make adequate financial provision to discharge the obligations of the licence.
Clearly, without bona fide access to the land, the person would not be in a position to
discharge the obligations of the licence.

1   While s 35(2) of the EPA 1990 requires that a site licence is only *granted* to a person in occupation of
    the land, there does not appear to be an analogous requirement in s 40 in relation to licence transfer.
2   EPA 1990, s 74(3)(c).

9.120   The fee for licence transfer is currently set at £250[1]. This amount, which has
been increased from £160 since 1994[2], is ludicrously low. A licence transfer is unlikely
to be straightforward matter. There is the need to assess a transferee's credentials as a

fit and proper person and ensure that financial provision is adequate. This is particularly important given that, once transferred, the transferor is no longer bound by the liabilities contained in the licence conditions. For example, McNair[3] has estimated that the cost to a regulatory body for one licence transfer for a household waste landfill site was £2,500. Given that the Environment Agency is now responsible for the Waste Management Licensing (Charges) Scheme[4], it surprising that a strong case has not been made for Treasury approval for a substantial increase. Given the sums involved in acquisitions of waste management facilities, a considerable increase in the level of transfer fee would hardly seem a burden on business.

1   Waste Management Licensing (Charges) Scheme 1999–2000; the amount for transfers in Scotland is
    £206 (see Waste Management Charging (Scotland) Scheme 1999).
2   See the Waste Management Licensing (Fees and Charges) Scheme 1994.
3   McNair D (1994) '"Fit and Proper Person": Assessment of Adequate Financial Provision', *Waste
    Planning*, September 1994, pp 34–37.
4   Environment Act 1995, s 41.

Defining licence transfer

9.121   Licence transfer is perhaps one of the more ambiguous concepts of Part II of the EPA 1990. While detailed provisions are set down in the procedures to effect a licence transfer, the nature of a licence transfer is not defined. The latter is not unimportant, particularly where licences are to pass between bodies corporate. Given that licences are intended to continue to bind a licensee until surrender is accepted by the Agency, it is vital that licence transfers are done correctly and in a manner which does not allow licensees to withdraw from their obligations with impunity.

9.122   In some circumstances, the nature of a licence transfer will be pretty self-evident and straightforward. An example might be Person A wishing to sell a facility to Person B or where Company A sold its waste management assets to Company B. However, matters appear to get difficult where companies are taken over. An example might involve Company A being purchased by Company B and becoming a subsidiary. Company A may retain its corporate identity and even its directors. Alternatively, Company B may gain control of Company A by way of a purchase of its shares. In such circumstances, it may not be apparent to the Agency that the assets are to be, or indeed have been, transferred until the takeover happened. One further and particularly awkward example concerns companies placed in receivership[1].

1   See para 9.104.

9.123   All these examples describe possible circumstances when a licence transfer is enacted. Although in certain types of corporate takeover, the name of the licensee will remain the same, what would appear to be crucial to the EPA 1990 is the identity of the organisation which exercises ultimate control[1]. Matters of controlling interest are particularly vital to the EPA 1990 as the Agency must be in a position to ensure that the requirements of the licence continue in the long term and that the licensee remains a fit and proper person. The question of the continued making of financial provision is particularly crucial. The importance of this matter is clearly evident from the EPA 1990 itself, whereby financial provision is a prime consideration in respect of a decision on licence transfer[2].

1   However, taken to its logical conclusion, this argument does appear to disintegrate. The nature of
    'control' will vary in many larger companies from time to time, being ultimately a matter of the
    shareholding.
2   EPA 1990, s 40(4).

9.124 Moreover, the EPA 1990 envisages the Agency's advance consent to any licence transfer. Without such consent, the waste management activities of the transferee would not be lawful[1] and hence would involve possible offences under s 33 of the EPA 1990[2]. However, what is not at all clear is what is to happen when a company has been purchased by another without a formal licence transfer being enacted. Although increasingly the Agency is consulted as part of the environmental due diligence searches on a company, it may well be that the Agency may be one of the last bodies to hear about a company take-over. Given the commercial sensitivity of company acquisitions, it may not receive prior consultation, let alone a request to commence formal licence transfers on all effected waste management assets. Finally, the EPA 1990 also requires both transferee and transferor to jointly apply for a transfer[3]. In the case of a 'hostile bid' by one company on another, it seems very unlikely that a transfer will be agreed between parties. Furthermore, receivership will be, by definition, equally problematic. Although no formal transfer is undertaken in the latter circumstances – until disposed of, the company name and assets remain the same – the control of the company is moved from current management to be vested in the receiver[4].

1   EPA 1990, s 35(10).
2   See Chapter 7; in addition, users of such a facility may well be causing offences in respect of the duty of care (EPA 1990, s 34): see para 3.49ff.
3   EPA 1990, s 40(2).
4   See para 9.104.

9.125 Overall, the more detailed the examination of the nature of licence transfer, the more it becomes apparent that the concept does not sit comfortably with the realities of commercial corporate transactions. These difficulties and unanswered questions – which seem unlikely to be readily solvable – do raise serious doubt about whether the EPA 1990 is capable of fulfilling its intentions of guaranteeing that licences are adequately resourced, particularly over long time periods.

APPEALS TO THE SECRETARY OF STATE

9.126 Section 43 of the EPA 1990[1] sets down a system of appeals to the Secretary of State in relation to the granting, modification, transfer, suspension, revocation and surrender of licences[2]. These provisions are supplemented by regs 6 to 9 of the Waste Management Licensing Regulations 1994[3] and by s 53 and s 114 of the Environment Act 1995. Guidance on appeals is to be found in Annex 10 of Circular 11/94 and in the document entitled 'Waste Management Licences The Appeals Procedure'[4].

1   As amended by the Environment Act 1995, Sch 22, para 77 and Sch 24.
2   There is no appeal in relation to partial licence revocation for the non-payment of subsistence charges under s 41 of the Environment Act 1995.
3   SI 1994/1056: reg 8 is amended by SI 1996/593, reg 10(2).
4   Department of the Environment (1996) *Waste Management Licences The Appeals Procedure*, Dept of the Environment, March 1996.

9.127 Appeals are always lodged in England and Wales with the Secretary of State who, since 1 May 1996, has delegated most[1] appeals to the Planning Inspectorate[2]. The lodging of an appeal may or may not cause the Agency's decision to be lifted. Where a licence application is refused or is granted subject to specific conditions, or where an application for licence modification, surrender or transfer is refused, the Agency's decision holds until any appeal to the Secretary of State has been determined. This is also the case with licence suspension[3] and with the immediate modification of a licence by the Agency or its immediate revocation (full or partial)[4] on the grounds of preventing or minimising pollution of the environment or harm to human health[5]. In other cases, the Agency's decision on licence modification or revocation is of no effect between the time when the appeal is lodged and when it is heard by the Secretary of State[6].

1   See Department of the Environment (1996) *Waste Management Licences The Appeals Procedure*, Dept of the Environment, March 1996, Appendix 4.
2   EPA 1990, s 43(2A) (as amended by the Environment Act 1995, Sch 22, para 77) and the Environment Act 1995, s 114: see Department of the Environment (1996) *Waste Management Licences The Appeals Procedure*, Dept of the Environment, March 1996.
3   EPA 1990, s 43(5).
4   EPA 1990, s 43(6).
5   The other criteria for licence modification under the EPA 1990, s 37(2)(a), serious detriment to amenity, does not provide grounds for immediate revocation. It is not referred to in s 43(6) of that Act.
6   EPA 1990, s 43(4).

9.128   Where a waste management licence has been subject to suspension or to an immediate modification or revocation, the licence holder is entitled to both appeal against the decision[1] and seek to have the suspension (etc) lifted prior to that appeal being heard[2]. The grounds for applying to have the Agency's decision lifted are that it is unreasonable[3]. An application for compensation can also be made where the appellant's assertion of unreasonableness is upheld by the Secretary of State[4]. The aggrieved party must apply to the Secretary of State both for a determination that the Agency acted unreasonably and for compensation[5]. An application to the Secretary of State that the Agency's action is unreasonable can be made separate to, and can be acted upon prior to, the actual appeal on the modification, revocation, etc, being heard. A successful application will result in the Secretary of State staying the Agency's action prior to hearing the substance of the appeal[6]. Disputes over the level of compensation payable must be settled by arbitration[7].

1   EPA 1990, s 43(7).
2   EPA 1990, s 43(7)(a).
3   EPA 1990, s 43(7).
4   EPA 1990, s 43(7)(b).
5   EPA 1990, s 43(7).
6   EPA 1990, see s 43(7)(a) and Circular 11/94, Annex 10, para 10.14.
7   EPA 1990, s 43(7).

9.129   Much of the detail of the provisions on appeals is contained in the Waste Management Licensing Regulations 1994. An appeal to the Secretary of State is to be made by notice in writing[1]. Such a notice is required to be accompanied by the following information[2]:

  (i)   a statement of the grounds for the appeal;
 (ii)   where an application was rejected by an Agency, a copy of the application and any supporting documents;
(iii)   a copy of the waste management licence, where the appeal relates to an existing licence;
 (iv)   copies of all relevant correspondence;
  (v)   copies of other relevant documents, such as a planning permission, certificate of lawful use etc; and
 (vi)   a statement indicating whether the appellant wishes the appeal to be determined by a hearing or by written representations.

The appeal can be made on forms which are available, in the case of England and Wales, from the Planning Inspectorate in Bristol[3]. The appellant is required to ensure that copies of all of the documentation, and the notice of appeal, have been served on the Agency[4].

1 SI 1994/1056, reg 6(1).
2 SI 1994/1056, reg 6(2).
3 Department of the Environment (1996) *Waste Management Licences The Appeals Procedure*, Dept of the Environment, March 1996, para 11.
4 SI 1994/1056, reg 6(3).

9.130   An appeal must be made within six months of the date of the decision which is the subject of the appeal[1]. Alternatively, in the case where the Agency is deemed to have rejected an application by failing to make a decision, the six-month period is triggered from the date at which the decision should have been made[2]. However, the Waste Management Licensing Regulations 1994[3] allow appeals to be lodged after the end of the six-month period. The Secretary of State has discretion over whether such an appeal should take place in the light of any explanation of why it is to be heard out of time[4].

1 SI 1994/1056, reg 7(1)(a)(i).
2 SI 1994/1056, reg 7(1)(a)(ii): ie at the end of the four-month decision period set down in the EPA 1990 for licence applications (s 36(9)) or the two-month period appropriate for a licence modification (s 37(6)).
3 SI 1994/1056, reg 7(2).
4 See Circular 11/94, Annex 10, para 10.20.

9.131   If an appellant wishes to withdraw, the Secretary of State must be notified, with the notification being copied to the Agency affected[1]. An appeal which is withdrawn allows the decision of the Agency to have immediate effect from the time and date of withdrawal[2].

1 SI 1994/1056, reg 6(4).
2 EPA 1990, s 43(4).

9.132   The Secretary of State can refer any matter concerning the appeal to a person appointed by him and can direct a person appointed by him to hear and/or determine the appeal[1]. Hence the involvement of the Planning Inspectorate in England and Wales.

1 EPA 1990, s 43(2A) (whose effect is to replace s 43(2)(a) and (b), with the latter being deleted by the Environment Act 1995, Sch 24) and the Environment Act 1995, s 114.

9.133   Usually, the appeal will be heard by written representations. However, the Agency, the appellant or the Secretary of State can require that the appeal takes the form of a hearing[1]. Circular 11/94[2] sets down the procedures for appeals by way of written representations and for hearings. Where the decision is by way of written representations, the Agency is given four weeks to respond to the material submitted by the appellant which triggered the appeal[3]. Copies of the Agency's response must also be sent to the appellant. Often the material submitted by both the parties at this stage will be sufficient for the Secretary of State to determine the appeal[4].

1 EPA 1990, s 43(2)(c).
2 Circular 11/94, Annex 10, para 10.22ff; see also Department of the Environment (1996) *Waste Management Licences The Appeals Procedure*, Dept of the Environment, March 1996.
3 Department of the Environment (1996) *Waste Management Licences The Appeals Procedure*, Dept of the Environment, March 1996, para 14: Circular 11/94 (Annex 10, para 10.23) indicates that this period is 42 days (six weeks). However, according to *The Appeals Procedure* document, this is an error (see para 14).
4 Circular 11/94, Annex 10, para 10.23.

9.134   However, if further material is needed, or where the Secretary of State considers that each party should be given the opportunity to comment upon the other's submitted material, the parties will be given 28 days in which to do so. Again, the parties should send copies of their responses to each other[1].

1   Circular 11/94, Annex 10, para 10.23.

9.135   In the case of hearings, the person appointed has considerable discretion on how it is to be conducted: somewhat of a contrast to planning appeals. This extends, *inter alia*, to receiving evidence from other persons[1] besides the appellant, the Agency and affected statutory consultees[2]. A person hearing the appeal also has the discretion to hold the hearing, or any part of it, in private[3]. Full hearing statements must be available three weeks prior to the commencement of the hearing[4].

1   Circular 11/94, Annex 10, para 10.26.
2   The 'appropriate planning authority' (see the EPA 1990, s 36(11) and para 8.17), the Health and Safety Executive and, where required, the 'appropriate nature conservation body' (see the EPA 1990, s 36(7) and para 8.19).
3   EPA 1990, s 43(2)(c).
4   Department of the Environment (1996) *Waste Management Licences The Appeals Procedure*, Dept of the Environment, March 1996, para 15.

9.136   Usually, a site visit will take place, being organised by the person determining the appeal[1]. Both parties will be invited to attend. However, if it has been agreed that the appeal is to be determined in writing, no further evidence can be given or discussed at the time of the visit[2].

1   Department of the Environment (1996) *Waste Management Licences The Appeals Procedure*, Dept of the Environment, March 1996, para 13.
2   Department of the Environment (1996) *Waste Management Licences The Appeals Procedure*, Dept of the Environment, March 1996, para 14.

9.137   Where a person is appointed to conduct a hearing, a report must be made to the Secretary of State and must include conclusions or recommendations[1]. The only exception is where that person – rather than the Secretary of State – is given the power to actually make the decision on the facts of the hearing[2].

1   SI 1994/1056, reg 8 as amended by SI 1996/593, reg 10(2).
2   SI 1994/1056, reg 8 (as amended by SI 1996/593, reg 10(2)) and Environment Act 1995, s 114.

9.138   The Secretary of State or any person appointed to determine the appeal is required to notify the appellant in writing of the decision and of the reasons[1]. Where the Secretary of State undertakes to make the decision after a hearing, any report made by the person conducting the hearing is also to be sent to the appellant[2]. The Agency must receive copies of any document sent to the appellant at the time of the decision[3]. In deciding the appeal, the Secretary of State will take particular account of any matter which impinges upon the 'statutory guidance' issued under s 35(8) and s 74(5) of the EPA 1990[4]. The Agency is required to give effect to any determination of the appeal which causes a previous decision to be altered[5].

1   SI 1994/1056, reg 9(1).
2   SI 1994/1056, reg 9(2).
3   SI 1994/1056, reg 9.
4   Circular 11/94, Annex 10, para 10.3. As outlined at para 8.231, such guidance includes Waste Management Papers 4, 4A, 26A and part of Circular 11/94.
5   EPA 1990, s 43(3).

9.139   Where appeals are considered by way of written representations, each party is expected to bear their own costs[1]. This principle also generally applies in the case of hearings. However, s 53 of the Environment Act 1995 allows costs to be awarded when an appeal has been caused by the unreasonable conduct of one of the parties which has resulted in unnecessary expense being incurred[2]. Unlike proceedings in respect of planning appeals, costs do not seem able to be awarded when a party withdraws prior to the hearing[3].

1   Department of the Environment (1996) *Waste Management Licences The Appeals Procedure*, Dept of the Environment, March 1996, para 21.
2   Environment Act 1995, s 52(2) and s 250(2) to (5) of the Local Government Act 1972; and see Circular 8/93 (in Scotland, Environment Act 1995, s 53(3) and s 210(2) to (8) of the Local Government (Scotland) Act 1973).
3   See a written answer to Parliamentary Question dated 20 March 1997.

9.140   The manner by which appeals have been managed in the past has left much to be desired[1]. Indeed, this has proved to be a significant deterrent upon regulatory bodies using their immediate licence modification or revocation powers or enacting licence suspension. As noted earlier, compensation is payable if the Secretary of State considers that a regulatory body has acted unreasonably[2]. Given that appeals have traditionally been taking one to two years to be heard[3], the amount of compensation which might be payable for the loss of a licence holder's business over that period is a significant deterrent to using such powers. Although there is evidence that appeal clear-up rates have improved recently, the amount of compensation potentially payable over even six months for a busy waste management site still places a constraint upon the widespread use of these powers by the Agency.

1   For example, Macrory has pointed out that the two-year period of one appeal constituted a comparable length of time to that taken by Sir Frank Layfield to produce his report on the acceptability of the Sizewell nuclear power station (see Macrory R (1987) 'Waste Disposal Licences and Appeals', *ENDS Report*, August 1987).
2   EPA 1990, s 43(7).
3   See for example, *ENDS Report* 231, April 1994, p 33, *ENDS Report*, January 1990, p 25 and see the then junior Minister, David Trippier's, comments in the Commons Committee stage of the Environmental Protection Bill (Official Report of Standing Committee H, Column 504, paragraph 6).

9.141   In addition, the fact that a licence may be subject to appeal may cause undesirable uncertainty to a licence holder. In *R v Secretary of State for the Environment, ex p Land Reclamation Co Ltd*[1], an order of mandamus was served upon the Secretary of State by an appellant. The order, which was granted, required that an appeal over the modification of a licence condition had to be heard by a date set down by the court.

1   (7 March 1983, unreported).

CHARGES FOR WASTE MANAGEMENT LICENCES

9.142   For the year 1999/2000, the Environment Agency is expecting to receive an income of £23 million[1] from licensees and licence applicants[2]. This sum is collected through s 41 of the Environment Act 1995[3], which allows the Agency to devise a statutory charging scheme. Charges are payable for licence applications, modifications, transfers and licence surrender under the EPA 1990[4]. Each Agency has the devolved responsibility for the production of annual licensing and other charges schemes[5], and accordingly, in England and Wales, this is published by the Environment Agency as the Waste Management Licensing (Charges) Scheme for the particular financial year[6]. Such a scheme needs the prior approval of the Secretary of State[7] and the consent of the Treasury[8]. Before its annual publication, the scheme must also be brought to the attention of persons likely to be affected by it[9]. The Secretary of State must consider representations from affected parties[10] and must have regard to the desirability that the amounts covered by the scheme relate directly to the costs of the Agency in the carrying out of its specified function[11].

1 The figure excludes Scotland and Northern Ireland.
2 Environment Agency (1998) *Environment Agency Corporate Plan 1999–2000 Our Forward Look to 2002*, Environment Agency, Bristol, Figure 8.9. The roughly equivalent figure for SEPA is £2.6m (SEPA (1999) *Corporate Plan 1999–2000*, SEPA, Stirling).
3 EPA 1990, s 41 was deleted by the Environment Act 1995: see Sch 22, para 75.
4 Environment Act 1995, s 41(2).
5 Environment Act 1995, s 41(3).
6 In Scotland, the Waste Management Charging (Scotland) Scheme 1999.
7 Environment Act 1995, s 41(9).
8 Environment Act 1995, s 42(7).
9 Environment Act 1995, s 42(1).
10 Environment Act 1995, s 42(2)(a).
11 Environment Act 1995, s 42(2)(b) and (3).

9.143 The Scheme for 1999–2000 covers both annual subsistence charges for licences, as well as charges to cover the Agency's costs of processing applications for licences, their modification, transfer and surrender. Such sums are supposedly set at the level which covers the inspection and administrative costs of the Agency for each licensed site.

9.144 Since the annual Charging Schemes were commenced in 1994, there has been a succession of variations, often involving clarification where ambiguity has arisen. Such clarification is contained in the detailed rules of the scheme for the particular year. Given that both the actual levels of charges, and also the rules by which they are levied, is altered yearly, reference should be made to the scheme for the particular financial year for an exact account.

9.145 As noted at paras 9.28 and 9.49 above, should the licence holder fail to pay the annual subsistence charge, the Agency can partially revoke or suspend a licence[1]. However, Circular 11/94 advises regulatory bodies[2] that:

'. . . [b]efore taking steps to revoke a licence under this section, the authority should give the licensee a reasonable opportunity to make good his failure to pay the subsistence charge,'

Besides the option of partial licence revocation, the monies outstanding can also be recovered as a debt.

1 Environment Act 1995, s 41(6).
2 Circular 11/94, Annex 4, para 4.58.

9.146 It should be emphasised that the system of charges is not intended to finance the Agency for the entirety of its waste regulation duties. It only covers its costs for such matters as licence applications, modifications and also charges for the subsistence of licences[1]. Other costs, such as for the enforcement action on unauthorised tipping, are met through central government funding.

1 Special waste (see para 4.69) and transfrontier waste shipment (see para 5.100) notifications, along with controlled waste carrier (see para 6.52), broker (see para 6.52) and metal recycling facility (see para 11.90) registrations are also subject to separate charges.

Chapter 10

Exemptions and exclusions from waste management licensing

INTRODUCTION

10.01 Chapter 1 has indicated that transactions involving substances defined as wastes are highly commonplace, very diverse and have varying potential environmental impacts. Given the richness of the variety of these transactions, coupled with the minimal environmental impact of a significant minority, it is not surprising that policymakers have deemed that certain disposal or recovery activities should not fall within the full rigidity of the waste management licensing system.

10.02 The system of exclusions and exemptions from licensing was enacted early on with the implementation of the Control of Pollution Act 1974. Since then there has been an observable trend for refinement[1], culminating in the Waste Management Licensing Regulations 1994[2] and, a year later, exemptions for metal recycling facilities in the Waste Management Licensing (Amendment etc) Regulations 1995[3]. Explanation of the current general exclusion and exemption system forms an extensive component of Circular 11/94[4], whilst a further Circular was issued in respect of exempt metal reclamation sites[5]. Although the Directive on Waste[6] also sets out a system whereby specified waste recovery activities can be subject to registrations as opposed to full permitting, it should be noted that the original British system of exemptions pre-dates the Directive's provisions by a number of years.

1   Exemptions from waste disposal site licensing under the Control of Pollution Act 1974 stemmed principally from the Control of Pollution (Licensing of Waste Disposal) Regulations 1976 (SI 1976/732; in Scotland, the Control of Pollution (Licensing of Waste Disposal) (Scotland) Regulations 1977 (SI 1977/2006)). Subsequently the 1976 Regulations were repealed and principally replaced by the Collection and Disposal of Waste Regulations 1988 (SI 1988/819) for England and Wales. In Scotland, the 1977 Regulations were instead amended by the Control of Pollution (Licensing of Waste Disposal) (Scotland) Amendment Regulations 1992 (SI 1992/1368).
2   SI 1994/1056, reg 17 and Sch 3, as amended by SI 1995/288, SI 1996/972 and SI 1998/606. The Waste Management Licensing Regulations 1994 also have application in Scotland.
3   SI 1995/288.
4   Department of the Environment (1994) *Environmental Protection Act 1990: Part II Waste on Land The Framework Directive on Waste*, Circular 11/94, HMSO, London, Annex 5 and 6.
5   Department of the Environment (1995) *Environmental Protection Act 1990: Part II Waste on Land The Framework Directive on Waste*, Circular 6/95, HMSO, London, paras 1 to 18 and Annex 1.
6   Council Directive of 15 July 1975 on Waste (75/442/EEC), (OJ L194/39 25.7.75) (as amended by Council Directive of 18 March 1991 amending Directive 75/442/EEC on Waste (91/156/EEC) (OJ L78/32 26.3.91) Article 11).

10.03 In certain cases, the wording of the exemptions continued throughout the three generations of British regulations. However, the number of paragraphs of exemptions contained in the Waste Management Licensing Regulations 1994 – 45 – is over double that found in the earlier statutory instruments. This was a direct result of the implementation of s 34 of the EPA 1990 and the duty of care. The concept of the duty of care inevitably raised questions to be raised about the legal status of certain activities with respect to the need to be licensed. Many of these activities were small-scale, and a significant number had little potential to cause environmental damage. They were often unknown to, or ignored by, the regulatory authority in whose functional area they were situated. However, s 34 of the EPA 1990 sets out the statutory requirement that a transferor of waste should verify the transferee's compliance with such matters as carrier registration and the EPA 1990's provisions[1]. This required the clarification of the legal status of many of these activities. To comply legitimately with the duty of care, all destinations for waste had to fall within the definition of 'authorised persons'[2]. Hence there was a need to set up a system which embraced many of the hitherto more environmentally trivial activities in a manner which satisfied the requirements of s 34 of the EPA 1990, but which was also much simpler than waste management licensing. For the financial year 1997/98, there were 28,541 facilities[3] in England and Wales subject to the exemptions described in this chapter[4].

1   See Chapter 3.
2   EPA 1990, s 34(1)(c)(i): see para 3.49ff.
3   This figure excludes metal recycling facilities.
4   Environment Agency (1998) *1997–98 Annual Report and Accounts*, Environment Agency, Bristol, Appendix 5: SEPA's Annual Report does not give figures in respect of Scotland.

10.04   In parallel to the increase in the number of exemptions, there was also a need to condense the responsibilities of regulatory bodies in order to avoid overlaps and duplication. As its name suggests, this was a theme of the system of Integrated Pollution Control (IPC), instigated by Part 1 of the EPA 1990. Prior to the implementation of the IPC regime, for example, the environmental implications of a major chemical waste incinerator were subject to at least three regulatory interests[1]. Inevitably, there was potential for the luckless operator to be subject to conflicting regulatory requirements[2]. The result was that, along with the system of exemptions, a parallel set of exclusions was also enacted by the Waste Management Licensing Regulations 1994[3]. The latter excluded certain activities entirely from the licensing requirements of Part II of the EPA 1990[4].

1   Air pollution was overseen by the then Industrial Air Pollution Inspectorate; aquatic discharges policed by the Regional Water Authority; the storage of wastes supervised by the then Waste Disposal Authority.
2   This matter was, of course, later addressed once more by the formation of the Environment Agency itself.
3   SI 1994/1056, reg 16 as amended by SI 1995/288, reg 3(4).
4   A further method used to exclude activities from the requirements of the EPA 1990 is to hold that certain wastes are not to be defined as 'controlled wastes' in specified circumstances: see para 2.219.

10.05   The remainder of this chapter will use the dual terminology outlined above. Exclusions emanate from reg 16 of the Waste Management Licensing Regulations 1994[1] and cover facilities which are subject to the provisions of other control regimes such as IPC. In this instance the principal offence under s 33 of the EPA 1990 does not apply at all[2]. Exemptions from waste management licences stem from reg 17 of the Waste Management Licensing Regulations 1994[3] and refer to instances when the offence provisions of s 33 of the EPA 1990 are partially disapplied[4]. The proviso in this instance is that the operation subject to the exemption accords with the particular terms set out in reg 17 and in Schedule 3 to the Waste Management Licensing Regulations 1994.

1   SI 1994/1056 as amended by SI 1995/288, reg 3(4).
2   See the EPA 1990, s 33(3) and SI 1994/1056, reg 16(1) (as amended by SI 1995/288, reg 3(4)).
3   SI 1994/1056 as amended by SI 1995/288, reg 3(5) and 3(6) and SI 1996/972, Sch 3.
4   EPA 1990, s 33(1)(a) and (b) are disapplied, but not s 33(1)(c).

10.06   This chapter will continue with a discussion of the relationship between the exclusions and exemptions contained in the Waste Management Licensing

Regulations 1994 and the Directive on Waste[1] and will then set out the requirements for registration and the manner by which enforcement can occur at exempt waste management facilities. A description of the exemptions themselves follows. However, the somewhat different system for exemptions which relate to metal reclamation facilities will be discussed separately in the next chapter.

1   Council Directive of 15 July 1975 on Waste (75/442/EEC) (OJ L194/39 25.7.75) (as amended by
    Council Directive of 18 March 1991 amending Directive 75/442/EEC on Waste (91/156/EEC)
    (OJ L78/32 26.3.91)).

THE RELATIONSHIP WITH THE DIRECTIVE ON WASTE

10.07   Up to the time the Directive on Waste[1] was amended in 1991, there was no leeway in the general requirement[2] that all waste management facilities subject to the Directive needed to possess permits. This was made clear by the European Court of Justice in *Ministère Public v Oscar Traen*[3]. It was determined that the one-off land-spreading of waste fell within the terms of the Directive and, given that the only option then available was to require the activity be subject to formal permitting, the court held accordingly.

1   Council Directive of 15 July 1975 on Waste (75/442/EEC) (OJ L194/39 25.7.75) (subsequently
    amended by Council Directive of 18 March 1991 amending Directive 75/442/EEC on Waste
    (91/156/EEC) (OJ L78/32 26.3.91)).
2   Council Directive of 15 July 1975 on Waste (75/442/EEC), (OJ L194/39 25.7.75) Article 8 (in the
    unamended Directive).
3   [1988] 3 CMLR 511.

10.08   Given that the Directive's permitting system was a rather heavy-handed way of authorising small-scale or one-off activities, a system of registration for specified waste management activities was introduced when the amendments[1] to the Directive were enacted in 1993. The result was a new Article 11 of the Directive, which allowed a member state the option of lifting the general requirement for permits in two stipulated circumstances. Both relate to activities which involve either the carrying out of 'their own waste disposal at the place of production' or the carrying out of 'recovery'. The term 'recovery' is defined by way of the list in Annex IIB as set out in Table 2.3 in Chapter 2. What should be noted is that, in contrast to recovery, the Directive holds that disposal activities[2] situated away from the place of waste production can only be subject to permits. Exemptions cannot be applied in this instance.

1   Council Directive of 18 March 1991 amending Directive 75/442/EEC on Waste (91/156/EEC)
    (OJ L78/32 26.3.91).
2   As defined by Annex IIA of the Directive on Waste (as amended by Commission Decision of 24 May
    1996 adapting Annexes IIA and IIB to Council Directive 75/442/EEC on Waste (OJ L135/32 6.6.96)):
    see Table 2.2 in Chapter 2.

10.09   For those activities involving either disposal at the place of production or waste recovery, Article 11 of the Directive on Waste requires member states to lay down 'general rules' on the types and quantities of waste 'and the conditions under which the activity in question may be exempted from the permit requirements'[1]. The nature of the activity covered by such general rules is also required to be compatible to the objectives of Article 4 of the Directive: namely that wastes are not disposed of or recovered in a manner which endangers human health or harms the environment. Finally, the Directive requires that establishments or undertakings which are subject to these general rules should register with the competent authority[2].

1   Council Directive of 15 July 1975 on Waste (75/442/EEC), (OJ L194/39 25.7.75) (as amended by
     Council Directive of 18 March 1991 amending Directive 75/442/EEC on Waste (91/156/EEC)
     (OJ L78/32 26.3.91) Article 11(1): discussed in *Inter-Environnement Wallonie ASBL v Region
     Wallone* [1998] Env LR 623.
2   Council Directive of 15 July 1975 on Waste (75/442/EEC), (OJ L194/39 25.7.75) (as amended by
     Council Directive of 18 March 1991 amending Directive 75/442/EEC on Waste (91/156/EEC)
     (OJ L78/32 26.3.91)) Article 11(2).

10.10   The Directive on Hazardous Waste[1] provides an additional constraint on the
scope of permissible disposal activities at the site of waste production. Where
hazardous wastes are involved, the derogation contained in the Directive on Waste in
respect of the need to hold permits does not apply to persons 'who carry out their own
waste disposal' at the place of production. The manner by which this term is to be
understood is not well explained in the Directive. It would appear to require that all
disposal activities listed in the Directive on Waste require permits when they occur on
the producer's premises and when hazardous waste is involved. However, this requirement excludes the storage of hazardous waste pending collection, given that this operation is explicitly left off the list of disposal activities contained in Annex IIA of the
Directive[2].

1   Council Directive of 12 December 1991 on Hazardous Waste (91/689/EEC) (OJ L377/20),
     Article 3(1).
2   See Council Directive of 15 July 1975 on Waste (75/442/EEC), (OJ L194/39 25.7.75) (as amended by
     Council Directive of 18 March 1991 amending Directive 75/442/EEC on Waste (91/156/EEC)
     (OJ L78/32 26.3.91) and by Commission Decision of 24 May 1996 adapting Annexes IIA and IIB to
     Council Directive 75/442/EEC on Waste (OJ L135/32 6.6.96)), Annex IIA, Item D15: see Table 2.2 in
     Chapter 2.

10.11   Obviously, the Directive on Waste's delineation between activities which can
be subject to permits or registrations provided a major constraint on the British legislators' ability to draft exemptions. Off-site disposal activities – as defined in Annex IIA
to the Directive – cannot be subject to exemptions[1]. Accordingly, the system of exemptions from waste management licences does mainly concentrate on recovery activities.
As waste storage may fall within the definition of a recovery activity[2], the exemptions
include waste storage prior to later recovery. However, outside the provisions of the
Directive, Circular 11/94 claims that other exemptions can be granted where the
Directive on Waste is silent on the particular matter[3]. An example is wastes produced
on the premises which are being stored awaiting collection – this circumstance fits in
neither Annex IIA nor Annex IIB to the Directive[4].

1   However, there are a small number of activities subject to the exemption system which appear to be
     closer to disposal than to recovery. As is discussed later in this chapter (see, for example, para 10.82),
     it appears to be questionable whether the particular provisions are completely in accordance with
     European Community law. In addition, not all exemptions contain quantity limits despite these being
     a requirement of Article 11 of the Directive.
2   Directive on Waste Annex IIB (as amended by Commission Decision of 24 May 1996 adapting
     Annexes IIA and IIB to Council Directive 75/442/EEC on Waste (OJ L135/32 6.6.96)), Item R13: see
     Table 2.3 in Chapter 2.
3   See Circular 11/94, Annex 5, para 5.10.
4   See Directive on Waste (as amended by Commission Decision of 24 May 1996 adapting Annexes IIA
     and IIB to Council Directive 75/442/EEC on Waste (OJ L135/32 6.6.96)) Annex IIA, Item D15 and
     Annex IIB, Item R13.

10.12   Finally, it should be appreciated that the Directive on Waste leaves member
states with discretion as to the manner by which its requirements are to be achieved. A
variety of different types of authorisation will therefore fulfil the provisions of the
Directive in respect of permits and registrations, as long as they comply with the

provisions contained in the relevant Articles of the Directive itself. As will be seen, the British provisions utilise a range of mechanisms for this purpose, which include integrated pollution control authorisations, water discharge consents and sea disposal licences, as well as waste management licences and the exemptions set out in Schedule 3 to the Waste Management Licensing Regulations 1994.

EXCLUSIONS FROM WASTE MANAGEMENT LICENSING FOR ACTIVITIES COVERED BY PART 1 OF THE EPA 1990 AND OTHER CONTROL REGIMES

10.13   Certain waste disposal or recovery activities are subject to control by legislation other than Part II of the EPA 1990. To avoid a duplication of controls, reg 16(1)[1] of the Waste Management Licensing Regulations 1994 entirely disapplies the offence provisions of s 33(1)(a), (b) and (c) of the EPA 1990 where such a facility satisfies the requirements of a separate environmental control regime, and therefore no waste management licence is needed. However to ensure compliance with the Directive on Waste[2], certain of these sites are required to keep records under Schedule 4 to the Waste Management Licensing Regulations 1994[3] and follow the Directive's 'relevant objectives'[4].

1   SI 1994/1056, reg 16(1) as amended by SI 1995/288, reg 3(4).
2   Council Directive of 15 July 1975 on Waste (75/442/EEC), (OJ L194/39 25.7.75) (as amended by Council Directive of 18 March 1991 amending Directive 75/442/EEC on Waste (91/156/EEC) (OJ L78/32 26.3.91)) Articles 4, 9 and 14.
3   SI 1994/1056, Sch 4, para 14.
4   SI 1994/1056, reg 17(4) and Sch 4(1)(a). Relevant objectives are discussed at paras 8.50ff and 12.13ff: in respect of their relationship to IPC facilities, see *R v Environment Agency and Redland Aggregates Ltd, ex p Gibson* [1999] Env LR 73.

Facilities subject to IPC[1]

10.14   The first type of separate control regime subject to the exclusions in the Waste Management Licensing Regulations 1994 is Integrated Pollution Control (IPC) under Part 1 of the EPA 1990. All of the industrial activities covered by IPC require an authorisation under s 6 of the EPA 1990. The full listing of the activities covered is contained in Schedule 1 to the Environmental Protection (Prescribed Processes and Substances) Regulations 1991[2]. The Schedule is divided up into sections which correspond to each major type of industrial activity, and each section is sub-divided into 'Part A' and 'Part B' lists of processes. Part A activities are regulated by the Environment Agency. Examples include hazardous waste incineration plants and solvent recovery facilities. Part B processes are those other activities which in England and Wales[3] are designated for control by the local authority[4]. Such activities are generally those that have a lower, or more localised, pollution potential; an example might be a pet crematorium.

1   As discussed at para 1.93ff of the system of IPC is due for major change in Autumn 1999, with the commencement of the Pollution Prevention and Control Act 1999. No doubt amendments will be made to set out exclusions from the EPA 1990 to that Act.
2   SI 1991/472, as amended by SI 1991/836, SI 1992/614, SI 1993/1749, SI 1993/2405, SI 1994/1271, SI 1994/1329, SI 1995/3247, SI 1996/2678 and SI 1998/767.
3   In Scotland, they are also the responsibility of the Scottish Environment Protection Agency.
4   See para 1.68.

10.15   Those Part A processes involving recovery or disposal of waste are expressly excluded from Part II of the EPA 1990 by reg 16(1)(a) of the Waste Management Licensing Regulations 1994. This extends to instances where the activity involves the 'deposit in or on land' of waste[1]. However, the latter refers only to temporary storage[2], for the reason that the IPC regime cannot address instances where the final deposit of waste in or on land occurs[3]. In addition, it should be emphasised that reg 16 only disapplies the offence provisions of s 33 of the EPA 1990. The duty of care, and the statutory requirements for transfer notes or for special waste notifications for wastes delivered to such plants still apply.

1   SI 1994/1056, reg 16(1) as amended by SI 1995/288, reg 3(4).
2   Para 7.16ff notes that the word 'deposit' can include the temporary setting down of waste.
3   SI 1994/1056, reg 16(2) and see the EPA 1990, s 28(1) as amended by the Environment Act 1995, Sch 22, para 61.

10.16   One of the most important waste management activities that is outside the scope of waste management licensing under Part II of the EPA 1990 is waste incineration. Such plants are included within Section 5.1 of the Environmental Protection (Prescribed Substances and Processes) Regulations 1991[1] and Parts A and B of Section 5.1 are shown in Table 10.1. It can be seen that the Agency deals with hazardous waste incinerators and other waste incinerators of over 1 tonne per hour capacity, while, in England and Wales[2], the local authority controls the air emission aspects of those that have a capacity of between 50 kgs and 1,000 kgs per hour. For those incinerators which have a capacity of less than 50 kgs per hour, the Agency is the main controlling body. In the latter case, a waste management licence may be required, unless the process features as one of the exemptions from waste management licensing contained in Schedule 3 to the Waste Management Licensing Regulations 1994. These exemptions are discussed at para 10.216ff.

1   SI 1991/472, as amended by SI 1992/614, reg 2, Sch 1, para 9(a) and (b); SI 1994/1271, reg 3, Sch 1, para 8 and reg 4(3), Sch 3, para 33, SI 1998/767, reg 2.
2   In Scotland, SEPA covers Part B processes as well.

Table 10.1

Environmental Protection (Prescribed Processes and Substances) Regulations 1991

Section 5.1 Incineration[1]

Part A
(a) The destruction by burning in an incinerator of any waste[2] chemicals or waste plastic arising from the manufacture of a chemical or the manufacture of a plastic;
(b) the destruction by burning in an incinerator, other than incidentally in the course of burning other waste, of any chemicals being, or comprising in elemental or compound form, of any of the following –
　　　bromine, cadmium, chlorine, fluorine, iodine, lead, mercury, nitrogen, phosphorous, sulphur or zinc;
(bb) the incineration of hazardous waste[3] in an incineration plant[4], other than in an exempt hazardous waste incineration plant[5];
(c) the destruction by burning of any other waste, including animal remains, otherwise than by a process related to and carried on as part of a Part B process, on premises where there is plant designed to incinerate such waste at a rate of 1 tonne or more per hour;
(d) the cleaning for reuse of metal containers used for the transport or storage of a chemical by burning out their residual content.

Part B
(a) The destruction by burning in any incinerator other than an exempt incinerator[6] of any waste, including animal remains, except where related to a Part A process;
(b) the cremation of human remains.

1   SI 1991/472, Sch 1, Section 5.1, as amended by SI 1992/614, reg 2, Sch 1, para 9(a) and (b); SI
    1994/1271, reg 3, Sch 1, para 8 and reg 4(3), Sch 3, para 33; SI 1998/767, reg 2(2).
2   'Waste' means solid, liquid or gaseous wastes (other than gas produced by biological degradation of
    waste).
3   'Hazardous waste' means solid or liquid waste which is covered by the Hazardous Waste Directive
    (91/689), excepting:
    (a)   combustible liquid wastes, including waste oil (provided that they do not contain significant
          quantities of PCBs or pentachlorinated phenol or do not contain constituents which cause the
          'relevant objectives' of the Directive on Waste (see paras 8.50ff and 12.13ff) to be breached or
          have a net calorific value in excess of 30 MJ per kg);
    (b)   combustible liquid wastes which, after combustion, result in emissions equivalent to the
          emissions from the combustion of primary gas oil;
    (c)   hazardous waste from on-board incineration on off-shore gas or oil platforms;
    (d)   municipal waste within the meaning of the two municipal waste incineration directives (89/369
          and 89/429);
    (e)   sewage sludge from municipal waste water treatment which is not hazardous under the
          Hazardous Waste Directive and which does not cause the 'relevant objectives' of the Directive on
          Waste to be breached.
4   'Incineration of hazardous waste in an incineration plant' means incineration of hazardous wastes by
    oxidation, with or without heat recovery, as well as pyrolysis or other thermal treatment processes and
    includes the incineration of hazardous waste as a fuel for an industrial process.
5   An 'exempt hazardous waste incineration plant' means an incinerator for (a) carcasses or animal
    remains, (b) for infectious clinical waste, provided such waste only has property C35 (infectious
    substances) and no other hazardous constituent listed on Annex II of the Hazardous Waste Directive
    (91/689) (an example might be pharmaceutical or veterinary compounds), (c) municipal wastes,
    where such an incinerator is used for burning infectious clinical waste (but where the clinical waste is
    not mixed with other wastes which have hazardous properties other than H9 (infectious) in Annex III
    of Directive 91/689).
6   An 'exempt incinerator' means any incinerator on premises where there is plant designed to incinerate
    waste, including animal remains at a rate of not more than 50 kgs per hour, not being an incinerator
    employed to incinerate clinical waste, sewage sludge, sewage screenings or municipal waste (as
    defined in Article 1 of EC Directive 89/369/EEC); and for the purposes of this section, the weight of
    waste is determined by reference to its weight as fed into the incinerator. Clinical waste in this
    context is given the same meaning as in reg 1 of the Controlled Waste Regulations 1992
    (SI 1992/588: see para 2.210), except that waste consisting wholly of animal remains is excluded.
    However, for the purposes only of SI 1991/472, clinical waste from farms and mines and quarries
    (which in SI 1992/588 is excluded by reg 1(4)) falls within this definition.

10.17   While all the processes covered by Part A of the Environmental Protection
(Prescribed Processes and Substances) Regulations 1991 are the responsibility of the
Agency, smaller incinerators which are Part B processes are jointly regulated in
England and Wales with the local authority[1]. The local control system through Part B
does not address those environmental impacts of the process that do not involve air
pollution. The other potential impacts, such as possible land contamination from plant
operations, are subject to waste management licensing and are the responsibility of the
Agency[2].

1   See SI 1994/1056, reg 16(1)(b): however, Part B processes in Scotland are entirely regulated by
    SEPA.
2   SI 1994/1056, reg 16(2); see also SI 1994/1056, Sch 4, para 2(3).

Disposal of liquid wastes under discharge consents

10.18   Besides those facilities subject to IPC, reg 16 of the Waste Management
Licensing Regulations 1994 also excludes the disposal of 'liquid waste'[1] where it is
subject to a consent issued under Chapter II of Part III of the Water Resources Act
1991 or under Part II of the Control of Pollution Act 1974[2]. It should be noted that the
discharge of liquid waste to a sewer which is subject instead to trade effluent consent
under Part IV of the Water Industry Act 1991 is not subject to this provision.

1 Discharges of industrial wastes to the sewers are claimed by Circular 11/94 not to be Directive
   wastes: see Circular 11/94, Annex 1, para 1.17(d) and see also para 2.62.
2 SI 1994/1056, reg 16(1)(c).

Sea disposal

10.19 Further exclusions from Part II of the EPA 1990 are countenanced in the Waste
Management Licensing Regulations 1994 where the 'recovery or disposal' of waste is
subject to a sea disposal licence issued under Part II of the Food and Environmental
Protection Act 1985. A similar exclusion pertains to those sea disposal sites which do
not require a licence but are described by an order made under s 7 of the Food and
Environmental Protection Act 1985[1]. The Deposits at Sea (Exemptions) Order[2] lists a
series of more minor activities which, *inter alia*, involve the deposit of waste on the
foreshore for construction or land reclamation purposes[3].

1 SI 1994/1056, reg 16(1)(d).
2 SI 1985/1699, as amended by SI 1994/1056, reg 21.
3 The definition of 'land' under the EPA 1990 (s 29(8)) and 'sea' under the Food and Environmental
   Protection Act 1985 (s 24) overlap (see para 7.45). Therefore, to be exempt from licensing under
   either of the Acts, an activity which straddles the foreshore must satisfy the requirements of the
   exemptions contained in both the Waste Management Licensing Regulations 1994 and the Deposits at
   Sea (Exemptions) Order 1985.

EXEMPTIONS FROM WASTE MANAGEMENT LICENCES

10.20 As well as the system of exclusions described above, there is a very extensive
series of exemptions contained in the Waste Management Licensing Regulations 1994.
These are set out in Schedule 3 to the Regulations, which was subsequently considerably extended in respect of exempt metal reclamation facilities by the Waste Management Licensing (Amendment etc) Regulations 1995[1]. Other amendments have been
made since then, principally by the Special Waste Regulations 1996[2].

1 SI 1995/288.
2 SI 1996/972, Sch 3.

10.21 In response to both Article 11 of the Directive on Waste and the former
government's ethos for deregulation, the exempt activities in Schedule 3 to the Waste
Management Licensing Regulations 1994 are typically subject to a low level of technical and administrative requirements. However, metal recycling sites such as scrapyards are treated somewhat differently[1].

1 See Chapter 11.

'Establishments and undertakings'

10.22 The Department of the Environment in Circular 11/94[1] makes much of the fact
that the Directive on Waste applies solely to 'establishments or undertakings'[2]. The
latter is the phrase utilised in the Directive, particularly in respect of Articles 9 and 10
which cover the requirements for permits. 'Establishments and undertakings' are
viewed by the Circular as quite distinct from the concept of individuals. The implication is that individuals do not need to register their exempt waste management activities.

1 See in particular Circular 11/94, Annex 5, para 5.10; see also Circular 6/95, para 1.4 and Circular
   11/94, para 8.11 (regarding establishments and undertakings and broker registration).
2 See SI 1994/1056, reg 18(1) as amended by SI 1995/288, reg 3(7).

10.23 However, there seems to be some doubt as to whether the Circular 11/94's distinction between establishments or undertakings and individuals is of merit. It would appear from European case law that anybody – even single employees such as office cleaners[1] and self-employed performing artistes[2] – may fall within the concept of an establishment or undertaking when they are acting in a commercial capacity. The only time when a person is not subject to that definition is when they are acting privately. Indeed, the Circular itself considers that an establishment and undertaking includes[3]:

'. . . any organisation, whether a company, partnership, authority, society, trust, club, charity or other organisation, but not private individuals.'

Even if the reference to establishments and undertakings was not contained in the Waste Management Licensing Regulations 1994, it is somewhat difficult to see many instances when individuals acting in their private capacity would need appropriate waste management licensing exemptions anyway. For example, the EPA 1990 itself holds that householders disposing of waste on their properties are already generally outside the scope of the principal offence in s 33 of the EPA 1990[4]. Overall, it would seem that Circular 11/94 is making a distinction of little practical relevance.

1　See *Christel Schmidt v Spar- und Leihkasse der früheren Amter Bordesholm, Kiel und Cronshagen* [1994] ECR I-1311.
2　See *Re Unitel Film- und Fernseh-Produktionsgesellschaft mbH & Co* [1978] 3 CMLR 306; see also *Gottfried Reuter v BASF AG* [1976] 2 CMLR D44 at para 35 .
3　Circular 11/94, Annex 6, para 6.19.
4　See EPA 1990, s 33(2) and para 7.04. An exception would seem to be the highly trivial instance when a deceased pet needs to be buried on the householder's premises. Being clinical waste (defined in SI 1992/588, reg 1(2)), such waste would not fall within s 33(2) of the EPA 1990, as that section only allows for the lifting of the offence provisions of s 33 in the case of household waste. Clinical waste is always industrial waste (see SI 1992/588, reg 3(1) and see para 2.210). Another example would concern waste from peat extraction activities generated by householders (see para 10.254).

Registration of exempt activities

10.24 The Waste Management Licensing Regulations 1994 take a somewhat tokenist approach to the Directive on Waste's requirements on the registration of exempt activities. With the exception of scrap metal recovery and vehicle dismantling facilities[1], 31 December 1994 was the final registration date for all existing activities claiming to be exempt from waste management licensing[2]. However, the requirements for registration apply only when the activity features in Annexes IIA and IIB of the Directive[3]. If they do not so feature, there is no need to register. In practice, this will mean that only the exempt waste management activities which are set down in stipulated paragraphs of Schedule 3 to the Waste Management Licensing Regulations 1994[4] will need to register. However, if not so registered, they will be subject to a fine of only £10 on summary conviction[5].

1　See Chapter 11.
2　SI 1994/1056, reg 18(1) as amended by SI 1995/288, reg 3(8).
3　See SI 1994/1056, regs 1(3) and 18(1) (as amended by SI 1995/288, reg 3(8)) and the reference to 'recovery or disposal'. See also Circular 11/94, Annex 6, para 6.20.
4　According to Circular 11/94 (Annex 6, para 6.21), these are paras 1–35, 38 and 39 of Sch 3: metal recovery facilities are discussed in Chapter 11.
5　SI 1994/1056, reg 18(6) as amended by SI 1995/288, reg 3(11) (originally the fine was £500 – level 2 on the standard scale).

10.25 In addition to the very low level of penalty, there are no grounds for refusing a registration, no fees to pay to the Agency, registration certificates are not issued and, once granted, a registration is indefinite[1]. This arrangement is in stark contrast to the requirements for registration of, for example, controlled waste carriers.

1   See Circular 11/94, Annex 6, para 6.5.

10.26   The Agency has a duty to establish a register of exempt activities[1]. Unlike waste carrier registration[2], the registration for exempt activities must relate to an individual site and be with the Agency responsible for the area where the activity takes place. So a major company will need to possess registrations for all the locations where its exempt activities are occurring.

1   SI 1994/1056, reg 18(2): registers are discussed at para 13.39ff.
2   See Chapter 6.

10.27   The nature and content of the register is set down in reg 18 of the Waste Management Licensing Regulations 1994[1]. These requirements are discussed alongside the other provisions on registers for waste management facilities at para 13.39ff. As is the case with the other registers held by the Agency, the exemption register is open to public inspection and copies of it can be supplied on request[2].

1   SI 1994/1056, reg 18(3).
2   SI 1994/1056, reg 18(8) as amended by SI 1996/593, Sch 2, para 10.

10.28   The Waste Management Licensing Regulations 1994 often provide for exemptions for the actual waste processing activity undertaken at the site and also for the separate storage of the waste. It appears from Circular 11/94[1] that, where the disposal or recovery process and the associated storage provision are contained in the same paragraph of Schedule 3 to the Waste Management Licensing Regulations 1994, one registration covers both the processing and the storage components. However, and by implication, where both the processing activity and storage occur at the same site, but where the exemptions for these activities are found in separate paragraphs of Schedule 3, separate registrations are necessary.

1   Circular 11/94, Annex 6, para 6.13(a).

10.29   No formal application for the registration of an exempt activity is needed. The duty on the Agency to establish a register is subject to reg 18(4)[1], which requires the registration authority to record the details of exempt activities on the register 'if it receives notice of them in writing or otherwise becomes aware of those activities'[2]. In all cases, only basic details are required and these are described with the other provisions on registration at para 13.39. This information, which includes the name of the establishment undertaking the exempt activity, the activity's location and so on, will often be in the hands of a regulatory authority already. For example, it may have been passed over as part of an application for an Authorisation under Part 1 of the EPA 1990. Hence reg 18(5) states that, if these details have already been provided, the controlling authority is deemed to have been made aware of the existence of the exempt activity, and no further action appears to be required of the operator of the facility. Indeed, the only regulatory body that needs to specifically establish a register of exempt activities is the Agency[3]. However, this register is itself partial. For example, it does not contain separate entries for IPC activities. The legislation treats the existence of the IPC authorisation as being sufficient to satisfy the Directive on Waste's requirements on registration.

1   As amended by SI 1994/288, reg 3(10).
2   SI 1994/1056, reg 18(4).
3   Circular 11/94, Annex 6, para 6.22.

10.30   The overall message from Circular 11/94 is that the system of registration 'is designed to be as little onerous both for business and for WRAs[1] as is consistent with the implementation of the Directive'[2]. This message could not be made more explicit when the procedure for registering exempt activities is analysed. As noted above, reg 18(4) of the Waste Management Licensing Regulations 1994 requires that an activity shall be registered by the Agency if it receives notice of it in writing or 'otherwise becomes aware of those particulars'. Consider the case where an Agency officer sees an exempt activity occurring at a particular premises. By simply looking through the site fence, it is possible to satisfy the three requirements of reg 18(3) by having available the name and address of the establishment or undertaking, the nature of the exempt activity and the place the activity is carried on. In these circumstances, reg 18(4) is worded in such a way that, once this information is in the hands of the officer, the activity is deemed to be registered from that moment onwards[3]. Hence no offence can occur under reg 18(1) in these circumstances[4]. This means that a person commits an offence for failing to register only up to the point when the Agency staff are actually able to decide who is responsible for the activity, where it is occurring and what is occurring at the particular location. Once these matters have been met, the requirements of reg 18(3) have been satisfied and registration under reg 18(4) is deemed to have occurred.

1   The Circular refers to the local authority Waste Regulation Authorities, which were later amalgamated into the Agency.
2   Circular 11/94, Annex 6, para 6.1.
3   See Circular 11/94, Annex 6, para 6.27.
4   SI 1994/1056, reg 18(4).

10.31   Finally, parallel to the cursory manner by which registration is approached in the Waste Management Licensing Regulations 1994, three further paragraphs of guidance are given in Circular 11/94 to indicate that registration is nothing less than a formality[1]. The Circular states that regard should be made to the objectives of both the Directive on Waste and waste management licensing. These objectives should be seen as focusing on the prevention and minimisation of pollution and harm[2]. Hence the Circular explicitly discourages enforcement action where, for example, a body has failed to register but no environmental or other damage has resulted. 'Authorities[3] should not expect to take enforcement action for such technical breaches, until and unless the establishment or undertaking concerned fails to cooperate with the reasonable actions open to the authority to secure a registration'[4]. If this is not enough, in the process of compiling a register, the Circular advises that waste regulation '[a]uthorities are advised to give the completion of registration a significantly lower priority than the licensing and regulation of licensable activities'[5].

1   Circular 11/94, Annex 6, paras 6.25 to 6.27.
2   Circular 11/94, Annex 6, para 6.25.
3   Local authority Waste Regulation Authorities, which were subsequently subsumed into the Agency.
4   Circular 11/94, Annex 6, para 6.25.
5   Circular 11/94, Annex 6, para 6.26.

Common statutory requirements for exempt facilities

10.32   Although the question of whether a person is actually registered is treated as a rather trivial matter in the Waste Management Licensing Regulations 1994, a much greater emphasis is placed upon ensuring adherence to the terms and conditions of a particular exemption. It has been noted that the mechanism by which the system of exemptions is enacted is contained in reg 17(1) of the Waste Management Licensing Regulations 1994. This disapplies the requirements of s 33(1)(a) and (b) of the EPA 1990 where an activity is one which fits into one of the 45 paragraphs contained in

Schedule 3 to the Waste Management Licensing Regulations 1994[1]. However, to be the subject of an exemption, the activity must take place in accordance with the terms set down by the relevant paragraphs of the Schedule. Should the activity be operated outside those terms, a waste management licence is needed and the person responsible is open to prosecution for contravention of s 33 of the EPA 1990[2]. As was found in *Environment Agency v Stanford*[3]:

'It is however plain that an exemption, even if registered, does not provide protection from prosecution if the activity carried on is not within the terms of the exemption and does not comply with its terms.'

1 As amended by SI 1995/288 and SI 1996/972.
2 Confirmed, for example, in Circular 6/95 (Annex 1, para 1.16 in respect of the metal reclamation facility exemptions) and also Department of the Environment (1996) *Waste Management the Duty of Care Code of Practice*, 2nd ed, HMSO. Annex 1, para A.1.
3 [1999] Env LR 286 at 292.

10.33 Besides operating within the terms set down in the relevant paragraph of Schedule 3 to the Waste Management Licensing Regulations 1994, four other conditions must be satisfied for an activity to remain exempt and immune from the penal provisions in s 33 of the EPA 1990:

(i) *Compliance with s 33(1)(c).* Section 33(1)(c) of the EPA 1990 still applies to exempt waste management activities[1]. Therefore, the treating, keeping or disposing of waste in a manner likely to cause pollution of the environment or harm to human health is an offence.

(ii) *Special Waste.* Unless Schedule 3 to the Waste Management Licensing Regulations 1994 states otherwise, the exemptions do not apply where special waste is being handled[2]. An implication of this is that, when the broader definition of special waste was enacted in 1996[3], the breadth of certain exemptions narrowed somewhat[4].

(iii) *Consent of Occupier.* For those specific paragraphs[5] to Schedule 3 to which reference is made by reg 17(2), an exemption is only valid where the activity is carried on by or with the consent of the occupier of the land where the activity is occurring[6]. Alternatively, the person carrying on the exempt activity must otherwise be entitled to do so on that land[7].

(iv) *Compliance with Relevant Objectives.* Immunity from the offence provisions of s 33 of the EPA 1990 is only retained[8] where the 'relevant objectives' in Article 4 of the Directive on Waste are satisfied[9]. Circular 11/94 notes[10] that, in respect of the need for an exempt activity to be consistent with the above objectives, this requirement overlaps somewhat with the others just described:

'... in practice this is unlikely to invalidate exemptions which would otherwise be permitted; inconsistent activities are likely to be already caught by other provisions. It is likely that carrying out an activity using methods of disposal or recovery inconsistent with the objectives would fall foul of section 33(1)(c)[11]. In other cases, where excessive quantities or dangerous or harmful types of waste were subject to the activity, they would exceed the limits as to types and quantities of wastes specified in individual exemptions in Schedule 3.'

1 SI 1994/1056, reg 17(1).
2 SI 1994/1056, reg 17(3): special waste is discussed in Chapter 4.
3 By way of SI 1996/972 as amended by SI 1996/2019.
4 A Consultation Paper published in April 1998 proposed certain adjustments to the wording of the exemptions to accommodate the effects of the new definition of special waste: DETR (1998)

Proposed Amendments to the Special Waste Regulations 1996 and the Waste Management Licensing Regulations 1994, DETR, London.
5 SI 1994/1056, Sch 3, paras 4, 7, 9, 11, 13, 14, 15, 17, 18, 19, 25, 37, 40, 41 and 45.
6 SI 1994/1056, reg 17(2)(a) as amended by SI 1995/288, reg 3(6).
7 SI 1994/1056, reg 17(2)(b) as amended by SI 1995/288, reg 3(6).
8 SI 1994/1056, reg 17(4).
9 SI 1994/1056, Sch 4, para 4(1): the following are 'relevant objectives':
   '(a) ensuring that waste is recovered or disposed of without endangering human health and without using processes or methods which could harm the environment and in particular without:
      (i) risk to water, air, soil, plants or animals; or
      (ii) causing nuisance through noise or odours; or
      (iii) adversely affecting the countryside or places of special interest;'.
   Relevant objectives are more extensively discussed in paras 8.50ff and 12.13ff.
10 Circular 11/95, Annex 5, paragraph 5.35.
11 EPA 1990, s 33(1)(c): see Chapter 7.

10.34 Besides the requirements described above, it should be emphasised that an activity which is subject to an exemption is only exempt from the requirements to obtain a waste management licence[1]. It is not exempt from the other provisions of the EPA 1990. The need to satisfy the requirements of s 33(1)(c) of the EPA 1990 has already been mentioned, but equally important are the provisions of s 34 of the EPA 1990 in respect of the duty of care. A person who accepts waste but has an exempt status is an authorised person under s 34(1)(c). A registered carrier (or a carrier who is exempt from the need to possess a registration) must usually be utilised[2]. Finally, any transactions of wastes to exempt sites should be documented with appropriate transfer notes[3] or, where appropriate, special waste[4] notifications[5].

1 SI 1994/1056, reg 17(1) only disapplies s 33(1)(a) and s 33(1)(b) of the EPA 1990, not s 33(1)(c).
2 See para 3.48ff.
3 See para 3.118ff.
4 See para 4.60ff.
5 Section 8 of the Environment Act 1995 requires nature conservation interests to be consulted by the Agency in respect of notified land which may be damaged by operations on them. However, this provision only applies in respect of 'consents or licences' issued by the Agency. As discussed at para 10.29, the registration process for exemptions does not involve the Agency consenting to the activity. Hence, it seems that s 8 of the Environment Act does not have application to the exempt activities discussed in this chapter. However, the Groundwater Regulations 1998 (SI 1998/2746) will apply to a very small number of facilities which – while exempt – may cause a direct or indirect discharge of List 1 or List 2 substances to groundwater. However – and rather perversely – if the activity is operated *outside* the terms of the exemption in the Waste Management Licensing Regulations 1994, the Groundwater Regulations 1998 do not apply. This is as a result of the wording of reg 2(1)(d) which states that the Groundwater Regulations 1999 do not apply when a waste management licence 'is required'. Clearly such a licence is only required when the terms of exemption are breached.

Points of general interpretation

10.35 Certain general approaches should be used for the interpretation of words and phrases which feature commonly in a number of the paragraphs of the Schedule which set out the exemptions. Somewhat confusingly, key terms are defined in three places in the Waste Management Licensing Regulations 1994. Certain definitions are found in reg 1(3) of the Waste Management Licensing Regulations 1994, some further interpretation is contained in reg 17, while additional definitions may be embedded into each of the relevant paragraphs of Schedule 3 to the Waste Management Licensing Regulations 1994.

'Secure container, lagoon or place'

10.36 A very common requirement of Schedule 3 to the Waste Management Licensing Regulations 1994 is that, for an activity to remain exempt from licensing, it must be carried out using a 'secure container, lagoon or place'. Regulation 17(5) states that a container, lagoon or place is to be regarded as secure in relation to the waste within it 'if all reasonable precautions[1] are taken to ensure that the waste cannot escape from it and members of the public are unable to gain access to the waste'. Similarly, it is held that any reference to 'secure storage' means storage in a secure container, lagoon or place. Circular 11/94 suggests that, although a container is secure when members of the public cannot obtain access to the waste, this does not prevent them from depositing waste in it where this is appropriate[2]. This allows public recycling centres to be exempt if 'secure' under the relevant exemption.

1 The term 'reasonable precautions' is discussed at para 7.145ff.
2 Circular 11/94, para 5.142.

The location of the exempt activity

10.37 Usually the wording of each exemption makes clear if the exempt activity can occur at any location, or only at the site where the waste is produced or is to be re-cycled/disposed of. However, there appear to be some variations to this general rule, which are the result of the relevant paragraph to Schedule 3 being silent on this requirement. An example is Schedule 3, paragraph 5, where burning waste in a small incinerator is granted an exemption. In contrast to virtually all the other paragraphs of Schedule 3, the paragraph does not set down a location for either the burning appliance or the associated storage. Indeed, it does not stipulate that the storage needs to be at the same location as the incinerator. A similar example can be found in Schedule 3, paragraph 6(2), which does not indicate the appropriate location for waste oil storage when such material is to be used as a fuel. In the absence of such a requirement, it could be assumed that the activity can occur at any place. Certainly this matter has yet to be judicially clarified.

Time and quantity limits

10.38 A number of the exemptions set time limits and maximum quantities for the wastes being stored, processed or otherwise treated. Circular 11/94 provides clarification on the manner in which these limits should be interpreted. For limits on the duration of storage, it is pointed out that this does not preclude the continuous use of a premises for storing less than the quantity of waste set down[1]: '... it is the turnover of waste at the site that must be within the time limit'.

1 Circular 11/94, Annex 5, para 5.39.

10.39 Circular 11/94 also indicates[1] that, should the quantity limit be exceeded, then the whole of the activity becomes one that should be licensed. This includes the quantity of waste that would have been excluded by the exemption if the limit had not been otherwise exceeded.

1 Circular 11/94, Annex 5, para 5.39.

Exemptions for the storage and processing of waste

10.40 In any interpretation of Schedule 3 to the Waste Management Licensing Regulations 1994, there is also a need to ensure that a distinction is being made between the exemptions which relate to the processing of waste and those that apply only to waste storage. In some cases, a different exemption applies to storage and these may be located in a separate paragraph from that which refers to the exempt processing activity. For example, waste glass can be subject to exempt storage under paragraph 17[1]; it can be sorted, crushed or washed under the exemption set out in paragraph 11[2];

and made back into primary glass under the provision of paragraph 1[3]. This distinction affects the requirements on registrations, as separate registrations may be required for the storage and processing activities even if they occur on the same site.

1   See para 10.83.
2   See para 10.177.
3   See para 10.187.

Permissible types of waste

10.41   Although the amount of detail varies, most of the exemptions specify the types of waste that can be dealt with under the relevant provision. An example is waste paper and cardboard, which can be sorted and baled at a depot without the need for the premises to have a waste management licence[1]. Should wastes other than those stipulated by the exemption be accepted at the premises, it may be reasonable to surmise that the exemption no longer applies. However, it is an inevitable part of many operations that 'contrary materials' are inadvertently accepted in the wastes brought in. On occasion such materials might well be outside the scope of the exemption, but, with the exception of exemptions relating to metal reclamation facilities[2], there is no provision in Schedule 3 to the Waste Management Licensing Regulations 1994 to address this type of occurrence. This may mean that, where contrary wastes are accepted, the exemption becomes disapplied and the site operator is open to a prosecution under s 33 of the EPA 1990. The only way of defending such a prosecution is by way of the statutory defences contained in s 33(7) of the EPA 1990. As discussed in Chapter 7, the most relevant of these is that the person 'took all reasonable precautions and exercised all due diligence' to avoid the commission of the offence[3]. With this in mind, it is important that all operators of exempt activities have appropriate procedures, staff training and record-keeping systems which will show that these criteria have been satisfied.

1   SI 1994/1056, Sch 3, para 11. See para 10.83.
2   See SI 1994/1056, Sch 3, para 45(5) and the reference to 'non-scrap waste': discussed at para 11.76ff.
3   EPA 1990, s 33(7)(a): see para 7.145ff.

The requirement to possess a licence and exemptions from licensing

10.42   Although the precise requirements of the exemptions are explored in detail later in this chapter and in the following chapters, it is sufficient to note at this stage that sites may switch between exempt and licensable status[1]. This may occur where the limits which confer exemption, such as quantities or types of waste stored, are exceeded. In the case of metal recycling facilities, the requisite infrastructure and record-keeping systems may deteriorate to such an extent that the terms of the exemption can no longer be sustained. If the particular requirements of the exemption are not complied with, a waste management licence is required and an offence may be committed in respect of s 33 of the EPA 1990[2].

1   Metal recycling sites are subject to an additional constraint due to the application of SI 1994/1056, reg 17(1A): see para 11.15ff.
2   See Chapter 7.

10.43   The implementation of the new system in the Waste Management Licensing Regulations 1994 presented a significant opportunity for a number of sites which were hitherto licensed under the Control of Pollution Act 1974 to seek exemption. In addition to other matters, fees and charges for the possession of a waste management licence were introduced at that time[1]. Sites operated by the utilities where wastes are imported from elsewhere and subject to incidental storage in containers[2] and many metal recycling sites[3] are examples of the types of facilities which were often licensed under the Control of Pollution Act 1974.

1   See para 9.142.
2   Exempted by SI 1994/1056, Sch 3, para 40: see para 10.65ff below.
3   Exempted primarily under Sch 3, para 45: see Chapter 11.

10.44   Precisely how the requirements of the EPA 1990 in respect of waste management licences and the system of exemptions interact is not considered in detail in Circular 11/94[1]. However, Circular 6/95 sets out the Department of the Environment's view on how the transition from licence to exemption should be approached. Although the context of the Circular relates to metal recycling sites, its sentiment applies to all Schedule 3 exemptions[2]:

> 'In the Departments' view, a waste management licence is a licence **authorising** the treatment, keeping or disposal of controlled waste. An activity is only **authorised** when the person in question would not otherwise have the right to do it and permission is granted. An activity which is exempt does not need to be authorised because the person in question has the right to carry on the activity without the licence' [emphasis in original].

Accordingly, this might suggest that a site can possess both a licence *and* qualify for an exemption. The licence does not become void when the exemption is conferred on the operator. Circular 6/95 goes on to state[3]:

> 'The fact that an activity satisfies the terms and conditions of an exemption does not mean that the site licence ceases to have effect. Rather, it means that the site licence[4] ceases to be of any practical utility. It follows that, so long as the operator fulfils the terms and conditions of the exemption, the conditions of the site licence are unenforceable.'

1   See Circular 11/94, Annex 4, para 4.80.
2   Circular 6/95, Annex 1, para 1.39.
3   Circular 6/95, Annex 1, para 1.40.
4   The quotation refers to licences which were granted under the Control of Pollution Act 1974, but it also applies equally to waste management licences.

10.45   If the argument in the latter quotation is correct, some quite fundamental issues suggest themselves. Where a site is covered by both an exemption and a dormant waste management licence[1], the licence appears to be 'activated' if the conditions of the exemption are breached. It therefore follows that an offence is committed in such a circumstance *only* where both the terms of the exemption *and* the terms and conditions of the licence are breached. It is certainly possible to conceive of circumstances where the terms of the exemption are breached but where those of the licence are not[2]. In respect of annual charges that are to be levied on licence-holders[3], this requirement does not apply whilst the site is exempt, but would appear to come into force when the terms of the exemption are breached. In contrast, where an exemption has been conferred on a site which has never been the subject of a licence at all, it seems that the site is open to prosecution as an unlicensed waste management facility as soon as the terms of the exemption are breached.

1   When sites become exempt, there is no requirement that the licence is formally surrendered under the procedures set down in s 39 of the EPA 1990 (described at para 9.93ff).
2   For example, whilst the maximum storage limit of a particular exemption may be exceeded, the storage limits in the 'dormant' licence may not be.
3   Environment Act 1995, s 41: see para 9.142.

10.46 Overall, the relationship between licences and exemptions does not seem to be clearly considered in the EPA 1990 and the Waste Management Licensing Regulations 1994. The somewhat anomalous position has peculiar effects in respect of the Agency as an enforcing authority and upon operators of exempt sites. In relation to the Agency, the prosecution's evidential requirements may be subtly different between the two classes of site. For an operator, it may be desirable to operate a site as an exempt facility but to retain, or even apply for[1], a licence. The licence can remain dormant whilst the facility operates within the terms of the exemption. As the existence of the licence has no effect in these circumstances, there would appear to be no requirement to pay a subsistence charge for the possession of the licence[2]. However, it would seem likely that, if the site is unlicensed, an application fee is payable in these, somewhat unusual, circumstances.

1 Precisely how the Agency is to respond to such a request is not clear.
2 See para 9.142.

Exemptions located on sites subject to waste management licences

10.47 In *London Waste Regulation Authority v Drinkwater Sabey Ltd*[1], the Divisional Court considered the problem where an activity which fell within an exemption set down in Schedule 3 to the Waste Management Licensing Regulations 1990 occurred at a site subject to a waste management licence. It was held that the conditions of the licence could not apply to any operation covered by a relevant exemption.

1 [1997] Env LR 137.

10.48 The *Drinkwater Sabey* case involved the importation onto a landfill of a large volume of dredging wastes which, when added to the quantity of other wastes accepted at the site, exceeded the daily waste input limit allowable under the licence. The exemption in question was contained in paragraph 13 of Schedule 3 to the Waste Management Licensing Regulations 1994, which permitted the manufacture of soil or soil substitutes from wastes arising from demolition or construction work, tunnelling or other excavations[1]. Also permitted under the exemption was the storage of these materials prior to soil substitute manufacture[2]. It was accepted by the court that the dredgings were being used as soil substitutes, the use of which would appear to have been the restoration of the filled areas of the landfill.

1 The applicable waste types are listed in SI 1994/1056, Sch 3, para 13(1); exempt soil substitute manufacture is allowable under para 13(2): see para 10.121.
2 SI 1994/1056, Sch 3, para 13(4).

10.49 Drinkwater Sabey Ltd pleaded not guilty to a summons alleging that it contravened the quantity limit set down in the landfill's licence. Under the EPA 1990, a breach of a licence condition is an offence under s 33(6)[1]. The Divisional Court looked at the relationship between the general requirement of s 33 to comply with the conditions of a licence[2] and the provisions in s 33(3) and (4), which allow regulations to be made to disapply that requirement in specified instances. Section 33(4) permits secondary legislation to be made to provide for exemptions or exclusions from the licensing provisions in the case of small or temporary deposits[3], means of treatment or disposal which are innocuous[4], and cases where adequate controls are provided in other legislation[5]. Having analysed these provisions, Smith J concluded that s 33(4)[6] 'provides a clear indication of the intention of Parliament to exempt some activities from licensing controls altogether'. The following conclusion was therefore reached[7]:

'In my judgment the position is clear. An activity which falls within one of the exemptions set out in Schedule 3 to the 1994 Regulations is exempted from any licensing requirement and is subject only to the requirement of registration. This does not mean ... that the premises on which the activity occurs are subject to no control or restraint at all in respect of such matters as the hours of opening, the number of vehicles attending and other such matters which might affect the amenities of the neighbourhood. Those matters can be properly controlled by the local planning authority.'[8]

1   See Chapter 7.
2   EPA 1990, s 33(1) and (6).
3   EPA 1990, s 33(4)(a).
4   EPA 1990, s 33(4)(b).
5   EPA 1990, s 33(4)(c).
6   [1997] Env LR 137 at 143.
7   [1997] Env LR 137 at 146.
8   The court also noted in passing that, a few months after the offence was alleged to have been committed – but prior to trial – a letter had been sent by the company to the London Waste Regulation Authority providing notification that the exempt activity was occurring at the licensed site. It would seem that, quite separately of the prosecution, a reply came back from the Authority, informing the company that the process was exempt under the Waste Management Licensing Regulations 1994.

10.50   The *Drinkwater Sabey* decision has certainly not made matters any easier in respect of the enforcement of waste management licences and their conditions[1]. Indeed, when faced with allegations concerning breaches of their licences, operators may wish to consider if the circumstances of the breach can be categorised by one or more of the exemptions listed in Schedule 3 to the Waste Management Licensing Regulations 1994. Precisely how the Agency is to respond to such an action is not immediately apparent, but the fact that no registration existed prior to summonses being issued may need to be put before any court. In the long term, it may be appropriate that the European Court should consider whether the Directive on Waste does in fact envisage that particular waste management operations occurring at sites subject to permits should be excluded from the permit's requirements. Alternatively, the Agency might look to the Department of the Environment for a possible amendment to the existing legislation.

1   It also appears to reverse many statements made in WMP 4A on the relationship between metal recycling facility licences and exemptions: see for example WMP 4A, paras 1.23 and 2.17.

The burden of proof

10.51   An interesting legal point arises in respect of the burden of proof when a person is claiming that the existence of an exemption absolves them from prosecution under s 33 of EPA 1990. This principle is codified in s 101 of the Magistrates' Courts Act 1980, but is also a general rule of construction at common law[1]. The relevant section of the Magistrates' Courts Act 1980 reads:

'Where the defendant to an information or complaint relies for his defence on any exception, *exemption*[2], proviso, excuse or qualification, whether or not it accompanies the description of the offence ... the burden of proving the exception, exemption, proviso, excuse or qualification shall be on him ... and this notwithstanding that the information or complaint contains ... an allegation negativing the exception, exemption, proviso, excuse or qualification.'

1   *R v Hunt* [1987] AC 352; see also *R v Edwards* [1975] QB 27 at 40A and, for example, *Reynolds v G H Austin & Sons Ltd* [1951] 2 KB 135 at 152.
2   Author's emphasis.

10.52 This does not, of course, mean that the burden of proof is reversed[1]. It means that a defendant must substantiate the nature of the exemption as part of that person's defence. It is then left to the prosecution to show that the exemption does not apply[2].

1 See *R v Edwards* [1975] QB 27 at 40D/E.
2 See *R v Clarke* [1969] 2 All ER 1008; *Saddleworth UDC v Aggregate and Sand Ltd* (1970) 69 LGR 103; *R v Edwards* [1975] QB 27; *R v Hunt* [1987] AC 352 and *Tandridge District Council v P & S Civil Engineering* [1995] Env LR 67; see also *Polychronakis v Richard & Jerrom Ltd* [1998] Env LR 346.

THE SCHEDULE 3 EXEMPTIONS[1]

10.53 As a general comment, the list of exemptions drafted in Schedule 3 to the Waste Management Licensing Regulations 1994 is, at best, confusing. There are some overlaps between a number of the exemptions, and it seems that the exemptions are listed in an order which, on detailed examination, appears not to have a strong internal logic or consistency. It is for this reason that the order of the exemptions in that Schedule is not followed closely below. Instead, the discussion of the exemptions has been organised in an attempt to place similar provisions together. They have also been grouped, on the basis of problem areas that are common in British waste regulation. It is hoped that the approach used allows accessibility, while providing a clear indication where different exemptions overlap.

1 Note that amendments are expected in late 1999 for certain exemptions: see DETR (1998) *Consultation Paper – Proposed Amendments to the Special Waste Regulations 1996 and the Waste Management Licensing Regulations 1998*, DETR, London, and see also *Hansard* 31 March 1999 col 767.

Waste produced on the premises

10.54 Many substances held on the premises of a waste producer will, by definition, not fall within the EPA 1990's concept of waste – particularly on the grounds that they are still wanted and have not been discarded. Only when producers discard the material or when, by way of their actions, it may be surmised that the material has been effectively discarded[1] do the provisions of the EPA 1990 come into play[2]. Alternatively, they apply when producers intend to discard materials or are required to discard them. Accordingly, for substances arising on the premises of waste producers, two matters should be settled: whether the material is waste in the first place; and if its storage on the premises needs a waste management licence or falls into one of the exemptions contained in Schedule 3 to the Waste Management Licensing Regulations 1994.

1 See SI 1994/1056, reg 1(3); an example might be rotting drums of process chemicals.
2 The definition of waste is discussed in Chapter 2.

Wastes awaiting collection[1]

10.55 Paragraph 41 of Schedule 3 to the Waste Management Licensing Regulations 1994 allows waste to be temporarily stored, 'on the site where it is produced' pending its collection[2]. There are certain exclusions for special wastes (see below) but, for non-special waste, paragraph 41(1) presents no time limit for keeping such wastes, nor does it suggest a maximum quantity that can be stored. Circular 11/94 also suggests[3] that the Regulations' concept of the site where the waste is produced extends to the street immediately outside the premises. Accordingly, it is asserted that the exemption is not restricted only to the storage of wastes within the curtilage of the premises. It is claimed that this provision, for example, allows skips to be left on the street outside the location of construction activities.

1   This exemption does not apply to the storage at a place 'designed or adapted' for the recovery of scrap metal or for motor vehicle dismantling (SI 1994/1056, Sch 3, para 41(1A) as amended by SI 1995/288, reg 3(13)). Activities at those locations are discussed in Chapter 11.
2   SI 1994/1056, Sch 3, para 41(1). The occupier's consent or other entitlement to carry on the activity on the land is needed (SI 1994/1056, reg 17(2) as amended by SI 1995/288, reg 3(6)).
3   Circular 11/94, Annex 5, para 5.233.

10.56   In the case where special wastes are to be stored on the premises of production, the exemption for storage awaiting collection stands but is much more restricted[1]. Firstly, this form of storage is allowable provided that the material is not stored for over 12 months[2]. Secondly, if the material is liquid special waste, then it must be stored in a secure container[3] and the total volume must not exceed 23,000 litres at any one time[4]. 23,000 litres is slightly above the capacity of one of the larger articulated waste tankers[5]. In the case of non-liquid special wastes awaiting collection, storage can involve the use of secure containers[3] and the total volume stored must not exceed 80 cubic metres. Alternatively, solid special waste may be stored in a 'secure place'[3] and the total volume must not exceed 50 cubic metres.

1   SI 1994/1056, Sch 3, para 41(2); a separate exemption relates to waste oil stored in these circumstances: see para 10.58 below.
2   SI 1994/1056, Sch 3, para 41(2)(a).
3   'Secure' is defined in SI 1994/1056, reg 17(5); see para 10.36 above.
4   SI 1994/1056, Sch 3, para 41(2)(b).
5   A change to the 23,000 litre limit, with the exception of waste oil storage, has been mooted: see DETR (1998) *Consultation Paper – Proposed Amendments to the Special Waste Regulations 1996 and the Waste Management Licensing Regulations 1994*, DETR, London, April 1998.

10.57   No registration is needed for establishments storing wastes prior to collection. This activity is excluded from Annexes IIA and IIB of the Directive on Waste[1], as the storage of waste awaiting collection on the premises of production is not classed as a disposal or recovery activity (see Tables 2.2 and 2.3 in Chapter 2).

1   See Circular 11/94, paras 6.20 and 6.21.

Waste oil awaiting collection

10.58   Waste oil awaiting off-site collection has been singled out for an exemption of its own[1]. The relevant provision can be found in Schedule 3, paragraph 3(c), which permits waste oil[2] to be held in secure[3] storage for up to 12 months at the place of production. However, to fall within this exemption, the oil must be intended to be burnt as a fuel[4]. As many waste oils are special waste[5], this provision is wider than the general exemption for special waste stored on the premises of production and awaiting collection[6]. There is no quantity limit and, in addition, there seems to be nothing to prevent this exemption applying to the storage of oil at a scrapyard or vehicle dismantler. This exemption does not require registration with the Agency.

1   Waste oil is defined in SI 1994/1056, reg 1(3) as meaning any mineral-based lubricating or industrial oil, which has become unfit for the use for which it was originally intended and, in particular, used combustion engine oil, gearbox oil, mineral lubricating oil, oil for turbines and hydraulic oil.
2   This exemption includes waste oil which is special waste: SI 1994/1056, Sch 3, para 3(c) as amended by SI 1996/972, reg 25 and Sch 3.
3   'Secure' is defined in SI 1994/1056, reg 17(5): see para 10.36 above.
4   SI 1994/1056, Sch 3, para 3(c) as amended by SI 1996/972, reg 25 and Sch 3.
5   See Circular 6/96, Annex B1, para 16; special wastes are the subject of Chapter 4.
6   SI 1994/1056, Sch 3, para 41(2): see para 10.56.

Waste processing infrastructure located on the producer's premises

10.59 A number of non-special waste processing activities are also exempt, so that items such as static compactors located in a factory's curtilage do not fall within the scope of waste management licensing. As well as compactors, operations involving the baling, crushing, shredding or pulverising of waste at the premises where it was produced are all exempt[1]. Similarly, the storage of wastes awaiting such processing is exempt[2] when they are kept on the premises where they have been produced. As with the exemption in respect of non-special wastes awaiting collection, no time or quantity limits have been laid down.

1 SI 1994/1056, Sch 3, para 27(1).
2 SI 1994/1056, Sch 3, para 27(2).

10.60 These activities need to be subject to a registration with the relevant Agency[1]. This includes every compactor or baler in the country situated on the premises of a waste producer.

1 SI 1994/1056, reg 18(10)(d).

The disposal or recovery of wastes integral to a production process

10.61 Besides the above exemptions relating to waste awaiting collection, the recovery or disposal of non-special waste on the premises on which it is produced, which is 'an integral part of the process that produces it'[1], is exempt from the requirement to possess a waste management licence. Similarly wastes can be stored on the premises prior to such integral recovery or disposal[2]. However, this exemption does not apply to any activity which might involve the 'final disposal of waste by deposit in or on land'[3]. All such activities need to be registered with the Agency[4].

1 SI 1994/1056, Sch 3, para 26(1).
2 SI 1994/1056, Sch 3, para 26(2).
3 SI 1994/1056, Sch 3, para 26(3).
4 SI 1994/1056, reg 18(10)(d).

10.62 It should be observed that the above exemption does not sit particularly comfortably with the definition of waste in the EPA 1990[1]. If substances are recovered in an integral manner on the premises of production, it seems doubtful that they are to be viewed as discarded. Therefore, they will not be defined as waste in the first place. Furthermore, the exemption does not appear to be necessary if the advice contained in Annex 2 of Circular 11/94 is correct. This indicates that surplus materials should not fall within the definition of waste when they are transferred as part of 'normal commercial cycles or chain of utility'[2]. However, in the light of the subsequent European Court of Justice's finding in *Inter-Environnement Wallonie ASBL*[3], there may be some, very limited, circumstances where it is possible that substances which are wastes are being integrally disposed of or recovered at the premises of production.

1 See Chapter 2.
2 See Circular 11/94, Annex 2, paras 2.20ff.
3 [1998] Env LR 623. See para 2.87ff.

Wastes arising on the premises of production: burning wastes and dealing with waste arising from construction work

10.63 Wastes may also be burnt on the premises where they were produced without a waste management licence being required. This exemption is discussed at para 10.216 below. Certain construction activities may also result in wastes needing to be processed on the premises of production. Again, the relevant exemptions are discussed at para 10.110ff.

Temporary storage of wastes other than at the site of production

10.64 The exemptions which allow waste to be kept at a site that is neither the premises of production nor the facility where the waste is to be disposed of or recovered are now considered. Schedule 3 to the Waste Management Licensing Regulations 1994 contains a number of provisions which exempt the storage of wastes prior to disposal or recovery. The majority only allow for storage at the site of production[1] or at the final destination[2], but only those exemptions which allow waste to be kept at intermediate holding points which are independent of a final disposal or recovery activity will be described here. However, it should be pointed out that in this context, Schedule 3 often uses the term 'at any place' when describing an acceptable location for exempt storage. Hence many of the exemptions covered below can pertain also to storage at licensed or exempt disposal and recovery sites.

1 See para 10.54.
2 These exemptions are described alongside the provisions which relate to the actual exempt disposal or recovery process itself.

Storage of solid waste in containers

10.65 Although metal reclamation facilities are excluded from this provision[1], Schedule 3, paragraph 40 of the Waste Management Licensing Regulations 1994 allows the exempt storage of non-liquid wastes at 'any place other than the premises where it was produced'[2], providing that the wastes are stored in secure[3] containers. To stay exempt, only non-special waste may be stored[4], the maximum quantity must not exceed 50 cubic metres, storage cannot exceed three months[5] and the person storing the waste must be the owner of the containers or must have obtained the owner's consent[6].

1 This exemption does not apply to the storage of waste at a site 'designed and adapted' for the recovery of scrap metal or the dismantling of motor vehicles: SI 1994/1056, Sch 3, para 40(1A) as amended by SI 1995/288, reg 3(13).
2 SI 1994/1056, Sch 3, para 40(1). The occupier's consent or other entitlement to carry on the activity on the land is needed (SI 1994/1056, reg 17(2)).
3 'Secure' is defined in SI 1994/1056, reg 17(5) (see para 10.36 above).
4 See SI 1994/1056, reg 17(3).
5 SI 1994/1056, Sch 3, para 40(1)(a).
6 SI 1994/1056, Sch 3, para 40(1)(b).

10.66 In addition, the exemption requires that the site of the storage cannot be one that has been 'designed or adapted for the reception of waste with a view to its being disposed of or recovered elsewhere'[1]. Finally, to fall within this exemption, the storage must be 'incidental' to the collection and transport of the waste.

1 SI 1994/1056, Sch 3, para 40(1)(c).
2 SI 1994/1056, Sch 3, para 40(1)(d).

10.67 It would appear that such facilities are required to register with the relevant Agency[1]. However, by contrast, Circular 11/94 indicates that no registration is necessary[2].

1 SI 1994/1056, reg 18(10)(d).
2 See Circular 11/94, Annex 5, Table 5.1 and Annex 6, para 6.21.

10.68   This exemption may parallel and extend the likely interpretation of the concept of 'keeping' waste as set down in s 33(1) of the EPA 1990[1]. Like the term 'keeping' waste, it is vital that this exemption is subject to careful consideration. Otherwise it is likely to cause a number of highly undesirable waste disposal activities to appear to fall out of the waste management licensing controls. Of particular importance is the interpretation of the terms 'designed or adapted' and 'incidental to'.

1   See para 7.26.

10.69   Circular 11/94 sets out the Department of the Environment's view on the nature and purpose of this exemption[1]:

'After it leaves its place of production, the storage of waste that is destined for disposal, in connection with that disposal, is itself a disposal operation and must be licensed; but some storage of waste, at the stage where it is being gathered together, is incidental to the collection and transport of the waste rather than incidental to its disposal. This latter form of storage, in places such as yards and depots where waste from different sources is brought together for temporary storage pending collection, is distinct from the licensable disposal operations of a transfer station. The terms of this exemption draw a distinction between these two forms of storage, based on exempting a modest quantity of waste that is gathered and stored for a short time incidental to its collection and transport.'

According to Circular 11/94, therefore, a waste transfer station should never be seen to be included within this exemption[2].

1   Circular 11/94, Annex 5, para 5.225.
2   See also Circular 11/94, Annex 5, para 5.229; this quotation was considered by the lower court in *North Yorkshire County Council v Boyne*: see below.

10.70   This exemption was subject to consideration by the Divisional Court in *North Yorkshire County Council v Peter Anthony Boyne*[1]. Mr Boyne operated a skip hire business, bringing the occasional full skip back to his premises for temporary storage prior to haulage to a landfill site 15 miles away. The land did not have the benefit of a waste management licence and the skips were placed in the yard for a limited period of time. There was no suggestion made to the court that any waste was processed in the yard, nor were smaller skips emptied into larger ones. The County Council laid charges against Mr Boyne, under s 33(1)(b) of the EPA 1990, to the effect that he was involved in keeping waste on land and did not possess a waste management licence. The allegations were subsequently rejected by a local magistrates' court. The Council appealed to the Divisional Court.

1   [1997] Env LR 91.

10.71   The case turned on whether Mr Boyne's operation satisfied specified requirements of Schedule 3, paragraph 40 to the Waste Management Licensing Regulations 1994[1]. These were whether the arrangement of the skips offered 'secure' storage[2]; if the yard had been 'adapted' for the reception of waste[3]; and if the waste storage activity was 'incidental to'[4] the other commercial activities of the skip hire business.

1   See [1997] Env LR 91 at 94.
2   SI 1994/1056, Sch 3, para 40(1)(a).
3   SI 1995/1056, Sch 3, para 40(1)(c).
4   SI 1994/1056, Sch 3, para 40(1)(d).

10.72   It is perhaps important in respect of the long-term ramifications of this judgment to note that the Divisional Court did not appear to be entirely happy with the manner in which the magistrates stated the case[1]. In particular, the evidence which lead the lower court to its decision was not set out in a manner which assisted the Divisional Court. The result is a significant caveat to Pill LJ's judgment which, whilst upholding the magistrates' decision, notes that the court felt that, in this particular case, the magistrates[2]:

'... were entitled to hold that the requirements of that paragraph[3] were satisfied. I would dismiss this appeal and answer the question by saying that the Justices were entitled to reach that conclusion. I put it in that way because a direct answer to the question actually posed[4] is not possible when this court does not know precisely what evidence was before them.'

Likewise Newman J states[5]:

'In view of the Appellant's[6] inability to impugn the Justices' findings of fact it has not been necessary to determine the precise meaning and effect of regulation[7] 40(1)(a) and regulation 17(5) ...'

1   See [1997] Env LR 91 per Pill LJ at 95 and 98 and Newman LJ at 98.
2   [1997] Env LR 91 at 98.
3   Ie the exemption contained in SI 1994/1056, Sch 3, para 40.
4   The question was ([1997] Env LR 91 at 95) 'Whether there was sufficient relevant evidence for us to properly conclude that the respondent came within the exemptions set out in Regulation [sic] 40(a) [sic], (c) and (d) of the Waste Management Regulations [sic] 1994.'
5   [1997] Env LR 91 at 98.
6   Ie North Yorkshire County Council.
7   This is in fact referring to SI 1994/1056, Sch 3, para 40(1)(a).

10.73   Having noted these caveats, it is useful to set out the manner by which the Divisional Court considered the elements which make up the exemption in paragraph 40(1). In respect of the requirement that waste must be stored in secure containers, the wording of the definition of 'secure' in reg 17(1) of the Waste Management Licensing Regulations 1994 was briefly considered. However, given the lack of clarity of the summary of the evidence passed to the Divisional Court, Pill LJ declined to rule on whether 'all reasonable precautions' had been taken to ensure that the waste was secure[1]. The Divisional Court's consideration is more illuminating in respect of the question of whether the site was 'adapted'[2] for the reception of waste which is subsequently taken elsewhere. A screening bund had been placed around the premises as a requirement of the site's planning permission. For the enforcing authority, it was argued that this earthwork caused the site to be adapted for the use to which it was put, namely the collection of full skips, their storage and their subsequent transportation to landfill. However, the Divisional Court held that this was not sufficient to 'adapt' a premises for the reception of waste prior to it being moved elsewhere[3]:

'There is nothing which irresistibly points to the purpose of the bund-building in this case being to conceal the storage of waste rather than a more general wish to prevent local complaint by enclosing an industrial use.'[4]

Accordingly, it would seem from this conclusion that a site is only adapted for waste reception when it is given purpose-built features which facilitate that function.

1   [1997] Env LR 91 at 96.
2   The court did not enter into to a detailed exposition of the term 'designed or adapted' and simply considered the latter term in apparent isolation.
3   As is required by SI 1994/1056, Sch 3, para 40(1)(c).
4   [1997] Env LR 91 at 96.

10.74   Finally, the Divisional Court considered the requirement of the exemption that storage was 'incidental' to the collection or transport of waste[1]. The court noted that there was no evidence that any recovery or disposal process was occurring at the site[2] and that the word 'storage' does contemplate something more than a momentary presence of waste on a site[3]. Overall, they felt that the facts of the case made it reasonable to conclude that the storage operation at the site was incidental to the business of the skip hire company.

1   As required by SI 1994/1056, Sch 3, para 40(1)(c).
2   [1997] Env LR 91 at 98.
3   [1997] Env LR 91 at 98.

10.75   It is perhaps fair to say that *Boyne* only constituted a partial review of the wording of the exemption and one which was constrained by the inadequate manner by which the case was stated by the lower court. Certainly, it would seem that there is more to the interpretation of this highly important exemption than that considered by either court. Of particular importance is the manner by which the phrase 'designed or adapted'[1] is to be interpreted, and also whether the scope of the exemption should viewed as being restricted by the wording of the Directive on Waste.

1   SI 1994/1056, Sch 3, para 40(1)(c).

10.76   The Department of the Environment's view of the nature of the interpretation of the words 'designed or adapted'[1] is set out in Circular 11/94. The relevant paragraph states[2] that:

'[t]he key is that the transfer of waste is the purpose of a transfer station, and it is designed or adapted for that purpose. The exemption is only to apply where the transfer of waste is merely ancillary to the operations of the site.'

1   SI 1994/1056, Sch 3, para 40(1)(c).
2   Circular 11/94, Annex 5, para 5.229.

10.77   However, this does not seem to be an entirely correct interpretation of the judicial meaning of 'designed or adapted'. The words have featured in a number of other statutes, including the Road Traffic Act 1960, the Caravan Sites and Control of Development Act 1960, the Town and Country Planning Act 1947 and in the Firearms Act 1968. Consequently, a series of judicial interpretations have been made over the years. These interpretations were brought together and reviewed in *R v Upton and R v Formosa*[1]. In this case, the defendants were found in possession of a washing up bottle containing hydrochloric acid. They were charged under s 5(1) of the Firearms Act 1968 and found guilty at the Crown Court. The relevant section of the Act makes it an offence to possess a firearm or other weapon, including one designed or adapted for the discharge of any noxious liquid.

1   [1991] 1 All ER 131.

10.78   The defendants successfully appealed, on the grounds that the washing up bottle was not 'designed or adapted' within the meaning of the Firearms Act 1968. The Court of Appeal was referred to *French v Champkin*[1], *Taylor v Mead*[2], *R v Titus*[3], *Maddox v Storer*[4] and *Backer v Secretary of State for the Environment*[5, 6]. Lloyd LJ concluded[7]:

'From these authorities there emerges this proposition, that the word "adapted" takes its colour and meaning from the context in which it appears. Where it is used on its own, it may bear a wide meaning. Thus in *Maddox v Storer* it was held that in

Sch 1 to the Road Traffic Act 1960 it meant simply apt or fit for the purpose in question. This meaning corresponds to the first of the two meanings contained in the Oxford English Dictionary. But where the word is used in conjunction with the word "constructed" in the phrase "constructed or adapted" it bears a narrower meaning. It imports then some physical alteration to the thing in question. This corresponds to the second of the two meanings in the Oxford English Dictionary. That was the meaning of the word given in *French v Champkin* ... and *Taylor v Mead* ...

...

Here[8] the word "adapted" is used in conjunction with the word "designed". On which side of the line does the present case come? We have no doubt that it comes on the same side as *French v Champkin*.

...

We conclude, therefore, that the word "adapted" in s 5(1)(b) must bear the narrower of the two meanings; in other words it must mean that the object has been altered so as to make it fit for the use in question.'

1 [1920] 1 KB 76.
2 [1961] 1 All ER 626, [1961] 1 WLR 435.
3 [1971] Crim LR 279.
4 [1963] 1 QB 451, [1962] 1 All ER 831.
5 [1983] 2 All ER 1021, [1983] 1 WLR 1485.
6 The following other cases also have relevance: *Wurzal v Addison* [1965] 2 QB 131; *Wilson v West Sussex County Council* [1963] 1 All ER 751; *Customs and Excise Comrs v Mechanical Services (Trailer Engineers) Ltd* [1978] 1 All ER 204; revsd [1979] 1 WLR 395, CA.
7 *R v Upton, R v Formosa*, [1991] 1 All ER 131 at 133.
8 Ie the Firearms Act 1968, s 5(1).

10.79 Following from Lloyd LJ's decision in *R v Upton*, it seems appropriate to surmise that a yard that has been taken over and operated as an occasional waste transfer station, but which is being used without any physical changes, is not 'a site designed or adapted for the reception of waste with a view to its being disposed of elsewhere'[1]. However, if the layout had been changed, by, for example, adding some bays for the transferring of waste, then the site clearly has been designed or adapted. But from *North Yorkshire County Council v Boyne* it would seem[2] that the changes made to the premises must be directly material to the manner by which waste is itself handled. If the Divisional Court's analysis in *Boyne* is to be followed, general site works – such as landscaping – do not provide significant enough alterations for a site to be 'designed or adapted' for the reception of waste.

1 As in SI 1994/1056, Sch 3, para 40(1)(c).
2 But this must be regarded as a somewhat tentative conclusion given the significant caveats contained in that judgment.

10.80 Besides the words 'designed or adapted' contained in this exemption, it seems that the requirement of the exemption – that storage is 'incidental to' the collection and transportation of waste[1] – has the purpose of differentiating between occasional waste storage and waste transfer station operations. The Department of the Environment's understanding of 'incidental to' is outlined in Circular 11/94[2]. The requirement that the storage of waste must be incidental to collection and transportation:

'... clearly distinguishes it [ie storage] from disposal or recovery operations. Such exempt storage might include gathering waste from multi-occupied premises into shared containers for collection; the gathering in a skip at a yard or depot of waste produced by a contractor in the course of work at other sites; and the storage of waste in mobile containers that are temporarily stationary during a journey.'

1   SI 1994/1056, Sch 3, para 40(1)(d).
2   Circular 11/94, Annex 5, para 5.230.

10.81   Despite the Department of the Environment's assertions above, precisely how the word 'incidental' should be interpreted seems open to some much greater doubt. The Concise Oxford Dictionary (1995 Edition) gives the word the following meanings:

'1.adj. . . . a) having a minor role in relation to a more important thing, event, etc b) not essential . . .'

The Collins Concise Dictionary (1997) gives a similar meaning:

'adj. 1. happening in connection with or resulting from something more important; casual or fortuitous. 2.(post positive; foll. by to) found in connection (with); related (to) . . . .'

From the Department of the Environment's quotation above and this analysis, it would appear allowable for a waste collection company to occasionally – but not regularly or frequently – store wastes in their general haulage yards prior to disposal[1]. The *Boyne* case is a classic example of such an instance. In this respect, it does seem rather doubtful that these practices are desirable, particularly as the exemption allows storage for up to three months[2]. Whilst it may be fair to provide exemptions which allow for temporary storage in respect of instances such as where all local landfill sites became shut due to sudden and unexpected inclement weather, or where a load of waste had been rejected by a site as unsuitable[3,4], this particular exemption seems open to abuse.

1   Provided, of course, that the premises had not been designed or adapted for the waste management activity.
2   SI 1994/1056, Sch 3, para 40(1)(a).
3   Although, if it was special waste, it could not be brought back and stored under this exemption.
4   These circumstances may be addressed by way of an interpretation of the offence of 'keeping' waste on land without a waste management licence: see para 7.26.

10.82   There also remains a significant question over whether this exemption is congruent with Community law. The Directive on Waste clearly holds that the intermediate storage of waste beyond the site of production is a waste disposal activity[1] in the instance when the final destination of the waste is itself to be disposal. Accordingly, being a disposal activity, a permit is always needed and the dispensation in respect of the lesser registration system does not apply[2]. Indeed, the only type of occasion when an exemption for intermediate storage is allowable is in respect of the incidental storage of waste prior to submission to a recovery activity. Regrettably this point did not feature in the argument of *Boyne*. However, the uncontested facts of that case clearly suggest that waste was being stored prior to disposal at a landfill 15 miles away. For this reason alone, a quite different judgment may have emerged if it had been suggested by the prosecution that the paragraph 40 exemption needs to be interpreted in the light of the requirements of the Directive on Waste.

1   See Council Directive of 15 July 1975 on Waste (75/442/EEC), (OJ L194/39 25.7.75) (as amended by Council Directive of 18 March 1991 amending Directive 75/442/EEC on Waste (91/156/EEC) (OJ L78/32 26.3.91) and by Commission Decision of 24 May 1996 adapting Annexes IIA and IIB to Council Directive 75/442/EEC on Waste (OJ L135/32 6.6.96)) Annex IIA, Item D15.
2   Council Directive of 15 July 1975 on Waste (75/442/EEC), (OJ L194/39 25.7.75) (as amended by Council Directive of 18 March 1991 amending Directive 75/442/EEC on Waste (91/156/EEC) (OJ L78/32 26.3.91)) Article 11(1).

Storage of materials prior to their recycling

10.83   Besides the off-site storage of waste which is incidental to waste collection or transportation, paragraphs 17 and 18 to Schedule 3 permit the exempt storage of certain specified materials in a secure[1] place[2] or in secure containers[3] where they are going to be re-used or recovered[4]. The range of permissible materials is shown in Table 10.2 and they are mainly ones that are likely to be destined for recycling. They are mainly limited to non-special wastes[5], with the exception of solvents, halons and refrigerants[6]. The categories of mammalian protein – otherwise known as bonemeal – and tallow were added to this Table by the Waste Management Licensing (Amendment) Regulations 1996[7]. This amendment is discussed separately at para 10.92 below.

1   'Secure' is defined in SI 1994/1056, reg 17(5), see para 10.36 above.
2   SI 1994/1056, Sch 3, para 17 as amended by SI 1996/1279, reg 2.
3   SI 1994/1056, Sch 3, para 18.
4   The occupier's consent or other entitlement to carry on the activity on the land is needed (SI 1994/1056, Sch 3, reg 17(2) as amended by SI 1995/288, reg 3(6)).
5   SI 1994/1056, reg 17(3).
6   SI 1994/1056, reg 17, Table 4: it is proposed to add waste paint (including paint which is special waste), waste from printing or photographic processing (including special waste), nickel cadmium batteries (including batteries which are special waste) to the list (see DETR (1998) *Consultation Paper – Proposed Amendments to the Special Waste Regulations 1996 and the Waste Management Licensing Regulations 1994*, DETR, London, April 1998).
7   SI 1996/1279.

Table 10.2

Waste Management Licensing Regulations 1994

Exempt Storage Limits for Materials Collected for Recycling[1]

Type of Waste	*Maximum Total Quantity*
Waste paper and cardboard	15,000 tonnes
Waste textiles	1,000 tonnes
Waste plastics	500 tonnes
Waste glass	5,000 tonnes
Waste steel or aluminium cans or aluminium foil	500 tonnes
Waste food and drink cartons	500 tonnes
Waste articles 'which are to be used for construction work which are capable of being so used in their existing state'	100 tonnes
Solvents (including solvents which are special waste)	5 cubic metres
Refrigerants[2] and halons (including refrigerants and halons which are special waste)	18 tonnes
Tyres	1,000 tyres
Waste mammalian protein	60,000 tonnes
Waste mammalian tallow	45,000 tonnes

1   SI 1994/1056, Sch 3, para 17, Table 4 (as amended by SI 1996/1279).
2   Defined in SI 1994/1056, Sch 3, para 17(2).

10.84   The materials shown in Table 10.2 can be stored 'on any premises'[1], and such premises can include the site where the wastes are recovered. According to Circular 11/94 the primary intention of the exemption 'is to permit the bulking up of the most important materials returned for recycling at intermediate deposits and stores between initial collection and final recovery points'[2].

1 SI 1994/1056, Sch 3, paras 17(1) and 18(1).
2 Circular 11/94, Annex 5, para 5.133.

10.85 The other requirement of the exemption in respect of the storage in a secure place is that the total amounts shown in Table 10.2 are not exceeded[1]. Each of the materials listed in the Table should be kept separately on the premises[2] and, accordingly, a mixture of such wastes is not allowed. It is also a requirement that the wastes have to be 're-used, or used for the purposes of' baling, sorting, shredding, densifying, washing, crushing, pulverising, compacting or 'any other recovery operation'[3]. A further proviso is that the wastes are not stored on the premises for a period longer than 12 months[4].

1 More than one substance in Table 10.2 can be stored on a premises, provided that the totals for each of the individual substances are not exceeded. In other words, 500 tonnes of cans can be stored with 5,000 tonnes of glass, as long as the materials are segregated (see Circular 11/94, Annex 5, para 5.135).
2 SI 1994/1056, Sch 3, para 17(1)(c).
3 SI 1994/1056, Sch 3, para 17(1)(b).
4 SI 1994/1056, Sch 3, para 17(1)(d) .

10.86 There are a number of items of note from Table 10.2. Firstly, unlike most of the exemptions, solvents and refrigerants which are special wastes can be stored under the exemption[1]. Secondly, the exemption for waste articles to be used in construction work is highly restricted. As discussed at para 10.131, this exemption is designed to permit architectural salvage to take place but not the general recovery of construction industry materials.

1 See SI 1994/1056, Sch 3, para 17, Table 4.

10.87 Oddly, this exemption permits the storage of up to 15,000 tonnes of 'paper and cardboard'[1]. However, as will be discussed later[2], the exemption in Schedule 3, paragraph 13, which relates to the storage prior to 'manufacture', only permits the storage of 'paper' – cardboard is not mentioned – and the maximum quantity stipulated is 20,000 tonnes.

1 SI 1994/1056, Sch 3, para 17.
2 See para 10.182.

10.88 In addition to the exemption which permits a person to hold wastes in a secure place, with the exception of solvents, refrigerants and halons, paragraph 18 to Schedule 3 allows these wastes to be also stored 'on any premises' in secure containers[1]. Besides the list of substances in Table 10.2, waste oils can also be stored under this exemption[2]. This exemption is principally aimed at recycling centres for household wastes, which contain such items as bottle and can banks, a waste oil container and so on. For this reason, the quantity limits set are based on the capacity of the containers and not on the total amount that can be stored at the site at any one time.

1 SI 1994/1056, Sch 3, para 18. 'Secure' is defined in SI 1994/1056, reg 17(5): see para 10.36 above.
2 SI 1994/1056, Sch 3, para 18(1)(b) and 18(2)(b) (as amended by SI 1996/972, reg 25 and Sch 3).

10.89 Accordingly, no waste management licence is needed, provided that the storage capacity of the containers does not collectively exceed 400 cubic metres[1]. These materials also have to be stored on a premises with the intention that the materials are to be processed by one of the exempt activities listed[2] in Table 10.5 (see para 10.177) or are to pass to any other type of recovery activity[3]. In addition, each type of waste must be stored separately[4]; no waste should be stored on the premises for longer than 12 months[5] and the person storing the waste must be the owner of the containers or have the consent of their owner[6].

1   SI 1994/1056, Sch 3, para 18(1)(a).
2   In SI 1994/1056, Sch 3, para 11: baling, sorting, shredding, densifying, washing, crushing, pulverising and compacting.
3   SI 1994/1056, Sch 3, para 18(1)(d).
4   SI 1994/1056, Sch 3, para 18(1)(e).
5   SI 1994/1056, Sch 3, para 18(1)(f).
6   SI 1994/1056, Sch 3, para 18(1)(g).

10.90   Finally, the exemption requires that there cannot be more than 20 such containers on the premises at any one time. Given that a typical builder's skip is about eight cubic metres, the limit on container numbers will be the main constraint. In the case of the larger 30 or 40 cubic metre roll-on-off containers, the requirement that no more than 400 cubic metres of capacity is available will be the principal restriction. For waste oil storage, Schedule 3, paragraph 18(1)(b) additionally requires that no more than three cubic metres is to be stored in total and that provision is made 'to prevent oil escaping into the ground or a drain'.

10.91   Establishments or undertakings operating facilities which are exempt under paragraphs 17 and 18 are required to have their locations registered with the relevant Agency[1].

1   SI 1994/1056, reg 18(10)(d).

Bonemeal and tallow storage

10.92   In the midst of the BSE crisis in 1996, provisions to exempt the temporary storage of bonemeal[1] and tallow[2] were added to the Waste Management Licensing Regulations 1994[3]. The general requirements for the exempt storage of bonemeal and tallow are the same as those set down for the other waste types covered at para 10.83ff above, with quantity limits being shown in Table 10.2. Storage can be at a secure place[4] or in secure containers[5], the waste must be segregated from other wastes[6] and storage must not exceed 12 months[7]. In the case of storage in containers, no more that 20 containers can be in place on the premises[8] and the storage capacity of the containers must not exceed 400 cubic metres in total[9]. Finally, it is essential to the exemption that the wastes are to be eventually recovered[10].

1   Termed in the exemptions 'mammalian protein', which is defined as meaning 'proteinaceous material . . . derived from the whole or part of any dead animal by a process of crushing, cooking or grinding' (SI 1994/1056, Sch 3, para 17(3) as amended by SI 1996/1279, reg 2(1)(b)).
2   Defined as meaning 'fat . . . derived from the whole or part of any dead animal by a process of crushing, cooking or grinding' (SI 1994/1056, Sch 3, para 17(3) as amended by SI 1996/1279, reg 2(b)).
3   SI 1994/1056, Sch 3, para 17 as amended by SI 1996/1279, reg 2(1).
4   SI 1994/1056, Sch 3, para 17.
5   SI 1994/1056, Sch 3, para 18.
6   SI 1994/1056, Sch 3, para 17(1)(c) and 18(1)(e).
7   SI 1994/1056, Sch 3, para 17(1)(d) and 18(1)(f).
8   SI 1994/1056, Sch 3, para 18(1)(c).
9   SI 1994/1056, Sch 3, para 18(1)(a). The person storing the waste must be the owner of the containers or have that person's consent: SI 1994/1056, Sch 3, para 18(1)(g).
10 SI 1994/1056, Sch 3, para 17(1)(b) and 18(1)(d).

10.93 The quantities permitted under this exemption are considerable and reflect the backlog of bonemeal and tallow which was awaiting disposal at that time. Although these provisions were no doubt an invaluable stop-gap measure to ensure the continued storage of the material without the requirement of a waste management licence, the exemption only applies where the stored materials are to be recovered later[1]. The most obvious recovery operation for these wastes is combustion as a fuel source in an incinerator equipped with energy reclamation capability[2]. Tallow has a relatively high calorific value and is most suitable. Bonemeal, by contrast, has a low calorific value of between 12–15 MJ/kg[3] and may be less attractive to operators of such plant. But it is essential to the exempt storage of this material that later recovery is guaranteed. Landfill or incineration without energy recovery are classified within the list of disposal facilities set out in the Waste Management Licensing Regulations 1994[4], hence a waste management licence is necessary for storage prior to the use of these other options. Similarly such a licence is needed if any of the other requirements of the exemption – such as the 12 month maximum storage period – are exceeded.

1 Temporary exempt storage at locations beyond the site of production is only allowable in respect of the eventual recovery of the stored materials (SI 1994/1056, Sch 3, para 17(1)(b)(ii) and 18(1)(d)(ii)).
2 In SI 1994/1056, recovery is held to include the use of waste as a fuel (see reg 1(3) and Sch 4, Pt IV, Item 9).
3 By contrast, an equivalent figure for household waste is between 7 and 10 MJ/kg: see for example Royal Commission on Environmental Pollution (1993) *Seventeenth Report. Incineration of Waste*, CMND 2181, HMSO, London, Chapter 5.
4 SI 1994/1056, reg 1(3) and Sch 4, Pt III, Items 1 and 10 respectively.

Storage of wastes prior to burning or use as a fuel

10.94 Straw, poultry litter[1], wood, and 'solid fuel which has been manufactured from waste by a process involving the application of heat' can be subject to secure[2] storage 'on any premises' without needing a waste management licence[3]. No quantity or time limits have been set to control this storage. However, to be exempt, they must be 'intended to be burned' in a plant which has a Part B authorisation granted under Part 1 of the EPA 1990[4]. It should be noted that Part A processes are excluded and hence the exemption does not apply to off-site storage prior to use in a Part A process.

1 Many such substances from an agricultural premises may not be controlled waste under the EPA 1990, see s 75(7) and see para 2.60.
2 'Secure' is defined in SI 1994/1056, reg 17(5): see para 10.36 above.
3 SI 1994/1056, Sch 3, para 3(b).
4 SI 1994/1056, Sch 3, para 3(b).

10.95 Tyres can also be stored prior to combustion and remain exempt under paragraph 3 to Schedule 3 of the Waste Management Licensing Regulations 1994[1]. This exemption appears to duplicate separate provisions for scrap tyre storage contained in paragraphs 17 and 18[2]. Under paragraph 3, tyres can be stored at any place, but the storage must be secure[3] and the tyres should be 'intended to be submitted to' burning as a fuel under the separate exemption in Schedule 3, paragraph 3(d)[4]. This exemption holds only where the tyres are stored separately[5]; where 'none of the tyres' are stored on the premises for over 12 months[6]; and where the total number stored does not 'at any time' exceed 1,000[7].

1 SI 1994/1056, Sch 3, para 3(e).
2 See para 10.83ff.
3 'Secure' is defined in SI 1994/1056, reg 17(5): see para 10.36 above.

4   See para 10.229ff.
5   SI 1994/1056, Sch 3, para 3(e)(ii): Circular 11/94 advises: '. . . separate storage does not preclude the use of the same site for waste tyres and other storage, but there must be some separation between them, whether a barrier or simply by distance' (see Annex 5, para 5.55).
6   SI 1994/1056, Sch 3, para 3(e)(iii).
7   SI 1994/1056, Sch 3, para 3(e)(iv).

10.96   It is notable that the exemption does not restrict storage to the location of the combustion process but refers to any place. However, this exemption only relates[1] to storage prior to burning in a process subject to an appropriate Part B authorisation[2]. Accordingly, it would appear that intermediate storage of tyres prior to consignment to a Part A combustion process is licensable or is limited to the quantities set down in the other exemptions contained elsewhere in paragraphs 17 and 18 to Schedule 3[3]. However, if the tyres are located on the premises where they are produced, the much wider limits contained in the paragraph 41 exemption apply[4].

1   SI 1994/1056, Sch 3, para 3(d).
2   The process must figure in SI 1991/472, Sch 1, Pt B, Section 1.3 (as amended by SI 1992/614, reg 2, Sch 1, para 7; SI 1994/1271, reg 3, Sch 1, para 2 and reg 4(3), Sch 3, para 6).
3   See para 10.83.
4   See para 10.55.

Waste oil intermediate storage

10.97   Waste oil[1] can be subject to exempt storage under Schedule 3, paragraph 6(2). However, to remain exempt, storage must be for the purposes of the subsequent use as a fuel in a combustion engine and must be secure[2] The amount that can be stored appears to be unlimited and the material can be stored at any place.

1   While the other references to waste oil in Schedule 3 have been amended (by SI 1996/972, reg 25 and Sch 3) to permit waste oil which is defined as special waste to be subject to exempt storage, no such change has been made to the wording of the exemption contained in para 6.
2   'Secure' is defined in SI 1994/1056, reg 17(5): see para 10.36 above.

10.98   In the case of waste oil storage prior to any other type of recovery process, the requirements on quantities are more restricted. Schedule 3 paragraph 18 allows for the exempt storage of no more than three cubic metres of waste oil[1]. This includes oil which is special waste[2]. Again, storage should be secure, but in addition, provision should be made to prevent the oil escaping onto the ground or into a drain[3]. Storage must not exceed a 12-month period[4] and a maximum of 20 containers are to be used[5].

1   SI 1994/1056, Sch 3, para 18(1)(b).
2   SI 1994/1056, Sch 3, para 18(2)(b) as amended by SI 1996/972, reg 25, Sch 3.
3   SI 1994/1056, Sch 3, para 18(1)(b).
4   SI 1994/1056, Sch 3, para 18(1)(f).
5   SI 1994/1056, Sch 3, para 18(1)(c).

Storage of returned goods

10.99   Many faulty or unsuitable goods sent back to the manufacturer or distributor would not generally be regarded as waste. Often there is no indication of discarding the item within such transactions. However, in a small number of circumstances, it is conceivable that the materials could be waste. Examples might be a product recall where the goods are so faulty as not to warrant repair, or where foodstuffs have been found to be contaminated. Accordingly, an exemption in Schedule 3, paragraph 28[1] has been devised for these, and other, circumstances.

1   SI 1994/1056, Sch 3, para 28 as amended by SI 1996/972, reg 25 and Sch 3.

10.100 The 'manufacturer, distributor or retailer' is allowed to store the 'returned goods that are waste' for a period of a month without the need to possess a waste management licence[1]. To be exempt, they must be being stored with the purpose of subsequent recovery or disposal[2]. The exemption covers special waste, provided that the storage is secure[3]. Interestingly, given its advice elsewhere on the nature of the definition of waste[4], Circular 11/94 envisages that trade-in goods would be covered by this exemption[5]. All such exempt activities require a registration with the relevant Agency[6].

1 Note that certain goods, such as textiles, bottles etc, might fall within the wider exemption contained in SI 1994/1056, Sch 3, paras 17 and 18 – see para 10.83 above.
2 SI 1994/1056, Sch 3, para 28 as amended by SI 1996/972, reg 25 and Sch 3.
3 'Secure' is defined in SI 1994/1056, reg 17(5): see para 10.36. However, the word 'secure' is used in conjunction with the words 'container, lagoon or place'. In the exemption contained in para 28 of Sch 3, the term 'secure' is used on its own. This may lead to some doubt about whether the more usual definition applies to this particular paragraph.
4 See Circular 11/94, Annex 2 and see para 2.103ff.
5 Circular 11/94, Annex 5, para 5.183: note that the Circular is referring to the wording in Sch 3, para 28 prior to its replacement by SI 1996/972, reg 25 and Sch 3. Perhaps significantly in respect of developments in the understanding of the definition of waste (see para 2.131ff), the word 're-use' in the exemption as originally drafted has not been continued.
6 SI 1994/1056, reg 18(10)(d).

Waste medicines stored at pharmacists, doctors, vets etc

10.101 Under paragraph 39 to Schedule 3, waste medicines[1] can be accepted by any[2] pharmacy. However, a proviso is that they must have been returned from either households or by individuals[3]. This appears to disallow waste medicines from factory sick rooms, for example, being returned and stored under this exemption, as well as other more commercial enterprises. The other provisos of the exemption are that the total amount of returned medicines does not exceed 5 cubic metres at the pharmacy; that each individual item of waste passes out of the premises within a six month period; and that the storage is secure[4].

1 Including special waste.
2 See Circular 11/94, Annex 5, para 5.223.
3 Sch 3, para 39(1).
4 SI 1994/1056, Sch 3, para 39(1)(a) and (b). 'Secure' is defined in SI 1994/1056, reg 17(5): see para 10.36 above.

10.102 This paragraph exempts pharmacists from the need to possess a waste management licence if they become involved in the return of out of date or surplus drugs. Some pharmacists offer such a service as a means of ensuring safe disposal.

10.103 Similar exempt storage can occur at the premises of a medical, nursing or veterinary practice for wastes 'produced in carrying out that practice'[1]. Again, up to 5 cubic metres can be stored, but any such wastes have to be moved on after three, rather than six months[2]. An additional contrast between these two provisions is that storage in a pharmacy must be 'secure'[3], but there is no such requirement for medical practitioners, vets etc.

1 Note the contrast to Sch 3, para 39(1) which applies to pharmacists but allows them to store only medicines returned from individuals and households.
2 SI 1994/1056, Sch 3, para 39(2). Circular 11/94 (Annex 5, para 5.224) erroneously states that the period is six months.
3 'Secure' is defined in SI 1994/1056, reg 17(5): see para 10.36 above.

10.104   All doctors, pharmacists, etc are required to register with the Agency which covers their premises when they are involved in the exempt activities described above[1].

1   SI 1994/1056, Sch 3, reg 18(10).

Storage of garbage and tank washings from ships[1]

10.105   Garbage and tank washings from ships are industrial waste under the Controlled Waste Regulations 1992[2]. Schedule 3 to the Waste Management Licensing Regulations 1994 provides that the temporary storage of wastes[3] consisting of garbage[4] at a reception facility located within a harbour area[5] is exempt from the need to possess a waste management licence[6]. Should wastes from ships which are not garbage or tank washings be stored, this exemption does not apply[7], while if the storage of such garbage and tank washings is not restricted to the harbour area[5], a waste management licence is also required[8]. Furthermore, to be exempt, the Waste Management Licensing Regulations 1994 require that the storage must be in accordance with the requirements of the Merchant Shipping (Reception Facilities for Garbage) Regulations 1988[9]. The latter Regulations, in fact, were revoked in 1998[10]. The exemption also requires storage to be 'incidental' to the collection or transport of the waste. According to Circular 11/94[11], this disallows the exemption where storage is undertaken pending treatment or disposal in the harbour area. An interpretation of 'incidental' has been described at para 10.74ff.

1   Provision has been made in s 130A to D of the Merchant Shipping Act 1995 by s 5 of the Merchant Shipping and Maritime Security Act 1997 to make regulations to require the provision of waste reception facilities in harbours and the making of waste management plans for such harbours. The resultant provisions were the Merchant Shipping (Port Waste Reception Facilities) Regulations 1997 (SI 1997/3018). There is also a draft directive on controlling ship waste at ports: Proposal for a Council Directive for Ship-Generated Waste and Cargo Residues (OJ C271/79 31.8.98).
2   SI 1992/588, reg 5(1) (as amended by SI 1994/1056, reg 24(4)) and Sch 3, para 18.
3   This includes garbage which is special waste: SI 1994/1056, Sch 3, para 36(1).
4   Defined by the now revoked Merchant Shipping (Reception Facilities for Garbage) Regulations 1988 (SI 1988/2293).
5   As defined in the Dangerous Substances in Harbour Areas Regulations 1987 (SI 1987/37). See para 4.118.
6   SI 1994/1056, Sch 3, para 36.
7   Circular 11/94, Annex 5, para 5.216.
8   Circular 11/94, Annex 5, para 5.208.
9   SI 1988/2293.
10 Being replaced by the Merchant Shipping (Port Waste Reception Facilities) Regulations 1997 (SI 1997/3018: see reg 16).
11 Circular 11/94, Annex 5, para 5.208.

10.106   The other requirements of this exemption are that the storage of garbage must not exceed a limit of 20 cubic metres 'for each ship[1] from which garbage has been landed'; and the garbage must not be stored for over seven days[2].

1   Defined as meaning 'a vessel of any type whatsoever operating in the marine environment including submersible craft, floating craft and any structure which is a fixed or floating platform' (SI 1994/1056, Sch 3, para 36(3)).
2   SI 1994/1056, Sch 3, para 36(1).

10.107   The 'temporary' storage of tank washings[1] is also exempt from licensing[2]. To be exempt, the storage must occur at reception facilities in the harbour area[3] in accordance with the Prevention of Pollution (Reception Facilities) Order 1984[4]. As was the case with marine garbage, the storage must be 'incidental' to the collection or transport of the waste[5]. In addition, the amount of tank washings 'consisting of dirty ballast' stored in the harbour must not exceed 30% of the total deadweight of the ships from which the washings have been landed[6], while the amount of tank washings consisting of 'waste mixtures containing oil' must not exceed 1% of the total deadweight of the ships from which the washings have been landed[7]. The latter may prove a rather difficult evidential requirement on the luckless Agency officer who has to enforce this provision.

1   Defined as meaning 'waste residues from tanks (other than fuel tanks) or holds of a ship or waste arising from the cleaning of such tanks or holds' (SI 1994/1056, Sch 3, para 36(3)). Tank washings may be special waste under SI 1996/972: see Chapter 4.
2   SI 1994/1056, Sch 3, para 36(2).
3   As defined in the Dangerous Substances in Harbour Areas Regulations 1987 (SI 1987/37): discussed at para 4.118.
4   SI 1984/862: revoked and replaced in 1998 by SI 1997/3018, reg 16.
5   SI 1994/1056, Sch 3, para 36(2): see para 10.74.
6   SI 1994/1056, Sch 3, para 36(2)(a).
7   SI 1994/1056, Sch 3, para 36(2)(b).

10.108   These activities do not need to be registered[1] under reg 18.

1   See SI 1994/1056, reg 18(10) and Circular 11/94, Annex 5, Table 5.1.

Storage of construction industry wastes and waste ash, slag, clinker, rock, wood and gypsum

10.109   These wastes can be stored under the terms of the exemption contained in Schedule 3, paragraph 19 of the Waste Mangement Licensing Regulations 1994. This exemption is discussed at para 10.125, alongside all the other exemptions which affect construction and demolition activities.

Exemptions for wastes created or used by the construction industry

10.110   A wide range of wastes for construction and demolition activities are covered by exemptions in the Waste Management Licensing Regulations 1994. These will be discussed below. In the case of demolition, particular care should be taken to ensure that no special wastes – such as asbestos or disused tanks containing chemicals – are involved. If they are, the exemptions discussed below may not apply.

10.111   In addition to a detailed consideration of the wording of the exemptions, there is a need to ensure that the material in question is waste in the first place. Certain construction industry materials will not be discarded[1]. As Circular 11/94 points out[2], no exemptions have been drafted for wastes arising from excavations or from boreholes constructed in connection with water supply or sewerage. If such excavations or boreholes are simply refilled with the displaced material, this material would never fall within the definition of waste under s 75 of the EPA 1990. Hence the temporary storage and the infilling process would not need a licence, nor would it require exemption.

1   Waste definitions and 'discarding' are discussed at para 2.75ff, and for example para 2.182.
2   Circular 11/94, Annex 5, para 5.204.

Using wastes in construction work

10.112   Under Schedule 3, paragraph 19 of the Waste Management Licensing Regulations 1994, exemptions are allowed for the use and temporary storage of waste from demolition and construction work[1]. Similarly, materials derived from tunnelling and excavation, or wastes which consist of ash, slag, clinker, rock, wood or gypsum can be used for the purposes of construction work. Such construction work can include the deposit of waste in connection with the provision of recreational facilities[2] or the construction, maintenance or improvement of a building, highway, railway, airport, dock or other transport facility[3]. However, 'the deposit of waste in any other circumstances or any work involving land reclamation' is excluded from the terms of this exemption[4]. The function of the latter requirement is explained in Circular 11/94[5]. The deliberate limitation of the construction waste exemption to the items stipulated above would exclude the piling of wastes in heaps or mounds which may be claimed as being part of the works, but are in reality a cheap way of disposing of excess construction or demolition material.

1   Note 'construction work' is defined in SI 1994/1056, reg 1(3) as including the repair, alteration or improvement of existing works. The use of the word 'include' should be noted; 'work' is viewed as including preparatory work.
2   Circular 11/94 gives the example of the landscaping of a golf course – see Annex 5, para 5.158.
3   All of the activities listed are defined as 'relevant work' in SI 1994/1056, Sch 3, para 19(4).
4   SI 1994/1056, Sch 3, para 19(4).
5   See Circular 11/94, Annex 5, para 5.159.

10.113   Where such wastes are to be used in construction work, the proviso is that the waste must be 'suitable for use for the purposes of relevant work[1] which will be carried on at the site'[2]. Therefore wastes contaminated with materials such as paper, cardboard and other biodegradable type refuse should not be viewed as suitable for the purpose of the construction of, for example, building foundations. In addition, it is submitted that each of the waste types stipulated in the exemption should also be suitable for the purpose to which it is put. Therefore waste wood can be used extensively for a range of construction industry applications under this exemption. An example might be the building of a temporary site fence or cabin. But that does not mean that wood is suitable for all construction works. It would not be appropriate to have large quantities of wood mixed with hardcore for use as foundations.

1   Relevant work means
        'construction work, including the deposit of waste on land in connection with –
        (a) the provision of recreational facilities on that land; or
        (b) the construction, maintenance or improvement of a building, highway, railway, airport, dock or other transport facility on that land,
        but not including either any deposit of waste in any other circumstances or any work involving land reclamation' (SI 1994/1056, Sch 3, para 19(4)).
2   SI 1994/1056, Sch 3, para 19(2); see also *Environment Agency v Short* [1999] Env LR 300.

10.114   In this respect, it should also be noted that waste wood is no longer classed as a suitable material to be sent to landfill sites accepting inert wastes[1]. A deep pile of wood covered by soil, ostensibly for a screening bund, will rot down and landfill gas or leachate may result. Given that Waste Management Paper No 4 advises against wood being deposited at landfills which are licensed only to accept inert waste, it seems to be quite inappropriate that wood can be deposited at a construction site under this exemption.

1   See Department of the Environment (1994) *Waste Management Paper No 4 Licensing of Waste Management Facilities* (3rd edn) HMSO paras 5.17ff. Wood is also excluded from the list of 'qualifying materials' to which the lower level of landfill tax applies (see Landfill Tax (Qualifying Material) Order 1996, SI 1996/1528 and see para 3.138). See also HM Customs and Excise (1997) Notice LFT1 *A General Guide to the Landfill Tax*, para 2.3.

10.115   All exemptions under the above provisions need to register with the relevant Agency[1].

1   SI 1994/1056, reg 18(10)(d).

The reclamation and re-use of construction wastes

10.116 Besides the direct usage of construction industry materials, many reclamation processes involving construction wastes are also exempt from needing a waste management licence.

10.117 The 'crushing, grinding or other size reduction' of waste bricks, tiles and concrete is exempt[1] where such plants are in possession of a relevant Part B authorisation[2]. Should the activity not have an authorisation, the exemption does not, of course, apply. However, if the crushing, grinding, etc operations occur elsewhere from where the waste was produced, the exemption only applies 'if those activities are carried on with a view to recovery or re-use of the waste'[3].

1 SI 1994/1056, Sch 3, para 24.
2 SI 1991/472, Sch 1, Section 3.4, Pt B, para (c): 'the crushing, grinding, or other size reduction, with machinery designed for that purpose, of bricks, tiles or concrete'.
3 SI 1994/1056, Sch 3, para 24(2).

10.118 Up to 20,000 tonnes of such materials can be stored at any one time at the place where the process is carried on[1]. By contrast to the other construction-related exemptions, which permit wastes to be stored prior to the operation actually starting, the wording of paragraph 24(3) does not allow the storage of materials before the crushing operation has commenced.

1 SI 1994/1056, Sch 3, para 24(3).

10.119 Being a process under local control by way of Part 1 of the EPA 1990, there is no need for this process to be separately registered with the Agency. The details contained in application for registration as a Part B process are deemed sufficient[1].

1 SI 1994/1056, reg 18(5).

10.120 The 'manufacture' of specified materials from construction industry wastes is also exempt[1] under Schedule 3, paragraph 13. Timber products, straw board, plasterboard, bricks, blocks, roadstone or aggregate can all be produced from specified wastes without the requirement to possess a waste management licence. The exemption holds provided that these products are derived from wastes arising from construction and demolition work, or from tunnelling and other excavation wastes, or from waste ash, slag, clinker, rock, wood or bark[2]. It should be pointed out that it is easy to misread paragraph 13(1) of Schedule 3 to the Waste Management Licensing Regulations 1994 and to overlook the fact that the final line is not indented. The exemption does *not* allow the exempt manufacture of items from waste timber products, straw board, plasterboard, bricks, blocks, roadstone or aggregate. It simply permits ash, slag, clinker, etc to be made into them. This is confirmed by the Circular 11/94[3].

1 The occupier's consent or other entitlement to carry on the activity on the land is needed
(SI 1994/1056, reg 17(2) as amended by SI 1995/288, reg 3(6)).
2 SI 1994/1056, Sch 3, para 13(1)(a). Waste paper, straw and gypsum can also be used to manufacture these materials under the terms of this exemption, but these are discussed elsewhere in this chapter as they are not strictly construction industry wastes.
3 See Annex 5, para 5.112.

10.121 Soil or soil substitute manufacture is also exempt[1] provided the soil arises from demolition, construction, excavation or tunnelling work or is derived from one of the substances in the inclusive list of wastes[2] set out in Schedule 3, paragraph 13(1)(b).

It should be noted that the manufacture of soil from other sources is not exempt[3]. The further requirements of the exemption are that soil manufacture can only occur where the waste is produced or where the soil or soil substitute is to be applied to the land[4]. Finally, the total amount manufactured should not exceed 500 tonnes per day[5].

1 SI 1994/1056, Sch 3, para 13(2).
2 Ash, slag, clinker, rock, wood, bark, paper, straw or gypsum.
3 Dredgings from a canal which were used to manufacture soil substitutes were considered in *London Waste Regulation Authority v Drinkwater Sabey Ltd* [1997] Env LR 137: see para 10.47.
4 SI 1994/1056, Sch 3, para 13(2)(a).
5 SI 1994/1056, Sch 3, para 13(2)(b)

10.122 The 'treatment' of waste 'soil or rock' is exempt under Schedule 3, paragraph 13(3) where these materials are to be later spread on agricultural land[1] under the exemption in paragraph 7 or on other land[2] under the exemption in Schedule 3, paragraph 9. A maximum of 100 tonnes per day is allowable[3]. However, to be exempt, the treatment can only be undertaken at the place where the waste is produced or where the treated product is to be spread[4]. In this respect, Circular 11/94 notes that the exemption for the treatment process is qualified by the requirements of the exemption relating to the actual spreading activity itself: particularly that the resultant spreading should satisfy the criteria of the separate spreading exemptions themselves[5]. Hence treatment prior to spreading for the purposes of the agricultural or ecological improvement of the land[6] will only be exempt if those benefits result. Clearly, if no agricultural or ecological improvement will result from the material that is treated under this exemption, the exemption for the treatment process itself does not hold.

1 Discussed at para 10.140.
2 Discussed at para 10.153.
3 SI 1994/1056, Sch 3, para 13(3)(b).
4 SI 1994/1056, Sch 3, para 13(3)(a).
5 Circular 11/94, Annex 5, para 5.115.
6 SI 1994/1056, Sch 3, para 7(3).

10.123 All of the exempt activities under Schedule 3, paragraph 13 need to be registered with the relevant Agency[1].

1 SI 1994/1056, reg 18(10)(d).

Storage of construction industry wastes

10.124 Like all other types of waste, construction and demolition waste can be stored at the site of production pending its collection for disposal or re-use without a waste management licence being needed[1]. In addition to this exemption, where construction or demolition wastes are to be sent for re-use or are to be imported onto a site to be re-utilised in other construction work, a range of other exemptions may apply. All such exempt activities need to register with the Agency[2].

1 SI 1994/1056, Sch 3, para 41: see para 10.55.
2 SI 1994/1056, reg 18(10)(d).

10.125 Waste from demolition and construction work[1], materials from tunnelling and excavation or waste which consists of ash, slag, clinker, rock, wood or gypsum can be stored 'on a site' for the purposes of construction work prior to the work commencing[2]. The proviso is that the waste must be 'suitable for use for the purposes of the relevant work[3] which will be carried on at the site'[4]. Where the waste was not produced on the site, it can only be stored for a period of three months before the work starts.

1 'Construction work' is defined as including 'repair, alteration or improvement of existing works', whilst 'work' includes preparatory work (SI 1994/1056, reg 1(3)).
2 SI 1994/1056, Sch 3, para 19(1). The occupier's consent or other entitlement to carry on the activity on the land is needed (SI 1994/1056, reg 17(2) as amended by SI 1995/288 reg 3(6)).
3 Relevant work
    'means construction work, including the deposit of waste on land in connection with –
    (a) the provision of recreational facilities on that land; or
    (b) the construction, maintenance or improvement of a building, highway, railway, airport, dock or other transport facility on that land,
    but not including either any deposit of waste in any other circumstances or any work involving land reclamation' (SI 1994/1056, Sch 3, para 19(4)).
4 The nature of 'suitable for use' is discussed at para 10.113ff.

10.126 Besides requiring that the waste is suitable for the purpose, according to Circular 11/94 the exemption only holds[1] if there is a designated construction project for the waste when it is used; if it is destined for the relevant work and nowhere else; or if the quantity of the waste is not excessive. Whilst no numerical quantity limit has been included in the exemption, the Circular points out[1] that the quantity that can be subject to prior storage is limited by the amount necessary to undertake the construction work.

1 Circular 11/94, Annex 5, para 5.154.

10.127 In the case of road planings, the exemption for storage is much wider. They can be stored prior to use for the purposes of relevant work[1], not just at the site of production or use but elsewhere, at quantities of no more than 50,000 tonnes, provided that such storage goes on for three months or less[2].

1 Relevant work
    'means construction work, including the deposit of waste on land in connection with –
    (a) the provision of recreational facilities on that land; or
    (b) the construction, maintenance or improvement of a building, highway, railway, airport, dock or other transport facility on that land,
    but not including either any deposit of waste in any other circumstances or any work involving land reclamation' (SI 1994/1056, Sch 3, para 19(4)).
2 SI 1994/1056, Sch 3, para 19(3).

10.128 It is of note that the words 'on a site' in Schedule 3, paragraph 19(1) do not allow exempt storage at any location. The context indicates that the 'site' being referred to is the construction site. Sub-paragraph 19(1)(a) refers to relevant work[1] being carried on 'at the site', and the exemption for the storage of road planings[2] allows such materials to be stored 'for the purposes of relevant work carried on elsewhere'. There would be no need, in the road planings exemption, to refer to relevant work being carried on elsewhere if the remainder of Schedule 3, paragraph 19 allowed the storage of construction and demolition wastes to occur at any premises.

1 Relevant work
    'means construction work, including the deposit of waste on land in connection with –
    (a) the provision of recreational facilities on that land; or
    (b) the construction, maintenance or improvement of a building, highway, railway, airport, dock or other transport facility on that land,
    but not including either any deposit of waste in any other circumstances or any work involving land reclamation' (SI 1994/1056, Sch 3, para 19(4)).
2 SI 1994/1056, Sch 3, para 19(3).

10.129 As well as the actual manufacturing process of construction industry wastes covered in paragraph 13, the storage of such wastes prior to processing into timber products, strawboard, plasterboard, bricks, blocks, roadstone or aggregate is also exempt from waste management licensing[1]. Where roadstone is to be manufactured from road planings, up to 50,000 tonnes can be stored[2]. For all the other specified types of waste[3], 20,000 tonnes can be stored without needing a waste management licence. In either case, the storage must occur 'where the activity is to be carried on'[4]. The use of the future tense here, it is submitted, indicates that all that is needed is an intention to process these construction wastes.

1   SI 1994/1056, Sch 3, para 13(4).
2   SI 1994/1056, Sch 3, para 13(4)(b)(i).
3   Waste arising from demolition or construction work, from tunnelling and other excavations, waste ash, slag, clinker, rock, wood, bark, paper, straw or gypsum (SI 1994/1056, Sch 3, para 13(1)).
4   SI 1994/1056, Sch 3, para 13(4)(a).

10.130   In addition, the Waste Management Licensing Regulations 1994 allow for the storage of bricks, tiles and concrete without a waste management licence prior to crushing, grinding or other size reduction operations[1]. Again the storage must occur 'at the place the process is carried on', and no more than 20,000 tonnes may be stored at any one time.

1   SI 1994/1056, Sch 3, para 24(3).

10.131   Somewhat confusingly, the above exemptions are augmented by two more in Schedule 3. The exempt storage is allowed of 'waste articles which are to be used for construction work which are capable of being so used in their existing state'[1]. According to Circular 11/94[2], 'waste articles which are to be used for construction work' means wastes that have, for example, been subject to architectural salvage. Excluded are wastes that will need further processing prior to use 'and wastes that are materials rather than articles'[3]. It appears therefore that the Department of the Environment is attempting to make a distinction between an ornamental gatepost, as an article, and clean used bricks, which are seen as materials. Schedule 3, paragraph 17 allows 100 tonnes of such articles to be stored 'on any premises' and in a secure[4] place. In addition, the wastes must be re-used or subject to baling, sorting, shredding, densifying washing or compacting[5]. The inclusion of the latter operations in this context seems a trifle odd as the subject of the exemption – wastes available to be used for construction work in their present state – are, by definition, highly unlikely to be subject to any of these operations, with the possible exception of sorting.

1   SI 1994/1056, Sch 3, para 17, Table 4, which is also referred to in respect of the exemptions under para 18: see Table 10.2.
2   Circular 11/94, Annex 5, para 5.140.
3   Circular 11/94, Annex 5, para 5.140.
4   See para 10.36.
5   SI 1994/1056, Sch 3, para 17(1)(b).

10.132   The exemption contained in Schedule 3, paragraph 18 also permits architectural salvage materials[1] to be stored in secure[2] containers, provided that the storage capacity of the containers does not exceed 400 cubic metres[3] and that there are no more than 20 of them on the premises[4]. This exemption is cast in terms of the capacity and the number of the containers: not whether they are full or empty. In addition, to be exempt, the waste articles to be used for construction work must be eventually re-used, or subject to baling, sorting, shredding, densifying, washing or compacting[5].

1   'Waste articles which are to be used for construction work which are capable of being so used in their existing state': SI 1994/1056, Sch 3, para 17, Table 4.

2   The nature of 'secure' is discussed at para 10.36.
3   SI 1994/1056, Sch 3, para 18(1)(a).
4   SI 1994/1056, Sch 3, para 18(1)(c).
5   SI 1994/1056, Sch 3, para 18(1)(d).

10.133   All the above exemptions need to register with the Agency[1].

1   SI 1994/1056, reg 18(10)(d).

10.134   Finally, paragraph 40 to Schedule 3 allows solid waste to be stored at premises other than those at which it was produced, hence the storage of construction wastes at a builder's yard does not require a waste management licence. However, these wastes need to be stored in 'a secure container or containers' – therefore they cannot be piled up on the ground. The other requirements of this exemption are discussed at para 10.65.

Borehole and mineral excavation wastes

10.135   The deposit of excavated materials from a 'borehole or other excavation for the purpose of mineral exploration'[1] is exempt under Schedule 3, paragraph 35. Such materials must be deposited on or in the land from which they were excavated[2] and the total quantity disposed of in a period of 24 months must not exceed 45,000 cubic metres per hectare[3]. However, the applicability of this exemption is highly restricted as it only applies if the development has planning permission under the Town and Country Planning General Development Order 1988[4] and if the conditions of the permission are observed[5]. In practice, many boreholes will not be subject to planning permissions. It should also be pointed out that, should the waste stem from a mine or quarry, it will not be covered by Part II of the EPA 1990 at all[6]. All the activities encompassed by this exemption need to register with the Agency[7].

1   Mineral exploration is defined in the Town and County Planning (General Development) Order 1988 or, in Scotland, by the Town and County Planning (General Permitted Development) (Scotland) Order 1992.
2   SI 1994/1056, Sch 3, para 35(1)(a).
3   SI 1994/1056, Sch 3, para 35(1)(b).
4   SI 1994/1056, Sch 3, para 35(2)(a). The permission must be granted by way of Article 3 and Class A or B of Part 22 to Schedule 2 of the Town and Country Planning (General Development) Order 1988; in Scotland, it must be permitted by Class 53, 54 or 61 to Schedule 1 of the Town and Country Planning (General Permitted Development) (Scotland) Order 1992.
5   SI 1994/1056, Sch 3, para 35(2)(b).
6   See EPA 1990, s 75(7) and para 2.55ff.
7   SI 1994/1056, reg 18(10)(d).

Spreading construction industry materials on land

10.136   Waste arising from construction and demolition work can be subject to 'spreading' on land 'in connection with the reclamation or improvement of that land' without a waste management licence[1]. This is discussed at para 10.153.

1   SI 1994/1056, Sch 3, para 9.

Bonfires at construction sites

10.137   Bonfires at construction sites are exempt from waste management licences[1] when they consist only of wood, bark and plant matter. This exemption is discussed at para 10.224.

1   SI 1994/1056, Sch 3, para 30.

Exemptions involving the application of wastes to agricultural and other land

10.138 The statutory approach to the environmental control of the landspreading of waste and related storage activities is split between two quite distinct items of legislation. The controls on the emplacement of most wastes in or on land are the subject of the EPA 1990. Where waste management licences are not needed, exemptions usually apply. Schedule 3 to the Waste Management Licensing Regulations 1994 allows for the exempt landspreading of a diverse range of mainly biodegradable industrial wastes for the purposes of agricultural or ecological improvement[1]. A separate provision covers the spreading of more inert materials, mainly from the construction industry, for the purposes of land reclamation[2]. The exempt storage of materials associated with these activities is also addressed. By contrast, the spreading of sewage sludge and septic tank sludge is subject to a rather different statutory approach. In the case of the spreading of these materials on agricultural land, the controls upon this activity are mainly contained in regulations which are both independent of, and quite separate to, the provisions of the EPA 1990: the Sludge (Use in Agriculture) Regulations 1989[3]. These Regulations specifically implement Directive 86/278[4] and, prior to the formation of the Agency, were the responsibility of the Ministry of Agriculture, Fisheries and Food. For these waste types, it is only where the Sludge (Use in Agriculture) Regulations 1989 do not apply that the EPA 1990 and the Waste Management Licensing Regulations 1994 come into effect.

1   SI 1994/1056, Sch 3, para 7.
2   SI 1994/1056, Sch 3, para 9.
3   SI 1989/1263, as amended by SIs 1990/880, 1996/593 and 1996/973.
4   Council Directive on the protection of the environment and in particular the soil, when sewage sludge is used in Agriculture (OJ L181/6 4.7.86).

10.139 As will be seen, the wording of certain of the exemptions is rather open-ended and the manner by which the Waste Management Licensing Regulations 1994 set out the system of registration with the Agency leaves much to be desired. When these difficulties are coupled with the financial incentive created by the landfill tax[1] on waste holders to keep as many wastes as possible away from licensed landfill sites, the result is an area of statutory control which is in urgent need of reform. In this respect, the existing provisions have received strong criticism from the Royal Commission on Environmental Pollution[2]. In early 1997 the then Conservative Government gave the Royal Commission the undertaking that a review of the legislation would occur and that research into the environmental effects of the landspreading of non-sewage sludge wastes has been commissioned[3]. While at the time of writing (Summer 1999) no concrete proposal has emerged, the findings of the research have been published[4], suggesting some fundamental gaps in both the statutory framework and in the scientific justification of many current landspreading practices[5]. Given these factors, it seems inevitable that the landspreading exemptions will be tightened in the near future.

1   See para 1.100ff.
2   Royal Commission on Environmental Pollution (1996) *Sustainable Use of Soil* 19th Report of the Commission, HMSO, London.
3   See *Sustainable Use of Soil: Government Response to the Nineteenth Report of the Royal Commission on Environmental Pollution* (1997) HMSO, paras 27–30.
4   Water Research Centre (1998) *Investigation of the Criteria for, and Guidance on, the Landspreading of Industrial Wastes*, Environment Agency, Bristol.
5   See also SEPA (1998) *Strategic Review of Organic Waste Spread on Land*, SEPA, Stirling.

Spreading wastes for beneficial conditioning of the land[1]

10.140 A wide range of non-special wastes can be subject to 'spreading'[2] on land 'which is used for agriculture'[3] without the need to obtain a waste management licence[4]. The wastes that can be spread are shown in Table 10.3. However, it is important to note that any wastes produced by an agricultural premises or a mine or quarry will not be controlled wastes[5] and hence no exemption from licensing is necessary to authorise the deposit of those materials.

1 Sewage sludge is discussed separately below.
2 An interpretation of the word 'spreading' is discussed later. It would seem that there is doubt as to whether the common practice of the injection of liquids into the soil surface is embraced by the concept of 'spreading' in the Waste Management Licensing Regulations 1994.
3 Agriculture has the same meaning as in the Agriculture Act 1947 or in Scotland, the Agriculture (Scotland) Act 1948: see para 10.167 below.
4 SI 1994/1056, Sch 3, para 7. The occupier's consent or other entitlement to carry on the activity on the land is needed (SI 1994/1056, reg 17(2)).
5 See the EPA 1990, s 75(7) and paras 2.55 and 2.60. However, as discussed at para 2.61, this exclusion is due for amendment.

Table 10.3

Waste Management Licensing Regulations 1994

Types of wastes that can be spread on land under Schedule 3, paragraph 7[1]

1	Waste soil or compost
2	Waste wood, bark or other plant matter
3	Waste food, drink or materials used in or resulting from the preparation of food or drink
4	Blood and gut contents from abattoirs
5	Waste lime
6	Lime sludge from cement manufacture or gas processing
7	Waste gypsum
8	Paper waste sludge, waste paper and de-inked paper pulp
9	Dredgings from any inland waters[2]
10	Textile waste
11	Septic tank sludge[3]
12	Sludge from biological treatment plants[4]
13	Waste hair and effluent sludge from a tannery

1 SI 1994/1056, Sch 3, para 7, Table 2.
2 Defined by reg 1(3) as having the same meaning as in s 221(1) of the Water Resources Act 1991 (in Scotland, s 30A of the Control of Pollution Act 1974 but including also a loch or pond whether or not it discharges into a river or watercourse).
3 Defined in reg 2(1) of the Sludge (Use in Agriculture) Regulations 1989, SI 1989/1263 (as amended by SI 1990/880) as meaning 'residual sludge from septic tanks and other similar installations for the treatment of sewage'.
4 This should be distinguished in the Waste Management Licensing Regulations 1994 from sludge from sewage treatment works. Although a sewage treatment works is a biological treatment facility, the word 'sludge' in this Table appears to be being used differently than in subsequent paragraphs of Sch 3. Under Sch 3, para 8(5), the word 'sludge' is given the same meaning as in the Sludge (Use in Agriculture) Regulations 1989 for those paragraphs specified (paras 8, 9, and 10). Accordingly, it is submitted that the word 'sludge' in Sch 3, para 7 should be seen to have its ordinary meaning and be viewed in its context. In addition, if the definition in the Sludge (Use in Agriculture) Regulations 1989 did apply, the exemption in para 7 would undermine the controls on sewage sludge spreading: particularly the requirements to assess sludge and the relevant land for heavy metals.

10.141 Although this exemption covers septic tank sludge, the legislative position in respect of that waste type is somewhat complex. When septic tank sludge is 'used'[1] in the manner set out by the Sludge (Use In Agriculture) Regulations 1989[2], the material is not a controlled waste at all[3]. Hence there is no need for any exemption from the EPA 1990. However, the scope of the Sludge (Use in Agriculture) Regulations 1989 are restricted only to certain types of agricultural land[4]. Hence for the spreading of septic tank sludge on other types of farm land, the system of exemptions contained in the Waste Management Licensing Regulations 1994 apply.

1   In other words, spread.
2   SI 1989/1263 as amended by SI 1990/880, SI 1996/593 and SI 1996/973.
3   See SI 1992/588, reg 7(1)(c) as amended by SI 1995/288, reg 2(2): see para 2.223ff.
4   See para 10.167 below.

10.142   Where it is proposed to undertake spreading on other, non-agricultural land, the range of wastes that can be spread under paragraph 7 of Schedule 3 is restricted to items (1) and (2) in Table 10.3 only[1]. In this case, such substances can only be spread on 'operational land'[2] of a railway, light railway, internal drainage board[3] or the Agency[4], or where the land constitutes a forest, woodland, park, garden, verge, landscaped area, sports ground, recreation ground, churchyard or cemetery[5].

1   SI 1994/1056, Sch 3, para 7(2).
2   Defined in SI 1994/1056, reg 1(3) as meaning the same as set down in ss 263 and 264 of the Town and County Planning Act 1990 (in Scotland ss 211 and 212 of the Town and Country Planning (Scotland) Act 1972): see also Circular 11/94, Annex 5, para 5.253.
3   Having the meaning given by s 1(1) of the Land Drainage Act 1991 and for the purposes of the definition of operational land, an internal drainage board shall be deemed to be a statutory undertaker (SI 1994/1056, Sch 3, para 7(9)).
4   SI 1994/1056, Sch 3, para 7(2)(a) refers to the 'National Rivers Authority': presumably this title transferred on the creation of the Agency.
5   SI 1994/1056, Sch 3, para 7(2)(b).

10.143   For both agricultural land and non-agricultural land, the maximum amount of the waste types 1–13 in Table 10.3 that can be spread is 250 tonnes per hectare in a period of 12 months[1]. This is a layer of about 2.5 cm in depth. For item (9) – dredgings – this allowance is increased to 5,000 tonnes per hectare[2]. Circular 11/94 advises that, when more than one type of waste is spread on the same land, 'the quantities applied must be taken together'[3].

1   SI 1994/1056, Sch 3, para 7(3)(a).
2   SI 1994/1056, Sch 3, para 7(3)(a).
3   Circular 11/94, Annex 5, para 5.73.

10.144   As the Circular notes, the quantities shown in Table 10.3 are absolute maxima and other constraints are likely to restrict the amounts spread to lower levels[1]. In particular, an important prerequisite is found in the wording of the exemption, which requires that the spreading activity must result 'in benefit to agriculture or ecological improvement'[2]. However, in the case where these substances are applied to non-agricultural land, only ecological improvement will be a relevant criterion[3].

1   Circular 11/94, Annex 5, para 5.73.
2   SI 1994/1056, Sch 3, para 7(3)(b).
3   Circular 11/94, Annex 5, para 5.74.

10.145   The Circular admits[1] that the phrase 'benefit to agriculture or ecological improvement' is lifted verbatim from the Waste Directive's Annex IIB, item R10[2]. It declines to provide a detailed interpretation, but states that '[t]he phrase is not defined[3] but bears the same meaning as in the Directive'[4]. However, it is also suggested that a bulk application of waste solely to raise land levels 'may' not be viewed as of benefit to agriculture or causing ecological improvement. In all cases, Circular 11/94 indicates that the exemption requires positive benefits to accrue and that '[i]n order to keep within the terms of the exemption it will be essential to establish on the basis of properly qualified advice what application rate is appropriate for each waste material, each soil and each site'[5]. A more recent report by the Water Research Centre sets out the nature of these terms in more detail[6].

1   Circular 11/94, Annex 5, para 5.74 .
2   See Table 2.3 in Chapter 2.
3   In the Waste Management Licensing Regulations 1994 or Circular 11/94.
4   Circular 11/94, Annex 5, para 5.74: there is no definition to be found in the Directive. This reference appears to be included to ensure that any interpretation of exemptions considers the purpose of the Directive.
5   Circular 11/94, Annex 5, para 5.74.
6   Water Research Centre (1998) *Investigation of the Criteria for, and Guidance on, the Landspreading of Industrial Wastes*, Environment Agency, Bristol.

10.146   At the first instance, the terminology used in Table 10.3 could be seen as very open-ended. For example, 'waste food, drink or materials used in or resulting from the preparation of food or drink' could be construed to encompass drink cans, cartons, packaging etc from the premises producing the food or drink. However, it should be recalled that the exemption also contains the requirement that the materials can only be spread under the exemption if benefit to agriculture or ecological improvement occurs. Clearly, this will not be satisfied if such patently unsuitable wastes were spread.

10.147   The Waste Management Licensing Regulations 1994 allow for the storage and pre-treatment of some of the substances discussed above without a waste management licence being needed. However, exemption applies only if the storage is done at the place where the spreading is to take place[1]. For solid wastes that are to be spread, Schedule 3 does not set down a maximum storage limit[2], but for liquid wastes being spread on land for the benefit of agriculture or ecological improvement – but not sludge from septic tanks[3] – the exemption only applies where they are stored in a secure[4] container or lagoon, with no more than 500 tonnes 'in any one container or lagoon'[5].

1   Storage at the place of production prior to collection is covered by the exemption contained in Sch 3, para 41 (discussed above).
2   SI 1994/1056, Sch 3, para 7(5).
3   SI 1994/1056, Sch 3, para 7(5).
4   Secure is defined in SI 1994/1056, reg 17(5): see para 10.36.
5   SI 1994/1056, Sch 3, para 7(6).

10.148   The requirements contained in Schedule 3 for the storage of septic tank sludge[1] appear to be slightly anomalous. Only the 'use' of such wastes is subject to the Sludge (Use in Agriculture) Regulations 1989[2]. Accordingly, transportation and storage of septic tank sludge is subject to the EPA 1990's provisions. Schedule 3 to the Waste Management Licensing Regulations 1994 allows for an unlimited amount to be stored in a secure container or lagoon (or for 'dewatered sludge'[3] in a secure[4] place) provided that it is intended to be spread 'in reliance upon the exemption conferred by sub-paragraph (1) above'[5]. Sub-paragraph (1) refers to the spreading of wastes on land used for agriculture. Spreading on other types of land, such as forestry, etc is covered by sub-paragraph (2), while spreading in accordance with the Sludge (Use in Agriculture) Regulations 1989 does not need an exemption at all[6]. Accordingly, it would seem that the storage of septic tank sludge that is to be spread on non-agricultural land is not covered by this exemption. Neither is storage prior to spreading under the Sludge (Use in Agriculture) Regulations 1989.

1   SI 1994/1056, Sch 3, para 7(7). Septic tank sludge is defined in reg 2(1) of the Sludge (Use in Agriculture) Regulations 1989 (SI 1989/1263) (as amended by SI 1990/880) as meaning 'residual sludge from septic tanks and other similar installations for the treatment of sewage'.
2   SI 1989/1263 (as amended by SI 1990/880), reg 4.
3   Undefined in the Waste Management Licensing Regulations 1994.
4   Secure is defined in SI 1994/1056, reg 17(5): see para 10.36.
5   SI 1994/1056, Sch 3, para 7(7).
6   Septic tank sludge is not a controlled waste when 'used' in accordance with the Sludge (Use in Agriculture) Regulations: see SI 1992/588, reg 7(1)(c) (as amended by SI 1995/288, reg 2(2)) and see also para 2.223ff.

10.149   Unlike the usual procedure set down for registration with the Agency for the other exemptions discussed in this chapter, the requirements for the notification of exempt landspreading under paragraph 7 are quite different[1]. Schedule 3, paragraph 7(3)(c) requires that, where spreading is undertaken on 'land used for agriculture'[2], details of the spreading are forwarded to the Agency which covers the location where the activity is taking place[3]. The activity is not exempt if the details have not been so forwarded.

1   SI 1994/1056, reg 18(7) and Sch 3, para 7(3)(c).
2   'Agriculture' is defined by the Agriculture Act 1947 and, in Scotland, the Agriculture (Scotland) Act 1948.
3   SI 1994/1056, Sch 3, para 7(3)(c).

10.150   Where the spreading is a one-off event, the details must be submitted in advance[1]. But where there is to be 'regular or frequent spreading of waste of a similar composition', details must be sent every six months. Should the waste be of a different description to that previously notified, the details of the predicted composition must be sent in advance[2]. The latter condition seems rather peculiar. For a new site where 'regular or frequent' spreading is to occur, no advance notice appears necessary. All that should be sent are the details at six monthly intervals. However, if the arrangements then change, the nature of the change has to be notified in advance.

1   SI 1994/1056, Sch 3, para 7(3)(c)(i): no definition is given of the required time period, and it would appear that ten minutes' notice would satisfy this provision.
2   SI 1994/1056, Sch 3, para 7(3)(c)(ii).

10.151   The details to be sent to the Agency are set down in Schedule 3, paragraph 7(4). These are the name, address, telephone and fax number of the establishment or undertaking, a description of the waste, details of the process which created the waste, the location where the waste is being stored before the spreading, an estimate of the total quantity of the waste to be spread and, finally, the location and date of the spreading. Where regular spreading is to occur, the details required to be sent to the Agency are slightly modified. The quantity of material spread has to be expressed in terms of an estimate of the amount to be spread over the six month period, while the date that spreading is to commence should be substituted by an indication of its intended frequency[1].

1   SI 1994/1056, Sch 3, paras 7(4)(d) and (e).

10.152   In either case, the Agency must include these details as part of their register of exempt activities[1].

1   SI 1994/1056, Sch 3, para 18(7): see para 13.39.

Other land improvement and land reclamation schemes

10.153 Besides the above exemptions for activities aimed at improving the bio-logical or ecological properties of land, waste arising from construction and demolition work, dredgings or waste soil, rock, ash or sludge[1] can also be subject to exempt 'spreading' on land[2]. In this case, to be exempt from the need for a waste management licence, such spreading must be undertaken 'in connection with the reclamation or improvement of that land'[3]. According to Circular 11/94, this reclamation or improvement 'may be for any subsequent land use, including development'[4].

1 SI 1994/1056, Sch 3, para 8(5): the word 'sludge' is given the same meaning as in the Sludge (Use in Agriculture) Regulations 1989. Sludge spreading is discussed further at para 10.163.
2 SI 1994/1056, Sch 3, para 9.
3 The occupier's consent or other entitlement to carry on the activity on the land is needed (SI 1994/1056, reg 17(2) as amended by SI 1995/288, reg 3(6)).
4 Circular 11/94, Annex 5, para 5.95.

10.154 The exemption for the reclamation or improvement of the land is subject to three requirements. Firstly, that 'by reason of industrial or other development the land is incapable of beneficial use without treatment'[1]. The second is that the spreading is carried out 'in accordance with a planning permission for the reclamation or improvement of the land' and that it results 'in benefit to agriculture or ecological improvement'[2]. Finally, no more than 20,000 cubic metres per hectare of waste can be spread on the land[3].

1 SI 1994/1056, Sch 3, para 9(1)(a).
2 SI 1994/1056, Sch 3, para 9(1)(b): see Water Research Centre (1998) *Investigation of the Criteria for, and Guidance on, the Landspreading of Industrial Wastes*, Environment Agency, Bristol.
3 SI 1994/1056, Sch 3, para 9(1)(c).

10.155 A number of matters are of note in relation to this exemption, particularly in relation to distinguishing between bona fide activities and blatant illegal tipping. These matters have become even more crucial given the spiralling cost of landfill due to the landfill tax[1]. Of particular note is the use of the word 'spreading'. Much of the EPA 1990 and the Waste Management Licensing Regulations 1994 is concerned with the 'disposal or deposit in or on land'. Clearly, there is a need to distinguish between 'depositing' wastes and 'spreading' them. While a distinction can be made on the basis of the choice of these contrasting words and their implied meanings in the EPA 1990 and the subsidiary regulations, such a distinction is also assisted by the juxtaposition of the terms in a separate exemption in Schedule 3, paragraph 25. The wording of paragraph 25 shows that a clear differentiation is envisaged between the exemptions which allow dredgings and plant matter to be 'deposited'[2] and those which permit such materials to be 'spread'[3].

1 See paras 1.46 and 1.100ff.
2 SI 1994/1056, Sch 3, para 25(5)(a).
3 SI 1994/1056, Sch 3, paras 25(5)(b) and (c).

10.156 Although undefined in the Waste Management Licensing Regulations 1994, it seems clear from its ordinary meaning that spreading involves placing a thin layer over a wide area[1]. The Collins Concise Dictionary[2] suggests 23 separate meanings including:

– to apply or be applied in a coating;
– to distribute or be distributed over an area or region
– Agriculture. a. to lay out (hay) in a relatively thin layer to dry. b. to scatter (seed, manure, etc) over an area.

In this respect, 20,000 cubic metres on a hectare of land would involve covering it uniformly with waste up to two metres deep. The two metre limit may have derived from the belief that waste spread to that depth would not produce landfill gas. The shallowness of the deposit might cause only the aerobic decomposition of any suitable materials. Generally, depths in excess of two metres may well result in anaerobic decomposition, for the reason that a sufficient supply of oxygen cannot be guaranteed further away from the surface, and hence landfill gas may result.

1　It would therefore seem doubtful that the injection of liquids into soils is covered by this exemption.
2　1997 edition.

10.157　The second requirement of the exemption is that the land where the waste is to be spread must be incapable of beneficial use 'by reason of industrial or other development'[1]. It therefore follows that, should there have been no development of the land, the exemption does not apply. Similarly, if the land is currently under some beneficial use, the exemption does not apply.

1　SI 1994/1056, Sch 3, para 9(1)(a).

10.158　Thirdly, the paragraph specifically refers to spreading being carried out 'in accordance with a planning permission for the reclamation or improvement of the land'. This requires, at first instance, the existence of a planning permission[1]. Neither the exemption from the need to have a planning permission nor the existence of a certificate of lawful use constitutes a planning permission. The wording also appears to suggest that the planning permission must relate to the reclamation or improvement of the land, and it would appear that, if the planning permission is silent on these matters, then the exemption does not apply. Furthermore, even if a planning permission does exist, the exemption requires that the spreading must still result in benefit to agriculture or ecological improvement[2].

1　Circular 11/94, Annex 5, para 5.95.
2　SI 1994/1056, Sch 3, para 9(1)(b). See Circular 11/94, Annex 5, para 5.95.

10.159　Finally, Schedule 3, paragraph 9(3) makes it clear that this exemption does not apply 'at a site designed or adapted for the final disposal of waste by landfill'. The nature of the interpretation of the term 'designed or adapted' has already been discussed at paras 10.73 and 10.76ff, but in summary, the term appears to require that a site has been physically changed and altered. Consequently, and despite Circular 11/94's assertion[1] that the words designed or adapted 'ensure that the exemption is not available for cases where waste disposal rather than land reclamation is the main purpose of the scheme', precisely when a site is designed and adapted for the use of landfill is less than immediately obvious. Clearly, no operator of an unlicensed site is going to put up a notice board and site office. The most obvious change needed to adapt a site as a landfill is to put an access road into it. However, building a suitable road access may also be a prerequisite prior to the spreading of waste on land as well. It therefore appears that Schedule 3, paragraph 9(3) is of little effect and that many disputes concerning this exemption will turn on the question of the precise nature and meaning of the word 'spreading'. The only time that the provision may have effect is to require that restoration works on closed landfill sites must always be carried out under a waste management licence. If anything, this may hinder, rather than assist, the reclamation and landscaping of old landfills.

1　Circular 11/94, Annex 5, para 5.97.

10.160   For those wastes which are to be spread under this exemption, there is no maximum permitted total relating to the storage of such materials in excess of which waste management licensing applies[1]. Nor is there a time limit over which the maximum amount specified in the exemption is to be spread. However, storage under this exemption must be restricted to the place where the waste is to be spread.

1   SI 1994/1056, Sch 3, para 9(2): presumably the maximum amount of waste that can be stored is constrained by the total quantity of waste which can be subject to exempt spreading. This relationship may present an inferential limit on storage capacity.

10.161   Finally, the exempt pretreatment of dredgings (but not plant matter associated with watercourse clearance) at the site of land reclamation is permissible under Schedule 3, paragraph 25(5)(c). The nature of the requirements of this exemption is spelt out at para 10.237 below.

10.162   In all cases where exempt spreading is done under Schedule 3, paragraph 9, the activity needs to register with the Agency in the usual way[1]. The more involved notification system, as set down in paragraph 7 in respect of the spreading of biodegradable waste, does not apply in this instance.

1   SI 1994/1056, reg 18(10)(d). See para 10.24.

The spreading of sewage sludge

10.163   Schedule 3 to the Waste Management Licensing Regulations 1994[1] permits sludge[2] to be 'spread' on agricultural and non-agricultural land without the need for a waste management licence. This spreading can be for the purposes of ecological improvement[3] or can be done for the reason of land reclamation or other improvement of the land[4].

1   SI 1994/1056, Sch 3, paras 8(2) and 9.
2   Required by SI 1994/1056, Sch 3, para 8(5) to have the same meaning as in reg 2(1) of the Sludge (Use in Agriculture) Regulations 1989 (SI 1989/1263): 'residual sludge from sewage treatment plants treating domestic or urban waste waters and from other sewage plants treating waste waters of a composition similar to domestic or urban waste waters'. The term 'sewage sludge' should be seen to be quite distinct from 'septic tank sludge'.
3   SI 1994/1056, Sch 3, para 8(2).
4   SI 1994/1056, Sch 3, para 9.

10.164   The spreading of sewage sludge on farmland is controlled principally by the Sludge (Use in Agriculture) Regulations 1989[1]. These set down a series of requirements to prevent sewage sludge with an elevated heavy metals content being disposed of by land spreading and also to preclude the build-up of heavy metals in the soils of such land. They also pertain to the spreading of septic tank sludge. However, while the following provisions in the Waste Management Licensing Regulations 1994 allow for exempt sewage sludge spreading on land not subject to the Sludge (Use in Agriculture) Regulations 1989, these provisions oddly do not apply to septic tank sludge spreading. This material can only be subject to exempt spreading under the provisions of Schedule 3, paragraph 7 of the Waste Management Licensing Regulations 1994[2].

1   SI 1989/1263 as amended by SI 1990/880, SI 1996/593 and SI 1996/973: see also Water Research Centre (1998) *A Review of the Scientific Evidence Relating to the Controls on the Agricultural Spreading of Sewage Sludge*, WRC.
2   See para 10.140ff.

10.165   Sewage sludge spreading on agricultural land under the Sludge (Use in Agriculture) Regulations 1989[1] does not require an exemption under Schedule 3 to the Waste Management Licensing Regulations 1994 for the reason that sewage sludge is not a controlled waste when it is 'supplied or used' in accordance with the Sludge (Use in Agriculture) Regulations 1989[2]. The Sludge (Use in Agriculture) Regulations 1989[3] set down the meaning of the words 'use' and 'used': with both terms meaning spreading on the soil or any other application on or in the soil. The word 'supply' – in the context of supplying sludge – is not defined, but it is assumed that it retains its ordinary meaning and covers transportation.

1   SI 1989/1263, as amended by SI 1990/880 and SI 1996/973.
2   See SI 1992/588, reg 7(1)(b) and para 2.223ff.
3   SI 1989/1263, reg 2(1).

10.166   However, sewage sludge *is* a controlled waste when it is subject to storage beyond the curtilage of a sewage works and up to the time that it is 'supplied or used'. The reason for this assertion is that a specific exemption from waste management licensing has been granted for the off-site storage of the material[1] prior to spreading under the Sludge (Use in Agriculture) Regulations 1989. To be exempt, such storage must occur in a secure[2] container, lagoon or, for dewatered sludge, place. It must also occur on land used for agriculture[3] and places where the storage occurs need to be registered with the relevant Agency[4].

1   SI 1994/1056, Sch 3, para 8(1).
2   Secure is defined in SI 1994/1056, reg 17(5): see para 10.36.
3   Defined by the Agriculture Act 1947 and not by the Sludge (Use in Agriculture) Regulations 1989.
4   SI 1994/1056, reg 18(10)(d).

10.167   Part II of the EPA 1990 only addresses those aspects of sewage sludge disposal which had not been subject to the Sludge (Use in Agriculture) Regulations 1989. In this instance, while the deposit or disposal of sewage sludge on land would require a waste management licence, the 'spreading' of the sludge on land mainly falls within the exemption contained in Schedule 3, paragraph 8 to the Waste Management Licensing Regulations 1994. In this respect, some care is needed in interpreting paragraph 8 of Schedule 3. This is because paragraph 8(2) seeks to control the spreading of sewage sludge on all land other than that covered by the Sludge (Use in Agriculture) Regulations 1989. What should be appreciated is that the spreading of sewage sludge on some agricultural land may not, in fact, be encompassed by the Sludge (Use in Agriculture) Regulations 1989. The definition of 'agriculture' used in the Sludge (Use in Agriculture) Regulations 1989 appears to have a narrower meaning than that given in the Agriculture Act 1947[1]. Thus, sewage sludge spreading on farmland outside the definition in the Sludge (Use in Agriculture) Regulations 1989 is covered by the exemptions contained within Schedule 3, paragraph 8, alongside the spreading of sludge on all other non-agricultural land.

1   'Agriculture' in the Sludge (Use in Agriculture) Regulations 1989 (SI 1989/1263, reg 2(1)) means 'the growing of all types of commercial food crops, including for stock-rearing purposes'. The Regulations also require that cognate words shall be construed accordingly. By contrast, the definition of agriculture in s 109(3) of the Agriculture Act 1947 (in Scotland, the Agriculture (Scotland) Act 1948) 'includes horticulture, fruit growing, seed growing, dairy farming and livestock breeding and keeping, the use of land as grazing land, meadow land, osier land, market gardens and nursery grounds, and the use of land for woodlands where that use is ancillary to the farming of land for other agricultural purposes'.

10.168   In addition Schedule 3, paragraph 8(2), requires sewage sludge to be spread under exemption only if it results in 'ecological improvement' and does not cause the concentration in the soil of those metals shown in the Table contained in Schedule 2 to the Sludge (Use in Agriculture) Regulations 1989 to be exceeded. This Table is reproduced as Table 10.4 below.

Table 10.4

Sewage Sludge: Metal Levels in Soils

Maximum Concentrations[1]

Element	Limit According to the pH of the Soil (mg/kg of dry matter)			
pH	5.0<5.5	5.5<6.0	6.0–7.0	>7.0
Zinc	200	250	300	450
Copper	80	100	135	200
Nickel	50	60	75	110
	For pH 5.0 and above			
Lead	300			
Cadmium	3			
Mercury	1			

1   Schedule 2 to the Sludge (Use in Agriculture) Regulations 1989 (SI 1989/1263).

10.169   In addition to the exemption for the storage of sewage sludge prior to its spreading on land covered by the Sludge (Use in Agriculture) Regulations 1989, a second exemption allows storage prior to the spreading activities covered by the above exemptions[1]. To be exempt, sewage sludge must be stored in a secure[2] container or lagoon[3]. Unlike the case with sludge storage prior to spreading under the Sludge (Use in Agriculture) Regulations 1989, the relevant sub-paragraph is silent as to the location where this storage can be undertaken. The exempt spreading or off-site storage of sewage sludge must be registered with the Agency[4].

1   SI 1994/1056, Sch 3, para 8(3).
2   Secure is defined in SI 1994/1056, reg 17(5): see para 10.36.
3   Or, where it has been dewatered, in a secure place.
4   SI 1994/1056, reg 18(10)(d).

10.170   The spreading of sewage sludge is also permissible 'on any land in connection with the reclamation or improvement of that land' under an exemption set out in paragraph 9[1]. This exemption has been discussed in respect of other wastes in para 10.153 above, but briefly, the exemption applies when the land, 'by reason of industrial or other development', is 'incapable of beneficial use without treatment'[2]. The spreading must also be in accordance with a planning permission for the reclamation or improvement of the land and agricultural or ecological improvements must accrue from it[3]. No more than 20,000 cubic metres of sewage sludge can be spread per hectare[4]. The exemption is disapplied where the waste is being disposed of at a site designed or adapted for the final disposal of waste by landfill[5]. It should be noted that, unlike the exemption under Schedule 3, paragraph 8 discussed above, there is no requirement in Schedule 3, paragraph 9 restricting the metals content of the sewage sludge spreading process. Although this may be acceptable at some land reclamation schemes where the after-use of the land is likely to be very restricted, it is less than desirable in other cases.

1   SI 1994/1056, Sch 3, para 9: 'sludge' is as defined in the Sludge (Use in Agriculture) Regulations 1989 (see SI 1994/1056, Sch 3, para 8(5)).
2   SI 1994/1056, Sch 3, para 9(1)(a).
3   SI 1994/1056, Sch 3, para 9(1)(b).
4   SI 1994/1056, Sch 3, para 9(1)(c).
5   SI 1994/1056, Sch 3, para 9(3).

10.171 Finally, sewage sludge can be stored at the land reclamation site where it is to be spread without the need for a licence[1]. In this case, no quantity limits are applicable and, in contrast to the other exemption on sewage sludge spreading and storage, there is no explicit requirement that the storage has to be secure[2]. The spreading of sewage sludge as a part of a land reclamation scheme must be registered with the Agency[3].

1 SI 1994/1056, Sch 3, para 9(2).
2 However, this deficiency could be addressed by the duty of care (EPA 1990, s 34) in relation to the 'escape of waste': see para 3.45.
3 SI 1994/1056, reg 18(10)(d).

Recycling and recovery of waste

10.172 The Waste Management Licensing Regulations 1994 make a clear distinction between the actual processing of waste and the storage of waste before undergoing processing. Both activities are treated as discrete activities, and exemptions need to be sought for both. In certain cases, storage is only exempt from licensing when it occurs at the site where the recycling or recovery activity takes place. In this instance, both the activity and the requirements on storage are covered below. However, for some of the other exemptions, the storage of recycled materials can occur 'at any place'. Accordingly, such storage can occur either independently of the recycling activity or at the site of the activity itself. In this case, the discussion of the storage element can be found at para 10.64ff above.

Packaging, container and drum recovery

10.173 Waste packaging and waste containers can be cleaned, washed, sprayed or coated in order that they can be re-used without the need to possess a waste management licence[1]. This is allowable provided that the total quantity of wastes processed does not exceed 1,000 tonnes in seven days[2]. However, the exemption only applies where neither the containers nor their residual contents are special wastes[3]. Accordingly, should residues in any of the containers exceed the toxicity thresholds contained in the Special Waste Regulations 1996[4], the exemption is disapplied.

1 SI 1994/1056, Sch 3, para 4. The occupier's consent or other entitlement to carry on the activity on the land is needed (SI 1994/1056, reg 17(2)).
2 SI 1994/1056, Sch 3, para 4(1).
3 SI 1994/1056, reg 17(3): in *Durham County Council v Thomas Swan & Co Ltd* [1995] Env LR 72 it was held that drums were 'empty' when less than 1% of their original volume remained, but this case involved the use of the word 'empty' in a licence condition. Outside that context, it cannot be correct to state that drums with less than 1% of their constituents are 'empty' and it is certainly incorrect to imply that chemical drum residues cannot fall within the definition of special waste for that reason. In respect of *Thomas Swan*, it should also be noted that neither SI 1994/1056, reg 17 nor Sch 3, para 4 uses the term 'empty' in relation to the contents of any container.
4 SI 1996/972 as amended by SI 1996/2019: see para 4.19ff.

10.174 Under this exemption, up to 1,000 tonnes of waste can be subject to exempt storage where recovery is going on[1]. For steel drums, the maximum quantity that can be stored is set at a level of less than one tonne of 'metal containers used for the transport or storage of any chemical' which are dealt with over a period of seven days[2]. The one tonne over seven days ceiling – which seems quite low – appears to apply only to the storage of the drums, not the washing (etc) processes.

1 SI 1994/1056, Sch 3, para 4(2)(a).
2 SI 1994/1056, Sch 3, para 4(2)(b).

10.175 Circular 11/94 points out that this exemption is intended to cover the recovery of whole containers and packaging. The recovery of materials from which the containers are made is not viewed as falling within this exemption[1]. However, exemptions under paragraphs 11 and 14 of Schedule 3 may apply in this circumstance: these are discussed at paras 10.177 and 10.185.

1   Circular 11/94, Annex 5, para 5.58.

10.176 Some drum recovery processes involving spraying or coating metal containers fall within Part B of the Environmental Protection (Prescribed Processes and Substances) Regulations 1991[1]. Accordingly, the details obtained from their Part B authorisation application are sufficient to constitute a registration[2]. However, all other exempt activities need to register with the Agency[3].

1   SI 1991/472, Sch 1, Section 6.5, Pt B, as amended by SI 1994/1271, reg 3, Sch 1, para 10 and
    reg 4(3), Sch 3, paras 41 and 42.
2   SI 1994/1056, reg 18(5).
3   SI 1994/1056, reg 18.

Baling, sorting, shredding, etc of recyclable materials

10.177 Certain types of wastes can be sorted and otherwise processed prior to recovery or re-use without a waste management licence being needed: see Table 10.5[1]. To be exempt, the maximum quantity limit must not be exceeded. Furthermore, the activity must be 'carried on with a view to the recovery or re-use of the waste'[2]. This exemption does not only apply to the site at which the waste is re-used, but can occur at any other place.

1   SI 1994/1056, Sch 3, para 11. The occupier's consent or other entitlement to carry on the activity on
    the land is needed (SI 1994/1056, reg 17(2)).
2   SI 1994/1056, Sch 3, para 11(a).

Table 10.5

Exempt Intermediate Processing Activities for Materials Destined for Recycling[1]

Type of waste	*Permitted exempt activity*	*Maximum permitted throughput (tonnes per week)*
Waste paper or cardboard	Baling, sorting or shredding	3,000
Waste textiles	Baling, sorting or shredding	100
Waste plastic	Baling, sorting shredding, densifying or washing	100
Waste glass	Sorting, crushing or washing	1,000
Waste steel cans, aluminium cans, aluminium foil	Sorting, crushing pulverising, shredding compacting or baling	100
Waste food or drink cartons	Sorting, crushing, pulverising, shredding compacting or baling	100

1   SI 1994/1056, Sch 3, para 11, Table 3.

10.178 In addition to this exemption, a separate, and much less onerous, exemption is permitted for baling, etc on the site of the production of the waste[1].

1 See SI 1994/1056, Sch 3, para 27 and para 10.59 above.

10.179 The exemption under Schedule 3, paragraph 11 is clearly designed to cover the processing activity only. The associated storage activity is not subject to exemption by that paragraph, which is entirely silent in this respect. The reason for this is that storage is intended to be covered by a separate exemption[1]. Accordingly, most storage associated with exempt recycling and recovery operations will be covered by exemptions contained in Schedule 3, paragraphs 17 and 18. These allow the storage of materials such as bottles, paper and textiles in a secure place or in secure containers to be exempt from waste management licensing. The nature of the statutory requirements is dealt with elsewhere in this chapter, at para 10.83ff.

1 See Circular 11/94, Annex 5, para 5.132.

10.180 The inclusion of the word 'sorting' as a permissible activity does raise some concerns that something close to a waste transfer station could be operated under this exemption. However, operations must be restricted to only the wastes set out in Table 10.5. Secondly, the associated storage exemptions[1] of Schedule 3 clearly indicate that wastes must be subject to segregated storage.

1 Principally SI 1994/1056, Sch 3, paras 17 and 18: see paras 10.84 and 10.88.

10.181 All of these exempt activities need to be registered with the Agency. This includes charitable organisations, such as scout groups and schools, who collect waste paper. Such organisations are included within Circular 11/94's view of the nature of an establishment or undertaking[1].

1 Circular 11/94, Annex 6, para 6.19: see also para 10.22 above.

Manufacturing items from wastes

10.182 As described at para 10.116[1], the manufacturing of materials from a range of construction and demolition wastes is exempt under Schedule 3, paragraph 13 of the Waste Management Licensing Regulations 1994. Paragraph 13 also permits exemptions for places where a wide range of other wastes are subject to 'manufacturing'. Such substances are waste ash, slag, clinker, rock, wood, bark, paper, straw or gypsum. The processing of these materials is exempt when they are to be made into timber products, straw board, plasterboard, bricks, blocks, roadstone or aggregate[2].

1 Which also covers the manufacture of soil from wastes and the treatment of soil or rock prior to land spreading.
2 SI 1994/1056, Sch 3, para 13(1)(b). The occupier's consent or other entitlement to carry on the activity on the land is needed (SI 1994/1056, reg 17(2)).

10.183 The storage of such materials prior to manufacture is also exempt[1], provided it is carried out at the place where manufacture is occurring and provided that the total quantity stored does not exceed 20,000 tonnes[2].

1 SI 1994/1056, Sch 3, para 13(4).
2 50,000 tonnes for road planings.

10.184 All of these activities need to be registered with the Agency[1].

1 SI 1994/1056, reg 18(10)(d).

10.185 The above range of wastes is further augmented by Schedule 3, paragraph 14, which exempts the manufacture from wastes of 'finished goods'[1]. The range of wastes falling within this exemption are waste metal, plastic, glass, ceramics, rubber, textiles, wood, paper or cardboard[2]. For the storage of such materials to be exempt, it must occur at the 'place of manufacture' and the amount stored at any one time must not exceed 15,000 tonnes[3]. All of these activities need to be registered with the Agency[4].

1 The occupier's consent or other entitlement to carry on the activity on the land is needed
   (SI 1994/1056, reg 17(2)).
2 SI 1994/1056, Sch 3, para 14(1).
3 SI 1994/1056, Sch 3, para 14(2).
4 SI 1994/1056, reg 18(10)(d).

10.186 It might be considered that these exemptions sit rather uncomfortably next to the EPA 1990's definition of waste and, in particular the 'concepts of normal commercial cycle' or 'chain of utility' as set out in Circular 11/94[1]. However, the Circular[2] attempts to clarify this by offering an interpretation of the words 'finished goods' in Schedule 3, paragraph 14(1). It suggests that many recovery processes will be composed of a series of stages and that, once a waste has passed the first stage, it becomes a feedstock (rather than a waste) for the further stages and before it has become finished goods[3]:

'If this is the case, then the final manufacturing process will be utilising feedstock that is no longer waste and no question of waste management licensing for manufacture arises. In other cases, however, a manufacturing process may take waste directly and transform it at one operation into finished goods. Such processes are the subject of this exemption. It should be noted, however, that the exemption only applies to manufacturing processes that end with finished goods, it does not apply to intermediate stages of processing waste even if these are recovery operations that produce materials that are no longer waste'[3].

It would seem therefore that this exemption is intended to prevent, for example, companies who make paper products out of waste paper requiring a waste management licence for the actual manufacturing process itself.

1 See Circular 11/94, Annex 2; see also paras 2.103ff and 2.131ff.
2 Circular 11/94, Annex 5, para 5.119.
3 Circular 11/94, Annex 5, para 5.119.

10.187 While waste glass features in the list of materials that can be used to manufacture 'finished goods' in Schedule 3, paragraph 14 of the Waste Management Licensing Regulations 1994, scrap glass is subject to a further, and much wider, exemption by way of Schedule 3, paragraph 1. The latter exempts any manufacturer receiving waste glass if the use of such glass is covered by the required Part B authorisation for glass manufacturing[1]. However, to be exempt, the total amount of waste glass 'used in that process' must not exceed 600,000 tonnes in 12 months[2]. The storage at the premises of the glass manufacturer is also exempt[3], with no storage quantity limit being set down.

1 SI 1991/472, Sch 1, Pt B, Section 3.5, as amended by SI 1994/1271, reg 4(3) Sch 3, para 21.
2 SI 1994/1056, Sch 3, para 1(1).
3 SI 1994/1056, Sch 3, para 1(2).

10.188 Being a Part B process, no separate registration is needed as the local enforcing authority is 'taken to be aware of' the activity[1].

1   SI 1994/1056, reg 18(4) and (10); similarly, in Scotland, the Agency itself is taken to 'be aware' of
    the activity.

10.189   A very wide-ranging exemption is granted by Schedule 3, paragraph 15. This
exempts all activities involved in the 'beneficial use of waste' where the waste can be
'put to that use without further treatment' and the use of the waste 'does not involve its
disposal'[1]. Similarly, wastes can be stored prior to this exempt activity without a
licence if the storage 'does not amount to disposal of the waste'[2]. Neither the type of
waste[3] nor the required location of the storage activity is specified. Therefore, storage
can occur at locations other than the place of beneficial use. In addition, no quantity
limits are set down.

1   SI 1994/1056, Sch 3, para 15(1)(a) and (b). The occupier's consent or other entitlement to carry on
    the activity on the land is needed (SI 1994/1056, reg 17(2)).
2   SI 1994/1056, Sch 3, para 15(2).
3   However, special waste cannot be accepted: SI 1994/1056, reg 17(3).

10.190   Circular 11/94 provides an interpretation[1] of the term 'does not involve its
disposal' in Schedule 3, paragraph 15. It points out that 'disposal' is defined in reg 1(3)
of the Waste Management Licensing Regulations 1994[2]:

'. . . as any of the disposal operations listed in Part III of Schedule 4, but does not
include any other form of disposal, notwithstanding its meaning in the 1990 Act.
"Treatment" has no definition particular to these Regulations[3], but under section 29
of the 1990 Act "waste is 'treated' when it is subjected to any process, including
making it re-usable or reclaiming substances from it". Accordingly the effect of
Schedule 3 paragraph 15(1)(a) and (b) is to disapply the exemption in any case
involving:

(a)   the subjecting of waste, before it is put to use, to any process including making
      it re-usable or reclaiming substances from it; or
(b)   a disposal operation.

What is left as being exempted by paragraph 15(1) is any beneficial use of waste
that may involve a recovery operation but no treatment.'

This exclusion is, of course, necessary to ensure compliance with the system of
permits and registrations envisaged by the Directive on Waste[4].

1   Circular 11/94, Annex 5, paras 5.125 and 5.126.
2   Circular 11/94, Annex 5, para 5.125. SI 1994/1056, reg 1(3) holds that '"Disposal" means any of the
    operations listed in Part III of Schedule 4, and any reference to waste being disposed of is a reference
    to its being submitted to any of those operations'. A copy of Sch 4 is provided in Table 2.5 of
    Chapter 2.
3   Waste Management Licensing Regulations 1994.
4   See para 10.08.

10.191   However, the exemption in Schedule 3, paragraph 15 does not apply[1] if the
activities have been covered by specified other paragraphs of the Schedule[2]. The
latter involve exemptions on spreading of waste on land[3]; storage of sludge and septic tank contents[4]; the use of construction, demolition, excavation or tunnelling
wastes and waste ash, slag, clinker, rock, wood or gypsum[5]; and the deposit of
dredging materials[6]. Although this 'exemption to the exemption' clause may appear
a little strange, it essentially requires that the limits set by one of the other exemptions should apply and therefore not be over-ruled by the wider exemption in paragraph 15.

1 SI 1994/1056, Sch 3, para 15(3).
2 SI 1994/1056, Sch 3, paras 7, 8, 9, 19 or 25.
3 SI 1994/1056, Sch 3, paras 7 and 9.
4 SI 1994/1056, Sch 3, para 8.
5 SI 1994/1056, Sch 3, para 19.
6 SI 1994/1056, Sch 3, para 25.

10.192 All exempt activities covered by Schedule 3, paragraph 15 need to be registered with the relevant Agency[1].

1 SI 1994/1056, reg 18(10)(d).

10.193 Soil or soil substitute manufacture is also exempt provided the soil is made from waste ash, slag, clinker, rock, wood, bark, paper, straw or gypsum[1]. The exemption also applies to soil manufacture from demolition, construction, tunnelling and other excavation wastes: these are discussed at para 10.121. It should be noted that the manufacture of 'soil' from other sources, such as foundry sand – a not-unknown activity by the less customer-conscious waste disposal contractor – is not exempt. In any case, to be exempt, soil manufacture can only occur where the waste is produced or where the soil or soil substitute is to be applied to the land[2]. Finally, the total amount manufactured should not exceed 500 tonnes per day[3]. This activity needs to be registered with the Agency[4].

1 SI 1994/1056, Sch 3, para 13(2).
2 SI 1994/1056, Sch 3, para 13(2)(a).
3 SI 1994/1056, Sch 3, para 13(2)(b).
4 SI 1994/1056, Sch 3, reg 18(10)(d).

Laundering textiles

10.194 The 'laundering or otherwise cleaning of textiles' with a view to their recovery or re-use is exempt[1]. There are no quantity or other requirements.

1 SI 1994/1056, Sch 3, para 20.

10.195 Besides the actual cleaning process itself, the storage of the textiles at the place of cleaning is also exempt. Waste textiles storage at other locations is covered by the exemption contained in the 1994 Regulations, Schedule 3, paragraph 41 of the Waste Management Licensing Regulations 1994[1], where the rags are awaiting collection and also by paragraphs 17 or 18[2] where they are being bulked up.

1 See para 10.55.
2 See para 10.83ff.

10.196 Should the rags be impregnated with cleaning materials such as solvents, they may reach the threshold set down for the definition of special waste[1]. If this is the case, these exemptions do not apply[2].

1 See Chapter 4.
2 SI 1994/1056, reg 17(3): however, a possible amendment to this requirement has been mooted –
   DETR 1998 *Consultation Paper – Proposed Amendments to the Special Waste Regulations 1996 and the Waste Management Licensing Regulations 1994*, DETR, London, April 1998.

Silver recovery

10.197 The recovery, and storage prior to recovery, of silver from the photographic or printing industry wastes is exempt under Schedule 3, paragraph 22. The caveat is that no more than 50,000 litres can be dealt with in any one day. Silver recovery can be undertaken at any premises[1]. The exempt storage of photographic processing solutions or printing wastes prior to silver recovery can occur only at premises where the recovery process is taking place, but no limit is provided on the quantity that can be stored. All exempt undertakings involved in these operations need to be registered with the Agency[2].

1 SI 1994/1056, Sch 3, para 22(1).
2 SI 1994/1056, Sch 3, reg 18(10)(d).

Composting

10.198 The composting[1] of 'biodegradable waste' is exempt[2] in tightly defined circumstances. The exemption is conditional on the fact that the composting process is undertaken on the site at which the waste is produced or where the compost is to be used, or at 'any other place occupied by the person producing the waste or using the compost'[3]. Circular 11/94 states that this phrasing disallows the exemption in the case where waste is taken from outside sources and the compost is then sent on to other users[4]: in this case a waste management licence is needed.

1 Defined in SI 1994/1056 (Sch 3, para 12(3)) as including 'any other biological transformation process that results in materials which may be spread on land for the benefit of agriculture or ecological improvement'.
2 SI 1994/1056, Sch 3, para 12.
3 This phrase would seem to disallow many community compost schemes to be set up under the exemption.
4 Circular 11/94, Annex 5, para 5.107.

10.199 The exemption is also subject to the restriction that, where mushroom compost is being produced, only 10,000 cubic metres of waste is composted[1]. For any other type of composting activity, the limit is 1,000 cubic metres at any one time[2]. The limit of 1,000 cubic metres is very low and appears to permit only the operation of small scale facilities, pilot composting plants or trials.

1 SI 1994/1056, Sch 3, para 12(1).
2 SI 1994/1056, Sch 3, para 12(1)(b): Circular 11/94 erroneously states (Annex 5, para 5.108) that the 1,000 tonne limit is a yearly threshold.

10.200 Storage of the biodegradable waste prior to composting can take place without a licence where the waste is produced or where the composting takes place[1]. No quantities or time limits appear to apply.

1 SI 1994/1056, Sch 3, para 12(2).

10.201 It should also be noted that, if the waste feedstock for composting is produced from an agricultural premises, it will not be controlled waste by virtue of s 75(7) of the EPA 1990[1].

1 See para 2.60ff.

10.202 The exempt composting activity itself, along with associated storage, will need to be registered with the relevant Agency.

Operations involving the processing of waste plant matter

10.203 Paragraph 21 of Schedule 3 exempts from licensing '[c]hipping, shredding, cutting or pulverising waste plant matter (including wood or bark)', along with the sorting and baling of sawdust and wood shavings. This applies to any premises. Circular 11/94 states the word 'premises' would 'include any place, including the street or open air'[1]. The provisos contained in the exemption are that the activity results in recovery or re-use, and that the throughput of the premises is less than 1,000 tonnes per week[2].

1 Circular 11/94, Annex 5, para 5.162.
2 SI 1994/1056, Sch 3, para 21(1).

10.204 The storage of these wastes prior to processing is also exempt, provided that no more than 1,000 tonnes is to be stored at any one time and that the storage occurs where the chipping, shredding, etc is carried on[1]. Circular 11/94[2] points out that some of the operations contained in the exemption, while changing the physical form of the material, will not change the fact that the material is still a waste after processing. Hence the exemption uses the phrase 'storage in connection with' the exempted processing activity. This allows the exemption for storage to extend to cover the storage of the waste materials after processing. All such exempt activities need to be registered with the relevant Agency[3].

1 SI 1994/1056, Sch 3, para 21(2).
2 Circular 11/94, Annex 5, para 5.164.
3 SI 1994/1056, Sch 3, reg 18(10)(d).

Recovery processes for sewage sludge, septic tank contents and wastes from water treatment works

10.205 As noted at para 10.165, the Controlled Waste Regulations 1992[1] contain provisions which cause sewage, sewage sludge or septic tank contents not to be controlled wastes when they are treated, kept or disposed of within the curtilage of a sewage treatment works 'as an integral part of the operation of those works'[2]. Given that s 29(6) of the EPA 1990 holds that recycling and reclamation is a form of waste treatment, many sewage-related recycling activities at sewage works will not fall within Part II of the EPA 1990 at all. In addition, many sewage sludge incinerators are excluded from Part II of the EPA 1990 on the grounds that they are subject to integrated pollution control authorisations[3]. But should a sewage treatment works accept other types of controlled waste, such as biologically treatable or recoverable industrial waste which is delivered by road, a waste management licence will be required.

1 SI 1992/588. See also para 2.223ff.
2 SI 1992/588, reg 7(1).
3 SI 1991/472, Sch 1, Section 5.1, Pt A, as amended by SI 1994/1271, reg 4(3) and Sch 3, para 33, and by SI 1998/767, reg 2.

10.206 Unless subject to spreading on agricultural land[1], sewage sludge and septic tank sludge are usually controlled wastes when transported beyond the curtilage of the sewage treatment works. Therefore, other recovery and treatment processes that are not integral to a sewage treatment works may need licensing or, more likely, will be covered by the exemption discussed below.

1 These materials are generally not controlled wastes when they are subject to the provisions of the Sludge (Use in Agriculture) Regulations 1989 (SI 1989/1263): see paras 2.223 and 10.165.

10.207 When they are moved from one works to another, an exemption applies[1] to sewage sludge and septic tank sludge[2] which is subject to any 'recovery operation' within the curtilage of the destination sewage works. The caveat is that no more than 10,000 cubic metres is imported into the works over a 12-month period. The exemption clearly specifies that a recovery process must be undertaken. Accordingly, the exemption only holds when sludge and septic tank contents are the subject of such a process (Circular 11/94 uses the example of fertiliser production[3]). Certainly, it does not hold when such wastes pass to a sewage works for disposal or for treatment prior to disposal.

1   SI 1994/1056, Sch 3, para 10(1).
2   The word 'sludge' is required by SI 1994/1056 (Sch 3, para 8(5)) to have the same meaning as in reg 2(1) of the Sludge (Use in Agriculture) Regulations 1989 (SI 1989/1263): 'residual sludge from sewage treatment plants treating domestic or urban waste waters and from other sewage plants treating waste waters of a composition similar to domestic or urban waste waters'. Similarly 'septic tank sludge' is required by Sch 3, para 7(10) to have the meaning of 'residual sludge from septic tanks and other similar installations for the treatment of sewage'.
3   Circular 11/94, Annex 5, para 5.99.

10.208   A separate exemption in Schedule 3 refers to the 'treatment' within the curtilage of a 'water treatment works'[1]. The treatment of waste arising at the works is exempt provided that a 10,000 cubic metre limit over 12 months is not exceeded. In addition, the exemption only applies for wastes generated within the curtilage of a water treatment works. It does not permit wastes to be brought in from outside the works for treatment. The distinction between paragraphs 10(1) and 10(2) should be noted. The former refers to the recovery of sludge at a sewage treatment works (ie where sewage is disposed of), whilst the latter refers to the treatment of waste at a water treatment works (ie where drinking or industrial water is treated prior to use).

1   SI 1994/1056, Sch 3, para 10(2).

10.209   The storage of 'waste' prior to exempt recovery at a sewage treatment works or prior to exempt treatment at a water treatment works is permitted without the need to possess a waste management licence[1]. While no quantity limits are included, the storage must occur where the recovery or treatment is to be carried on and must relate to that activity.

1   SI 1994/1056, Sch 3, para 10(3).

10.210   In the case of both sewage treatment and water treatment works, a registration with the Agency is required[1].

1   SI 1994/1056, reg 18(10)(d).

Burning wastes and using wastes as fuel sources

Use of wastes as a fuel

10.211   Provided that an authorisation under Part 1 of the EPA 1990 has been granted, it is allowable to burn[1] straw, poultry litter, wood, waste oil[2] or 'solid fuel which has been manufactured from waste by a process involving the application of heat' without a waste management licence being required. However, such activities must be, or form part of, 'any section of' Part B of Schedule 1 to the Environmental Protection (Prescribed Processes and Substances) Regulations 1991[3].

1   SI 1994/1056, Sch 3, para 3(a).
2   Waste oil is defined as meaning 'any mineral based lubricating or industrial oil which has become unfit for the use for which it was originally intended and, in particular, used combustion engine oil, gearbox oil, mineral lubricating oil, oil for turbines and hydraulic oil' (SI 1994/1056, reg 1(3)). The exemption includes waste oil which is special waste: SI 1994/1056, Sch 3, para 3(a)(ii) (as amended by SI 1996/972, Sch 3).

3 SI 1991/472, as amended by SI 1991/836, SI 1992/614, SI 1993/1749, SI 1993/2405, SI 1994/1271, SI 1994/1329, SI 1995/3247, SI 1996/2678 and SI 1998/767; Pt A processes are excluded from licensing altogether by SI 1994/1056, reg 16(1)(a): see para 10.14.

10.212 With the exception of waste oil, the storage of the other materials listed above 'on any premises' prior to burning is also exempt[1], as is the 'feeding of such wastes into an appliance in which they are to be burned'[2]. There appears to be no quantity limit. While waste oil can be stored at the place where it is produced[3], intermediate storage of waste oil prior to burning or the storage at the premises of waste oil disposal or recovery appears to be licensable in general[4]. However, there is a minor exception to this general principle: when less than three cubic metres of waste oil is stored, the storage will be subject to the exemption contained in Schedule 3, paragraph 18(1)(b)[5].

1 SI 1994/1056, Sch 3, para 3(b): it is not clear whether the exemption for storage applies in respect of storage prior to submission to a Pt A process. Paragraph 3 only refers to storage and subsequent combustion in a Pt B process; Pt A processes are not mentioned.
2 SI 1994/1056, Sch 3, para 3(b).
3 SI 1994/1056, Sch 3, para 3(c).
4 These provisions have a somewhat odd contrast to those contained in Sch 3, para 6(2), which appear to allow unlimited quantities of waste oil to be stored prior to use as a fuel in a small combustion engine (see para 10.97).
5 See paras 10.88 and 10.89.

10.213 For those wastes listed above that are to be burnt in a Part B process, the requirement to possess a registration under the Directive on Waste is deemed to be satisfied by the information provided in the Part B application[1]. This appears to apply also to off-site storage, despite the fact that the local enforcing authority may be totally unaware of the location of this storage. This is a consequence of the wording of regs 18(5) and 18(10)(a)(i). Regulation 18(5) states that the local enforcing authority 'shall be taken to be aware' for registration purposes of those activities stated in reg 18(10), which includes the exemption contained in Schedule 3, paragraph 3. While Schedule 3, paragraph 3 covers the burning activity itself, with the exception of waste oil, it also covers 'secure storage on any premises'.

1 SI 1994/1056, reg 18(5) and (10).

10.214 Waste oil can also be burnt 'as a fuel in an engine' of any aircraft, hovercraft, vehicle, railway locomotive, ship or other vessel if the total amount burnt in one hour is less than 2,500 litres[1]. This is below the threshold required for authorisation as a Part B process[2]. Should the amount be over that threshold, the exemption contained in Schedule 3, paragraph 3(a) takes over. This activity needs to be registered with the Agency. Compliance with reg 18 of the Waste Management Licensing Regulations 1994 may prove difficult in respect of the need to indicate the place at which the combustion is to take place given that mobile plant is also embraced by the exemption[3].

1 SI 1994/1056, Sch 3, para 6(1).
2 SI 1991/472, Sch 1, Section 1.3, Pt B, as amended by SI 1992/614, reg 2, Sch 1, para 7 and SI 1994/1271, reg 3, Sch 1, para 2 and reg 4(3), Sch 3, para 6.
3 See SI 1994/1056, reg 18(3).

10.215 Allied to the exemption for the burning of waste in a small combustion engine, waste oil can be stored anywhere 'if it is intended to be so burned'[1]. No maximum quantity is set down and the only caveat is that the oil must be located in a secure[2] container. However, such storage must relate to the use of the oil in an engine with a capacity of less than 2,500 litres per hour.

1   SI 1994/1056, Sch 3, para 6(2): no specific location is set down in this provision.
2   Secure is defined in SI 1994/1056, reg 17(5): see para 10.36 above.

Small incinerators

10.216   Two exemptions apply to incinerators which do not fall within Schedule 1 to the Environmental Protection (Prescribed Processes and Substances) Regulations 1991[1]. Under Schedule 3 to the Waste Management Licensing Regulations 1994, wastes can be burnt at any place as a fuel under paragraph 5 of Schedule 3[2], while wastes can be disposed of in a small incinerator on the premises of production under exemptions contained in paragraph 29.

1   SI 1991/472, Sch 1, Section 5.1, as amended by SI 1992/614, reg 2, Sch 1, para 9(a) and (b);
    SI 1994/1271, reg 3, Sch 1, para 8 and SI 1996/767, reg 2(2).
2   SI 1994/1056, Sch 3, para 5 as amended by SI 1995/288, reg 3(12).

10.217   Waste can be burnt as a fuel in an 'appliance' without a waste management licence being needed if the appliance has a net rated thermal input[1] of less than 0.4 MW[2]. This threshold is set on the grounds that an appliance over 0.4 MW would be one that requires an authorisation as a Part B process[3]. However, appliances burning straw, poultry litter, wood, tyres and waste oil do not have such a tight restriction and are covered by a separate exemption[4].

1   Defined as meaning 'the rate at which fuel can be burned at the maximum continuous rating of the
    appliance by the net calorific value of the fuel and expressed as megawatts thermal' (SI 1994/1056,
    Sch 3, para 5(3)).
2   SI 1994/1056, Sch 3, para 5(1) (as amended by SI 1995/288, reg 3(12)): where more than one
    appliance is used at the same time, 0.4 MW is a collective threshold for all appliances.
3   SI 1991/472, Sch 1, Section 5.1, Pt B, as amended by SI 1992/614, reg 2, Sch 1, para 9(a) and (b);
    SI 1994/1271, reg 3, Sch 1, para 8 and reg 4(3), Sch 3, para 33; SI 1998/767, reg 2(2).
4   SI 1994/1056, Sch 3, para 3: see para 10.211.

10.218   For appliances under 0.4 MW which are covered by the exemption contained in Schedule 3, paragraph 5, it would appear that, excluding special waste[1], any suitable type of waste can be burnt under this provision. However, a constraint will be the requirement of the exemption that waste is burnt as a fuel[2] – therefore many small rubbish incinerators are not covered by this exemption. The latter are burning waste to dispose of it – not using waste as a fuel. What seems less certain is the use of a rubbish incinerator to heat a building or part of it. The fact that a wide range of wastes can be burnt under this exemption is in contrast to the exemption in respect of bonfires[3], which is restricted to a much more limited range of wastes.

1   See SI 1994/1056, reg 17(3): this would preclude the burning of most waste oil under this exemption.
2   SI 1994/1056, Sch 3, para 5(1) as amended by SI 1995/288, reg 3(12).
3   SI 1994/1056, Sch 3, para 30: see para 10.224.

10.219   Waste can also be subject to exempt storage prior to the burning referred to above[1]. The only requirement is that the storage is secure[2]. It should be noted that there is no limit on how much waste can be so stored, nor is there an indication of the permissible types of waste. Finally, the paragraph is silent on where the storage should occur.

1   SI 1994/1056, Sch 3, para 5(2).
2   Secure is defined in SI 1994/1056, reg 17(5): see para 10.36 above.

10.220   Both the combustion appliance and storage are required to be registered with the Agency[1].

1   SI 1994/1056, reg 18(10)(d).

10.221   Wastes can also be incinerated on the premises where they were produced without a licence under the exemption contained in Schedule 3, paragraph 29. This activity is exempt provided that the waste is burnt in equipment which constitutes an incinerator which is exempt from Part A and B authorisations under the Environmental Protection (Prescribed Processes and Substances) Regulations 1991[1]. These state that an exempt incinerator is defined as an incinerator of a capacity of less than 50 kgs per hour that is not used to incinerate hazardous waste[2], clinical waste (except animal carcasses), sewage sludge, sewage screenings or municipal waste.

1   SI 1991/472, Sch 1, Section 5.1, as amended by SI 1992/614, reg 2, Sch 1, para 9(a) and (b);
    SI 1994/1271, reg 3, Sch 1, para 8 and reg 4(3), Sch 3, para 33, and SI 1998/767, reg 2(2).
2   In any case, the wording of the exemption itself does not permit special waste to be burnt. See
    SI 1994/1056, reg 17(3).

10.222   However, there is a caveat in the exemption contained in Schedule 3, paragraph 29(1), which requires that the incineration of waste must be undertaken 'where it is produced' and 'by the person producing it'. This appears to disallow from the exemption a communal incinerator served by a number of small industrial units and, for example, operated on the tenants' behalf by the landlord.

10.223   Materials being stored prior to incineration on the premises of production are also exempt[1]. However, unlike the other on-site storage exemptions in Schedule 3, paragraphs 26[2] and 27[3], such waste must be subject to 'secure[4] storage'. Both the incineration process and the associated storage will need to be registered with the Agency[5].

1   SI 1994/1056, Sch 3, para 29(2).
2   See para 10.61.
3   See para 10.59
4   Secure is defined in SI 1994/1056, reg 17(5): see para 10.36 above.
5   SI 1994/1056, reg 18(10)(d).

Bonfires

10.224   Under Schedule 3, paragraph 30, waste can be burnt on land 'in the open' where it was produced if it consists of 'wood, bark or other plant matter'. However, it must be produced on 'operational' land of a railway[1], tramway, internal drainage board[2] or the Agency[3]. Alternatively, it must have arisen from a forest or woodland, park, garden, verge, landscaped area, sports or recreation ground, churchyard or cemetery or have been 'produced on other land[4] as the result of demolition work'[5]. In all cases, the exemption only holds where persons responsible for the burning are burning their own waste[6]. In addition, such waste can be burnt in the open only if the total quantity burned in 24 hours does not exceed 10 tonnes[7].

1   Including a light railway.
2   Given the meaning (by SI 1994/1056, Sch 3, para 7(9)) contained in s 1(1) of the Land Drainage Act
    1991 'and for the purposes of operational land, an internal drainage board shall be deemed a statutory
    undertaker' (see also Circular 11/94, Annex 5, para 5.253).
3   SI 1994/1056, Sch 3, para 30 refers to the Agency as the 'National Rivers Authority'.
4   'Other land' should be taken to mean land that does not form part of a railway, internal drainage
    board, forest, woodland, etc (discussed further below).
5   SI 1994/1056, Sch 3, para 30(1)(b).
6   SI 1994/1056, Sch 3, para 30(2).
7   SI 1994/1056, Sch 3, para 30(1)(d).

10.225   The provisions in respect of the combustion of waste from 'demolition work'[1] are worded slightly differently. This causes something of a contrast between Schedule 3, paragraph 30(1)(c) – which set down the requirement of the exemption that the waste must be burned in the open on the site where it was produced – and paragraph 30(1)(b) – which allows demolition waste to be burned if 'it is produced on other land'. However, the 'other land' being referred to is land that is operational land of a railway, forest, park, etc and which is listed in paragraph 30(1)(b). Therefore the exemption still prevents the importation from a different site of demolition waste for burning. In addition, this exemption is not to be seen as a carte blanche to burn any waste at demolition sites. As noted, the exemption holds only for burning wood, bark and other plant matter[2].

1   Note that 'construction work' is not mentioned.
2   SI 1994/1056, Sch 3, para 30(1)(a).

10.226   As noted at para 10.22, the Waste Management Licensing Regulations 1994 make the distinction, supposedly in line with the wording of the Directive on Waste, between the application of the requirements upon individuals and upon 'establishments or undertakings'. Circular 11/94 indicates that this phrase has a particular significance in respect of the exemptions for burning wastes in Schedule 3, paragraph 30. As noted, it is stated that the exemption described above 'only' applies to the 'burning of waste by an establishment or undertaking where the waste burned is the establishment or undertaking's own waste'[1]. Circular 11/94 states[2] that this means that '[p]ersons other than establishments and undertakings may burn waste from any source provided that the other limitations on the exemption are met'. However, as noted at para 10.23, it is less than clear if this – or indeed any other – exemption applies to the activities of persons acting in their capacity as individuals.

1   SI 1994/1056, Sch 3, para 30(2).
2   Circular 11/94, Annex 5, para 5.188.

10.227   Besides the actual bonfire itself, the exemption permits waste to be stored 'on the land where it is to be burned' prior to the burning actually taking place[1]. All exempt burning activities by establishments or undertakings need to register with the Agency[2].

1   SI 1994/1056, Sch 3, para 30(3).
2   SI 1994/1056, Sch 3, reg 18(10)(d).

Burning tyres

10.228   A tyre incinerator of over 3 MW output would constitute a Part A process in Section 1.3 to Schedule 1 of the Environmental Protection (Prescribed Processes and Substances) Regulations 1991[1] and is excluded from waste management licensing for that reason[2].

1   SI 1991/472, Sch 1, Section 1.3, Pt A, as amended by SI 1992/614, reg 2, Sch 1, para 6;
    SI 1994/1271, reg 4(3), Sch 3, para 5; SI 1995/3247, reg 2, Sch 1, para 2(a), (b) and (c).
2   SI 1994/1056, reg 16: see para 10.14.

10.229   A tyre incinerator of between 0.4 MW and 3 MW is exempt from waste management licensing, provided that the appliance has a Part B authorisation under the EPA 1990[1]. Unlike other Part B incinerators[2], the exemption applies to the plant in its totality, as opposed to exempting solely the atmospheric emissions from such controls. A second provision exempts the shredding and feeding of the tyres into such an appliance[3].

1   SI 1991/472, Sch 1, Section 1.3, Pt B, as amended by SI 1992/614, reg 2, Sch 1, para 7;
    SI 1994/1271, reg 3, Sch 1, para 2 and reg 4(3), Sch 3, para 6.
2   See para 10.216.
3   SI 1994/1056, Sch 3, para 3(d).

10.230   Such plants would not need to register with the Agency, as the details provided within their Part B authorisation are deemed sufficient[1].

1   SI 1994/1056, reg 18(5) and (10).

10.231   An exemption is also possible where tyres are stored in a secure[1] place and 'are intended to be submitted to' the exempt operation referred to above[2]. As the exemption refers to storage 'at any premises', tyres can be held not only at the premises of the incinerator, but anywhere else. However, the exemption holds good only where the tyres are stored separately from other wastes[3]; where 'none of the tyres' is stored on the premises for over 12 months[4]; and where the total stored does not 'at any time' exceed 1,000 in number[5]. There is no requirement that this storage is registered as it is excluded from the need to have a separate registration by reg 18(5) of the Waste Management Licensing Regulations 1994. By contrast, the Directive on Waste[6] would require that the off-site storage of tyres at a location other than that of the incinerator itself would need a separate registration.

1   Secure is defined in SI 1994/1056, reg 17(5): see para 10.36 above.
2   SI 1994/1056, Sch 3, para 3(e).
3   SI 1994/1056, Sch 3, para 3(e)(ii). See Circular 11/94, Annex 5, para 5.55.
4   SI 1994/1056, Sch 3, para 3(e)(iii).
5   SI 1994/1056, Sch 3, para 3(e)(iv).
6   Council Directive of 15 July 1975 on Waste (75/442/EEC), (OJ L194/39 25.7.75) (as amended by Council Directive of 18 March 1991 amending Directive 75/442/EEC on Waste (91/156/EEC) (OJ L78/32 26.3.91)) Article 11: see para 10.08.

Other miscellaneous exemptions

Dead pets

10.232   In the last ten years, a small industry has grown up around the wish of pet owners to have deceased animals disposed of in a fitting manner. Accordingly, a number of pet incinerators and graveyards are now in existence. The more substantial incinerators are Part B processes[1], with the emissions subject to control by the local authority[2] and the remaining operation of the plant subject to a waste management licence[3]. Incinerators of a capacity below the threshold for the application of Part B authorisations, along with animal cemeteries, fall totally within the regulatory ambit of the Agency.

1   SI 1991/472, Sch 1, Section 5.1, Pt B, as amended by SI 1992/614, reg 2, Sch 1, para 9(a) and (b); SI 1994/1271, reg 3, Sch 1, para 8 and reg 4(3), para 33.
2   This applies in England and Wales, in Scotland the Agency is responsible for Part B processes.
3   SI 1994/1056, reg 16(1)(b).

10.233   However, a separate exemption, under paragraph 37 of Schedule 3 of the Waste Management Licensing Regulations 1994, allows owners to dispose of their pet 'in the garden of a domestic property where the pet lived'[1]. This exemption is subject to two restrictions. The first[2] is that the exemption is disapplied if the dead pet 'may prove hazardous to anyone who may come into contact with it'. The second is that the burial must be done by an individual, not by an establishment or undertaking. The latter bodies are explicitly precluded from such exempt burial activities. Circular

11/94 adds that the exemption allows an individual to bury the pet even if it did not die on the property. However, the Circular states that an establishment or undertaking could not arrange a burial in similar circumstances and be subject to the exemption, since 'this follows the strictly literal interpretation of the Directive[3], however, given that the exemption is concerned only with burials at domestic property by or with the permission of the occupier, it is not envisaged that any "establishment or undertaking" will be involved, so that this final proviso should not prevent any pet burials'[4]. There is no requirement to register such burials with the Agency[5].

1   SI 1994/1056, Sch 3, para 37(1): the deceased pet – falling within the definition of clinical waste (see SI 1992/588, reg 3(1) and para 2.210) – is not 'household waste' under s 75(5) of the EPA 1990. Hence its internment is not excluded from the requirement for a waste management licence by s 33(2) of the EPA 1990. The occupier's consent or other entitlement to carry on the activity on the land is needed (SI 1994/1056, reg 17(2)).
2   SI 1994/1056, Sch 3, para 37(2)(a).
3   Council Directive of 15 July 1975 on Waste (75/442/EEC), (OJ L194/39 25.7.75) (as amended by Council Directive of 18 March 1991 amending Directive 75/442/EEC on Waste (91/156/EEC) (OJ L78/32 26.3.91)).
4   Circular 11/94, Annex 5, para 5.219.
5   Circular 11/94, Annex 5, Table 5.1.

Samples of waste

10.234   Paragraph 38 allows samples of waste, including special waste, to be stored at any place 'where they are being or are to be tested or analysed'. However, the samples must be taken 'in the exercise of any power under' the Radioactive Substances Act 1993, the Sewerage (Scotland) Act 1968, the Control of Pollution Act 1974, the Environmental Protection Act 1990, the Water Industry Act 1991 and the Water Resources Act 1991[1]. Samples can be stored where they are to be analysed under this exemption if taken by or on behalf of:

–   a waste management licence holder 'in pursuance of the conditions of that licence'[2];
–   a person whose facility is excluded from the requirement for a waste management licence[3] under reg 16(1) of the Waste Management Licensing Regulations 1994;
–   an owner of the land from which the samples were taken[4];
–   a person subject to the duty of care and s 34 of the EPA 1990 'in connection with his duties under that section'[5];
–   for the purposes of research[6].

It would seem that this exemption does not apply to a concerned resident living by a waste management facility or to an environmental pressure group who have taken and stored waste samples for their own purposes.

1   SI 1994/1056, Sch 3, para 38(a). There is no mention of samples taken by the Agency through powers under s 108 and Sch 18 of the Environment Act 1995: see para 12.65.
2   SI 1994/1056, Sch 3, para 38(b).
3   SI 1994/1056, Sch 3, para 38(c).
4   SI 1994/1056, Sch 3, para 38(d).
5   SI 1994/1056, Sch 3, para 38(e).
6   SI 1994/1056, Sch 3, para 38(f).

10.235   Although the temporary storage of samples is exempt, the testing and analysis of samples is neither exempt nor licensable. Circular 11/94 states that[1] '[i]n the view of the Departments, the testing and analysis of samples taken from waste is neither a disposal or recovery operation within the scope of those terms and the lists in Parts III and IV of Schedule 4'[2]. All exempt locations for the storage of samples need to be registered with the Agency[3].

1   Circular 11/94, Annex 5, para 5.220.
2   SI 1994/1056, Sch 4: see Tables 2.5 and 2.6 in Chapter 2.
3   SI 1994/1056, reg 18(10)(d): see also Circular 11/94, Annex 5, Table 5.1.

Operations under the Diseases of Animals (Waste Food) Order 1973[1]

10.236   Articles 7 and 8 of the Diseases of Animals (Waste Food) Order 1973[2] introduced a licensing system for places processing waste food, or receiving it with the intention of feeding it to animals. The relevant licensing authority is the Ministry of Agriculture, Fisheries and Food in England, and the Secretaries of State for Scotland and Wales. To be exempt from needing a waste management licence[3], the relevant premises must have both a licence under the Diseases of Animals (Waste Food) Order 1973 and be abiding with its conditions. No separate registration is required with the Agency; the details given in the permit applications under the Diseases of Animals (Waste Food) Order 1973 are considered sufficient to satisfy the requirements on registration[4].

1   Note that the Diseases of Animals (Waste Food) Order 1973 was revoked in 1999, being replaced by the Animal By-Products Order 1999 (SI 1999/646). The Waste Management Licensing Regulations 1994 have not been changed to reflect this revocation. The discussion in this section follows the Waste Management Licensing Regulations 1994 as currently worded.
2   SI 1973/1936.
3   SI 1994/1056, Sch 3, para 16.
4   SI 1994/1056, reg 18(5) and (10)(b).

Deposit, treatment and spreading of dredgings and plant matter from inland waters

10.237   The deposit of waste from dredging inland waters[1] or from clearing plant matter in inland waters is exempt from the requirement to have a waste management licence under Schedule 3, paragraph 25 of the Waste Management Licensing Regulations 1994. The requirements[2] are that the waste must be 'deposited' along the bank or towpath 'of the waters where the dredging or clearing takes place'[3]. The exemption only applies where the material deposited is an establishment or undertaking's own waste[4].

1   Inland waters are defined in SI 1994/1056, reg 1(3) as having the meaning in contained in s 221(1) of the Water Resources Act 1991 (in Scotland s 30A of the Control of Pollution Act 1974, but including any loch or pond whether or not it discharges into a river or watercourse).
2   The occupier's consent or other entitlement to carry on the activity on the land is needed (SI 1994/1056, reg 17(2)).
3   SI 1994/1056, Sch 3, para 25(1)(a).
4   SI 1994/1056, Sch 3, para 25(4).

10.238   The deposit of dredgings or plant matter in a lagoon or container is explicitly excluded from this exemption[1]. According to Circular 11/94, the purpose of this requirement is to prevent lagoons becoming final resting places for dredgings under this exemption and to 'permit the deposit of waste from dredgings or of waste from clearing plant matter only as these operations proceed'[2].

1   SI 1994/1056, Sch 3, para 25(3).
2   Circular 11/94, Annex 5, para 5.173.

10.239   However, if the dredgings or plant matter were awaiting shipment off-site for subsequent disposal or recovery, their temporary storage would seem to be covered by the general exemption for the wastes stored on the site of production which are awaiting collection[1]. Despite the statement in Circular 11/94[2] that, under Schedule 3, paragraph 25(3), dredgings cannot be placed in lagoons at all and still be exempt, it appears quite legitimate to place them in temporary lagoons prior to collection. Furthermore, when such lagoons act to allow dewatering, they appear to be allowable under a further exemption[3]. However, it is vital to the validity of any of these exemptions that any lagoon does not become a final resting place for the deposited materials. Such a disposal site would need a waste management licence.

1   SI 1994/1056, Sch 3, para 41: see para 10.55. However, storage under that paragraph must always be 'secure' (see para 10.36 above). Hence only lagoons which are containments are allowable and must not be accessible to the public.
2   Circular 11/94, Annex 5, Para 5.173.
3   See SI 1994/1056, Sch 3, para 25(5) and para 10.241.

10.240   As an alternative to the immediate placing of dredgings in proximity to the place where the activity is occurring, dredgings and cleared plant matter may be deposited under exemption along the bank or towpath 'of any inland waters' 'so as to result in benefit to agriculture or ecological improvement'[1]. In either case the maximum amount of material deposited must not exceed 50 tonnes per metre of bank or towpath[2].

1   SI 1994/1056, Sch 3, para 25(1)(b).
2   SI 1994/1056, Sch 3, para 25(2).

10.241   Dredgings and plant matter can also be subject to pre-treatment by 'screening or dewatering' without a licence being required[1]. This is allowable provided that it is done on the bank or towpath where the activity is taking place and prior to these materials being deposited under the exemption discussed above[2].

1   SI 1994/1056, Sch 3, para 25(5).
2   SI 1994/1056, Sch 3, para 25(5)(a).

10.242   Dredgings and plant matter which are to be spread under the exemptions contained in Schedule 3, paragraphs 7(1) and 7(2) of the Waste Management Licensing Regulations 1994, can also be subject to dewatering or screening at the location where they are to be spread[1]. The nature of the exemptions for spreading are discussed at para 10.138ff, but briefly they allow the spreading of dredgings and plant matter on land used for agriculture[2]. However, for other land[3] – for example forestry, recreation grounds, etc – only the spreading of plant matter appears allowable. Schedule 3, paragraph 7(2) is cast in a manner which prevents the exempt spreading of dredgings to other non-agricultural land[4].

1   SI 1994/1056, Sch 3, para 25(5)(b).
2   SI 1994/1056, Sch 3, para 7(1). Agriculture is defined by the Agriculture Act 1947.
3   SI 1994/1056, Sch 3, para 7(2).
4   The exemption for spreading on non-agricultural land is contained in Sch 3, para 7(2) which refers to a list of permissible materials set down in Part I of Sch 3's Table 2. This list includes plant matter. By contrast, dredgings feature only on Pt II of that Table and hence this exemption does not apply.

10.243   However, and rather perversely in the light of the above, dredgings – but not plant matter – can be spread on the land for the purposes of land reclamation under Schedule 3, paragraph 9(1) of the Waste Management Licensing Regulations 1994. Again, the nature of this exemption is discussed fully at para 10.153 above. Associated with this provision is an exemption[1] for the treatment of dredgings (but not plant matter), either on the towpath or bank or where the wastes are to be spread, prior to spreading for land reclamation purposes.

1   SI 1994/1056, Sch 3, para 25(5)(c).

10.244 Most of the above treatment and storage activities require registration with the Agency. This also applies to spreading dredgings for land reclamation purposes under Schedule 3, paragraph 9 of the Waste Management Licensing Regulations 1994. However, the spreading of dredgings and plant matter under Schedule 3, paragraph 7 needs to conform to the requirements of paragraph 7(3)(c). The latter requires that details of the spreading activities are sent to the relevant Agency in accordance with the general procedures for exempt landspreading[1]. These requirements must be adhered to in order to retain the benefit of the exemption.

1   The nature of these requirements is discussed at para 10.149 above.

Keeping or treating waste under the Animal By-Products Order 1992[1]

10.245 Any place which treats or keeps wastes 'in accordance with'[2] the requirements of the Animal By-Products Order 1992[3] is exempt from waste management licensing[4]. Animal by-products are defined in the Order as meaning 'any carcase or part of any animal or product of animal origin not intended for direct human consumption but does not include animal excreta or catering waste or meat cooked or denatured at a knacker's yard for use as food for animals whose flesh is not intended for human consumption'[5]. However, it should be noted that many such wastes will stem from farms and hence will not be controlled wastes under s 75(7) of the EPA 1990. In addition, other transactions involving such materials may be closer to 'normal commercial cycle' movements and hence may not fall within Circular 11/94's concept of waste[6].

1   Note that the Animal By-Products Order 1992 was revoked in April 1999, being replaced by the Animal By-Products Order 1999 (SI 1999/646). The Waste Management Licensing Regulations 1994 have not been amended to reflect this change. The discussion below follows the current wording of the Waste Management Licensing Regulations 1994.
2   Should the waste not be treated or kept in accordance with the Animal By-Products Order 1992, the exemption falls. Hence both s 33 of the EPA 1990 and the Animal By-Products Order 1992 itself are contravened in such circumstances.
3   SI 1992/3303 as amended by SI 1996/827 and SI 1997/2894.
4   SI 1994/1056, Sch 3, para 23.
5   SI 1994/1056, Sch 3, para 23(2) holds that the definition of animal by-products contained in SI 1992/3303, Art 3(1) (as amended by SI 1996/827, Art 2(2)) applies for the purposes of this exemption. Note that the Animal By-Products Order 1999 (SI 1999/646, Art 3(1)) holds that 'animal by-products' means (a) animal carcases; (b) parts of animal carcases (including blood); or (c) products of animal origin; not intended for human consumption, with the exception of animal excreta and catering waste.
5   See paras 2.60 and 2.103ff.

10.246 Briefly, the Animal By-Products Order requires that animal by-products are disposed of by rendering at approved premises or by incineration. Since the Animal By-Products Order 1992 was amended in the light of the BSE crisis[1], burial of animal by-products is being discouraged and now needs to be justified as a special case. The alternative to these options for some wastes is specified re-use, with such premises needing to be registered. In addition to the requirement for a registration, such facilities also need to conform with the conditions set down in the Order.

1   By SI 1997/2894, Art 3.

10.247 According to Circular 11/94[1], the provisions on exemptions go hand-in-hand with regs 23(3) and 24(7) of the Waste Management Licensing Regulations 1994 which disapply the requirements of the duty of care and the requirement that controlled waste carriers should possess registrations[2] in respect of animal by-products.

1   Circular 11/94, Annex 4, para 4.91ff; Annex 5, para 5.167.
2   See Chapters 3 and 6.

10.248   It is important to note that, due to the exemption only referring to the 'treating or keeping' of wastes under s 33(1)(b) of the EPA 1990, the exemption does not apply to the 'disposal' of by-products which are outside the Animal By-Products Order. Hence waste management facilities accepting carcasses and associated flesh, etc, for disposal may need licensing, when such materials are not subject to the provisions of the Order.

10.249   The bodies responsible for administrating the Animal By-Products Order are the Ministry of Agriculture and local authorities. In these cases, the Waste Management Licensing Regulations 1994 indicate that the information already held by these bodies is sufficient to constitute a deemed registration[1]. Accordingly, no registration with the Agency is needed.

1   SI 1994/1056, reg 18(5) and (10)(c).

Discharges from railway carriages

10.250   Most types of sewage are not controlled wastes under s 75(8) of the EPA 1990[1] or are excluded by the Controlled Waste Regulations 1992[2]. However, these provisions do not apply to discharges of sewage from railway vehicles. Accordingly, Schedule 3, paragraph 31 to the Waste Management Licensing Regulations 1994 exempt from waste management licensing the discharge of waste onto the track of a railway from a toilet or sink located in a railway carriage. However, to be exempt, the discharge must not exceed 25 litres. Although perhaps a rather trivial matter, the fact that this material does require an exemption for its disposal raises certain other questions. The most obvious is over the application of s 33(1)(c) of the EPA 1990 in relation to possible harm to human health from the deposited materials upon rail track gangs. If nothing else, contravening s 33(1)(c) disallows the exemption[3]. Further issues might arise in respect of compliance with the provisions of the duty of care in relation to an escape of waste[4] and over precisely how the required details in respect of written descriptions of the waste transfer are to be recorded and sent between parties. The latter seems all the more pertinent since rail privatisation, as a separate company will be operating the carriages which produce the wastes, whilst the material is deposited on the property of Railtrack. It is perhaps significant in this respect that the exemption does not require the consent of the occupier of the land on which the discharge is made. Such discharges need to be registered with the Agency.

1   EPA 1990, s 75(8): see para 2.223ff.
2   SI 1992/588, reg 7 and Sch 3, para 7(a).
3   See SI 1994/1056, reg 17(1) and para 10.33 above.
4   EPA 1990, s 34(1)(b): see para 3.45ff.

Railway ballast

10.251   'Spent ballast' can be kept or deposited 'at the place it is produced' without the need to possess a waste management licence[1]. The exemption only holds if the place on which the materials are kept or deposited is 'operational land'[2] of a railway, light railway or tramway. In addition, the total amount kept or deposited should not exceed '10 tonnes for each metre of track from which the ballast derives'[3]. Circular 11/94 advises[4] that '[i]n calculating this limit, each track of a multiple track line may contribute its quota of 10 tonnes for each metre'. The exemption only applies where the waste in question has been produced by an establishment or undertaking and has been treated or disposed of by that body[5]. In all cases, registration with the Agency is required[6].

1 SI 1994/1056, Sch 3, para 34.
2 Defined in SI 1994/1056, reg 1(3) as having the same meaning as in ss 263 and 264 of the Town and Country Planning Act 1990 or in Scotland, ss 211 and 212 of the Town and Country Planning (Scotland) Act 1972.
3 SI 1994/1056, Sch 3, para 34(1).
4 Circular 11/94, Annex 5, para 5.196.
5 SI 1994/1056, Sch 3, para 34(2).
6 SI 1994/1056, reg 18(10)(d).

Scrap rails

10.252 Scrap rails can be subject to 'temporary storage' on operational land[1] of a railway, light railway or tramway without the need for a waste management licence[2]. The other provisos are that the total quantity of rails 'in any one place' does not exceed ten tonnes and that the storage is 'incidental'[3] to the collection and transport of such rails. As Circular 11/94 points out[4], rails stored on the trackside awaiting removal would be covered by the exemption in respect of storage, pending collection, on the premises they were produced[5]. The exempt temporary storage of scrap rails away from the site where they were produced needs to be registered with the Agency[6].

1 Defined in SI 1994/1056, reg 1(3) as having the same meaning as in ss 263 and 264 of the Town and Country Planning Act 1990 or, in Scotland, ss 211 and 212 of the Town and Country Planning (Scotland) Act 1972.
2 SI 1994/1056, Sch 3, para 40(2).
3 The nature and meaning of 'incidental' is discussed at para 10.80ff.
4 Circular 11/94, Annex 5, para 5.231.
5 See Sch 3, para 41 and para 10.55.
6 SI 1994/1056, reg 18(10)(d).

Burial of waste from portable or temporary toilets

10.253 Circular 11/94 states[1] that this exemption permits the burial of latrine wastes from temporary entertainment sites and non-residential camp sites. Waste arising from a sanitary convenience which is equipped with a 'removable receptacle' can be buried without the need for a waste management licence[2]. This exemption applies only where the total amount buried within 12 months does not exceed 5 cubic metres. These exempt activities need to be registered with the relevant Agency. The Directive on Waste[3] requires that, like all the other registered activities, they should be inspected periodically by the Agency.

1 Circular 11/94, Annex 5, para 5.193.
2 SI 1994/1056, Sch 3, para 32.
3 Council Directive of 15 July 1975 on Waste (75/442/EEC), (OJ L194/39 25.7.75) (subsequently amended by Council Directive of 18 March 1991 amending Directive 75/442/EEC on Waste (91/156/EEC) (OJ L78/32 26.3.91)) Article 13.

The keeping or deposit of waste from peatworking

10.254 Excavated materials arising from peatworking can be kept and deposited 'at the place where that activity takes place'[1]. In the case of an establishment or undertaking, the exemption is only allowable where such a body's own waste is involved[2]. Registration with the Agency is required in the case of establishments and undertakings[3]. This is perhaps one of the few exemptions where the distinction made in the Circular between individuals and establishments or undertakings[4] is valid.

Persons cutting peat for their own domestic fires would be acting as individuals, for the reason that they are acting in a personal capacity, and therefore do not need to register.

1 SI 1994/1056, Sch 3, para 33.
2 SI 1994/1056, Sch 3, para 33(2).
3 SI 1994/1056, reg 18(10)(d).
4 See Circular 11/94, Annex 5, para 5.10 and see para 10.22.

Chapter 11

Exemptions for scrapyards and vehicle dismantlers

INTRODUCTION

11.01   The Waste Management Licensing Regulations 1994[1] contain provisions which permit certain scrapyards and motor vehicle dismantlers to operate without the need to possess waste management licences. Instead a system of registered exemptions apply. As a concept, the exemptions are little different in style from the others contained in Schedule 3 to the Waste Management Licensing Regulations 1994[2] and which are discussed in Chapter 10. Like those exemptions, they derive from reg 17 of the Waste Management Licensing Regulations 1994, by virtue of s 33(3) of the EPA 1990 and, ultimately, from the requirements of Article 11 of the Directive on Waste[3]. However, in comparison to the other provisions contained in Schedule 3, the exemptions in relation to scrapyards and vehicle dismantlers are much more complex. They also apply to a large section of the UK's waste management industry. Scrapyards and vehicle dismantlers make up nearly 25% of all licensed sites in England and Wales, with 1,404 further sites[4] being subject to the exemptions from licensing described below. It is for these reasons that this chapter is solely devoted to discussing the exemptions in respect of such facilities.

1   SI 1994/1056 as amended by SI 1995/288 and SI 1998/606.
2   SI 1994/1056.
3   Council Directive of 15 July 1975 on Waste (75/442/EEC) (OJ L194/39 25.7.75), as amended by Council Directive of 18 March 1991 on Waste (91/156/EEC) (OJ L78/32 26.3.91): discussed further at para 10.07ff.
4   Environment Agency (1998) *1997–98 Annual Report and Accounts*, Environment Agency, Bristol, Appendix 5 (no equivalent figure is contained in SEPA's Annual Report for Scotland).

11.02   While the nature of the exemptions will be explored extensively below, the Agency[1] is given certain specific duties in relation to the inspection of exempt scrapyards and vehicle dismantlers[2]. These are discussed at para 12.32ff.

1   The Environment Agency in England and Wales and, in Scotland, the Scottish Environment Protection Agency.
2   SI 1994/1056, Sch 4, para 13 as amended by SI 1995/288, reg 3(18).

11.03   It should be made clear at the outset that, in most cases, scrapyards and vehicle dismantlers need waste management licences. Only a limited number of the yards satisfy the complex and stringent requirements of the exemptions. Given the long legacy of uncontrolled activities by this sector of the materials reclamation industry, many sites will not have sufficient infrastructure or record-keeping systems to qualify. Accordingly, the provisions relating to waste management licences described in Chapter 8 will apply in the majority of cases.

11.04   Scrapyards and car dismantlers entered the waste licensing regime at a rather late stage, and hence their position in comparison to other waste management facilities has been a little anomalous. While permits for reclamation facilities were required by the Directive on Waste[1] in its unamended form, only in the 1990s were Waste Regulation Authorities encouraged by the Department of the Environment to licence them. Until 1995, the Waste Management Paper series was notable for the omission of any guidance on the requirements of such licences[2]. Although the need to licence such yards became a higher priority in the later 1980s, licensing was sporadic. Besides the lack of Department of the Environment lead, other factors included the scale of the task, limited regulatory resources, difficulties in the planning status of many yards[3], and the awkwardness of a minority of the yard operators. Hence the licensing of scrapyards and car dismantlers spread slowly between 1988 and 1995, but did gather pace considerably in the early 1990s. However, figures published in November 1998 suggested that between 1,000–1,500 sites were operating illegally in England and Wales[4]. As a convenient shorthand to describe activities involving the recovery of scrap metal and vehicle dismantling, the remainder of this chapter will use the term 'metal recycling sites' where it is appropriate to do so.

1   OJ L194/39 27.7.75: see also *Vessoso and Zanetti* [1990] ECR I-1461 and see para 2.78.
2   See Department of the Environment (1995) *Licensing of Metal Recycling Sites, Waste Management Paper 4A*, HMSO, London.
3   Many yards did not have planning permissions, but were able to apply for a certificate of established use. Later such certificates were replaced by certificates of lawful use. Only once s 10 of the Planning and Compensation Act 1991 was implemented could certificates of *lawful use* be regarded as a 'planning permission' for the purposes of s 5(2) of the Control of Pollution Act 1974. It was only then that a waste disposal licence could be issued for such a site. However many yards already had the earlier certificates of *established use*. These were not sufficient to satisfy the requirements of s 5 and to allow a licence to be issued under the Control of Pollution Act 1974. Only when s 36 of the EPA 1990 was implemented in May 1994 was it possible to issue a licence for yards which had the benefit of either type of certificate.
4   'Agency to Clamp Down on Scrap Yards', *Ends Report* 286, November 1998, p 16.

THE IMPLEMENTATION OF THE EPA 1990 FOR METAL RECYCLING SITES

11.05   Scrap metal and scrap vehicles accepted at metal recycling sites are controlled waste[1]. Section 33 of the EPA 1990 requires sites receiving controlled wastes to possess waste management licences or have a valid reason to be excluded or exempted from such a requirement[2]. Metal recycling sites are deemed to be recovery facilities under the Waste Management Licensing Regulations 1994 as they fall within Items 3 and 13 of the Table contained in Part IV to Schedule 4 to the Waste Management Licensing Regulations 1994[3].

1   See Chapter 2.
2   See paras 7.05 and 10.05.
3   SI 1994/1056, reg 1(3): see also Table 2.6 in Chapter 2, Circular 6/95, para 8 and Annex 1, para 1.23.

11.06   The following section describes the manner by which the relevant statutory provisions apply to metal recycling sites, since different requirements apply depending upon the nature of the site and its past compliance with the EPA 1990 or the Control of Pollution Act 1974. It is also the intention of this section to summarise the options available to a proprietor of a site in relation to whether possession of a licence or registration under exemption is possible. As will be seen, the position is somewhat complex, principally due to the convoluted manner by which the relevant statutory provisions have been drafted. Although the statutory deadlines for compliance have passed, the implementation of controls on the metal reclamation industry has been patchy, and not all sites are yet under statutory control. In addition, proprietors of sites subject to the existing provisions may be licensed, but desire exemption (or vice versa).

Metal recycling sites licensed under the Control of Pollution Act 1974: transitional provisions

11.07   Although waste management licensing and the EPA 1990 came into force on 1 May 1994, this did not apply to the metal reclamation industry[1]. This was due to the government having a significant – and late – re-think on the desirable level of environmental controls appropriate to such sites. One important effect of this re-think is illustrated by a series of statutory deadlines which, whilst purporting to indicate when waste management licensing would apply, were subsequently changed and extended[2].

1   Environmental Protection Act 1990 (Commencement No 15) Order 1994, SI 1994/1096.
2   See SI 1994/1096, SI 1994/2487 and SI 1994/3234.

11.08   An operator of a metal recycling site could apply for a licence under the Control of Pollution Act 1974 up to 1 April 1995[1]. The criteria for deciding applications made under the Control of Pollution Act 1974 were much less stringent that those emanating from the EPA 1990[2]. While an application under the Control of Pollution Act 1974 was being determined, the facility could claim a temporary exemption from the need to possess a licence under Schedule 3, paragraph 42 of the Waste Management Licensing Regulations 1994[3]. Such a provision should be viewed as quite distinct from the more permanent exemptions conferred by paragraph 45 of Schedule 3 to the amended Waste Management Licensing Regulations 1994[4].

1   SI 1994/1096, Article 3(2)(c) as amended by SI 1994/3234, Article 2.
2   Control of Pollution Act 1974, s 5.
3   SI 1994/1056 as amended by SI 1995/288, reg 3(14).
4   SI 1994/1056 as amended by SI 1995/288, reg 3(16). The nature of paragraph 45 exemptions are discussed in detail at para 11.49ff.

11.09   In the end, waste disposal licences granted under the Control of Pollution Act 1974 for scrapyards and vehicle dismantlers became waste management licences on 1 April 1995[1]. Licence applications made under the Control of Pollution Act 1974 which had not been decided by that date, became waste disposal licences for one day only after being granted. On the following day they converted into waste management licences[2]. The transitional provisions contained in s 77(2) of the EPA 1990 and Commencement Order 15[3] applied. Hence the operator of a site which was subject to the transitional provisions was deemed to be a 'fit and proper person'[4].

1   EPA 1990, s 77(2) and SI 1994/1096, Article 3(2)(c) as amended by SI 1994/3234, Article 2.
2   SI 1994/1096, Article 3(2)(a) as amended by SI 1994/3234, Article 2.
3   SI 1994/1096.
4   See para 9.82ff.

The relationship between the exemptions and sites already licensed by 1 April 1995

11.10   The provisions describing the exemptions for metal recycling sites finally emerged in the Spring of 1995 in the form of the Waste Management Licensing (Amendment etc) Regulations 1995[1]. These enlarged the scope of the Schedule 3 exemptions to address metal recycling sites[2]. Implementation was spread over a period from April to October 1995.

1   SI 1995/288.
2   Further amendments were made by SI 1996/634, regs 2(5) and 2(7) and by SI 1998/606, reg 2(2).

11.11   In the months immediately prior to 1 April 1995, a number of operators of scrapyards and car dismantlers returned licences granted under the Control of

Pollution Act 1974[1]. Most then re-applied for a licence. This action was considered advantageous, as it made use of the Schedule 3, paragraph 42 exemption referred to above[2]. It made the site temporarily exempt until the fresh application had been determined. Licence surrender and re-application meant that the affected operators no longer needed to abide by the conditions of the licence originally issued. They could therefore stall the requirements for stricter environmental controls for a number of months.

1   Under the Control of Pollution Act 1974, the WRA did not have the power to object to a surrender of
    a waste disposal licence as is now possible under s 39 of the EPA 1990: see para 9.93ff.
2   SI 1994/1056 as amended by SI 1995/288, reg 3(14).

11.12   Other site operators surrendered their licences before April 1995 and later registered the site's possible exemption with the then local government-based Waste Regulation Authorities under paragraph 45 of Schedule 3 to the amended Waste Management Licensing Regulations 1994. The nature of these provisions will be described at para 11.49 below. The proprietors of such sites had up to 30 September 1995 to obtain exempt status[1], as the offence in reg 18(6)[2] of operating an unregistered vehicle dismantler or scrapyard came into force from that date.

1   SI 1994/1056, reg 18(1A) as amended by SI 1995/288, reg 3(8).
2   SI 1994/1056, reg 18(6) as amended by SI 1995/288, reg 18(11).

Exemptions and sites which had not applied for licences by 1 April 1995

11.13   Existing metal recycling sites which had not applied for a licence before 1 April 1995 had to be the subject of a full waste management licence application. Alternatively, they had to have sufficient infrastructure and record keeping in place by 30 September 1995 to qualify for exemption.

11.14   The waste management licence application process is fully described in Chapter 8. Briefly, the most important hurdle is the submission of satisfactory proposals to demonstrate that the yard's infrastructure will not cause pollution of the environment or harm to human health[1]. This information must be augmented by a clear indication that the operator satisfies the requirements of s 74 of the EPA 1990 with respect of being a 'fit and proper person'[2].

1   Serious detriment to the amenity of the locality is also a criteria if the site's planning permission was
    issued prior to 1 May 1994 or if the site does not require a planning permission due to its possession
    of certificates of lawful or established use (EPA 1990, s 36(3) and SI 1994/1056, Sch 4, Pt I, para
    9(7): see para 8.49).
2   See para 8.112ff.

11.15   It is important to understand that a metal recycling site subject to a waste management licence application made *after* 31 March 1995 would seem to face a significant obstacle in subsequently attaining exempt status. This is in spite of the fact that it may have both infrastructure and record-keeping which would otherwise make it qualify. The reason for this is the wording of reg 17(1A) of the amended Waste Management Licensing Regulations 1994[1]. Regulation 17(1) confers exemption on all sites which satisfy the terms of reg 17 and the appropriate paragraphs of Schedule 3. For metal recycling sites the relevant part of Schedule 3 is paragraph 45. Regulation 17(1A) disapplies the requirement that activities which satisfy the requirements of reg 17 and paragraph 45 are exempt from the need to possess a waste management licence. Regulation 17(1A) states:

'Paragraph (1)[2] above does not apply to the carrying on of an exempt activity falling withat paragraph 45(1), (2) or (5) of Schedule 3 where the carrying on of that activity is authorised by a waste management licence granted upon an application made *after 31st March 1995*[3] under section 36 of the 1990 Act.'[4]

1 SI 1994/1056, reg 17(1A) as amended by SI 1995/288, reg 3(5).
2 Ie SI 1994/1056, reg 17(1).
3 Author's emphasis.
4 Regulation 17(1A) has application only to scrapyards and vehicle dismantlers described in para 45, not to the exemptions on metal scrap furnaces (SI 1994/1056, Sch 3, para 2) nor to scrap cleaning processes (1994/1056, Sch 3, para 44 as amended by SI 1995/288, reg 3(16)).

11.16   This restriction appears to have important consequences as it affects a significant number of facilities which had neither applied for a licence before 31 March 1995 nor qualified for exempt status by 30 September 1995. The wording would suggest that such facilities cannot easily obtain exemption if, as an interim measure, they applied for a waste management licence after 31 March 1995. The goal of exempt status might not be achievable for a number of years until sufficient funds are available to put the required site infrastructure into place. However, unless the site was granted a waste management licence *before* 31 March 1995, it would seem that no exemption can be conferred later[1,2].

1 This appears to be confirmed by the final line of Circular 6/95, Annex 1, para 1.41.
2 It would have been impossible for a metal recycling site to have been subject to a waste management licence before 31 March 1995. Until 1 April 1995 a licence application for a metal recycler was made was under the Control of Pollution Act 1974 (SI 1994/1096, Article 3(2)(c) as amended by SI 1994/3234, Article 2) and applicants applied for a 'disposal licence': not a 'waste management licence' as is required by reg 17(1A).

11.17   A second problem affected those operators who intended to obtain exemption by 30 September 1995, but whose efforts were deemed by the regulatory authorities as insufficient to satisfy the requirements of the exemption. A full waste management licence application is needed if the notification of exemption to the Waste Regulation Authority/Agency[1] was not accepted as meeting the requirements of the Waste Management Licensing Regulations 1994[2]. Again, reg 17(1A) would seem to prevent such sites from subsequently moving directly from the possession of a waste management licence to exemption.

1 The site would become an unauthorised facility as soon as registration was refused. An offence under s 33 of the EPA 1990 would be committed immediately. If any scrap materials of commercial or industrial origin were accepted, then s 34 also would be contravened.
2 Principally SI 1994/1056, Sch 3, para 45.

11.18   If the above analysis is correct, there appears only one way in which a licensed site subject to a waste management licence application made after 31 March 1995 can progress to exemption. This is via the procedures set down in the EPA 1990 with regard to the surrender of the licence[1]. This is the only option which will satisfy the requirements of reg 17(1A). When the licence has been surrendered, the activity referred to in reg 17(1A) is no longer authorised by a waste management licence. Hence reg 17(1A) no longer applies. As is explained at para 9.93, licence surrender is not easy to attain and requires the approval of the Agency[2].

1 EPA 1990, s 39. The transition to exempt status for sites with licences which were subject to applications *before* 31 March 1995 is explained at para 11.10.
2 See also Appendix D of WMP 4.

Sites which qualify for an exemption but wish to possess a waste management licence

11.19 Circular 6/95 acknowledges that a proprietor of a metal recycling site may prefer to possess a waste management licence rather than be subject to registration as an exempt activity[1]. For example, the operator may not wish to be constrained by the quantity limits set down by the exemption for the storage of materials. Although the site may be within those limits at present, and have adequate infrastructure and record-keeping to comply with the other terms of the exemption, it may be that flexibility is needed to permit the storage of larger quantities of materials when business conditions so dictate. This can only be done by way of the possession of a valid waste management licence.

1 Circular 6/95, Annex 1, para 1.41.

11.20 It seems from Circular 6/95 that the primary purpose of reg 17(1A) of the Waste Management Licensing Regulations 1994[1] was to allow a waste management licence to be applied for and lawfully issued at a site which in all other respects would qualify for exemption[2]. As noted above, reg 17(1A) causes reg 17(1) not to apply in the case of a facility which has been authorised by a waste management licence resultant from an application made after 31 March 1995[3]. In the absence of reg 17(1A), reg 17(1) would always automatically confer exemption upon a site which was managed within the terms set out in the appropriate paragraphs of Schedule 3 to the Waste Management Licensing Regulations 1994.

1 SI 1994/1056 as amended by SI 1995/288, reg 3(5).
2 Circular 6/95, Annex 1, para 1.41.
3 Regulation 17(1A) has application only to scrapyards and vehicle dismantlers, not to the exemptions on scrap metal furnaces (SI 1994/1056, Sch 3, para 2) nor to scrap cleaning processes (SI 1994/1056, Sch 3, para 44 as amended by SI 1995/288, reg 3(16)).

Metal recycling sites at new locations

11.21 The possession of either a waste management licence or registration of exemption are options available for operators of metal recycling sites setting up at 'greenfield' locations. A full waste management licence application which fulfils the requirements of s 36 of the EPA 1990 can be made to the Agency[1]. Alternatively, the site can be provided with the infrastructure and record-keeping needed to satisfy the requirements for exemption. As has been noted, these are contained in reg 17 and paragraph 45 of Schedule 3 to the Waste Management Licensing Regulations 1994[2]. The detailed requirements of these provisions are discussed at para 11.49 below.

1 See para 8.29ff.
2 SI 1994/1056 as amended by SI 1995/288 and by SI 1998/606.

11.22 It would appear, however, that a successful application for a waste management licence made after 31 March 1995 considerably forecloses the possibility that a site can later attain exemption. These difficulties stem from the wording of reg 17(1A) of the Waste Management Licensing Regulations 1994[1]. The nature of these problems is discussed at para 11.15 above. It also appears that operators who decide that a waste management licence is preferable to registration as an exempt facility cannot change their mind. This may have certain implications if the operator wishes to sell the site or reduce the scale of the business to levels that would otherwise qualify for exemption.

1   SI 1994/1056 as amended by SI 1995/288, reg 3(5). Regulation 17(1A) has application only to
     scrapyards and vehicle dismantlers, not to the exemptions on metal scrap furnaces (SI 1994/1056,
     Sch 3, para 2) nor to scrap cleaning processes (1994/1056, Sch 3, para 44 as amended by
     SI 1995/288, reg 3(16)).

Selling a metal recycling site to a third party or closing it

11.23   A metal recycling site which has an exemption can be sold to another operator
at its proprietor's behest. It can also be closed. In neither instance can the Agency
influence the decision. However, this is not the case when a site is subject to a waste
management licence. In this instance, there are only three ways in which proprietors of
metal recycling sites can divest themselves of their licences. The first two apply to all
licensed sites, but the third appears to be subject to a rather perverse constraint which
limits its application to only some metal recycling sites.

11.24   The first way by which proprietors of metal recycling sites can divest themselves of their licences is by arranging the transfer of the site and the licence to another
party[1]. The second way is by surrendering the licence[2]. For either of these courses of
action to occur, the Agency must be satisfied that the proposed action is appropriate
and that it complies with the relevant statutory provisions and associated guidance.
Otherwise, the proposed change cannot go ahead.

1   Under the requirements of the EPA 1990, s 40: see para 9.114ff.
2   Under the EPA 1990, s 39: see para 9.93ff and see also Appendix D of WMP 4.

11.25   The third option is the rather obvious route of obviating the need to possess a
licence by arranging for the site's infrastructure and record-keeping to qualify for
exemption. Once exempt, it can then be closed or sold without the Agency being able
to influence the decision. However, this may not always be possible under the Waste
Management Licensing Regulations 1994. It would appear that exemption can only be
attained by a metal recycling site which was subject to a waste management licence
application *after* 31 March 1995 by undertaking the formal process of licence
surrender[1]. Conversely, those other sites which already possessed waste disposal
licences – or which had applied for them – *prior to* 31 March 1995 can arrange suitable site infrastructure and record-keeping and are able to notify the Agency of their
exemption. Once exempt, they can be sold or shut down as required.

1   EPA 1990, s 39 and see para 9.93ff. This is a consequence of SI 1994/1056, reg 17(1A) (as amended
     by SI 1995/288, reg 3(5)): see para 11.15 above. However, reg 17(1A) has application only to
     scrapyards and vehicle dismantlers, not to the exemptions on metal scrap furnaces (SI 1994/1056,
     Sch 3, para 2) nor to scrap cleaning processes (1994/1056, Sch 3, para 44 as amended by
     SI 1995/288, reg 3(16)).

The duty of care and sites receiving scrap metal

11.26   Besides being the deadline for operators to notify the Waste Regulation
Authority of the exempt nature of their facilities, the date of 30 September 1995 was
also the day by which scrap metal became defined as industrial, commercial or household waste for the purposes of the duty of care[1]. Circular 11/94 explains the purpose of
inserting this deadline into the Controlled Waste Regulations 1992[2]. Should no licence
application have been received by this deadline:

> 'It will then become a breach of section 34[3] to consign scrap metal that is controlled
> waste to an unlicensed waste manager in a case where a licence is required. This
> will, as intended, cut off the supply of waste for unlawful treatment.'

1   By way of the Controlled Waste Regulations 1992: SI 1992/588, regs 3(2) and 7(2) as amended by
    reg 2(1) of SI 1995/288.
2   Circular 11/94, Annex 5, para 5.240: note that the deadlines referred to in the remainder of that
    paragraph were extended by SI 1995/288.
3   EPA 1990, s 34: see para 3.39ff.

11.27 Circular 11/94 claims that case law has indicated that motor vehicles
consigned for dismantling do not fall within the legal definition of scrap metal[1]. It
therefore suggests that the duty of care[2] has always applied to transactions involving
such vehicles[3].

1   Circular 11/94, Annex 5, para 5.242 and see also Department of the Environment (1996) *Waste
    Management – the Duty of Care Code of Practice* (2nd edn), HMSO, para 7.14.
2   EPA 1990, s 34.
3   Although the legal authority referred to in the circular for this authority is less than clear, it may be
    Such v Gibbons ([1981] RTR 126), which is discussed at para 11.32.

11.28 The duty of care Code of Practice contains detailed information on the requirements of the duty of care[1] in respect of operators of metal recycling sites. These are
discussed with the other provisions on the duty in Chapter 3.

1   EPA 1990, s 34: Department of the Environment (1996) *Waste Management – the Duty of Care Code
    of Practice* (2nd edn) HMSO.

THE DEFINITION OF 'SCRAP METAL RECOVERY' AND 'VEHICLE DISMANTLING'

11.29 Businesses involved in scrap metal recovery and vehicle dismantling have
quite distinct legal definitions in relation to Part II of the EPA 1990. The former is
defined statutorily, while the term 'motor vehicle dismantler' (and the variety of
synonymous phrases used in the Waste Management Licensing Regulations 1994) is
left with its common, ordinary English meaning.

11.30 Under the Waste Management Licensing Regulations 1994[1], the term 'scrap
metal' is given the meaning contained in s 9(2) of the Scrap Metal Dealers Act 1964.
Section 9(2) of the 1964 Act states that:

'"scrap metal" includes any old metal, and any broken, worn out, defaced or partly
manufactured articles made wholly or partly of metal, and any metallic wastes, and
also includes old, broken, worn out or defaced tooltips or dies made of any of the
materials commonly known as hard metal or of cemented or sintered metallic
carbides.'

1   SI 1994/1056, reg 1(3).

11.31 The Waste Management Licensing Regulations 1994[1] also require that
'carrying on business as a scrap metal dealer' has the meaning given in s 9(1) of the
Scrap Metal Dealers Act 1964[2]. Section 9(1) of the Scrap Metal Dealers Act 1964
states that:

'. . . a person carries on business as a scrap metal dealer if he carries on a business
which consists wholly or partly of buying and selling scrap metal, whether the scrap
metal sold is in the form in which it was bought or otherwise, other than a business
in the course of which scrap metal is not bought except as materials for the manufacture of other articles and is not sold except as a by-product of such manufacture
or as surplus materials bought but not required for such manufacture; and "scrap

metal dealer" . . . means a person who (in accordance with the preceding provisions of this subsection) carries on business as a scrap metal dealer.'

Somewhat oddly, in the light of the use of the above definition, the term 'scrap metal dealer' is only used once in relation to exemptions found in the original Waste Management Licensing Regulations 1994[3] and is not utilised at all in the Waste Management Licensing (Amendment etc) Regulations 1995[4]. Instead, the Regulations typically utilise the terms 'treatment, keeping or disposal of scrap metal'[5] or the 'recovery of scrap metal'[6].

1   SI 1994/1056, reg 1(4).
2   In Scotland, a metal dealer has the meaning given in s 37(2) of the Civic Government (Scotland) Act 1982.
3   SI 1994/1056, Sch 3, para 2: exempt scrap metal furnaces.
4   SI 1995/288.
5   SI 1994/1056, Sch 3, para 42(1).
6   SI 1994/1056, Sch 3, paras 45(1), 45(2) and 45(5) as amended by SI 1995/288, reg 3(16).

11.32   There is precedent to indicate that many vehicle dismantlers do not fall within the Scrap Metal Dealers Act 1964. In *Such v Gibbons*[1] it was held that a person who solely dismantles motor vehicles for the re-sale of parts is not a 'scrap metal dealer' under the Scrap Metal Dealers Act 1964. As noted, a scrap metal dealer is defined in that Act as a business which exists wholly or partly for the purposes of buying scrap metal. Woolf J found that this was not the role of someone whose business involved the sale of components from the 'used' vehicles. Conversely, if the person only sells vehicles on for their metal content, then that person is dealing in scrap metal. He held:

'I make a very real distinction between a business exclusively of the type carried on by . . . [the defendant], that is buying worn out cars for their parts, and the business of what I will call a car breaker, who . . . as part of the business removes usable parts but is also buying the cars for their metal. That seems to me to be a situation where one can, in common parlance, say that the person is carrying on a business as a scrap metal dealer. There are obviously going to be very many variations which do not fall clearly on one side of the fence or the other. In those different situations the magistrates will have to apply their minds to the facts.'

1   [1981] RTR 126.

11.33   This, rather rarefied, distinction in *Such v Gibbons* between a scrap metal dealer and a vehicle dismantler may present difficulties in determining where specific exemptions apply. Indeed, it could be argued that Woolf J had omitted to acknowledge that a consequence of any vehicle dismantling activity is that, when there are no re-saleable parts left on a vehicle, it is inevitable that the remaining metal will be sold as scrap metal[1]. That this type of activity is clearly envisaged as being encompassed by the definition contained in the Scrap Metal Dealers Act 1964[2] is indicated by the wording used: a person who carries on a business 'which consists wholly or *partly* of buying and selling scrap metal' is a scrap metal dealer[3]. Indeed, it is somewhat surprising that this aspect was not addressed by Woolf J.

1   This is particularly likely where a dismantler processes old vehicles and/or those which are accident damaged.
2   Scrap Metal Dealers Act 1964, s 9(1).
3   Author's emphasis.

11.34   In respect of the exemptions contained in the Waste Management Licensing Regulations 1994, of particular importance is that different quantity limits apply to the processing of scrap metal and to the dismantling of vehicles. Whilst these are discussed in detail at para 11.51 below, it is sufficient to point out that *Such v Gibbons* might appear to suggest that a 'car breaker' – to use Woolf J's term – should be viewed as a scrap metal dealer and not as a vehicle dismantler under the Waste Management Licensing Regulations 1994. Such an interpretation may not be wholly appropriate in the context of the 1994 Regulations and may be less than logical from the point of view of the manner in which the exemptions have been drafted[1].

1   However, Waste Management Paper 4A (Department of the Environment 1995 *The Licensing of Metal Recycling Sites*, HMSO, London) explicitly confirms that the Scrap Metal Dealers Act 1964 does not apply to many vehicle dismantlers: see para 1.29.

11.35   The term 'dismantling of waste motor vehicles' is not defined in the Waste Management Licensing Regulations 1994. Due to the fact that it is juxtaposed with the term 'recovery of scrap metal' it is quite clear that the meaning is different and, perhaps, is intended to reflect the distinction made in *Such v Gibbons*[1].

1   [1981] RTR 126.

11.36   While the word 'dismantling' may most readily be interpreted by way of its ordinary meaning, the definition of the term 'motor vehicle' in the Waste Management Licensing Regulations 1994 may be more problematic. At first sight, the adoption of the definition of 'motor vehicle' from other enactments may be attractive. An example is s 185(1) of the Road Traffic Act 1988, which states that a motor vehicle is a 'mechanically propelled vehicle intended or adapted for use on roads'. But extreme caution should be used in the cross-application of such a definition into this, quite different, statute[1]. Although the definition in the Road Traffic Act 1988 is in accordance with its ordinary meaning, certain judicial decisions have restricted the use of the term. Of particular pertinence in this context is *Smart v Allan*[2], where it was held that a private car purchased by a scrap metal dealer and stored on the public highway did not fall within the definition of 'motor vehicle' in the Road Traffic Act 1988. This was because the vehicle was in such a dilapidated condition that it had no reasonable prospect of ever becoming mobile again. It did not, therefore, fall within the Road Traffic Act 1988's concept of a mechanically propelled vehicle. Clearly, the application of such a meaning into the Waste Management Licensing Regulations 1994[3] would rule out many vehicle dismantlers from being exempt from licensing[4].

1   '. . . it would be a new terror in the construction of Acts of Parliament if we were required to limit a word to an unnatural sense because in some Act which is not incorporated or referred to such an interpretation is given to it for the purposes of that Act alone' *Macbeth and Co v Chislett* [1910] AC 220 at 223.
2   [1963] 1 QB 291.
3   SI 1995/1056 as amended by SI 195/288.
4   Note also that under the Road Traffic Act 1988 the term 'motor vehicle' is to be viewed as quite distinct from 'trailers' (s 185(1)). The importation of this definition into the Waste Management Licensing Regulations 1994 would appear to rule out the exemption of many dismantlers of heavy goods vehicles. Such sites often receive scrap vehicle trailers either separately or as a composite with the tractor unit. However, under the Road Traffic Act 1988, 'trailers' are not motor vehicles: see s 185(1).

THE NATURE OF THE EXEMPTIONS APPROPRIATE TO METAL RECYCLING SITES

11.37   As was the case with many of the other exemptions contained in Schedule 3 to the Waste Management Licensing Regulations 1994[1], all activities involving scrap processing or vehicle dismantling, along with associated storage, are required to fulfil certain general criteria set down in reg 17. They have also to address additional, and more specific, criteria set down in the relevant paragraphs of Schedule 3. In terms of reg 17, exemption is conditional on the site operator having the consent of the occupier of the land[2]. Alternatively, if there is no occupier, the person must be otherwise entitled to carry on the business on the relevant land[3]. If these criteria are not fulfilled, the site is not exempt, and the operator is open to prosecution under s 33 of the EPA 1990[4]. Furthermore, correct compliance with an exemption only offers immunity from s 33(1)(a) and s 33(1)(b) of the EPA 1990[5]. Hence a facility is open to prosecution under s 33(1)(c) if it is operated in a manner which causes pollution of the environment or harm to human health[6].

1 See para 10.32ff.
2 SI 1994/1056, reg 17(2)(a) as amended by SI 1995/288, reg 3(6).
3 SI 1994/1056, reg 17(2)(b).
4 See Chapter 7.
5 SI 1994/1056, reg 17(1).
6 See paras 7.03, 8.40 and 10.33ff.

11.38 Subject only to minor exclusions in respect of scrap vehicles, no special waste[1] is permitted on any exempt metal recycling site[2]. Where motor vehicles are concerned, the Waste Management Licensing Regulations 1994[3] allow for the acceptance of both the vehicle battery and 'any substance which is special waste and which forms part of, or is contained in, a vehicle and was necessary for the normal operation of vehicle'. Petrol, oil and brake fluid best fit within the latter category, but the presence of other special wastes at a metal recycling site will cause the exemption to no longer apply.

1 Defined in SI 1996/972 as amended by SI 1996/2019: see Chapter 4. Oil is now usually a special waste.
2 SI 1994/1056, reg 17(3).
3 SI 1994/1056, Sch 3, Tables 4A and 4B as amended by SI 1995/288, reg 3(16).

11.39 Finally, all exempt facilities must comply[1] with the relevant objectives of Article 4 of the Directive on Waste[2]. These require that waste is subject to recovery and disposal with the objective of:

'... ensuring that waste is recovered or disposed of without endangering human health and without using processes or methods which could harm the environment and in particular without –

(i) risk to water, air, soil, plants or animals; or
(ii) causing nuisance through noise or odours; or
(iii) adversely affecting the countryside or places of special interest.'

Such relevant objectives are considered further at para 10.33.

1 SI 1994/1056, reg 17(4).
2 OJ L149/39 25.7.75 as amended by Directive 91/156 (OJ L78/32 26.3.91) as set down in Sch 4, para 4(1)(a) to the Waste Management Licensing Regulations 1994.

11.40 Besides these criteria, Schedule 3 to the Waste Management Licensing Regulations 1994 sets down a number of specific requirements which relate to individual metal reclamation processing and storage activities. These relate to infrastructural requirements, record-keeping, annual fees and the registration process and are all discussed below.

Scrap furnaces and heating processes

11.41 Two exemptions apply to scrap furnaces and heating processes. Both of these relate to activities covered by authorisations for processes falling within Part 1 of the

EPA 1990 and the Environmental Protection (Prescribed Processes and Substances) Regulations 1991[1]. The first exemption was contained in the original Waste Management Licensing Regulations 1994[2], while the second was introduced into those regulations by the Waste Management Licensing (Amendment etc) Regulations 1995[3].

1 SI 1991/472 as amended by SI 1993/2405, SI 1994/1271 and SI 1995/3247.
2 SI 1994/1056.
3 SI 1995/288.

Ferrous and non-ferrous scrap metal furnaces

11.42 A scrap metal furnace of less than 25 tonnes capacity is generally exempt[1] if it is covered by relevant Part B authorisation[2]. However, not all of the listed activities in each of the Parts of the Environmental Protection (Prescribed Processes and Substances) Regulations 1991 are exempt[3]. Also covered by the exemption is the loading and unloading of such a furnace[4] and the storage of metal scrap on the premises where the furnace is located. In this respect, it should be noted that the exemption for storage only applies to the scrap that is to be loaded into the furnace, and does not apply to the general storage of scrap at a scrap metal dealers' premises[5,6].

1 SI 1994/1056, Sch 3, para 2(1).
2 SI 1991/472, Sch 1, Section 2.1 or 2.2, Pt B as amended by SI 1993/2405, SI 1994/1271 and SI 1995/3247. Facilities subject to equivalent Part A authorisations are excluded from needing a waste management licence by SI 1994/1056, reg 16(1)(a) (see para 10.14ff).
3 Only processes subject to paragraphs (a), (b) and (d) of Part B of Section 2.1 of SI 1991/472 (as amended by SI 1994/1271, reg 4(3)) and paragraphs (a), (b) and (e) of Section 2.2 (as amended by SI 1994/1271, reg 4(3) and SI 1995/3247, reg 2) are affected by the exemption.
4 SI 1994/1056, Sch 3, para 2(2).
5 A metal dealer in Scotland.
6 See Circular 11/94, Annex 5, para 5.48.

11.43 Being a process under the control of a local authority, there is no separate requirement to register with the Agency. The details submitted to the authority as part of an application for a Part B authorisation[1] are deemed sufficient[2].

1 Discussed at para 10.29.
2 SI 1994/1056, reg 18(5) and 18(10)(a).

Cleaning ferrous and non-ferrous metals by the application of heat

11.44 An exemption applies where 'iron, steel or any ferrous alloy[1], non-ferrous metal or non-ferrous metal alloy' is heated 'for the purpose of removing grease, oil or any other non-metallic contaminant'[2]. To be exempt, the primary combustion chamber of the furnace must have a net rated thermal input[3] of less than 0.2 MW[4]. This 0.2 MW threshold should be seen as an aggregate limit where more than one combustion chamber of the furnace is used.

1 Defined as meaning 'an alloy of which iron is the largest constituent, or equal to the largest constituent, by weight, whether or not that alloy also has a non-ferrous metal content greater than any percentage specified in Section 2.2 of Schedule 1 to the 1991 Regulations, and "non-ferrous metal alloy" shall be construed accordingly' (SI 1994/1056, Sch 3, para 44(7) as amended by SI 1995/288, reg 3(16)).
2 SI 1994/1056, Sch 3, para 44 as amended by SI 1995/288, reg 3(16).
3 Defined as meaning 'the rate at which fuel can be burned at the maximum continuous rating of the appliance multiplied by the net calorific value of the fuel and expressed as megawatts thermal'.
4 SI 1994/1056, Sch 3, para 44(6) as amended by SI 1995/288, reg 3(16).

11.45 The exemption does not apply to a process which uses heat to remove plastic or rubber coverings from scrap cables or for the removal of any asbestos contaminant[1].

It also does not apply where the heating process is related to certain other stipulated iron and steel, non-ferrous metal or ferrous and non-ferrous metal alloy production processes[2].

1 SI 1994/1056, Sch 3, para 44(2) as amended by SI 1995/288, reg 3(16).
2 SI 1994/1056, Sch 3, para 44(3) and (4): the paragraphs stipulated from Sch 1 of the Environmental Protection (Prescribed Process and Substances) Regulations 1991 (SI 1991/472 as amended by SI 1994/1271 and SI 1995/3247) are paras (a) to (h) and (j) to (m) of Part A of Section 2.1; paras (a) to (c) and (e) or (f) of Part B of Section 2.1; paras (a) to (g) or (i) to (k) of Part A of Section 2.2.

11.46 Some of the processes which are set down in the exemption are Part A processes under the Environmental Protection (Prescribed Substances and Processes) Regulations 1991. Precisely why they need to be referred to in Schedule 3 to the Waste Management Licensing Regulations 1994 is not immediately obvious. It would seem that reg 16 of the Waste Management Licensing Regulations 1994 has already excluded such operations from Part II of the EPA 1990 altogether[1]. This does not, of course, apply to the listed Part B processes.

1 See para 10.14ff: however, see Circular 6/95, Annex 2, para 2.21ff.

11.47 Along with the actual contaminant removal processes, the associated waste storage areas are also exempt from licensing[1]. However, to fall within the exemption, the material stored must be 'intended to be submitted to' the heating process. In addition, storage must be arranged in a 'secure'[2] manner. Finally, any waste in the storage facility or located in any container must be situated on 'an impermeable pavement which is provided with a sealed drainage system'[3]: it is clearly insufficient that any container should itself be leak-proof. Unfortunately, the location of the exempt storage site is not specified in Schedule 3 to the Waste Management Licensing Regulations 1994. Hence it appears that such storage can take place quite separately from the metal cleaning process.

1 SI 1994/1056, Sch 3, para 44(5) as amended by SI 1995/288, reg 3(16).
2 Defined in SI 1994/1056, reg 17(5) as when '. . . all reasonable precautions are taken to ensure that the waste cannot escape from it and members of the public are unable to gain access to the waste . . .'.
3 A 'sealed drainage system' is defined as constituting 'a drainage system with impermeable components which does not leak and which will ensure that –
   (a) no liquid will run off the pavement otherwise than via the system; and
   (b) except where they may be lawfully discharged, all liquids entering the system are collected in a sealed sump'.
   (SI 1994/1056, Sch 3, para 45(7) as amended by SI 1995/288, reg 3(16).)

11.48 The Waste Management Licensing Regulations 1994 require that both the heating process and associated storage must be registered. In all cases – even at sites controlled by local authorities as Part B processes – the registration authority is the Agency[1].

1 SI 1994/1056, reg 18(10)(d).

Processing operations at scrapyards and vehicle dismantlers

11.49 The exemptions for these metal recycling sites split into three components. It is possible that two or three of these exempt activities can occur at any site. The components are:

(1) the actual scrap processing or vehicle dismantling activity;
(2) the storage of scrap metal or scrap vehicles; and
(3) the storage of 'non-scrap waste' accepted with the scrap or vehicles brought onto the site.

The first two categories are principally defined by two Tables[1] and by the contents of paragraph 45 of Schedule 3 to the Waste Management Licensing Regulations 1994[2]. The Tables are reproduced here as Tables 11.1 and 11.2. The third category of non-scrap waste is subject to those limits contained in paragraph 45(5) to the Waste Management Licensing Regulations 1994.

1   Table 4A and 4B of para 45 of SI 1994/1056 as amended by SI 1995/288, reg 3(16).
2   SI 1994/1056 as amended by SI 1995/288 and SI 1998/606, reg 2(3).

11.50   The wording of Schedule 3 makes explicit[1] the fact that the exempt storage of waste at a metal recycling site can also occur at a licensed waste management facility or at a premises subject to a Part I authorisation under the EPA 1990[2]. Notwithstanding this provision, since the Divisional Court's findings in *London Waste Regulation Authority v Drinkwater Sabey Ltd*[3], this arrangement can apply to all of the Schedule 3 exemptions anyway. Accordingly, it is possible to have the scrap storage area covered by the exemption but the actual processing unit regulated by a waste management licence or by a Part I authorisation. Conversely, processing activities may themselves be subject to the exemption, but a waste management licence needed for the storage of the materials prior to handling. Such a circumstance may occur, for example, at a site which is operated with a very extensive waste storage capability. In all cases, the Agency – not the body responsible for any Part B authorisation – is always the registration authority[4].

1   Sch 3, para 45(2)(a) of SI 1994/1056 as amended by SI 1995/288, reg 3(16).
2   In practice this would mainly be a Part B authorisation: processes subject to a relevant Part A authorisation are excluded from waste management licences by SI 1994/1056, reg 16(1)(a): see para 10.14ff.
3   [1997] Env LR 137: see para 10.47ff.
4   SI 1994/1056, reg 18(10)(d).

Scrap metal processing and vehicle dismantling activities

11.51   For those processing activities at metal recycling sites, the terms and conditions of any exemption are principally set down in Table 4A of the Waste Management Licensing Regulations 1994[1] (see Table 11.1).

1   Sch 3, para 45(1) of SI 1994/1056 as amended by SI 1995/288, reg 3(16).

11.52   It can be seen that Table 11.1 is split into three columns. The first describes the kind of waste covered by the exemption; the second sets out the allowable processing activities; and the third establishes a maximum quantity limit for waste processed by each activity. Throughout paragraph 45(1) of Schedule 3, the word 'activity' is defined in terms of the second column of the table. Accordingly, any processing operations occurring at a site which are not covered by the activity stipulated in the table result in the exemption falling. For example, the mechanical crushing of dismantled vehicles is not covered by the activities listed in relation to motor vehicle dismantling. Should such an activity occur at a premises used for vehicle dismantling, a waste management licence would be required.

11.53   Many of the words found in the table are undefined. They will therefore retain the ordinary meanings which are appropriate and standard practice to the industry as a whole[1]. As will be seen, this approach is less than helpful at times. The Waste Management Licensing Regulations 1994, for some reason, define the word 'shearing'. Shearing is held to mean 'the cold cutting of metal by purpose-made shears'[2]. The interpretation of the term 'motor vehicle' has already been discussed above at para 11.36.

1   See in the context of the Scrap Metal Dealers Act 1964 *Jenkins v A Cohen & Co Ltd* [1971] 2 All ER 1384 at 1388B/C.
2   SI 1994/1056, Sch 3, para 45(6) as amended by SI 1995/288, para 3(16). In Table 4A, the relevant phrase used is 'shearing by manual feed'. Circular 6/95 states that (Annex 1, para 1.30):
   '... the Departments understand that in the industry manually-operated grabs or cranes which feed scrap metal into shearers are known as "manual feeds". This description is consistent with the ordinary meaning of "manual" which distinguishes between hand-operated devices or machines and those which operate automatically. In the Departments' view, therefore, scrap metal fed into a shearer by a manually operated grab or crane falls within the scope of the term "shearing by manual feed"'.

Table 11.1

Exempt Metal Recycling Processing Activities

Waste Management Licensing Regulations 1994, Sch 3, para 45

Kind of Waste	Activities	Seven day limit
Ferrous metals or ferrous alloys in metallic non-dispersible form (but not turnings, shavings or chippings of those metals or alloys)	Sorting; grading; baling; shearing by manual feed; compacting; crushing; cutting by hand-held equipment	8,000 tonnes
The following non-ferrous metals, namely copper, aluminium, nickel, lead, tin, tungsten, cobalt, molybdenum, vanadium, chromium, titanium, zirconium, manganese or zinc, or non-ferrous alloys, in metallic non-dispersible form, of any of those metals (but not turnings, shavings or chippings of those metals or alloys)	Sorting; grading; baling; shearing by manual feed; compacting; crushing; cutting by hand-held equipment	400 tonnes
Turnings, shavings or chippings of any of the metals or alloys listed in either of the above categories	Sorting; grading; baling; shearing by manual feed; compacting; crushing; cutting by hand-held equipment	300 tonnes
Motor vehicles (including any substance which is special waste and which forms part of, or is contained in, a vehicle and was necessary for the normal operation of the vehicle)	Dismantling, rebuilding, restoring or reconditioning, but, in relation to lead acid batteries, only their removal from motor vehicles	40 vehicles
Lead acid motor vehicle batteries (including those whose contents are special waste), whether or not forming part of, or contained in, a motor vehicle	Sorting (including removal from motor vehicles)	20 tonnes

11.54   The manner by which the 'kind of waste' is classified in Table 4A has some important limitations on exempt operations at scrapyards. Under that heading, the table lists various types of ferrous and non-ferrous scrap as well as the category 'motor vehicles'. The range of permissible activities set down in the table appears to cause particular restriction in respect of dismantling. The table would suggest that only motor vehicles can be subject to exempt dismantling: the word 'dismantling' only appears in that context. If interpreted strictly, this would preclude other, non-motor vehicle, scrap equipment being dismantled under exemption.

11.55   The final column in Table 11.1 sets out maximum quantity limits. It is required that these limits should be interpreted in terms of whether 'the total quantity of any particular kind of waste so dealt with at that place does not in any period of seven days exceed the limit specified . . .'[1]. Accordingly, most sites subject to exemption will be quite small. This applies particularly to exempt motor vehicle dismantling. Only 40 vehicles can be involved in the process of 'dismantling, rebuilding, restoring or reconditioning' over seven days.

1   SI 1994/1056, Sch 3, para 45(1)(a) as amended by SI 1995/288, reg 3(16).

11.56   Paragraph 45(1) of Schedule 3 to the Waste Management Licensing Regulations 1994 also sets down a series of further specific conditions. Again if they are not complied with the exemption does not hold. The conditions are that:

(a)   the premises where the exempt activity takes place must be a 'secure place'[1];
(b)   the location of the exempt activity must be one which is 'designed or adapted for the recovery of scrap metal or the dismantling of waste motor vehicles'[2];
(c)   the activity referred to in the second column of Table 11.1 must be 'carried on with a view to the recovery of the waste (whether or not by the person carrying on the activity listed in that Table)'[3]. According to Circular 6/95, this provision allows the actual process which finally reclaims the scrap materials to occur elsewhere, or to be operated by a third party[4].

1   SI 1994/1056, reg 17(5): see para 10.36.
2   SI 1994/1056, Sch 3, para 45(1) as amended by SI 1995/288, reg 3(16).
3   SI 1994/1056, Sch 3, para 45(1)(b) as amended by SI 1995/288, reg 3(16).
4   See Circular 6/95, Annex 1, para 1.26(b).

11.57   The meaning of the words 'designed or adapted' in (b) above is discussed at para 10.77ff and clearly indicates that a site must be physically changed to facilitate the particular waste recovery activity which is being undertaken[1]. The requirement that a site is designed or adapted would appear to prevent a person attaining exemption when taking over a premises for metal recycling purposes, which in all other aspects satisfies the requirements of the exemption, but where no physical changes were necessary to its layout to allow scrap metal or scrap vehicles to be processed. It would seem that placing scrap or vehicles on a site is not sufficient to design or adapt it.

1   See *R v Upton* and *R v Formosa* [1991] 1 All ER 131 and also *North Yorkshire County Council v Boyne* [1997] Env LR 91. In certain respects, the words 'designed or adapted' in the context of paragraph 45(1) of Sch 3 to the Waste Management Licensing Regulations 1994 are the mirror image to their use in the exemption contained in paragraph 40. In paragraph 40 (see para 10.65ff), a site is exempt when, *inter alia*, it is not 'designed or adapted' for the reception of waste which is to be disposed of or recovered elsewhere. In paragraph 45, the reverse is true: an exemption only holds when a site is 'designed or adapted' for scrap metal recovery or motor vehicle dismantling.

11.58   Given the potential of many scrapyards and car dismantlers to contaminate the soil and sub-soil beneath the premises, there are also requirements which relate to surfacing and drainage[1]. For a premises to be exempt from the need for a waste management licence, the Waste Management Licensing Regulations 1994 require that 'every part of that place on which the activity is carried out is surfaced with an impermeable pavement . . .'[2]. Given that the word 'activity' relates to the processing operations set down in Table 4A of the regulations, it follows that all of the sorting, shearing, crushing, dismantling, rebuilding etc activities shown in Table 11.1 should occur only on this impermeable pavement. The term 'impermeable pavement' is not defined in the regulations and hence retains its ordinary meaning. However, Circular 6/95 states that[3]:

'... an impermeable pavement for the purposes of the exemption is one which is constructed and maintained to a standard sufficient to prevent the transmission of liquids beyond the pavement surface. To fulfil this purpose, the pavement should be constructed to an appropriate density and thickness.'

1   SI 1994/1056, Sch 3, para 45(1)(c) as amended by SI 1995/288, reg 3(16).
2   SI 1994/1056, Sch 3, para 45(1)(c) as amended by SI 1995/288, reg 3(16).
3   Circular 6/95, Annex 1, para 1.29.

11.59   As well as an impermeable pavement being required, the exempt processing activity must also be 'provided with a sealed drainage system'[1]. The term 'sealed drainage system' is defined in the Waste Management Licensing Regulations 1994[2] as constituting:

'a drainage system with impermeable components which does not leak and which will ensure that –

(a)   no liquid will run off the pavement otherwise than via the system; and
(b)   except where they may be lawfully discharged, all liquids entering the system are collected in a sealed sump.'

Accordingly, the drainage system must be arranged so that all liquids falling on the impermeable pavement will be drawn towards it. Once the liquids enter the drainage system, the most obvious choice is for them to be 'lawfully' discharged[3]. Usually, this discharge will be to the trade sewerage system and may be subject to a consent[4] from the local water company. In order to satisfy the water company's requirements, it is likely that the discharge will be arranged to occur through a tank known as an interceptor. This will be needed to ensure that oil and other materials do not enter the sewerage system and breach the consent. An alternative arrangement might involve the discharge via an interceptor to a watercourse. In this case, a consent under the Water Resources Act 1991 would be necessary.

1   SI 1994/1056, Sch 3, para 45(1)(c) as amended by SI 1995/288, reg 3(16).
2   SI 1994/1056, Sch 3, para 45(7) as amended by SI 1995/288, reg 3(16).
3   SI 1994/1056, Sch 3, para 45(7)(b) as amended by SI 1995/288, reg 3(16).
4   Under the Water Industry Act 1991, s 118.

11.60   Where no suitable sewer or surface water outlet exists in the locality of the exempt facility, it is a condition of the exemption that the contaminated drainage must pass to the 'sealed sump' referred to above[1]. Such a sump will need to be regularly emptied by a waste disposal contractor and the contents taken off-site for lawful disposal.

1   SI 1994/1056, Sch 3, para 45(7) as amended by SI 1995/288, reg 3(16).

11.61   It should be noted that the requirement for a sealed drainage system relates to all facilities processing scrap metal or dismantling vehicles, even those metal reclaimers located entirely within industrial buildings. Despite the fact that the nature of such buildings may mean that a sealed drainage system is not always environmentally warranted, the absence of such infrastructure at any site will disallow the exemption, and the site would therefore require a waste management licence.

11.62   The final caveat of the exemption for scrap and vehicle processing is that the plant or equipment which constitute the exempt activity is required to be maintained 'in reasonable working order'[1]. Precisely, how this highly subjective test is to be applied in practice remains less than clear. Certainly Circular 6/95 provides no guidance.

1   SI 1994/1056, Sch 3, para 45(1)(d) as amended by SI 1995/288, reg 3(16).

Storage of motor vehicles or metal scrap

11.63   The requirements for the storage element of the exemption are set down in the Waste Management Licensing Regulations 1994 by way of Table 4B. This is reproduced as Table 11.2. It will be apparent that, in comparison to the scrap processing activities set down in Table 4A of the regulations (see Table 11.1), Table 4B uses a somewhat different style in expressing the maximum quantities of waste which can be stored at exempt sites. The quantity limits are expressed as a maximum which must not be exceeded at any one time[1]. Should they be exceeded, the exemption no longer holds and a waste management licence is required. The limits are set quite low in some instances, for example, only 1,500 tonnes of non-ferrous metal can be stored at any one time.

1   SI 1994/1056, Sch 3, para 45(2)(b) as amended by SI 1995/288, reg 3(16).

Table 11.2

Exempt Metal Recycling Storage Activities

Waste Management Licensing Regulations 1994, Sch 3, para 45

Kind of Waste	**Maximum total quantity**
Ferrous metals or ferrous alloys in metallic non-dispersible form (but not turnings, shavings or chippings of those metals or alloys)	50,000 tonnes
The following non-ferrous metals, namely copper, aluminium, nickel, lead, tin, tungsten, cobalt, molybdenum, vanadium, chromium, titanium, zirconium, manganese or zinc, or non-ferrous alloys, in metallic non-dispersible form, of any of those metals (but not turnings, shavings or chippings of those metals or alloys)	1,500 tonnes
Turnings, shavings or chippings of any of the metals or alloys listed in either of the above categories	1,000 tonnes
Motor vehicles (including any substance which is special waste and which forms part of, or is contained in, a vehicle and was necessary for the normal operation of the vehicle):	
— where any such vehicle is stored on a hardstanding which is not an impermeable pavement:	100 vehicles
— where all such vehicles are stored on an impermeable pavement:	1,000 vehicles
Lead acid motor vehicle batteries (including those whose contents are special waste), whether or not forming part of, or contained in, a motor vehicle	40 tonnes

11.64   There are also other caveats in relation to exempt waste storage. They are that:

(a)   no waste scrap or vehicles can be allowed to remain at the exempt site for a period in excess of 12 months[1]; and

(b)   only two configurations of exempt storage infrastructure are possible in respect of motor vehicles awaiting dismantling[2].

In respect of item (b) above, the choice between the two options is determined by the quantity of motor vehicles that are to be stored. A less rigorous requirement applies where less than 100 vehicles are stored at the site. In this case, they can be 'stored on a hardstanding which is not an impermeable pavement' and so extensive concreting under the storage area is not required in this instance.

1   SI 1994/1056, Sch 3, para 45(2)(c) as amended by SI 1995/288, reg 3(16).
2   See Table 11.2 and amended para 45(2)(f).

11.65   Where between 100 and 1,000 scrap vehicles are to be stored, all the vehicles must be placed on an 'impermeable pavement'. As noted at para 11.58 above, the term 'impermeable pavement' is not defined but clearly should be seen as contradistinct from the notion of a hardstanding: the intention is that 'hardstanding' should not to be viewed as impermeable.

11.66   The exemption requires that all scrap and vehicle storage on impermeable pavements must have an associated sealed drainage system[1]. However, no such drainage system is needed for the smaller sites where only 100 vehicles or less are to be stored on a hardstanding[2].

1   SI 1994/1056, Sch 3, para 45(2)(g) as amended by SI 1995/288, reg 3(16).
2   SI 1994/1056, Sch 3, para 45(2)(f) as amended by SI 1995/288, reg 3(16).

11.67   The exemption for storage also appears to state that only waste motor vehicles 'from which all fluids have been drained' can be stored on impermeable pavements or hardstanding[1]. The requirement for the drainage of all fluids is a tough one as the words 'all fluids' refer not only to oil and coolant but also to other fluids, including brake and clutch fluids, windscreen wash etc. The wording may also require the battery, which inevitably will contain liquid, to be removed. Otherwise the presence of the battery acid would not satisfy the requirement that all fluids are drained prior to storage. However, such an assertion needs to be set against what is said in Table 4B to the Waste Management Licensing Regulations 1994 (see Table 11.2), which appears to be somewhat contradictory. Here a limit for the storage of lead acid motor vehicle batteries is set at 40 tonnes 'whether or not forming part of, *or contained in*, a motor vehicle' (Author's emphasis)[2]. In addition, Table 4B allows motor vehicles to be stored on pavements or hardstanding 'including any substance which is special waste *and* which forms part of, or is contained in, a vehicle and was necessary for the normal operation of the vehicle' (Author's emphasis). Battery acid, petrol, oil and brake fluid all appear to fit this criteria since the Special Waste Regulations 1996 were revised[3]. However – and somewhat perversely – coolant and screenwash may not do so. Such apparent contradictions introduce ambiguities which are difficult to reconcile in practice.

1   SI 1994/1056, Sch 3, para 45(2)(f) as amended by SI 1994/288, reg 3(16). This interpretation is confirmed by Circular 6/95, Annex 1, para 1.32(f).
2   As such an activity is excluded by Table 4A, such batteries cannot, of course, be emptied at an exempt site.
3   SI 1996/972 as amended by SI 1996/2019: see Chapter 4.

11.68   The third caveat contained in the storage exemption is that each 'kind of waste'[1] must be stored separately[2] or must be kept in separate containers. However, where loads consisting of more than one kind[3] of waste are received, they can be stored in an unseparated fashion 'at that place pending sorting' for no more than two months[4].

1   As defined by Table 4B: see the left hand column of Table 11.2.
2   SI 1994/1056, Sch 3, para 45(2)(d) as amended by SI 1995/288, reg 3(16).
3   As defined in Table 4B: see Table 11.2.
4   SI 1994/1056, Sch 3, para 45(2)(d) as amended by SI 1995/288, reg 3(16).

11.69   As was the case with the exempt metal scrap and vehicle processing activities, the place where the storage is to occur must be 'secure'[1] and 'designed or adapted'[2] for the recovery of scrap metal or for the dismantling of waste motor vehicles[3].

1   Defined in SI 1994/1056, reg 17(5): see para 10.36.
2   See para 10.77ff and *R v Upton* and *R v Formosa* [1991] 1 All ER 131 and *North Yorkshire County Council v Boyne* [1997] Env LR 91.
3   SI 1994/1056, Sch 3, para 45(2) as amended by SI 1995/288, reg 3(16).

11.70   Where the waste is stored in liquid form[1] or where it consists of motor vehicle batteries, the storage of such materials must also be in a secure[2] container[3]. The maximum total quantity for the storage of batteries is 40 tonnes (see Table 11.2) 'whether or not forming part of, or contained in, a motor vehicle'. As a rough guide, a car battery weighs about 12–14 kgs.

1   Which will be resultant from the recovery or dismantling activities set down in Table 4A of the Waste Management Licensing Regulations 1994.
2   Defined in SI 1994/1056, reg 17(5): see para 10.36.
3   SI 1994/1056, Sch 3, para 45(2)(e) as amended by SI 1995/288, reg 3(16).

11.71   Containers for these materials, along with any other container in which waste is stored[1], must only be located on impermeable pavements with associated sealed drainage systems.

1   See SI 1994/1056, Sch 3, para 45(2)(g) as amended by SI 1995/288, reg 3(16) and Circular 6/95, Annex 1, para 1.32(g).

11.72   Further conditions also apply for the storage activity to be exempt. The waste stored must be intended 'to be submitted to any of the activities specified in Table 4A[1] in relation to that kind of waste'[2]. Alternatively, it must be submitted to a 'recycling or reclamation' (sic) operation authorised by a waste management licence or covered by an authorisation under Part I of the EPA 1990[3].

1   Ie Table 11.1 above.
2   SI 1994/1056, Sch 3, para 45(2)(a) as amended by SI 1995/288, reg 3(16).
3   It is of note that the words used here are 'recycling and reclamation operation' and not 'waste recovery operation'. Accordingly, the range of activities to which the waste is to be submitted is broader than in Part IV of Schedule 4 of SI 1994/1056 (see Table 2.6 in Chapter 2). It would also seem that the waste cannot be submitted to further storage at a separate location as would be possible if the word 'recovery' had been used. In common parlance, a recycling or reclamation operation does not encompass the word 'storage'.

11.73   The final requirement for the exempt storage of scrap or vehicles awaiting dismantling is that the height of 'any pile or stack of waste' must not exceed five metres[1]. This condition is likely to prove a significant constraint at many of the larger yards dealing in ferrous scrap. Certainly it will off-set the very generous quantity limit set down in the table, which permits the storage of 50,000 tonnes of such scrap at any one time.

1   SI 1994/1056, Sch 3, para 45(2)(h) as amended by SI 1995/288, reg 3(16).

11.74   The wording of paragraph 45(2) of Schedule 3 to the Waste Management Licensing Regulations 1994 does beg the question of whether exempt storage can occur at a place separate from any scrap or vehicle processing operation. Certain operators possess separate storage compounds at locations different to the actual processing facilities themselves, whilst others deal in scrap metal and, particularly, scrap vehicles, without actually undertaking any processing activities such as sorting or dismantling. An example is a person who deals in damaged vehicles after they have been written off by an insurance company. Paragraph 45(2) of Schedule 3 allows 'the storage, at any secure place designed or adapted for the recovery of scrap metal or the dismantling of waste motor vehicles' to be exempt. At first reading, the wording would appear to indicate that the storage and processing activity must be located together. However, the use of the word 'recovery' in this phrase should be interpreted by way of its definition in reg 1(3) of the Waste Management Licensing Regulations 1994[1]. This suggests that it is possible to store waste motor vehicles at sites independent of dismantling activities under the exemptions. In addition, and in contrast to many of the exemptions contained in Schedule 3 to the Waste Management Licensing Regulations 1994[2], there is no use of the phrase '. . . storage at the place where the process is carried on . . .' in paragraph 45(2).

1   SI 1994/1056, reg 1(3) see Item 13 in Table 2.6 in Chapter 2. This approach to the word 'recovery' is confirmed by Circular 6/95, Annex 1, para 1.32(j).
2   See for example, SI 1994/1056, Sch 3, paras 1(2), 2(3), 4(2), 7(5), 7(7), 9(2), 10(3), 13(4), 20(2), 21(2), 24(2), and so on.

11.75   However, a second difficulty then emerges due to the use of the words 'designed or adapted'. Case law indicates that a site is only designed or adapted when it is physically changed[1], and it seems that these changes must facilitate the particular waste management process taking place. Hence a person wishing to arrange exemption for separate scrap or vehicle storage compounds will need to demonstrate that changes have been made to arrangements on the site. Otherwise, it would seem that the site cannot be regarded as designed or adapted and hence exempt from a waste management licence. It appears that this was not taken into account when the Waste Management Licensing (Amendment) Regulations 1995[2] were drafted.

1   *R v Upton* and *R v Formosa* [1991] 1 All ER 131; *North Yorkshire County Council v Boyne* [1997] Env LR 91: see para 10.70ff.
2   SI 1995/288.

Storage of other waste at scrapyards and vehicle dismantlers

11.76   The storage of non-special waste at the site where it is produced is subject to a general exemption under Schedule 3 to the Waste Management Licensing Regulations 1994[1]. However, that exemption does not apply in relation to places which are 'designed or adapted for the recovery of scrap metal or the dismantling of waste motor vehicles'[2]. Instead, a separate exemption covers the temporary storage of wastes derived from metal scrap or from waste motor vehicles delivered to such sites[3]. Such materials are termed, for the purposes of that paragraph, 'non-scrap waste' and are composed of any waste *not* listed in Table 4B of the Waste Management Licensing Regulations 1994 (see Table 11.2)[4]. The wording of the reference to motor vehicles in that table means that non-scrap waste can only be composed of materials which do not constitute special waste. Petrol, brake fluid, lead acid batteries and oil do not, therefore, fall under this term.

1   SI 1994/1056, Sch 3, para 41: see para 10.55ff.
2   SI 1994/1056, Sch 3, para 41A as amended by SI 1995/288, reg 3(13).
3   SI 1994/1056, Sch 3, para 45(5) as amended by SI 1995/288, reg 3(16).
4   SI 1994/1056, Sch 3, para 45(5)(a) as amended by SI 1995/288, reg 3(16).

11.77   The principal requirement for the exempt storage of non-scrap waste is that it is subject to 'temporary storage . . . pending its collection' and that such storage is done 'at a secure place designed or adapted for the recovery of scrap metal or the dismantling of waste motor vehicles'[1]. Again, if these fail to apply to a facility, the site is not exempt.

1   SI 1994/1056, Sch 3, para 45(5) as amended by SI 1995/288, reg 3(16).

11.78 To retain the exemption, the 'non-scrap waste' delivered to the site must also have been part of a consignment of waste of which at least 70% by weight comprised waste motor vehicles[1], or of which at least 95% by weight was waste of any other kind as described in Table 4B (see Table 11.2)[2]. In either case, the exemption requires that the material must be 'capable of being separated from that waste by sorting or hand dismantling'. It should be noted that the phrase that is used is not '*hand* sorting or hand dismantling'. Accordingly, metal scrap could be subject to mechanical sorting processes to remove the contraries.

1　SI 1994/1056, Sch 3, para 45(5)(b)(i) as amended by SI 1994/288, reg 3(16).
2　SI 1994/1056, Sch 3, para 45(5)(b)(ii) as amended by SI 1995/288, reg 3(16).

11.79 The non-scrap waste must be stored on the site for no more than three months for the exemption to apply[1]. If it is liquid[2], then it must only be stored in a secure[3] container[4].

1　SI 1994/1056, Sch 3, para 45(5)(c) as amended by SI 1995/288, reg 3(16).
2　It is rather unlikely that non-scrap waste which is liquid can be stored under exemption now that the term 'special waste' includes oil and brake fluid.
3　Defined in SI 1994/1056, reg 17(5).
4　SI 1994/1056, Sch 3, para 45(5)(d) as amended by SI 1995/288, reg 3(16).

11.80 Finally, the exemption only holds where the non-scrap waste, along with any container in which it is held, is stored on 'an impermeable pavement which is provided with a sealed drainage system'[1]. It should be noted that this requirement applies to premises where vehicles have been drained of liquids. For example, whilst 100 vehicles 'from which all the fluids have been drained'[2] can be stored on a hard-standing, the drained and collected fluids must be stored on an impermeable pavement with an integral sealed drainage system[3].

1　SI 1994/1056, Sch 3, para 45(5)(e) as amended by SI 1995/288, reg 3(16): see Circular 6/95, Annex 1, para 1.33. 'In relation to an impermeable pavement' (SI 1994/1056, Sch 3, para 45(7) as amended by SI 1995/288, reg 3(16)), a sealed drainage system constitutes 'a drainage system with impermeable components which does not leak and which will ensure that –
　(a) no liquid will run off the pavement otherwise than via the system; and
　(b) except where they may be lawfully discharged, all liquids entering the system are collected in a sealed sump.'
2　SI 1994/1056, Sch 3, para 45(2)(f) as amended by SI 1995/288, reg 3(16).
3　See SI 1994/1056 Sch 3 para 45(5)(e) as amended by SI 1995/288, reg 3(16).

Requirements on the operators of scrapyards and vehicle dismantlers for site audits and record-keeping

11.81 The above discussion has covered the statutory requirements which relate to the infrastructural arrangements necessary at exempt metal recycling sites. Such requirements are substantiated by further provisions which require site audits by the operator and record-keeping[1]. Again, if the operator does not satisfy these require-ments, the exemption for the particular site fails[2].

1　SI 1994/1056, Sch 3, para 45(3) as amended by SI 1995/288, reg 3(16) and by SI 1998/606, reg 2(3).
2　SI 1994/1056, Sch 3, paras 45(1) and 45(2) as amended by SI 1995/288, reg 3(16).

11.82 The 'person responsible for the management' of the exempt activity is required to establish 'administrative arrangements' to ensure that the waste accepted at the site is of a kind listed in Tables 4A and 4B of the Waste Management Licensing Regula-tions 1994[1] (see Tables 11.1 and 11.2). Such arrangements should also ensure that no waste is accepted at the site in such a quantity as to breach the terms of the exemption[2].

The person responsible for the management also has to carry out a monthly audit to confirm that the site complies with the terms and conditions of the exemption[3]. The precise nature of such an audit is not made clear in the regulations nor in Circular 6/95.

1　SI 1994/1056, Sch 3, para 45(3)(a)(i)(A) as amended by SI 1995/288, reg 3(16).
2　SI 1994/1056, Sch 3, para 45(3)(a)(i)(B) as amended by SI 1995/288, reg 3(16).
3　SI 1994/1056, Sch 3, para 45(3)(ii) as amended by SI 1995/288, reg 3(16).

11.83　As noted at para 8.234ff, all waste management licence holders are required to keep records under Schedule 4, paragraph 14 to the Waste Management Licensing Regulations 1994[1]. This requirement does not, in general, apply to operators of facilities which are exempt under Schedule 3 to the Waste Management Licensing Regulations 1994[2]. However, the requirement for record-keeping does apply where records are kept at exempt metal recycling sites[3].

1　SI 1994/1056, Sch 4, para 14(1) as amended by SI 1995/288, reg 3(19).
2　SI 1994/1056, Sch 4, Pt 1, para 14(2) as amended by SI 1995/288, reg 3(20).
3　SI 1994/1056, Sch 4, Pt 1, para 14(3) as amended by SI 1995/288, reg 3(21).

11.84　The nature of the records to be kept at metal recycling sites is set out in paragraph 45[1] of Schedule 3 to the Waste Management Licensing Regulations 1994, as well as in Schedule 4, paragraph 14. They must be kept 'in such a form as to show, for each month, the total quantity of each kind of waste recovered during that month at that place'. They must also give[2] the 'quantity, nature, origin and, where relevant, the destination, frequency of collection, mode of transport and treatment method' of any waste recovered. It should be noted that reference is made to records which provide information on waste 'recovered'. As Circular 6/95 states[3], this includes waste received through the gate and stored on the site. The words 'recovery' and 'recovered' embrace storage sites[4], including sites where no processing activities take place.

1　SI 1994/1056, Sch 3, para 45(3)(b) as amended by SI 1995/288, reg 3(16).
2　SI 1994/1056, Sch 4, Pt 1, para 14(1) as amended by SI 1995/288, reg 3(19).
3　Circular 6/95, Annex 1, para 1.32(j).
4　SI 1994/1056, reg 1(3) and Sch 4, Pt IV (see Table 2.6).

11.85　Much of the information required is already necessary for sites subject to the Scrap Metal Dealers Act 1964. Section 2(1) of that Act requires that all scrap received, processed and dispatched from the premises is entered into a book kept at the site[1]. The following details must be recorded for wastes received at the site[2]:

(a)　a description[3] of the metal and its weight;
(b)　the date and time of receipt of the metal;
(c)　the name and address of the person who delivered it;
(d)　the price paid (or the value of the metal);
(e)　the registration mark of the vehicle delivering the scrap metal to the site.

For wastes being despatched from the site, the following must be recorded[4]:

(a)　the description and weight of the metal;
(b)　the date of dispatch and, if processed[5], the process applied;
(c)　where sold or exchanged, the full name and address of the recipient and the price paid[6].

1　When the book is complete it can be kept elsewhere: *W Houston & Sons Ltd v Armstrong* [1969] 1 WLR 1864.
2　Scrap Metal Dealers Act 1964, s 2(2).
3　For what constitutes an adequate description see *Jenkins v A Cohen & Co Ltd* [1971] 2 All ER 1384.
4　Scrap Metal Dealers Act 1964, s 2(3).

5 'Processing' includes melting down but not dismantling or breaking up: Scrap Metal Dealers Act
   1964, s 2(7).
6 If not sold or exchanged, the value of the metal.

11.86 The duty of care[1] also requires that certain records are kept in the form of the
retained copies of the transfer notes which document transactions of waste[2]. With
certain minor exceptions, the requirements of the duty[3] duplicate the records needed
under the Scrap Metal Dealers Act 1964. It therefore appears that the requirements for
record keeping of the Waste Management Licensing Regulations 1994, the Scrap
Metal Dealers Act 1964 and the duty of care[4] might be best satisfied by a combined
system.

1 EPA 1990, s 34.
2 See Chapter 3.
3 EPA 1990, s 34 and the Environment Protection (Duty of Care) Regulations 1991, SI 1991/2839.
4 See Department of the Environment (1996) *Waste Management – the Duty of Care Code of Practice*
   (2nd edn) HMSO, London, para 7.7.

11.87 A person who fails to comply with the record-keeping provisions contained in
the Waste Management Licensing Regulations 1994 is subject to two separate sets of
penalties. These involve whether:

(a) the terms of the exemption are breached due to non-compliance with Schedule 3,
    paragraph 45(3)(b);
(b) non-compliance in respect of the requirements of paragraph 14 of Schedule 4 to
    the Regulations.

In the former case there is an offence under s 33 of the EPA 1990[1]. The latter case
involves an offence separate to s 33 of the EPA 1990[2], with the only available defence
being that an emergency prevented the records being kept[3] – a rather unlikely scenario.
The falsification of records is also an offence[4] and there are the usual provisions in
respect of directors' liability and where offences have been caused by the default of
others[5]. The penalties are those contained in the Special Waste Regulations 1996[6]. On
summary conviction, a fine not exceeding level 5[7] on the standard scale can be levied,
while the maximum penalty on indictment is imprisonment of up to two years, a fine,
or both.

1 See Chapter 7.
2 SI 1994/1056, Sch 4, para 14(4) as amended by SI 1996/972, reg 25 and Sch 3.
3 SI 1994/1056, Sch 4, para 14(5) as amended by SI 1996/972, reg 25 and Sch 3.
4 SI 1994/1056, Sch 4, para 14(6) and (7) as amended by SI 1996/972, reg 25 and Sch 3: see para
   12.218ff.
5 SI 1994/1056, Sch 4, para 14(8) (as amended by SI 1996/972, reg 25 and Sch 3), which cross-refers
   to SI 1996/972, reg 18(5) and (6): discussed at paras 7.156ff and 7.173ff.
6 SI 1994/1056, Sch 4, para 14(8) (as amended by SI 1996/972, reg 25 and Sch 3) and SI 1996/972, reg
   18(8).
7 Currently £5,000.

THE REGISTRATION OF EXEMPT SCRAPYARDS, VEHICLE DISMANTLERS AND SCRAP MELTING AND CLEANING PROCESSES

Obtaining registration

11.88 Exempt activities need to be registered under the provisions of reg 18 of the
Waste Management Licensing Regulations 1994. The registration body for the exempt
scrap processing, vehicle dismantling and associated storage is always the Agency[1].

The same applies to those exempt metal contamination removal processes covered by paragraph 44 of Schedule 3 to the Regulations[2]. However, this does *not* apply to the registration of exempt scrap metal furnaces, nor the associated storage described in paragraph 2 of that Schedule[3]. In this case, the information provided in the application for a Part B authorisation to the local authority[4] is deemed sufficient to ensure registration[5].

1 See SI 1994/1056, reg 18(10)(d) and Circular 6/95, Annex 1, paras 1.8(f) and 1.85.
2 See SI 1994/1056, reg 18(10).
3 SI 1994/1056, Sch 3, para 2(1) and reg 18(10)(a)(i): see para 11.43 above.
4 In Scotland, the Scottish Environment Protection Agency.
5 See para 10.29.

11.89 The system for the registration of exempt scrap yards and vehicle dismantlers is somewhat different to all other exempt activities listed in the Waste Management Licensing Regulations 1994[1]. The system was instigated by way of amendments made to reg 18 by the Waste Management Licensing (Amendment etc) Regulations 1995[2]. The normal requirement on other exempt activities, that the Agency registers activities 'if it received notice of them in writing or otherwise becomes aware of those particulars'[3], does not apply[4]. In the case of metal recycling sites, the Agency can only register the activity if it has received the requisite information from the site operator and the required fee. Notice of the registered activity must be made in writing to the Agency[5] by the establishment or undertaking operating the site[6]. The notice must be accompanied by a plan of the place where the exempt activity is being carried on, which should show[7] the site's boundaries, the locations where the exempt activities are being carried on within those boundaries, the location of any secure[8] containers, and the location and specification of any impermeable pavement, drainage system or hardstanding. Registration lasts for a year, after which it must be renewed[9].

1 It also contrasts with the registration of those furnaces covered by SI 1994/1056, Sch 3, para 2 and scrap metal cleaning processes described in para 44.
2 SI 1995/288, reg 3; further minor amendments were made by SI 1996/593, SI 1996/634 and SI 1998/606.
3 SI 1994/1056, reg 18(4) as amended by SI 1995/288, reg 3(9).
4 SI 1994/1056, reg 18(4A) as amended by SI 1995/288, reg 3(10).
5 Strictly, the regulations only require the Agency to be formerly notified of exemption – there is no application process *per se*. However, the Agency has available 'application' forms, albeit that there is no statutory requirement to use them.
6 SI 1994/1056, reg 18(4A)(a) and (b) as amended by SI 1995/288, reg 3(10).
7 SI 1994/1056, reg 18(4A)(c) as amended by SI 1995/288, reg 3(10).
8 Defined in SI 1994/1056, reg 17(5): see para 10.36.
9 SI 1994/1056, Sch 3, para 45(4) as amended by SI 1995/288, reg 3(16).

11.90 The requisite fee[1] is to be enclosed with the other required information 'in respect of *each place* where any such exempt activity is carried on' (author's emphasis). Hence one fee is payable for each location where the exempt scrap processing activities, exempt storage, or both, are taking place[2]. The purpose of the fee is to defray the Agency's costs of visiting the site to decide if it fulfils the criteria which make an exemption applicable[3]. Since April 1998, the required fee is set down in the Charging Scheme current for the financial year[4].

1 SI 1994/1056, reg 18(4A)(d) as amended by SI 1995/288, reg 3(10) and SI 1998/606, reg 2(2).
2 See Circular 6/95, Annex 1, para 1.26(h).
3 Circular 6/95, Annex 1, para 1.21.
4 SI 1994/1056, reg 18(4A)(d) as amended by SI 1995/288, reg 3(10) and SI 1998/606, reg 2(2). The fee for 1999/2000 was £552: Waste Management Licensing (Charges) Scheme 1999/2000, para 5.1 (in Scotland the fee is £495: Waste Management Charging (Scotland) Scheme 1999, para 6(1)).

11.91   In comparison to the provisions in respect of site records[1], it is not immediately clear from the Waste Management Licensing Regulations 1994 if the provision of false information in respect of a metal recycling site registration is an offence[2]. However, it is covered by s 44 of the EPA 1990[3].

1   See para 11.87 above.
2   See para 12.209ff.
3   See para 12.236.

11.92   Although the Agency must be notified of the wish of a site operator to obtain exempt status, there is no requirement on the Agency to issue any form of certificate of registration. The lack of certification is in immediate contrast to the carrier registration certificates required under the Control of Pollution (Amendment) Act 1989[1]. The absence of such a certificate will inevitably make compliance with the requirements of the duty of care[2] more difficult, as it will be less easy for users to check that the site is duly and appropriately authorised.

1   See Chapter 6.
2   EPA 1990, s 34: see Chapter 3.

Renewing a registration

11.93   As registration lasts for only one year, the Agency is required to notify registered sites when renewal is due[1]. This must be done one month prior to the anniversary of the date when the notice of registration, plan and fee were submitted to the registration authority[2]. The notice can be served on the exempt site operator by post under the terms set down in s 160 of the EPA 1990[3].

1   SI 1994/1056, Sch 3, para 45(4)(a) as amended by SI 1995/288, reg 3(16).
2   SI 1994/1056, Sch 3, para 45(4)(b) as amended by SI 1995/288, reg 3(16).
3   Circular 6/95, Annex 1, para 1.36.

11.94   The notification must include details of the amount of payment needed, the method of payment, the date of the anniversary of the receipt of the registration details, and statements to the effect that payment is due one month after the latter date and which concerns 'the effect of payment not being made by the date on which it is due'[1]. It should be noted that the annual registration is triggered by the date that the Agency receives the original notice from the applicant: it does not commence from the date on which the exemption was processed or accepted.

1   SI 1994/1056, Sch 3, para 45(4)(b) as amended by SI 1995/288, reg 3(16).

11.95   The requirements for the continuation of registration are set down in reg 18(4B) and Schedule 3, paragraphs 45(3) and 45(4) of the Waste Management Licensing Regulations 1994. Once registered, a fee must be paid for the exemption to continue beyond the initial year[1]. The annual fee is set out in the annual Charging Scheme[2] current for the particular financial year[3], being intended to cover the cost of the Agency visiting the site in order to verify its continued exempt status[4].

1   SI 1994/1056, Sch 3, para 45(3) as amended by SI 1995/288, reg 3(16) and SI 1998/606, reg 2(3).
2   SI 1994/1056, Sch 3, para 45(3)(d) as amended by SI 1995/288, reg 3(16) and SI 1998/606, reg 2(3).
3   The fee for 1999/2000 was £207: Waste Management Licensing (Charges) Scheme 1999/2000, para 5.2 (in Scotland the charge is £185: Waste Management Charging (Scotland) Scheme 1999, para 6(2)).
4   Circular 6/95, Annex 1, para 1.21.

11.96 The fee must be received within two months of the due date given in the notice[1]. Along with the fee, an annual summary of the site's records and an up-to-date plan of the site must be sent to the Agency[2]. The plan must show[3]:

(a) the site's boundaries;
(b) the locations where exempt activities are being carried out;
(c) the location and specification of impermeable pavements, drainage systems and hardstandings;
(d) the location of any secure containers containing liquids or motor vehicle batteries.

If these details are not submitted, the exemption fails[4].

1   SI 1994/1056, reg 18(4B) as amended by SI 1995/288, reg 3(10).
2   SI 1994/1056, Sch 3, para 45(3)(c) as amended by SI 1995/288, reg 3(10).
3   SI 1995/1056, Sch 3, para 45(3)(c) as amended by SI 1995/288, reg 3(10) cross-referenced to the requirement of the amended reg 18(4A)(c)(i)–(iv).
4   SI 1995/1056, Sch 3, para 45(3) as amended by SI 1995/288, reg 3(16) and by SI 1998/606, reg 2(3).

11.97 If an operator of one or more exempt activities has not paid the annual fee, the registration of all the activities is to be cancelled and their details removed from the register[1]. Where a partial payment has been received for some sites but not for others, the registration is to be cancelled in relation to any location where the fee is unpaid[2]. In either case, the Agency should notify the operator of the deregistration[3].

1   SI 1994/1056, reg 18(4B)(a) as amended by SI 1995/288, reg 3(10).
2   SI 1994/1056, reg 18(4B)(b) as amended by SI 1995/288, reg 3(10).
3   SI 1994/1056, reg 18(4B) as amended by SI 1995/288, reg 3(10).

11.98 The powers in the Waste Management Licensing Regulations 1994 to cancel registration are potentially problematic as they seem only explicitly to address the matter of non-payment of the required fee. It is conceivable that a site operator may pay the fee but, on inspection, the site is deemed not to fulfil the requirements of the exemption. Due to the absence of an appropriate mechanism for the cancellation of a registration for these other reasons, it might seem that the details of the registration must remain in the register until the next year's fee has not been paid. This may be in spite of the fact that the site is operating outside the terms of the exemption and, even, has been successfully prosecuted in that year. The continued presence of details of the site on the register may be potentially misleading to other parties who wish to check up on the site's status as part of the requirements of the duty of care[1]. It therefore seems desirable that the Agency should amend the entry. Whilst an explicit power to this effect appears to have been omitted from the Regulations, reg 18(2) requires the Agency to 'establish and maintain' the register. The correction of inaccurate information may fall within the provision requiring the register's maintenance.

1   EPA 1990, s 34: see para 3.48ff.

OFFENCES COMMITTED BY UNREGISTERED SCRAPYARDS AND VEHICLE DISMANTLERS

11.99 By comparison to all the other exemptions, the offence relating to the operation of an unregistered metal recycling site is somewhat more substantial[1]. It became an offence to operate an unregistered metal recycling site after 30 September 1995[2], with the maximum penalty being fixed at a fine of level 2 on the standard scale[3]. In addition, many unregistered metal recycling sites which are not subject to a waste management licence are also likely face a prosecution under s 33(1) of the EPA 1990[4] and face a fine of up to £20,000. The latter is certainly the case where the physical infrastructure or record-keeping at the site is deficient and hence where the require-ments of reg 17(1) and Schedule 3 cannot be met.

1 All activities other than those metal recycling sites covered by para 45 are subject to SI 1994/1056, reg 18(6)(b) (as amended by SI 1995/288, reg 3(11)): this includes furnaces subject to SI 1994/1056, Sch 3, para 2 and cleaning processes covered by para 44.
2 SI 1994/1056, reg 18(1A) as amended by SI 1995/288, reg 3(8).
3 Currently £500. SI 1994/1056, reg 18(6)(a) as amended by SI 1995/288, para 3(11).
4 See Chapter 7.

11.100 However, the Waste Management Licensing Regulations 1994 contain two peculiar anomalies which affect the offence provisions. Firstly, while the fine for oper-ating a totally unregistered premises is currently £500[1] maximum on summary convic-tion, the maximum penalty in respect of an operator of an exempt metal recycling site who fails to submit to the Agency the required annual records is £5,000[2]. In the latter case, the offence is also indictable and hence, besides an unlimited fine, a custodial sentence of up to two years' imprisonment can be levied.

1 SI 1994/1056, Sch 3, para 18(6)(a): level 2 on the standard scale.
2 SI 1994/1056, Sch 4, Pt 1, para 14(1), (3), (4) and (8) in conjunction with SI 1996/972, reg 18(9).

11.101 The second oddity concerns the non-payment of registration fees. This may affect the applicability of the offence provisions of s 33 of the EPA 1990 in respect of unregistered metal recycling sites. When a site initially notifies the Agency for regis-tration it is required to pay the required registration fee. Such a requirement stems from reg 18(4A)(d)[1]. However, the following year and each year thereafter, a separate continuation fee is to be paid to keep up the registration. This requirement stems from paragraph 45(3)(d) of Schedule 3[2], which is subsidiary to reg 17(1) of the Waste Management Licensing Regulations 1994. It is therefore apparent that the require-ments for payment stem from two, quite separate, elements of the Waste Management Licensing Regulations 1994.

1 SI 1994/1056, reg 18(4A)(d) as amended by SI 1995/288, reg 3(10) and by SI 1998/606, reg 2(2).
2 SI 1994/1056, Sch 3, para 45(3)(d) as amended by SI 1995/288, reg 3(16) and by SI 1998/606, reg 2(3).

11.102 This is significant, as the terms of the exemption are only breached when the requirements of either reg 17 or Schedule 3, paragraph 45 are breached. The terms are unaffected by any breach of reg 18. The result is that paragraph 45(3)(d) is not complied with if the fee for continuation of registration is not paid. This means that the exemption has fallen and that the site can be prosecuted under s 33(1) of the EPA 1990. By definition, this contravention can only occur in the second and subsequent years of registration.

11.103 Conversely, if a site has never been registered, there is, by definition, no need to pay the continuation of registration fee. Instead, the more substantial initial regis-tration fee is to be submitted to the Agency – along with the other required details, plans and so forth. But the initial registration fee is required by reg 18, not by reg 17. If a site operator refuses to pay or to register, it is possible that reg 17 and paragraph 45 may still be satisfied by the site's infrastructure and record-keeping. Whether or not the fee has been paid is irrelevant to reg 17. Hence the outcome is that there is no offence under s 33(1) of the EPA 1990, because the requirements of reg 17(1) are fulfilled, and the site is only open to prosecution under reg 18(6). Such an offence is much less serious than that contained in s 33 of the EPA 1990.

11.104   Circular 6/95 claims that the Agency can prosecute under s 33 if an exempt operator neglects to pay the required fees on the grounds that payment of the registration fees is a condition of registration[1]. However, this seems only partially correct, as it does not apply to a site which has never been registered but which has sufficient infrastructure and record-keeping to comply with reg 17. What is said in Circular 6/95 only relates to a site with adequate infrastructure and record-keeping that has been registered in the past but whose operator has allowed the payment of the registration fee to lapse. It should also be noted that those metal recycling sites which possess neither suitable infrastructure nor record-keeping to satisfy reg 17 and paragraph 45, nor possess valid registrations, can be charged under both s 33(1) of the EPA 1990 and reg 18(6) of the amended Waste Management Licensing Regulations 1994. Such differences and subtleties may need to be addressed by the enforcing authorities in their prosecution policy.

1   Circular 6/95, Annex 1, paras 1.38 and 1.16.

Chapter 12

Statutory duties and powers of the Agency

INTRODUCTION

12.01   The purpose of this chapter is to describe the Agency's statutory duties and statutory powers in controlling waste management activities. The chapter is divided into two principal sections, with the first considering the nature of the Agency's duties. As will be shown, these emanate from both British and EC law. Many of these had application to waste regulation authorities prior to the Agency's formation in April 1996, but some of them have been substantiated or formalised by the Environment Act 1995 which created the Agency. The discussion here will be restricted to the general duties which affect the manner in which the Agency undertakes its overall waste regulatory functions. Those more specific duties which apply to particular types of waste management activity are to be found elsewhere in this book. For this reason, the general requirements of the Directive on Waste[1] are considered here where they relate to the regulation of the entire waste management infrastructure of a member state. However, provisions of Community law which are specific to one class of waste management facility are to be found in other chapters[2].

1   Council Directive of 15 July 1975 on Waste (75/442/EEC) (OJ L194/39 25.7.75) (as amended by Council Directive of 18 March 1991 amending Directive 75/442/EEC on Waste (91/156/EEC) (OJ L78/32 26.3.91) and Commission Decision of 24 May 1996 adapting Annexes IIA and IIB to Council Directive 75/442/EEC on Waste (96/350/EC) (OJ L135/32 6.6.96)).
2   For example, the Groundwater Directive is subject to a detailed evaluation at paras 8.70, 8.247 and 9.65.

12.02   The second half of this chapter will consider the nature of the Agency's statutory powers, concentrating upon the Agency's day-to-day inspection functions and general enforcement powers. Powers of entry will be considered in detail, along with provisions relating to emergencies and situations where wastes are unlawfully deposited. The Agency's enforcement powers in respect of controlled waste carriers are considered, as well as general powers to obtain information. The chapter ends with an evaluation of legislative provisions relating to the obstruction of the Agency's staff undertaking their duties and to the submission of false information. Evidential provisions will also be discussed.

DUTIES OF THE AGENCY

12.03   The Agency has a number of duties in respect of the enforcement of the relevant legislation at waste management facilities. These duties stem from European Community law, particularly the requirements of the Directive on Waste, and from Part II of the EPA 1990 and the Environment Act 1995. The EC provisions do not directly require the Agency to undertake particular courses of action. However, a successful complaint to the Commission concerning the non-implementation by Britain of particular Community provisions may well reflect badly on the Agency's competence and public image in the long term.

Duties emanating from European law

Waste management facilities

12.04   Although the British provisions do not set down an explicit requirement to ensure that each and every waste management facility is subject either to a licence or to registration, this matter is much clearer under Community law. Article 9 of the Directive on Waste[1] requires that all member states should provide permits for 'any' disposal operation described in the Directive's Annex IIA[2]. Similarly, Articles 10 and 11 of the Directive require that 'any' facility undertaking one or more of the waste recovery operations set down in Annex IIB[3] should either obtain a permit[4] or a registration[5] from the competent authority.

1   Council Directive of 15 July 1975 on Waste (75/442/EEC) (OJ L194/39 25.7.75 (as amended by Council Directive of 18 March 1991 amending Directive 75/442/EEC on Waste (91/156/EEC) (OJ L78/32 26.3.91) and Commission Decision of 24 May 1996 adapting Annexes IIA and IIB to Council Directive 75/442/EEC on Waste (96/350/EC) (OJ L135/32 6.6.96)).
2   Annex IIA is reproduced as Table 2.2 in Chapter 2.
3   Annex IIB is contained in Table 2.3 in Chapter 2.
4   Directive 75/442, Article 10.
5   Directive 75/442, Article 11.

12.05   The question of the application of the provisions of the Directive on Waste in respect of permits was addressed by the European Court in the case of *Ministère Public v Oscar Traen*[1]. The *Traen* case involved a number of persons who were discovered spreading waste over land. The wastes included materials removed from septic tanks and from interceptors located at industrial premises. It was argued unsuccessfully that, because the spreading activities were generally one-off incidents on particular fields, no permit was required under the Directive[2]. Accordingly, the court held[3]:

'. . . the essential objective of the [Waste] directive . . ., namely the protection of human health and the environment, would in any event be endangered if the application of measures for the control and supervision of such activities were conditional upon distinctions based on criteria such as the company objects [sic] of the undertaking, whether the disposal of waste is a main or subsidiary activity or the foreseeable impact on the environment.

It must therefore be stated . . . that any operator engaging in any of the activities referred to in Articles 8 to 12 of Directive 75/442[4] is subject to the measures provided for in those provisions.'

The *Traen* judgment therefore makes it clear that the Agency has only three options in respect of any unlawful waste management activities: to use the enforcement provisions of the EPA 1990 to prosecute and require cessation; to require that an appropriate licence is applied for; or, if applicable, to register the activity as exempt from licensing[5].

1   [1988] 3 CMLR 511.
2   Note that the *Traen* case involves the Directive on Waste in its unamended form, prior to changes made by Directive 91/156. Hence the term 'disposal' also covered recovery operations: see the wording of Article 1(b) of the Directive prior to amendment.
3   *Traen* at 519, para 9/10.
4   Note that these articles have been replaced by Directive 91/156. However, the objectives and requirements are broadly similar to the Directive in its unamended form.
5   Exemptions are covered in Chapters 10 and 11.

12.06   Finally, it should be noted that, while Article 4 of the Directive on Waste sets down certain requirements in respect of the protection of the environment from waste management activities, the European Court of Justice has held that these constitute only general objectives which a member state must follow in the wording of its own legislation or by way of implementation[1]. Given that the kernel of Article 4 is contained in the Waste Management Licensing Regulations 1994[2], the Regulations themselves set out the nature of the Agency's duties in these respects[3].

1 *Comitato di Coordinamento per la Difesa della Cava v Regione Lombardia* [1996] 8 JEL, 2 313.
2 SI 1994/1056, Sch 4, para 4(1)(a).
3 When transposed into British law, they become 'relevant objectives': see para 12.13 below.

Waste carriers and waste brokers

12.07 Article 13 of the Directive on Waste requires that establishments and undertakings[1] which collect or transport waste on a professional basis are to be authorised or registered with the competent authority. A similar requirement applies to dealers and brokers involved in waste transactions. In this instance, it would seem that the principles of the *Traen*[2] judgment can be applied by analogy. Once the Agency is aware of an unregistered carrier or broker, it cannot be selective as to whether it wishes to require an appropriate registration.

1 The definition of establishments and undertakings is considered at para 10.22.
2 [1988] 3 CMLR 511: see para 12.05 above.

Duty to carry out inspections

12.08 Article 13 of the Directive on Waste requires that all establishments or undertakings involved in waste disposal, recovery, haulage, and brokerage should be subject to 'appropriate periodic inspection'. In the case of hazardous waste, the requirement to undertake appropriate periodic inspections is extended to the producers of such waste[1].

1 Council Directive of 12 December 1991 on Hazardous Waste (91/689) (OJ L377/20), Article 4(1). In December 1998, the European Commission published a proposal on environmental inspections 'Proposal for a Council Recommendation Providing for Minimum Criteria for Environmental Inspections in the Member States' (16.12.98 com (1998) 772 Final). However, an earlier proposal for a Directive on inspections has been dropped.

Duties under Part II of the EPA 1990

Waste management facilities

12.09 The EPA 1990 itself contrasts with the Directive on Waste in that it does not explicitly require the Agency to take any particular action when the Agency becomes aware of the existence of an unauthorised waste management activity. However, in respect of those activities which are exempt from waste management licensing[1], the Waste Management Licensing Regulations 1994 approach this matter differently. Provided that the activity falls within the terms of one of the exemptions in Schedule 3 to the Regulations, the Agency is required to register it when it has been brought to its attention[2]. There are, however, a number of exceptions to this general rule – the most prominent being exempt scrapyards and vehicle dismantlers[3].

1 See Chapters 10 and 11.
2 SI 1994/1056, reg 18(4): see para 10.24ff.
3 See para 11.88ff.

12.10 For sites which are, or should be, the subject of waste management licences, the principal statutory duty of the Agency is that any application for a waste management licence should be either accepted or rejected within the statutory time period. It must be rejected where the applicant is not a fit and proper person or when the proposed activities may cause pollution of the environment or harm to human health[1]. In certain circumstances, these grounds are extended to include whether the site will cause a serious detriment to the amenities of the locality[2]. Further, the requirements in relation to the 'relevant objectives' of the Directive on Waste must be complied with[3] and the provisions contained in the Waste Management Licensing Regulations 1994 in respect of groundwater protection[4] met. Similar statutory duties apply when licences are subject to modification[5], transfer[6] or surrender[7].

1 EPA 1990, s 36(3): see para 8.40ff.
2 EPA 1990, s 36(3): see para 8.49.
3 As set down in SI 1994/1056, Sch 4, Pt 1: see para 8.50ff.
4 SI 1994/1056, reg 15: see para 8.70ff.
5 EPA 1990, s 37: see para 9.03ff.
6 EPA 1990, s 40: see para 9.114ff.
7 EPA 1990, s 39: see para 9.93ff.

12.11 Once a waste management licence has been granted, the Agency's obligations under the EPA 1990 are more explicit. Section 42(1) requires the Agency 'to take the steps needed' to ensure that the activities authorised by the licence do not cause pollution of the environment, harm to human health or become seriously detrimental to the amenities of the locality[1]. The Agency also has a statutory duty to take the required steps to ensure compliance with any condition of a waste management licence[2].

1 EPA 1990, s 42(1).
2 EPA 1990, s 42(1)(b).

Waste carriers and waste brokers

12.12 In respect of controlled waste carriers and brokers, the Agency has duties similar to those pertaining to waste management licence applications. The legislation is explicit on the requirements of the Agency once an application has been made, but leaves the enforcement of the need to register to the Agency's discretion[1].

1 Waste carrier and broker registration is discussed in Chapter 6.

Relevant objectives

12.13 The concept of 'relevant objectives' has been partially covered in Chapters 8[1] and 9[2] in the context of waste management licences. The objectives are set out in the Waste Management Licensing Regulations 1994[3], being derived from Articles 3, 4 and 5 of the Directive on Waste[4]. Three sets of objectives can be identified, of which only the first[5] is significant in the context of the Agency's overall waste regulation functions.

1 See para 8.50.
2 See para 9.88ff.
3 SI 1994/1056, reg 19 and Sch 4, paras 2 to 4.
4 Council Directive of 15 July 1975 on Waste (75/442/EEC) (OJ L194/39 25.7.75) (as amended by Council Directive of 18 March 1991 amending Directive 75/442/EEC on Waste (91/156/EEC) (OJ L78/32 26.3.91) and Commission Decision of 24 May 1996 adapting Annexes IIA and IIB to Council Directive 75/442/EEC on Waste (96/350/EC) (OJ L135/32 6.6.96)).
5 SI 1994/1056, Sch 4, para 4(1) (discussed below). The other objectives relate principally to development control matters of waste disposal installations (Sch 4 para 4(2): see in the context of licence applications, para 8.55ff) and waste management plans (Sch 4, para 4(3)).

12.14 The key relevant objective in this context is contained in Schedule 4, Part I, paragraph 4(1) to the Waste Management Licensing Regulations 1994, which is a copy of the kernel of Article 4 of the Directive on Waste. For the disposal and recovery[1] of waste the Agency must ensure[2]:

'... that waste is recovered or disposed of without endangering human health and without using processes or methods which could harm the environment and in particular without –

(i)   risk to water, air, soil, plants or animals; or

(ii) causing nuisance through noise or odours; or

(iii) adversely affecting the countryside or places of special interest.'

1   'Disposal' and 'recovery' are defined by reg 1(3) as falling within the lists contained in Schedule 4 to the Waste Management Licensing Regulations 1994 (see para 2.42).
2   SI 1994/1056, Pt I, Sch 4, para 4(1)(a).

12.15   In order to understand how the objectives relate to the Agency's overall functions it is important to appreciate two precepts: their conceptual nature and their relationship to the other statutory provisions. As will be seen, the objectives only apply to certain functions and not to others.

12.16   It needs to be clear what is envisaged by the term 'relevant objectives'. Circular 11/94 indicates that there is a distinction between 'objectives' (ie matters relating to goals or aims) and absolute requirements[1]. Hence, while following the objectives, the exact manner by which they should be implemented is left to the Agency's discretion[2].

1   See Circular 11/94 Annex 1, paras 1.26 to 1.28, para 1.31 and see PPG 23, Annex 6.
2   See Circular 11/94, Annex 1, para 1.48.

12.17   The European Court's ruling on Article 4 of the Directive on Waste[1] forms the rationale for including relevant objectives within the Waste Management Licensing Regulations 1994. The court determined that the provisions of Article 4 of the Directive on Waste are not 'directly effective', as they did fulfil the well-known test of 'unconditionality nor sufficient precision'[2]. However, this does not mean that Article 4 has no function. The court found that Article 4[3]:

'... indicates a programme to be followed and sets out the objectives which the Member States must observe in their performance of the specific obligations imposed on them by Articles 5 to 11 of the directive concerning planning, supervision and monitoring of waste disposal operations. ... Thus, the provision at issue[4] must be regarded as defining the framework for the action to be taken by the Member States regarding the treatment of waste and not as requiring, in itself, the adoption of specific measures or a particular method of waste disposal[5].'

Accordingly, the transposition of Article 4 into the Waste Management Licensing Regulations 1994[6] should be viewed as an attempt to make the British waste regulation system reflect not only the content of the Directive on Waste but also its purpose.

1   *Comitato di Coordinamento per la Difesa della Cava and Regione Lombardia* [1996] 8 JEL 313.
2   The requirements for direct effect are set down in *Van Gend en Loos* [1963] ECR 1 at 12/13, *Becker v Finanzamt Münster-Innenstadt* [1982] ECR 53 at 70; *Marshall v Southampton Health Authority* [1986] 1 CMLR 688; *Foster v British Gas plc* [1990] 2 CMLR 833.
3   *Regione Lombardia* [1996] 8 JEL 2, 313 at 322, para 12–14.
4   Article 4 of the Directive on Waste.
5   Note that this judgment refers to the Directive on Waste prior to subsequent amendment.
6   SI 1994/1056, Sch 4, para 4(1).

12.18 However, it would seem from Circular 11/94 that these objectives must not be followed too rigidly. The Circular acknowledges[1] that the Directive's requirement that waste is recovered or disposed of 'without risk to water, soil, plants or animals'[2] is potentially problematic[3]. Regulatory bodies:

'... would have difficulty in permitting any operations if they had to be sure that there would be no risk to air, soil, plants or animals.'

The Circular therefore points out that the preamble to the Directive requires that disposal and recovery sites are to be provided and that Article 5 encourages the establishment of an integrated network of such installations in the Community. Accordingly, the implication is that there is a need to balance what appears to be the absolute requirement contained in Article 4[4] against the other purposes of the Directive[5]. This is all very well, but it does beg the question of why there was need to write the requirement that disposal or recovery should be done 'without risk' to water, soil, plants, etc directly into a statutory instrument.

1 Circular 11/94, Annex 1, para 1.26.
2 SI 1994/1056, Sch 4, para 4(1).
3 See also Department of Environment (1994) *Planning Policy Guidance: Planning and Pollution Control*, (PPG 23) HMSO, London, Annex 6, para 4.
4 Which is transposed by SI 1994/1056, Sch 4, para 4(1)(a).
5 This is confirmed by PPG 23, Annex 6, para 4.

12.19 The scope of application of the relevant objectives holds only in relation to those 'specified functions' identified in the Waste Management Licensing Regulations 1994[1]. If those functions are not so specified, then there is no compulsion to uphold the objectives[2]. The functions which have been identified are those which implement particular provisions of the Directive on Waste. Other statutory functions which are not set down in the Directive do not need to accord to the objectives.

1 SI 1994/1056, Sch 4, para 3 and Table 5 (with Table 5 being amended by SI 1998/2746, reg 17).
2 See Circular 11/94, Annex 1, para 1.47: however, the waste management licensing exemption system also needs to uphold the objectives: see SI 1994/1056, reg 17(4) and see para 10.33.

12.20 The result is that the statutory duties of the Agency in relation to waste management facilities subject to Part II of the EPA 1990 must be discharged in accordance with the relevant objectives solely in terms of the[1]:

' ... respective functions under Part II of the 1990 Act in relation to waste management licences, including preparing plans or modifications of them under s 50 of the 1990 Act'.

The objectives therefore need to be considered in relation to both licence applications and also licence subsistence[2]. From elsewhere in the Waste Management Licensing Regulations 1994[3], they also need to be applied in respect of activities exempt from waste management licences. In this case, exemption is conditional on compliance with the objectives. But other regulatory matters, including duties which emanate from the Control of Pollution (Amendment) Act 1989, regulations made under the European Communities Act 1972[4], etc are not specified functions, and therefore are to be excluded from the requirements of the relevant objectives.

1 SI 1994/1056, Sch 4, Pt I, para 3(1), Table 5.
2 Eg inspections and their outcomes in terms of licence modification, revocation, suspension, etc; see also para 9.88.
3 SI 1994/1056, reg 17(4): see para 10.33.
4 Under which much Community environmental legislation is transposed as statutory instruments.

12.21   The application of the relevant objectives is also restricted[1] to those recovery and disposal installations covered by Annexes IIA and IIB of the Directive on Waste[2]. These are repeated[3] in the Waste Management Licensing Regulations 1994 by Part III and Part IV of Schedule 4 – see Tables 2.5 and 2.6 in Chapter 2. Given that not all waste management activities are portrayed in these tables, the objectives do not apply to a minority of waste management operations, such as waste stored on the site of production awaiting collection.

1   SI 1994/1056, Sch 4, Part I, para 2(1) and reg 1(3).
2   Council Directive of 15 July 1975 on Waste (75/442/EEC) (OJ L194/39 25.7.75) (as amended by Council Directive of 18 March 1991 amending Directive 75/442/EEC on Waste (91/156/EEC) (OJ L78/322 6.3.91) and Commission Decision of 24 May 1996 adapting Annexes IIA and IIB to Council Directive 75/442/EEC on Waste (96/350/EC) (OJ L135/32 6.6.96)); see Tables 2.2 and 2.3 in Chapter 2.
3   But they do not reflect the amendments made to the Directive on Waste by Commission Decision of 24 May 1996 adapting Annexes IIA and IIB to Council Directive 75/442/EEC on Waste (96/350/EC) (OJ L135/32 6.6.96).

12.22   Finally, it must be appreciated that the provisions on relevant objectives in Schedule 4 are not only addressed to the Agency's regulatory activities under Part II of the EPA 1990. They impinge upon all other environmental control authorities which have a role in implementing the Directive on Waste's provisions. Hence they apply to waste management activities subject to Integrated Pollution Control authorisations[1], as well as local planning authorities[2], the Ministry of Agriculture, Fisheries and Food in relation to sea disposal activities, and also to the Secretary of State. Which body is responsible for which 'specified function' is set out in Schedule 4 to the Waste Management Licensing Regulations 1994[3]. All affected statutory bodies have the duty to discharge their functions according to the relevant objectives when dealing with the waste management operations subject to the Directive[4].

1   *R v Environment Agency and Redland Aggregates Ltd, ex p Gibson* [1999] Env LR 73.
2   Particularly in their functions of the granting of planning permissions: see *R v Bolton Metropolitan Borough Council, ex p Kirkham* [1998] Env LR 719.
3   SI 1994/1056, Sch 4, para 3: note that the words 'specified function' in Schedule 4 should be seen as distinct from 'specified action'. The former term is defined in Schedule 4, Pt I, para 3, while the term 'specified action' relates solely to the development control system and is defined in Schedule 4, Pt I, para 1. Table 5 of para 3 has been amended by SI 1998/2746, reg 17.
4   SI 1994/1056, Sch 4, para 2(1).

Duties to carry out inspections

12.23   The Agency has certain explicit duties under the EPA 1990 and associated regulations to undertake inspections of waste management facilities. In the year 1997/98, the Agency carried out 140,000 inspections at facilities subject to waste management licences[1]. As will be shown, the duty to undertake site inspections extends to other waste facilities as well as those subject to licences.

1   Environment Agency (1998) *1997/98 Report and Accounts*, Environment Agency, Bristol, Appendix V (the equivalent figure for inspections in Scotland is about 16,000: SEPA (1998) *Corporate Plan 1998/99*, SEPA, Stirling, p 12).

12.24   Section 42 of the EPA 1990 sets down the statutory duty of the Agency to supervise activities subject to waste management licences. The nature of this super-vision has been described at para 12.11 above, but it includes ensuring that facilities comply with the conditions of their waste management licences[1]. In addition, the Special Waste Regulations 1996[2] make the Agency responsible for 'supervising the persons and activities' subject to those regulations. This will include waste producers, waste carriers and disposal or recovery facilities.

1   EPA 1990, s 42(1)(b).
2   SI 1996/972, reg 19.

12.25   These duties are bolstered by the Waste Management Licensing Regulations 1994[1], which enact Article 13 of the Directive on Waste[2]. The Waste Management Licensing Regulations 1994 require the Agency to undertake the 'appropriate periodic inspection' of 'any' establishment or undertaking which carries out the recovery or disposal of controlled waste. Given that this requirement relates to all sites, not just those licensed under Part II of the EPA 1990, it applies to exempt sites and unauthorised facilities as well as sites subject to waste management licences and Part I authorisations. Similar inspections have to be made wherever persons collect or transport waste on a professional basis. Hence the Waste Management Licensing Regulations 1994 indicate that there is a duty to visit controlled waste carriers. Dealers or brokers also need to be inspected, along with producers of special waste[3].

1   SI 1994/1056, reg 19, Sch 4, para 13.
2   Council Directive of 15 July 1975 on Waste (75/442/EEC) (OJ L194/39 25.7.75) (as amended by Council Directive of 18 March 1991 amending Directive 75/442/EEC on Waste (91/156/EEC) (OJ L78/32 26.3.91) and Commission Decision of 24 May 1996 adapting Annexes IIA and IIB to Council Directive 75/442/EEC on Waste (96/350/EC) (OJ L135/32 6.6.96)): see para 12.08.
3   The reference to special waste producers was added to SI 1994/1056 by SI 1996/972, reg 25 and Sch 3.

12.26   Circular 11/94 provides the following advice on how these requirements can be met[1]:

'Authorities should note that the duty is to carry out *appropriate* periodic inspections. In practice, this should not require them to do any more than they would otherwise have expected to do in the proper exercise of their functions in relation to the various control regimes. The frequency and extent of inspections should in general be related to the potential for causing pollution of the environment or harm to human health, and inspections should not be carried out for the sake of it, where the authority do not consider there would be any benefit.'

1   Circular 11/94 Annex 1, para 1.87: emphasis in original.

Inspection frequencies at sites subject to waste management licences

12.27   The required inspection frequencies for licensed waste management facilities[1] are currently as set down in Waste Management Paper No 4[2]. This document constitutes 'statutory guidance'[3]. It falls within the requirement, contained in s 35(8) of the EPA 1990, that the Agency must have regard to guidance issued by the Secretary of State 'with respect to the discharge of their functions in relation to licences'[4].

1   For facilities subject to authorisations under Part 1 of the EPA 1990 which process controlled waste, there is no required inspection frequency. However, certain of the facilities now subject to IPC were under the jurisdiction of the local authorities in the 1980s. The inspection frequency required of a local authority was set down in the now-superseded second edition of Waste Management Paper 4. Four visits a month were envisaged for household waste and merchant incinerators: see *Waste Management Paper No 4 The Licensing of Waste Facilities* (1988) 2nd edn, HMSO, London, p 41, Appendix C.
2   *Waste Management Paper No 4 The Licensing of Waste Management Facilities* (1994) 3rd edn, HMSO, London.
3   See WMP 4, para 1.4.
4   EPA 1990, s 35(8): the nature of 'statutory guidance' is considered at para 8.231ff.

12.28   The Waste Management Paper envisages that the Agency should undertake routine inspections of licensed facilities, as well as longer duration audits 'which might extend over several days for a large site'[1]. The Waste Management Paper also states that[2]:

'Inspections should include random visits to sites over the whole working day including early morning, evening and weekends as appropriate. Sites should also be visited outside their licensed hours to monitor compliance with operational hours and security . . .'.

1   WMP 4, para B7.
2   WMP 4, Appendix B, para B6.

12.29   The Waste Management Paper sets out frequencies of inspection for particular classes of site. These are shown in Table 12.1. The inspection rates are described by the Paper as an 'overall minimum':

'. . . any reduction in frequency should only be justified on the basis of a high and sustained quality of site management . . . The frequency and rigour of inspection should increase when any facility is not, or is in danger of not, operating to the required standards'[1].

Accordingly, these inspection frequencies can only be varied 'to reflect the quality and success of operational site management' or 'for rare cases' where sites are so small and remote as to make it impractical to adhere to the inspection frequencies[2]. Circular 11/94 makes it clear that the inspection frequencies set down in Waste Management Paper 4 are in line with the principles of regulatory 'proportionality'[3].

1   WMP 4, para B9.
2   WMP 4, Para B9.
3   Circular 11/94, para 12: 'proportionality' is discussed at para 12.34.

Table 12.1

Minimum Inspection Frequencies[1]

Type of Facility	No of Inspections per Month
Co-disposal landfill site taking difficult and special wastes	8
Household, commercial and/or industrial waste landfill	4
Treatment plant	4
Household, commercial and/or industrial waste transfer station	4
Landfill/transfer station taking non-biodegradable wastes	2
Industrial waste landfill (factory curtilage)	1
Metal recycling facility	1
In-House storage facilities	0.25

1   WMP 4, p 62.

12.30   Although the inspection frequencies portrayed in Waste Management Paper 4 are described as minimum levels, the Agency does not achieve them. For the financial year, 1997/98 the overall figure for England and Wales was 75% of the levels set in the Waste Management Paper[1]. The Agency had gone on record to the effect that 100% compliance with the targets was to be achieved by the financial year 2000/2001[2]. However, the inspection targets have been subject to recent negotiation between the Agency and the Department of the Environment[3], with proposals for a more selective approach. However, they still stand as part of the statutory guidance of Waste Management Paper No 4[4].

1   Environment Agency (1998) *Corporate Plan 1999–2000 Our Forward Look to 2002*, Environment Agency, Bristol, p 15, fig 3.1.
2   Environment Agency (1997) *Environment Agency Corporate Plan 1998–99 Our Forward Look to 2000–01*, Environment Agency, Bristol, p 36.
3   Environment Agency (1998) *Corporate Plan 1999–2000 Our Forward Look to 2002*, Environment Agency, Bristol, pp 48, 50.
4   Proposals for changes can be found in DETR (1999) *Waste Management Licensing Risk Assessment Inspection Frequencies Operator Pollution Risk Appraisal* 'OPRA for Waste' A Consultation Paper, DETR, London.

12.31   From Circular 11/94, it would be apparent that, when inspections of waste management facilities are undertaken by the Agency, it is the expectation that reports are usually written of these visits[1]. Such reports will need to be placed in the Agency's public register of activities[2].

1   Circular 11/94, Annex 9, para 9.29.
2   SI 1994/1056, reg 10(1)(g): see para 13.31.

Inspection frequencies at exempt scrapyards and vehicle dismantlers

12.32   The Waste Management Licensing Regulations 1994 contain one additional statutory requirement for Agency inspections. This only applies to registered metal recycling facilities where such activities are exempt from waste management licences[1]. These sites must be subject to an inspection within two months of the Agency's receipt of a notice from the operator that the site is to be viewed as exempt[2]. In addition to this requirement, a registered exempt site is required to be revisited by the Agency at 12 monthly intervals[3].

1   By way of SI 1994/1056, reg 17: see Chapter 11 and see Circular 6/95, Annex 1, paras 1.12–1.15.
2   SI 1994/1056, Sch 4, para 13(3)(a) as amended by SI 1995/288, reg 3(18).
3   SI 1994/1056, Sch 4, para 13(3)(b) as amended by SI 1995/288, reg 3(18).

12.33   The purpose of these inspections is to ensure that the terms and conditions of the exemption still apply. As explained in Chapter 11, the registration for this type of waste management activity is renewed on a yearly basis. Accordingly, the provisions ensure that the Agency checks that the continuation of the exemption is appropriate. It should be noted that the frequency set down in the regulations is a bare minimum. Normally, many scrapyards and vehicle dismantlers will warrant more frequent visits to ensure that site operations are continuing within the terms of the exemption[1].

1   SI 1994/1056, Sch 4, para 13(5)(a) (as amended by SI 1995/288, reg 3(18)) makes it clear that more frequent visits can be countenanced.

PROPORTIONALITY AND WEIGHING THE COSTS AND BENEFITS OF REGULATORY ACTION

12.34   The guidance associated with the implementation of the EPA 1990, as well as the Environment Act 1995 itself, attempts to set out the context within which the Agency should operate, particularly where regulatory activities may hamper business[1]. The approach of the Environment Act 1995 is firmer than that associated with Part II of the EPA 1990, but in either case the requirements are loosely cast, making it difficult to judge, outside the general statements set down, the points at which the Agency is overstepping the required boundary.

1   The effects on commercial activities of particular regulatory actions are stressed also in various Circulars: see Circular 11/94, para 10ff, Circular 6/95, para 14 and Circular 6/96, Annex A, para 82; see also in respect of transfrontier waste shipments, Department of the Environment (1996) *United Kingdom Management Plan for Exports and Imports of Waste*, para 2.22ff.

12.35   Section 39 of the Environment Act 1995 requires that the Agency must have regard to the costs and benefits of its activities prior to embarking on a particular course of action. However, this requirement only applies in respect of statutory powers, not statutory duties[1]. Accordingly, the duties outlined above are unaffected by s 39. Hence there remains the requirement to enforce licence conditions[2] and to prevent, register or appropriately licence any waste management activity which the Agency discovers[3].

1   Environment Act 1995, s 39(2).
2   EPA 1990, s 42(1)(a).
3   See *Ministère Public v Oscar Traen and Others* [1988] 3 CMLR 511: discussed at para 12.07 above.

12.36   Section 39(1) of the Environment Act 1995 applies when the Agency is considering exercising any of its statutory powers or when determining the manner by which the power is to be exercised[1]. In respect of any of its powers, the Agency must 'take into account the likely costs and benefits of the exercise or non-exercise of the power or its exercise in the manner in question'. The term 'costs and benefits' is defined[2] as including both financial and environmental costs. The only point at which such a consideration is inappropriate is where, 'in view of the nature or purpose of the power or in the circumstances of the particular case', it is unreasonable for the Agency to consider this matter[3].

1   Environment Act 1995, s 39(1).
2   Environment Act 1995, s 46(1).
3   Environment Act 1995, s 39(1).

12.37   As noted, s 39 of the Environment Act 1995 applies to the Agency's statutory powers. However, the guidance associated with Part II of the EPA 1990 purports to apply not only to powers but also to the Agency's statutory duties – a somewhat questionable matter. However, central to this guidance is the requirement that regulatory activities should be 'proportionate'[1] to the benefits and risks involved. Circular 11/94 contains the most prominent and explicit statement of this principle[2]. It reminds enforcement authorities that their actions should be determined at a level appropriate to the matter in question and that the waste industry's societal contribution should be weighed against the possible environmental effects of industry's activities.

1   See, for example, *R v Chief Constable of Sussex, ex p International Trader's Ferry Ltd* [1997] 2 All ER 65 at 80 G/H.
2   Circular 11/94, para 10ff.

12.38   The requirements for proportionality are set down in paragraph 10 of Circular 11/94:

'It is . . . the Government's more general policy that where regulation is necessary:

(a)   it should be proportionate to the risks involved and the benefits to be obtained;

(b)   it should be goal based. That is to say, it should have an objective and a means of ensuring the fulfilment of that objective;

(c)   it **should not** serve as an end to itself;

(d)   it **should not** be over-prescriptive; and

(e)   it **should not** impose an unjustifiable or disproportionate burden on those regulated – especially small businesses.'

Paragraph 14 of the circular requires that regulatory bodies should have regard to the principles of proportionality in developing policies necessary to fulfil the aims of Part II of the EPA 1990 and subsidiary regulations. The principles should equally be considered in 'the practical application of those policies in individual cases'[1]. However, it is acknowledged that the requirements of proportionality do not over-ride the inspection frequencies set down in Waste Management Paper No 4 for licensed waste management facilities[2].

1   Circular 11/94, para 14(b).
2   See Circular 11/94, paras 12 and 13: inspection frequencies are discussed at para 12.27.

12.39   Similar sentiments are repeated later in Circular 11/94[1] and in Circular 6/95 in respect of scrapyards and vehicle dismantlers[2]. Regulatory bodies[3]:

'(a)   should have regard to the fact that waste management facilities are a source of benefit to the environment and sustainable development. This is a consideration which is particularly important in relation to facilities carrying out the recovery of waste;

(b)   should strike an appropriate balance between advice and encouragement and regulation and legal enforcement. Again this is a consideration which is particularly important in relation to facilities carrying out the recovery of waste; and

(c)   should distinguish between and act proportionately in relation to "technical" breaches of the Regulations[4] or Part II of the 1990 Act where there is no threat of pollution to the environment or harm to human health. In the former case . . . [the Agency's] main aim should be to ensure that the person responsible is made aware of his legal responsibilities and that steps are taken by the . . . [Agency] or the person concerned to prevent the commission of any further "technical" offences.'

1   Circular 11/94, para 17.
2   Circular 6/95, para 14.
3   Circular 11/94, para 17.
4   Ie SI 1994/1056.

12.40   The principles of proportionality also apply[1] to the supervision by the Agency of the Special Waste Regulations 1996[2]. However, the relevant circular[3] would appear to suggest that an over-riding principle is that special waste is 'soundly managed'.

1   Circular 6/96, Annex A, para 82.
2   SI 1996/972: see Chapter 4.
3   Circular 6/96, Annex A, para 82.

12.41   Like s 39 of the Environment Act 1995, which requires the Agency to weigh the costs and benefits of its regulatory activities and their outcomes, it would seem that proportionality should be applied principally to the Agency's statutory powers. It should have less effect, for reasons which will be readily apparent, on the Agency's statutory duties, and even less application where the Agency is implementing Community law. Although this distinction is not made in the relevant guidance, the contents of the circulars are, of course, of much less significance than the words of the relevant legislation. Hence the duties contained in s 42 of the EPA 1990, for example, should be of prime consideration. Accordingly, the Agency must ensure that environmental pollution or harm to human health is not created by any sites subject to waste management licences[1]. Similarly, the Agency must take the steps needed to ensure that the conditions of the licences are complied with[2]. These considerations appear much more important than the guidance contained in the relevant circulars[3].

1 EPA 1990, s 42(1)(a).
2 EPA 1990, s 42(1)(b).
3 See Baldwin R and Houghton J 'Circular Arguments: the Status and Legitimacy of Administrative Rules', [1986] *Public Law* 239.

THE AGENCY'S ENFORCEMENT POLICY

12.42 The Agency has had a formalised Enforcement and Prosecution Policy since November 1998. The policy sets out a general framework within which decisions on enforcement action are to be made. It also seems that this Policy will spawn a series of sub-documents which provide '. . . guidance for staff in respect of each of the Agency's functions'[1].

1 Environment Agency (1998) *Enforcement and Prosecution Policy*, Environment Agency, Bristol, para 5.

12.43 A series of 'Principles for Enforcement' are set out in the Policy. They emphasise the need for proportionality, consistency and transparency. Proportionality – as is discussed at para 12.34 – involves the need to balance the action necessary to protect the environment against risks and cost, taking into account the seriousness of any breach of the law[1]. The need for consistency over the implementation of all of the Agency's powers is stressed, including in respect of their operational use and in decisions over whether to prosecute[2]. Transparency is considered important so that all parties understand what is expected: '[i]t also means making clear why an officer intends to, or has taken enforcement action'[3]. Hence, should remedial actions be required, the Policy states that an explanation as to why it is needed will be provided. An opportunity will also be given to discuss what is required '. . . before formal enforcement action is taken . . .', unless the matter justifies an urgent response[4]. In the latter case, the Policy states that a written explanation will be furnished after the event[5].

1 Environment Agency (1998) *Enforcement and Prosecution Policy*, Environment Agency, Bristol, para 10.
2 Environment Agency (1998) *Enforcement and Prosecution Policy*, Environment Agency, Bristol, para 12.
3 Environment Agency (1998) *Enforcement and Prosecution Policy*, Environment Agency, Bristol, para 14.
4 Environment Agency (1998) *Enforcement and Prosecution Policy*, Environment Agency, Bristol, para 15.
5 the Policy states that the explanation will also embrace any rights of appeal. However as set out in Chapter 9, an explanation of the method of appeal is usually an essential component of any valid statutory notice under the EPA 1990.

12.44 When considering a possible prosecution, the Policy states that regard will be had to the Code for Crown Prosecutions[1]. Besides the availability of evidence[2], a decision on whether to prosecute will involve the consideration of the following matters[3]:

– the environmental effect of the offence;
– its foreseeability;
– the intent of the offender;
– a person's past offending history;
– the offender's attitude;

- the deterrent effect of a prosecution;
- the personal circumstances of an offender.

Where companies are involved, the Policy states that the Agency will look to the use of powers concerning the liability of directors, managers etc[4] where such individuals were directly involved in the commission of an offence[5]. The Policy states that this will include seeking their disqualification under the Companies Act.

1   Environment Agency (1998) *Enforcement and Prosecution Policy*, Environment Agency, Bristol, para 20.
2   Environment Agency (1998) *Enforcement and Prosecution Policy*, Environment Agency, Bristol, para 21.
3   Environment Agency (1998) *Enforcement and Prosecution Policy*, Environment Agency, Bristol, para 22.
4   See para 7.156ff.
5   Environment Agency (1998) *Enforcement and Prosecution Policy*, Environment Agency, Bristol, para 24.

12.45   Finally, the Policy sets out the instances when the Agency will 'normally prosecute'[1]. These are where:

- breaches have potentially serious environmental consequences;
- activities occur without a relevant licence;
- persistent breaches occur at a facility;
- there is a failure to comply with remedial requirements;
- there has been reckless disregard for management or quality standards;
- information has not been produced when requested or where false information has been supplied;
- staff of the Agency have been subject to obstruction;
- there has been impersonation of Agency staff.

Conversely, the Agency will also look to alternatives to prosecution where such action is considered appropriate, including warnings or formal cautions[2].

1   Environment Agency (1998) *Enforcement and Prosecution Policy*, Environment Agency, Bristol, para 28.
2   Environment Agency (1998) *Enforcement and Prosecution Policy*, Environment Agency, Bristol, para 29.

POWERS OF AGENCY OFFICERS

12.46   The main body of statutory powers for officers of the Agency is contained in s 108 of the Environment Act 1995. These powers supersede the provisions of s 69 of the EPA 1990[1]. They are common to both Environment Agencies in Britain[2] and relate to functions being carried out under the enactments set out in s 108(15) of the Environment Act 1995. The enactments listed include Part II of the EPA 1990, the Control of Pollution (Amendment) Act 1989 and regulations implementing Community law by way of the European Communities Act 1972. The latter covers the provisions of waste broker registration[3] and transfrontier waste shipments[4].

1   Environment Act 1995, s 120(3) and Sch 24.
2   Environment Act 1995, s 108(15): they also apply to local authorities in respect of their enforcement powers on Part B processes (EPA 1990, Pt 1), the new contaminated land regime (EPA 1990, Pt IIA as amended by the Environment Act 1995, s 57) and local air quality management plans (Environment Act 1995, Pt IV).
3   Causing the provision in SI 1994/1056, reg 20(8) and in Sch 4, Pt I, para 13(2) to become superfluous. The purpose of these two provisions is explained in Circular 11/94, Annex 1, para 1.86.
4   SI 1994/1137: see Chapter 6.

12.47 The Agency also has additional powers under the EPA 1990. As described elsewhere[1], the Agency can modify, suspend and revoke waste management licences. It can also serve notices on persons requiring specified actions, or can enter land, undertake particular works and recoup the cost from the persons responsible[2]. There are also powers to obtain information[3] and, under the relevant secondary legislation, to obtain copies of the transfer notes under the provisions on the duty of care[4] and to require transfrontier waste shipments to be returned[5]. Finally, extended powers are contained in the Control of Pollution (Amendment) Act 1989 in respect of the policing of the system of registered waste carriers[6]. The latter permit Agency officers and police constables to stop and seize vehicles in defined circumstances[7].

1 See Chapter 9.
2 EPA 1990, s 59: see para 12.103ff.
3 EPA 1990, s 71: see para 12.174ff.
4 SI 1991/2839, reg 4: see para 12.182ff.
5 SI 1994/1137, regs 8 and 9: see para 12.128ff.
6 However the powers of entry in s 7 of the Control of Pollution (Amendment) Act 1989 have been superseded by those contained in the Environment Act 1995: EPA 1990, Sch 15, para 31(4)(a) as amended by the Environment Act 1995, Sch 22, para 37(5).
7 See paras 12.139ff and 12.151ff below.

12.48 It should be noted that the powers contained in these enactments are potentially very broad. The Environment Act 1995 states that information obtained under the s 108 powers is admissible against any person[1]. However, notwithstanding this provision on general admissibility, the Environment Act 1995 places limits upon the general common law principle that permits suspects to exercise their right of silence and not to make self-incriminatory statements[2]. From the face of the legislation, both the EPA 1990 and the Environment Act 1995 appear able to permit the Agency to compel persons to make statements or produce documents which may be self-incriminatory. There is little protection built into the statute, other than that in the Environment Act 1995 concerning documents protected by professional legal privilege[3]. In respect of the provisions in the EPA 1990[4] which enable a notice to be served on a person to obtain information, there is not even this safeguard. Although somewhat clarified by *R v Hertfordshire County Council, ex p Green Environmental Industries*[5], the uncertainty is potentially problematic, particularly with respect of evidence admissibility.

1 This is made explicit in respect of s 108 powers by Environment Act 1995, Sch 18, para 4(1). In other cases, see *R v Hertfordshire County Council, ex p Green Environmental Industries* [1998] Env LR 153. The only exception in this respect is s 108(4)(j): see s 108(12) and para 12.74 below.
2 See paras 12.49 and 12.74.
3 Environment Act 1995, s 108(13).
4 EPA 1990, s 71: see para 12.174ff.
5 [1998] Env LR 153.

12.49 The difficulty stems from the question of whether the provisions of the Environment Act 1995 should be seen in the context of developments in other fields of law where rights of silence are being limited in order to assist investigations of, particularly, corporate crime. For example, s 236 of the Insolvency Act 1986 can, on pain of penalty, cause persons to be placed before the courts and be required to account for their actions and to produce written records about a company. But this matter is additionally complicated by the fact that questions have been raised about whether such provisions accord to the principle of Article 6 of the European Convention for the Protection of Human Rights and Fundamental Freedoms[1]. The relevant section of that Article states that:

'In the determination of . . . any criminal charge against him, everyone is entitled to a fair . . . hearing . . . by an independent and impartial tribunal . . .'

Perhaps the most prominent case in this respect was *Saunders v United Kingdom*[2], a case taken to the European Court of Human Rights. The case mainly concerned the use of written statements made by Mr Ernest Saunders, hitherto Chief Executive of Guinness PLC, at his trial. These statements had been taken, under the threat of penalty for non-cooperation, under s 436 of the Companies Act 1985, prior to trial and were extensively used to illustrate discrepancies in Mr Saunders' verbal evidence. The Court of Human Rights found for Mr Saunders, holding that the right not to incriminate oneself was central to the fair workings of a country's criminal justice system and that the use made of the statements contravened that principle.

1   To be incorporated fully into UK law by the Human Rights Act 1998.
2   (1996) 23 EHRR 313.

12.50   Although there remains uncertainty over the matter of admissibility in the context of the EPA 1990 and Environment Act 1995, it may be that the over-riding principle is the right of individuals not to incriminate themselves is paramount. However, this only relates to the admissibility of the evidence, this right does not preclude the Agency obtaining the information in the first place[1]. Furthermore, it would seem that, whilst individuals may retain rights of silence and against self-incrimination, these rights do not apply so strictly to bodies corporate. Considering *Orkem SA v EC Commission*[2] approvingly, Lord Justice Waller indicated in *R v Hertfordshire County Council, ex p Green Environmental Industries* that[3] '... the right not to give evidence against oneself is basically a right of an individual, not a legal entity or company'. However, this does not extend to providing evidence which causes the defence to virtually admit the existence of the offence[4].

1   *R v Hertfordshire County Council, ex p Green Environmental Industries* [1998] Env LR 153 at 167.
2   [1991] 4 CMLR 502.
3   *R v Hertfordshire County Council, ex p Green Environmental Industries* [1998] Env LR 153 at 168.
4   *R v Hertfordshire County Council, ex p Green Environmental Industries* [1998] Env LR 153 at 168,
    CA; *Orkem SA v EC Commission* [1991] 4 CMLR 502 at 553ff.

12.51   Finally, it will become apparent that a number of the powers in both the EPA 1990 and the Environment Act 1995 overlap. It has been held that these overlaps do not cause the particular powers to be mutually exclusive[1]. But even within the Environment Act 1995, it would seem that there is potential duplication. For example, persons who fail to undertake particular actions required of them by Agency officers, acting under powers contained in s 108 of the Environment Act 1995, commit offences quite separate from the general offence of obstruction[2]. In respect of the obtaining of records, there are also overlaps between the s 108 powers[3] and the powers contained in the EPA 1990[4]. The existence of these overlaps needs careful consideration by the Agency as evidential requirements, the scope of the powers and the penalties may be different.

1   Environment Act 1995, see s 108, Sch 18, para 4(1) and *R v Hertfordshire County Council, ex p Green Environmental Industries* [1998] Env LR 153 at 167.
2   Non-compliance with any requirements under s 108 of the Environment Act 1995 is made an offence under s 110(2), but obstruction of an officer is an offence under s 110(1). Obstruction is considered in para 12.195 below.
3   Environment Act 1995, s 108(4)(k): see para 12.71.
4   EPA 1990, s 71, in respect of obtaining information by notices, and SI 1991/2839, reg 4, in relation to obtaining copies of duty of care transfer notes. See para 12.173ff.

Powers of authorised persons

12.52   The Agency[1] is given powers to appoint authorised persons under s 108(1) of the Environment Act 1995. Both Agency staff and other persons – for example contractors working on the behalf of the Agency – can be duly authorised. The authorisation must always be in writing[2]. As discussed below, the main purpose of the authorisation is to allow legitimate entry onto private land, but authorisation also permits the use of powers relating to the seizure of items, the establishment of monitoring equipment on private property, and so on.

1   Or other enforcing authority, which includes local authorities' activities in respect of such matters as integrated pollution control, contaminated land and air quality management plans.
2   Environment Act 1995, s 108(1).

12.53   Authorised Agency officers are subject to protection from any civil or criminal proceedings, provided that the court is satisfied that the act was done in good faith and that there were reasonable grounds for doing it[1].

1   Environment Act 1995, Sch 18, para 6(4).

12.54   The purposes of the authorisation are specified in the Environment Act 1995[1]. Primarily, they involve the determination of compliance with pollution control enactments[2] and the performing of pollution control functions[3]. For licensed waste management facilities, these powers need to be read in conjunction with s 42 of the EPA 1990. As discussed at para 12.11, s 42 provides an explicit requirement on the Agency to undertake inspections of sites subject to waste management licences in order to ensure condition compliance[4].

1   Environment Act 1995, s 108(1).
2   Environment Act 1995, s 108(1)(a).
3   Environment Act 1995, s 108(1)(b). 'Pollution control enactments' and 'pollution control functions' are defined in the Environment Act 1995, s 108(15) and include Part II of the EPA 1990, the Control of Pollution (Amendment) Act 1989 and any regulations made by way of the European Communities Act 1972. The latter covers the Transfrontier Shipment of Waste Regulations 1994 (SI 1994/1137): see Chapter 5.
4   See Circular 11/94, Annex 9, para 9.36.

12.55   Authorisation under the Environment Act 1995 also covers functions not immediately connected to compliance monitoring. It permits access onto land for the purposes of determining how other functions of the Agency should be exercised or performed[1], such as the collection of background data for environmental quality assessment purposes, waste surveys as part of waste management planning, and so on.

1   Environment Act 1995, s108(1)(c).

12.56   In all cases where s 108 powers are used, including those requiring general access to land[1], an Agency officer must 'produce' evidence of authorisation prior to the power being exercised[2]. In respect of police powers, it has been held that 'produce' means making the authorisation available in a manner by which a land occupier can inspect it[3]. However, whether or not the occupier does, in fact, inspect the authorisation does not affect the legality of the power being enacted.

1   Environment Act 1995, s 108(4)(a).
2   Environment Act 1995, s 108, Sch 18, para 3.
3   *R v Longman* [1988] 1 WLR 619 at 627A/D.
4   *R v Longman* at 627D.

12.57   Under the Environment Act 1995, persons who 'falsely pretend' to be authorised persons commit an offence. The offence is only triable summarily, with a maximum fine of level 5[1] being imposed[2].

1   Currently £5,000.
2   Environment Act, s 110(3) and (5).

Powers of entry, sampling, etc

12.58   The powers under which duly authorised persons can operate on private land vary in degree, being dependent on whether routine investigations are taking place or whether an 'emergency' has arisen. The routine powers will be considered below. The Agency's emergency powers are considered separately at para 12.92ff. Warrants can be applied for when problems obtaining entry to premises are envisaged[1].

1   Environment Act 1995, s 108(7) and Sch 18: warrants are discussed at para 12.79 below.

12.59   An Agency inspector can enter 'at any reasonable time' any premises which the inspector has 'reason to believe it is necessary for him to enter'[1]. What constitutes 'a reasonable time' will vary. It would usually be regarded as normal business hours. Certainly, 4 o'clock in the morning is not a reasonable time[2]. Sunday afternoon might be, but this would depend upon circumstances[3]. Unless an emergency occurs, entry must always be at a reasonable time, even when warrants are used.

1   Environment Act 1995, s 108(4)(a).
2   *Davies v Winstanley* (1930) 144 LT 433.
3   *Small v Bickley* (1875) 32 LT 726.

12.60   The wording of s 108 requires that legitimate access to private land can only occur where Agency officers have reason to believe that it is necessary for them to make an entry[1]. In other words, prior to enacting their entry, the officers must have clear grounds or reasons[2]. The fact that they are allowed to enter premises does not mean that they can demand entry randomly or on a whim. On the other hand, the wording does not require formal evidence to be obtained prior to entry[3]; a belief is a much more abstract concept[4]. It would appear that the statutory duty on the Agency in respect of ensuring compliance with waste management licence conditions[5] would be a sufficient reason to allow access to any land subject to a waste management licence. Alternatively, and perhaps usefully in respect of unauthorised waste management activities, the provision in s 108(1) which requires the Agency to ensure compliance with any pollution control enactment, would appear to be an applicable rationale.

1   *R v Banks* [1916–17] All ER Rep 356 at 357C, *Registrar of Restrictive Trading Agreements v W H Smith and Son Ltd* [1969] 3 All ER 1065 at 1070D and see also *R v Harrison* [1938] 3 All ER 134.
2   See *Nakkuda Ali v Jayaratne* [1951] AC 66 at 77; *Wimbledon UDC v Hastings* (1902) 87 LT 118 per Channel J at 121.
3   *Nakkuda Ali v Jayaratne* [1951] AC 66 at 77.
4   *Hicks v Faulkner* (1881) 8 QBD 167 at 173.
5   EPA 1990, s 42(2).

12.61   Force can be used to gain access to premises in emergencies[1]. However, it would seem that forceable entry can be countenanced in non-emergency situations only with the possession of a warrant[2].

1   Environment Act 1995, s 108(4)(a).
2   Environment Act 1995, s 108(7): warrants are discussed at para 12.79; see also *Grove v Eastern Gas Board* [1951] 2 All ER 1051.

12.62   As noted, the powers of entry are exercisable in respect of 'premises'[1]. The term 'premises' is defined[2] as including land, vehicles, vessels or mobile plant[3]. A definition of land is contained in the Interpretation Act 1978[4] and encompasses buildings and other structures, and land covered by water[5].

1   Environment Act 1995, s 108(4)(a).
2   Environment Act 1995, s 108(15).

3 Mobile plant means plant which is designed to move or to be moved, whether on roads or otherwise: the Environment Act 1995, s 108(15).
4 Interpretation Act 1978, Sch 1.
5 That the Interpretation Act 1978's definition of land is appropriate in the context of waste regulation is confirmed by the Scottish case of *Gotech Industrial and Environmental Services Ltd and James Pitcairn v James Friel* [1995] SCCR 22: see para 7.45.

12.63 In general, the powers of entry allow immediate access, with penalties for refusal[1]. As noted, entry must usually occur at reasonable times[2], but special provisions apply where it is proposed to enter a residential property or where it is proposed to take 'heavy equipment' onto any premises. In these instances, seven days' notice must be given to the occupier of the premises[3]. These circumstances also require that either the occupier's consent must be sought or entry must be made by way of a warrant[4]. These restrictive provisions do not apply in cases which are emergencies[5]. When warrants have been issued, seven days' notice is still required in relation to heavy equipment[6]. However, immediate entry under the warrant can occur when the site is temporarily or permanently unoccupied or where prior warning would defeat the purpose of the warrant[7].

1 Penalties are discussed at paras 12.77 and 12.81ff below.
2 Environment Act 1995, s 108(4)(a).
3 Environment Act 1995, s 108(6)(a): an Agency inspector who makes entry prior to the end of the required period of notice will be acting unlawfully: see, for example, *Stroud v Bradbury* [1952] 2 All ER 76.
4 Environment Act 1995, s 108(6)(b): warrants are discussed at para 12.79 below.
5 See para 12.92ff below.
6 Environment Act 1995, s 108(6) and Sch 19, para 2(3).
7 Environment Act 1995, Sch 18, para 2(2).

12.64 Authorised Agency staff entering premises are allowed to take with them other persons – provided that such persons are themselves duly authorised – and, if necessary, a police constable[1]. In addition, equipment or materials can be brought on to the premises. Once on the premises, for the purposes of ensuring compliance with the relevant legislation[2], the Agency is allowed to carry out experimental borings or other works and to install, keep and maintain monitoring equipment or other apparatus[3]. Data obtained by way of monitoring equipment or other apparatus[4] placed on a person's premises, with or without their consent is admissible in court[5].

1 Environment Act 1995, s 108(4)(b).
2 But not, it would seem, for other reasons such as ambient environmental monitoring.
3 EPA 1990, s 108(5).
4 A gas monitor or a hidden video camera perhaps.
5 Environment Act 1995, Sch 18, para 4(2).

12.65 The authorised person can also undertake a range of other actions as set down in s 108(4)[1]. Examinations and investigations can be undertaken as may be necessary[2]. This can include the taking of measurements, photographs[3] and samples of any articles or substances[4]. The latter samples can be of air, water and land[5] 'in, on or in the vicinity of' the premises in which the power of entry is exercised[6].

1 The actions listed can be supplemented by additional powers by way of regulations made by the Secretary of State: the Environment Act 1995, s 108(4)(m).
2 Environment Act 1995, s 108(4)(c).
3 Environment Act 1995, s 108(4)(e).
4 Environment Act 1995, s 108(4)(f).
5 The definition of 'land' is considered at para 7.45: for samples taken from land, see *Polymeric Treatments Ltd v Walsall Metropolitan Borough Council* [1993] Env LR 427.
6 Environment Act 1995, s 108(4)(f).

12.66   The Secretary of State has powers to make regulations which set out procedures to be followed when samples are to be taken[1]. However, none have yet been made.

1   Environment Act 1995, s 108(9).

12.67   An authorised person can direct that a premises or any part of it is left undisturbed[1]. Presumably this could be done verbally or by other means, such as fax. The premises or part of it can be required to be left untouched for 'as long as is reasonably necessary'.

1   Environment Act 1995, s 108(4)(d).

12.68   Where the authorised person considers that an article or substance 'appears to him' to have caused or is likely to cause pollution of the environment or harm to human health[1], it can be dismantled or subject to any process or test. However, it should not be damaged or destroyed unless that action is necessary[2]. Such articles and substances can be removed from the site 'for as long as necessary' for specified reasons. The latter include removal for the purposes of later examination[3], to ensure that it is not tampered with or when it is to be used in legal proceedings[4].

1   Note the words are 'pollution of the environment' not *'serious* pollution of the environment'. The term 'harm to human health' is constructed similarly. 'Pollution of the environment' and 'harm to human health' do not appear to be defined in the Environment Act 1995. However, a definition is contained in the EPA 1990 (s 29(3): see para 8.40ff). An identical power of entry to that contained in s 108(4)(d) of the Environment Act 1995 was contained in s 69(3)(g) of the EPA 1990. This continuity of statutory function may allow the interpretation of these terms in the context of the definition set down in the EPA 1990.
2   Environment Act 1995, s 108(4)(g).
3   Including dismantling or subjecting it to a process or test.
4   Including those relating to licence enforcement or variation notices: see Chapter 9. See also Environment Act 1995, s 108(4)(h).

12.69   Where articles or substances are to be dismantled or removed under this power, a person with responsibility for the premises can request to be present to witness the action being carried out[1]. Furthermore, the Agency officer is required to consult appropriate persons on the premises in order to ascertain the possible existence of any danger in the dismantling or removal operation[2].

1   Environment Act 1995, s 108(10).
2   Environment Act 1995, s 108(11).

12.70   The power to dismantle, remove and/or subject substances or articles to processes or tests should be distinguished from the normal powers of sampling under s 108(4)(e) of the Environment Act 1995. Normal sampling under those powers does not require the activity to be witnessed. However, if items are to be dismantled (etc) under the powers contained in s 108(4)(g), a refusal by an Agency official to allow the operation to be witnessed would appear to cause any test results to be inadmissible in any subsequent proceedings[1].

1   See *Laws v Keane* 1983 SLT 40 and also *Tudhope v Laws* [1982] SLT 85.

12.71   Authorised persons can also require records to be produced and this includes extracts from information stored on a computer[1]. The records covered are those which are required to be kept by any of the relevant legislation[2] and other records which relate to the matters under investigation. Agency staff are allowed to inspect these records and take copies of them. The Environment Act 1995 contains penalties for failures to accede to requests for copies of such records[3].

1 Environment Act 1995, s 108(4)(k).
2 For waste management, these will include records as required by a condition of waste management licences, special waste and transfrontier waste notifications, transfer notes, information to be kept at exempt sites, etc.
3 Environment Act 1995, s 110(2)(a); such records are admissible against any person: the Environment Act 1995, Sch 18, para 4(1).

12.72 There would appear to be two significant restrictions on the powers[1] to obtain records and require them to be copied. Should no copying facility be available, the power does not allow the record to be taken away for copying elsewhere[2]. But a hand-written copy could be made[3]. Secondly, the nature of a 'record' seems subject to a restrictive definition. For example, in *R v Tirado*[4] the Divisional Court had 'at least some hesitation' in declaring that a file of correspondence or its individual documents is embraced by the concept of a record. That a file of correspondence is not a record was subsequently confirmed by *R v Jones*[5]. However, it would seem that bills of lading or consignment notes constitute records[6], as do cash books or ledgers[7]. But reports culled from secondary sources[8] or which contain opinion[9] (an environmental consultant's report might be an example) are not records. This does not, of course, mean that these materials cannot be obtained at all. A notice served under s 71 of the EPA 1990[10] can be used for this purpose.

1 Environment Act 1995, s 108(4)(k).
2 See *Barge v British Gas Board* (1982) 81 LGR 53.
3 *Barge v British Gas Board* (1982) 81 LGR 53 at 58. In circumstances where no copier was available, it would also seem that information could be copied down by hand in a manner which clearly identifies the record. The record could subsequently be obtained in full by a statutory notice under s 71 of the EPA 1990 (see para 12.174ff).
4 *R v Tirado* (1974) 59 Cr App Rep 80 at 90; see also *R v Gwilliam* [1968] 1 WLR 1839; but in relation to *Gwilliam* see *R v Jones* [1978] 1 WLR 195 at 198G/H.
5 *R v Jones* [1978] 1 WLR 195 at 199A.
6 *R v Jones* [1978] 1 WLR 195 at 199C.
7 *R v Tirado* (1974) 59 Cr App Rep 80 at 90.
8 *H v Schering Chemicals* [1983] 1 WLR 143: scientific papers are not records
9 *Savings and Investment Bank Ltd v Gasco Investments (Netherlands) BV* [1984] 1 WLR 271 at 285A.
10 EPA 1990, s 71(2): discussed at para 12.174 below.

12.73 In order to assist with enquiries, an Agency official can require any person to help them[1]. The only limit to this assistance is that it must be necessary to enable the inspector to carry out any of the functions set out in s 108 of the Environment Act 1995.

1 'To afford him such facilities and assistance with respect to any matters or things within that person's control or in relation to which that person has responsibilities': Environment Act 1995, s 108(4)(l).

12.74 Where there is 'reasonable cause to believe'[1] that any person has information, the Agency may require that person to answer any questions thought fit to ask and to sign a declaration as to the truth of the answers provided[2]. However, care must be exercised in this respect. The Environment Act 1995 states that answers given to questioning under these powers are not admissible in legal proceedings in court against the person providing them[3].

1 See para 12.59 above.
2 Environment Act 1995, s 108(4)(j).
3 Environment Act 1995, s 108(12): see also Sch 18, para 4(1).

12.75 In *R v Hertfordshire County Council, ex p Green Environmental Industries*, Waller LJ considered a similarly worded power in s 69(8) of the EPA 1990[1] in the following terms[2]:

'. . . it is clear that Parliament considered what protection should be given and provided a complete embargo on the use in evidence of questions answered by an individual against that individual if s 69 powers were used. The thinking behind that may have been that Inspectors might have to act with great speed and get answers from individuals with great haste and that it was only fair in those circumstances to provide that degree of protection to those individuals.'

However, he also stated that this provision only gave protection to the individual who answered questions, and did not protect other persons or bodies corporate which might be affected[3]. Finally, this safeguard was held to relate only to oral answers given to the Agency, not to documentation[4].

1 Which was replaced by the Environment Act 1995, s 108(4)(j) (see Sch 22, para 85).
2 [1998] Env LR 153 at 170.
3 *R v Hertfordshire County Council, ex p Green Environmental Industries* [1998] Env LR 153 at 166; see also *Walkers Snack Foods Ltd v Coventry City Council* [1998] 3 All ER 163 but note that in the latter case, the defence in s 33(3) of the Food Safety Act 1990 is differently constructed.
4 *R v Hertfordshire County Council, ex p Green Environmental Industries* [1998] Env LR 153 at 166/167.

12.76 However, while Waller LJ's judgment has been of considerable assistance in squaring the powers of the Agency against such matters as rights of silence, potential difficulties remain. Section 108 of the Environment Act 1995 does not appear to provide a clear boundary between the use of this power and the 'normal' questioning of suspects. Accordingly, it may be possible to assume that, when suspects are formally cautioned, the provision in s 108 of the Environment Act 1995 which compels them to answer is not being invoked. It should therefore be apparent to suspects that they can remain silent[1]. The Agency will need to make it clear when the powers to assist on penalty of refusal are being invoked.

1 But inference of this silence can be taken into account in subsequent proceedings.

12.77 Non-compliance with these provisions is an offence under s 110 of the EPA 1990[1]. This is an offence entirely separate from that of obstruction[2]. As to whether an employee was in fact acting as a representative of an employer when providing oral or written statements, it is up to the employer to provide evidence to the contrary. Unless such evidence is available, persons with apparent seniority – such as a depot manager – are to be assumed to be acting on behalf of their employer[3].

1 Discussed at para 12.81 below.
2 Obstruction is dealt with at para 12.195 below.
3 *Edwards v Brookes (Milk) Ltd* [1963] 1 WLR 795; see also *London Borough of Barnet v Network Sites Ltd* [1997] JPL B90.

12.78 Oddly, there does not appear to be a section in the Environment Act 1995 which makes it an offence to provide false or misleading information to the Agency[1]. However, this is certainly an offence under the EPA 1990 (see para 12.209 below). In the absence of specific provisions in the Environment Act 1995, it is assumed that the provision of such information could be construed to constitute obstruction[2].

1 While s 112 and Sch 19 of the Environment Act 1995 cause the insertion of a series of amendments to other enactments, such as the Control of Pollution (Amendment) Act 1989 and Pt II of the EPA 1990, it does not pertain to the Environment Act 1995 itself.
2 See *Rice v Connolly* [1966] 2 QB 414 and para 12.202 below.

Warrants

12.79 It has been noted earlier that warrants can be used in circumstances where entry has been or is expected to be refused and where the use of force may be necessary to gain entry[1]. The procedures for the issuing of warrants are contained in Schedule 18 of the Environment Act 1995[2]. To obtain a warrant, an authorised officer of the Agency must present a justice of the peace[3] with sworn written information[4]. The information must show to the justice's satisfaction that there are 'reasonable grounds' for exercising the proposed action and that at least one of the following conditions has been satisfied[5]:

(a) that the expressed desire of an Agency officer to exercise a power[6] at a premises has been refused;
(b) that such a refusal is 'reasonably apprehended';
(c) that the premises are unoccupied;
(d) that the occupier is temporarily absent and that the case is of urgency[7];
(e) that an application for admission would defeat the objective of the proposed entry[8].

1 Environment Act 1995, s 108(7); however, the need to obtain a warrant is dispensed with in an emergency, with the term 'emergency' being defined in the Environment Act 1995, s 108(15): discussed at para 12.92.
2 Environment Act 1995, s 108(14).
3 In Scotland a sheriff or justice of the peace.
4 Environment Act 1995, Sch 18, para 2(1).
5 Environment Act 1995, Sch 18, para 2(2). See also *R v Marylebone Magistrates' Court and Metropolitan Police Comr, ex p Amorell Ltd (t/a Get Stuffed Ltd)* [1999] Env LR D11.
6 This can be any of the s 108 powers, not just those which relate to entry onto private premises.
7 Note that the term 'emergency' is not used: if an emergency occurred, a warrant is not necessary.
8 For example, because evidence may be destroyed or relevant operations cease.

12.80 The warrant designates a particular person from the Agency to be authorised to execute it[1]. Immediately prior to the use of the warrant, the person so designated must produce evidence of authorisation[2]. Once issued, the warrant continues to be in force until its purposes have been fulfilled[3].

1 Environment Act 1995, Sch 18, para 2(1).
2 Environment Act 1995, Sch 18, para 3: the occupier should be given the opportunity to inspect the warrant (*R v Longman* [1988] 1 WLR 619 at 627A/D).
3 Environment Act 1995, Sch 18, para 2(4).

Offences in respect of powers of entry

12.81 Many of the powers contained in s 108 of the Environment Act 1995 attract penalties. These offences are separate to those involving the obstruction of Agency officers[1]. They should also be viewed as distinct from the additional provisions contained in the EPA 1990 and associated regulations[2].

1 Environment Act 1995, s 110(1): see para 12.195ff below.
2 The latter usually contain their own offence provisions.

12.82 Section 110 of the Environment Act 1995 makes it an offence, 'without reasonable excuse'[1], to fail to comply with any of the requirements of s 108[2]. In addition, and no doubt overlapping with this provision, it is also an offence to fail or refuse to provide 'facilities or assistance or any information or to permit any inspection reasonably required by an authorised person in the execution of his powers or duties

...'[3]. Finally, persons who prevent others from answering questions put to them by Agency staff under s 108(4) also commit an offence[4].

1   See para 12.109.
2   Environment Act 1995, s 110(2)(a).
3   Environment Act 1995, s 110(2)(b).
4   Environment Act 1995, s 110(2)(c): note that obstruction (see para 12.195) is dealt with separately under s 110(1), which is distinct from s 110(2).

12.83   Persons found guilty of these offences are liable on summary conviction to a fine not exceeding level 5[1] on the standard scale[2]. Unlike the provisions in respect of obstruction[3] under s 110(1), the offence is not one which is indictable.

1   Currently £5,000.
2   Environment Act 1995, s 110(5).
3   See the Environment Act 1995, s 110(4).

Compensation when powers of entry are exercised

12.84   In certain circumstances, the Agency may be liable to pay compensation to any person who has sustained 'loss or damage' when the powers of entry[1] were exercised. Such a payment will only occur if an Agency officer failed to resecure an unoccupied premises against trespassers[2]. However, compensation is not payable when the loss or damage is attributable to the person who sustained it[3,4]. Disputes of compensation are to be settled by way of arbitration; in default of an agreement, they pass to the Secretary of State for determination[5].

1   Under Environment Act 1995, s 108(4)(a), (b) and (5) only.
2   Environment Act 1995, Sch 18, para 6(1): as noted earlier, the required level of security is only that which was encountered prior to entry of the premises (Sch 18, para 5).
3   Or where compensation provisions are contained in other enactments affecting the Agency: an example would be s 35A of the EPA 1990; see para 8.23ff.
4   Environment Act 1995, Sch 18, para 6(2).
5   Environment Act 1995, Sch 18, para 6(3).

Injunctions

12.85   Both the EPA 1990 and the Environment Act 1995 contain provisions which allow the Agency to obtain injunctions. In the past, injunctions have provided a useful way of causing the cessation of waste management activities by the more stubborn regular offender. For example, Lancashire County Council successfully applied for an injunction against a local skip vehicle operator. The continuation of the operator's illegal activities resulted in him receiving a prison sentence of three months for contempt of court[1]. When the responsibilities for waste regulation rested with the local authorities, injunctions were obtained under s 222 of the Local Government Act 1972.

1   See Burns S (1993) 'High Court Injunctions: An Alternative for WRAs' *Wastes Management*, Feb 1993, pp 12–13.

12.86   Since the enactment of the Environment Act 1995, the Agency is given injunctive powers. However, they appear to be more restrictive than was the case hitherto with s 222 of the Local Government Act 1972. Injunctive powers stem from s 38(13)[1] and s 42(6A)[2] of the EPA 1990 and, possibly, s 37(1) of the Environment Act 1995.

1   As amended by the Environment Act 1995, Sch 22, para 72(2).
2   As amended by the Environment Act 1995, Sch 22, para 76(7).

12.87   The EPA 1990 itself only allows injunctions in respect of sites subject to waste management licences[1]. It does not permit injunctions to be sought in the arena where they are most needed – at unlicensed facilities. However, the powers in the Environment Act 1995 may help to plug this gap.

1   EPA 1990, s 38(13) as amended by the Environment Act 1995, s 120 and Sch 22, para 72(2); s 42(6A) as amended by the Environment Act 1995, s 120, Sch 22, para 76(7): see paras 9.36 and 9.57.

12.88   Under s 38 of the EPA 1990, the Agency can suspend a waste management licence on the grounds that the site is no longer managed by a technically competent person or that serious pollution of the environment or harm to human health is threatened by the continuation of waste disposal activities[1]. In order to mitigate the environmental problems which caused the licence to be suspended, the Agency can require specified works to be undertaken[2] by way of a notice[3]. Failure to comply with such a requirement is an offence under s 38(10) or (11) of the EPA 1990.

1   EPA 1990, s 38(6): see para 9.40.
2   EPA 1990, s 38(9): see para 9.53.
3   EPA 1990, s 38(12).

12.89   The injunctive provisions relate to the continued failure of the licence holder to comply with the notice. Section 38(13) of the EPA 1990 allows the Agency to take proceedings in the High Court[1] where the Agency is of the opinion that proceedings for an offence under s 38(10) or (11) of the EPA 1990 'would afford an ineffectual remedy' against the person.

1   In Scotland, 'any court of competent jurisdiction'.

12.90   Section 42 of the EPA 1990 allows the Agency to serve a notice on the licensee requiring the compliance with one or more conditions[1]. Non-compliance with the notice can cause the licence to be revoked – either fully or partially – or suspended[2]. Should this route prove an effectual remedy, the Agency can apply to the High Court in a manner similar to that described above in respect of s 38 of the EPA 1990[3].

1   EPA 1990, s 42(5)(a) as amended by the Environment Act 1995, s 120, Sch 22, para 76(5): see para 9.26.
2   EPA 1990, s 42(6).
3   EPA 1990, s 42(6A) as amended by the Environment Act 1995, s 120, Sch 22, para 76(7).

12.91   The question of the Agency obtaining injunctions in respect of activities at sites not subject to waste management licences is, unfortunately, less than clear. Section 37(1) of the Environment Act 1995 allows the Agency to:

'. . . do anything which, in its opinion, is calculated to facilitate, or is conducive or incidental to, the carrying on of its functions . . .'

It would seem that the obtaining of an injunction would be within the scope of this requirement. However, oddly, the final line of s 37(1) states that the Agency 'may institute criminal proceedings in England and Wales'. Although this is a general power to instigate proceedings, what should be noted is that there is no reference to civil proceedings, under which injunctions are sought. Whether the reference only to criminal proceedings affects the breadth of the earlier requirements of s 37(1) is not clear. But it seems difficult to imagine that Parliament would have wished to fetter the Agency's powers with a provision which restricted injunctions to only licensed facilities. However, the drafting would suggest that some doubt may exist over whether s 37 allows the Agency to obtain injunctions under this provision. Indeed, the amendments made to the EPA 1990 in respect of injunctions which relate to licensed sites would seem to have little purpose if there is a general injunctive power contained in s 37 of the Environment Act 1995.

POWERS TO DEAL WITH EMERGENCIES OR OTHER DANGERS

Emergency powers of entry

12.92 Section 108 of the Environment Act 1995 allows the Agency to gain access to a premises[1] at any time in the case of an 'emergency'. If necessary, entry can be made by force[2]. There is also no need to obtain a warrant[3].

1 Defined in the Environment Act 1995, s 108(15): see para 12.62 above.
2 Environment Act 1995, s 108(4)(a).
3 Environment Act 1995, s 108(6) and (7).

12.93 For the purposes of this provision, the Environment Act 1995 provides a definition of circumstances which constitute an 'emergency'[1]:

'. . . a case in which it appears to the authorised person in question –

(a) that there is an immediate risk of serious pollution of the environment or serious harm to human health, or
(b) that circumstances exist which are likely to endanger life or health, and that immediate entry to any premises is necessary to verify the existence of that risk or those circumstances or to effect a remedy'[2].

It should be noted that this provision requires that there must be a risk of 'serious' pollution of the environment or 'serious' harm to health.

1 Environment Act 1995, s 108(15).
2 The term 'emergency' is also considered in other contexts at para 7.154.

12.94 Finally, it should be noted that the provision in the Environment Act 1995 allowing emergency access refers to 'an immediate risk' of serious pollution of the environment (etc) occurring. The concept of risk has been judicially considered in the case of *R v Board of Trustees of the Science Museum*[1]. It was held that the word 'risk' conveys the idea of a possibility of danger and did not require the existence of actual danger[2].

1 *R v Board of Trustees of the Science Museum* [1993] 3 All ER 853.
2 [1993] 3 All ER 853 at 858J/859A.

Emergency powers to carry out works at licensed facilities

12.95 In the case of an emergency, s 42 of the EPA 1990 allows an authorised person to carry out works on the land or on plant or equipment 'to which the licence relates'[1]. Where the Agency has incurred expenditure in the undertaking of this task, it can be recovered[2]. If the amount of expenditure is contested, the burden of proof is upon the licensee to show that either there was, in fact, no emergency or that the expenditure[3] was unnecessary.

1 EPA 1990, s 42(3).
2 EPA 1990, s 42(4) as amended by the Environment Act 1995, s 120(1) and Sch 22, para 76(3).
3 Or part of it.

12.96   Unlike the Environment Act 1995, the EPA 1990 does not define the term 'emergency' in the context of s 42[1]. But it must relate to the need for the site not to cause pollution to the environment, harm to human health, or serious detriment to the amenity of locality[2]. Alternatively, the emergency must result from the operator's non-compliance with the waste management licence's conditions[3]. It should be noted that, in contrast to the Agency's general powers under the Environment Act 1995, this provision does not require these matters to be 'serious' before the powers can be invoked.

1   And hence will retain its ordinary meaning: see para 7.154.
2   EPA 1990, s 42(1) and (3): these terms are discussed at para 8.40ff.
3   EPA 1990, s 42(1) and (3): in practice it would seem hard to envisage circumstances where non-compliance with the licence conditions created an emergency which was not also likely to cause pollution of the environment or harm to human health (etc).

12.97   As a further contrast to the Environment Act 1995[1] – under which there are penalties separate to the general offence of obstruction for persons who fail to undertake actions required by Agency staff utilising their powers of entry – failing to permit access in the circumstances envisaged by the EPA 1990 can only be dealt with as obstruction[2].

1   See the Environment Act 1995, s 110(2).
2   Under the Environment Act 1995, s 110(1): obstruction is discussed at para 12.195.

Powers of seizure of goods and articles

12.98   The Environment Act 1995 contains additional powers which relate to instances where, on exercising the normal powers of entry, substances or articles are discovered which themselves may give rise to imminent danger. As these powers emanate from the Environment Act 1995, they relate to any type of land, including land unconnected with waste management activities. Should an inspector have 'reasonable cause to believe[1] that, in the circumstances in which he finds it' the article or substance 'is a cause of imminent danger of serious pollution of the environment or serious harm to human health' that person can seize it or otherwise cause it to be rendered harmless[2]. If necessary the substance or object can be destroyed.

1   See para 12.60.
2   Environment Act 1995, s 109(1).

12.99   There are three restrictions upon the utility of these powers, and hence the Agency may wish to invoke some of the other provisions in the EPA 1990 at first instance. Firstly, the Agency inspector must have reasonable cause to believe[1] that the substance or object is dangerous. Secondly, the substance or object must already constitute a danger. The sub-section does not address the *possibility* of a danger and hence excludes circumstances which involve risks. Finally, pollution or harm to human health must not only be manifest but must be 'serious' for the powers to be invoked.

1   See para 12.60.

12.100   Once a substance or object has been seized or rendered harmless under these powers, the Agency officer must prepare a written report setting down the circumstances in which the substance or object was seized[1]. It must be signed and a copy given to the 'responsible person' at the premises from which the seizure took place. If the responsible person is different from the owner of the substance or object, then the owner must also be provided with the report. If the owner cannot be found, the second copy is passed to the person responsible for the premises.

1   Environment Act 1995, s 109(2).

AGENCY POWERS TO REMOVE WASTE OR MITIGATE ITS EFFECTS

12.101   The Agency[1] has range of powers under s 59 of the EPA 1990 in relation to the unauthorised deposit of controlled waste. Notices can be used to cause the removal or elimination of the effects of the deposited waste[2]. However, in respect of immediate environmental problems, this provision has the considerable disadvantage of an appeal mechanism. This allows the notice to be held in abeyance in the appeal period. The Agency can also enter land and undertake the required actions itself. Depending upon the circumstances, any costs can be recovered by the Agency. Each of these provisions will be discussed in turn below.

1   And the waste collection authorities.
2   EPA 1990, s 59(1).

12.102   Finally, the Agency has supplementary powers in relation to transfrontier waste shipments. Like the s 59 powers, the primary tool is a system of statutory notices. Depending upon the circumstances, the notice can require the return of waste consigned out of the UK and/or its disposal or recovery.

Statutory notices in respect of waste unlawfully deposited

12.103   The notice to effect the removal of waste or the reduction of its consequences must be served in respect of any land[1] on or in which waste has been 'deposited'[2] in contravention of s 33(1)[3]. The EPA 1990 restricts the notice to 'occupiers'[4] of land: such a notice cannot be used on other parties who undertook the activity of depositing waste[5]. To be valid, the notice must also apply to occupiers of land who have deposited the waste or have knowingly caused or knowingly permitted its deposit[6].

1   Defined in the EPA 1990, s 29(8): see para 7.45.
2   See para 7.16
3   EPA 1990, s 59(1): circumstances when s 33(1) is contravened will be returned to.
4   The nature of an 'occupier' is considered below.
5   This is somewhat of a contrast to the powers in Part IIA of the EPA 1990 (as amended by the Environment Act 1995, s 57), where remediation notices can be addressed to any person who 'caused or knowingly permitted' substances to result in land contamination (EPA 1990, ss 78E and 78F).
6   EPA 1990, s 59(3).

12.104   The notice can require the occupier to remove the waste within a specified time period but not less than 21 days from date of service[1]. Alternatively, the notice can require the occupier 'to take ... specified steps with a view to eliminating or reducing the consequences of the deposit of the waste'[2]. The recipient can be required to both reduce the consequences of the waste and remove it if necessary. To be valid, the notice must include information which sets out the manner by which an appeal is to be made, along with the requisite appeal time period[3].

1   EPA 1990, s 59(1)(a).
2   EPA 1990, s 59(1)(b).
3   EPA 1990, s 73(4).

12.105   It should be noted that the wording of the EPA 1990 appears to allow a notice to require the immediate reduction or elimination of the consequences of the waste: the requirement in respect of 21-day period only relates to the separate provision requiring waste to be removed[1]. Reducing or eliminating the consequences of the waste, for example, may involve the covering or capping of waste where its removal is impractical or undesirable. It may even stretch to requiring environmental monitoring to be undertaken in the locality of the unauthorised waste. Should no adverse effects be discovered by such monitoring, it may be considered preferable to leave the waste where it is. Alternatively, monitoring may detect leachate or landfill gas being produced by biodegradation, and hence the occupier could then be required to remove the waste. These requirements would, of course, all need to be set down in the notice itself.

1   Ie the EPA 1990, s 59(1)(a), not s 59(1)(b).

12.106   The recipient of the notice is allowed 21 days from the date of service in which to appeal to a magistrates' court[1]. At appeal, the notice can be quashed on two grounds[2]. The first is when the court is satisfied that the appellant did not deposit, knowingly cause or knowingly permit[3] the deposit of the waste[4]. The second ground on which to quash the notice is that it is subject to a material defect[5]. The court is also allowed to modify the notice's requirements, for example, by extending the compliance deadlines set down in it[6]. Either party can appeal the magistrates' decision to the Crown Court[7].

1   Sheriff's court in Scotland: the EPA 1990, s 59(2): precisely how this squares with s 59(1)(b)'s requirement which appears to permit the notice to instigate an immediate reduction or elimination of the consequences of the waste is not clear.
2   EPA 1990, s 59(3).
3   The definition of these terms is discussed in Chapter 7.
4   EPA 1990, s 59(3)(a).
5   EPA 1990, s 59(3)(b): it should be noted that the additional requirements in respect of contents of notices, as contained in s 73(4) of the EPA 1990, are easily overlooked.
6   EPA 1990, s 59(4).
7   EPA 1990, s 73(1): Court of Session in Scotland: the EPA 1990, s 73(2).

12.107   Where an appeal has been lodged either in respect of the original notice or in relation to the magistrates' court's decision, the requirements of the notice are held in abeyance pending the subsequent hearing[1].

1   EPA 1990, s 59(4) and s 73(3).

12.108   Notices served under EPA 1990, s 59(1) have effect only in relation to occupiers – not to other land users[1]. Often an occupier of land will be the actual owner of it. However, in *Southern Water Authority v Nature Conservancy Council*[2], it was held that the expression 'occupier' in relation to ss 28 and 29 of the Wildlife and Countryside Act 1981 encompasses[3]:

'... someone who, although lacking the title of an owner, nevertheless stands in such a comprehensive and stable relationship with the land as to be, in company with the actual owner, someone to whom the mechanisms [of the relevant sections of the 1981 Act] can sensibly be made to apply.'

However, care must be taken, given an extensive caveat expressed by Lord Mustill in parallel to the above definition. It was held that the word 'occupier' in any statute draws its meaning from the purpose of the statute and its context[4] and that definitions extracted from judgments relating to one particular enactment will not necessarily apply to other, unconnected, legislation. However, the above definition is a useful starting point, and given Lord Mustill's observations about definitions being statute- and context-specific, it should be observed that the definition set down in *Southern Water Authority* may be deliberately narrow as a consequence of the wording and provisions of the Wildlife and Countryside Act 1981[5]. This would suggest that, for the purposes of the EPA 1990, a somewhat broader approach may be appropriate. This may extend the term 'occupier' to embrace a person who takes over some unused land for waste disposal purposes and secures the gates so that that person has exclusive access to the land[6]. However, it does seem certain that someone who enters land for the purposes of transitory fly-tipping cannot be held to be in occupation of it[7].

1   In *Wheat v E Lacon & Co Ltd* [1966] 1 All ER 582 at 594b and 595f it was noted that more than one person can be an occupier and that occupiers' responsibilities can be shared; see also *Jackson v Hall* [1980] 1 All ER 177 at 185B.
2   [1992] 3 All ER 481.
3   [1992] 3 All ER 481 at 488D.
4   [1992] 3 All ER 481 at 487J: see also *Madrassa Anjuman Islamia of Kholwad v Johannesburg Municipal Council* [1922] 1 AC 500 at 504; *Wheat v E Lacon & Co Ltd* [1966] 1 All ER 582 at 593E and 596I; *H & N Emanuel Ltd v Greater London Council* [1971] 2 All ER 835 at 839F; *R v Tao* [1976] 3 All ER 65 at 67D/G. In certain cases, receivers have been held to be acting as occupiers: see *Meigh v Wickenden* [1942] 2 KB 160 and *Lord Advocate v Aero Technologies Ltd* 1991 SLT 134.
5   The provisions in the Act in respect of compliance notices juxtapose the words 'owner and occupier': see *Southern Water Authority* [1992] 3 All ER 481 per Lord Mustill at 488C/D. By contrast, s 59 of the EPA 1990 refers solely to 'occupiers'.
6   This type of circumstance would appear to satisfy the two tests set down by Lord Justice Edmund Davies in *Stevens v Bromley London Borough Council* [1972] 1 All ER 712 at 720G, that occupation is a matter of (a) the degree of control a person exercises over a piece of land and (b) the duration of that control (see also *R v St Pancras Assessment Committee* (1877) 2 QBD 581 at 588/589). In *Woodcock v South Western Electricity Board* [1975] 2 All ER 545 squatters were not held to be 'occupiers' under the Electric Lighting (Clauses) Act 1899, which required all occupiers to be supplied with electricity. However, Mr Justice Dunn makes clear that this finding is specific only to the circumstances of this Act (at 549A/B) and notes that, for example, squatters as occupiers are required to pay rates. See also *In Re Briant Colour Printing Co* [1977] 1 WLR 942.
7   See Lord Mustill in *Southern Water Authority* [1992] 3 All ER 481 at 489C.

12.109   A contravention of the notice under s 59 of the EPA 1990 'without reasonable excuse' will result in a fine, on summary conviction, of up to level 5 on the standard scale[1]. The offence is not indictable. The nature of what constitutes a 'reasonable excuse' appears to be a question of fact, not law[2]. Certainly, ignorance of the law does not constitute a reasonable excuse[3] nor does the right of suspects not to provide information which incriminates themselves[4]. In *Saddleworth UDC v Aggregate and Sand Ltd*[5] the lack of availability of funds to undertake specified works was not a reasonable excuse. However, in *Saddleworth*, Lord Parker of Waddington left open the question of whether the reliance upon the erroneous advice of experts, such as consultants, does or does not pass as a reasonable excuse[6]. This will be dependent on the '. . . nature of the advice given, the circumstances in which it is given and all the other facts of the case [which] have . . . to be taken into account . . .'[7].

1   EPA 1990, s 59(5): currently £5,000.
2   *Leck v Epsom RDC* [1922] All ER Rep 784.
3   *Aldridge v Warwickshire Coal Co Ltd* [1925] 133 LT 439; *R v Reid* [1973] 3 All ER 1020 at 1289 B/E.
4   *R v Hertfordshire County Council, ex p Green Environmental Industries* [1998] Env LR 153 at 169; however, self-incriminatory material may not be admissible in proceedings (see para 12.48ff).
5   (1970) 69 LGR 103; see also *Greenwich London Borough Council v Millcroft Construction Ltd* (1986) 150 JP 645; *R v Reid* [1973] 1 WLR 1283.
6   *Saddleworth UDC v Aggregate and Sand Ltd* (1970) 69 LGR 103 at 107.
7   *Walkers Snack Foods Ltd v Coventry City Council* [1998] 3 All ER 163 at 174B.

12.110   In *A Lambert Flat Management Ltd v Lomas*[1], it was held that the phrase 'without reasonable excuse' was designed to cover any special circumstances of the recipient of a notice, such as if the person could not comply due to illness or being away from his property[2]. It is also important to distinguish between the nature of a reasonable excuse and circumstances which are, in fact, mitigating factors which should be considered at the time of sentencing[3].

1   [1981] 1 WLR 898.
2   See *Lambert Flat* at 904E/F and H, 907C and D. *Lambert Flat* also held that the appropriate forum for a challenge to the validity of a noise abatement notice served under s 58 of the Control of Pollution Act 1974 was within the appeal period set down in the statute. Such a challenge did not fall within scope of the phrase 'without reasonable excuse'. For the principles of a collateral challenge of such a notice see, for example, *Francis v Yiewsley and West Drayton UDC* [1957] 3 All ER 529; the joined cases of *R v Crown Court at Reading, ex p Hutchinson* and *R v Devizes Justices, ex p Lee* [1988] 1 All ER 333; and *R v Ettrick Trout Co Ltd and Baxter* [1994] Env LR 165.
3   See *Wellingborough District Council v Gordon* (1990) 155 JP 494.

12.111   While it is up to a defendant to present the nature of the excuse to the court[1], the burden of proving that an accused person did not have a reasonable excuse is upon the prosecution. Defendants are not required to provide conclusive proof that their explanation of the events falls within the concept of a 'reasonable excuse'[2]. They must set out the nature of the excuse to the Court and it is left to the prosecution to displace it.

1   *Aldridge v Warwickshire Coal Co Ltd* (1925) 133 LT 439 at 442.
2   *R v Clarke* [1969] 2 All ER 1008 at 1011A/C; see also *R v Hunt* [1987] AC 352 and *Polychonakis v Richards and Jerrom Ltd* [1998] Env LR 346.

12.112   Should the requirements of the notice still not be met after an initial conviction under s 59, the EPA 1990 presents the Agency with two options. The Agency can undertake the work itself and attempt to recover the cost from the occupier[1]. Alternatively, it can return to the court and request that further penalties are imposed. The former action of recovering costs is discussed separately later[2]. For the option for the Agency to return to the court, the Act allows for a further fine to be levied, which is set at a current maximum of £500 per day[3].

1   EPA 1990, s 59(6).
2   See para 12.115ff below.
3   Defined in s 59(5) of the EPA 1990 as 1/10th of a level 5 fine per day; the level 5 fine is currently £5,000.

12.113   When a fine such as this is to be calculated, certain rules must be taken into account. Firstly, as the offence can only be dealt with by way of summary trial[1], it is under the usual time limits which apply to the magistrates' courts. Hence the magistrates are prevented from hearing a case which involves any information relating to events beyond the requisite time limit of six months[2]. The ability to fine for continuing non-compliance should be construed as allowing a magistrates' court to impose a fine of up to £500 per day for every day on which an offence triable by the court was committed. A continuing offence will be committed the day after conviction, but since offences are triable by magistrates within six months, in practice this period places a cap on the maximum fine that can be imposed[3]. Secondly, the time during which a daily fine can be levied continues up to the day of the actual trial, rather than to the day the information was laid or served[4]. Alternatively, the period over which the daily fine builds up is between the first date of the offence to its final day, where a notice is complied with prior to trial.

1   EPA 1990, s 59(5).
2   Magistrates Courts Act 1980, s 127(1).
3   *R v Chertsey Justices, ex p Franks* [1961] 1 All ER 825 at 828I/829A: see also *R v Slade, ex p Saunders* [1895] 2 QB 247.
4   *Grice v Needs* [1979] 3 All ER 501.

12.114   One further point should be made in respect of s 59 notices. The requirements of a notice only relate to persons who deposit waste or knowingly cause or knowingly permit its deposit. While these provisions are worded to protect occupiers who are innocent of the disposal activities and who suffer from the actions of third parties, this protection is not absolute. For example, it would seem that a s 59 notice could be served on a person whose land was subject to third party fly-tipping in certain circumstances, even if the individual had taken no action to encourage the perpetrators. An example might be when an occupier has manifestly failed to prevent further unauthorised activities by improving site security. In these circumstances, if the matter was brought to the occupier's attention by the Agency, the occupier subsequently may be held to be in contravention of s 33(1) of the EPA 1990 if inaction allows the continuation of third party tipping activities[1] – the occupier could be held to be 'knowingly permitting' the deposit. Knowingly permitting is discussed extensively in Chapter 7, but briefly, a person who does nothing when in a position to forbid an action has been held to permit it[2]. This matter may be of considerable interest to persons in possession of empty buildings or unused land, such as land agents, mortgagees or receivers[3].

1 Note also that s 59 only requires that s 33(1) is contravened, it does not make reference to the statutory defences contained in s 33(7). Accordingly, although it may be possible that a person involved in a contravention of s 33(1) might be covered by a statutory defence, this would appear irrelevant in respect of s 59 of the EPA 1990. All s 59 requires is for s 33(1) to be contravened, not for that contravention to be mitigated by s 33(7).
2 See *Goodbarne v Buck* [1940] 1 All ER 613 and, for example, *Nuttall v Vehicle Inspectorate* [1999] 1 WLR 629: discussed at para 7.80ff.
3 'For my part I am inclined to think that in certain circumstances a man may permit the continuance of an act if he can prevent it by taking legal proceedings and refrains from doing so': *Berton v Alliance Economic Investment Co* [1922] 1 KB 742 at 761. However, this matter would be primarily a function of whether there is a possibility that proceedings would be successful: *Barton v Reed* [1932] 1 Ch 362; see also *Atkin v Rose* [1923] 1 Ch 522.

Other powers in respect of waste unlawfully deposited

12.115   While notices can be served on occupiers of land under s 59 of the EPA 1990, that section also permits the Agency to enter land and undertake the required work itself. If an occupier has not complied with a valid s 59 notice, the Agency may decide to fulfil the requirements of the notice. It is then permitted to recover any expenses 'reasonably incurred' from the occupier[1].

1 EPA 1990, s 59(6). Note that there is no facility to attach a statutory charge on the land, unlike the case with contaminated land and Part IIA of the EPA 1990: see the EPA 1990, s 78P (as amended by the Environment Act 1995, s 57).

12.116   Alternatively, s 59 allows the Agency to remove waste or reduce its consequences immediately and without serving notice[1]. However, this type of action is restricted to instances where it is necessary:

'... in order to remove or prevent pollution of land, water or air or harm to human health ...'[2].

If the occupier deposited or knowingly caused or knowingly permitted the deposit of the waste, that person subsequently can be required to reimburse the Agency for the costs involved in removing the waste, reducing its consequences and also its final disposal[3].

1 EPA 1990, s 59(7).
2 EPA 1990, s 59(7)(a): note that the usual phrase contained in Part II of the EPA 1990, concerning 'pollution of the environment', is not used in this sub-section. Instead 'pollution of land, water or air' is used. Unlike 'pollution of the environment', there is no definition of 'pollution' in the manner set down in s 59. It will therefore hold its ordinary meaning.

3   EPA 1990, s 59(8)(a): it should be noted that, in contrast to s 59(8), the requirement to dispose of the
     waste does not feature in relation to the statutory notices issued under s 59(1) and which were
     discussed at para 12.103ff above.

12.117   It is often the case that a person in occupation of land has not deposited the
waste, nor knowingly caused or knowingly permitted its deposit[1]. In other instances,
there may be no occupier of the land. Section 59(7)(b) and (c) of the EPA 1990 allows
the Agency to deal directly with the responsible parties[2]. The Agency can remove the
waste and/or reduce its consequences and then recover its costs from the person who
'deposited' the waste or 'knowingly caused or knowingly permitted'[3] its deposit[4].

1   But see *H & N Emanuel Ltd v Greater London Council* [1971] 2 All ER 835, where a landowner, as
     occupier, was held responsible for contractors when the latter caused a fire which spread onto other
     persons' property. However, also note Lord Mustill's warning about the pitfalls of translating the
     definition of occupier from one statute to another in *Southern Water Authority*: see para 12.108
     above.
2   This can, of course, be as an adjunct to any prosecution under s 33 of the EPA 1990: see Chapter 7.
3   See paras 7.16 and 7.52ff.
4   EPA 1990, s 59(8)(b).

12.118   This provision relates to any waste, not just that which may result in pollution of the environment or harm to human health[1]. Like the rest of s 59, it affects land
subject to waste management licences as well as other land. Again, the person faced
with the requirement to reimburse the Agency is not required to pay any costs which
are shown to have been incurred unnecessarily[2].

1   Section 59(7)(a), (b) and (c) of the EPA 1990 are separated by the word 'or'.
2   EPA 1990, s 59(8).

12.119   There is a curious contrast in the manner in which s 59 of the EPA 1990
impinges upon different types of offenders. In respect of occupiers of land, the cost of
removing the waste can be recovered only in relation to waste which causes pollution
or harm to human health[1]. But where the occupier is innocent or where there is no
occupier, the persons who deposited the waste or knowingly caused or knowingly
permitted its deposit can be required to pay the cost of its removal. In this instance,
there is no caveat which requires that costs of removal can be recovered only where
pollution or harm to human health may occur[2]. Accordingly, if an occupier is responsible for the waste being deposited *and* the deposit is not likely to cause pollution or
harm to human health, the notice route through s 59(1) is the only method of restitu-
tion. While the Agency can undertake the work itself, it would seem that it cannot get
the occupier to pay for it directly.

1   EPA 1990, s 59(7)(a).
2   EPA 1990, s 59(7)(b) and (c).

Scope of application of notices under s 59 of the EPA 1990

12.120   In all cases, s 59 applies only where the deposit has been made 'in contravention of s 33(1)' of the EPA 1990. It will be apparent from the discussion in Chapter
7 that certain activities are excluded from the ambit of s 33(1) by way of regulations
made under s 33(2) and (3)[1]. In certain other instances, activities may only be partially
excluded from some elements of s 33. These subtleties require that care is taken in
analysing the application of the Agency's powers under s 59 in certain circumstances.
These problems become particularly acute where wastes have been deposited by
householders on their property or at sites subject to exclusions or exemptions from
waste management licences. In addition, the wording of s 59 of the EPA 1990 may

present problems in effecting the removal of waste at sites subject to waste management licences.

1   See para 7.04 and Chapters 10 and 11.

Domestic properties

12.121   The wording of both s 59(1) and s 33(2) of the EPA 1990 ensures that s 59 does not apply where 'household waste' has been deposited in the curtilage of a domestic property by the occupier[1]. Hence the Agency can neither issue a notice to effect actions such as having the waste removed nor use s 59 to step in and cause the material to be removed. However, this restriction only applies specifically to 'household waste'[2] and this term has a constrained meaning in relation to s 33 of the EPA 1990[3]. 'Household waste' in this context excludes mineral oil or grease, asbestos and clinical waste generated at domestic properties[4]. These are always classified as industrial wastes under the Controlled Waste Regulations 1992. Similarly, any construction and demolition waste arising in these circumstances is also industrial waste, not 'household waste'[5]. Hence s 59 notices can effect the removal of waste such as asbestos roofing sheeting and rubble dumped by the more anti-social householder on their own land.

1   Or where the deposit is knowingly caused or knowingly permitted by the occupier.
2   EPA 1990, s 33(2).
3   See paras 7.04 and 2.200ff.
4   See SI 1992/588, reg 3(1) and para 2.205ff.
5   See SI 1992/588, reg 5(2)(a) and para 2.202.

Facilities subject to integrated pollution control authorisations

12.122   A second area of potential difficulty concerns facilities which are excluded from the need to possess a waste management licence. Such exclusions stem from s 33(3) of the EPA 1990 and reg 16 of the Waste Management Licensing Regulations 1994[1]. Generally, facilities excluded by these provisions will be waste management operations subject to Part I of the EPA 1990 and the Integrated Pollution Control (IPC) regime[2]. Hazardous waste incinerators and solvent recovery plants are examples[3].

1   SI 1994/1056: see para 10.13.
2   SI 1994/1056, reg 16(1)(a) as amended by SI 1995/288, reg 3(4).
3   This only applies to Part A processes; facilities subject to authorisations under Part B are not subject to this difficulty. In this case, s 59 of the EPA 1990 applies; such plants are only partially excluded from the provisions of s 33 in respect of their air emissions (see SI 1994/1056, reg 16(1)(b)).

12.123   In relation to the possible application of s 59 notices to these types of activity, the wording of reg 16 of the Waste Management Licensing Regulations 1994 must be carefully considered. On the one hand, reg 16(1) states that s 33(1) of the EPA 1990 is not to apply to the activities specified[1]. However, reg 16(2) overrules this provision 'insofar as the activity involves the final disposal of waste by deposit in or on land'. This would suggest that, for example, a s 59 notice can be validly served at an IPC facility where 'final disposal' of some inappropriate controlled waste has occurred. Similarly, the Agency appears to have the right under s 59 to enter these premises, cause the clean-up of the waste[2], and attempt to recoup the cost from those responsible. However, the temporary storage of wastes in an unsafe manner on an IPC site could not be addressed by these powers. In the latter circumstances, there is no 'final disposal' and hence the exclusion under reg 16(1) of the Waste Management Licensing Regulations 1994 applies.

1   See also the EPA 1990, s 28, as amended by the Environment Act 1990, Sch 22, para 61(1).
2   Ie remove it and/or reduce its consequences.

Sites subject to exemptions

12.124   The third problematic area concerns the application of s 59 of the EPA 1990 to sites subject to exemption from waste management licences[1]. Under reg 17(1) of the Waste Management Licensing Regulations 1994, these sites are excluded from s 33(1)(a) and (b) of the EPA 1990, but not from s 33(1)(c). Accordingly, there is only a partial exclusion from s 33. Furthermore, the exclusion from s 33(1)(a) and (b) only holds while a particular facility is operated within the terms of the exemption as set down in reg 17 and Schedule 3 to the Waste Management Licensing Regulations 1994[2].

1   Under SI 1994/1056, reg 17: see Chapters 10 and 11.
2   See para 10.33.

12.125   This means that the s 59 powers are applicable to this type of site when it is operated outside the terms of the exemption. This is because the usual requirements of s 33(1)(a) and (b) of the EPA 1990 in respect of the need to possess a waste management licence are only lifted when the terms of the particular exemption are complied with. Therefore, s 33(1) applies as soon as the terms of the exemption are breached. Once that section has application, the s 59 powers can be invoked as necessary. Similarly, because exempt facilities are not excluded from s 33(1)(c), as soon as pollution of the environment or harm to human health is 'likely to' arise, the Agency can use its s 59 powers to address the problem.

Sites subject to waste management licences

12.126   It has been noted that s 59 of the EPA 1990 has application to deposits of waste on land, including at sites subject to waste management licences. The application of s 59 to licensed sites would mean that the Agency could require the removal of wastes unlawfully accepted at a landfill or treatment facility. However, s 59 only relates to waste which is deposited in 'contravention of s 33(1)' of the EPA 1990. The nature of s 33(1) is extensively described in Chapter 7. It should be noted that s 59 does not also refer to waste deposited in contravention with s 33(6)[1]: in other words it does not explicitly make reference to waste deposited in breach of the conditions of the waste management licence. At first reading, it might appear possible to argue that s 59 does not have application where offences under s 33(6) are concerned, but there are number of reasons to suggest that this approach is incorrect.

1   See para 7.08.

12.127   As is noted in Chapter 7[1], there is a somewhat confusing overlap between s 33(1) and s 33(6) of the EPA 1990, in that s 33(1)(a) and (b) require that waste is deposited, kept, treated or disposed of at licensed waste management facilities 'in accordance with the licence'. Clearly, waste deposited not 'in accordance with the licence' contravenes s 33(1) as much as s 33(6). For that reason, it appears that an explicit cross-reference to s 33(6) is not required. The focusing of s 59 to s 33(1) at the expense of s 33(6) does not mean that a notice can be challenged as materially defective when waste is deposited in breach of a condition of a waste management licence.

1   See para 7.103ff.

Supplementary powers in respect of transfrontier waste shipments

12.128   The Transfrontier Shipment of Waste Regulations 1994[1] contain a series of powers which enable the Agency to meet specified obligations under EC Regulation

259/93[2]. The Regulations and Regulation 259/93 are fully explained in Chapter 5 but, briefly, the Agency is granted powers to issue notices in respect of cross-border shipments which have got into difficulties and need to be returned to Britain or where notifiers[3] or consignees have been responsible for 'illegal traffic' under the Regulation. Illegal traffic includes[4] instances where, for example, waste is imported or exported without the required notification document and/or without the required approvals from the member states covering the notifier, consignee and any states of transit.

1 SI 1994/1137, regs 8 and 9.
2 Council Regulation (EEC) No 259/93 of 1 February 1993 on the supervision and control of shipments of waste within, into and out of the European Community (OJ L30/1 6.2.93).
3 This term is explained at para 5.79.
4 See para 5.188.

12.129   Depending upon who is responsible for a shipment getting into difficulties, the Transfrontier Shipment of Waste Regulations 1994 allow the Agency to serve one or more notices to ensure the waste's return and/or 'environmentally sound' disposal or recovery[1].

1 SI 1994/1137, regs 8 and 9.

Requirements on a notifier

12.130   Under Regulation 259/93, the Agency is obliged to ensure that transfrontier waste shipments which are in difficulties should be returned to Britain[1]. Usually this will be done under the terms of the commercial contract between notifier and consignee. However, the Transfrontier Shipment of Waste Regulations 1994[2] allow a return to be enacted by the Agency serving a notice on the notifier[3]. This notice requires the notifier to return the waste to 'an area within the United Kingdom' by a specified date[4]. This date must allow the notifier 'reasonable time to comply . . . having regard, in particular, to the location of the waste at the time the notice is served'[5]. A non-compliance with the notice is an offence[6].

1 Regulation 259/93, Article 25(1) or 26(2).
2 SI 1994/1137.
3 SI 1994/1137, reg 8(1).
4 SI 1994/1137, reg 8(2). It is not the function of the notice to require alternative recovery or disposal arrangements as set out in Article 25(1) of Regulation 259/93. Presumably, an attempt would be made to negotiate on these arrangements, with the notice requiring the return being an option of last resort.
5 SI 1994/1137, reg 8(3).
6 SI 1994/1137, reg 12(9). Offences and penalties are discussed at para 12.137.

12.131   If the notifier fails to comply with the notice, a second notice can be sent. The second notice must state that the Agency intends to act as an agent of the notifier[1]. The Agency can act as an agent[2] 'so far as is necessary to effect the return of the waste'[3]. According to Circular 13/94, this allows a regulatory body to act out of its area of jurisdiction on the notifier's deemed authority[4]. Costs of this action can be set against the financial guarantee[5] if the latter remains available and accessible. However, Article 33 of Regulation 259/93 allows for charges to be made for all regulatory costs and therefore a claim can be made independently of the guarantee[6]. The Transfrontier Shipment of Waste Regulations 1994 require the notifier to provide the Agency with 'such information and assistance as the authority may reasonably request in writing' to enable the waste to be returned[7].

1 SI 1994/1137, reg 8(4).
2 SI 1994/1137, reg 8(6).
3 SI 1994/1137, reg 8(5).

4   Circular 13/94, para 127.
5   Financial guarantees are explained at para 5.85.
6   See Circular 13/94, para 127.
7   SI 1994/1137, reg 8(5).

Requirements on a consignee

12.132   The Agency may also serve a notice on a British consignee when that individual is responsible for illegal traffic[1] under Regulation 259/93[2]. The notice should require the consignee to ensure the environmentally sound disposal or recovery of the waste 'in accordance with the notice'[3] and by a specified date[4].

1   As defined by Regulation 259/93, Article 26(1): see para 5.188.
2   SI 1994/1137, reg 9(1).
3   Presumably this allows the notice to stipulate in some detail the disposal and recovery method proposed for the waste.
4   SI 1994/1137, reg 9(2).

12.133   The date contained in the notice must permit the consignee a 'reasonable time' to comply[1]. However, Circular 13/94 states[2] that '... this requirement is subject to the [Agency's] over-riding obligation to ensure the disposal or recovery of the waste within the timescale specified by Article 26(3)'. Article 26(3) sets this timescale at a maximum of 30 days. However, it also permits this period to be extended by way of agreement by the affected competent authorities.

1   SI 1994/1137, reg 9(3).
2   Circular 13/94, para 128.

12.134   If the consignee fails to comply with the notice, a second notice can be served[1]. This notice must state that powers conferred on Agency staff under reg 9(6) of the Transfrontier Shipment of Waste Regulations 1994 will be exercised in respect of the non-compliance with the earlier notice[2]. It would appear that the regulations require the notice to indicate that these powers will be exercised 'so far as is necessary to enable ... [the Agency] to effect the disposal or recovery of the waste' in order to fulfil the relevant obligations of Article 26(3) of the Regulations[3]. The nature of these obligations is summarised at para 5.179.

1   SI 1994/1137, reg 9(4).
2   SI 1994/1137, reg 9(4).
3   SI 1994/1137, reg 9(4).

12.135   Non-compliance with the notice is an offence under the Transfrontier Shipment of Waste Regulations 1994[1], as is obstruction of inspectors by a consignee[2]. Offences in respect of notices are discussed below.

1   SI 1994/1137, reg 12(9).
2   SI 1994/1137, reg 12(10). Obstruction is discussed at para 12.195ff.

12.136   Finally, it should be noted that the Transfrontier Shipment of Waste Regulations 1994 contain separate powers of entry provisions specific to the circumstances when a consignee fails to comply with the notice[1]. These appear to overlap with the general powers that can be exercised by duly appointed Agency staff under s 108 of the Environment Act 1995[2]. Whether they are still necessary is not clear. Briefly, the regulations include provisions for Agency staff to remove the waste and arrange for its disposal and recovery[3]. It would seem that costs can be set against the financial guarantee[4] but, additionally, Article 33 of Regulation 259/93 allows a competent authority to make charges on the consignee for any other costs it incurs[5]. The consignee is required to provide the Agency with information which its staff may 'reasonably request' to enable it to fulfil the obligations on a member state under Regulation 259/93 for the removal and subsequent disposal or recovery of the waste in question[6].

1   SI 1994/1137, reg 9(5) and (6) as amended by SI 1996/593, reg 11(3)(a) and (b).
2   See para 12.52ff above: the Environment Act 1995 classes the Transfrontier Shipment of Waste Regulations 1994 as one of the Agency's 'pollution control functions' (see the Environment Act 1995, s 108(15)).
3   SI 1994/1137, reg 9(6) and 9(7) as amended by SI 1996/593, reg 11(3)(b) and (c).
4   Financial guarantees are discussed at para 5.85.
5   See Circular 13/94, para 128.
6   SI 1994/1137, reg 9(7) as amended by SI 1996/593, reg 11(3)(c).

Offences with respect to the contravention of a notice requiring a transfrontier shipment to be returned, recovered or disposed of

12.137   As noted at para 12.130 above, UK notifiers may be required to effect the return of a shipment which has got into difficulties[1]. Likewise, UK consignees can be required to ensure alternative disposal or recovery of waste imported into this country[2]. These provisions are enforced by notices. Non-compliance with the notice is an offence[3], with the penalty on summary conviction being a fine up to the statutory maximum[4]. On conviction on indictment, a maximum prison sentence of two years and/or a fine can be levied[5].

1   SI 1994/1137, reg 8.
2   SI 1994/1137, reg 9.
3   SI 1994/1137, reg 12(9).
4   SI 1994/1137, reg 15(1): currently £5,000: in Northern Ireland, the maximum fine is £2,000.
5   SI 1994/1137, reg 15(1).

12.138   A person charged with failing to comply with the notice has the statutory defence[1] that all reasonable steps were taken and all due diligence[2] exercised to avoid the commission of the offence.

1   SI 1994/1137, reg 14(1).
2   Discussed at para 7.145ff.

POWERS TO REQUIRE CONTROLLED WASTE CARRIERS TO PRODUCE EVIDENCE OF REGISTRATION

12.139   The Control of Pollution (Amendment) Act 1989 contains powers which allow a person transporting controlled waste to be stopped and permit the searching of vehicles carrying such waste[1]. These powers can be exercised by police constables in uniform and, on a more restricted basis, by duly authorised officers of an Agency. They can only be invoked where it 'reasonably appears' to such officers that s 1 of the Control of Pollution (Amendment) Act 1989 is being breached by the transportation[2] of controlled waste. Section 1 of the Control of Pollution (Amendment) Act 1989 is fully considered at para 6.36, but briefly it establishes the offence of transporting waste without the possession of a valid controlled waste carrier registration. As discussed at para 6.08ff, all those involved with moving waste on behalf of third parties, and most bodies transporting building and demolition waste, need such a registration.

1   Control of Pollution (Amendment) Act 1989, s 5. Controlled waste carrier registration is discussed in Chapter 6.
2   'Transport' includes transport of waste by road, rail, air, sea or by inland waterway, but transport by pipeline is excluded (s 9(1)).

Stopping waste carriers

12.140   As noted, the stop powers contained in the Control of Pollution (Amendment) Act 1989 only relate to instances where it 'reasonably appears' to a constable or duly authorised Agency officer that s 1 of the Control of Pollution (Amendment) Act 1989 is being breached. This power does not, of course, allow the random flagging down of any vehicle used for waste management purposes. There must be some indication to the enforcing authorities that the carrier is unregistered and hence non-compliant with s 1 of the Control of Pollution (Amendment) Act 1989. Moreover, the fact that the statute only refers to s 1 of the Act appears to prevent vehicles being stopped for the purposes of checking other documentation such as duty of care transfer notes[1] and special waste[2] or transfrontier waste shipment notifications[3]. Finally, it would seem that the requirement that a vehicle can only be stopped when it 'reasonably appears' that the carrier is unregistered is a quite stringent test. Certainly, it would seem to require more concrete evidence than would be the case if, for example, the term in the statute used instead was 'reasonable cause to suspect'. Something more than just a suspicion by an Agency officer seems needed prior to a vehicle being stopped.

1   Discussed at para 3.118ff.
2   Discussed at para 4.60ff.
3   See para 5.69ff, whilst Council Regulation 259/93 refers to 'spot checks of shipments' (Article 30), there is at least doubt as to whether this entitles Agency officers to randomly stop vehicles outside the powers set out in the Control of Pollution (Amendment) Act 1989.

12.141   The powers to stop waste carriers relate to transporters who appear 'to be or to have been engaged in' carrying waste[1] and hence they may apply to empty as well as loaded vehicles. Once stopped, the person responsible for the transportation can be required to produce evidence that either a valid registration exists[2] or that a registration certificate is not required[3]. Evidence of registration does not have to be produced immediately. The Controlled Waste (Registration of Carriers and Seizure of Vehicles) Regulations 1991[4] allow evidence of registration to be produced within seven days of the day on which the initial request was made. A person so required can take the certificate to an office of the Agency[5] 'for the area in which he is stopped' or send it there by post.

1   Control of Pollution (Amendment) Act 1989, s 5(1)(a).
2   Proof of registration can be established by the production of a valid certificate of registration. See Figure 6.1 in Chapter 6. Alternatively, where an Agency has issued copies of certificates of registration under reg 9, the copy can be regarded as such a proof: SI 1991/1624, reg 14(2). See para 6.59.
3   Control of Pollution (Amendment) Act 1989, s 5(1)(a) and (6): the most common reason why registration will not be required is when the person stopped is carrying waste produced by that person's own activities (see para 6.08ff). However, this exemption from registration does not apply to the carrying of building and demolition waste. Other reasons why a certificate is not required include cases where a certificate has expired and the renewal is under appeal (Circular 11/91, Annex 1, para 1.86).
4   SI 1991/1624, reg 14(1).
5   The wording of SI 1991/1624, reg 14(1) was amended by SI 1996/593, reg 9(3).

12.142   Only a police constable in uniform can stop a vehicle on 'any road'[1]. As the Act is silent on this matter, it seems that persons engaged in the non-road transportation of waste can be stopped by any duly authorised Agency officer. However, in the case of wastes transported by vehicle, the meaning in the statute of the term 'road' may be potentially problematic.

1   Control of Pollution (Amendment) Act 1989, s 5(2).

12.143 The term 'road' in the Control of Pollution (Amendment) Act 1989 is given the same meaning as in the Road Traffic Act 1988[1]. Under the Road Traffic Act[2], the word 'road':

'... means any highway and any other road to which the public has access, and includes bridges over which a road passes'.

It should be noted that the definition used is not the same as what is generally taken to be encompassed by the term 'public highway'. Hence rights of way on private land which constitute a road may fall within this definition since public access is possible[3].

1   Control of Pollution (Amendment) Act 1989, s 9(1).
2   Road Traffic Act 1988, s 192(1), as amended by the Road Traffic Act 1991, s 48, Sch 4, para 78.
3   For example, in *Bugge v Taylor* [1941] 1 KB 198 a hotel forecourt was held to fall within the meaning of a road as it was used as a general short-cut, besides permitting access to the hotel itself. Conversely, in *Buchanan v Motor Insurers' Bureau* [1955] 1 All ER 607, the internal highway of a port was held not to fall within the statutory meaning of a 'road', as the port itself was protected by manned security barriers.

12.144 Whether a place falls within the definition of a 'road' is generally a question of fact[1]. But it is clear that care must be taken by Agency officers wishing to stop vehicles to check carrier registrations. If the location where the vehicle is stopped is held to fall within the definition of a 'road' under the Control of Pollution (Amendment) Act 1989, then stopping a vehicle may be unlawful unless the Agency officer was accompanied by a constable in uniform[2]. In this respect, Lord Clyde makes a useful distinction in *Harrison v Hill*[3] with reference to how the phrase 'road to which the public has access' should be viewed:

'I think that, when the statute speaks of "the public" in this connection, what is meant is the public generally, and not the special class of members of the public who have occasion for business or social purposes to go to the farmhouse or to any part of the farm itself; were it otherwise, the definition might just as well have included all private roads as well as all public highways.'[4]

Accordingly, a member of the public using a landfill or a household waste centre's access road solely for the purposes of waste disposal should be viewed in Lord Clyde's phrase as 'a special class of members of the public'. The person would be a lawful invitee in these circumstances, rather than having any general right of access. Accordingly, an Agency officer can legitimately stop a vehicle on an access road to this type of facility. Conversely, if a site road was used as a general footway for other, perhaps recreational, purposes, then the definition of 'road' contained in the Road Traffic Act 1988 would apply.

1   See, for example, *Griffin v Squires* [1958] 3 All ER 468 at 470I.
2   However, it seems that, if the vehicle stopped was found to contravene s 1 of the Control of Pollution (Amendment) Act 1989, a conviction could still be successful if it can be shown that, although acting somewhat outside their powers, the officers were acting in good faith (see for example *R v Fox* [1985] 1 WLR 1126).
3   1932 SC (J) 13 at 16.
4   See also *Thomas v Dando* [1951] 1 All ER 1010 and *Griffin v Squires* [1958] 3 All ER 468.

Searching vehicles involved in controlled waste transportation

12.145 Besides requiring a transporter of waste to stop and to produce evidence of registration, a constable or an Agency officer can search 'any vehicle'[1], carry out tests on anything found in the vehicle and take away samples of anything so found[2]. Again, this applies to a vehicle which is being used to transport controlled waste and also one that reasonably appears to have been so used. However, unlike the stop powers, such search powers only pertain to 'vehicles', despite a registration being required for the transportation[3] of waste by road, rail, air, sea or inland waterway[4].

1 Defined as meaning any motor vehicle or trailer within the meaning of the Road Traffic Regulation Act 1984 (Control of Pollution (Amendment) Act 1989, s 9(1)).
2 Control of Pollution (Amendment) Act 1989, s 5(1)(b).
3 As defined by the Control of Pollution (Amendment) Act 1989, s 9(1).
4 Registration is discussed in full at para 6.45ff.

Offences

12.146 The general offence of transporting controlled waste without a carrier registration is considered in Chapter 6[1]. In respect of the powers discussed in this section, there are additional offence provisions in respect of obstruction[2] and the failure to produce evidence of registration.

1 See para 6.35ff.
2 Control of Pollution (Amendment) Act 1989, s 5(4)(a). The nature of the concept of obstruction is discussed at para 12.202.

12.147 An offence is also committed by a person who fails 'without reasonable excuse'[1] to produce evidence of registration within the time period allowed[2]. The burden of establishing that there was a reasonable excuse is upon the person accused. The prosecution is not required to show that there was no such excuse[3]. However, a person is not to be held guilty of such an offence 'unless it is shown' that the waste in question was controlled waste and that it was in fact transported to or from a place in Great Britain[4]. The burden of proof here is on the prosecution and clearly requires significant evidence that controlled waste had been transported by an unregistered carrier.

1 Discussed at para 12.109.
2 Control of Pollution (Amendment) Act 1989, s 5(4)(b).
3 Control of Pollution (Amendment) Act 1989, s 5(4).
4 Control of Pollution (Amendment) Act 1989, s 5(5).

12.148 A person found guilty of contravening these provisions may be subject to a fine on summary conviction of up to level 5 on the standard scale[1]. The offence is not one which is indictable.

1 Control of Pollution (Amendment) Act 1989, s 5(7): currently £5,000.

12.149 The Control of Pollution (Amendment) Act 1989 also contains provisions which allow the prosecution of persons other than those directly responsible for the offence, when the offence was caused by their act or default[1]. Similarly, managers, directors or other officers of bodies corporate can be charged with offences committed by the body corporate[2].

1 Control of Pollution (Amendment) Act 1989, s 7(5). Similar provisions are contained in the EPA 1990: see para 7.173ff.
2 Control of Pollution (Amendment) Act 1989, ss 6 and 7. See, in the context of the EPA 1990, para 7.156ff.

12.150 Finally, a person who submits information which 'he knows is false or misleading'[1] in a material particular, or recklessly provides information which is false in a material particular may be subject to a fine of up to level 5 on summary conviction[2]. The nature of this offence is more fully discussed at para 12.221.

1 The words 'or misleading' were added by the Environment Act 1995, Sch 19, para 3.
2 Control of Pollution (Amendment) Act 1989, s 7(3) and (4).

POWERS TO SEIZE VEHICLES INVOLVED IN THE CONTRAVENTION OF S 33 OF THE EPA 1990

12.151   The Control of Pollution (Amendment) Act 1989 allows a vehicle[1] involved in illegal disposal activities to be impounded[2]. The power can be enacted at licensed or unlicensed sites, but it is essential that it is only used against persons who have contravened s 33 of the EPA 1990[3]. Accordingly, the vehicle does not necessarily need to have been concerned with the transportation of waste: all the statute requires is for it to be involved in a breach of s 33. As will be shown below, the term 'vehicles' may encompass loading shovels and bulldozers.

1   Defined as meaning a motor vehicle or trailer within the meaning of the Road Traffic Regulation Act 1984 (Control of Pollution (Amendment) Act 1989, s 9(1)).
2   Control of Pollution (Amendment) Act 1989, s 6.
3   Control of Pollution (Amendment) Act 1989, s 6(1)(a) as amended by the EPA 1990, Sch 15, para 31(3): it should be noted that the amendment inserts the words 'deposit, treatment or' after the word 'unlicensed' in the bracketed phrase '(prohibition on unlicensed disposal of waste)'. Oddly, the word 'keeping' has been omitted. However, whether this is significant is not clear. It may well be that the purpose of the phrase is simply to provide an explanation of s 33 of the EPA 1990, not to cause any limit on the application of the section.

12.152   It should be noted that the Control of Pollution (Amendment) Act 1989 is drafted in a manner which means that vehicle seizure is very much a last resort[1]. Seizure is only possible when all other methods of finding out the details of the identity of the person who committed the offence have failed. Hence the purpose of vehicle seizure is solely to obtain the name and address of the user of the vehicle at the time an offence was committed; it is not to cause the permanent confiscation of the vehicle. Indeed, once the user turns up to claim the vehicle, the vehicle must be returned.

1   It needs to be differentiated from the general power – under s 43 of the Powers of Criminal Courts Act 1973 – which allows a defendant to be deprived of property used for the purposes of crime. The latter has been used to cause vehicles to be forfeited by the Agency (see *ENDs Report* 289, September 1998, p 48). Powers of confiscation of the proceeds of crime are also contained in the Criminal Justice Act 1988 (as amended by the Proceeds of Crime Act 1995).

What can be seized?

12.153   The Control of Pollution (Amendment) Act 1989 permits the seizure of 'vehicles' which have been involved with a contravention of s 33 of the EPA 1990. The reference to s 33 may mean that it is possible to secure the seizure of vehicles involved in the disposal of waste but not its transportation. It is not unknown for a vehicle such as a loading shovel to be left at an unauthorised waste disposal facility[1]. Such vehicles are often difficult to trace as they may not have a registration mark, while the site may be being operated sporadically and it may be difficult – or resource intensive – for the enforcing authority to catch the individuals responsible. Hence it is eminently appropriate that the authority looks to the powers available to seize the vehicle and to wait for the keeper to come forward.

1   Similarly trailers are often left unattended. Trailers fall within the definition of 'vehicle' under the Control of Pollution (Amendment) Act 1989 (see s 9(1)).

12.154   Some care needs to be taken to ensure that what is to be seized is in fact 'a vehicle' within the meaning of the Control of Pollution (Amendment) Act 1989. Under the 1989 Act[1] the term 'vehicle' is defined as meaning:

'. . . any motor vehicle or trailer within the meaning of the Road Traffic Regulation Act 1984'.

The Road Traffic Regulation Act 1984 defines 'motor vehicle' and 'trailer' as meaning[2]:

'. . . a mechanically propelled vehicle intended or adapted for use on roads, and "trailer" means a vehicle drawn by a motor vehicle'.

Case law has provided some clarification on the instances where a motor vehicle falls within the definition of a mechanically propelled vehicle intended or adapted for use on roads. This becomes important with respect to equipment such as bulldozers which have been involved with a contravention of s 33 of the EPA 1990. Not all such equipment falls within the statutory definition. In *Burns v Currell*[3] it was held that the test of whether a vehicle was 'intended' for use on roads revolved around whether a reasonable person looking at the vehicle would say that one of its functions would be road use[4]. It was up to the prosecution to show that the vehicle was 'intended or adapted' for use on roads[5].

1 Control of Pollution (Amendment) Act 1989, s 9(1).
2 Road Traffic Regulation Act 1984, s 136(1).
3 [1963] 2 All ER 297 at 300E.
4 Affirmed in *Chief Constable of Avon and Somerset v Fleming* [1987] 1 All ER 318 at 322D.
5 *Burns v Currell* [1963] 2 All ER 297 at 301B.

12.155   In the case of rubber-tyred loading shovels – particularly those which are often generically referred to as 'JCBs' – it would seem inevitable that a reasonable person would conclude that road use is one of their functions. Evidence such as lights, indicators, etc all point to such a function. However, there may be some uncertainty about equipment which has been taken to a site by way of a separate transporter. An example might be a track-laying bulldozer. It does seem somewhat doubtful that such equipment satisfies the test of being intended or adapted for use on roads[1].

1 In *Daley v Hargreaves* [1961] 1 All ER 552 it was held that dump trucks which were used for off-highway road construction were not to be viewed as motor vehicles. This was due to the manufacturer's specifications which omitted the normal requirements for road vehicles such as headlights, horns, number plates, indicators, etc, and the one-off nature of their road use. It was made clear, both in that judgment (at 556F and I) and subsequently in *Burns v Currell* ([1963] 2 All ER 297, at 299E and I and again at 300A) that this decision was specific to the facts of *Daley v Hargreaves* and was not to be applied to other possible instances involving dump trucks.

12.156   Even if a vehicle is unable to move under its own power, it can still be impounded. Hence a lorry with the engine missing is still a 'mechanically propelled vehicle', provided that there is a possibility that the engine may be readily replaced[1]. However, the equipment must not be so dilapidated or otherwise immobilised as to be no longer a 'mechanically propelled vehicle'[2].

1 *Newberry v Simmonds* [1961] 2 All ER 318 at 320 D/E.
2 See *MacLean v Hall* 1961 77 SCR 161 and *Smart v Allan* [1962] 3 All ER 893; see also *Reader v Bunyard* [1987] RTR 406.

12.157   Finally, it will have been noted that vehicle trailers fall within the definition of 'a vehicle' under the Control of Pollution (Amendment) Act 1989 and the Road Traffic Regulation Act 1984. The word 'trailer' is to be construed very widely and appears to include anything on wheels which is drawn by a motor vehicle[1].

1 See *Garner v Burr* [1950] 2 All ER 683, when a chicken shed on tow was found to constitute a vehicle under the Road Traffic Act 1930.

Procedures of vehicle seizure

12.158 To obtain a seizure, a sworn information must be submitted to a justice of the peace[1]. Before such an information can be placed before the justice of peace, the Agency must have already undertaken certain prescribed steps. These steps involve attempting, by means other than vehicle seizure, to obtain the name and address of the person 'using' the vehicle at the time the offence was committed[2]. The prescribed steps are set down in Regulation 20 of the Controlled Waste (Registration of Carriers and Seizure of Vehicles) Regulations 1991[3].

1 Control of Pollution (Amendment) Act 1989, s 6(1): in Scotland, a sheriff or justice of the peace.
2 The identity and address of this person is 'prescribed information' under s 6(1)(c) of the Control of Pollution (Amendment) Act 1989. The nature of such information is contained in SI 1991/1624, reg 19.
3 SI 1991/1624.

12.159 The first prescribed step concerns the vehicle registration plate. If it has a GB registration, the Agency has the duty to attempt to obtain from the Secretary of State[1] the identity of the 'keeper and user of the vehicle' by way of its registration mark[2].

1 The Secretary of State for Transport: ie the Driver and Vehicle Licensing Agency (DVLA) at Swansea (Circular 11/91, Annex 2, paras 2.11 and 2.12).
2 SI 1991/1624, reg 20(2)(a): in the case of vehicles registered in Northern Ireland, the Secretary of State for Transport must be approached and asked to provide the information prescribed (SI 1991/1624, reg 20(2)(b)). If the vehicle has a foreign registration plate, details of the offence have to be sent to the chief officer of police in the area where the offence was committed and a request issued for that person's assistance in tracing the vehicle (SI 1991/1624, reg 20(2)(c)).

12.160 The second prescribed step requires the Agency to serve[1] a notice under s 71 of the EPA 1990 on 'any person who they consider . . . may be able to provide' the name and address of the user of the vehicle. Section 71 notices are described more fully at para 12.174. The service of the notice may be undertaken in the light of information obtained from the vehicle's registration details, or may be undertaken in response to information obtained from other sources. The information requested by the notice can be wider than the name and address of the user at the time of the offence[2].

1 Service can be done by post: SI 1991/1624, reg 26 and the EPA 1990, s 160. Service of notices is discussed at para 12.185.
2 Circular 11/91, Annex 2, para 2.9. It should be pointed out that the failure to reply to the s 71 notice (see para 12.174 below), or the provision of false information in the reply (EPA 1990, s 44 (as amended by s 112 and Sch 19, para 4 of the Environment Act 1995): see para 12.236 below) is an offence. Unlike the offences under the Control of Pollution (Amendment) Act 1989, conviction on indictment is possible under either s 44 or s 71 of the EPA 1990 and may involve an unlimited fine or imprisonment for up to two years.

12.161 Only when both the above steps have failed to discover the identity of the user of the vehicle can a justice of the peace be approached for a warrant to enact vehicle seizure[1]. To grant such a warrant, the justice of the peace must be satisfied that there are reasonable grounds for believing that an offence under s 33 of the EPA 1990 has been committed[2] and that the identified vehicle was involved. In addition, the justice of the peace must be satisfied that proceedings in relation to the offence have not been brought against any person[3]. Finally, the Agency has to provide a convincing case that the two prescribed steps outlined above have failed to obtain the name and address of any person who can identify the user of the vehicle at the time the offence was committed[4].

1 Control of Pollution (Amendment) Act 1989, s 6(1)(c) and see Circular 11/91, Annex 2, para 2.15.

2   Control of Pollution (Amendment) Act 1989, s 6(1)(a)(i) as amended by the EPA 1990, Sch 15.
3   Control of Pollution (Amendment) Act 1989, s 6(1)(b).
4   Control of Pollution (Amendment) Act 1989, s 6(1)(c) and SI 1991/1624, regs 19 and 20.

12.162   When obtained, the warrant lasts until its purpose has been fulfilled[1]. To enforce the warrant, only a police constable in uniform can stop the vehicle named in the warrant on any road[2]. A duly authorised Agency officer can stop the vehicle when not on a road[3]. However, only when accompanied by a constable in uniform can the Agency officer subsequently seize the vehicle and its contents[4].

1   Control of Pollution (Amendment) Act 1989, s 6(4).
2   Control of Pollution (Amendment) Act 1989, s 6(2) and (3). A 'road' is defined as having the same meaning as under the Road Traffic Act 1988 (Control of Pollution (Amendment) Act 1989, s 9(1)): see para 12.143 above.
3   Control of Pollution (Amendment) Act 1989, s 6(3).
4   Control of Pollution (Amendment) Act 1989, s 6(3): described at para 12.153ff above.

12.163   When seized, the vehicle can be driven, towed or removed by other means. To facilitate its removal, 'any necessary steps may be taken'[1]. The contents[2] of the vehicle can be removed[3]. They may be stored separately if this facilitates the removal of the vehicle, if there is 'good reason' for storing them at a different place to the vehicle, or 'if their condition requires them to be disposed of without delay'.

1   SI 1991/1624, reg 21(2). These steps may include gaining access to the vehicle when the keys are not available (Circular 11/91, Annex 2, para 2.18).
2   See Circular 11/91, Annex 2, para 2.19.
3   SI 1991/1624, reg 21(2).

12.164   A person who 'intentionally' obstructs a constable or a duly authorised Agency officer in enforcing the warrant commits an offence[1]. A person found guilty of such an offence may be fined up to level 5 on the standard scale[2] on summary conviction.

1   Control of Pollution (Amendment) Act 1989, s 6(9). Obstruction is considered further at para 12.197.
2   Currently £5,000.

12.165   The Agency is required to take 'such steps as are reasonably necessary for the safe custody of that property'[1] while it is in its care.

1   Control of Pollution (Amendment) Act 1989, s 6(8).

12.166   The vehicle and its contents can only be kept by the Agency until a person appears who is able to establish that 'he is entitled to it'[1]. To be so entitled, the person must produce satisfactory evidence of his entitlement and of his identity and address[2]. Alternatively, if that person is an agent of a third party, both persons' identities and addresses need to be produced, along with the agent's authority to act and evidence of the third party's entitlement to the property[3]. The registration book also must be produced[4]. Once entitlement to the vehicle has been established, entitlement to the contents of the vehicle must also be granted[5]. The only exception is where there is more than one claim on the property. Such a dispute must be adjudicated by the Agency 'on the basis of the evidence provided'[6].

1   Control of Pollution (Amendment) Act 1989, s 6(5).
2   SI 1991/1624, reg 22(1)(a).
3   SI 1991/1624, reg 22(1)(b).
4   SI 1991/1624, reg 22(1)(c).
5   SI 1991/1624, reg 22(2).
6   SI 1991/1624, reg 22(3).

12.167 The vehicle does not, however, need to be released as soon as evidence to entitlement has been established. Circular 11/91[1] states that the Agency can take time to consider the evidence and to make appropriate enquiries with regard to its authenticity.

1   Circular 11/91, Annex 2, para 2.24.

12.168 If no one claims the vehicle, the property can be disposed of[1]. To do this, the Agency must have published 'in a newspaper circulating in the area' a notice which includes the authority's name, description of the property and vehicle registration mark. The notice must also indicate the time, place and powers under which the vehicle was seized. Finally, the notice must indicate the time and place where the vehicle can be claimed and a deadline for such a claim. The latter must be set at least 28 days after the notice's publication[2]. A statement to the effect that the property will be disposed of after that date must also be included[3].

1   Control of Pollution (Amendment) Act 1989, s 6(6) as amended by the Environment Act 1995, Sch 22, para 37(4).
2   SI 1991/1624, reg 23(2).
3   SI 1991/1624, reg 23(1)(a).

12.169 A copy of this notice must be served on the person to whom the s 71 notice was originally sent, the chief police officer covering the location at which the property was seized, the Secretary of State for Transport[1] and HP Information Ltd[2].

1   Ie DVLA at Swansea: Circular 11/91, Annex 2, para 2.26.
2   HP Information Ltd, Dolphin House, New Street, Salisbury, Wilts, SP1 2TB (Circular 11/91, Annex 2, para 2.26).

12.170 Generally, 28 days must lapse from the publication of the notice and its service on the bodies stipulated in the Controlled Waste (Registration of Carriers and Seizure of Vehicles) Regulations 1991 before the property can be disposed of[1]. But it can be got rid of before that date if 'the condition of the property requires it to be disposed of without delay'[2]. The latter refers more to the contents of the vehicle than the vehicle itself. However, even then, the notice must be published first[3].

1   SI 1991/1624, reg 23(1)(b).
2   SI 1991/1624, reg 23(1)(c).
3   Circular 11/91, Annex 2, para 2.27.

12.171 Notice of the eventual disposal of the vehicle should be given to the chief police officer, the Secretary of State for Transport and to HP Information Ltd[1]. Any proceeds from the sale can be used by the Agency to reimburse their costs of attaining a vehicle's seizure[2]. Alternatively, if the keeper appears after the property has been disposed of, the keeper can apply for the proceeds of the sale. However, the amount which can be returned is limited to what is left after the costs of seizure have been taken into account. To apply for the proceeds of the sale, the keeper must present evidence which would have caused the return of the property had it not been sold[3]. In other words, satisfactory information must be supplied as to the name and address of the user when the offence was committed.

1   SI 1991/1624, reg 24.
2   SI 1991/1624, reg 25(1).
3   SI 1991/1624, reg 25(2).

12.172 It should be noted that the relevant sections of the Control of Pollution (Amendment) Act 1989 refer only to 'vehicles'[1]. Hence other equipment used for the transportation of wastes cannot be seized. This is in spite of the fact that carrier registration applies also to the transportation of controlled waste by rail, air, sea or inland waterway[2].

1   Defined as meaning any motor vehicle or trailer within the meaning of the Road Traffic Regulation Act 1984 (Control of Pollution (Amendment) Act 1989, s 9(1)).
2   Control of Pollution (Amendment) Act 1989, s 9(1).

NOTICES TO PROVIDE INFORMATION AND DOCUMENTATION

12.173   The EPA 1990 contains two powers which allow information, including documentation, to be obtained by the Agency using statutory notices. Section 71 of the EPA 1990 provides for a notice to be served on a person requiring 'information' to be submitted to the Agency. By contrast, a separate provision contained in the Environmental Protection (Duty of Care) Regulations 1991[1] is more specific, involving the requirement to submit copies of transfer notes[2] to the Agency[3]. That transfer notes are singled out as the subject of a notice provision which is separate from the general power under s 71 appears a little odd[4]. No equivalent power exists for the obtaining of other types of statutory documentation on waste movements, such as special waste consignment notes[5], transfrontier shipment notifications[6] or associated written materials such as contracts. Presumably, s 71 notices need to be utilised in these circumstances.

1   SI 1991/2839.
2   The nature of transfer notes is discussed at para 3.118ff.
3   SI 1991/2839, reg 4.
4   However, Circular 19/91 states that a s 71 notice cannot be used to require the furnishing of transfer notes under the duty of care (see Circular 19/91, para 36). Instead, notices are served under powers contained in the Environmental Protection (Duty of Care) Regulations 1991 (SI 1991/2839, reg 4). The basis of this assertion is not clear. There does not appear to be an explicit exclusion in the statute which forbids the use of s 71 notices for these purposes.
5   See Chapter 4.
6   See Chapter 5.

Section 71 notices

12.174   The EPA 1990's powers which allow the Agency[1] to obtain information[2] by statutory notice stem from s 71(2). Although these provisions apply specifically to Part II of the EPA 1990, they have been extended to encompass subsidiary regulations and/or other enactments relating to waste. Hence a notice under s 71 can be used to require information in relation to the Control of Pollution (Amendment) Act 1989[3]. This allows information to be obtained in relation to the activities of registered and unregistered controlled waste carriers[4].

1   And the Secretary of State.
2   For whether the written response of an employee can be held to represent the response of an employer charged with an offence, see *London Borough of Barnet v Network Sites Ltd* [1997] JPL B90 and also *Edwards v Brookes (Milk) Ltd* [1963] 1 WLR 795.
3   Control of Pollution (Amendment) Act 1989, s 7(1) as amended by the EPA 1990, Sch 15, para 31(4)(a) and by the Environment Act 1995, s 120(1), Sch 22, para 37(5).
4   See para 12.160.

12.175   Similarly, notices can be used to assist in the enactment of the duty contained in the Waste Management Licensing Regulations 1994 which requires the Agency to supervise all waste management activities embraced by the Directive on Waste[1], such as waste brokers and producers of special waste[2]. Copies of records, for example, can be obtained in respect of these activities. This provision appears to be included to address instances where there is doubt that a s 71 notice may be valid due to questions of whether Part II of the EPA 1990 or the Control of Pollution (Amendment) Act 1989, actually apply[3].

1   Council Directive of 15 July 1975 on Waste (75/442/EEC) (OJ L194/39 25.7.75) (as amended by Council Directive of 18 March 1991 amending Directive 75/442/EEC on Waste (91/156/EEC) (OJ L78/32 26.3.91) and Commission Decision of 24 May 1996 adapting Annexes IIA and IIB to Council Directive 75/442/EEC on Waste (96/350/EC) (OJ L135/32 6.6.96)).
2   SI 1994/1056, reg 19 and Sch 4, para 13(2).
3   See Circular 11/94, Annex 1, para 1.86.

12.176   The EPA 1990 requires that the s 71 notice must be in writing and can require the recipient[1]:

'. . . to furnish such information specified in the notice [as the Agency] . . . reasonably considers . . . it needs[2], in such form and within such period following service as is so specified.'

Should the recipient fail to comply with the requirement of the notice 'without reasonable excuse'[3], that person will be liable to a fine on summary conviction of up to the statutory maximum[4]. On conviction on indictment, an unlimited fine can be levied or imprisonment of up to two years imposed, or both[5].

1   EPA 1990, s 71(2).
2   This means, *inter alia*, that the information must not already be in the hands of the Agency: see *R v Hertfordshire County Council, ex p Green Environmental Industries* [1998] Env LR 153 at 169.
3   See para 12.109. The failure to provide information on grounds of self-incrimination is not a reasonable excuse: see *R v Hertfordshire County Council, ex p Green Environmental Industries* [1998] Env LR 153 at 169.
4   Currently £5,000.
5   EPA 1990, s 71(3).

12.177   It is an offence under s 44 of the EPA 1990 to furnish false or misleading information in response to such a notice[1]. This provision is discussed at para 12.236ff below.

1   EPA 1990, s 44(1)(a) as amended by the Environment Act 1995, s 112, Sch 19, para 4(1). The reference in s 71(3) to false statements has been deleted by the Environment Act 1995, Sch 19, para 4(2).

12.178   In *J B and M Motor Haulage Ltd v London Waste Regulation Authority*[1] a series of notices served under s 93 of the Control of Pollution Act 1974 were judicially considered. Section 71(2) of the EPA 1990 closely follows the wording of s 93(1) of the Control of Pollution Act 1974. It was held that, in order to secure a conviction for failing to comply with a notice, the court must have put before it evidence to show why the Waste Regulation Authority 'reasonably considered' that the information specified in the notice was required. It is insufficient to use the matters raised on the face of the notice to illustrate the reason for requiring the information[2]. For a notice to be valid, there must be admissible evidence that the relevant legislation[3] had not been complied with and that the recipients of the notice were somehow implicated[4]. This may not be as onerous as it seems, as Watkins LJ notes[5]:

'It may be that, in certain circumstances, what justices need only be satisfied with before they can find that an authority reasonably considered [that the information was wanted] . . . is that the person upon whom the notice was served was the prime suspect in relation to the primary offence which evidence established on a prima facie basis had been committed.'

But in the absence of any such evidence being placed before the court – as was the case in *J B and M Motor Haulage* – a conviction for failing to comply with the notices cannot be sustained.

1   *J B and M Motor Haulage* [1993] Env LR 243.
2   *J B and M Motor Haulage* per Otton J at 247.
3   Then s 3 of the Control of Pollution Act 1974; now replaced by s 33 of the EPA 1990.
4   *J B and M Motor Haulage* [1993] Env LR 243 at 246.
5   *J B and M Motor Haulage* at 246–247.

12.179   It also appears, perhaps unintentionally, from *J B and M Motor Haulage* that the notice can only be served on prime suspects. Accordingly, this judgment may create some doubt about whether it is appropriate to use such a notice on other persons, for example in an attempt to compel a third party to provide information. However, it would also seem that this doubt may be displaced by considering the utility of information obtained from such notices and the argument about self-incrimination.

12.180   Since *R v Hertfordshire County Council, ex p Green Environmental Industries*[1], it is clear that the provisions of s 71 of the EPA 1990 over-ride the common law right of a person not to be compelled to provide information which incriminates themselves. Waller LJ found that[2]:

'Provided the information is "reasonably needed" by a Waste Regulation Authority it is my view that the intention of Parliament was that requisitions demanding such information should be answered even if, in the result, evidence would be provided against the person or entity that provided it.'

However, what is less clear is the admissibility of certain evidence obtained in this fashion[3]. Hence while s 71 notices can provide a valuable tool in the investigation of environmental crime, it may be prudent for the Agency to play safe and exercise care about using the responses to the notice as key evidence against a suspect.

1   [1998] Env LR 153.
2   *R v Hertfordshire County Council, ex p Green* [1998] Env LR 153 at 170.
3   See para 12.48ff.

12.181   The procedures for serving notices under s 71 fall within the ambit of s 160 of the EPA 1990. This provision is discussed at para 12.185 below.

Notices to furnish transfer notes

12.182   The Environmental Protection (Duty of Care) Regulations 1991 allow the Agency to serve a notice on a person 'specifying or describing' a written description or transfer note and requiring the production of such a document within a specified period[1]. A minimum period of seven days is allowed for document production. The document must be furnished 'at the authority's office'[2] within the period stipulated. The notice is served on either the transferor or transferee of a waste transaction. It must pertain to a transfer note which must be retained for two years under reg 3[3].

1   SI 1991/2839, reg 4.
2   Ie the Agency as waste regulation authority: it is not clear if the meaning of this term has been
    changed by the Environment Act 1995 to mean the relevant Agency's office.
3   SI 1991/2839, reg 4.

12.183   Circular 19/91 states[1] that the provisions of s 160 of the EPA 1990 apply to the service of notices. However, as a contrast to the Waste Management Licensing

Regulations 1994[2], there is no explicit cross reference to this section in the Environmental Protection (Duty of Care) Regulations 1991[3]. The procedures on the service of notices are discussed at para 12.185.

1 Circular 19/91, para 23.
2 SI 1994/1056, reg 1(7) as amended by SI 1995/288, reg 3.
3 SI 1991/2839.

12.184 It should be noted that Circular 19/91 states that the usual manner by which the Agency[1] obtains information – by way of a notice served under s 71 of the EPA 1990 – cannot be used in relation to s 34 of that Act[2]. The power to use a notice to obtain transfer notes under reg 4 of the Duty of Care Regulations 1991 is to be employed instead. Unfortunately, the Circular does not make clear why s 71 notices cannot be used in these circumstances.

1 As waste regulation authority.
2 Circular 19/91, para 36.

SERVICE OF NOTICES[1]

12.185 The EPA 1990 and associated regulations frequently require that the powers and duties of the Agency are enacted by way of a notice served on a particular person. Examples include the statutory notices described in this chapter, but extend to notices covering such matters as waste management licence suspension or revocation. In other cases, a person may need to serve notice on the Agency. The manner by which notices are served is set down in s 160 of the EPA 1990[2]. Section 160 also applies to notices served by way of subsidiary legislation such as the Waste Management Licensing Regulations 1994[3] and the Controlled Waste (Registration of Carriers and Seizure of Vehicles) Regulations 1991[4].

1 The word 'notice' also covers other documents which are required to be served (EPA 1990, s 160(6)).
2 In addition, s 123 of the Environment Act 1995 also contains provisions in respect of notices served under that Act. These are broadly similar in terms and content to s 160 of the EPA 1990, although s 123(5) provides additional embellishment. For the purposes of waste management, most notices are served under the EPA 1990. The main instance where s 123 of the Environment Act 1995 needs to be considered is in respect of notices served under the provisions on powers of entry under s 108 (see para 12.58ff above) and notices in relation to the non-payment of licence subsistence charges (Environment Act 1995, s 41(6) and SI 1996/508: see paras 9.28 and 9.49). Further procedures applicable to both the EPA 1990 and the Environment Act 1995 concerning the service of notices are contained in the Interpretation Act 1978.
3 SI 1995/1056, reg 1(7) as amended by SI 1995/288, reg 3(2).
4 SI 1991/1624, reg 26.

12.186 The mechanism for the service of notices is contained in s 160(2) of the EPA 1990[1]. A notice can be served by handing it to a person directly, delivering it to that person's office or by sending it by post[2]. In the case of bodies corporate, such a notice 'may' be served on or given to that organisation's 'secretary or clerk'[3]. Where partnerships are concerned, a notice 'may' be served on or given to a partner or a person 'having the control or management of the partnership'[4].

1 Section 160(1) refers to instances when the Act requires notice to be served on 'an inspector'. There does not appear to be a requirement for persons to serve such notices in Part II of the EPA 1990. In any case, the provisions by which 'inspectors' were appointed (EPA 1990, s 68(3)) have been deleted by the Environment Act 1995 (s 120(1) and Sch 22, para 85). The Environment Act 1995's system, which ensures that Agency staff are duly authorised, does not use the term 'inspector'.
2 EPA 1990, s 160(2); obviously, for the notice to be valid, it has to be made out correctly identifying the recipient. Care is particularly necessary with sister companies: see *AMEC Building Ltd v London Borough of Camden* [1997] Env LR 330.

3   EPA 1990, s 160(3)(a).
4   EPA 1990, s 160(3)(b).

12.187   In respect of the service of notices relating to transfrontier waste shipments subject to EC Regulation 259/93[1], there are separate provisions. These are contained in the Transfrontier Shipment of Waste Regulations 1994[2]. While the requirements on the service of notices are broadly similar in wording to s 160 of the EPA 1990, there is one significant difference. This relates to the nature of a person's 'proper address' for the receipt of a notice. This difference is discussed further below.

1   See para 12.128ff.
2   SI 1994/1137, reg 17.

12.188   In terms of personal service, the requirement of s 160 of the EPA 1990 is that a notice is to be served at a person's 'proper address'. From *Lord Newborough v Jones*[1], it would seem irrelevant whether a person residing at the address actually had their attention drawn to the notice[2]. Russell LJ held[3]:

'   . . . if [a notice is] served by leaving it at the proper address of the person to be served, it must be left there in a proper way; that is to say, in a manner which a reasonable person, minded to bring the document to the attention of the person to whom the notice is addressed, would adopt. This is, to my mind, the only qualification (or gloss, if you please) proper to be placed on the express language of the statutory provision.'

1   [1974] 3 All ER 17; see also *Lambeth London Borough Council v Mullins* (1990) Times, 16 January 1990, p 33.
2   In *Lord Newborough* a notice was viewed as correctly served when it was pushed under a back door of a house, despite the claim that it had lain concealed under the linoleum located behind the door for some months.
3   *Lord Newborough* at 19D.

12.189   Special provisions relate to the service of notices and other documents by post. The requirements in this instance are principally contained in the Interpretation Act 1978[1]. But these are substantiated by s 160(4) of the EPA 1990. Under the Interpretation Act 1978[2], service is deemed to have been effected by 'properly addressing, pre-paying and posting a letter containing the document'. The time by which it was effected, 'unless the contrary is proved'[3] is 'the time at which the letter would be delivered in the ordinary course of post'. Despite the Interpretation Act 1978 not explicitly referring to registered post, this option can be used to effect service[4].

1   The provisions on notices served under the Transfrontier Shipment of Waste Regulations 1994 (SI 1994/1137, reg 17(3)) make reference to the Interpretation Act 1978.
2   Interpretation Act 1978, s 7.
3   Hence if a notice is, for example, returned by the Post Office marked 'gone away' it has not been served: see *R v Appeal Committee of the London Quarter Sessions, ex p Rossi* [1956] 1 All ER 670; *Beer v Davies* [1958] 2 All ER 255; *White v Weston* [1968] 2 All ER 842; *Hewitt v Leicester City Council* [1969] 2 All ER 802; *A/S Cathrineholm v Norequipment Trading Ltd* [1972] 2 All ER 538; and *Maltglade Ltd v St Albans District Council* [1972] 3 All ER 129. But see also *Moody v Godstone RDC* [1966] 2 All ER 696. The burden of proof is upon the defendant in this instance.
4   *T O Supplies Ltd v Jerry Creighton Ltd* [1951] 2 All ER 992.

12.190   Under the EPA 1990, the 'proper address' of an individual is 'his last known address'[1]. For bodies corporate, it is the address of the registered or principal office. In the case of partnerships, the proper address is the principal office of the partnership. For a non-UK registered company or a partnership carrying on business outside the United Kingdom, the proper address is the principal office of the organisation within the UK.

1   EPA 1990, s 160(4).

12.191   There are two exceptions to the above definition of a 'proper address'. The first applies generally to all notices served under s 160 of the EPA 1990. In the instance where a person has specified a different location as the place where notices are to be accepted, the alternative location is to be the person's 'proper address'[1].

1   EPA 1990, s 160(5).

12.192   The second relates to notices in respect of transfrontier waste shipments. Like s 160 of the EPA 1990, the Transfrontier Shipment of Waste Regulations 1994[1] require that a notice may be served by personal delivery, or by leaving it at the person's 'proper address' or by posting it to that address[2]. However, in this instance, the nature of a person's 'proper address' has a slightly different meaning. It is defined as the address given on the transfrontier shipment notification document relating to the shipment of waste which is the subject of the notice[3].

1   SI 1994/1137, reg 17(1).
2   SI 1994/1137, reg 17(1).
3   SI 1994/1137, reg 17(3).

12.193   In certain cases it may be necessary to serve a notice on a person involved in an international waste shipment who was not named in any notification document. The most obvious occasion is when a shipment has been effected without such a document. These circumstances are not specifically provided for in the Transfrontier Shipment of Waste Regulations 1994's procedures for the service of notices. Presumably, the requirements of the Interpretation Act 1978 in respect of a 'proper address' of a person apply instead.

12.194   Problems may arise where an individual or body corporate has moved premises and this fact has not been communicated to the relevant authorities. Certainly notices sent by post to an out-of-date address were held to be served when they were successfully re-directed by the Post Office to the new address[1]. However, where a person has moved and genuinely did not receive the notice, it cannot be held to have been validly served[2]. In general, therefore, it may be a sound principle for Agency staff to effect personal service wherever possible.

1   *Stylo Shoes v Prices Tailors Ltd* [1959] 3 All ER 901.
2   See, for example, *White v Weston* [1968] 2 All ER 842.

OBSTRUCTION OF AGENCY OFFICERS

The offence

12.195   Section 110 of the Environment Act 1995 sets down a general offence involving persons who obstruct the Agency staff in the carrying out of their duties[1]. To be an offence the obstruction must be intentional[2] and the Agency staff must have been duly authorised[3]. Section 110 replaces the offence of obstruction which was contained in s 69 of the EPA 1990[4].

1   This includes powers and duties exercised by way of warrants (see para 12.79): the Environment Act 1995, s 110(6).
2   Environment Act 1995, s 110(1).
3   See para 12.52ff above.
4   Environment Act 1995, s 120(3) and Sch 24.

12.196   Two levels of penalties are envisaged in the Environment Act 1995. These are dependent on which of the Agency's particular duties were subject to obstruction.

A more serious penalty[1] relates to the obstruction of Agency officers when they enter premises believing that 'immediate danger of serious pollution of the environment or serious harm to human health' may occur[2]. In this instance, a fine up to the statutory maximum[3] can be levied on summary conviction[4]. On indictment, sentencing may involve an unlimited fine and/or imprisonment of up to two years[5]. In any other case involving the obstruction of Agency staff, the question of obstruction is dealt with summarily, with the Environment Act 1995 setting down a maximum fine of up to level 5 on the standard scale[6].

1   Environment Act 1995, s 110(4)(a).
2   Environment Act 1995, s 109(1): see para 12.92 above.
3   Currently £5,000.
4   Environment Act 1995, s 110(4)(a)(i).
5   Environment Act 1995, s 110(4)(a)(ii).
6   Currently £5,000.

12.197   The Control of Pollution (Amendment) Act 1989 contains separate provisions relating to the obstruction of Agency staff involved in policing controlled waste carrier registrations[1]. This offence applies also to obstruction of police constables[2]. Again, the obstruction must be intentional. Such an offence is only triable summarily, with a maximum fine of level 5[3] being levied[4].

1   Control of Pollution (Amendment) Act 1989, s 5(4).
2   As only constables in uniform can stop a vehicle on the highway: see para 12.142.
3   Currently £5,000.
4   Control of Pollution (Amendment) Act 1989, s 5(7).

12.198   Obstruction is also addressed by the Transfrontier Shipment of Waste Regulations 1994[1]. In this instance, more serious penalties can apply. However, there is only an offence of obstruction where a UK *consignee* is required to ensure alternative disposal of a waste which has been the subject of illegal traffic[1]. There is no similar requirement in respect of *notifiers* involved in exports from the UK. This is because the obstruction provision contained in reg 12(10) of the Transfrontier Shipment of Waste Regulations 1994 only refers to the provisions in the Regulations on notices served on consignees[2], not to the equivalent provisions in respect of notifiers[3]. Whether this deficiency is mopped up by the general provision in the Environment Act 1995[4] in respect of obstruction of Agency staff undertaking their other duties is not clear.

1   SI 1994/1137, reg 12(10): see para 12.128ff and Chapter 5.
2   SI 1994/1137, reg 9.
3   SI 1994/1137, reg 8.
4   Environment Act 1995, s 110(1): see para 12.195.

12.199   In respect of persons found guilty of obstruction under the Transfrontier Shipment of Waste Regulations 1994, a fine up to the statutory maximum[1] can be levied on summary conviction. On indictment, sentencing involving an unlimited fine, imprisonment of up to two years or both is envisaged[2]. However, by contrast to the provisions of the Environment Act 1995 and Control of Pollution (Amendment) Act 1989, the regulations grant an offender a rather strange statutory defence. This is that persons are allowed to to prove that they took all reasonable precautions and exercised all due diligence to avoid the commission of obstruction[3].

1   Currently £5,000.
2   SI 1994/1137, reg 15(1).
3   SI 1994/1137, reg 14(1). A similarly worded defence is discussed at para 7.145ff.

12.200   Since the Environment Act 1995 was enacted, it is not clear why it is strictly necessary to have a separate offence of obstruction remaining in the Transfrontier Shipment of Waste Regulations 1994. It may be that this provision should have been deleted when the Environment Act 1995 came into force.

12.201   Finally, it should be noted that a person can only be convicted of obstruction where an officer of the Agency is acting lawfully. Accordingly, an official who has not been duly authorised or is acting outside of the powers described in this chapter, cannot be obstructed[1].

1   See, for example, *Consett UDC v Crawford* [1903] 2 KB 183. See also *Stroud v Bradbury* [1952] 2 All ER 76.

The nature of obstruction

12.202   Obstruction is, of course, a well known concept in criminal law[1]. Cases of obstruction of inspectors at waste management facilities are by no means unknown: see *Polymeric Treatments Ltd v Walsall Metropolitan Borough Council*[2]. The courts have held that the nature of 'obstruction' involves actions which prevent authorised persons from carrying out their duties, or otherwise make it more difficult for them[3]. Obstruction contains three elements[4]. It has to be shown that obstruction took place; that the obstructed person was undertaking their lawful duties; and that the act of obstruction was intended to prevent the carrying out of those duties.

1   However, it would seem that the term 'wilful obstruction' has been more generally used in the past. For example, the term was used in s 92(6) of the Control of Pollution Act 1974 and is contained in many police powers. By contrast, the EPA 1990 and the other provisions, such as the Control of Pollution (Amendment) Act 1989, uses the phrase 'intentional obstruction'. This change may be due to a number of judgments construing 'wilful obstruction' as requiring some element or component of hostility towards the person obstructed: see for example, *Willmott v Atack* [1976] 3 All ER 794 at 798J.
2   [1993] Env LR 427: a case involving the deliberate destruction of environmental monitoring boreholes.
3   *Hinchliffe v Sheldon* [1955] 3 All ER 406 at 408F; see also *Lewis v Cox* [1984] 3 All ER 672 at 674G.
4   *Rice v Connolly* [1966] 2 QB 414 at 419, affirmed by *Green v Moore* [1982] 1 All ER 428 at 432.

12.203   The final category is particularly important. Accidental or inadvertent prevention of persons carrying out their duties would not be obstruction[1]. In addition, officers of a statutory body subject to obstruction must be acting reasonably and within the boundaries of their sanctioned powers[2].

1   See *Willmott v Atack* [1976] 3 All ER 794 at 798-799; *Arrowsmith v Jenkins* [1963] 2 All ER 210 at 211f; and see also *R v Senior* [1899] 1 QB 283 at 291.
2   See *Wershof v Metropolitan Police Comr* [1978] 3 All ER 540.

12.204   The question of motive is irrelevant to the offence of obstruction, as is whether the perpetrators realised beforehand that their actions might amount to obstruction[1]. As McCullough J states[2] 'What matters is intention, that is what state of affairs the defendant intended to bring about'[3]. In other words, the outcome of the action is of prime consideration, with obstruction only occurring when a person sets out to make life difficult for the enforcing authorities[4].

1   See *Hills v Ellis* [1983] 1 All ER 667 at 671A, J, and 672(a).
2   [1987] 1 All ER 667 at 671A.
3   See also *Lewis v Cox* [1984] 3 All ER 672.
4   Hence in *Willmott v Atack* a person charged with obstruction was acquitted when, whilst getting in the way of a police officer, he was in fact trying to remonstrate with a person who was refusing to get into a police car.

12.205 In common usage, there is a tendency to consider that obstruction involves a physical act, such as the blocking of a person's path or the refusal to permit entry[1]. However, obstruction is, in fact, a somewhat broader concept. An important case is *Hinchliffe v Sheldon*[2]. On returning to the premises late at night, a son of a licensee of a public house shouted a warning to those inside which indicated that the police were outside. This warning was sufficient for the person to be convicted of obstruction.

1 Refusal of entry without force is obviously obstruction: see for example *Borrow v Howland* (1896) 74 LT 787.
2 [1955] 3 All ER 406.

2.206 Indeed, the offence of obstruction can be found proven even if no other crime has been committed. Hence in *Hinchliffe v Sheldon*[1], there was, in fact, no evidence to suggest that late night drinking was taking place. Similarly, in *Green v Moore*[2] and *Moore v Green*[3] it was held that a probationary police officer committed obstruction when he tipped off an hotel landlord that a raid was expected[4].

1 [1955] 3 All ER 406.
2 [1982] 1 All ER 428.
3 [1983] 1 All ER 663.
4 *Green v Moore* and *Moore v Green* will make salutary reading for disaffected Agency staff.

12.207 A person standing by and doing nothing does not constitute obstruction, provided that the statute does not set down that the person is under a duty to undertake a particular action[1]. However, as noted at para 12.48, the powers of entry under s 108 of the Environment Act 1995 are very wide. For example, a person is required to assist Agency officials in respect of 'any matters or things within that person's control' which enables the official to fulfil any of the other powers so conferred[2]. Accordingly, for example, if access is required by Agency staff to stacked chemical waste drums for sampling purposes, a refusal to assist with a forklift truck would constitute obstruction[3].

1 *Swallow v LCC* [1914–15] All ER Rep 403.
2 Environment Act 1995, s 108(4)(l).
3 This example shows the effect of the odd duplication of offences in s110 of the Environment Act 1995. A person is required to assist an Agency inspector by way of s 108 and a refusal to assist would be an offence under s 110(2)(a). However, such an act would appear to also constitute obstruction, which is subject to a separate offence provision under s 110(1). See also *Walkers Snack Foods Ltd v Coventry City Council* [1998] 3 All ER 163.

12.208 But there are limits to the extent of possible obstruction offences. Of crucial importance is the fact that all defendants have a common law right to silence. Accordingly, refusing to answer questions put to them by Agency staff investigating an offence would usually not constitute obstruction[1]. However, such a refusal would be a matter which the prosecution could bring to the court's attention in any proceedings.

1 See *Rice v Connolly* [1966] 2 QB 414: unless of course s 108(4)(j) of the Environment Act 1995 was being invoked – see para 12.74. But in this instance, the information would not be admissible in court against the person questioned (Environment Act 1995, s 108(12)), whilst a refusal would be subject to the separate penalty set down in s 110(2)(a) of the Environment Act 1995. The provision of false information has been held to constitute obstruction: see *Rice v Connolly* [1966] 2 QB 414. However, the provision of false information is dealt with separately in the EPA 1990 (see s 44 and see para 12.209).

THE PROVISION OF FALSE INFORMATION

12.209 False information provided by persons involved in waste management is treated in two different ways by the EPA 1990. Firstly, there is a general offence concerning the fraudulent use of a waste management licence[1]. This use can be in any context, of which the purported compliance with requirements of the duty of care[2] is the most obvious example. Secondly, both the EPA 1990[3] and the Control of Pollution (Amendment) Act 1989[4] contain offences in respect of persons making false statements to the Agency. Certain subsidiary or related regulations also incorporate similar provisions[5]. The nature of these requirements are discussed below. Having covered the nature of the various statutory provisions, an interpretation of common terminology is presented.

1   EPA 1990, s 35(7B)(b) (as amended by the Environment Act 1995, s 120, Sch 22, para 66(2)).
2   EPA 1990, s 34: see Chapter 3.
3   EPA 1990, s 44.
4   Control of Pollution (Amendment) Act 1989, s 7.
5   For example, SI 1994/1056, Sch 4, para 14; SI 1994/1137, reg 15; SI 1996/972, reg 18.

12.210   It will become apparent that some of the provisions on false statements overlap. There are also subtle variations in the wording used, which may have a significant effect on their practical application. Finally, it may be that the offence of submitting false statements does not, in fact, cover all the associated regulations which require information to be submitted to the Agency or that documents are filled out for other reasons. Regulatory bodies faced with such a problem may benefit from a careful trawl through all the provisions, as the existence of overlaps may mean that prosecution is better pursued under one of the other regulations[1]. Where no offence is located in respect of falsified statements, it may be that the provision of such a statement may constitute obstruction[2].

1   For example, there is a requirement in the Waste Management Licensing Regulations 1994 that all waste management facilities, including those subject to Part 1 of the Act and all exempt sites, keep specified records. The falsification of those records is an offence: see para 12.217 below.
2   See *Rice v Connolly* [1966] 2 QB 414: obstruction is discussed at para 12.195ff.

12.211   In all cases, the EPA 1990 and relevant regulations contain provisions affecting the personal liability of managers, directors etc, so that they, as well as their companies, are open to prosecution when they have personally arranged for false statements to be submitted. The liability of these individuals in under these provisions is discussed at para 7.156ff.

Fraudulent use of a waste management licence

12.212   The Environment Act 1995 makes an amendment to s 35 of the EPA 1990 which addresses the case where waste management licences are forged[1]. This affects a person who

'. . . with intent to deceive, forges or uses a licence or makes or has in his possession a document so closely resembling a licence as to be likely to deceive.'

1   EPA 1990, s 35(7B)(b) as amended by the Environment Act 1995, s 120, Sch 22, para 66(2).

12.213   A person found guilty of an offence under this section can, on summary conviction, be sentenced to fine not exceeding the statutory maximum[1]. On conviction on indictment, a fine and or a custodial sentence of up to two year can be imposed.

1   Currently £5,000: the EPA 1990, s 35(7C)(a) as amended by the Environment Act 1995, s 120, Sch 22, para 66(2).

False statements in respect of the waste management licences

Waste management licence applications

12.214   A general offence of making false statements in relation to licence applications is set down in s 44 of the EPA 1990[1]. An offence is committed in relation to a waste management licence application, or an application for modification, surrender or transfer, when the person[2]:

'... makes a statement which he knows[3] to be false[4] or misleading in a material particular, or recklessly[5] makes any statement which is false in a material particular ....'

1   EPA 1990, s 44(1)(b) as amended by the Environment Act 1995s s 112 and Sch 19, para 4.
2   EPA 1990, s 44(1)(b).
3   See para 12.239 below.
4   See para 12.238 below.
5   See para 12.240 below.

12.215   On summary conviction, the penalty for the contravention of s 44 of the EPA 1990 is a fine up to the statutory maximum[1]. A conviction on indictment can result in a maximum prison sentence of two years and/or an unlimited fine[2].

1   Currently £5,000: the EPA 1990, s 44(3)(a).
2   EPA 1990, s 44(3)(b).

12.216   It should be noted that this provision not only encompasses persons who make false statements so that they themselves can gain[1] a waste management licence. The section embraces actions by persons who attempt to cause others to gain[2] the licence[3]. Hence, the offence extends beyond the applicant or licence holder to individuals such as an applicant's agent or environmental consultant.

1   Or modify, transfer or surrender.
2   Or modify, transfer or surrender.
3   See the wording of the amended s 44(1) of the EPA 1990.

Information required to be kept by way of a licence condition

12.217   A person who 'intentionally' makes a 'false[1] entry'[2] in any record required to be kept by way of a licence commits an offence under s 44(2) of the EPA 1990[3]. The penalty is the same as that which relates to false statements submitted in licence applications[4]. This provision may overlap with the general requirement in respect of falsified information contained in the records of waste management facilities[5]. It is also oddly duplicated by s 35(7B)(a) of the EPA 1990[6].

1   See para 12.238.
2   Not a 'false or misleading entry' as is the case in s 44(1) of the EPA 1990: see above.
3   As amended by s 112 and Sch 19, para 4 of the Environment Act 1995: unlike s 44(1), there is no additional offence in s 44(2) in respect of entries which are recklessly made.
4   EPA 1990, s 44(3) see para 12.214 above.
5   See para 12.218 below.
6   EPA 1990, s 35(7B)(a) as amended by the Environment Act 1995, s 120, Sch 22, para 66(2). Section 35(7C) makes this an offence, allowing a fine up to the statutory maximum at summary conviction. On conviction on indictment a fine, a custodial sentence of up to two years, or both can be levied.

False entries made to site records at licensed facilities and metal recycling sites

12.218   The Waste Management Licensing Regulations 1994[1] require that establishments and undertakings subject to waste management licences or exemptions as metal recycling sites retain specified records[2]. These records may be kept by way of a licence condition, but this may not always be the case. Furthermore, this requirement is entirely separate from the provisions of the duty of care[3] and the Special Waste Regulations 1996[4].

1   SI 1994/1056, reg 19 and Sch 4, para 14, as amended by SI 1995/288, reg 3(19)–(21) and SI 1996/972, reg 25 and Sch 3.
2   SI 1994/1056, reg 19, Sch 4, para 14(1) and 14(3) (the latter as amended by SI 1995/288, reg 3(21). It also applies to sites subject to authorisations under Part I of the EPA 1990.
3   See Chapter 3.
4   See Chapter 4.

12.219   The Waste Management Licensing Regulations 1994 make the provision of information to the Agency[1] which a person 'knows'[2] to be 'false[3] or misleading in a material particular' an offence[4]. Similarly, an offence occurs if the information in a statement is made which is false or misleading and which has been submitted 'recklessly'[5]. Finally, a person who 'intentionally' makes a 'false entry' on any record which is required by these provisions to be kept commits an offence[6].

1   And to other persons: Sch 4, para 14(1)(b) requires that information on special waste is to be furnished to users of the site: see para 4.172ff.
2   See para 12.239.
3   See para 12.238 below.
4   SI 1994/1056, Sch 4, para 14(6) as amended by SI 1996/972, reg 25 and Sch 3.
5   See para 12.240 below.
6   SI 1994/1056, Sch 4, para 14(7) as amended by SI 1996/972, reg 25 and Sch 3.

12.220   These provisions are subject[1] to the penalties contained in the Special Waste Regulations 1996[2]. On summary conviction, a person may be subject to a fine up to level 5[3]. On conviction on indictment, a fine, imprisonment or both penalties can be imposed[4].

1   SI 1994/1056, Sch 4, para 14(8) as amended by SI 1996/972, reg 25 and Sch 3.
2   SI 1996/972, reg 18(5) to 18(9).
3   Currently £5,000: SI 1996/972, reg 18(9)(a).
4   SI 1996/972, reg 18(9)(b).

False statements in respect of waste carrier and broker registrations

12.221   In respect of the system of registration of controlled waste carriers[1], the Control of Pollution (Amendment) Act 1989 contains it own provisions in respect of the provision of 'false[2] or misleading'[3] statements[4]. Like s 44 of the EPA 1990, the offence requires that they are provided either knowingly[5] or recklessly[6]. However, in this instance, the offence under the Control of Pollution (Amendment) Act 1989 is only triable summarily[7], with a maximum fine being level 5[8].

1   See Chapter 6.
2   See para 12.238.
3   The words 'or misleading' were added by the Environment Act 1995, Sch 19, para 3.
4   Control of Pollution (Amendment) Act 1989, s 7(3).
5   See para 12.239.

6   See para 12.240.
7   Control of Pollution (Amendment) Act 1989, s 7(4).
8   Currently £5,000.

12.222   It is not immediately clear if an offence will occur in the case of false or misleading information submitted in respect of the provisions relating to waste broker registration[1]. Regulation 20(8) of the Waste Management Licensing Regulations 1994[2] requires that certain stipulated sub-sections in Part II of the EPA 1990[3] shall apply to the registration of waste brokers. However, this refers to a provision in the EPA 1990 in respect of the submission of false information[4] which has been repealed by the Environment Act 1995[5].

1   See SI 1994/1056, reg 20, Sch 4 para 12 and Sch 5; see para 6.28ff.
2   SI 1994/1056.
3   EPA 1990, s 68(3)–(5), s 69, s 71(2) and (3).
4   EPA 1990, s 71(3).
5   Environment Act 1995, Sch 19, para 4(2).

False statements in duty of care transfer notes

12.223   The nature of transfer notes under the provisions of the EPA 1990 in respect of the duty of care[1] is explained at para 3.118ff. What should be noted is that the content of a transfer note is governed by two, quite separate, provisions. Firstly, there is the written description required by s 34 of the EPA 1990[2]. Secondly, there is the remainder of the information on the note, which is prescribed by the Environmental Protection (Duty of Care) Regulations 1991[3]. It may be important to bear this distinction in mind in the discussion below.

1   EPA 1990, s 34.
2   EPA 1990, s 34(1)(c)(ii).
3   SI 1991/2839, reg 2.

12.224   The provision by a person of information which is 'false or misleading in a material particular' in respect of a written description is an offence. Such a matter falls within the general offence contained in s 44(1)(a) of the EPA 1990[1].

1   As amended by the Environment Act 1995, s 112 and Sch 19, para 4.

12.225   In respect of the information other than written descriptions on transfer notes, the provision of false information is less obviously addressed. Section 44 is clear that falsifying information in respect of a requirement of Part II of the EPA 1990 is an offence. It is assumed that this applies as much to written descriptions, which are a requirement of s 34(1), as it does to any regulations made under Part II. Hence it embraces any information required by the Environmental Protection (Duty of Care) Regulations 1991. However, the fact that the 1991 Regulations do not explicitly contain provisions on false information provides an odd contrast to, for example, the Special Waste Regulations 1996[1], whereby Regulation 18(3) sets out an offence of falsifying or providing misleading information on special waste consignment notes[2].

1   SI 1996/972. It may be possible that the Special Waste Regulations 1996 required a separate provision for the reason that the regulations emanate from powers delegated to the Secretary of State by the EPA 1990 and also by the European Communities Act 1972. By contrast, the Environmental Protection (Duty of Care) Regulations 1991 stem solely from powers contained in s 34(5) of the EPA 1990. Certainly s 44 of the EPA has been used by the Agency in the context of the duty of care (see *ENDs Report* 291, April 1999 p 55).
2   See also SI 1994/1056, Sch 4, para 14(6) which contains its own provisions on false information in the context of record keeping (see para 12.218ff).

False statements in respect of special waste consignments

12.226   The Special Waste Regulations 1996[1] contain an offence provision in respect of making false statements[2]. This affects persons who, in purported compliance with the requirement 'to furnish any information', makes a statement which they know[3] to be 'false[4] or misleading' in a material particular[5]. Similarly, a person commits an offence when any statement is made recklessly[6] which is false or misleading.

1   SI 1996/972: see Chapter 4.
2   SI 1996/972, reg 18(3).
3   See para 12.239 below.
4   See para 12.238.
5   SI 1996/972, reg 18(3).
6   See para 12.240.

12.227   In addition, persons who 'intentionally' make a 'false' entry in any record or register required to be kept by the Special Waste Regulations 1996 commit an offence[1]. This provision would probably cover the completion of consignment notes, albeit that the requirement is only satisfied when 'false' entries have been made. There is no reference to misleading entries.

1   SI 1996/972, reg 18(4).

12.228   A person found guilty of these offences is liable on summary conviction to a fine not exceeding level 5[1]. On indictment, a fine, imprisonment of up to two years, or both sentences, can be levied[2].

1   Currently £5,000.
2   SI 1996/972, reg 18(9)(a) and (b).

False statements in respect of transfrontier waste shipment notifications

12.229   The provisions which create offences for the supply of false or misleading statements in respect of transfrontier waste shipments are somewhat different in their construction to the other requirements discussed above. This is because the transfrontier waste control system is primarily implemented by Community Regulation 259/93[1] and, being a Regulation, the articles contained therein are directly applicable[2]. Penalties for non-compliance with the Regulation are contained in the Transfrontier Shipment of Waste Regulations 1994[3], which itself also presents two additional provisions in respect of persons submitting false information in specified circumstances.

1   Council Regulation (EEC) No 259/93 of 1 February 1993 on the supervision and control of shipments of waste within, into and out of the European Community (OJ L30/1 6.2.93).
2   See para 5.28.
3   SI 1994/1137, reg 15.

12.230   Article 26 of Regulation 259/93 sets down circumstances which are held to be 'illegal traffic'[1]. One of these concerns shipments of waste effected 'with the consent obtained from the competent authorities concerned through falsification, misrepresentation or fraud'[2]. Obviously, this would cover falsified notification documents or, in the case of Green List waste[3], the required transport document. A further instance of illegal traffic is where a shipment of waste is effected 'which is not specified in a material way in the consignment note'[4]. Actions constituting illegal traffic under Article 26 of the Regulation are made offences in UK[5] law by the Transfrontier Shipment of Waste Regulations 1994[6].

1   See para 5.188.
2   Regulation 259/93, Article 26(1)(c).
3   Green List waste is explained at paras 5.47ff and 5.136ff.
4   Regulation 259/93, Article 26(1)(d): note that this does not apply to Green List waste transport documents.
5   The Regulation also applies to Northern Ireland.
6   SI 1994/1137, reg 12(1).

12.231   It should be noted that Article 26 of the Regulation defines illegal traffic as occurring when a shipment is 'effected'. Accordingly, if the shipment was not effected, but information was falsified, there would seem to be no offence.

12.232   The Transfrontier Shipment of Waste Regulations 1994 themselves contain the additional requirement[1] that no shipment[2] should commence until the Agency has provided a certificate that a financial guarantee is in place[3]. A person who supplies information which is 'false'[4] in a material particular to obtain a certificate commits an offence[5]. This sub-section may, to a certain extent, plug the gap alluded to above, which precludes the submission of false information being an offence if the transfrontier shipment ends up not going ahead.

1   SI 1994/1137, reg 7.
2   Other than Green List waste: see para 5.136.
3   Financial guarantees are explained at para 5.85ff.
4   Not 'false or misleading'.
5   SI 1994/1137, reg 12(5).

12.233   A second provision on false information in the Transfrontier Shipment of Waste Regulations 1994 relates to where a transfrontier shipment has been completed. As explained in para 5.69, recipients of shipments are required to certify, within 180 days of its arrival at their premises[1], that the waste has been processed, on the Transfrontier Waste Consignment Note. Should a person send a certificate which is 'false'[2] in a material particular, an offence is committed[3].

1   As required by Regulation 259/93, Articles 5(6), 8(6) and 20(9).
2   Not 'false or misleading'.
3   SI 1994/1137, reg 12(3).

12.234   Somewhat oddly, persons charged with submitting false information in respect of any of these provisions – including the contravention of Regulation 259/93 itself – are permitted to invoke the statutory defence that they took all reasonable precautions and exercised all due diligence[1] to avoid the commission of the offence[2]. None of the other provisions discussed here contain such a requirement. As an additional contrast to these other enactments, it should also be noted that the Transfrontier Shipment of Waste Regulations 1994 do not address false statements which are made recklessly.

1   This phrase is discussed at para 7.145ff.
2   SI 1994/1137, reg 14(1).

12.235   Where the provisions of Regulation 259/93 or the Transfrontier Shipment of Waste Regulations 1994 have been contravened, summary conviction can involve a fine of up to the statutory maximum[1]. On indictment, a fine, imprisonment of up to two years or both can be levied[2].

1   Currently £5,000: in Northern Ireland this is £2,000.
2   SI 1994/1137, reg 15(1).

False statements in other information submitted to the Agency[1]

12.236   Section 44 of the EPA 1990[2] contains provisions on statements made in respect of those elements of Part II of the EPA 1990 which require information to be furnished to the Agency. In certain circumstances, these are likely to overlap with some of the other provisions just described. Section 44 sets down that an offence is committed by a person who 'in purported compliance with a requirement to furnish any information imposed by or under any provision of this Part' submits falsified information[3]. Again the requirement[4] is either that the person makes a statement which is known[5] to be false[6] or misleading or which is made recklessly[7].

1   There appears to be no provision in the Environment Act 1995 in respect of falsified information submitted to the Agency by way of the powers contained in s 108 of the Environment Act 1995.
2   As amended by s 112 and Sch 19, para 4(1) of the Environment Act 1995.
3   Ie Part II of the EPA 1990.
4   EPA 1990, s 44(1) as amended by the Environment Act 1995, s 112 and Sch 19, para 4.
5   See para 12.239.
6   See para 12.238.
7   See para 12.240.

12.237   This provision will find use in respect of notices issued under s 71 of the EPA 1990[1]. These notices require persons to supply specified information to the Agency. It is to be assumed that it also has application in relation to the Waste Management Licensing Regulations 1994 and the need for exempt sites to submit specified information to the Agency as part of the exemption registration process. Scrapyards and motor vehicle dismantlers are required to submit specified details, such as site plans and specifications of drainage systems[2]. It is distinctly possible that the information submitted in these circumstances may not always be truthful.

1   See para 12.174ff above: the sub-section on false statements in s 71 itself was deleted by the Environment Act 1995 (see Sch 19, para 4(2)).
2   SI 1994/1056, reg 18(4A)(a) and (b), Sch 3, para 45(3)(c): as amended by SI 1995/288, reg 3(10): see paras 11.83ff, 11.89 and 11.96.

False statements: general interpretation

12.238   Being 'economical with the truth' by omitting relevant information has been held to constitute the making of a false statement, despite the presence in the statement of facts which are, themselves, true[1]. Accordingly, a false statement can be one which contains '. . . such a partial and fragmentary statement of facts that the withholding of that which is not stated makes that which is stated false'[2].

1   *R v Lord Kylsant* [1931] 1 All ER Rep 179.
2   *R v Bishirgian* [1936] 1 All ER 586, at 591. See also *Curtis v Chemical Cleaning and Dyeing Co Ltd* [1951] 1 All ER 631, at 634.

12.239   With the exception of the provisions contained in Regulation 259/93 on transfrontier waste shipments, all of the other enactments discussed above require that the statement furnished not only must be false, but that the prosecution must show that the defendant knows that it is false. Obviously, a person can deliberately set out to produce a false statement. But in addition, a person can be found to 'know' that such a statement is false when there is evidence that the person shut their eyes to the obvious or refrained from making appropriate enquiries[1].

1   See *Westminster City Council v Croyalgrange* [1986] 2 All ER 353, at 359C: see para 7.57ff and see *James and Son v Smee* [1954] 3 All ER 273 at 278G/H.

12.240   Certain of the offences discussed above include a provision which covers a person making a false or misleading statement recklessly. 'Recklessly' has been held to describe a situation where a person, prior to doing an act which had an obvious risk of harmful consequences, either fails to give any thought to the possibility of there being such a risk or, having acknowledged there was such a risk, goes ahead and does it anyway[1]. Whether a risk should be viewed as obvious is adjudicated on the basis of whether a reasonably prudent person would consider it to be so: not whether the particular defendant so considered it[2].

1   *R v Lawrence* [1981] 1 All ER 974 at 982F; *Metropolitan Police Comr v Caldwell* [1982] AC 341 at 354F/G.
2   *Elliott v C (a minor)* [1983] 2 All ER 1005 at 1008E and 1009H/J.

12.241   A person can be prosecuted under the provisions of making false or misleading statements regardless of whether a material advantage was accrued by the defendant by way of the statement[1].

1   *Jones v Meatyard* [1939] 1 All ER 140; *Stevens v Steeds Ltd and Evans v King* [1943] 1 All ER 314; *Barrass v Reeve* [1980] 3 All ER 705.

12.242   Finally, it has been held that the time the offence was committed was when the falsified document was received by the statutory authorities. In other words, the offence occurred when the person to whom the statement was made acquired it, not when it was written[1]. This finding is important, given the statutory time periods for taking cases to the magistrates' court.

1   *Lawrence v Ministry of Agriculture Fisheries and Food* (1992) Independent, 27 April.

EVIDENTIAL REQUIREMENTS

12.243   This is not the place to undergo a detailed exposition of the nature of evidence and the requirements affecting its legitimate collection. However, the Environment Act 1995 contains certain provisions in respect of evidence which deserve highlighting. In addition, mention should be made of the requirements of the Police and Criminal Evidence Act 1984 in respect of the Agency's powers of entry and when suspects are to be interviewed.

12.244   The Environment Act 1995 set down certain evidential provisions in s 111. Any information obtained by way of a condition[1] of a 'relevant licence' is admissible in any proceedings[2]. A relevant licence is defined[3] as including a controlled waste carrier registration[4]; a waste management licence; a controlled waste broker registration[5]; and a registration as an exempt scrapyard or motor vehicle dismantler[6]. The Environment Act 1995 requires that any apparatus[7] which is used to provide information in respect of a requirement of a 'relevant licence' is to be assumed to be functioning correctly 'unless the contrary is shown'[8]. Therefore, the burden of proving that monitoring equipment was not correctly functioning lies with the defence, being discharged on the balance of probabilities.

1   Defined as including 'any requirement to which a person is subject under, by virtue of or in consequence of a relevant licence': the Environment Act 1995, s 111(5).
2   Environment Act 1995, s 111(2).
3   Environment Act 1995, s 111(5) and s 56(1).
4   But only in respect of a registration under s 2 of the Control of Pollution (Amendment) Act 1989: Environment Act 1995, s 56(1).
5   By way of the Waste Management Licensing Regulations 1994.
6   Environment Act 1995, s 56(1) explicitly refers to para 45(1) and (2) of Sch 3 of SI 1994/1056: other types of registered exemptions are not mentioned.

7 'Apparatus' includes any meter or other device 'for measuring, assessing, determining, recording or enabling to be recorded, the volume, temperature, radioactivity, rate, nature, origin, composition or effect of any substance, flow, discharge, emission, deposit or abstraction': the Environment Act 1995, s 111(5).
8 Environment Act 1995, s 111(3).

12.245 Finally, if a condition of a 'relevant licence' requires that entries are to be made in any record, evidence of non-compliance with the condition can be admissibly submitted to a court when the need for such an entry was neglected[1]. Oddly, this provision is also duplicated by an amendment made by the Environment Act 1995 to s 35 of the EPA 1990[2].

1 Environment Act 1995, s 111(4).
2 EPA 1990, s 35(7A) as amended by the Environment Act 1995, s 120, Sch 22, para 66(2).

12.246 In respect of the Police and Criminal Evidence Act 1984, the Code of Practice[1] has application to Agency officers by way of s 67(9). The Code applies the Agency's activities where the cautioning and interviewing of offenders is to be undertaken[2].

1 *Police and Criminal Evidence Act 1984 Codes of Practice Revised Edition* (1995) HMSO, London.
2 See also *Walkers Snack Foods Ltd v Coventry City Council* [1998] 3 All ER 163.

12.247 Of particular significance is the applicability of the Code to the Agency's enforcement activities. While the Code will apply as soon as an officer has cause to suspect that an offence has been committed, it does not apply to the Agency's day-to-day routine inspection and monitoring function. This is made clear in Code B[1] which states that:

'This code does not apply to the exercise of a statutory power to enter premises or to inspect goods, equipment or procedures if the exercise of that power is not dependent on the existence of reasonable grounds for suspecting that an offence may have been committed and the person exercising the power has no reasonable grounds for such suspicion.'

1 PACE Codes of Practice Code B, page 14, para 1.3B.

12.248 The wording of s 108 of the Environment Act 1995 does not contain a provision which allows entry to be made by Agency officers only where there is reasonable grounds to suspect that an offence is committed. This goes hand in hand with s 42 of the EPA 1990, which requires officers to ensure that pollution of the environment or harm to human health does not occur at sites subject to waste management licence and that licence conditions are not breached[1].

1 These matters are discussed at para 12.11 above.

12.249 Code B of the Police and Criminal Evidence Act 1984 is now in its second edition. That edition – unlike the first – contains the paragraph quoted verbatim above. Prior to the publication of the second edition, the Divisional Court considered the requirements of the Code in its unamended form in the trading standards case of *Dudley Metropolitan Borough Council v Debenhams plc*[1]. In this case, trading standards officers entered a branch of Debenhams and requested sight of certain computer records. The relevant managers of the store were not cautioned. The records handed over were used to charge the company with offences under the Consumer Protection Act 1987 in respect of providing misleading price labels.

1 (1994) 159 JP 18.

12.250 The Divisional Court held that the evidence was inadmissible as the store staff should be have been cautioned prior to the handing over of the records. More importantly, the court appears to suggest that shop staff should be cautioned as soon as trading standards officers enter the premises. By analogy, it seemed that the *Debenhams* principles might have had application to waste regulatory staff in respect of their routine inspection function.

12.251 Within a few months of the *Debenhams* judgment the Police and Criminal Evidence Act's Code of Practice was amended in the manner described above. It seems likely that the timing of the amendment was not coincidental. The amendment would indicate that the procedures set down in Code B are not applicable on routine visits or inspections and only come into force when the statute explicitly requires that persons should have grounds for suspecting an offence. The amendment to the Code would appear to dis-apply much of the *Debenhams* judgment, in the sense that there may be no need for trading standards officers to caution shop staff on entry. However, there remains the requirement to apply the caution when computer records are requested or in other instances when an offence appears to have been committed. These principles would appear to apply equally to the activities of the Agency's staff.

Chapter 13

Public registers

REGISTERS AND ACCESS TO INFORMATION

13.01 The Agency is required to maintain a register of public information on specified waste management activities. Although a key objective of the Agency is to apply a unified, multi-environmental media approach across its main pollution control functions, the arrangements for public registers generally follow the more 'traditional' single environmental media boundaries.

13.02 The statutory powers by which registers of information on waste management activities are maintained remain those that were hitherto used by waste regulation authorities when they were part of local government. For those waste management activities which are subject to Part II of the EPA 1990, the requirements for registers mainly stem from s 64. Other enactments contain separate provisions which operate in parallel to the s 64 register. Examples include the register of activities which are exempt from waste management licences[1] and the register of waste brokers[2]. Further provisions are contained in the Controlled Waste (Registration of Carriers and Seizure of Vehicles) Regulations 1991[3] in respect of registered controlled waste carriers[4]. These provisions have only been subject to minor amendment by the Environment Act 1995.

1 SI 1994/1056, reg 18: see Circular 11/94, Annex 9, para 9.34: see para 13.39.
2 SI 1994/1056, reg 20.
3 SI 1991/1624, reg 3.
4 See para 13.43 below.

13.03 The statutory requirements for public information registers are found in a variety of legislative provisions. Information on facilities such as chemical waste incinerators, which are subject to Integrated Pollution Control (IPC) authorisations under Part I of the EPA 1990, is held under separate provisions[1]. The register of premises exempt from waste management licences is even more fragmented. While the main bulk of these activities are subject to a register established under the Waste Management Licensing Regulations 1994[2], others will be instead contained in the IPC register. But details of some exempt activities are not held by the Agency at all. These are the Part B processes under the EPA 1990 which in England and Wales remain under local authority control in respect of their air emissions[3]. Being a Part B process, the possessor of the appropriate public register is the district council[4].

1 EPA 1990, s 20 as amended by the Environment Act 1995, s 120(1), Sch 22, para 57, and SI 1991/507, as amended by SIs 1991/836, 1992/614, 1993/1749, 1996/667, 1996/979 and 1996/2678.
2 SI 1994/1056, reg 18.
3 Part B processes are discussed at para 10.14ff.
4 Or, where formed, a unitary authority: in Scotland, Part B processes are within SEPA's domain.

13.04 It will prove a challenging task to the Agency to establish a single, unified register out of these provisions. This task is not made any easier by the fact that the contents of much of the register has been inherited from the Agency's predecessor organisations. Naturally, these will vary in format and in such matters as ordering and indexing.

13.05 The statutory requirements in respect of registers are quite separate from the more general public right for information under the Environmental Information Regulations 1992[1]. The latter transpose Council Directive 91/313 on the Freedom of Access to Information on the Environment[2], being amended in 1998[3]. While it is not the purpose of this chapter to explore the wider issue of the provision of information under such provisions as the Environmental Information Regulations 1992[4], certain general matters arise due to the parallel approaches of the EPA 1990's register system and the rather wider right of access to information under the Environmental Information Regulations 1992. For example, potentially different rights of access and degrees of protection are built into the legislation. Information which has been 'volunteered'[5] to the Agency is subject to some protection from access by third parties under the Environmental Information Regulations 1992. A significant amount of this may not fall within the EPA 1990's requirements on registers. Hence the Agency needs to exercise caution to ensure that it is correctly empowered to hand over the requested material. The relevant guidance states[6] that statutory '[b]odies will need to be careful when handling requests for commercially confidential information to avoid the possibility of legal action through wrongful release'[7]. While this point is somewhat obvious, it should be borne in mind that not all of the Agency's predecessor waste regulation authorities kept a register which was separate from their general files.

1 SI 1992/3240. They are also distinct from the general right of access contained in the yet to be commenced Freedom of Information Act 1999. The scope of access may need also to be changed to fully implement the European Convention on Access to Information, Public Participation in Decision Making and Access to Justice in Environmental Matters (The 'Aarhus Convention'). It should also be noted that the European Convention on Human Rights – which is to be put into effect in British law by the Human Rights Act 1998 – refers to the right of 'freedom . . . to receive . . . information . . .' (Art 10). These new provisions are beyond the scope of this chapter. Procedures for access to information for environmental searches have been issued by the Agency (see Law Society's Gazette, 9 September 1998).
2 Council Directive on the Freedom of Access to Information on the Environment (91/313) (OJ L158/56 23.6.90).
3 SI 1998/1447.
4 See House of Lords Select Committee on the European Communities (1989) *Freedom of Access to Information on the Environment* HMSO, London; House of Lords Select Committee on the European Communities (1996) *Freedom of Access to Information on the Environment* Stationery Office, London.
5 SI 1992/3240, reg 4(3)(c): in other words, a person who hitherto held the information is not required by law to pass it over.
6 Department of the Environment (1992) *Guidance on the Implementation of the Environmental Information Regulations 1992 in Great Britain*, para 61.
7 See also John E (1995) 'Access to Environmental Information: Limitations of the UK Radioactive Substances Registers' 7 JEL 11 at 22.

13.06 The Environmental Information Regulations 1992 usually allow a much broader level of access to information which extends beyond the boundaries of the Agency's register. However, the Environmental Information Regulations 1992 concern solely 'any information which relates to the environment'[1]. Whether the names of directors of a waste management company, for example, constitute such information seems doubtful, hence recourse may be necessary to the Agency's register where such information may be present[2]. In addition, the viewing of the contents of the Agency's register is free of charge[3], whereas the Environmental Information Regulations 1992 give the Agency discretion to charge for the supply of information. Furthermore, access to information on the register is more or less automatic[4], whereas the 1992 Regulations set a maximum disclosure deadline of two months[5]. Finally, the content of the Agency's register is made explicit under the EPA 1990 and in the other regulations. By contrast, the Environmental Information Regulations 1992 permit access to unspecified documentation[6]. Hence a person wishing to view information on the register will always have a reasonably clear picture of what they are entitled to see.

1　SI 1992/3240, reg 2(1)(a). Environmental information is defined in reg 2(2): see Case C-312/96 *Wilhelm Mecklenberg & Kreis Pinneberg – Der Landrat* (17 June 1998, unreported), ECJ; *R v British Coal Corpn, ex p Ibstock Brick Building Products Ltd* [1995] JPL 836; *R v Secretary of State for the Environment, Transport and the Regions and Midland Expressway Ltd, ex p Alliance Against the Birmingham Northern Relief Road* [1999] Env LR 447.
2　This information is required as part of the controlled waste broker or carrier registration process (see para 6.49) and is also needed to be submitted as part of a waste management licence application (see para 8.134).
3　EPA 1990, s 65(6)(a) as amended by the Environment Act 1995, s 120(1) and Sch 22, para 82.
4　The EPA 1990, s 64(6)(a) (as amended by the Environment Act 1995, s 120(1) and Sch 22, para 82) states that the register must be open for '... inspection ... at all reasonable times ...'. 'Reasonable times' would normally be office opening hours: see para 12.59.
5　SI 1992/3240, reg 3(2).
6　Excluded from the principal requirements of the Environmental Information Regulations 1992 is information which is already in the public domain by way of other statutory rights of access: see SI 1992/3240, reg 2(1)(c).

13.07　It should also be noted that the register provided under s 64 of the EPA 1990 contains only very limited information in respect of consignment notes passed to the Agency by way of the Special Waste Regulations 1996[1]. Similarly, little information is held on the register in relation to notification documents under the Transfrontier Shipment of Waste Regulations 1994[2]. The exact nature of the register in these respects is explored further at para 13.36 below, but public access to virtually all current documentation on these matters can only be obtained by way of a request under the Environmental Information Regulations 1992. Questions of commercial sensitivity on the information contained in such documents may arise in this context[3] and requests for access may be refused for this reason[4].

1　SI 1996/972: see Chapter 4.
2　SI 1994/1137: see Chapter 5.
3　See, in the case of transfrontier waste shipment notification documents, Circular 13/94, paras 162–164.
4　As noted, the Environmental Information Regulations 1992 concern solely 'information which relates to the environment'. There may be a question over whether, for example, information on special waste movements, in particular that which relates to particular waste producers (as opposed to disposal or recovery facilities), falls within this concept.

THE s 64 REGISTER

The form of the register

13.08　The Agency's main register of public information on waste management facilities stems from powers contained in s 64 of the EPA 1990. Section 64 contains enabling powers which establish the scope of the information which can be required, by way of subsidiary regulations, to be included in a register. The requirements of s 64 are typically specific to the particular provisions referred to. However, a catch-all provision is also included, allowing other prescribed matters relating to the treatment, keeping or disposal of waste or any pollution of the environment[1] caused by such facilities to be included as part of the register[2].

1　Oddly, 'harm to human health' is not mentioned.
2　EPA 1990, s 64(1)(m).

13.09   The main provisions on the actual content of registers are contained in the Waste Management Licensing Regulations 1994[1]. This register encompasses such items as copies of waste management licences, licence applications, statutory notices, inspection reports, environmental monitoring data, limited information on special waste, etc. Generally, the register is oriented towards activities subject to waste management licences. Accordingly, little information is found on this – or any other – register in relation to the Agency's activities concerning the policing of unauthorised waste management facilities.

1   SI 1994/1056, reg 10.

13.10   The register created by way of s 64 of the EPA 1990 can be kept in any form[1], allowing it to be contained on computer or microfiche. However, Circular 11/94 recommends that the register should be clearly indexed or otherwise ordered so that information can be readily accessible to users[2]. In certain cases, various elements of the statutory provisions may appear to cause possible duplication of information being held on the register[3]. Where this duplication arises there is no need for multiple entries to be contained in the register[4].

1   EPA 1990, s 64(7).
2   Circular 11/94, Annex 9, para 9.11.
3   An example is SI 1994/1056, reg 10(1)(f), which requires that a licence holder's convictions under the EPA 1990 must be held on the register. However, reg 10(1)(b) requires that a copy of the application for the licence must also be retained, and such convictions would need to be disclosed in the application.
4   See Circular 11/94, Annex 9, para 9.21.

13.11   Any information which is superseded by subsequent material can be removed from the register[1]. However, it must remain on the register for a four-year period prior to removal. The EPA 1990 no longer states where the register is to be held[2]; instead the Secretary of State can prescribe places where the register is to be maintained[3].

1   SI 1994/1056, reg 11(2)(b).
2   This was deleted from s 64(6) by SI 1996/593 reg 3, Sch 2, para 6.
3   EPA 1990, s 66(6) as amended by the Environment Act 1995, s 120(1) and Sch 22, para 82(5).

13.12   The Agency must ensure that the register 'is open to inspection' by members of the public at 'all reasonable times'[1] and free of charge[2]. The fact that the EPA 1990 requires that the register is 'open for inspection' would appear to suggest that a person is permitted free and unhindered access to it. It would also imply that the register must be separate from the normal files of the Agency. The Agency is also required to allow members of the public access to 'reasonable facilities' for obtaining copies of the entries on the register. Such copies can be supplied on payment of 'reasonable charges'[3].

1   See *Davies v Winstanley* (1930) 144 LT 433: see para 12.59.
2   EPA 1990, s 64(6)(a), as amended by the Environment Act 1995, s 120(1) and Sch 22, para 82.
3   EPA 1990, s 64(5)(b), as amended by the Environment Act 1995, s 120(1) and Sch 22, para 82(5).

13.13   While there is no time limit on the Agency to ensure that information is initially placed on the register, Circular 11/94[1] indicates that the register should be updated as soon as possible. Furthermore, the Environmental Information Regulations 1992[2] separately set down certain general requirements in respect of information which is required to be provided on registers such as that maintained under the EPA 1990[3]. Requests for information should be met 'as soon as possible'[4] and refusals to allow access to information must be communicated in writing and contain reasons[5].

1   Circular 11/94, Annex 9, para 9.9.
2   SI 1992/3240, reg 5.

3 As information contained on public registers established by other statutes is not 'environmental information' under the Environmental Information Regulations 1992, the main provisions of these regulations do not apply. However, reg 5 sets down separate requirements in respect of persons who maintain information on registers which are not subject to the Environmental Information Regulations 1992.
4 SI 1992/3240, reg 5(a).
5 SI 1992/3240, reg 5(c): reg 5 also requires that requests are responded to within two months: this would appear to be over-ridden by the requirement in s 64(6)(a) of the EPA 1990, which allows access to registers at all reasonable times. Similarly, the regulations provide that no charge exceeding a reasonable amount is made for the supply of the information: again s 64(6)(a) indicates that no charge should be made.

13.14 As the content of the register is set down in the Waste Management Licensing Regulations 1994[1], these provisions were enacted in May 1994. Given the changes brought about by the establishment of the Agency in 1996, it will be apparent that certain of the provisions of the Waste Management Licensing Regulations 1994 refer to sections of the EPA 1990 which have been repealed[2]. The continuation of these cross-references presumably ensures the retention of information on the register which was supplied prior to April 1996, the date when the EPA 1990 was amended.

1 SI 1994/1056, reg 10 and 11.
2 Principally by the Environment Act 1995, Schs 22 and 24.

Registers of waste management licences

Licences and licence applications[1]

13.15 The Waste Management Licensing Regulations 1994 require all current licences granted by the Agency[2] to be placed on the public register. This includes licences[3] which have ceased to be in force in the last 12 months[4]. The Waste Management Licensing Regulations 1994 make clear that the requirement for licences to be present on the register includes copies of the associated working plans[5]. However, when working plans are superseded, the earlier copy can be removed from the register after four years[6].

1 Superseded resolutions for public waste management facilities in Scotland are also required to be held on SEPA's register. Also included must be 'proposals' for resolutions, the draft conditions, any written representations, references to the Secretary of State and emergency situations which involved the postponement of consultations: SI 1994/1056, reg 10(1)(n).
2 Or prior to the Agency's formation, the local government waste regulation authorities.
3 SI 1994/1056, reg 10(1)(a).
4 SI 1994/1056, reg 10(4).
5 SI 1994/1056 reg 10(1)(a): the nature of working plans is discussed at para 8.218.
6 By way of reg 11(2)(b) of SI 1994/1056: see Circular 11/94, Annex 4, para 9.46.

13.16 All licence applications which are pending determination or which relate to existing licences need to be held[1], including applications[2] which have been rejected in the last 12 months. This requirement also encompasses other documents submitted to the Agency which contain information supporting the application[3]. Licence applications may contain details of any criminal convictions of applicants and their associates[4]. Circular 11/94 reminds the Agency that these convictions will become 'spent' under the Rehabilitation of Offenders Act 1974[5]. Hence these details will need to be removed from the register at the end of the required period set down by the Rehabilitation of Offenders Act 1974. Whilst the Rehabilitation of Offenders Act 1974 does not apply to convictions received by bodies corporate, the Circular recommends that these convictions are to be treated in the same manner as convictions accrued by individuals.

1   SI 1994/1056, reg 10(1)(b).
2   SI 1994/1056, reg 10(4).
3   SI 1994/1056, reg 10(1)(b)(i).
4   As material submitted in respect of an applicant being a fit and proper person (EPA 1990, s 74): see para 8.112ff.
5   Circular 11/94, Annex 9, para 9.24.

13.17   Responses submitted as part of the application process from the statutory consultees, such as the Health and Safety Executive, the planning authority[1] and the Nature Conservancy Council[2], must be included. Prior to the Agency's formation, the National Rivers Authority (NRA) was also a consultee. While the reference to consultation with the NRA in the EPA 1990 has been deleted by the Environment Act 1995[3], the register must still retain the NRA's consultation responses which took place prior to the date of the change[4]. Details of any emergencies which took place which required that the consultation process is postponed[5] must be recorded[6]. Finally, notices issued by the Agency rejecting an application[7] must be placed on the register[8].

1   Under the EPA 1990, s 36(4)(b).
2   EPA 1990, s 36(7): in Wales the Countryside Council for Wales; for Scotland, Scottish Natural Heritage.
3   See the Environment Act 1995, s 120(1) and Sch 22, para 68.
4   Similarly, decisions made by the relevant Secretary of State on appeal under s 36(5) or (6) of the EPA 1990 must be entered (SI 1994/1056 reg 10(1)(b)(iii)). Both of these sub-sections have been deleted by the Environment Act 1995. It should be noted that the wording of the Waste Management Licensing Regulations 1994 (SI 1994/1056, reg 10(1)(b)(ii)) only requires the inclusion of copies of consultees' responses made under powers contained in the EPA 1990. This therefore excludes responses given before 1 May 1994, as they stemmed instead from the Control of Pollution Act 1974.
5   EPA 1990, s 37(5)(a): see para 9.07.
6   SI 1994/1056, reg 10(1)(b)(v).
7   Under powers contained in the EPA 1990, s 36(9).
8   SI 1994/1056, reg 10(1)(b)(iv).

Licence modification and transfer

13.18   The register must contain copies of notices giving effect to a licence modification instigated by the Agency or those which provide an affirmative response to a request from the licence holder for a modification[1]. In contrast to the requirements in respect of licences themselves and licence applications, the Waste Management Licensing Regulations 1994 only make explicit reference to modifications made under the EPA 1990. If interpreted strictly, an effect of this would be to require that only those modification decision notices issued since 1 May 1994 need to be placed on the register. The wording of the Waste Management Licensing Regulations 1994 does not extend to notices issued under the earlier powers stemming from the Control of Pollution Act 1974, but these are usually included.

1   See EPA 1990, s 37(4) and SI 1994/1056, reg 10(1)(c); see para 9.03ff.

13.19   In addition to decision notices in respect of licence modifications, copies of applications made for modifications and licence transfers[1] need to be included. The wording of the Waste Management Licensing Regulations 1994 does, in this instance, cause applications made under the Control of Pollution Act 1974 to be included. However, in the case of applications for modification which were unsuccessful or where the licence itself is no longer is extant, these only need to stay on the register for 12 months[2].

1   In respect of licence transfer, only applications are required to be placed on the register. Unlike licence modifications, no formal notice is issued by the Agency to state that a transfer is enacted (see the EPA 1990, s 40). Instead, the licence is endorsed to that effect (see para 9.114ff).
2   SI 1994/1056, reg 10(4).

13.20   As was the case with licence applications, copies of the consultation replies submitted by the Health and Safety Executive, the planning authority[1] and, where affected, the appropriate nature conservation body, also need to be included[2]. Similarly, the register must incorporate responses made by the National Rivers Authority up to 1 April 1996.

1   EPA 1990, s 37(5): as amended by the Environment Act 1995, s 120(1), Sch 22, para 70(2).
2   SI 1994/1056, reg 10(1)(b)(ii).

13.21   Notices rejecting applications for licence modifications must be included[1], along with details of any emergency situation which caused a suspension of the consultation process for the determination of a modification[2].

1   SI 1994/1056, reg 10(1)(b)(iv).
2   SI 1994/1056, reg 10(1)(b)(v).

Licence surrender

13.22   Applications for licence surrender need to be placed on the register[1]. These remain on the register indefinitely, unlike the surrendered licence and its supporting documents[2]. Supporting information submitted by the applicant must be included, along with copies of the Agency's investigations of the relevant land in response to the surrender application[3] and any representation made by the planning authority[4]. Consultations from the National Rivers Authority prior to 1 April 1996 must be included[5], as must the Agency's notice of determination and any certificate of completion[6].

1   SI 1994/1056, reg 10(1)(l). Licence surrender is discussed at para 9.93ff.
2   Contrast SI 1994/1056, reg 10(1)(a) to reg 10(1)(l). Furthermore reg 11(2) would not apply in these circumstances, as it would seem unlikely that this information would ever become superseded.
3   By way of powers contained in the EPA 1990, s 39(4).
4   Made under EPA 1990, s 39(7)(b) as amended by the Environment Act 1995, s 120(1) and Sch 22, para 73(3): see para 9.102.
5   EPA 1990, s 39(7): a similar provision applies to the river purification authority and district planning authority in Scotland: the EPA 1990, s 39(8): repealed by the Environment Act 1995, s 120(3) and Sch 24. Decisions by the Secretary of State on disputes between the earlier local government waste regulation authorities and these bodies must be included: however, this appeal mechanism (EPA 1990, s 39(7) and (8)) was deleted by the Environment Act 1995 in 1996.
6   SI 1994/1056, reg 10(1)(l)(v): issued by way of powers contained in the EPA 1990, s 39: see para 9.103.

Notices in respect of licence compliance, revocation, suspension and remedial works[1]

13.23   The register must contain all notices relating to licence suspension or revocation[2]. The wording of the Waste Management Licensing Regulations 1994 excludes any revocation notices issued under the Control of Pollution Act 1974. Notices requiring operators to comply with licence conditions[3] must be included[4]. Also to be placed on the register is any correspondence made prior to 1 April 1996 with the National Rivers Authority[5] in respect of inspections by waste regulation authorities which indicated that pollution of water was occurring at a licensed facility[6]. Finally, the register should contain details of any remedial or preventative measures taken by the Agency[7] under powers contained in s 42(3) of the EPA 1990 for the mitigation of pollution[8].

1   Note that the register only contains notices in respect of facilities subject to waste management licences. It also excludes notices issued under s 59 of the EPA 1990: s 59 notices require waste which is unlawfully deposited to be removed or otherwise mitigated. They can be used at both licensed and unlicensed premises (see para 12.101ff).
2   SI 1994/1056, reg 10(1)(d). Licence suspension and revocation are considered at paras 9.17 and 9.40.
3   Issued under s 42(5) of the EPA 1990: see paras 9.26 and 9.48.
4   SI 1994/1056, reg 10(1)(g)(iii): oddly this sub-article refers primarily to the requirement to place 'reports' on the register. However, the word extends to a copy of the actual notice itself.
5   Or river purification authority in Scotland.
6   SI 1994/1056, reg 10(1)(g)(i), under the EPA 1990, s 42(2): s 42(2) was repealed by the Environment Act 1995, s 120(3) and Sch 24.
7   Or its predecessors.
8   SI 1994/1056, reg 10(1)(g)(ii): see para 12.95ff.

Details of appeals

13.24   The register should contain notices of all appeals made to the Secretary of State in respect of waste management licence applications, modifications, transfers, suspensions, revocations and surrender[1]. This must include all other documentation submitted[2] in support of the appeal. The register must contain any notice of the appeal's withdrawal[3]. A copy of the Secretary of State's decision notice and information supporting that decision – such as an inspector's report – should also be included[4].

1   Appeals are made under s 43 of the EPA 1990: see para 9.126ff.
2   As prescribed under SI 1994/1056, reg 6(2): see para 9.129.
3   Under SI 1994/1056, reg 6(4).
4   Under SI 1994/1056, reg 9(3): see paras 9.133 and 9.134.

13.25   Circular 11/94 indicates that copies of appeal applications can be removed from the register[1]. This can only be done after a period of four years and on the grounds that the material has been superseded[2].

1   Circular 11/94, Annex 9, para 9.46.
2   SI 1994/1056, reg 11(2)(b).

Licence holders' convictions

13.26   All convictions against licence holders[1] for offences 'under Part II of the EPA 1990' need to be placed on the register. While these convictions are not so broad as those listed as 'relevant offences' under the Waste Management Licensing Regulations 1994[2], they must be included whether or not they relate to any particular licences. Details to be retained on the register are the name of the offender, the date of conviction, the penalty imposed and the name of the court. After the periods set down in the Rehabilitation of Offenders Act 1974, information on convictions must be removed from the register[3].

1   SI 1994/1056, reg 10(1)(f).
2   SI 1994/1056, reg 3: see para 8.117.
3   Circular 11/94, para 9.24: including information relating to convictions of bodies corporate.

Environmental monitoring information

13.27   The provisions in the EPA 1990 require that 'any monitoring information' furnished to the Agency by way of a licence condition or resulting from the Agency's activities at licensed sites must be contained in the register[1]. This requirement also extends to monitoring information[2] supplied to the Agency by way of a notice under s 71(2) of the EPA 1990[3].

1   SI 1994/1056, reg 10(1)(h).
2   But not to other data collected by a s 71 notice that does not relate to monitoring.
3   SI 1994/1056, reg 10(1)(h): s 71 notices are discussed at para 12.174ff.

13.28   How far the term 'monitoring information' stretches is not clear. Many waste management licence conditions require that both the monitoring data and an interpretation of its significance is submitted to the Agency. It is not immediately clear from the Waste Management Licensing Regulations 1994 whether interpretations of the data fall within the term 'monitoring information'. However, Circular 11/94 advises that the requirement of the Waste Management Licensing Regulations 1994 is satisfied when 'all raw monitoring data, analysis of information obtained and completed reports' are placed on the register[1]. Working drafts and preliminary reports are, however, considered to be excluded.

1   Circular 11/94, Annex 9, para 9.27.

13.29   Where monitoring information is entered on the register, it is only required to remain in place for four years[1]. All of it can be removed after that date[2]. Oddly, while reg 11 of the Waste Management Licensing Regulations 1994 requires that specified information is to be excluded from the register where legal proceedings are pending[3], the requirement to place monitoring data on the register[4] is not lifted by this provision.

1   SI 1994/1056, reg 11(2)(a).
2   SI 1994/1056, reg 11(2)(a) does not, unlike reg 11(2)(b), require that the data must be superseded before removal can occur.
3   SI 1994/1056, reg 11(1), which refers to information specified under reg 10(1)(g), (m) or reg 10(2).
4   SI 1994/1056, reg 10(1)(h).

Directions by the Secretary of State

13.30   Any directions to the Agency from the Secretary of State in respect of waste management licences[1] need to be added to the register when they are made in respect of specified sections of Part II of the EPA 1990[2].

1   Directions under the EPA 1990, ss 35(7), 37(3), 38(7) and ss 42(8) (and 54(11) and (15), 58 in Scotland). Directions under ss 50(9) and 66(7) are also required to be included: s 50 and s 66 have been repealed by the Environment Act 1995 (s 120(3) and Sch 24).
2   SI 1994/1056, reg 10(1)(i).

Reports of inspections/other visits by staff of the Agency

13.31   The Waste Management Licensing Regulations 1994 set down significant requirements in respect of the placing on the register of inspection reports[1] and written details of the Agency's inspectors' other visits to premises[2]. To a certain extent, the provisions overlap and cause duplication. But the principal reason why there is differentiation in respect of these provisions is that the Waste Management Licensing Regulations 1994 would appear to treat the inspection of licensed sites[3] separately to information on inspections of other premises[4]. Information which relates to pending criminal proceedings is excluded[5]. But, at the end of the proceedings, the omitted material must be incorporated into the register.

1   SI 1994/1056, reg 10(2).
2   SI 1994/1056, reg 10(1)(g) and (m).

3   SI 1994/1056, reg 10(1)(g).
4   SI 1994/1056, reg 10(2).
5   SI 1994/1056, reg 11(1).

13.32   Under s 108(4) of the Environment Act 1995, Agency inspectors can enter any premises at any reasonable time and undertake such examinations, inspections etc as are deemed necessary[1]. Where staff of the Agency exercise any of the powers contained in s 108[2], 'a record showing when the power was exercised' must be placed on the register[3]. The record must also indicate 'what information was obtained, and what action was taken' when the powers were exercised. Similar records must be kept in relation to inspections undertaken by way of the now superseded powers of entry contained in s 69(3) of the EPA 1990. Hence inspection reports up to 1 April 1996 must be included[4].

1   These powers are discussed at para 12.46ff.
2   However, for information to be placed on the register under s 64, the power must be exercised in respect of Part II of the EPA 1990.
3   SI 1994/1056, reg 10(2)(aa): as inserted by SI 1996/593, reg 10(3).
4   SI 1994/1056, reg 10(2)(a); but not those stemming from the operation of the Control of Pollution Act 1974.

13.33   The Waste Management Licensing Regulations 1994 also require that 'reports' produced when the Agency has discharged any function under s 42 of the EPA 1990 need to be placed on the register[1]. Functions under s 42 include the duty on the Agency to ensure that licensed facilities do not cause pollution of the environment or harm to human health and that there is compliance with licence conditions[2]. Accordingly, it would seem that the Agency's routine inspection role at licensed waste management facilities emanates from the need to ensure that s 42 is complied with[3]. The material placed on the register should include any remedial or preventive measures taken under s 42(5) of the EPA 1990[4] and any notices issued under s 42(5)[5]. In relation to any reports produced under this provision prior to April 1994, correspondence with the National Rivers Authority[6] needs to be included[7].

1   SI 1994/1056, reg 10(1)(g).
2   EPA 1990, s 42(1): see paras 12.11 and 12.23.
3   See Circular 11/94, Annex 9, para 9.36.
4   SI 1994/1056, reg 10(1)(g)(ii).
5   SI 1994/1056, reg 10(1)(g)(iii).
6   Oddly, in respect of Scotland, the reference to the river purification authority has been deleted (see SI 1996/973, reg 2, Sch 1, para 17(1)). No equivalent provision has a similar effect in respect of the reference to the National Rivers Authority in relation to England and Wales.
7   SI 1994/1056, reg 10(1)(g)(i): s 42(2) was deleted by the Environment Act 1995, s 120(1) and Sch 22, para 76(2).

13.34   'Written reports' emanating from instances when powers have been used to seize and render harmless certain articles must be placed on the register[1].

1   SI 1994/1056, reg 10(1)(m): these powers are contained in s 109 of the Environment Act 1995, with the requirement to produce written reports contained in s 109(2). They are discussed in more detail at para 12.98. Prior to the enactment of the Environment Act 1995, the reports for this purpose were contained in s 70(3) of the EPA 1990. These need to remain on the register: SI 1994/1056, reg 10(1)(m).

13.35   Circular 11/94 recommends that inspection reports should remain on the register for a period of four years, after which they can be removed[1]. The Waste Management Licensing Regulations 1994 allow material which is 'superseded' to be removed from the register after four years[2]. The Circular considers that old inspection reports fall into this category[3].

1   Circular 11/94, Annex 9, para 9.45.
2   SI 1994/1056, reg 11(2)(b).
3   Circular 11/94, Annex 9, para 9.45. Para 9.45 refers to ss 69 and 70 of the EPA 1990. These have been replaced by ss 108 and 109 of the Environment Act 1995: see para 12.52ff.

Special waste and transfrontier waste shipments

13.36   In respect of special waste[1] certain requirements relating to registers are contained in s 64 of the EPA 1990 and in the Waste Management Licensing Regulations 1994[2]. However, these provisions need to be read in conjunction with the Special Waste Regulations 1996[3]. It also should be noted that specified requirements of the Special Waste Regulations 1996 apply to wastes transported internationally under transfrontier shipment notifications[4], and therefore the provisions on the contents of the s 64 register will embrace wastes defined as special wastes which are moved in the latter circumstances.

1   See Chapter 4.
2   SI 1994/1056, reg 10(1)(k).
3   SI 1996/972, previously SI 1980/1709.
4   See Chapter 5 and Circular 6/96, para 19.

13.37   The Waste Management Licensing Regulations 1994 require the public register to contain 'any summary data' prepared by the Agency[1] on the amount of special waste produced or disposed of in its area[2]. Although there is no statutory requirement on the Agency to produce summary data on an annual basis, statistics are collated at the Department of the Environment's behest in order to provide information to the European Commission[3].

1   Or previously by the local authority waste regulation authorities.
2   SI 1994/1056, reg 10(1)(j).
3   As required under Commission Decision concerning questionnaires of member states on the implementation of Certain Directives in the Waste Sector (Decision 97/622) (OJ L256/13 19.9.97) or under Council Regulation on the Supervision and Control of Shipments with, into and out of the European Community (Regulation 259/93) (OJ L30/1 6.2.93) Article 41.

13.38   The Special Waste Regulations 1996[1] require that, where a waste management licence has been surrendered or fully revoked, the operator must hand over to the Agency all retained special waste consignment notes[2]. The Agency itself must then keep them for not less than three years[3]. Similarly, where special waste is deposited in or on any land, the site operator must ensure that location plans of these deposits are made[4]. These plans must be handed over to the Agency. Provisions similar to those just described also existed in respect of the earlier Control of Pollution (Special Waste) Regulations 1980[5]. The Waste Management Licensing Regulations 1994 require that, once handed to the Agency, the above documents and plans are retained in the register[6].

1   SI 1996/972, reg 15(5): see para 4.159.
2   And carrier's schedules: see Chapter 4.
3   SI 1996/972, reg 15(5).
4   As required by SI 1996/972, reg 16(1).
5   SI 1980/1709, regs 13(5) and 14(1).
6   SI 1994/1056, reg 10(1)(k) as amended by SI 1996/972, reg 25 and Sch 3.

REGISTERS OF ACTIVITIES EXEMPT FROM WASTE MANAGEMENT LICENCES

13.39   The Agency is required to maintain a register of the details of many of those activities which are exempt from the need to possess a waste management licence[1]. This registration requirement stems from the Waste Management Licensing Regulations 1994, and is separate to the register under s 64 of the EPA 1990. For this reason, they are also not subject to the provisions of the EPA 1990 in respect of exclusions for commercial confidentiality[2].

1   SI 1994/1056, reg 18: the system of exemptions is the subject of Chapters 10 and 11.
2   See para 13.65.

13.40   The Agency is required to set up the exemption register under reg 18(2) of the Waste Management Licensing Regulations 1994[1]. It should be noted that not all the exempt activities are to be recorded on this register. Details of certain of them are contained on the separate registers held by the Agency in respect of IPC facilities. In addition, some other exemptions are only to be found on registers held by the local authorities. Chapters 10 and 11 indicate which particular activity needs to be placed on the register established by way of reg 18.

1   SI 1994/1056.

13.41   The following details need to be placed on the register under reg 18[1]:

–   the name and address of the establishment or undertaking;
–   a description of the exempt activity; and
–   the place at which the activity is occurring.

In the case where the exempt landspreading of specified wastes occurs[2], the above information is substituted by[3] the name, fax, phone number and address of the person undertaking the activity; a description of the waste[4]; an estimate of the total quantity to be spread or, if there are frequent spreadings, an estimate of the next six months' rate of application; the location of the spreading activity; and the commencement date or, for frequent spreading, an estimate of the frequency of spreading.

1   SI 1994/1056, reg 18(3).
2   See SI 1994/1056, Sch 3, para 7(3)(c) and para 10.149ff.
3   SI 1994/1056, reg 18(7) and Sch 3, para 7(4).
4   Which must include the process from which it arises.

13.42   Like the register established under s 64 of the EPA 1990, the Agency must ensure that its register of exemptions is open to inspection by members of the public free of charge and at all reasonable times[1]. Where copies of entries are required, they should be provided on payment of reasonable charges. The Waste Management Licensing Regulations 1994 allow this register to be kept in any form, permitting the use of such methods as computer information systems[2].

1   SI 1994/1056, reg 18(8) as amended by SI 1996/972, reg 3 and Sch 2, para 10(4): see paras 12.59 and 13.12.
2   SI 1994/1056, reg 18(9).

REGISTERS OF CONTROLLED WASTE CARRIERS AND BROKERS

13.43   Under the Controlled Waste (Registration of Carriers and Seizure of Vehicles) Regulations 1991, the Agency is given a duty to establish and maintain a register of controlled waste carriers[1]. As is described at para 6.05, separate provisions relate to the registration of the waste disposal authority, waste collection authority, the Agency[2], charities and voluntary groups and subsidiaries of British Rail when they are involved in waste carriage[3]. The latter types of waste carriers are excluded from the Control of Pollution (Amendment) Act 1989, but are subject to a separate registration by way of Schedule 4 to the Waste Management Licensing Regulations 1994[4]. Finally, the Agency is also given a further duty to maintain a register of controlled waste brokers[5]. While the register of waste carriers subject to the Control of Pollution (Amendment) Act 1989 and the broker register are essentially similar, the requirements which apply to the registration of bodies such as the waste collection authority are much less onerous. Accordingly, the provisions described below relate to only the main carrier and broker registers: the simplified register for the collection authority and other bodies is described separately at the end of this section.

1 SI 1991/1624, reg 3(1).
2 As Waste Regulation Authority: see the EPA 1990, s 30(1) as amended by the Environment Act 1995, s 120(1) Sch 22, para 62.
3 SI 1994/1056, Sch 4, Pt I, para 12.
4 SI 1994/1056, Sch 4, Pt I, para 12(5): see para 6.105.
5 SI 1994/1056, Sch 5, para 2(1).

13.44 The Agency has assumed responsibility for the Co-ordinated Local Authority Database of Waste Carriers (CLADWAC). Although prior to the Agency's formation, not all waste regulation authorities entered information on to CLADWAC, all the details contained in the carrier register are now entered onto this database. Hence any Agency officer is able to check up on the central register whether a carrier or broker possesses a valid registration.

Carrier registers under the Control of Pollution (Amendment) Act 1989 and broker registers

13.45 For carrier registration applications made under the Control of Pollution (Amendment) Act 1989, the Agency must ensure that the register contains a copy of the application for registration or for a renewal of registration[1]. A similar requirement applies to controlled waste brokers[2].

1 SI 1991/1624, reg 4(10).
2 SI 1994/1056, Sch 5, para 3(12). The Transfrontier Shipment of Waste Regulations 1994 (SI 1994/1137, reg 20) contain certain requirements in respect of brokers involved in international waste shipments. These powers were solely transitional provisions to ensure that brokers wishing to act as notifiers were to be regarded as registered whilst their applications were pending after January 1995. The provision only applied to broker applications received prior to that date (see SI 1994/1137, reg 20(3)).

13.46 If the Agency accepts a carrier or broker application, it must enter prescribed details in the carrier register. This should also be done when the Agency has been directed to accept a registration following a successful appeal to the Secretary of State[1]. The information to be placed on the register must contain[2]:

–   an entry which indicates that the person is a registered waste carrier or broker;
–   a registration number;
–   the date of registration taking effect and its expiry;
–   the business name[3] and address of the principal place of business or the name of person or partnership who is a registered carrier;
–   the date(s) of birth of the applicant or of all partners in a partnership;

- in the case of a body corporate, the names of 'each director, manager, secretary or other similar officer'[4] and their dates of birth;
- in the case of a company registered under the Companies Acts[5], details of the country of incorporation and Companies Acts' registration number;
- appropriate details relating to the carrier and 'another relevant person'[6] where they have been convicted of prescribed offences; and
- where the applicant or 'any company in the same group[7] of companies' holds a waste management licence, the name of the licence holder and the regulatory authority who granted.

In the case of a partnership, the details of all the partners need to be included on the register as one entry[8].

1   SI 1991/1624, reg 6(1); SI 1994/1056, Sch 5, para 4(1).
2   SI 1991/1624, reg 6(1)(a)–(g); SI 1994/1056, Sch 5, para 4(1).
3   Defined as 'a name under which a person carries on business and by virtue of which the Business Names Act 1979 applies' (SI 1991/1624, reg 6(4)).
4   The definition of these terms is discussed at para 7.156ff.
5   Given the same meaning as s 744 of the Companies Act 1985 (SI 1991/1624, reg 6(4)).
6   See para 6.65.
7   A group of companies is as defined by s 53(1) of the Companies Act 1989 (SI 1991/1624, reg 6(4)).
8   SI 1991/1624, reg 6(2); SI 1994/1056, Sch 5, para 4(2).

13.47   The Agency is required to keep copies of both the application for a registration and any subsequent renewal on the register for at least six years[1]. Afterwards, its details can be deleted from the register at the Agency's discretion if the carrier is no longer registered[2].

1   SI 1991/1624, reg 4(11); SI 1994/1056, Sch 5, para 3(17).
2   See Circular 11/91, Annex 1, para 1.26; Circular 11/94, Annex 8, para 8.96.

13.48   Should an applicant appeal after the refusal by the Agency to accept the registration, the Agency must 'as soon as reasonably practicable' enter the date of the appeal and its result on the register[1]. If registration is refused, but no appeal has been lodged, a record to that effect must entered into the register[2]. These entries can only be removed after six years from the date of cessation of registration[3].

1   SI 1991/1624, reg 5(3); SI 1994/1056, Sch 5, para 3(15).
2   SI 1991/1624, reg 5(4); SI 1994/1056, Sch 5, para 3(16).
3   SI 1991/1624, reg 5(5) and 12(2); SI 1994/1056, Sch 5, para 8.

13.49   When a registration has been renewed, or where an appeal has been upheld, the Agency is required to place on the register[1]:

- the date when the renewal takes effect and the new expiry date;
- any changes disclosed on the renewal application form; and
- the date when these amendments were made.

Similarly, when a registered person requests that amendments are made to the entries – for example when the details of a partnership change – the Agency must make appropriate changes to the register and note the date when the amendments were made[2].

1   SI 1991/1624, reg 7(1)(a)–(c); SI 1994/1056, Sch 5, para 4(4).
2   SI 1991/1624, reg 8(2)(i) and (ii); SI 1994/1056, Sch 5, para 4(7)(i) and (ii).

13.50   For controlled waste carriers, Table 1.4 of Circular 11/91 provides a useful summary of the somewhat complex requirements relating to when entries pertaining to the carrier register have to be subject to alteration. There is, however, no equivalent Table in Circular 11/94 in relation to waste brokers.

13.51 The information contained in the register must be kept up to date and, in this respect, it appears easy for slippage to occur. As noted at para 6.80, partnerships are vulnerable to inadvertently voiding their registration if partners change and the change is not communicated to the Agency[1]. This is likely to be a particular problem in the construction industry, as these rules are unlikely to be at the top of the mind of many small builders. Similarly, waste disposal contractors need to be careful that details of *all* their licensed sites are kept on the register and remain current[2].

1 SI 1991/1624, reg 11(6); SI 1994/1056, Sch 5, para 7(9).
2 SI 1991/1624, regs 6(1) and 8(1); SI 1994/1056, Sch 5, para 4(1) and (6).

13.52 Inevitably the details of individuals' prescribed offences which were initially placed on the register at the time of application will become 'spent' for the purposes of the Rehabilitation of Offenders Act 1974. Both Circulars 11/91 and 11/94 note[1] that it is not unlawful to retain such details on the register after the Act's prescribed period. However, it is recommended that they are removed from the register. The Agency therefore should regularly review the convictions on the register and delete those that have become 'spent'.

1 Circular 11/91, Annex 1, para 1.50; Circular 11/94, Annex 8, para 8.59.

13.53 The Controlled Waste (Registration of Carriers and Seizure of Vehicles) Regulations 1991 and Schedule 5 to the Waste Management Licensing Regulations 1994 stipulate a number of matters concerned with public access to the carrier and broker register. The Agency must permit the public to be able to inspect the register free of charge and at all reasonable hours[1]. The public must also be granted reasonable facilities for obtaining copies of the entries on the register on payment of reasonable charges[2]. To facilitate public access, the controlled waste carrier register 'may be kept in any form but shall be indexed and arranged so that members of the public can readily trace information contained within it'[3]. In contrast, the broker register is required solely to be 'kept in any form'[4].

1 SI 1991/1624, reg 3(1)(a); SI 1994/1056, Sch 5, para 2(1)(a). See paras 12.59 and 13.12.
2 SI 1991/1624, reg 3(1)(b); SI 1994/1056, Sch 5, para 2(1)(b).
3 SI 1991/1624, reg 3(2). It should be noted that, in respect of the register established under s 64 of the EPA 1990, the requirement for indexing is only contained in the non-statutory guidance in Circular 11/94: see Circular 11/94, Annex 9, para 9.11.
4 SI 1994/1056, Sch 5, para 2(2); but see, in relation to waste brokers, Circular 11/94, Annex 8, para 8.21.

Registration of the waste collection authority and other waste carriers

13.54 It has been mentioned that certain, mainly public sector, organisations are required to register under separate provisions when they wish to be involved in the carriage of controlled waste[1]. The requirements for the Agency's register for the waste disposal authority, waste collection authority, the Agency itself[2], charities and voluntary groups and subsidiaries of British Rail[3] are much less complex: 'It is designed to place the minimum burden consistent with the implementation of the Directive[4] on both the organisation concerned and on WRAs'[5]. The Agency is required to register these bodies if it receives notice of them in writing 'or otherwise becomes aware of those particulars'[6]. The latter requirement means that the Agency has the duty to register the activity if it simply knows of its existence[7].

1 SI 1994/1056, Sch 4, Pt I, para 12: see para 6.105.

2   As 'waste regulation authority': see the EPA 1990, s 30(1) as amended by the Environment Act 1995, s 120(1), Sch 22, para 62.
3   SI 1994/1056, Sch 4, Pt I, para 12.
4   Council Directive of 15 July 1975 on Waste (75/442/EEC) (OJ L194/39 25.7.75 (as amended by Council Directive of 18 March 1991 amending Directive 75/442/EEC on Waste (91/156/EEC) (OJ L78/32 26.3.91)) Article 12.
5   Circular 11/94, Annex 1, para 1.74.
6   SI 1994/1056 Sch 4, Pt I, para 12(7).
7   See para 6.110.

13.55   The following details need to be contained in the register in respect of these bodies: the name of the establishment or undertaking, its principal place of business, and the address of any other place from which it undertakes its business[1]. The register can be kept in any form[2]. Circular 11/94 notes that, '[p]rovided it contains the necessary information, the register may simply consist of the originals of any notices received from an establishment or undertaking together with added details of other cases that have come to the Authority's notice'[3].

1   SI 1994/1056, Sch 4, Pt I, para 12(6).
2   SI 1994/1056, Sch 4, Pt I, para 12(10).
3   Circular 11/94, Annex 1, para 1.84.

13.56   Like the register established under the Control of Pollution (Amendment) Act 1989, this register is required to be open to public inspection free of charge and at all reasonable hours. Copies of entries on the register must be supplied on the payment of reasonable charges[1].

1   SI 1994/1056, Sch 4, Pt I, para 9.

COPIES OF THE REGISTER TO BE HELD BY THE WASTE COLLECTION AUTHORITY

13.57   A proportion of the Agency's register must also be duplicated and sent to each waste collection authority[1] in England and Wales[2]. Additional information must also be sent out as and when the Agency is required to add information to its own register.

1   The District Council or, where created, the unitary authority.
2   EPA 1990, s 64(5) as amended by the Environment Act 1995, s 120(1), Sch 22, para 82(4): extended to cover Wales by Sch 22, para 82(3). It would appear that no equivalent arrangement exists for Scotland.

13.58   The particulars to be passed on to the collection authorities are set down in reg 10 of the Waste Management Licensing Regulations 1994[1]. The Regulations require that each collection authority's register must contain all current waste management licences for facilities in its area[2]. This includes licences which have been either surrendered or fully revoked in the last 12 months[3]. In addition, notices relating to the modification of those licences, their revocation or suspension and certificates of completion on licence surrender also need to be kept[4]. However, no other information needs to be provided beyond these details.

1   SI 1994/1056, reg 10(3).
2   SI 1994/1056, reg 10(3)(a).
3   SI 1994/1056, reg 10(3)(a) and reg 10(4).
4   SI 1994/1056, reg 10(3)(b), (c) and (d).

13.59   The waste collection authorities have the duty to establish a register of the information furnished to them[1] and to ensure that the register is open for inspection at all reasonable times and at no charge[2]. The authorities are also subject to the requirement to provide and maintain reasonable facilities to allow copies to be made of entries of the register on payment of reasonable charges[3]. Like the Agency's main register, this register can be maintained 'in any form'[4], allowing microfiche and computer storage to be used.

1 EPA 1990, s 64(4).
2 EPA 1990, s 64(6)(a) as amended by the Environment Act 1995, Sch 22, para 82(5).
3 EPA 1990, s 64(6)(b) as amended by the Environment Act 1995, Sch 22, para 82(5).
4 EPA 1990, s 64(7).

13.60 The purpose of this provision would appear to be to ensure that public access to the register is possible without inordinate travelling. However, this arrangement is a little odd in the sense that, in areas other than unitary authorities, the district council – as waste collection authority – will possess the register of waste management licences, but any person wanting information about planning permissions for a particular facility will have to go also to the County Council[1].

1 As explained at para 8.33, with the exception of metropolitan areas or where unitary authorities have been established, planning applications in respect of waste management facilities are 'county matters'.

13.61 In addition, given the very limited particulars which need to be kept on the collection authority's register, it seems likely that most persons requiring access to the register will need a much wider range of information. However, the collection authority's register may prove to be useful to persons subject to the duty of care[1] who are required to verify the existence of appropriate licences. But details of the registers of controlled waste carriers, brokers and most[2] exempt activities remain solely within the premises of the Agency.

1 EPA 1990, s 34: see Chapter 3.
2 Other than those required to be placed on the local authority's register: see para 13.40.

EXCLUSIONS FROM THE PUBLIC REGISTER

13.62 The legislation discussed below concerns only information excluded from the system of registers relating to the EPA 1990 and subsidiary provisions. It has been noted earlier that other environmental information may be obtainable under the Environmental Information Regulations 1992[1]. In respect of the latter, different confidentiality provisions apply[2]. Hence the Agency needs to be aware of which legislative provisions apply to whatever information is being requested and also the need, ultimately, to follow the spirit of the Directive on Access to Information[3] when deciding such matters.

1 SI 1992/3240, as amended by SI 1998/1447. See para 13.05.
2 Contrast SI 1992/3240, reg 4 (as amended by SI 1998/1447, reg 2) to the EPA 1990, ss 65 and 66.
3 Council Directive on the Freedom of Access to Information on the Environment (91/313) (OJ L158/56 23.6.90).

13.63 The EPA 1990 allows certain commercially confidential information to be excluded from the public register. But this only applies to the register established under s 64 of the EPA 1990[1]. Information can also be left off that register on grounds of national security[2]. There are no equivalent provisions in respect of the registers of exempt activities and controlled waste carriers and brokers. Hence the content of the latter registers are available in their totality. This contrast means that the following discussion relates solely to exclusions from the register set up under s 64 of the EPA 1990.

1 EPA 1990, s 66.
2 EPA 1990, s 65.

13.64   In respect of requests that information is left off the s 64 register on grounds of commercial confidentiality, it is the Agency who makes the decision at first instance[1]. The Secretary of State can also direct that certain information should be removed from the register. The latter power relates to information which is neither prescribed as being required to be present on the register or where, for national security or commercial confidentiality reasons, an appeal has deemed that it is necessary that it should be excluded[2].

1   EPA 1990, s 66(1).
2   EPA 1990, s 64(2A): as amended by the Environment Act 1995, s 120(1) and Sch 22, para 82. There would appear to be mistake in the drafting of this provision: the amended sub-section allows the Secretary of State to require '. . . the removal from any register *of its of any* specified information . . .'

Commercially confidential information

13.65   Section 66 of the EPA 1990 requires that 'commercially confidential' information relating to individuals or businesses should be only contained in the register with those persons' consent[1]. The only exception is where such information is directed to be put on the register by the Secretary of State. Commercially confidential information is defined as information which 'would prejudice to an unreasonable degree the commercial interests' of an individual or person[2].

1   EPA 1990, s 66(1).
2   EPA 1990, s 66(11).

13.66   In general, there is a presumption in favour of disclosure. In respect of the EPA 1990, Circular 11/94 makes this point clear[1]:

'The overriding principle governing access to information, and informing these legislative provisions, is that all information that affects the environment should be freely available unless it is genuinely commercially confidential. In that case, the amount of information excluded should be kept to the minimum necessary to safeguard the commercial advantage.'

1   Circular 11/94, Annex 9, para 9.39.

13.67   By definition, confidential information must not be information which is public property or public knowledge[1]. In *Thomas Marshall (Exporters) Ltd v Guinle*[2], it was 'tentatively' suggested that, in relation to information or secrets in a trade or industrial setting, four elements can be identified when particular information is to be held to be confidential:

'First, . . . the information must be information the release of which the owner believes would be injurious to him or of advantage to his rivals or others. Second, . . . the owner must believe that the information is confidential or secret, ie that it is not already in the public domain. It may be that some or all of his rivals already have the information: but as long as the owner believes it to be confidential . . . he is entitled to try and protect it. Third, . . . the owner's belief under the two previous heads must be reasonable. Fourth, . . . the information must be judged in the light of the usage and practices of a particular industry or trade concerned. It may be that information which does not satisfy all these requirements may be entitled to protection as confidential information or trade secrets: but . . any information which does satisfy them must be of a type which is entitled to protection'[3].

1   *Saltman Engineering Co Ltd v Campbell Engineering Co Ltd* (1948) 65 RPC 203 at 215/10: however see also *Coco v A N Clark (Engineers) Ltd* [1969] RPC 41 at 47/20 per Megarry J.

2   [1978] 3 WLR 116 at 136A.
3   Similarly, in *Coco v A N Clark (Engineers) Ltd* [1969] RPC 41 at 47/12), Megarry J identified three
    elements: that the information was not already in the public domain; that it had been imparted in
    circumstances involving an obligation of confidence; and that its unauthorised use by the recipient
    had caused detriment to the party which communicated it.

13.68   One of the most sensitive areas in respect of commercial confidentiality is the
requirement of the EPA 1990 that any waste management licence holder or licence
applicant makes financial provision[1]. A significant amount of financial information
must be supplied to the Agency as part of this process, much of which will be commercially sensitive. In addition, the Agency may wish to impose a particular type of financial provision mechanism such as a bond in order to ensure that a licensee will have
long-term funds available to satisfy the requirements of the licence and to address
unexpected events. Third parties, such as local action groups, may wish to review the
material submitted and the wording of bonds or other mechanisms imposed. For
obvious reasons, the information is also of considerable interest to the applicant's or
licensee's competitors.

1   EPA 1990, s 74: the requirements in respect of financial provision are discussed at para 8.172ff.

13.69   It would seem that the general information submitted by applicants on their
financial standing would probably not be commercially confidential. Usually company accounts are requested by the Agency for this purpose. For many of the larger
waste management companies, this information is already in the public domain being
lodged in Companies House. However, matters become more complicated in respect
of other information submitted, including more recent accounts which have yet to be
lodged with Companies House, business plans for individual facilities[1] and information relating to other bodies corporate, such as partnerships. The Agency is placed in a
somewhat difficult dilemma in these respects. On the one hand, it would seem legitimate for a person neighbouring a proposed landfill to need to be satisfied that what is
proposed is fully costed and that the wording of any legal agreements in respect of
financial provision is watertight. However, on the other hand, this information – particularly business plans and the wording of legal agreements – might be of considerable use to competitors. No doubt this dilemma will take time to be resolved in favour
of one or the other party. Indeed, the seemingly wider access contained within the
Environmental Information Regulations 1992[2] may cause at least some of this information to be open to public scrutiny[3].

1   See para 8.185ff.
2   SI 1992/3240 as amended by SI 1998/1447.
3   See *R v British Coal Corpn, ex p Ibstock Building Products Ltd* [1995] JPL 836, where the name of a
    person able to provide verification of information supplied was held to fall within the concept of
    'information which relates to the environment' in SI 1992/3430, reg 2(1)(a).

13.70   Where commercially sensitive information is excluded from the register, the
EPA 1990 requires that it is replaced by a statement 'indicating the existence of information of that description'[1]. In the case where commercially confidential information
is excluded which relates directly to compliance with any condition of a waste
management licence, a statement must be placed on the register indicating whether or
not there has been compliance with the condition[2].

1   EPA 1990, s 64(2).
2   SI 1994/1056, reg 10(2)(b): see Circular 11/94, Annex 9, para 9.44.

13.71   The EPA 1990 approaches the question of commercial confidentiality in two,
quite different, ways[1]. As will be described, the first way requires that a person should

actively request that information is to be regarded as confidential. However, this appears to be allowed only in respect of information specified in the Waste Management Licensing Regulations 1994 which is passed to the Agency. In all other cases, the onus is on the Agency to approach the person to ask if certain material is to be treated as confidential.

1 See the EPA 1990, s 66(2) and (4).

13.72 The circumstances when the EPA 1990 explicitly allows individuals and businesses to apply directly to the Agency[1] relates only to specific prescribed instances. These are where confidential information has been passed to the Agency in respect of applications for waste management licences or for their modification[2] or in compliance with either the requirements of licence conditions or notices issued under s 71(2) of the EPA 1990[3].

1 EPA 1990, s 66(2).
2 Licence transfer appears to be excluded as it is not mentioned.
3 See para 12.174ff.

13.73 Circular 11/94 emphasises that the onus is upon the applicant to justify any claim of commercial confidentiality[1]:

'An application in respect of commercial confidentiality is unlikely to be sufficiently justified by a general claim that if the information were in the public domain the reputation of the operator and hence his commercial competitiveness would be adversely affected. The ... [Agency] should require cogent and specific evidence to demonstrate that the inclusion of the information on the register would negate or significantly diminish a commercial advantage. [The Agency] ... should also consider to what extent the information about which they are being asked to make a determination is available elsewhere or can be inferred from other sources.'

1 Circular 11/94, Annex 9, para 9.40.

13.74 However, the Circular singles out certain recovery operations as a possible special case on the grounds that high value materials may be being stored at the site[1]:

'Provided that this is in a form that is unlikely to cause pollution or harm to health, the amounts stored, where they are stored and the relevant security precautions will have no environmental implications; and these details should not be published on a register as they could seriously prejudice the security and commercial future of the scrap metal merchant'.

1 Circular 11/94, Annex 9, para 9.41.

13.75 The Agency has 14 days in which to determine an application that commercial confidentiality is to apply[1] and, should no decision be made at the end of this period, the information is automatically treated as confidential[2].

1 'Beginning with the date of the application': the EPA 1990, s 66(3).
2 EPA 1990, s 66(3): this time period can be modified by way of regulations (EPA 1990, s 66(10)).

13.76 Besides containing a mechanism to process requests for confidentiality, s 66 of the EPA 1990 also contains provisions which require the Agency to alert a third party that information of a potentially sensitive nature has been submitted. This applies only to information obtained by the Agency 'under or by virtue of any provision' of Part II of the EPA 1990 which the Agency considers 'might' be commercially confidential[1].

As part of the notification process, the Agency is required to give notice that the information will pass to the register unless it is to be excluded. A 'reasonable opportunity' is then to be given for the person to object on the grounds of commercial confidentiality and to make representations justifying this requirement. The Agency must take the representations into account and then must determine the issue[2].

1 EPA 1990, s 66(4). This provision excludes information submitted under s 66(2) and therefore does not apply to licence applications or applications for modifications or in respect of s 71 notices: the EPA 1990, s 66(4).
2 EPA 1990, s 66(4).

13.77 After the Agency has come to a decision over whether information is to be held to be commercially confidential under either of the two provisions described above, an aggrieved person has 21 days in which to lodge an appeal to the Secretary of State[1]. The 21-day period commences on the date by which the person received notification[2]. Any disputed information must not be entered on the register in this period. If the appeal is either upheld or withdrawn, seven days must lapse prior to the information being finally put on the register[3].

1 EPA 1990, s 66(5)(b): see SI 1994/1056, reg 7(1)(b).
2 EPA 1990, s 66(5)(a).
3 EPA 1990, s 66(5) as amended by the Environment Act 1995, Sch 22, para 83(1).

13.78 Appeals on confidentiality are dealt with under the same mechanism as appeals in respect of other Agency functions in the EPA 1990[1]. Either party – or the Secretary of State – can request that the appeal be heard by way of a hearing[2]. This must always be heard in private[3]. The Secretary of State is allowed discretion to delegate the holding of appeals[4].

1 EPA 1990, s 43 as amended by the Environment Act 1995, s 120(1) and Sch 22, para 77: see para 9.126ff.
2 EPA 1990, s 43(2)(c).
3 EPA 1990, s 43(2)(c) as subject to s 66(6)(a): note that s 66(6) has been amended by Sch 22, para 83 of the Environment Act 1995. This amendment superseded the statement made in Circular 11/94 that, unless the applicant requests otherwise, these hearings will always be held in private (Circular 11/94, Annex 10, para 10.27).
4 EPA 1990, s 66(6)(b) (as amended by the Environment Act 1995, Sch 22, s 83(2)) by way of s 114 of the Environment Act 1995.

13.79 Where the Agency has decided, or has been required by the Secretary of State to determine, that confidentiality should apply, the information is required to be left off the register for four years[1]. This period starts with the date of determination of its confidential nature. Towards the end of the four-year period, the person who furnished the information must re-apply for the continued exclusion of the information from the register[2]. The Agency must then reconsider the application in the manner already set out above[3].

1 EPA 1990, s 66(8).
2 Note that the onus this time is always on the holder of the information, not the Agency.
3 EPA 1990, s 66(9).

13.80 It should be noted that the Secretary of State also has the power to give the Agency directions as to information which the 'public interest' requires to be included on the register, notwithstanding that the information falls within the definition of being commercially confidential[1].

1 EPA 1990, s 66(7).

Confidential information and national security

13.81   Persons wishing to have information excluded from registers for reasons of national security are required to make such a request directly to the Secretary of State[1]. The Agency must be notified to that effect by the applicant. When notified, the information is to be withheld from the register until a determination has been made[2].

1   EPA 1990, s 65(4).
2   EPA 1990, s 65(4).

13.82   Information is to be excluded from the register when, in the opinion of the Secretary of State, the inclusion of that information would be 'contrary to the interests of national security'[1]. If the Secretary so considers, the Agency will receive a direction that the information be excluded or removed from the register if already present on it[2]. Any direction is to be made in writing[3] and can be subsequently varied or revoked as necessary[4]. The Agency is under a duty to notify the Secretary of State that the direction has been responded to[5].

1   EPA 1990, s 65(1).
2   EPA 1990, s 65(2).
3   EPA 1990, s 161(6).
4   EPA 1990, s 161(5).
5   EPA 1990, s 65(3).

Appendices

Appendix I

Waste Management Papers[1]

No 1   A Review of Options: A Memorandum providing Guidance on the Options available for Waste Treatment and Disposal, HMSO, 2nd Edn, 1992.

No 2   Waste Disposal Surveys, HMSO 1976.

No 3   Guideline for the Preparation of a Waste Disposal Plan, HMSO 1976.

No 4   Licensing of Waste Management Facilities, HMSO 1994.

No 4A   Licensing of Metal Recycling Sites, HMSO 1995.

No 5   The Relationship between Waste Disposal Authorities and Private Industry, HMSO 1976.

No 6   Polychlorinated Biphenyl (PCB) Wastes—A Technical Memorandum on Reclamation, Treatment and Disposal Including a Code of Practice, HMSO 1995 (replacing 1976 text).

No 7   Mineral Oil Wastes—A Technical Memorandum on Arisings, Treatment and Disposal Including a Code of Practice, HMSO 1976.

No 8   Heat-treatment Cyanide Wastes—A Technical Memorandum on Arisings, Treatment and Disposal Including a Code of Practice, HMSO 1976.

No 9   Halogenated Hydrocarbon Solvent Wastes from Cleaning Processes—A Technical Memorandum on Reclamation and Disposal Including a Code of Practice, HMSO 1976.

No 10   Local Authority Waste Disposal Statistics 1974/75, HMSO 1976.

No 11   Metal Finishing Wastes—A Technical Memorandum on Arisings, Treatment and Disposal Including a Code of Practice, HMSO 1976.

No 12   Mercury Bearing Wastes—A Technical Memorandum on Storage, Handling, Treatment and Recovery of Mercury Including a Code of Practice, HMSO 1977.

No 13   Tarry and Distillation Wastes and Other Chemical Based Residues—A Technical Memorandum on Arisings, Treatment and Disposal Including a Code of Practice, HMSO 1977.

No 14   Solvent Wastes (excluding Halogenated Hydrocarbons)—A Technical Memorandum on Reclamation and Disposal Including a Code of Practice, HMSO 1977.

No 15   Halogenated Organic Wastes—A Technical Memorandum on Arisings, Treatment and Disposal Including a Code of Practice, HMSO 1978.

No 16   Wood Preserving Wastes—A Technical Memorandum on Arisings, Treatment and Disposal Including a Code of Practice, HMSO 1978.

No 17   Wastes from Tanning, Leather Dressing and Fellmongering—A Technical Memorandum on Recovery, Treatment and Disposal Including a Code of Practice, HMSO 1978.

No 18   Asbestos Wastes—A Technical Memorandum on Arisings and Disposal Including a Code of Practice, HMSO 1978.

No 19   Wastes from the Manufacture of Pharmaceuticals, Toiletries and Cosmetics—A Technical Memorandum on Arisings, Treatment and Disposal Including a Code of Practice, HMSO 1978.

No 20   Arsenic-bearing Wastes: A Technical Memorandum on Recovery, Treatment and Disposal, Including a Code of Practice, HMSO 1980.

No 21   Pesticide Wastes: A Technical Memorandum on Arisings and Disposal Including a Code of Practice, HMSO 1980.

No 22   Local Authority Waste Disposal Statistics, 1974–75 to 1977–78: Second Analysis of Annual Returns from English Waste Disposal Authorities, HMSO 1980.

No 23   Special Wastes: A Technical Memorandum Providing Guidance on their Definition, HMSO 1983.

No 25   Clinical Wastes: A Technical Memorandum on Arisings, Treatment and Disposal, Including a Code of Practice, HMSO 1983.

No 26   Landfilling Wastes: A Technical Memorandum for the Disposal of Wastes on Landfill Sites, HMSO 1986.

No 26A   Landfill Completion, HMSO 1994.

No 26B   Landfill Design Construction and Operational Practice, HMSO 1995.

No 27   The Control of Landfill Gas: A Technical Memorandum on the Monitoring and Control of Landfill Gas, HMSO 1989, revised 1991.

No 28   Recycling: A Memorandum Providing Guidance to Local Authorities on Recycling, HMSO 1991.

1   While this is a complete list, it should be appreciated that some of these documents contain totally out of date information, being published in the 1970s. Waste Management Paper 23 has been superseded by Environment Agency (1999) *Special Wastes: a Technical guidance Note on their Definition and Classification*, Environment Agency, Bristol. However, unlike the usual practice with Department of the Environment Circulars, whether the guidance still retains currency is not formally drawn to readers' attention.

Appendix II

European Waste Catalogue and Hazardous Waste List

The European Waste Catalogue[1] is reproduced below. The entries shown in bold are those European Waste Catalogue waste codes which feature on the Hazardous Waste List contained in Council Decision 94/904[2].

Index

01 00 00   WASTE RESULTING FROM EXPLORATION, MINING, DRESSING AND FURTHER TREATMENT OF MINERALS AND QUARRYING

01 01 00   *waste from mineral excavation*
01 01 01   waste from mineral metalliferous excavation
01 01 02   waste from mineral non-metalliferous excavation

01 02 00   *waste from mineral dressing*
01 02 01   waste from the dressing of metalliferous minerals
01 02 02   waste from the dressing of non-metalliferous minerals

01 03 00   *waste from further physical and chemical processing of metalliferous minerals*
01 03 01   tailings
01 03 02   dusty and powdery waste
01 03 03   red mud from the alumina production
01 03 99   wastes not otherwise specified

01 04 00   *waste from further physical and chemical processing of non metalliferous minerals*
01 04 01   waste gravel and crushed rocks
01 04 02   waste sand and clays
01 04 03   dusty and powdery waste
01 04 04   waste from potash and rock salt processing
01 04 05   waste from washing and cleaning of minerals
01 04 06   waste from stone cutting and sawing
01 04 99   wastes not otherwise specified

01 05 00   *drilling muds and other drilling wastes*
01 05 01   oil containing drilling muds and wastes
01 05 02   barite containing drilling muds and wastes
01 05 03   chloride containing drilling muds and wastes
01 05 04   fresh water drilling muds and wastes
01 05 99   wastes not otherwise specified

---

1   Commission Decision of 20 December 1993 establishing a list of wastes pursuant to Article 1(a) of Council Directive 75/442/EEC on Waste (Decision 94/3/EC, OJ L5/15 7.1.94): see para 2.22ff.
2   Council Decision of 22 December 1994 establishing a list of Hazardous Waste pursuant to Article 1(4) of Council Directive 91/689/EEC on Hazardous Waste (Decision 94/904/EC, OJ L356/14 31.12.94): see para 4.15ff.

02 00 00   WASTE FROM AGRICULTURAL, HORTICULTURAL, HUNTING, FISHING
AND AQUACULTURE PRIMARY PRODUCTION, FOOD PREPARATION
AND PROCESSING

02 01 00   *primary production waste*
02 01 01   sludges from washing and cleaning
02 01 02   animal tissue waste
02 01 03   plant tissue waste
02 01 04   waste plastics (excluding packaging)
02 01 05   **agrochemical waste**
02 01 06   animal faeces, urine and manure (including spoiled straw), effluent, collected
separately and treated off-site
02 01 07   waste from forestry exploitation
02 01 99   wastes not otherwise specified

02 02 00   *wastes from the preparation and processing of meat, fish and other foods of
animal origin*
02 02 01   sludges from washing and cleaning
02 02 02   animal tissue waste
02 02 03   materials unsuitable for consumption or processing
02 02 04   sludges from on-site effluent treatment
02 02 99   wastes not otherwise specified

02 03 00   *wastes from fruit, vegetables, cereals, edible oils, cocoa, coffee and tobacco
preparation, processing; conserve production; tobacco processing*
02 03 01   sludges from washing, cleaning, peeling, centrifuging and separation
02 03 02   wastes from preserving agents
02 03 03   wastes from solvent extraction
02 03 04   materials unsuitable for consumption or processing
02 03 05   sludges from on-site effluent treatment
02 03 99   wastes not otherwise specified

02 04 00   *wastes from sugar processing*
02 04 01   soil from cleaning and washing beet
02 04 02   off specification calcium carbonate
02 04 03   sludges from on-site effluent treatment
02 04 99   wastes not otherwise specified

02 05 00   *wastes from the dairy products industry*
02 05 01   materials unsuitable for consumption or processing
02 05 02   sludges from on-site effluent treatment
02 05 99   wastes not otherwise specified

02 06 00   *wastes from the baking and confectionery industry*
02 06 01   materials unsuitable for consumption or processing
02 06 02   wastes from preserving agents
02 06 03   sludges from on site effluent treatment
02 06 99   wastes not otherwise specified

02 07 00   *wastes from the production of alcoholic and non-alcoholic beverages (excluding
coffee, tea and cocoa)*
02 07 01   wastes from washing, cleaning and mechanical reduction of the raw material
02 07 02   wastes from spirits distillation
02 07 03   waste from chemical treatment
02 07 04   materials unsuitable for consumption or processing
02 07 05   sludges from on-site effluent treatment
02 07 99   wastes not otherwise specified

03 00 00	WASTES FROM WOOD PROCESSING AND THE PRODUCTION OF PAPER, CARDBOARD, PULP, PANELS AND FURNITURE

03 01 00	*wastes from wood processing and the production of panels and furniture*
03 01 01	waste bark and cork
03 01 02	sawdust
03 01 03	shavings, cuttings, spoiled timber/particle board/veneer
03 01 99	wastes not otherwise specified

03 02 00	*wood preservation waste*
03 02 01	**non-halogenated organic wood preservatives**
03 02 02	**organochlorinated wood preservatives**
03 02 03	**organometallic wood preservatives**
03 02 04	**inorganic wood preservatives**

03 03 00	*wastes from pulp, paper and cardboard production and processing*
03 03 01	bark
03 03 02	dregs and green liquor sludge (from black liquor treatment)
03 03 03	bleaching sludges from hypochlorite and chlorine processes
03 03 04	bleaching sludges from other bleaching processes
03 03 05	de-inking sludges from paper recycling
03 03 06	fibre and paper sludge
03 03 07	rejects from paper and cardboard recycling
03 03 99	wastes not otherwise specified

04 00 00	WASTES FROM THE LEATHER AND TEXTILE INDUSTRIES

04 01 00	*wastes from the leather industry*
04 01 01	fleshings and lime split waste
04 01 02	liming waste
04 01 03	**degreasing wastes containing solvents without a liquid phase**
04 01 04	tanning liquor containing chromium
04 01 05	tanning liquor free of chromium
04 01 06	sludges containing chromium
04 01 07	sludges free of chromium
04 01 08	waste tanned leather (blue sheetings, shavings, cuttings, buffing dust) containing chromium
04 01 09	wastes from dressing and finishing
04 01 99	wastes not otherwise specified

04 02 00	*wastes from textile industry*
04 02 01	wastes from unprocessed textile fibres and other natural fibrous substances mainly of vegetable origin
04 02 02	wastes from unprocessed textile fibres mainly of animal origin
04 02 03	wastes from unprocessed textile fibres mainly artificial or synthetic
04 02 04	wastes from unprocessed mixed textile fibres before spinning and weaving
04 02 05	wastes from processed textile fibres mainly of vegetable origin
04 02 06	wastes from processed textile fibres mainly of animal origin
04 02 07	wastes from processed textile fibres mainly of artificial or synthetic origin
04 02 08	wastes from processed mixed textile fibres
04 02 09	wastes from composite materials (impregnated textile, elastomer, plastomer)
04 02 10	organic matter from natural products (eg grease, wax)
04 02 11	**halogenated wastes from dressing and finishing**
04 02 12	non-halogenated wastes from dressing and finishing
04 02 13	dyestuffs and pigments
04 02 99	wastes not otherwise specified

05 00 00	WASTES FROM PETROLEUM REFINING, NATURAL GAS PURIFICATION AND PYROLYTIC TREATMENT OF COAL
05 01 00	*oily sludges and solid wastes*
05 01 01	sludges from on-site effluent treatment
05 01 02	desalter sludges
05 01 03	**tank bottom sludges**
05 01 04	**acid alkyl sludges**
05 01 05	**oil spills**
05 01 06	sludges from plant, equipment and maintenance operations
05 01 07	**acid tars**
05 01 08	**other tars**
05 01 99	wastes not otherwise specified
05 02 00	*non-oily sludges and solid wastes*
05 02 01	boiler feedwater sludges
05 02 02	waste from cooling columns
05 02 99	wastes not otherwise specified
05 03 00	*spent catalysts*
05 03 01	spent catalysts containing precious metals
05 03 02	other spent catalysts
05 04 00	*spent filter clays*
05 04 01	**spent filter clays**
05 05 00	*oil desulphurisation waste*
05 05 01	waste containing sulphur
05 05 99	wastes not otherwise specified
05 06 00	*waste from the pyrolytic treatment of coal*
05 06 01	**acid tars**
05 06 02	asphalt
05 06 03	**other tars**
05 06 04	waste from cooling columns
05 06 99	wastcs not otherwise specified
05 07 00	*wastes from natural gas purification*
05 07 01	**sludges containing mercury**
05 07 02	wastes containing sulphur
05 07 99	wastes not otherwise specified
05 08 00	*wastes from oil regeneration*
05 08 01	**spent filter clays**
05 08 02	**acid tars**
05 08 03	**other tars**
05 08 04	**aqueous liquid waste from oil regeneration**
05 08 99	wastes not otherwise specified
06 00 00	WASTES FROM INORGANIC CHEMICAL PROCESSES
06 01 00	*waste acidic solutions*
06 01 01	**sulphuric acid and sulphurous acid**
06 01 02	**hydrochloric acid**
06 01 03	**hydrofluoric acid**
06 01 04	**phosphoric and phosphorous acid**
06 01 05	**nitric acid and nitrous acid**
06 01 99	**waste not otherwise specified**

06 02 00	*waste alkaline solutions*
06 02 01	**calcium hydroxide**
06 02 02	**soda**
06 02 03	**ammonia**
06 02 99	**wastes not otherwise specified**

06 03 00	*waste salts and their solutions*
06 03 01	carbonates (except 02 04 02 and 19 10 03)
06 03 02	saline solutions containing sulphates, sulphites or sulphides
06 03 03	solid salts containing sulphates, sulphites or sulphides
06 03 04	saline solutions containing chlorides, fluorides and halides
06 03 05	solid salts containing chlorides, fluorides and other halogenated solid salts
06 03 06	saline solutions containing phosphates and related solid salts
06 03 07	phosphates and related solid salts
06 03 08	saline solutions containing nitrates and related compounds
06 03 09	solid salts containing nitrides (nitrometallic)
06 03 10	solid salts containing ammonium
06 03 11	**salts and solutions containing cyanides**
06 03 12	salts and solutions containing organic compounds
06 03 99	wastes not otherwise specified

06 04 99	*metal-containing wastes*
06 04 01	metallic oxides
06 04 02	**metallic salts (except 06 03 00)**
06 04 03	**wastes containing arsenic**
06 04 04	**wastes containing mercury**
06 04 05	**wastes containing heavy metals**
06 04 99	wastes not otherwise specified

06 05 00	*sludges from on-site effluent treatment*
06 05 01	sludges from on-site effluent treatment

06 06 00	*wastes from sulphur chemical processes (production and transformation) and desulphurisation processes*
06 06 01	waste containing sulphur
06 06 99	wastes not otherwise specified

06 07 00	*wastes from halogen chemical processes*
06 07 01	**wastes containing asbestos from electrolysis**
06 07 02	**activated carbon from chlorine production**
06 07 99	wastes not otherwise specified

06 08 00	*wastes from production of silicon and silicon derivatives*
06 08 01	wastes from production of silicon and silicon derivatives

06 09 00	*wastes from phosphorus chemical processes*
06 09 01	phosphogypsum
06 09 02	phosphorous slag
06 09 99	wastes not otherwise specified

06 10 00	*wastes from nitrogen chemical processes and fertilizer manufacture*
06 10 01	wastes from nitrogen chemical processes and fertilizer manufacture

06 11 00	*wastes from the manufacturing of inorganic pigments and opacifiers*
06 11 01	gypsum from titanium dioxide production
06 11 99	wastes not otherwise specified

06 12 00	*wastes from production, use and regeneration of catalysts*
06 12 01	spent catalysts containing precious metals
06 12 02	other spent catalysts
06 13 00	*wastes from other inorganic chemical processes*
06 13 01	**inorganic pesticides, biocides and wood preserving agents**
06 13 02	**spent activated carbon (except 06 07 02)**
06 13 03	carbon black
06 13 99	wastes not otherwise specified
07 00 00	WASTES FROM ORGANIC CHEMICAL PROCESSES
07 01 00	*waste from the manufacture, formulation, supply and use (MFSU) of basic organic chemicals*
07 01 01	**aqueous washing liquids and mother liquors**
07 01 02	sludges from on-site effluent treatment
07 01 03	**organic halogenated solvents, washing liquids and mother liquors**
07 01 04	**other organic solvents, washing liquids and mother liquors**
07 01 05	spent catalysts containing precious metals
07 01 06	other spent catalysts
07 01 07	**halogenated still bottoms and reaction residues**
07 01 08	**other still bottoms and reaction residues**
07 01 09	**halogenated filter cakes, spent absorbents**
07 01 10	**other filter cakes, spent absorbents**
07 01 99	wastes not otherwise specified
07 02 00	*waste from the MFSU of plastics, synthetic rubber and man-made fibres*
07 02 01	**aqueous washing liquids and mother liquors**
07 02 02	sludges from on-site effluent treatment
07 02 03	**organic halogenated solvents, washing liquids and mother liquors**
07 02 04	**other organic solvents, washing liquids and mother liquors**
07 02 05	spent catalysts containing precious metals
07 02 06	other spent catalysts
07 02 07	**halogenated still bottoms and reaction residues**
07 02 08	**other still bottoms and reaction residues**
07 02 09	**halogenated filter cakes, spent absorbents**
07 02 10	**other filter cakes, spent absorbents**
07 02 99	wastes not otherwise specified
07 03 00	*waste from the MFSU of organic dyes and pigments (excluding 06 11 00)*
07 03 01	**aqueous washing liquids and mother liquors**
07 03 02	sludges from on-site effluent treatment
07 03 03	**organic halogenated solvents, washing liquids and mother liquors**
07 03 04	**other organic solvents, washing liquids and mother liquors**
07 03 05	spent catalysts containing precious metals
07 03 06	other spent catalysts
07 03 07	**halogenated still bottoms and reaction residues**
07 03 08	**other still bottoms and reaction residues**
07 03 09	**halogenated filter cakes, spent absorbents**
07 03 10	**other filter cakes, spent absorbents**
07 03 99	wastes not otherwise specified
07 04 00	*waste from the MFSU of organic pesticides (except 02 01 05)*
07 04 01	**aqueous washing liquids and mother liquors**
07 04 02	sludges from on-site effluent treatment
07 04 03	**organic halogenated solvents, washing liquids and mother liquors**
07 04 04	**other organic solvents, washing liquids and mother liquors**

07 04 05	spent catalysts containing precious metals
07 04 06	other spent catalysts
07 04 07	**halogenated still bottoms and reaction residues**
07 04 08	**other still bottoms and reaction residues**
07 04 09	**halogenated filter cakes, spent absorbents**
07 04 10	**other filter cakes, spent absorbents**
07 04 99	wastes not otherwise specified
07 05 00	*waste from the MFSU of pharmaceuticals*
07 05 01	**aqueous washing liquids and mother liquors**
07 05 02	sludges from on-site effluent treatment
07 05 03	**organic halogenated solvents, washing liquids and mother liquors**
07 05 04	**other organic solvents, washing liquids and mother liquors**
07 05 05	spent catalysts containing precious metals
07 05 06	other spent catalysts
07 05 07	**halogenated still bottoms and reaction residues**
07 05 08	**other still bottoms and reaction residues**
07 05 09	**halogenated filter cakes, spent absorbents**
07 05 10	**other filter cakes, spent absorbents**
07 05 99	wastes not otherwise specified
07 06 00	*waste from the MFSU of fats, grease, soaps, detergents, disinfectants and cosmetics*
07 06 01	**aqueous washing liquids and mother liquors**
07 06 02	sludges from on-site effluent treatment
07 06 03	**organic halogenated solvents, washing liquids and mother liquors**
07 06 04	**other organic solvents, washing liquids and mother liquors**
07 06 05	spent catalysts containing precious metals
07 06 06	other spent catalysts
07 06 07	**halogenated still bottoms and reaction residues**
07 06 08	**other still bottoms and reaction residues**
07 06 09	**halogenated filter cakes, spent absorbents**
07 06 10	**other filter cakes, spent absorbents**
07 06 99	wastes not otherwise specified
07 07 00	*waste from the MFSU of fine chemicals and chemical products not otherwise specified*
07 07 01	**aqueous washing liquids and mother liquors**
07 07 02	sludges from on-site effluent treatment
07 07 03	**organic halogenated solvents, washing liquids and mother liquors**
07 07 04	**other organic solvents, washing liquids and mother liquors**
07 07 05	spent catalysts containing precious metals
07 07 06	other spent catalysts
07 07 07	**halogenated still bottoms and reaction residues**
07 07 08	**other still bottoms and reaction residues**
07 07 09	**halogenated filter cakes, spent absorbents**
07 07 10	**other filter cakes, spent absorbents**
07 07 99	wastes not otherwise specified
08 00 00	WASTES FROM THE MANUFACTURE, FORMULATION, SUPPLY AND USE (MFSU) OF COATINGS (PAINTS, VARNISHES AND VITREOUS ENAMELS), ADHESIVE, SEALANTS AND PRINTING INKS
08 01 00	*wastes from MFSU of paint and varnish*
08 01 01	**waste paints and varnish containing halogenated solvents**
08 01 02	**waste paints and varnish free of halogenated solvents**
08 01 03	waste from water-based paints and varnishes

08 01 04	powder paints
08 01 05	hardened paints and varnishes
08 01 06	**sludges from paint or varnish removal containing halogenated solvents**
08 01 07	**sludges from paint or varnish removal free of halogenated solvents**
08 01 08	aqueous sludges containing paint or varnish
08 01 09	waste from paint or varnish removal (except 08 01 05 and 08 01 06)
08 01 10	aqueous suspensions containing paint or varnish
08 01 99	wastes not otherwise specified
08 02 00	*wastes from MFSU of other coating (including ceramic materials)*
08 02 01	waste coating powders
08 02 02	aqueous sludges containing ceramic materials
08 02 03	aqueous suspensions containing ceramic materials
08 02 99	wastes not otherwise specified
08 03 00	*waste from MFSU of printing inks*
08 03 01	**waste ink containing halogenated solvents**
08 03 02	**waste ink free of halogenated solvents**
08 03 03	waste from water-based ink
08 03 04	dried ink
08 03 05	**ink sludges containing halogenated solvents**
08 03 06	**ink sludges free of halogenated solvents**
08 03 07	aqueous sludges containing ink
08 03 08	aqueous liquid waste containing ink
08 03 09	waste printing toner (including cartridges)
08 03 99	wastes not otherwise specified
08 04 00	*wastes from MFSU of adhesives and sealants (including waterproofing products)*
08 04 01	**waste adhesives and sealants containing halogenated solvents**
08 04 02	**waste adhesive and sealants free of halogenated solvents**
08 04 03	waste from water-based adhesives and sealants
08 04 04	hardened adhesives and sealants
08 04 05	**adhesives and sealants sludges containing halogenated solvents**
08 04 06	**adhesives and sealants sludges free of halogenated solvents**
08 04 07	aqueous sludges containing adhesives and sealants
08 04 08	aqueous liquid wastes containing adhesives and sealants
08 04 99	wastes not otherwise specified
09 00 00	WASTES FROM THE PHOTOGRAPHIC INDUSTRY
09 01 00	*wastes from photographic industry*
09 01 01	**water-based developer and activator solutions**
09 01 02	**water-based offset plate developer solutions**
09 01 03	**solvent based developer solutions**
09 01 04	**fixer solutions**
09 01 05	**bleach solutions and bleach fixer solutions**
09 01 06	**waste containing silver from on-site treatment of photographic waste**
09 01 07	photographic film and paper containing silver or silver compounds
09 01 08	photographic film and paper free of silver or silver compounds
09 01 09	single-use cameras with batteries
09 01 10	single-use cameras without batteries
09 01 99	wastes not otherwise specified
10 00 00	INORGANIC WASTES FROM THERMAL PROCESSES
10 01 00	*wastes from power station and other combustion plants (except 19 00 00)*
10 01 01	bottom ash

10 01 02	coal fly ash
10 01 03	peat fly ash
10 01 04	**oil fly ash**
10 01 05	calcium-based reaction wastes from flue gas desulphurisation in solid form
10 01 06	other solid wastes from gas treatment
10 01 07	calcium-based reaction wastes from flue gas desulphurisation in sludge form
10 01 08	other sludges from gas treatment
10 01 09	**sulphuric acid**
10 01 10	spent catalysts eg from removal of NOx
10 01 11	aqueous sludges from boiler cleansing
10 01 12	spent linings and refractories
10 01 99	wastes not otherwise specified
10 02 00	*wastes from the iron and steel industry*
10 02 01	waste from the processing of slag
10 02 02	unprocessed slag
10 02 03	solid wastes from gas treatment
10 02 04	sludges from gas treatment
10 02 05	other sludges
10 02 06	linings and refractories
10 02 99	wastes not otherwise specified
10 03 00	*wastes from aluminium thermal metallurgy*
10 03 01	**tars and other carbon-containing wastes from anode manufacture**
10 03 02	anode scraps
10 03 03	**skimmings**
10 03 04	**primary smelting slags/white drosses**
10 03 05	alumina dust
10 03 06	used carbon strips and fireproof materials from electrolysis
10 03 07	**spent pot linings**
10 03 08	**salt slags from secondary smelting**
10 03 09	**black drosses from secondary smelting**
10 03 10	**waste from treatment of salt slags and black drosses treatment**
10 03 11	flue gas dust
10 03 12	other particulates and dust (including ball mill dust)
10 03 13	solid waste from gas treatment
10 03 14	sludges from gas treatment
10 03 99	wastes not otherwise specified
10 04 00	*wastes from lead thermal metallurgy*
10 04 01	**slags (1st and 2nd smelting)**
10 04 02	**dross and skimmings (1st and 2nd smelting)**
10 04 03	**calcium arsenate**
10 04 04	**flue gas dust**
10 04 05	**other particulates and dust**
10 04 06	**solid waste from gas treatment**
10 04 07	**sludges from gas treatment**
10 04 08	spent linings and refractories
10 04 99	wastes not otherwise specified
10 05 00	*wastes from zinc thermal metallurgy*
10 05 01	**slags (1st and 2nd smelting)**
10 05 02	**dross and skimmings (1st and 2nd smelting)**
10 05 03	**flue gas dust**
10 05 04	other particulates and dust
10 05 05	**solid waste from gas treatment**
10 05 06	**sludges from gas treatment**

| 10 05 07 | spent linings and refractories |
| 10 05 99 | wastes not otherwise specified |

10 06 00	*wastes from copper thermal metallurgy*
10 06 01	slags (1st and 2nd smelting)
10 06 02	dross and skimmings (1st and 2nd smelting)
10 06 03	**flue gas dust**
10 06 04	other particulates and dust
10 06 05	**waste from electrolytic refining**
10 06 06	**solid waste from gas treatment**
10 06 07	**sludges from gas treatment**
10 06 08	spent linings and refractories
10 06 99	wastes not otherwise specified

10 07 00	*wastes from silver, gold and platinum thermal metallurgy*
10 07 01	slags (1st and 2nd smelting)
10 07 02	dross and skimmings (1st and 2nd smelting)
10 07 03	solid waste from gas treatment
10 07 04	other particulates and dust
10 07 05	sludges from gas treatment
10 07 06	spent linings and refractories
10 07 99	waste not otherwise specified

10 08 00	*wastes from other non-ferrous thermal metallurgy*
10 08 01	slags (1st and 2nd smelting)
10 08 02	dross and skimmings (1st and 2nd smelting)
10 08 03	flue gas dust
10 08 04	other particulates and dust
10 08 05	solid waste from gas treatment
10 08 06	sludges from gas treatment
10 08 07	spent linings and refractories
10 08 99	wastes not otherwise specified

10 09 00	*wastes from casting of ferrous pieces*
10 09 01	casting cores and moulds containing organic binders which have not undergone pouring
10 09 02	casting cores and moulds containing organic binders which have undergone pouring
10 09 03	furnace slag
10 09 04	furnace dust
10 09 99	wastes not otherwise specified

10 10 00	*wastes from casting of non-ferrous pieces*
10 10 01	casting cores and moulds containing organic binders which have not undergone pouring
10 10 02	casting cores and moulds containing organic binders which have undergone pouring
10 10 03	furnace slag
10 10 04	furnace dust
10 10 99	wastes not otherwise specified

10 11 00	*wastes from manufacture of glass and glass products*
10 11 01	waste preparation mixture before thermal processing
10 11 02	waste glass
10 11 03	waste glass-based fibrous materials
10 11 04	flue gas dust
10 11 05	other particulates and dust

10 11 06	solid waste from gas treatment
10 11 07	sludges from gas treatment
10 11 08	spent linings and refractories
10 11 99	wastes not otherwise specified

10 12 00 *wastes from manufacture of ceramic goods, bricks, tiles and construction products*

10 12 01	waste preparation mixture before thermal processing
10 12 04	flue gas dust
10 12 05	other particulates and dust
10 12 06	solid waste from gas treatment
10 12 07	sludges from gas treatment
10 12 08	discarded moulds
10 12 08	spent linings and refractories
10 12 99	wastes not otherwise specified

10 13 00 *wastes from manufacture of cement, lime and plaster and articles and products made from them*

10 13 01	waste preparation mixture before thermal processing
10 13 02	wastes from asbestos-cement manufacture
10 13 03	wastes from other cement-based composite materials
10 13 04	waste from calcination and hydration of lime
10 13 05	solid waste from gas treatment
10 13 06	other particulates and dust
10 13 07	sludges from gas treatment
10 13 08	spent linings and refractories
10 13 99	wastes not otherwise specified

11 00 00 INORGANIC WASTE WITH METALS FROM METAL TREATMENT AND THE COATING OF METALS; NON-FERROUS HYDRO-METALLURGY

11 01 00 *liquid wastes and sludges from metal treatment and coating of metals (eg galvanic processes, zinc coating processes, pickling processes, etching, phosphatizing, alkaline degreasing)*

11 01 01	**cyanidic (alkaline) wastes containing heavy metals other than chromium**
11 01 02	**cyanidic (alkaline) wastes which do not contain heavy metal**
11 01 03	**cyanide-free wastes containing chromium**
11 01 04	cyanide-free wastes not containing chromium
11 01 05	**acidic pickling solutions**
11 01 06	**acids not otherwise specified**
11 01 07	**alkalis not otherwise specified**
11 01 08	**phosphatizing sludges**

11 02 00 *wastes and sludges from non-ferrous hydro-metallurgical processes*

11 02 01	sludges from copper hydro-metallurgy
11 02 02	**sludges from zinc hydro-metallurgy (incl jarosite, goethite)**
11 02 03	wastes from the production of anodes for aqueous electrolytic processes
11 02 04	sludges not otherwise specified

11 03 00 *sludges and solids from tempering processes*

11 03 01	**wastes containing cyanide**
11 03 02	**other wastes**

11 04 00 *other inorganic wastes with metals not otherwise specified*

11 04 01	other inorganic wastes with metals not otherwise specified

12 00 00   WASTES FROM SHAPING AND SURFACE TREATMENT OF METALS AND PLASTICS

12 01 00   *wastes from shaping (including forging, welding, pressing, drawing, turning, cutting and filing)*
12 01 01   ferrous metal filings and turnings
12 01 02   other ferrous metals particles
12 01 03   non-ferrous metal filings and turnings
12 01 04   other non-ferrous metal particles
12 01 05   plastic particles
12 01 06   **waste machining oils containing halogens (not emulsioned)**
12 01 07   **waste machining oils free of halogens (not emulsioned)**
12 01 08   **waste machining emulsions containing halogens**
12 01 09   **waste machining emulsions free of halogens**
12 01 10   **synthetic machining oils**
12 01 11   **machining sludges**
12 01 12   **spent waxes and fats**
12 01 13   welding wastes
12 01 99   wastes not otherwise specified

12 02 00   *wastes from mechanical surface treatment processes (blasting, grinding, honing, lapping, polishing)*
12 02 01   spent blasting grit
12 02 02   sludges from grinding, honing and lapping
12 02 03   polishing sludges
12 02 99   wastes not otherwise specified

12 03 00   *wastes from water and steam degreasing processes (except 11 00 00)*
12 03 01   **aqueous washing liquids**
12 03 02   **steam degreasing wastes**

13 00 00   OIL WASTES (except edible oils, 05 00 00 and 12 00 00)

13 01 00   *waste hydraulic oils and brake fluids*
13 01 01   **hydraulic oils, containing PCBs or PCTs**
13 01 02   **other chlorinated hydraulic oils (not emulsions)**
13 01 03   **non-chlorinated hydraulic oils (not emulsions)**
13 01 04   **chlorinated emulsions**
13 01 05   **non-chlorinated emulsions**
13 01 06   **hydraulic oils containing only mineral oil**
13 01 07   **other hydraulic oils**
13 01 08   **brake fluids**

13 02 00   *waste engine, gear and lubricating oils*
13 02 01   **chlorinated engine, gear and lubricating oils**
13 02 02   **non-chlorinated engine, gear and lubricating oils**
13 02 03   **other engine, gear and lubricating oils**

13 03 00   *waste insulating and heat transmission oils and other liquids*
13 03 01   **insulating or heat transmission oils and other liquids containing PCBs or PCTs**
13 03 02   **other chlorinated insulating and heat transmission oils and other liquids**
13 03 03   **non-chlorinated insulating and heat transmission oils and other liquids**
13 03 04   **synthetic insulating and heat transmission oils and other liquids**
13 03 05   **mineral insulating and heat transmission oils**

13 04 00	*bilge oils*
13 04 01	**bilge oils from inland navigation**
13 04 02	**bilge oils from jetty sewers**
13 04 03	**bilge oils from other navigation**

13 05 00	*oil/water separator contents*
13 05 01	**oil/water separator solids**
13 05 02	**oil/water separator sludges**
13 05 03	**interceptor sludges**
13 05 04	**desalter sludges or emulsions**
13 05 05	**other emulsions**

13 06 00	*oil waste not otherwise specified*
13 06 01	**oil waste not otherwise specified**

14 00 00	WASTES FROM ORGANIC SUBSTANCES EMPLOYED AS SOLVENTS (except 07 00 00 and 08 00 00)

14 01 00	*wastes from metal degreasing and machinery maintenance*
14 01 01	**chlorofluorocarbons**
14 01 02	**other halogenated solvents and solvent mixes**
14 01 03	**other solvents and solvent mixes**
14 01 04	**aqueous solvent mixes containing halogens**
14 01 05	**aqueous solvent mixes free of halogens**
14 01 06	**sludges or solid wastes containing halogenated solvents**
14 01 07	**sludges or solid wastes free of halogenated solvents**

14 02 00	*wastes from textile cleaning and degreasing of natural products*
14 02 01	**halogenated solvents and solvent mixes**
14 02 02	**solvent mixes or organic liquids free of halogenated solvents**
14 02 03	**sludges or solid wastes containing halogenated solvents**
14 02 04	**sludges or solid wastes containing other solvents**

14 03 00	*wastes from the electronic industry*
14 03 01	**chlorofluorocarbons**
14 03 02	**other halogenated solvents**
14 03 03	**solvents and solvent mixes free of halogenated solvents**
14 03 04	**sludges or solid wastes containing halogenated solvents**
14 03 05	**sludges or solid wastes containing other solvents**

14 04 00	*wastes from coolants, foam/aerosol propellents*
14 04 01	**chlorofluorocarbons**
14 04 02	**other halogenated solvents and solvent mixes**
14 04 03	**other solvents and solvent mixes**
14 04 04	**sludges or solid wastes containing halogenated solvents**
14 04 05	**sludges or solid wastes containing other solvents**

14 05 00	*wastes from solvent and coolant recovery (still bottoms)*
14 05 01	**chlorofluorocarbons**
14 05 02	**halogenated solvents and solvent mixes**
14 05 03	**other solvents and solvent mixes**
14 05 04	**sludges containing halogenated solvents**
14 05 05	**sludges containing other solvents**

15 00 00   PACKAGING; ABSORBENTS, WIPING CLOTHS, FILTER MATERIALS
AND PROTECTIVE CLOTHING NOT OTHERWISE SPECIFIED

15 01 00   packaging
15 01 01   paper and cardboard
15 01 02   plastic
15 01 03   wooden
15 01 04   metallic
15 01 05   composite packaging
15 01 06   mixed

15 02 00   absorbents, filter materials, wiping cloths and protective clothing
15 02 01   absorbents, filter materials, wiping cloths and protective clothing

16 00 00   WASTE NOT OTHERWISE SPECIFIED IN THE CATALOGUE

16 01 00   end of life vehicles
16 01 01   catalysts removed from vehicles containing precious metals
16 01 02   other catalysts removed from vehicles
16 01 03   used tyres
16 01 04   discarded vehicles
16 01 05   light fraction from automobile shredding
16 01 99   wastes not otherwise specified

16 02 00   discarded equipment and shredder residues
16 02 01   transformers and capacitors containing PCB or PCTs
16 02 02   other discarded electronic equipment (eg printed circuit boards)
16 02 03   equipment containing chlorofluorocarbons
16 02 04   discarded equipment containing free asbestos
16 02 05   other discarded equipment
16 02 06   wastes from the asbestos processing industry
16 02 07   waste from the plastic convertor industry
16 02 08   shredder residues

16 03 00   off-specification batches
16 03 01   inorganic off-specification batches
16 03 02   organic off-specification batches

16 04 00   waste explosives
16 04 01   waste ammunition
16 04 02   fireworks waste
16 04 03   other waste explosives

16 05 00   chemicals and gases in containers
16 05 01   industrial gases in high pressure cylinders, LPG containers and industrial aerosol
containers (including halons)
16 05 02   other waste containing inorganic chemicals, eg lab chemicals not otherwise
specified, fire extinguishing powders
16 05 03   other waste containing organic chemicals, eg lab chemicals not otherwise
specified

16 06 00   batteries and accumulators
16 06 01   lead batteries
16 06 02   Ni-Cd batteries
16 06 03   mercury dry cells

16 06 04	alkaline batteries
16 06 05	other batteries and accumulators
16 06 06	**electrolyte from batteries and accumulators**

16 07 00	*waste from transport and storage tank cleaning (except 05 00 00 and 12 00 00)*
16 07 01	**waste from marine transport tank cleaning, containing chemicals**
16 07 02	**waste from marine transport tank cleaning, containing oil**
16 07 03	**waste from railway and road transport tank cleaning containing oil**
16 07 04	**waste from railway and road transport tank cleaning containing chemicals**
16 07 05	**waste from storage tank cleaning, containing chemicals**
16 07 06	**waste from storage tank cleaning, containing oil**
16 07 07	solid wastes from ship cargoes
16 07 99	waste not otherwise specified

17 00 00	CONSTRUCTION AND DEMOLITION WASTE (INCLUDING ROAD CONSTRUCTION)

17 01 00	*concrete, bricks, tiles, ceramics, and gypsum-based materials*
17 01 01	concrete
17 01 02	bricks
17 01 03	tiles and ceramics
17 01 04	gypsum-based construction materials
17 01 05	asbestos-based construction materials

17 02 00	*wood, glass and plastic*
17 02 01	wood
17 02 02	glass
17 02 03	plastic

17 03 00	*asphalt, tar and tarred products*
17 03 01	asphalt containing tar
17 03 02	asphalt (not containing tar)
17 03 03	tar and tar products

17 04 00	*metals (including their alloys)*
17 04 01	copper, bronze, brass
17 04 02	aluminium
17 04 03	lead
17 04 04	zinc
17 04 05	iron and steel
17 04 06	tin
17 04 07	mixed metals
17 04 08	cables

17 05 00	*soil and dredging spoil*
17 05 01	soil and stones
17 05 02	dredging spoil

17 06 00	*insulation materials*
17 06 01	**insulation materials containing asbestos**
17 06 02	other insulation materials

17 07 00	*mixed construction and demolition waste*
17 07 01	mixed construction and demolition waste

18 00 00   WASTES FROM HUMAN OR ANIMAL HEALTHCARE AND/OR RELATED
            RESEARCH (excluding kitchen and restaurant wastes which do not arise from
            immediate health care)

18 01 00   *waste from natal care, diagnosis, treatment or prevention of disease in humans*
18 01 01   sharps
18 01 02   body parts and organs including blood bags and blood preserves
18 01 03   **other wastes whose collection and disposal is subject to special requirements**
            in view of the prevention of infection
18 01 04   wastes whose collection and disposal is not subject to special requirements in
            view of the prevention of infection (eg dressings, plaster casts, linen, disposable
            clothing, diapers)
18 01 05   discarded chemicals and medicines

18 02 00   *waste from research, diagnosis, treatment or prevention of disease involving*
            animals
18 02 01   sharps
18 02 02   **other wastes whose collection and disposal is subject to special requirements**
            in view of the prevention of infection
18 02 03   wastes whose collection and disposal is not subject to special requirements in
            view of the prevention of infection
18 02 04   **discarded chemicals**

19 00 00   WASTES FROM WASTE TREATMENT FACILITIES, OFF SITE WASTE
            WATER TREATMENT PLANTS AND THE WATER INDUSTRY

19 01 00   *wastes from incineration or pyrolysis of municipal and similar commercial,*
            industrial and institutional wastes
19 01 01   bottom ash and slag
19 01 02   ferrous materials removed from bottom ash
19 01 03   **fly ash**
19 01 04   **boiler dust**
19 01 05   **filter cake from gas treatment**
19 01 06   **aqueous liquid waste from gas treatment and other aqueous liquid waste**
19 01 07   **solid waste from gas treatment**
19 01 08   pyrolysis wastes
19 01 09   spent catalysts eg from NOx removal
19 01 10   **spent activated carbon from flue gas treatment**
19 01 99   wastes not otherwise specified

19 02 00   *wastes from specific physico/chemical treatments of industrial wastes (eg*
            dechromatation, decyanidation, neutralisation)
19 02 01   **metal hydroxide sludges and other sludges from metal insolubilisation**
            treatment
19 02 02   premixed wastes for final disposal

19 03 00   *stabilised/solidified wastes*
19 03 01   wastes stabilised/solidified with hydraulic binders
19 03 02   wastes stabilised/solidified with organic binders
19 03 03   wastes stabilised by biological treatment

19 04 00   *vitrified wastes and wastes from vitrification*
19 04 01   vitrified wastes
19 04 02   **fly ash and other flue gas treatment wastes**
19 04 03   **non-vitrified solid phase**
19 04 04   aqueous liquid waste from vitrified waste tempering

19 05 00	*wastes from aerobic treatment of solid wastes*
19 05 01	non-composted fraction of municipal and similar wastes
19 05 02	non-composted fraction of animal and vegetable wastes
19 05 03	off-specification compost
19 05 99	wastes not otherwise specified
19 06 00	*wastes from anaerobic treatment of wastes*
19 06 01	anaerobic treatment sludges of municipal and similar wastes
19 06 02	anaerobic treatment sludges of animal and vegetal wastes
19 06 99	wastes not otherwise specified
19 07 00	*landfill leachate*
19 07 00	landfill leachate
19 08 00	*wastes from waste water treatment plants not otherwise specified*
19 08 01	screenings
19 08 02	wastes from desanding
19 08 03	**grease and oil mixture from oil/waste water separation**
19 08 04	sludges from the treatment of industrial waste water
19 08 05	sludges from treatment of urban waste water
19 08 06	**saturated or spent ion exchange resins**
19 08 07	**solutions and sludges from regeneration of ion exchangers**
19 08 99	wastes not otherwise specified
19 09 00	*wastes from the preparation of drinking water or water for industrial use*
19 09 01	solid wastes from primary filtration and screenings
19 09 02	sludges from water clarification
19 09 03	sludges from decarbonation
19 09 04	spent activated carbon
19 09 05	saturated or spent ion exchange resins
19 09 06	solutions and sludges from regeneration of ion exchangers
19 09 99	wastes not otherwise specified
20 00 00	MUNICIPAL WASTES AND SIMILAR COMMERCIAL, INDUSTRIAL AND INSTITUTIONAL WASTES INCLUDING SEPARATELY COLLECTED FRACTIONS
20 01 00	*separately collected fractions*
20 01 01	paper and cardboard
20 01 02	glass
20 01 03	small plastics
20 01 04	other plastics
20 01 05	small metals (cans etc)
20 01 06	other metals
20 01 07	wood
20 01 08	organic compostable kitchen waste (including frying oil and kitchen waste from canteens and restaurants)
20 01 09	oil and fat
20 01 10	clothes
20 01 11	textiles
20 01 12	**paint, inks, adhesives and resins**
20 01 13	**solvents**
20 01 14	acids
20 01 15	alkalines
20 01 16	detergents
20 01 17	**photo chemicals**
20 01 18	medicines

20 01 19	**pesticides**
20 01 20	batteries
20 01 21	**fluorescent tubes and other mercury containing waste**
20 01 22	aerosols
20 01 23	equipment containing chlorofluorocarbons
20 01 24	electronic equipment (eg printed circuit boards)
20 02 00	*garden and park waste (including cemetery waste)*
20 02 01	compostable wastes
20 02 02	soil and stones
20 02 05	other non-compostable wastes
20 03 00	*other municipal waste*
20 03 01	mixed municipal waste
20 03 02	waste from markets
20 03 03	street cleaning residues
20 03 04	septic tank sludge
20 03 05	end of life vehicles

Appendix III

Transfrontier Waste Shipments

Table 1

Green List of Wastes[1]

Annex II   Council Regulation 259/93

Regardless of whether or not wastes are included on this list, they may not be moved as green wastes if they are contaminated by other materials to an extent which (*a*) increases the risks associated with the waste sufficiently to render it appropriate for inclusion in the amber or red lists, or (*b*) prevents the recovery of the waste in an environmentally sound manner.

GA Metal and metal-alloy wastes in metallic, non dispersible form[2]

The following waste and scrap of precious metals and their alloys:

GA 010 ex 7112 10	— Of gold	
GA 020 ex 7112 20	— Of platinum (the expression 'platinum' includes platinum, iridium, osmium, palladium, rhodium and ruthenium)	
GA 030 ex 7112 90	— Of other precious metal, eg silver	
	NB: Mercury is specifically excluded as a contaminant of these metals or their alloys or amalgams.	

The following ferrous waste and scrap of iron or steel:

GA 040	7204 10	Waste and scrap of cast iron
GA 050	7204 21	Waste and scrap of stainless steel
GA 060	7204 29	Waste and scrap of other alloy steels
GA 070	7204 30	Waste and scrap of tinned iron or steel
GA 080	7204 41	Turnings, shavings, chips, milling waste, filings, trimmings and stampings, whether or not in bundles
GA 090	7204 49	Other ferrous waste and scrap
GA 100	7204 50	Re-melting scrap ingots
GA 110 ex 7302 10		Used iron and steel rails

The following waste and scrap of non-ferrous metals and their alloys:

GA 120	7404 00	Copper waste and scrap
GA 130	7503 00	Nickel waste and scrap
GA 140	7602 00	Aluminium waste and scrap
GA 150	7802 00	Lead waste and scrap
GA 160	7902 00	Zinc waste and scrap
GA 170	8002 00	Tin waste and scrap
GA 180 ex 8101 91		Tungsten waste and scrap
GA 190 ex 8102 91		Molybdenum waste and scrap
GA 200 ex 8103 10		Tantalum waste and scrap
GA 210	8104 20	Magnesium waste and scrap (excluding those listed in AA 190)
GA 220 ex 8105 10		Cobalt waste and scrap
GA 230 ex 8106 00		Bismuth waste and scrap
GA 240 ex 8107 10		Cadmium waste and scrap
GA 250 ex 8108 10		Titanium waste and scrap
GA 260 ex 8109 10		Zirconium waste and scrap
GA 270 ex 8110 00		Antimony waste and scrap
GA 280 ex 8111 00		Manganese waste and scrap
GA 290 ex 8112 11		Beryllium waste and scrap
GA 300 ex 8112 20		Chromium waste and scrap
GA 310 ex 8112 30		Germanium waste and scrap

701

Table 1 – *contd*

Green List of Wastes[1]

Annex II   Council Regulation 259/93

GA 320 ex 8112 40	Vanadium waste and scrap	
ex 8112 91	Wastes and scrap of:	
GA 330	— Hafnium	
GA 340	— Indium	
GA 350	— Niobium	
GA 360	— Rhenium	
GA 370	— Gallium	
GA 400 ex 2804 90	Selenium waste and scrap	
GA 410 ex 2804 50	Tellurium waste and scrap	
GA 420 ex 2805 30	Rare earth waste and scrap	

GB Metal bearing wastes arising from melting, smelting and refining of metals

GB 010 2620 11	Hard zinc spelter
GB 020	Zinc containing drosses:
GB 021	— Galvanising slab zinc top dross (>90% Zn)
GB 022	— Galvanising slab zinc bottom dross (>92% Zn)
GB 023	— Zinc die cast dross (>85% Zn)
GB 024	— Hot dip galvanisers slab zinc dross (batch) (>92% Zn)
GB 025	— Zinc skimmings
GB 030	Aluminium skimmings
GB 040 ex 2620 90	Slags from precious metals and copper processing for further refining
GB 050 ex 2620 90	Tantalum bearing tin slags with less than 0.5% tin

GC Other wastes containing metals

GC 010	Electrical assemblies consisting only of metals or alloys
GC 020	Electronic scrap (eg printed circuit boards, electronic components, wire, etc) and reclaimed electronic components suitable for base and precious metal recovery
GC 030 ex 8908 00	Vessels and other floating structures for breaking up, properly emptied of any cargo and other materials arising from the operation of the vessel which may have been classified as a dangerous substance or waste
GC 040	Motor vehicle wrecks, drained of liquids
GC 050	Spent fluid catalytic cracking (FCC) catalysts (eg aluminium oxide, zeolites)
GC 060	Spent metal bearing catalysts containing any of: — Precious metals: gold, silver — Platinum-group metals: ruthenium, rhodium, palladium, osmium, iridium, platinum — Transition metals: scandium, vanadium, manganese, cobalt, copper, yttrium, niobium, hafnium, tungsten, titanium, chromium, iron, nickel, zinc, zirconium, molybdenum, tantalum, rhenium — Lanthanides (rare earth metals): lanthanum, praseodymium, samarium, gadolinium, dysprosium, erbium, ytterbium, cerium, neodymium, europium, terbium, holmium, thulium, lutetium
GC 070 ex 2619 00	Slags arising from the manufacture of iron and carbon steel (including low alloy steel) excluding those slags which have been specifically produced to meet both national and relevant international requirements and standards[3]
GC 080	Mill scale (ferrous metal)

GD Wastes from mining operations: these wastes to be in non-dispersible form

GD 010 ex 2504 90	Natural graphite waste

Table 1 – *contd*

Green List of Wastes[1]

Annex II   Council Regulation 259/93

GD 020 ex 2514 00   Slate waste, whether or not roughly trimmed or merely cut, by sawing
           or otherwise
GD 030   2525 30   Mica waste
GD 040 ex 2529 30   Leucite, nepheline and nepheline syenite waste
GD 050 ex 2529 10   Feldspar waste
GD 060 ex 2529 21   Fluospar waste
       ex 2529 22
GD 070 ex 2811 22   Silica wastes in solid form excluding those used in foundry operations

GE Glass waste in non-dispersible form
GE 010 ex 7001 00   Cullet and other waste and scrap of glass except for glass from
           cathode-ray tubes and other activated glasses
GE 020   Fibre glass wastes

GF Ceramic wastes in non-dispersible form
GF 010   Ceramic wastes which have been fired after shaping, including
           ceramic vessels (before and/or after use)
GF 020 ex 8113 00   Cermet waste and scrap (metal ceramic composites)
GF 030   Ceramic based fibres not elsewhere specified or included

*GG Other wastes containing principally inorganic constituents, which may contain metals
and organic materials*
GG 010   Partially refined calcium sulphate produced from flue gas
           desulphurisation (FGD)
GG 020   Waste gypsum wallboard or plasterboard arising from the demolition
           of buildings
GG 030 ex 2621   Bottom ash and slag tap from coal-fired power plants
GG 040 ex 2621   Coal-fired power plants fly ash
GG 050   Anode butts of petroleum coke and/or bitumen
GG 060 ex 2803   Spent activated carbon, resulting from the treatment of potable water
           and processes of the food industry and vitamin production
GG 080 ex 2621 00   Slag from copper production, chemical stabilised, having a high iron
           content (above 20%) and processed according to industrial
           specifications (eg DIN 4301 and DIN 8201) mainly for construction
           and abrasive applications
GG 090   Sulphur in solid form
GG 100   Limestone from the production of calcium cyanamide (having a pH
           less than 9)
GG 110 ex 2621 00   Neutralised red mud from alumina production
GG 120   Sodium, potassium, calcium chlorides
GG 130   Carborundum (silicon carbide)
GG 140   Broken concrete
GG 150 ex 2620 90   Lithium-tantalum and lithium-niobium containing glass scraps

GH Solid plastic wastes

Including, but not limited to:
GH 010   3915   Waste, parings and scrap of plastics of:
GH 011 ex 3915 10   — Polymers of ethylene
GH 012 ex 3915 20   — Polymers of styrene
GH 013 ex 3915 30   — Polymers of vinyl chloride
GH 014 ex 3915 90   — Polymerized or co-polymers: for example:
                — Polypropylene
                — Polyethylene terephthalate
                — Acrylonitrile copolymer

Table 1 – *contd*

Green List of Wastes[1]

Annex II   Council Regulation 259/93

		— Butadiene copolymer
		— Styrene copolymer
		— Polyamides
		— Polybutylene terephthalates
		— Polycarbonates
		— Polyphenylene sulphides
		— Acrylic polymers
		— Paraffins (C10–C13)[4]
		— Polyurethane (not containing chlorofluorocarbons)
		— Polysiloxalanes (silicones)
		— Polymethyl methacrylate
		— Polyvinyl alcohol
		— Polyvinyl butyral
		— Polyvinyl acetate
		— Polymers of fluorinated ethylene (Teflon, PTFE)
GH 015 ex 3915 90		— Resins or condensation products, for example:
		— Urea formaldehyde resins
		— Phenol formaldehyde resins
		— Melamine formaldehyde resins
		— Epoxy resins
		— Alkyd resins
		— Polyamides

GI Paper, paperboard and paper product wastes

GI 010	4707	Waste and scrap of paper or paperboard:
GI 011	4707 10	— Of unbleached kraft paper or paperboard or of corrugated paper or paperboard
GI 012	4707 20	— Of other paper or paperboard, made mainly of bleached chemical pulp, not coloured in the mass
GI 013	4707 30	— Of paper or paperboard made mainly of mechanical pulp (for example, newspapers, journals and similar printed matter)
GI 014	4707 90	— Other, including but not limited to: 1. Laminated paperboard 2. Unsorted waste and scrap

GJ Textile wastes

GJ 010	5003	Silk waste (including cocoons unsuitable for reeling, yarn waste and garnetted stock):
GJ 011	5003 10	— Not carded or combed
GJ 012	5003 90	— Other
GJ 020	5103	Waste of wool or of fine or coarse animal hair, including yarn waste but excluding garnetted stock
GJ 021	5103 10	— Noils of wool or of fine animal hair
GJ 022	5103 20	— Other waste of wool or of fine animal hair
GJ 023	5103 30	— Waste of coarse animal hair
GJ 030	5202	Cotton waste (including yarn waste and garnetted stock)
GJ 031	5202 10	— Yarn waste (including thread waste)
GJ 032	5202 91	— Garnetted stock
GJ 033	5202 99	— Other
GJ 040	5301 30	Flax tow and waste
GJ 050 ex 5302 90		Tow and waste (including yarn waste and garnetted stock) of true hemp (*Cannabis sativa* L)

Table 1 – *contd*

Green List of Wastes[1]

Annex II   Council Regulation 259/93

GJ 060 ex 5303 90   Tow and waste (including yarn waste and garnetted stock) of jute and other textile bast fibres (excluding flax, true hemp and ramie)

GJ 070 ex 5304 90   Tow and waste (including yarn waste and garnetted stock) of sisal and other textile fibres of the genus *Agave*

GJ 080 ex 5305 19   Tow, noils and waste (including yarn waste and garnetted stock) of coconut

GJ 090 ex 5305 29   Tow, noils and waste (including yarn waste and garnetted stock) of abaca (Manila hemp or *Musa textilis* Nee)

GJ 100 ex 5305 99   Tow, noils and waste (including yarn waste and garnetted stock) of ramie and other vegetable textile fibres, not elsewhere specified or included

GJ 110   5505   Waste (including noils, yarn waste and garnetted stock) of man-made fibres

GJ 111   5505 10   — Of synthetic fibres
GJ 112   5505 20   — Of artificial fibres
GJ 120   6309 00   Worn clothing and other worn textile articles
GJ 130 ex 6310   Used rags, scrap twine, cordage, rope and cables and worn out articles of twine, cordage, rope or cables of textile materials
GJ 131 ex 6310 10 — Sorted
GJ 132 ex 6310 90 — Other

GK Rubber wastes
GK 010   4004 00   Waste, parings and scrap of rubber (other than hard rubber) and granules obtained therefrom
GK 020   4012 20   Used pneumatic tyres
GK 030 ex 4017 00   Waste and scrap of hard rubber (for example, ebonite)

GL Untreated cork and wood wastes
GL 010 ex 4401 30   Wood waste and scrap, whether or not agglomerated in logs, briquettes, pellets or similar forms
GL 020   4501 90   Cork waste; crushed, granulated or ground cork

GM Wastes arising from agro-food industries
GM 070 ex 2307   Wine lees
GM 080 ex 2308   Dried and sterilised vegetable waste, residues and by-products, whether or not in the form of pellets, of a kind used in animal feeding, not elsewhere specified or included
GM 090   1522   Degras; residues resulting from the treatment of fatty substances or animal or vegetable waxes
GM 100   0506 90   Waste of bones and horn-cones, unworked, defatted, simply prepared (but not cut to shape), treated with acid or degelatinised
GM 110 ex 0511 91   Fish waste
GM 120   1802 00   Cocoa shells, husks, and other cocoa waste
GM 130   Waste from the agro-food industry excluding by-products which meet national and international requirements and standards for human or animal consumption

GN Wastes arising from tanning and fellmongery operations and leather use
GN 010 ex 0502 00   Waste of pigs', hogs' or boars' bristles and hair or of badger hair and other brushmaking hair
GN 020 ex 0503 00   Horsehair waste, whether or not put up as a layer with or without supporting material

Table 1 – *contd*

Green List of Wastes[1]

Annex II   Council Regulation 259/93

GN 030 ex 0505 90   Waste of skins and other parts of birds, with their feathers or down, of feathers and parts of feathers (whether or not with trimmed edges) and down, not further worked than cleaned, disinfected or treated for preservation

GN 040 ex 4110 00   Parings and other waste of leather or of composition leather, not suitable for the manufacture of leather articles, excluding leather sludges

GO Other wastes containing principally organic constituents, which may contain metals and inorganic materials

GO 010 ex 0501 00   Waste of human hair

GO 020   Waste straw

GO 030   Deactivated fungus mycelium from penicillin production to be used as animal feed

GO 040   Waste photographic film base and waste photographic film not containing silver

GO 050   Single-use cameras without batteries

Notes – Annex II Council Regulation 259/93

1   Wherever possible, the code number of the Harmonised Commodity Description and Coding System, established by the Brussels Convention of 14 June 1983 under the auspices of the Customs Cooperation Council (Harmonised System) is listed opposite an entry. This code may apply to both wastes and products. This Regulation does not include items which are not wastes. Therefore, the code – used by customs officials in order to facilitate their procedures as well as by others – is only provided here to help in identifying wastes that are listed and subject to this Regulation. However, corresponding official Explanatory Notes as issued by the Customs Cooperation Council should be used as interpretative guidance to identify wastes covered by generic headings.

The indicative 'ex' identifies a specific item contained within a heading of the Harmonised System code.

The code in bold in the first column is the OECD code: it consists of two letters (one for the list: Green, Amber or Red and one for the category of waste: A, B, C ...) followed by a number.

2   'Non-dispersible' does not include any wastes in the form of powder, sludge, dust or solid items containing encased hazardous waste liquids.

3   This entry covers the use of such slags as a source of titanium dioxide and vanadium.

4   These cannot be polymerised and are used as plasticisers.

Table 2

Amber List of Wastes[1]

Annex III   Council Regulation 259/93

Regardless of whether or not wastes are included on this list, they may not be moved as amber wastes if they are contaminated by other materials to an extent which (*a*) increases the risks associated with the waste sufficiently to render it appropriate for inclusion in the red list, or (*b*) prevents the recovery of the waste in an environmentally sound manner.

AA Metal bearing wastes

AA 010 ex 2619 00	Dross, scalings and other wastes from the manufacture of iron and steel[2]
AA 020 ex 2620 19	Zinc ashes and residues[2]
AA 030 2620 20	Lead ashes and residues[2]
AA 040 ex 2620 30	Copper ashes and residues[2]
AA 050 ex 2620 40	Aluminium ashes and residues[2]
AA 060 ex 2620 50	Vanadium ashes and residues[2]
AA 070 2620 90	Ashes and residues[2] containing metals or metal compounds not elsewhere specified or included
AA 080 ex 8112 91	Thallium waste scrap and residues[2]
AA 090 ex 2804 80	Arsenic waste and residues[2]
AA 100 ex 2805 40	Mercury waste and residues[2]
AA 110	Residues from alumina production not elsewhere specified or included
AA 120	Galvanic sludges
AA 130	Liquors from the pickling of metals
AA 140	Leaching residues from zinc processing, dusts and sludges such as jarosite, hematite, goethite, etc
AA 150	Precious metal bearing residues in solid form which contain traces of inorganic cyanides
AA 160	Precious metal ash, sludge, dust and other residues such as:
AA 161	— Ash from incineration of printed circuit boards
AA 162	— Photographic film ash
AA 170	Lead-acid batteries, whole or crushed
AA 180	Used batteries or accumulators, whole or crushed, other than lead-acid batteries, and waste and scrap arising from the production of batteries and accumulators, not otherwise specified or included
AA 190 8014 20	Magnesium waste and scrap that is flammable, pyrophoric or emits, upon contact with water, flammable gases in dangerous quantities.

AB Wastes containing principally inorganic constituents, which may contain metals and organic materials

AB 010 2621 00	Slag, ash and residues[2], not elsewhere specified or included
AB 020	Residues arising from the combustion of municipal/household wastes
AB 030	Wastes from non-cyanide based systems which arise from surface treatment of metals
AB 040 ex 7001 00	Glass waste from cathode-ray tubes and other activated glasses
AB 050 ex 2529 21	Calcium fluoride sludge
AB 060	Other inorganic fluorine compounds in the form of liquids or sludges
AB 070	Sands used in foundry operations
AB 080	Spent catalysts not on the green list
AB 090	Waste hydrates of aluminium
AB 100	Waste alumina
AB 110	Basic solutions
AB 120	Inorganic halide compounds, not elsewhere specified or included
AB 130	Used blasting grit
AB 140	Gypsum arising from chemical industry processes

Table 2 – *contd*

Amber List of Wastes[1]

Annex III   Council Regulation 259/93

AB 150	Unrefined calcium sulphite and calcium sulphate from flue gas desulphurisation (FGD)

AC Wastes containing principally organic constituents, which may contain metals and inorganic materials

AC 010 ex 2713 90	Wastes from the production/processing of petroleum coke and bitumen, excluding anode butts
AC 020	Asphalt cement wastes
AC 030	Waste oils unfit for their originally intended use
AC 040	Leaded petrol (gasoline) sludges
AC 050	Thermal (heat transfer) fluids
AC 060	Hydraulic fluids
AC 070	Brake fluids
AC 080	Antifreeze fluids
AC 090	Waste from production, formulation and use of resins, latex, plasticizers, glues and adhesives
AC 100 ex 3915 90	Nitrocellulose
AC 110	Phenols, phenol compounds including chlorophenol in the form of liquids or sludges
AC 120	Polychlorinated naphtalenes
AC 130	Ethers
AC 140	Triethylamine catalyst for setting foundry sands
AC 150	Chlorofluorocarbons
AC 160	Halons
AC 170	Treated cork and wood wastes
AC 180 ex 4110 00	Leather dust, ash, sludges and flours
AC 190	Fluff — light fraction from automobile shredding
AC 200	Organic phosphorous compounds
AC 210	Non-halogenated solvents
AC 220	Halogenated solvents
AC 230	Halogenated or unhalogenated non-aqueous distillation residues arising from organic solvent recovery operations
AC 240	Wastes arising from the production of aliphatic halogenated hydrocarbons (such as chloromethanes, dichloro-ethane, vinyl chloride, vinylidene chloride, allyl chloride and epichlorhydrin)
AC 250	Surface active agents (surfactants)
AC 260	Liquid pig manure; faeces
AC 270	Sewage sludge

AD Wastes which may contain either inorganic or organic constituents

AD 010	Wastes from the production and preparation of pharmaceutical products
AD 020	Wastes from the production, formulation and use of biocides and phytopharmaceuticals
AD 030	Wastes from the manufacture, formulation and use of wood preserving chemicals
AD 040	Wastes that contain, consist of or are contaminated with any of the following: — Inorganic cyanides, excepting precious metal-bearing residues in solid form containing traces of inorganic cyanides
AD 050	— Organic cyanides
AD 060	Waste oils/water, hydrocarbons/water mixtures, emulsions

Table 2 – *contd*

Amber List of Wastes[1]

Annex III   Council Regulation 259/93

AD 070	Wastes from production, formulation and use of inks, dyes, pigments, paints, lacquers, varnish
AD 080	Wastes of an explosive nature, when not subject to specific other legislation
AD 090	Wastes from production, formulation and use of reprographic and photographic chemicals and materials not elsewhere specified or included
AD 100	Wastes from non-cyanide based systems which arise from surface treatment of plastics
AD 110	Acidic solutions
AD 120	Ion exchange resins
AD 130	Single-use cameras with batteries
AD 140	Wastes from industrial pollution control devices for cleaning of industrial off-gases, not elsewhere specified or included
AD 150	Naturally occurring organic material used as a filter medium (such as bio-filters)
AD 160	Municipal/household wastes
AD 170 ex 2803	Spent activated carbon having hazardous characteristics and resulting from its use in the inorganic chemical, organic chemical and pharmaceutical industries, waste water treatment, gas/air cleaning processes and similar applications.

Notes – Annex III Council Regulation 259/93

1   Wherever possible, the code number of the Harmonised Commodity Description and Coding System, established by the Brussels Convention of 14 June 1983 under the auspices of the Customs Cooperation Council (Harmonised System) is listed opposite an entry. This code may apply to both wastes and products. This Regulation does not include items which are not wastes. Therefore, the code – used by customs officials in order to facilitate their procedures as well as by others – is only provided here to help in identifying wastes that are listed and subject to this Regulation. However, corresponding official Explanatory Notes as issued by the Customs Cooperation Council should be used as interpretative guidance to identify wastes covered by generic headings.

The indicative 'ex' identifies a specific item contained within a heading of the Harmonised System code.

The code in bold in the first column is the OECD: it consists of two letters (one for the list: Green; Amber or Red and one for the category of waste: A, B, C, ...) followed by a number.

2   This listing includes wastes in the form of ash, residue, slag, dross, skimming, scaling, dust, powder, sludge and cake, unless a material is expressly listed elsewhere.

Table 3

Red List of Wastes

Annex IV   Council Regulation 259/93

'Containing' or 'contained with', when used in this list, means that the substance referred to is present to an extent which (*a*) renders the waste hazardous, or (*b*) renders it not suitable for submission to a recovery operation.

RA Wastes containing principally organic constituents, which may contain metals and inorganic materials

RA 010	Wastes, substances and articles containing, consisting of or contaminated with polychlorinated biphenyl (PCB) and/or polychlorinated terphenyl (PCT) and/or polybrominated biphenyl (PBB), including any other polybrominated analogues of these compounds, at a concentration level of 50 mg/kg or more
RA 020	Waste tarry residues (excluding asphalt cements) arising from refining, distillation and any pyrolitic treatment

RB Wastes containing principally inorganic constituents, which may contain metals and organic materials

RB 010	Asbestos (dusts and fibres)
RB 020	Ceramic-based fibres of physico-chemical characteristics similar to those of asbestos

RC Wastes which may contain either inorganic or organic constituents

	Wastes that contain, consist of or are contaminated with any of the following:
RC 010	— Any congenor of polychlorinated dibenzo-furan
RC 020	— Any congenor of polychlorinated dibenzo-dioxin
RC 030	Leaded anti-knock compounds sludges
RC 040	Peroxides other than hydrogen peroxide

Table 4

Council Regulation 1420/1999 – Annexes A and B. Restrictions on Green List Shipments to Non-OECD States

ANNEX A

Countries and territories which have indicated to the Commission that they do not wish to receive shipments for recovery of certain types of waste listed in Annex II to Council Regulation (EEC) No 259/93

ALBANIA

All types except:

1. In Section GA ('Metal and metal-alloy wastes in metallic, no-dispersible form'):

    (a) the following ferrous waste and scrap of iron and steel:

GA 040	7204 10	Waste and scrap of cast iron
GA 050	7204 21	Waste and scrap of stainless steel
GA 060	7204 29	Waste and scrap of other alloy steels
GA 070	7204 30	Waste and scrap of tinned iron or steel
GA 080	7204 41	Turnings, shavings, chips, milling waste, filings, trimmings and stampings, whether or not in bundles
GA 090	7204 49	Other ferrous scrap and waste
GA 100	7204 50	Remelting scrap ingots
GA 110	ex 7302 10	Used iron and steel rails

    (b) the following waste and scrap of non-ferrous metals and their alloys:

GA 120	7404 00	Copper waste and scrap
GA 150	7802 00	Lead waste and scrap
GA 160	7902 00	Zinc waste and scrap
GA 170	8002 00	Tin waste and scrap.

2. All types included in section GB ('Metal bearing wastes arising from melting, smelting and refining of metals'):

3. All types included in section GE ('Glass waste in non-dispersible form').

4. In section GG ('Other wastes containing principally inorganic constituents, which may contain metals and organic materials'):

GG 080	ex 2621 00	Slag from copper production, chemically stabilised, having a high iron content (above 20%) and processed according to industrial specifications (e.g. DIN 4301 and DIN 8201) mainly for construction and abrasive applications.

5. All types in section GI ('Paper, paperboard and paper product wastes').

6. In section GJ ('Textile wastes'):

GJ 020	5103	Waste of wool or of fine or coarse animal hair, including yarn waste but excluding garnetted stock:
GJ 021	5103 10	— Noils of wool or of fine animal hair
GJ 022	5103 20	— Other waste of wool or of fine animal hair
GJ 023	5103 30	— Waste of coarse animal hair
GJ 030	5202	Cotton waste (including yarn waste and garnetted stock):
GJ 031	5202 10	— Yarn waste (including thread waste)
GJ 032	5202 91	— Garnetted stock
GJ 033	5202 99	— Other.

Table 4 – *contd*

Council Regulation 1420/1999 – Annexes A and B. Restrictions on Green List Shipments to Non-OECD States

ANDORRA

All types

ANTIGUA and BARBUDA

All types

ARUBA

All types

BAHAMAS

All types

BARBADOS

All types

BELIZE

All types

BHUTAN

All types

BOLIVIA

All types

BOTSWANA

All types

BRAZIL

All types except:

1. In Section GA ('Metal and metal-alloy wastes in metallic, non-dispersible form'):

    (a) the following ferrous waste and scrap of iron and steel:

GA 040	7204 10	Waste and scrap of cast iron
GA 050	7204 21	Waste and scrap of stainless steel
GA 060	7204 29	Waste and scrap of other alloy steels
GA 070	7204 30	Waste and scrap of tinned iron or steel
GA 080	7204 41	Turnings, shavings, chips, milling waste, filings, trimmings and stampings, whether or not in bundles
GA 090	7204 49	Other ferrous scrap and waste
GA 100	7204 50	Remelting scrap ingots

    (b) the following waste and scrap of non-ferrous metals and their alloys:

GA 120	7404 00	Copper waste and scrap
GA 130	7503 00	Nickel waste and scrap
GA 140	7602 00	Aluminium waste and scrap
GA 150	7802 00	Lead waste and scrap

Table 4 – *contd*

Council Regulation 1420/1999 – Annexes A and B. Restrictions on Green List Shipments to
Non-OECD States

GA 160	7902 00	Zinc waste and scrap
GA 170	8002 00	Tin waste and scrap
GA 180	ex 8101 91	Tungsten waste and scrap
GA 190	ex 8102 91	Molybdenum waste and scrap
GA 200	ex 8103 10	Tantalum waste and scrap
GA 210	8104 20	Magnesium waste and scrap (excluding those listed in AA 190) (*)
GA 220	ex 8105 10	Cobalt waste and scrap
GA 230	ex 8106 00	Bismuth waste and scrap
GA 240	ex 8107 10	Cadmium waste and scrap
GA 250	ex 8108 10	Titanium waste and scrap
GA 260	ex 8109 10	Zirconium waste and scrap
GA 270	ex 8110 00	Antimony waste and scrap
GA 280	ex 8111 00	Manganese waste and scrap
GA 290	ex 8112 11	Beryllium waste and scrap
GA 300	ex 8112 20	Chromium waste and scrap
GA 310	ex 8112 30	Germanium waste and scrap
GA 320	ex 8112 40	Vanadium waste and scrap
	ex 8112 91	Waste and scrap of:
GA 330		— Hafnium
GA 340		— Indium
GA 350		— Niobium
GA 360		— Rhenium
GA 370		— Gallium
GA 400	ex 2804 90	Selenium waste and scrap
GA 410	ex 2804 50	Tellurium waste and scrap
GA 420	ex 2805 30	Rare earth waste and scrap

(*) See Annex III of Commission Decision 98/368/EC of 18 May 1998 (OJ L 165, 10.6.1998, p. 20).

2. In section GB ('Metal bearing wastes arising from melting, smelting and refining of metals'):

GB 040	ex 2620 90	Slags from precious metals and copper processing for further refining

3. In section GC ('Other wastes containing metals'

[...]

GC 070 [...]	ex 2619 00	Slag arising from the manufacture of iron and carbon steel (including low alloy steel) excluding those slags which have been specifically produced to meet both national and relevant international requirements and standards (*)

(*) This entry covers the use of such slags as a source of titanium dioxide and vanadium.

4. In section GD ('Wastes from mining operations: these wastes to be in non-dispersible form').

GD 040	ex 2529 30	Leucite, nepheline and nepheline syenite waste
GD 050	ex 2529 10	Feldspar waste
GD 060	ex 2529 21	Fluorspar waste
	ex 2529 22	

Table 4 – *contd*

Council Regulation 1420/1999 – Annexes A and B. Restrictions on Green List Shipments to Non-OECD States

5. In section GG ('Other wastes containing principally inorganic constituents, which mas contain metals and organic materials')

GG 030	ex 2621	Bottom ash and slag tap from coal-fired power plants
GG 040	ex 2621	Coal-fired power plants fly ash
GG 060	ex 2803	Spent activated carbon, resulting from the treatment of potable water and processes of the food industry and vitamin production
GG 080	ex 2621 00	Slag from copper production, chemically stabilised, having a high iron content (above 20%) and processed according to industrial specifications (e.g. DIN 4301 and DIN 8201) mainly for construction and abrasive applications
GG 100		Limestone from the production of calcium cyanamide (having a pH less than 9)

6. In section GH ('Solid plastic wastes'):

GH 013	ex 3915 30	Waste, parings and scrap of plastics of — Polymers of vinyl chloride
GH 015	ex 3915 90	Waste, parings and scrap of plastics of — Resins or condensation products, for example: — Urea formaldehyde resins — Phenol formaldehyde resins — Melamine formaldehyde resins — Epoxy resins — Alkyd resins — Polyamides

7. In section GJ ('Textile wastes')

GJ 050	ex 5302 90	Tow and waste (including yarn waste and garnetted stock) of true hemp (*Cannabis sativa* L.)

8. In section GK ('Rubber wastes'):

GK 020	4012 20	Used pneumatic tyres
GK 030	ex 4017 00	Waste and scrap of hard rubber (for example, ebonite)

9. In section GO ('Other wastes containing principally organic constituents, which may contain metals and inorganic materials'):

GO 040		Waste photographic film base and photographic film not containing silver
GO 050		Single-use cameras without batteries

BULGARIA

All types except:

1. In Section GA ('Metal and metal-alloy wastes in metallic, non-dispersible form'):

 (a) The following waste and scrap of precious metals and their alloys:

GA 010	ex 7112 10	— of gold
GA 030	ex 7112 90	— of other precious metals, e.g. silver

 N.B.: Mercury is specifically excluded as a contaminant of these metals or their alloys or amalgams

Table 4 – *contd*

Council Regulation 1420/1999 – Annexes A and B. Restrictions on Green List Shipments to Non-OECD States

(b) The following ferrous waste and scrap of iron or steel:

GA 040	7204 10	Waste and scrap of cast iron
GA 060	7204 29	Waste and scrap of other alloy steels
GA 070	7204 30	Waste and scrap of tinned iron or steel
GA 080	7204 41	Turnings, shavings, chips, milling waste, filings, trimmings and stampings, whether or not in bundles
GA 090	7204 49	Other ferrous waste and scrap
GA 100	7204 50	Re-melting scrap ingots
GA 110	ex 7302 10	Used iron and steel rails

(c) The following waste and scrap of non-ferrous metals and their alloys:

GA 120	7404 00	Copper waste and scrap
GA 140	7602 00	Aluminium waste and scrap
GA 150	7802 00	Lead waste and scrap
GA 160	7902 00	Zinc waste and scrap
GA 170	8002 00	Tin waste and scrap

2. In section GB ('Metal bearing wastes arising from melting, smelting and refining of metals'):

GB 010	2620 11	Hard zinc spelter
GB 020		Zinc containing drosses:
GB 021		— Galvanising slab zinc top dross (> 90% Zn)
GB 022		— Galvanising slab zinc bottom dross (> 92% Zn)
GB 023		— Zinc die cast dross (> 85% Zn)
GB 024		— Hot dip galvanisers slab zinc dross (batch) (> 92% Zn)
GB 025		— Zinc skimmings
GB 030		Aluminium skimmings
GB 040	ex 2620 90	Slags from precious metals and copper processing for further refining

3. In section GC ('Other wastes containing metals')

GC 060	Spent metal bearing catalysts containing any of:
	— Precious metals: gold, silver
	— Platinum-group metals: ruthenium, rhodium, palladium, osmium, iridium, platinum
	— Transition metals: scandium, vanadium, manganese, cobalt, copper, yttrium, nionium, hafnium, tungsten, titanium, chromium, iron, nickel, zinc, zirconium, molybdenum, tantalum, rhenium
	— Lanthanides (rare earth metals): lanthanum, praesodymium, samarium, gadolinium, dysprosium, erbium, ytterbium, cerium, neodymium, europium, terbium, holmium, thulium, lutetium

4. In section GH ('Solid plastic wastes'):

GH 010	3915	Waste, parings and scrap of plastics of:
GH 011	ex 3915 10	— Polymers of ethylene
GH 012	ex 3915 20	— Polymers of styrene
GH 013	ex 3915 30	— Polymers of vinyl chloride

5. All types in section GI ('Paper, paperboard and paper product wastes').

Table 4 – *contd*

Council Regulation 1420/1999 – Annexes A and B. Restrictions on Green List Shipments to Non-OECD States

BURKINA FASO

All types except:

All types in section GA ('Metal and metal-alloy wastes in metallic, non-dispersible (¹) from')

CAMEROON

All types except:

1. In section GA ('Metal and metal-alloy wastes in metallic, non-dispersible form')

    (a) The following waste and scrap of precious metals and their alloys:

GA 010	ex 7112 10	— Of gold
GA 020	ex 7112 20	— Of platinum (the expression 'platinum' includes platinum, iridium, osmium, palladium, rhodium and ruthenium)
GA 030	ex 7112 90	— Of other precious metals, e.g. silver

    N.B. Mercury is specifically excluded as a contaminant of these metals or their alloys or amalgams

    (b) The following ferrous waste and scrap of iron or steel:

GA 040	7204 10	— Waste and scrap of cast iron
GA 050	7204 21	— Waste and scrap of stainless steel
GA 060	7204 29	— Waste and scrap of other alloy steels
GA 070	7204 30	— Waste and scrap of tined iron or steel
GA 080	7204 41	— Turnings, shavings, chips, milling waste, filings, trimmings and stampings, whether or not in bundles
GA 090	7204 49	— Other ferrous waste and scrap
GA 100	7204 50	— Re-melting scrap ingots
GA 110	ex 7302 10	— Used iron and steel rails
GA 120	7404 00	Copper waste and scrap
GA 130	7503 00	Nickel waste and scrap
GA 150	7802 00	Lead waste and scrap
GA 160	7902 00	Zinc waste and scrap
GA 170	8002 00	Tin waste and scrap
GA 210	8104 20	Magnesium waste and scrap (excluding those listed in AA 190) (*)
GA 220	ex 8105 10	Cobalt waste and scrap
GA 280	ex 8111 00	Manganese waste and scrap
GA 300	ex 8112 20	Chromium waste and scrap

    (*) See Annex III of Decision 98/368/EC.

2. In section GB ('Metal bearing wastes arising from melting, smelting and refining of metals')

GB 050	ex 2620 90	Tantalum bearing tin slags with less than 0,5% tin

---

(¹) 'Non-dispersible' does not include any wastes in the form of powder, sludge, dust or solid items containing encased hazardous waste liquids.

Table 4 – *contd*

Council Regulation 1420/1999 – Annexes A and B. Restrictions on Green List Shipments to Non-OECD States

3. In section GC ('Other wastes containing metals')

GC 030	ex 8908 00	Vessels and other floating structures for breaking up, properly emptied of any cargo and other materials arising from the operation of the vessel which may have been classified as a dangerous substance or waste
GC 040		Motor vehicle wrecks, drained of liquids

4. In section GE ('Glass waste in non-dispersible form')

GE 010	ex 7001 00	Cullet and other waste and scrap of glass except for glass from cathode-ray tubes and other activated glasses

5. In section GF ('Ceramic wastes in non-dispersible form')

GF 010		Ceramic wastes which have been fired after shaping, including ceramic vessels (before and/or after use)

6. In section GH ('Solid plastic wastes')

GH 010	3915	Waste, parings and scrap of plastics of:
GH 011	ex 3915 10	— Polymers of ethylene
GH 012	ex 3915 20	— Polymers of styrene
GH 013	ex 3915 30	— Polymers of vinyl chloride

7. All types in section GI ('Paper, paperboard and paper product wastes')

8. In section GJ ('Textile wastes')

GJ 010	5003	Silk waste (including cocoons unsuitable for reeling, yarn waste and garnetted stock):
GJ 011	5003 10	— Not carded or combed
GJ 012	5003 90	— Other
GJ 020	5103	Waste of wool or of fine or coarse animal hair, including yarn waste but excluding garnetted stock:
GJ 021	5103 10	— Noils of wool of fine animal hair
GJ 022	5103 20	— Other waste of wool or of fine animal hair
GJ 023	5103 30	— Waste of coarse animal hair
GJ 030	5202	Cotton waste (including yarn waste and garnetted stock):
GJ 031	5202 10	— Yarn waste (including thread waste)
GJ 032	5202 91	— Garnetted stock
GJ 033	5202 99	— Other
GJ 090	ex 5305 29	Tow, noils and waste (including yarn waste and garnetted stock) of abaca (Manila hemp or Musa textilis Nee)
GJ 110	5505	Waste (including noils, yarn waste and garnetted stock) of man-made fibres:
GJ 111	5505 10	— Of synthetic fibres
GJ 112	5505 20	— Of artificial fibres
GJ 120	6309 00	Worn clothing and other worn textile articles
GJ 130	ex 6310	Used rags, scrap twine, cordage, rope and cables and worn out articles of twine, cordage, rope or cables of textile materials:

Table 4 – *contd*

Council Regulation 1420/1999 – Annexes A and B. Restrictions on Green List Shipments to Non-OECD States

| | GJ 131 | ex 6310 10 | — Sorted |
| | GJ 132 | ex 6310 90 | — Other |

9. In section GK ('Rubber wastes')

| | GK 020 | 4012 20 | Used pneumatic tyres |

10. All types in section GL ('RUntreated cork and wood wastes')

11. In section GM ('Wastes arising from agro-food industries')

| | GM 080 | ex 2308 | Dried and sterilised vegetable waste, residues and by-products, whether or not in the form of pellets, of a kind used in animal feeding, not elsewhere specified or included |

CAPE VERDE

All types

COLOMBIA

1. In section GA ('Metal and metal-alloy wastes in metallic, non-dispersible (¹) form'):

    All types of waste and scrap of non-ferrous metals and their alloys:

    [. . .]

2. In section GB ('Metal bearing wastes arising from melting, smelting and refining of metals'):

    | GB 040 | ex 2620 90 | Slags from precious metals and copper processing for further refining. |

3. In section GC ('Other wastes containing metals'):

    | GC 070 | ex 2619 00 | Slags arising from the manufacture of iron and steel (including low alloy steel) excluding those slags which have been specifically produced to meet both national and relevant international requirements and standards (*) |

    (*) This entry covers the use of such slags as a source of titanium dioxide and vanadium.

4. In section GD ('Wastes from mining operations: these wastes to be in non-dispersible form'):

    | GD 040 | ex 2529 30 | Leucite, nepheline and nepheline syenite waste |
    | [...] | | |
    | GD 060 | ex 2529 21 | Fluorspar waste |
    | | ex 2529 22 | |

5. In section GG ('Other wastes containing principally inorganic constituents, which may contain metals and organic materials'):

    | GG 030 | ex 2621 | Bottom ash and slag tap from coal-fired power plants |
    | GG 040 | ex 2621 | Coal-fired power plants fly ash |

(¹) 'Non-dispersible'does not include any wastes in the form of powder, sludge, dust or solid items containing encased hazardous waste liquids.

Table 4 – *contd*

Council Regulation 1420/1999 – Annexes A and B. Restrictions on Green List Shipments to Non-OECD States

GG 060	ex 2803		Spent activated carbon, resulting from the treatment of potable water and processes of the food industry and vitamin production
GG 080	ex 2621 00		Slag from copper production, chemically stabilised, having a high iron content (above 20%) and processed according to industrial specifications (e.g. DIN 4301 and DIN 8201) mainly for construction and abrasive applications
GG 100			Limestone from production of calcium cyanamide (having a pH less than 9)

6. In section GH ('Solid plastic wastes'):

GH 013	ex 3915 30	Waste, parings and scrap of plastics of polymers of vinyl chloride
GH 015	ex 3915 90	— Resins or condensation products, for example: — Urea formaldehyde resins — Phenol formaldehyde resins — Melamine formaldehyde resins — Epoxy resins — Alkyd resins — Polyamides

7. In section GJ ('Textile wastes'):

GJ 050	ex 5302 90	Tow and waste (including yarn waste and garnetted stock of true hemp (Cannabis sativa L.)

8. In section GK ('Rubber wastes'):

GK 020	4012 20	Used pneumatic tyres
GK 030	ex 4017 00	Waste and scrap of hard rubber (for example, ebonite)

9. In section GO ('Other wastes containing principally organic constituents, which may contain metals and inorganic materials'):

GO 040		Waste photographic film base and waste photographic film not containing silver
GO 050		Single-use cameras without batteries

COMOROS, Federal Islamic republic

All types except:

In section GJ ('Textile wastes'):

GJ 120	6309 00	Worn clothing and other worn textile articles

COSTA RICA

All types

DOMINICA

All types

DOMINICAN REPUBLIC

All types

Table 4 – *contd*

Council Regulation 1420/1999 – Annexes A and B. Restrictions on Green List Shipments to Non-OECD States

DJIBOUTH

All types

EGYPT

All types except:

1. All types in section GA ('Metal and metal-alloy wastes in metallic non-dispersible form').
2. All types in section GI ('Paper, paperboard and paper product wastes').
3. All types in section GJ ('Textile wastes').

FIJI

All types

GAMBIA

All types except:

In section GJ ('Textile wastes'):

> GJ 120   6309 00   Worn clothing and other worn textile articles

GHANA

All types

GRENADA

All types except:

In section GK ('Rubber wastes'):

> GK 020   4012 20   Used pneumatic tyres

GUYANA

All types

KIRIBATI

All types

KUWAIT

All types except:

In section GH ('Solid plastic wastes'):

> GH 011   ex 3915 10   Waste, parings and scrap of plastics of
>   — Polymers of ethylene

LEBANON

All types except:

In section GJ ('Textile wastes'):

> GJ 120   6309 00   Worn clothing and other worn textile articles

Table 4 – *contd*

Council Regulation 1420/1999 – Annexes A and B. Restrictions on Green List Shipments to Non-OECD States

MALAWI

All types excepts:

1. All types in section GA ('Metal and metal-alloy wastes in metallic, non-dispersible form').

2. All types in section GE ('Glass waste in non-dispersible form').

3. All types in section GI ('Paper, paperboard and paper product wastes').

4. In section GJ ('Textile wastes'):

    GJ 120   6309 00   Worn clothing and other worn textile articles

MALDIVES

All types

MALI

1. In section GA ('Metal and metal-alloy wastes in metallic, non dispersible (¹) form')

    All types of waste and scrap of non-ferrous metals and their alloys.

2. All types in section GE ('Glass waste in non-dispersible form').

3. All types in section GF ('Ceramic wastes in non-dispersible form')

4. All types in section GH ('Solid plastic wastes')

5. All types in section GN ('Wastes arising from tanning and fellmongery operations and leather use')

MOLDOVA

All types

MONGOLIA

All types

MYANMAR

All types

NICRAGUA

All types

NIGER

All types except:

1. In section GJ ('Textile wastes')

    GJ 120   6309 00   Worn clothing and other worn textile articles

2. In section GK ('Rubber wastes')

    GK 020   4012 20   Used pneumatic tyres

Table 4 – *contd*

Council Regulation 1420/1999 – Annexes A and B. Restrictions on Green List Shipments to Non-OECD States

NIGERIA

All types except:

All types in section GH ('Solid plastic wastes')

PAKISTAN

1. In section GK ('Rubber wastes'):

    GK 020   4012 20   Used pneumatic tyres

2. In section GM ('Wastes arising from agro-food industries'):

    GM 070   ex 2307   Wine lees

3. In section GN ('Wastes arising from tanning and fellmongery operations and leather use'):

    GN 010   ex 0502 00   Waste of pigs', hogs' or boars' bristles and hair or of badger hair and other brush-making hair

PAPUA NEW GUINEA

All types

PARAGUAY

All types except:

1. All types included in section GI ('Paper, paperboard and paper product wastes')

2. In section GJ ('Textile wastes'):

GJ 010	5003	Silk waste (including cocoons unsuitable for reeling, yarn waste and garnetted stock):
GJ 011	5003 10	— Not carded or combed
GJ 030	5202	Cotton waste (including yarn waste and garnetted stock)
GJ 031	5202 10	Yarn waste (including thread waste)
GJ 032	5202 91	Garnetted stock

3. In section GL ('Untreated cork and wood wastes'):

    GL 020   4501 90   Cork waste; crushed, granulated or ground cork.

PERU

All types

SÃO TOMÉ AND PRÍNCIPE

All types except:

1. In section GJ ('Textile wastes'):

GJ 111	5505 10	Waste (including noils, yarn waste and garnetted stock) of man-made fibres: — Of synthetic fibres
GJ 120	6309 00	Worn clothing and other worn textile articles

([1]) 'Non-dispersible' does not include any wastes in the form of powder, sludge, dust or solid items containing encased hazardous waste liquids.

Table 4 – *contd*

Council Regulation 1420/1999 – Annexes A and B. Restrictions on Green List Shipments to Non-OECD States

GJ 130	ex 6310	Used rags, scrap twine, cordage, rope and cables and worn out articles of twine, cordage, rope or cables of textile materials:
GJ 131	ex 6310 10	— Sorted
GJ 132	ex 6310 90	— Other

2.   In section GK ('Rubber wastes'):

GK 020	4012 20	Used pneumatic tyres

SAUDIA ARABIA

All types

SENEGAL

All types

SEYCHELLES

All types

SINGAPORE

All types except:

1.   In section GA ('Metal and metal-alloy wastes in metallic, non-dispersible form'):

(a)   The following waste and scrap of precious metals and their alloys:

GA 010	ex 7112 10	— Of gold
GA 020	ex 7112 20	— Of platinum (the expression 'platinum' includes platinum, iridium, osmium, palladium, rhodium and ruthenium)
GA 030	ex 7112 90	— Other precious metals, e.g. silver

N.B.: Mercury is specifically excluded as a contaminant of these metals or their alloys or amalgams

(b)   the following ferrous waste and scrap of iron or steel:

GA 040	7204 10	— Waste and scrap of cast iron
GA 050	7204 21	— Waste and scrap of stainless steel
GA 060	7204 29	— Waste and scrap of other alloy steels

(c)   the following waste and scrap of non-ferrous metals and their alloys:

GA 120	7404 00	Copper waste and scrap
GA 130	7503 00	Nickel waste and scrap
GA 140	7602 00	Alluminium waste and scrap
GA 150	7802 00	Lead waste and scrap
GA 170	8002 00	Tin waste and scrap
GA 190	ex 8102 91	Molybdenum waste and scrap
GA 250	ex 8108 10	Titanium waste and scrap
GA 260	ex 8109 10	Zirconium waste and scrap
GA 280	ex 8111 00	Manganese waste and scrap
GA 300	ex 8112 20	Chromium waste and scrap
GA 320	ex 8112 91	Vanadium waste and scrap
	ex 8112 91	Waste and scrap of:
GA 350		Niobium

Table 4 – *contd*

Council Regulation 1420/1999 – Annexes A and B. Restrictions on Green List Shipments to Non-OECD States

2. In section GC ('Other wastes containing metals'):

GC 070   ex 2619 00   Slags arising from the manufacture of iron and carbon steel (including low alloy steel) excluding those slags which have been specifically produced to meet both national and relevant international requirements and standards (*)

(*) This entry covers the use of such slags as a source of titanium dioxide and vanadium.

3. In section GD ('Wastes from mining operations: these wastes to be in non-dispersible form'):

GD 020   ex 2514 00   Slate waste, whether or not roughly trimmed or merely cut by sawing or otherwise.

4. In section GH ('Solid plastic wastes'):

GH 013   ex 3915 30   Waste, parings and scrap of plastics of:
     — Polymers of vinyl chloride

ST. KITTS AND NEVIS

All types

ST LUCIA

All types

ST VINCENT AND THE GRENADINES

All types

TANZANIA

All types except:

In section GJ ('Textile wastes'):

GJ 120   6309   Worn clothing and other worn textile articles

UGANDA

All types except:

1. In section GA ('Metal and metal-alloy wastes in metallic, non-dispersible form')

GA 050   7204 21   Waste and scrap of stainless steel
GA 060   7204 29   Waste and scrap of other alloy steels

2. In section GJ ('Textile wastes')

GJ 120   6309 00   Worn clothing and other worn textile articles

TUVALU

All types

VANUATU

All types

WESTERN SAMOA

All types

Table 4 – *contd*

Council Regulation 1420/1999 – Annexes A and B. Restrictions on Green List Shipments to Non-OECD States

ANNEX B

Countries and territories which have not responded to the Commission's communications on shipments for recovery of certain types of waste listed in Annex II to Council Regulation (EEC) No 259/93

AFGHANISTAN

All types

ALGERIA

All types

ANGOLA

All types except:

1. All types in section GA ('Metal and metal alloy wastes in metallic, non-dispersible form').
2. All types in section GE ('Glass wastes in non-dispersible form').
3. All types in section GI ('Paper, paperboard and paper product wastes').
4. All types in section GJ ('Textile wastes').
5. All types in section GK ('Rubber wastes').

ARMENIA

All types

AZERBAIJAN

All types

BAHRAIN

All types

BANGLADESH

All types

BRUNEI

All types

BURUNDI

All types

CAMBODIA

All types

ECUADOR

All types

Table 4 – *contd*

Council Regulation 1420/1999 – Annexes A and B. Restrictions on Green List Shipments to Non-OECD States

EL SALVADOR

All types

EQUATORIAL GUINEA

All types

ERITREA

All types

ETHIOPIA

All types

FORMER YUGOSLAV REPUBLIC OF MACEDONIA

All types

GABON

All types

GUATEMALA

All types

GUINEA

All types except:

In section GJ ('Textile wastes'):

      GJ 120   6309 00   Worn clothing and other worn textile articles

HAITI

All types

HONDURAS

All types

IVORY COAST

All types

KAZAKHSTAN

All types

KYRGYSTAN

All types

Table 4 – *contd*

Council Regulation 1420/1999 – Annexes A and B. Restrictions on Green List Shipments to Non-OECD States

LAOS

All types

LESOTHO

All types

MOROCCO

All types

MOZAMBIQUE

All types

NAMIBIA

All types

NEPAL

All types

OMAN

All types

PANAMA

All types

QATAR

All types

RUSSIAN FEDERATION

All types except:

1. In section GA ('Metal and metal-alloy wastes in metallic, non-dispersible form'):

    (a) The following waste and scrap of non-ferrous metals and their alloys:

GA 150		7802 00	Lead waste and scrap
GA 160		7902 00	Zinc waste and scrap
GA 170		8002 00	Tin waste and scrap
GA 180	ex	8101 91	Tungsten waste and scrap
GA 190	ex	8102 91	Molybdenum waste and scrap
GA 200	ex	8103 10	Tantalum waste and scrap
GA 210		8104 20	Magnesium waste and scrap (excluding those listed in AA 190) (*)
GA 220	ex	8105 10	Cobalt waste and scrap
GA 230	ex	8106 00	Bismuth waste and scrap
GA 240	ex	8107 10	Cadmium waste and scrap
GA 250	ex	8108 10	Titanium waste and scrap
GA 260	ex	8109 10	Zirconium waste and scrap

Table 4 – *contd*

Council Regulation 1420/1999 – Annexes A and B. Restrictions on Green List Shipments to Non-OECD States

GA 270	ex 8110 00	Antimony waste and scrap
GA 280	ex 8111 00	Manganese waste and scrap
GA 290	ex 8112 11	Beryllium waste and scrap
GA 300	ex 8112 20	Chromium waste and scrap
GA 310	ex 8112 30	Germanium waste and scrap
GA 320	ex 8112 40	Vanadium waste and scrap
	ex 8112 91	Wastes and scrap of:
GA 330		— Hafnium
GA 340		— Indium
GA 350		— Niobium
GA 400	ex 2804 90	Selenium waste and scrap
GA 410	ex 2804 50	Tellurium waste and scrap.

(*) See Annex III of Decision 98/368/EC of 18 May 1998 (OJ L 165, 10.6.1998, p. 20).

2. In section GB ('Metal bearing wastes arising from melting, smelting and refining of metals'):

GB 010	2620 11	Hard zinc spelter
GB 025		— Zinc skimmings.

3. In section GC ('Other wastes containing metals'):

GC 030	ex 8908 00	Vessels and other floating structures for breaking up, properly emptied of any cargo and other materials arising from the operation of the vessel which may have been classified as a dangerous substance or waste.
GC 070	ex 2619 00	Slag arising from the manufacture of iron and carbon steel (including low alloy steel) excluding those slags which have been specifically produced to meet both national and relevant international requirements and standards (*)

(*) This entry covers the use of such slags as a source of titanium dioxide and vanadium.

4. In section GD ('Waste from mining operations: these wastes to be in non-dispersible form'):

GD 020	ex 2514 00	Slate waste, whether or not roughly trimmed or merely cut, by sawing or otherwise
GD 030	2525 30	Mica waste
GD 070	ex 2811 22	Silica wastes in solid form excluding those used in foundry operations.

5. In section GG ('Other wastes containing principally inorganic constituents, which may contain metals and organic metals'):

GG 030	ex 2621	Bottom ash and slag tap from coal fired power plants
GG 040	ex 2621	Coal fired power plants fly ash
GG 060	ex 2803	Spent activated carbon, resulting from the treatment of potable water and processes of the food industry and vitamin production
GG 110	ex 2621 00	Neutralised red mud from alumina production.

6. All types included in section GH ('Solid plastic wastes').

Table 4 – *contd*

Council Regulation 1420/1999 – Annexes A and B. Restrictions on Green List Shipments to Non-OECD States

7. In section GJ ('Textile wastes'):

GJ 110	5505	Waste (including noils, yarn waste and garnetted stock) of man-made fibres
GJ 111	5505 10	— Of synthetic fibres
GJ 112	5505 20	— Of artificial fibres.

8. All types included in section GK ('Rubber wastes').

9. In section GM ('Wastes arising from agro-food industries'):

GM 090	1522	Degras; residues resulting from the treatment of fatty substances or animal or vegetable waxes
GM 100	0506 90	Waste of bones and horn-cones, unworked, defatted, simply prepared (but not cut to shape), treated with acid or degelatinised
GM 110	ex 0511 91	Fish waste.

10. In section GN ('Wastes arising from tanning and fellmongery operations and leather use'):

GN 010	ex 0502 00	Waste of pigs', hogs' or boars' bristles and hair or of badger hair and other brush-making hair
GN 020	ex 0503 00	Horsehair waste, whether or not put up as a layer or without supporting material
GN 030	ex 0505 90	Waste of skins and other parts of birds, with their feathers or down of feathers and parts of feathers (whether or not with trimmed edges) and down, not further worked than cleaned, disinfected or treated for preservation.

11. In section GO ('Other wastes containing principally organic constituents, which may contain metals and inorganic materials'):

GO 010	ex 0501 00	Waste of human hair

SOLOMON ISLANDS

All types

SUDAN

All types

SWAZILAND

All types

SYRIA

All types

TAJIKISTAN

All types

TONGA

All types

Table 4 – *contd*

Council Regulation 1420/1999 – Annexes A and B. Restrictions on Green List Shipments to Non-OECD States

TUNISIA

All types in Annex II except:

1. In section GA ('Metal and metal-alloy wastes in metallic, non-dispersible form'):

    (a) The following ferrous waste and scrap of iron and steel:

    | GA 110 | ex 7302 10 | Used iron and steel rails |

    (b) The following waste and scrap of non-ferrous metals and their alloys:

    | GA 120 | 7404 00 | Copper waste and scrap |
    | GA 140 | 7602 00 | Aluminium waste and scrap |
    | GA 170 | 8002 00 | Tin waste and scrap. |

2. In section GC ('Other wastes containing metals'):

    | GC 030 | ex 8908 00 | Vessels and other floating structures for breaking up, properly emptied of any cargo and other materials arising from the operation of the vessel which may have been classified as a dangerous substance or waste. |

3. All types in section GH ('Solid plastic wastes').

4. All types in section GI ('Paper, paperboard and paper product wastes').

5. In section GJ ('Textile wastes'):

    | GJ 010 | 5003 | Silk waste (including cocoons unsuitable for reeling, yarn waste and garnetted stock |
    | GJ 012 | 5003 90 | — Other |
    | GJ 020 | 5103 | Waste of wool or of fine or coarse animal hair, including yarn waste but excluding garnetted stock |
    | GJ 030 | 5202 | Cotton waste (including yarn waste and garnetted stock) |
    | GJ 060 | ex 5303 90 | Tow and waste (including yarn waste and garnetted stock) of jute and other textile bast fibres (excluding flax, true hemp and ramie) |
    | GJ 070 | ex 5304 90 | Tow and waste (including yarn waste and garnetted stock) of sisal and other textile fibres of the genus Agave |
    | GJ 111 | 5505 10 | Waste (including noils, yarn waste and garnetted stock) of man-made fibres — Of synthetic fibres |
    | GJ 120 | 6309 00 | Worn clothing and other worn textile articles |
    | GJ 130 | ex 6310 | Used rags, scrap twine, cordage, rope and cables and worn out articles of twine, cordage, rope or cables of textile materials. |

6. All types in section GK ('Rubber wastes').

7. In section GM ('Wastes arising from agro-food industries'):

    | GM 080 | ex 2308 | Dried and sterilised vegetable waste, residues and by-products, whether or not in the form of pellets, of a kind used in animal feeding, not elsewhere specified or included |

Table 4 – *contd*

Council Regulation 1420/1999 – Annexes A and B. Restrictions on Green List Shipments to Non-OECD States

GM 130		Waste from the agro-food industry excluding by-products which meet national and international requirements and standards for human or animal consumption.

8.   In section GN ('Wastes arising from tanning and fellmongery operations and leather use')

GN 010	ex 0502 00	Waste of pigs', hogs' or boars' bristles and hair or of badger hair and other brush making hair
GN 020	ex 0503 00	Horsehair waste, whether or not put up as a layer with or without supporting material
GN 040	ex 4110 00	Parings and other leather waste of leater or of composition leather, not suitable for the manufacture of leather articles, excluding leather sludges.

TURKMENISTAN

All types

UZBEKISTAN

All types

VATICAN CITY

All types

VENEZUELA

All types

VIETNAM

All types

YEMEN

All types

ZIMBABWE

All types

Table 5

Commission Regulation 1547/1999 – Annexes A–D. Restrictions on Green List Shipments to Countries where OECD Decision C(92)39 Final does not Apply

ANNEX A

Countries to which shipments of certain categories of waste listed in Annex II (the 'green' list) of Regulation (EEC) No 259/93, should be carried out under the control procedure applying to waste listed in Annex III (the 'amber' list) to the same Regulation are set out below. The categories of waste listed in Annex II which are covered are also given.

BULGARIA

1. In section GA ('Metal and metal-alloy wastes in metallic, non dispersible (¹) form')

    (a) The following waste and scrap of precious metals and their alloys:

GA 010	ex 7112 10	— Of gold
GA 030	ex 7112 90	— Of other precious metals, e.g. silver

    NB. Mercury is specifically excluded as a contaminant of these metals or their alloys or amalgams.

    (b) The following ferrous waste and scrap of iron or steel:

GA 040	7204 10	Waste and scrap of cast iron
GA 060	7204 29	Waste and scrap of other alloy steels
GA 070	7204 30	Waste and scrap of tinned iron or steel
GA 080	7204 41	Turnings, shavings, chips, milling waste, filings, trimmings and stampings, whether or not in bundles
GA 090	7204 49	Other ferrous waste and scrap
GA 100	7204 50	Re-melting scrap ingots
GA 110	ex 7302 10	Used iron and steel rails.

    (c) The following waste and scrap of non-ferrous metals and their alloys:

GA 120	7404 00	Copper waste and scrap
GA 140	7602 00	Aluminium waste and scrap
GA 150	7802 00	Lead waste and scrap
GA 160	7902 00	Zinc waste and scrap
GA 170	8002 00	Tin waste and scrap.

2. In sectin GB ('Metal bearing wastes arising from melting, smelting and refining of metals')

GB 010	2620 11	Hard zinc spelter
GB 020		Zinc containing drosses:
GB 021		— Galvanising slab zinc top dross (> 90% Zn)
GB 022		— Galvanising slab zinc bottom dross (> 92% Zn)
GB 023		— Zinc die cast dross (> 85% Zn)
GB 024		— Hot dip galvanisers slab zinc dros(batch) (> 92% Zn)
GB 025		— Zinc skimmings
GB 030		— Aluminium skimmings
GB 040	ex 2620 90	Slags from precious metals and copper processing for further refining.

3. In section GC ('Other wastes containing metals')

GC 060		Spent metal bearing catalysts containing any of:
		— Precious metals: gold, silver,

(¹) 'Non-dispersible' does not include any wastes in the form of powder, sludge, dust or solid items containing encased hazardous waste liquids.

Table 5 – *contd*

Commission Regulation 1547/1999 – Annexes A–D. Restrictions on Green List Shipments to Countries where OECD Decision C(92)39 Final does not Apply

       — Platinum-group metals: ruthenium, rhodium, palladium, osmium, iridium, platinum
       — Transition metals: scandium, vanadium, manganese, cobalt, copper, yttrium, niobium, hafnium, tungsten, titanium, chromium, iron, nickel, zinc, zirconium, molybdenum, tantalum, rhenium
       — Lanthanides (rare earth metals): lanthanum, praseodymium, samarium, gadolinium, dysprosium, erbium, ytterbium, cerium, neodymium, europium, terbium, holmium, thulium, lutetium.

4.   In section GH ('Solid plastic wastes')

GH 010	3915	Waste, parings and scrap of plastics of:
GH 011	ex 3915 10	— Polymers of ethylene
GH 012	ex 3915 20	— Polymers of styrene
GH 013	ex 3915 30	— Polymers of vinyl chloride.

CYPRUS

All types in Annex II except those listed in Annex D.

HUNGARY ([1])

All types in Annex II except those listed in Annex B.

INDONESIA

In section GA ('Metal and metal-alloy waste in metallic, non-dispersible ([2]) form')

(a)   The following ferrous waste and scrap of iron or steel:

GA 080	7204 41	Turnings, shavings, chips, milling waste, filings, trimmings and stampings, whether or not in bundles
GA 090	7204 49	Other ferrous waste and scrap
GA 100	7204 50	Re-melting scrap ingots.

(b)   The following waste and scrap of non-ferrous metals and their alloys:

GA 120	7404 00	Copper waste and scrap
GA 130	7503 00	Nickel waste and scrap
GA 150	7802 00	Lead waste and scrap
GA 160	7902 00	Zinc waste and scrap
GA 170	8002 00	Tin waste and scrap
GA 180	ex 8101 91	Tungsten waste and scrap
GA 190	ex 8102 91	Molybdenum waste and scrap
GA 200	ex 8103 10	Tantalum waste and scrap
GA 210	8104 20	Magnesium waste and scrap (excluding those listed in AA 190) (*)
GA 220	ex 8105 10	Cobalt waste and scrap
GA 230	ex 8106 00	Bismuth waste and scrap

([1]) Although this country is a member of the OECD, it does not apply OECD Council Decision C(92) 39 Final. When this country implements Decision C(92) 39 Final, this Regulation will no longer be applicable to it.
([2]) 'Non-dispersible' does not include any wastes in the form of powder, sludge, dust or solid items containing encased hazardous waste liquids.

Table 5 – *contd*

Commission Regulation 1547/1999 – Annexes A–D. Restrictions on Green List Shipments to Countries where OECD Decision C(92)39 Final does not Apply

GA 240	ex	8107 10	Cadmium waste and scrap
GA 250	ex	8108 10	Titanium waste and scrap
GA 260	ex	8109 10	Zirconium waste and scrap
GA 270	ex	8110 00	Antimony waste and scrap
GA 280	ex	8111 00	Manganese waste and scrap
GA 290	ex	8112 11	Beryllium waste and scrap
GA 300	ex	8112 20	Chromium waste and scrap
GA 310	ex	8112 30	Germanium waste and scrap
GA 320	ex	8112 40	Vanadium waste and scrap.

(*) See Annex III of Decision 98/368/EC (OJ L 165, 10.6.1998, p. 20).

JAMAICA

1. All types included in section GA ('Metal and metal-alloy waste in metallic, non dispersible ([1]) form').

2. All types included in section GB ('Metal bearing wastes arising from melting, smelting and refining of metals').

3. All types included in section GD ('Wastes from mining operations: these wastes to be in non-dispersible form').

4. All types included in section GE ('Glass waste in non-dispersible form').

5. All types included in section GF ('Ceramic waste in non-dispersible form').

6. All types included in section GI ('Paper, paperboard and paper product wastes').

7. All types included in section GJ ('Textile wastes').

8. All types included in section GL ('Untreated cork and wood wastes').

MACAU

All types in Annex II.

POLAND ([2])

All types in Annex II.

SINGAPORE

1. In section GA ('Metal and metal-alloy wastes in metallic, non-dispersible ([1]) form')

    (a) The following waste and scrap of precious metals and their alloys:

GA 010	ex 7112 10	— Of gold
GA 020	ex 7112 20	— Of platinum (the expression 'platinum' includes platinum, iridium, osmium, palladium, rhodium and ruthenium)
GA 030	ex 7112 90	— Other precious metals, e.g. silver

    NB. Mercury is specifically excluded as a contaminant of these metals or their alloys or amalgams.

([1]) 'Non-dispersible' does not include any wastes in the form of powder, sludge, dust or solid items containing encased hazardous waste liquids.
([2]) Although this country is a member of the OECD, it does not apply OECD Council Decision C(92) 39 Final. When this country implements Decision C(92) 39 Final, this Regulation will no longer be applicable to it.

Table 5 – *contd*

Commission Regulation 1547/1999 – Annexes A–D. Restrictions on Green List Shipments to
Countries where OECD Decision C(92)39 Final does not Apply

(b) The following waste and scrap of non-ferrous metals and their alloys:

GA 120	7404 00	Copper waste and scrap
GA 130	7503 00	Nickel waste and scrap
GA 140	7602 00	Aluminium waste and scrap
GA 170	8002 00	Tin waste and scrap
GA 190	ex 8102 91	Molybdenum waste and scrap
GA 250	ex 8108 10	Titanium waste and scrap
GA 260	ex 8109 10	Zirconium waste and scrap
GA 280	ex 8111 00	Manganese waste and scrap
GA 300	ex 8112 20	Chromium waste and scrap
GA 320	ex 8112 40	Vanadium waste and scrap
	ex 8112 91	Wastes and scrap of:
GA 350		Niobium

2. In section GC ('Other wastes containing metals')

GC 070	ex 2619 00	Slags arising from the manufacture of iron and carbon steel (including low alloy steel) excluding those slags which have been specifically produced to meet both national and relevant international requirements and standards (*).

(*) This entry covers the use of such slags as a source of titanium dioxide and vanadium.

3. In section GD ('Wastes from mining operations: these wastes to be in non-dispersible form')

GD 020	ex 2514 00	Slate waste, whether or not roughly trimmed or merely cut, by sawing or otherwise.

THAILAND:

1. In section GA ('Metal and metal-alloy wastes in metallic, non-dispersible (¹) form')

(a) The following waste and scrap of non-ferrous metals and their alloys:

GA 130	7503 00	Nickel waste and scrap
GA 150	7802 00	Lead waste and scrap
GA 220	ex 8105 10	Cobalt waste and scrap
GA 240	ex 8107 10	Cadmium waste and scrap
GA 270	ex 8110 00	Antimony waste and scrap
GA 290	ex 8112 11	Beryllium waste and scrap
GA 300	ex 8112 20	Chromium waste and scrap
GA 320	ex 8112 40	Vanadium waste and scrap
	ex 8112 91	Wastes and scrap of:
GA 330		— Hafnium
GA 340		— Indium
GA 350		— Niobium
GA 360		— Rhenium
GA 370		— Gallium
GA 400	ex 2804 90	Selenium waste and scrap
GA 410	ex 2804 50	Tellerium waste and scrap
GA 420	ex 2805 30	Rare earth waste and scrap.

(¹) 'Non-dispersible' does not include any wastes in the form of powder, sludge, dust or solid items containing encased hazardous waste liquids.

Table 5 – *contd*

Commission Regulation 1547/1999 – Annexes A–D. Restrictions on Green List Shipments to Countries where OECD Decision C(92)39 Final does not Apply

2. All types in section GB ('Metal bearing wastes arising from melting, smelting and refining of metals').

3. In section GC ('Other wastes containing metals')

GC 050		Spent fluid catalytic cracking (FCC) catalysts (e.g. aluminium oxide, zeolites)
GC 060		Spent metal bearing catalysts containing any of: — Precious metals: gold, silver — Platinum-group metals: ruthenium, rhodium, palladium, osmium, iridium, platinum — Transition metals: scandium, vanadium, manganese, cobalt, copper, yttrium, niobium, hafnium, tungsten, titanium, chromium, iron, nickel, zinc, zirconium, molybdenum, tantalum, rhenium — Lanthanides (rare earth metals): lanthanum, praseodymium, samarium, gadolinium, dysprosium, erbium, ytterbium, cerium, neodymium, europium, terbium, holmium, thulium, lutetium
GC 070	ex 2619 00	Slags arising from the manufacture of iron and carbon steel (including low alloy steel) excluding those slags which have been specifically produced to meet both national and relevant international requirements and standards (*).

(*) This entry covers the use of such slags as a source of titanium dioxide and vanadium.

4. In section GD ('Wastes from mining operations: these wastes to be in non-dispersible form')

GD 040	ex 2529 30	Leucite, nepheline and nepheline syenite waste
GD 050	ex 2529 10	Feldspar waste
GD 060	ex 2529 21 ex 2529 22	Fluospar waste.

5. All types in section GE ('Glass waste in non-dispersible form').

6. All types in section GF ('Ceramic wastes in non-dispersible form').

7. In section GG ('Other wastes containing principally inorganic constituents, which may contain metals and organic material')

GG 030	ex 2621	Bottom ash and slag tap from coal-fired powder plants
GG 040	ex 2621	Coal-fired power plants fly ash
GG 060	ex 2803	Spent activated carbon, resulting from the treatment of potable water and processes of the food industry and vitamin production
GG 080	ex 2621 00	Slag from copper production, chemically stabilised, having a high iron content (above 20%) and processed according to industrial specifications (e.g. DIN 4301 and DIN 8201), mainly for construction and abrasive applications
GG 090		Sulphur in solid form
GG 110	ex 2621 00	Neutralised red mud from alumina production
GG 140		Broken concrete.

Table 5 – *contd*

Commission Regulation 1547/1999 – Annexes A–D. Restrictions on Green List Shipments to Countries where OECD Decision C(92)39 Final does not Apply

8. All types in section GH ('Solid plastic wastes')

9. All types in section GK ('Rubber wastes').

10. In section GO ('Other wastes containing principally organic constituents, which may contain metals and inorganic materials')

GO 020	Waste straw
GO 030	Deactivated fungus mycelium from penicillin production to be used as animal feed.

TUNISIA:

1. In section GA ('Metal and metal-alloy wastes in metallic, non-dispersible ([1]) form')

GA 170	8002 00	Tin waste and scrap.

2. In section GC ('Other wastes containing metals')

GC 030	ex 8908 00	Vessels and other floating structures for breaking up, properly emptied of any cargo and other materials arising from the operation of the vessel which may have been classified as a dangerous substance or waste.

3. All types in section GH ('Solid plastic wastes').

4. All types in section GI ('Paper, paperboard and paper product wastes').

5. In section GJ ('Textile wastes')

GJ 070	ex 5304 90	Tow and waste (including yarn waste and garnetted stock) of sisal and other textile fibres of the genus Agave
GJ 111	5505 10	Waste (including noils, yarn waste and garnetted stock) of man-made fibres — of synthetic fibres.

6. All types in section GK ('Rubber wastes').

7. In section GM ('Wastes arising from agro-food industries')

GM 130		Waste from the agro-food industry excluding by-products which meet national and international requirements and standards for human or animal consumption.

ANNEX B

Countries to which shipments of certain categories of waste listed in Annex II (the 'green' list) to Regulation (EEC) No 259/93 should be carried out under the control procedure applying to waste listed in Annex IV (the 'red' list) of the same Regulation are set out below. The categories of waste listed in Annex II which are covered are also given:

ARGENTINA

All types in Annex II.

([1]) 'Non-dispersible' does not include any wastes in the form of powder, sludge, dust or solid items containing encased hazardous waste liquids.

Table 5 – *contd*

Commission Regulation 1547/1999 – Annexes A–D. Restrictions on Green List Shipments to Countries where OECD Decision C(92)39 Final does not Apply

BOSNIA AND HERZEGOVINA

All types in Annex II.

BRAZIL

1. In section GA ('Metal and metal-alloy wastes in metallic non-dispersible (^{1}) form')

    (a) The following waste and scrap of non-ferrous metals and their alloys:

GA 130	7503 00	Nickel waste and scrap
GA 150	7802 00	Lead waste and scrap
GA 160	7902 00	Zinc waste and scrap
GA 170	8002 00	Tin waste and scrap
GA 180	ex 8101 91	Tungsten waste and scrap
GA 190	ex 8102 91	Molybdenum waste and scrap
GA 200	ex 8103 10	Tantalum waste and scrap
GA 220	ex 8105 10	Cobalt waste and scrap
GA 230	ex 8106 00	Bismuth waste and scrap
GA 240	ex 8107 10	Cadmium waste and scrap
GA 250	ex 8108 10	Titanium waste and scrap
GA 260	ex 8109 10	Zirconium waste and scrap
GA 270	ex 8110 00	Antimony waste and scrap
GA 280	ex 8111 00	Manganese waste and scrap
GA 290	ex 8112 11	Beryllium waste and scrap
GA 300	ex 8112 20	Chromium waste and scrap
GA 310	ex 8112 30	Germanium waste and scrap
GA 320	ex 8112 40	Vanadium waste and scrap
	ex 8112 91	Waste and scrap of:
GA 330		— Hafnium
GA 340		— Indium
GA 350		— Niobium
GA 360		— Rhenium
GA 370		— Gallium
GA 400	ex 2804 90	Selenium waste and scrap
GA 410	ex 2804 50	Tellurium waste and scrap
GA 420	ex 2805 30	Rare earth waste and scrap.

2. In section GB ('Metal bearing wastes arising from melting, smelting, and refining of metals')

    GB 040   ex 2620 90   Slags from precious metals and copper processing for further refining.

3. In section GC ('Other wastes containing metals')

    GC 070   ex 2619 00   Slag arising from the manufacture of iron and carbon steel (including low alloy steel) excluding those slags which have been specifically produced to meet both national and relevant international requirements and standards (*).

(*) This entry covers the use of such slags as a source of titanium dioxide and vanadium.

(^{1}) 'Non-dispersible' does not include any wastes in the form of powder, sludge, dust or solid items containing encased hazardous waste liquids.

Table 5 – *contd*

Commission Regulation 1547/1999 – Annexes A–D. Restrictions on Green List Shipments to Countries where OECD Decision C(92)39 Final does not Apply

4. In section GD ('Wastes from mining operations: these wastes to be in non-dispersible form')

GD 040	ex 2529 30	Leucite, nepheline and nepheline syenite waste
GD 050	ex 2529 10	Feldspar waste
GD 060	ex 2529 21	Fluospar waste.
	ex 2529 22	

5. In section GG ('Other wastes containing principally inorganic constituents, which may contain metals and organic materials')

GG 030	ex 2621	Bottom ash and slag tap from coal-fired power plants
GG 040	ex 2621	Coal-fired power plants fly ash
GG 060	ex 2803	Spent activated carbon, resulting from the treatment of potable water and processes of the food industry and vitamin production
GG 080	ex 2621 00	Slag from copper production, chemically stabilised, having a high iron content (above 20%) and processed according to industrial specifications (e.g. DIN 4301 and DIN 8201) mainly for construction and abrasive applications
GG 100		Limestone from the production of calcium cyanamide (having a pH less than 9).

6. In section GH ('Solid plastic wastes')

GH 013	ex 3915 30	Waste, parings and scrap of plastics of polymers of vinyl chloride
GH 015	ex 3915 90	Waste, parings and scrap of plastics of resins or condensation products, for example: — urea formaldehyde resins — phenol formaldehyde resins — melamine formaldehyde resins — epoxy resins — alkyd resins — polyamides.

7. In section GJ ('Textile wastes')

GJ 050	ex 5302 90	Tow and waste (including yarn waste and garnetted stock) of true hemp (*Cannabis sativa* L.).

8. In section GK ('Rubber wastes')

GK 020	4012 20	Used pneumatic tyres
GK 030	ex 4017 00	Waste and scrap of hard rubber (for example, ebonite).

9. In section GO ('Other wastes containing principally organic constituents, which may contain metals and inorganic materials')

GO 040		Waste photographic film base and photographic film not containing silver
GO 050		Single-use cameras without batteries.

CHINA

All types in Annex II except those listed in Annex D.

Table 5 – *contd*

Commission Regulation 1547/1999 – Annexes A–D. Restrictions on Green List Shipments to
Countries where OECD Decision C(92)39 Final does not Apply

COLOMBIA

All types in Annex II except:

1. In section GA ('Metal and metal-alloy wastes in metallic, non-dispersible (^{1}) form')

    All types of waste and scrap of non-ferrous metals and their alloys.

2. In section GB ('Metal bearing wastes arising from melting, smelting and refining of
    metals')

GB 040	ex 2620 90	Slags from precious metals and copper processing for further refining.

3. In section GC ('Other wastes containing metals')

GC 070	ex 2619 00	Slags arising from the manufacture of iron and carbon steel (including low alloy steel) excluding those slags which have been specifically produced to meet both national and relevant international requirements and standards (*).

    (*) This entry covers the use of such slags as a source of titanium dioxide and vanadium.

4. In section GD ('Wastes from mining operations: these wastes to be in non-dispersible
    form')

GD 040	ex 2529 30	Leucite, nepheline and nepheline syenite waste
GD 050	ex 2529 10	Feldspar waste
GD 060	ex 2529 21	Fluospar waste.
	ex 2529 22	

5. In section GG ('Other wastes containing principally inorganic constituents, which may
    contain metals and organic materials')

GG 030	ex 2621	Bottom ash and slag tap from coal-fired power plants
GG 040	ex 2621	Coal-fired power plants fly ash
GG 060	ex 2803	Spent activated carbon, resulting from the treatment of potable water and processes of the food industry and vitamin production
GG 080	ex 2621 00	Slag from copper production, chemically stabilised, having a high iron content (above 20%) and processed according to industrial specifications (e.g. DIN 4301 and DIN 8201) mainly for construction and abrasive applications
GG 100		Limestone from production of calcium cyanamide (having a pH less than 9).

6. In section GH ('Solid plastic wastes')

GH 013	ex 3915 30	Waste, parings and scrap of plastics of — Polymers of vinyl chloride
GH 015	ex 3915 90	— Resins or condensation products, for example: — Urea formaldehyde resins — Phenol formaldehyde resins

(^{1}) 'Non-dispersible' does not include any wastes in the form of powder, sludge, dust or solid items
containing encased hazardous waste liquids.

Table 5 – *contd*

Commission Regulation 1547/1999 – Annexes A–D. Restrictions on Green List Shipments to Countries where OECD Decision C(92)39 Final does not Apply

		— Melamine formaldehyde resins
		— Epoxy resins
		— Alkyd resins
		— Polyamides.

7. In section GJ ('Textile wastes')

GJ 050	ex 5302 90	Tow and waste (including yarn waste and garnetted stock) of true hemp (Cannabis sativa L.).

8. In section GK ('Rubber wastes')

GK 020	4012 20	Used pneumatic tyres
GK 030	ex 4017 00	Waste and scrap of hard rubber (for example, ebonite).

9. In section GO ('Other wastes containing principally organic constituents, which may contain metals and inorganic materials')

GO 040		Waste photographic film base and waste photographic film not containing silver
GO 050		Single-use cameras without batteries.

CUBA

1. In section GA ('Metal and metal-alloy wastes in metallic, non-dispersible (^{1}) form')

(a) The following waste and scrap of non-ferrous metals and their alloys:

GA 120	7404 00	Copper waste and scrap
GA 150	7802 00	Lead waste and scrap
GA 160	7902 00	Zinc waste and scrap
GA 240	ex 8107 10	Cadmium waste and scrap
GA 270	ex 8110 00	Antimony waste and scrap
GA 290	ex 8112 11	Beryllium waste and scrap
GA 300	ex 8112 20	Chromium waste and scrap
GA 400	ex 2804 90	Selenium waste and scrap
GA 410	ex 2804 50	Tellurium waste and scrap
GA 420	ex 2805 30	Rare earth waste and scrap.

2. All types in section GB ('Metal bearing wastes arising from melting, smelting and refining of metals').

3. All types in section GC ('Other wastes containing metals').

4. In section GD ('Wastes from mining operations: these wastes to be in non-dispersible form')

GD 060	ex 2529 21	Fluospar waste.
	ex 2529 22	

5. All types in section GF ('Ceramic wastes in non-dispersible form').

6. All types in section GG ('Other wastes containing principally inorganic constituents, which may contain metals and organic material').

7. All types in section GH ('Solid plastic wastes').

8. All types in section GN ('Wastes arising from tanning and fellmongery operations and leather use').

Table 5 – *contd*

Commission Regulation 1547/1999 – Annexes A–D. Restrictions on Green List Shipments to Countries where OECD Decision C(92)39 Final does not Apply

9. All types in section GO ('Other wastes containing principally organic constituents, which may contain metals and inorganic materials').

ESTONIA

1. In section GA ('Metal and metal-alloy wastes in metallic, non-dispersible (¹) form')

    (a) The following waste and scrap of non-ferrous metals and their alloys:

GA 150	7802 00	Lead waste and scrap
GA 240	ex 8107 10	Cadmium waste and scrap
GA 270	ex 8110 00	Antimony waste and scrap
GA 290	ex 8112 11	Beryllium waste and scrap
GA 400	ex 2804 90	Selenium waste and scrap
GA 410	ex 2804 50	Tellurium waste and scrap
GA 420	ex 2805 30	Rare earth waste and scrap.

2. In section GC ('Other wastes containing metals')

GC 040		Motor vehicle wrecks, drained of liquids
GC 050		Spent fluid catalytic cracking (FCC) catalysts (e.g. aluminium oxide, zeolites)
GC 060		Spent metal bearing catalysts containing any of: — Precious metals: gold, silver — Platinum metals: ruthenium, rhodium, palladium, osmium, iridium, platinum, — Transition metals: scandium, vanadium, manganese, cobalt, copper, yttrium, niobium, hafnium, tungsten, titanium, chromium, iron, nickel, zinc, zirconium, molybdenum, tantalum, rhenium — Lanthanides (rare earth metals): lanthanum, praseodymium, samarium, gadolinium, dysprosium, crbium, ytterbium, cerium, neodymium, europium, terbium, holmium, thulium, lutetium.
GC 070	ex 2619 00	Slags arising from the manufacture of iron and carbon steel (including low alloy steel) excluding those slags which have been specifically produced to meet both national and relevant international requirements and standards (*).

(*) This entry covers the use of such slags as a source of titanium dioxide and vanadium.

3. In section GG ('Other wastes containing principally inorganic constituents, which may contain metals and organic materials')

GG 010		Partially refined calcium sulphate produced from flue gas desulphurisation (FGD)
GG 030	ex 2621	Bottom ash and slag tap from coal-fired power plants
GG 040	ex 2621	Coal-fired power plants fly ash
GG 050		Anode butts of petroleum coke and/or bitumen

(¹) 'Non-dispersible' does not include any wastes in the form of powder, sludge, dust or solid items containing encased hazardous waste liquids.

Table 5 – *contd*

Commission Regulation 1547/1999 – Annexes A–D. Restrictions on Green List Shipments to Countries where OECD Decision C(92)39 Final does not Apply

GG 060	ex 2803	Spent activated carbon, resulting from the treatment of potable water and processes of the food industry and vitamin production
GG 080	ex 2621 00	Slag from copper production, chemically stabilised, having a high iron content (above 20%) and processed according to industrial specifications (e.g. DIN 4301 and DIN 8201), mainly for construction and abrasive applications
GG 090		Sulphur in solid form
GG 110	ex 2621 00	Neutralised red mud from alumina production
GG 120		Sodium, potassium, calcium chlorides.

4. In section GH ('Solid plastic wastes')

   (a) Waste, parings and scrap of plastics of:

GH 013	ex 3915 30	— Polymers of vinyl chloride
GH 015	ex 3915 90	— Resins or condensation products, for example:
		— urea formaldehyde resins
		— phenol formaldehyde resins
		— melamine formaldehyde resins
		— epoxy resins
		— alkyd resins
		— polyamides.

5. In section GK ('Rubber wastes')

GK 020	4012 20	Used pneumatic tyres.

GUINEA

In section GJ ('Textile wastes')

GJ 120	6309 00	Worn clothing and other worn textile articles

GUINEA-BISSAU

All types in Annex II.

HUNGARY

1. In section GA ('Metal and metal-alloy wastes in metallic, non-dispersible ([1]) form')

   (a) The following waste and scrap of non-ferrous metals and their alloys:

GA 160	7902 00	Zinc waste and scrap
GA 290	ex 8112 11	Beryllium waste and scrap.

2. In section GC ('Other wastes containing metals')

GC 050		Spent fluid catalytic cracking (FCC) catalysts (e.g. aluminium oxide, zeolites)
GC 060		Spent metal bearing catalysts containing any of:
		— Precious metals: gold, silver
		— Platinum-group metals: ruthenium, rhodium, palladium, osmium, iridium, platinum

---

([1]) 'Non-dispersible' does not include any wastes in the form of powder, sludge, dust or solid items containing encased hazardous waste liquids.

Table 5 – *contd*

Commission Regulation 1547/1999 – Annexes A–D. Restrictions on Green List Shipments to Countries where OECD Decision C(92)39 Final does not Apply

		— Transition metals: scandium, vanadium, manganese, cobalt, copper, yttrium, niobium, hafnium, tungsten, titanium, chromium, iron, nickel, zinc, zirconium, molybdenum, tantalum, rhenium
		— Lanthanides (rare earth metals): lanthanum, praseodymium, samarium, gadolinium, dysprosium, erbium, ytterbium, cerium, neodymium, europium, terbium, holmium, thulium, lutetium.

3. In section GG ('Other wastes containing principally inorganic constituents, which may contain metals and organic materials')

GG 060	ex 2803	Spent activated carbon, resulting from the treatment of potable water and processes of the food industry and vitamin production
GG 110	ex 2621 00	Neutralised red mud from alumina production.

4. In section GH ('Solid plastic wastes')

GH 015	ex 3915 90	Waste, parings and scrap of plastics of: — resins or condensation products, for example: — urea formaldehyde resins — phenol formaldehyde resins — melamine formaldehyde resins — epoxy resins — alkyd resins — polyamides.

5. In section GM ('Wastes arising from agro-food industries')

GM 090	1522	Degras; residues resulting from the treatment of fatty substances or animal or vegetable waxes
GM 100	0506 90	Waste of bones and horn-cones, unworked, defatted, simply prepared (but not cut to shape), treated with acid or degelatinised
GM 110	ex 0511 91	Fish waste.

6. In section GN ('Wastes arising from tanning and fellmongery operations and leather use')

GN 030	ex 0505 90	Waste of skins and other parts of birds, with their feathers or down, of feathers and parts of feathers (whether or not with trimmed edges) and down, not further worked than cleaned, disinfected or treated for preservation.

INDIA

1. In section GA ('Metal and metal-alloy wastes in metallic, non-dispersible ([1]) form')

(a) The following waste and scrap of non-ferrous metals and their alloys:

GA 240	ex 8107 10	Cadmium waste and scrap
GA 270	ex 8110 00	Antimony waste and scrap
GA 290	ex 8112 11	Beryllium waste and scrap
GA 300	ex 8112 20	Chromium waste and scrap
GA 400	ex 2804 90	Selenium waste and scrap

([1]) 'Non-dispersible' does not include any wastes in the form of powder, sludge, dust or solid items containing encased hazardous waste liquids.

Table 5 – *contd*

Commission Regulation 1547/1999 – Annexes A–D. Restrictions on Green List Shipments to Countries where OECD Decision C(92)39 Final does not Apply

| GA 410 | ex 2804 50 | Tellurium waste and scrap. |

2. In section GB ('Metal bearing wastes arising from melting, smelting and refining of metals')

| GB 010 | 2620 11 | Hard zinc spelter |
| GB 040 | ex 2620 90 | Slags from precious metals and copper processing for further refining. |

3. All types in section GH ('Solid plastic wastes') except

| GH 014 | ex 3915 90 | Polymerized or co-polymers (polyethylene terephthalate). |

4. In section GJ ('Textile wastes')

| GJ 130 | ex 6310 | Used rags, scrap twine, cordage, rope and cables and worn out articles of twine, cordage, rope or cables of textile materials |
| GJ 132 | ex 6310 90 | — other. |

INDONESIA

All types in Annex II except those listed in Annex A or Annex D.

JAMAICA

1. All types in section GC ('Other wastes containing metals').

2. All types in section GG ('Other wastes containing principally inorganic constituents, which may contain metals and organic materials').

3. All types in section GH ('Solid plastic wastes').

4. All types in section GK ('Rubber wastes').

5. All types in section GM ('Wastes arising from agro-food industries').

6. All types in section GN ('Wastes arising from tanning and fellmongery operations and leather use').

7. All types in section GO ('Other wastes containing principally organic constituents, which may contain metals and inorganic materials').

LITHUANIA

1. In section GA ('Metal and metal-alloy wastes in metallic, non-dispersible ([1]) form')

   (a) The following waste and scrap of non-ferrous metals and their alloys:

GA 130	7503 00	Nickel waste and scrap
GA 150	7802 00	Lead waste and scrap
GA 190	ex 8102 91	Tungsten waste and scrap
GA 200	ex 8103 10	Tantalum waste and scrap
GA 210	8104 20	Magnesium waste and scrap (excluding those listed in AA 190) (*)
GA 220	ex 8105 10	Cobalt waste and scrap
GA 240	ex 8107 10	Cadmium waste and scrap
GA 270	ex 8110 00	Antimony waste and scrap

([1]) 'Non-dispersible' does not include any wastes in the form of powder, sludge, dust or solid items containing encased hazardous waste liquids.

Table 5 – *contd*

Commission Regulation 1547/1999 – Annexes A–D. Restrictions on Green List Shipments to Countries where OECD Decision C(92)39 Final does not Apply

GA 290	ex 8112 11	Beryllium waste and scrap
GA 300	ex 8112 20	Chromium waste and scrap
GA 320	ex 8112 40	Vanadium waste and scrap
GA 400	ex 2804 90	Selenium waste and scrap
GA 410	ex 2804 50	Tellurium waste and scrap.

(*) Annex III to Decision 98/368/EC.

2. In section GC ('Other wastes containing metals')

GC 040		Motor vehicle wrecks, drained of liquids
GC 050		Spent fluid catalytic cracking (FCC) catalysts (e.g. aluminium oxide, zeolites)
GC 060		Spent metal bearing catalysts containing any of: — Precious metals: gold, silver — Platinum-group metals: ruthenium, rhodium, palladium, osmium, iridium, platinum — Transition metals: scandium, vanadium, manganese, cobalt, copper, yttrium, niobium, hafnium, tungsten, titanium, chromium, iron, nickel, zinc, zirconium, molybdenum, tantalum, rhenium — Lanthanides (rare earth metals): lanthanum, praseodymium, samarium, gadolinium, dysprosium, erbium, ytterbium, cerium, neodymium, europium, terbium, holmium, thulium, lutetium.
GC 070	ex 2619 00	Slags arising from the manufacture of iron and carbon steel (including low alloy steel) excluding those slags which have been specifically produced to meet both national and relevant international requirements and standards (*).

(*) This entry covers the use of such slags as a source of titanium dioxide and vanadium.

3. In section GD ('Wastes from mining operations: these wastes to be in non-dispersible form')

GD 040	ex 2529 30	Leucite, nepheline and nepheline syenite waste
GD 050	ex 2529 10	Feldspar waste
GD 060	ex 2529 21 ex 2529 22	Fluospar waste.

4. In section GG ('Other wastes containing principally inorganic constituents, which may contain metals and organic materials')

GG 010		Partially refined calcium sulphate produced from flue gas desulphurisation (FGD)
GG 040	ex 2621	Coal-fired power plants fly ash
GG 050		Anode butts of petroleum coke and/or bitumen
GG 060	ex 2803	Spent activated carbon, resulting from the treatment of potable water and processes of the food industry and vitamin production
GG 080	ex 2621 00	Slag from copper production, chemically stabilised, having a high iron content (above 20%) and processed according to industrial specifications (e.g. DIN 4301 and DIN 8201) mainly for construction and abrasive applications

Table 5 – *contd*

Commission Regulation 1547/1999 – Annexes A–D. Restrictions on Green List Shipments to Countries where OECD Decision C(92)39 Final does not Apply

GG 090	Sulphur in solid form
GG 120	Sodium, potassium, calcium chlorides
GG 140	Broken concrete.

5. All types in section GH ('Solid plastic wastes') except

   GH 011 ex 3915 10 Polymers of ethylene.

6. All types in section GK ('Rubber wastes').

7. In section GO ('Other wastes containing principally organic constituents, which may contain metals and inorganic materials')

   GO 040 Waste photographic film base and waste photographic film not containing silver.

MADAGASCAR

All types in Annex II except those listed in Annex D.

MALAYSIA

All types in Annex II except those listed in Annex D.

MALTA

All types in Annex II.

MAURITIUS

All types in Annex II.

NIGERIA

All types included in section GH ('Solid plastic wastes').

RUSSIA

1. In section GA ('Metal and metal-alloy wastes in metallic, non-dispersible ([1]), form')

   (a) The following waste and scrap of non-ferrous metals and their alloys:

GA 150	7802 00	Lead waste and scrap
GA 160	7902 00	Zinc waste and scrap
GA 170	8002 00	Tin waste and scrap
GA 180	ex 8101 91	Tungsten waste and scrap
GA 190	ex 8102 91	Molybdenum waste and scrap
GA 200	ex 8103 10	Tantalum waste and scrap
GA 210	8104 20	Magnesium waste and scrap (excluding those listed in AA 190) (*)
GA 220	ex 8105 10	Cobalt waste and scrap
GA 230	ex 8106 00	Bismuth waste and scrap
GA 240	ex 8107 10	Cadmium waste and scrap
GA 250	ex 8108 10	Titanium waste and scrap
GA 260	ex 8109 10	Zirconium waste and scrap
GA 270	ex 8110 00	Antimony waste and scrap

([1]) 'Non-dispersible' does not include any wastes in the form of powder, sludge, dust or solid items containing encased hazardous waste liquids.

Table 5 – *contd*

Commission Regulation 1547/1999 – Annexes A–D. Restrictions on Green List Shipments to Countries where OECD Decision C(92)39 Final does not Apply

GA 280	ex 8111 00	Manganese waste and scrap
GA 290	ex 8112 11	Beryllium waste and scrap
GA 300	ex 8112 20	Chromium waste and scrap
GA 310	ex 8112 30	Germanium waste and scrap
GA 320	ex 8112 40	Vanadium waste and scrap
	ex 8112 91	Wastes and scrap of
GA 330		— Hafnium
GA 340		— Indium
GA 350		— Niobium
GA 400	ex 2804 90	Selenium waste and scrap
GA 410	ex 2804 50	Tellurium waste and scrap.

(*) This entry covers the use of such slags as a source of titanium dioxide and vandium.

2. In section GB ('Metal bearing wastes arising from melting, smelting and refining of metals')

GB 010	2620 11	Hard zinc spelter.
GB 025		— Zinc skimmings.

3. In section GC ('Other wastes containing metals')

GC 030	ex 8908 00	Vessels and other floating structures for breaking up, properly emptied of any cargo and other materials arising from the operation of the vessel which may have been classified as a dangerous substance or waste.
GC 070	ex 2619 00	Slag arising from the manufacture of iron and carbon steel (including low alloy steel) excluding those slags which have been specifically produced to meet both national and relevant international requirements and standards (*).

(*) This entry covers the use of such slags as a source of titanium dioxide and vanadium.

4. In section GD ('Wastes from mining operations: these wastes to be in non-dispersible form')

GD 020	ex 2514 00	Slate waste, whether or not roughy trimmed or merely cut, by sawing or otherwise
GD 030	2525 30	Mica waste
GD 070	ex 2811 22	Silica wastes in solid form excluding those used in foundry operations.

5. In section GG ('Other wastes containing principally inorganic constituents, which may contain metals and organic metals')

GG 030	ex 2621	Bottom ash and slag tap from coal-fired power plants
GG 040	ex 2621	Coal-fired power plants fly ash
GG 060	ex 2803	Spent activated carbon, resulting from the treatment of potable water and processes of the food industry and vitamin production
GG 110	ex 2621 00	Neutralised red mud from alumina production.

6. All types included in section GH ('Solid plastic wastes'

7. In section GJ ('Textile wastes')

Table 5 – *contd*

Commission Regulation 1547/1999 – Annexes A–D. Restrictions on Green List Shipments to Countries where OECD Decision C(92)39 Final does not Apply

GJ 110	5505	Waste (including noils, yarn waste and garnetted stock) of man-made fibres
GJ 111	5505 10	— of synthetic fibres
GJ 112	5505 20	— of artificial fibres.

8. All types included in section GK ('Rubber wastes').

9. In section GM ('Wastes arising from agro-food industries')

GM 090	1522	Degras; residues resulting from the treatment of fatty substances or animal or vegetable waxes
GM 100	0506 90	Waste of bones and horn-cones, unworked, defatted, simply prepared (but not cut to shape), treated with acid or degelatinised
GM 110	ex 0511 91	Fish waste.

10. In section GN ('Wastes arising from tanning and fellmongery operations and leather use')

GN 010	ex 0502 00	Waste of pigs', hogs', or boars' bristles and hair or of badger hair and other brushmaking hair
GN 020	ex 0503 00	Horsehair waste, whether or not put up as a layer with or without supporting material
GN 030	ex 0505 90	Waste of skins and other parts of birds, with their feathers or down, of feathers and parts of feathers (whether or not with trimmed edges) and down, not further worked than cleaned, disinfected or treated for preservation.

11. In section GO ('Other wastes containing principally organic constituents, which may contain metal and inorganic materials')

GO 010	ex 0501	Waste of human hair.

SÃO TOMÉ E PRÍNCIPE

1. In section GJ ('Textile wastes')

GJ 120	6309 00	Worn clothing and other worn textile articles
GJ 130	ex 6310	Used rags, scrap twine, cordage, rope and cables and worn out articles of twine, cordage, rope or cables of textile materials
GJ 131	ex 6310 10	— Sorted
GJ 132	ex 6310 90	— Other.

SINGAPORE

1. In section GA ('Metal and metal-alloy wastes in metallic, non-dispersible ([1]), form')

    (a) The following waste and scrap of non-ferrous metals and their alloys:

GA 150	7802 00	Lead waste and scrap.

2. In section GH ('Solid plastic wastes')

Waste, parings and scrap of plastics of:

GH 013	ex 3915 30	polymers of vinyl cloride.

([1]) 'Non-dispersible' does not include any wastes in the form of powder, sludge, dust or solid items containing encased hazardous waste liquids.

Table 5 – *contd*

Commission Regulation 1547/1999 – Annexes A–D. Restrictions on Green List Shipments to Countries where OECD Decision C(92)39 Final does not Apply

SLOVAKIA

All types in Annex II except those listed in Annex D.

TOGO

All types in Annex II.

TRINIDAD AND TOBAGO

All types in Annex II.

UKRAINE

All types in Annex II.

ZAMBIA

All types in Annex II except those listed in Annex D.

ANNEX C

Countries to which shipments of certain categories of waste in Annex II (the 'green' list) to Regulation (EEC) No 259/93 should be carried out under the control procedure laid down in Article 15 of the same Regulation are set out below. The categories of waste listed in Annex II which are covered are also given.

BELARUS

All types in Annex II.

LATVIA

All types in Annex II.

PHILIPPINES

1. All types in section GA ('Metals and metal-alloy wastes in metallic, non-dispersible (¹) form')

2. In section GB ('Metal bearing wastes arising from melting, smelting and refining of metals')

GB 010	2620 11	Hard zinc spelter
GB 020		Zinc containing drosses:
GB 021		— Galvanising slab zinc top dross (> 90% Zn)
GB 022		— Galvanising slab zinc bottom dross (> 92% Zn)
GB 023		— Zinc die cast dross (> 85% Zn)
GB 024		— Hot dip galvanisers slab zinc dross(batch)(> 92% Zn)
GB 025		— Zinc skimmings
GB 030		Aluminium skimmings
GB 040	ex 2620 90	Slags from precious metals and copper processing for further refining
GB 050	ex 2620 90	Tantalum bearing tin slags with less than 0,5% tin.

(¹) 'Non-dispersible' does not include any wastes in the form of powder, sludge, dust or solid items containing encased hazardous waste liquids.

Table 5 – *contd*

Commission Regulation 1547/1999 – Annexes A–D. Restrictions on Green List Shipments to Countries where OECD Decision C(92)39 Final does not Apply

3.   In section GC ('Other wastes containing metals')

GC 020   Electronic scrap (e.g. printed circuit boards, electronic components, wire, etc) and reclaimed electronic components suitable for base and precious metal recovery

4.   All types in section GH ('Solid plastic wastes')

ROMANIA

All types in Annex II.

TAIWAN

In section GA ('Metal and metal-alloy wastes in metallic, non-dispersible (¹) form')
The following waste and scrap of non-ferrous metals and their alloys:

GA 150	7802 00	Lead waste and scrap
GA 240	ex 8107 10	Cadmium waste and scrap
GA 300	ex 8112 20	Chromium waste and scrap.

URUGUAY

All types in Annex II.

ANNEX D

Countries to which shipments of certain categories of waste listed in Annex II (the 'green' list) to Council Regulation (EEC) No 259/93 will be accepted from the EC without recourse to any of the control procedures provided for in the Regulation. Shipments of these wastes to these countries may continue under the same conditions applying to normal commercial transactions. The categories of waste listed in Annex II which are covered are also given:

ALBANIA

1.   In section GA ('Metal and metal-alloy wastes in metallic, non-dispersible (¹) form')

(a)   The following ferrous waste and scrap of iron or steel:

GA 040	7204 10	Waste and scrap of cast iron
GA 050	7204 21	Waste and scrap of stainless steel
GA 060	7204 29	Waste and scrap of other alloy steels
GA 070	7204 30	Waste and scrap of tinned iron or steel
GA 080	7204 41	Turnings, shavings, chips, milling waste, filings, trimmings and stampings, whether or not in bundles
GA 090	7204 49	Other ferrous waste and scrap
GA 100	7204 50	Re-melting scrap ingots
GA 110	ex 7302 10	Used iron and steel rails.

(b)   The following waste and scrap of non-ferrous metals and their alloys:

GA 120	7404 00	Copper waste and scrap
GA 150	7802 00	Lead waste and scrap
GA 160	7902 00	Zinc waste and scrap

(¹) 'Non-dispersible' does not include any wastes in the form of powder, sludge, dust or solid items containing encased hazardous waste liquids.

Table 5 – *contd*

Commission Regulation 1547/1999 – Annexes A–D. Restrictions on Green List Shipments to Countries where OECD Decision C(92)39 Final does not Apply

GA 170	8002 00	Tin waste and scrap.

2. All types included in section GB ('Metal bearing wastes arising from melting, smelting and refining of metals').

3. All types included in section GE ('Glass waste in non-dispersible form').

4. In section GG ('Other wastes containing principally inorganic constituents, which may contain metals and organic materials')

GG 080	ex 2621 00	Slag from copper production, chemically stabilised, having a high iron content (above 20%) and processed according to industrial specifications (e.g. DIN 4301 and DIN 8201) mainly for construction and abrasive applications.

5. All types in section GI ('Paper, paperboard and paper product wastes').

6. In section GJ ('Textile wastes')

GJ 020	5103	Waste of wool or of fine or coarse animal hair, including yarn waste but excluding garnetted stock
GJ 021	5103 10	— Noils of wool or of fine animal hair
GJ 022	5103 20	— Other waste of wool or of fine animal hair
GJ 023	5103 30	— Waste of coarse animal hair
GJ 030	5202	Cotton waste (including yarn waste and garnetted stock)
GJ 031	5202 10	— Yarn waste (including thread waste)
GJ 032	5202 91	— Garnetted stock
GJ 033	5202 99	— Other.

ANGOLA

1. All types in section GA ('Metal and metal alloy wastes in metallic, non-dispersible ([1]) form').

2. All types in section GE ('Glass wastes in non-dispersible form').

3. All types in section GI (Paper, paperboard and paper product wastes).

4. All types in section GJ ('Textile wastes').

5. All types in section GK ('Rubber wastes').

BENIN

All types in Annex II.

BRAZIL

1. In section GA ('Metal and metal-alloy wastes in metallic, non-dispersible form')

   (a) The following ferrous waste and scrap of iron or steel:

GA 040	7204 10	Waste and scrap of cast iron
GA 050	7204 21	Waste and scrap of stainless steel
GA 060	7204 29	Waste and scrap of other alloy steels

([1]) 'Non-dispersible' does not include any wastes in the form of powder, sludge, dust or solid items containing encased hazardous waste liquids.

Table 5 – *contd*

Commission Regulation 1547/1999 – Annexes A–D. Restrictions on Green List Shipments to Countries where OECD Decision C(92)39 Final does not Apply

GA 070	7204 30	Waste and scrap of tinned iron or steel
GA 080	7204 41	Turnings, shavings, chips, milling waste, filings, trimmings and stampings, whether or not in bundles
GA 090	7204 49	Other ferrous waste and scrap
GA 100	7204 50	Re-melting scrap ingots.

(b) The following waste and scrap of non-ferrous metals and their alloys:

GA 120	7404 00	Copper waste and scrap
GA 140	7602 00	Aluminium waste and scrap
GA 210	8104 20	Magnesium waste and scrap (excluding those listed in AA 190) (*).

(*) Annex III to Decision 98/368/EC (OJ L 165, 10.6.1998, p. 20).

BULGARIA

All types in section GI ('Paper, paperboard and paper product wastes')

BURKINA FASO

All types in section GA ('Metal and metal alloy wastes in metallic, non-dispersible ([1]) form')

CAMEROON

1. In section GA ('Metal and metal-alloy wastes in metallic, non-dispersible ([1]) form')

(a) The following waste and scrap of precious metals and their alloys:

GA 010	ex 7112 10	Of gold
GA 020	ex 7112 20	Of platinum (the expression 'platinum' includes platinum, iridium, osmium, palladium, rhodium and ruthenium)
GA 030	ex 7112 90	Of other precious metal e.g. silver,

N.B. Mercury is specifically excluded as a contaminant of these metals or their alloys or amalgams.

(b) The following ferrous waste and scrap of iron or steel:

GA 040	7204 10	Waste and scrap of cast iron
GA 050	7204 21	Waste and scrap of stainless steel
GA 060	7204 29	Waste and scrap of other alloy steels
GA 070	7204 30	Waste and scrap of tinned iron or steel
GA 080	7204 41	Turnings, shavings, chips, milling waste, filings, trimmings and stampings, whether or not in bundles
GA 090	7204 49	Other ferrous waste and scrap
GA 100	7204 50	Re-melting scrap ingots
GA 110	ex 7302 10	Used iron and steel rails
GA 120	7204 00	Copper waste and scrap
GA 130	7503 00	Nickel waste and scrap
GA 150	7802 00	Lead waste and and scrap
GA 160	7902 00	Zinc waste and scrap
GA 170	8002 00	Tin waste and scrap

([1]) 'Non-dispersible' does not include any wastes in the form of powder, sludge, dust or solid items containing encased hazardous waste liquids.

Table 5 – *contd*

Commission Regulation 1547/1999 – Annexes A–D. Restrictions on Green List Shipments to Countries where OECD Decision C(92)39 Final does not Apply

GA 210	8104 20	Magnesium waste and scrap (excluding those listed in AA 190) (*)
GA 220	ex 8105 10	Cobalt waste and scrap
GA 280	ex 8111 00	Manganese waste and scrap
GA 300	ex 8112 20	Chromium waste and scrap.

(*) Annex III to Decision 98/368/EC (OJ L 165, 10.6.1998, p.20).

2. In section GB ('Metal bearing wastes arising from melting, smelting and refining of metals')

GB 050	ex 2620 90	Tantalum bearing tin slags with less than 0.5% tin.

3. In section GC ('Other wastes containing metals')

GC 030	ex 8908 00	Vessels and other floating structures for breaking up, properly emptied of any cargo and other materials arising from the operation of the vessel which may have been classified as a dangerous substance or waste.
GC 040		Motor vehicle wrecks, drained of liquids.

4. In section GE ('Glass waste in non-dispersible form')

GE 010	ex 7001 00	Cullet and other waste and scrap of glass except for glass from cathode-ray tubes and other activated glasses.

5. In section GF ('Ceramic wastes in non-dispersible form')

GF 010		Ceramic wastes which have been fired after shaping, including ceramic vessels (before and/or after use).

6. In section GH ('Solid plastic wastes')

GH 010	3915	Waste, parings and scrap of plastics of:
GH 011	ex 3915 10	— polymers of ethylene
GH 012	ex 3915 20	— polymers of styrene
GH 013	ex 3915 30	— polymers of vinyl chloride.

7. All types in section GI ('Paper, paperboard and paper product wastes').

8. In section GJ ('Textile wastes')

GJ 010	5003	Silk waste (including cocoons unsuitable for reeling, yarn waste and garnetted stock)
GJ 011	5003 10	— Not carded or combed
GJ 012	5003 90	— Other
GJ 020	5103	Waste of wool or of fine or coarse animal hair, including yarn waste but excluding garnetted stock
GJ 021	5103 10	— noils of wool or of fine animal hair
GJ 022	5103 20	— other waste of wool or of fine animal hair
GJ 023	5103 30	— waste of coarse animal hair
GJ 030	5202	Cotton waste (including yarn waste and garnetted stock)
GJ 031	5202 10	— yarn waste (including thread waste)
GJ 032	5202 91	— garnetted stock
GJ 033	5202 99	— other

Table 5 – *contd*

Commission Regulation 1547/1999 – Annexes A–D. Restrictions on Green List Shipments to Countries where OECD Decision C(92)39 Final does not Apply

GJ 090	ex 5305 29	Tow, noils and waste (including yarn waste and garnetted stock) of abaca (Manila hemp or Musa textilis Nee)
GJ 110	5505	Waste (including noils, yarn waste and garnetted stock) of man-made fibres
GJ 111	5505 10	— of synthetic fibres
GJ 112	5505 20	— of artificial fibres
GJ 120	6309 00	Worn clothing and other worn textile articles
		Used rags, scrap twine, cordage, rope and cables and worn out articles of twine, cordage, rope or cables of textile materials
GJ 131	ex 6310 10	— Sorted
GJ 132	ex 6310 90	— Other.

9. In section GK ('Rubber wastes')

GK 020	4012 20	Used pneumatic tyres.

10. All types in section GL ('Untreated cork and wood wastes').

11. In section GM ('Wastes arising from agro-food industries')

GM 080	ex 2308	Dried and sterilised vegetable waste, residues and by-products, whether or not in the form of pellets, of a kind used in animal feeding, not elsewhere specified or included.

CENTRAL AFRICAN REPUBLIC

All types in Annex II.

CHAD

All types in Annex II.

CHILE

All types in Annex II.

CHINA

Obligatory pre-inspection shipment by CCIC (China National Import and Export Commodities Inspection Corporation) before shipment

1. In section GA ('Metal and metal alloy wastes in metallic, non-dispersible (¹) form')

(a) The following ferrous waste and scrap of iron or steel:

GA 040	7204 10	Waste and scrap of cast iron
GA 050	7204 21	Waste and scrap of stainless steel
GA 060	7204 29	Waste and scrap of other alloy steels
GA 070	7204 30	Waste and scrap of tinned iron or steel
GA 080	7204 41	Turnings, shavings, chips, milling waste, filings, trimmings and stampings, whether or not in bundles
GA 090	7204 49	Other ferrous waste and scrap
GA 100	7204 50	Re-melting scrap ingots.

(¹) 'Non-dispersible' does not include any wastes in the form of powder, sludge, dust or solid items containing encased hazardous waste liquids.

Table 5 – *contd*

Commission Regulation 1547/1999 – Annexes A–D. Restrictions on Green List Shipments to Countries where OECD Decision C(92)39 Final does not Apply

(b)   The following waste and scrap of non-ferrous metals and their alloys:

GA 120	7404 00	Copper waste and scrap
GA 130	7503 00	Nickel waste and scrap
GA 140	7620 00	Aluminium waste and scrap
GA 160	7902 00	Zinc waste and scrap
GA 170	8002 00	Tin waste and scrap
GA 200	ex 8103 10	Tantalum waste and scrap.

2.   In section GC ('Other wastes containing metals')

GC 010		Electrical assemblies consisting only of metals or alloys
GC 020		Electronic scrap (e.g. printed circuit boards, electronic components, wire etc) and reclaimed electronic components suitable for base and precious metal recovery
GC 030	ex 8908 00	Vessels and other floating structures for breaking up, properly emptied of any cargo and other materials arising from the operation of the vessel which may have been classified as a dangerous substance or waste
GC 070	ex 2619 00	Slags arising from the manufacture of iron and steel, (including low alloy steel) excluding those slags which have been specifically produced to meet both national and relevant international requirements and standards (*).

(*) This entry covers the use of such slags as a source of titanium dioxide and vanadium.

3.   All types in section GI ('Paper, paperboard and paper product wastes').

4.   In section GJ ('Textile wastes')

GJ 031	5202 10	— Yarn waste (including thread waste)
GJ 033	5202 99	— Other.

5.   All types in section GL ('Untreated cork and wood wastes').

6.   In section GM ('Wastes arising from agro-food industries')

GM 100	0506 90	Waste of bones and horn-cones, unworked, defatted, simply prepared (but not cut to shape), treated with acid or degelatinised.

COMORES

In section GJ ('Textile wastes')

GJ 120	6309 00	Worn clothing and other worn textile articles.

CONGO

All types in Annex II.

CONGO, DEMOCRATIC REPUBLIC OF

All types in Annex II.

Table 5 – *contd*

Commission Regulation 1547/1999 – Annexes A–D. Restrictions on Green List Shipments to Countries where OECD Decision C(92)39 Final does not Apply

CROATIA

All types in Annex II.

CUBA

All types in Annex II except those listed in Annex B.

CYPRUS

1. In section GA ('Metal and metal-alloy wastes in metallic, non-dispersible ([1]) form')

    (a) The following waste and scrap of precious metals and their alloys:

GA 010	ex 7112 10	— Of gold
GA 020	ex 7112 20	— Of platinum (the expression 'platinum' includes platinum, iridium, osmium, palladium, rhodium and ruthenium)
GA 030	ex 7112 90	— Of other precious metals, e.g. silver

    NB: Mercury is speciafically excluded as a contaminant of these metals or their alloys or amalgams.

    (b) The following ferrous waste and scrap of iron or steel:

GA 040	7204 10	Waste and scrap of cast iron
GA 050	7204 21	Waste and scrap of stainless steel
GA 060	7204 29	Waste and scrap of other alloy steels
GA 070	7204 30	Waste and scrap of tinned iron or steel
GA 080	7204 41	Turnings, shavings, chips, milling waste, filings, trimmings and stampings, whether or not in bundles
GA 090	7204 49	Other ferrous waste and scrap
GA 100	7204 50	Re-melting scrap ingots
GA 110	ex 7302 10	Used iron and steel rails.

    (c) The following waste and scrap of non-ferrous metals and their alloys:

GA 140	7602 00	Aluminium waste and scrap.

2. In section GK ('Rubber wastes'):

GK 010	4004 00	Waste, parings and scrap of rubber (other than hard rubber) and granules obtained therefrom

3. In section GM ('Wastes arising from agro-food industries')

GM 080	ex 2308	Dried and sterilised vegetable waste, residues and by-products, whether or not in the form of pellets, of a kind used in animal feeding, not elsewhere specified or included
GM 100	0506 90	Waste of bones and horn-cones, unworked, defatted, simply prepared (but not cut to shape), treated with acid or degelatinised
GM 110	ex 0511 91	Fish waste

([1]) 'Non-dispersible' does not include any wastes in the form of powder, sludge, dust or solid items containing encased hazardous waste liquids.

Table 5 – *contd*

Commission Regulation 1547/1999 – Annexes A–D. Restrictions on Green List Shipments to Countries where OECD Decision C(92)39 Final does not Apply

EGYPT

1. All types in section GA ('Metal and metal-alloy wastes in metallic, non-dispersible (¹) form').

2. All types in section GI ('Paper, paperboard and paper product wastes').

3. All types in section GJ ('Textile wastes').

ESTONIA

All types in Annex II except those listed in Annex B.

GAMBIA

In section GJ ('Textile wastes')

GJ 120	6309 00	Worn clothing and other worn textile articles.

GEORGIA

All types in Annex II.

GRENADA

In section GK ('Rubber wastes')

GK 020	4012 20	Used pneumatic tyres.

HONG KONG

All types in Annex II.

INDIA

All types in Annex II except those listed in Annex B.

INDONESIA

1. In section GA ('Metal and metal-alloy wastes in metallic, non-dispersible (¹) form')

    The following ferrous waste and scrap of iron or steel:

GA 040	7204 10	— Waste and scrap of cast iron
GA 050	7204 21	— Waste and scrap of stainless steel
GA 060	7204 29	— Waste and scrap of other alloy steels
GA 070	7204 30	— Waste and scrap of tinned iron or steel.

2. All types in section GI ('Paper, paperboard and paper product wastes')

3. In section GJ ('Textile wastes')

GJ 010	5003	Silk waste (including cocoons unsuitable for reeling, yarn waste and garnetted stock)
GJ 012	5003 90	— Other
GJ 020	5103	Waste of wool or of fine or coarse animal hair, including yarn waste but excluding garnetted stock

---

(¹) 'Non-dispersible' does not include any wastes in the form of powder, sludge, dust or solid items containing encased hazardous waste liquids.

Table 5 – *contd*

Commission Regulation 1547/1999 – Annexes A–D. Restrictions on Green List Shipments to Countries where OECD Decision C(92)39 Final does not Apply

GJ 021	5103 10	— Noils of wool or of fine animal hair
GJ 022	5103 20	— Other waste of wool or of fine animal hair
GJ 030	5202	Cotton waste (including yarn waste and garnetted stock)
GJ 031	5202 10	— Yarn waste (including thread waste).

ISRAEL

All types in Annex II.

JORDAN

All types in Annex II.

KENYA

All types in Annex II.

KUWAIT

In section GH ('Solid plastic wastes').

Waste, parings and scrap of plastics of:

GH 011	ex 3915 10	— Polymers of ethylene.

LEBANON

In section GJ ('Textile wastes')

GJ 120	6309 00	Worn clothing and other worn textile articles.

LIECHTENSTEIN

All types in Annex II.

LITHUANIA

All types in Annex II except those listed in Annex B.

MADAGASCAR

1. In section GA ('Metal and metal-alloy wastes in metallic, non-dispersible ([1]) form')

   (a) The following waste and scrap of iron and steel:

GA 060	7204 29	Waste and scrap of other alloy steels
GA 080	7204 41	Turnings, shavings, chips, milling waste, filings, trimmings and stampings, whether or not in bundles
GA 090	7204 49	Other ferrous waste and scrap
GA 110	ex 7302 10	Used iron and steel rails.

   (b) The following waste and scrap of non-ferrous metals and their alloys:

GA 140	7602 00	Aluminium waste and scrap
GA 230	ex 8106 00	Bismuth waste and scrap
GA 270	ex 8110 00	Antimony waste and scrap

([1]) 'Non-dispersible' does not include any wastes in the form of powder, sludge, dust or solid items containing encased hazardous waste liquids.

Table 5 – *contd*

Commission Regulation 1547/1999 – Annexes A–D. Restrictions on Green List Shipments to Countries where OECD Decision C(92)39 Final does not Apply

GA 280	ex 8111 00	Manganese waste and scrap.

2.   In section GC ('Other wastes containing metals')

GC 030	ex 8908 00	Vessels and other floating structures for breaking up, properly emptied of any cargo and other materials arising from the operation of the vessel which may have been classified as a dangerous substance or waste
GC 070	ex 2619 00	Slags arising from the manufacture of iron and carbon steel (including low alloy steel) excluding those slags which have been specifically produced to meet both national and relevant international requirements and standards (*).

(*) This entry covers the use of such slags as a source of titanium dioxide and vanadium.

3.   In section GD ('Wastes from mining operations: These wastes to be in non-dispersible form')

GD 020	ex 2514 00	Slate waste, whether or not roughly trimmed or merely cut, by sawing or otherwise.

4.   In section GE ('Glass waste in non-dispersible form'):

GE 010	ex 7001 00	Cullet and other waste and scrap of glass except for glass from cathode-ray tubes and other activated glasses.

5.   In section GF ('Ceramic wastes in non-dispersible form')

GF 020	ex 8113 00	Cermet waste and scrap (metal ceramic composites).

6.   In section GG ('Other wastes containing principally inorganic constituents, which may contain metals and organic materials')

GG 100	Limestone from the production of calcium cyanamide (having a pH less than 9)
GG 130	Carborundum (silicon carbide).

7.   In section GH ('Solid plastic wastes')

GH 014	ex 3915 90	Waste, parings and scrap of plastics of: — Polymerised or co-polymers for example.: — polypropylene — polyethylene terephthalate — acrylonitrile copolymer — butadiene copolymer — styrene copolymer — polyamides — polybutylene terephthalates — polycarbonates — acrylic polymers — paraffins (C10-C13)

(¹) 'Non-dispersible' does not include any wastes in the form of powder, sludge, dust or solid items containing encased hazardous waste liquids.

Table 5 – *contd*

Commission Regulation 1547/1999 – Annexes A–D. Restrictions on Green List Shipments to Countries where OECD Decision C(92)39 Final does not Apply

		— polyurethane (not containing chlorofluorocarbons)
		— polysiloxalanes (silicones)
		— polymethyl methacrylate
		— polyvinyl alcohol
		— polyvinyl butyral
		— polyvinyl acetate
		— polymers of fluorinated ethylene (Teflon, PTFE)
GH 015	ex 3915 90	Resins or condensation products, for example:
		— urea formaldehyde resins
		— phenol formaldehyde resins
		— melamine formaldehyde resins
		— epoxy resins
		— alkyd resins
		— polyamides.

8. All types included in section GI ('Paper, paperboard and paper product wastes').

9. In section GJ ('Textile wastes')

GJ 022	5103 20	— Other waste of wool or of fine animal hair
GJ 023	5103 30	— Waste of coarse animal hair
GJ 031	5202 10	— Yarn waste (including thread waste)
GJ 032	5202 91	— Garnetted stock
GJ 040	5301 30	Flax tow and waste
GJ 050	ex 5302 90	Tow and waste (including yarn waste and garnetted stock) of true hemp (*Cannabis sativa L.*)
GJ 110	5505	Waste (including noils, yarn waste and garnetted stock) of man-made fibres
GJ 111	5505 10	— of synthetic fibres
GJ 112	5505 20	— of artifical fibres
GJ 120	6309 00	Worn clothing and other worn textile articles
GJ 130	ex 6310	Used rags, scrap twine, cordage, rope and cables and worn out articles of twine, cordage, rope or cables of textile materials
GJ 131	ex 6310 10	— sorted
GJ 132	ex 6310 90	— other.

10. In section GK ('Rubber wastes')

GK 020	4012 20	Used pneumatic tyres
GK 030	ex 4017 00	Waste and scrap of hard rubber (for example, ebonite).

MALAWI

1. All types in section GA ('Metal and metal-alloy wastes in metallic, non-dispersible ([1]) form')

2. All types in section GE ('Glass waste in non-dispersible form').

3. All types in section GI ('Paper, paperboard and paper product wastes').

4. In section GJ ('Textile wastes')

GJ 120	6309 00	Worn clothing and other worn textile articles.

Table 5 – *contd*

Commission Regulation 1547/1999 – Annexes A–D. Restrictions on Green List Shipments to
Countries where OECD Decision C(92)39 Final does not Apply

MALAYSIA

1. In section GA ('Metal and metal-alloy wastes in metallic, non-dispersible (^{1}) form')

    GA 050   7204 21   Waste and scrap of stainless steel.

2. Obligatory pre-inspection shipment required:

All types in section GI ('Paper, paperboard and paper product wastes').

MALI

All types in Annex II except:

1. In section GA ('Metal and metal-alloy wastes in metallic, non-dispersible (^{1}) form')

    All types of waste and scrap of non-ferrous metals and their alloys.

2. All types in section GE ('Glass waste in non-dispersible form').

3. All types in section GF ('Ceramic wastes in non-dispersible form').

4. All types in section GH ('Solid plastic wastes').

5. All types in section GN ('Wastes arising from tanning and fellmongery operations and
    leather use').

MAURITANIA

All types in Annex II.

MONACO

All types in Annex II.

NETHERLANDS ANTILLES

All types in Annex II.

NIGER

1. In section GJ ('Textile wastes')

    GJ 120   6309 00   Worn clothing and other worn textile articles.

2. In section GK ('Rubber wastes')

    GK 020   4012 20   Used pneumatic tyres.

PAKISTAN

1. All types in section GA ('Metal and metal-alloy wastes in metallic, non-dispersible (^{1})
    form').

2. All types in section GB ('Metal bearing wastes arising from smelting and refining of
    metals').

3. All types in section GC ('Other wastes containing metals').

(^{1}) 'Non-dispersible' does not include any wastes in the form of powder, sludge, dust or solid items
containing encased hazardous waste liquids.

Table 5 – *contd*

Commission Regulation 1547/1999 – Annexes A–D. Restrictions on Green List Shipments to Countries where OECD Decision C(92)39 Final does not Apply

4. All types in section GD ('Wastes from mining operations: these wastes to be in non-dispersible form').

5. All types in section GE ('Glass waste in non-dispersible form').

6. All types in section GF ('Ceramic wastes in non-dispersible form').

7. All types in section GG ('Other wastes containing principally inorganic constituents, which may contain metals and organic materials').

8. All types in section GH ('Solid plastic wastes').

9. All types in section GI ('Paper, paperboard and paper product wastes').

10. All types in section GJ ('Textile wastes').

11. In section GK ('Rubber wastes')

GK 010	4004 00	Waste, parings and scrap of rubber (other than hard rubber) and granules obtained therefrom
GK 030	ex 4017 00	Waste and scrap of hard rubber (for example, ebonite).

12. All types in section GL ('Untreated cork and wood wastes').

13. In section GM ('Wastes arising from the agro-food industry')

GM 080	ex 2308	Dried and sterilised vegetable waste, residues and by-products, whether or not in the form of pellets, of a kind used in animal feeding, not elsewhere specified or included
GM 090	1522	Degras; residues resulting from the treatment of fatty substances or animal or vegetable waxes
GM 100	0506 90	Waste of bones and horn-cores, unworked, defatted, simply prepared (but not cut to shape), treated with acid or degelatinised
GM 110	ex 0511 91	Fish waste
GM 120	1802 00	Cocoa shells, husks, and other cocoa waste
GM 130		Wastes from the agro-food industry excluding by-products which meet national and international requirements and standards for human or animal consumption.

14. In section GN ('Wastes arising from tanning and fellmongery operations and leather use')

GN 020	ex 0503 00	Horsehair waste, whether or not put up as a layer with or without supporting material.
GN 030	ex 0505 90	Waste of skins and other parts of birds, with their feathers or down , of feathers and parts of feathers (whether or not with trimmed edges) and down, not further worked than cleaned, disinfected or treated for preservation.
GN 040	ex 4110 00	Parings and other waste of leather or of composition leather, not suitable for the manufacture of leather articles, excluding leather sludges.

15. All types in section GO ('Other wastes containing principally organic constituents, which may contain metals and inorganic materials').

Table 5 – *contd*

Commission Regulation 1547/1999 – Annexes A–D. Restrictions on Green List Shipments to Countries where OECD Decision C(92)39 Final does not Apply

PARAGUAY

1. All types included in section GI ('Paper, paperboard and paper product wastes').
2. In section GJ ('Textile wastes')

    Silk waste (including cocoons unsuitable for reeling, yarn waste and garnetted stock)

GJ 012	5003 90	— other

    Cotton waste (including yarn waste and garnetted stock)

GJ 031	5202 10	— Yarn waste (including thread waste)
GJ 032	5202 91	— Garnetted stock.

3. In section GL ('Untreated cork and wood wastes')

GL 020	4501 90	Cork waste; crushed, granulated or ground cork.

PHILIPPINES

All types in Annex II except those listed in Annex C.

RWANDA

All types in Annex II.

SAN MARINO

All types in Annex II.

SÃO TOMÉ E PRÍNCIPE

1. In section GJ ('Textile wastes')

GJ 111	5505 10	Waste (including noils, yarn waste and garnetted stock) of man-made fibres — Of synthetic fibres.

2. In section GK ('Rubber wastes').

GK 020	4012 20	Used pneumatic tyres.

SIERRA LEONE

All types in Annex II.

SINGAPORE

1. In section GA ('Metal and metal-alloy wastes in metallic, non-dispersible (¹) form')

    The following ferrous waste and scrap of iron or steel:

GA 040	7204 10	Waste and scrap of cast iron
GA 050	7204 21	Waste and scrap of stainless steel
GA 060	7204 29	Waste and scrap of other alloy steels.

Table 5 – *contd*

Commission Regulation 1547/1999 – Annexes A–D. Restrictions on Green List Shipments to Countries where OECD Decision C(92)39 Final does not Apply

SLOVAKIA

1. In section GA ('Metal and metal-alloy wastes in metallic, non-dispersible (¹) form')

    (a) The following ferrous waste and scrap of iron and steel:

GA 040	7204 10	Waste and scrap of cast iron
GA 050	7204 21	Waste and scrap of stainless steel
GA 060	7204 29	Waste and scrap of other alloy steels
GA 070	7204 30	Waste and scrap of tinned iron or steel
GA 080	7204 41	Turnings, shavings, chips, milling waste, filings, trimming and stampings, whether or not in bundles
GA 090	7204 49	Other ferrous waste and scrap
GA 100	7204 50	Re-melting scrap ingots
GA 110	ex 7302 10	Used iron and steel rails.

    (b) The following waste and scrap of non-ferrous metals and their alloys:

    GA 120 7404 00 Copper waste and scrap
    GA 140 7602 00 Aluminium waste and scrap
    GA 160 7902 00 Zinc waste and scrap.

2. In section GE ('Glass waste in non-dispersible form')

GE 010	ex 7001 00	Cullet and other waste and scrap of glass except for glass from cathode-ray tubes and other activated glass.
GE 020		Fibre glass wastes.

3. In section GI ('Paper, paperboard and paper product wastes')

GI 011	4707 10	— of unbleached kraft paper or paperboard or of corrugated paper or paperboard
GI 012	4707 20	— of other paper or paperboard, made mainly of bleached chemical pulp, not coloured in the mass
GI 013	4707 30	— of paper or paperboard made mainly of mechanical pulp (for example, newspapers, journals and similar printed matter).

SLOVENIA

All types in Annex II.

SOUTH AFRICA

All types in Annex II.

SRI LANKA

All types in Annex II.

SURINAME

All types in Annex II.

(¹) 'Non-dispersible' does not include any wastes in the form of powder, sludge, dust or solid items containing encased hazardous waste liquids.

Table 5 – *contd*

Commission Regulation 1547/1999 – Annexes A–D. Restrictions on Green List Shipments to Countries where OECD Decision C(92)39 Final does not Apply

TAIWAN

All types in Annex II except those listed in Annex C.

TANZANIA

In section GJ ('Textile wastes')

GJ 120	6309 00	Worn clothing and other worn textile articles.

THAILAND

All types in Annex II except those listed in Annex A.

TUNISIA

1. In section GA ('Metal and metal-alloy wastes in metallic, non-dispersible (¹) form')

   (a) The following ferrous waste and scrap of iron and steel:

GA 110	ex 7302 10	Used iron and steel rails.

   (b) The following waste and scrap of non-ferrous metals and their alloys:

GA 120	7404 00	Copper waste and scrap
GA 140	7602 00	Aluminium waste and scrap.
GJ 010	5003	Silk waste (including cocoons unsuitable for reeling, yarn waste and garnetted stock)
GJ 012	5003 90	— Other
GJ 020	5103	Waste of wool or of fine or coarse animal hair, including yarn waste but excluding garnetted stock
GJ 030	5202	Cotton waste (including yarn waste and garnetted stock)
GJ 060	ex 5303 90	Tow and waste (including yarn waste and garnetted stock) of jute and other textile bast fibres (excluding flax, true hemp and ramie)
GJ 120	6309 00	Worn clothing and other worn textile articles.
GJ 130	ex 6310	Used rags, scrap twine, cordage, rope and cables and worn out articles of twine, cordage, rope or cables of textile materials.

3. In section GM ('Wastes arising from agro-food industries')

GM 080	ex 2308	Dried and sterilised vegetable waste, residues and by-products, whether or not in the form of pellets, of a kind used in animal feeding, not elsewhere specified or included.

4. In section GN ('Wastes arising from tanning and fellmongery operations and leather use')

GN 010	ex 0502 00	Waste of pigs', hogs' or boars' bristles and hair or of badger hair and other brush making hair
GN 020	ex 0503 00	Horsehair waste, whether or not put up as a layer with or without supporting material

---

(¹) 'Non-dispersible' does not include any wastes in the form of powder, sludge, dust or solid items containing encased hazardous waste liquids.

Table 5 – *contd*

Commission Regulation 1547/1999 – Annexes A–D. Restrictions on Green List Shipments to Countries where OECD Decision C(92)39 Final does not Apply

GN 040	ex 4110 00	Parings and other leather waste of leather or of composition leather, not suitable for the manufacture of leather articles, excluding leather sludges.

UGANDA

1. In section GA ('Metal and metal-alloy wastes in metallic, non-dispersible ([1]) form')

GA 050	7204 21	Waste and scrap of stainless steel
GA 060	7204 29	Waste and scrap of other alloy steels.

2. In section GJ ('Textile wastes')

GJ 120	6309 00	Worn clothing and other worn textile articles.

ZAMBIA

1. All types in section GA ('Metal and metal-alloy wastes in metallic, non-dispersible ([1]) form').

2. All types in section GE ('Glass waste in non-dispersible form').

3. All types in section GI ('Paper, paperboard and paper product wastes').

4. All types in section GJ ('Textile wastes').

5. All types in section GK ('Rubber wastes').

([1]) 'Non-dispersible' does not include any wastes in the form of powder, sludge, dust or solid items containing encased hazardous waste liquids.

Table 6

Regulation 259/93 – Substances Covered by the Export Ban – Annex V, Part I

List A (Annex VIII to the Basel Convention)

[A1] Metal and metal-bearing wastes

[A1010]	Metal wastes and waste consisting of alloys of any of the following: — Antimony — Arsenic — Beryllium — Cadmium — Lead — Mercury — Selenium — Tellurium — Thallium but excluding such waste specifically listed on List B.
[A1020]	Waste having as constituents or contaminants, excluding metal waste in massive form, any of the following: — Antimony; antimony compounds — Beryllium; beryllium compounds — Cadmium; cadmium compounds — Lead; lead compounds — Selenium; selenium compounds — Tellurium; tellurium compounds
[A1030]	Wastes having as constituents or contaminants any of the following: — Arsenic; arsenic compounds — Mercury; mercury compounds — Thallium; thallium compounds
[A1040]	Wastes having as consistuents any of the following: — Metal carbonyls — Hexavalent chromium compounds
[A1050]	Galvanic sludges
[A1060]	Waste liquors from the pickling of metals
[A1070]	Leaching residues from zinc processing, dust and sludges such as jarosite, hematite, etc.
[A1080]	Waste zinc residues not included on List B, containing lead and cadmium in concentrations sufficient to exhibit Annex III characteristics
[A1090]	Ashes from the incineration of insulated copper wire
[A1100]	Dusts and residues from gas cleaning systems of copper smelters
[A1110]	Spent electrolytic solutions from copper electro-refining and electro-winning operations
[A1120]	Waste sludges, excluding anode slimes, from electrolyte purification systems in copper electro-refining and electro-winning operations
[A1130]	Spent etching solutions containing dissolved copper
[A1140]	Waste cupric chloride and copper cyanide catalysts
[A1150]	Precious metal ash from incineration of printed circuit boards not included on List B[1]
[A1160]	Waste lead-acid batteries, whole or crushed
[A1170]	Unsorted waste batteries excluding mixtures of only List B batteries. Waste batteries not specified on List B containing Annex I constituents to an extent to render them hazardous
[A1180]	Waste electrical and electronic assemblies or scrap[2] containing components such as accumulators and other batteries included on List A, mercury-switches, glass from cathode-ray tubes and other activated glass and PCB capacitors, or contaminated with Annex I constituents (e.g. cadmium, mercury, lead, polychlorinated biphenyl) to an extent that they possess any of the characteristics contained in Annex III (note the related entry on List B [B1110])[3]

Table 6 – *contd*

Regulation 259/93 – Substances Covered by the Export Ban – Annex V, Part I

List A (Annex VIII to the Basel Convention)

[A2] Wastes containing principally inorganic constituents, which may contain metals and organic materials

[A2010]   Glass waste from cathode-ray tubes and other activated glasses
[A2020]   Waste inorganic fluorine compounds in the form of liquids or sludges but excluding such wastes specified on List B
[A2030]   Waste catalysts but excluding such wastes specified on List B
[A2040]   Waste gypsum arising from chemical industry processes, when containing Annex I constituents to the extent that it exhibits an Annex III hazardous characteristic (note the related entry on List B [B2080])
[A2050]   Waste asbestos (dusts and fibres)
[A2060]   Coal-fired power plant fly-ash containing Annex I substances in concentrations sufficient to exhibit Annex III characteristics (note the related entry on List B [B2050])

[A3] Wastes containing principally organic constituents, which may contain metals and inorganic materials

[A3010]   Waste from the production or processing of petroleum coke and bitumen
[A3020]   Waste mineral oils unfit for their originally intended use
[A3030]   Wastes that contain, consist of or are contaminated with leaded anti-knock compound sludges
[A3040]   Waste thermal (heat transfer) fluids
[A3050]   Wastes from production, formulation and use of resins, latex, plasticizers, glues/adhesives excluding such wastes specified on List B (note the related entry on List B [B4020])
[A3060]   Waste nitrocellulose
[A3070]   Waste phenols, phenol compounds including chlorophenol in the form of liquids or sludges
[A3080]   Waste ethers not including those specified on List B
[A3090]   Waste leather dust, ash, sludges and flours when containing hexavalent chromium compounds or biocides (note the related entry on List B [B3100])
[A3100]   Waste paring and other waste of leather or of composition leather not suitable for the manufacture of leather articles containing hexavalent chromium compounds or biocides (note the related entry on List B [3090])
[A3110]   Fellmongery wastes containing hexavalent chromium compounds or biocides or infectious substances (note the related entry on List B [3110])
[A3120]   Fluff – light fraction from shredding
[A3130]   Waste organic phosphorous compounds
[A3140]   Waste non-halogenated organic solvents but excluding such wastes specified on List B
[A3150]   Waste halogenated organic solvents
[A3160]   Waste halogenated or unhalogenated non-aqueous distillation residues arising from organic solvent recovery operations
[A3170]   Wastes arising from the production of aliphatic halogenated hydrocarbons (such as chloro-methane, dichloro-ethane, vinyl chloride, vinylidene chloride, allyl chloride and epichlorhydrin)
[A3180]   Wastes, substances and articles containing, consisting of or contaminated with polychlorinated biphenyl (PCB), polychlorinated terphenyl (PCT), polychlorinated naphthalene (PCN) or polybrominated biphenyl (PBB), or any other polybrominated analogues of these compounds, at a concentration level of 50 mg/kg or more[4]

Table 6 – *contd*

Regulation 259/93 – Substances Covered by the Export Ban – Annex V, Part I

List A (Annex VIII to the Basel Convention)

[A3190] Waste tarry residues (excluding asphalt cements) arising from refining, distillation and any pyrolitic treatment of organic materials

[A4] Wastes which may contain either inorganic or organic constituents

[A4010] Wastes from the production, preparation and use of pharmaceutical products but excluding such wastes specified on List B

[A4020] Clinical and related wastes; that is wastes arising from medical, nursing, dental, veterinary, or similar practices, and wastes generated in hospitals or other facilities during the investigation or treatment of patients, or research projects

[A4030] Wastes from the production, formulation and use of biocides and phytopharmaceuticals, including waste pesticides and herbicides which are off-specification, out-dated[5], or unfit for their originally intended use

[A4040] Wastes from the manufacture, formulation and use of wood-preserving chemicals[6]

[A4050] Wastes that contain, consist of or are contaminated with any of the following:
— Inorganic cyanides, excepting precious-metal-bearing residues in solid form containing traces of inorganic cyanides
— Organic cyanides

[A4060] Waste oils/water, hydrocarbons/water mixtures, emulsions

[A4070] Wastes from the production, formulation and use of inks, dyes, pigments, paints, lacquers, varnish excluding any such waste specified on List B (note the related entry on List B [B4010])

[A4080] Wastes of an explosive nature (but excluding such wastes specified on List B)

[A4090] Waste acidic or basic solutions, other than those specified in the corresponding entry on List B (note the related entry on List B [B2120])

[A4100] Wastes from industrial pollution control devices for cleaning of industrial off-gases but excluding such wastes specified on List B

[A4110] Wastes that contain, consist of or are contaminated with any of the following:
— any congenor of polychlorinated dibenzo-furan
— any congenor of polychlorinated dibenzo-dioxin

[A4120] Wastes that contain, consist of or are contaminated with peroxides

[A4130] Wastes packages and containers containing Annex I substances in concentrations sufficient to exhibit Annex III hazard characteristics

[A4140] Waste consisting of or containing off-specification or out-dated[5] chemicals corresponding to Annex I categories and exhibiting Annex III hazard characteristics

[A4150] Waste chemical substances arising from research and development or teaching activities which are not identified and/or are new and whose effects on human health and/or the environment are not known

[A4160] Spent activated carbon not included on List B (note the related entry on List B [B2060])

Notes – Annex V, Part I Council Regulation 259/93
1 Note that the mirror entry on List B ([B1160]) does not specify exceptions.
2 This entry does not include scrap assemblies from electric power generation.
3 PCBs are at a concentration level of 50 mg/kg or more.
4 The 50 mg/kg level is considered to be an internationally practical level for all wastes. However, many individual countries have established lower regulatory levels (e.g. 20 mg/kg) for specific wastes.
5 'Out-dated' means unused within the period recommended by the manufacturer.
6 This entry does not include wood treated with wood-preserving chemicals.

Table 7

Regulation 259/93 – Substances not Covered by the Export Ban – Annex V, Part I

List B (Annex IX to the Basel Convention)

[B1] Metal and metal-bearing wastes

[B1010]   Metal and metal-alloy wastes in metallic, non-dispersible form:
     — Precious metals (gold, silver, the platinum group, but not mercury)
     — Iron and steel scrap
     — Copper scrap
     — Nickel scrap
     — Aluminium scrap
     — Zinc scrap
     — Tin scrap
     — Tungsten scrap
     — Molybdenum scrap
     — Tantalum scrap
     — Magnesium scrap
     — Cobalt scrap
     — Bismuth scrap
     — Titanium scrap
     — Zirconium scrap
     — Manganese scrap
     — Germanium scrap
     — Vanadium scrap
     — Scrap of hafnium, indium, niobium, rhenium and gallium
     — Thorium scrap
     — Rare earths scrap

[B1020]   Clean, uncontaminated metal scrap, including alloys, in bulk finished form (sheet, plate, beams, rods, etc.):
     — Antimony scrap
     — Beryllium scrap
     — Cadmium scrap
     — Lead scrap (but excluding lead-acid batteries)
     — Selenium scrap
     — Tellurium scrap

[B1030]   Refractory metals containing residues

[B1040]   Scrap assemblies from electrical power generation not contaminated with lubricating oil, PCB or PCT to an extent to render them hazardous

[B1050]   Mixed non-ferrous metal, heavy fraction scrap, not containing Annex I materials in concentrations sufficient to exhibit Annex III characteristics[1]

[B1060]   Waste selenium and tellurium in metallic elemental form including powder

[B1070]   Waste of copper and copper alloys in dispersible form, unless than contain [sic] Annex I constituents to an extent that they exhibit Annex III characterists

[B1080]   Zinc ash and residues including zinc alloys residues in dispersible form unless containing Annex I constituents in concentration such as to exhibit Annex III characteristics or exhibiting hazard characteristic H4.3[2]

[B1090]   Waste batteries conforming to a specification, excluding those made with lead, cadmium or mercury

[B1100]   Metal-bearing wastes arising from melting, smelting and refining of metals:
     — Hard zinc spelter
     — Zinc-containing drosses:
          — galvanizing slab zinc top dross (>90% Zn)
          — galvanizing slab zinc bottom dross (>92% Zn)
          — zinc die casting dross (>85% Zn)
          — hot dip galvanizers slab zinc dross (batch) (>92% Zn)
          — zinc skimmings

Table 7 – *contd*

Regulation 259/93 – Substances not Covered by the Export Ban – Annex V, Part I

List B (Annex IX to the Basel Convention)

       — Aluminium skimmings (or skims) excluding salt slag
       — Slags from copper processing for further processing or refining not containing arsenic, lead or cadmium to an extent that they exhibit Annex III hazard characteristics
       — Wastes of refractory linings, including crucibles, originating from copper smelting
       — Slags from precious metals processing for further refining
       — Tantalum bearing tin slags with less than 0,5% tin

[B1110]   Electrical and electronic assemblies:
       — Electronic assemblies consisting only of metals or alloys
       — Waste electrical and electronic assemblies or scrap[3] (including printed circuit boards) not containing components such as accumulators and other batteries included on List A, mercury-switches, glass from cathode-ray tubes and other activated glass and PCB capacitors, or not contaminated with Annex I constituents (e.g. cadmium, mercury, lead, polychorinated biphenyl) or from which these have been removed, to an extent that they do not possess any of the characteristics contained in Annex III (note the related entry on List A [A1180])
       — Electrical and electronic assemblies (including printed circuit boards, electronic components and wires) destined for direct re-use[4] and not for recycling or final disposal[5]

[B1120]   Spent catalysts excluding liquids used as catalysts, containing any of:
       — Transition metals, excluding waste catalysts (spent catalysts, liquid used catalysts or other catalysts) on List A: scandium, vanadium, manganese, cobalt, copper, yttrium, niobium, hafnium, tungsten, titanium, chromium, iron, nickel, zinc, zirconium, molybdenum, tantalum, rhenium
       — Lanthanides (rare earth metals): lanthanum, praseodymium, samarium, gadolinium, dysprosium, erbium, ytterbium, cerium, neody, europium, terbium, holmium, thulium, lutetium

[B1130]   Cleaned spent precious-metal-bearing catalysts
[B1140]   Precious-metal-bearing residues in solid form which contain traces of inorganic cyanides
[B1150]   Precious metals and alloy wastes (gold, silver, the platinum group, but not mercury) in a dispersible, non-liquid form with appropriate packaging and labelling
[B1160]   Precious-metal ash from the incineration of printed circuit boards (note the related entry on List A [A1150])
[B1170]   Precious-metal ash from the incineration of photographic film
[B1180]   Waste photographic film containing silver halides and metallic silver
[B1190]   Waste photographic paper containing silver halides and metallic silver
[B1200]   Granulated slag arising from the manufacture of iron and steel
[B1210]   Slag arising from the manufacture of iron and steel including slags as a source of TiO_2 and vanadium
[B1220]   Slag from zinc production, chemically stabilised, having a high iron content (above 20%) and processed according to industrial specifications (e.g. DIN 4301) mainly for construction
[B1230]   Mill scaling arising from the manufacture of iron and steel
[B1240]   Copper oxide mill-scale

[B2] Wastes containing principally inorganic constituents, which may contain metals and organic materials

[B2010]   Wastes from mining operations in non-dispersible form:

Table 7 – *contd*

Regulation 259/93 – Substances not Covered by the Export Ban – Annex V, Part I

List B (Annex IX to the Basel Convention)

  — Natural graphite waste
  — Slate waste, whether or not roughly trimmed or merely cut, by sawing or otherwise
  — Mica waste
  — Leucite, nepheline and nepheline syenite waste
  — Feldspar waste
  — Fluospar waste
  — Silica wastes in solid form excluding those used in foundry operations

[B2020]   Glass waste in non-dispersible form:
  — Cullet and other waste and scrap of glass except for glass from cathode-ray tubes and other activated glasses

[B2030]   Ceramic wastes in non-dispersible form:
  — Cermet waste and scrap (metal ceramic composites)
  — Ceramic based fibres not elsewhere specified or included

[B2040]   Other wastes containing principally inorganic constituents:
  — Partially refined calcium sulphate produced from flue-gas desulphurisation (FGD)
  — Waste gypsum wallboard or plasterboard arising from the demolition of buildings
  — Slag from copper production, chemically stabilised, having a high iron content (above 20%) and processed according to industrial specifications (eg DIN 4301 and DIN 8201) mainly for construction and abrasive applications
  — Sulphur in solid form
  — Limestone from the production of calcium cyanamide (having a pH less than 9)
  — Sodium, potassium, calcium chlorides
  — Carborundum (silicon carbide)
  — Broken concrete
  — Lithium-tantalum and lithium-niobium containing glass scraps

[B2050]   Coal-fired power plant fly-ash, not included on List A (note the related entry on List A [A2060])

[B2060]   Spent activated carbon resulting from the treatment of potable water and processes of the food industry and vitamin production (note the related entry on List A [A4160])

[B2070]   Calcium fluoride sludge

[B2080]   Waste gypsum arising from chemical industry processes not included on List A (note the related entry on List A [A2040])

[B2090]   Waste anode butts from steel or aluminium production made of petroleum coke or bitumen and cleaned to normal industry specifications (excluding anode butts from chlor alkali electrolyses and from metallurgical industry)

[B2100]   Waste hydrates of aluminium and waste alumina and residues from alumina production excluding such materials used for gas cleaning, flocculation or filtration processes

[B2110]   Bauxite residue ('red mud') (pH moderated to less than 11,5)

[B2120]   Waste acidic or basic solutions with a PH greater than 2 and less than 11,5, which are not corrosive or otherwise hazardous (note the related entry on List A [A4090])

[B3] Wastes containing principally organic constituents, which may contain metals and inorganic materials

[B3010]   Solid plastic waste:
  The following plastic or mixed plastic materials, provided they are not mixed with other wastes and are prepared to a specification:

Table 7 – *contd*

Regulation 259/93 – Substances not Covered by the Export Ban – Annex V, Part I

List B (Annex IX to the Basel Convention)

— Scrap plastic of non-halogenated polymers and co-polymers, including but not limited to the following[6]:
  — ethylene
  — styrene
  — polypropylene
  — polyethylene terephthalate
  — acrylonitrile
  — butadiene
  — polyacetals
  — polyamides
  — polybutylene terephthalate
  — polycarbonates
  — polyethers
  — polyphenylene sulphides
  — acrylic polymers
  — alkanes C10–C13 (plasticiser)
  — polyurethane (not containing CFCs)
  — polysiloxanes
  — polymethyl methacrylate
  — polyvinyl alcohol
  — polyvinyl butyral
  — polyvinyl acetate
— Cured waste resins or condensation products including the following:
  — urea formaldehyde resins
  — phenol formaldehyde resins
  — melamine formaldehyde resins
  — epoxy resins
  — alkyd resins
  — polyamides
— The following fluorinated polymer wastes[7]:
  — Perfluoroethylene/propylene (FEP)
  — Perfluoroalkoxy alkane (PFA)
  — Perfluoroalkoxy alkane (MFA)
  — Polyvinylfluoride (PVF)
  — Polyvinylidenefluoride (PVDF)

[B3020] Paper, paperboard and paper product wastes
The following materials, provided they are not mixed with hazardous wastes:
Waste and scrap of paper or paperboard of:
— unbleached paper or paperboard or of corrugated paper or paperboard
— other paper or paperboard, made mainly of bleached chemical pulp, not coloured in the mass
— paper or paperboard made mainly of mechanical pulp (for example, newspapers, journals and similar printed matter)
— other, including but not limited to 1. laminated paperboard; 2. unsorted scrap

[B3030] Textile wastes
The following materials, provided they are not mixed with other wastes and are prepared to a specification:
— Silk waste (including cocoons unsuitable for reeling, yarn waste and garnetted stock):
  — not carded or combed
  — other

Table 7 – *contd*

Regulation 259/93 – Substances not Covered by the Export Ban – Annex V, Part I

List B (Annex IX to the Basel Convention)

— Waste of wool or of fine or coarse animal hair, including yarn waste but
excluding garnetted stock:
— noils of wool or of fine animal hair
— other waste of wool or of fine animal hair
— waste of coarse animal hair
— Cotton waste (including yarn waste and garnetted stock):
— yarn waste (including thread waste)
— garnetted stock
— other
— Flax tow and waste
— Tow and waste (including yarn waste and garnetted stock) of true hemp
(*Cannabis sativa* L.)
— Tow and waste (including yarn waste and garnetted stock) of jute and other
textile bast fibres (excluding flax, true hemp and ramie)
— Tow and waste (including yarn waste and garnetted stock) of sisal and other
textile fibres of the genus Agave
— Tow, noils and waste (including yarn waste and garnetted stock) of coconut
— Tow, noils and waste (including yarn waste and garnetted stock) of abaca
(Manila hemp or *Musa textilis* Nee)
— Tow, noils and waste (including yarn waste and garnetted stock) of ramie and
other vegetable textile fibres, not elsewhere specified or included
— Waste (including noils, yarn waste and garnetted stock) of man-made fibres:
— of synthetic fibres
— of artificial fibres
— Worn clothing and other worn textile articles
— Used rags, scrap twine, cordage, rope and cables and worn out articles of
twine, cordage, rope or cables of textile:
— sorted
— other

[B3040] Rubber wastes
The following materials, provided they are not mixed with other wastes:
— Waste and scrap of hard rubber (e.g. ebonite)
— Other rubber wastes (excluding such wastes specified elsewhere)

[B3050] Untreated cork and wood waste:
— Wood waste and scrap, whether or not agglomerated in logs, briquettes, pellets
or similar forms
— Cork waste: crushed, granulated or ground cork

[B3060] Wastes arising from agro-food industries provided it is not infectious:
— Wine lees
— Dried and sterilised vegetable waste, residues and by-products, whether or not
in the form of pellets, or a kind used in animal feeding, not elsewhere specified
or included
— Degras; residues resulting from the treatment of fatty substances or animal or
vegetable waxes
— Waste of bones and horn-cones, unworked, defatted, simply prepared (but not
cut to shape), treated with acid or degelatinised
— Fish waste
— Cocoa shells, husks, and other cocoa waste
— Other wastes from the agro-food industry excluding by-products which meet
national and international requirements and standards for human or animal
consumption

Table 7 – *contd*

Regulation 259/93 – Substances not Covered by the Export Ban – Annex V, Part I

List B (Annex IX to the Basel Convention)

[B3070] The following wastes:
— Waste of human hair
— Waste straw
— Deactivated fungus mycelium from penicillin production to be used as animal feed
[B3080] Waste parings and scrap of rubber
[B3090] Paring and other wastes of leather or of composition leather not suitable for the manufacture of leather articles, excluding leather sludges, not containing hexavalent chromium compounds and biocides (note the related entry on List A [A3100])
[B3100] Leather dust, ash, sludges or flours not containing hexavalent chromium compounds or biocides (note the related entry on List A [A3090])
[B3110] Fellmongery wastes not containing hexavalent chromium compounds or biocides or infectious substances (note the related entry on List A [A3110])
[B3120] Wastes consisting of food dyes
[B3130] Waste polymer ethers and waste non-hazardous monomer ethers incapable of forming peroxides
[B3140] Waste pneumatic tyres, excluding those destined for Annex IV.A operations

[B4] Wastes which may contain either inorganic or organic constituents

[B4010] Wastes consisting mainly of water-based/latex paints, inks and hardened varnishes not containing organic solvents, heavy metals or biocides to an extent to render them hazardous (note the related entry on List A [A4070])
[B4020] Wastes from production, formulation and use of resins, latex, plasticisers, glues/adhesives, not listed on List A, free of solvents and other contaminants to an extent that they do not exhibit Annex III characteristics, e.g. water based, or glues based on casein starch, dextrin, cellulose ethers, polyvinyl alcohols (note the related entry on List A [A3050])
[B4030] Used single use cameras, with batteries not included on List A

Notes – Annex V, Part I Council Regulation 259/93
1 Note that even where low level contamination with Annex I materials initially exists, subsequent processes, including recycling processes, may result in separated fractions containing signficantly enhanced concentrations of those Annex I materials.
2 The status of zinc ash is currently under review and there is a recommendation with United Nations Conference on Trade and Development (UNCTAD) that zinc ashes should not be dangerous goods.
3 This entry does not include scrap from electrical power generation.
4 Re-use can include repair, refurbishment or upgrading, but not major reassembly.
5 In some countries these materials destined for direct re-use are not considered wastes.
6 It is understood that such scraps are completely polymerized.
7 — Post-consumer wastes are excluded from this entry.
— Wastes shall not be mixed.
— Problems arising from open-burning practices to be considered.

Index

Brokers – *continued*
  registration of – *continued*
    Waste Management Licensing
      Regulations 1994 and, 6.28
  responsibilities of, 3.106–3.110
  transfer notes and, 3.107
  unregistered, 3.108, 6.35
  waste collection authorities as, 3.102,
    3.110, 6.30
  waste disposal authorities as, 3.102,
    3.110, 6.30
  written descriptions and, 3.107
Building waste. *See* Construction waste
Burden of proof
  exemptions from waste management
    licences and, 10.51, 10.52
  monitoring equipment not correctly
    functioning, 12.244
  section 33 defences and, 7.155
  whether or not material is waste, 2.33, 2.46
Business plans
  financial provision requirements of
    licence and, 8.187

Captives
  financial provision requirements of
    licence and, 8.194–8.197,
    8.210–8.212
Carriage of waste. *See* Carriers of
  controlled waste; Transfer of waste
Carriers of controlled waste
  Co-ordinated Local Authority Database of
    Waste Carriers (CLADWAC), 6.60,
    13.44
  definition of carrier, 3.94, 3.95
  Environment Agency's duties/powers as
    to, 12.07, 12.12, 12.07, 12.139 *ff*
  see also registration *below*
  number of registered carriers, 1.79, 6.02
  register of. *See* Registers, public
  registration of—
    amendment of registration details—
      additional registration as broker,
        6.78, 6.83–6.85
      generally, 6.78–6.82
    animal by-products/carcasses
      transporters, exclusion, 6.14–6.21
    appeals—
      documentary requirements, 6.101
      generally, 6.02, 6.99–6.104
      refusal of registration, against, 6.67
      revocation, against, 6.96, 6.97
    applications for registration—
      copy to be entered in register, 6.53
      details of form, 6.49
      false/misleading information and,
        6.50, 12.221

Carriers of controlled waste – *continued*
  registration of – *continued*
    applications for registration – *continued*
      fees, 6.52
      information to be provided by
        applicant, 6.50
      joint carrier/broker applications, 6.49
      multiple applications, 6.47
      place of business and, 6.46
      refusal of. *See* refusal *below*
      time limits for processing, 6.48
    certificate of registration, 6.53, 6.57, 6.59
    charities and, 6.25, 6.105, 6.106–6.110
    Circular guidance, 6.02
    Control of Pollution (Amendment) Act
      1989 provisions, 6.02 *ff*
    Controlled Waste (Registration of
      Carriers and Seizure of Vehicles)
      Regulations 1991 and, 6.07
    criminal convictions and. *See*
      'prescribed offences' *below*
    Directive on Waste and, 6.05
    Environment Agency and, 6.105,
      6.106–6.110, 12.07, 12.12
    evidence of, requirement to produce—
      generally, 6.02, 12.139
      offences as to, 12.146–12.150
      stop powers of Environment Agency,
        12.140–12.144
    exclusions from requirement, 6.08–6.25
    exportation of waste by air or sea,
      exclusion, 6.22
    false/misleading information and, 6.50,
      12.221
    ferry operator exclusion, 6.25
    generally, 6.02
    groups of companies and, 6.55
    hiring of vehicles to third parties and,
      6.26, 6.27
    householder exclusion, 6.09
    importation of waste to point of
      landing, exclusion, 6.22
    joint registration as broker, 6.01, 6.49,
      6.78, 6.86
    local authority waste disposal
      companies and, 6.24
    national application of registration, 6.59
    obstruction of officers and, 6.64, 12.197
    offences—
      bodies corporate, involving, 6.39
      defences, 6.41, 6.42
      directors' etc liability, 6.39
      false/misleading information in
        application form, 6.50
      generally, 6.35, 6.36–6.40
      HGV licences and, 6.40
      obstruction of officers, 12.197

Environmental Protection Act 1990 –
continued
 section 33 – *continued*
  'depositing' and 'disposing' of
   controlled waste, 7.16–7.24,
   7.31–7.44, 7.135–7.139
  duplicity and 7.104–7.108
  duty of care under section 34, overlap
   with section 33, 7.12
  employees, causation by, 7.75
  exclusions/exemptions made by
   regulations and, 7.05
  extraordinary events and, 7.76, 7.77
  fly-tipping prevention and, 7.06, 7.15
  generally, 7.01, 7.02
  household waste and, 7.04
  in the alternative, offences charged,
   7.107, 7.108
  interpretation of terms, 7.14 *ff*
  'keeping' controlled waste, 7.26–7.30,
   7.31–7.44, 7.135–7.139
  'knowingly', 7.52–7.54, 7.55–7.61,
   7.117
  'knowingly causing', 7.52–7.54,
   7.93–7.102, 7.117, 7.126, 7.127
  'knowingly permitting', 7.52–7.54,
   7.88–7.92, 7.117, 7.126, 7.127
  'land', 7.45–7.51
  liability of directors etc 7.13
  main provisions of, 7.03–7.13
  mens rea and, 7.55, 7.109, 7.110,
   7.117, 7.122–7.126
  multiple causes, 7.73, 7.74
  overlaps between offence provisions,
   7.15, 7.103, 7.105, 7.142, 7.143
  penalties, 7.11, 7.12
  'permitting', 7.78–7.86
  provisos, 7.04, 7.05
  strict liability and, 7.14, 7.109, 7.110,
   7.114–7.116, 7.126, 7.135
  'treating' controlled waste, 7.25,
   7.31–7.44, 7.135–7.139
  Waste Management Licensing
   Regulations 1994 and, 7.14,
   7.31–7.44
 section 158, 7.13
Escape of waste
 duty of care, 3.11, 3.16, 3.45–3.47
Escrow accounts
 financial provision requirements of
  licence and, 8.190, 8.194–8.197,
  8.200–8.203
'Establishments and undertakings',
 10.22, 10.23
European Community
 Community Strategy on Waste
  Management, 1.16, 1.17, 1.26

European Community – *continued*
 cross-border waste movements. *See*
  Transfrontier waste movements
 Dangerous Substances Directive, 2.63,
  4.12
 definition of waste etc, 1.21, 1.24, 1.30
 Directives—
  *see also individual Directives above
   and below*
  precision of, 1.21, 1.22, 1.24
  problems with original Directives, 1.21
  transposition into national law, 1.22,
   1.121, 1.122
 disposal policy, 1.17, 1.21
 electronic waste, proposed Directive, 1.29
 end of life vehicles, proposed Directive,
  1.29
 Environmental Action Programmes—
  generally, 1.12, 1.16
  need for, 1.12–1.15
 Environmental Assessment Directive,
  4.06
 European Waste Catalogue, 1.30, 2.22,
  4.15, 4.16, 4.26
 generation of waste, 1.13, 1.17
 Groundwater Directive—
  applications for waste management
   licences and, 8.101–8.111
  Circular guidance, 8.70, 8.71
  conditions of waste management
   licences and, 8.246–8.252
  de minimis discharges, exclusion for,
   8.81–8.84
  definition of groundwater, 8.79, 8.80
  direct/indirect discharges, 8.76–8.78
  'discharges' subject to, 8.86–8.90
  exclusion of substances from List I,
   8.75
  generally, 8.70
  implementation of, 8.70, 8.71
  List I and List II substances, 8.74–8.78
  regulation 15 of Waste Management
   Licensing Regulations 1994 and,
   8.70 *ff*
  review of discharges, 9.65–9.69
  scope of, 8.78, 8.80
  waste management facilities subject to,
   8.85–8.100
 Hazardous Waste Directive—
  definition of hazardous waste, 1.24,
   4.07, 4.08–4.18
  'domestic waste' excluded from, 4.09
  generally, 4.08
  list of hazardous waste, 4.07, 4.08–4.18
  Special Waste Regulations and, 4.01
 Hazardous Waste Incineration Directive,
  4.06

Peatworking
keeping/deposit of waste from, exemption, 10.254
'Permitting', 7.52–7.54, 7.78–7.86
Pets
burial/cremation, 10.232, 10.233
Planning authorities
role of, 1.59–1.61
Planning Inspectorate
appeals and, 1.55, 6.102, 9.127, 9.132
Planning permission
waste management licences and, 8.29, 8.31–8.39, 8.49, 8.54
Planning policy guidance, 8.35 *ff*
'Poisonous or noxious wastes', 2.212
Police and Criminal Evidence Act 1984
Code of Practice, applicability of, 12.246–12.251
Pollution Prevention and Control Act 1999
Environmental Protection Act and, 1.95, 1.96, 1.97, 1.98
existing facilities and, 1.95, 1.96
generally, 1.93
industrial processes affected by, 1.97
Integrated Pollution Prevention and Control (IPPC) Directive and, 1.94, 1.95
landfills and, 1.97
new facilities and, 1.95, 1.96, 1.98
Scotland and, 1.94
secondary legislation, 1.93, 1.94, 1.96
time-limited waste management licences, provisions as to, 1.99
Wales and, 1.94
waste management activities affected by, 1.97
Pollution of the environment
applications for licences and, 8.29, 8.40–8.47, 8.52, 8.69
emergencies and, power to carry out works, 12.95–12.97
Environment Agency's statutory duties, 9.63, 9.64, 12.11, 12.14
exemptions from waste management licensing and, 10.33
financial provision reviews and, 9.76
metal recycling sites and, 11.14, 11.37, 11.39
modification of licences and, 9.05, 9.15
obstruction of officers and, 12.196
removal/elimination of effects of waste and, 12.119
revocation of licences and, 9.17, 9.25, 9.30
seizure of goods and articles and, 12.98–12.100

Pollution of the environment – *continued*
'serious pollution', 9.46, 9.47
suspension of licences and, 9.45–9.47, 9.53
Power of entry
compensation and, 12.84
emergencies and, 12.61, 12.92–12.94
generally, 12.58–12.64
offences relating to, 12.81–12.83
transfrontier waste shipment notices and, 12.136
warrants to gain, 12.58, 12.61, 12.79, 12.80
Pre-sorting, 1.46, 2.174–2.178
Prescription medicines. *See* Medicines
'Process', 7.25
Producer responsibility scheme
Environment Agency oversight, 1.53
Production of waste
carrier registration and, 6.10–6.13
definition of waste producer—
carrier registration and, 6.13
definition of waste and, 2.157–2.159, 2.164, 2.165
duty of care and ,3.13, 3.80, 3.84
'discarding' of waste, producer's role. *See* Definition of waste
duty of care and, 3.79–3.93
hierarchy of waste producers, 2.168
identity of producer, 3.79–3.89
legislative overview, 1.77, 1.78
responsibilities of waste producer, 3.90–3.93
Proportionality principle
Environment Agency and, 12.38–12.41
Public registers. *See* Registers, public

Quarries. *See* Mines and quarries waste
Questioning of persons
authorised persons' powers as to, 12.75–12.78, 12.82

Radioactive waste
Directive waste, exclusion from definition of, 2.50, 2.53, 2.54
special waste, as, 4.53
Rails, scrap
exemption from waste management licensing, 10.252
Railway ballast
exemption from waste management licensing, 10.251
Railway carriages
discharges from, exemption from waste management licensing, 10.250
Reclamation. *See* Recovery of waste

Waste management papers
  Environment Agency responsibility for
      producing, 1.54
  licences and, 1.87
  list of, Appendix 1
  statutory guidance, 8.232
Waste oils. *See* Oils
Waste production. *See* Production of
  waste
Waste regulation authorities
  bodies constituting, 1.52
  transfer of functions to Environment
      Agency, 1.51
  use of term, 1.52
Water
  Groundwater Directive. *See* European
      Community

Water – *continued*
  inland waters, deposit etc of
      dredgings/plant matter from,
      exemption, 10.237–10.244
  treatment works, recovery processes
      exemption, 10.205–10.210
  waste water, exclusion from definition of
      waste, 2.50, 2.62–2.72
'Without reasonable excuse', 12.109 *ff*
Working plans
  changes to, modification of licences and,
      9.04
  register to hold copy of, 13.15
  waste management licences and,
      8.217–8.224, 9.04
Written descriptions of waste. *See*
  Transfer of waste